MISSOURI

HOLT

Elements of LITERATURE

Third Course

correlated to

Missouri

Communication Arts Course Level Expectations

CONTENTS

HOLT, RINEHART AND WINSTON

Missouri
The Show Me State

COVER PHOTO CREDITS: (c), © Macduff Everton/The Image Bank/Getty Images; (b), c Sot/Photodisc/Getty Images; (bc), c Siede Preis/Photodisc/Getty Images; (bkgd), c Bill Stevenson/Aurora/Getty Images; (inset), c Jason Horowitz/zefa/CORBIS.

Acknowledgments and other credits appear on pages 1323–1331, which are an extension of the copyright page.

Printed in the United States of America

ISBN-13: 978-0-55-401457-9
ISBN-10: 0-55-401457-2

1 2 3 4 5 048 11 10 09 08

Bluebird, state bird

White hawthorn, state flower

Missouri Communication Arts Course Level Expectations

>9.R.1 Develop and apply skills and strategies to the reading process

- **9.R.1.C Phonics**

  >9.R.1.C.1 Problem-solve" unknown words when reading when needed.

What does it mean? Learn how to use what you already know about words to figure out the meaning of new words.

EXAMPLES: Many of the Vocabulary Skills Review sections give you practice in determining the meaning of a word from its context. See, for example, the exercise on page 519.

The Language Coach on page 841 gives strategies to find context clues in "Romeo and Juliet."

Pages 1306-1308 discuss commonly used roots, prefixes and suffixes, with a guide to word construction.

The Language Coach on page 456 provides practice in recognizing jargon and technical vocabulary.

See the Vocabulary Development lesson on pages 1103-1104 for help with names and terms from Greek and Roman mythology.

Rock Bridge State Park

- **9.R.1.D Fluency**
  - **>9.R.1.D.1** Read grade-level instructional text
    - **a** with fluency: accuracy, comprehension, and appropriate expression
    - **b** adjusting reading rate to difficulty and type of text

What does it mean? Read accurately, understand what you read, and use an appropriate tone of voice to convey your understanding. Speed up or slow down your pace depending on what type of text you're reading.

EXAMPLES: The Reading Focus on page 445 shows a graphic organizer for use in paraphrasing and gives guidance in reading aloud with a passage by Mark Twain (pages 447-455).

The Reading Focus activities on pages 1205-1209 help you adjust your reading rate in a series of informational texts.

- **9.R.1.E Vocabulary**

  >9.R.1.E.1 Develop vocabulary through text, using

  a roots and affixes

  b context clues

  c glossary, dictionary, and thesaurus

What does it mean? Learn new words by studying the word parts, looking for other words and phrases that can help you guess meaning, and using reference books.

EXAMPLES: Understanding Vocabulary
Several Vocabulary Development exercises help you develop your reading vocabulary. You'll find practice activities that show you how to map unfamiliar words on page 294. The Vocabulary Development on page 709 discusses multiple-meaning words, and the Your Turn gives practice with charting vocabulary in a passage.

A Language Coach on page 929 deals with Latin roots, and an overview of roots, prefixes, and suffixes can be found on pages 1306-1307 of the Language Handbook.

Gateway Arch and Mississippi River

Missouri
The Show Me State

Old Spillway, Finley River

- **9.R.1.F Pre-Reading**
  - **>9.R.1.F.1** Apply pre-reading strategies to aid comprehension
    - **a** access prior knowledge
    - **b** preview
    - **c** predict with text support or rationale
    - **d** set a purpose and rate for reading

What does it mean? Use tools before you even begin reading, such as thinking about what you already know and guessing what will happen based on the title, to help you understand.

EXAMPLES: Reading Focus sections give note-taking guidelines. For examples, see "Making Predictions" on page 17 and "Making Connections to Characters" on page 175.

- **9.R.1.G During Reading**
  - **>9.R.1.G.1** During reading, utilize strategies to
    - **a** determine meaning of unknown words
    - **b** self-monitor comprehension
    - **c** question the text
    - **d** infer
    - **e** visualize
    - **f** paraphrase
    - **g** summarize

What does it mean? Use tools during reading, such as learning new words, asking questions, making guesses (inferences), "seeing" the action in your mind, and restating text in your own words.

EXAMPLES: Pages 1162-1164 of the Writing Workshop on research papers shows how to evaluate a variety of sources and prepare note cards for writing.

The Reading Focus essay "What Skills Help You Understand Symbolism and Irony?" (pages 324-325) discusses active reading techniques and a graphic organizer for understanding supporting details.

Margin notes throughout The Tragedy of Romeo and Juliet (pages 804-949) ask you to examine how the characters' dialogue and diction create tone and mood. See, for example, the prompts that accompany Act I, scene 1, line 41 (Staging the Play, page 809); Act I, scene 4, line 53 (Elements of Drama, page 830); and Act I, scene 5, lines 1–15 (Staging the Play, page 833).

- **9.R.1.H Post-Reading**
  - **>9.R.1.H.1** Apply post-reading skills to comprehend, interpret, analyze, and evaluate text:
    - **a** identify and explain the relationship between the main idea and supporting details
    - **b** question to clarify
    - **c** reflect
    - **d** draw conclusions
    - **e** paraphrase
    - **f** summarize

What does it mean? After you read, ask yourself questions, draw conclusions, identify the most important (main) idea and details and write a summary, a short version of the text that includes the main idea and important details.

EXAMPLES: The Reading Focus essay "What Skills Help You Read Functional Documents?" (pages 1186-1187) discusses taking notes and asking questions in response to the text.

Many Literary Focus sections introduce literary devices to accompany a selection. Questions after reading then ask you to analyze and evaluate the author's use of the literary device. See "Suspense and Foreshadowing" (page 17) before the story "The Most Dangerous Game" and questions that follow the story (page 37).

Constructed Response sections trace main and supporting ideas in model texts (page 111).

Choices activities encourage creative writing in response to texts. See page 657 for an example.

- **9.R.1.I Making Connections**
  - >**9.R.1.I.1** Compare, contrast, and analyze connections:
    - **a** text to text (information and relationships in various fiction and non-fiction works)
    - **b** text to self (text ideas and own experience)
    - **c** text to world (text ideas and the world by identifying how literature reflects a culture and historic time frame)

What does it mean? Put what you read in context: connect it to other works you've read, to your own life, and to the time and culture in which it was written.

EXAMPLES: Cross-Curricular Links encourage reading across subject areas. The Science Link on page 29 focuses on ecosystems and page 343 links science to the story "The Scarlet Ibis."

Several Language Coach sections assist with dialect. See page 804 for "Shakespeare's Language," and page 535 for writing about dialect in "Ain't I a Woman" by Sojourner Truth.

See the Vocabulary Development lesson on pages 1103-1104 for a discussion of Greek and Roman myths and their influence on the English language.

Eads Bridge

>9.R.2 Develop and apply skills and strategies to comprehend, analyze, and evaluate fiction, poetry and drama from a variety of cultures and times

- **9.R.2.A Text Features**

  >9.R.2.A.1 Analyze and evaluate the text features in grade-level text

What does it mean? Read the title of a work to learn more about it. Then, learn the text features of fiction, poetry, and drama (plays)

EXAMPLES: Each literary collection is introduced by a Literary Focus essay that explains the elements of that genre. Literary and Reading Focus activities outline individual elements and example texts follow with guidelines for note-taking and reflection. See Collection 4 (pages 320-395) for examples concerning symbolism and irony.

The Reading Focus "Reading a Play" discusses the use of dialogue and stage directions in drama and gives "The Frog Prince" as an example (pages 775-794).

- **9.R.2.B Literary Techniques**

  >9.R.2.B.1 Identify and explain literary techniques, in text emphasizing

  a irony

  b imagery

  c repeated sound, line or phrase and

  d analyze literary techniques already introduced

What does it mean? Find and describe irony (a contrast between what appears to be and actually is), imagery, repetition, and other types of literary techniques, such as symbolism, metaphor, and similes.

EXAMPLES: Language Focus essays teach the elements of a particular genre. "What is the Language of Poetry?" on pages 616-619 deals with figurative language as well as sound devices such as rhyme and meter.

A comparison of diction in two catalog poems can be found on pages 646-651. Imagery is the focus of pages 652-656, and figurative language such as personification and similes are discussed on pages 669-678.

Castle ruins, Ha Ha Tonka State Park

Missouri
The Show Me State

• **9.R.2.C Literary Elements**

> **9.R.2.C.1**

a demonstrate comprehension skills previously introduced

b analyze character, plot, setting, point of view

c analyze the development of theme across genres

d evaluate the effect of the author's style

What does it mean? Analyze the characters by looking at their motivations (reasons for acting), their words, and their actions; the plot by studying how the events progress; and the point of view by identifying who is telling the story. Theme is the general idea about life the author is conveying through the story—it is generally inferred rather than stated directly. The author's style is his or her unique voice—created by word choice, sentence structure, and the use of literary techniques.

Aerial view, Kansas City

EXAMPLES: The Essay "What Do You Need to Know About Plot and Setting?" (pages 4-5) sets a foundation for approaching literature and models skills for reading the following texts.

Reading Focus activities outline individual elements and follow with example texts and guidelines for note-taking and reflection. See Collection 4 (pages 320-395) for examples concerning symbolism and irony.

Writing Focus sections give topics for responding critically to text, while the Choices sections encourage creative writing and discussion. See page 501 for essay, poem, and informal letter prompts in response to the works of Maya Angelou.

Literary Focus questions also accompany many example texts, such as those that focus on dialogue and characterization in Langston Hughes's short story "Thank You Ma'am" (pages 134-141).

>9.R.3 Develop and apply skills and strategies to comprehend, analyze, and evaluate nonfiction (such as biographies, newspapers, technical manuals) from a variety of cultures and times

- **9.R.3.A Text Features**

  >9.R.3.A.1 Explain, analyze, and evaluate the author's use of text features to clarify meaning

What does it mean? Nonfiction text features include titles, headings, subheads; studying these can help you understand the nonfiction you read.

EXAMPLES: "The Handbook of Reading and Informational Terms (pages 1253-1262) provides definitions and discussions of terms related to the structure of informational materials.

The Informational Text Focus on pages 1204-1211 guides readers through the functions of four types of workplace documents. Alternate sections focus on other informational texts.

The Reading Model on pages 1188-1191 gives practice in reading consumer documents.

Pages 1271-1273 show examples of informational graphics and visuals.

- **9.R.3.B Literary Techniques**
  - **>9.R.3.B.1** Identify and explain literary techniques in nonfiction text, emphasizing
    - **a** irony
    - **b** imagery
    - **c** repeated sound, line or phrase and
    - **d** sound devices previously introduced

What does it mean? Nonfiction text features many techniques used in fiction. Find and describe irony (a contrast between what appears to be and actually is), imagery, repetition, and other types of literary techniques, such as symbolism, metaphor, and similes.

EXAMPLES: Functional documents such as workplace and consumer documents are outlined on pages 1182-1183, with strategies on pages 1186-1187 for adjusting reading speed and various texts for practice.

The Literary Focus on pages 524-525 shows an author's various methods of persuasion.

The Comparing Texts section "Comparing Themes and Topics Across Genres" on pages 1114-1133 offers students opportunities to compare fiction and nonfiction texts about life in Mexico.

Sunrise on Lake of the Ozarks

- **9.R.3.C Text Structures**
  - **>9.R.3.C.1** Use details from informatonal text to
    - **a** identify and explain the organizational pattern
    - **b** analyze and evaluate effectiveness of word choice
    - **c** analyze and evaluate the accuracy and adequacy of evidence
    - **d** analyze and evaluate point of view
    - **e** evaluate proposed solutions

What does it mean? Respond actively to nonfiction texts: identify how the text is organized—for example, chronologically (by time) or by order of importance; critique the author's choice of words and the support he or she uses for his ideas; evaluate the author's point of view, or perspective, and the suggested solutions to problems.

EXAMPLES: The Informational Text Focus on pages 1182-1183 analyzes various informational texts, including workplace documents, public documents and technical directions.

The Skills in Action that follows (pages 1188-1190) gives practice in reading four types of consumer documents about product and safety information.

The Informational Text Focus "Four Readings About Poe's Death" (pages 296-307) guides you in evaluating and synthesizing information from four different sources that explore the same topic. Finding and evaluating essential ideas uses reading skills such as predicting, questioning, visualizing, retelling, and finding implicitly stated main ideas.

- **9.R.3.D Understanding Directions**
  - **>9.R.3.D.1** Read and follow multi-step directions to perform complex procedures and/or tasks.

What does it mean? Learn to follow written directions so that you can complete even the most challenging assignments.

EXAMPLES: The Writing Workshops "Autobiographical Narrative" (pages 416-427) and "Response to Literature" (pages 734-743) both give step-by-step instructions for writing pieces that follow the conventions of each genre.

Pages 1194-1196 give step-by-step instructions for adding graphics to your web site.

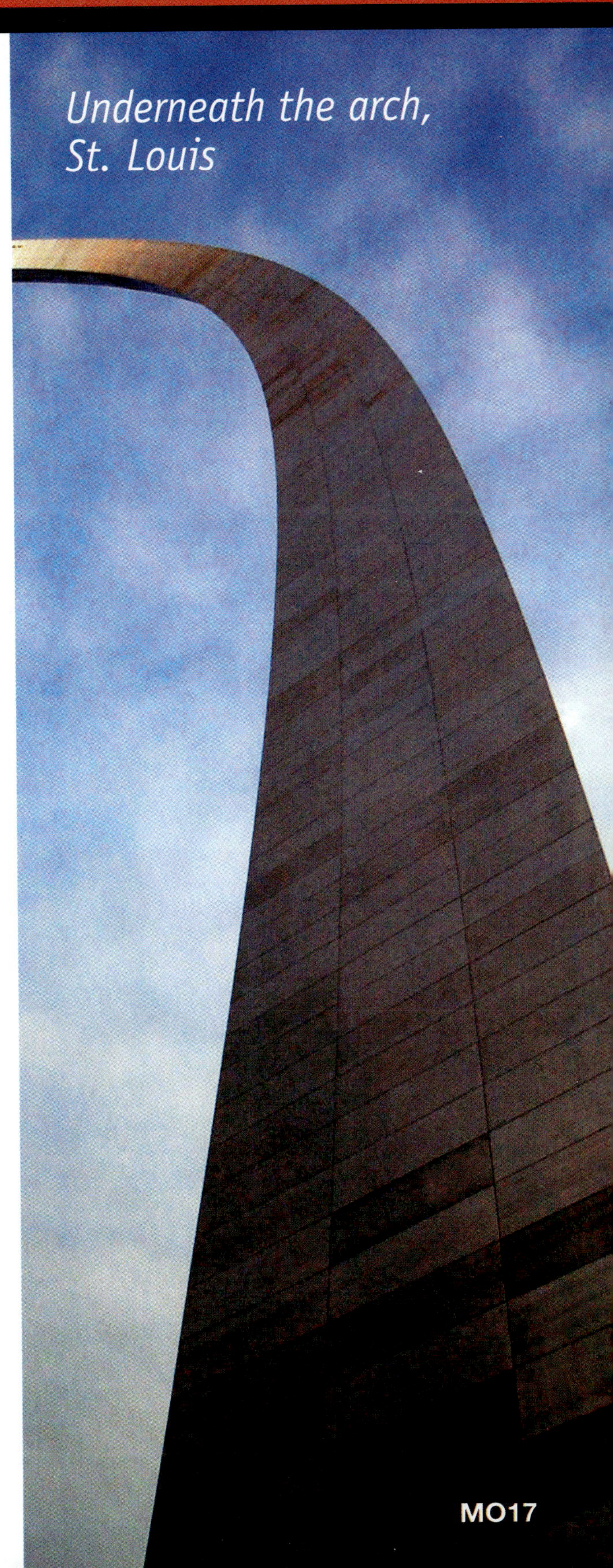

Underneath the arch, St. Louis

>9.W.1 Apply a writing processing in composing text

- **9.W.1.A Writing Process**

>9.W.1.A.1 Follow a writing process to

a use appropriate prewriting strategies as needed

b generate a draft

c revise in response to feedback (peer and/or teacher)

d edit for conventions

e share writing

What does it mean? Following a clear writing process will help you plan, write, revise, and edit papers that successfully address your topic, your audience (or readers), and your purpose. Use feedback from your classmates or teachers to make your papers even better.

EXAMPLES: Each Writing Workshop contains tips for revising a topic, considering form and audience, gathering information and self-evaluating the finished product. See "Response to Literature" (pages 734-743).

Every Writing Workshop suggests an order for prewriting, including a traditional outline format for main and supporting ideas on page 1166.

See pages 1270-1273 of the Writer's Handbook, "Designing Your Writing," for ideas on format and design. Note especially the chart "Design Elements" on page 1270.

All of the Writing Workshops contain suggestions for where and how to share, present, or publish various kinds of writing. See "Publishing" on page 999, for example.

Outlet at Alley Springs

>9.W.2 Compose well-developed text

• 9.W.2.A Audience and Purpose

>9.W.2.A.1 Compose text

a showing awareness of audience

b choosing a form and point of view appropriate to purpose and audience

What does it mean? When you write, you should always keep your audience, or readers, in mind. You should choose a form of writing (such as a letter or memo) and a perspective (how you view about the topic) that suits your purpose (your reason for wrting) and your audience.

EXAMPLES: Each writing workshop contains a section entitled "Think About Purpose and Audience" and focuses on the audience for that genre of writing. See page 735 for an example.

The Informational Text Focus "Main Idea, Audience, and Purpose" on pages 198-213 guides readers in understanding these literary elements with writing practice included.

• 9.W.2.B Ideas and Content

>9.W.2.B.1 Compose text with

a strong controlling idea

b relevant, specific details

c complex ideas

d freshness of thought

What does it mean? Your papers should have a controlling, or main, idea that is supported with details, such as examples, facts, expert opinions, and statistics. Your ideas should be complex, rather than simplistic, and new.

EXAMPLES: See "Revising to Improve Style" (pages 1268-1269) of the Writer's Handbook for many aspects of style. These pages show you what and how to revise as you re-read your first draft.

The Writing Workshop "Informative Essay" (pages 992-1001) gives details about gathering information to support a thesis and organizing writing with transition words.

The story "To Da-duh, in Memoriam," by Paule Marshall (pages 146-159), focuses on dialect as a feature of style.

Missouri
The Show Me State

Missouri Botanical Garden, St. Louis

- **9.W.2.C Organization and Sentence Structure**
  - **>9.W.2.C.1** Compose text with
    - **a** an effective beginning, middle, and end
    - **b** a logical order
    - **c** effective paragraphing
    - **d** cohesive devices
    - **e** varied sentence structure
    - **f** clarity of expression
    - **g** active voice

What does it mean? Your papers should have an introduction, a body, and a conclusion that grab your readers' attention, keep them entertained, and help them understand your point of view. Events and ideas should be expressed in an order that makes sense, and you should use transitions to connect ideas. You should include different types of sentences to keep your paper interesting, and an active, rather than passive voice.

EXAMPLES: See "Writing Effective Sentences" on pages 1294-1295 for help combining related sentences, varying sentence structure, and improving sentence style.

Grammar Links in each Writing Workshop (as found on page 1231) focus on revising sentences.

For a list of organizational patterns such as chronological, spatial, and cause and effect, see "Text Structures" (page 1261) of the Handbook of Reading and Informational Terms.

The Writer's Handbook describes effective body paragraphs and developing main ideas on pages 1264-1266. A list of transitional words and phrases appears on page 1267.

- **9.W.2.D Word Choice**
  - >**9.W.2.D.1** Compose text using
    - **a** precise and vivid language
    - **b** writing techniques, such as imagery, humor, voice, and figurative language

What does it mean? The words you choose should be precise, meaning they state exactly what you mean, and vivid, or colorful. One way to make your writing colorful is to use imagery (language that describes the scene), humor, voice (your unique way of expressing your ideas) and figurative language, such as metaphors.

EXAMPLES: The Writer's Handbook (pages 1264-1267) gives examples of vivid supporting sentences (sensory details, facts and statistics, examples, and several other kinds of evidence).

The Glossary of Usage (pages 1309-1311) in the Language Handbook lists, defines, and explains words and expressions that are standard, nonstandard, formal, or informal usage.

Grammar Links guide writers through word choice. The example on page 39 deals with powerful verbs. Page 547 focuses on active and passive voice.

• **9.W.2.E Conventions**

> **9.W.2.E.1** In written text apply

a conventions of capitalization

b conventions of punctuation

c standard usage

What does it mean? Using correct capitalization, punctuation, and grammar ensures your readers will focus on your ideas, not your mistakes.

EXAMPLES: The Language Handbook on pages 1274–1311 serves as a ready reference for all aspects of spelling, capitalization, punctuation, grammar, and sentence structure.

Grammar Links give practice in correcting sentence structure. See the example on page 457 that discusses complex sentences.

Guidelines for proofreading and proofreading marks are found in the Writer's Handbook (page 1264), as well as notes on editing sentences for content and style.

>9.W.3 Write effectively in various forms and types of writing

• **9.W.3.A Forms/Types/Modes of Writing**

> **9.W.3.A.1** Compose a variety of texts,

a using narrative, descriptive, expository, and/or persuasive features

b in various formats, including workplace communication

c including summary

d including literary analysis

e including reflective writing

What does it mean? Narrative writing tells a story; descriptive writing describes a place, event, or person; expository writing informs or explains, and persuasive writing convinces. When you use workplace communication, such as a business letter or e-mail, you should use certain conventions to ensure your writing is clear. When you write a summary, you tell another writer's main ideas. A literary analysis is an essay that explores the elements and ideas in a piece of literature. When you write reflectively, you look back and identify the significance of an experience, generally one you have had or witnessed.

EXAMPLES: Several of the Choices activities encourage creative writing in various genres. Page 547 focuses on scripting speeches from a story, and several entries encourage the writing of poetry. See page 501 for a writing prompt in response to the work of Maya Angelou.

The Writing Workshop "Persuasive Essay" on pages 598-607 takes you step-by-step through the process of writing with persuasion, including developing and supporting a position.

The Writing Workshop "Autobiographical Narrative" (pages 416-425) will help you to create a written record of an important and memorable personal experience.

Missouri meadow

>9.LS.1 Develop and apply effective listening skills and strategies

- **9.LS.1.A Purpose for Listening**

>9.LS.1.A.1 Listen

a for enjoyment

b for information

c for directions

d critically to summarize and evaluate communications that inform, persuade, and entertain

e to evaluate own and others' effectiveness in presentations and group discussions, using provided criteria

f to evaluate the validity and reliability of speaker's message

What does it mean? We listen to others for many different reasons. For example, you might listen for enjoyment to your friend telling a funny story, to learn something new, or to learn how to do something. You might also listen to tell and critique what you've heard. You might use standards provided by your teacher to help you critique your own and others' oral presentations and participation in group discussions. You might also tell how reliable and reasonable you think a speaker's ideas are.

EXAMPLES: On pages 1225-1230 you'll find tips on taking meeting notes and drafting clear and logical minutes.

The Listening and Speaking Workshop "Analyzing and Evaluating Speeches" outlines various types of persuasive arguments and gives guidelines for evaluating content (pages 1002-1005).

You can listen to many of the textbook's nonfiction and fiction selections on audio recordings.

The Listening and Speaking Workshop on pages 744-745 gives you practice in listening to poems.

- **9.LS.1.B Listening Behavior**
  - > **9.LS.1.B.1** Use active-listening behaviors (e.g., asks questions of speaker and uses body language and facial expressions to indicate agreement, disagreement or confusion)

What does it mean? When you listen actively, you ask questions about what you have heard, and you give the speaker feedback using your body language and your facial expressions.

EXAMPLE: Step-by-step guidelines in "Do-It-Yourself Interview" (pages 506-510) demonstrate the active listening and questioning techniques that are used to conduct interviews.

Old St. Louis Courthouse reflection

>9.LS.2 Develop and apply effective speaking skills and strategies for various audiences and purpose

- **9.LS.2.A Discussion and Presentation**

  >9.LS.2.A.1 In discussions and presentations,

  a create concise presentations on a variety of topics

  b incorporate appropriate media or technology

  c respond to feedback

  d defend ideas

  e demonstrate poise and self-control

What does it mean? When you speak in class discussions or when giving a presentation, be sure to stick to the topic, to wisely use media or technology to support your ideas, respond to the feedback or evaluation you get from classmates, use facts to support your ideas, and show poise, or self-confidence.

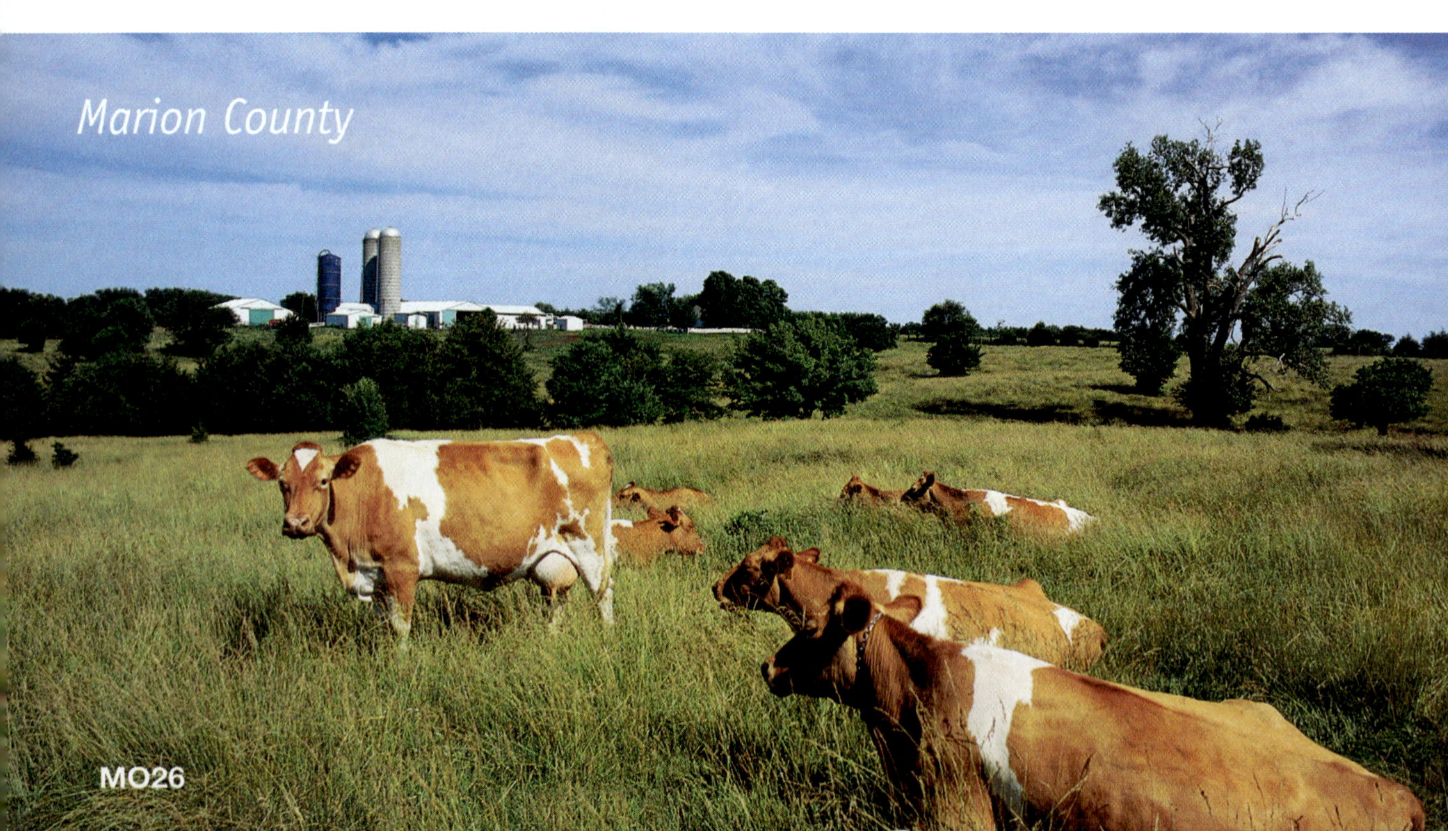

Marion County

EXAMPLES: The Listening and Speaking Workshops identify the skills used by successful speakers. See "Deliver Your Narrative" on page 427 for three key verbal techniques. "Deliver Your Speech" on page 609 includes a chart of vocal effects and also several nonverbal techniques.

All of the Literary Focus questions that follow the passages give ideas for classroom discussion. (See, for example, the questions about "The Scarlet Ibis" on page 345.)

Talk About sections also follow several texts. See page 533 for discussion questions about "An Indian's Views of Indian Affairs."

The Listening and Speaking Workshop "Debating an Issue" (pages 1234-1237) gives an outline for conducting a formal debate.

- **9.LS.2.B Giving Directions**
  - **9.LS.2.B.1** Give clear and concise multi-step oral directions to perform complex procedures and/or tasks.

What does it mean? You want to tell someone how to do a complicated task. You will be successful if you provide clear (easy-to-understand) and concise (short and to-the-point) directions.

EXAMPLES: Giving Oral Directions The Informational Text Focus on page 1213 shares guidance for logical sequencing of instruction.

"Documents for Life" discusses technical directions and following steps with diagrams and visual aids.

>9.IL.1 Develop and apply research process skills to gather, analyze and evaluate information

- **9.IL.1.A**

  >9.IL.1.A.1 Develop an appropriate research plan to guide investigation and research of focus questions

What does it mean? Write a list of questions about your topic and use them to develop a plan for how you will conduct your research.

EXAMPLES: The Writing Workshop "Research Paper" on pages 1161-1162 provides instruction on selecting a topic, considering audience and writing research questions.

The Preparing to Read on page 721 teaches how to generate research questions. A newspaper article and web page follow on pages 722-724 to give practice.

- **9.IL.1.B Acquire Information**

  >9.IL.1.B.1 Locate and use multiple primary and secondary sources to
  - ❍ select relevant and credible information
  - ❍ evaluate reliability of information
  - ❍ evaluate reliability of sources

What does it mean? As you conduct research, find primary sources, such as letters, and secondary sources, such as newspaper articles and books. Use only sources that have reliable, or trustworthy, information: ones that have a knowledgeable author, quotations from experts, and facts to support opinions.

EXAMPLES: On pages 1163-1165 the Writing Workshop "Research Paper" shows how to find and evaluate sources, prepare works cited information, and organize facts with note cards.

The Informational Text Focus on pages 1198-1203 focuses on Internet sources and using notecards.

- **9.IL.1.C Record Information**
  - **>9.IL.1.C.1** Record relevant from multiple primary and secondary sources

What does it mean? As you conduct research, you will write and organize information that supports your ideas. Use both primary and secondary sources to find this information.

EXAMPLE: See the Writing Workshop "Research Paper" on pages 1160-1173. You will be guided in taking notes, preparing source cards, developing a thesis statement, organizing information, and giving credit by means of footnotes and works cited.

The Informational Text Focus "Main Idea and Supporting Details" (page 106) shares guidelines for evaluating and organizing support from within a text.

The Informational Text Focus on pages 972-979 gives two nonfiction examples and guidance in researching and responding to literature with primary and secondary sources.

Formations in Bridal Cave

• **9.IL.1.D Sources Consulted**

> **9.IL.1.D.1** Document sources of information using a standard citation format

What does it mean? Use a Work's Cited list, or another citation format, to show your readers where you found your information. In your paper, use quotation marks, authors' last names or article titles, and page numbers to tell where specific information came from.

EXAMPLE: A Style Manual on pages 1200-1201 shows how to cite Internet sources.

> **9.IL.2 Develop and apply effective skills and strategies to analyze and evaluate oral and visual media**

• **9.IL.2.A Media Messages**

> **9.IL.2.A.1** Analyze, describe and evaluate the elements of messages projected in various media (e.g,, videos, pictures, web-sites, artwork, plays and/or news programs)

What does it mean? Different media use different techniques to convey information: pictures use color, lines, shapes; videos use images taken from different angles, along with audio; and news programs use anchor scripts along with video clips. Use what you know to study, describe, and critique the messages in different media.

EXAMPLES: The *Elements of Literature* web site provides supporting materials for the core literature in a variety of formats, including audio recordings and video segments.

Media tutorials are available on the *Elements of Literature* Internet site (go.hrw.com).

The Ozarks

Source of Big Springs near Van Buren

Black River

Kansas City Country Club Plaza

Snow covered maples, Rock Bridge State Park

James River

HOLT

Elements of LITERATURE

Third Course

How To Use Your READER/WRITER Notebook

You've been in school long enough to know that you can't write in your textbooks. But, many times, you need a place to capture your thoughts about what you are reading or write your ideas down on paper. Your *Reader/Writer Notebook* is a place where you can do just that.

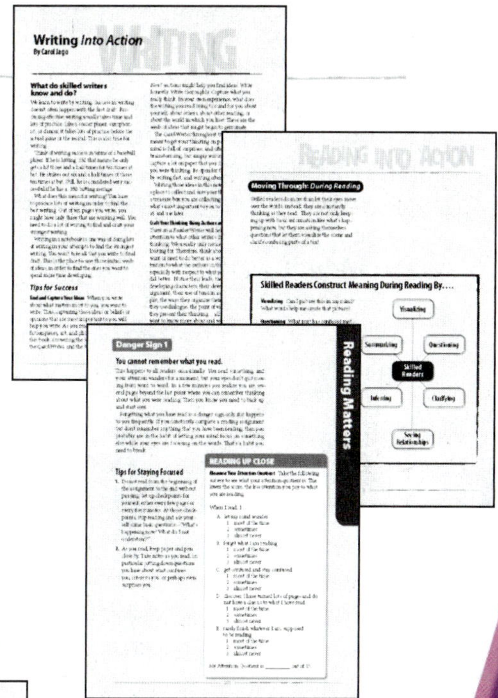
Writing *Into Action*

By Carol Jago

What do skilled writers know and do?

Tips for Success

READING INTO ACTION

Moving Through: *During Reading*

Skilled Readers Construct Meaning During Reading By....

Visualizing

Summarizing

Questioning

Skilled Readers

Inferring

Clarifying

Seeing Relationships

Danger Sign 1

You cannot remember what you read.

Tips for Staying Focused

READING UP CLOSE

Reading Matters

Want to improve your skills?

By now, you can read and write, but are you as strong as you want to be? In your *Reader/Writer Notebook*, you'll find helpful tips from real experts on how to become a better reader and writer. You can also take a survey to help you see how you think as a reader and as a writer.

Thinking like a Reader

In your notebook, you can track how much you read, what you read, and how you react to each piece. This habit helps you understand what you like or don't like to read, but more importantly, you can chart how reading changes you. Just as musicians can quickly tell you music that they enjoy playing and athletes can reaccount their victories, you can know what makes you a reader.

Your teachers probably tell you to take notes about what you are reading, but that task is easier said than done! A blank piece of paper doesn't tell you how to take notes, but your *Reader/Writer Notebook* outlines space for you to take notes on up to 30 different reading selections.

How To Use Your READER/WRITER Notebook continued

Thinking like a Writer

When you read, you are also learning how to be a writer, so your *Reader/Writer Notebook* makes space to take your writing notes within your reading notes. There is lots of space for sketching out your ideas and trying out drafts, too. You can work on the Writing Workshops and Your Turn activities from your textbook in your RWN notebook.

Finding the Right Words

You can't read or write without words. As you read, you run across new words or words that you know that are used in a new way. As you write, you try to find the best way to express what you want to say. For both of these reasons, vocabulary is an important part of being a reader/writer. Your notebook helps you increase your personal vocabulary by helping you take better notes as you read and write. It also has a handy reference list of all the word parts and academic vocabulary found in your textbook and graphic organizers to help you tackle new words.

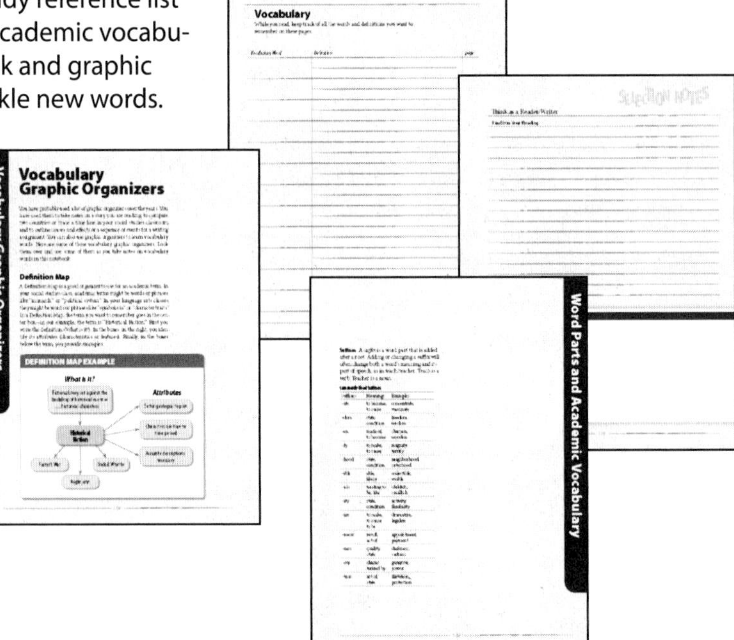

Program Authors

Kylene Beers is the senior program author for *Elements of Literature.* A former middle school teacher, she is now Senior Reading Advisor to Secondary Schools for Teachers College Reading and Writing Project at Columbia University. She is the author of *When Kids Can't Read: What Teachers Can Do* and co-editor (with Linda Rief and Robert E. Probst) of *Adolescent Literacy: Turning Promise into Practice*. The former editor of the National Council of Teachers of English (NCTE) literacy journal *Voices from the Middle*, Dr. Beers assumed the NCTE presidency in 2008. With articles in *English Journal, Journal of Adolescent and Adult Literacy, School Library Journal, Middle Matters,* and *Voices from the Middle,* she speaks both nationally and internationally as a recognized authority on struggling readers. Dr. Beers has served on the review boards of *English Journal, The ALAN Review,* the Special Interest Group on Adolescent Literature of the International Reading Association, and the Assembly on Literature for Adolescents of the NCTE. She is the 2001 recipient of the Richard W. Halley Award given by NCTE for outstanding contributions to middle school literacy.

Carol Jago is a teacher with thirty-two years of experience at Santa Monica High School in California. The author of nine books on education, she continues to share her experiences as a writer and as a speaker at conferences and seminars across the country. Her wide and varied experience in standards assessment and secondary education in general has made her a sought-after speaker. As an author, Ms. Jago also works closely with Heinemann Publishers and with the National Council of Teachers of English. Her long-time association with NCTE led to her June 2007 election to a four-year term on the council's board. During that term she will serve for one year as president of the council. She is also active with the California Association of Teachers of English (CATE) and has edited CATE's scholarly journal *California English* since 1996. Ms. Jago served on the planning committees for the 2009 NAEP Reading Framework and the 2011 NAEP Writing Framework.

Deborah Appleman is professor and chair of educational studies and director of the Summer Writing Program at Carleton College in Northfield, Minnesota. Dr. Appleman's primary research interests include adolescent response to literature, multicultural literature, and the teaching of literary theory in high school. With a team of classroom teachers, she co-edited *Braided Lives,* a multicultural literature anthology. In addition to many articles and book chapters, she is the author of

Linda Rief, Alfred Tatum, Kylene Beers, Patrick Schwarz, and Carol Jago

PROGRAM AUTHORS continued

Critical Encounters in High School English: Teaching Literary Theory to Adolescents and co-author of *Teaching Literature to Adolescents*. Her most recent book, *Reading for Themselves,* explores the use of extracurricular book clubs to encourage adolescents to read for pleasure. Dr. Appleman was a high school English teacher, working in both urban and suburban schools. She is a frequent national speaker and consultant and continues to work weekly in high schools with students and teachers.

Leila Christenbury is a former high school English teacher and is currently professor of English education at Virginia Commonwealth University, Richmond. The former editor of *English Journal,* she is the author of ten books, including *Writing on Demand, Making the Journey,* and *Retracing the Journey: Teaching and Learning in an American High School.* Past president of the National Council of Teachers of English, Dr. Christenbury is also a former member of the steering committee of the National Assessment of Educational Progress (NAEP). A recipient of the Rewey Belle Inglis Award for Outstanding Woman in English Teaching, Dr. Christenbury is a frequent speaker on issues of English teaching and learning and has been interviewed and quoted on CNN and in the *New York Times, USA Today, Washington Post, Chicago Tribune,* and *U.S. News & World Report*.

Leila Christenbury, Héctor Rivera, Sara Kajder, Eric Cooper, and Deborah Appleman

Sara Kajder, author of *Bringing the Outside In: Visual Ways to Engage Reluctant Readers* and *The Tech-Savvy English Classroom,* is an assistant professor at Virginia Polytechnic Institute and State University (Virginia Tech). She has served as co-chair of NCTE's Conference on English Education (CEE) Technology Commission and of the Society for Information Technology and Teacher Education (SITE) English Education Committee. Dr. Kajder is the recipient of the first SITE National Technology Leadership Fellowship in English Education; she is a former English and language arts teacher for high school and middle school.

Linda Rief has been a classroom teacher for twenty-five years. She is author of *The Writer's-Reader's Notebook, Inside the Writer's-Reader's Notebook, Seeking Diversity, 100 Quickwrites,* and *Vision and Voice* as well as the co-author (with Kylene Beers and Robert E. Probst) of *Adolescent Literacy: Turning Promise into Practice*. Ms. Rief has written numerous chapters and journal articles, and she co-edited the first five years of *Voices from the Middle*. During the summer she teaches graduate courses at the University of New Hampshire and Northeastern University. She is a national and international consultant on adolescent literacy issues.

Program Consultants

Isabel L. Beck is professor of education and senior scientist at the University of Pittsburgh. Dr. Beck has conducted extensive research on vocabulary and comprehension and has published well over one hundred articles and several books, including *Improving Comprehension with Questioning the Author* (with Margaret McKeown) and *Bringing Words to Life: Robust Vocabulary Instruction* (with Margaret McKeown and Linda Kucan). Dr. Beck's numerous national awards include the Oscar S. Causey Award for outstanding research from the National Reading Conference and the William S. Gray Award from the International Reading Association for lifetime contributions to the field of reading research and practice.

Margaret G. McKeown is a senior scientist at the University of Pittsburgh's Learning Research and Development Center. Her research in reading comprehension and vocabulary has been published extensively in outlets for both research and practitioner audiences. Recognition of her work includes the International Reading Association's (IRA) Dissertation of the Year Award and a National Academy of Education Spencer Fellowship. Before her career in research, Dr. McKeown taught elementary school.

Amy Benjamin is a veteran teacher, literacy coach, consultant, and researcher in secondary-level literacy instruction. She has been recognized for excellence in teaching from the New York State English Council, Union College, and Tufts University. Ms. Benjamin is the author of several books about reading comprehension, writing instruction, grammar, and differentiation. Her most recent book (with Tom Oliva) is *Engaging Grammar: Practical Advice for Real Classrooms,* published by the National Council of Teachers of English. Ms. Benjamin has had a long association and leadership role with the NCTE's Assembly for the Teaching of English Grammar (ATEG).

Eric Cooper is the president of the National Urban Alliance for Effective Education (NUA) and co-founder of the Urban Partnership for Literacy with the IRA. He currently works with the NCTE to support improvements in urban education and collaborates with the Council of the Great City Schools. In line with his educational mission to support the improvement of education for urban and minority students, Dr. Cooper writes, lectures, and produces educational documentaries and talk shows to provide advocacy for children who live in disadvantaged circumstances.

Mabel Rivera, Harvey Daniels, Margaret McKeown, and Isabel Beck

Harvey Daniels is a former college professor and classroom teacher, working in urban and suburban Chicago schools. Known for his pioneering work on student book clubs, Dr. Daniels is author and co-author of many books, including *Literature Circles: Voice and Choice in Book Clubs and Reading Groups* and *Best Practice: Today's Standards for Teaching and Learning in America's Schools.*

Ben Garcia is associate director of education at the Skirball Cultural Center in Los Angeles, California, where he oversees school programs and teacher professional development. He is a board member of the Museum Educators of Southern California and presents regularly at conferences in the area of visual arts integration across curricula. Prior to the Skirball, he worked with classroom teachers for six years in the Art and Language Arts program at the J. Paul Getty Museum. Recent publications include *Art and Science: A Curriculum for K-12 Teachers* and *Neoclassicism and the Enlightenment: A Curriculum for Middle and High School Teachers.*

PROGRAM CONSULTANTS continued

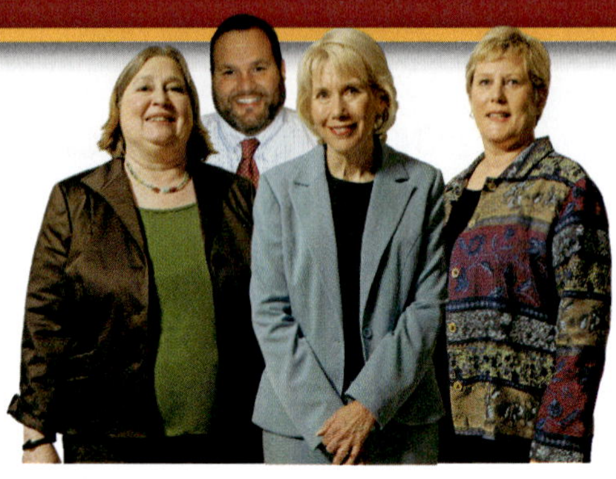

Amy Benjamin, Ben Garcia, Robin Scarcella, and Judith Irvin

Judith L. Irvin taught middle school for several years before entering her career as a university professor. She now teaches courses in curriculum and instructional leadership and literacy at Florida State University. Dr. Irvin's many publications include *Reading and the High School Student: Strategies to Enhance Literacy* and *Integrating Literacy and Learning in the Content Area Classroom*. Her latest book, *Taking Action: A Leadership Model for Improving Adolescent Literacy*, is the result of a Carnegie-funded project and is published by the Association for Supervision and Curriculum Development.

Victoria Ramirez is the interim education director at the Museum of Fine Arts, Houston, Texas, where she plans and implements programs, resources, and publications for teachers and serves as liaison to local school districts and teacher organizations. She also chairs the Texas Art Education Association's museum division. Dr. Ramirez earned a doctoral degree in curriculum and instruction from the College of Education at the University of Houston and an M.A.T. in museum education from George Washington University. A former art history instructor at Houston Community College, Dr. Ramirez currently teaches education courses at the University of Houston.

Héctor H. Rivera is an assistant professor at Southern Methodist University, School of Education and Human Development. Dr. Rivera is also the director of the SMU Professional Development/ESL Supplemental Certification Program for Math and Science Teachers of At-Risk Middle and High School LEP Newcomer Adolescents. This federally funded program develops, delivers, and evaluates professional development for educators who work with at-risk newcomer adolescent students. Dr. Rivera is also collaborating on school reform projects in Guatemala and with the Institute of Arctic Education in Greenland.

Mabel Rivera is a research assistant professor at the Texas Institute for Measurement, Evaluation, and Statistics at the University of Houston. Her current research interests include the education of and prevention of reading difficulties in English-language learners. In addition, Dr. Rivera is involved in local and national service activities for preparing school personnel to teach students with special needs.

Robin Scarcella is a professor at the University of California at Irvine, where she also directs the Program in Academic English/English as a Second Language. She has a Ph.D. in linguistics from the University of Southern California and an M.A. degree in education–second language acquisition from Stanford University. She has taught all grade levels. She has been active in shaping policies affecting language assessment, instruction, and teacher professional development. In the last four years, she has spoken to over ten thousand teachers and administrators. She has written over thirty scholarly articles that appear in such journals as the *TESOL Quarterly* and *Brain and Language*. Her most recent publication is *Accelerating Academic English: A Focus on the English Learner*.

Patrick Schwarz is professor of special education and chair of the Diversity in Learning and Development Department for National-Louis University, Chicago, Illinois. He is author of *From Disability to Possibility* and *You're Welcome* (co-written with Paula Kluth), texts that have inspired teachers worldwide to reconceptualize inclusion to help all children. Other books co-written with Paula

Kluth include *Just Give Him the Whale* and *Inclusion Bootcamp*. Dr. Schwarz also presents and consults worldwide through Creative Culture Consulting.

Alfred W. Tatum is an associate professor in the Department of Curriculum and Instruction at the University of Illinois at Chicago (UIC), where he earned his Ph.D. He also serves as the director of the UIC Reading Clinic. He began his career as an eighth-grade teacher, later becoming a reading specialist. Dr. Tatum has written more than twenty-five articles, chapters, and monographs and is the author of *Teaching Reading to Black Adolescent Males: Closing the Achievement Gap*. His work focuses on the literacy development of African American adolescent males, particularly the impact of texts on their lives.

UNIT INTRODUCTION WRITERS ON WRITING

UNIT 1 SHORT STORIES

Joyce Carol Oates

"If you read carefully, return to the beginning and read again, you may be inspired to invent your own stories. For no one else can tell your stories, except you."

UNIT 2 NONFICTION

Andrew Lam

"The writer's voice [in nonfiction], when honest and frank, provides an emotional intimacy with the reader no other genre can."

UNIT 3 POETRY

Judith Ortiz Cofer

"The poem is a territory that is open to all; no passports are necessary."

UNIT 4 DRAMA

Anna Deavere Smith

"Regardless of the gifts of the artist, the greatest gift given to the drama maker is the audience."

UNIT 5 EPIC

Ian Johnston

"I first started reading epic poems because I loved the grand adventures of brave heroes in wild and often magical places."

UNIT 6 CONSUMER & WORKPLACE DOCUMENTS

Carol Jago

"Writing that letter helped us feel a lot better. Setting out our complaint on paper . . . allowed us to begin to laugh about it all."

Critical Reviewers

Noreen L. Abdullah
Chicago Public Schools
Chicago, Illinois

Martha Armenti
Baltimore City College High School
Baltimore, Maryland

Jessica J. Asmis-Carvajal
Coronado High School
El Paso, Texas

Susan Beechum
Apopka High School
Apopka, Florida

Nilda Benavides
Del Rio High School
Del Rio, Texas

Melissa Bowell
Ft. Walton Beach High School
Ft. Walton Beach, Florida

Stacey Chisolm
Meridian High School
Meridian, Mississippi

Vincent Contorno
L. C. Anderson High School
Austin, Texas

Rita Curington
Athens High School
Athens, Texas

Melinda Fulton
Leon High School
Tallahassee, Florida

Holly Hillgardner
South Bronx Preparatory
New York, New York

Anna Yoccabel Horton
Highland Middle School
Gilbert, Arizona

Elizabeth Ignatius
Paul R. Wharton High School
Tampa, Florida

Tim King
Mason High School
Mason, Ohio

Barbara Kimbrough
Kane Area High School
Kane, Pennsylvania

Jennifer Moore Krievs
Midlothian High School
Midlothian, Virginia

Lynn V. Mason
Newark High School
Newark, Ohio

Vivian Nida
University of Oklahoma
Norman, Oklahoma

John Kevin M. Perez
Hampton Bays Secondary High School
Hampton Bays, New York

Judd Pfeiffer
Bowie High School
Austin, Texas

Aimee Riordan
Sun Valley High School
Monroe, North Carolina

Celia Rocca
Western High School
Baltimore, Maryland

Kelly L. Self
Alexandria Senior High School
Alexandria, Louisiana

Kelly Southern
Ouachita Parish High School
Monroe, Louisiana

Jody Steinke
Quincy Senior High School
Quincy, Illinois

Kelly Swifney
Zeeland West High School
Zeeland, Michigan

Nichole Wilson
Mason High School
Mason, Ohio

Dr. Bernard Zaidman
Greenville Senior High School Academy of Academic Excellence
Greenville, South Carolina

FIELD-TEST PARTICIPANTS

Linda Brescia
HS for Health Professions and Human Services
New York, New York

Katherine Burke
Timber Creek High School
Orlando, Florida

Greg Cantwell
Sheldon High School
Eugene, Oregon

Cheryl Casbeer
Del Rio High School
Del Rio, Texas

Ms. Linda Chapman
Colonel White High School
Dayton, Ohio

Kim Christiernsson
Durango High School
Las Vegas, Nevada

Amanda Cobb
Timber Creek High School
Orlando, Florida

Marylea Erhart-Mack
University High School
Orlando, Florida

Yolanda Fernandez
Del Rio High School
Del Rio, Texas

Angela Ferreira
Hoover High School
San Diego, California

Dan Franke
Lemont High School
Lemont, Illinois

Ellen Geisler
Mentor High School
Mentor, Ohio

Luanne Greenberg
Coronado High School
El Paso, Texas

Colleen Hadley
Abilene High School
Abilene, Texas

Leslie Hardiman
Hoover High School
San Diego, California

Sandra Henderson
Lemont High School
Lemont, Illinois

Lee Ann Hoffman
Southeast High School
Bradenton, Florida

Jennifer Houston
Timber Creek High School
Orlando, Florida

Eva M. Lazear
Springfield North High School
Springfield, Ohio

Phil Lazzari
Lemont High School
Lemont, Illinois

Jacquelyn McLane
Cypress Creek High School
Orlando, Florida

Kathleen Mims
H. Grady Spruce High School
Dallas, Texas

Julie Moore
Monroe High School
Monroe, Wisconsin

Denise Morris
Rich Central High School
Olympia Fields, Illinois

Bunny Petty
Florence High School
Florence, Texas

Valerie Pfeffer
Durango High School
Las Vegas, Nevada

Bernadette Poulos
Reavis High School
Burbank, Illinois

Ann L. Rodgers
Currituck County High School
Barco, North Carolina

Narima Shahabudeen
East Orange Campus 9
East Orange, New Jersey

Shari Simonds
Valley High School
Las Vegas, Nevada

Gail Tuelon
University High School
Orlando, Florida

Mandy Unruh
Brownsburg High School
Brownsburg, Indiana

Vanessa Vega
Irving High School
Irvin, Texas

Elizabeth Weaver
Cypress Creek High School
Orlando, Florida

Tamera West
McQueen High School
Reno, Nevada

Erica White
Sherando High School
Stephens City, Virginia

Contents in Brief

Missouri Communication Arts Course Level Expectations for each collection can be found in the full Table of Contents on pages A4, A6, A8, A10, A12, A14, A16, A20, A22, and A24.

UNIT 3 Poetry

UNIT 4 Drama

UNIT 5 Epic

UNIT 6 Consumer and Workplace Documents

RESOURCE CENTER

UNIT 1

Short Stories

COLLECTION 1 Plot and Setting

"All the best stories in the world are but one story in reality—the story of escape."
—**A. C. Benson**

What Do You Think? Why are stories of escape so interesting and timeless?

Missouri Communication Arts Course Level Expectations

Reading 9.R.1.C.1; 9.R.1.E.1.a; 9.R.1.E.1.b; 9.R.1.E.1.c; 9.R.1.F.1.a; 9.R.1.F.1.c; 9.R.1.F.1.d; 9.R.1.G.1.a; 9.R.1.G.1.e; 9.R.1.H.1.a; 9.R.2.C.1.b; 9.R.3.C.1.a;

Writing 9.W.1.A.1.a; 9.W.1.A.1.b; 9.W.2.B.1.b; 9.W.2.D.1.a; 9.W.2.E.1.c; 9.W.3.A.1.a; 9.W.3.A.1.b; 9.W.3.A.1.d; 9.W.3.A.1.e

Comparing Texts

Informational Text Focus

Focus on English II Course Level Expectations

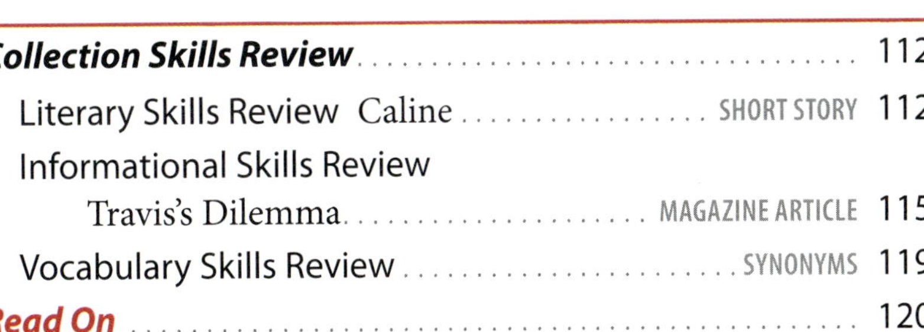

UNIT 1

Short Stories

COLLECTION 2 Character

"I am the person I know best." —**Frida Kahlo**

What Do You Think? How do other people affect the way we think about ourselves?

Missouri Communication Arts Course Level Expectations

Reading 9.R.1.C.1; 9.R.1.E.1.a; 9.R.1.E.1.b; 9.R.1.E.1.c; 9.R.1.F.1.a; 9.R.1.F.1.d; 9.R.1.G.1.a; 9.R.1.G.1.d; 9.R.1.H.1.a; 9.R.1.I.1.a; 9.R.1.I.1.b; 9.R.2.C.1.a; 9.R.2.C.1.b; 9.R.2.C.1.d;

Writing 9.W.2.A.1.b; 9.W.2.D.1.a; 9.W.2.D.1.b; 9.W.2.E.1.c; 9.W.3.A.1.a; 9.W.3.A.1.d; 9.W.3.A.1.e

Literary Selections

Comparing Texts

Informational Text Focus

Focus on English II Course Level Expectations 

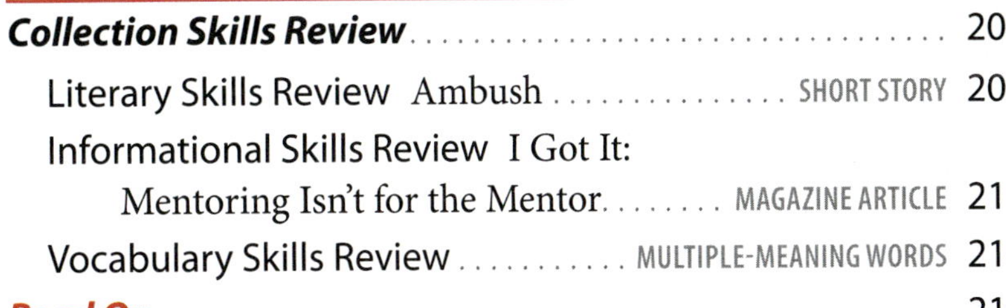

UNIT 1

Short Stories

COLLECTION 3 Narrator and Voice

"Only enemies speak the truth. Friends lie endlessly, caught in the web of duty." —**Stephen King**

What Do You Think? Who are our friends, and who are our enemies? How can we tell the difference?

Missouri Communication Arts Course Level Expectations

Reading 9.R.1.C.1; 9.R.1.E.1.b; 9.R.1.E.1.c; 9.R.1.F.1.d; 9.R.1.G.1.a; 9.R.1.G.1.c; 9.R.1.H.1.a; 9.R.1.H.1.b; 9.R.1.H.1.c; 9.R.1.H.1.d; 9.R.1.I.1.a; 9.R.1.I.1.b; 9.R.1.I.1.c; 9.R.2.B.2.a; 9.R.2.B.2.b; 9.R.2.C.1.a; 9.R.2.C.1.b; 9.R.2.C.1.d; 9.R.3.A.1; 9.R.3.B.1.b; 9.R.3.C.1.c; 9.R.3.C.1.d;

Writing 9.W.2.D.1.b; 9.W.2.E.1.c; 9.W.3.A.1.a; 9.W.3.A.1.b; 9.W.3.A.1.d; 9.W.3.A.1.e

Comparing Texts

Informational Text Focus

UNIT 1

Short Stories

COLLECTION 4 Symbolism and Irony

"When you cannot make up your mind which of two evenly balanced courses of action you should take—choose the bolder."

—**Ezra Pound**

What Do You Think? How do we make hard choices?

Missouri Communication Arts Course Level Expectations

Reading 9.R.1.D.1.a; 9.R.1.E.1.c; 9.R.1.F.1.a; 9.R.1.F.1.c; 9.R.1.F.1.d; 9.R.1.G.1.a; 9.R.1.G.1.b; 9.R.1.G.1.c; 9.R.1.H.1.a; 9.R.1.H.1.b; 9.R.1.H.1.e; 9.R.2.A.1; 9.R.2.B.2.a; 9.R.2.B.2.b; 9.R.2.B.2.c; 9.R.2.B.2.d; 9.R.2.C.1.a; 9.R.2.C.1.b; 9.R.2.C.1.c; 9.R.2.C.1.d; 9.R.3.B.1.a; 9.R.3.B.1.b; 9.R.3.B.1.c; 9.R.3.C.1.a;

Writing 9.W.1.A.1.a; 9.W.1.A.1.b; 9.W.1.A.1.c; 9.W.1.A.1.d; 9.W.1.A.1.e; 9.W.2.A.1.a; 9.W.2.A.1.b; 9.W.2.B.1.d; 9.W.2.C.1.a; 9.W.2.C.1.b; 9.W.2.C.1.c; 9.W.2.C.1.d; 9.W.2.C.1.e; 9.W.2.C.1.f; 9.W.2.C.1.g; 9.W.2.D.1.b; 9.W.2.E.1.a; 9.W.2.E.1.b; 9.W.2.E.1.c; 9.W.3.A.1.a; 9.W.3.A.1.d; 9.W.3.A.1.e

Literary Selections

UNIT 2

Nonfiction

COLLECTION 5 Form and Style

"Memories of our lives, of our works and our deeds will continue in others."
—**Rosa Parks**

What Do You Think? What do you have to say to the world?

Missouri Communication Arts Course Level Expectations

Reading 9.R.1.C.1; 9.R.1.E.1.b; 9.R.1.E.1.c; 9.R.1.F.1.d; 9.R.1.G.1.a; 9.R.1.G.1.e; 9.R.1.G.1.f; 9.R.1.H.1.a; 9.R.1.H.1.c; 9.R.1.H.1.d; 9.R.1.I.1.c; 9.R.2.B.2.b; 9.R.2.B.2.c; 9.R.2.C.1.a; 9.R.2.C.1.b; 9.R.2.C.1.c; 9.R.2.C.1.d; 9.R.3.A.1; 9.R.3.B.1.b; 9.R.3.C.1.a;

Writing 9.W.1.A.1.b; 9.W.2.A.1.b; 9.W.2.C.1.b; 9.W.2.D.1.b; 9.W.2.E.1.b; 9.W.2.E.1.c; 9.W.3.A.1.a; 9.W.3.A.1.d; 9.W.3.A.1.e

UNIT 2

Nonfiction

COLLECTION 6 Persuasion

"First we have to believe, and then we believe." —**Martha Graham**

What Do You Think? What do you believe in, and why?

Missouri Communication Arts Course Level Expectations

Reading 9.R.1.D.1.a; 9.R.1.E.1.c; 9.R.1.F.1.a; 9.R.1.F.1.d; 9.R.1.G.1.a; 9.R.1.G.1.c; 9.R.1.G.1.g; 9.R.1.H.1.a; 9.R.1.H.1.b; 9.R.1.H.1.d; 9.R.1.H.1.f; 9.R.2.B.2.c; 9.R.2.C.1.d; 9.R.3.C.1.a; 9.R.3.C.1.c; 9.R.3.C.1.d; 9.R.3.C.1.e;

Writing 9.W.1.A.1.a; 9.W.1.A.1.b; 9.W.1.A.1.c; 9.W.1.A.1.d; 9.W.1.A.1.e; 9.W.2.A.1.a; 9.W.2.A.1.b; 9.W.2.B.1.a; 9.W.2.B.1.b; 9.W.2.C.1.a; 9.W.2.C.1.b; 9.W.2.C.1.c; 9.W.2.C.1.d; 9.W.2.C.1.e; 9.W.2.C.1.f; 9.W.2.C.1.g; 9.W.2.E.1.a; 9.W.2.E.1.b; 9.W.2.E.1.c; 9.W.3.A.1.a; 9.W.3.A.1.b

Literary Selections

Comparing Texts

Informational Text Focus

Focus on English II Course Level Expectations MO

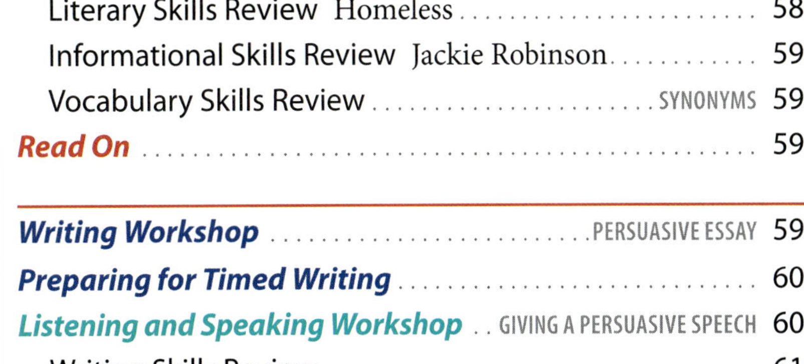

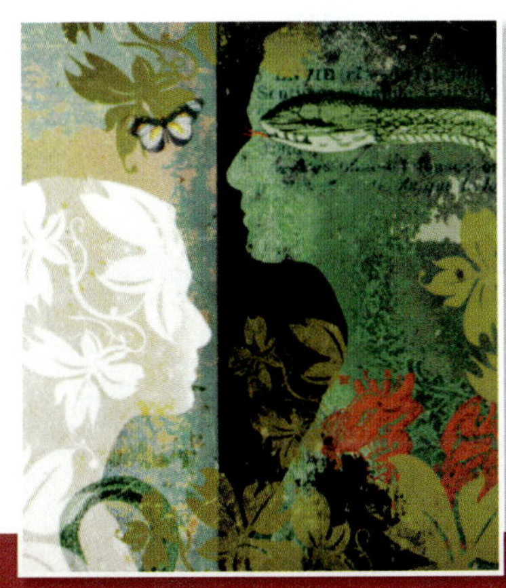

UNIT 3

Poetry

COLLECTION 7 Poetry

"The man who has no imagination has no wings." —**Muhammad Ali**

What Do You Think? What are the limits of the imagination?

Missouri Communication Arts Course Level Expectations

Reading 9.R.1.C.1; 9.R.1.D.1.a; 9.R.1.E.1.b; 9.R.1.E.1.c; 9.R.1.F.1.d; 9.R.1.G.1.a; 9.R.1.G.1.b; 9.R.1.G.1.c; 9.R.1.G.1.e; 9.R.1.G.1.f; 9.R.1.H.1.a; 9.R.1.I.1.a; 9.R.1.I.1.c; 9.R.2; 9.R.2.A.1; 9.R.2.B.2.a; 9.R.2.B.2.b; 9.R.2.B.2.c; 9.R.2.B.2.d; 9.R.2.C.1.a; 9.R.2.C.1.b; 9.R.2.C.1.c; 9.R.2.C.1.d; 9.R.3.B.1.a; 9.R.3.B.1.b; 9.R.3.B.1.c; 9.R.3.C.1.b;

Writing 9.W.1.A.1.a; 9.W.1.A.1.b; 9.W.1.A.1.c; 9.W.1.A.1.d; 9.W.1.A.1.e; 9.W.2.A.1.a; 9.W.2.A.1.b; 9.W.2.B.1.a; 9.W.2.C.1.a; 9.W.2.C.1.b; 9.W.2.C.1.c; 9.W.2.C.1.d; 9.W.2.C.1.e; 9.W.2.C.1.f; 9.W.2.C.1.g; 9.W.2.D.1.a; 9.W.2.E.1.a; 9.W.2.E.1.b; 9.W.2.E.1.c; 9.W.3.A.1.a; 9.W.3.A.1.d; 9.W.3.A.1.e

Literary Selections

UNIT 3

Poetry CONTINUED

Informational Text Focus

UNIT 4

Drama

COLLECTION 8 Drama

"Love the actor, for he gives you his heart." —**Bela Lugosi**

What Do You Think? In what way are both comedies and tragedies about love?

Missouri Communication Arts Course Level Expectations

Reading 9.R.1.C.1; 9.R.1.D.1.a; 9.R.1.E.1.a; 9.R.1.E.1.b; 9.R.1.E.1.c; 9.R.1.F.1.c; 9.R.1.F.1.d; 9.R.1.G.1.a; 9.R.1.G.1.d; 9.R.1.G.1.e; 9.R.1.G.1.f; 9.R.1.H.1.a; 9.R.1.H.1.f; 9.R.1.I.1.a; 9.R.2; 9.R.2.A.1; 9.R.2.C.1.a; 9.R.2.C.1.b; 9.R.2.C.1.c; 9.R.2.C.1.d; 9.R.3.B.1.a; 9.R.3.C.1.a; 9.R.3.C.1.c; 9.R.3.D.1; Writing 9.W.1.A.1.a; 9.W.1.A.1.b; 9.W.1.A.1.c; 9.W.1.A.1.d; 9.W.1.A.1.e; 9.W.2.A.1.a; 9.W.2.A.1.b; 9.W.2.B.1.a; 9.W.2.B.1.b; 9.W.2.B.1.c; 9.W.2.C.1.a; 9.W.2.C.1.b; 9.W.2.C.1.c; 9.W.2.C.1.d; 9.W.2.C.1.e; 9.W.2.C.1.f; 9.W.2.C.1.g; 9.W.2.E.1.a; 9.W.2.E.1.b; 9.W.2.E.1.c; 9.W.3.A.1.a; 9.W.3.A.1.c; 9.W.3.A.1.d

Literary Selections

UNIT 5

Epic

COLLECTION 9 Epic and Myth

"It is good to have an end to journey toward, but it is the journey that matters in the end." —**Ursula K. Le Guin**

What Do You Think? In what ways can life be thought of as a journey?

Missouri Communication Arts Course Level Expectations

Reading 9.R.1.C.1; 9.R.1.D.1.a; 9.R.1.E.1.a; 9.R.1.E.1.b; 9.R.1.E.1.c; 9.R.1.F.1.d; 9.R.1.G.1.a; 9.R.1.G.1.f; 9.R.1.G.1.g; 9.R.1.H.1.a; 9.R.1.H.1.b; 9.R.1.H.1.d; 9.R.1.H.1.f; 9.R.1.I.1.a; 9.R.1.I.1.b; 9.R.2; 9.R.2.A.1; 9.R.2.B.2.b; 9.R.2.B.2.d; 9.R.2.C.1.a; 9.R.2.C.1.b; 9.R.2.C.1.c; 9.R.2.C.1.d; 9.R.3.B.1.a; 9.R.3.B.1.c; 9.R.3.C.1.a;

Writing 9.W.1.A.1.a; 9.W.1.A.1.b; 9.W.1.A.1.c; 9.W.1.A.1.d; 9.W.1.A.1.e; 9.W.2.A.1.a; 9.W.2.A.1.b; 9.W.2.B.1.a; 9.W.2.B.1.b; 9.W.2.C.1.a; 9.W.2.C.1.b; 9.W.2.C.1.c; 9.W.2.C.1.d; 9.W.2.C.1.e; 9.W.2.C.1.f; 9.W.2.C.1.g; 9.W.2.E.1.a; 9.W.2.E.1.b; 9.W.2.E.1.c; 9.W.3.A.1.a; 9.W.3.A.1.d; 9.W.3.A.1.e

Comparing Texts

Informational Text Focus

UNIT 6

Consumer and Workplace Documents

COLLECTION 10 Reading for Life

"Ninety percent of leadership is the ability to communicate something people want." —**Dianne Feinstein**

What Do You Think? What does it take to succeed in the world?

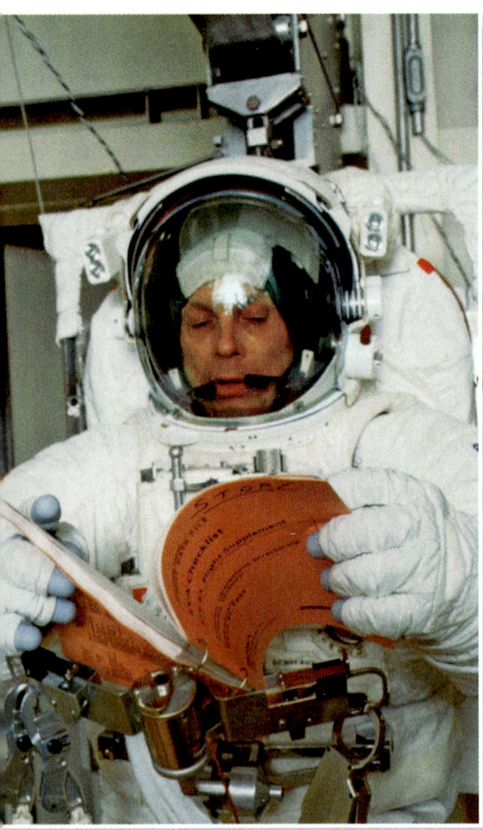

Missouri Communication Arts Course Level Expectations

Reading 9.R.1.C.1; 9.R.1.D.1.a; 9.R.1.D.1.b; 9.R.1.E.1.b; 9.R.1.E.1.c; 9.R.1.F.1.b; 9.R.1.F.1.d; 9.R.1.G.1.a; 9.R.1.G.1.b; 9.R.1.G.1.c; 9.R.1.H.1.b; 9.R.3.A.1; 9.R.3.C.1.c; 9.R.3.D.1

Writing 9.W.1.A.1.a; 9.W.1.A.1.b; 9.W.1.A.1.c; 9.W.1.A.1.d; 9.W.1.A.1.e; 9.W.2.A.1.a; 9.W.2.A.1.b; 9.W.2.C.1.a; 9.W.2.C.1.b; 9.W.2.C.1.c; 9.W.2.C.1.d; 9.W.2.C.1.e; 9.W.2.C.1.f; 9.W.2.C.1.g; 9.W.2.D.1.a; 9.W.2.E.1.a; 9.W.2.E.1.b; 9.W.2.E.1.c; 9.W.3.A.1.a; 9.W.3.A.1.b

Informational Text Focus

Focus on English II Course Level Expectations 

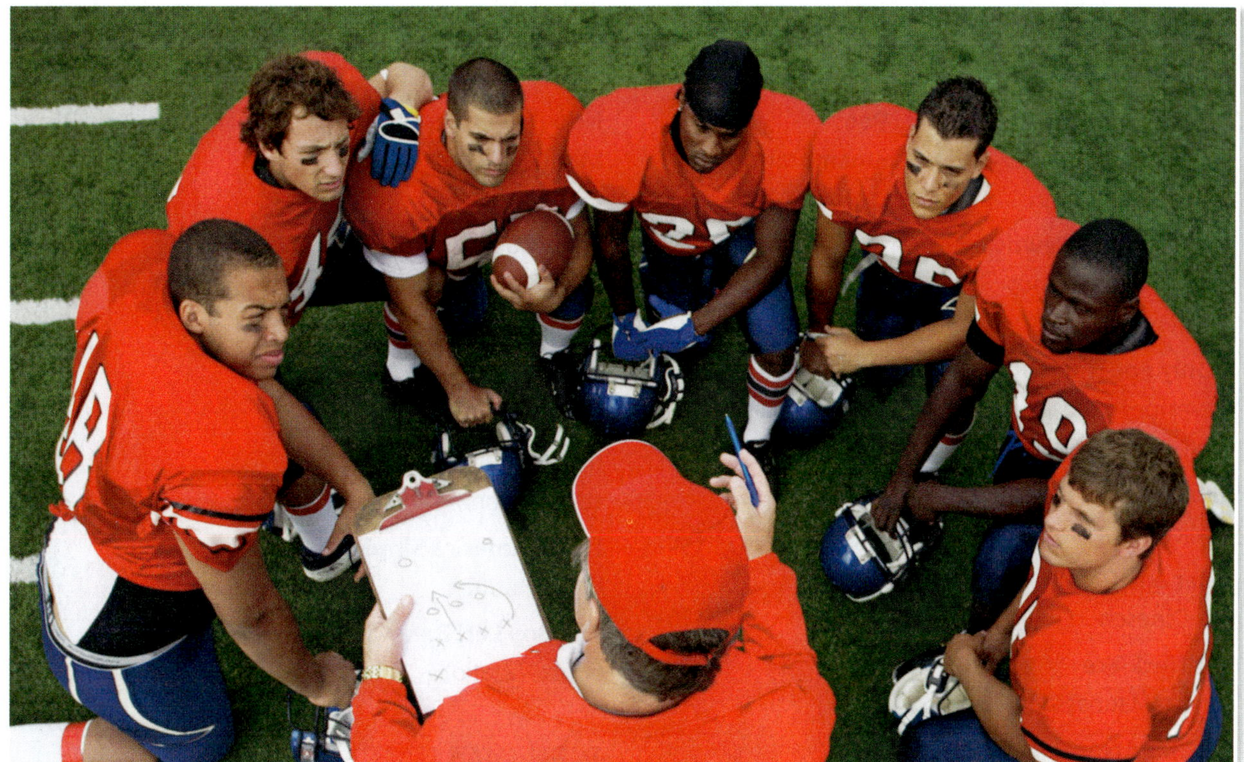

RESOURCE CENTER

Selections by Alternative Themes

Selections are listed here in alternative theme groupings.

APPEARANCE VS. REALITY

HOPES AND DREAMS

THE HUMAN SPIRIT

IDEALS AND VALUES

SELECTIONS BY ALTERNATIVE THEMES continued

IDENTITY

INNOCENCE AND EXPERIENCE

JOURNEYS

LOYALTY AND BETRAYAL

NATURE

PASSAGES

SELECTIONS BY ALTERNATIVE THEMES continued

FAMILY TIES

WAR AND PEACE

Skills, Workshops, and Features

SKILLS

LITERARY FOCUS ESSAYS BY CAROL JAGO

INFORMATIONAL TEXT FOCUS ESSAY BY CAROL JAGO

READING FOCUS ESSAYS BY KYLENE BEERS

LITERARY SKILLS

SKILLS, WORKSHOPS, AND FEATURES continued

READING SKILLS FOR LITERARY TEXTS

READING SKILLS FOR INFORMATIONAL TEXTS

INFORMATIONAL TEXT SKILLS

ACADEMIC VOCABULARY

LANGUAGE COACH

VOCABULARY DEVELOPMENT

WORKSHOPS

WRITING WORKSHOPS

PREPARING FOR TIMED WRITING

LISTENING AND SPEAKING WORKSHOPS

FEATURES

ANALYZING VISUALS

CROSS-CURRICULAR LINKS

LITERARY PERSPECTIVES

GRAMMAR LINKS

SKILLS REVIEW

LANGUAGE HANDBOOK

WRITER'S HANDBOOK

Why Be a Reader/Writer?

by **Kylene Beers**

Family Photos

When my son Baker was about five years old, he decided his dad and I weren't his parents. (In fact, he even seemed pretty hopeful about this—as in, "Perhaps these people really aren't my parents!") He shared this news with his ten-year-old sister, Meredith, who, using our family photo albums, set about explaining to him why he was wrong. Since his and her baby photos looked exactly alike, she reasoned with him, they had to be brother and sister. Using this evidence, however, Baker decided that Meredith was adopted, too.

Meredith had shown Baker some important family photos, but he hadn't seen them all. He had an incomplete image of himself. If I hadn't talked with him and shown him more pictures, his belief that he was adopted would have shaped how he thought about himself, his family, and his place in the world.

Capture A MOMENT

As you've moved through life, your mind has created a kind of **reading/writing photo album**—a collection of different views or pictures of your reading and writing experiences. Those pictures shape how you think and feel about reading and writing.

Some of the pictures in that album are like **school photos**—showing you how important skillful reading and effective writing are to success in school. If you had only these "school photo" images, you might think that the only reason to read and write is to make good grades and pass tests.

Other pictures you have in your reading/writing photo album are **personal, informal images** of friends and family. They've captured the times when you've used reading and writing to interact with others—through text messages, e-mails, letters, and even notes passed in the hall. These images show you that there's more to reading and writing than good grades.

Your reading/writing photo album would be incomplete if it didn't have some **pictures of you.** Through reading and writing, you have explored your own thoughts and feelings. The more you know about yourself, the sharper your self-image becomes.

Ways you've explored your thoughts and feelings:

- keeping a journal
- writing poetry
- composing song lyrics
- writing editorials to your school or local newspaper
- writing a blog entry about something you've seen on TV

SEEING the Whole Picture

Our goal, as the writers and editors of this book, is to make sure you see ALL the pictures in your reading/writing photo album. We want you to reach well-founded conclusions about reading and writing. Making good grades, passing tests, and connecting to others are all very important, but so is learning more about yourself. Throughout this book, you'll find activities that strengthen the skills you need to be successful in school. You'll work collaboratively with your peers, to connect with others. You'll also answer questions and complete assignments that ask you what YOU think and how YOU feel.

As you work with this book this year, you will be building images of yourself as a reader and a writer—BIG-PICTURE images. We hope your journey with this text will bring clarity, sharpness, and rich color to those images.

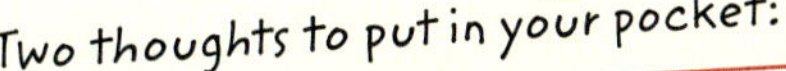

Two thoughts to put in your pocket:

- As you read, you learn about your own thoughts and feelings as you compare them with those of the characters and people you're reading about.
- As you write, you explore and clarify your own thoughts and feelings about what you're writing about, from school assignments to personal experiences.

Kylene Beers
Senior Author
Elements of Literature

How to Use Your Textbook

Getting to know a new textbook is like getting to know a new video game. In each case, you have to figure out how the game or book is structured, as well as its rules. Knowing how your book is structured, you can be successful from the start.

UNIT 1

Short Stories

Writers on Writing

Joyce Carol Oates on Short Stories Joyce Carol Oates is one of the most prolific authors in the United States today. In her award-winning fiction for adults and teens, she often explores the way people act when strange or terrible things happen.

"The stories you read in school, in books, were not originally in printed form but began as ideas in someone's imagination. The authors in your books did not begin as authors but as readers, when they were children. Some of you, reading these words, will grow up to become authors and you will look back upon your childhood, and middle school, as a rich source of material stored in your memory. All you need is to pull it out: a provocative title will begin this process.

The story writers you will be reading began with such ideas, and memories, and the self-imposed query: What if—? And, Why—? Finally, the query is: What does this mean?

You are not likely to know what your story "means" until you have written it, and perhaps rewritten it. You will need to think over any story—one you read in a book, or one you have written yourself—to speculate on its meaning.

A real story does have meaning. A brief anecdote or news article only reports facts, and ends. It does not convey meaning.

All of us tell stories, all of the time. Usually these stories are meant to amuse or inform our friends or relatives; they are not embellished with literary meaning, nor are they likely to be elegant constructs. A serious fiction writer begins with wisps of stories, likely to be personal memories, anecdotes, events he has heard of, haunting images in dreams. The writer then invests these kernels of stories with atmosphere, through language; there is a plot—a sequence of events.

Though I have written many short stories, my earliest stories were not in words but in drawings: I was too young to write! These childish, awkward yet somehow recognizable drawings were of chickens and cats, standing upright like people. (We lived on a small farm in upstate New York, south of Lake Ontario in the region ominously known as the Snow Belt. One week this past year, seven feet of snow fell in this region, in less than 48 hours.)

In time, when I learned to read, my favorite book was Lewis Carroll's *Alice's Adventures in Wonderland* and *Alice's Adventures Through the Looking-Glass.*

Any story, any work of fiction, can be your doorway into the imagination. At first, you may think that this landscape is very strange; but, as you continue onward, you will discover that it is like the interior of your own imagination. If you read carefully, return to the beginning and read again, you may be inspired to invent your own stories. For no one else can tell your stories, except you."

Think as a Writer

In her essay, Oates says that fiction can be a "doorway into the imagination." What short stories have you read that have inspired you?

Writers on Writing

If you think about the authors of the selections in your book, you may think they are a rare breed like astronauts or underwater explorers. **Writers on Writing** introduces you to authors whose stories, poems, plays, or articles began with experiences that were transformed by their words.

Collection Opener

What is the focus of each collection, or section of the book? What does the image suggest about what the collection will cover? On the right, you'll see a bold heading that says "Plot and Setting" or "Character." The heading lists the **literary skills** you will study in the collection. Also in bold type is the **Informational Text Focus** for the collection. This lists skills you might use when reading a newspaper, Web site, or other infomational text. Keep the **What Do You Think?** question in mind as you go through the collection. Your answers may even surprise you.

COLLECTION 2

Character

INFORMATIONAL TEXT FOCUS

Synthesizing Sources: Main Idea, Audience, and Purpose

"I am the person I know best."

—Frida Kahlo

What Do You Think? How do other people affect the way we think about ourselves?

Learn It Online

Character 123

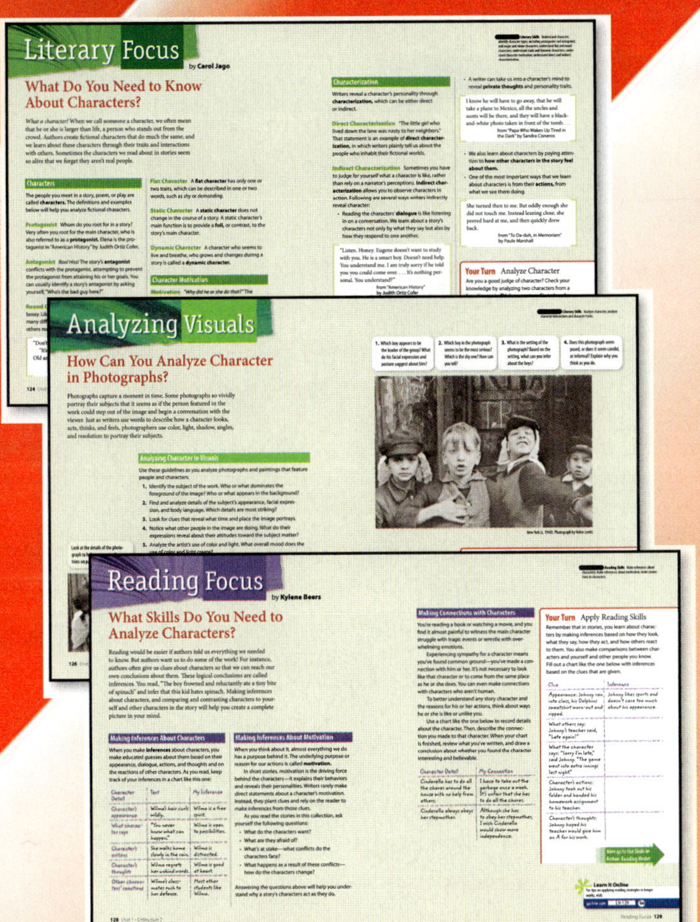

Literary Focus

Like a set of rules or a map, the **Literary Focus** shows you how literary elements work in stories and poems, helping you navigate through selections more easily. The Literary Focus will help you get to your destination—understanding and enjoying the selection.

Analyzing Visuals

Visuals are all around you: murals on buildings, magazine ads, or video game graphics. Because you see images daily, you probably know a lot about analyzing them. **Analyzing Visuals** helps you apply these skills to understand the literary elements that drive the selections.

Reading Focus

Your mind is working all the time as you read, even if you're not aware of it. Still, all readers, even very good ones, sometimes don't understand what they have read. **Reading Focus** gives you the skills to help you improve your reading.

Reading Model

You tend to do things more quickly and easily if you have a model to follow. The **Reading Model** shows you the literary and reading skills that you will practice in the collection so that you can learn them more quickly and easily.

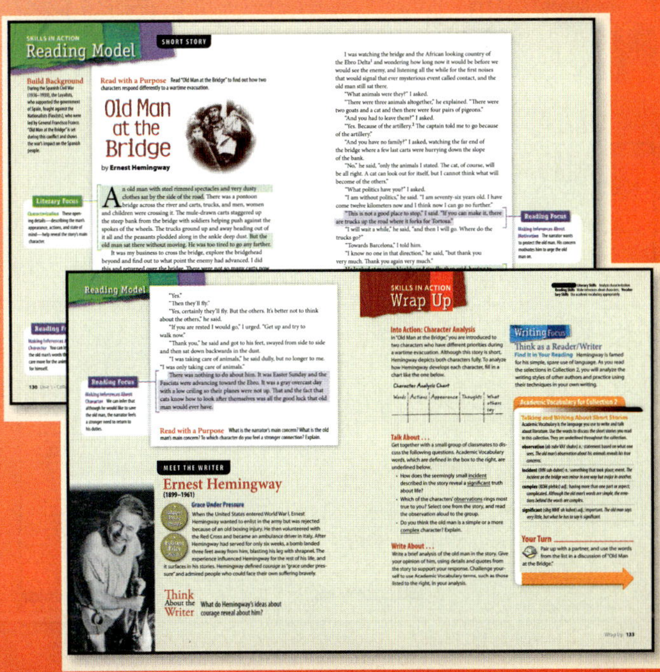

Wrap Up

Think of **Wrap Up** as a bridge that gives you a chance to practice the skills on which the collection will focus. It also introduces you to the **Academic Vocabulary** you will study in the collection: the language of school, business, and standardized tests. To be successful in school, you'll need to understand and use this language in an academic setting.

How to Use Your Textbook

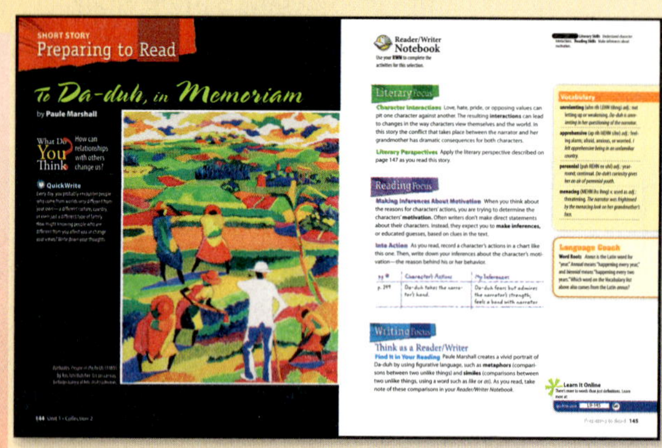

Literary Selection Pages

Preparing to Read

If you have ever done something complicated, you know that things go more smoothly with some preparation. It's the same with reading. The **Preparing to Read** page gives you a boost by presenting the literary, reading, and writing skills you'll learn about and use as you read the selection. The list of **Vocabulary** words gives the words you need to know for reading both the selection and beyond the selection. **Language Coach** explains the inner workings of English—like looking at the inside of a clock.

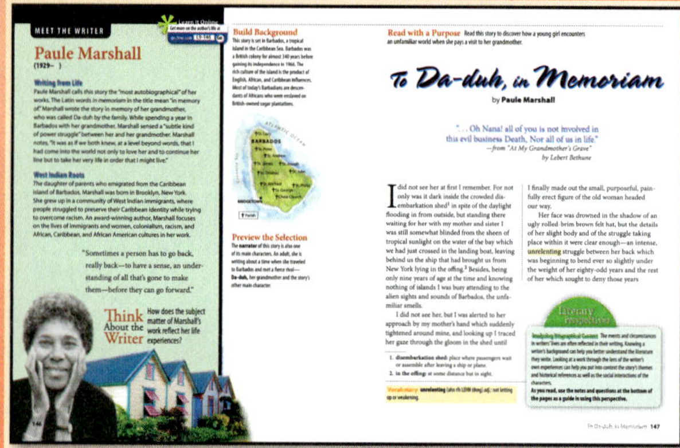

Selection

Meet the Writer gives you all kinds of interesting tidbits about the authors who wrote the selections in this book. **Build Background** provides information you sometimes need when a selection deals with unfamiliar times, places, and situations. **Preview the Selection** presents the selection's main character, like a movie trailer that hints at what is to come. **Read with a Purpose** helps you set a goal for your reading. It helps you answer the question, "What's the point of this selection?"

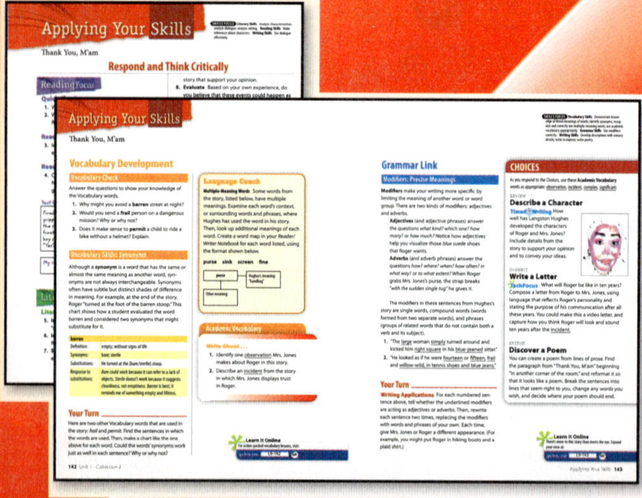

Applying Your Skills

If you have a special talent or hobby, you know that you have to practice to master it. In **Applying Your Skills**, you will apply the reading, literary, vocabulary, and language skills from the Preparing to Read page that you practiced as you read the selection. This gives you a chance to check on how well you are mastering these skills.

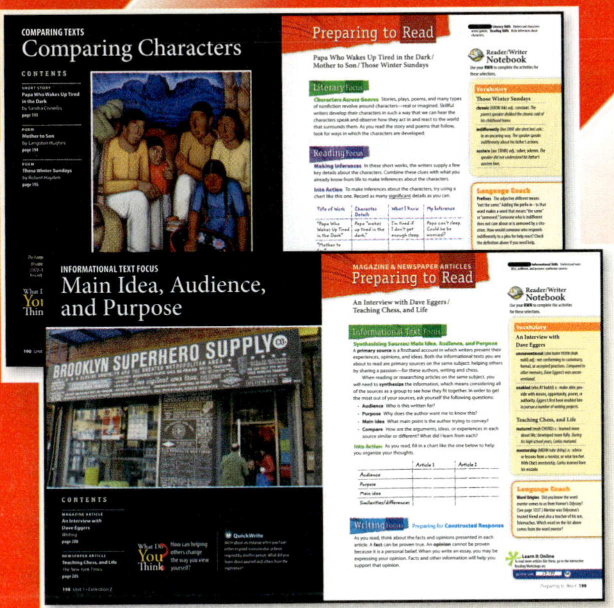

COMPARING TEXTS

Comparing Characters

Preparing to Read

Papa Who Wakes Up Tired in the Dark / Mother to Son / Those Winter Sundays

INFORMATIONAL TEXT FOCUS

Main Idea, Audience, and Purpose

MAGAZINE & NEWSPAPER ARTICLES

Preparing to Read

An Interview with Dave Eggers / Teaching Chess, and Life

Comparing Texts

You probably compare people, places, and things all the time, such as a favorite singer's new songs with her previous album. In **Comparing Texts,** you will compare different works—sometimes by the same author, sometimes by different authors—that have something in common.

Informational Text Focus

If you've ever read a Web site or followed a technical manual, you've been reading informational text. The skills you use in this type of reading are different from the ones you use for literary text. **Informational Text Focus** helps you gain the skills that will enable you to be a more successful reader in daily life and on standardized tests.

Preparing for Standardized Tests

Do you dread test-taking time? Do you struggle over reading the passage and then choosing the correct answer? **Preparing for Standardized Tests** can reduce your "guesses" and give you the practice you need to feel more confident during testing.

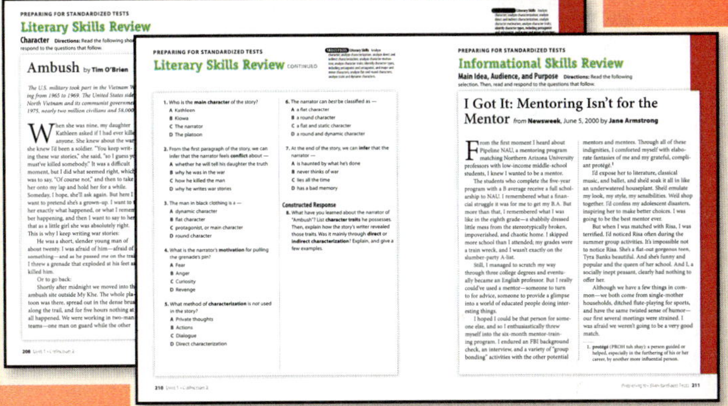

PREPARING FOR STANDARDIZED TESTS

Literary Skills Review

Ambush by Tim O'Brien

Literary Skills Review CONTINUED

Informational Skills Review

I Got It: Mentoring Isn't for the Mentor from Newsweek, June 5, 2000 by Jane Armstrong

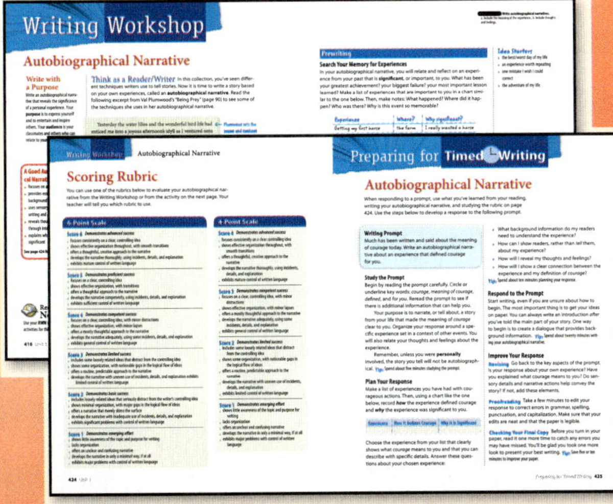

Writing Workshop

Autobiographical Narrative

Scoring Rubric

Preparing for Timed Writing

Autobiographical Narrative

Writing Workshop

Does a blank piece of paper send shivers up your spine? The **Writing Workshop** will help you tackle the page. It takes you step-by-step through developing an effective piece of writing. Models, annotations, graphic organizers, and charts take the "What now?" out of writing for different purposes and audiences.

Preparing for Timed Writing

What's your idea of a nightmare? Maybe it's trying to respond to a writing prompt. **Preparing for Timed Writing** helps you practice for on-demand, or timed, writing so that you can realize your dreams of success.

UNIT 1

Short Stories

Writers on Writing

Joyce Carol Oates on Short Stories Joyce Carol Oates is one of the most prolific authors in the United States today. In her award-winning fiction for adults and teens, she often explores the way people act when strange or terrible things happen.

"The stories you read in school, in books, were not originally in printed form but began as ideas in someone's imagination. The authors in your books did not begin as authors but as readers, when they were children. Some of you, reading these words, will grow up to become authors and you will look back upon your childhood, and middle

school, as a rich source of material stored in your memory. All you need is to pull it out: a provocative title will begin this process.

The story writers you will be reading began with such ideas, and memories, and the self-imposed query: What if—? And, Why—? Finally, the query is: What does this mean?

You are not likely to know what your story "means" until you have written it, and perhaps rewritten it. You will need to think over any story—one you read in a book, or one you have written yourself—to speculate on its meaning.

A real story does have meaning. A brief anecdote or news article only reports facts, and ends. It does not convey meaning.

All of us tell stories, all of the time. Usually these stories are meant to amuse or inform our friends or relatives; they are not embellished with literary meaning, nor are they likely to be elegant constructs. A serious fiction writer begins with wisps of stories, likely to be personal memories, anecdotes, events he has heard of, haunting images in dreams. The writer then invests these kernels of stories with atmosphere, through language; there is a plot—a sequence of events.

Though I have written many short stories, my earliest stories were not in words but in drawings: I was too young to write! These childish, awkward yet somehow recognizable drawings were of chickens and cats, standing upright like people. (We lived on a small farm in upstate New York, south of Lake Ontario in the region ominously known as the Snow Belt. One week this past year, seven feet of snow fell in this region, in less than 48 hours.)

In time, when I learned to read, my favorite book was Lewis Carroll's *Alice's Adventures in Wonderland* and *Alice's Adventures Through the Looking-Glass.*

Any story, any work of fiction, can be your doorway into the imagination. At first, you may think that this landscape is very strange; but, as you continue onward, you will discover that it is like the interior of your own imagination. If you read carefully, return to the beginning and read again, you may be inspired to invent your own stories. For no one else can tell your stories, except you. ”

Think as a Writer

In her essay, Oates says that fiction can be a "doorway into the imagination." What short stories have you read that have inspired you?

COLLECTION 1

Plot and Setting

INFORMATIONAL TEXT FOCUS

Understand Main Idea

"All the best stories in the world are but one story in reality—the story of escape."

—A. C. Benson

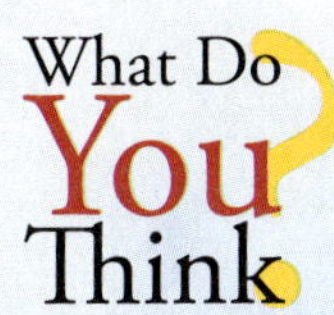

Why are stories of escape so interesting and timeless?

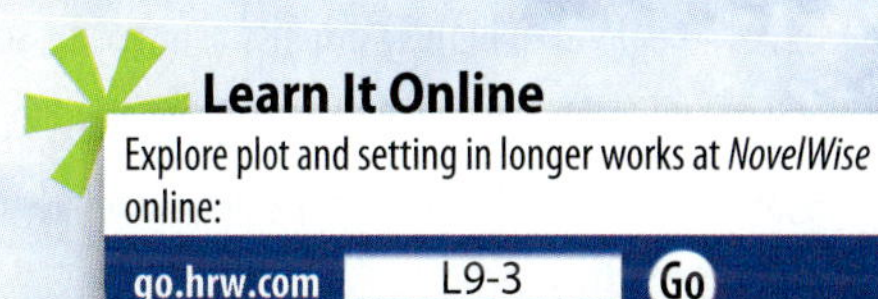

Learn It Online
Explore plot and setting in longer works at *NovelWise* online:
go.hrw.com
L9-3
Go

Literary Focus

by **Carol Jago**

What Do You Need to Know About Plot and Setting?

"What happened?" You often ask friends this question when you want to know what is going on. In a story, the answer to "What happened?" is the plot. Like a travel agent, a storyteller can help move us from where we are, putting us in another setting on earth or, for that matter, on another planet or the moon. Setting tells us where and when a story takes place.

Plot

Just as life can be described as a series of events, a story's **plot** is a series of events. One event triggers another event, and so on. When you describe the major events of a movie or TV show to a friend, you are summarizing its plot.

Most plots have a basic structure like this:

Exposition: part of the story in which the basic situation is outlined and the characters and main conflict are introduced

Rising Action: chain of events that takes place as the main character struggles to achieve his or her goal

Climax: the point of highest emotional intensity; sometimes the point at which we learn the outcome of the conflict

Resolution: events following the climax in which any remaining issues are resolved

Conflict The struggle or clash between opposing characters, forces, or emotions is referred to as **conflict.** Here are the basic types of conflicts:

- **Internal conflict** An internal conflict is created when the main character undergoes an emotional struggle. The conflict is within the character's own heart or mind.
- **External conflict** An external conflict is created when a person or outside force prevents the main character from achieving his or her goal. For example, a secret agent or a blizzard might threaten a person's life.

> With a violent effort, he tore loose. He knew where he was now. Death Swamp and its quicksand.
>
> from "The Most Dangerous Game" by Richard Connell

Flashback Sometimes a story's main action is interrupted in order to tell of events that took place in the past. Any scene that presents events that happened before the main time frame of a story is called a **flashback.** Through the use of flashback, storytellers provide us with background about the main events of the story or share a character's past.

The last station sped behind her. The overhead light went out, and the fluorescent flashes from the subway tunnel gleamed in the darkness behind her eyelids, pane after pane like frames of a movie.

Mrs. Chen, then just a girl named Lai Fong, was in China again.

from "Disguises"
by Jean Fong Kwok

Foreshadowing A story character is unaware of wolves howling in the distance, but the reader wonders about them. Later, that character is pursued by those wolves and the reader realizes that the howling foreshadowed the character's now-desperate situation. **Foreshadowing** is the use of such clues to hint at what is going to happen later in a story.

"The old charts call it Ship-Trap Island," Whitney replied. "A suggestive name, isn't it? Sailors have a curious dread of the place."

from "The Most Dangerous Game"
by Richard Connell

Suspense When your heart races and you become anxious about what might happen next in a story, it's because the writer has created suspense. **Suspense** is the feeling of uncertainty or anxiety about what is going to happen next. Writers create suspense by hinting at what may happen.

George Bergeron correctly identified the earthquake, and well he might have—for many was the time his own home had danced to the same crashing tune. "My God—" said George, "that must be Harrison!"

from "Harrison Bergeron"
by Kurt Vonnegut

Setting

The time period and place in which the action of a story takes place is called its **setting.** A historical period or social beliefs and customs may also be part of a story's setting. Sometimes a story's setting can have a direct impact on how the characters act and the conflicts the characters face.

She looked around. No one had followed her. A desolate avenue lined with streetlamps stretched before her, the concrete buildings smothered in graffiti, interrupted by long alleys.

from "Disguises"
by Jean Fong Kwok

Mood Stories often convey a **mood,** or atmosphere, affecting the way we feel as we read. Mood is created by a writer's word choice and by details of setting. Some details may make us fearful or anxious while others make us feel happy. Mood can be described by words like *eerie, romantic,* and so on.

Eckels glanced across the vast office at a mass and tangle, a snaking and humming of wires and steel boxes, at an aurora that flickered now orange, now silver, now blue.

from "A Sound of Thunder"
by Ray Bradbury

Your Turn Analyze Plot and Setting

Fill in a plot diagram with events from a movie, TV show, or story familiar to you. Note instances in which the story's setting affects its plot.

Learn It Online
To understand the role of literary elements in novels, visit *NovelWise* at:
go.hrw.com
L9-5
Go

Analyzing Visuals

How Can You Recognize Setting and Mood in Art?

Some paintings, like stories, convey a powerful sense of place. While a writer uses imagery and figurative language to establish a **setting,** an artist uses color, line, and form to bring a setting to life. The artist's color choices, use of light and dark contrasts, brushstrokes, and other techniques help establish **mood**—the overall emotional impact of the painting.

Analyzing a Painting

Use these guidelines to help you read paintings:

1. Identify the subject of the painting. An artist centers a painting around a focal point, or the most dramatic point of interest.
2. Find details that help locate the scene in a particular time or place.
3. Study the way the artist created the setting. Is the setting highly detailed or more abstract?
4. Analyze the importance of setting in the painting. Is the setting simply part of the background, or does it take on a more dominant role?
5. Think about how the colors and shapes in the painting help create a mood.

Look at the details of the painting below to help you answer the questions on page 7.

Details from *The Gulf Stream.*

1. The Gulf Stream is an ocean current that produces harsh weather patterns dangerous for sailing. How does Homer portray the ocean **setting** in this painting?

2. Notice the red flecks in the water near the sharks. What **mood** does this **setting** detail convey?

3. How does the presence of the ship in the background contribute to the **mood** of the painting or provide a clue to what is happening? Explain.

4. The thick cords near the man's feet are sugar cane. What does this detail tell you about the painting's **setting** and what is taking place?

The Gulf Stream (1899) by Winslow Homer (1836–1910). Oil on canvas (28 1/8" x 49 1/8").

Your Turn Write About Setting and Mood

Flip through this book, and find a painting or photograph that is set in a specific time and place. Study the artwork, and write a brief description of its setting. Then, describe what the artist did with colors and shapes to create a mood.

Reading Focus

by **Kylene Beers**

What Reading Skills Help You Understand Plot and Setting?

What if every time your attention wandered while you read a story, a story character yelled "Listen up!" Now, that would probably get your attention quickly. But story characters can't do that, so you must shout that to yourself. Keeping yourself focused on what you're reading is part of being an active reader. Using these reading skills can help you understand a story's plot and setting.

Making Predictions

Writers often provide hints, or clues, about where a text is heading. Sometimes those clues are clear and direct—you can predict that a book titled *How to Be a Better Skateboarder* will be about skateboarding. Within a text, though, the clues may not be quite so obvious. Use the clues listed below to help you make predictions as you read.

Clues for Predicting When you read a suspenseful story, you make predictions about what is going to happen, sometimes without thinking about it. A **prediction** is a type of inference, a guess based on evidence. As a reader, you can base your predictions on

- clues the writer plants, such as in dialogue or action
- your own experience of life
- your understanding of how stories work

Asking Questions Another way to make predictions is to ask questions about what is happening. As you read, pause from time to time to ask yourself, "Why has the author chosen to include this detail?" and "Is this detail important?" Your answers to these questions help you predict upcoming events.

Tracing a Sequence of Events

Story characters' lives may entertain, shock, horrify, or enchant us. Pay attention to what a character experiences in a story by pausing from time to time to summarize, or briefly restate, what has just happened. Doing so will help you keep track of stories that contain flashbacks and complex plots.

Story Time Line As you read any of the action-packed stories in this collection, fill out a chart like this one to track the story's events. Such a chart will help you keep the story's chronological order, or time order, clear. This story time line contains two story events from "The Most Dangerous Game." Add to the chart as necessary.

Story Event 1	Story Event 2	Story Event 3	Story Event 4
Rainsford talks to Whitney on the deck of a ship.	Rainsford is knocked over-board.		

Visualizing

Characters' worlds and lives are as full as our own. If, as you read, you can't visualize what is happening and where it is happening, you may be missing out on half the story. When you **visualize,** you create mental images of the story's characters, setting, and action. Use the tips below to help you get to know the characters you read about.

Tips for Visualizing Improve your ability to visualize text by doing the following as you read:

- Read a passage, and then describe what is happening.
- As you read, sketch what is happening and where it is happening.
- Read aloud, and pay special attention to the descriptive words the author uses.

Descriptive details and sensory details—those describing how something looks, feels, smells, sounds, or tastes—are underlined in this passage. Details such as these help you visualize the scene being described.

> Papi came home with a dog whose kind we had never seen before. A black-and-white-speckled electric current of energy. It was a special breed with papers, like a person with a birth certificate. Mami just kept staring at the puppy with a cross look on her face. "It looks like a mess!" she said. "Take it back."
>
> from "Liberty"
> by Julia Alvarez

You might use a graphic organizer, like the one below, to keep track of details describing an image.

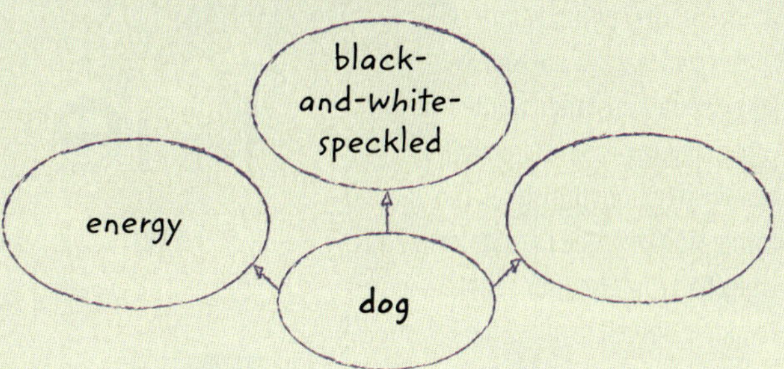

Your Turn Apply Reading Skills

Read this passage from "The Sniper," and identify details that help you understand the sequence of events. Then, identify details that help you visualize the action. Finally, make a prediction based on clues in the passage and your own life experience.

> Just then an armored car came across the bridge and advanced slowly up the street. It stopped on the opposite side of the street, fifty yards ahead. The sniper could hear the dull panting of the motor. His heart beat faster. It was an enemy car. He wanted to fire, but he knew it was useless. His bullets would never pierce the steel that covered the gray monster.
>
> Then round the corner of a side street came an old woman, her head covered by a tattered shawl.
>
> from "The Sniper"
> by Liam O'Flaherty

Now go to the Skills in Action: Reading Model

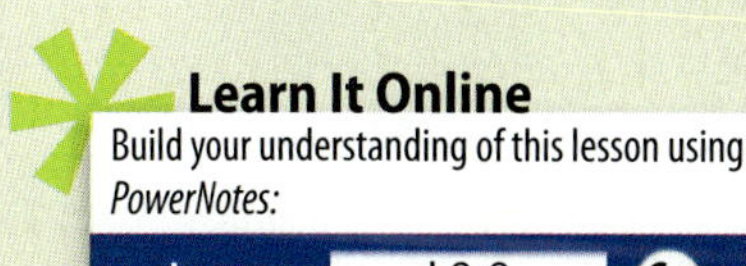

Learn It Online
Build your understanding of this lesson using *PowerNotes:*
go.hrw.com
L9-9
Go

SKILLS IN ACTION

Reading Model

SHORT STORY

Build Background

This story is set in Dublin, Ireland, in the 1920s, during a time of bitter civil war. On one side were the Republicans; they wanted all of Ireland to become a republic, totally free from British rule. On the other side were the Free Staters; they had compromised with Britain and had agreed to allow the British to continue to rule six counties in the northern province of Ulster.

Read with a Purpose As you read "The Sniper," think about what motivates the sniper's actions and whether or not you think the result is worth the cost.

The Sniper

by **Liam O'Flaherty**

The long June twilight faded into night. Dublin lay enveloped in darkness but for the dim light of the moon that shone through fleecy clouds, casting a pale light as of approaching dawn over the streets and the dark waters of the Liffey.[1] Around the beleaguered Four Courts[2] the heavy guns roared. Here and there through the city, machine guns and rifles broke the silence of the night, spasmodically, like dogs barking on lone farms. Republicans and Free Staters were waging civil war.

Literary Focus

Setting and Mood Writers often create mood, the overall feeling a story conveys, through setting and word choice. The descriptive words in this passage help create a dark, serious mood.

On a rooftop near O'Connell Bridge, a Republican sniper lay watching. Beside him lay his rifle and over his shoulders was slung a pair of field glasses. His face was the face of a student, thin and ascetic,[3] but his eyes had the cold gleam of the fanatic. They were deep and thoughtful, the eyes of a man who is used to looking at death.

He was eating a sandwich hungrily. He had eaten nothing since morning. He had been too excited to eat. He finished the sandwich, and, taking a flask of whiskey from his pocket, he took a short draft. Then he returned the flask to his pocket. He paused for a moment, considering whether he should risk a smoke. It was dangerous. The flash might be seen in the darkness, and there were enemies watching. He decided to take the risk.

Placing a cigarette between his lips, he struck a match, inhaled the smoke hurriedly, and put out the light. Almost immediately, a bullet flattened itself against the parapet[4] of the roof. The sniper took another whiff and put out the cigarette. Then he swore softly and crawled away to the left.

1. **Liffey:** river that runs through Dublin.
2. **Four Courts:** government buildings in Dublin.
3. **ascetic** (uh SEHT ihk): severe; self-disciplined.
4. **parapet** (PAR uh peht): low wall or railing.

Sniper at the foot of Nelson's column in Dublin, Ireland.

Cautiously he raised himself and peered over the parapet. There was a flash and a bullet whizzed over his head. He dropped immediately. He had seen the flash. It came from the opposite side of the street.

He rolled over the roof to a chimney stack in the rear and slowly drew himself up behind it, until his eyes were level with the top of the parapet. There was nothing to be seen—just the dim outline of the opposite housetop against the blue sky. His enemy was under cover.

Just then an armored car came across the bridge and advanced slowly up the street. It stopped on the opposite side of the street, fifty yards ahead. The sniper could hear the dull panting of the motor. His heart beat faster. It was an enemy car. He wanted to fire, but he knew it was useless. His bullets would never pierce the steel that covered the gray monster.

Then round the corner of a side street came an old woman, her head covered by a tattered shawl. She began to talk to the man in the turret[5] of the car. She was pointing to the roof where the sniper lay. An informer.

The turret opened. A man's head and shoulders appeared, looking toward the sniper. The sniper raised his rifle and fired. The head fell heavily on the turret wall. The woman darted toward the side street. The sniper fired again. The woman whirled round and fell with a shriek into the gutter.

Suddenly from the opposite roof a shot rang out and the sniper dropped his rifle with a curse. The rifle clattered to the roof. The sniper thought the noise would wake the dead. He stooped to pick

Literary Focus

Plot The main conflict of the story, sniper versus sniper, is introduced here.

Reading Focus

Predicting These story events may lead you to predict that the sniper will be shot or captured.

5. **turret** (TUR iht): low, usually revolving structure for guns on a tank or warship.

the rifle up. He couldn't lift it. His forearm was dead. "I'm hit," he muttered.

Dropping flat onto the roof, he crawled back to the parapet. With his left hand he felt the injured right forearm. The blood was oozing through the sleeve of his coat. There was no pain—just a deadened sensation, as if the arm had been cut off.

Quickly he drew his knife from his pocket, opened it on the breastwork[6] of the parapet, and ripped open the sleeve. There was a small hole where the bullet had entered. On the other side there was no hole. The bullet had lodged in the bone. It must have fractured it. He bent the arm below the wound. The arm bent back easily. He ground his teeth to overcome the pain.

Then taking out his field dressing, he ripped open the packet with his knife. He broke the neck of the iodine bottle and let the bitter fluid drip into the wound. A paroxysm[7] of pain swept through him. He placed the cotton wadding over the wound and wrapped the dressing over it. He tied the ends with his teeth.

Then he lay still against the parapet, and, closing his eyes, he made an effort of will to overcome the pain.

In the street beneath all was still. The armored car had retired speedily over the bridge, with the machine gunner's head hanging lifeless over the turret. The woman's corpse lay still in the gutter.

The sniper lay still for a long time nursing his wounded arm and planning escape. Morning must not find him wounded on the roof. The enemy on the opposite roof covered his escape. He must kill that enemy and he could not use his rifle. He had only a revolver to do it. Then he thought of a plan.

Taking off his cap, he placed it over the muzzle of his rifle. Then he pushed the rifle slowly upward over the parapet, until the cap was visible from the opposite side of the street. Almost immediately there was a report,[8] and a bullet pierced the center of the cap. The sniper slanted the rifle forward. The cap slipped down into the street. Then, catching the rifle in the middle, the sniper dropped his left hand over the roof and let it hang, lifelessly. After a few moments he let the rifle drop to the street. Then he sank to the roof, dragging his hand with him.

Reading Focus

Tracing a Sequence of Events Transitional words such as *then* and *after* help you follow the sequence of events. Because he is under fire, the sniper has thought of a plan to fool the other sniper.

Crawling quickly to the left, he peered up at the corner of the roof. His ruse[9] had succeeded. The other sniper, seeing the cap and

6. **breastwork:** low wall put up as a military defense.
7. **paroxysm** (PAR uhk sihz uhm): sudden attack; fit.
8. **report** (rih PAWRT): loud noise; in this case, from a gunshot.
9. **ruse** (rooz): trick.

rifle fall, thought that he had killed his man. He was now standing before a row of chimney pots, looking across, with his head clearly silhouetted against the western sky.

The Republican sniper smiled and lifted his revolver above the edge of the parapet. The distance was about fifty yards—a hard shot in the dim light, and his right arm was paining him like a thousand devils. He took a steady aim. His hand trembled with eagerness. Pressing his lips together, he took a deep breath through his nostrils and fired. He was almost deafened with the report and his arm shook with the recoil.

Then when the smoke cleared he peered across and uttered a cry of joy. His enemy had been hit. He was reeling over the parapet in his death agony. He struggled to keep his feet, but he was slowly falling forward, as if in a dream. The rifle fell from his grasp, hit the parapet, fell over, bounded off the pole of a barber's shop beneath, and then clattered on the pavement.

Then the dying man on the roof crumpled up and fell forward. The body turned over and over in space and hit the ground with a dull thud. Then it lay still.

The sniper looked at his enemy falling and he shuddered. The lust of battle died in him. He became bitten by remorse.[10] The sweat stood out in beads on his forehead. Weakened by his wound and the long summer day of fasting and watching on the roof, he revolted from the sight of the shattered mass of his dead enemy. His teeth chattered, he began to gibber to himself, cursing the war, cursing himself, cursing everybody.

Literary Focus

Conflict The sniper has succeeded in killing his enemy. Now the sniper faces an internal conflict.

He looked at the smoking revolver in his hand, and with an oath he hurled it to the roof at his feet. The revolver went off with the concussion and the bullet whizzed past the sniper's head. He was frightened back to his senses by the shock. His nerves steadied. The cloud of fear scattered from his mind and he laughed.

Taking the whiskey flask from his pocket, he emptied it at a draft. He felt reckless under the influence of the spirit. He decided to leave the roof now and look for his company commander, to report. Everywhere around was quiet. There was not much danger in going through the streets. He picked up his revolver and put it in his pocket. Then he crawled down through the skylight to the house underneath.

When the sniper reached the laneway on the street level, he felt a sudden curiosity as to the identity of the enemy sniper whom he had

10. **remorse** (rih MAWRS): deep guilt.

killed. He decided that he was a good shot, whoever he was. He wondered did he know him. Perhaps he had been in his own company before the split in the army. He decided to risk going over to have a look at him. He peered around the corner into O'Connell Street. In the upper part of the street there was heavy firing, but around here all was quiet.

The sniper darted across the street. A machine gun tore up the ground around him with a hail of bullets, but he escaped. He threw himself face downward beside the corpse. The machine gun stopped.

Then the sniper turned over the dead body and looked into his brother's face.

Literary Focus

Plot This shocking event functions both as the climax and resolution of the story.

Read with a Purpose What do you think motivates the sniper to kill others and to risk his own life? Do you think the sniper will come to regret his actions? Why or why not?

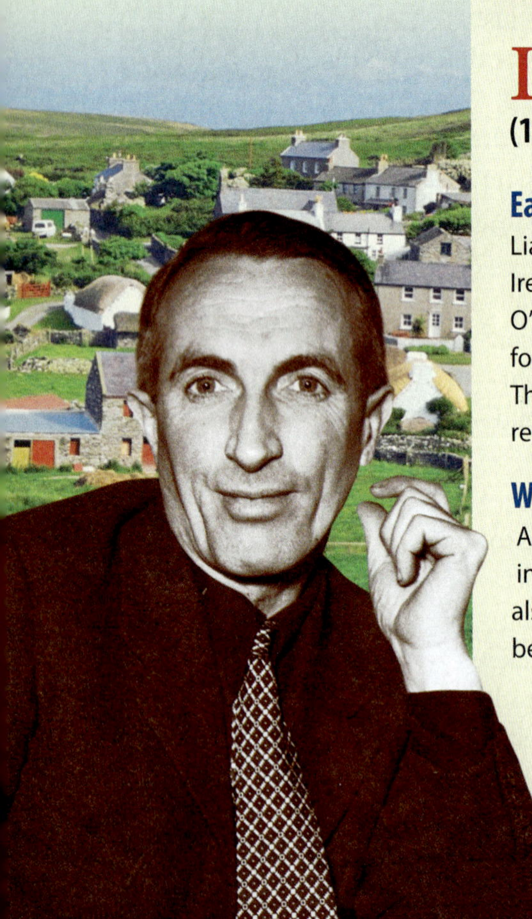

MEET THE WRITER

Liam O'Flaherty

(1896–1984)

Early Hardships

Liam O'Flaherty was born into a large, impoverished family on one of Ireland's Aran Islands. The family faced great hardships—several of O'Flaherty's siblings died when they were quite young, and money and food were scarce. The O'Flaherty home was rich, instead, with stories. The Aran Islands have a long tradition of oral storytelling, and neighbors regularly gathered at the family's home to share tales and songs.

Writing Inspirations

As a storyteller in his own right, O'Flaherty turned to the Aran Islands for inspiration, writing frequently about Irish peasant life. In his fiction he also captured the struggles of the Irish Civil War. *The Informer* (1925), his best-known novel, is a tale of betrayal set during the Irish "Troubles."

Think About the Writer O'Flaherty fought on the Republican side of the Irish Civil War. How might O'Flaherty's personal experiences have influenced his writing?

SKILLS IN ACTION
Wrap Up

Into Action: Storyboard

Imagine you are planning to film "The Sniper" and want to capture the story's key plot events. Fill in a storyboard like this one to plan the movie's main sequence of events.

Event 1	Event 2	Event 3
The sniper eats a sandwich on the rooftop of a building in Dublin.		

Talk About . . .

1. With a partner, discuss the plot and setting of "The Sniper." Try to use each Academic Vocabulary word listed at the right at least once in your discussion.

Write About . . .

Answer the following questions about "The Sniper." For definitions of Academic Vocabulary words, see the column at the right.

2. What conflicts does the sniper face? Support your ideas with details from the story.
3. What excerpt shows what happens during the story's climax?
4. What idea about war does the story's outcome convey?

Writing Focus

Think as a Reader/Writer

O'Flaherty uses short, simple sentences to describe the story's action and create suspense. In Collection 1, you will read short stories and examine the writers' use of language. You will then have a chance to practice those techniques in your own writing.

Academic Vocabulary for Collection 1

Talking and Writing About Short Stories

Academic Vocabulary is the language you use to write and talk about literature. Use these words to discuss the short stories you read in this collection. The words are underlined throughout the collection.

convey (kuhn VAY) *v.:* suggest; communicate. *In this story, O'Flaherty tries to convey an idea about war.*

effect (uh FEHKT) *n.:* result. *Describe one effect of the sniper's actions.*

excerpt (EHK surpt) *n.:* passage; part of a longer work. *Choose an excerpt from the story that proves your point.*

support (suh PAWRT) *v.:* back up; strengthen by giving evidence. *Support your ideas about "The Sniper" by giving examples.*

outcome (OWT kuhm) *n.:* result; ending. *The outcome of the story's conflict was revealed in the climax.*

Your Turn

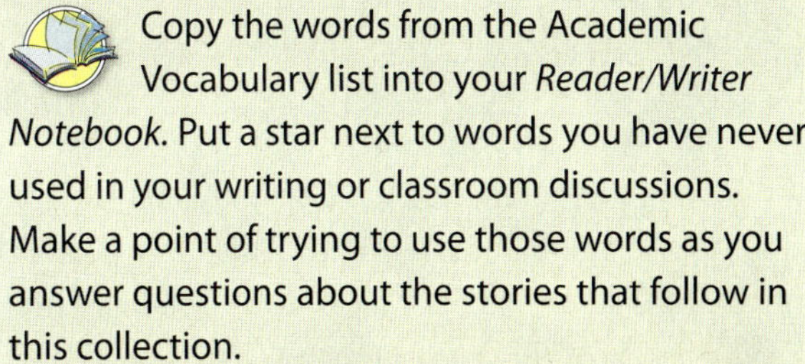

Copy the words from the Academic Vocabulary list into your *Reader/Writer Notebook.* Put a star next to words you have never used in your writing or classroom discussions. Make a point of trying to use those words as you answer questions about the stories that follow in this collection.

SHORT STORY

Preparing to Read

The Most Dangerous Game

by **Richard Connell**

Mr. Kurtz (1999) by Paul Sierra (1944–). Oil on canvas (12" x 14").

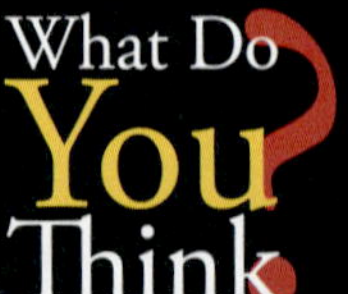

How might you escape from a game that could prove deadly?

QuickWrite

Think about a movie or a TV show you've seen where the hero ha landed in a dangerous situation. What special skills did he or she use to escape? Tell what happened.

Reader/Writer Notebook

Use your **RWN** to complete the activities for this selection.

MO **9.R.2.C.1.b** Use details from text(s): to analyze character, plot, setting, point of view **9.R.1.F.1.c** Apply pre-reading strategies to aid comprehension: predict with text support or rationale

Literary Focus

Suspense and Foreshadowing **Suspense** is the feeling of anxiety or dread you feel about what will happen next in a story, especially when you are concerned for a character. One way writers build suspense is through **foreshadowing,** or planting clues in the text to hint at events that occur later in the plot. Foreshadowing makes you curious, even anxious, to know what will happen next.

Reading Focus

Making Predictions A **prediction** is a type of inference, a guess based on evidence. You can base your predictions on clues the writer plants, your own experience of life, and your understanding of how stories work.

Into Action As you read "The Most Dangerous Game," record examples of clues that lead you to predict what will happen next.

Pg #	Clue	My Prediction	Yes	No
19	"Ship-Trap Island"; "Sailors . . . curious dread"	The ship will crash into the island.		
19	"The place has a reputation—a bad one."			

Writing Focus

Think as a Reader/Writer

Find It in Your Reading Like all good storytellers, Richard Connell captures your attention at the beginning of the story. Record in your *Reader/Writer Notebook* the ways Connell introduces the exotic setting, using vivid details to create suspense.

TechFocus As you read this story, think about how you might create an interactive map of the story. Take note of places and settings that you might plot on a map.

Vocabulary

receding (rih SEED ihng) *v.* used as *adj.:* moving into the distance. *Rainsford tried to call to the receding yacht.*

disarming (dihs AHR mihng) *adj.:* removing suspicion or fear; charming. *At first glance the man looked scary, but his disarming smile made Rainsford think he was friendly.*

imprudent (ihm PROO duhnt) *adj.:* unwise; foolish. *It was imprudent for the sailors to sail on rough seas during such a dark night.*

surmounted (suhr MOWN tihd) *v.:* overcame. *Whitney forgave the sailors who surmounted their fears and agreed to complete the voyage.*

invariably (ihn VAIR ee uh blee) *adv.:* without exception. *The sailors invariably got spooked at the sight of the island, no matter how many times they had sailed past it.*

Language Coach

Prefixes A **prefix** is one or more letters or syllables added to the beginning of a word or word part to create a new word. Write the Vocabulary words in your *Reader/Writer Notebook*, and circle any prefixes that you see.

Learn It Online
For a story preview, see the video introduction on:
go.hrw.com
L9-17
Go

Richard Connell

(1893–1949)

After working at his father's Poughkeepsie newspaper while still in high school, Connell was hired as the city editor for sixteen dollars a week. He began college at Georgetown University while also working as a secretary for his father, who had been elected to Congress. When his father died in 1912, Connell transferred to Harvard.

From Harvard to Hollywood

During his student days at Harvard, Connell wrote for two college newspapers. He moved to New York after graduation but left for a brief stint in the army during World War I. Connell eventually returned to writing and published hundreds of short stories and a number of novels. In 1925, Connell moved to Los Angeles and began to write screenplays for the major Hollywood movie studios.

An Adventure Story for All Time

Despite Connell's tremendous output, only one story—"The Most Dangerous Game" (1924)—is still widely read. The story has not only fascinated readers for decades but has also intrigued filmmakers. This suspenseful tale has inspired more than a dozen movies since its publication and is probably the most frequently anthologized American story ever written.

"My first writing was done for the daily newspaper my father edited. . . . I was ten years old. . . . I have been a professional writer ever since."

Think About the Writer How might Connell's experience writing screenplays have affected his writing of short stories?

Build Background

"The Most Dangerous Game" was written more than eighty years ago, when big-game hunting was considered a glamorous sport. Many well-to-do travelers in the early 1900s hunted exotic game—wild or unusual animals—in foreign locales.

Preview the Selection

Sanger Rainsford, a big-game hunter from New York who is traveling at sea, is one of the story's main characters. As the story begins, he and his companion, **Whitney,** sail by an island on a muggy tropical night.

Read with a Purpose Read the following story to find out what one hunter thinks is the most dangerous game.

The Most Dangerous Game

by **Richard Connell**

"Off there to the right—somewhere—is a large island," said Whitney. "It's rather a mystery—"

"What island is it?" Rainsford asked.

"The old charts call it Ship-Trap Island," Whitney replied. "A suggestive name, isn't it? Sailors have a curious dread of the place. I don't know why. Some superstition—"

"Can't see it," remarked Rainsford, trying to peer through the dank tropical night that was palpable as it pressed its thick warm blackness in upon the yacht.

"You've good eyes," said Whitney, with a laugh, "and I've seen you pick off a moose moving in the brown fall bush at four hundred yards, but even you can't see four miles or so through a moonless Caribbean night."

"Nor four yards," admitted Rainsford. "Ugh! It's like moist black velvet."

"It will be light in Rio," promised Whitney. "We should make it in a few days. I hope the jaguar guns have come from Purdey's.[1] We should have some good hunting up the Amazon. Great sport, hunting."

"The best sport in the world," agreed Rainsford.

"For the hunter," amended Whitney. "Not for the jaguar."

"Don't talk rot, Whitney," said Rainsford. "You're a big-game hunter, not a philosopher. Who cares how a jaguar feels?"

"Perhaps the jaguar does," observed Whitney.

"Bah! They've no understanding."

"Even so, I rather think they understand one thing—fear. The fear of pain and the fear of death."

"Nonsense," laughed Rainsford. "This hot weather is making you soft, Whitney. Be a realist. The world is made up of two classes—the hunters and the huntees. Luckily, you and I are the hunters. Do you think we've passed that island yet?" **A**

"I can't tell in the dark. I hope so."

"Why?" asked Rainsford.

"The place has a reputation—a bad one."

"Cannibals?" suggested Rainsford.

"Hardly. Even cannibals wouldn't live in such a Godforsaken place. But it's gotten into sailor lore, somehow. Didn't you notice that the crew's nerves seemed a bit jumpy today?"

1. **Purdey's:** British manufacturer of hunting equipment.

A **Reading Focus** **Predicting** Restate in your own words Rainsford's opinion about hunting. Then, make a prediction about what might happen to change Rainsford's mind.

"They were a bit strange, now you mention it. Even Captain Nielsen—"

"Yes, even that tough-minded old Swede, who'd go up to the devil himself and ask him for a light. Those fishy blue eyes held a look I never saw there before. All I could get out of him was: 'This place has an evil name among seafaring men, sir.' Then he said to me, very gravely: 'Don't you feel anything?'—as if the air about us was actually poisonous. Now, you mustn't laugh when I tell you this—I did feel something like a sudden chill.

"There was no breeze. The sea was as flat as a plate-glass window. We were drawing near the island then. What I felt was a—a mental chill, a sort of sudden dread."

"Pure imagination," said Rainsford. "One superstitious sailor can taint the whole ship's company with his fear."

"Maybe. But sometimes I think sailors have an extra sense that tells them when they are in danger. Sometimes I think evil is a tangible thing—with wavelengths, just as sound and light have. An evil place can, so to speak, broadcast vibrations of evil. Anyhow, I'm glad we're getting out of this zone. Well, I think I'll turn in now, Rainsford." **B**

"I'm not sleepy," said Rainsford. "I'm going to smoke another pipe on the afterdeck."

"Good night, then, Rainsford. See you at breakfast."

"Right. Good night, Whitney."

There was no sound in the night as Rainsford sat there but the muffled throb of the engine that drove the yacht swiftly through the darkness, and the swish and ripple of the wash of the propeller.

Rainsford, reclining in a steamer chair, indolently puffed on his favorite brier.[2] The sensuous drowsiness of the night was on him. "It's so dark," he thought, "that I could sleep without closing my eyes; the night would be my eyelids—"

An abrupt sound startled him. Off to the right he heard it, and his ears, expert in such matters, could not be mistaken. Again he heard the sound, and again. Somewhere, off in the blackness, someone had fired a gun three times.

Rainsford sprang up and moved quickly to the rail, mystified. He strained his eyes in the direction from which the reports had come, but it was like trying to see through a blanket. He leapt upon the rail and balanced himself there, to get greater elevation; his pipe, striking a rope, was knocked from his mouth. He lunged for it; a short, hoarse cry came from his lips as he realized he had reached too far and had lost his balance. The cry was pinched off short as the blood-warm waters of the Caribbean Sea closed over his head. **C**

He struggled up to the surface and tried to cry out, but the wash from the speeding yacht slapped him in the face and the salt water in his open mouth made him gag and strangle. Desperately he struck out with strong strokes after the receding lights of the yacht, but he stopped before he had swum fifty feet. A certain coolheadedness had come to him; it was not the first time he had been in a tight place. There

2. **puffed on his favorite brier:** smoked on a tobacco pipe made from the root of a brier bush.

B **Literary Focus** **Foreshadowing** What might this statement of Whitney's foreshadow?

C **Reading Focus** **Predicting** Rainsford just fell into the "blood-warm waters" of the Caribbean. Do you think he'll make it back to the boat? Why or why not?

Vocabulary **receding** (rih SEED ihng) *v.* used as *adj.:* moving into the distance.

was a chance that his cries could be heard by someone aboard the yacht, but that chance was slender and grew more slender as the yacht raced on. He wrestled himself out of his clothes and shouted with all his power. The lights of the yacht became faint and ever-vanishing fireflies; then they were blotted out entirely by the night.

Rainsford remembered the shots. They had come from the right, and doggedly he swam in that direction, swimming with slow, deliberate strokes, conserving his strength. For a seemingly endless time he fought the sea. He began to count his strokes; he could do possibly a hundred more and then—

Rainsford heard a sound. It came out of the darkness, a high screaming sound, the sound of an animal in an extremity of anguish and terror.

He did not recognize the animal that made the sound; he did not try to; with fresh vitality he swam toward the sound. He heard it again; then it was cut short by another noise, crisp, staccato.

"Pistol shot," muttered Rainsford, swimming on.

Ten minutes of determined effort brought another sound to his ears—the most welcome he had ever heard—the muttering and growling of the sea breaking on a rocky shore. He was almost on the rocks before he saw them; on a night less calm he would have been shattered against them. With his remaining strength he dragged himself from the swirling waters. Jagged crags appeared to jut into the opaqueness.[3]

Mexico Jungle (1831) by Johann Moritz Rugendas. Oil on board.

Analyzing Visuals **Viewing and Interpreting** What dangers might Rainsford face in a jungle landscape such as this?

He forced himself upward, hand over hand. Gasping, his hands raw, he reached a flat place at the top. Dense jungle came down to the very edge of the cliffs. What perils that tangle of trees and underbrush might hold for him did not concern Rainsford just then. All he knew

3. **opaqueness** (oh PAYK nuhs): here, darkness. Something opaque does not let light pass through.

was that he was safe from his enemy, the sea, and that utter weariness was on him. He flung himself down at the jungle edge and tumbled headlong into the deepest sleep of his life.

When he opened his eyes he knew from the position of the sun that it was late in the afternoon. Sleep had given him new vigor; a sharp hunger was picking at him. He looked about him, almost cheerfully.

"Where there are pistol shots, there are men. Where there are men, there is food," he thought. But what kind of men, he wondered, in so forbidding a place? An unbroken front of snarled and ragged jungle fringed the shore.

He saw no sign of a trail through the closely knit web of weeds and trees; it was easier to go along the shore, and Rainsford floundered along by the water. Not far from where he had landed, he stopped.

Some wounded thing, by the evidence a large animal, had thrashed about in the underbrush; the jungle weeds were crushed down and the moss was lacerated; one patch of weeds was stained crimson. A small, glittering object not far away caught Rainsford's eye and he picked it up. It was an empty cartridge.

> Some wounded thing, by the evidence a large animal, had thrashed about in the underbrush.

"A twenty-two," he remarked. "That's odd. It must have been a fairly large animal too. The hunter had his nerve with him to tackle it with a light gun. It's clear that the brute put up a fight. I suppose the first three shots I heard was when the hunter flushed his quarry[4] and wounded it. The last shot was when he trailed it here and finished it." **D**

He examined the ground closely and found what he had hoped to find—the print of hunting boots. They pointed along the cliff in the direction he had been going. Eagerly he hurried along, now slipping on a rotten log or a loose stone, but making headway; night was beginning to settle down on the island.

Bleak darkness was blacking out the sea and jungle when Rainsford sighted the lights. He came upon them as he turned a crook in the coastline, and his first thought was that he had come upon a village, for there were many lights. But as he forged along, he saw to his great astonishment that all the lights were in one enormous building—a lofty structure with pointed towers plunging upward into the gloom. His eyes made out the shadowy outlines of a palatial château; it was set on a high bluff, and on three sides of it cliffs dived down to where the sea licked greedy lips in the shadows.

"Mirage," thought Rainsford. But it was no mirage, he found, when he opened the tall spiked iron gate. The stone steps were real enough; the massive door with a leering gargoyle for a knocker was real enough; yet about it all hung an air of unreality.

He lifted the knocker, and it creaked up stiffly, as if it had never before been used. He let it fall, and it startled him with its booming loudness. He thought he heard steps within; the door remained closed. Again Rainsford lifted the heavy knocker and let it fall. The door

4. **flushed his quarry:** drove the animal he was hunting out of its hiding place.

D Literary Focus Foreshadowing Rainsford comments that the bullet is small, although it was used to kill a large animal. What might this detail tell you about the hunter?

opened then, opened as suddenly as if it were on a spring, and Rainsford stood blinking in the river of glaring gold light that poured out. The first thing Rainsford's eyes discerned was the largest man Rainsford had ever seen—a gigantic creature, solidly made and black-bearded to the waist. In his hand the man held a long-barreled revolver, and he was pointing it straight at Rainsford's heart.

Out of the snarl of beard two small eyes regarded Rainsford. **E**

"Don't be alarmed," said Rainsford, with a smile which he hoped was disarming. "I'm no robber. I fell off a yacht. My name is Sanger Rainsford of New York City."

The menacing look in the eyes did not change. The revolver pointed as rigidly as if the giant were a statue. He gave no sign that he understood Rainsford's words or that he had even heard them. He was dressed in uniform, a black uniform trimmed with gray astrakhan.[5]

"I'm Sanger Rainsford of New York," Rainsford began again. "I fell off a yacht. I am hungry."

The man's only answer was to raise with his thumb the hammer of his revolver. Then Rainsford saw the man's free hand go to his forehead in a military salute, and he saw him click his heels together and stand at attention. Another man was coming down the broad marble steps, an erect, slender man in evening clothes. He advanced to Rainsford and held out his hand.

In a cultivated voice marked by a slight accent that gave it added precision and deliberateness, he said: "It is a very great pleasure and honor to welcome Mr. Sanger Rainsford, the celebrated hunter, to my home."

Automatically Rainsford shook the man's hand.

"I've read your book about hunting snow leopards in Tibet, you see," explained the man. "I am General Zaroff."

Rainsford's first impression was that the man was singularly handsome; his second was that there was an original, almost bizarre quality about the general's face. He was a tall man past middle age, for his hair was a vivid white; but his thick eyebrows and pointed military moustache were as black as the night from which Rainsford had come. His eyes, too, were black and very bright. He had high cheekbones, a sharp-cut nose, a spare, dark face, the face of a man used to giving orders, the face of an aristocrat. Turning to the giant in uniform, the general made a sign. The giant put away his pistol, saluted, withdrew.

"Ivan is an incredibly strong fellow," remarked the general, "but he has the misfortune to be deaf and dumb. A simple fellow, but, I'm afraid, like all his race, a bit of a savage."

"Is he Russian?"

"He is a Cossack,"[6] said the general, and his smile showed red lips and pointed teeth. "So am I. **F**

"Come," he said, "we shouldn't be chatting here. We can talk later. Now you want clothes, food, rest. You shall have them. This is a most

5. **astrakhan** (AS truh kuhn): curly furlike wool of very young lambs.

6. **Cossack** (KAHS ak): member of a group from Ukraine, many of whom served as horsemen to the Russian czars and were famous for their fierceness in battle.

E Literary Focus Suspense How do the details about the man who answers the door add to the suspense?

Vocabulary disarming (dihs AHR mihng) *adj.:* removing suspicion or fear; charming.

F Reading Focus Predicting Re-read the description of General Zaroff. What details about his physical appearance seem bizarre to you? What kind of man do you think he is?

restful spot."

Ivan had reappeared, and the general spoke to him with lips that moved but gave forth no sound.

"Follow Ivan, if you please, Mr. Rainsford," said the general. "I was about to have my dinner when you came. I'll wait for you. You'll find that my clothes will fit you, I think."

It was to a huge, beam-ceilinged bedroom with a canopied bed big enough for six men that Rainsford followed the silent giant. Ivan laid out an evening suit, and Rainsford, as he put it on, noticed that it came from a London tailor who ordinarily cut and sewed for none below the rank of duke.

The dining room to which Ivan conducted him was in many ways remarkable. There was a medieval magnificence about it; it suggested a baronial hall of feudal times, with its oaken panels, its high ceiling, its vast refectory table where two-score men could sit down to eat. About the hall were the mounted heads of many animals—lions, tigers, elephants, moose, bears; larger or more perfect specimens Rainsford had never seen. At the great table the general was sitting, alone.

"You'll have a cocktail, Mr. Rainsford," he suggested. The cocktail was surpassingly good; and, Rainsford noted, the table appointments were of the finest—the linen, the crystal, the silver, the china.

They were eating borscht, the rich red soup with sour cream so dear to Russian palates. Half apologetically General Zaroff said: "We do our best to preserve the amenities[7] of civilization here. Please forgive any lapses. We are well off the beaten track, you know. Do you think the champagne has suffered from its long ocean trip?"

"Not in the least," declared Rainsford. He was finding the general a most thoughtful and affable host, a true cosmopolite.[8] But there was one small trait of the general's that made Rainsford uncomfortable. Whenever he looked up from his plate he found the general studying him, appraising him narrowly.

"Perhaps," said General Zaroff, "you were surprised that I recognized your name. You see, I read all books on hunting published in English, French, and Russian. I have but one passion in my life, Mr. Rainsford, and it is the hunt."

"You have some wonderful heads here," said Rainsford as he ate a particularly well-cooked filet mignon. "That Cape buffalo is the largest I ever saw."

"Oh, that fellow. Yes, he was a monster."

"Did he charge you?"

"Hurled me against a tree," said the general. "Fractured my skull. But I got the brute."

"I've always thought," said Rainsford, "that the Cape buffalo is the most dangerous of all big game."

For a moment the general did not reply; he was smiling his curious red-lipped smile. Then he said slowly: "No. You are wrong, sir. The Cape buffalo is not the most dangerous big game." He sipped his wine. "Here in my preserve on this island," he said in the same slow tone, "I hunt more dangerous game."

Rainsford expressed his surprise. "Is there big game on this island?"

The general nodded."The biggest."

"Really?"

"Oh, it isn't here naturally, of course. I have to stock the island."

"What have you imported, general?" Rainsford asked. "Tigers?"

The general smiled. "No," he said. "Hunting tigers ceased to interest me some years ago. I exhausted their possibilities, you see. No thrill

7. **amenities** (uh MEHN uh teez): comforts and conveniences.

8. **cosmopolite** (koz MAHP ah lyt): knowledgeable citizen of the world.

left in tigers, no real danger. I live for danger, Mr. Rainsford."

The general took from his pocket a gold cigarette case and offered his guest a long black cigarette with a silver tip; it was perfumed and gave off a smell like incense.

"We will have some capital hunting, you and I," said the general. "I shall be most glad to have your society."

"But what game—" began Rainsford.

"I'll tell you," said the general. "You will be amused, I know. I think I may say, in all modesty, that I have done a rare thing. I have invented a new sensation. May I pour you another glass of port, Mr. Rainsford?"

"Thank you, general."

The general filled both glasses and said: "God makes some men poets. Some He makes kings, some beggars. Me He made a hunter. My hand was made for the trigger, my father said. He was a very rich man, with a quarter of a million acres in the Crimea, and he was an ardent[9] sportsman. When I was only five years old, he gave me a little gun, specially made in Moscow for me, to shoot sparrows with. When I shot some of his prize turkeys with it, he did not

9. **ardent** (AHR duhnt): dedicated; enthusiastic.

Analyzing Visuals **Viewing and Interpreting** What similarities do you see between the man in the painting and Zaroff?

Casanova (1987) by Julio Larraz. Oil on canvas (60" x 69"). Courtesy of the Marlborough Gallery, New York.

punish me; he complimented me on my marksmanship. I killed my first bear in the Caucasus when I was ten. My whole life has been one prolonged hunt. I went into the army—it was expected of noblemen's sons—and for a time commanded a division of Cossack cavalry, but my real interest was always the hunt. I have hunted every kind of game in every land. It would be impossible for me to tell you how many animals I have killed."

The general puffed at his cigarette.

"After the debacle[10] in Russia I left the country, for it was imprudent for an officer of the czar to stay there. Many noble Russians lost everything. I, luckily, had invested heavily in American securities, so I shall never have to open a tearoom in Monte Carlo or drive a taxi in Paris. Naturally, I continued to hunt—grizzlies in your Rockies, crocodiles in the Ganges, rhinoceroses in East Africa. It was in Africa that the Cape buffalo hit me and laid me up for six months. As soon as I recovered I started for the Amazon to hunt jaguars, for I had heard they were unusually cunning. They weren't." The Cossack sighed. "They were no match at all for a hunter with his wits about him and a high-powered rifle. I was bitterly disappointed. I was lying in my tent with a splitting headache one night when a terrible thought pushed its way into my mind. Hunting was beginning to bore me! And hunting, remember, had been my life. I have heard that in America businessmen often go to pieces when they give up the business that has been their life."

"Yes, that's so," said Rainsford.

10. **debacle** (dih BAH kuhl): sudden downfall. Zaroff is referring to the Russian Revolution of 1917, in which the czar and his government were overthrown.

The general smiled. "I had no wish to go to pieces," he said. "I must do something. Now, mine is an analytical mind, Mr. Rainsford. Doubtless that is why I enjoy the problems of the chase."

"No doubt, General Zaroff."

"So," continued the general, "I asked myself why the hunt no longer fascinated me. You are much younger than I am, Mr. Rainsford, and have not hunted as much, but you perhaps can guess the answer."

"What was it?"

"Simply this: Hunting had ceased to be what you call a sporting proposition. It had become too easy. I always got my quarry. Always. There is no greater bore than perfection."

The general lit a fresh cigarette.

"No animal had a chance with me anymore. That is no boast; it is a mathematical certainty. The animal had nothing but his legs and his instinct. Instinct is no match for reason. When I thought of this, it was a tragic moment for me, I can tell you."

Rainsford leaned across the table, absorbed in what his host was saying.

"It came to me as an inspiration what I must do," the general went on. **G**

"And that was?"

The general smiled the quiet smile of one who has faced an obstacle and surmounted it with success. "I had to invent a new animal to hunt," he said.

"A new animal? You're joking."

"Not at all," said the general. "I never joke about hunting. I needed a new animal. I found one. So I bought this island, built this house, and here I do my hunting. The island is perfect for my purposes—there are jungles with a maze

G Reading Focus Predicting What do you think Zaroff will say to Rainsford?

Vocabulary **imprudent** (ihm PROO duhnt) *adj.:* unwise; foolish. **surmounted** (suhr MOWN tihd) *v.:* overcame.

of trails in them, hills, swamps—"

"But the animal, General Zaroff?"

"Oh," said the general, "it supplies me with the most exciting hunting in the world. No other hunting compares with it for an instant. Every day I hunt, and I never grow bored now, for I have a quarry with which I can match my wits."

Rainsford's bewilderment showed in his face.

"I wanted the ideal animal to hunt," explained the general. "So I said: 'What are the attributes of an ideal quarry?' And the answer was, of course: 'It must have courage, cunning, and, above all, it must be able to reason.'" **H**

"But no animal can reason," objected Rainsford.

"My dear fellow," said the general, "there is one that can."

"But you can't mean—" gasped Rainsford.

"And why not?"

"I can't believe you are serious, General Zaroff. This is a grisly joke."

"Why should I not be serious? I am speaking of hunting."

"Hunting? Good God, General Zaroff, what you speak of is murder."

The general laughed with entire good nature. He regarded Rainsford quizzically. "I refuse to believe that so modern and civilized a young man as you seem to be harbors romantic ideas about the value of human life. Surely your experiences in the war—"

"Did not make me condone coldblooded murder," finished Rainsford stiffly.

Laughter shook the general. "How extraordinarily droll you are!" he said. "One does not expect nowadays to find a young man of the educated class, even in America, with such a naive, and, if I may say so, mid-Victorian point of view. It's like finding a snuffbox in a limousine. Ah, well, doubtless you had Puritan ancestors. So many Americans appear to have had. I'll wager you'll forget your notions when you go hunting with me. You've a genuine new thrill in store for you, Mr. Rainsford."

"Thank you, I'm a hunter, not a murderer."

"Dear me," said the general, quite unruffled, "again that unpleasant word. But I think I can show you that your scruples[11] are quite ill-founded."

"Yes?"

> "But no animal can reason," objected Rainsford.

"Life is for the strong, to be lived by the strong, and if need be, taken by the strong. The weak of the world were put here to give the strong pleasure. I am strong. Why should I not use my gift? If I wish to hunt, why should I not? I hunt the scum of the earth—sailors from tramp ships—lascars,[12] blacks, Chinese, whites, mongrels—a thoroughbred horse or hound is worth more than a score of them."

"But they are men," said Rainsford hotly.

"Precisely," said the general. "That is why I use them. It gives me pleasure. They can reason, after a fashion. So they are dangerous."

"But where do you get them?"

The general's left eyelid fluttered down in a wink. "This island is called Ship-Trap," he answered. "Sometimes an angry god of the high seas sends them to me. Sometimes, when Providence is not so kind, I help Providence a

11. **scruples** (SKROO puhlz): feelings of doubt or guilt about a suggested action.

12. **lascars** (LAS kuhrz): sailors from the East Indies who worked on European ships.

H **Reading Focus** **Predicting** What animal is Zaroff describing?

bit. Come to the window with me."

Rainsford went to the window and looked out toward the sea.

"Watch! Out there!" exclaimed the general, pointing into the night. Rainsford's eyes saw only blackness, and then, as the general pressed a button, far out to sea Rainsford saw the flash of lights.

The general chuckled. "They indicate a channel," he said, "where there's none; giant rocks with razor edges crouch like a sea monster with wide-open jaws. They can crush a ship as easily as I crush this nut." He dropped a walnut on the hardwood floor and brought his heel grinding down on it. "Oh, yes," he said, casually, as if in answer to a question, "I have electricity. We try to be civilized here."

"Civilized? And you shoot down men?"

A trace of anger was in the general's black eyes, but it was there for but a second, and he said, in his most pleasant manner: "Dear me, what a righteous young man you are! I assure you I do not do the thing you suggest. That would be barbarous. I treat these visitors with every consideration. They get plenty of good food and exercise. They get into splendid physical condition. You shall see for yourself tomorrow." **I**

"What do you mean?"

"We'll visit my training school," smiled the general. "It's in the cellar. I have about a dozen pupils down there now. They're from the Spanish bark *San Lucar* that had the bad luck to go on the rocks out there. A very inferior lot, I regret to say. Poor specimens and more accustomed to the deck than to the jungle."

He raised his hand, and Ivan, who served as waiter, brought thick Turkish coffee. Rainsford, with an effort, held his tongue in check.

"It's a game, you see," pursued the general blandly. "I suggest to one of them that we go hunting. I give him a supply of food and an excellent hunting knife. I give him three hours' start. I am to follow, armed only with a pistol of the smallest caliber and range. If my quarry eludes me for three whole days, he wins the game. If I find him"—the general smiled—"he loses."

"Suppose he refuses to be hunted?"

"Oh," said the general, "I give him his option, of course. He need not play that game if he doesn't wish to. If he does not wish to hunt, I turn him over to Ivan. Ivan once had the honor of serving as official knouter[13] to the Great White Czar, and he has his own ideas of sport. Invariably, Mr. Rainsford, invariably they choose the hunt." **J**

"And if they win?"

The smile on the general's face widened. "To date I have not lost," he said.

Then he added, hastily: "I don't wish you to think me a braggart, Mr. Rainsford. Many of them afford only the most elementary sort of problem. Occasionally I strike a tartar.[14] One almost did win. I eventually had to use the dogs."

"The dogs?"

"This way, please. I'll show you."

The general steered Rainsford to a window. The lights from the windows sent a flickering illumination that made grotesque patterns on

---

13. **knouter** (NOWT uhr): person who beats criminals with a knout, a kind of leather whip.

14. **strike a tartar:** to take on someone stronger than you. A tartar is a violent, unmanageable person.

I **Reading Focus** **Predicting** What do you think will happen tomorrow?

J **Literary Focus** **Suspense** Why would the men choose to be hunted? How does this sentence add to the suspense?

Vocabulary **invariably** (ihn VAIR ee uh blee) *adv.:* without exception.

SCIENCE LINK

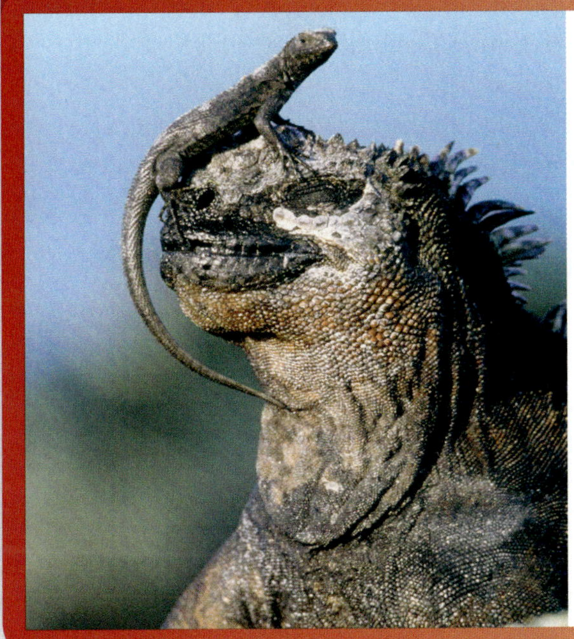

Islands and Ecosystems

Being stranded on a desert island is a popular theme in literature and in our culture—in classic novels, such as *The Swiss Family Robinson* and *Robinson Crusoe,* and in films and television series, such as *Cast Away* and *Lost.* Islands are like little worlds in which plant and animal life develop their own rhythms and relationships. Scientists find it rewarding to study island ecosystems, such as the Galapagos Islands off the coast of Ecuador. Although there might be a limited number of plants and animals to study, scientists gain many insights about their interdependency.

Ask Yourself

In what way has Zaroff shown that he, too, has studied animal behavior?

the courtyard below, and Rainsford could see moving about there a dozen or so huge black shapes; as they turned toward him, their eyes glittered greenly.

"A rather good lot, I think," observed the general. "They are let out at seven every night. If anyone should try to get into my house—or out of it—something extremely regrettable would occur to him." He hummed a snatch of song from the Folies-Bergère.

"And now," said the general, "I want to show you my new collection of heads. Will you come with me to the library?" **K**

"I hope," said Rainsford, "that you will excuse me tonight, General Zaroff. I'm really not feeling at all well."

"Ah, indeed?" the general inquired solicitously.[15] "Well, I suppose that's only natural, after your long swim. You need a good, restful night's sleep. Tomorrow you'll feel like a new man, I'll wager. Then we'll hunt, eh? I've one rather promising prospect—"

Rainsford was hurrying from the room.

"Sorry you can't go with me tonight," called the general. "I expect rather fair sport—a big, strong black. He looks resourceful— Well, good night, Mr. Rainsford; I hope you have a good night's rest."

The bed was good and the pajamas of the softest silk, and he was tired in every fiber of his being, but nevertheless Rainsford could not quiet his brain with the opiate[16] of sleep. He lay, eyes wide open. Once he thought he heard stealthy steps in the corridor outside his room. He sought to throw open the door; it would not

15. **solicitously** (suh LIHS uh tuhs lee): in a concerned manner.

16. **opiate** (OH pee iht): anything that tends to soothe or calm someone. An opiate may also be a medicine containing opium or a drug used to relieve pain.

K **Reading Focus** **Predicting** Will Rainsford go see Zaroff's new collection of heads? Why or why not?

open. He went to the window and looked out. His room was high up in one of the towers. The lights of the château were out now, and it was dark and silent, but there was a fragment of sallow moon, and by its wan light he could see, dimly, the courtyard; there, weaving in and out in the pattern of shadow, were black, noiseless forms; the hounds heard him at the window and looked up, expectantly, with their green eyes. Rainsford went back to the bed and lay down. By many methods he tried to put himself to sleep. He had achieved a doze when, just as morning began to come, he heard, far off in the jungle, the faint report of a pistol.

General Zaroff did not appear until luncheon. He was dressed faultlessly in the tweeds of a country squire. He was solicitous about the state of Rainsford's health.

"As for me," sighed the general, "I do not feel so well. I am worried, Mr. Rainsford. Last night I detected traces of my old complaint."

To Rainsford's questioning glance the general said: "Ennui. Boredom."

Then, taking a second helping of crêpes suzette, the general explained: "The hunting was not good last night. The fellow lost his head. He made a straight trail that offered no problems at all. That's the trouble with these sailors; they have dull brains to begin with, and they do not know how to get about in the woods. They do excessively stupid and obvious things. It's most annoying. Will you have another glass of Chablis, Mr. Rainsford?"

"General," said Rainsford firmly, "I wish to leave this island at once."

The general raised his thickets of eyebrows; he seemed hurt. "But, my dear fellow," the general protested, "you've only just come. You've had no hunting—"

"I wish to go today," said Rainsford. He saw the dead black eyes of the general on him, studying him. General Zaroff's face suddenly brightened.

He filled Rainsford's glass with venerable Chablis from a dusty bottle.

"Tonight," said the general, "we will hunt—you and I."

Rainsford shook his head. "No, general," he said. "I will not hunt."

The general shrugged his shoulders and delicately ate a hothouse grape. "As you wish, my friend," he said. "The choice rests entirely with you. But may I not venture to suggest that you will find my idea of sport more diverting[17] than Ivan's?"

He nodded toward the corner where the giant stood, scowling, his thick arms crossed on his hogshead of chest.

"You don't mean—" cried Rainsford. **L**

"My dear fellow," said the general, "have I not told you I always mean what I say about hunting? This is really an inspiration. I drink to a foeman worthy of my steel—at last."

The general raised his glass, but Rainsford sat staring at him.

"You'll find this game worth playing," the general said enthusiastically. "Your brain against mine. Your woodcraft against mine. Your strength and stamina against mine. Outdoor chess! And the stake is not without value, eh?"

"And if I win—" began Rainsford huskily.

"I'll cheerfully acknowledge myself defeated if I do not find you by midnight of the third day," said General Zaroff. "My sloop will place you on the mainland near a town."

17. **diverting** (duh VUR tihng): amusing.

L **Reading Focus** **Predicting** What *does* Zaroff mean?

Untitled (1992) by Paul Sierra (1944–). Oil on canvas (70" x 54").

The general read what Rainsford was thinking.

"Oh, you can trust me," said the Cossack. "I will give you my word as a gentleman and a sportsman. Of course you, in turn, must agree to say nothing of your visit here."

"I'll agree to nothing of the kind," said Rainsford.

"Oh," said the general, "in that case— But why discuss that now? Three days hence we can discuss it over a bottle of Veuve Clicquot, unless—"

The general sipped his wine.

Then a businesslike air animated him. "Ivan," he said to Rainsford, "will supply you with hunting clothes, food, a knife. I suggest you wear moccasins; they leave a poorer trail. I suggest too that you avoid the big swamp in the southeast corner of the island. We call it Death Swamp. There's quicksand there. One foolish fellow tried it. The deplorable part of it was that Lazarus followed him. You can imagine my feelings, Mr. Rainsford. I loved Lazarus; he was the finest hound in my pack. Well, I must beg you to excuse me now. I always take a siesta after lunch. You'll hardly have time for a nap, I fear. You'll want to start, no doubt. I shall not follow till dusk. Hunting at night is so much more exciting than by day, don't you think? Au revoir,[18] Mr. Rainsford, au revoir."

General Zaroff, with a deep, courtly bow, strolled from the room.

From another door came Ivan. Under one arm he carried khaki hunting clothes, a haversack of food, a leather sheath containing a long-bladed hunting knife; his right hand rested on a cocked revolver thrust in the crimson sash about his waist. . . .

18. au revoir (oh ruh VWAR): French for "goodbye."

Rainsford had fought his way through the bush for two hours. "I must keep my nerve. I must keep my nerve," he said through tight teeth.

He had not been entirely clearheaded when the château gates snapped shut behind him. His whole idea at first was to put distance between himself and General Zaroff, and, to this end, he had plunged along, spurred on by the sharp rowels of something very like panic. Now he had got a grip on himself, had stopped, and was taking stock of himself and the situation.

He saw that straight flight was futile; inevitably it would bring him face to face with the sea. He was in a picture with a frame of water, and his operations, clearly, must take place within that frame.

"I'll give him a trail to follow," muttered Rainsford, and he struck off from the rude paths he had been following into the trackless wilderness. He executed a series of intricate loops; he doubled on his trail again and again, recalling all the lore of the fox hunt and all the dodges of the fox. Night found him leg-weary, with hands and face lashed by the branches, on a thickly wooded ridge. He knew it would be insane to blunder on through the dark, even if he had the strength. His need for rest was imperative and he thought: "I have played the fox; now I must play the cat of the fable." A big tree with a thick trunk and outspread branches was nearby, and taking care to leave not the slightest mark, he climbed up into the crotch and stretching out on one of the broad limbs, after a fashion, rested. Rest brought him new confidence and almost a feeling of security. Even so zealous a hunter as General Zaroff could not trace him there, he told himself; only the devil himself could follow that complicated trail through the jungle after dark. But, perhaps, the general was a devil—

An apprehensive night crawled slowly by like a wounded snake, and sleep did not visit Rainsford, although the silence of a dead world was on the jungle. Toward morning, when a dingy gray was varnishing the sky, the cry of some startled bird focused Rainsford's attention in that direction. Something was coming through the bush, coming slowly, carefully, coming by the same winding way Rainsford had come. He flattened himself down on the limb, and through a screen of leaves almost as thick as tapestry, he watched. The thing that was approaching was a man.

It was General Zaroff. He made his way along with his eyes fixed in utmost concentration on the ground before him. He paused, almost beneath the tree, dropped to his knees and studied the ground. Rainsford's impulse was to hurl himself down like a panther, but he saw the general's right hand held something metallic—a small automatic pistol.

The hunter shook his head several times, as if he were puzzled. Then he straightened up and took from his case one of his black cigarettes; its pungent incenselike smoke floated up to Rainsford's nostrils.

Rainsford held his breath. The general's eyes had left the ground and were traveling inch by inch up the tree. Rainsford froze there, every muscle tensed for a spring. But the sharp eyes of the hunter stopped before they reached the limb where Rainsford lay; a smile spread over his brown face. Very deliberately he blew a smoke ring into the air; then he turned his back on the tree and walked carelessly away, back along the trail he had come. The swish of the underbrush against his hunting boots grew fainter and fainter. **M**

Then pent-up air burst hotly from Rainsford's lungs. His first thought made him feel sick and numb. The general could follow a trail through the woods at night; he could follow an extremely difficult trail; he must have uncanny powers; only by the merest chance had the Cossack failed to see his quarry.

> Something was coming through the bush, coming slowly, carefully, coming by the same winding way Rainsford had come.

Rainsford's second thought was even more terrible. It sent a shudder of cold horror through his whole being. Why had the general smiled? Why had he turned back? **N**

Rainsford did not want to believe what his reason told him was true, but the truth was as evident as the sun that had by now pushed through the morning mists. The general was playing with him! The general was saving him for another day's sport! The Cossack was the cat; he was the mouse. Then it was that Rainsford knew the full meaning of terror. **O**

"I will not lose my nerve. I will not."

He slid down from the tree and struck off again into the woods. His face was set and he forced the machinery of his mind to function. Three hundred yards from his hiding place he

---

M **Literary Focus** **Suspense** Re-read this paragraph. How does Connell create suspense here?

N **Reading Focus** **Predicting** Sometimes when characters ask themselves questions, the reader is left to wonder about the answer. What predictions can you make based on these questions?

O **Literary Focus** **Foreshadowing** Rainsford compares his situation to that of a mouse being hunted by a cat. Where in the story was this feeling foreshadowed?

stopped where a huge dead tree leaned precariously on a smaller living one. Throwing off his sack of food, Rainsford took his knife from its sheath and began to work with all his energy.

The job was finished at last, and he threw himself down behind a fallen log a hundred feet away. He did not have to wait long. The cat was coming again to play with the mouse.

Following the trail with the sureness of a bloodhound came General Zaroff. Nothing escaped those searching black eyes, no crushed blade of grass, no bent twig, no mark, no matter how faint, in the moss. So intent was the Cossack on his stalking that he was upon the thing Rainsford had made before he saw it. His foot touched the protruding bough that was the trigger. Even as he touched it, the general sensed his danger and leapt back with the agility of an ape. But he was not quite quick enough; the dead tree, delicately adjusted to rest on the cut living one, crashed down and struck the general a glancing blow on the shoulder as it fell; but for his alertness, he must have been smashed beneath it. He staggered, but he did not fall; nor did he drop his revolver. He stood there, rubbing his injured shoulder, and Rainsford, with fear again gripping his heart, heard the general's mocking laugh ring through the jungle.

"Rainsford," called the general, "if you are within the sound of my voice, as I suppose you are, let me congratulate you. Not many men know how to make a Malay man-catcher. Luckily for me, I too have hunted in Malacca. You are proving interesting, Mr. Rainsford. I am going now to have my wound dressed; it's only a slight one. But I shall be back. I shall be back."

When the general, nursing his bruised shoulder, had gone, Rainsford took up his flight again. It was flight now, a desperate, hopeless flight, that carried him on for some hours. Dusk came, then darkness, and still he pressed on. The ground grew softer under his moccasins; the vegetation grew ranker, denser; insects bit him savagely. Then, as he stepped forward, his foot sank into the ooze. He tried to wrench it back, but the muck sucked viciously at his foot as if it were a giant leech. With a violent effort, he tore loose. He knew where he was now. Death Swamp and its quicksand.

His hands were tight closed as if his nerve were something tangible that someone in the darkness was trying to tear from his grip. The softness of the earth had given him an idea. He stepped back from the quicksand a dozen feet or so, and, like some huge prehistoric beaver, he began to dig.

Rainsford had dug himself in in France, when a second's delay meant death. That had been a placid pastime compared to his digging now. The pit grew deeper; when it was above his shoulders, he climbed out and from some hard saplings cut stakes and sharpened them to a fine point. These stakes he planted in the bottom of the pit with the points sticking up. With flying fingers he wove a rough carpet of weeds and branches and with it he covered the mouth of the pit. Then, wet with sweat and aching with tiredness, he crouched behind the stump of a lightning-charred tree.

He knew his pursuer was coming; he heard the padding sound of feet on the soft earth, and the night breeze brought him the perfume of the general's cigarette. It seemed to Rainsford that the general was coming with unusual swiftness; he was not feeling his way along, foot by foot. Rainsford, crouching there, could not see the general, nor could he see the pit. He lived a year in a minute. Then he felt an impulse to cry aloud with joy, for he heard the sharp crackle of the breaking branches as the cover of the pit gave way; he heard the sharp scream of pain as the pointed stakes found their mark. He leapt up from his place of concealment. Then he cow-

Analyzing Visuals

Viewing and Interpreting In what way is the dog pictured here similar to and different from the hounds described in the story?

ered back. Three feet from the pit a man was standing, with an electric torch in his hand.

"You've done well, Rainsford," the voice of the general called. "Your Burmese tiger pit has claimed one of my best dogs. Again you score. I think, Mr. Rainsford, I'll see what you can do against my whole pack. I'm going home for a rest now. Thank you for a most amusing evening."

At daybreak Rainsford, lying near the swamp, was awakened by the sound that made him know that he had new things to learn about fear. It was a distant sound, faint and wavering, but he knew it. It was the baying of a pack of hounds.

Rainsford knew he could do one of two things. He could stay where he was and wait. That was suicide. He could flee. That was postponing the inevitable. For a moment he stood there, thinking. An idea that held a wild chance came to him, and, tightening his belt, he headed away from the swamp. **P**

The baying of the hounds drew nearer, then still nearer, nearer, ever nearer. On a ridge Rainsford climbed a tree. Down a watercourse, not a quarter of a mile away, he could see the bush moving. Straining his eyes, he saw the lean figure of General Zaroff; just ahead of him Rainsford made out another figure whose wide shoulders surged through the tall jungle weeds. It was the giant Ivan, and he seemed pulled forward by some unseen force. Rainsford knew that Ivan must be holding the pack in leash.

They would be on him any minute now. His

P **Literary Focus** **Suspense** What choice does Rainsford face? How has the tension of his situation increased?

mind worked frantically. He thought of a native trick he had learned in Uganda. He slid down the tree. He caught hold of a springy young sapling and to it he fastened his hunting knife, with the blade pointing down the trail; with a bit of wild grapevine he tied back the sapling. Then he ran for his life. The hounds raised their voices as they hit the fresh scent. Rainsford knew now how an animal at bay feels.

He had to stop to get his breath. The baying of the hounds stopped abruptly, and Rainsford's heart stopped too. They must have reached the knife.

He shinnied excitedly up a tree and looked back. His pursuers had stopped. But the hope that was in Rainsford's brain when he climbed died, for he saw in the shallow valley that General Zaroff was still on his feet. But Ivan was not. The knife, driven by the recoil of the springing tree, had not wholly failed.

"Nerve, nerve, nerve!" he panted, as he dashed along. A blue gap showed between the trees dead ahead. Ever nearer drew the hounds. Rainsford forced himself on toward that gap. He reached it. It was the shore of the sea. Across a cove he could see the gloomy gray stone of the château. Twenty feet below him the sea rumbled and hissed. Rainsford hesitated. He heard the hounds. Then he leapt far out into the sea. . . .

When the general and his pack reached the place by the sea, the Cossack stopped. For some minutes he stood regarding the blue-green expanse of water. He shrugged his shoulders. Then he sat down, took a drink of brandy from a silver flask, lit a perfumed cigarette, and hummed a bit from *Madama Butterfly*. **Q**

General Zaroff had an exceedingly good dinner in his great paneled dining hall that evening. With it he had a bottle of Pol Roger and half a bottle of Chambertin. Two slight annoyances kept him from perfect enjoyment. One was the thought that it would be difficult to replace Ivan; the other was that his quarry had escaped him; of course the American hadn't played the game—so thought the general as he tasted his after-dinner liqueur. In his library he read, to soothe himself, from the works of Marcus Aurelius. At ten he went up to his bedroom. He was deliciously tired, he said to himself as he locked himself in. There was a little moonlight, so before turning on his light, he went to the window and looked down at the courtyard. He could see the great hounds, and he called: "Better luck another time," to them. Then he switched on the light.

A man, who had been hiding in the curtains of the bed, was standing there.

"Rainsford!" screamed the general. "How in God's name did you get here?"

"Swam," said Rainsford. "I found it quicker than walking through the jungle."

The general sucked in his breath and smiled. "I congratulate you," he said. "You have won the game."

Rainsford did not smile. "I am still a beast at bay," he said, in a low, hoarse voice. "Get ready, General Zaroff." **R**

The general made one of his deepest bows. "I see," he said. "Splendid! One of us is to furnish a repast[19] for the hounds. The other will sleep in this very excellent bed. On guard, Rainsford. . . ."

He had never slept in a better bed, Rainsford decided.

19. **repast** (rih PAST): meal.

Q **Reading Focus** **Predicting** What do you think has happened to Rainsford? What will Zaroff do now?

R **Literary Focus** **Foreshadowing** Rainsford has always been described as a polite, well-mannered gentleman. Here, he calls himself a beast. What might this description foreshadow?

Applying Your Skills

MO **9.R.2.C.1.b** Use details from text(s): to analyze character, plot, setting, point of view **9.R.1.F.1.c** Apply pre-reading strategies to aid comprehension: predict with text support or rationale **9.W.3.A.1.e** Compose a variety of texts: including reflective writing

The Most Dangerous Game

Respond and Think Critically

Reading Focus

Quick Check

1. Why is it fitting that Zaroff's island is called Ship-Trap Island?
2. Why is Zaroff glad that Rainsford has come to the island?
3. How does the game between Zaroff and Rainsford end?

Read with a Purpose

4. What is the most dangerous game?

Reading Skills: Making Predictions

5. While reading, you made predictions about what might happen next using the chart from page 17. Now, indicate which of your predictions were correct and which were not. Then, compare your chart with a partner's to see how your predictions differed.

Pg #	Clue	My Prediction	Yes	No
19	"Ship-Trap Island"; . . .	The ship will crash into the island.		X
19	"The place has a reputation—a bad one."	Something bad will happen on the island.	X	

Literary Focus

Literary Analysis

6. **Analyze** Think about the conflicts Rainsford faces beginning with his fall off the boat. Which conflicts are external, and which are internal?
7. **Evaluate** Re-read Zaroff's arguments for hunting men. What is your opinion of his comments?
8. **Interpret** In the end, do you think that Rainsford changes his mind about hunting? Explain.

Literary Skills: Suspense and Foreshadowing

9. **Identify** What clues at the beginning of the story foreshadow danger for Rainsford?
10. **Evaluate** What part of the story did you find most suspenseful? Identify key words or phrases that kept you reading.

Literary Skills Review: Climax

11. **Analyze** The **climax** of a story is a moment of emotional intensity, when we learn how the conflict will be resolved. At what point in the story do we learn the outcome of the conflict between Rainsford and Zaroff?

Writing Focus

Think as a Reader/Writer

Use It in Your Writing The descriptive words Connell uses in this story conjure up images of a tropical island full of danger. Write your own description of a setting that poses potential dangers. Choose words that not only help convey the setting but also create a mood.

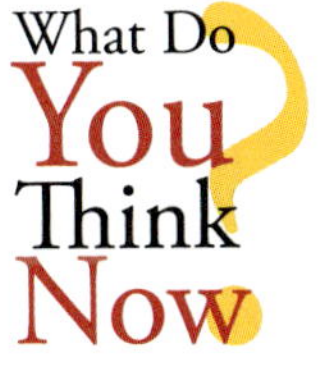

What skills helped Rainsford escape an untimely death? What skills of Zaroff's made escape difficult?

Applying Your Skills

The Most Dangerous Game

Vocabulary Development

Vocabulary Check

An **antonym** is a word that means the opposite of another word. Choose the best antonym for each boldface Vocabulary word below.

1. **receding** — a. wise
2. **surmounted** — b. approaching
3. **invariably** — c. scary
4. **imprudent** — d. surrendered
5. **disarming** — e. occasionally

Vocabulary Skills: Prefixes

What's the difference between *net* and *Internet?* The difference is just a **prefix**—a few letters added to the beginning of a word that can greatly change a word's meaning. Knowing what a prefix means can help you define a new word. The chart below contains a list of common prefixes, many of which you'll find in the Vocabulary words for this story.

Prefix	Meaning	Example
di–, dis–	no; not; away	dishonest; discontinue
im–, in–	no; not	improper; inevitable
pre–	before	prehistory
re–	back; again	return; redo
sur–	over; above	surpass

Your Turn

Use the prefix chart to answer these questions:

1. What's the difference between *preceding* and **receding**? (Hint: The root *–cede–* means "to go.")
2. How might a **disarming** smile affect you? (To *arm* means "to provide with weapons.")
3. Give an example of an **imprudent** decision.
4. Use the meanings of the prefixes *sur–* and *dis–* to explain the difference between **surmounted** and *dismounted.*
5. If Zaroff **invariably** catches his prey, what are the chances of his prey escaping?

Language Coach

Prefixes Look back at the prefixes you circled in the Vocabulary words. What other words do you know that start with these same prefixes? Write down these words in your *Reader/Writer Notebook.*

Academic Vocabulary

Write About . . .

1. Did you predict the story's outcome? Explain.
2. What idea about life do you think Connell was trying to convey in this story?

Learn It Online
Focus on prefixes with *WordSharp:*
go.hrw.com L9-38 Go

MO **9.R.2.C.1.b** Use details from text(s): to analyze character, plot, setting, point of view **9.W.3.A.1.a** Compose a variety of texts: using narrative, descriptive, expository, and/or persuasive features **9.R.1.E.1.c** Develop vocabulary through text: using glossary, dictionary and thesaurus **9.R.1.E.1.a** Develop vocabulary through text: using roots and affixes

Grammar Link

Powerful Verbs

Verbs help give writing power and color. Richard Connell's verbs help us visualize very specifically what is happening. Compare Connell's vivid verb choices below to the tamer ones at left.

Tame Verbs	Connell's Vivid Verbs
He jumped upon the rail and stood there. . . .	"He leapt upon the rail and balanced himself there. . . ."
. . . His pipe fell from his mouth. He tried to catch it. . . .	". . . His pipe . . . was knocked from his mouth. He lunged for it. . . ."
. . . The wash from the speeding yacht hit him in the face and the salt water in his open mouth made him choke.	". . . The wash from the speeding yacht slapped him in the face and the salt water in his open mouth made him gag and strangle."

Your Turn

Replace the tame, general verbs in these sentences with more vivid, powerful verbs.

1. Rainsford *went* to the cellar.
2. Whitney *said* something under his breath.
3. Zaroff *looked* around.
4. An animal *called* in the night.
5. Rainsford and Zaroff *looked* at each other.

Writing Applications Review the description you wrote in the Think as a Reader/Writer activity on page 37. See if you can replace tame verbs with more vivid verbs to add excitement to your writing.

CHOICES

As you respond to the Choices, use these **Academic Vocabulary** words as appropriate: convey, effect, excerpt, support, outcome.

REVIEW

Map the Story

TechFocus Use presentation software to create an interactive map of the story, showing the locations for the major scenes. First, find a digital image of an island (preferably an aerial view) for the first slide. Then, create a slide for each location, including an image and text from the story. Finally, link the location slides to numbers on the map.

CONNECT

Persuade Zaroff

Timed Writing Rainsford is horrified when he learns that Zaroff hunts humans, but he fails to convince Zaroff to change his ways. Write a persuasive paragraph in which you try to persuade Zaroff that human life is too precious to be used as "game." Use reasons and evidence in your argument that you think Zaroff will find convincing.

EXTEND

Write a Sequel

It is morning, and Rainsford has just awakened in Zaroff's excellent bed. What happens next? Write the next episode in Rainsford's adventure. (Does he stay on Ship-Trap Island and turn it into a theme park, or does he go home and work on behalf of endangered species? Or does he do something even more surprising?) You might let Rainsford tell his story, using "I."

Learn It Online
Create an eye-popping multimedia presentation! Visit the MediaScope minisite at:
go.hrw.com
L9-39
Go

SHORT STORY

Preparing to Read

Disguises

by **Jean Fong Kwok**

How might you escape from a place in which you are lost?

QuickWrite

Imagine that you are lost in a foreign country where you do not speak the local language. How would you find your way home? Write down your ideas.

Self Portrait (2000) by Diana Ong (1940–). Computer graphics.

Use your **RWN** to complete the activities for this selection.

MO **9.R.2.C.1.b** Use details from text(s): to analyze character, plot, setting, point of view **9.R.3.C.1.a** Use details from informational text: to identify and explain the organizational pattern

Literary Focus

Flashback Interrupting the present action of a plot to tell of events that took place in the past is called **flashback**. Flashbacks provide readers with background information that explains the events taking place in the present. As you read "Disguises," think about Jean Fong Kwok's reasons for using flashbacks.

Reading Focus

Identifying Sequence of Events Most stories follow **chronological order,** in which the story events occur in time order. In some stories, however, the writer interrupts the present time with flashbacks. As you read, look for clues that clarify the sequence of events and reveal the time and place in which the events take place.

Into Action Use a chart like the one below to follow the sequence of events in "Disguises." Evaluate each event to determine if it is part of a flashback, and note how the writer signals the beginning and end of each flashback.

Page	Event	Flashback? Yes or No	Flashback Signal
43	Mrs. Chen counts subway stops.	Yes	Continuation of numbers, 1, 2, 3 . . .; setting changes

Writing Focus

Think as a Reader/Writer

Find It in Your Reading Many authors create a backstory for their characters that explains why and how the characters came to be who they are. Although backstories are not usually part of the published story, they sometimes do surface in published stories. In "Disguises," for example, Mrs. Chen's backstory is revealed in flashbacks. Use your *Reader/Writer Notebook* to record notes about Mrs. Chen's past.

Vocabulary

lurched (lurcht) *v.:* swayed suddenly. *The train lurched violently to the left.*

rancid (RAN sihd) *adj.:* having a disgusting smell or taste. *The food thrown on the subway tracks was rancid.*

compassion (kuhm PASH uhn) *n.:* sympathy; pity. *The boy showed compassion for the woman who was lost and upset.*

desolate (DEHS uh liht) *adj.:* deserted; lonely. *The city streets at night can be desolate.*

insistently (ihn SIHST uhnt lee) *adv.:* in a demanding manner; persistently. *The lost woman tapped on the window insistently to get the clerk's attention.*

Language Coach

Derivations Many words from different languages have the same origin.For example, four of the Vocabulary words above share the same roots as their Spanish counterparts. Which Vocabulary words have the same origins as these Spanish words: *rancio, compasión, desolado, insistentemente?* Consult a Spanish-English dictionary if you need help.

Learn It Online
Elevate your vocabulary skills with Word Watch:
go.hrw.com L9-41 Go

MEET THE WRITER

Jean Fong Kwok

(1968–)

Jean Fong Kwok, the youngest of seven children, was born in Hong Kong, China. She was only five years old when her family immigrated to the United States. Like the Chen family in the story, Kwok's family struggled to learn a new language and new customs. When she entered kindergarten at a public school in Queens, New York, she spoke no English. "Like most other immigrants, my family came to make a better life for themselves, and especially for the children. It was quite a difficult time for all of us. I think I had it the easiest because I was so young and I could learn English fairly quickly."

Writing from Life

Much of Kwok's writing is based on her own experiences. In fact, "Disguises" is based on real-life events. Kwok's mother, who speaks no English, once got lost on the subway. A young man helped Mrs. Kwok get back to her stop. Of the young man, Kwok says, "We don't know who he is, of course, but to me, this is an example of how much kindness can mean and of how generous people can be. It reminds me to try to err on the side of kindness when I can."

Think About the Writer What does the quote "to err on the side of kindness" suggest about Jean Fong Kwok?

Build Background

The story's main character works in a type of factory that is sometimes referred to as a sweatshop. Sweatshops are places in which people work at low wages, for long hours, and often under dangerous conditions. Workers in such places are not backed by unions who help ensure safe conditions and fair wages. People who own sweatshops typically rely on immigrants for their workforce.

Preview the Selection

Mrs. Chen is an immigrant from China caught between the world she left behind and the world of her new country. Mrs. Chen's ideas and beliefs come from the practices of Chinese Buddhism and from cultural and family traditions in which gods, goddesses, and demons help determine one's fate.

Read with a Purpose In this story, discover how Mrs. Chen receives unlikely help in a foreign land.

Disguises

by **Jean Fong Kwok**

On the night Mrs. Chen got lost, she was wearing a golden amulet of the goddess Kuan Yin underneath her clothes, for protection. She took the subway home from the factory in Chinatown. Sitting on the long seat with her feet lightly grazing the floor, she felt the weight of sleep drag her head forward, her permed curls sinking toward the small neat hands cupped politely in her lap. As the half-empty subway car lurched through the tunnel, its movement sporadically flung her head upward. She caught herself from sleep in those moments, looking about her, alarmed, only to have exhaustion fall over her again like a blanket. The swaying of the subway threw her back and forth against the hard seat, the thin fabric of her flowered pants brushed against the shopping bag full of sewing.

Sculpture of Kuan Yin Bodhisattva of Compassion.

One . . . two . . . she had to take the subway fourteen stops to get home. The conductor's voice in English was a river of sound in her ear, noise following noise like the falling of water over rocks. Three . . . four . . . **A**

Mrs. Chen lifted her heavy head. Five . . . six . . . the door opened and her factory supervisor strolled out of the elevator with her polyester skirt flicking about her legs, stepping quickly and fastidiously, as though the clumps of fabric dust on the sewing room floor dirtied her high-heeled shoes. As she walked, she waved one wide hand in front of her mouth to clear away the dust in the air—the other gripped a wadded piece of clothing. The supervisor only came into the work area when there was a problem; otherwise, she stayed in the air-conditioned offices upstairs. Mrs. Chen could feel the supervisor's presence passing through the rows of silent women bent over their Singer sewing machines; no one dared look up, their needles racing, piercing the fabric.

A Literary Focus Flashback Mrs. Chen is on her way home. What phrases in this paragraph suggest that a flashback is about to begin?

Vocabulary **lurched** (lurcht) *v.:* swayed suddenly.

Girl kneels at an altar during a Chinese festival honoring ancestors.

Analyzing Visuals **Viewing and Interpreting** Read page 45 and tell in what way this photograph captures the essence of Mrs. Chen's childhood memories.

The supervisor threaded her way through the pack of women, bright in her silver-toned suit; its light gray material stretched across her fat stomach like the skin of a snake. She stopped next to Mrs. Chen and with fingers thick with rings of jade, snapped open the garment she had been holding—a skirt. Mrs. Chen, knowing it was not her place to meet the supervisor's eyes, cautiously raised her gaze to the round collar of her shirt, while everyone about her seemed to busy themselves with their work.

"Your seams are crooked," the supervisor announced, wrenching her mouth around the crisp Cantonese words. "This is not acceptable." She always attempted to speak Cantonese, one of the so-called "sophisticated" dialects, although her accent was painfully rural. She told everyone that she had been born in Hong Kong where the cleanest Cantonese is spoken, but, Mrs. Chen thought, her peasant roots shone clearly through her words.

Mrs. Chen stood up.

"I am so sorry," she said, her pronunciation flawless. She knew the supervisor resented her for the breeding that meant so little in this country. She could see the skirt was one she had labored over at night, sewing between the soft breaths of her sleeping family.

"May I see it?" she asked, taking a step closer.

The supervisor held it away from her. "If this ever happens again, just one more time, you will no longer be allowed to bring work home," she said. "Please remember, Mrs. Chen, you are very new to this country—we have had much trouble with recent arrivals—and my uncle is doing you a great favor to allow you to take home extra sewing, and indeed to work here at all. I do not like to see ungrateful employees. You will, of course, not be paid for that entire bundle."

Then, before Mrs. Chen could reach for the skirt, the supervisor took one corner of it in her teeth and the other in her hands, and tore it down the seams, in half. She tossed the pieces onto Mrs. Chen's table as she turned on her heel and stalked from the room. **B**

Mrs. Chen sank into her seat, spreading her fingers to shield her hot face. What crime have I committed, in which past life, to deserve these evil winds of fate that blow at my back,[1] she wondered. She realized that everyone was watching her out of the corners of their eyes, pretending they had noticed nothing. No one said anything to her. The subway doors closed and her head nodded forward.

The last station sped behind her. The overhead light went out, and the fluorescent flashes from the subway tunnel gleamed in the darkness behind her eyelids, pane after pane like frames of a movie.

Mrs. Chen, then just a girl named Lai Fong, was in China again. She was wearing green silk, preparing with her mother the ceremony for the seven goddesses who protected virginal maidens; it was the last time she would do this, because she was soon to be married. She bent to kneel on the cushion before the goddesses at the altar. Her mother, already kneeling, stopped her with a touch on her arm. Slowly, her mother gazed up at her, and her small rounded features, so much like Lai Fong's, were filled with grief and tenderness.

"My only daughter," she said, "before you pray with me this final time, you must remember this: It is said, one who is human must kneel only before the gods." She paused, and then said fiercely, "Never before anyone else." **C**

The screech of the subway rang in her ears, startling her. Mrs. Chen brushed her forehead three times, to clear away painful memories. She touched the amulet of Kuan Yin hanging from the gold chain around her neck; its shape underneath her blouse reassured her. Everyone knew that pure gold protected you from evil, but even more important, the monks at Shaolin Temple[2] had "opened it to the light," so that the goddess could truly live in it, as though it were her temple. The amulet was the only part of her mother Mrs. Chen had been able to take with her when she left China.

More people filled the subway car than she remembered. Two well-dressed black women across from her chatted, and as one laughed,

1. **crime have I committed . . . blow at my back:** Some Chinese people believe the course of one's life is determined by the "good winds" and "evil winds" that blow as a person travels along the road of life.

2. **monks at Shaolin Temple:** Monks are men who, living apart from society, devote themselves to the practices of their religion—in this case, Buddhism. The Shaolin Temple is known throughout China for its religious significance to Buddhists and for the martial-arts skills of its monks.

B **Reading Focus** **Identifying Sequence of Events** What events take place within this flashback?

C **Literary Focus** **Flashback** Why do you think that this flashback follows the flashback with the supervisor? What details about Mrs. Chen are revealed in this flashback?

the long yellow feather on her hat wiggled. A homeless man wearing a cardboard sign with English writing on it had wrapped himself around a pole near Mrs. Chen.

He gingerly peeled his hands from the pole, as if it caused him pain, and holding out his left palm, began to make his way through the car. His rancid smell, like sour milk, reached her before he did, and she tried not to breathe too deeply. Spittle clung to the sides of his mouth, suspended in droplets in his rough beard, but his lips were full and red, as though they alone had not lost their hold on life. When he stood in front of her, she studied his dirty face, and she was not afraid. It is said, she thought, we must all be beggars for one life, we only hope that that life has already past.

She opened her change purse and pressed a quarter into his palm. She had none to spare, but in this world, she mused, the times when you are able to give are so few that when you can, you must; the gods always view compassion kindly.

"Haf nice day," Mrs. Chen said, smiling. This was one of the few English phrases she had managed to learn.

The homeless man closed his fingers around the coin, his stare not leaving her smile as though it surprised him more than the quarter. He turned to the two women sitting across from her. They had stopped talking to watch Mrs. Chen. Now, they also took out their purses and gave him some change. As the homeless man went on his way, Mrs. Chen nodded to the women and they smiled back before resuming their conversation. **D**

Mrs. Chen settled into her seat and closed her eyes. The subway car clattered; it was as though she and the women and the homeless man were all in a carriage together, riding to the same place. But where were they going? We are the Monkey King, the monk, and their two companions, seeking enlightenment[3] on a road filled with demons and goddesses in disguise, she thought, and the voice of the English-speaking conductor sounded like her father's voice in China when he would tell her stories that she was too tired to understand. Then it seemed to her that the homeless man had put his head on her shoulder and they were resting together, sleeping, with the women across the way looking on.

Suddenly, she sat up. What stop was this? This must be number fourteen! This should be the right one but why did everything seem so unfamiliar? Where should she get off? The black women were gone; there was no sign of the homeless man. Mrs. Chen grabbed her shopping bag and hurried out of the train just before the doors closed, hoping this was indeed her station. Mr. Chen always scolded her for being overly imaginative. But as she stood on the platform, she realized that she had never seen this place before. **E**

She watched the few passengers make their way to the stairs. Then, from behind her, she

3. **the Monkey King, the monk, and their two companions, seeking enlightenment:** reference to *The Monkey King*, a famous sixteenth-century Chinese novel telling of a monk and his companions who travel far and wide searching for spiritual insight, or "enlightenment."

D Reading Focus Identifying Sequence of Events What do the other women on the subway do when Mrs. Chen gives the homeless man a quarter?

E Reading Focus Identifying Sequence of Events What happens while Mrs. Chen sleeps?

Vocabulary **rancid** (RAN sihd) *adj.:* having a disgusting smell or taste.
compassion (kuhm PASH uhn) *n.:* sympathy; pity.

Inside a New York City subway car.

heard the sound of footsteps. She panicked and fled for the exit, the shopping bag bumping against her legs. She had been mugged only a few weeks ago; she was the last one leaving the subway platform and a teenager in a leather jacket had blocked her way. He pulled out a long knife and held it in front of his body, half-hidden by the folds of his coat. His eyes horrified her. They were pale blue, blue as she'd only seen in the eyes of those blinded by cataracts in China, yet this man was able to see, as if he were some sort of demon. Without a word, he gestured with his knife. She gave him her purse; he took it and ran. **F**

Mrs. Chen reached the token booth, passed it, and raced up to the street. She stood outside gulping in the cool night air, holding onto the stair rail. She looked around. No one had followed her. A desolate avenue lined with streetlamps stretched before her, the concrete buildings smothered in graffiti, interrupted by long alleys. In the distance, a dark figure walked down the block, only to quickly disappear around a corner. A skeleton of a car, windshield broken, stripped of all four wheels, loomed next to the subway entrance. She did not recognize anything.

This was a terrible place. She took the amulet out of her blouse and clutched it. A low wind whistled through the avenue, setting stray pieces of litter skittering across the concrete. She went back to the token booth.

F **Reading Focus** **Identifying Sequence of Events** Why is Mrs. Chen so scared? What previous event caused her to be so frightened?

Vocabulary **desolate** (DEHS uh liht) *adj.:* deserted; lonely.

She was relieved to see the clerk, a heavy man with a gray goatee, through the murky glass; he was an official, he could help her. She went around to the front of the booth and rapped on the glass with her knuckles.

"Hello? Hello?" she said.

He was talking on the phone, and when he saw her, shifted so that his back was to her. She tapped on the booth more insistently. He waved for her to wait. She searched through her purse to find the piece of paper with her street address on it. Her son had written it out for her, just in case she got lost.

"Hello, hello," she said, her voice growing shriller.

Hunching over the phone, the clerk ignored her.

"HELLO!" she screamed.

He turned around. Mrs. Chen quickly pushed the crumpled paper toward him. He studied it, and said some words to her in English.

"No," she said, "no understand."

He repeated what he'd said, only louder. She shook her head. The man ran his fingers across the top of his puffy hair, then pointed at the receiver he was holding, like she was keeping him from something. She pressed her ear as close to the glass as she could. She tried to understand even one word of what he said, but it was just babble to her.

"Dank you," she said. "Bye bye." The man shrugged and returned to his phone conversation.

She slowly climbed to the street. *Please, Kuan Yin, let me get home to my child and husband . . .* she prayed. There was a pay telephone on the corner. She walked to it as fast as she could, put down her bag, fumbled for a quarter, and dialed her home number. Her husband answered on the first ring.

"Big Brother Chen?" she said. She never called him by his first name because that would be disrespectful, even though they had been married more than ten years.

"Where have you been?" he asked angrily.

"I don't know—I'm lost." She leaned against the side of the phone booth and began to sob.

"How could you be so stupid?" he yelled, as he always did when he was afraid. "Your son is here, waiting for his dinner—why don't you ever pay attention to where you're going? Where are you?"

"I don't know."

"You have to stop that crying," Mr. Chen said. His voice grew more quiet. "Listen, don't be afraid. We have to find out where you are and then we will come get you. Let me put Sonny on the line."

She wiped her eyes on her sleeve and tried to pull herself together. Her child must not know how upset she was.

His voice seemed much higher over the phone. "Mommy, where are you?"

"You have to help Mommy," she said. Sonny was only nine years old but he was as smart as the boys a grade ahead of him. He was learning English so rapidly. She described her surroundings but he did not recognize them.

"I know," Sonny said. "Can you spell the name of the street by you? Can you see the street sign?"

She found it but the word was very long. She had never been that good with the English alphabet.

"M . . . I . . . no, E . . . and then A . . . no, R . . ." she began. In the middle of her spelling, she had to put another coin in the telephone. Finally, she came up with something that Sonny thought could be the name of a street.

Vocabulary **insistently** (ihn SIHST uhnt lee) *adv.:* in a demanding manner; persistently.

CULTURE LINK

Buddhism

Buddhism is based on the teachings of Siddhartha Gautama, the son of a prince of Nepal, who was born around 563 B.C. Although Gautama had experienced little suffering in his own life, he was troubled by the suffering of others. At age 29, Gautama set out on a journey across India to find the meaning of life and the reason for human suffering. One day while meditating, Gautama realized that the origin of human suffering was desire. From this realization, Gautama believed he had achieved a state of enlightenment, or nirvana. Gautama became known to his followers as the Buddha, or "the enlightened one." The Buddha taught his followers that if they practiced the Eightfold Path, they would achieve a state of enlightenment that would ease their suffering.

The Eightfold Path

Right Views Seeing life as it really is

Right Intentions Living a life of good will; striving toward perfection

Right Speech Avoiding lies and gossip

Right Action Trying to be law-abiding and honest

Right Living Avoiding work that harms others

Right Effort Seeking to prevent evil

Right Mindfulness Being in constant awareness of one's self

Right Concentration Directing the mind in meditation

Ask Yourself **How does Mrs. Chen's behavior reflect Buddhist ideals?**

"But I don't know where it is," he said.

"Do you have any maps?" she asked.

"Yeah," he said. "Let me check in my geography book. That has maps."

She could hear him getting off the chair and running to his books. He was gone for a few minutes. Mrs. Chen looked at her amulet, glinting brightly against her dark blouse. She brought the golden goddess to her face and laid it against her cheek.

She heard shuffling, then Sonny came back on the phone.

"Mommy?" he said. "I can't find it. It's not in my book. I'm sorry." He started to sniffle.

"When are you going to come home, Mommy?" he asked.

"Shhh . . . don't cry," she said, trying to sound calm. She could hear Mr. Chen cursing in the background. "Mommy will be fine. I will walk around and maybe I will recognize something. Just tell your father that I will call soon."

She hung up before she had to speak to Mr. Chen again. It would be more frightening to talk to her husband; he was just as helpless as she, and he would not be as easily comforted as Sonny. Her quarters were almost gone and she did not want to waste another. Perhaps she shouldn't have given one to the homeless man, she thought. What was kindness in this world? She rested her head against the telephone for a moment. *I invite the goddess Kuan Yin,* she said under her breath, *from the Shaolin Temple in the hills of Canton, to come to me now; so soon as I . . .*

She felt a hand close to her ear reach for the amulet, as though it were trying to take it before she could finish her prayer. Mrs. Chen screamed and ducked at the same time. Grasping the shopping bag, she swung it in a circle, felt it hit, heard the sides rip. She hugged the bag and fled toward the subway station, hampered by its bulk. Someone seemed to race away in the opposite direction. *So soon as I call her,* she gasped, running, *so soon will she appear. . . .*

As Mrs. Chen rushed to the steps, she

Exterior of a moving subway car.

Analyzing Visuals **Viewing and Interpreting**
How does this image reflect Mrs. Chen's emotions at this point of the story?

caught a glimpse of features that looked Chinese. She skidded to a stop.

"Mister! Mister!" she shouted.

The young man turned, surprised. "Yes?" He was Chinese. He must be a student, with his thick glasses and a green bookbag slung over his narrow shoulder.

Mrs. Chen almost cried from relief. "I am lost," she said, breathing hard, "and someone just tried to take my necklace."

"My Cantonese is very bad," he said in Mandarin.[4]

"We are both Chinese," Mrs. Chen said, part in Mandarin and part in Cantonese, "please help me."

She explained the situation to him, her voice breaking—how she was lost and almost robbed, how she couldn't follow the token booth clerk, how her son and husband couldn't help her—using as much Mandarin as she remembered and filling in the rest with Cantonese. She put her bag on the ground and took out the piece of paper with her address on it. The young man listened and nodded; he seemed to understand her story. He took the slip of paper and the two of them went into the subway station. As they approached the token booth, the clerk recognized Mrs. Chen and rolled his eyes. **G**

The young man spoke to the clerk in English and showed him her address. Then he said to Mrs. Chen, "The train you were on must have been re-routed. They probably announced the change but you did not understand. What you must do now is take the train over here for two stops and then switch . . ."

But Mrs. Chen was frantic. She clutched his arm, shaking her head.

He stopped speaking and looked at her fingers buried in his jacket. "I will go with you," he said.

4. **Mandarin** (MAN duhr ihn): official, most widely spoken language of China.

G **Reading Focus** **Identifying Sequence of Events** Why does the subway clerk roll his eyes when he sees Mrs. Chen? What happened earlier that gave the clerk such an opinion of Mrs. Chen?

Analyzing Visuals

Viewing and Interpreting
Which story setting does this photograph capture?

An abandoned alley in lower Manhattan.

Mrs. Chen sighed in relief and then offered to pay for his token, but he put one in the slot as he waved her hand away. When they got on the subway, the young man took out a book and began to study, only peering at her occasionally to check that she was all right. She was too exhausted to even try to make conversation. *Kuan Yin, thank you for your aid. . . .* The student escorted her the entire way to her own station. Mrs. Chen asked him to come to her house, so she could at least give him something to eat to repay his kindness, but when she passed through the gate, he did not follow.

She turned back to him. "Thank you," she said.

The young man grinned and bowed, his schoolbag slipping off his shoulder. She bowed in response[5] but by the time she straightened, he was gone.

When Mrs. Chen got home, Sonny threw himself at her and cried, while Mr. Chen roughly patted her on the arm. They were quiet as she told them how the young man had helped her, how he must have been sent by the gods. Mrs. Chen lit incense at the altar[6] in their kitchen to formally give thanks and noticed there were extra incense stubs in the holder—Mr. Chen had also prayed for her.

"We were afraid for you," he said. "We thought we might have lost you."

Later that night, she had to stay awake to do her work. She bent to sew the pieces of the torn skirt, joining again the severed parts with thread.

5. **The young . . . bowed in response:** reference to the Chinese custom of bowing to express respect for another person.

6. **lit incense at the altar:** Incense is a substance that has a pleasant smell when burned. The burning of incense is a gesture of respect and gratitude in several religions.

Applying Your Skills

9.R.2.C.1.b Use details from text(s): to analyze character, plot, setting, point of view 9.R.3.C.1.a Use details from informational text: to identify and explain the organizational pattern *Also covered* 9.W.3.A.1.a; 9.R.1.G.1.a

Disguises

Respond and Think Critically

Reading Focus

Quick Check

1. Why do you think Mrs. Chen dreams of her past while on the subway?
2. What contributes to Mrs. Chen's fear when she discovers she is lost?

Read with a Purpose

3. How does Mrs. Chen find her way home?

Reading Skills: Identifying Sequence of Events

4. Complete your sequence chart and compare it with a partner's to see if your events match up. With a partner, make a time line that shows the events taking place in the present and the events that took place in the past.

Page	Event	Flashback? Yes or No	Flashback Signal
43	Mrs. Chen counts subway stops.	Yes	Continuation of numbers 1, 2, 3 . . .; setting changes

Vocabulary Check

Match each Vocabulary word with its definition.

5. **lurched** — a. persistently
6. **rancid** — b. having a bad smell or taste
7. **compassion** — c. deserted
8. **desolate** — d. swayed suddenly
9. **insistently** — e. pity

Literary Focus

Literary Analysis

10. **Analyze** Mrs. Chen becomes lost in a busy urban environment. In what way does the setting contribute to Mrs. Chen's challenges?
11. **Interpret** At the end of the story, Mrs. Chen is back at home, sewing the torn skirt. What does this action reveal about her life or her character?
12. **Interpret** Why do you think this story is titled "Disguises"?

Literary Skills: Flashback

13. **Analyze** Flashbacks can reveal a character's past or convey a present event's cause. What purposes do the flashbacks serve in this story?

Literary Skills Review: Conflict

14. **Analyze** A **conflict** is a struggle between opposing forces and can be external (against an outside force) or internal (within a character's mind). What conflict(s) does Mrs. Chen experience? What is the outcome?

Writing Focus

Think as a Reader/Writer

Use It in Your Writing What do you think Kwok's backstory, or character history, for Mrs. Chen's supervisor might be? Write a brief description of the supervisor's past.

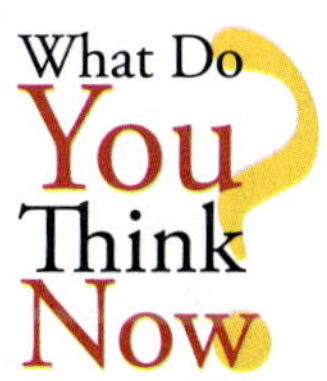

In what way is "Disguises" a story about escape?

SHORT STORY

Preparing to Read

Liberty

by **Julia Alvarez**

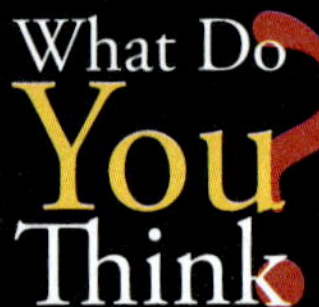

Why might a person or a family need to escape from their homeland?

QuickWrite

People often have mixed feelings about leaving a place, even when they are leaving to escape danger. Write down some reasons people might have for leaving their homes, and describe how they might feel.

Ferry passengers look at the Statue of Liberty.

Reader/Writer Notebook

Use your **RWN** to complete the activities for this selection.

MO **9.R.2.C.1.b** Use details from text(s): to analyze character, plot, setting, point of view

Literary Focus

Setting and Conflict The **setting** of a story is more than just a place. It is also the social and historical conditions in which characters live. For example, in a story taking place before women had the right to vote, the story's characters may have certain attitudes about women and their place in society. Those attitudes may in turn spark conflict as a character struggles against the expectations of society.

TechFocus People sometimes take pictures or make videos to help them remember special places. As you read "Liberty," make a list of what the narrator might want to remember.

Reading Focus

Analyzing Details The details a writer uses in a story can tell you many things. For example, details about a time or place help to create a specific setting. Details describing a character's thoughts or feelings often help you understand the conflicts a character is facing.

Into Action As you read, create a chart such as this one to record and analyze details in "Liberty."

Detail	What It Tells Me
Papi and Mami look scared when talking about leaving their country.	The situation is dangerous; they are worried about what might happen.
Mami would rather have visas than a puppy.	

Writing Focus

Think as a Reader/Writer

Find It in Your Reading In "Liberty," Julia Alvarez not only brings people to life, but she also brings one special dog to life through her powers of description. As you read, write down in your *Reader/Writer Notebook* the details describing the narrator's dog, Liberty.

Vocabulary

elect (ih LEHKT) *v.:* choose as a course of action. *I hate to waste my time, so I elect to schedule my week very carefully.*

distracted (dih STRAKT ihd) *adj.:* not able to concentrate; unfocused. *She was so distracted I had to shout to get her attention.*

admonitions (ad muh NIHSH uhnz) *n.:* scoldings; warnings. *When Mami forgot her admonitions to me about doing my homework, I knew something was wrong.*

impression (ihm PREHSH uhn) *n.:* idea; notion. *I had a strong impression that my father was keeping something secret.*

inconsolable (ihn kuhn SOHL uh buhl) *adj.:* unable to be comforted; brokenhearted. *I was inconsolable and could not stop crying when they told me we had to leave.*

resort (rih ZAWRT) *v.:* turn to something when in need. *When the rain started, we had to resort to our backup plan.*

Language Coach

Multiple Meanings Some words, including three on the list above, have more than one meaning. For example, a person who impersonates others is said to do *impressions.* The word *impression* can also refer to a pattern made by pressing. What definition does *impression* have as used in the list above?

Look through the list again. What other words on the list have multiple meanings?

Learn It Online

See the *PowerNotes* introduction to this story on:

go.hrw.com L9-55 

MEET THE WRITER

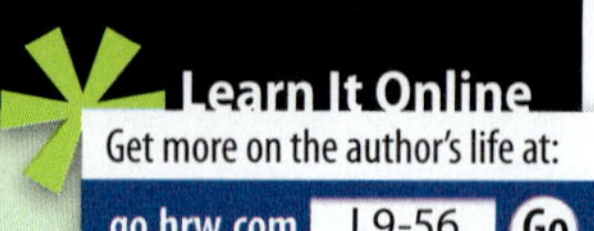

Learn It Online
Get more on the author's life at:
go.hrw.com L9-56 Go

Julia Alvarez
(1950–)

Witness to Terror

Like the girl in "Liberty," Julia Alvarez knows political terror and exile firsthand. Her family fled from the Dominican Republic when she was ten. Perhaps that is why Alvarez says she "can't shut up" about important human events. Her novel *In the Time of the Butterflies* (1994) was inspired by the true story of the 1960 murders of three sisters who were wives of political prisoners in her homeland.

"Magic Happened in My Life"

When Alvarez first arrived in the United States, she remembers "feeling out of place, feeling that I would never belong in this world. . . . And then, magic happened in my life. . . . An English teacher asked us to write little stories about ourselves." Writing has helped her understand both her new and old worlds. Having two cultures and two languages is central to Alvarez's work. Her novels *How the Garcia Girls Lost Their Accents* (1991) and *¡Yo!* (1997) follow four sisters who grow up in America speaking Spanglish, a mixture of Spanish and English.

"I am a Dominican, hyphen, American. As a fiction writer, I find that the most exciting things happen in the realm of that hyphen, the place where two worlds collide or blend together."

Think About the Writer How might Alvarez's life have been different without writing?

Build Background

Although the setting of "Liberty" is not directly stated, it most likely takes place in the Dominican Republic. Julia Alvarez lived there until her family was forced to leave because of her father's opposition to the dictator Rafael Trujillo. During Trujillo's time in power (1930–1961), Dominicans had limited civil rights, and the secret police dealt brutally with anyone who opposed Trujillo.

Preview the Selection

In this story you'll meet a unnamed young girl who lives with her family in an unnamed island country that is undergoing political upheaval.

Read with a Purpose Read this story to find out what a young girl learns about freedom from a dog named Liberty.

Liberty

by **Julia Alvarez**

Papi came home with a dog whose kind we had never seen before. A black-and-white-speckled electric current of energy. It was a special breed with papers, like a person with a birth certificate. Mami just kept staring at the puppy with a cross look on her face. "It looks like a mess!" she said. "Take it back."

"Mami, it is a gift!" Papi shook his head. It would be an insult to Mister Victor, who had given us the dog. The American consul[1] wanted to thank us for all we'd done for him since he'd been assigned to our country.

"If he wanted to thank us, he'd give us our visas,"[2] Mami grumbled. For a while now, my parents had been talking about going to the United States so Papi could return to school. I couldn't understand why a grown-up who could do whatever he wanted would elect to go back to a place I so much wanted to get out of.

On their faces when they talked of leaving there was a scared look I also couldn't understand. **A**

"Those visas will come soon," Papi promised. But Mami just kept shaking her head about the dog. She had enough with four girls to take on puppies, too. Papi explained that the dog would stay at the end of the yard in a pen. He would not be allowed in the house. He would not be pooping in Mami's orchid garden. He would not be barking until late at night. "A well-behaved dog," Papi concluded. "An American dog."

The little black-and-white puppy yanked at Papi's trouser cuff with his mouth. "What shall we call you?" Papi asked him.

"Trouble," Mami suggested, kicking the puppy away. He had left Papi's trousers to come slobber on her leg.

"We will call him Liberty. Life, liberty, and the pursuit of happiness." Papi quoted the U.S.A. Constitution. "Eh, Liberty, you are a lucky sign!"

Liberty barked his little toy barks and all us kids laughed. "Trouble." Mami kept shaking her head as she walked away. Liberty trotted behind her as if he agreed that that was the better name for him.

Mami was right, too—Liberty turned out to be trouble. He ate all of Mami's orchids, and that little hyperactive baton of a tail knocked things off the low coffee

---

1. **American consul** (KAHN suhl): person appointed by the United States government to represent American interests and provide assistance to Americans living in a foreign country.
2. **visas** (VEE zuhz): certificates granting official approval to enter a country.

A **Literary Focus** **Setting and Conflict** How does the story's setting contribute to the conflict the family faces?

Vocabulary **elect** (ih LEHKT) *v.:* choose as a course of action.

table whenever Liberty climbed on the couch to leave his footprints in among the flower prints. He tore up Mami's garden looking for buried treasure. Mami screamed at Liberty and stamped her foot. "Perro sin vergüenza!"[3] But Liberty just barked back at her.

"He doesn't understand Spanish," Papi said lamely. "Maybe if you correct him in English, he'll behave better!"

Mami turned on him, her slipper still in midair. Her face looked as if she'd light into him after she was done with Liberty. "Let him go be a pet in his own country if he wants instructions in English!" In recent weeks, Mami had changed her tune about going to the United States. She wanted to stay in her own country. She didn't want Mister Victor coming around our house and going off into the study with Papi to talk over important things in low, worried voices.

"All liberty involves sacrifice," Papi said in a careful voice. Liberty gave a few perky barks as if he agreed with that.

Mami glared at Papi. "I told you I don't want trouble—" She was going to say more, but her eye fell on me and she stopped herself. "Why aren't you with the others?" she scolded. It was as if I had been the one who had dug up her lily bulbs.

The truth was that after Liberty arrived, I never played with the others. It was as if I had found my double in another species. I had always been the tomboy, the live wire, the troublemaker, the one who was going to drive Mami to drink, the one she was going to give away to the Haitians. While the sisters dressed pretty and stayed clean in the playroom, I was out roaming the world looking for trouble. And now I had found someone to share my adventures.

"I'll take Liberty back to his pen," I offered. There was something I had figured out that Liberty had yet to learn: when to get out of Mami's way.

She didn't say yes and she didn't say no. She seemed distracted, as if something else was on her mind. As I led Liberty away by his collar, I could see her talking to Papi. Suddenly she started to cry, and Papi held her. **B**

"It's okay," I consoled Liberty. "Mami doesn't mean it. She really does love you. She's just nervous." It was what my father always said when Mami scolded me harshly.

At the back of the property stood Liberty's pen—a chain-link fence around a dirt square at the center of which stood a doghouse. Papi had built it when Liberty first came, a cute little house, but then he painted it a putrid green that reminded me of all the vegetables I didn't like. It was always a job to get Liberty to go into that pen.

Sure enough, as soon as he saw where we were headed, he took off, barking, toward the house, then swerved to the front yard to our favorite spot. It was a grassy knoll[4] surrounded by a tall hibiscus hedge. At the center stood a tall, shady samán tree. From there, no one could see you up at the house. Whenever I did something wrong, this was where I hid out until the punishment winds blew over. That was where Liberty headed, and I was fast behind on his trail.

Inside the clearing I stopped short. Two

3. **"Perro sin vergüenza!"**: Spanish for "shameless dog."

4. **knoll** (nohl): small hill.

B **Reading Focus** **Analyzing Details** Mami seems distracted, and then she suddenly starts to cry. What do these details tell you about Mami and the family's situation?

Vocabulary **distracted** (dih STRAKT ihd) *adj.:* not able to concentrate; unfocused.

A colorful house catches the shadow of a passerby.

Analyzing Visuals

Viewing and Interpreting What mood does this photograph create? Does it reflect the narrator's feelings? Explain.

strange men in dark glasses were crouched behind the hedge. The fat one had seized Liberty by the collar and was pulling so hard on it that poor Liberty was almost standing on his hind legs. When he saw me, Liberty began to bark, and the man holding him gave him a yank on the collar that made me sick to my stomach. I began to back away, but the other man grabbed my arm. "Not so fast," he said. Two little scared faces—my own—looked down at me from his glasses.

"I came for my dog," I said, on the verge of tears.

"Good thing you found him," the man said. "Give the young lady her dog," he ordered his friend, and then he turned to me. "You haven't seen us, you understand?"

I didn't understand. It was usually I who was the one lying and grown-ups telling me to tell the truth. But I nodded, relieved when the man released my arm and Liberty was back in my hands. **C**

"It's okay, Liberty." I embraced him when I put him back in his pen. He was as sad as I was. We had both had a hard time with Mami, but this was the first time we'd come across mean and scary people. The fat man had almost broken Liberty's neck, and the other one had left his fingerprints on my arm. After I locked up the pen, I watched Liberty wander back slowly to his house and actually go inside, turn around, and stick his little head out the door. He'd always avoided that ugly doghouse before. I walked back to my own house, head down, to find my parents and tell them what I had seen.

C **Literary Focus** **Setting and Conflict** The two strange men do not have names. In what way do these men help reveal the story's setting? What conflict do they trigger?

Overnight, it seemed, Mister Victor moved in. He ate all his meals with us, stayed 'til late, and when he had to leave, someone from the embassy was left behind "to keep an eye on things." Now, when Papi and Mister Victor talked or when the *tíos*[5] came over, they all went down to the back of the property near Liberty's pen to talk. Mami had found some wires in the study, behind the portrait of Papi's great-grandmother fanning herself with a painted fan. The wires ran behind a screen and then out a window, where there was a little box with lots of other wires coming from different parts of the house.

Mami explained that it was no longer safe to talk in the house about certain things. But the only way you knew what things those were was when Mami leveled her eyes on you as if she were pressing the off button on your mouth. She did this every time I asked her what was going on. **D**

"Nothing," she said stiffly, and then she urged me to go outside and play. Forgotten were the admonitions to go study or I would flunk out of fifth grade. To go take a bath or the *microbios*[6] might kill me. To drink my milk or I would grow up stunted and with no teeth. Mami seemed absent and tense and always in tears. Papi was right—she was too nervous, poor thing.

I myself was enjoying a heyday of liberty. Several times I even got away with having one of Mister Victor's Coca-Colas for breakfast instead of my boiled milk with a beaten egg, which Liberty was able to enjoy instead.

"You love that dog, don't you?" Mister Victor asked me one day. He was standing by the pen with Papi waiting for the uncles. He had a funny accent that sounded like someone making fun of Spanish when he spoke it.

I ran Liberty through some of the little tricks I had taught him, and Mister Victor laughed. His face was full of freckles—so that it looked as if he and Liberty were kin. I had the impression that God had spilled a lot of his colors when he was making American things.

Soon the uncles arrived and the men set to talking. I wandered into the pen and sat beside Liberty with my back to the house and listened. The men were speaking in English, and I had picked up enough of it at school and in my parents' conversations to make out most of what was being said. They were planning some hunting expedition for a goat with guns to be delivered by Mister Charlie. Papi was going to have to leave the goat to the others because his tennis shoes were missing. Though I understood the words—or thought I did—none of it made sense. I knew my father did not own a pair of tennis shoes, we didn't know a Mister Charlie, and who ever heard of hunting a goat? **E**

As Liberty and I sat there with the sun baking the tops of our heads, I had this sense that the world as I knew it was about to end. The image of the two men in mirror glasses flashed through my head. So as not to think about them, I put my arm around Liberty and buried my face in his neck.

5. ***tíos:*** Spanish for "uncles."

6. ***microbios:*** Spanish for "germs."

D **Reading Focus** **Analyzing Details** Mami finds wires in the house. What might this detail signify?

E **Reading Focus** **Analyzing Details** The narrator hears the men talk about hunting a goat and thinks their conversation is strange. How might her reaction be a clue to what the men are really saying?

Vocabulary **admonitions** (ad muh NIHSH uhnz) *n.:* scoldings; warnings.
impression (ihm PREHSH uhn) *n.:* idea; notion.

Late one morning Mami gave my sisters and me the news. Our visa had come. Mister Victor had arranged everything, and that very night we were going to the United States of America! Wasn't that wonderful! She flashed us a bright smile, as if someone were taking her picture.

We stood together watching her, alarmed at this performance of happiness when really she looked like she wanted to cry. All morning aunts had been stopping by and planting big kisses on our foreheads and holding our faces in their hands and asking us to promise we would be very good. Until now, we hadn't a clue why they were so worked up.

As Liberty and I sat there with the sun baking the tops of our heads, I had this sense that the world as I knew it was about to end.

Mami kept smiling her company smile. She had a little job for each of us to do. There would not be room in our bags for everything. We were to pick the one toy we wanted to take with us to the United States.

I didn't even have to think twice about my choice. It had suddenly dawned on me we were leaving, and that meant leaving *everything* behind. "I want to take Liberty."

Mami started shaking her head no. We could not take a dog into the United States of America. That was not allowed.

"Please," I begged with all my might. "Please, please, Mami, please." Repetition sometimes worked—each time you said the word, it was like giving a little push to the yes that was having a hard time rolling out of her mouth.

"I said no!" The bright smile on Mami's face had grown dimmer and dimmer. "*N-O.*" She spelled it out for me in case I was confusing no with another word like yes. "I said a toy, and I mean a toy."

I burst into tears. I was not going to the United States unless I could take Liberty! Mami shook me by the shoulders and asked me between clenched teeth if I didn't understand we had to go to the United States or else. But all I could understand was that a world without Liberty would break my heart. I was inconsolable. Mami began to cry. **F**

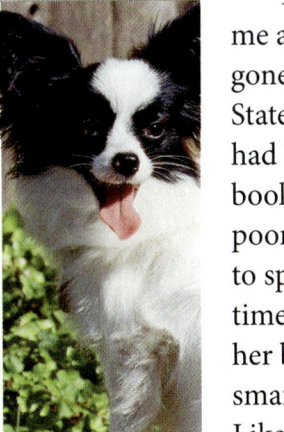

Tía[7] Mimi took me aside. She had gone to school in the States and always had her nose in a book. In spite of her poor taste in how to spend her free time, I still loved her because she had smart things to say. Like telling Mami that punishment was not the way to make kids behave. "I'm going to tell you a little secret," she offered now. "You're going to find liberty when you get to the United States."

"Really?" I asked.

She hesitated a minute, and then she gave me a quick nod. "You'll see what I mean," she said. And then, giving me a pat on the butt, she added, "Come on, let's go pack. How about taking that wonderful book I got you on the Arabian Nights?"

Late in the night someone comes in and shakes us awake. "It's time!"

Half asleep, we put on our clothes,

7. *tía:* Spanish for "aunt."

F **Literary Focus** **Setting and Conflict** The narrator and Mami battle over what will happen to Liberty. In what way does this conflict relate to the setting of the story?

Vocabulary **inconsolable** (ihn kuhn SOHL uh buhl) *adj.:* unable to be comforted; brokenhearted.

hands helping our arms to go into the right sleeves, buttoning us up, running a comb through our hair.

We were put to sleep hours earlier because the plane had not come in.

But now it's time.

"Go sit by the door," we are ordered, as the hands, the many hands that now seem to be in control, finish with us. We file out of the bedroom, one by one, and go sit on the bench where packages are set down when Mami comes in from shopping. There is much rushing around. Mister Victor comes by and pats us on the head like dogs. "We'll have to wait a few more minutes," he says.

In that wait, one sister has to go to the bathroom. Another wants a drink of water. I am left sitting with my baby sister, who is dozing with her head on my shoulder. I lay her head down on the bench and slip out.

Through the dark patio down the path to the back of the yard I go. Every now and then a strange figure flashes by. I have said good-bye to Liberty a dozen times already, but there is something else I have left to do.

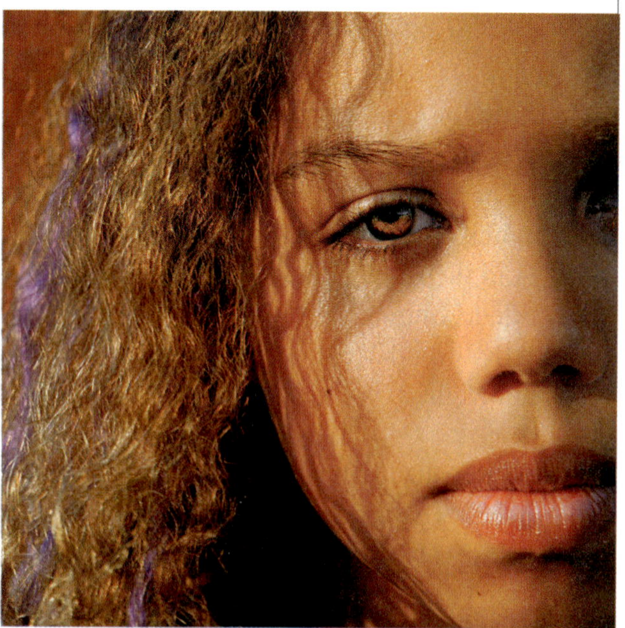

Sitting on the bench, I had an image again of those two men in mirror glasses. After we are gone, they come onto the property. They smash the picture of Papi's great-grandmother fanning herself. They knock over the things on the coffee table as if they don't know any better. They throw the flowered cushions on the floor. They smash the windows. And then they come to the back of the property and they find Liberty.

Quickly, because I hear calling from the big house, I slip open the door of the pen. Liberty is all over me, wagging his tail so it beats against my legs, jumping up and licking my face.

"Get away!" I order sharply, in a voice he is not used to hearing from me. I begin walking back to the house, not looking around so as not to encourage him. I want him to run away before the gangsters come.

He doesn't understand and keeps following me. Finally I have to resort to Mami's techniques. I kick him, softly at first, but then, when he keeps tagging behind me, I kick him hard. He whimpers and dashes away toward the front yard, disappearing in areas of darkness, then reappearing when he passes through lighted areas. At the front of the house, instead of turning toward our secret place, he keeps on going straight down the drive, through the big gates, to the world out there. G

He will beat me to the United States is what I am thinking as I head back to the house. I will find Liberty there, like Tía Mimi says. But I already sense it is a different kind of liberty my aunt means. All I can do is hope that when we come back—as Mami has promised we will—my Liberty will be waiting for me here.

G Literary Focus Setting and Conflict How are the narrator and Liberty in conflict at the end of the story?

Vocabulary resort (rih ZAWRT) *v.:* turn to something when in need.

Applying Your Skills

MO 9.R.2.C.1.b Use details from text(s): to analyze character, plot, setting, point of view 9.R.1.H.1.a Apply post-reading skills to comprehend, interpret, analyze, and evaluate text: identify and explain the relationship between the main idea and supporting details

Liberty

Respond and Think Critically

Reading Focus

Quick Check

1. How does Liberty come to live with the family? What happens to Liberty at the story's end?
2. What do the two strangers do when they visit the family's house? What events does their visit set in motion?

Read with a Purpose

3. What does Liberty teach the narrator about both personal and political freedom?

Reading Skills: Analyzing Details

4. Analyzing story details may help you follow a story's conflict and its resolution. Review the chart you made as you read the story. Which details hint at the conflicts the story's characters face? Circle those details.

Detail	What It Tells Me
Papi and Mami look scared when talking about leaving their country.	The situation is dangerous; they are worried about what might happen.

Literary Focus

Literary Analysis

5. **Compare** The narrator describes Liberty as her "double in another species." Describe her character. What traits do she and her dog share?
6. **Interpret** The word *liberty* is central to this story: It is the title, the dog's name, and a central story idea. Explain how the story's **theme,** or insight about life, relates to the idea of liberty.
7. **Evaluate** What effect did the writer's decision to tell this story from a child's point of view create? Would the story be equally effective if it were told from the point of view of the mother or the father? Explain.

Literary Skills: Setting and Conflict

8. **Draw Conclusions** How does the political setting of the story create conflict for the narrator? Why might the author have decided not to directly reveal the setting of the story?

Literary Skills Review: Exposition

9. **Evaluate** Many stories begin with a brief exposition that introduces the story's setting, its main character, and his or her conflict. Alvarez chooses to skip the exposition and immediately launch into the action. Do you think Alvarez's choice is effective? Explain why or why not, supporting your ideas with details from the text.

Writing Focus

Think as a Reader/Writer

Use It in Your Writing Alvarez uses descriptive details to bring the dog, Liberty, to life for readers. How does the depiction of the dog help to highlight the idea or concept of liberty? Write a brief essay describing your ideas. Use details from the story to support the points you make.

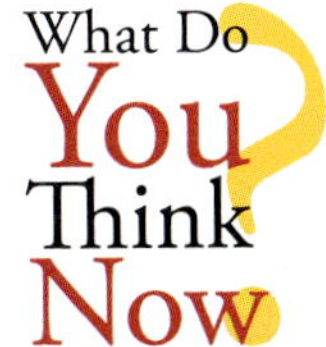

What sacrifice does the narrator make so that she and her family can escape from a difficult situation? Did she have a choice?

Applying Your Skills

Liberty

Vocabulary Development

Vocabulary Check

Answer each of the questions below using the boldface Vocabulary word in your answer.

1. What might make a star athlete **inconsolable**?
2. How can you tell if someone is **distracted** during a class?
3. What is your strongest **impression** of what it is like to go to college?
4. Why might someone who is normally very quiet **resort** to shouting?
5. How do you decide which of two weekend activities you will **elect** to do?
6. What kind of book might include **admonitions** to the reader?

Vocabulary Skills: Using a Thesaurus

A **synonym** is a word that has the same, or nearly the same, meaning as another word. To find synonyms, you can use a **thesaurus,** which is a reference source that lists synonyms, often based on a word's different shades of meaning. You can then follow the cross-references given until you find the exact meaning you want to convey.

This chart shows how one student used a thesaurus to find synonyms for *admonition.*

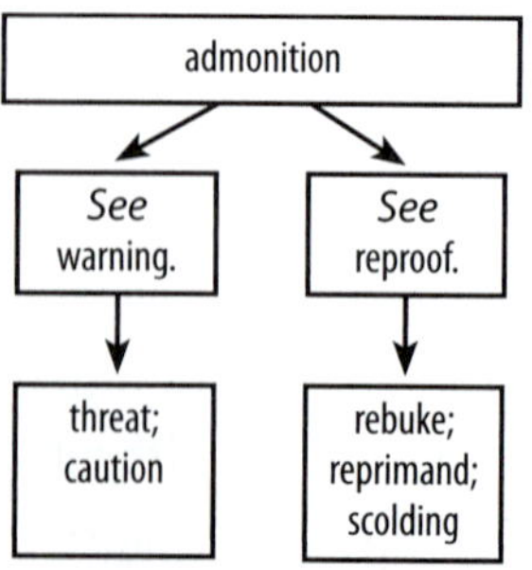

Your Turn

Use a thesaurus to make charts for the other Vocabulary words in this selection: *elect, distracted, impression, inconsolable,* and *resort.* Follow the format shown in the left-hand column. Then, write a sentence for each synonym. If there are slight (or not so slight) differences in meanings among the synonyms, or differences in connotation, try to make your sentences show that.

Language Coach

Multiple Meanings Copy these words from the story into your *Reader/Writer Notebook,* and find two other meanings for each. Write a pair of sentences in which you demonstrate the different meanings of the words. Use a dictionary if you need help.

1. light
2. tears
3. mouth
4. hands
5. finish

Academic Vocabulary

Talk About . . .

Work with a partner to answer the following question about "Liberty."

1. What effect does the parents' decision to flee their homeland have on the story's narrator?

MO 9.W.3.A.1.d Compose a variety of texts: including literary analysis 9.W.3.A.1.e Compose a variety of texts: including reflective writing 9.W.2.E.1.c In written text apply: standard usage 9.R.1.G.1.a During reading, utilize strategies: to determine meaning of unknown words *Also covered* **9.R.1.E.1.c; 9.W.3.A.1.a; 9.R.1.E.1.b; 9.W.3.A.1.b**

Grammar Link

Pronouns and Antecedents

When you use pronouns in your writing, *you* know to whom you're referring when you use *he*, *she*, or *they*, but your readers may think you mean someone else. Inexact pronoun reference is a common mistake and can cause confusion.

A pronoun should refer clearly to its **antecedent** (the noun or pronoun to which a pronoun refers). Avoid unclear, or **ambiguous,** pronoun references. Such references occur when a pronoun can refer to more than one antecedent. Usually you can make your meaning clear by replacing the pronoun with the noun to which it refers.

UNCLEAR: Papi and Mister Victor are fluent in two languages, but he speaks Spanish with an accent.

CLEAR: Papi and Mister Victor are fluent in two languages, but Mister Victor speaks Spanish with an accent.

CLEAR: Papi and Mister Victor, who speaks Spanish with an accent, are fluent in two languages.

Your Turn

Writing Applications Rewrite the following sentences to correct the inexact pronoun references.

1. Papi brought home a puppy, and he caused a lot of trouble.
2. When I spotted Liberty and the strange man with sunglasses, he looked frightened.
3. All morning, aunts stopped by to kiss the sisters because they were leaving for America.
4. Tía Mimi said that Mami was upset, and she had a secret.

CHOICES

As you respond to the Choices, use these **Academic Vocabulary** words as appropriate: convey, effect, excerpt, support, outcome.

REVIEW

Write a Letter to the Author

Write a letter to Julia Alvarez in which you describe your reaction to "Liberty." In your letter, identify the story details that helped bring to life the story's setting and the conflict the narrator and her family faced. Your letter should conform to standard letter format. Begin with the date and then write a greeting, the body of the letter, and your sign-off.

CONNECT

Pay Tribute

TechFocus Review the list you made as you read about things and people the narrator might miss when she moves to the United States. Now, think about what would be most difficult for *you* to leave behind if you had to leave your homeland. Write a personal essay in which you pay tribute to what's best about home and use your essay as a script to create a digital story or short video showcasing what you like best about home.

EXTEND

Explore the Idea of Liberty

Timed Writing Julia Alvarez chose to give the dog in the story a name, yet opted to have the narrator herself remain nameless. Alvarez may have chosen to do so in order to emphasize the idea of liberty. Write a brief essay in which you define, describe, and explain the concept of liberty.

Learn It Online
Tell your personal essay in a whole new way. Find out how at the Digital Storytelling site:
go.hrw.com
L9-65
Go

SHORT STORY

Preparing to Read

Harrison Bergeron

by **Kurt Vonnegut**

© Ed Paschke, 1996.

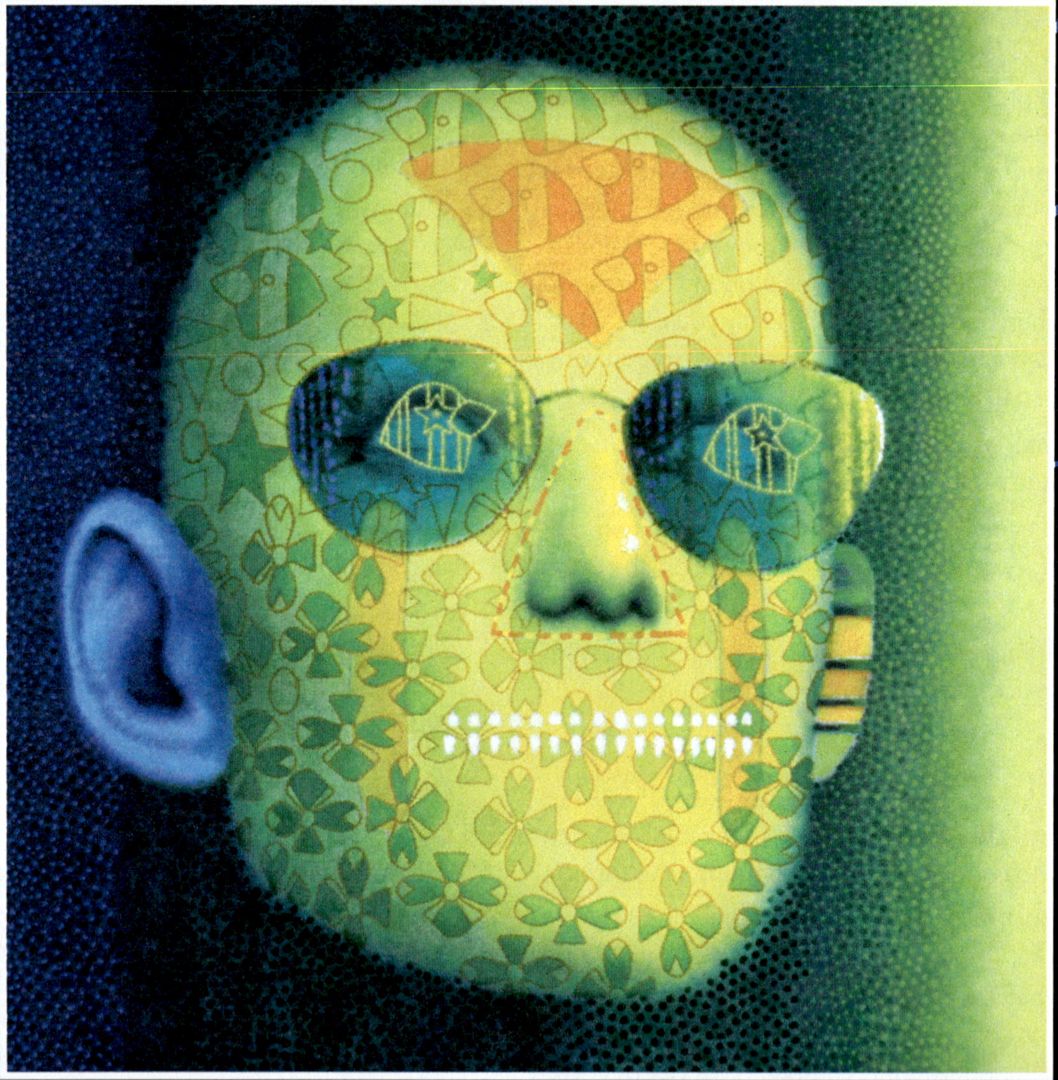

Bird Eye (1996) by Edward Paschke (1939–2004). Oil on linen (36" x 40").

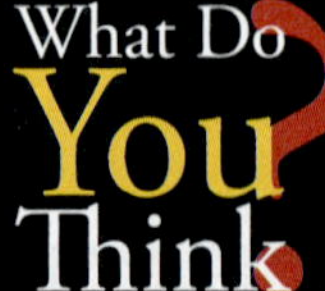

What Do You Think? Why do people sometimes seek to escape the rules of society?

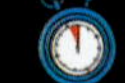

QuickTalk

When, if ever, is rebelling the right thing to do? Discuss your ideas with a partner.

Reader/Writer Notebook

Use your **RWN** to complete the activities for this selection.

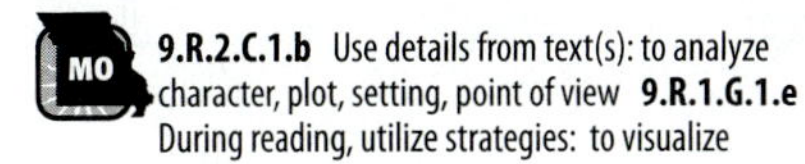

9.R.2.C.1.b Use details from text(s): to analyze character, plot, setting, point of view **9.R.1.G.1.e** During reading, utilize strategies: to visualize

Literary Focus

Setting and Mood **Setting** refers to the world in which a story takes place. Details that describe the story's location, weather, time of day, time of year, time in history, and even a society's beliefs contribute to the setting. The writer's use of language helps to set the **mood**—the emotional effect or feeling a story creates. A story's mood can be described by adjectives such as *upbeat, gloomy,* and *serious.*

Literary Perspectives Apply the literary perspective described on page 69 as you read this story.

Reading Focus

Visualizing When you **visualize** a story's setting, events, or characters, you take note of sensory details the writer includes and picture what is being described. Visualizing helps put you in the time and place of the story's action, making you more of a participant in the story rather than a distant observer.

Into Action As you read "Harrison Bergeron," fill out the chart below with story passages that create a strong sense of time and place. Then, describe what you visualize as you read those excerpts.

Story Passage	What I Visualize
"George and Hazel were watching television. There were tears on Hazel's cheeks. . . ."	I visualize a couple sitting in silence in their home, watching a television set.

Writing Focus

Think as a Reader/Writer

Find It in Your Reading Kurt Vonnegut creates a bleak, or grim, mood in "Harrison Bergeron" by describing very simply and bluntly the society in which Harrison lives. As you read, record in your *Reader/Writer Notebook* details that help set the story's mood.

Vocabulary

vigilance (VIHJ uh luhns) *n.:* state of being alert; watchfulness. *The vigilance of the inspector made escaping notice difficult.*

hindrances (HIHN druhns ihs) *n.:* obstacles; things that restrain or prevent an activity. *Wearing hindrances such as weights and heavy masks made it hard for people to move.*

cowered (KOW uhrd) *v.:* drew back in fear; cringed. *People in the television studio cowered when gunshots rang out.*

synchronizing (SIHNG kruh ny zihng) *v.:* causing to occur at the same time or rate; coordinating. *Synchronizing their movements was difficult for the masked dancers.*

Language Coach

Word Origins The Greek word *chronos* means "time." Words built on the word *chronos* include *chronology*, which is a kind of time line, and *chronicle*, which is a historical record arranged in time order. Which Vocabulary word on the list above is related to these words?

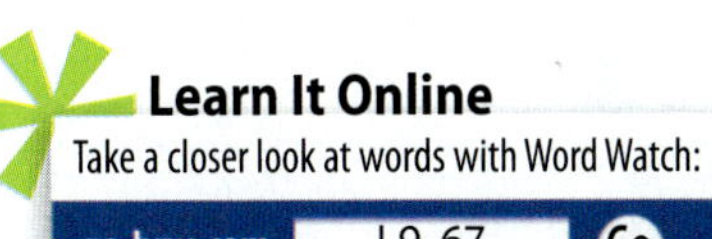

Learn It Online

Take a closer look at words with Word Watch:

go.hrw.com L9-67 Go

MEET THE WRITER

Kurt Vonnegut
(1922–2007)

A Good Citizen
Although once thought of as primarily a science-fiction writer, Kurt Vonnegut is now recognized for his novels—works that raise tough questions about morality, freedom, and values in a high-tech world. "I consider writing an act of good citizenship," he has said.

A Writer from the Beginning
Born in Indiana, Kurt Vonnegut started writing for his high school newspaper. After graduation, he attended Cornell University and studied biochemistry in order to please his father. During World War II, Vonnegut served as a battalion scout for the United States Army. In December 1944, near the end of the war, he was captured by German troops and held prisoner in the underground meat locker of a slaughterhouse in Dresden, Germany. In February 1945, British and American troops fiercely bombed the city; although Vonnegut and other prisoners of war survived, most of the local residents did not. Vonnegut used that experience in his most famous novel, *Slaughterhouse-Five, or the Children's Crusade* (1969).

"When I used to teach creative writing, I would tell the students to make their characters want something right away—even if it's only a glass of water."

Think About the Writer How might Vonnegut's experience as a prisoner of war in WWII have shaped him as a writer?

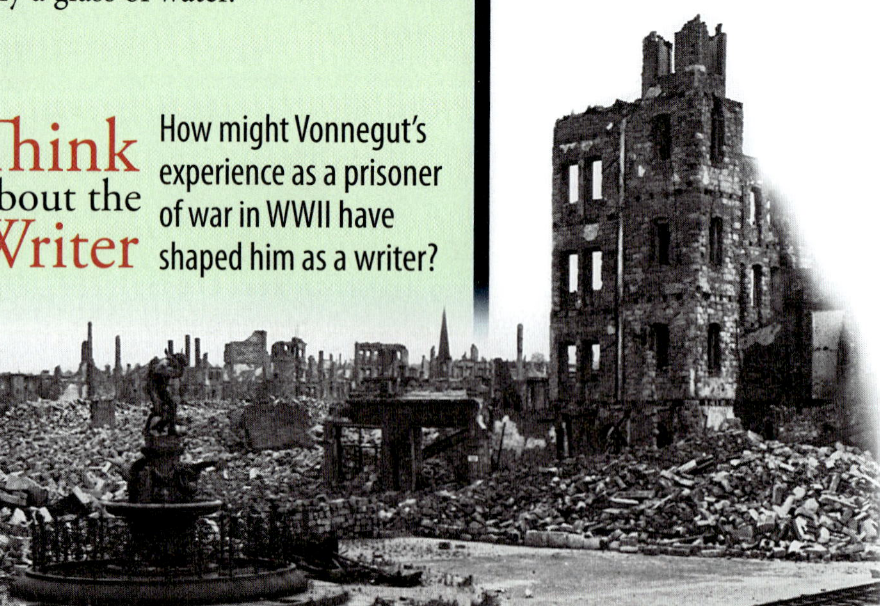

Build Background
Kurt Vonnegut once wrote, "I can't be sure, but there is a possibility that my story 'Harrison Bergeron' is about the envy and self-pity I felt in an overachievers' high school in Indianapolis quite a while ago."

Preview the Selection
In this story, you'll meet a young man named **Harrison Bergeron** who lives in a society that enforces extraordinary control over its citizens. He has been taken away from his parents, **George** and **Hazel Bergeron,** and put in jail because the government feels that Harrison is a threat to society.

Read with a Purpose As you read this story, look for ways in which Harrison differs from his parents, especially his father.

Harrison Bergeron

by **Kurt Vonnegut**

The year was 2081, and everybody was finally equal. They weren't only equal before God and the law. They were equal every which way. Nobody was smarter than anybody else. Nobody was better looking than anybody else. Nobody was stronger or quicker than anybody else. All this equality was due to the 211th, 212th, and 213th Amendments to the Constitution, and to the unceasing vigilance of agents of the United States Handicapper General. **A**

Some things about living still weren't quite right, though. April, for instance, still drove people crazy by not being springtime. And it was in that clammy month that the H-G men took George and Hazel Bergeron's fourteen-year-old son, Harrison, away.

It was tragic, all right, but George and Hazel couldn't think about it very hard. Hazel had a perfectly average intelligence, which meant she couldn't think about anything except in short bursts. And George, while his intelligence was way above normal, had a little mental handicap radio in his ear. He was required by law to wear it at all times. It was tuned to a government transmitter. Every twenty seconds or so, the transmitter would send out some sharp noise to keep people like George from taking unfair advantage of their brains.

George and Hazel were watching television. There were tears on Hazel's cheeks, but she'd forgotten for the moment what they were about.

On the television screen were ballerinas.

A buzzer sounded in George's head. His thoughts fled in panic, like bandits from a burglar alarm.

"That was a real pretty dance, that dance they just did," said Hazel.

"Huh?" said George.

A **Reading Focus** **Visualizing** So far we have learned that the year is 2081 and that everyone is equal in this world. What might the world look like in 2081?

Vocabulary **vigilance** (VIHJ uh luhns) *n.:* state of being alert; watchfulness.

Literary Perspectives

Analyzing Historical Context When you analyze the historical context of a selection, you consider how the events of the time in which the story was written may have affected the story's characters, plot, or theme. As you read this story, pay attention to the notes at the bottom of the pages and keep the following in mind:

In the early 1960s, when this story was written, the United States and the Soviet Union were engaged in a cold war. The nations' opposing political philosophies of democracy and communism created an atmosphere of suspicion and distrust. Also at this time, memories of McCarthyism, in which Americans who were suspected of being communist sympathizers were interrogated and stripped of their status, were also fresh.

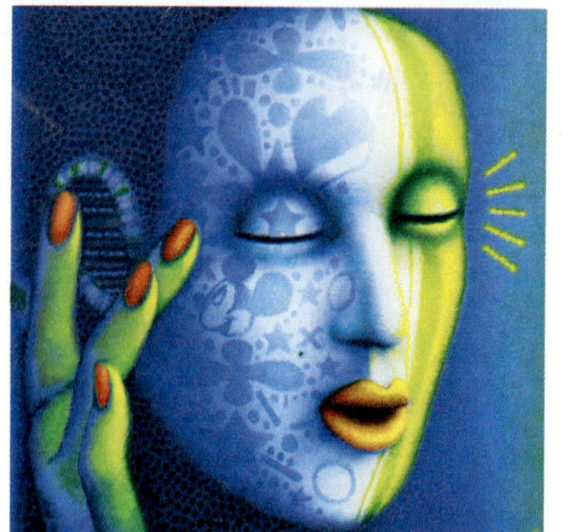

Pause (1996) by Edward Paschke (1939–2004). Oil on canvas (28" x 35"). © Ed Paschke, 1996.

"That dance—it was nice," said Hazel.

"Yup," said George. He tried to think a little about the ballerinas. They weren't really very good—no better than anybody else would have been, anyway. They were burdened with sash weights and bags of birdshot, and their faces were masked, so that no one, seeing a free and graceful gesture or a pretty face, would feel like something the cat drug in. George was toying with the vague notion that maybe dancers shouldn't be handicapped. But he didn't get very far with it before another noise in his ear radio scattered his thoughts.

George winced. So did two out of the eight ballerinas. **B**

Hazel saw him wince. Having no mental handicap herself, she had to ask George what the latest sound had been.

"Sounded like somebody hitting a milk bottle with a ball-peen hammer,"[1] said George.

"I'd think it would be real interesting, hearing all the different sounds," said Hazel, a little envious. "All the things they think up."

"Um," said George.

"Only, if I was Handicapper General, you know what I would do?" said Hazel. Hazel, as a matter of fact, bore a strong resemblance to the Handicapper General, a woman named Diana Moon Glampers. "If I was Diana Moon Glampers," said Hazel, "I'd have chimes on Sunday—just chimes. Kind of in honor of religion."

"I could think, if it was just chimes," said George.

"Well—maybe make 'em real loud," said Hazel. "I think I'd make a good Handicapper General."

"Good as anybody else," said George.

"Who knows better'n I do what normal is?" said Hazel.

"Right," said George. He began to think glimmeringly about his abnormal son who was now in jail, about Harrison, but a twenty-one-gun salute in his head stopped that.

"Boy!" said Hazel, "that was a doozy, wasn't it?"

It was such a doozy that George was white and trembling, and tears stood on the rims of his red eyes. Two of the eight ballerinas had collapsed to the studio floor and were holding their temples.

"All of a sudden you look so tired," said Hazel. "Why don't you stretch out on the sofa, so's you can rest your handicap bag on the pillows, honeybunch." She was referring to the forty-seven pounds of birdshot in a canvas bag which was padlocked around George's neck. "Go on and rest the bag for a little while," she said. "I don't care if you're not equal to me for a while."

George weighed the bag with his hands. "I don't mind it," he said. "I don't notice it anymore. It's just a part of me."

"You been so tired lately—kind of wore out," said Hazel. "If there was just some way we could make a little hole in the bottom of the bag, and

1. **ball-peen hammer:** hammer with a ball-shaped head.

B Literary Perspectives Analyzing Historical Context What does the Handicapper General do to make everyone equal? What kind of power does she seem to have over others?

just take out a few of them lead balls. Just a few."

"Two years in prison and two thousand dollars fine for every ball I took out," said George. "I don't call that a bargain."

"If you could just take a few out when you came home from work," said Hazel. "I mean—you don't compete with anybody around here. You just set around."

"If I tried to get away with it," said George, "then other people'd get away with it—and pretty soon we'd be right back to the Dark Ages again, with everybody competing against everybody else. You wouldn't like that, would you?"

"I'd hate it," said Hazel.

"There you are," said George. "The minute people start cheating on laws, what do you think happens to society?"

If Hazel hadn't been able to come up with an answer to this question, George couldn't have supplied one. A siren was going off in his head.

"Reckon it'd fall all apart," said Hazel.

"What would?" said George blankly.

"Society," said Hazel uncertainly. "Wasn't that what you just said?"

"Who knows?" said George. **C**

The television program was suddenly interrupted for a news bulletin. It wasn't clear at first as to what the bulletin was about, since the announcer, like all announcers, had a serious speech impediment. For about half a minute, and in a state of high excitement, the announcer tried to say, "Ladies and gentlemen——"

He finally gave up, handed the bulletin to a ballerina to read.

> "The minute people start cheating on laws, what do you think happens to society?"

"That's all right——" Hazel said of the announcer, "he tried. That's the big thing. He tried to do the best he could with what God gave him. He should get a nice raise for trying so hard."

"Ladies and gentlemen——" said the ballerina, reading the bulletin. She must have been extraordinarily beautiful, because the mask she wore was hideous. And it was easy to see that she was the strongest and most graceful of all the dancers, for her handicap bags were as big as those worn by two-hundred-pound men. **D**

And she had to apologize at once for her voice, which was a very unfair voice for a woman to use. Her voice was a warm, luminous, timeless melody. "Excuse me——" she said, and she began again, making her voice absolutely uncompetitive.

"Harrison Bergeron, age fourteen," she said in a grackle squawk,[2] "has just escaped from jail, where he was held on suspicion of plotting to overthrow the government. He is a genius and an athlete, is under-handicapped, and should be regarded as extremely dangerous."

A police photograph of Harrison Bergeron was flashed on the screen—upside down, then sideways, upside down again, then right side up. The picture showed the full length of Harrison against a background calibrated[3] in feet and inches. He was exactly seven feet tall.

The rest of Harrison's appearance was

2. **grackle squawk:** loud, harsh cry, like that of a grackle (blackbird).
3. **calibrated:** marked with measurements.

C Literary Focus Mood What mood is Vonnegut creating? How does the dialogue in this passage contribute to the story's mood?

D Reading Focus Visualizing Pause for a moment to visualize the ballerina described in this excerpt. In what way is her appearance a result of the society in which she lives?

Halloween and hardware. Nobody had ever borne heavier handicaps. He had outgrown hindrances faster than the H-G men could think them up. Instead of a little ear radio for a mental handicap, he wore a tremendous pair of earphones, and spectacles with thick wavy lenses. The spectacles were intended not only to make him half blind, but to give him whanging headaches besides.

Scrap metal was hung all over him. Ordinarily, there was a certain symmetry,[4] a military neatness to the handicaps issued to strong people, but Harrison looked like a walking junkyard. In the race of life, Harrison carried three hundred pounds.

And to offset his good looks, the H-G men required that he wear at all times a red rubber ball for a nose, keep his eyebrows shaved off, and cover his even white teeth with black caps at snaggletooth random.

"If you see this boy," said the ballerina, "do not—I repeat, do not—try to reason with him."

There was the shriek of a door being torn from its hinges.

Screams and barking cries of consternation[5] came from the television set. The photograph of Harrison Bergeron on the screen jumped again and again, as though dancing to the tune of an earthquake.

George Bergeron correctly identified the earthquake, and well he might have—for many was the time his own home had danced to the same crashing tune. "My God—" said George, "that must be Harrison!"

The realization was blasted from his mind instantly by the sound of an automobile collision in his head.

When George could open his eyes again, the photograph of Harrison was gone. A living, breathing Harrison filled the screen.

Clanking, clownish, and huge, Harrison stood in the center of the studio. The knob of the uprooted studio door was still in his hand. Ballerinas, technicians, musicians, and announcers cowered on their knees before him, expecting to die.

"I am the Emperor!" cried Harrison. "Do you hear? I am the Emperor! Everybody must do what I say at once!" He stamped his foot and the studio shook.

"Even as I stand here—" he bellowed, "crippled, hobbled, sickened—I am a greater ruler than any man who ever lived! Now watch me become what I *can* become!"

Harrison tore the straps of his handicap harness like wet tissue paper, tore straps guaranteed to support five thousand pounds.

Harrison's scrap-iron handicaps crashed to the floor.

Harrison thrust his thumbs under the bar of the padlock that secured his head harness. The bar snapped like celery. Harrison smashed his headphones and spectacles against the wall.

He flung away his rubber-ball nose, revealed a man that would have awed Thor, the god of thunder. **E**

"I shall now select my Empress!" he said, looking down on the cowering people. "Let the first woman who dares rise to her feet claim her mate and her throne!"

A moment passed, and then a ballerina arose, swaying like a willow.

---

4. **symmetry:** balanced arrangement.

5. **consternation:** fear; bewilderment.

E **Reading Focus** **Visualizing** What details does Vonnegut include to help you visualize Harrison's appearance?

Vocabulary **hindrances** (HIHN druhns ihs) *n.:* obstacles; things that restrain or prevent an activity.
cowered (KOW uhrd) *v.:* drew back in fear; cringed.

Harrison plucked the mental handicap from her ear, snapped off her physical handicaps with marvelous delicacy. Last of all, he removed her mask.

She was blindingly beautiful.

"Now—" said Harrison, taking her hand, "shall we show the people the meaning of the word *dance*? Music!" he commanded.

The musicians scrambled back into their chairs, and Harrison stripped them of their handicaps, too. "Play your best," he told them, "and I'll make you barons and dukes and earls."

The music began. It was normal at first—cheap, silly, false. But Harrison snatched two musicians from their chairs, waved them like batons as he sang the music as he wanted it played. He slammed them back into their chairs.

The music began again and was much improved.

Harrison and his Empress merely listened to the music for a while—listened gravely, as though synchronizing their heartbeats with it.

They shifted their weights to their toes.

Harrison placed his big hands on the girl's tiny waist, letting her sense the weightlessness that would soon be hers.

And then, in an explosion of joy and grace, into the air they sprang!

Vocabulary **synchronizing** (SIHNG kruh ny zihng) *v.:* causing to occur at the same time or rate; coordinating.

Analyzing Visuals **Viewing and Interpreting** How might this image reflect the society Vonnegut describes in the story?

Cyborg and Binary Digits (2000) by Darren Winter.

Not only were the laws of the land abandoned, but the law of gravity and the laws of motion as well.

They reeled, whirled, swiveled, flounced, capered, gamboled,[6] and spun.

They leaped like deer on the moon.

The studio ceiling was thirty feet high, but each leap brought the dancers nearer to it.

It became their obvious intention to kiss the ceiling.

They kissed it.

La Nuit (1983) by Edward Paschke (1939–2004). Oil on paper (1.01 meters x 1.52 meters). Musee National d'Art Moderne, Centre Georges Pompidou, Paris.

And then, neutralizing gravity with love and pure will, they remained suspended in air inches below the ceiling, and they kissed each other for a long, long time.

It was then that Diana Moon Glampers, the Handicapper General, came into the studio with a double-barreled ten-gauge shotgun. She fired twice, and the Emperor and the Empress were dead before they hit the floor.

Diana Moon Glampers loaded the gun again. She aimed it at the musicians and told them they had ten seconds to get their handicaps back on.

It was then that the Bergerons' television tube burned out.

Hazel turned to comment about the blackout to George. But George had gone out into the kitchen for a can of beer.

George came back in with the beer, paused while a handicap signal shook him up. And then he sat down again. "You been crying?" he said to Hazel.

"Yup," she said.

"What about?" he said.

"I forget," she said. "Something real sad on television."

"What was it?" he said.

"It's all kind of mixed up in my mind," said Hazel.

"Forget sad things," said George.

"I always do," said Hazel.

"That's my girl," said George. He winced. There was the sound of a riveting-gun in his head.

"Gee—I could tell that one was a doozy," said Hazel.

"You can say that again," said George.

"Gee—" said Hazel, "I could tell that one was a doozy." F

6. **gamboled:** frolicked; romped.

F **Literary Focus** **Mood** Back in the setting of the Bergerons' home, life goes on as usual. How would you describe the mood at the story's end?

Applying Your Skills

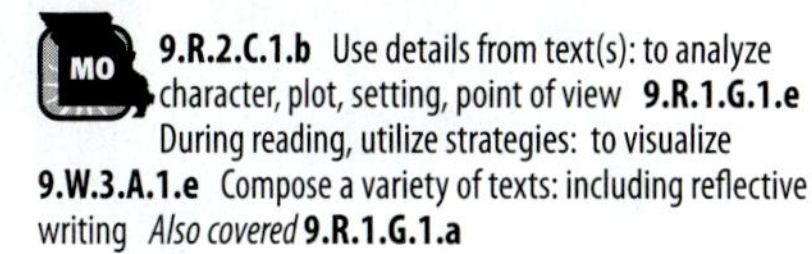

MO
9.R.2.C.1.b Use details from text(s): to analyze character, plot, setting, point of view 9.R.1.G.1.e During reading, utilize strategies: to visualize
9.W.3.A.1.e Compose a variety of texts: including reflective writing Also covered 9.R.1.G.1.a

Harrison Bergeron

Respond and Think Critically

Reading Focus

Quick Check

1. What happens when George tries to think for himself? Why is he so heavily "handicapped"?
2. Why was Harrison imprisoned?

Read with a Purpose

3. What choices does Harrison make that his father would not or could not make?

Reading Skills: Visualizing

4. Review the entries you made on the visualizing chart you began on page 67, and add a row in which you describe the story's overall mood.

Story Passage	What I Visualize
"George and Hazel . . ."	I visualize a couple . . .

Overall Mood:

Vocabulary Check

Identify each statement as true (T) or false (F).

5. **Hindrances** help people get things done.
6. Being a successful security guard requires **vigilance.**
7. A person who **cowered** might be called brave.
8. **Synchronizing** dance steps is key to a good performance.

Literary Focus

Literary Analysis

9. **Speculate** Why is Harrison taking such risky action? Is he trying to free others, or might he have a more selfish reason? Explain.
10. **Literary Perspectives** Is this story one of hope or one that cautions or warns us? Support your ideas with examples from the text. In your response, discuss ways in which Vonnegut may have been influenced by events of his time.

Literary Skills: Setting and Mood

11. **Analyze** When and where does this story take place? Could this story have taken place in a different time and place? Explain.
12. **Analyze** How would the mood of the story change if Vonnegut had made the characters less familiar and more "futuristic"?

Literary Skills Review: Resolution

13. **Interpret** During a story's **resolution,** lingering questions are answered and loose ends are tied up. What is unusual about the way George and Hazel react to the events that end the story? What idea about life does this ending suggest?

Writing Focus

Think as a Reader/Writer

Use It in Your Writing Write a paragraph describing an imaginary place in the future. In your story, strive to create a specific mood (lighthearted or eerie perhaps). Like Vonnegut, use descriptive details that will help you create this mood.

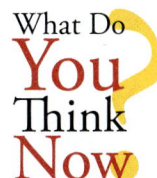

What Do You Think Now?

From what do you think Harrison was escaping, prison or the rules of society? Was Harrison's quest to escape justified? Explain.

Comparing Plot and Setting

CONTENTS

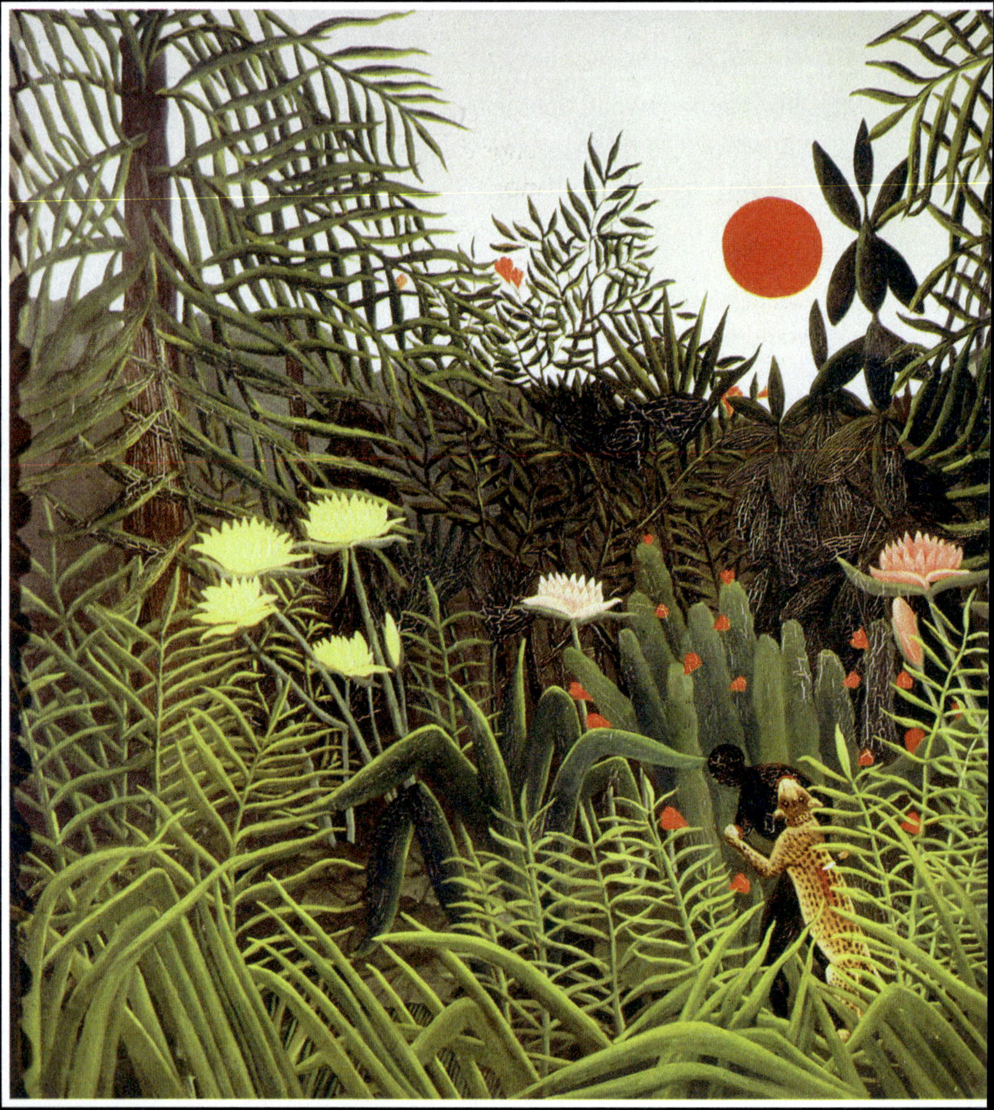

Virgin forest with setting sun (c. 1910) by Henri Rosseau (1844–1910).

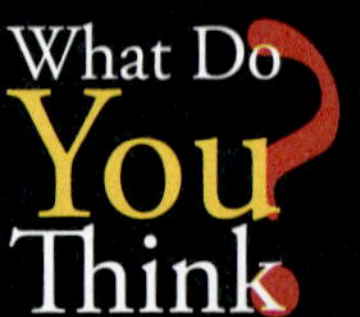

How would you escape from a wild animal that is intent on taking your life?

QuickWrite

What stories have you heard that involve an escape from a wild animal? Briefly summarize one of those stories, describing the means of escape.

Preparing to Read

A Sound of Thunder / Being Prey

MO 9.R.2.C.1.b Use details from text(s): to analyze character, plot, setting, point of view 9.R.3.C.1.a Use details from informational text: to identify and explain the organizational pattern

Literary Focus

Plot and Setting Across Genres The stories you are about to read differ in that one is fiction and the other is nonfiction. They both, however, contain exciting settings that have a strong effect on what happens in the stories. Remember that **setting** refers to the time of, place of, and social and historical conditions present during a story. As you read the stories that follow, pay attention to the dangers lurking in the settings. Then, think about how the time and place of the story helps to move the **plot,** the action of the story, forward.

Reading Focus

Analyzing Sequence of Events As you read the stories that follow, take note of important plot events. Also think about how each story's setting contributes to the characters' actions.

Into Action Use an organizer such as the one below to keep track of plot events and to see how one event triggers the next.

A Sound of Thunder	Being Prey
Eckels arrives at the Time Safari offices.	The author goes out onto the lagoon in a canoe.
And then . . .	And then . . .

Writing Focus

Think as a Reader/Writer

Find It in Your Reading Good descriptions help readers visualize story settings and put themselves into the action. By describing the sounds, smells, and images of a place, writers draw you into the world of the story. In your *Reader/Writer Notebook,* write down the descriptive details that draw you into each of the following stories.

Reader/Writer Notebook

Use your **RWN** to complete the activities for these selections.

Vocabulary

A Sound of Thunder

annihilate (uh NY uh layt) *v.:* destroy; wipe out. *Eckels must not annihilate any of the protected animals.*

delirium (dih LIHR ee uhm) *n.:* extreme mental disturbance, often accompanied by hallucinations (seeing things that are not there). *The jungle seemed unreal, as if it were a product of his delirium.*

revoke (rih VOHK) *v.:* cancel; withdraw. *Time Safari threatened to revoke the hunter's license if he broke any rules.*

Being Prey

menacing (MEHN ihs ihng) *v.* used as an *adj.:* threatening. *The menacing clouds indicated that a rainstorm would soon begin.*

incredulous (ihn KREHJ uh luhs) *adj.:* doubting; here, prompting disbelief. *She was incredulous upon seeing a set of huge teeth rise up from the water.*

Language Coach

Word Origins The Latin word *vocare* means "to call." Words built on this root include *provoke, vocal,* and *convocation.* Which Vocabulary word listed above also contains the root *vocare?* How can you tell?

Learn It Online
There is more to words than just definitions. Get the whole story at:

go.hrw.com L9-77 

MEET THE WRITERS

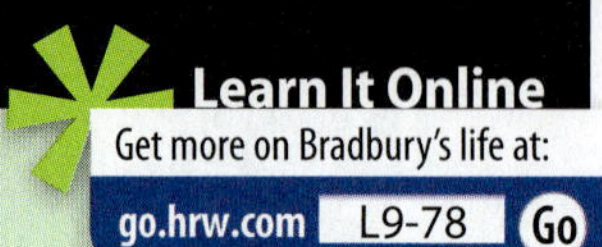

Learn It Online
Get more on Bradbury's life at:
go.hrw.com L9-78 Go

Ray Bradbury
(1920–)

Teller of Tales

Ray Bradbury calls himself a teller of tales and a magical realist. He also claims to remember everything—every book he's read, every movie he's seen, all the events of his life back to and including his birth, in Waukegan, Illinois, on August 22, 1920. All those memories and a big imagination are the materials for the fiction and poetry he's been writing for more than fifty years. Bradbury gives credit for his writing to his boyhood self: "I don't know if I believe in previous lives; I'm not sure I can live forever. But that young boy believed in both, and I have let him have his head. He has written my stories and books for me."

For another Bradbury story, turn to page 375.

Val Plumwood
(1939–)

A Serious Nature-Lover

An Australian professor and author, Val Plumwood is a prominent environmentalist who has written four books and more than a hundred papers. She specializes in ecofeminism, the study of the relationship between women, animals, and nature. As a child in Australia, she spent a lot of time in the Australian wilderness and a lot of time reading *Alice in Wonderland.* The narrative you are about to read describes in detail her near-death experience with one of nature's most fearsome creatures. Plumwood remarks that her story is "a humbling and cautionary tale about our relationship with the earth."

Think About the Writers

Why do you think these writers are driven to share their tales of suspense?

Preview the Selections

In "A Sound of Thunder", you'll meet **Eckels,** a man who has dreamed his whole life about traveling back in time to hunt dinosaurs.

At the start of "Being Prey," the narrator, **Val Plumwood,** describes in lush detail her surroundings in an Australian national park, where dangers may lurk.

SHORT STORY

A SOUND OF THUNDER

by **Ray Bradbury**

Read with a Purpose

Read "A Sound of Thunder" to find out about the effects of one person's actions.

Build Background

The *Tyrannosaurus rex*, or "king of the tyrant lizards," is one of the best-known dinosaurs. At 15,000 pounds and 45 feet long, a large adult would have stood more than 21 feet tall if it had been able to stand upright. Fierce and strong, the *Tyrannosaurus rex* would have been able to bite through a car roof, just as in the movie *Jurassic Park*.

The sign on the wall seemed to quaver under a film of sliding warm water. Eckels felt his eyelids blink over his stare, and the sign burned in this momentary darkness:

Time Safari, Inc.
Safaris to any
year in the past.
You name the animal.
We take you there.
You shoot it.

A warm phlegm gathered in Eckels's throat; he swallowed and pushed it down. The muscles around his mouth formed a smile as he put his hand slowly out upon the air, and in that hand waved a check for ten thousand dollars to the man behind the desk.

"Does this safari guarantee I come back alive?"

"We guarantee nothing," said the official, "except the dinosaurs." He turned. "This is Mr. Travis, your Safari Guide in the Past. He'll tell you what and where to shoot. If he says no shooting, no shooting. If you disobey instructions, there's a stiff penalty of another ten thousand dollars, plus possible government action, on your return."

Eckels glanced across the vast office at a mass and tangle, a snaking and humming of wires and steel boxes, at an aurora[1] that flickered now orange, now silver, now blue. There was a sound like a gigantic bonfire burning all of Time, all the years and all the parchment calendars, all the hours piled high and set aflame. **A**

A touch of the hand and this burning would, on the instant, beautifully reverse itself. Eckels remembered the wording in the advertisements to the letter. Out of chars and ashes, out of dust and coals, like golden salamanders, the old years, the green years, might leap; roses sweeten the air, white hair turn Irish-black, wrinkles vanish; all, everything fly back to seed, flee death, rush down to their beginnings, suns rise in western skies and set in glorious easts,

1. **aurora** (aw RAWR uh): Bradbury is comparing the glow coming from the time machine to an aurora, a colorful display of light that appears at night in the skies near the North and South Poles.

A **Literary Focus** **Setting** When does the story take place? What details help reveal the setting?

moons eat themselves opposite to the custom, all and everything cupping one in another like Chinese boxes,[2] rabbits into hats, all and everything returning to the fresh death, the seed death, the green death, to the time before the beginning. A touch of a hand might do it, the merest touch of a hand.

"Unbelievable." Eckels breathed, the light of the Machine on his thin face. "A real Time Machine." He shook his head. "Makes you think. If the election had gone badly yesterday, I might be here now running away from the results. Thank God Keith won. He'll make a fine President of the United States."

"Yes," said the man behind the desk. "We're lucky. If Deutscher had gotten in, we'd have the worst kind of dictatorship. There's an anti-everything man for you, a militarist, anti-Christ, anti-human, anti-intellectual. People called us up, you know, joking but not joking. Said if Deutscher became President they wanted to go live in 1492. Of course it's not our business to conduct Escapes, but to form Safaris. Anyway, Keith's President now. All you got to worry about is—"

"Shooting my dinosaur," Eckels finished it for him.

"A *Tyrannosaurus rex*. The Tyrant Lizard, the most incredible monster in history. Sign this release. Anything happens to you, we're not responsible. Those dinosaurs are hungry."

Eckels flushed angrily. "Trying to scare me!"

"Frankly, yes. We don't want anyone going who'll panic at the first shot. Six Safari leaders were killed last year, and a dozen hunters. We're here to give you the severest thrill a *real* hunter ever asked for. Traveling you back sixty million years to bag the biggest game in all of Time. Your personal check's still there. Tear it up."

Mr. Eckels looked at the check. His fingers twitched.

"Good luck," said the man behind the desk. "Mr. Travis, he's all yours."

They moved silently across the room, taking their guns with them, toward the Machine, toward the silver metal and the roaring light.

First a day and then a night and then a day and then a night, then it was day-night-day-night-day. A week, a month, a year, a decade! A.D. 2055. A.D. 2019. 1999! 1957! Gone! The Machine roared. **B**

They put on their oxygen helmets and tested the intercoms.

Eckels swayed on the padded seat, his face pale, his jaw stiff. He felt the trembling in his arms, and he looked down and found his hands tight on the new rifle. There were four other men in the Machine. Travis, the Safari Leader; his assistant, Lesperance; and two other hunters, Billings and Kramer. They sat looking at each other, and the years blazed around them.

"Can these guns get a dinosaur cold?" Eckels felt his mouth saying.

"If you hit them right," said Travis on the helmet radio. "Some dinosaurs have two brains, one in the head, another far down the spinal column. We stay away from those. That's stretching luck. Put your first two shots into the eyes, if you can, blind them, and go back into the brain."

The Machine howled. Time was a film run backward. Suns fled and ten million moons fled after them. "Think," said Eckels. "Every hunter that ever lived would envy us today. This makes Africa seem like Illinois."

2. **Chinese boxes:** set of boxes, each of which fits into the next-largest one.

B **Reading Focus** **Analyzing Sequence of Events** What happened to six Safari leaders last year? What is taking place now?

The Machine slowed; its scream fell to a murmur. The Machine stopped.

The sun stopped in the sky.

The fog that had enveloped the Machine blew away and they were in an old time, a very old time indeed, three hunters and two Safari Heads with their blue metal guns across their knees.

"Christ isn't born yet," said Travis. "Moses has not gone to the mountain to talk with God. The Pyramids are still in the earth, waiting to be cut out and put up. *Remember* that. Alexander, Caesar, Napoleon, Hitler—none of them exists."

The men nodded.

"That"—Mr. Travis pointed—"is the jungle of sixty million two thousand and fifty-five years before President Keith."

He indicated a metal path that struck off into green wilderness, over streaming swamp, among giant ferns and palms.

"And that," he said, "is the Path, laid by Time Safari for your use. It floats six inches above the earth. Doesn't touch so much as one grass blade, flower, or tree. It's an anti-gravity

Analyzing Visuals

Viewing and Interpreting
In what way does this image convey the idea of time travel as it takes place in the story?

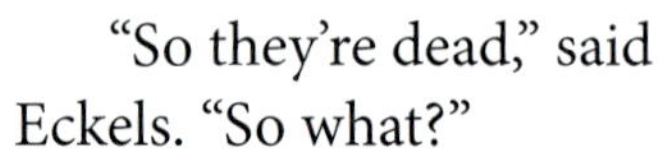

metal. Its purpose is to keep you from touching this world of the Past in any way. Stay on the Path. Don't go off it. I repeat. *Don't go off*. For *any* reason! If you fall off, there's a penalty. And don't shoot any animal we don't okay." **C**

"Why?" asked Eckels.

They sat in the ancient wilderness. Far birds' cries blew on a wind, and the smell of tar and an old salt sea, moist grasses, and flowers the color of blood.

"We don't want to change the Future. We don't belong here in the Past. The government doesn't *like* us here. We have to pay big graft[3] to keep our franchise. A Time Machine is finicky business. Not knowing it, we might kill an important animal, a small bird, a roach, a flower even, thus destroying an important link in a growing species."

"That's not clear," said Eckels.

"All right," Travis continued, "say we accidentally kill one mouse here. That means all the future families of this one particular mouse are destroyed, right?"

"Right."

"And all the families of the families of the families of that one mouse! With a stamp of your foot, you annihilate first one, then a dozen, then a thousand, a million, a *billion* possible mice!"

"So they're dead," said Eckels. "So what?"

"So what?" Travis snorted quietly. "Well, what about the foxes that'll need those mice to survive? For want of ten mice, a fox dies. For want of ten foxes, a lion starves. For want of a lion, all manner of insects, vultures, infinite billions of life forms are thrown into chaos and destruction. Eventually it all boils down to this: Fifty-nine million years later, a cave man, one of a dozen in the *entire world,* goes hunting wild boar or saber-toothed tiger for food. But you, friend, have *stepped* on all the tigers in that region. By stepping on *one* single mouse. So the cave man starves. And the cave man, please note, is not just *any* expendable man, no! He is an *entire future nation.* From his loins would have sprung ten sons. From *their* loins one hundred sons, and thus onward to a civilization. Destroy this one man, and you destroy a race, a people, an entire history of life. It is comparable to slaying some of Adam's grandchildren. The stomp of your foot, on one mouse, could start an earthquake, the effects of which could shake our earth and destinies down through Time, to their very foundations. With the death of that one cave man, a billion others yet unborn are throttled in the womb. Perhaps Rome never rises on its seven hills. Perhaps Europe is forever a dark forest, and only Asia waxes

3. **graft:** bribes.

C **Literary Focus** **Setting** What modern element of setting has Time Safari introduced into the setting of the ancient jungle?

Vocabulary **annihilate** (uh NY uh layt) *v.:* destroy; wipe out.

healthy and teeming.[4] Step on a mouse and you crush the Pyramids. Step on a mouse and you leave your print, like a Grand Canyon, across Eternity. Queen Elizabeth might never be born, Washington might not cross the Delaware, there might never be a United States at all. So be careful. Stay on the Path. *Never* step off!" **D**

"I see," said Eckels. "Then it wouldn't pay for us even to touch the *grass*?"

"Correct. Crushing certain plants could add up infinitesimally.[5] A little error here would multiply in sixty million years, all out of proportion. Of course maybe our theory is wrong. Maybe Time *can't* be changed by us. Or maybe it can be changed only in little subtle ways. A dead mouse here makes an insect imbalance there, a population disproportion later, a bad harvest further on, a depression, mass starvation, and, finally, a change in *social* temperament in far-flung countries. Something much more subtle, like that. Perhaps only a soft breath, a whisper, a hair, pollen on the air, such a slight, slight change that unless you looked close you wouldn't see it. Who knows? Who really can say he knows? We don't know. We're guessing. But until we do know for certain whether our messing around in Time *can* make a big roar or a little rustle in history, we're being careful. This Machine, this Path, your clothing and bodies, were sterilized, as you know, before the journey. We wear these oxygen helmets so we can't introduce our bacteria into an ancient atmosphere."

"How do we know which animals to shoot?"

"They're marked with red paint," said Travis. "Today, before our journey, we sent Lesperance here back with the Machine. He came to this particular era and followed certain animals."

"Studying them?"

"Right," said Lesperance. "I track them through their entire existence, noting which of them lives longest. Very few. How many times they mate. Not often. Life's short. When I find one that's going to die when a tree falls on him, or one that drowns in a tar pit, I note the exact hour, minute, and second. I shoot a paint bomb. It leaves a red patch on his side. We can't miss it. Then I correlate our arrival in the Past so that we meet the Monster not more than two minutes before he would have died anyway. This way, we kill only animals with no future, that are never going to mate again. You see how *careful* we are?" **E**

"But if you came back this morning in Time," said Eckels eagerly, "you must've bumped into *us*, our Safari! How did it turn out? Was it successful? Did all of us get through—alive?"

Travis and Lesperance gave each other a look.

"That'd be a paradox,"[6] said the latter. "Time doesn't permit that sort of mess—a man meeting himself. When such occasions threaten, Time steps aside. Like an airplane hitting an air pocket. You felt the Machine jump just before we stopped? That was us passing ourselves on the way back to the Future. We saw nothing. There's no way of telling *if* this expedition was a success, *if we* got our monster, or whether all of us—meaning *you,* Mr. Eckels—got out alive."

Eckels smiled palely.

---

4. **teeming:** swarming; overflowing.
5. **infinitesimally** (ihn fih nuh TEHS uh muhl lee): in amounts too small to be measured.
6. **paradox** (PAR uh dahks): something that has or seems to have contradictory qualities.

D **Reading Focus** **Analyzing Sequence of Events** Summarize the Safari Leader's explanation of the importance of the Path. How could straying from the Path affect the plot of the story?

E **Reading Focus** **Analyzing Sequence of Events** By preselecting animals about to die, what events do the Time Safari people prevent from happening?

"Cut that," said Travis sharply. "Everyone on his feet!"

They were ready to leave the Machine.

The jungle was high and the jungle was broad and the jungle was the entire world forever and forever. Sounds like music and sounds like flying tents filled the sky, and those were pterodactyls soaring with cavernous gray wings, gigantic bats of delirium and night fever. Eckels, balanced on the narrow Path, aimed his rifle playfully. F

"Stop that!" said Travis. "Don't even aim for fun, blast you! If your guns should go off—"

Eckels flushed. "Where's our *Tyrannosaurus*?"

Lesperance checked his wristwatch. "Up ahead. We'll bisect his trail in sixty seconds. Look for the red paint! Don't shoot till we give the word. Stay on the Path. *Stay on the Path!*"

They moved forward in the wind of morning.

"Strange," murmured Eckels. "Up ahead, sixty million years, Election Day over. Keith made President. Everyone celebrating. And here we are, a million years lost, and they don't exist. The things we worried about for months, a lifetime, not even born or thought of yet."

"Safety catches off, everyone!" ordered Travis. "You, first shot, Eckels. Second, Billings. Third, Kramer."

"I've hunted tiger, wild boar, buffalo, elephant, but now, this is *it*," said Eckels. "I'm shaking like a kid."

"Ah," said Travis.

Everyone stopped.

Travis raised his hand. "Ahead," he whispered. "In the mist. There he is. There's His Royal Majesty now."

The jungle was wide and full of twitterings, rustlings, murmurs, and sighs.

Suddenly it all ceased, as if someone had shut a door.

Silence.

A sound of thunder.

Out of the mist, one hundred yards away, came *Tyrannosaurus rex*. G

"It," whispered Eckels. "It . . ."

"Sh!"

It came on great oiled, resilient, striding legs. It towered thirty feet above half of the trees, a great evil god, folding its delicate watchmaker's claws close to its oily reptilian chest. Each lower leg was a piston, a thousand pounds of white bone, sunk in thick ropes of muscle, sheathed over in a gleam of pebbled skin like the mail[7] of a terrible warrior. Each thigh was a ton of meat, ivory, and steel mesh. And from the great breathing cage of the upper body those two delicate arms dangled out front, arms with hands which might pick up and examine men like toys, while the snake neck coiled. And the head itself, a ton of sculptured stone, lifted easily upon the sky. Its mouth gaped, exposing a fence of teeth like daggers. Its eyes rolled, ostrich eggs, empty of all expression save hunger. It closed its mouth in a death grin. It ran, its pelvic bones crushing aside trees and bushes, its taloned feet clawing damp earth, leaving prints six inches deep wherever it settled its weight. It ran with a gliding ballet step, far too poised and balanced for its ten tons. It moved into a sunlit arena warily, its beautifully reptilian hands feeling the air.

"Why, why," Eckels twitched his mouth. "It

7. **mail:** here, flexible metal armor.

F **Literary Focus** **Setting** What details in this passage help you visualize the setting?

Vocabulary **delirium** (dih LIHR ee uhm) *n.:* extreme mental disturbance, often accompanied by hallucinations (seeing things that are not there).

G **Literary Focus** **Setting** How would you describe the mood, or overall feeling, created by the details of the setting?

could reach up and grab the moon."

"Sh!" Travis jerked angrily. "He hasn't seen us yet."

"It can't be killed." Eckels pronounced this verdict quietly, as if there could be no argument. He had weighed the evidence and this was his considered opinion. The rifle in his hands seemed a cap gun. "We were fools to come. This is impossible."

"Shut up!" hissed Travis.

"Nightmare."

"Turn around," commanded Travis. "Walk quietly to the Machine. We'll remit one half your fee."

"I didn't realize it would be this *big*," said Eckels. "I miscalculated, that's all. And now I want out."

"It *sees* us!"

"There's the red paint on its chest!"

The Tyrant Lizard raised itself. Its armored flesh glittered like a thousand green coins. The coins, crusted with slime, steamed. In the slime, tiny insects wriggled, so that the entire body seemed to twitch and undulate, even while the monster itself did not move. It exhaled. The stink of raw flesh blew down the wilderness.

"Get me out of here," said Eckels. "It was never like this before. I was always sure I'd come through alive. I had good guides, good safaris, and safety. This time, I figured wrong. I've met my match and admit it. This is too much for me to get hold of." **H**

"Don't run," said Lesperance. "Turn around. Hide in the Machine."

"Yes." Eckels seemed to be numb. He looked at his feet as if trying to make them move. He gave a grunt of helplessness.

"Eckels!"

He took a few steps, blinking, shuffling.

"Not *that* way!"

The Monster, at the first motion, lunged forward with a terrible scream. It covered one hundred yards in six seconds. The rifles jerked up and blazed fire. A windstorm from the beast's mouth engulfed them in the stench of slime and old blood. The Monster roared, teeth glittering with sun.

Eckels, not looking back, walked blindly to the edge of the Path, his gun limp in his arms, stepped off the Path, and walked, not knowing it, in the jungle. His feet sank into green moss. His legs moved him, and he felt alone and remote from the events behind. **I**

The rifles cracked again. Their sound was lost in shriek and lizard thunder. The great level of the reptile's tail swung up, lashed sideways. Trees exploded in clouds of leaf and branch. The Monster twitched its jeweler's hands down to fondle at the men, to twist them in half, to crush them like berries, to cram them into its teeth and its screaming throat. Its boulder-stone

---

H **Literary Focus** **Plot** Eckels is terrified of the *Tyrannosaurus.* What conflict develops between Eckels and Travis?

I **Reading Focus** **Analyzing Sequence of Events** What causes Eckels to step off the Path?

eyes leveled with the men. They saw themselves mirrored. They fired at the metallic eyelids and the blazing black iris.

Like a stone idol, like a mountain avalanche, *Tyrannosaurus* fell. Thundering, it clutched trees, pulled them with it. It wrenched and tore the metal Path. The men flung themselves back and away. The body hit, ten tons of cold flesh and stone. The guns fired. The Monster lashed its armored tail, twitched its snake jaws, and lay still. A fount of blood spurted from its throat. Somewhere inside, a sac of fluids burst. Sickening gushes drenched the hunters. They stood, red and glistening.

The thunder faded.

The jungle was silent. After the avalanche, a green peace. After the nightmare, morning.

Billings and Kramer sat on the pathway and threw up. Travis and Lesperance stood with smoking rifles, cursing steadily.

In the Time Machine, on his face, Eckels lay shivering. He had found his way back to the Path, climbed into the Machine.

Travis came walking, glanced at Eckels, took cotton gauze from a metal box, and returned to the others, who were sitting on the Path.

"Clean up."

They wiped the blood from their helmets. They began to curse too. The Monster lay, a hill of solid flesh. Within, you could hear the sighs and murmurs as the furthest chambers of it died, the organs malfunctioning, liquids running a final instant from pocket to sac to spleen, everything shutting off, closing up forever. It was like standing by a wrecked locomotive or a steam shovel at quitting time, all valves being released or levered tight. Bones cracked; the tonnage of its own flesh, off balance, dead weight, snapped the delicate forearms, caught underneath. The meat settled, quivering.

Another cracking sound. Overhead, a gigantic tree branch broke from its heavy mooring, fell. It crashed upon the dead beast with finality.

"There." Lesperance checked his watch. "Right on time. That's the giant tree that was scheduled to fall and kill this animal originally." He glanced at the two hunters. "You want the trophy picture?" **J**

"What?"

"We can't take a trophy back to the Future. The body has to stay right here where it would have died originally, so the insects, birds, and bacteria can get at it, as they were intended to. Everything in balance. The body stays. But we *can* take a picture of you standing near it."

The two men tried to think, but gave up, shaking their heads.

They let themselves be led along the metal Path. They sank wearily into the Machine cushions. They gazed back at the ruined Monster, the stagnating mound, where already strange reptilian birds and golden insects were busy at the steaming armor.

A sound on the floor of the Time Machine stiffened them. Eckels sat there, shivering.

"I'm sorry," he said at last.

"Get up!" cried Travis.

Eckels got up.

"Go out on that Path alone," said Travis. He had his rifle pointed. "You're not coming back in the Machine. We're leaving you here!"

Lesperance seized Travis's arm. "Wait—"

"Stay out of this!" Travis shook his hand away. "This fool nearly killed us. But it isn't *that* so much, no. It's his *shoes*! Look at them! He ran off the Path. That *ruins* us! We'll forfeit! Thousands of dollars of insurance! We guar-

---

J **Reading Focus** **Analyzing Sequence of Events** Why doesn't the hunters' killing of the dinosaur affect the future?

antee no one leaves the Path. He left it. Oh, the fool! I'll have to report to the government. They might revoke our license to travel. Who knows *what* he's done to Time, to History!"

"Take it easy, all he did was kick up some dirt."

"How do we *know*?" cried Travis. "We don't know anything! It's all a mystery! Get out of here, Eckels!"

Eckels fumbled his shirt. "I'll pay anything. A hundred thousand dollars!"

Travis glared at Eckels's checkbook and spat. "Go out there. The Monster's next to the Path. Stick your arms up to your elbows in his mouth. Then you can come back with us."

"That's unreasonable!"

"The Monster's dead, you idiot. The bullets! The bullets can't be left behind. They don't belong in the Past; they might change anything. Here's my knife. Dig them out!"

Like a stone idol, like a mountain avalanche, *Tyrannosaurus* fell.

The jungle was alive again, full of the old tremorings and bird cries. Eckels turned slowly to regard the primeval garbage dump, that hill of nightmares and terror. After a long time, like a sleepwalker he shuffled out along the Path.

He returned, shuddering, five minutes later, his arms soaked and red to the elbows. He held out his hands. Each held a number of steel bullets. Then he fell. He lay where he fell, not moving.

"You didn't have to make him do that," said Lesperance.

"Didn't I? It's too early to tell." Travis nudged the still body. "He'll live. Next time he won't go hunting game like this. Okay." He jerked his thumb wearily at Lesperance. "Switch on. Let's go home."

1492. 1776. 1812.

They cleaned their hands and faces. They changed their caking shirts and pants. Eckels was up and around again, not speaking. Travis glared at him for a full ten minutes.

"Don't look at me," cried Eckels. "I haven't done anything."

"Who can tell?"

"Just ran off the Path, that's all, a little mud on my shoes—what do you want me to do—get down and pray?"

"We might need it. I'm warning you, Eckels, I might kill you yet. I've got my gun ready."

"I'm innocent. I've done nothing!"

1999. 2000. 2055.

The Machine stopped.

"Get out," said Travis.

The room was there as they had left it. But not the same as they had left it. The same man sat behind the same desk. But the same man did not quite sit behind the same desk.

Travis looked around swiftly. "Everything okay here?" he snapped.

"Fine. Welcome home!"

Travis did not relax. He seemed to be looking at the very atoms of the air itself, at the way the sun poured through the one high window.

"Okay, Eckels, get out. Don't ever come back."

Eckels could not move.

"You heard me," said Travis. "What're you *staring* at?"

Eckels stood smelling of the air, and there was a thing to the air, a chemical taint so subtle, so slight, that only a faint cry of his subliminal senses warned him it was there. The colors,

Vocabulary **revoke** (rih VOHK) *v.:* cancel; withdraw.

white, gray, blue, orange, in the wall, in the furniture, in the sky beyond the window, were . . . were . . . And there was a *feel.* His flesh twitched. His hands twitched. He stood drinking the oddness with the pores of his body. Somewhere, someone must have been screaming one of those whistles that only a dog can hear. His body screamed silence in return. Beyond this room, beyond this wall, beyond this man who was not quite the same man seated at this desk that was not quite the same desk . . . lay an entire world of streets and people. What sort of world it was now, there was no telling. He could feel them moving there, beyond the walls, almost, like so many chess pieces blown in a dry wind. . . .

But the immediate thing was the sign painted on the office wall, the same sign he had read earlier today on first entering.

Somehow, the sign had changed:

Tyme Sefari Inc.
Sefaris tu any yeer en the past.
Yu naim the animall.
Wee taekyuthair.
Yu shoot itt. K

Eckels felt himself fall into a chair. He fumbled crazily at the thick slime on his boots. He held up a clod of dirt, trembling, "No, it *can't* be. Not a *little* thing like that. No!"

Embedded in the mud, glistening green and gold and black, was a butterfly, very beautiful and very dead.

"Not a little thing like *that*! Not a butterfly!" cried Eckels.

It fell to the floor, an exquisite thing, a small thing that could upset balances and knock down a line of small dominoes and then big dominoes and then gigantic dominoes, all down the years across Time. Eckels's mind whirled. It *couldn't* change things. Killing one butterfly couldn't be *that* important! Could it?

His face was cold. His mouth trembled, asking: "Who—who won the presidential election yesterday?"

The man behind the desk laughed. "You joking? You know very well. Deutscher, of course! Who else? Not that fool weakling Keith. We got an iron man now, a man with guts!" The official stopped. "What's wrong?"

Eckels moaned. He dropped to his knees. He scrabbled at the golden butterfly with shaking fingers. "Can't we," he pleaded to the world, to himself, to the officials, to the Machine, "can't we take it *back,* can't we *make* it alive again? Can't we start over? Can't we—"

He did not move. Eyes shut, he waited, shivering. He heard Travis breathe loud in the room; he heard Travis shift his rifle, click the safety catch, and raise the weapon.

There was a sound of thunder.

K **Literary Focus Plot and Setting** What does this setting detail tell you? What happened during the safari to cause this event to occur?

Applying Your Skills

A Sound of Thunder

9.R.2.C.1.b Use details from text(s): to analyze character, plot, setting, point of view **9.R.3.C.1.a** Use details from informational text: to identify and explain the organizational pattern **9.W.3.A.1.e** Compose a variety of texts: including reflective writing **9.R.1.G.1.a** During reading, utilize strategies: to determine meaning of unknown words

Respond and Think Critically

Reading Focus

Quick Check

1. How does Eckels react when he confronts the dinosaur?
2. Why is Eckels killed at the story's end?

Read with a Purpose

3. What earth-changing events happen as a result of Eckels's actions?

Reading Skills: Analyzing Sequence of Events

4. Review the chart that you created to record the major events in this story. Think about how each event triggered the next. Then, identify the story's **turning point,** during which a critical action takes place that determines the outcome of the story.

A Sound of Thunder

Eckels arrives at the Time Safari offices.

And then . . .

Vocabulary Check

Use the Vocabulary words to correctly complete these sentences.

annihilate
delirium
revoke

5. In my ________, I thought I saw a snake in the grass.
6. The attack was meant to ________ the enemy.
7. We will ________ his fee if he fails to finish the job.

Literary Focus

Literary Analysis

8. **Interpret** Might the title of the story have more than one meaning? Explain.
9. **Interpret** What is the significance of the misspellings in the Time Safari, Inc., sign that Eckels sees at the end of the story?
10. **Evaluate** Are there any flaws in Bradbury's logic in the telling of this story? If so, do those flaws lessen your enjoyment of the story? Explain.
11. **Interpret** What do you think is Bradbury's purpose for telling this story? What **theme,** or idea about life, is he trying to convey? Explain.

Literary Skills: Plot and Setting Across Genres

12. **Identify** When the characters travel between the present and the past, how does the setting change? When they cross back into the present, what further change has taken place?
13. **Analyze** Which scene do you think is the climax of the story? Explain.

Literary Skills Review: Suspense

14. **Analyze** What does Bradbury do to build suspense, as the story leads to its climax?

Writing Focus

Think as a Reader/Writer

Use It in Your Writing Re-read the descriptions of Bradbury's dangerous setting that you wrote down in your *Reader/Writer Notebook.* Then, write a paragraph describing the place that the time travelers return to at the end of the story. Use descriptive details to liven up your description.

AUTOBIOGRAPHY

BEING PREY

by **Val Plumwood**

Read with a Purpose

Read this autobiographical narrative to discover how the author's outlook on life changes.

Preparing to Read for this selection is on page 77.

Build Background

This gripping real-life adventure story is set in Kakadu National Park, the largest national park in Australia. The Aborigines, the native peoples of Australia, have lived in the region for tens of thousands of years, and the park is famous for its Aboriginal cave paintings and rock carvings. The park's diverse habitats, such as its wetlands and grasslands, are home to numerous species of mammals, birds, and reptiles.

In the early wet season, Kakadu's paperbark wetlands are especially stunning, as the water lilies weave white, pink, and blue patterns of dreamlike beauty over the shining thunderclouds reflected in their still waters. Yesterday, the water lilies and the wonderful bird life had enticed me into a joyous afternoon's idyll[1] as I ventured onto the East Alligator Lagoon for the first time in a canoe lent by the park service. "You can play about on the backwaters," the ranger had said, "but don't go onto the main river channel. The current's too swift, and if you get into trouble, there are the crocodiles. Lots of them along the river!" I followed his advice and glutted myself on the magical beauty and bird life of the lily lagoons, untroubled by crocodiles. **A**

Today, I wanted to repeat that experience despite the drizzle beginning to fall as I neared the canoe launch site. I set off on a day trip in search of an Aboriginal rock art site across the lagoon and up a side channel. The drizzle turned to a warm rain within a few hours, and the magic was lost. The birds were invisible, the water lilies were sparser, and the lagoon seemed even a little menacing. I noticed now how low the 14-foot canoe sat in the water, just a few inches of fiberglass between me and the great saurians,[2] close relatives of the ancient dinosaurs. Not long ago, saltwater crocodiles were considered endangered, as virtually all mature animals in Australia's north were shot by commercial hunters. But after a decade and more of protection, they are now the most plentiful of the large animals of Kakadu National Park. I was actively involved in preserving such places, and for me, the crocodile was a symbol of the power and integrity of this place and the incredible richness of its aquatic habitats. **B**

1. **idyll** (Y duhl): peaceful or pleasant outing.

2. **saurians** (SAWR ee uhnz): lizards and related animals.

A Reading Focus **Analyzing Sequence of Events** What did Plumwood do the day before?

B Literary Focus **Setting** What details in this paragraph convey that "the magic" of the scene "was lost"?

Vocabulary **menacing** (MEHN ihs ihng) *v.* used as an *adj.:* threatening.

Analyzing Visuals **Viewing and Interpreting** Does the mood of this photograph match the mood of the story? Explain.

Kakadu National Park in Northern Territory, Australia.

After hours of searching the maze of shallow channels in the swamp, I had not found the clear channel leading to the rock art site, as shown on the ranger's sketch map. When I pulled my canoe over in driving rain to a rock outcrop for a hasty, sodden lunch, I experienced the unfamiliar sensation of being watched. Having never been one for timidity, in philosophy or in life, I decided, rather than return defeated to my sticky trailer, to explore a clear, deep channel closer to the river I had traveled along the previous day.

The rain and wind grew more severe, and several times I pulled over to tip water from the canoe. The channel soon developed steep mud banks and snags. Farther on, the channel opened up and was eventually blocked by a large sandy bar. I pushed the canoe toward the bank, looking around carefully before getting out in the shallows and pulling the canoe up. I would be safe from crocodiles in the canoe—I had been told—but swimming and standing or wading at the water's edge were dangerous. Edges are one of the crocodile's favorite food-capturing places. I saw nothing, but the feeling of unease that had been with me all day intensified. **C**

The rain eased temporarily, and I crossed a sandbar to see more of this puzzling place. As I crested a gentle dune, I was shocked to glimpse the muddy waters of the East Alligator River gliding silently only 100 yards away. The channel had led me back to the main river. Nothing stirred along the riverbank, but a great tumble of escarpment cliffs up on the other side caught my attention. One especially striking rock formation—a single large rock balanced precariously on a much smaller one—held my gaze. As I looked, my whispering sense of unease turned into a shout of danger. The strange formation put me sharply in mind of two things: of the indigenous[3] Gagadgu owners of Kakadu, whose advice about coming here I had not sought, and of the precariousness of my own life, of human lives. As a solitary specimen of a major prey species of the saltwater crocodile, I was standing in one of the most dangerous places on earth.

I turned back with a feeling of relief. I had not found the rock paintings, I rationalized, but it was too late to look for them. The strange rock formation presented itself instead as a telos[4] of the day, and now I could go, home to trailer comfort. **D**

As I pulled the canoe out into the main current, the rain and wind started up again. I had not gone more than five or ten minutes down the channel when, rounding a bend, I saw in midstream what looked like a floating stick—one I did not recall passing on my way up. As the current moved me toward it, the stick developed eyes. A crocodile! It did not look like a large one. I was close to it now but was not especially afraid; an encounter would add interest to the day.

Although I was paddling to miss the crocodile, our paths were strangely convergent.[5] I knew it would be close, but I was totally unprepared for the great blow when it struck the canoe. Again it struck, again and again, now from behind, shuddering the flimsy craft. As I paddled furiously, the blows continued. The unheard of was happening; the canoe was under attack! For the first time, it came to me fully that I was prey. I realized I had to get out of the canoe or risk being capsized.

The bank now presented a high, steep face of slippery mud. The only obvious avenue of escape was a paperbark tree near the muddy bank wall. I made the split-second decision to leap into its lower branches and climb to safety. I steered to the tree and stood up to jump. At the same instant, the crocodile rushed up alongside the canoe, and its beautiful, flecked golden eyes looked straight into mine. Perhaps I could bluff it, drive it away, as I had read of British tiger hunters doing. I waved my arms and shouted, "Go away!" (We're British here.) The golden eyes glinted with interest. I tensed for the jump and leapt. Before my foot even tripped the first branch, I had a blurred, incredulous vision of great toothed jaws bursting from the water. Then I was seized between

3. **indigenous** (ihn DIHJ uh nuhs): native; born in a particular place.
4. **telos** (TEE lahs): goal; purpose.
5. **convergent** (kuhn VUR juhnt): directed toward each other; coming together.

C Literary Focus Plot and Setting What mood does the setting create? What foreshadowing clues hint at danger to come?

D Reading Focus Analyzing Sequence of Events What does Plumwood decide to do here?

Vocabulary incredulous (ihn KREHJ uh luhs) *adj.:* doubting; here, prompting disbelief.

the legs in a red-hot pincer grip and whirled into the suffocating wet darkness. . . .

Few of those who have experienced the crocodile's death roll have lived to describe it. It is, essentially, an experience beyond words of total terror. The crocodile's breathing and heart metabolism are not suited to prolonged struggle, so the roll is an intense burst of power designed to overcome the victim's resistance quickly. The crocodile then holds the feebly struggling prey underwater until it drowns. The roll was a centrifuge[6] of boiling blackness that lasted for an eternity, beyond endurance, but when I seemed all but finished, the rolling suddenly stopped. My feet touched bottom, my head broke the surface, and, coughing, I sucked at air, amazed to be alive. The crocodile still had me in its pincer grip between the legs. I had just begun to weep for the prospects of my mangled body when the crocodile pitched me suddenly into a second death roll.

When the whirling terror stopped again I surfaced again, still in the crocodile's grip next to a stout branch of a large sandpaper fig growing in the water. I grabbed the branch, vowing to let the crocodile tear me apart rather than throw me again into that spinning, suffocating hell. For the first time I realized that the crocodile was growling, as if angry. I braced myself for another roll, but then its jaws simply relaxed; I was free. I gripped the branch and pulled away, dodging around the back of the fig tree to avoid the forbidding mud bank, and tried once more to climb into the paperbark tree.

As in the repetition of a nightmare, the horror of my first escape attempt was repeated.

As in the repetition of a nightmare, the horror of my first escape attempt was repeated. As I leapt into the same branch, the crocodile seized me again, this time around the upper left thigh, and pulled me under. Like the others, the third death roll stopped, and we came up next to the sandpaper fig branch again. I was growing weaker, but I could see the crocodile taking a long time to kill me this way. I prayed for a quick finish and decided to provoke it by attacking it with my hands. Feeling back behind me along the head, I encountered two lumps. Thinking I had the eye sockets, I jabbed my thumbs into them with all my might. They slid into warm, unresisting holes (which may have been the ears, or perhaps the nostrils), and the crocodile did not so much as flinch. In despair, I grabbed the branch again. And once again, after a time, I felt the crocodile jaws relax, and I pulled free.

I knew I had to break the pattern; up the slippery mud bank was the only way. I scrabbled for a grip, then slid back toward the waiting jaws. The second time I almost made it before again sliding back, braking my slide by grabbing a tuft of grass. I hung there, exhausted. I can't make it, I thought. It'll just have to come and get me. The grass tuft began to give way. Flailing to keep from sliding farther, I jammed

6. **centrifuge** (SEHN truh fyooj): machine that spins items to separate materials or parts.

my fingers into the mud. This was the clue I needed to survive. I used this method and the last of my strength to climb up the bank and reach the top. I was alive! **E**

Escaping the crocodile was not the end of my struggle to survive. I was alone, severely injured, and many miles from help. During the attack, the pain from the injuries had not fully registered. As I took my first urgent steps, I knew something was wrong with my leg. I did not wait to inspect the damage but took off away from the crocodile toward the ranger station.

After putting more distance between me and the crocodile, I stopped and realized for the first time how serious my wounds were. I did not remove my clothing to see the damage to the groin area inflicted by the first hold. What I could see was bad enough. The left thigh hung open, with bits of fat, tendon, and muscle showing, and a sick, numb feeling suffused my entire body. I tore up some clothing to bind the wounds and made a tourniquet[7] for my bleed-

7. **tourniquet** (TUR nuh keht): bandage or device used to stop bleeding or prevent blood from flowing to part of the body.

E **Reading Focus** **Analyzing Sequence of Events** Summarize what has just happened to Plumwood and how she escapes.

ing thigh, then staggered on, still elated from my escape. I went some distance before realizing with a sinking heart that I had crossed the swamp above the ranger station in the canoe and could not get back without it.

I would have to hope for a search party, but I could maximize my chances by moving downstream toward the swamp edge, almost two miles away. I struggled on, through driving rain, shouting for mercy from the sky, apologizing to the angry crocodile, repenting to this place for my intrusion. I came to a flooded tributary and made a long upstream detour looking for a safe place to cross.

My considerable bush experience served me well, keeping me on course (navigating was second nature). After several hours, I began to black out and had to crawl the final distance to the swamp's edge. I lay there in the gathering dusk to await what would come. I did not expect a search party until the following day, and I doubted I could last the night.

The rain and wind stopped with the onset of darkness, and it grew perfectly still. Dingoes howled, and clouds of mosquitoes whined around my body. I hoped to pass out soon, but consciousness persisted. There were loud swirling noises in the water, and I knew I was easy meat for another crocodile. After what seemed like a long time, I heard the distant sound of a motor and saw a light moving on the swamp's far side. Thinking it was a boat, I rose up on my elbow and called for help. I thought I heard a faint reply, but then the motor grew fainter and the lights went away. I was as devastated as any castaway who signals desperately to a passing ship and is not seen. **F**

The lights had not come from a boat. Passing my trailer, the ranger noticed there was no light inside it. He had driven to the canoe launch site on a motorized trike and realized I had not returned. He had heard my faint call for help, and after some time, a rescue craft appeared. As I began my 13-hour journey to Darwin Hospital, my rescuers discussed going upriver the next day to shoot a crocodile. I spoke strongly against this plan: I was the intruder, and no good purpose could be served by random revenge. The water around the spot where I had been lying was full of crocodiles. That spot was under six feet of water the next morning, flooded by the rains signaling the start of the wet season.

In the end I was found in time and survived against many odds. A similar combination of good fortune and human care enabled me to overcome a leg infection that threatened amputation or worse. I probably have Paddy Pallin's incredibly tough walking shorts to thank for the fact that the groin injuries were not as severe as the leg injuries. I am very lucky that I can still walk well and have lost few of my previous capacities. The wonder of being alive after being held—quite literally—in the jaws of death has never entirely left me. For the first year, the experience of existence as an unexpected blessing cast a golden glow over my life, despite the injuries and the pain. The glow has slowly faded, but some of that new gratitude for life endures, even if I remain unsure whom I should thank. **G**

F **Literary Focus** **Setting** What changes have taken place in the setting?

G **Literary Focus** **Plot** How was Plumwood finally found and rescued?

Applying Your Skills

Being Prey

9.R.2.C.1.b Use details from text(s): to analyze character, plot, setting, point of view 9.R.3.C.1.a Use details from informational text: to identify and explain the organizational pattern 9.W.2.D.1.a Compose text using: precise and vivid language 9.R.1.G.1.a During reading, utilize strategies: to determine meaning of unknown words

Respond and Think Critically

Reading Focus

Quick Check

1. What is the purpose of the crocodile's death roll?
2. How was Plumwood able to survive the attack?

Read with a Purpose

3. How does Plumwood's adventure change her outlook on life?

Reading Skills: Analyzing Sequence of Events

4. Review the story events that you recorded on a chart. Then, think about how each event caused the next to happen, and in doing so, built suspense. What changes in the sequence of events may have prevented Plumwood's encounter with the crocodile?

Being Prey
The author goes out onto the lagoon in a canoe . . .
And then . . .

Vocabulary Check

Match each Vocabulary word below with its definition.

5. **menacing** a. unbelievable
6. **incredulous** b. threatening

Literary Focus

Literary Analysis

7. **Interpret** Who is the prey in this story? What is the significance of the title of this selection?
8. **Infer** Why is Plumwood against the plan to kill the crocodile that attacked her? Why does she refer to herself as an "intruder"?

Literary Skills: Plot and Setting Across Genres

9. **Speculate** An **autobiographical narrative** is a true story that tells of an event the writer experienced. Do you think "Being Prey" would lose its impact if it were fiction, or made up? Explain, citing details to support your opinion.

Clue	What Happened Next

10. **Analyze** Why is the setting such an important part of this story? Explain.
11. **Compare** Although the narrators of these two selections are very different, they face similar dangers. Describe the similarities and differences in the plots of these two selections.

Literary Skills Review: Foreshadowing

12. **Analyze** Writers often use **foreshadowing,** or clues that hint at future events, to create suspense. Go back to the story and find two examples of foreshadowing.

Writing Focus

Think as a Reader/Writer

Use It in Your Writing Review the descriptive details in your *Reader/Writer Notebook*. Think of another dangerous situation from which it may be difficult to escape. Then, write a short description of this setting. Like Bradbury and Plumwood, use vivid details to enliven the description of your setting.

COMPARING TEXTS

Wrap Up

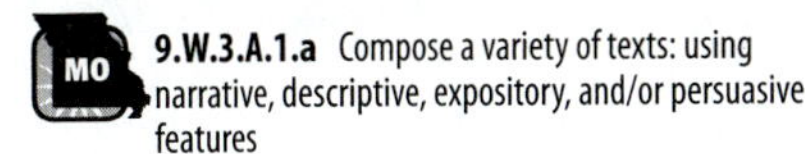

MO
9.W.3.A.1.a Compose a variety of texts: using narrative, descriptive, expository, and/or persuasive features

A Sound of Thunder / Being Prey

Writing Focus

Writing a Comparison-Contrast Essay

"A Sound of Thunder" and "Being Prey" are both stories of escape, though one is fiction and the other is nonfiction. What similarities can you find between the two texts? Review the items below to come up with some ideas for a comparison-contrast essay.

Prewriting

Select one of the following writing topics to explore in a comparison-contrast essay.

- How does each of the writers build suspense? What details in the texts foreshadow the danger to come?
- How do the settings in each story contribute to the conflicts the characters face? Think about the specifics each writer gives you about the time and place in which the story occurs.
- What is the theme, or message about life, conveyed in each selection? How does each writer explore the idea of escape?

Review the Elements of the Writing

Once you've chosen a topic, review the elements that help make a successful comparison-contrast essay.

An effective comparison-contrast essay—

- clearly states what is being compared in the essay's opening paragraph
- conveys a clear main idea
- is organized logically and consistently
- uses details from the text to support ideas
- has a concluding paragraph in which the main ideas are summarized

Gathering Details

Create a simple T-chart to organize your ideas. In the first column, write details that relate to "A Sound of Thunder." Use the second column to record details from "Being Prey."

A Sound of Thunder	Being Prey

Drafting

Choose an organization method for your essay. Most comparison-contrast essays are organized in either of these ways:

Point-by-Point Method	Block Method
Body paragraph: • Subject 1 detail • Subject 2 detail Body paragraph: • Subject 1 detail • Subject 2 detail	Body paragraph: • All Subject 1 details Body paragraph: • All Subject 2 details

Revising and Editing

- Re-read your opening paragraph to be sure you have fully introduced your topic to your readers. Re-read your conclusion to make sure your main idea is clearly stated.
- Add details to support the points you make. Add transitions such as *both, but,* and *like* to help readers follow your ideas.
- Proofread your essay and correct errors in grammar and spelling.

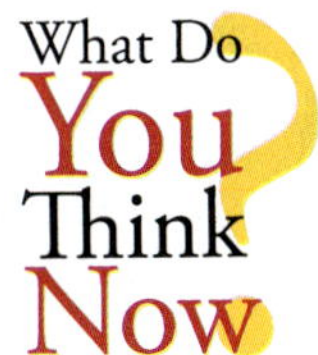

You just read about characters who felt fear while battling wild creatures. What do such experiences teach us about the world?

INFORMATIONAL TEXT FOCUS

Understand Main Idea

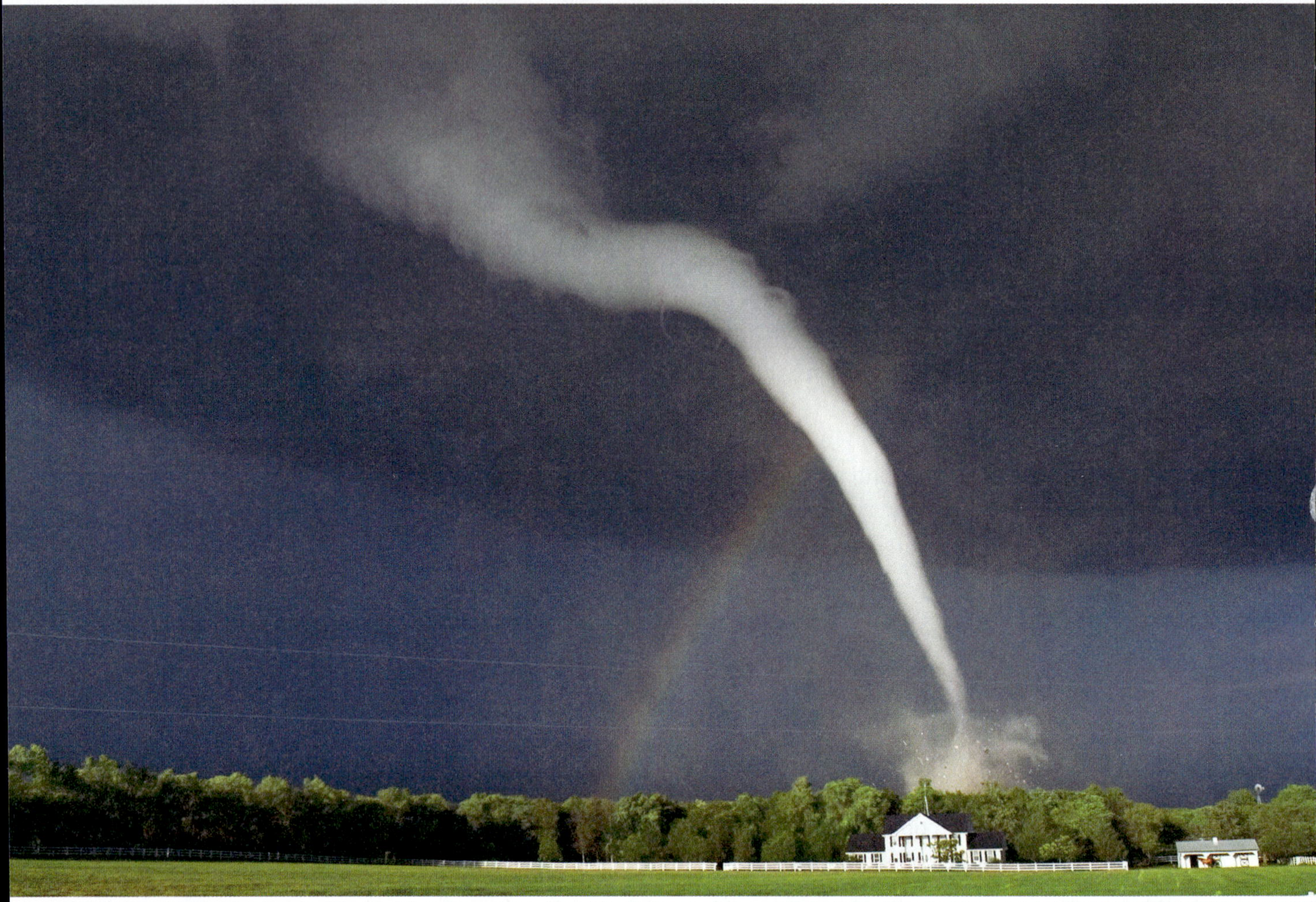

A beautiful yet violent tornado destroys a house near Mulvane, Kansas, on June 12, 2004.

CONTENTS

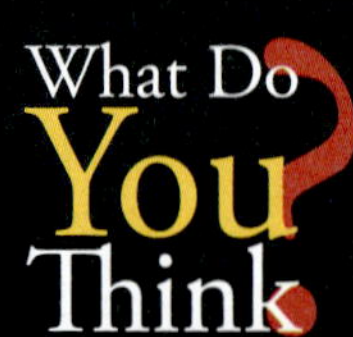

What Do You Think? Is the need for escape one of instinct or intellect?

QuickWrite

Think of a movie or television show in which the main character devises an escape plan. Briefly describe the situation. Is this desire for escape propelled by a physical need, an intellectual need, or both?

MAGAZINE ARTICLE

Preparing to Read

The Great Escape

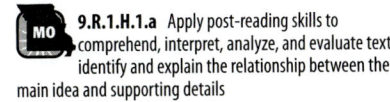

9.R.1.H.1.a Apply post-reading skills to comprehend, interpret, analyze, and evaluate text: identify and explain the relationship between the main idea and supporting details

Reader/Writer Notebook

Use your **RWN** to complete the activities for this selection.

Informational Text Focus

Main Idea When you read informational texts, two important questions to ask are "What is the writer trying to say?" and "Why is the author making that point?" The answers to those questions will reveal the writer's main idea and his or her purpose for writing. The most important point or central message in a nonfiction text is called the **main idea.** To develop the main idea, an author might use a variety of details, such as facts, quotations, and statistics (number facts).

Tips for Finding the Main Idea

- Read the article's title and scan the headings to see if they provide clues about the important points in the article.
- Read the article's introduction to see if it states a main idea.
- Look for the repetition of key phrases or ideas within the article.
- Re-read the article's conclusion to see if the writer has restated his or her main idea there.

Into Action Use the chart below to record information from the article that may help you identify the main idea.

Text Feature	My Comments
Title of Article	The Great Escape
Headings	
Repetition of Ideas	
Conclusion	

Vocabulary

prowled (prowld) *v.:* hunted; stalked. *The guards prowled the campgrounds, looking for escapees.*

pursued (puhr SOOD) *v.:* followed; chased. *After word of the escape got out,troops pursued the prisoners.*

Language Coach

Word Forms Both of the Vocabulary words above are verbs with corresponding noun forms. Use a dictionary to find the noun form of each Vocabulary word. Then, write a sentence for each word, using its noun form.

Writing Focus

Preparing for **Constructed Response**

As you read "The Great Escape," use your *Reader/Writer Notebook* to record notes about the prisoners' actions that particularly impressed you.

Learn It Online

Explore main idea through *PowerNotes* online:

go.hrw.com L9-99 Go

THE GREAT ESCAPE

from Boys' Life
by **Thomas Fleming**

Read with a Purpose

Read this article to discover why this particular escape is still considered "great" today.

Build Background

The article you are about to read recounts one of the most famous real-life escape stories of the last century: the Great Escape of World War II in which 76 prisoners of war, from many different countries, escaped from a Nazi prisoner-of-war (POW) camp in Poland.

The seven hundred fliers in the prisoner of war camp called Stalag Luft III came from many countries—the United States, England, Canada, Poland, Czechoslovakia, Australia, South Africa. They had two things in common. All had been shot down fighting Germany during World War II in the early 1940s.

And all were determined to escape.

They had tried to escape from many other camps and had been caught. That was why these prisoners had ended up in Stalag Luft III, deep in eastern Germany. It was supposed to be escape-proof. **A**

Two nine-foot-high barbed wire fences surrounded the camp. Between the fences were big towers equipped with searchlights and machine guns. The prisoners called the towers "goon boxes." Day and night specially trained groups of Germans, whom the fliers called "ferrets," prowled inside the camp, looking for escape activity.

Anyone the ferrets caught planning an escape was sent to "the cooler"—a block of solitary confinement[1] cells where the prisoner would live on nothing but bread and water.

The Escape Genius

The Germans seemed to have thought of everything. But they did not count on facing Roger Bushell. This South African was an escape genius. He was called Big X by the rest of the

1. **solitary confinement:** imprisonment in a cell isolated from all other prisoners.

A **Informational Reading Focus** **Main Idea** What background does the author provide about the time and place of the escape? What information does he provide about the POWs?

Vocabulary **prowled** (prowld) *v.:* hunted; stalked.

prisoners. He transformed Stalag Luft III into the "X Organization," announcing to his fellow prisoners that they were going to pull off the greatest escape in history.

Big X's plan called for the prisoners to start three tunnels—called Tom, Dick and Harry. The men cut trapdoors through the stone floors of three huts and inserted removable slabs made from stolen concrete. "Tunnel rats" dropped through the trapdoors and began digging.

Big X wanted deep tunnels. If they were too shallow, the Germans would be able to hear the men working in them. So, despite the danger of the tunnels collapsing and burying them alive, the tunnel rats went down thirty feet before they started for the fences. **B**

The Escape Factory

The tunnels were only the beginning. "I want each escaping man to be equipped with a set of forged documents that will fool the German police," Big X said. "I want them to be wearing civilian clothes or fake German uniforms. I want them to have compasses and maps that

---

B **Informational Reading Focus** **Main Idea** Why did Bushell want the prisoners to dig the tunnels so deep?

Map of Eastern Europe during World War II.

The tunnel was to come up in the woods beyond the guard box, Stalag Luft III (1945) by A. H. Comber.
Australian War Memorial Negative Number ART34781.021

Another tunnel: Stalag Luft III: coming up after the day's work in "Dick" (1945) by A. H. Comber.
Australian War Memorial Negative Number ART34781.017

will help them reach the borders of neutral countries."

The X Organization spotted weaklings among the ferrets and bribed them with chocolate from their Red Cross aid packages. Soon they had ink and pens, a camera and a set of official documents. A forgery factory ran day and night.

In other huts prisoners created civilian clothes by cutting and reshaping prisoners' uniforms, the linings of winter coats and other pieces of cloth. An Australian flight lieutenant ran a factory that made two hundred compasses out of melted phonograph records. The compass needles were slices of magnetized razor blades.

An engineering factory built air pumps so the tunnel rats could breathe. The engineers also made small flatbed trolleys from wooden bed boards. They even stole light bulbs and wiring for the tunnels.

The diggers lay on their stomachs in the two-foot-wide tunnels and filled boxed on the trolleys with sand. Other prisoners poured the sand into bags made from towels—bags that could be inserted under a man's pants.

Fifty Americans worked as sand carriers. They were called "penguins" because they had to spend most of their time outside, walking up and down, waiting for the right moment to pull a string on the bags and let the sand run out.

All around the camp were dozens of "stooges" who signaled when a ferret approached. This gave the forgers, tailors, penguins and the others time to hide their work or take cover. Thirty feet underground, the tunnel rats kept digging.

Pretending Defeat

Then disaster struck. The Germans discovered the trapdoor for Tom, the longest tunnel. The diggers had gotten past the wire fence and were only one hundred feet from the woods around the camp. Big X ordered a halt to all digging for more than a month. He wanted the Germans to think they had given up.

Extending the tunnel at the working face, Stalag Luft III (1945) by A. H. Comber.

Australian War Memorial Negative Number ART34781.016

Then Big X ordered an all-out push in Harry. Soon they were under the wire and—they thought—into the woods. It was time for "the great escape." Big X was hoping to spring no fewer that 250 men. Not even a six-inch snowfall was going to stop them. **C**

At 9 P.M. on March 24, 1944, the break-out began. Men wearing German uniforms, business suites and tattered workers' outfits crowded into the hut containing Harry's trap-door. At the other end, the tunnel rats finished the thirty-foot shaft to the surface.

They finally broke through and stared around in horror. They were ten feet short of the trees!

After a frantic conference, Big X decided they had to keep going. All their forged documents were dated. If they dug another ten feet and waited a month for the next moonless night, the forgery factory would have to do its work all over again.

They stretched a rope from the hole to the trees. The first man out lay in the trees and pulled the rope to signal when the guard in the nearest goon box was not looking. Over the next seven hours, seventy six men scuttled through the woods towards freedom.

It was almost dawn when a German sentry patrolling outside the barbed wire discovered the hole. The guard raised his rifle to shoot the man crawling out. The rope controller leaped from the woods crying: *"Nicht schiessen!"* ("Don't shoot!"). The startled guard's shot went wild.

By this time Big X and his friends were far away from Stalag Luft III.

The German dictator, Adolf Hitler, was furious. He ordered one of the biggest manhunts in history. More than 70,000 policemen and troops pursued the fugitives. Big X's plan to humiliate the Germans and make them worry about escapees—and not the war front—was successful. **D**

But only three men—Peter Bergsland, Jens Mueller and Bram van der Stok—made it to freedom. Fifty of the captured men, including Big X, were shot by the German secret police, the Gestapo, at Hitler's order. This was an outrageous violation of the rules of war. The bodies were cremated to hide the murders.

C **Informational Reading Focus** **Main Idea** How might snow hinder the escape? Why does the author provide this detail?

D **Informational Reading Focus** **Main Idea** Re-read the last paragraph. What new information about Big X's reasons for orchestrating the escape is given here?

Vocabulary **pursued** (puhr SOOD) *v.:* followed; chased.

The rest of the escapers were returned to Stalag Luft III and other camps for long stays in the cooler. A year later, Allied tanks[2] freed the survivors as Germany surrendered.

After the war, the British sent a team of investigators to Germany. They tracked down those who had carried out Hitler's order.

2. **Allied tanks:** tanks belonging to the Allied counties (including the United States, Great Britain, France, and Russia), those countries battling the Axis powers (Germany, Italy, and Japan) in World War II.

Twenty-one were hanged for murder, seventeen received prison terms.

What had the great escape accomplished? One writer summed it up this way: It proved that "there is nothing that can stop a group of men, regardless of race, creed, color or nationality, from achieving a goal once they agree to what that goal is." **E**

Read with a Purpose

Why do so many people regard the prisoners' escape as "great"?

E **Informational Reading Focus** **Main Idea** Why does the author provide this quote in the last paragraph?

Escapee Peter Bergsland.

Escapee Jens Muller.

Escapee Bram van der Stok.

MAGAZINE ARTICLE

Applying Your Skills

MO **9.R.1.H.1.a** Apply post-reading skills to comprehend, interpret, analyze, and evaluate text: identify and explain the relationship between the main idea and supporting details **9.W.3.A.1.e** Compose a variety of texts: including reflective writing

The Great Escape

Practicing the Standards

Informational Text and Vocabulary

1. What is the **main idea** of the article?

A World War II should never have been allowed to happen.

B The prisoners in Stalag Luft III showed that by working together, they could accomplish their goal.

C The prisoners in Stalag Luft III proved that they could outsmart the guards.

D It's easy to escape from a prison camp.

2. Which of the following **details** in the article suggest that the writer admired Roger Bushell (Big X)?

A The Germans seemed to have thought of everything. But they did not count on Roger Bushell.

B Big X ordered a halt to all digging for more than a month.

C Big X was hoping to spring no fewer than 250 men.

D Big X called for the prisoners to start three tunnels—Tom, Dick, and Harry.

3. What is the **main idea** of the section of text with the heading "The Escape Factory"?

A There the prisoners became friendly with the guards.

B The prisoners were well-organized and resourceful.

C The camps were easy to escape.

D The prisoners had a fighting spirit.

4. The word *prowled* means

A celebrated.

B revered.

C ousted.

D hunted.

5. When someone is *pursued,* he or she is

A injured.

B followed.

C captured.

D discovered.

Writing Focus Constructed Response

Think of another event in history in which someone or a group of people fought against all odds in order to gain their freedom. What is most impressive to you about this person or group? Share your ideas in a brief essay.

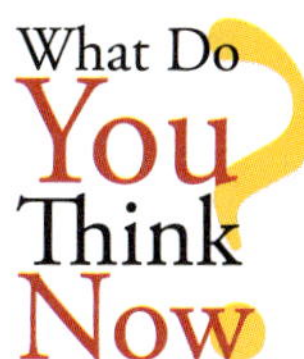

Why did the prisoners plan to escape? Were they trying to outsmart their captors or motivated by a deeper need? Explain.

MAGAZINE ARTICLE

Preparing to Read

Did Animals Sense Tsunami Was Coming?

Informational Text Focus

Main Idea and Supporting Details A **main idea** is the writer's most important message. To help determine the main idea, ask yourself, "What is the author's purpose for writing? What message is he or she trying to convey?"

A successful text contains details that support a writer's main idea. These details may include—

- **facts** (statements that can be proved)
- **statistics** (facts in the form of numbers)
- **quotations** (a person's exact words or statement)
- **evidence** (examples)

Into Action As you read, fill in a chart like the one below to help you identify the main idea and its supporting details. In the ovals, fill in key details you find within the article. Those key details may be found in headings, captions, or topic sentences of paragraphs. Review those details, and identify the main idea those details support.

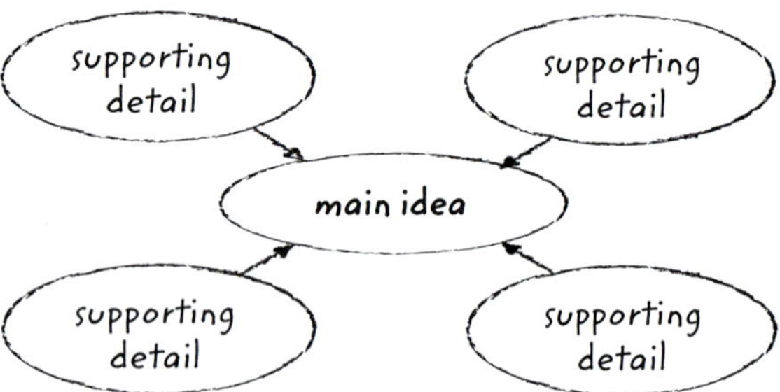

Writing Focus

Preparing for **Constructed Response**

News articles are informational in nature. If writers of news articles fail to clearly convey information to readers, they are not doing their jobs well. As you read this article, look for ways the writer presents and supports important ideas. Pay attention to the way the writer uses headings, paragraphs, and lists to convey ideas.

MO **9.R.1.H.1.a** Apply post-reading skills to comprehend, interpret, analyze, and evaluate text: identify and explain the relationship between the main idea and supporting details

Reader/Writer Notebook

Use your **RWN** to complete the activities for this selection.

Vocabulary

domestic (duh MEHS tihk) *adj.:* not wild; tame. *Even domestic animals retain their wild instincts.*

impending (ihm PEHN dihng) *adj.:* about to happen; looming. *No one knew the damage the impending tsunami would eventually cause.*

emigrated (EHM uh grayt ihd) *v.:* moved to another country. *The researcher emigrated to the United States from Pakistan ten years ago.*

Language Coach

Related Words The word *migrate* means "to move from one place to another." *Immigrate* (which means "come into a new country") and *immigrant* ("someone who has moved to a new country") are built on the word *migrate.*

- Which word on the list above is also built on *migrate?*
- How do the meanings of the words *emigrate* and *immigrate* differ? Consult a dictionary if you need help.

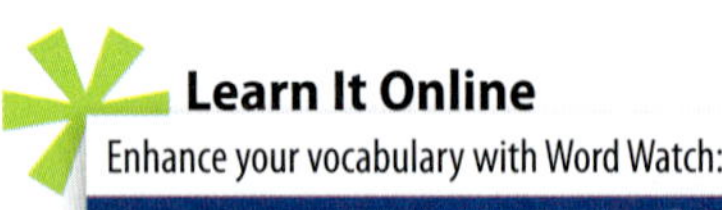

Learn It Online

Enhance your vocabulary with Word Watch:

go.hrw.com L9-106 

MAGAZINE ARTICLE

Did ANIMALS Sense Tsunami Was Coming?

from National Geographic News

Read with a Purpose
Read the following selection to learn how animals escaped the tsunami of 2004.

Build Background
On December 26, 2004, an undersea earthquake estimated to register 9.0 on the Richter scale triggered several tsunamis in the Indian Ocean. The tsunamis, gigantic ocean waves, flooded coastal areas of South and Southeast Asia, devastating entire communities and causing the deaths of more than 225,000 people.

Before giant waves slammed into Sri Lanka and India coastlines in 2004, wild and domestic animals seemed to know what was about to happen and fled to safety.

According to eyewitness accounts, the following events happened:

- Elephants screamed and ran for higher ground.
- Dogs refused to go outdoors.
- Flamingos abandoned their low-lying breeding areas.
- Zoo animals rushed into their shelters and could not be enticed to come back out. **A**

The belief that wild and domestic animals possess a sixth sense—and know in advance when the earth is going to shake—has been around for centuries.

Wildlife experts believe animals' more acute hearing and other senses might enable them to hear or feel the Earth's vibration, tipping them off to approaching disaster long before humans realize what's going on.

The massive tsunami was trigged by a magnitude 9 temblor[1] off the coast of northern Sumatra island on December 26, 2004. The giant waves rolled through the Indian Ocean, killing more than 225,000 people in a dozen countries.

Relatively few animals have been reported dead, however, reviving speculation that animals somehow sense impending disaster. **B**

Ravi Corea, president of the Sri Lanka Wildlife Conservation Society, which is based

1. **magnitude 9 temblor:** an earthquake measuring 9.0 on the Richter scale.

A **Informational Focus** **Supporting Details** What main idea do these details support? What kind of details are they?

B **Informational Focus** **Main Idea** What led researchers to question how animals sense danger?

Vocabulary **domestic** (duh MEHS tihk) *adj.:* not wild; tame.
impending (ihm PEHN dihng) *adj.:* about to happen; looming.

in Nutley, New Jersey, was in Sri Lanka when the massive waves struck.

Afterward, he traveled to the Patanangala beach inside Yala National Park, where some 60 visitors were washed away.

The beach was one of the worst hit areas of the 500-square-mile (1,300-square-kilometer) wildlife reserve, which is home to a variety of animals, including elephants, leopards, and 130 species of birds.

Corea did not see any animal carcasses nor did the park personnel know of any, other than two water buffaloes that had died, he said.

Along India's Cuddalore coast, where thousands of people perished, the Indo-Asian News service reported that buffaloes, goats, and dogs were found unharmed.

Flamingos that breed this time of year at the Point Calimere wildlife sanctuary in India flew to higher ground beforehand, the news service reported.

Strange Animal Behavior

Accounts of strange animal behavior have also started to surface.

About an hour before the tsunami hit, Corea said, people at Yala National Park observed three elephants running away from the Patanangala beach. . . .

Corea, a Sri Lankan who emigrated to the United States 20 years ago, said two of his friends noticed unusual animal behavior before the tsunami.

One friend, in the southern Sri Lankan town of Dickwella, recalls bats frantically flying away just before the tsunami struck. Another friend, who lives on the coast near Galle, said his two dogs would not go for their daily run on the beach.

"They are usually excited to go on this outing," Corea said. But on this day they refused to go and most probably saved his life.

Alan Rabinowitz, director for science and exploration at the Bronx Zoo-based Wildlife

Vocabulary **emigrated** (EHM uh grayt ihd) *v.:* moved to another country.

Conservation Society in New York, says animals can sense impending danger by detecting subtle or abrupt shifts in the environment.

"Earthquakes bring vibrational changes on land and in water while storms cause electromagnetic changes in the atmosphere," he said. "Some animals have an acute sense of hearing and smell that allow them to determine something coming towards them long before humans might know that something is there." **C**

Did Humans Lose Their Sixth Sense?

At one time humans also had this sixth sense, Rabinowitz said, but lost the ability when it was no longer needed or used.

Joyce Poole is director of the Savanna Elephant Vocalization Project, which has its headquarters in Norway. She has worked with African elephants in Kenya for 25 years. She said the reports of Sri Lanka's elephants fleeing to higher ground didn't surprise her.

Research on both acoustic and seismic communication[2] indicates that elephants could easily pick up vibrations generated from the massive earthquake-tsunami, she said.

Poole has also experienced this firsthand. "I have been with elephants during two small tremors, and on both occasions the elephants ran in alarm several seconds before I felt the tremor," she said. **D**

One of the world's most earthquake-prone countries is Japan, where devastation has taken

2. **acoustic and seismic communication:** related to sound and related to earthquakes or earth tremors.

C **Informational Focus** **Main Idea** According to this passage, why might animals sense oncoming storms and earthquakes before humans do?

D **Informational Focus** **Supporting Details** What kind of supporting detail does Poole provide here?

Residents walk through debris of a destroyed market after tidal waves hit the capital of Banda Aceh, Aceh province, on Indonesia's Sumatra island.

property. Researchers there have long studied animals in hopes of discovering what they hear or feel before the earth shakes. They hope that animals may be used as a prediction tool.

Some U.S. seismologists, on the other hand, are skeptical. There have been documented cases of strange animal behavior prior to earthquakes. But the United States Geological Survey [USGS], a government agency that provides scientific information about the Earth, says a reproducible connection between a specific behavior and the occurrence of a quake has never been made.

"What we're faced with is a lot of anecdotes,"[3] said Andy Michael, a geophysicist at USGS. "Animals react to so many things—being hungry, defending their territories, mating, predators—so it's hard to have a controlled study to get that advanced warning signal."

In the 1970s a few studies on animal prediction were done by the USGS, "but nothing concrete came out of it," Michael said. Since that time the agency has made no further investigations into the theory.

Read with a Purpose What special abilities might animals possess that enable them to escape natural disasters such as tsunamis?

3. **anecdotes:** stories; short accounts.

MAGAZINE ARTICLE

Applying Your Skills

MO **9.R.1.H.1.a** Apply post-reading skills to comprehend, interpret, analyze, and evaluate text: identify and explain the relationship between the main idea and supporting details **9.W.3.A.1.a** Compose a variety of texts: using narrative, descriptive, expository, and/or persuasive features *Also covered* **9.W.2.B.1.b; 9.R.1.G.1.a**

Did Animals Sense Tsunami Was Coming?

Practicing the Standards

Informational Text and Vocabulary

1. What is the **main idea** of the article?
   - **A** Animals can sense danger even when humans cannot.
   - **B** Tsunamis kill both humans and animals.
   - **C** Only animals are able to survive natural disasters.
   - **D** Scientists ignore lessons animals can teach us.

2. What kind of **supporting detail** is the following: "Another friend, who lives on the coast near Galle, said his two dogs would not go for their daily run on the beach."
   - **A** statistic
   - **B** definition
   - **C** fact
   - **D** quotation

3. Which of the following details *does not* support the writer's **main idea** that animal instinct helped many animals escape during the tsunami?
   - **A** Elephants screamed and ran for higher ground.
   - **B** Corea did not see any animal carcasses.
   - **C** The massive tsunami was trigged by a magnitude 9 temblor.
   - **D** One friend, in the southern Sri Lankan town of Dickwella, recalls bats frantically flying away just before the tsunami struck.

4. A *domestic* animal is —
   - **A** wild
   - **B** friendly
   - **C** hardworking
   - **D** tame

5. Which of the following is the best definition for *impending*?
   - **A** frightening
   - **B** oncoming
   - **C** costly
   - **D** heavy

6. If someone has recently *emigrated,* he or she has —
   - **A** gone on a trip
   - **B** become a citizen
   - **C** relocated to another country
   - **D** signed up for the military

Writing Focus Constructed Response

Identify the details that support the writer's main idea that animals may have successfully escaped the devastation of the tsunami by running to safer ground. In your response, be sure to make your own main ideas clear and support them with details.

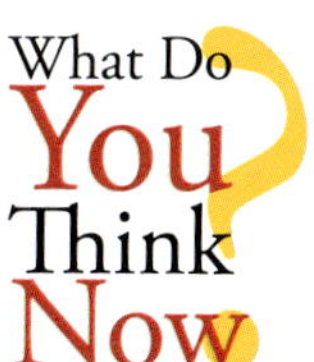

What might humans learn from animals about escaping natural disasters such as tsunamis?

FOCUS ON MISSOURI COURSE LEVEL EXPECTATIONS

Literary Skills Review

Plot and Setting

Directions: Read the following selection. Then, read and respond to the questions that follow.

Caline by **Kate Chopin**

The sun was just far enough in the west to send inviting shadows. In the center of a small field, and in the shade of a haystack which was there, a girl lay sleeping. She had slept long and soundly, when something awoke her as suddenly as if it had been a blow. She opened her eyes and stared a moment up in the cloudless sky. She yawned and stretched her long brown legs and arms, lazily. Then she arose, never minding the bits of straw that clung to her black hair, to her red bodice,[1] and the blue cotonade[2] skirt that did not reach her naked ankles.

The log cabin in which she dwelt with her parents was just outside the enclosure in which she had been sleeping. Beyond was a small clearing that did duty as a cotton field. All else was dense wood, except the long stretch that curved round the brow of the hill, and in which glittered the steel rails of the Texas and Pacific road.

When Caline emerged from the shadow she saw a long train of passenger coaches standing in view, where they must have stopped abruptly. It was that sudden stopping which had awakened her; for such a thing had not happened before within her recollection, and she looked stupid, at first, with astonishment. There seemed to be something wrong with the engine; and some of the passengers who dismounted went forward to investigate the trouble. Others came strolling along in the direction of the cabin, where Caline stood under an old gnarled mulberry tree, staring. Her father had halted his mule at the end of the cotton row, and stood staring also, leaning upon his plow.

There were ladies in the party. They walked awkwardly in their high-heeled boots over the rough, uneven ground, and held up their skirts mincingly.[3] They twirled parasols[4] over their shoulders, and laughed immoderately at the funny things which their masculine companions were saying.

They tried to talk to Caline, but could not understand the French patois[5] with which she answered them.

One of the men—a pleasant-faced youngster—drew a sketch book from his pocket and began to make a picture of the girl. She stayed motionless, her hands behind her, and her wide eyes fixed earnestly upon him.

Before he had finished there was a summons from the train; and all went scampering hurriedly away. The engine screeched, it sent a few lazy puffs into the still air, and in another

1. **bodice** (BAHD ihs): fitted upper part of a dress.
2. **cotonade** (kaht uhn AYD): coarse cotton fabric.
3. **mincingly:** done in an elegant or dainty manner to impress people.
4. **parasols:** lightweight umbrellas that provide protection from the sun.
5. **patois** (PAT wah): form of a language that differs from the accepted standard; dialect.

9.R.2.C.1.b Use details from text(s): to analyze character, plot, setting, point of view

moment or two had vanished, bearing its human cargo with it.

Caline could not feel the same after that. She looked with new and strange interest upon the trains of cars that passed so swiftly back and forth across her vision, each day; and wondered whence these people came, and whither they were going.

Her mother and father could not tell her, except to say that they came from "loin là bas,"[6] and were going "Djieu sait é où."[7]

One day she walked miles down the track to talk with the old flagman,[8] who stayed down there by the big water tank. Yes, he knew. Those people came from the great cities in the north, and were going to the city in the south. He knew all about the city; it was a grand place. He had lived there once. His sister lived there now; and she would be glad enough to have so fine a girl as Caline to help her cook and scrub, and tend the babies. And he thought Caline might earn as much as five dollars a month, in the city.

So she went; in a new cotonade, and her Sunday shoes; with a sacredly guarded scrawl that the flagman sent to his sister.

The woman lived in a tiny, stuccoed house, with green blinds, and three wooden steps leading down to the banquette.[9] There seemed to be hundreds like it along the street. Over the house tops loomed the tall masts of ships, and the hum of the French market could be heard on a still morning.

Caline was at first bewildered.[10] She had to readjust all her preconceptions to fit the reality of it. The flagman's sister was a kind and gentle task-mistress. At the end of a week or two she wanted to know how the girl liked it all. Caline liked it very well, for it was pleasant, on Sunday afternoons, to stroll with the children under the great, solemn sugar sheds; or to sit upon the compressed cotton bales, watching the stately steamers, the graceful boats, and noisy little tugs that plied the waters of the Mississippi. And it filled her with agreeable excitement to go to the French market, where the handsome Gascon[11] butchers were eager to present their compliments and little Sunday bouquets to the pretty Acadian girl; and to throw fistfuls of *lagniappe*[12] into her basket.

When the woman asked her again after another week if she were still pleased, she was

6. **loin là bas:** French dialect for "far away; over there."
7. **Djieu sait é où:** French dialect for "God knows where."
8. **flagman:** years ago, a man who signaled a train with a flag or lantern.
9. **banquette** (bang KEHT): Southern term for "sidewalk."
10. **bewildered:** hopelessly confused; puzzled.
11. **Gascon:** from Gascony, in southwestern France.
12. **lagniappe** (lan YAP): Southern term for "small present."

Literary Skills Review CONTINUED

9.R.2.C.1.b Use details from text(s): to analyze character, plot, setting, point of view *Also covered* **9.R.2.B.1.d; 9.R.2.C.1.a; 9.R.2.C.1.d; 9.R.1.H.1.f**

not so sure. And again when she questioned Caline the girl turned away, and went to sit behind the big, yellow cistern,[13] to cry unobserved. For she knew now that it was not the great city and its crowds of people she had so eagerly sought; but the pleasant-faced boy, who had made her picture that day under the mulberry tree.

13. **cistern** (SIHS tuhrn): large container or tank for holding water.

1. How do you know the story is set in the past?

A Caline is a young girl.

B Caline encounters a sketch artist.

C Caline travels to New Orleans.

D Caline encounters a flagman.

9.R.2.C.1.d

2. All of the following details from the story establish the **setting** *except* —

A Caline and her family live in a log cabin

B the women on the train carry parasols

C Caline goes to New Orleans

D tall ships are moored in the harbor

9.R.2.C.1.d

3. What event **foreshadows** the fact that Caline will go to the city?

A The family lives in a rural area.

B Caline leaves her house to watch the stranded passengers.

C The train passengers do not understand what Caline is saying to them.

D Caline asks the flagman where the train she had seen is going.

9.R.2.B.1.d

4. When Caline first arrives in the city, she —

A is bewildered by the change in environment

B cannot find a place to live

C gets hopelessly lost

D realizes she made a mistake

9.R.1.H.1.f

5. Which word *best* captures the story's overall **mood**?

A Lighthearted

B Tense

C Somber

D Angry

9.R.2.B.1.d

6. At the end of the story, what **internal conflict** does Caline experience?

A She still yearns to find the man who sketched her picture.

B She misses her family and wants to come home.

C She does not like the woman for whom she is working.

D She does not like living in the busy city.

9.R.2.C.1.a

Constructed Response

7. Describe the **setting** of the story. Then, list two or three words you would use to describe the story's **mood.** Use images and details from the story to explain why you chose these words.

9.R.2.C.1.d

Informational Skills Review

MO **9.R.1.H.1.a** Apply post-reading skills to comprehend, interpret, analyze, and evaluate text: identify and explain the relationship between the main idea and supporting details

Main Idea and Details

Directions: Read the following selection. Then, read and respond to the questions that follow.

Travis's Dilemma

from **New York Times Upfront**
by **Charlie LeDuff** and **Patricia Smith**

College freshman Travis Warner has to decide whether or not to take over his father's farm. As the number of family farms in the U.S. has fallen, the population of the rural Great Plains has gone into a steep decline. In 1960, farmers made up 18 percent of the U.S. labor force. In 2006, that figure was 2 percent.

A few weeks before 18 year-old Travis Warner started college in August, he was busy doing what he was raised to do: working sunup to sundown on his family's farm in Lebanon, Kan. As they'd done countless times before, Travis and his father fed the pigs and sprayed fly repellent on the cattle. As they worked, a question hung in the air.

"Do you think you'll come back to rural America? And farm? Raise cattle? Raise pigs?" Randall Warner asked his son.

"Depends if I find something better in the next couple years," Travis replied.

"What could be better?" his father pressed. "What could be better than life on the Great Plains where the wind blows and you catch fresh air every day?"

"That's what I'm going to look for," Travis said.

The exchange between father and son speaks volumes about what is happening across the region.

From the Dakotas to the Texas Panhandle, the rural Great Plains have been losing people for 75 years—a slow demographic collapse. In nearly 70 percent of the counties on the Plains, there are fewer people now than there were in 1950. Population continued to plunge in the 1990s and has fallen even faster since the 2000 Census. In fact, of all the regions of the U.S., the Great Plains has by far the highest proportion of residents older than 85.

The reason is simply that young people like Travis are moving away.

"Over the last 100 years or so, many of these counties have been losing 50 or 60 percent of their young people each generation," says Kenneth M. Johnson, a sociology professor at Loyola University Chicago. The departure of young people means that a community also loses the next generation, Johnson explains.

And over time, the effects are magnified.

This is how a town like Lebanon dies. The school closed 15 years ago. The old Lebanon bank has caved in. Main Street is a peeling veneer. The average age of town residents is 52.

Informational Skills Review CONTINUED

The Next Generation

As towns like Lebanon fade, some places are trying to reinvent themselves. In 2000, Iowa tried recruiting immigrants to stem its population decline. Last year, it considered abolishing its income tax for residents under 30 as a way to attract and keep more young people.

And in a modern-day version of the 1862 Homestead Act,[1] in which the federal government gave land away to encourage the settlement of the frontier, some towns are offering land at little or no cost to families willing to build a house and move in. In Washington, Senators Byron Dorgan of North Dakota and Chuck Hagel of Nebraska are sponsoring the New Homestead Act, a federal program based on the same idea.

"Twenty-five years ago, there were 350,000 farmers and ranchers under the age of 35," says John Crabtree of the Center for Rural Affairs in Lyons, Neb. "Now, there's only 70,000. We're not creating opportunities for the next generation of farmers and ranchers to get into the business."

Travis's dad doesn't understand the ins and outs of the international trade policies and government subsidies[2] that are changing the economics of farming, but he does see that large corporate farmers are taking over. And he knows that to make it nowadays "you work harder—sunup past sundown."

Travis wants to know more people than his dad and the salesman at the John Deere dealership. When he's at the farm, he says, the nearest pretty girl is 20 miles away.

"I like to work with people, I guess," Travis says, sitting in the cab of an old pickup truck. "Be around people. And we come out here every day. It's Dad and myself; that's not working with people."

He continues: "I told my dad he could retire and cash-rent the land to the big farmer, but then what's he going to do with his time? This is all he knows. Come out here and work daylight to dark. I don't want that."

"Best Kind of Life"

Travis is now a freshman at Hutchinson Community College in Hutchinson, Kan., 180 miles from home. He likes school, but it took some getting used to at first. Even small things were culture shock for him, like being able to walk 10 steps to the apartment next door to see his neighbors.

"At home, the nearest neighbors are four miles away," he says with a laugh.

The biggest difference between college and the farm is that for the first time in his life, he has free time. At home, when he finished with school and sports practice, there were still plenty of chores to do. By the time he was done, it was time for bed.

1. **Homestead Act:** a law instated to promote the sale of government land in order to raise revenue and give settlers free ownership of land for the purpose of cultivation in the Midwest, Great Plains, and the West.
2. **subsidies** (SUHB suh deez): aid or support; a grant of money.

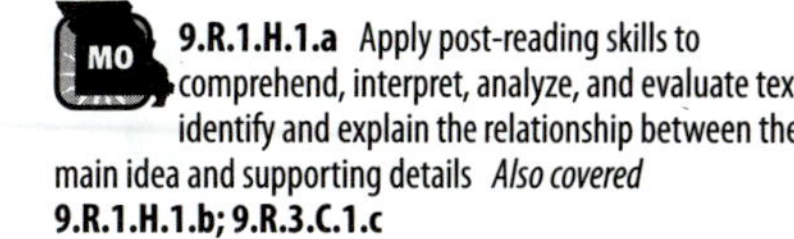
9.R.1.H.1.a Apply post-reading skills to comprehend, interpret, analyze, and evaluate text: identify and explain the relationship between the main idea and supporting details *Also covered* **9.R.1.H.1.b; 9.R.3.C.1.c**

Will he return to Lebanon? He just doesn't know yet. His 24-year-old brother is an engineer in Germany, and his 22-year-old sister is a senior at Kansas State University, studying to be a physician's assistant.

If Travis doesn't return to the farm, his father says he'll start selling it off in pieces to the farmer down the road.

Randall Warner sums up his values: "God. Family. Work," as he counts them on his fingertips. "Heritage." That's what he's worried will be lost if Travis doesn't take over the farm.

"My whole life is wrapped up in this," he says while baling hay. "To tell you the truth, it can get a little monotonous.[3] I've had four vacations my whole life."

Still, Randall Warner says, it's a good life. "The best kind of life there is."

3. **monotonous** (muh NAHT uh nuhs): having little variation or variety.

1. The main idea of the article is —
   - **A** the population in the rural Great Plains is increasing
   - **B** the population in the rural Great Plains is decreasing
   - **C** students should go away to college
   - **D** students should stay at home and work with their families

   9.R.1.H.1.a

2. What type of **evidence** do the authors of the article use to support the claim that the population of the rural Great Plains is decreasing?
   - **A** Ballpark figures
   - **B** Personal accounts
   - **C** Statistical information and interviews
   - **D** Maps and graphs

   9.R.3.C.1.c

3. According to the article, why are young people leaving the rural Great Plains?
   - **A** Young people are tired of working on family farms.
   - **B** Young people do not think farming is important work.
   - **C** Young people want greater opportunities to work and socialize.
   - **D** Young people want to live in dormitories with their friends.

   9.R.1.H.1.a

4. Which of the following details supports the article's **main idea**?
   - **A** Communities have lost 50 to 60 percent of their young people each generation.
   - **B** Population numbers have risen since the 2000 Census.
   - **C** Income tax has been abolished for residents under 30.
   - **D** The number of farmers in the United States has risen from 2 to 18 percent.

   9.R.1.H.1.a

Informational Skills Review CONTINUED

5. According to the article, one way small towns are trying to attract young people is to —

A offer classes on international trade policies

B give away government land at little or no cost

C offer government jobs to new residents

D open new schools for local families

9.R.1.H.1.a

6. Travis is thinking about moving away from Lebanon, Kansas, because —

A farm life is too difficult

B his father wants him to move to the city

C his father is going to sell the farm

D he wants to see what other options are available

9.R.1.H.1.a

7. Which of the following is the *best* follow-up question to the article?

A Why do older people stay in the rural Great Plains?

B Have the efforts to attract new residents to the rural Great Plains been successful?

C How much did Travis's father get for the sale of his land?

D How many students attend college in the rural Great Plains?

9.R.1.H.1.b

Constructed Response

8. According to the article, what does Travis's father want from life? What does Travis want from life? Do Travis and his father share any of the same goals? Explain.

9.R.1.H.1.a

FOCUS ON MISSOURI COURSE LEVEL EXPECTATIONS

Vocabulary Skills Review

MO
9.R.1.E.1.c Develop vocabulary through text: using glossary, dictionary and thesaurus

Synonyms

Directions: Choose the *best* synonym for the italicized word in each sentence.

1. In "The Most Dangerous Game," Rainsford knows he is in trouble when he sees the *receding* yacht speed away.

A hurrying
B advancing
C retreating
D enduring

9.R.1.E

2. Rainsford gives Ivan a *disarming* smile, hoping to put the threatening servant at ease.

A reassuring
B nasty
C nervous
D broad

9.R.1.E

3. In "Disguises," Mrs. Chen is lost on a *desolate* avenue at night in the city.

A crowded
B blocked
C scattered
D deserted

9.R.1.E

4. In "Disguises," a stranger treats Mrs. Chen with *compassion.*

A anguish
B disgust
C pity
D anger

9.R.1.E

5. The narrator in "Liberty" is *inconsolable* because she must leave her dog behind.

A overjoyed
B surprised
C heartbroken
D excited

9.R.1.E

6. In "Harrison Bergeron," the agents working for the Handicapper General show *vigilance* as they scan the crowds for rule-breakers.

A carelessness
B watchfulness
C intelligence
D helplessness

9.R.1.E

7. After Harrison escapes, it is clear that the *hindrances* placed upon him cannot stop him from achieving his goals.

A duties
B blessings
C responsibilities
D restraints

9.R.1.E

Academic Vocabulary

Directions: Choose the *best* synonym for the italicized Academic Vocabulary word in the sentence.

8. I wrote many letters but could not seem to *convey* my message clearly.

A mail
B communicate
C dispute
D convince

9.R.1.E

Read On

FICTION

The Hobbit

In J.R.R. Tolkien's fantasy *The Hobbit,* Bilbo Baggins is just a little guy—a hobbit—who is minding his own business. Then one day the wizard Gandalf and a gang of thirteen dwarfs arrive at his door and carry him off. So begins Bilbo's great adventure, an adventure with some big challenges for a little guy: bee pastures, giant spiders, icy waterfalls, and the dreaded dragon Smaug.

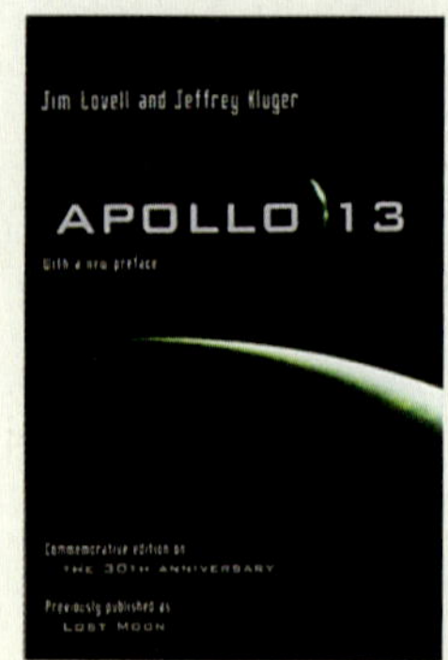

NONFICTION

Apollo 13

It was a routine journey—the fifth time U.S. astronauts had set out for the moon. But on April 13, 1970, Jim Lovell, Fred Haise, and Jack Swigert felt a strange explosion in their spacecraft. The lights dimmed, and the air got thinner. The three astronauts abandoned ship—for a tiny lunar module with room and supplies for only two. *Apollo 13,* co-written by Jim Lovell and Jeffrey Kluger, tells the story of the epic journey.

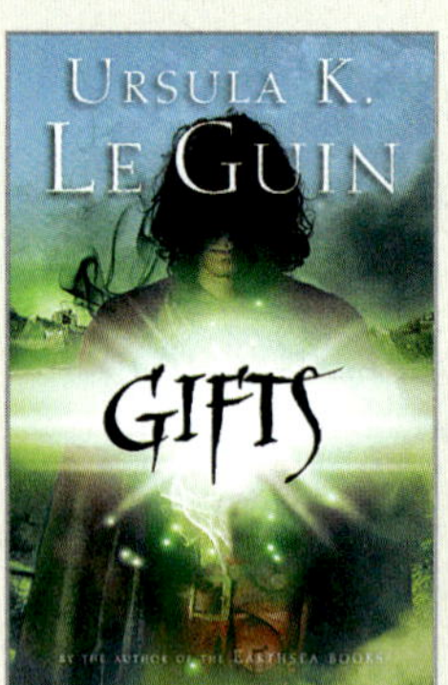

FICTION

Gifts

In Ursula K. Le Guin's thrilling novel *Gifts,* all is not what it seems. Scattered among poor, desolate farms, the clans of the Uplands possess wondrous gifts—the ability to summon animals, bring forth fire, move the land. They can twist a limb, change a mind, inflict a wasting illness. Two young people, friends since childhood, decide not to use their gifts. One, a girl, refuses to bring animals to their death in the hunt. The other, a boy, wears a blindfold lest his eyes and his anger kill.

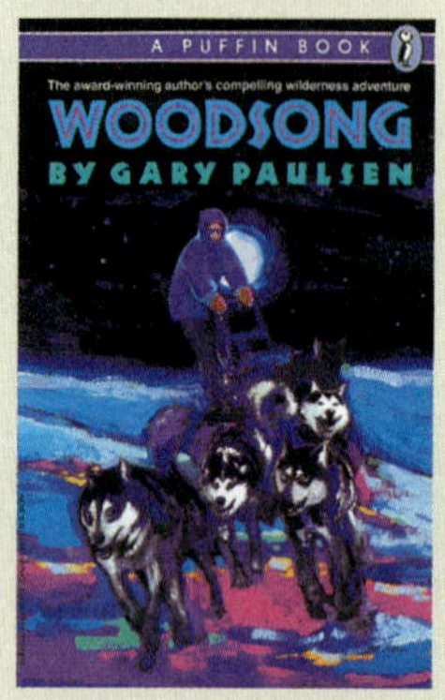

NONFICTION

Woodsong

Can you imagine enduring a temperature of –50°F—or lower—on a dog-sled race that covers more than a thousand miles? Gary Paulsen brings an adventure like this to life in his book *Woodsong.* In this account of his experiences during the Iditarod, a dog-sled race through Alaska, Paulsen whisks us along on his long and lonely journey. His only companions are a team of dogs, and they turn out to be the best friends he has ever had.

y Hyacinth Manning (1954–). Acrylic on canvas.

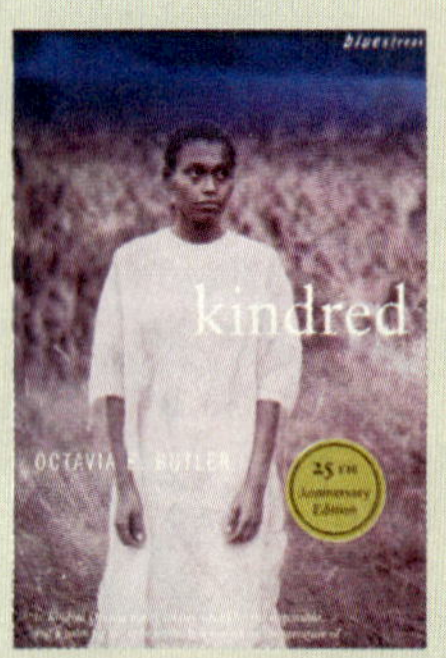

FICTION

Kindred

Dana, a young African American woman living in present-day California, is suddenly and mysteriously transported back through time to a Maryland slave plantation where she saves the life of a white boy named Rufus. Each time Rufus is in danger, she returns to save him, but she is also forced to endure the horrors of slavery—both emotional and physical. Part science fiction, part history and mystery (Who is Rufus, and why must Dana save him?), this novel is Octavia E. Butler's most famous work.

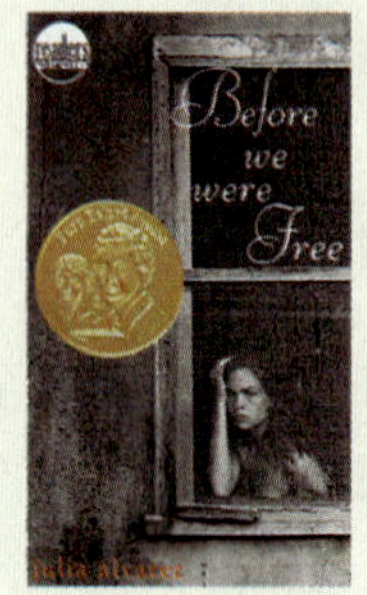

FICTION

Before We Were Free

Julia Alvarez and her family were forced to flee the Dominican Republic when she was ten, but in this novel of suspense and political intrigue, she imagines what life was like for friends who stayed. At first, the novel's young narrator, Anita de la Torre, is protected by her parents from the harsh realities of life in the Dominican Republic, but everything changes suddenly when her father and uncle are arrested for plotting to overthrow the dictator, Rafael Trujillo. Anita and her mother are forced to go into hiding, and Anita begins keeping a diary just like Anne Frank did. Will Anita suffer the same fate as Anne, or will she and her mother escape?

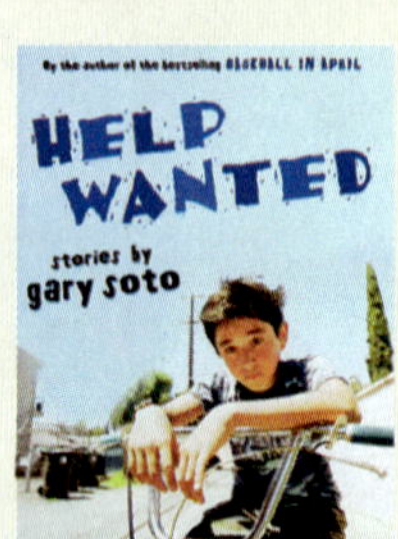

FICTION

Help Wanted

With good humor and heart Gary Soto takes readers into the lives of young people. In these stories you will meet Carolina, who writes to the columnist Miss Manners for help not just with etiquette but with bigger messes in her life; Ronnie and Joey, who feel so alienated from their world that they spend their days as "Teenage Chimps"; Javier, who knows the stories his friend Veronica tells him are lies, but can't find a way to prove it; Adan, who to his own shame and horror watches as his dad becomes a victim of the "Raiders nation"; and many other characters, each of them caught up in difficulties of coping with friends and adults.

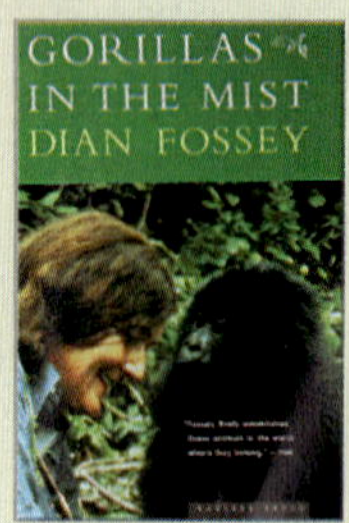

NONFICTION

Gorillas in the Mist

For years, Dian Fossey studied the behavior of endangered mountain gorillas in Africa. They learned to accept Fossey and even allowed her to sit with them and play with their young. She came to realize that gorillas are nothing like the ferocious King Kong image depicted in movies and fiction. *Gorillas in the Mist* is Fossey's account of how she devoted her life to protect these shy, gentle creatures from poachers who often dismember and mutilate gorillas. Tragically, Fossey would learn that although she had little to fear from gorillas, she had everything to fear from her fellow human beings.

Learn It Online

Explore other novels—and find tips for choosing, reading, and studying works—at:

go.hrw.com L9-121

COLLECTION 2

Character

INFORMATIONAL TEXT FOCUS

Synthesizing Sources: Main Idea, Audience, and Purpose

"I am the person I know best."

—Frida Kahlo

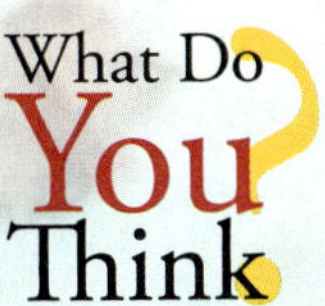

How do other people affect the way we think about ourselves?

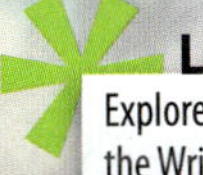

Learn It Online

Explore the lives of the authors in this collection at the Writers' Lives site online:

go.hrw.com L9-123 

Literary Focus

by **Carol Jago**

What Do You Need to Know About Characters?

What a character! When we call someone a character, we often mean that he or she is larger than life, a person who stands out from the crowd. Authors create fictional characters that do much the same, and we learn about these characters through their traits and interactions with others. Sometimes the characters we read about in stories seem so alive that we forget they aren't real people.

Characters

The people you meet in a story, poem, or play are called **characters.** The definitions and examples below will help you analyze fictional characters.

Protagonist Whom do you root for in a story? Very often you root for the main character, who is also referred to as a **protagonist.** Elena is the protagonist in "American History" by Judith Ortiz Cofer.

Antagonist *Boo! Hiss!* The story's **antagonist** conflicts with the protagonist, attempting to prevent the protagonist from attaining his or her goals. You can usually identify a story's antagonist by asking yourself, "Who's the bad guy here?"

Round Character Warm . . . funny . . . brainy . . . bossy. Like a real person, a **round character** has many different character traits, some admirable and others not so admirable.

> "Don't cry," I say. . . . "You're too old for that."
> "It's because," she hiccups, "I *am* too old. Old and funny."
>
> from "A Christmas Memory"
> by Truman Capote

Flat Character A **flat character** has only one or two traits, which can be described in one or two words, such as *shy* or *demanding.*

Static Character A **static character** does not change in the course of a story. A static character's main function is to provide a **foil,** or contrast, to the story's main character.

Dynamic Character A character who seems to live and breathe, who grows and changes during a story is called a **dynamic character.**

Character Motivation

Motivation *"Why did he or she do that?"* The reason a character behaves a certain way is called **motivation.** A character's motives may arise from feelings, experiences, or others' actions.

> I felt her fear of the lorry with its asthmatic motor (a fear and distrust, I later learned, she held of all machines) beating like a pulse in her rough palm.
>
> from "To Da-duh, in Memoriam"
> by Paule Marshall

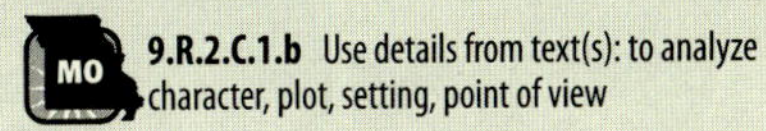

Characterization

Writers reveal a character's personality through **characterization,** which can be either direct or indirect.

Direct Characterization "The little girl who lived down the lane was nasty to her neighbors." That statement is an example of **direct characterization,** in which writers plainly tell us about the people who inhabit their fictional worlds.

Indirect Characterization Sometimes you have to judge for yourself what a character is like, rather than rely on a narrator's perceptions. **Indirect characterization** allows you to observe characters in action. Following are several ways writers indirectly reveal character:

- Reading the characters' **dialogue** is like listening in on a conversation. We learn about a story's characters not only by what they say but also by how they respond to one another.

> "Listen. Honey. Eugene doesn't want to study with you. He is a smart boy. Doesn't need help. You understand me. I am truly sorry if he told you you could come over. . . . It's nothing personal. You understand?"
>
> from "American History" by Judith Ortiz Cofer

- A few well-placed descriptions of a character's physical **appearance** can help bring him or her to life.

> She was a large woman with a large purse that had everything in it but a hammer and nails.
>
> from "Thank You, M'am" by Langston Hughes

- A writer can take us into a character's mind to reveal **private thoughts** and personality traits.

> I know he will have to go away, that he will take a plane to Mexico, all the uncles and aunts will be there, and they will have a black-and-white photo taken in front of the tomb . . .
>
> from "Papa Who Wakes Up Tired in the Dark" by Sandra Cisneros

- We also learn about characters by paying attention to **how other characters in the story feel about them.**
- One of the most important ways that we learn about characters is from their **actions,** from what we see them doing.

> She turned then to me. But oddly enough she did not touch me. Instead leaning close, she peered hard at me, and then quickly drew back.
>
> from "To Da-duh, in Memoriam" by Paule Marshall

Your Turn Analyze Character

Are you a good judge of character? Check your knowledge by analyzing two characters from a favorite movie, TV show, or story. First, describe the character types. Is one a protagonist? Are they round or flat characters? Then, write a brief character sketch of each, and share with a partner.

Learn It Online
Use PowerNotes as a visual aid to boost your learning at:
go.hrw.com
L9-125
Go

Analyzing Visuals

How Can You Analyze Character in Photographs?

Photographs capture a moment in time. Some photographs so vividly portray their subjects that it seems as if the person featured in the work could step out of the image and begin a conversation with the viewer. Just as writers use words to describe how a character looks, acts, thinks, and feels, photographers use color, light, shadow, angles, and resolution to portray their subjects.

Analyzing Character in Visuals

Use these guidelines as you analyze photographs and paintings that feature people and characters.

1. Identify the subject of the work. Who or what dominates the foreground of the image? Who or what appears in the background?
2. Find and analyze details of the subject's appearance, facial expression, and body language. Which details are most striking?
3. Look for clues that reveal what time and place the image portrays.
4. Notice what other people in the image are doing. What do their expressions reveal about their attitudes toward the subject matter?
5. Analyze the artist's use of color and light. What overall mood does the use of color and light create?

Look at the details of the photograph to help you answer the questions on page 127.

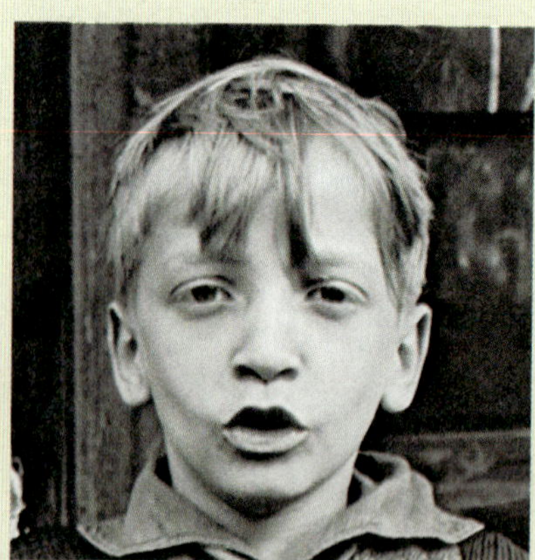

MO **9.R.2.C.1.b** Use details from text(s): to analyze character, plot, setting, point of view

1. Which boy appears to be the leader of the group? What do his facial expression and posture suggest about him?

2. Which boy in the photograph seems to be the most serious? Which is the shy one? How can you tell?

3. What is the setting of the photograph? Based on the setting, what can you infer about the boys?

4. Does this photograph seem posed, or does it seem candid, or informal? Explain why you think as you do.

New York (c. 1940). Photograph by Helen Levitt.
© Helen Levitt, courtesy Frankel Gallery, San Francisco.

Your Turn Write About Characters in Art

Flip ahead in this book, and choose a painting or photograph that features one or more people. Then, answer these questions:

1. What do you notice first about this photograph or painting? Who is the subject?
2. Does the person or group of people in the work seem real? Explain why or why not.
3. What can you learn about the person or people from their poses, expressions, and clothing? What do the subjects' eyes reveal about them?
4. Would you like to meet the person or people shown in the work? Why or why not?

Reading Focus

by **Kylene Beers**

What Skills Do You Need to Analyze Characters?

Reading would be easier if authors told us everything we needed to know. But authors want us to do some of the work! For instance, authors often give us clues about characters so that we can reach our own conclusions about them. These logical conclusions are called inferences. You read, "The boy frowned and reluctantly ate a tiny bite of spinach" and infer that this kid hates spinach. Making inferences about characters, and comparing and contrasting characters to yourself and other characters in the story, will help you create a complete picture in your mind.

Making Inferences About Characters

When you make **inferences** about characters, you make educated guesses about them based on their appearance, dialogue, actions, and thoughts and on the reactions of other characters. As you read, keep track of your inferences in a chart like this one:

Character Detail	Text	My Inference
Character's appearance	Wilma's hair curls wildly.	Wilma is a free spirit.
What character says	"You never know what can happen."	Wilma is open to possibilities.
Character's actions	She walks home slowly in the rain.	Wilma is distracted.
Character's thoughts	Wilma regrets her unkind words.	Wilma is good at heart.
Other characters' reactions	Wilma's classmates rush to her defense.	Most other students like Wilma.

Making Inferences About Motivation

When you think about it, almost everything we do has a purpose behind it. The underlying purpose or reason for our actions is called **motivation.**

In short stories, motivation is the driving force behind the characters—it explains their behaviors and reveals their personalities. Writers rarely make direct statements about a character's motivation. Instead, they plant clues and rely on the reader to make inferences from those clues.

As you read the stories in this collection, ask yourself the following questions:

- What do the characters want?
- What are they afraid of?
- What's at stake—what conflicts do the characters face?
- What happens as a result of these conflicts—how do the characters change?

Answering the questions above will help you understand why a story's characters act as they do.

9.R.1.G.1.d During reading, utilize strategies: to infer 9.R.1.I.1.b Compare, contrast, analyze and evaluate connections: text to self

Making Connections with Characters

You're reading a book or watching a movie, and you find it almost painful to witness the main character struggle with tragic events or wrestle with overwhelming emotions.

Experiencing sympathy for a character means you've found common ground—you've made a connection with him or her. It's not necessary to look like that character or to come from the same place as he or she does. You can even make connections with characters who aren't human.

To better understand any story character and the reasons for his or her actions, think about ways he or she is like or unlike you.

Use a chart like the one below to record details about the character. Then, describe the connection you made to that character. When your chart is finished, review what you've written, and draw a conclusion about whether you found the character interesting and believable.

Character Detail	My Connection
Cinderella has to do all the chores around the house with no help from others.	I have to take out the garbage once a week. It's unfair that she has to do all the chores.
Cinderella always obeys her stepmother.	Although she has to obey her stepmother, I wish Cinderella would show more independence.

Your Turn Apply Reading Skills

Remember that in stories, you learn about characters by making inferences based on how they look, what they say, how they act, and how others react to them. You also make comparisons between characters and yourself and other people you know. Fill out a chart like the one below with inferences based on the clues that are given.

Clue	Inference
Appearance: Johnny ran into class, his Dolphins sweatshirt worn-out and ripped.	Johnny likes sports and doesn't care too much about his appearance.
What others say: Johnny's teacher said, "Late again!"	
What the character says: "Sorry I'm late," said Johnny. "The game went into extra innings last night."	
Character's actions: Johnny took out his folder and handed his homework assignment to his teacher.	
Character's thoughts: Johnny hoped his teacher would give him an A for his work.	

Now go to the Skills in Action: Reading Model

Learn It Online

Find out how to analyze characters in longer works online at *NovelWise:*

go.hrw.com L9-129 Go

SKILLS IN ACTION

Reading Model

SHORT STORY

Build Background

During the Spanish Civil War (1936–1939), the Loyalists, who supported the government of Spain, fought against the Nationalists (Fascists), who were led by General Francisco Franco. "Old Man at the Bridge" is set during this conflict and shows the war's impact on the Spanish people.

Read with a Purpose Read "Old Man at the Bridge" to find out how two characters respond differently to a wartime evacuation.

Old Man at the Bridge

by **Ernest Hemingway**

An old man with steel rimmed spectacles and very dusty clothes sat by the side of the road. There was a pontoon bridge across the river and carts, trucks, and men, women and children were crossing it. The mule-drawn carts staggered up the steep bank from the bridge with soldiers helping push against the spokes of the wheels. The trucks ground up and away heading out of it all and the peasants plodded along in the ankle deep dust. But the old man sat there without moving. He was too tired to go any farther.

Literary Focus

Characterization These opening details—describing the man's appearance, actions, and state of mind—help reveal the story's main character.

It was my business to cross the bridge, explore the bridgehead beyond and find out to what point the enemy had advanced. I did this and returned over the bridge. There were not so many carts now and very few people on foot, but the old man was still there.

"Where do you come from?" I asked him.

"From San Carlos," he said, and smiled.

That was his native town and so it gave him pleasure to mention it and he smiled.

"I was taking care of animals," he explained.

"Oh," I said, not quite understanding.

"Yes," he said, "I stayed, you see, taking care of animals. I was the last one to leave the town of San Carlos."

Reading Focus

Making Inferences About Character You can infer from the old man's words that he may care more for the animals than for himself.

He did not look like a shepherd nor a herdsman and I looked at his black dusty clothes and his gray dusty face and his steel rimmed spectacles and said, "What animals were they?"

"Various animals," he said, and shook his head. "I had to leave them."

I was watching the bridge and the African looking country of the Ebro Delta[1] and wondering how long now it would be before we would see the enemy, and listening all the while for the first noises that would signal that ever mysterious event called contact, and the old man still sat there.

"What animals were they?" I asked.

"There were three animals altogether," he explained. "There were two goats and a cat and then there were four pairs of pigeons."

"And you had to leave them?" I asked.

"Yes. Because of the artillery.[2] The captain told me to go because of the artillery."

"And you have no family?" I asked, watching the far end of the bridge where a few last carts were hurrying down the slope of the bank.

"No," he said, "only the animals I stated. The cat, of course, will be all right. A cat can look out for itself, but I cannot think what will become of the others."

"What politics have you?" I asked.

"I am without politics," he said. "I am seventy-six years old. I have come twelve kilometers now and I think now I can go no further."

"This is not a good place to stop," I said. "If you can make it, there are trucks up the road where it forks for Tortosa."

"I will wait a while," he said, "and then I will go. Where do the trucks go?"

"Towards Barcelona," I told him.

"I know no one in that direction," he said, "but thank you very much. Thank you again very much."

He looked at me very blankly and tiredly, then said, having to share his worry with some one, "The cat will be all right, I am sure. There is no need to be unquiet about the cat. But the others. Now what do you think about the others?"

"Why they'll probably come through it all right."

"You think so?"

"Why not," I said, watching the far bank where now there were no carts.

"But what will they do under the artillery when I was told to leave because of the artillery?"

"Did you leave the dove cage unlocked?" I asked.

Reading Focus

Making Inferences About Motivation The narrator wants to protect the old man. His concern motivates him to urge the old man on.

Literary Focus

Character In this passage of dialogue, the old man's words reveal his inner conflict. The man knows he should leave, but he is worried about the animals.

---

1. **Ebro Delta:** land at the mouth of the Ebro, the largest river entirely in Spain.
2. **artillery** (awr TIHL uhr ee): mounted guns, such as cannons.

"Yes."

"Then they'll fly."

"Yes, certainly they'll fly. But the others. It's better not to think about the others," he said.

"If you are rested I would go," I urged. "Get up and try to walk now."

"Thank you," he said and got to his feet, swayed from side to side and then sat down backwards in the dust.

"I was taking care of animals," he said dully, but no longer to me. "I was only taking care of animals."

There was nothing to do about him. It was Easter Sunday and the Fascists were advancing toward the Ebro. It was a gray overcast day with a low ceiling so their planes were not up. That and the fact that cats know how to look after themselves was all the good luck that old man would ever have.

Reading Focus

Making Inferences About Character We can infer that although he would like to save the old man, the narrator feels a stronger need to return to his duties.

Read with a Purpose What is the narrator's main concern? What is the old man's main concern? To which character do you feel a stronger connection? Explain.

MEET THE WRITER

Ernest Hemingway

(1899–1961)

Pulitzer Prize WINNER

Grace Under Pressure

When the United States entered World War I, Ernest Hemingway wanted to enlist in the army but was rejected because of an old boxing injury. He then volunteered with the Red Cross and became an ambulance driver in Italy. After Hemingway had served for only six weeks, a bomb landed three feet away from him, blasting his leg with shrapnel. The experience influenced Hemingway for the rest of his life, and it surfaces in his stories. Hemingway defined *courage* as "grace under pressure" and admired people who could face their own suffering bravely.

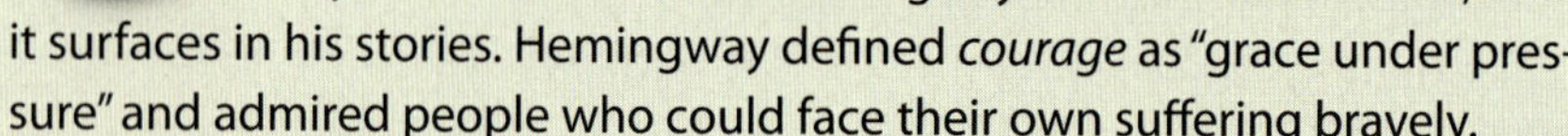

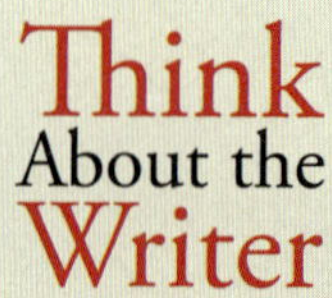

What do Hemingway's ideas about courage reveal about him?

SKILLS IN ACTION
Wrap Up

9.R.2.C.1.b Use details from text(s): to analyze character, plot, setting, point of view **9.R.1.G.1.d** During reading, utilize strategies: to infer **9.R.1.E.1.c** Develop vocabulary through text: using glossary, dictionary and thesaurus

Into Action: Character Analysis

In "Old Man at the Bridge," you are introduced to two characters who have different priorities during a wartime evacuation. Although this story is short, Hemingway depicts both characters fully. To analyze how Hemingway develops each character, fill in a chart like the one below.

Character Analysis Chart

Words	Actions	Appearance	Thoughts	What others say

Talk About . . .

Get together with a small group of classmates to discuss the following questions. Academic Vocabulary words, which are defined in the box to the right, are underlined below.

- How does the seemingly small incident described in the story reveal a significant truth about life?
- Which of the characters' observations rings most true to you? Select one from the story, and read the observation aloud to the group.
- Do you think the old man is a simple or a more complex character? Explain.

Write About . . .

Write a brief analysis of the old man in the story. Give your opinion of him, using details and quotes from the story to support your response. Challenge yourself to use Academic Vocabulary terms, such as those listed to the right, in your analysis.

Writing Focus

Think as a Reader/Writer

Find It in Your Reading Hemingway is famed for his simple, spare use of language. As you read the selections in Collection 2, you will analyze the writing styles of other authors and practice using their techniques in your own writing.

Academic Vocabulary for Collection 2

Talking and Writing About Short Stories

Academic Vocabulary is the language you use to write and talk about literature. Use the words to discuss the short stories you read in this collection. They are underlined throughout the collection.

observation (ahb zuhr VAY shuhn) *n.:* statement based on what one sees. *The old man's observation about his animals reveals his true concerns.*

incident (IHN suh duhnt) *n.:* something that took place; event. *The incident on the bridge was minor in one way but major in another.*

complex (KAHM plehks) *adj.:* having more than one part or aspect; complicated. *Although the old man's words are simple, the emotions behind the words are complex.*

significant (sihg NIHF uh kuhnt) *adj.:* important. *The old man says very little, but what he has to say is significant.*

Your Turn

Pair up with a partner, and use the words from the list in a discussion of "Old Man at the Bridge."

SHORT STORY

Preparing to Read

Thank You, M'am

by **Langston Hughes**

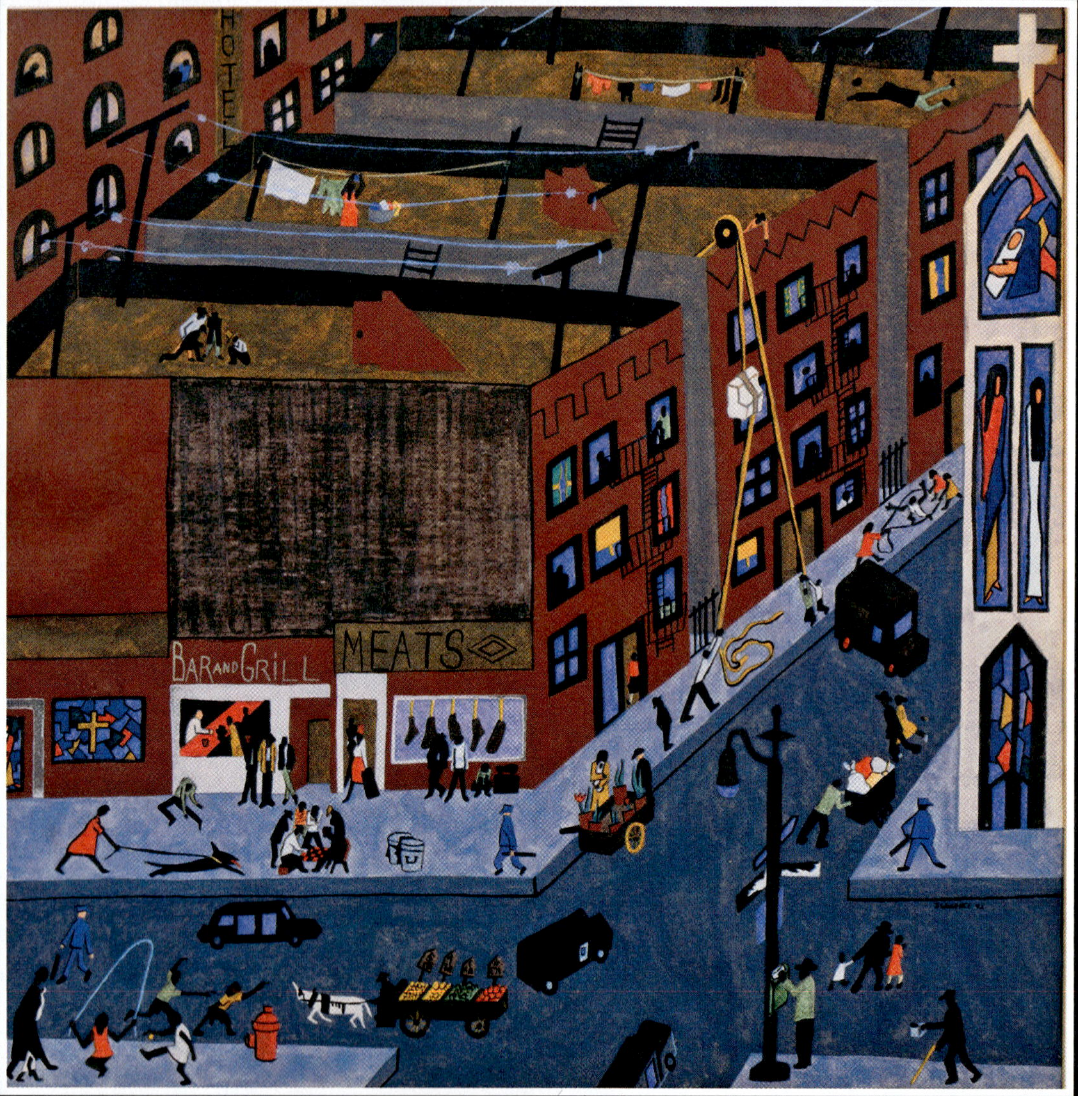

Harlem Street Scene (1942) by Jacob Lawrence (1917–2000). Gouache on paper (21"x 20 ¾").

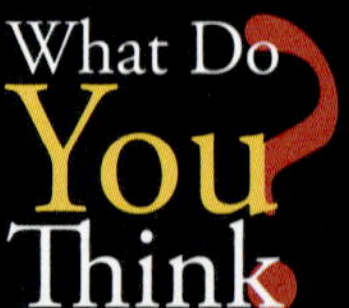

What Do You Think? What life lessons change the way you think about yourself?

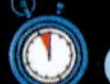

QuickTalk

Think about this common expression: "When the going gets tough, the tough get going." Discuss with a partner what you think this saying means.

Reader/Writer Notebook

Use your **RWN** to complete the activities for this selection.

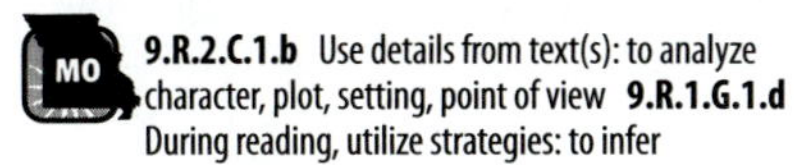

9.R.2.C.1.b Use details from text(s): to analyze character, plot, setting, point of view **9.R.1.G.1.d** During reading, utilize strategies: to infer

Literary Focus

Character and Dialogue Writers often develop characters by telling us how they look and act. Sometimes, writers let characters reveal themselves through **dialogue,** or conversation. As a reader, you listen in on those conversations and form opinions about the characters. Notice what the two characters in "Thank You, M'am" say to each other—and what they don't say.

Reading Focus

Making Inferences Writers often don't tell you directly what their characters are like. Instead, writers describe what characters say and do, allowing you to make your own inferences about them. When you make an inference, you use your observations and prior experience to make an educated guess.

Into Action Identify three or four places in the text where a character's words or actions, plus your own ideas, help you to make an inference about that character. Complete a chart like this one:

Text Clue		My Ideas		My Inference
Firmly gripped by his shirt front, the boy said, "Yes'm."	+	This is a respectful way to talk. Roger is not rude.	=	

Writing Focus

Think as a Reader/Writer

Find It in Your Reading Notice how Hughes uses dialogue to bring characters to life. In your *Reader/Writer Notebook,* collect examples of dialogue that strongly reflect each character.

TechFocus As you read this story, think about how the dialogue might sound if you were to speak the characters' lines. Would the characters sound the same ten years from now? Why or why not?

Vocabulary

permit (puhr MIHT) *v.:* allow. *The old woman would not permit the boy to commit a crime.*

frail (frayl) *adj.:* thin and weak; delicate. *The underfed boy looked frail and scared.*

barren (BAR uhn) *adj.:* empty; deserted. *By midnight everyone had gone home, and the streets were barren.*

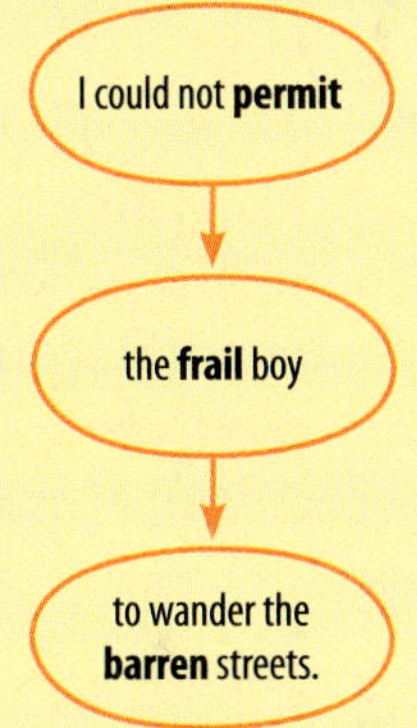
I could not **permit**
the **frail** boy
to wander the **barren** streets.

Language Coach

Multiple-Meaning Words Some words function as verbs (describing an action) as well as nouns (naming a person, place, thing, or idea). Which word from the Vocabulary list above is also a noun that means "license" or "document that gives permission"? Use a dictionary if you need help.

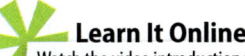

Learn It Online
Watch the video introduction to familiarize yourself with this story:

go.hrw.com L9-135 Go

MEET THE WRITER

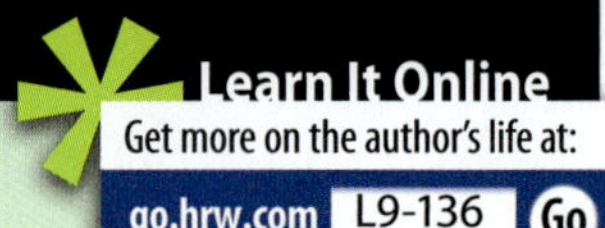
Learn It Online
Get more on the author's life at:
go.hrw.com L9-136 Go

Langston Hughes

(1902–1967)

A Lonely Child

Langston Hughes was a lonely child who moved often and felt distant from his parents, who eventually divorced. His father tried to discourage his son's "impractical" dream of being a writer by sending him to study engineering at Columbia University in New York City. Unhappy at college, Hughes left school and joined a ship's crew, sailing to Europe and Africa. He later graduated from Lincoln University in Pennsylvania and held a variety of jobs to support his writing: He was a cook, sailor, launderer, doorman, and busboy.

A Place in the City

Hughes is chiefly associated with Harlem, in New York City. In the 1920s, Hughes was a key figure in the movement of African American art and writing known as the Harlem Renaissance. His most creative work was done at his typewriter, near a third-floor rear-apartment window overlooking a Harlem backyard. There he wrote both stories and poetry, often using dialect and slang to capture the everyday voices of ordinary people.

"I have discovered in life that there are ways of getting almost anywhere you want to go, if you really want to go."

Think About the Writer How might the voices of ordinary people have inspired Hughes?

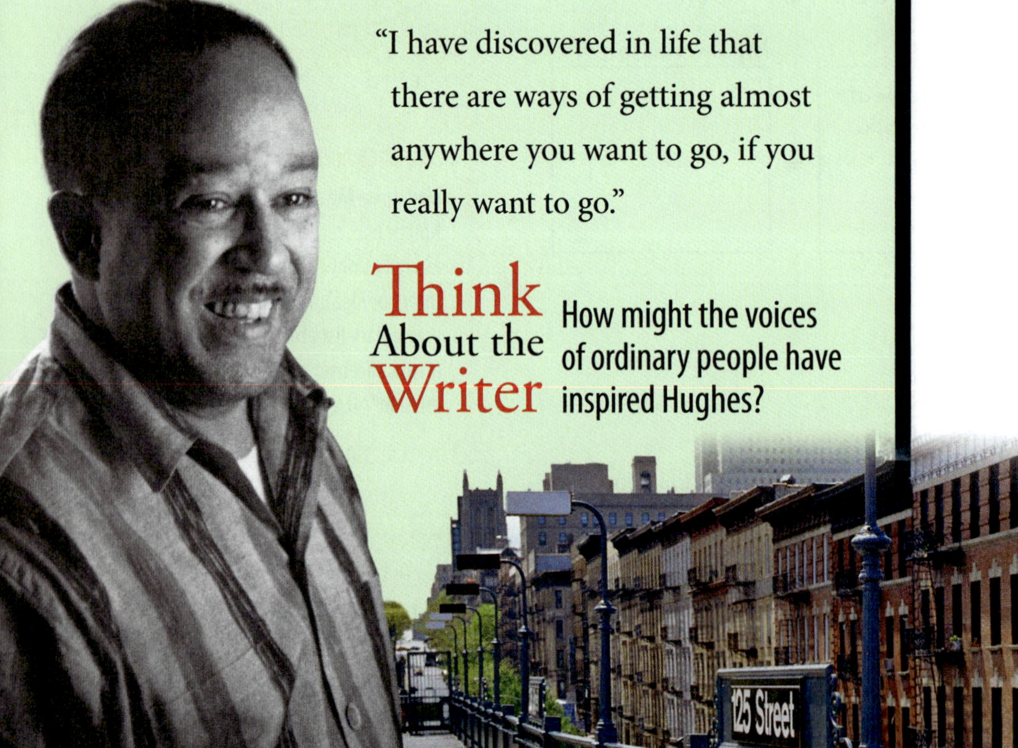
125 Street

Build Background

Harlem is a neighborhood in New York City in which most of the residents are African American. When Hughes lived there, he saw his neighbors struggling against poverty, crime, and overcrowding. More than 215,000 people lived within a square mile. These packed conditions led to some conflicts but also to the richly varied urban culture that Hughes documented in his writing.

Preview the Selection

One night, a teenager named **Roger** tries to steal the purse of a woman who is walking home alone. His attempt to steal leads him down a much different path than he expected.

Read with a Purpose Read this story to find out what happens when a boy unexpectedly meets his match.

Thank You, M'am

by **Langston Hughes**

Analyzing Visuals **Viewing and Interpreting**
Compare the two paintings. Which details do you find most significant? What do these details suggest about each character?

(right) *Woman in Calico* (1944) by William H. Johnson (1901–1970). Oil on paperback. (left) *Jim* (1930) by William H. Johnson (1901–1970). Oil on canvas (21 5/8" x 18 ¼").

She was a large woman with a large purse that had everything in it but a hammer and nails. It had a long strap, and she carried it slung across her shoulder. It was about eleven o'clock at night, dark, and she was walking alone, when a boy ran up behind her and tried to snatch her purse. The strap broke with the sudden single tug the boy gave it from behind. But the boy's weight and the weight of the purse combined caused him to lose his balance. Instead of taking off full blast as he had hoped, the boy fell on his back on the sidewalk and his legs flew up. The large woman simply turned around and kicked him right square in his blue-jeaned sitter. Then she reached down, picked the boy up by his shirt front, and shook him until his teeth rattled.

After that the woman said, "Pick up my pocketbook, boy, and give it here."

She still held him tightly. But she bent down enough to permit him to stoop and pick up her purse. Then she said, "Now ain't you ashamed of yourself?"

Firmly gripped by his shirt front, the boy said, "Yes'm."

The woman said, "What did you want to do it for?"

The boy said, "I didn't aim to."

She said, "You a lie!"

By that time two or three people passed, stopped, turned to look, and some stood watching.

"If I turn you loose, will you run?" asked the woman.

"Yes'm," said the boy. **A**

"Then I won't turn you loose," said the woman. She did not release him.

"Lady, I'm sorry," whispered the boy.

"Um-hum! Your face is dirty. I got a great mind to wash your face for you. Ain't you got nobody home to tell you to wash your face?"

"No'm," said the boy.

"Then it will get washed this evening," said the large woman starting up the street, dragging the frightened boy behind her.

He looked as if he were fourteen or fifteen, frail and willow-wild, in tennis shoes and blue jeans.

The woman said, "You ought to be my son. I would teach you right from wrong. Least I can do right now is to wash your face. Are you hungry?"

"No'm," said the being-dragged boy. "I just want you to turn me loose."

"Was I bothering *you* when I turned that corner?" asked the woman.

"No'm."

"But you put yourself in contact with *me*," said the woman. "If you think that that contact is not going to last awhile, you got another thought coming. When I get through with you, sir, you are going to remember Mrs. Luella Bates Washington Jones." **B**

Sweat popped out on the boy's face and he began to struggle. Mrs. Jones stopped, jerked him around in front of her, put a half nelson about his neck, and continued to drag him up the street. When she got to her door, she dragged the boy inside, down a hall, and into a large kitchenette-furnished room at the rear of the house. She switched on the light and left the door open. The boy could hear other roomers laughing and talking in the large house. Some of their doors were open, too, so he knew he and the woman were not alone. The woman still had him by the neck in the middle of her room.

She said, "What is your name?"

"Roger," answered the boy.

"Then, Roger, you go to that sink and wash your face," said the woman, whereupon she turned him loose—at last. Roger looked at the door—looked at the woman—looked at the door—*and went to the sink.*

"Let the water run until it gets warm," she said. "Here's a clean towel."

"You gonna take me to jail?" asked the boy, bending over the sink.

"Not with that face, I would not take you

A **Reading Focus** **Making Inferences** What does the boy say when the woman asks him if he'll run? What does his response tell you about his personality?

B **Literary Focus** **Character and Dialogue** What do you learn about Mrs. Jones from the way she speaks to the boy?

Vocabulary **permit** (puhr MIHT) *v.:* allow.
frail (frayl) *adj.:* thin and weak; delicate.

SOCIAL STUDIES LINK

The Great Migration

Beginning in 1915, African Americans seeking to escape the Jim Crow laws that enforced racial segregation in the rural South began to migrate to other U.S. cities. In addition, during World Wars I and II, an expanded labor force was needed to create materials for the wars. The need for workers created greater job opportunities for African Americans in cities such as New York, Detroit, Chicago, and Cleveland. From 1915 to 1970, it is estimated that six million black Americans migrated to urban areas. The Great Migration was one of the largest population shifts in U.S. history.

Yet urban life introduced new obstacles. African Americans continued to face racism and were segregated into ghettos. In New York City, many black families lived in Harlem where the creative movement known as the Harlem Renaissance was born.

Ask Yourself

Judging from this photograph, what did the city have to offer African Americans who lived there?

nowhere," said the woman. "Here I am trying to get home to cook me a bite to eat, and you snatch my pocketbook! Maybe you ain't been to your supper either, late as it be. Have you?"

"There's nobody home at my house," said the boy.

"Then we'll eat," said the woman. "I believe you're hungry—or been hungry—to try to snatch my pocketbook."

"I want a pair of blue suede shoes," said the boy.

"Well, you didn't have to snatch *my* pocketbook to get some suede shoes," said Mrs. Luella Bates Washington Jones. "You could've asked me."

"M'am?"

The water dripping from his face, the boy looked at her. There was a long pause. A very long pause. After he had dried his face and not knowing what else to do, dried it again, the boy turned around, wondering what next. The door was open. He could make a dash for it down the hall. He could run, run, run, *run*!

The woman was sitting on the daybed. After a while she said, "I were young once and I wanted things I could not get."

There was another long pause. The boy's mouth opened. Then he frowned, not knowing he frowned.

The woman said, "Um-hum! You thought I was going to say *but,* didn't you? You thought I was going to say, *but I didn't snatch people's pocketbooks*. Well, I wasn't going to say that." Pause. Silence. "I have done things, too, which I would not tell you, son—neither tell God, if He didn't already know. Everybody's got something in common. So you set down while I fix us something to eat. You might run that comb through your hair so you will look presentable." **C**

In another corner of the room behind a screen was a gas plate and an icebox. Mrs. Jones got up and went behind the screen. The woman did not watch the boy to see if he was going to run now, nor did she watch her purse, which she left behind her on the daybed. But the boy took care to sit on the far side of the room, away from the purse, where he thought she could easily see him out of the corner of her eye if she wanted to. He did not trust the woman *not* to trust him. And he did not want to be mistrusted now.

"Do you need somebody to go the store," asked the boy, "maybe to get some milk or something?" **D**

"Don't believe I do," said the woman, "unless you just want sweet milk yourself. I was going to make cocoa out of this canned milk I got here."

"That will be fine," said the boy.

She heated some lima beans and ham she had in the icebox, made the cocoa, and set the table. The woman did not ask the boy anything about where he lived, or his folks, or anything else that would embarrass him. Instead, as they ate, she told him about her job in a hotel beauty shop that stayed open late, what the work was like, and how all kinds of women came in and out, blondes, redheads, and Spanish. Then she cut him a half of her ten-cent cake.

"Eat some more, son," she said.

When they were finished eating, she got up and said, "Now here, take this ten dollars and buy yourself some blue suede shoes. And next time, do not make the mistake of latching onto *my* pocketbook *nor nobody else's*—because shoes got by devilish ways will burn your feet. I got to get my rest now. But from here on in, son, I hope you will behave yourself."

She led him down the hall to the front door and opened it. "Good night! Behave yourself, boy!" she said, looking out into the street as he went down the steps.

The boy wanted to say something other than "Thank you, m'am" to Mrs. Luella Bates Washington Jones, but although his lips moved, he couldn't even say that as he turned at the foot of the barren stoop and looked up at the large woman in the door. Then she shut the door. **E**

C **Literary Focus** **Character and Dialogue** What does the dialogue reveal about Mrs. Jones's character?

D **Reading Focus** **Making Inferences** Why does Roger offer to go to the store?

E **Reading Focus** **Making Inferences** Why do you think Mrs. Jones gives Roger ten dollars?

Vocabulary **barren** (BAR uhn) *adj.:* empty; deserted.

Applying Your Skills

9.R.2.C.1.b Use details from text(s): to analyze character, plot, setting, point of view 9.R.1.G.1.d During reading, utilize strategies: to infer 9.W.2.D.1.b Compose text using: writing techniques, such as imagery, humor, voice, and figurative language

Thank You, M'am

Respond and Think Critically

Reading Focus

Quick Check

1. Why does Roger want money?
2. What does Mrs. Jones give Roger? How does Roger feel when he leaves Mrs. Jones's house?

Read with a Purpose

3. In what way is Mrs. Jones tougher than Roger expects?

Reading Skills: Making Inferences

4. Complete the chart you started on page 135. Now add a row to your chart and make a general inference about Roger and Mrs. Jones.

Text Clue		My Ideas		My Inference
Firmly gripped by his shirt front, the boy said, "Yes'm."	+	This is a respectful way to talk. Roger is not rude.	=	Although his actions are aggressive, Roger seems polite.

My inference about Roger and Mrs. Jones:

Literary Focus

Literary Analysis

5. **Interpret** What does Mrs. Jones mean by "shoes got by devilish ways will burn your feet"?
6. **Infer** At the end of the story, what do you think Roger wants to say, besides "Thank you, m'am"?
7. **Speculate** Will Roger change as a result of his encounter with Mrs. Jones? Find clues in the story that support your opinion.
8. **Evaluate** Based on your own experience, do you believe that these events could happen as Hughes describes them? Why or why not?

Literary Skills: Character and Dialogue

9. **Analyze** Mrs. Jones's personality comes through in her unique dialogue. Choose two statements of hers from the story, and explain how they reflect her character.
10. **Analyze** What characters *don't* say can be as important as what they *do* say. What do you learn about Roger and Mrs. Jones from their silences? Find points in the story when Mrs. Jones and Roger are silent, and explain why you think they choose not to speak.

Literary Skills Review: Setting

11. **Connect** How does the **setting** of Mrs. Jones's home—her furnished room, the gas plate, the ten-cent cake, the noisy building—contribute to your sense of who she is?

Writing Focus

Think as a Reader/Writer

Use It in Your Writing Hughes uses dialogue to describe most of the story's events and to develop his characters. Write a scene in which two characters meet for the first time. Like Hughes, use dialogue to reveal something about each character.

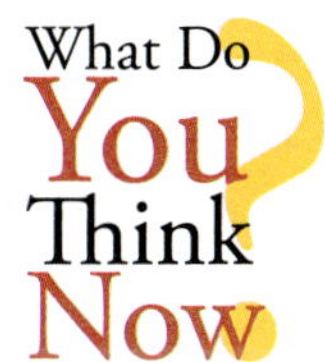

What lesson does Mrs. Jones teach Roger? What do you think he is really thanking her for?

Applying Your Skills

Thank You, M'am

Vocabulary Development

Vocabulary Check

Answer the questions to show your knowledge of the Vocabulary words.

1. Why might you avoid a **barren** street at night?
2. Would you send a **frail** person on a dangerous mission? Why or why not?
3. Does it make sense to **permit** a child to ride a bike without a helmet? Explain.

Vocabulary Skills: Synonyms

Although a **synonym** is a word that has the same or almost the same meaning as another word, synonyms are not always interchangeable. Synonyms often have subtle but distinct shades of difference in meaning. For example, at the end of the story, Roger "turned at the foot of the barren stoop." This chart shows how a student evaluated the word *barren* and considered two synonyms that might substitute for it.

barren	
Definition:	empty; without signs of life
Synonyms:	bare; sterile
Substitutions:	He turned at the [bare/sterile] stoop.
Response to substitutions:	*Bare* could work because it can refer to a lack of objects. *Sterile* doesn't work because it suggests cleanliness, not emptiness. *Barren* is best; it reminds me of something empty and lifeless.

Your Turn

Here are two other Vocabulary words that are used in the story: *frail* and *permit*. Find the sentences in which the words are used. Then, make a chart like the one above for each word. Could the words' synonyms work just as well in each sentence? Why or why not?

Language Coach

Multiple-Meaning Words Some words from the story, listed below, have multiple meanings. Examine each word's context, or surrounding words and phrases, where Hughes has used the word in his story. Then, look up additional meanings of each word. Create a word map in your *Reader/Writer Notebook* for each word listed, using the format shown below.

purse sink screen fine

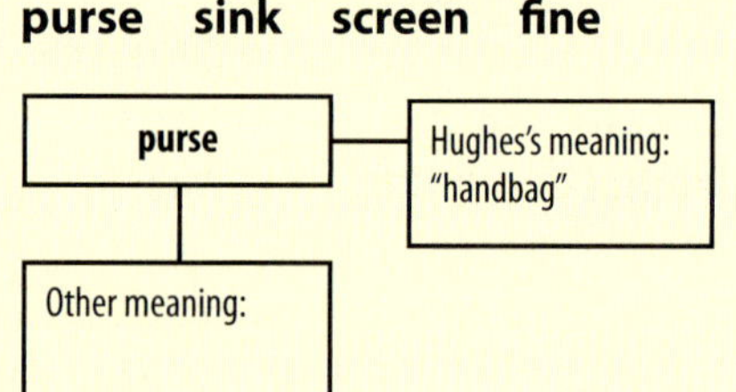

Academic Vocabulary

Write About . . .

1. Identify one observation Mrs. Jones makes about Roger in this story.
2. Describe an incident from the story in which Mrs. Jones displays trust in Roger.

Learn It Online
Explore synonyms with *WordSharp:*
go.hrw.com
L9-142
Go

MO **9.W.3.A.1.a** Compose a variety of texts: using narrative, descriptive, expository, and/or persuasive features **9.W.2.D.1.a** Compose text using: precise and vivid language **9.W.3.A.1.e** Compose a variety of texts: including reflective writing **9.W.2.E.1.c** In written text apply: standard usage *Also covered* **9.R.1.G.1.a; 9.R.1.E.1.c; 9.R.1.E.1.b**

Grammar Link

Modifiers: Precise Meanings

Modifiers make your writing more specific by limiting the meaning of another word or word group. There are two kinds of modifiers: adjectives and adverbs.

Adjectives (and adjective phrases) answer the questions *what kind? which one? how many?* or *how much?* Notice how adjectives help you visualize those *blue suede* shoes that Roger wants.

Adverbs (and adverb phrases) answer the questions *how? where? when? how often? in what way?* or *to what extent?* When Roger grabs Mrs. Jones's purse, the strap breaks *"with the sudden single tug"* he gives it.

The modifiers in these sentences from Hughes's story are single words, compound words (words formed from two separate words), and phrases (groups of related words that do not contain both a verb and its subject).

1. "The large woman simply turned around and kicked him right square in his blue-jeaned sitter."
2. "He looked as if he were fourteen or fifteen, frail and willow-wild, in tennis shoes and blue jeans."

Your Turn

Writing Applications For each numbered sentence above, tell whether the underlined modifiers are acting as adjectives or adverbs. Then, rewrite each sentence two times, replacing the modifiers with words and phrases of your own. Each time, give Mrs. Jones or Roger a different appearance. (For example, you might put Roger in hiking boots and a plaid shirt.)

CHOICES

As you respond to the Choices, use these **Academic Vocabulary** words as appropriate: observation, incident, complex, significant.

REVIEW

Describe a Character

Timed Writing How well has Langston Hughes developed the characters of Roger and Mrs. Jones? Include details from the story to support your opinion and to convey your ideas.

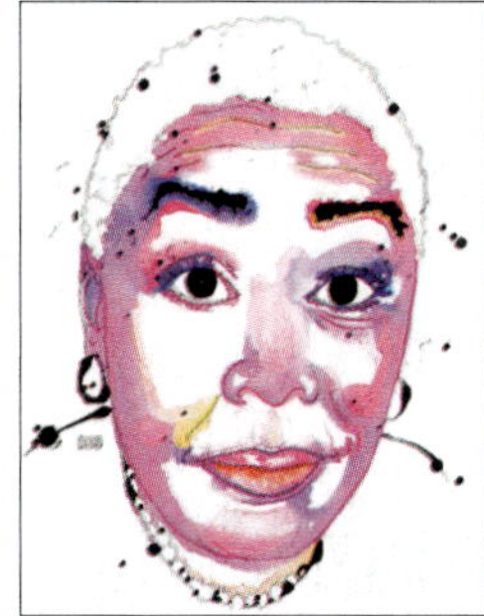

CONNECT

Write a Letter

TechFocus What will Roger be like in ten years? Compose a letter from Roger to Mrs. Jones, using language that reflects Roger's personality and stating the purpose of his communication after all these years. You could make this a video letter and capture how you think Roger will look and sound ten years after the incident.

EXTEND

Discover a Poem

You can create a poem from lines of prose. Find the paragraph from "Thank You, M'am" beginning "In another corner of the room," and reformat it so that it looks like a poem. Break the sentences into lines that seem right to you, change any words you wish, and decide where your poem should end.

Learn It Online

There's more to this story than meets the eye. Expand your view at:

SHORT STORY

Preparing to Read

To Da-duh, in Memoriam

by **Paule Marshall**

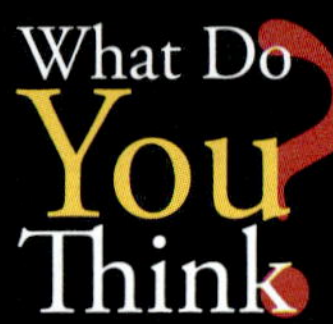

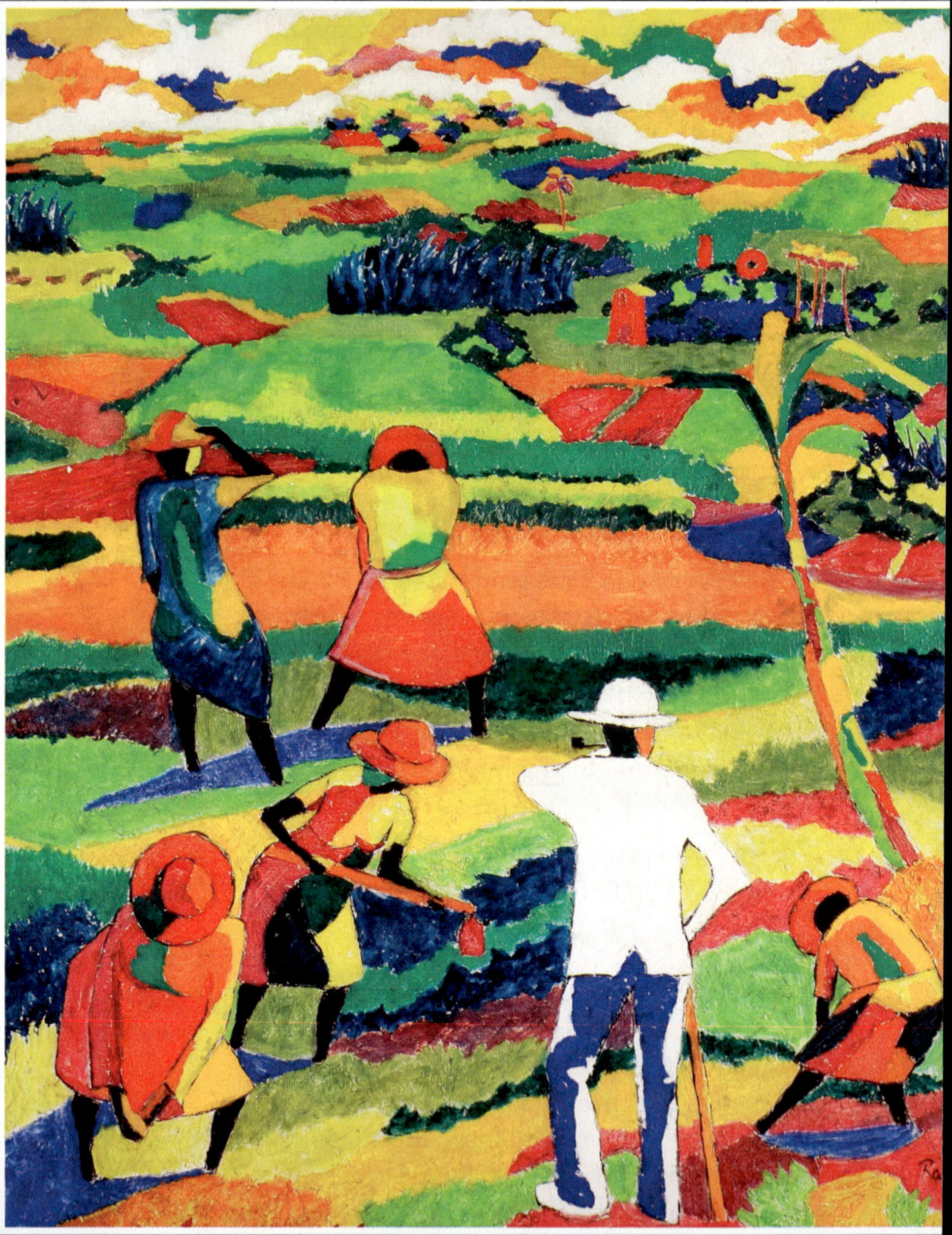

How can relationships with others change us?

QuickWrite

Every day, you probably encounter people who come from worlds very different from your own—a different culture, country, or even just a different type of family. How might knowing people who are different from you affect you or change your views? Write down your thoughts.

Variegation (1985) by Ras Ishi Butcher. Oil on canvas. Barbados Gallery of Arts (BGA) Collection.

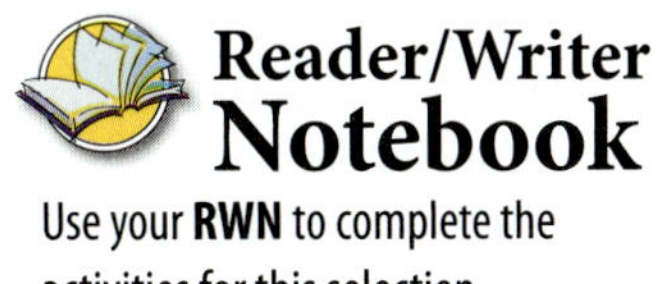

Use your **RWN** to complete the activities for this selection.

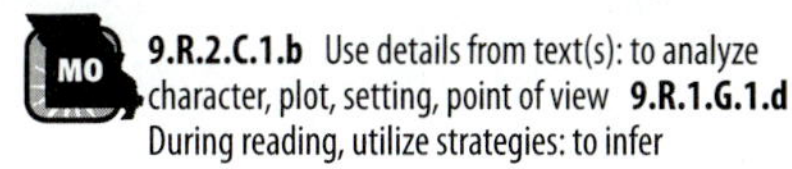

Literary Focus

Character Interactions Love, hate, pride, or opposing values can pit one character against another. The resulting **interactions** can lead to changes in the way characters view themselves and the world. In this story the conflict that takes place between the narrator and her grandmother has dramatic consequences for both characters.

Literary Perspectives Apply the literary perspective described on page 147 as you read this story.

Reading Focus

Making Inferences About Motivation When you think about the reasons for characters' actions, you are trying to determine the characters' **motivation.** Often writers don't make direct statements about their characters. Instead, they expect you to **make inferences,** or educated guesses, based on clues in the text.

Into Action As you read, record a character's actions in a chart like this one. Then, write down your inferences about the character's motivation—the reason behind his or her behavior.

pg #	Character's Actions	My Inferences
p. 149	Da-duh takes the narrator's hand.	Da-duh fears but admires the narrator's strength; feels a bond with narrator

Writing Focus

Think as a Reader/Writer

Find It in Your Reading Paule Marshall creates a vivid portrait of Da-duh by using figurative language, such as **metaphors** (comparisons between two unlike things) and **similes** (comparisons between two unlike things, using a word such as *like* or *as*). As you read, take note of these comparisons in your *Reader/Writer Notebook.*

Vocabulary

unrelenting (uhn rih LEHN tihng) *adj.:* not letting up or weakening. *Da-duh is unrelenting in her questioning of the narrator.*

apprehensive (ap rih HEHN sihv) *adj.:* feeling alarm; afraid, anxious, or worried. *I felt apprehensive being in an unfamiliar country.*

perennial (puh REHN ee uhl) *adj.:* year-round; continual. *Da-duh's curiosity gives her an air of perennial youth.*

menacing (MEHN ihs ihng) *v.* used as *adj.:* threatening. *The narrator was frightened by the menacing look on her grandmother's face.*

Language Coach

Word Roots *Annus* is the Latin word for "year." *Annual* means "happening every year," and *biennial* means "happening every two years." Which word on the Vocabulary list above also comes from the Latin *annus*?

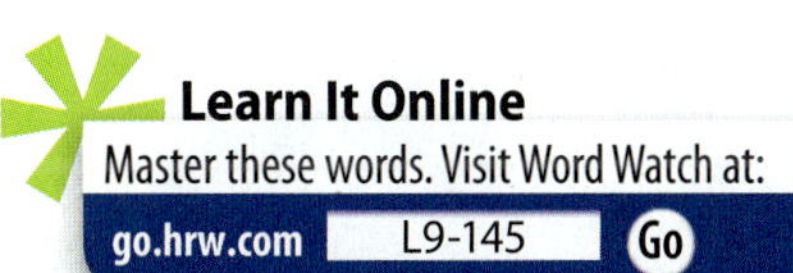

Learn It Online
Master these words. Visit Word Watch at:
go.hrw.com
L9-145
Go

MEET THE WRITER

Paule Marshall

(1929–)

Writing from Life

Paule Marshall calls this story the "most autobiographical" of her works. The Latin words *in memoriam* in the title mean "in memory of." Marshall wrote the story in memory of her grandmother, who was called Da-duh by the family. While spending a year in Barbados with her grandmother, Marshall sensed a "subtle kind of power struggle" between her and her grandmother. Marshall notes, "It was as if we both knew, at a level beyond words, that I had come into the world not only to love her and to continue her line but to take her very life in order that I might live."

West Indian Roots

The daughter of parents who emigrated from the Caribbean island of Barbados, Marshall was born in Brooklyn, New York. She grew up in a community of West Indian immigrants, where people struggled to preserve their Caribbean identity while trying to overcome racism. An award-winning author, Marshall focuses on the lives of immigrants and women, colonialism, racism, and African, Caribbean, and African American cultures in her work.

"Sometimes a person has to go back, really back—to have a sense, an understanding of all that's gone to make them—before they can go forward."

Think About the Writer How does the subject matter of Marshall's work reflect her life experiences?

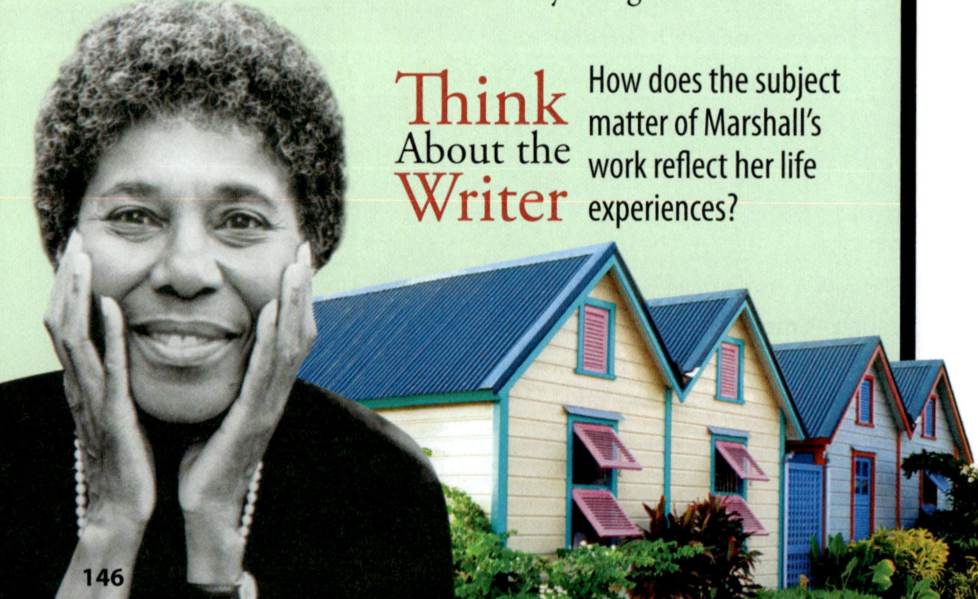

Build Background

This story is set in Barbados, a tropical island in the Caribbean Sea. Barbados was a British colony for almost 340 years before gaining its independence in 1966. The rich culture of the island is the product of English, African, and Caribbean influences. Most of today's Barbadians are descendants of Africans who were enslaved on British-owned sugar plantations.

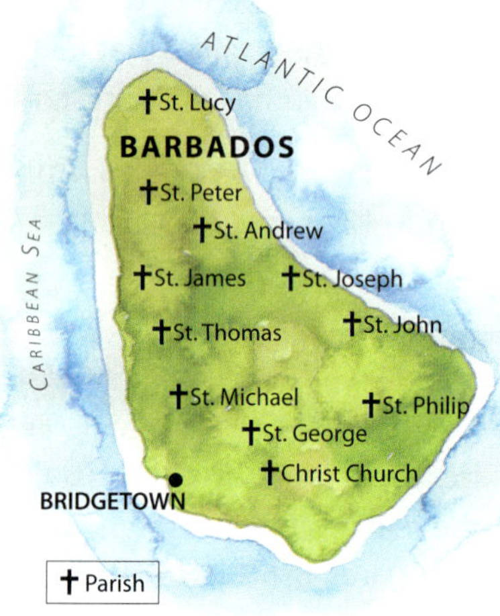

Preview the Selection

The **narrator** of this story is also one of its main characters. An adult, she is writing about a time when she traveled to Barbados and met a fierce rival—**Da-duh,** her grandmother and the story's other main character.

Read with a Purpose Read this story to discover how a young girl encounters an unfamiliar world when she pays a visit to her grandmother.

To Da-duh, in Memoriam

by **Paule Marshall**

"... Oh Nana! all of you is not involved in this evil business Death, Nor all of us in life."

—*from "At My Grandmother's Grave" by Lebert Bethune*

I did not see her at first I remember. For not only was it dark inside the crowded disembarkation shed[1] in spite of the daylight flooding in from outside, but standing there waiting for her with my mother and sister I was still somewhat blinded from the sheen of tropical sunlight on the water of the bay which we had just crossed in the landing boat, leaving behind us the ship that had brought us from New York lying in the offing.[2] Besides, being only nine years of age at the time and knowing nothing of islands I was busy attending to the alien sights and sounds of Barbados, the unfamiliar smells.

I did not see her, but I was alerted to her approach by my mother's hand which suddenly tightened around mine, and looking up I traced her gaze through the gloom in the shed until I finally made out the small, purposeful, painfully erect figure of the old woman headed our way.

Her face was drowned in the shadow of an ugly rolled-brim brown felt hat, but the details of her slight body and of the struggle taking place within it were clear enough—an intense, unrelenting struggle between her back which was beginning to bend ever so slightly under the weight of her eighty-odd years and the rest of her which sought to deny those years

1. **disembarkation shed:** place where passengers wait or assemble after leaving a ship or plane.
2. **in the offing:** at some distance but in sight.

Vocabulary **unrelenting** (uhn rih LEHN tihng) *adj.:* not letting up or weakening.

Literary Perspectives

Analyzing Biographical Context The events and circumstances in writers' lives are often reflected in their writing. Knowing a writer's background can help you better understand the literature he or she writes. Looking at a work through the lens of the writer's own experiences can help you put into context the story's themes and historical references as well as the social interactions of the characters. As you read, use the notes and questions at the bottom of the pages as a guide in using this perspective.

Border detail from *Barbados. People in the fields* (1985) by Ras Ishi Butcher.

and hold that back straight, keep it in line. Moving swiftly toward us (so swiftly it seemed she did not intend stopping when she reached us but would sweep past us out the doorway which opened onto the sea and like Christ walk upon the water!), she was caught between the sunlight at her end of the building and the darkness inside—and for a moment she appeared to contain them both: the light in the long severe old-fashioned white dress she wore which brought the sense of a past that was still alive into our bustling present and in the snatch of white at her eye; the darkness in her black high-top shoes and in her face which was visible now that she was closer. **A**

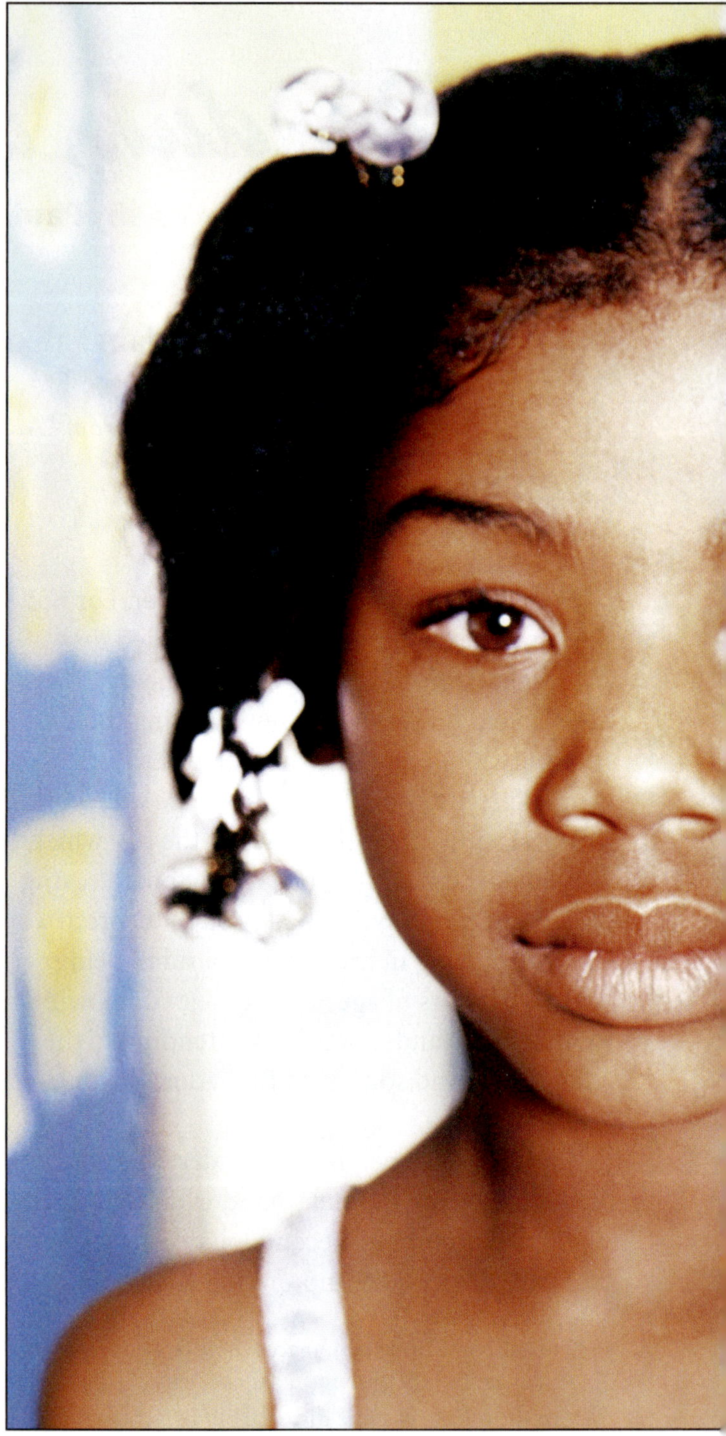

It was as stark and fleshless as a death mask, that face. The maggots might have already done their work, leaving only the framework of bone beneath the ruined skin and deep wells at the temple and jaw. But her eyes were alive, unnervingly so for one so old, with a sharp light that flicked out of the dim clouded depths like a lizard's tongue to snap up all in her view. Those eyes betrayed a child's curiosity about the world, and I wondered vaguely seeing them, and seeing the way the bodice of her ancient dress had collapsed in on her flat chest (what had happened to her breasts?), whether she might not be some kind of child at the same time that she was a woman, with fourteen children, my mother included, to prove it. Perhaps she was both, both child and woman, darkness and light, past and present, life and death—all the opposites contained and reconciled in her.

A Literary Perspectives Analyzing Biographical Context
How does the biography provided in the Meet the Writer on page 146 help you understand the narrator's first encounter with Da-duh?

"My Da-duh," my mother said formally and stepped forward. The name sounded like thunder fading softly in the distance.

"Child," Da-duh said, and her tone, her quick scrutiny of my mother, the brief embrace in which they appeared to shy from each other rather than touch, wiped out the fifteen years my mother had been away and restored the old relationship. My mother, who was such a formidable figure in my eyes, had suddenly with a word been reduced to my status.

"Yes, God is good," Da-duh said with a nod that was like a tic. "He has spared me to see my child again."

We were led forward then, apologetically because not only did Da-duh prefer boys but she also liked her grandchildren to be "white," that is, fair-skinned; and we had, I was to discover, a number of cousins, the outside children of white estate managers and the like, who qualified. We, though, were as black as she.

My sister being the oldest was presented first. "This one takes after the father," my mother said and waited to be reproved.

Frowning, Da-duh tilted my sister's face toward the light. But her frown soon gave way to a grudging smile, for my sister with her large mild eyes and little broad winged nose, with our father's high-cheeked Barbadian cast to her face, was pretty.

"She's goin' be lucky," Da-duh said and patted her once on the cheek. "Any girl child that takes after the father does be lucky."

She turned then to me. But oddly enough she did not touch me. Instead leaning close, she peered hard at me, and then quickly drew back. I thought I saw her hand start up as though to shield her eyes. It was almost as if she saw not only me, a thin truculent child who it was said took after no one but myself, but something in me which for some reason she found disturbing, even threatening. We looked silently at each other for a long time there in the noisy shed, our gaze locked. She was the first to look away.

"But Adry," she said to my mother and her laugh was cracked, thin, apprehensive. "Where did you get this one here with this fierce look?"

"We don't know where she came out of, my Da-duh," my mother said, laughing also. Even I smiled to myself. After all I had won the encounter. Da-duh had recognized my small strength—and this was all I ever asked of the adults in my life then. **B**

"Come, soul," Da-duh said and took my hand. "You must be one of those New York terrors you hear so much about."

She led us, me at her side and my sister and mother behind, out of the shed into the sunlight that was like a bright driving summer rain and over to a group of people clustered beside a decrepit lorry.[3] They were our relatives, most of them from St. Andrews although Da-duh herself lived in St. Thomas,[4] the women wearing

3. **lorry:** British for "truck."

4. **St. Andrews . . . St. Thomas:** two different parishes, or neighborhoods, in Barbados.

B **Literary Focus** **Character Interactions** When they first meet, the narrator and Da-duh come into conflict. Why does the narrator feel that she has "won the encounter"?

Vocabulary **apprehensive** (ap rih HEHN sihv) *adj.:* feeling alarm; afraid, anxious, or worried.

bright print dresses, the colors vivid against their darkness, the men rusty black suits that encased them like straitjackets. Da-duh, holding fast to my hand, became my anchor as they circled round us like a nervous sea, exclaiming, touching us with their calloused hands, embracing us shyly. They laughed in awed bursts: "But look Adry got big-big children!" / "And see the nice things they wearing, wrist-watch and all!" / "I tell you, Adry has done all right for herself in New York. . . ."

Da-duh, ashamed at their wonder, embarrassed for them, admonished them the while. . . . She said, "Why you all got to get on like you never saw people from 'Away' before? You would think New York is the only place in the world to hear wunna. That's why I don't like to go anyplace with you St. Andrews people, you know. You all ain't been colonized."

We were in the back of the lorry finally, packed in among the barrels of ham, flour, cornmeal, and rice and the trunks of clothes that my mother had brought as gifts. We made our way slowly through Bridgetown's clogged streets, part of a funereal procession of cars and open-sided buses, bicycles and donkey carts. The dim little limestone shops and offices along the way marched with us, at the same mournful pace, toward the same grave ceremony—as did the people, the women balancing huge baskets on top their heads as if they were no more than hats they wore to shade them from the sun. Looking over the edge of the lorry I watched as their feet slurred the dust. I listened, and their voices, raw and loud and dissonant in the heat, seemed to be grappling with each other high overhead.

Da-duh sat on a trunk in our midst, a monarch amid her court. She still held my hand, but it was different now. I had suddenly become her anchor, for I felt her fear of the lorry with its asthmatic motor (a fear and distrust, I later learned, she held of all machines) beating like a pulse in her rough palm. **C**

As soon as we left Bridgetown behind though, she relaxed, and while the others around us talked she gazed at the canes[5] standing tall on either side of the winding marl road. "C'dear," she said softly to herself after a time. "The canes this side are pretty enough."

They were too much for me. I thought of them as giant weeds that had overrun the island, leaving scarcely any room for the small tottering houses of sun-bleached pine we passed or the people, dark streaks as our lorry hurtled by. I suddenly feared that we were journeying, unaware that we were, toward some dangerous place where the canes, grown as high and thick as a forest, would close in on us and run us through with their stiletto blades. I longed then for the familiar: for the street in Brooklyn where I lived, for my father who had refused to accompany us ("Blowing out good money on foolishness," he had said of the trip), for a game of tag with my friends under the chestnut tree outside our aging brownstone house.

"Yes, but wait till you see St. Thomas canes," Da-duh was saying to me. "They's canes father, bo," she gave a proud arrogant nod. "Tomorrow, God willing, I goin' take you out in the ground and show them to you."

5. **canes:** tall stems of sugar-cane plants.

C **Reading Focus** **Making Inferences** Why might Da-duh fear the lorry and other machines, prompting her to hold the narrator's hand?

Grandma by Clifford Hobbs. Color lithograph.

Analyzing Visuals **Viewing and Interpreting** What aspects of this portrait are similar to the description of Da-duh in the story? Explain.

True to her word Da-duh took me with her the following day out into the ground. It was a fairly large plot adjoining her weathered board-and-shingle house and consisting of a small orchard, a good-sized cane piece, and behind the canes, where the land sloped abruptly down, a gully. She had purchased it with Panama money sent by her eldest son, my uncle Joseph, who had died working on the canal. We entered the ground along a trail no wider than her body and as devious and complex as her reasons for showing me her land. Da-duh strode briskly ahead, her slight form filled out this morning by the layers of sacking petticoats she wore under her working dress to protect her against the damp. A fresh white cloth, elaborately arranged around her head, added to her height, and lent her a vain, almost roguish air.

Her pace slowed once we reached the orchard, and glancing back at me occasionally over her shoulder, she pointed out the various trees.

"This here is a breadfruit," she said. "That one yonder is a papaw. Here's a guava. This is a mango. I know you don't have anything like these in New York. Here's a sugar apple." (The fruit looked more like artichokes than apples to me.) "This one bears limes. . . ." She went on for some time, intoning the names of the trees as though they were those of her gods. Finally, turning to me, she said, "I know you don't have anything this nice where you come from." Then, as I hesitated: "I said I know you don't have anything this nice where you come from. . . ." D

"No," I said and my world did seem suddenly lacking.

Da-duh nodded and passed on. The orchard ended and we were on the narrow cart road that led through the cane piece, the canes clashing like swords above my cowering head. Again she turned and her thin muscular arms spread wide, her dim gaze embracing the small field of canes, she said—and her voice almost broke under the weight of her pride, "Tell me, have you got anything like these in that place where you were born?"

"No."

"I din' think so. I bet you don't even know that these canes here and the sugar you eat is one and the same thing. That they does throw the canes into some machine at the factory and squeeze out all the little life in them to make sugar for you all so in New York to eat. I bet you don't know that."

"I've got two cavities and I'm not allowed to eat a lot of sugar."

But Da-duh didn't hear me. She had turned with an inexplicably angry motion and was making her way rapidly out of the canes and down the slope at the edge of the field which led to the gully below. Following her apprehensively down the incline amid a stand of banana plants whose leaves flapped like elephants' ears in the wind, I found myself in the middle of a small tropical wood—a place dense and damp and gloomy and tremulous with the fitful play of light and shadow as the leaves high above moved against the sun that was almost hidden from view. It was a violent place, the tangled foliage fighting each other for a chance at the sunlight, the branches of the trees locked in what seemed an immemorial struggle, one

---

D Reading Focus Making Inferences Why do you think Da-duh points out the trees in the orchard and says to the narrator, "I know you don't have anything this nice where you come from"?

both necessary and inevitable. But despite the violence, it was pleasant, almost peaceful in the gully, and beneath the thick undergrowth the earth smelled like spring.

This time Da-duh didn't even bother to ask her usual question, but simply turned and waited for me to speak.

"No," I said, my head bowed. "We don't have anything like this in New York."

"Ah," she cried, her triumph complete. "I din' think so. Why, I've heard that's a place where you can walk till you near drop and never see a tree."

"We've got a chestnut tree in front of our house," I said.

"Does it bear?" She waited. "I ask you, does it bear?"

"Not anymore," I muttered. "It used to, but not anymore."

She gave the nod that was like a nervous twitch. "You see," she said. "Nothing can bear there." Then, secure behind her scorn, she added, "But tell me, what's this snow like that you hear so much about?"

> "But tell me, what's this snow like that you hear so much about?"

Looking up, I studied her closely, sensing my chance, and then I told her, describing at length and with as much drama as I could summon not only what snow in the city was like, but what it would be like here, in her perennial summer kingdom.

". . . And you see all these trees you got here," I said. "Well, they'd be bare. No leaves, no fruit, nothing. They'd be covered in snow. You see your canes. They'd be buried under tons of snow. The snow would be higher than your head, higher than your house, and you wouldn't be able to come down into this here gully because it would be snowed under. . . ."

She searched my face for the lie, still scornful but intrigued. "What a thing, huh?" she said finally, whispering it softly to herself.

"And when it snows you couldn't dress like you are now," I said. "Oh no, you'd freeze to death. You'd have to wear a hat and gloves and galoshes and earmuffs so your ears wouldn't freeze and drop off, and a heavy coat. I've got a Shirley Temple[6] coat with fur on the collar. I can dance. You wanna see?" **E**

Before she could answer I began, with a dance called the Truck which was popular back then in the 1930s. My right forefinger waving, I trucked around the nearby trees and around Da-duh's awed and rigid form. After the Truck I did the Suzy-Q, my lean hips swishing, my sneakers sidling zigzag over the ground. "I can sing," I said and did so, starting with "I'm Gonna Sit Right Down and Write Myself a Letter," then without pausing, "Tea for Two," and ending with "I Found a Million Dollar Baby in a Five and Ten Cent Store."

For long moments afterwards Da-duh stared at me as if I were a creature from Mars, an emissary from some world she did not know but which intrigued her and whose power she both felt and feared. Yet something

6. **Shirley Temple:** child movie star popular during the 1930s.

E Reading Focus **Making Inferences** Why does the narrator present such a dramatic description of what would happen if it snowed in Barbados?

Vocabulary **perennial** (puh REHN ee uhl) *adj.:* year-round; continual.

Analyzing Visuals **Viewing and Interpreting** Here is a photograph of a setting that Da-duh knows well. How does it contrast with the tales of the city that the narrator tells Da-duh?

about my performance must have pleased her, because bending down she slowly lifted her long skirt and then, one by one, the layers of petticoats until she came to a drawstring purse dangling at the end of a long strip of cloth tied round her waist. Opening the purse she handed me a penny. "Here," she said half-smiling against her will. "Take this to buy yourself a sweet at the shop up the road. There's nothing to be done with you, soul."

From then on, whenever I wasn't taken to visit relatives, I accompanied Da-duh out into the ground, and alone with her amid the canes or down in the gully I told her about New York. It always began with some slighting remark on her part: "I know they don't have anything this nice where you come from," or "Tell me, I hear those foolish people in New York does do such and such. . . ." But as I answered, recreating my towering world of steel and concrete and machines for her, building the city out of words, I would feel her give way. I came to know the signs of her surrender: the total stillness that would come over

her little hard dry form, the probing gaze that like a surgeon's knife sought to cut through my skull to get at the images there, to see if I were lying; above all, her fear, a fear nameless and profound, the same one I had felt beating in the palm of her hand that day in the lorry. **F**

Over the weeks I told her about refrigerators, radios, gas stoves, elevators, trolley cars, wringer washing machines, movies, airplanes, the cyclone at Coney Island,[7] subways, toasters, electric lights: "At night, see, all you have to do is flip this little switch on the wall and all the lights in the house go on. Just like that. Like magic. It's like turning on the sun at night."

"But tell me," she said to me once with a faint mocking smile, "do the white people have all these things too or it's only the people looking like us?"

I laughed. "What d'ya mean," I said. "The white people have even better." Then: "I beat up a white girl in my class last term."

"Beating up white people!" Her tone was incredulous.

"How you mean!" I said, using an expression of hers. "She called me a name."

For some reason Da-duh could not quite get over this and repeated in the same hushed, shocked voice, "Beating up white people now! Oh, the lord, the world's changing up so I can scarce recognize it anymore."

One morning toward the end of our stay, Da-duh led me into a part of the gully that we had never visited before, an area darker and more thickly overgrown than the rest, almost

7. **cyclone at Coney Island:** roller-coaster ride in an amusement park in Brooklyn, New York.

F **Reading Focus** **Making Inferences** Why do you think Da-duh says to the narrator, "Tell me, I hear those foolish people in New York does do such and such. . . ."?

impenetrable. There in a small clearing amid the dense bush, she stopped before an incredibly tall royal palm which rose cleanly out of the ground, and drawing the eye up with it, soared high above the trees around it into the sky. It appeared to be touching the blue dome of sky, to be flaunting its dark crown of fronds right in the blinding white face of the late morning sun.

Da-duh watched me a long time before she spoke, and then she said very quietly, "All right, now, tell me if you've got anything this tall in that place you're from." G

I almost wished, seeing her face, that I could have said no. "Yes," I said. "We've got buildings hundreds of times this tall in New York. There's one called the Empire State Building that's the tallest in the world. My class visited it last year and I went all the way to the top. It's got over a hundred floors. I can't describe how tall it is. Wait a minute. What's the name of that hill I went to visit the other day, where they have the police station?"

"You mean Bissex?"

"Yes, Bissex. Well, the Empire State Building is way taller than that."

"You're lying now!" she shouted, trembling with rage. Her hand lifted to strike me.

"No, I'm not," I said. "It really is, if you don't believe me I'll send you a picture postcard of it soon as I get back home so you can see for yourself. But it's way taller than Bissex."

All the fight went out of her at that. The hand poised to strike me fell limp to her side, and as she stared at me, seeing not me but the building that was taller than the highest hill she knew, the small stubborn light in her eyes (it was the same amber as the flame in the kerosene lamp she lit at dusk) began to fail. Finally, with a vague gesture that even in the midst of her defeat still tried to dismiss me and my world, she turned and started back through the gully, walking slowly, her steps groping and uncertain, as if she were suddenly no longer sure of the way, while I followed triumphant yet strangely saddened behind.

The next morning I found her dressed for our morning walk but stretched out on the Berbice chair in the tiny drawing room where she sometimes napped during the afternoon heat, her face turned to the window beside her. She appeared thinner and suddenly indescribably old.

"My Da-duh," I said.

"Yes, nuh," she said. Her voice was listless

> And in the midst of my mother's tearful protracted farewell, she leaned down and whispered in my ear, "Girl, you're not to forget now to send me the picture of that building, you hear."

G **Literary Focus** **Character Interactions** Why has Da-duh taken the narrator to see this palm? What do you predict will happen between Da-duh and the narrator?

and the face she slowly turned my way was, now that I think back on it, like a Benin mask,[8] the features drawn and almost distorted by an ancient abstract sorrow.

"Don't you feel well?" I asked.

"Girl, I don't know."

"My Da-duh, I goin' boil you some bush tea," my aunt, Da-duh's youngest child, who lived with her, called from the shed-roof kitchen.

"Who tell you I need bush tea?" she cried, her voice assuming for a moment its old authority. "You can't even rest nowadays without some malicious person looking for you to be dead. Come girl," she motioned me to a place beside her on the old-fashioned lounge chair, "give us a tune." **H**

I sang for her until breakfast at eleven, all my brash irreverent Tin Pan Alley songs,[9] and then just before noon we went out into the ground. But it was a short, dispirited walk. Da-duh didn't even notice that the mangoes were beginning to ripen and would have to be picked before the village boys got to them. And when she paused occasionally and looked out across the canes or up at her trees, it wasn't as if she were seeing them but something else. Some huge, monolithic shape had imposed itself, it seemed, between her and the land, obstructing her vision. Returning to the house she slept the entire afternoon on the Berbice chair. **I**

She remained like this until we left, languishing away the mornings on the chair at the window gazing out at the land as if it were already doomed; then, at noon, taking the brief stroll with me through the ground during which she seldom spoke, and afterwards returning home to sleep till almost dusk sometimes.

On the day of our departure she put on the austere, ankle-length white dress, the black shoes and brown felt hat (her town clothes she called them), but she did not go with us to town. She saw us off on the road outside her house and in the midst of my mother's tearful protracted farewell, she leaned down and whispered in my ear, "Girl, you're not to forget now to send me the picture of that building, you hear."

By the time I mailed her the large colored picture postcard of the Empire State Building, she was dead. She died during the famous '37 strike,[10] which began shortly after we left. On the day of her death England sent planes flying low over the island in a show of force—so low, according to my aunt's letter, that the downdraft from them shook the ripened mangoes

8. **Benin mask:** reference to the beautiful ivory-and-wood masks carved in the West African kingdom of Benin, which flourished from the fourteenth to the seventeenth centuries.
9. **Tin Pan Alley songs:** Tin Pan Alley is a district in New York City, associated since the late nineteenth century with popular songwriters. Tin Pan Alley songs were "brash" (bold) and "irreverent" (mocking; disrespectful).
10. **famous '37 strike:** Political factors and economic hardships led Barbadian workers to riot against the British in 1937.

H Literary Focus **Character Interactions** Review the last few paragraphs in which the narrator describes Da-duh on the morning after their conflict over the Empire State Building. Has Da-duh completely surrendered? Explain.

I Literary Focus **Character Interactions** As a result of Da-duh's conflict with the narrator, a "huge, monolithic shape" blocks Da-duh's vision of the land. What might this huge shape represent?

from the trees in Da-duh's orchard. Frightened, everyone in the village fled into the canes. Except Da-duh. She remained in the house at the window so my aunt said, watching as the planes came swooping and screaming like monstrous birds down over the village, over her house, rattling her trees and flattening the young canes in her field. It must have seemed to her lying there that they did not intend pulling out of their dive, but like the hardback beetles which hurled themselves with suicidal force against the walls of the house at night, those menacing silver shapes would hurl themselves in an ecstasy of self-immolation[11] onto the land, destroying it utterly.

When the planes finally left and the villagers returned, they found her dead on the Berbice chair at the window.

She died and I lived, but always, to this day even, within the shadow of her death. For a brief period after I was grown I went to live alone, like one doing penance,[12] in a loft above a noisy factory in downtown New York and there painted seas of sugar cane and huge, swirling van Gogh[13] suns and palm trees striding like brightly-plumed Tutsi[14] warriors across a tropical landscape, while the thunderous tread of the machines downstairs jarred the floor beneath my easel, mocking my efforts. **J**

Analyzing Visuals **Viewing and Interpreting**
Which character in the story do you think this photo might represent? Explain.

11. **self-immolation** (sehlf ihm muh LAY shuhn): violent self-destruction, usually by fire.
12. **penance** (PEHN uhns): action done to make up for wrong behavior.
13. **van Gogh:** Dutch artist Vincent van Gogh (1853–1890) painted suns that seemed to roll through skies filled with swirling colors.
14. **Tutsi** (TOOT see): Watusi (or Watutsi), a people of Burundi and Rwanda, in central Africa.

J Reading Focus **Making Inferences** What do you think motivates the narrator to paint sugar cane, suns, and palm trees? Why is it significant that the machines in the factory below her loft mock her efforts to paint?

Vocabulary **menacing** (MEHN ihs ihng) *v.* used as *adj.:* threatening.

Applying Your Skills

9.R.2.C.1.b Use details from text(s): to analyze character, plot, setting, point of view **9.R.2.C.1.d** Use details from text(s): to evaluate the effect of author's style **9.R.1.G.1.d** During reading, utilize strategies: to infer *Also covered* **9.W.2.D.1.b; 9.R.1.G.1.a**

To Da-duh, in Memoriam

Respond and Think Critically

Reading Focus

Quick Check

1. Why is Da-duh so frightened of the narrator's stories of New York?
2. What causes "all the fight" to go out of Da-duh?

Read with a Purpose

3. Why is Barbados so foreign to the narrator?

Reading Skills: Making Inferences About Motivation

4. Review the inference chart you filled in as you read. What do you think motivates Da-duh and the narrator to try to triumph over each other?

Vocabulary Check

Tell whether each statement is true or false, and then explain why.

5. During an **unrelenting** storm, rivers might flood.
6. A kitten might seem **menacing.**
7. An injured animal might become **apprehensive.**
8. A **perennial** plant lives for only a short time.

Literary Focus

Literary Analysis

9. **Interpret** What "borders" does the narrator cross when she visits her grandmother?
10. **Interpret** Why, once her grandmother is defeated, does the narrator feel "triumphant yet strangely saddened"?
11. **Analyze** Re-read the description of Da-duh in the beginning of the story. In what ways does she represent both life and death?
12. **Literary Perspectives** In her biography on page 146, Marshall describes her own relationship with her grandmother as a "subtle kind of power struggle." Using evidence from the story, show how the relationship between the narrator and Da-duh might reflect the author's actual relationship with her grandmother.

Literary Skills: Character Interactions

13. **Contrast** List the opposites that the narrator and Da-duh represent. Then, explain the conflict that develops during their interactions.

Da-duh	Narrator	Conflict
lives in the country	lives in the city	

Literary Skills Review: Mood

14. **Analyze** How would you describe the story's **mood**—the feeling evoked by the setting?

Writing Focus

Think as a Reader/Writer

Use It in Your Writing Marshall uses figurative language to tell us not only what Da-duh looks like but also what kind of person she is. Write a description of a person, either real or imaginary, using metaphors or similes to bring the person to life.

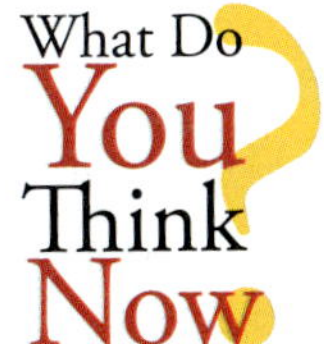

How does the relationship between the narrator and Da-duh affect each character's view of herself and the world?

SHORT STORY

Preparing to Read

American History

by **Judith Ortiz Cofer**

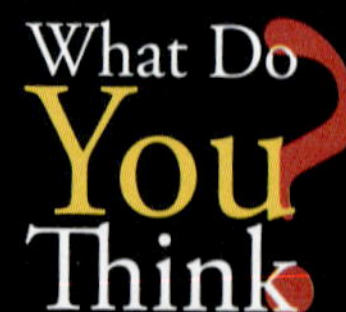

What are the consequences of judging other people?

QuickWrite

On a daily basis, we make judgments about people, and we are judged in turn. List the factors we use to evaluate people. When are such judgments helpful? When are they harmful? Write down your thoughts.

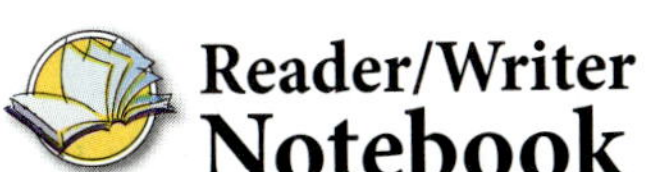

Use your **RWN** to complete the activities for this selection.

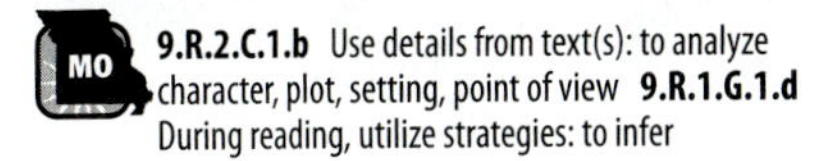

MO
9.R.2.C.1.b Use details from text(s): to analyze character, plot, setting, point of view 9.R.1.G.1.d During reading, utilize strategies: to infer

Literary Focus

Round and Flat Characters The story characters we most identify with are usually **round characters,** who have several sides to their personalities. In contrast, **flat characters,** who are often subordinate, or minor, characters, have only one or two traits. "American History" focuses on one round character, Elena (the narrator), but the minor characters, such as her neighbor Eugene, play a crucial role in her life.

Literary Perspectives Apply the literary perspective described on page 163 as you read this story.

Reading Focus

Making Inferences About Characters When characters narrate their own stories, they often tell you a lot about themselves upfront. Often, though, you need to determine a character's personality by **making inferences,** or educated guesses, based on the character's words, thoughts, and actions.

Into Action As you read, record your inferences about the narrator to help you understand her personality.

Pg #	Narrator's Words, Thoughts, and Actions	My Inferences
p. 164	"I was miserable, since I had forgotten my gloves...."	The narrator is forgetful and doesn't like the cold.
p. 164	The narrator's cheeks burn.	

Writing Focus

Think as a Reader/Writer

Find It in Your Reading Although the author employs dialogue sparingly in this story, she uses it to great effect to reveal information about her characters. As you read, comment in your *Reader/Writer Notebook* about the purpose of dialogue in the story.

Vocabulary

discreet (dihs KREET) *adj.:* careful; showing good judgment. *Elena's mother is worried that her daughter's behavior is not discreet.*

infatuated (ihn FACH oo ay tihd) *adj.:* carried away by shallow or foolish love. *Elena's mother thinks her daughter is infatuated with the boy next door.*

vigilant (VIHJ uh luhnt) *adj.:* watchful. *In charge of discipline at the school, Mr. DePalma is a vigilant teacher.*

elation (ih LAY shuhn) *n.:* great joy. *Elena's friendship with Eugene fills her with elation.*

solace (SAHL ihs) *n.:* comfort; easing of grief. *Saddened by life, Elena's mother finds solace in her dreams of the future.*

Someone who is	
infatuated	
might	
need **solace** if love is not returned	show **elation** if love is returned

Language Coach

Word Origins The Latin word *fatuus* means "foolish." Something that is fatuous (FACH oo uhs) is "silly" or "idiotic." In what way might someone who is infatuated with someone display silliness or idiocy?

Learn It Online
Get to know this story with the video online:
go.hrw.com
L9-161
Go

MEET THE WRITER

Learn It Online
Get more on the author's life at:
go.hrw.com L9-162 Go

Judith Ortiz Cofer
(1952–)

El Building

Judith Ortiz Cofer was born in Puerto Rico, but her family came to the mainland United States when she was a toddler. Her family moved to Paterson, New Jersey, and lived in a large apartment building that was known as El Building. Her father had encountered prejudice while looking for an apartment, but in El Building the family joined a community of fellow Puerto Rican immigrants. Cofer says of her early home, "The walls were thin, and voices speaking and arguing in Spanish could be heard all day."

Personal and Political

It was a challenge for Cofer to master English in her new home. Ultimately, however, she became an English professor and an award-winning author of poetry, fiction, and nonfiction. Cofer's stories often reflect the issues of her time. However, she explains that this does not make her a "political writer": "I am not a political writer in that I never take an issue and write a story about it. The people in my stories deal with political issues but only in accordance with the needs of their personal lives."

"My politics are imbedded in my work as part of the human experience."

Think About the Writer What distinction does Cofer make between political writers and herself?

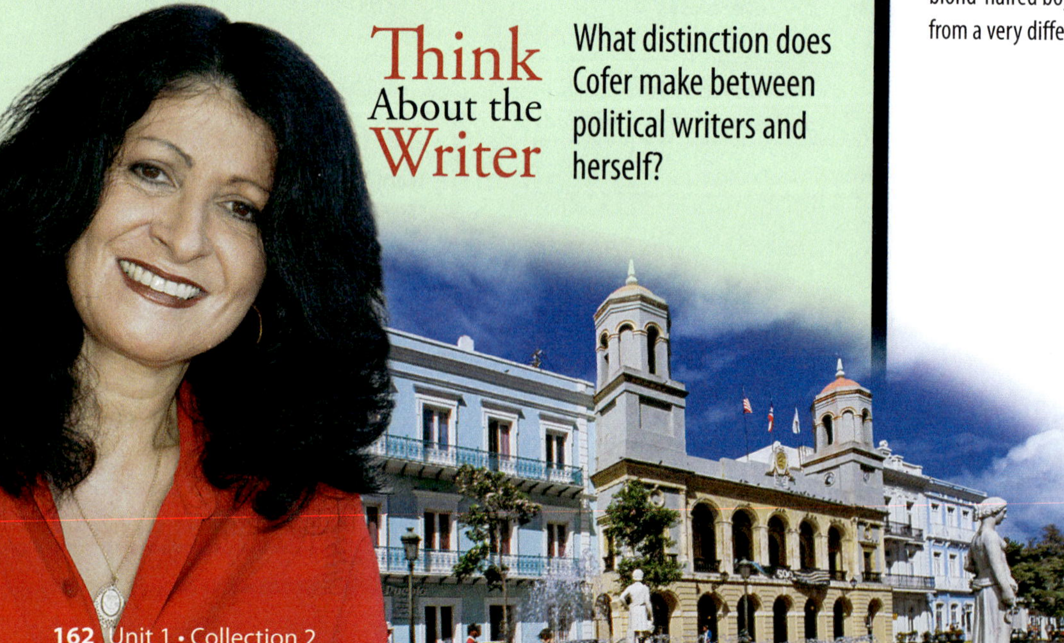

Build Background

President John F. Kennedy was assassinated on November 22, 1963, while riding in a motorcade in Dallas, Texas. Kennedy was committed to eliminating prejudice and establishing equal rights for all Americans. His assassination marked a loss of innocence in this country—it showed that dreams can be destroyed in one horrible moment. Even today, people still share stories about where they were when Kennedy was killed.

Preview the Selection

Elena, the story's narrator and main character, is a fourteen-year-old Puerto Rican girl whose mother worries about her. **Eugene,** the object of her affections, is a blond-haired boy from Georgia who comes from a very different world.

Read with a Purpose Read this story to discover what lesson the narrator learned on the day President Kennedy was shot.

American History

by **Judith Ortiz Cofer**

I once read in a "Ripley's Believe It or Not" column that Paterson, New Jersey, is the place where the Straight and Narrow (streets) intersect. The Puerto Rican tenement known as El Building was one block up on Straight. It was, in fact, the corner of Straight and Market; not "at" the corner, but *the* corner. At almost any hour of the day, El Building was like a monstrous jukebox, blasting out salsas[1] from open windows as the residents, mostly new immigrants just up from the island, tried to drown out whatever they were currently enduring with loud music. But the day President Kennedy was shot, there was a profound silence in El Building; even the abusive tongues of viragoes,[2] the cursing of the unemployed, and the screeching of small children had been somehow muted. President Kennedy was a saint to these people. In fact, soon his photograph would be hung alongside the Sacred Heart and over the spiritist altars[3] that many women kept in their apartments. He would become part of the hierarchy of martyrs[4] they prayed to for favors that only one who had died for a cause would understand. **A**

Literary Perspectives

Analyzing Historical Context When you analyze historical context, you consider what was happening during the time in which the author set his or her story. Sometimes an author's story is a reaction to a social, political, or cultural situation that he or she experienced. Judith Ortiz Cofer lived during the period she writes about—the civil rights movement and President Kennedy's assassination—and her story reflects these historical events and perhaps her reaction to them. Cofer said of "American History": "The story doesn't end with a speech on prejudice but with the heartbreak of a girl still unable to comprehend that it all comes together and affects her life: the death of a president, life in America, prejudice, the plight of the immigrant."

As you read, be sure to look at the notes and questions at the bottom of the pages, which will guide you in using this perspective.

1. **salsas** (SAHL sahz): lively dance music from Latin America.
2. **viragoes** (vuh RAY gohz): quarrelsome women.
3. **the Sacred Heart . . . altars:** The Sacred Heart is an image depicting the wounded heart of Jesus, often encircled by a crown of thorns. "Spiritist altars" most likely refers to memorials for dead relatives.
4. **hierarchy** (HY uh rahr kee) **of martyrs** (MAHR tuhrz): *Hierarchy* means "ranking in order of importance." Martyrs are people who have suffered or died rather than give up their faith or principles.

A Literary Perspectives Analyzing Historical Context According to the narrator, how does the community view President Kennedy and react to his assassination?

Analyzing Visuals **Viewing and Interpreting** What overall mood is conveyed in this photograph? How do the girls' expressions contribute to this mood?

On the day that President Kennedy was shot, my ninth-grade class had been out in the fenced playground of Public School Number 13. We had been given "free" exercise time and had been ordered by our PE teacher, Mr. DePalma, to "keep moving." That meant that the girls should jump rope and the boys toss basketballs through a hoop at the far end of the yard. He in the meantime would "keep an eye" on us from just inside the building.

It was a cold gray day in Paterson. The kind that warns of early snow. I was miserable, since I had forgotten my gloves and my knuckles were turning red and raw from the jump rope. I was also taking a lot of abuse from the black girls for not turning the rope hard and fast enough for them.

"Hey, Skinny Bones, pump it, girl. Ain't you got no energy today?" Gail, the biggest of the black girls who had the other end of the rope yelled, "Didn't you eat your rice and beans and pork chops for breakfast today?"

The other girls picked up the "pork chop" and made it into a refrain: "Pork chop, pork chop, did you eat your pork chop?" They entered the double ropes in pairs and exited without tripping or missing a beat. I felt a burning on my cheeks and then my glasses fogged up so that I could not manage to coordinate the jump rope with Gail. The chill was doing to me what it always did: entering my bones, making me cry, humiliating me. I hated the city, especially in winter. I hated Public School Number 13. I hated my skinny, flat-chested body, and I envied the black girls, who could jump rope so fast that their legs became a blur. They always seemed to be warm, while I froze.

There was only one source of beauty and light for me that school year—the only thing I had anticipated at the start of the semester. That was seeing Eugene. In August, Eugene and his family had moved into the only house on the block that had a yard and trees. I could see his place from my window in El Building. In fact, if I sat on the fire escape I was literally suspended above Eugene's backyard. It was my favorite spot to read my library books in the summer. Until that August the house had been occupied by an old Jewish couple. Over the years I had become part of their family, without their knowing it, of course. I had a view of their kitchen and their backyard, and though I could not hear what they said, I knew when they were arguing, when one of them was sick, and many other things. I knew all this by watching them at mealtimes. I could see their kitchen table, the sink, and the stove. During good times, he sat at the table and read his newspapers while she fixed the meals. If they argued, he would leave and the old woman would sit and stare at nothing for a long time. When one of them was sick, the other would come and get things from the kitchen and carry them out on a tray. The old man had died in June. The last week of school I had not seen him at the table at all. Then one day I saw that there was a crowd in the kitchen. The old woman had finally emerged from the house on the arm of a stocky middle-aged woman, whom I had seen there a few times before, maybe her daughter. Then a man had carried out suitcases. The house had stood empty for weeks. I had had to resist the temptation to climb down into the yard and water the flowers the old lady had taken such good care of. **B**

By the time Eugene's family moved in, the yard was a tangled mass of weeds. The father had spent several days mowing, and when he finished, from where I sat I didn't see the red, yellow, and purple clusters that meant flowers to me. I didn't see this family sit down at the kitchen table together. It was just the mother, a redheaded, tall woman who wore a white uniform—a nurse's, I guessed it was; the father was gone before I got up in the morning and was never there at dinner time. I only saw him on weekends, when they sometimes sat on lawn chairs under the oak tree, each hidden behind a section of the newspaper; and there was Eugene. He was tall and blond, and he wore glasses. I liked him right away because he sat at the kitchen table and read books for hours. That summer, before we had even spoken one word to each other, I kept him company on my fire escape.

Once school started, I looked for him in all my classes, but PS 13 was a huge, overpopulated place and it took me days and many discreet questions to discover that Eugene was in honors classes for all his subjects, classes that were not open to me because English was not my first language, though I was a straight-A student. After much maneuvering I managed to "run into him" in the hallway where his locker was—on the other side of the building from mine—and in study hall at the library, where he first seemed to notice me but did not speak, and finally, on the way home after school one day when I decided to approach him directly, though my stomach was doing somersaults. **C**

I was ready for rejection, snobbery, the worst. But when I came up to him, practically panting in my nervousness, and blurted out: "You're Eugene. Right?" he smiled, pushed his glasses up on his nose, and nodded. I saw then that he was blushing deeply. Eugene liked me, but he was shy. I did most of the talking that day. He

---

B **Reading Focus** **Making Inferences** What can you infer about the narrator from her description of the elderly couple?

C **Reading Focus** **Making Inferences** Note how the narrator takes action to meet Eugene. What do these actions reveal about her?

Vocabulary **discreet** (dihs KREET) *adj.:* careful; showing good judgment.

nodded and smiled a lot. In the weeks that followed, we walked home together. He would linger at the corner of El Building for a few minutes, then walk down to his two-story house. It was not until Eugene moved into that house that I noticed that El Building blocked most of the sun and that the only spot that got a little sunlight during the day was the tiny square of earth the old woman had planted with flowers.

I did not tell Eugene that I could see inside his kitchen from my bedroom. I felt dishonest, but I liked my secret sharing of his evenings, especially now that I knew what he was reading since we chose our books together at the school library. **D**

One day my mother came into my room as I was sitting on the windowsill staring out. In her abrupt way she said: "Elena, you are acting 'moony.'" "Enamorada" was what she really said, that is—like a girl stupidly infatuated. Since I had turned fourteen . . . , my mother had been more vigilant than ever. She acted as if I was going to go crazy or explode or something if she didn't watch me and nag me all the time about being a señorita[5] now. She kept talking about virtue, morality, and other subjects that did not interest me in the least. My mother was unhappy in Paterson, but my father had a good job at the bluejeans factory in Passaic and soon, he kept assuring us, we would be moving to our own house there. Every Sunday we drove out to the suburbs of Paterson, Clifton, and Passaic, out to where people mowed grass on Sundays in the summer and where children made snowmen in the winter from pure white snow, not like the gray slush of Paterson, which seemed to fall from the sky in that hue. I had learned to listen to my parents' dreams, which were spoken in Spanish, as fairy tales, like the stories about life in the island paradise of Puerto Rico before I was born. I had been to the island once as a little girl, to Grandmother's funeral, and all I remembered was wailing women in black, my mother becoming hysterical and being given a pill that made her sleep two days, and me feeling lost in a crowd of strangers all claiming to be my aunts, uncles, and cousins. I had actually been glad to return to the city. We had not been back there since then, though my parents talked constantly about buying a house on the beach someday, retiring on the island—that was a common topic among the residents of El Building. As for me, I was going to go to college and become a teacher. **E**

But after meeting Eugene I began to think of the present more than of the future. What I wanted now was to enter that house I had watched for so many years. I wanted to see the other rooms where the old people had lived and where the boy spent his time. Most of all I wanted to sit at the kitchen table with Eugene like two adults, like the old man and his wife had done, maybe drink some coffee and talk about books. I had started reading *Gone with the Wind.* I was enthralled by it, with the daring and the passion of the beautiful girl living in a mansion, and with her devoted parents and the slaves who did everything for them. I didn't

5. **señorita** (say nyoh REE tah): Spanish for "unmarried woman."

D **Literary Focus** **Round Character** Explain the complicated feelings the narrator expresses in this paragraph.

E **Reading Focus** **Making Inferences** What do Elena's statements in this passage suggest about her ties to Puerto Rico?

Vocabulary **infatuated** (ihn FACH oo ay tihd) *adj.:* carried away by shallow or foolish love.
vigilant (VIHJ uh luhnt) *adj.:* watchful.

believe such a world had ever really existed, and I wanted to ask Eugene some questions since he and his parents, he had told me, had come up from Georgia, the same place where the novel was set. His father worked for a company that had transferred him to Paterson. His mother was very unhappy, Eugene said, in his beautiful voice that rose and fell over words in a strange, lilting way. The kids at school called him "the Hick" and made fun of the way he talked. I knew I was his only friend so far, and I liked that, though I felt sad for him sometimes. "Skinny Bones and the Hick" was what they called us at school when we were seen together.

The day Mr. DePalma came out into the cold and asked us to line up in front of him was the day that President Kennedy was shot. Mr. DePalma, a short, muscular man with slicked-down black hair, was the science teacher, PE coach, and disciplinarian at PS 13. He was the teacher to whose homeroom you got assigned if you were a troublemaker, and the man called out to break up playground fights and to escort violently angry teenagers to the office. And Mr. DePalma was the man who called your parents in for "a conference."

That day, he stood in front of two rows of mostly black and Puerto Rican kids, brittle from their efforts to "keep moving" on a November day that was turning bitter cold. Mr. DePalma, to our complete shock, was crying. Not just silent adult tears, but really sobbing. There were a few titters from the back of the line where I stood shivering.

"Listen," Mr. DePalma raised his arms over his head as if he were about to conduct an

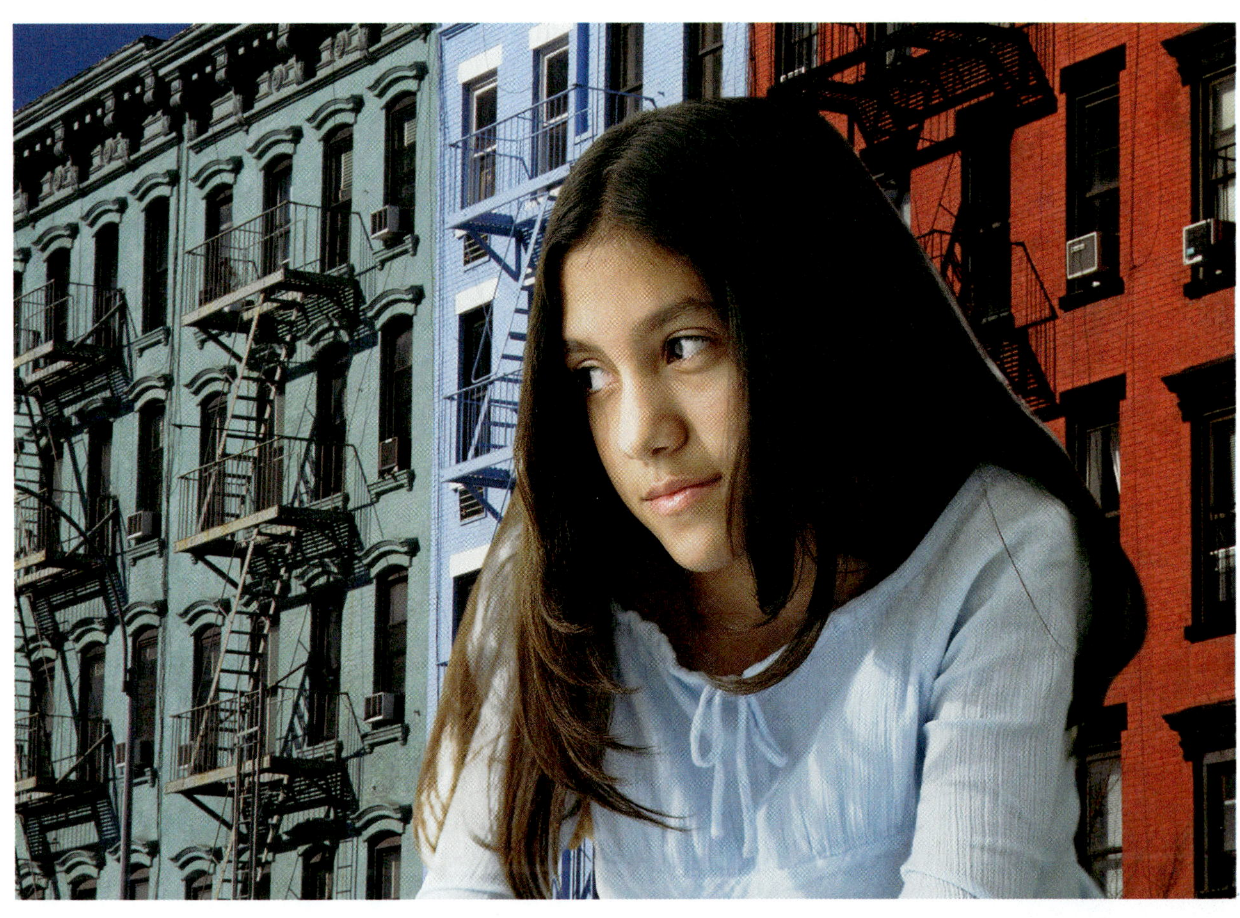

orchestra. His voice broke, and he covered his face with his hands. His barrel chest was heaving. Someone giggled behind me.

"Listen," he repeated, "something awful has happened." A strange gurgling came from his throat, and he turned around and spat on the cement behind him.

"Gross," someone said, and there was a lot of laughter.

"The president is dead, you idiots. I should have known that wouldn't mean anything to a bunch of losers like you kids. Go home." He was shrieking now. No one moved for a minute or two, but then a big girl let out a "Yeah!" and ran to get her books piled up with the others against the brick wall of the school building. The others followed in a mad scramble to get to their things before somebody caught on. It was still an hour to the dismissal bell. F

A little scared, I headed for El Building. There was an eerie feeling on the streets. I looked into Mario's drugstore, a favorite hangout for the high school crowd, but there were only a couple of old Jewish men at the soda bar talking with the short-order cook in tones that sounded almost angry, but they were keeping their voices low. Even the traffic on one of the busiest intersections in Paterson—Straight Street and Park Avenue—seemed to be moving slower. There were no horns blasting that day. At El Building, the usual little group of unemployed men was not hanging out on the front stoop making it difficult for women to enter the front door. No music spilled out from open doors in the hallway. When I walked into our apartment, I found my mother sitting in front of the grainy picture of the television set.

She looked up at me with a tear-streaked face and just said: "Dios mío,"[6] turning back to the set as if it were pulling at her eyes. I went into my room.

Though I wanted to feel the right thing about President Kennedy's death, I could not fight the feeling of elation that stirred in my chest. Today was the day I was to visit Eugene in his house. He had asked me to come over after school to study for an American history test with him. We had also planned to walk to the public library together. I looked down into his yard. The oak tree was bare of leaves and the ground looked gray with ice. The light through the large kitchen window of his house told me that El Building blocked the sun to such an extent that they had to turn lights on in the middle of the day. I felt ashamed about it. But the white kitchen table with the lamp hanging just above it looked cozy and inviting. I would soon sit there, across from Eugene, and I would tell him about my perch just above his house. Maybe I should. G

In the next thirty minutes I changed clothes, put on a little pink lipstick, and got my books together. Then I went in to tell my mother that I was going to a friend's house to study. I did not expect her reaction.

"You are going out *today*?" The way she said "today" sounded as if a storm warning had been

---

6. **Dios mío** (DEE ohs MEE oh): Spanish for "Oh, my God."

F **Literary Focus** **Flat Character** What is Mr. DePalma's role in the story? What point is the author trying to convey through Mr. DePalma's reaction to Kennedy's death?

G **Literary Perspectives** **Analyzing Historical Context** Why is it significant that Elena and Eugene are planning to study for an American history test together?

Vocabulary **elation** (ih LAY shuhn) *n.:* great joy.

Analyzing Visuals **Viewing and Interpreting** This photograph was taken the day that President Kennedy died. How are the people's reactions similar to those that Cofer records in her story?

issued. It was said in utter disbelief. Before I could answer, she came toward me and held my elbows as I clutched my books.

"Hija,[7] the president has been killed. We must show respect. He was a great man. Come to church with me tonight."

She tried to embrace me, but my books were in the way. My first impulse was to comfort her, she seemed so distraught, but I had to meet Eugene in fifteen minutes.

"I have a test to study for, Mama. I will be home by eight."

"You are forgetting who you are, Niña.[8] I have seen you staring down at that boy's house. You are heading for humiliation and pain." My mother said this in Spanish and in a resigned tone that surprised me, as if she had no intention of stopping me from "heading for humiliation and pain." I started for the door. She sat in front of the TV holding a white handkerchief to her face.

I walked out to the street and around the chain-link fence that separated El Building from Eugene's house. The yard was neatly edged around the little walk that led to the door. It always amazed me how Paterson, the inner core of the city, had no apparent logic to its architecture. Small, neat single residences like this one could be found right next to huge, dilapidated apartment buildings like El Building. My guess was that the little houses had been there first, then the immigrants had come in droves, and the monstrosities had been raised for them—the Italians, the Irish, the Jews, and now us, the Puerto Ricans and the blacks. The door was

7. **hija** (EE hah): Spanish for "daughter."

8. **niña** (NEE nyah): Spanish for "girl."

painted a deep green: verde, the color of hope. I had heard my mother say it: verde-esperanza.

I knocked softly. A few suspenseful moments later the door opened just a crack. The red, swollen face of a woman appeared. She had a halo of red hair floating over a delicate ivory face—the face of a doll—with freckles on the nose. Her smudged eye makeup made her look unreal to me, like a mannequin[9] seen through a warped store window.

"What do you want?" Her voice was tiny and sweet sounding, like a little girl's, but her tone was not friendly.

"I'm Eugene's friend. He asked me over. To study." I thrust out my books, a silly gesture that embarrassed me almost immediately.

"You live there?" She pointed up to El Building, which looked particularly ugly, like a gray prison, with its many dirty windows and rusty fire escapes. The woman had stepped halfway out and I could see that she wore a white nurse's uniform with "St. Joseph's Hospital" on the name tag.

"Yes. I do."

She looked intently at me for a couple of heartbeats, then said as if to herself, "I don't know how you people do it." Then directly to me: "Listen. Honey. Eugene doesn't want to study with you. He is a smart boy. Doesn't need help. You understand me. I am truly sorry if he told you you could come over. He cannot study with you. It's nothing personal. You understand? We won't be in this place much longer, no need for him to get close to people—it'll just make it harder for him later. Run back home now."

9. **mannequin** (MAN uh kihn): life-size model of a person.

I couldn't move. I just stood there in shock at hearing these things said to me in such a honey-drenched voice. I had never heard an accent like hers, except for Eugene's softer version. It was as if she were singing me a little song. **H**

"What's wrong? Didn't you hear what I said?" She seemed very angry, and I finally snapped out of my trance. I turned away from the green door and heard her close it gently.

Our apartment was empty when I got home. My mother was in someone else's kitchen, seeking the solace she needed. Father would come in from his late shift at midnight. I would hear them talking softly in the kitchen for hours that night. They would not discuss their dreams for the future, or life in Puerto Rico, as they often did; that night they would talk sadly about the young widow and her two children, as if they were family. For the next few days, we would observe luto in our apartment; that is, we would practice restraint and silence—no loud music or laughter. Some of the women of El Building would wear black for weeks. **I**

That night, I lay in my bed trying to feel the right thing for our dead president. But the tears that came up from a deep source inside me were strictly for me. When my mother came to the door, I pretended to be sleeping. Sometime during the night, I saw from my bed the streetlight come on. It had a pink halo around it. I went to my window and pressed my face to the cool glass. Looking up at the light, I could see the white snow falling like a lace veil over its face. I did not look down to see it turning gray as it touched the ground below.

H Literary Focus Flat Character What does the description of Eugene's mother's voice tell you about her personality?

Vocabulary solace (SAHL ihs) *n.:* comfort; easing of grief.

I Literary Perspectives Analyzing Historical Context "The young widow and her two children" is a reference to the president's wife, Jacqueline, and their children. Why is it significant that Elena's parents talk about them "as if they were family"?

Applying Your Skills

MO **9.R.2.C.1.b** Use details from text(s): to analyze character, plot, setting, point of view **9.R.1.G.1.d** During reading, utilize strategies: to infer **9.W.3.A.1.a** Compose a variety of texts: using narrative, descriptive, expository, and/or persuasive features

American History

Respond and Think Critically

Reading Focus

Quick Check

1. What do Elena and Eugene have in common?
2. What personal disappointment does Elena experience on the day Kennedy was shot?

Read with a Purpose

3. Why is Elena turned away from Eugene's house? What discovery does she make as a result?

Reading Skills: Making Inferences About Characters

4. Add a row to the bottom of your chart, and list three adjectives describing Elena's most important character traits.

pg #	Narrator's Words, Thoughts, and Actions	My Inferences
p. 164	"I was miserable, since I had forgotten my gloves. . . ."	The narrator is forgetful.

Three Important Character Traits:

Literary Focus

Literary Analysis

5. **Interpret** Re-read the last sentence of the story. Why doesn't Elena want to see the snow turning gray?
6. **Literary Perspectives** Review the Build Background on page 162. Why is it significant that the story events take place on the day that Kennedy was shot? Why do you think Cofer chose "American History" as the story's title?

Literary Skills: Round and Flat Characters

7. **Analyze** Round characters often experience internal conflicts, or struggles. What is Elena's conflict concerning her reaction to the president's death? Does she resolve this conflict at the end of the story? Explain.
8. **Interpret** Although Eugene is a minor, or subordinate, character, he is crucial to the story. What does he represent for Elena?
9. **Analyze** Elena's mother is not essential to the story's plot, but she serves an important purpose. How does she contribute to our understanding of Elena's character and experiences?

Literary Skills Review: Flashback

10. **Analyze** A **flashback** is a scene that interrupts the present action of the plot to show what happened in the past. Find the places in the story where a flashback begins and ends. What purpose(s) does the flashback serve?

Writing Focus

Think as a Reader/Writer

Use It in Your Writing Write a short scene for a story set on the day of a historic event. Before you begin writing, decide which ideas are best conveyed through narration and which through dialogue. How will you let the reader know what has happened?

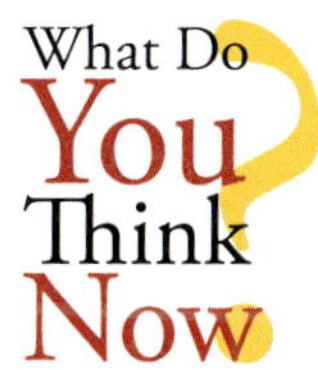

How is Elena affected by Eugene's mother's judgment of her?

Applying Your Skills

American History

Vocabulary Development

Vocabulary Check

Match the Vocabulary word on the left with the correct definition on the right.

1. discreet	**a.** great joy
2. infatuated	**b.** watchful
3. vigilant	**c.** comfort
4. elation	**d.** careful
5. solace	**e.** filled with feelings of love

Vocabulary Skills: Analogies

An **analogy** is two pairs of words that express the same relationship. Follow this example for completing analogies:

TERRIFIED : AFRAID :: hot : ___________

a. cold **b.** warm **c.** dry **d.** thirsty

To figure out the analogy, read the statement above as "*Terrified* is to *afraid* as *hot* is to ___________."

1. The relationship between the first pair of words is one of degree. *Terrified* describes a more intense, overwhelming type of fear than the word *afraid* implies.
2. In the second pair, *hot* refers to having a high temperature. The one word choice that indicates less intense heat is *warm*.

The chart below shows some relationships often used in analogies.

Type of Relationship	Example
Synonyms	HELP : AID :: speak : talk
Degree	PRETTY : BEAUTIFUL :: disappointed : heartbroken
Object (or thing) to a characteristic of it	APPLE : CRISP :: lemon : sour
Cause and effect	COLD : SHIVER :: happiness : smile

Your Turn

Complete each analogy below with the Vocabulary word that fits best.

discreet infatuated vigilant elation solace

1. LABOR : FATIGUE :: victory : ___________
2. CHILLY : FREEZING :: attracted : ___________
3. LOYAL : FAITHFUL :: careful : ___________
4. ARTIST : CREATIVE :: guard : ___________
5. WRITER : AUTHOR :: comfort : ___________

Language Coach

Word Origins Understanding the origin of a word can help you understand word meanings and recognize related words. Match these Vocabulary words with their roots.

1. solace	**a.** Latin *vigilia*, "watch"
2. vigilant	**b.** Latin *solari*, "to comfort"
3. elation	**c.** Latin *efferre*, "to bring out" or "lift up"

Academic Vocabulary

Talk About . . .

With a partner, discuss your responses to the following questions.

1. Which incident in the story did you find most amusing? Which did you find most sad?
2. Which event is more significant to Elena, the assassination of Kennedy or Eugene's mother's treatment of her? How can you tell?

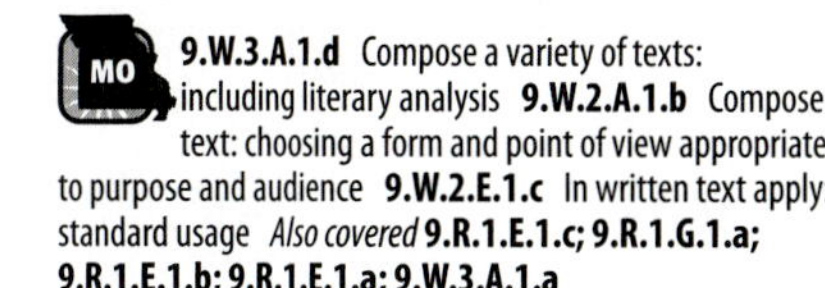

9.W.3.A.1.d Compose a variety of texts: including literary analysis **9.W.2.A.1.b** Compose text: choosing a form and point of view appropriate to purpose and audience **9.W.2.E.1.c** In written text apply: standard usage *Also covered* **9.R.1.E.1.c; 9.R.1.G.1.a; 9.R.1.E.1.b; 9.R.1.E.1.a; 9.W.3.A.1.a**

Grammar Link

Coordinating Conjunctions

A **coordinating conjunction** is a word such as *and, but, for, nor, or, so,* or *yet* that joins words, phrases, or clauses of equal importance. Suppose the following phrases are from notes that Judith Ortiz Cofer prepared:

> Mr. DePalma calls students together. He tells them that Kennedy was shot.

Here is how she puts these notes together in one sentence using coordinating conjunctions:

> The day that Mr. DePalma came out into the cold *and* asked us to line up in front of him was the day that President Kennedy was shot.

Here are two other sentences from "American History" that use coordinating conjunctions. Break these sentences into shorter ones to see how many details the writer combines:

1. "They entered the double ropes in pairs *and* exited without tripping *or* missing a beat."
2. "Her voice was tiny *and* sweet sounding, like a little girl's, *but* her tone was not friendly."

Your Turn

Now, go back to "American History" and find three sentences that contain a coordinating conjunction listed below. Work with a partner to break those sentences into shorter ones. What effect do the combined sentences have on you as a reader?

Coordinating Conjunctions						
and	or	yet	so	for	nor	but

CHOICES

As you respond to the Choices, use these **Academic Vocabulary** words as appropriate: observation, incident, complex, significant.

REVIEW

Conduct an Interview

Imagine that you're interviewing Elena about the events that occurred on the day President Kennedy was shot. With a partner, create a list of questions you could ask to explore Elena's thoughts and feelings. Then, write down the answers you think she would give. Make sure that the answers are consistent with her character and the details in the story.

CONNECT

Write an Essay

Timed Writing Explain the ways in which "American History" is a fictional tale that revolves around a historical incident. Do you find the characters' reactions believable, given the story's setting and historical context? Explain, and support your ideas by citing passages from the text.

EXTEND

Discuss a Different Viewpoint

Group Discussion "American History" presents Eugene through Elena's eyes. He isn't given even one line of dialogue in the story. What would have happened if Cofer had let you know more about him? How would he have seen the events around him? In a small group, discuss how you would turn Eugene into a round character—one with thoughts, feelings, and reactions consistent with what the story already tells you about him.

Learn It Online
Dig deeper into the story using these Internet links:
go.hrw.com
L9-173
Go

SHORT STORY

Preparing to Read

A Christmas Memory

by **Truman Capote**

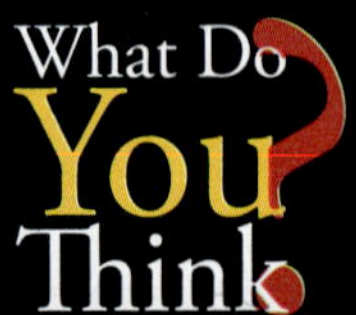

How does having a good friend help you to know yourself better?

QuickWrite

Think of a friendship that helped you learn something about yourself. Perhaps your friend built up your self-confidence. Maybe you discovered that you are more patient—or impatient—than you thought. Write down your ideas about what discoveries you made.

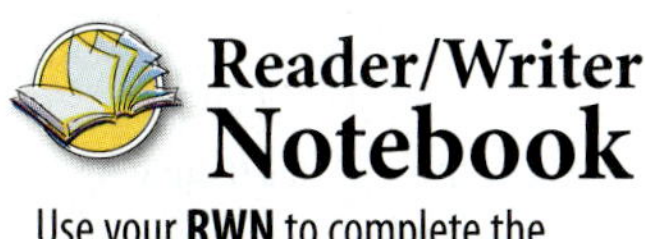

Use your **RWN** to complete the activities for this selection.

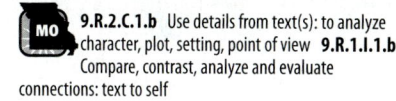

MO **9.R.2.C.1.b** Use details from text(s): to analyze character, plot, setting, point of view **9.R.1.I.1.b** Compare, contrast, analyze and evaluate connections: text to self

Literary Focus

Indirect Characterization Most modern writers avoid direct characterization—they don't *tell* you about their characters' personalities. Instead, they use **indirect characterization** to *show* you the story's characters. In "A Christmas Memory," Truman Capote shares with us his characters' words, actions, and appearance. As you read, pay attention to these character clues to discover for yourself what the characters are like.

Reading Focus

Making Connections to Characters You will understand characters better if you make connections as you read. To do so, ask yourself if the people in the story remind you of yourself or someone else in your life. Also, think about what motivates the characters. Would you ever think or act as they do?

Into Action As you read, record your reactions to the characters by creating a double-entry journal like the one below.

What the Text Says	My Connections
Buddy is seven and lives with his older cousin.	My grandmother lives with us.
Every November, they gather ingredients for fruitcake.	

Writing Focus

Think as a Reader/Writer

Find It in Your Reading Although "A Christmas Memory" is a work of fiction, it was inspired by Truman Capote's own childhood. In your *Reader/Writer Notebook,* write down some precise details Capote uses to describe Buddy's cousin. As you read, think about how those details create a vivid character.

Vocabulary

inhabit (ihn HAB iht) *v.:* live in. *Buddy and his relatives inhabit the same house.*

inaugurating (ihn AW gyuh ray tihng) *v.:* formally beginning. *The November snows seemed to be inaugurating the holiday season.*

dilapidated (duh LAP uh day tihd) *adj.:* shabby; falling apart. *Although the cart was dilapidated, we still managed to use it on our trip to the store.*

disposition (dihs puh ZIHSH uhn) *n.:* usual frame of mind; temperament. *Her tired disposition was obvious from her complete lack of energy.*

noncommittal (nahn kuh MIHT uhl) *adj.:* not agreeing or disagreeing. *Because my friend preferred to be noncommittal, she did not answer the question directly.*

Language Coach

Derivations The word *inhabit* means "to live in." Related words include *habitat,* or a place where an animal or plant grows naturally, and *inhabitable,* meaning "fit to be lived in." What do you think the word *uninhabitable* means?

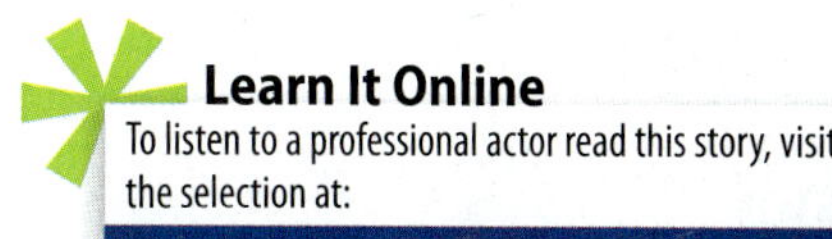

Learn It Online
To listen to a professional actor read this story, visit the selection at:
go.hrw.com
L9-175
Go

MEET THE WRITER

Learn It Online
Get more on the author's life at:
go.hrw.com L9-176 Go

Truman Capote

(1924–1984)

"A Turtle on Its Back"

Truman Capote said he was "sort of dragged up" by assorted relatives in "dirt-road Alabama." His father deserted the family, and the boy was moved from place to place while his mother lived in New York. For several years, Capote attended military schools, which he disliked. When he was seventeen, he abandoned formal schooling and moved to New York City to learn to write. Looking back on his frustrating early years, Capote said he felt "like a turtle on its back."

Combining Fiction and Fact

Capote's first novel, *Other Voices, Other Rooms* (1948), brought him to national prominence. Another of his works was made into a movie, *Breakfast at Tiffany's* (1958), which starred Audrey Hepburn as Holly Golightly, the story's unpredictable heroine. Capote's most famous book, *In Cold Blood* (1965), which has also been adapted for the big screen, is an account of a mass murder that took place in Kansas. Capote researched the book for six years, interviewing survivors, investigators, and the murderers themselves. He called the book a nonfiction novel—it reads like a novel but relates events that are true.

"I always felt that nobody was going to understand me, going to understand what I felt about things. I guess that's why I started writing."

Think About the Writer Why do you think Capote decided to leave the rural life of his youth to live in New York City?

The Granger Collection, New York.

Build Background

Capote spent years living in a remote Alabama home that he later called a very strange household. He said, "It consisted of three elderly ladies and an elderly uncle." He spun details from his life into the tale "A Christmas Memory." He said that this was his only work that "depended on its southern setting. . . . The moment I wrote that story, I knew I would never write another word about the South."

Preview the Selection

"A Christmas Memory" is about two unlikely friends—a seven-year old boy named **Buddy** and his cousin who is more than sixty years old. As you read, think about what this story reveals about the enduring power of love.

Read with a Purpose Read to discover why a young boy and his elderly cousin are best friends.

A Christmas Memory

by **Truman Capote**

Imagine a morning in late November. A coming of winter morning more than twenty years ago. Consider the kitchen of a spreading old house in a country town. A great black stove is its main feature; but there is also a big round table and a fireplace with two rocking chairs placed in front of it. Just today the fireplace commenced its seasonal roar.

A woman with shorn white hair is standing at the kitchen window. She is wearing tennis shoes and a shapeless gray sweater over a summery calico dress. She is small and sprightly, like a bantam hen; but, due to a long youthful illness, her shoulders are pitifully hunched. Her face is remarkable—not unlike Lincoln's, craggy like that, and tinted by sun and wind; but it is delicate too, finely boned, and her eyes are sherry-colored and timid. "Oh my," she exclaims, her breath smoking the windowpane, "it's fruitcake weather!" **A**

The person to whom she is speaking is myself. I am seven; she is sixty-something. We are cousins, very distant ones, and we have lived together—well, as long as I can remember. Other people inhabit the house, relatives; and though they have power over us, and frequently make us cry, we are not, on the whole, too much aware of them. We are each other's best friend. She calls me Buddy, in memory of a boy who was formerly her best friend. The other Buddy died in the 1880s, when she was still a child. She is still a child.

"I knew it before I got out of bed," she says, turning away from the window with a purposeful excitement in her eyes. "The courthouse bell sounded so cold and clear. And there were no birds singing; they've gone to warmer country, yes indeed. Oh, Buddy, stop stuffing biscuit and fetch our buggy. Help me find my hat. We've thirty cakes to bake."

It's always the same: A morning arrives in November, and my friend, as though officially inaugurating the Christmas time of year that exhilarates her imagination and fuels the blaze of her heart, announces: "It's fruitcake weather! Fetch our buggy. Help me find my hat."

The hat is found, a straw cartwheel corsaged with velvet roses out-of-doors has faded; it once belonged to a more fashionable relative. Together, we guide our buggy, a dilapidated baby carriage, out to the garden and into a grove of pecan trees. The buggy is mine; that

A **Literary Focus** **Indirect Characterization** What do you learn about this woman from the way she looks?

Vocabulary **inhabit** (ihn HAB iht) *v.:* live in.
inaugurating (ihn AW gyuh ray tihng) *v.:* formally beginning.
dilapidated (duh LAP uh day tihd) *adj.:* shabby; falling apart.

is, it was bought for me when I was born. It is made of wicker, rather unraveled, and the wheels wobble like a drunkard's legs. But it is a faithful object; springtimes, we take it to the woods and fill it with flowers, herbs, wild fern for our porch pots; in the summer, we pile it with picnic paraphernalia and sugar-cane fishing poles and roll it down to the edge of the creek; it has its winter uses, too: as a truck for hauling firewood from the yard to the kitchen, as a warm bed for Queenie, our tough little orange and white rat terrier who has survived distemper and two rattlesnake bites. Queenie is trotting beside it now.

Three hours later we are back in the kitchen hulling a heaping buggyload of windfall pecans. Our backs hurt from gathering them: How hard they were to find (the main crop having been shaken off the trees and sold by the orchard's owners, who are not us) among the concealing leaves, the frosted, deceiving grass. Caarackle! A cheery crunch, scraps of miniature thunder sound as the shells collapse and the golden mound of sweet, oily, ivory meat mounts in the milk-glass bowl. Queenie begs to taste, and now and again my friend sneaks her a mite, though insisting we deprive ourselves. "We mustn't, Buddy. If we start, we won't stop. And there's scarcely enough as there is. For thirty cakes." The kitchen is growing dark. Dusk turns the window into a mirror: Our reflections mingle with the rising moon as we work by the fireside in the firelight. At last, when the moon is quite high, we toss the final hull into the fire and, with joined sighs, watch it catch flame. The buggy is empty; the bowl is brimful. **B**

We eat our supper (cold biscuits, bacon, blackberry jam) and discuss tomorrow. Tomorrow the kind of work I like best begins: buying. Cherries and citron, ginger and vanilla and canned Hawaiian pineapple, rinds and raisins and walnuts and whiskey and oh, so much flour, butter, so many eggs, spices, flavorings: Why, we'll need a pony to pull the buggy home.

But before these purchases can be made, there is the question of money. Neither of us has any. Except for skinflint sums persons in the house occasionally provide (a dime is considered very big money); or what we earn ourselves from various activities: holding rummage sales, selling buckets of handpicked blackberries, jars of homemade jam and apple jelly and peach preserves, rounding up flowers for funerals and weddings. Once we won seventy-ninth prize, five dollars, in a national football contest. Not that we know a fool thing about football. It's just that we enter any contest we hear about: At the moment our hopes are centered on the fifty-thousand-dollar Grand Prize being offered to name a new brand of coffee (we suggested "A.M."; and, after some hesitation, for my friend thought it perhaps sacrilegious, the slogan "A.M.! Amen!"). To tell the truth, our only *really* profitable enterprise was the Fun and Freak Museum we conducted in a backyard woodshed two summers ago. The Fun was a stereopticon[1] with slide views of Washington and New York lent us by a relative who had been to those places (she was furious when she discovered why we'd borrowed it); the Freak was a three-legged biddy chicken hatched by one of our own hens. Everybody hereabouts wanted to see that biddy: We charged grown-ups a nickel, kids two cents. And took in a good

1. **stereopticon** (stehr ee AHP tuh kuhn): old-fashioned slide projector.

B Reading Focus Making Connections Buddy and his cousin are tired but happy at what they've accomplished. In what way can working together as they do foster a strong friendship?

twenty dollars before the museum shut down due to the decease of the main attraction.

But one way and another we do each year accumulate Christmas savings, a Fruitcake Fund. These moneys we keep hidden in an ancient bead purse under a loose board under the floor under a chamber pot[2] under my friend's bed. The purse is seldom removed from this safe location except to make a deposit, or, as happens every Saturday, a withdrawal; for on Saturdays I am allowed ten cents to go to the picture show. My friend has never been to a picture show, nor does she intend to: "I'd rather hear you tell the story, Buddy. That way I can imagine it more. Besides, a person my age shouldn't squander their eyes. When the Lord comes, let me see Him clear." In addition to never having seen a movie, she has never: eaten in a restaurant, traveled more than five miles from home, received or sent a telegram, read anything except funny papers and the Bible, worn cosmetics, cursed, wished someone harm, told a lie on purpose, let a hungry dog go hungry. Here are a few things she has done, does do: killed with a hoe the biggest rattlesnake ever seen in this county (sixteen rattles), dip snuff[3] (secretly), tame hummingbirds (just try it) till they balance on her finger, tell ghost stories (we both believe in ghosts) so tingling they chill you in July, talk to herself, take walks in the rain, grow the prettiest japonicas in town, know the recipe for every sort of old-time Indian cure, including a magical wart-remover.

Now, with supper finished, we retire to the room in a faraway part of the house where my friend sleeps in a scrap-quilt-covered iron bed

2. **chamber pot:** Before indoor plumbing and toilets, people used pots, usually kept in their bedrooms, or chambers.

3. **snuff:** powdered tobacco inhaled by sniffing.

painted rose pink, her favorite color. Silently, wallowing in the pleasures of conspiracy, we take the bead purse from its secret place and spill its contents on the scrap quilt. Dollar bills, tightly rolled and green as May buds. Somber fifty-cent pieces, heavy enough to weight a dead man's eyes. Lovely dimes, the liveliest coin, the one that really jingles. Nickels and quarters, worn smooth as creek pebbles. But mostly a hateful heap of bitter-odored pennies. Last summer others in the house contracted to pay us a penny for every twenty-five flies we killed. Oh, the carnage of August: the flies that flew to heaven! Yet it was not work in which we took pride. And, as we sit counting pennies, it is as though we were back tabulating dead flies. Neither of us has a head for figures; we count slowly, lose track, start again. According to her calculations, we have $12.73. According to mine, exactly $13. "I do hope you're wrong, Buddy. We can't mess around with thirteen. The cakes will fall. Or put somebody in the cemetery. Why, I wouldn't dream of getting out of bed on the thirteenth." This is true: She always spends thirteenths in bed. So, to be on the safe side, we subtract a penny and toss it out the window. **C**

They call him Haha because he's so gloomy, a man who never laughs.

Of the ingredients that go into our fruitcakes, whiskey is the most expensive, as well as the hardest to obtain: State laws forbid its sale. But everybody knows you can buy a bottle from Mr. Haha Jones. And the next day, having completed our more prosaic shopping, we set out for Mr. Haha's business address, a "sinful" (to quote public opinion) fish-fry and dancing cafe down by the river. We've been there before, and on the same errand; but in previous years our dealings have been with Haha's wife, an iodine-dark Indian woman with brassy peroxided hair and a dead-tired disposition. Actually, we've never laid eyes on her husband, though we've heard that he's an Indian too. A giant with razor scars across his cheeks. They call him Haha because he's so gloomy, a man who never laughs. As we approach his cafe (a large log cabin festooned inside and out with chains of garish-gay naked light bulbs and standing by the river's muddy edge under the shade of river trees where moss drifts through the branches like gray mist) our steps slow down. Even Queenie stops prancing and sticks close by. People have been murdered in Haha's cafe. Cut to pieces. Hit on the head. There's a case coming up in court next month. Naturally these goings-on happen at night when the colored lights cast crazy patterns and the Victrola[4] wails. In the daytime Haha's is shabby and deserted. I knock at the door, Queenie barks, my friend calls: "Mrs. Haha, ma'am? Anyone to home?"

Footsteps. The door opens. Our hearts overturn. It's Mr. Haha Jones himself! And he *is* a giant; he *does* have scars; he *doesn't* smile. No, he glowers at us through Satan-tilted eyes and demands to know: "What you want with Haha?"

For a moment we are too paralyzed to tell. Presently my friend half finds her voice,

4. **Victrola:** old term for record player.

C Reading Focus Making Connections Do you know of anyone who avoids the number thirteen, as Buddy's cousin does? What do Buddy's cousin's superstitions reveal about her?

Vocabulary disposition (dihs puh ZIHSH uhn) *n.:* usual frame of mind; temperament.

HISTORY LINK

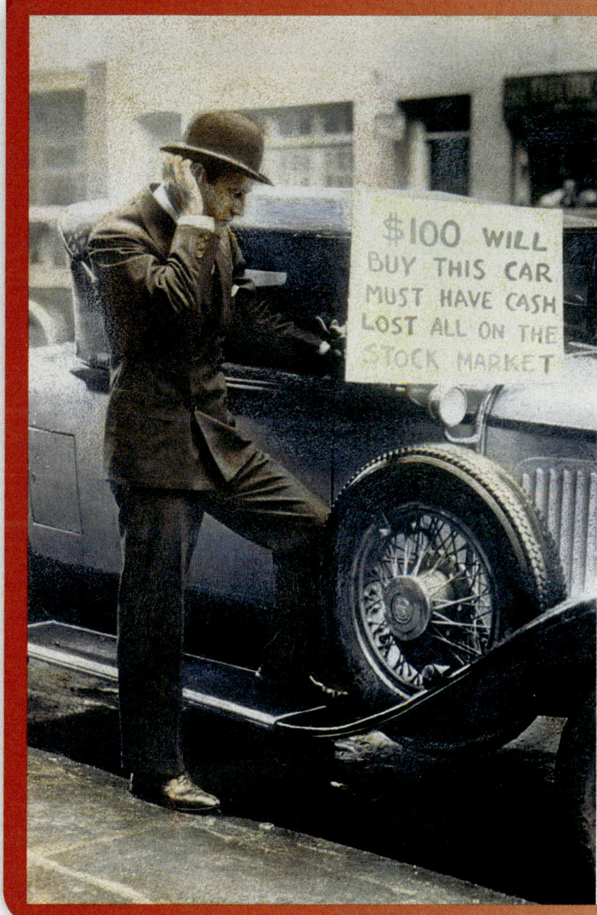

The Granger Collection, New York.

The Great Depression

In the 1920s, the U.S. stock market and businesses were booming. Americans felt confident about their financial futures and purchased appliances, cars, and other items on credit, which the government encouraged in order to keep interest rates low. Borrowing promoted new businesses and allowed consumers to buy goods without having the cash to pay for them.

The increase in borrowing made investors nervous and put a strain on the financial markets. On October 29, 1929, the U.S. stock market crashed. That day became known as Black Tuesday, and it triggered the Great Depression, which placed a tremendous burden on Americans. Businesses closed, and work was nearly impossible to find. Borrowers defaulted on loans, resulting in bank closures; between 1930 and 1932, more than 3,000 banks closed. Families had to take in relatives and stretch what little money they had.

Ask Yourself

What details in the story provide clues that it takes place during the Great Depression?

a whispery voice at best: "If you please, Mr. Haha, we'd like a quart of your finest whiskey."

His eyes tilt more. Would you believe it? Haha is smiling! Laughing, too. "Which one of you is a drinkin' man?"

"It's for making fruitcakes, Mr. Haha. Cooking."

This sobers him. He frowns. "That's no way to waste good whiskey." Nevertheless, he retreats into the shadowed cafe and seconds later appears carrying a bottle of daisy-yellow unlabeled liquor. He demonstrates its sparkle in the sunlight and says: "Two dollars."

We pay him with nickels and dimes and pennies. Suddenly, jangling the coins in his hand like a fistful of dice, his face softens. "Tell you what," he proposes, pouring the money back into our bead purse, "just send me one of them fruitcakes instead." D

"Well," my friend remarks on our way home, "there's a lovely man. We'll put an extra cup of raisins in *his* cake."

The black stove, stoked with coal and firewood, glows like a lighted pumpkin. Eggbeaters

---

D **Literary Focus** **Indirect Characterization** The narrator describes Mr. Haha as gloomy. How do Mr. Haha's words and actions prove this characterization wrong?

whirl, spoons spin round in bowls of butter and sugar, vanilla sweetens the air, ginger spices it; melting, nose-tingling odors saturate the kitchen, suffuse the house, drift out to the world on puffs of chimney smoke. In four days our work is done. Thirty-one cakes, dampened with whiskey, bask on window sills and shelves.

Who are they for?

Friends. Not necessarily neighbor friends: Indeed, the larger share are intended for persons we've met maybe once, perhaps not at all. People who've struck our fancy. Like President Roosevelt. Like the Reverend and Mrs. J. C. Lucey, Baptist missionaries to Borneo who lectured here last winter. Or the little knife grinder who comes through town twice a year. Or Abner Packer, the driver of the six o'clock bus from Mobile, who exchanges waves with us every day as he passes in a dust-cloud whoosh. Or the young Wistons, a California couple whose car one afternoon broke down outside the house and who spent a pleasant hour chatting with us on the porch (young Mr. Wiston snapped our picture, the only one we've ever had taken). Is it because my friend is shy with everyone *except* strangers that these strangers, and merest acquaintances, seem to us our truest friends? I think yes. Also, the scrapbooks we keep of thank-you's on White House stationery, time-to-time communications from California and Borneo, the knife grinder's penny postcards, make us feel connected to eventful worlds beyond the kitchen with its views of a sky that stops.

Now a nude December fig branch grates against the window. The kitchen is empty, the cakes are gone; yesterday we carted the last of them to the post office, where the cost of stamps turned our purse inside out. We're broke. That rather depresses me, but my friend insists on celebrating—with two inches of whiskey left in Haha's bottle. Queenie has a spoonful in a bowl of coffee (she likes her coffee chicory-flavored and strong). The rest we divide between a pair of jelly glasses. We're both quite awed at the prospect of drinking straight whiskey; the taste of it brings screwed-up expressions and sour shudders. But by and by we begin to sing, the two of us singing different songs simultaneously. I don't know the words to mine, just: *Come on along, come on along, to the dark-town strutters' ball.* But I can dance: That's what I mean to be, a tap-dancer in the movies. My dancing shadow rollicks on the walls; our voices rock the chinaware; we giggle as if unseen hands were tickling us. Queenie rolls on her back, her paws plow the air, something like a grin stretches her black lips. Inside myself, I feel warm and sparky as those crumbling logs, carefree as the wind in the chimney. My friend waltzes round the stove, the hem of her poor calico skirt pinched between her fingers as though it were a party dress: *Show me the way to go home,* she sings, her tennis shoes squeaking on the floor. *Show me the way to go home.*

Enter: two relatives. Very angry. Potent with eyes that scold, tongues that scald. Listen to what they have to say, the words tumbling together into a wrathful tune: "A child of seven! whiskey on his breath! are you out of your mind? feeding a child of seven! must be loony! road to ruination! remember Cousin Kate? Uncle Charlie? Uncle Charlie's brother-in-law? shame! scandal! humiliation! kneel, pray, beg the Lord!"

Queenie sneaks under the stove. My friend gazes at her shoes, her chin quivers, she lifts her skirt and blows her nose and runs to her room. Long after the town has gone to sleep and the house is silent except for the chimings of clocks and the sputter of fading fires, she is weeping into a pillow already as wet as a widow's handkerchief. **E**

"Don't cry," I say, sitting at the bottom of her bed and shivering despite my flannel nightgown that smells of last winter's cough syrup, "don't cry," I beg, teasing her toes, tickling her feet, "you're too old for that."

"It's because," she hiccups, "I *am* too old. Old and funny."

"Not funny. Fun. More fun than anybody. Listen. If you don't stop crying you'll be so tired tomorrow we can't go cut a tree."

She straightens up. Queenie jumps on the bed (where Queenie is not allowed) to lick her cheeks. "I know where we'll find real pretty trees, Buddy. And holly, too. With berries big as your eyes. It's way off in the woods. Farther than we've ever been. Papa used to bring us Christmas trees from there: carry them on his shoulder. That's fifty years ago. Well, now: I can't wait for morning."

Morning. Frozen rime[5] lusters the grass; the sun, round as an orange and orange as hot-weather moons, balances on the horizon, burnishes the silvered winter woods. A wild turkey calls. A renegade hog grunts in the undergrowth. Soon, by the edge of knee-deep, rapid-running water, we have to abandon the buggy. Queenie wades the stream first, paddles across, barking complaints at the swiftness of the current, the pneumonia-making coldness of it. We follow, holding our shoes and equipment (a hatchet, a burlap sack) above our heads. A mile more: of chastising thorns, burs and briers that catch at our clothes; of rusty pine needles brilliant with gaudy fungus and molted feathers. Here, there, a flash, a flutter, an ecstasy of shrillings remind us that not all the birds have flown south. Always, the path unwinds through lemony sun pools and pitch vine tunnels. Another creek to cross: A disturbed armada[6] of speckled trout froths the water round us, and frogs the size of plates practice belly flops; beaver workmen are building

5. **rime** (rym): frost.
6. **armada** (ahr MAH duh): group, as of warships.

E Literary Focus Indirect Characterization How does Buddy's friend react to the other relatives? What details does Capote include to characterize her?

a dam. On the farther shore, Queenie shakes herself and trembles. My friend shivers, too: not with cold but enthusiasm. One of her hat's ragged roses sheds a petal as she lifts her head and inhales the pine-heavy air. "We're almost there; can you smell it, Buddy?" she says, as though we were approaching an ocean.

And, indeed, it is a kind of ocean. Scented acres of holiday trees, prickly-leafed holly. Red berries shiny as Chinese bells: Black crows swoop upon them screaming. Having stuffed our burlap sacks with enough greenery and crimson to garland a dozen windows, we set about choosing a tree. "It should be," muses my friend, "twice as tall as a boy. So a boy can't steal the star." The one we pick is twice as tall as me. A brave, handsome brute that survives thirty hatchet strokes before it keels with a creaking, rending cry. Lugging it like a kill, we commence the long trek out. Every few yards we abandon the struggle, sit down, and pant. But we have the strength of triumphant huntsmen; that and the tree's virile, icy perfume revive us, goad us on. Many compliments accompany our sunset return along the red clay road to town; but my friend is sly and noncommittal when passersby praise the treasure perched in our buggy: What a fine tree and where did it come from? "Yonderways," she murmurs vaguely. Once a car stops and the rich mill owner's lazy wife leans out and whines: "Giveya twobits cash for that ol tree." Ordinarily my friend is afraid of saying no; but on this occasion she promptly shakes her head: "We wouldn't take a dollar." The mill owner's wife persists. "A dollar, my foot! Fifty cents. That's my last offer. Goodness, woman, you can get another one." In answer, my friend gently reflects: "I doubt it. There's never two of anything." F

Home: Queenie slumps by the fire and sleeps till tomorrow, snoring loud as a human.

A trunk in the attic contains: a shoe box of ermine tails[7] (off the opera cape of a curious lady who once rented a room in the house), coils of frazzled tinsel gone gold with age, one silver star, a brief rope of dilapidated, undoubtedly dangerous candylike light bulbs. Excellent decorations, as far as they go, which isn't far enough: My friend wants our tree to blaze "like a Baptist window," droop with weighty snows of ornament. But we can't afford the made-in-Japan splendors at the five-and-dime. So we do what we've always done: sit for days at the kitchen table with scissors and crayons and stacks of colored paper. I make sketches and my friend cuts them out: lots of cats, fish too (because they're easy to draw), some apples, some watermelons, a few winged angels devised from saved-up sheets of Hershey-bar tinfoil. We use safety pins to attach these creations to the tree; as a final touch, we sprinkle the branches with shredded cotton (picked in August for this purpose). My friend, surveying the effect, clasps her hands together. "Now honest, Buddy. Doesn't it look good enough to eat?" Queenie tries to eat an angel.

After weaving and ribboning holly wreaths for all the front windows, our next project is the fashioning of family gifts. Tie-dye scarves for the ladies, for the men a home-brewed lemon and licorice and aspirin syrup to be taken "at the first Symptoms of a Cold and after Hunting." But when it comes time for making each other's gift, my friend and I separate to work secretly. I would like to buy her a pearl-handled knife,

7. **ermine** (UR muhn) **tails:** black-tipped white tails of certain kinds of weasels, used to trim clothes.

F **Literary Focus** **Indirect Characterization** What do you learn about Buddy's cousin from her response to the rich mill owner's wife?

Vocabulary **noncommittal** (nahn kuh MIHT uhl) *adj.:* not agreeing or disagreeing.

a radio, a whole pound of chocolate-covered cherries (we tasted some once and she always swears: "I could live on them, Buddy, Lord yes I could—and that's not taking His name in vain"). Instead, I am building her a kite. She would like to give me a bicycle (she's said so on several million occasions: "If only I could, Buddy. It's bad enough in life to do without something *you* want; but confound it, what gets my goat is not being able to give somebody something you want *them* to have. Only one of these days, I will, Buddy. Locate you a bike. Don't ask how. Steal it, maybe"). Instead, I'm fairly certain that she is building me a kite—the same as last year, and the year before: The year before that we exchanged slingshots. All of which is fine by me. For we are champion kite-fliers who study the wind like sailors; my friend, more accomplished than I, can get a kite aloft when there isn't enough breeze to carry clouds. G

"I guess I hate to see you grow up. When you're grown up, will we still be friends?"

Christmas Eve afternoon we scrape together a nickel and go to the butcher's to buy Queenie's traditional gift, a good gnawable beef bone. The bone, wrapped in funny paper, is placed high in the tree near the silver star. Queenie knows it's there. She squats at the foot of the tree, staring up in a trance of greed: When bedtime arrives she refuses to budge. Her excitement is equaled by my own. I kick the covers and turn my pillow as though it were a scorching summer's night. Somewhere a rooster crows: falsely, for the sun is still on the other side of the world.

"Buddy, are you awake?" It is my friend, calling from her room, which is next to mine; and an instant later she is sitting on my bed holding a candle. "Well, I can't sleep a hoot," she declares. "My mind's jumping like a jack rabbit. Buddy, do you think Mrs. Roosevelt will serve our cake at dinner?" We huddle in the bed, and she squeezes my hand I-love-you. "Seems like your hand used to be so much smaller. I guess I hate to see you grow up. When you're grown up, will we still be friends?" I say always. "But I feel so bad, Buddy. I wanted so bad to give you a bike. I tried to sell my cameo Papa gave me. Buddy—" she hesitates, as though embarrassed. "I made you another kite." Then I confess that I made her one, too; and we laugh. The candle burns too short to hold. Out it goes, exposing the starlight, the stars spinning at the window like a visible caroling that slowly, slowly daybreak silences. Possibly we doze; but the beginnings of dawn splash us like cold water: We're up, wide-eyed and wandering while we wait for others to waken. Quite deliberately my friend drops a kettle on the kitchen floor. I tap-dance in front of closed doors. One by one the household emerges, looking as though they'd like to kill us both; but it's Christmas, so they can't. First, a gorgeous breakfast: just everything you can imagine—from flapjacks and fried squirrel to hominy grits and honey-in-the-comb. Which puts everyone in a good humor except my friend and me. Frankly, we're so impatient to get at the presents we can't eat a mouthful. H

Well, I'm disappointed. Who wouldn't be? With socks, a Sunday school shirt, some

---

G Reading Focus Making Connections Buddy and his cousin make each other presents for Christmas. What do you think motivates them to do so?

H Literary Focus Indirect Characterization How do Buddy and his cousin's actions on Christmas morning reflect their different personalities?

handkerchiefs, a hand-me-down sweater, and a year's subscription to a religious magazine for children, *The Little Shepherd*. It makes me boil. It really does.

My friend has a better haul. A sack of satsumas,[8] that's her best present. She is proudest, however, of a white wool shawl knitted by her married sister. But she *says* her favorite gift is the kite I built her. And it *is* very beautiful; though not as beautiful as the one she made me, which is blue and scattered with gold and green Good Conduct stars; moreover, my name is painted on it, "Buddy."

"Buddy, the wind is blowing."

The wind is blowing, and nothing will do till we've run to a pasture below the house where Queenie has scooted to bury her bone (and where, a winter hence, Queenie will be bur-

8. **satsumas** (sat SOO muhz): oranges.

Analyzing Visuals **Viewing and Interpreting** Buddy and his cousin are perfectly content and happy to be together. How does the photo below convey that feeling?

ied, too). There, plunging through the healthy, waist-high grass, we unreel our kites, feel them twitching at the string like sky fish as they swim into the wind. Satisfied, sun-warmed, we sprawl in the grass and peel satsumas and watch our kites cavort. Soon I forget the socks and hand-me-down sweater. I'm as happy as if we'd already won the fifty-thousand-dollar Grand Prize in that coffee-naming contest.

"My, how foolish I am!" my friend cries, suddenly alert, like a woman remembering too late she has biscuits in the oven. "You know what I've always thought?" she asks in a tone of discovery, and smiling not at me but a point beyond. "I've always thought a body would have to be sick and dying before they saw the Lord. And I imagined that when He came it would be like looking at the Baptist window: pretty as colored glass with the sun pouring through, such a shine you don't know it's getting dark. And it's been a comfort: to think of that shine taking away all the spooky feeling. But I'll wager it never happens. I'll wager at the very end a body realizes the Lord has already shown Himself. That things as they are"—her hand circles in a gesture that gathers clouds and kites and grass and Queenie pawing earth over her bone—"just what they've always seen, was seeing Him. As for me, I could leave the world with today in my eyes."

This is our last Christmas together.

Life separates us. Those who Know Best decide that I belong in a military school. And so follows a miserable succession of bugle-blowing prisons, grim reveille-ridden[9] summer camps. I have a new home too. But it doesn't count. Home is where my friend is, and there I never go.

And there she remains, puttering around the kitchen. Alone with Queenie. Then alone. ("Buddy dear," she writes in her wild hard-to-read script, "yesterday Jim Macy's horse kicked Queenie bad. Be thankful she didn't feel much. I wrapped her in a Fine Linen sheet and rode her in the buggy down to Simpson's pasture

9. **reveille-ridden** (REHV uh lee RIHD uhn): ruled by the drum or bugle signal used to wake sleeping people in a military or summer camp. The writer uses this phrase to suggest a tightly disciplined camp.

where she can be with all her Bones. . . .") For a few Novembers she continues to bake her fruitcakes single-handed; not as many, but some: And, of course, she always sends me "the best of the batch." Also, in every letter she encloses a dime wadded in toilet paper: "See a picture show and write me the story." But gradually in her letters she tends to confuse me with her other friend, the Buddy who died in the 1880s; more and more, thirteenths are not the only days she stays in bed: A morning arrives in November, a leafless birdless coming of winter morning, when she cannot rouse herself to exclaim: "Oh my, it's fruitcake weather!"

And when that happens, I know it. A message saying so merely confirms a piece of news some secret vein had already received, severing from me an irreplaceable part of myself, letting it loose like a kite on a broken string. That is why, walking across a school campus on this particular December morning, I keep searching the sky. As if I expected to see, rather like hearts, a lost pair of kites hurrying toward heaven. **I**

I **Literary Focus** **Indirect Characterization** What do Buddy's memories of his cousin reveal about him?

Applying Your Skills

9.R.2.C.1.b Use details from text(s): to analyze character, plot, setting, point of view **9.R.2.C.1.d** Use details from text(s): to evaluate the effect of author's style **9.R.1.I.1.b** Compare, contrast, analyze and evaluate connections: text to self *Also covered* **9.W.3.A.1.a; 9.R.1.G.1.a**

A Christmas Memory

Respond and Think Critically

Reading Focus

Quick Check

1. What obstacles must Buddy and his cousin overcome to make their gifts?
2. What does Buddy's friend discover after flying her kite on Christmas Day?

Read with a Purpose

3. What do Buddy and his cousin give to each other, and what do they get in return?

Reading Skills: Making Connections

Review the connections chart you began on page 175, and answer the following questions.

4. Which character, Buddy or his cousin, do you connect with more? Why?
5. Which story events could you connect with a situation from real life? Explain.

Vocabulary Check

Match each Vocabulary word with its definition.

6. **inhabit** — a. state of mind
7. **dilapidated** — b. marking a beginning
8. **inaugurating** — c. not agreeing or disagreeing
9. **disposition** — d. live in
10. **noncommittal** — e. shabby; run down

Literary Focus

Literary Analysis

11. **Interpret** Which details in the description of Mr. Haha's cafe make it seem threatening?
12. **Interpret** Re-read the last paragraph of the story. What do kites represent for Buddy? What does the final image suggest about how Buddy feels about his friend's death?

Literary Skills: Indirect Characterization

13. **Analyze** How is indirect characterization used to show what Buddy is like? Give examples.
14. **Evaluate** Do you think Capote's indirect portrait of Buddy's cousin is more effective than a direct description? Explain, using details from the story. Use the chart below to gather details.

Buddy's Cousin	Examples
What she says	
How she is described	
What she does	
How others respond to her	

Literary Skills Review: Mood

15. **Interpret** Look carefully at the sensory details in Capote's descriptions of the kitchen. What **mood**—or feeling—do these details convey?

Writing Focus

Think as a Reader/Writer

Use It in Your Writing Choose an important person from your own life, and write a short description of him or her. Like Capote, choose precise details to make that person come to life for the reader.

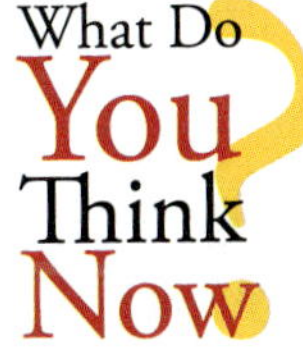

What does Buddy learn about himself as a result of his friendship with his cousin?

Comparing Characters

CONTENTS

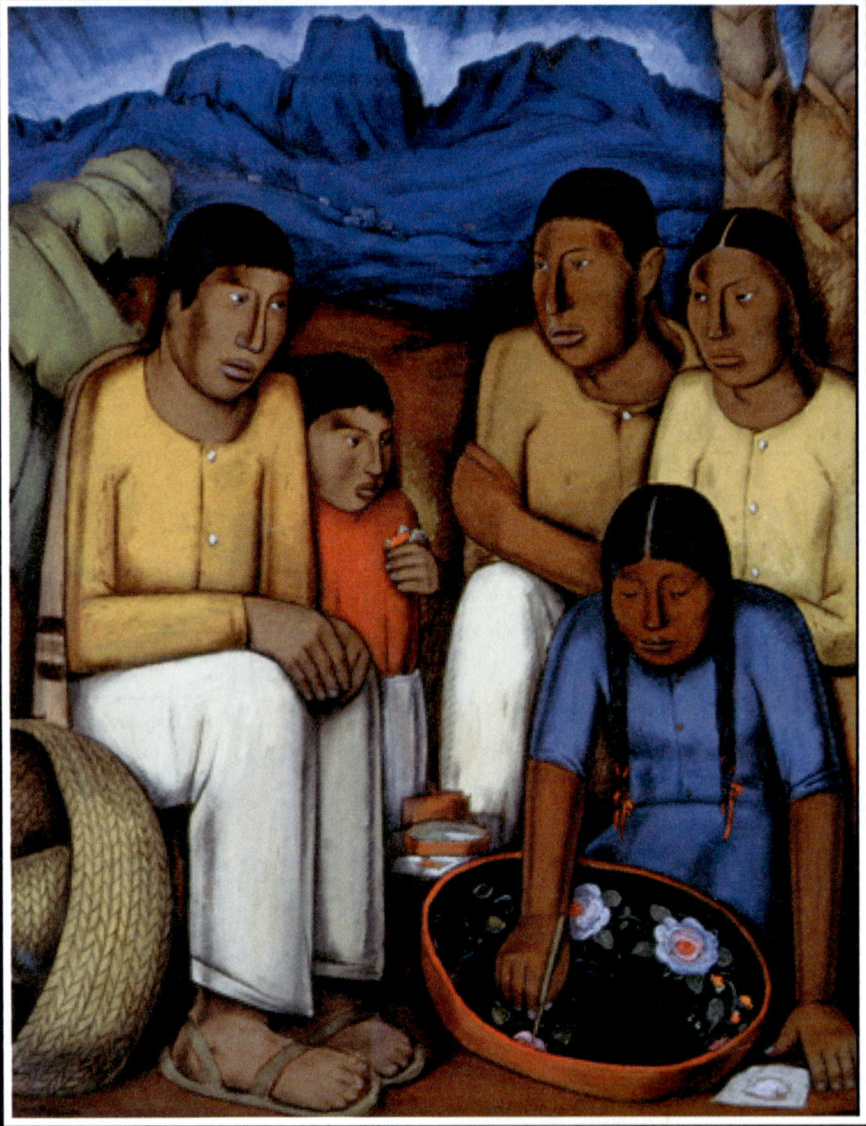

The Painter from Uruapan (La Pintora de Uruapan) by Alfredo Ramos Martinez (1872–1946) © Alfredo Ramos Martinez Research Project, reproduced by permission.

What Do You Think?

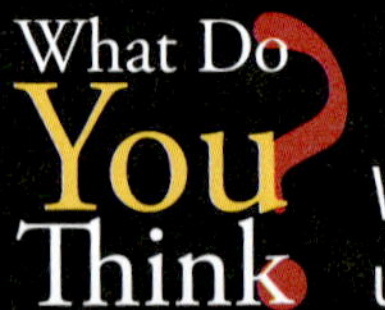

What do the people around us teach us about life?

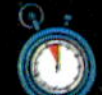

QuickWrite

Think of an influential person who helps others see things in a new way. Describe that person and the ways he or she shares life lessons with others—maybe even with you.

Preparing to Read

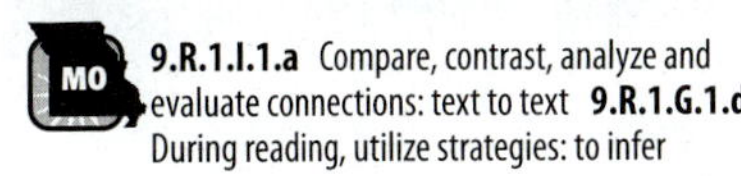

9.R.1.I.1.a Compare, contrast, analyze and evaluate connections: text to text **9.R.1.G.1.d** During reading, utilize strategies: to infer

Papa Who Wakes Up Tired in the Dark / Mother to Son / Those Winter Sundays

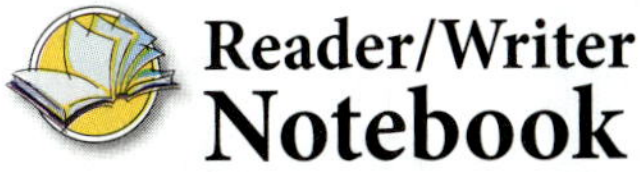

Use your **RWN** to complete the activities for these selections.

Literary Focus

Characters Across Genres Stories, plays, poems, and many types of nonfiction revolve around characters—real or imagined. Skillful writers develop their characters in such a way that we can hear the characters speak and observe how they act in and react to the world that surrounds them. As you read the story and poems that follow, look for ways in which the characters are developed.

Reading Focus

Making Inferences In these short works, the writers supply a few key details about the characters. Combine these clues with what you already know from life to make inferences about the characters.

Into Action To make inferences about the characters, try using a chart like this one. Record as many significant details as you can.

Title of Work	Character Details	What I Know	My Inference
"Papa Who Wakes Up Tired in the Dark"	Papa "wakes up tired in the dark."	I'm tired if I don't get enough sleep.	Papa can't sleep. Could he be worried?
"Mother to Son"			
"Those Winter Sundays"			

Writing Focus

Think as a Reader/Writer

Find It in Your Reading These writers use different writing styles to bring their characters to life. Note in your *Reader/Writer Notebook* the use of contractions in each piece, such as *can't* and *you're.* Which writer avoids contractions? Which uses nonstandard contractions? What effect do the writers' choices have on your reading experience?

Vocabulary

Those Winter Sundays

chronic (KRAHN ihk) *adj.:* constant. *The poem's speaker disliked the chronic cold of his childhood home.*

indifferently (ihn DIHF uhr uhnt lee) *adv.:* in an uncaring way. *The speaker speaks indifferently about his father's actions.*

austere (aw STIHR) *adj.:* sober; solemn. *The speaker did not understand his father's austere love.*

Language Coach

Prefixes The adjective *different* means "not the same." Adding the prefix *in–* to that word makes a word that means "the same" or "unmoved." Someone who is indifferent does not care about or is unmoved by a situation. How would someone who responds indifferently to a plea for help react? Check the definition above if you need help.

MEET THE WRITERS

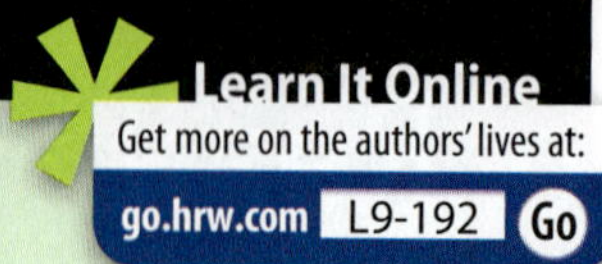

Learn It Online
Get more on the authors' lives at:
go.hrw.com L9-192 Go

Sandra Cisneros

(1954–)

Sandra Cisneros grew up as the only daughter in a family with seven children. Her father believed that daughters should worry only about getting husbands. Cisneros struggled in school, but a teacher encouraged her to write; and after graduating from college and earning her master's degree, Cisneros wrote *The House on Mango Street,* the book for which she is best known. Cisneros eventually showed her father one of her stories that had been translated into Spanish. He was so thrilled that he asked, "Where can we get more copies of this for the relatives?"

Langston Hughes

(1902–1967)

For biographical information about Langston Hughes, see page 136.

Robert Hayden

(1913–1980)

Originally named Asa Bundy Sheffey, Robert Hayden was passed between his parents and foster parents, who eventually changed Sheffey's name to their own. Hayden's bad eyesight kept him from participating in sports, and he turned to books instead. As a young adult, Hayden joined the Federal Writers' Project, a government program supplying jobs to out-of-work writers during the Great Depression. In the years he worked for the project, Hayden researched the historical roots of the Underground Railroad in Michigan and other aspects of African American history.

Think About the Writers

What obstacles did these writers need to overcome in their efforts to be accepted and successful?

Preview the Selections

In these three short works, you'll meet three very different narrators and the important people in their lives.

SHORT STORY

Papa Who Wakes Up Tired in the Dark

by **Sandra Cisneros**

Read with a Purpose

Read this story to find out how the death of a beloved grandfather affects the narrator's father.

Build Background

In Cisneros's short story "Papa Who Wakes Up Tired in the Dark," the narrator describes how her father deals with his own father's death. The story appears simple, but the rich language gives it a striking impact.

Young Man Desires Position (c. 1930) by Gordon Samstag (1906–1990). Oil on canvas (50 ¼" x 47 ¼"). Sheldon Swope Art Museum, Terre Haute, Indiana (1944.08).

Your *abuelito*[1] is dead, Papa says early one morning in my room. *Está muerto,*[2] and then as if he just heard the news himself, crumples like a coat and cries, my brave Papa cries. I have never seen my Papa cry and don't know what to do. **A**

I know he will have to go away, that he will take a plane to Mexico, all the uncles and aunts will be there, and they will have a black-and-white photo taken in front of the tomb with flowers shaped like spears in a white vase because this is how they send the dead away in that country.

Because I am the oldest, my father has told me first, and now it is my turn to tell the others. I will have to explain why we can't play. I will have to tell them to be quiet today.

My Papa, his thick hands and thick shoes, who wakes up tired in the dark, who combs his hair with water, drinks his coffee, and is gone before we wake, today is sitting on my bed. **B**

And I think if my own Papa died what would I do. I hold my Papa in my arms. I hold and hold and hold him.

1. ***abuelito*** (ah bwehl EE toh): Spanish for "grandpa."
2. ***Está muerto*** (ehs TAH MWEHR toh): Spanish for "He is dead."

A **Reading Focus** **Making Inferences** The narrator says she has never seen her Papa cry. What might that detail lead you to infer about his character?

B **Literary Focus** **Character** What do these details tell you about Papa?

POEM

Mother to Son

by **Langston Hughes**

Read with a Purpose

Read this poem to find out what advice the speaker has for her son.

Preparing to Read for this selection is on page 191.

Build Background

In Hughes's poem "Mother to Son," a mother is talking to her son. The poem is an example of a **dramatic monologue,** a poem in which a speaker addresses one or more silent listeners. During the course of a dramatic monologue, the speaker reveals important thoughts and feelings.

Well, son, I'll tell you:
Life for me ain't been no crystal stair.
It's had tacks in it,
And splinters,
And boards torn up,
And places with no carpet on the floor—
Bare. **A**
But all the time
I'se been a-climbin' on,
And reachin' landin's,
And turnin' corners,
And sometimes goin' in the dark
Where there ain't been no light.
So boy, don't you turn back.
Don't you set down on the steps
'Cause you finds it's kinder hard.
Don't you fall now—
For I'se still goin', honey,
I'se still climbin',
And life for me ain't been no crystal stair. **B**

Proletarian (1934) by Gordon Samstag (1906–1990). Oil on canvas (48 5/16" x 42"). The Toledo Museum of Art, Toledo, Ohio. Museum Purchase Fund (1935.34).

A **Literary Focus** **Character** What do the speaker's words tell you about her?

B **Reading Focus** **Making Inferences** The character is speaking to her son—perhaps responding to a question he asked her. What is the speaker's message to her son? What does she want him to do?

POEM

Those Winter Sundays

by **Robert Hayden**

Read with a Purpose

As you read, think about the relationship between the speaker and his father.

Preparing to Read for this selection is on page 191.

Build Background

In Hayden's poem "Those Winter Sundays," a son remembers his father. Notice how his father communicates in gestures rather than words.

Sundays too my father got up early
and put his clothes on in the blueblack cold,
then with cracked hands that ached
from labor in the weekday weather made
banked fires blaze. No one ever
thanked him. **A**

I'd wake and hear the cold splintering,
breaking.
When the rooms were warm, he'd call, **B**
and slowly I would rise and dress,
fearing the chronic angers of that house,

Speaking indifferently to him,
who had driven out the cold
and polished my good shoes as well.
What did I know, what did I know
of love's austere and lonely offices?

The Guardian by Ben Watson III. Watercolor. Private collection.

A **Literary Focus** **Character** What do these details reveal about the father?

B **Reading Focus** **Making Inferences** Why does the father wait until the rooms are warm to call his son?

Vocabulary **chronic** (KRAHN ihk) *adj.:* constant.
indifferently (ihn DIHF uhr uhnt lee) *adv.:* in an uncaring way.
austere (aw STIHR) *adj.:* sober; solemn.

Applying Your Skills

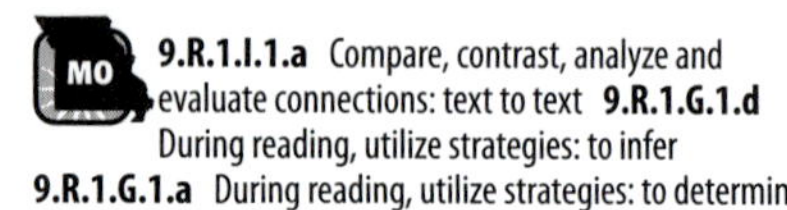

9.R.1.I.1.a Compare, contrast, analyze and evaluate connections: text to text **9.R.1.G.1.d** During reading, utilize strategies: to infer **9.R.1.G.1.a** During reading, utilize strategies: to determine meaning of unknown words

Papa Who Wakes Up Tired in the Dark / Mother to Son / Those Winter Sundays

Respond and Think Critically

Reading Focus

Quick Check

1. In "Papa Who Wakes Up Tired in the Dark," why must the narrator give the news to her family?
2. What does the speaker say her life has *not* been in "Mother to Son"?
3. In "Those Winter Sundays," what does the father get up early to do? Why?

Read with a Purpose

4. How is the father affected by the death of his father in "Papa Who Wakes Up . . ."?
5. What advice does the speaker in "Mother to Son" give to her son?
6. Describe the relationship between the speaker and his father in "Those Winter Sundays."

Reading Skills: Making Inferences

7. Review the inference chart that you created (see page 191). What similarities and differences among the characters were you able to infer? Cite details from the texts to support your ideas.

Vocabulary Check

Match each Vocabulary word to its definition.

8. **chronic** — a. solemn
9. **austere** — b. uncaringly
10. **indifferently** — c. constant

Literary Focus

Literary Analysis

11. **Analyze** At the end of both "Papa Who Wakes Up . . ." and "Those Winter Sundays," how do the children feel about their fathers? In "Mother to Son," how does the mother feel about her son?
12. **Interpret** What does the speaker of "Mother to Son" mean when she says life hasn't been "no crystal stair"?

Literary Skills: Characters Across Genres

13. **Compare and Contrast** Describe the narrator of "Papa Who Wakes Up . . ." and the speaker of "Those Winter Sundays." How are they similar or different?
14. **Analyze** In "Papa Who Wakes Up . . . ," the narrator's father cries in front of her for the first time. What does this tell you about him? What does the narrator learn about her father as a result?
15. **Analyze** In "Mother to Son," the mother speaks in **dialect,** a way of speaking that is particular to a region. Examples of dialect she uses are "a-climbin'" and "kinder hard." How do the mother's words help reveal her character?

Writing Focus

Think as a Reader/Writer

Use It in Your Writing In your *Reader/Writer Notebook,* you took notes about the ways in which these writers brought their characters to life. Choose one selection to imitate in style, and write a poem or a story in which you use descriptive details and dialogue to characterize the narrator or speaker.

COMPARING TEXTS
Wrap Up

MO **9.R.1.I.1.a** Compare, contrast, analyze and evaluate connections: text to text **9.W.3.A.1.a** Compose a variety of texts: using narrative, descriptive, expository, and/or persuasive features

Papa Who Wakes Up Tired in the Dark / Mother to Son / Those Winter Sundays

Writing Focus

Writing a Comparison-Contrast Essay

Now that you have read "Papa Who Wakes Up Tired in the Dark," "Mother to Son," and "Those Winter Sundays," write a comparison-and-contrast essay in which you tell about similarities (comparisons) and differences (contrasts) between the works.

Gather and Organize Your Ideas

All of the selections you have just read focus on the relationship between a parent and a child. However, each parent is characterized differently. To organize your ideas for this essay, fill out a chart like this one:

	"Papa Who . . ."	"Mother to Son"	"Those Winter Sundays"
Narrator or Speaker	The story is told by young girl.	The mother is the speaker.	
Characters We Learn About	Papa	Mother	Father
Methods of Characterization			

Use Three-Part Structure Most essays have three basic parts: **(1)** Your essay's introduction tells the reader what works you will compare, including titles, authors, and background information. The introduction should end with a thesis statement in which you state how the works are similar or different. **(2)** The body of your essay consists of paragraphs supporting your thesis statement with evidence from the works—the information listed in your chart. **(3)** Your conclusion sums up your major points and ends with a new (but related) thought.

Use the Block Method Comparison-and-contrast essays can be organized by the point-by-point method or the block method. You'll use the block method to write this essay.

When you use the **block method,** you discuss the works one at a time. First, write about the elements of one work in the order you think is most effective. Then, following the same order, discuss the same elements in the other works. The following chart provides an example.

Work 1: "Papa Who . . ."	Work 2: "Mother to Son"
Element 1: Parent character and situation	**Element 1:** Parent character and situation
Element 2: Method(s) of characterization	**Element 2:** Method(s) of characterization
Element 3: What child learns	**Element 3:** What child learns

Develop Your Ideas

Be sure to develop and elaborate general statements in your essay. Provide examples, details, or quotations from the texts to support your thesis.

Proofread Your Essay

Re-read your essay and correct any errors you find in grammar, spelling, and punctuation.

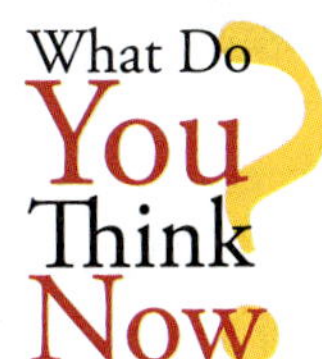

What ideas about life does each of the narrators impart? In what way are those ideas formed by the narrators' relationships with others?

INFORMATIONAL TEXT FOCUS

Main Idea, Audience, and Purpose

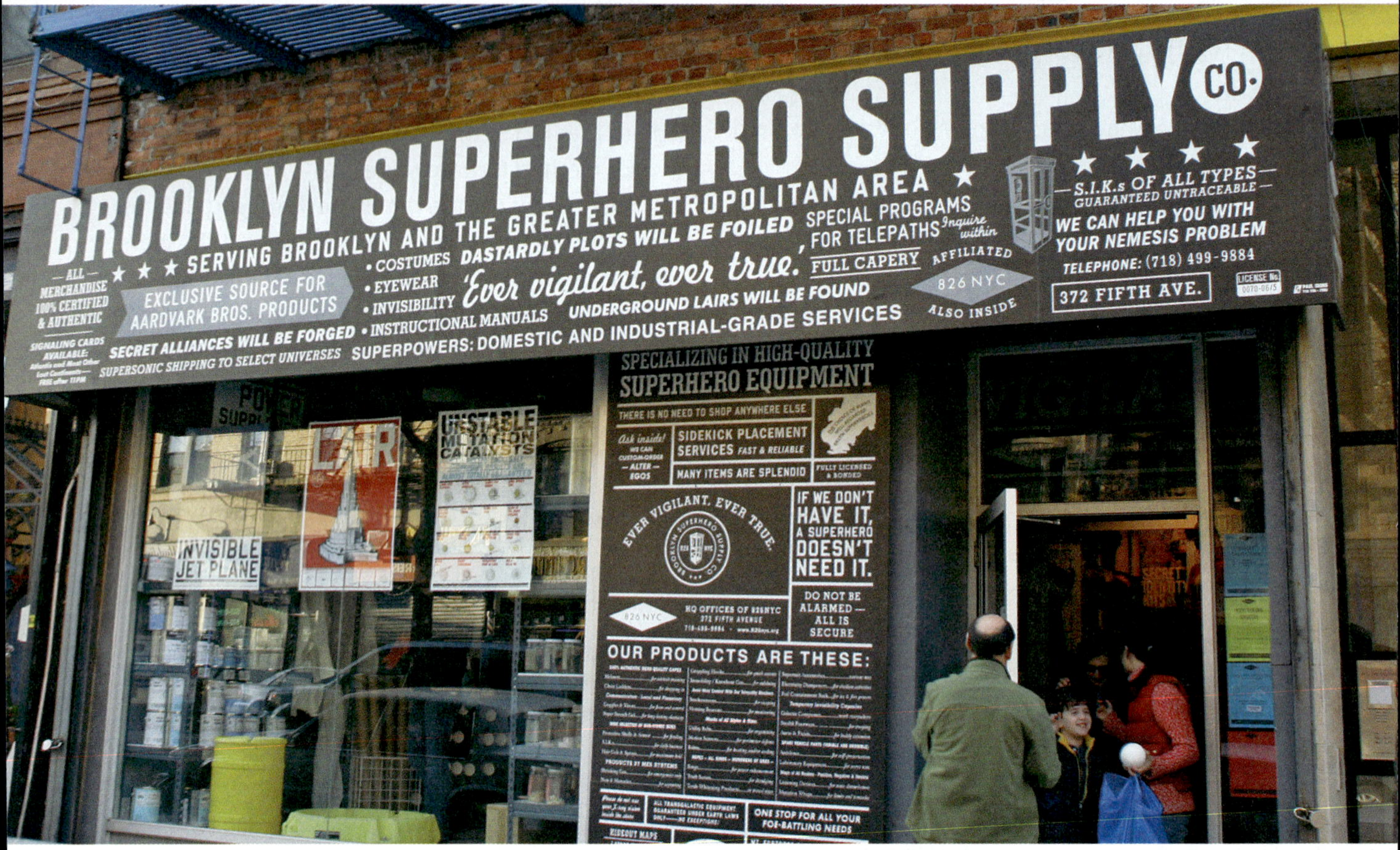

CONTENTS

What Do You Think?

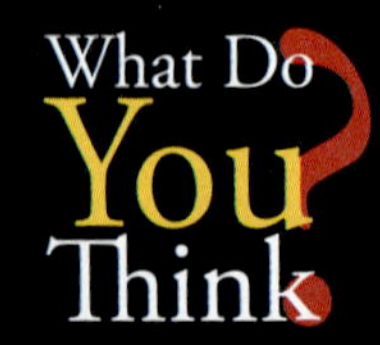

How can helping others change the way you view yourself?

QuickWrite

Write about an instance when you have either inspired someone else or been inspired by another person. What did you learn about yourself and others from the experience?

MAGAZINE & NEWSPAPER ARTICLES

Preparing to Read

An Interview with Dave Eggers / Teaching Chess, and Life

MO **9.R.1.H.1.a** Apply post-reading skills to comprehend, interpret, analyze, and evaluate text: identify and explain the relationship between the main idea and supporting details *Also covered* **9.R.1.I.1.a**

Reader/Writer Notebook

Use your **RWN** to complete the activities for these selections.

Informational Text Focus

Synthesizing Sources: Main Idea, Audience, and Purpose

A **primary source** is a firsthand account in which writers present their experiences, opinions, and ideas. Both the informational texts you are about to read are primary sources on the same subject: helping others by sharing a passion—for these authors, writing and chess.

When reading or researching articles on the same subject, you will need to **synthesize** the information, which means considering all of the sources as a group to see how they fit together. In order to get the most out of your sources, ask yourself the following questions:

- **Audience** Who is this written for?
- **Purpose** Why does the author want me to know this?
- **Main Idea** What main point is the author trying to convey?
- **Compare** How are the arguments, ideas, or experiences in each source similar or different? What did I learn from each?

Into Action As you read, fill in a chart like the one below to help you organize your thoughts.

	Article 1	Article 2
Audience		
Purpose		
Main idea		
Similarities/differences		

Writing Focus

Preparing for **Constructed Response**

As you read, think about the facts and opinions presented in each article. A **fact** can be proven true. An **opinion** cannot be proven because it is a personal belief. When you write an essay, you may be expressing your opinion. Facts and other information will help you support that opinion.

Vocabulary

An Interview with Dave Eggers

unconventional (uhn kuhn VEHN shuh nuhl) *adj.:* not conforming to customary, formal, or accepted practices. *Compared to other memoirs, Dave Eggers's was unconventional.*

enabled (ehn AY buhld) *v.:* made able; provided with means, opportunity, power, or authority. *Eggers's first book enabled him to pursue a number of writing projects.*

Teaching Chess, and Life

matured (muh CHURD) *v.:* learned more about life; developed more fully. *During his high school years, Carlos matured.*

mentorship (MEHN tuhr shihp) *n.:* advice or lessons from a mentor, or wise teacher. *With Chia's mentorship, Carlos learned from his mistake.*

Language Coach

Word Origins Did you know the word *mentor* comes to us from Homer's *Odyssey*? (See page 1037.) Mentor was Odysseus's trusted friend and also a teacher of his son, Telemachus. Which word on the list above comes from the word *mentor*?

Learn It Online

To learn more on synthesizing sources, go to the interactive Reading Workshops on:

go.hrw.com L9-199 

An Interview with Dave Eggers

from Writing

Read with a Purpose

Read the following selection to learn about award-winning author Dave Eggers's volunteer work and his love of reading and writing.

Build Background

Dave Eggers (pictured above) is an author, editor, and publisher who has also created a number of drop-in tutoring organizations around the country. In the following interview from the magazine *Writing,* Eggers talks about his passion for writing and the organization he founded.

A "Staggering Genius" Talks About Writing, Fame, and . . . Trout

When Dave Eggers was 21, he lost his parents to cancer. Each died within five weeks of the other, leaving Eggers to raise his 7-year-old brother, Christopher, or "Toph," on his own. A few years later, Eggers published his story in a highly unconventional, funny-sad memoir called *A Heartbreaking Work of Staggering Genius* (2000). The title hints at the self-mocking tone of the book, but it's not kidding—at least not totally. Critics called Eggers "refreshingly honest," "an original new voice," and oh, yes, "a staggering genius."

The success of his first book, which he refers to as *AHWOSG,* enabled Eggers to pursue a number of writing projects, including the creation of the superhip online literary journal *McSweeney's* (www.mcsweeneys.net). He has written several novels; edits an annual anthology of nonfiction, *The Best American Nonrequired Reading;* and recently published a book of short stories, *How We Are Hungry.* He also founded 826 Valencia, a writing center for kids in San Francisco. Recently, *Writing* caught up with Eggers and tossed him a few questions.

Vocabulary **unconventional** (uhn kuhn VEHN shuh nuhl) *adj.:* not conforming to customary, formal, or accepted practices.
enabled (ehn AY buhld) *v.:* made able; provided with means, opportunity, power, or authority.

Writing: **First, let's talk a little about you. What kind of student were you in school?** **A**

Dave Eggers: I guess I always liked school. I wasn't all about school—I didn't go running to the bus stop every day—but I did well in school, and I had a string of great teachers and enjoyed my time there. English and art were my favorite subjects, and I would take after-school art classes to learn more. I wanted to be a cartoonist.

Writing: **When and why did you start writing?**

Eggers: At various points—fifth grade, seventh grade, eighth grade—we were asked to create books, where we would write and illustrate them and spend a lot of time making them look official and spiffy, and I remember those books sparking in me an interest in writing. I still wanted, first and foremost, to be a comic-book artist, but I was doing well in English classes and started thinking I could combine my interest in art and in writing. It wasn't until college, though—not until my junior year—that I really thought about writing for a living. I studied painting for three years in college and switched to the journalism program my last year.

Writing: **So many people today seem to think fame is the ultimate goal in life. What's the deal with fame anyway?**

Eggers: The aspect of being well known that's important is that sometimes you can use your fame to help people or to change those things that need changing. Because people read my books, I can sometimes raise money for good causes easier than I could when I was younger and not known. I can write about an issue—like the need to pay teachers better—and people will listen to me in a way they wouldn't have before I had some success. I'm really happy that I can help that way. That's the main upshot of any measure of fame. **B**

Writing: **A little about the writing process: How do you write? Do you, like some writers, sit down and write for a set amount of time every day? Or do you write only when inspiration hits?**

Eggers: I write most days. Sometimes I write for about 10 hours a day, sometimes only a few hours. Sometimes I sit at the computer and stall forever; sometimes the words shoot onto the page at lightning speed. But I do write pretty much every day, even weekends. And I usually write late at night, from about 10 P.M. to 3 A.M.

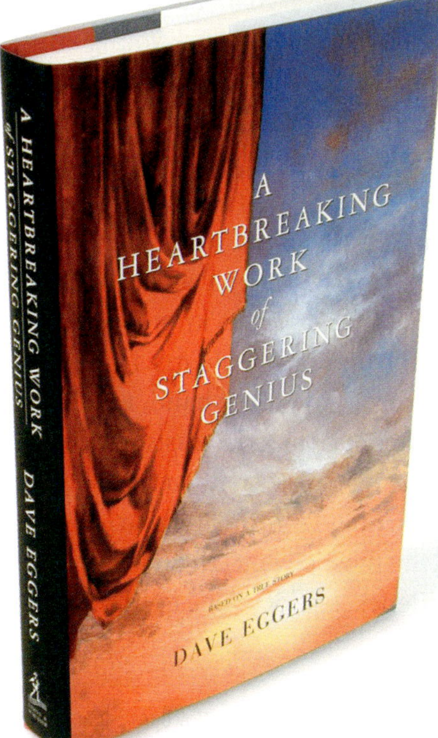

A **Informational Focus Audience** Based on the first question the interviewer asks, who do you think is the intended audience for this interview?

B **Informational Focus Main Idea** What is the main idea in this paragraph? What does Eggers say about being famous?

***Writing:* Tell us about your work with 826 Valencia.**

Eggers: 826 Valencia is a drop-in tutoring, writing, and publishing center in San Francisco. We help local students with writing-related homework, and we teach classes in tons of different fields: journalism, radio, film, poetry, and bookmaking—you name it. We also publish student work in various collections that are then sold in bookstores all over the city and on Amazon.

***Writing:* Why did you want to help young people learn to write?**

Eggers: Over the years, I'd worked with the YMCA and other groups, teaching middle school and high school students about cartooning, writing, and publishing, and we always had a great time. I learned a lot of what I know about writing and design while I was in high school, so I think if we at 826 Valencia can help aspiring writers when they're very young and if we can introduce them to actual writers who have been successful, then those students can get a clear idea of a writer's life, and how to get from *A* to *Z*. I meet hundreds of students every year who could be successful writers—as novelists, journalists, poets. Our goal at 826 Valencia is to make sure these aspirants know that they can actually do it and to give them as many tools as possible. On the other hand, we also help tons of students who need assistance with the basics—lots of students new to this country who are just learning English. So it varies, from the basics to the most advanced. That's what makes 826 Valencia a good place to be. **C**

***Writing:* A lot of people complain that kids today don't read. Some blame TV, computers, fast food. (Just kidding, but who knows?) What are your thoughts about it?**

Eggers: I watched a whole lot of TV when I was growing up. I lived in a house where the TV was on most of the day and night, but I still found a lot of time to read, and I spent most of my time outside, running around in the woods. I think there's a balance—you have to get out there and see the world, learn from books, and also know what's happening via the TV, the Web, and other media. Any young person who's interested in writing should be reading (outside of school) about 10 books a year. That's only one a month—you could definitely read more—but 10 a year is a guideline. I still keep track of my reading, making sure I'm reading a book every week or two. Again, it's part of the balance, because I still love TV. **D**

***Writing:* What books would you recommend to young people?**

Eggers: I recommend any book that grabs you, any book you can't put down. There are millions of books in the world, so I don't feel like we should spend too much time slogging our way through books we feel no connection to. I don't like Jane Austen very much. After reading a few of her books and feeling no particular connection to that world, I've decided I probably won't read any more. If you don't consider yourself a big reader, start by reading books about things you're interested in, like fishing. Maybe you're like LeBron James and you love trout, but you don't like reading so much, because you think

C **Informational Focus** **Purpose** Why does Eggers want to help students with their writing?

D **Informational Focus** **Main Idea** What main idea does Eggers convey about reading?

826 VALENCIA
FREE TUTORING
WE OFFER FREE ONE-ON-ONE TUTORING IN WRITING-RESEARCH PAPERS, CREATIVE WRITING, ESSAYS, POETRY, WHAT-HAVE-YOU.
KARL→
TUTORS HERE 3-7PM M-TH
AGES 7-18 WELCOME

Dave's Advice for Young Writers

Wear a helmet. Write every day. Keep a journal—buy one small enough to keep in your pocket. Listen to people, to the way they talk. Get lost in the woods or in new neighborhoods, explore. Swim a lot. Come up with new and better names for llamas. Listen to a lot of music, loud. Read as much as you can. Watch *Time Bandits* and *Napoleon Dynamite*. Don't let any one person discourage you. Don't count on your friends' liking your work. Maybe you like to write about zombies, and none of your friends like zombies—this doesn't mean there aren't thousands of people all over the world who are just dying (excuse the pun) to read your work about zombies. And when you write about zombies or anything else, try to describe them in ways never before done by humankind. A writer's job is to make the world new, to charge it full of new life, so you have to start over, from scratch; you can't rehash stories that have been told a hundred times. You have to give readers something brand-spanking new. Especially if it involves trout. E

books are always about people in the 19th century eating cucumber sandwiches. So go find some books about trout and trout fishing, trout preparation, trout eating. The point is to begin to love books. I guarantee there are at least 100 books out there for everyone—100 books that will knock you over and change your life—so get started looking for those. (That doesn't mean you shouldn't finish the books you're reading in class. Your teachers know why they're asking you to read a certain book. You have to trust them.) Sometimes a book will bore the life out of you for 50 pages, then get really interesting. You have to have patience, but if you're reading a book for fun and you're not having fun, maybe it's time to try something else.

Read with a Purpose What advice does Eggers give his readers? Which piece of advice is most significant to you?

E **Informational Focus** **Purpose** For what purpose does Eggers write his advice for young writers?

NEWSPAPER ARTICLE

Teaching Chess, and Life

by CARLOS CAPELLAN

from an essay adapted by *The New York Times,* September 3, 2000

Read with a Purpose

Read the following article to find out how playing chess helped change a student's life for the better.

Build Background

A **primary source** is a firsthand account of a writer's experiences, opinions, and ideas. Other examples of primary sources are interviews (like the one you just read), autobiographies, letters, oral histories, eyewitness news reports, and speeches. This article is an autobiographical essay, a primary source.

If you were to walk down West 160th Street in Washington Heights, New York, you would see drug dealers whistling to people in cars and handing off small packages to passersby. As you walk further down the block, you would see residents who are too scared to sit and talk to their neighbors on the front steps. These families stay inside most of the time. You would see parents pick up their children from P.S. 4 and hurry off the block before trouble can start. This is my block and this is my neighborhood. **A**

Many kids my age in Washington Heights wind up in gangs, as drug dealers, in jail, or dead. I decided long ago that I would not end up in one of those situations because of the consequences I saw others suffer. I have stuck by this decision with help from several important people. One of the most influential people in my life is my former chess coach and current boss, Jeremy Chiappetta, who has taught me a lot about chess and more about life. **B**

As an eighth-grader at a gang-infested junior high school, I joined the chess team as a way to stay out of trouble. I already knew the coach, Mr. Chiappetta, because he was my social studies teacher.

As a ninth- and tenth-grader, I volunteered to help Chia with his chess team at Intermediate School 90 on West 168th Street. During these years, I matured. I learned how to present myself in a

A **Informational Focus** **Main Idea** What main idea about his West 160th Street neighborhood does the writer convey?

B **Informational Focus** **Audience and Purpose** Who is the author's audience? What is the author's purpose in writing the article?

Vocabulary **matured** (muh CHURD) *v.:* learned more about life; developed more fully.

positive way: taking off my hat inside buildings, judging when it was appropriate to make jokes (I had to learn this lesson a few times), and knowing how to speak in certain situations.

At one tournament I learned an important lesson from Chia. It was the last round of the U.S. Amateur Team East. I was playing for a top prize and was nervous. In the middle of the game I found a winning combination and I began to slam the pieces out of happiness. Then a big hand stopped the game clock and pulled me away. It was Chia. I could tell that he was angry, but I did not realize what I had done wrong. We talked about the meaning of sportsmanship. I apologized for my rudeness to my opponent and forfeited the game. I didn't win a prize. **C**

With Chia's mentorship, I learned from my mistake. As a coach at I.S. 90, I've had to teach the same lesson to others. It makes me feel good about myself because I like helping the younger kids learn the game Chia taught me to love.

Carlos Capellan, an assistant chess coach, shares a laugh with students during chess practice at Intermediate School 90.

Chia left I.S. 90 the year I became an eleventh-grader. He recommended me as an assistant chess coach, for which I am paid. This is my second year at I.S. 90 as an assistant coach. My responsibilities include teaching chess strategies and tactics three days a week. I also chaperone the team at tournaments almost every weekend. **D**

All of this would not have been possible if not for Mr. Chiappetta. He turned me to chess and kept me involved. He gave me the opportunity to earn money doing something I love. Chess has kept me off the streets. It has challenged me and taught me to think in new ways. Because of chess, I was recently honored by the *Daily News* as one of the "21 New Yorkers to Watch in the 21st Century." Chess has made me a mentor to younger students, giving me the chance to become their Chia.

Read with a Purpose How did learning to play chess change Carlos's life?

C **Informational Focus** **Main Idea** What did Carlos learn from the competition?

Vocabulary **mentorship** (MEHN tuhr shihp) *n.:* advice or lessons from a mentor, or wise teacher.

D **Informational Focus** **Main Idea** How have Carlos's chess and life skills helped him find a career path?

MAGAZINE & NEWSPAPER ARTICLES

Applying Your Skills

MO 9.R.1.I.1.a Compare, contrast, analyze and evaluate connections: text to text 9.R.1.H.1.a Apply post-reading skills to comprehend, interpret, analyze, and evaluate text: identify and explain the relationship between the main idea and supporting details 9.R.1.G.1.a During reading, utilize strategies: to determine meaning of unknown words

An Interview with Dave Eggers / Teaching Chess, and Life

Practicing the Standards

Informational Text and Vocabulary

1. The **main idea** of the Eggers interview is —

A students should try to read one new book each week
B not all students should become writers
C students should follow their passion
D students should write about topics with which they are familiar

2. What is the author's **purpose** for writing "Teaching Chess, and Life"?

A To encourage others to play chess
B To show others that there are ways to stay out of trouble
C To praise Mr. Chiappetta
D To teach others about chess competitions

3. What conclusion can be drawn from **synthesizing** the interview and the article?

A Students should practice writing every day.
B Students should join clubs.
C Sharing a personal passion can help others.
D Sharing past experiences will not keep others out of trouble.

4. Which is the best definition for *unconventional*?

A Not influential
B Not ordinary
C Not noteworthy
D Not difficult

5. When something is *enabled,* it is —

A made difficult
B made easy
C made possible
D made impossible

6. A person who has *matured* —

A is very smart
B is very young
C has completed school
D has become more fully developed

7. Which is the best definition of *mentorship*?

A Advice from an older, wiser person
B Being in the company of others
C A gathering of elders
D An ability to work with others

Writing Focus Constructed Response

Both Dave Eggers and Carlos Capellan are passionate about helping others. What hobbies or interests inspire you? How could you share your enthusiasm with others? In a brief essay, describe what you are passionate about and how you might share your enthusiasm with others.

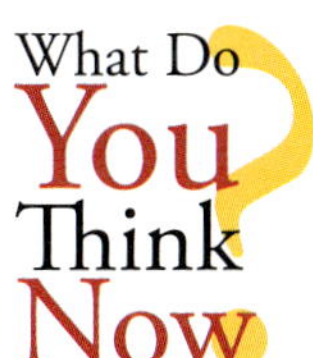

In what ways might people change as a result of helping others?

FOCUS ON MISSOURI COURSE LEVEL EXPECTATIONS

Literary Skills Review

Character **Directions:** Read the following short story. Then, read and respond to the questions that follow.

Ambush by **Tim O'Brien**

The U.S. military took part in the Vietnam War, most actively participating from 1965 to 1969. The United States sided with South Vietnam against North Vietnam and its communist government. When the war ended in 1975, nearly two million civilians and 58,000 military personnel had died.

When she was nine, my daughter Kathleen asked if I had ever killed anyone. She knew about the war; she knew I'd been a soldier. "You keep writing these war stories," she said, "so I guess you must've killed somebody." It was a difficult moment, but I did what seemed right, which was to say, "Of course not," and then to take her onto my lap and hold her for a while. Someday, I hope, she'll ask again. But here I want to pretend she's a grown-up. I want to tell her exactly what happened, or what I remember happening, and then I want to say to her that as a little girl she was absolutely right. This is why I keep writing war stories:

He was a short, slender young man of about twenty. I was afraid of him—afraid of something—and as he passed me on the trail I threw a grenade that exploded at his feet and killed him.

Or to go back:

Shortly after midnight we moved into the ambush site outside My Khe. The whole platoon was there, spread out in the dense brush along the trail, and for five hours nothing at all happened. We were working in two-man teams—one man on guard while the other slept, switching off every two hours—and I remember it was still dark when Kiowa shook me awake for the final watch. The night was foggy and hot. For the first few moments I felt lost, not sure about directions, groping for my helmet and weapon. I reached out and found three grenades and lined them up in front of me; the pins had already been straightened for quick throwing. And then for maybe half an hour I kneeled there and waited. Very gradually, in tiny slivers, dawn began to break through the fog, and from my position in the brush I could see ten or fifteen meters up the trail. The mosquitoes were fierce. I remember slapping at them, wondering if I should wake up Kiowa and ask for some repellent, then thinking it was a bad idea, then looking up and seeing the young man come out of the fog. He wore black clothing and rubber sandals and a gray ammunition belt. His shoulders were slightly stooped, his head cocked to the side as if listening for something. He seemed at ease. He carried his weapon in one hand, muzzle down, moving without any hurry up the center of the trail. There was no sound at all—none that I can remember. In a way, it seemed, he was part of the morning fog, or

MO **9.R.2.C.1.b** Use details from text(s): to analyze character, plot, setting, point of view

my own imagination, but there was also the reality of what was happening in my stomach. I had already pulled the pin on a grenade. I had come up to a crouch. It was entirely automatic. I did not hate the young man; I did not see him as the enemy; I did not ponder issues of morality or politics or military duty. I crouched and kept my head low. I tried to swallow whatever was rising from my stomach, which tasted like lemonade, something fruity and sour. I was terrified. There were no thoughts about killing. The grenade was to make him go away—just evaporate—and I leaned back and felt my mind go empty and then felt it fill up again. I had already thrown the grenade before telling myself to throw it. The brush was thick and I had to lob it high, not aiming, and I remember the grenade seeming to freeze above me for an instant, as if a camera had clicked, and I remember ducking down and holding my breath and seeing little wisps of fog rise from the earth. The grenade bounced once and rolled across the trail. I did not hear it, but there must've been a sound, because the young man dropped his weapon and began to run, just two or three quick steps, then he hesitated, swiveling to his right, and he glanced down at the grenade and tried to cover his head but never did. It occurred to me then that he was about to die. I wanted to warn him. The grenade made a popping noise—not soft but not loud either—not what I'd expected—and there was a puff of dust and smoke—a small white puff—and the young man seemed to jerk upward as if pulled by invisible wires. He fell on his back. His rubber sandals had been blown off. There was no wind. He lay at the center of the trail, his right leg bent beneath him, his one eye shut, his other eye a huge star-shaped hole.

It was not a matter of live or die. There was no real peril. Almost certainly the young man would have passed by. And it will always be that way.

Later, I remember, Kiowa tried to tell me that the man would've died anyway. He told me that it was a good kill, that I was a soldier and this was a war, that I should shape up and stop staring and ask myself what the dead man would've done if things were reversed.

None of it mattered. The words seemed far too complicated. All I could do was gape at the fact of the young man's body.

Even now I haven't finished sorting it out. Sometimes I forgive myself, other times I don't. In the ordinary hours of life I try not to dwell on it, but now and then, when I'm reading a newspaper or just sitting alone in a room, I'll look up and see the young man coming out of the morning fog. I'll watch him walk toward me, his shoulders slightly stooped, his head cocked to the side, and he'll pass within a few yards of me and suddenly smile at some secret thought and then continue up the trail to where it bends back into the fog.

Literary Skills Review CONTINUED

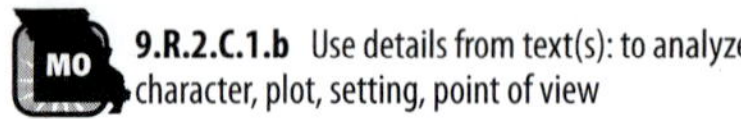

1. Who is the **main character** of the story?

A Kathleen

B Kiowa

C The narrator

D The platoon

9.R.2.C.1.b

2. From the first paragraph of the story, we can infer that the narrator feels **conflict** about —

A whether he will tell his daughter the truth

B why he was in the war

C how he killed the man

D why he writes war stories

9.R.2.C.1.b

3. The man in black clothing is a —

A dynamic character

B flat character

C protagonist, or main character

D round character

9.R.2.C.1.b

4. What is the narrator's **motivation** for pulling the grenade's pin?

A Fear

B Anger

C Curiosity

D Revenge

9.R.2.C.1.b

5. What method of **characterization** is *not* used in the story?

A Private thoughts

B Actions

C Dialogue

D Direct characterization

9.R.2.C.1.b

6. The narrator can *best* be classified as —

A a flat character

B a round character

C a flat and static character

D a round and dynamic character

9.R.2.C.1.b

7. At the end of the story, we can **infer** that the narrator —

A is haunted by what he's done

B never thinks of war

C lies all the time

D has a bad memory

9.R.2.C.1.b

Constructed Response

8. What have you learned about the narrator of "Ambush"? List **character traits** he possesses. Then, explain how the story's writer revealed those traits. Was it mainly through **direct** or **indirect characterization**? Explain, and give a few examples.

9.R.2.C.1.b

FOCUS ON MISSOURI COURSE LEVEL EXPECTATIONS

Informational Skills Review

Main Idea, Audience, and Purpose **Directions:** Read the following selection. Then, read and respond to the questions that follow.

I Got It: Mentoring Isn't for the Mentor *from* **Newsweek**, June 5, 2000, by **Jane Armstrong**

From the first moment I heard about Pipeline NAU, a mentoring program matching Northern Arizona University professors with low-income middle-school students, I knew I wanted to be a mentor.

The students who complete the five-year program with a B average receive a full scholarship to NAU. I remembered what a financial struggle it was for me to get my B.A. But more than that, I remembered what I was like in the eighth grade—a shabbily dressed little mess from the stereotypically broken, impoverished, and chaotic home. I skipped more school than I attended; my grades were a train wreck, and I wasn't exactly on the slumber-party A-list.

Still, I managed to scratch my way through three college degrees and eventually became an English professor. But I really could've used a mentor—someone to turn to for advice, someone to provide a glimpse into a world of educated people doing interesting things.

I hoped I could be that person for someone else, and so I enthusiastically threw myself into the six-month mentor-training program. I endured an FBI background check, an interview, and a variety of "group bonding" activities with the other potential mentors and mentees. Through all of these indignities, I comforted myself with elaborate fantasies of me and my grateful, compliant protégé.[1]

I'd expose her to literature, classical music, and ballet, and she'd soak it all in like an underwatered houseplant. She'd emulate my look, my style, my sensibilities. We'd shop together. I'd confess my adolescent disasters, inspiring her to make better choices. I was going to be the best mentor ever.

But when I was matched with Risa, I was terrified. I'd noticed Risa often during the summer group activities. It's impossible not to notice Risa. She's a flat-out gorgeous teen, Tyra Banks beautiful. And she's funny and popular and the queen of her school. And I, a socially inept peasant, clearly had nothing to offer her.

Although we have a few things in common—we both come from single-mother households, ditched flute-playing for sports, and have the same twisted sense of humor—our first several meetings were strained. I was afraid we weren't going to be a very good match.

1. **protégé** (PROH tuh zhay): a person guided or helped, especially in the furthering of his or her career, by another more influential person.

Informational Skills Review CONTINUED

Risa hated to read. Risa hated classical music. Risa hated the ballet. Risa never had any homework I could help her with. The only thing Risa seemed to care about was talking to her friends on the phone. I was not her friend. She wouldn't return my calls.

After three months, I was ready to give up. Spending two hours a week with someone who obviously didn't like me wasn't what I had in mind. I already had classes full of college students who serve that purpose.

I was sobbing daily, thinking of the big, fat "L" for loser burning itself into my forehead when I had this simple thought: mentoring isn't for the mentor. I signed up to do a job. A child was depending on me, whether she realized it or not. Whether I liked it or not.

So I dragged Risa to "The Nutcracker." I forced her to have afternoon tea with me. I tricked her into a Shakespeare lesson by taking her to see "Ten Things I Hate About You."[2] And I suspected she was starting to like these things, but I couldn't tell for sure. Risa didn't say much.

I asked Risa about her career goals, and she told me she wants to be a pediatric nurse because she "loves babies." I heard the unintended teen-pregnancy siren shrieking, so I set up a job shadow with a local pediatrician.

2. **"Ten Things I Hate About You"**: A 1999 movie based on Shakespeare's play *The Taming of the Shrew.*

I dropped Risa off at the doctor's office, and when I picked her up a few hours later, she was bouncing her legs up and down and clapping her exquisite hands and saying again and again, "That was so cool! I am so excited!" And she rattled off a litany of factoids about strep cultures, influenza viruses, and the relationship between dairy products and mucus.

I'd never seen this version of Risa before, and I thought, "This is it—my big mentoring moment." I didn't want to blow it so I tried to stay calm and keep listening, but I couldn't help saying, "So, Risa, do you think you might want to be a doctor?" And she said "yeah" in the way kids do, with a question mark at the end of the word.

I looked over at Risa's beautiful face. I wanted to hit the brakes, pull the car over, stare at her, and expand time because I knew nothing before or since in my shaky career as a mentor would ever come close to this moment.

Risa's world had just opened up, had become huge and complicated and full of possibilities, and I was there to see it happen.

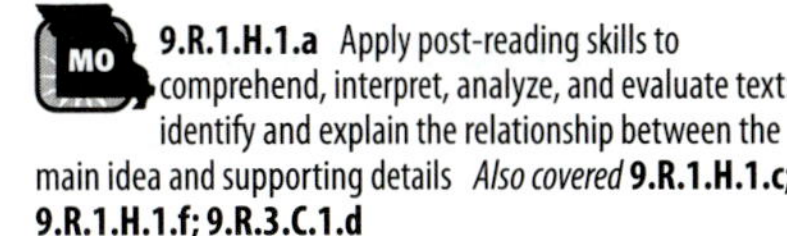
9.R.1.H.1.a Apply post-reading skills to comprehend, interpret, analyze, and evaluate text: identify and explain the relationship between the main idea and supporting details *Also covered* **9.R.1.H.1.c; 9.R.1.H.1.f; 9.R.3.C.1.d**

1. The **audience** for this article is —

A potential mentors

B potential professors

C NAU alumni

D future medical professionals

9.R.3

2. Why does the author want to become a mentor?

A To expose youngsters to literature and music

B To earn more money

C To share advice and experiences

D To help students earn scholarships

9.R.1.H.1.a

3. The **main idea** of the article is that a mentor should —

A expose the student to new experiences

B teach the student to imitate the mentor

C consider the student's needs and interests

D become the student's confidant and companion

9.R.1.H.1.a

4. In describing Risa, the author provides —

A facts

B opinions

C facts and opinions

D none of the above

9.R.1.H.1.a

5. Why does Armstrong almost give up her position as mentor?

A She and Risa get into an argument.

B She feels that mentoring takes up too much time.

C She thinks that Risa does not need a mentor.

D She feels like she isn't being a good mentor.

9.R.1.H.1.a

6. The **purpose** of Armstrong's article is to —

A persuade all adults to become mentors

B persuade all students to join mentoring programs

C share a personal experience about mentoring

D inform professors about mentoring programs

9.R.3.C.1.d

Constructed Response

7. What does Armstrong learn from her mentoring experience? What does Risa learn? Do you agree with the author's statement that "mentoring isn't for the mentor"? Explain why or why not.

9.R.1.H.1.c *9.R.1.H.1.f*

FOCUS ON MISSOURI COURSE LEVEL EXPECTATIONS

Vocabulary Skills Review

Multiple-Meaning Words

Directions: Choose the answer in which the italicized word is used in the same way it is used in the sentence from "A Christmas Memory."

1. "Together, we *guide* our buggy, a dilapidated baby carriage, out to the garden and into a grove of pecan trees."

A Our tour *guide* carried a flashlight.

B Let your conscience be your *guide*.

C This dog is trained as a *guide*.

D I will *guide* the car through the snowstorm.

9.R.1.E.1.b

2. "These moneys we keep hidden in an ancient *bead* purse under a loose board under the floor under a chamber pot under my friend's bed."

A Layla likes to *bead* necklaces.

B My mother's favorite piece of jewelry is a *bead* ring.

C I see a *bead* of water on the ladybug.

D The hunter drew a *bead* on the deer.

9.R.1.E.1.b

3. "Neither of us has a *head* for figures; we count slowly, lose track, start again."

A Hugo does not have a *head* for business; he gives money away.

B After five years, she became *head* coach.

C It's time for me to *head* home.

D She is at the *head* of her class.

9.R.1.E.1.b

4. "There's a case coming up in *court* next month."

A Let's meet at the tennis *court*.

B Those two girls are both trying to *court* him.

C The lawyers have to go to *court*.

D The king's *court* laughed at the jester.

9.R.1.E.1.b

5. "Indeed, the larger *share* are intended for persons we've met maybe once, perhaps not at all."

A We are taught to *share* our toys.

B He hates to *share* with his sister.

C Estaban wants his *share* of the cashews.

D I want to buy a stock *share*.

9.R.1.E.1.b

6. "Or Abner Packer, the driver of the six o'clock bus from Mobile, who exchanges *waves* with us every day as he passes in a dust-cloud whoosh."

A She *waves* her hair with a curling iron.

B The ocean's *waves* are treacherous today.

C See all the people on deck giving *waves* goodbye.

D There have been *waves* of crime in the city.

9.R.1.E.1.b

7. "Now a nude December fig branch *grates* against the window."

A Watch out for the subway *grates*.

B My uncle *grates* cheese for the sauce.

C To annoy me, he *grates* his fingernail against the chalkboard.

D That noise *grates* on her nerves.

9.R.1.E.1.b

8. "Queenie rolls on her back, her paws *plow* the air, something like a grin stretches her black lips."

A His arms *plow* through the water when he swims.

B The farmers *plow* the fields in the spring.

C Sometimes oxen are harnessed to a *plow*.

D They are ready to *plow* into the food.

9.R.1.E.1.b

9.R.1.E.1.c Develop vocabulary through text: using glossary, dictionary and thesaurus 9.R.1.E.1.b Develop vocabulary through text: using context clues

9. ". . . The sun, *round* as an orange and orange as hot-weather moons, balances on the horizon, burnishes the silvered winter woods."

A He lost in the second *round*.

B I like how *round* you made the basket.

C We went *round* trip to California.

D When doing percentages, we *round* the numbers up or down.

9.R.1.E.1.b

10. "On the farther shore, Queenie *shakes* herself and trembles."

A We celebrated the victory with strawberry *shakes*.

B The politician is scared of germs and never *shakes* hands.

C After swimming, she *shakes* the water out of her hair.

D J. R. always *shakes* at horror movies.

9.R.1.E.1.b

11. "Christmas Eve afternoon we *scrape* together a nickel and go to the butcher's."

A They have to *scrape* off the old paint before applying the new.

B When skating, it's easy to *scrape* a knee.

C That dog really got us into a *scrape* this time.

D Let's *scrape* some wood together, so we can build a fire.

9.R.1.E.1.b

12. "Somewhere a rooster *crows*: falsely, for the sun is still on the other side of the world."

A The *crows* are after the corn.

B I hate how she *crows* after winning a game.

C We woke up because of the birds' *crows*.

D *Crows* used to live in this area.

9.R.1.E.1.b

Academic Vocabulary

Directions: Choose the best definition for the italicized word in each sentence.

13. The character Sherlock Holmes is known for picking up on *significant* details.

A fallacious

B incomprehensible

C important

D unnecessary

9.R.1.E.1.b

14. Holmes's careful attention to detail helps him solve the most *complex* crimes.

A complicated

B dangerous

C easily solved

D idiotic

9.R.1.E.1.b

Read On

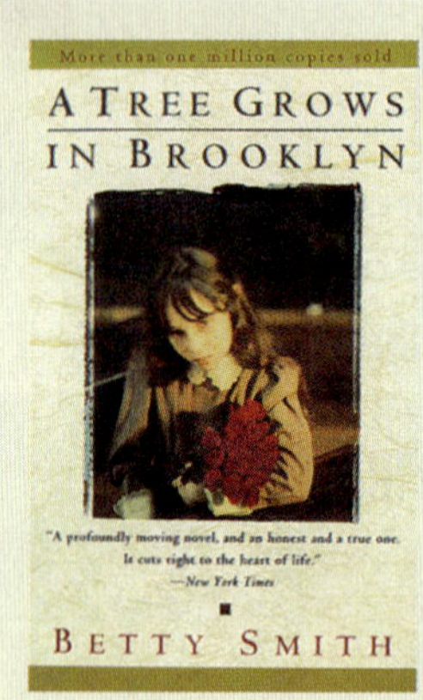

FICTION

A Tree Grows in Brooklyn

In Betty Smith's novel, a tree grows in Brooklyn—and so does young Francie Nolan. Living in a poor neighborhood with her parents and her brother, Francie finds joys and an assortment of troubles as she comes of age. Her experiences are sometimes painful, but they become the building blocks of wisdom. *A Tree Grows in Brooklyn* takes place between 1902 and 1919, but don't be surprised if Francie and the Nolan family remind you of people you know.

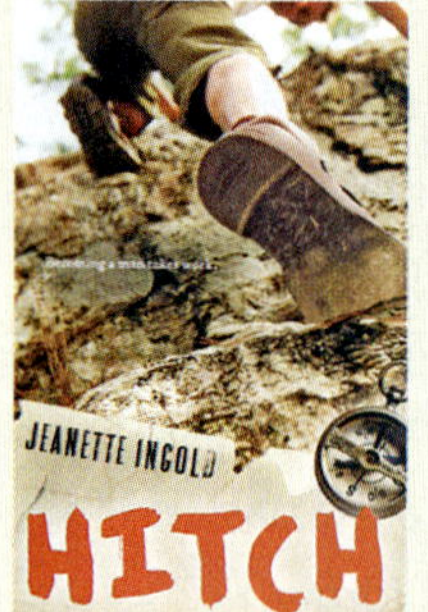

FICTION

Hitch

Seventeen-year-old Moss Trawnley is in desperate need of work, so he decides to head out west as a member of President Roosevelt's Civilian Conservation Corps to help protect Montana's wildlife from devastating erosion and wildfires. Despite the grueling work, Moss has time to play baseball, make lifelong friends, and rediscover what he almost lost in the Great Depression: himself. Jeannette Ingold brings an important era of U.S. history to life in this riveting coming-of-age story that will appeal to any teen who has dreamed of adventure and survival in the great outdoors.

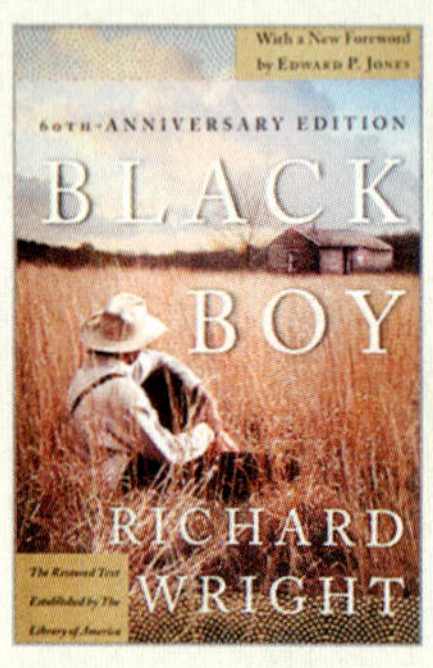

NONFICTION

Black Boy

Richard Wright's early years were plagued with hunger—for food, for knowledge, and for respect. He wrote stories filled with imagination and longing, and his intelligence left those around him feeling puzzled and threatened. After all, a black boy living in rural Mississippi in the 1920s couldn't go far in life—or could he? Wright's autobiography *Black Boy* is the stunning account of a young man who rose above oppression to live out his dreams.

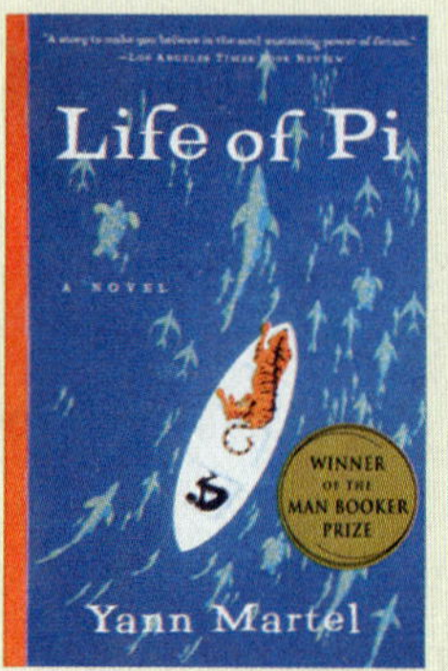

FICTION

Life of Pi

The son of a zookeeper, Pi Patel has an encyclopedic knowledge of animal behavior and a love of stories. When Pi is sixteen, his family emigrates from India to North America aboard a cargo ship, along with zoo animals bound for new homes. When the ship sinks, Pi finds himself alone in a lifeboat—his only companions a hyena, an orangutan, a wounded zebra, and Richard Parker, a 450-pound Bengal tiger. Yann Martel's award-winning novel *Life of Pi* is at once a rousing adventure and a reflection on what it means to live and to believe.

FICTION

I, Robot

Isaac Asimov is famous for his robot novels, which show the complex interactions between human beings and robots. He is equally famous for devising the three fundamental Laws of Robotics that are designed to protect both humans and robots. In this collection of stories connected by comments and detective work from "Robopsychologist" Susan Calvin, we see how robots gradually develop more and more human characteristics, becoming both increasingly helpful and dangerous as the history of humans and robots moves to a surprising but logical end.

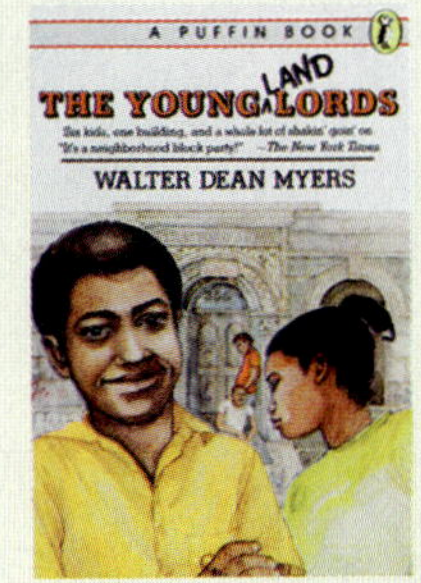

FICTION

The Young Landlords

Fifteen-year-old Paul Williams and his friends decide to form an Action Group to get things done in their neighborhood. They confront an absentee landlord and demand that he improve conditions in his run-down apartment building. To Paul's surprise, the landlord sells him the building for one dollar. Paul and the Action Group are now the new landlords and find it's not an easy job. This upbeat novel shows how the young landlords deal with problem tenants, endless repairs, utility bills, and suspicious activities in their building. In the process they rapidly mature as they take on these adult responsibilities.

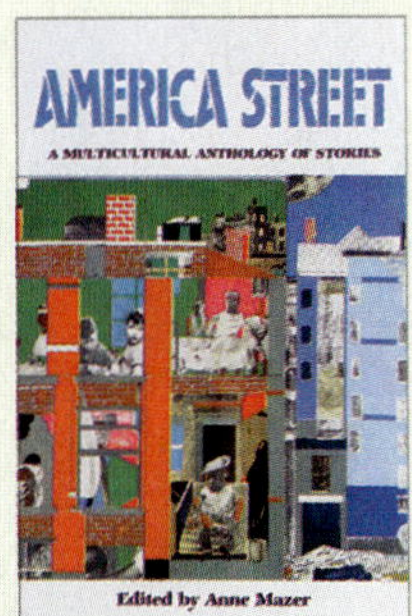

FICTION

America Street

Reading the stories in *America Street* is like taking a walk in fourteen neighborhoods. On one street Toni Cade Bambara will introduce you to Squeaky, who's determined to win the neighborhood race if it kills her. On another street you'll meet Gary Soto's Fausto, who's busy scraping pennies together to buy a guitar. Duane Big Eagle will take you to Raoul's neighborhood, where he is boarding a train in search of his mysterious medicine-woman aunt. Why not go for a walk and meet your neighbors?

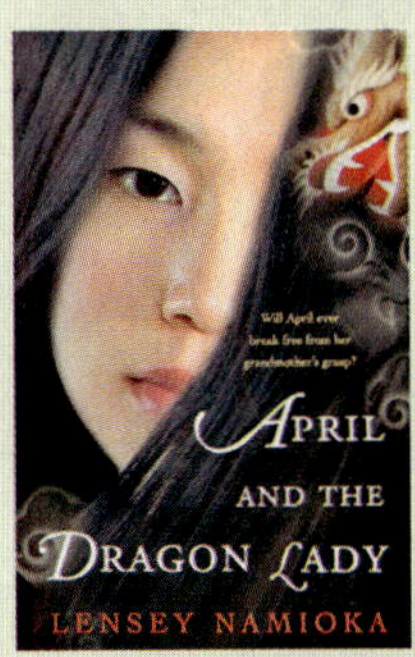

FICTION

April and the Dragon Lady

April Chen is happily planning to go away to college, and she has a new boyfriend, Steve. But as the only girl in her Chinese American family, April is expected to take care of her eccentric and demanding grandmother. Grandma, or "The Dragon Lady," hates Steve because he is Caucasian and she has other plans for April. Torn between her duty to her family and her desire for independence, April realizes that she must find a way to define herself on her own terms before she is torn apart in a culture clash.

Learn It Online
Find tips for exploring novels with *NovelWise* at:
go.hrw.com L9-217 Go

COLLECTION 3

Narrator and Voice

INFORMATIONAL TEXT FOCUS

Synthesizing Sources: Drawing Conclusions

"Only enemies speak the truth. Friends lie endlessly, caught in the web of duty."

—Stephen King

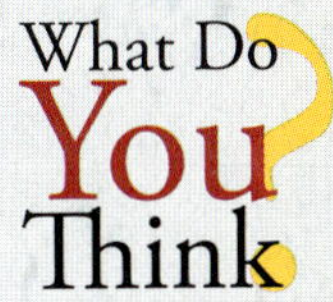

Who are our friends, and who are our enemies? How can we tell the difference?

Four Masks by Noma. Mixed media (5" x 5"). Private Collection.

Learn It Online
Listen to the selections in this collection come alive online:
go.hrw.com
L9-219
Go

Literary Focus

by **Carol Jago**

What Do You Need to Know About Narrator and Voice?

Have you ever listened to a story and wondered if you were getting the whole story? Have you ever told the same story differently? Writers choose particular narrators and voices to achieve particular effects. Sometimes a narrator can be depended upon to give you the whole story. At other times you need to beware of an unreliable narrator, who will not—or cannot—tell it like it is.

Narrator

Narrator Simply put, a narrator is a storyteller. The narrator controls everything we know about the characters and events in a story. We see the story through his or her point of view. There are three main types of **narrators,** or points of view: omniscient (ahm NIHSH uhnt), first person, and third-person limited.

Omniscient Narrator In real life, you can guess what others think and feel, but you don't know for sure. Writers have the option of knowing all: Since they create the characters, they can choose to tell us everything about all of the characters.

When the **omniscient point of view** is used, the narrator is not a story character and almost never refers to himself or herself directly. *Omniscient* means "all knowing," and the omniscient narrator is able to tell us what every character thinks and feels.

> The two enemies stood glaring at one another for a long silent moment. Each had a rifle in his hand, each had hate in his heart and murder uppermost in his mind.
>
> from "The Interlopers"
> by Saki

First-Person Narrator Unlike the omniscient narrator, the **first-person narrator** is a character in the story who talks to us, using the first-person pronoun *I*. (Literary critics sometimes use the term *persona* to refer to a first-person narrator.)

We get a very personal view of what is happening from a first-person narrator, but we know *only* what he or she thinks and experiences and is able—or chooses—to tell us.

> When I think of the hometown of my youth, all that I seem to remember is dust—the brown, crumbly dust of late summer—arid, sterile dust that gets into the eyes and makes them water, gets into the throat and between the toes of bare brown feet.
>
> from "Marigolds"
> by Eugenia W. Collier

Unreliable Narrator Have you ever heard people say they need to hear both sides of the story? They mean that they need to make a judgment about who is more credible, or believable. When reading, always question whether a first-person narrator can be trusted. An **unreliable narrator** is biased about or ignorant of what has actually occurred.

MO 9.R.2.C.1.b Use details from text(s): to analyze character, plot, setting, point of view 9.R.2.C.1.d Use details from text(s): to evaluate the effect of author's style

Third-Person-Limited Narrator A **third-person-limited narrator** plays no part in the story—he or she just tells it. In the third-person-limited point of view, the storyteller focuses on just one character but talks about that character in the third person, using *he* or *she*. When the story is told from this point of view, we share one character's reactions, but what we know about the other characters is limited.

> The basement room was dark and warm, like the inside of a sealed jar, Millicent thought, her eyes getting used to the strange dimness.
>
> from "Initiation"
> by Sylvia Plath

Tone and Voice

Tone A story's tone can be described in a single word, such as *humorous, serious,* or *ironic*. **Tone** is the attitude a speaker or writer takes toward a subject, character, or audience. Notice the loving tone the narrator has toward her mother in "Marigolds."

> My mother's voice was like a cool, dark room in summer—peaceful, soothing, quiet. I loved to listen to it; it made things seem all right somehow.
>
> from "Marigolds"
> by Eugenia W. Collier

Voice When you really know someone, you recognize his or her voice on the phone. In the same way, a writer's **voice** is his or her unique use of language and style. Often you can identify the author of a work from the voice of the writing. At times, writers may purposely alter their voice, but usually a writer's voice remains recognizable from work to work.

In fiction, narrators are often described as having a voice created by their manner of speaking, word choice, and tone. A narrator's voice affects our view of characters and plot events and shapes the tone of the story as a whole.

I remember well my sensation as we first entered the house. I knew instantly that something was very wrong. I realized that my father's chair had been sat in, as well as my mother's and my own. The porridge we had left on the table to cool had been partially eaten. None of this, however, prepared me for what we were about to discover upstairs. . . .

> He was a good husband, a good father. I don't understand it. I don't believe in it. I don't believe that it happened. I saw it happen but it isn't true.
>
> from "The Wife's Story"
> by Ursula K. Le Guin

Your Turn Analyze Point of View

With a partner, pick a favorite fairy tale, such as "Cinderella." Take turns telling parts of the story as a first-person narrator, as an unreliable narrator, as a third-person-limited narrator, and as an omniscient narrator. With each retelling, discuss how the change in point of view affects your experience of the story.

Learn It Online
Use *NovelWise* to increase your understanding of points of view. Visit:
go.hrw.com L9-221 Go

Analyzing Visuals

How Can You Analyze Point of View and Tone in Art?

In a sense, painters are like narrators of the pictures they create. The artist chooses what you see, and the work comes from his or her point of view. Some works, such as abstract art, don't present an obvious point of view. Others show one only in a literal sense—where the artist stood and what he or she saw. Yet some paintings with recognizable images hint at the artist's unique point of view. You just have to know what to look for.

1. Thomas Cordell once worked as an architect. From what **point of view** does he depict the structures and action of 7th Avenue?

2. What **tone** does this work convey? How does Thomas Cordell create that tone?

7th Avenue (2002) by Thomas Cordell (1951–). Oil on canvas (68.5 cm x 68.5 cm). Private Collection.

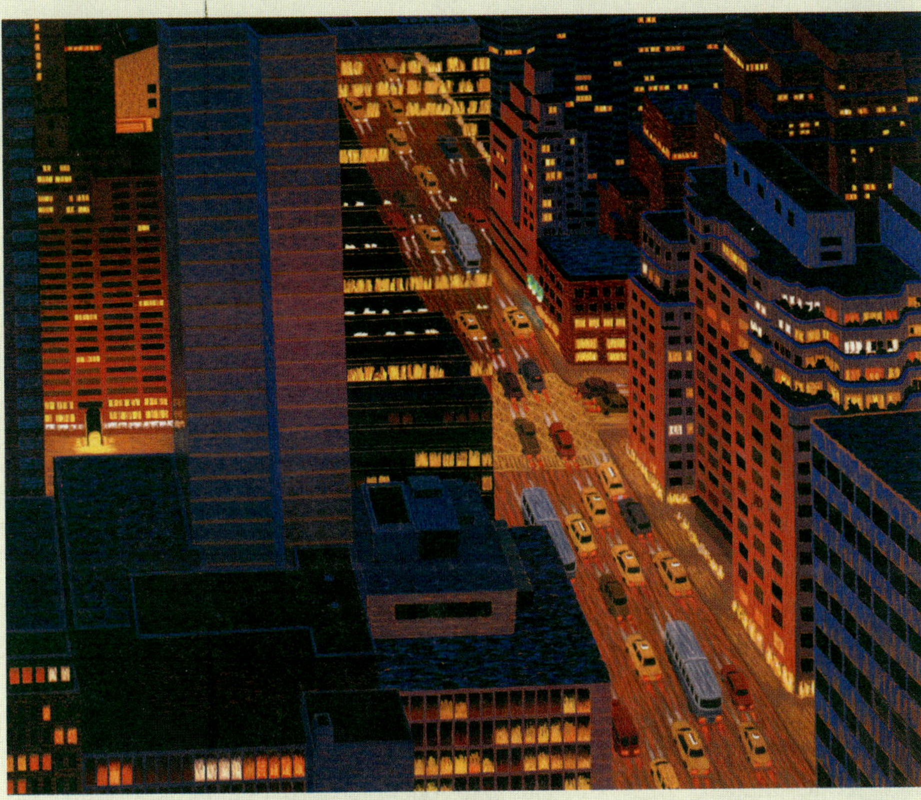

3. How does the **point of view** in this painting differ from Cordell's point of view?

4. What effect do you think that Yvonne Jacquette was striving to create by using this **point of view**?

Third Avenue (with reflection) II (2004) by Yvonne Jacquette (1934–). Oil on canvas (63" x 77"). Courtesy of the DC Moore Gallery, New York.

Analyzing Paintings

Use these guidelines to help you identify point of view in a painting.

1. Identify the painting's subject, its visual content. Does the artist present it crisply and clearly, or is the subject presented more imaginatively?
2. Note the vantage point of the artist. Are we looking at things from within the scene? from just outside it? from some detached place?
3. Interpret **tone,** or the artist's attitude toward the topic. Are the colors realistic? optimistic? negative? Are the lines flowing or jagged? Is the paint smooth or textured?
4. Analyze the artist's intentions. Ask yourself why the artist chose to present the subject the way he or she did. What purpose for painting might the artist have had?

Your Turn Write About Point of View

One of these paintings drops you in the thick of things, on the street; the other lifts you to the sky. Which point of view do you think evokes a deeper emotional reaction? Explain.

Reading Focus

by **Kylene Beers**

What Skills Help You Analyze Narrator and Point of View?

Sometimes, to understand something, you answer questions. Other times, though, what you need to do is *ask* questions. Questioning the text as you read is an important reading habit. Occasionally, your questions will focus on details (*Who said what to whom?*), but more often they will probably be questions that help you draw conclusions (*So what does all this really mean?*). Many times, the conclusions you reach will be influenced by the narrator's perspective of story events and characters. For this reason, questioning characters as well as events is sometimes the best approach.

Asking Questions

A friend repeats a story you find too incredible to believe. You probably ask, "Who told you that?" or "Where did you hear that?" Your **questions** are geared toward finding out who originally told the story and whether that person is to be trusted.

You should do the same thing when you read narratives. Don't simply accept what a story's narrator has to say; think about the story first. The following questions will help you identify and begin thinking about a story's narrator.

Question	My Response
Who is the narrator?	Lizabeth
Is the narrator taking part in the story?	
Does the narrator zoom in on one story character or focus on them all?	

Drawing Conclusions

Don't jump to conclusions! That's a phrase many of us have heard. What it means is, "Don't rush to form an opinion before you examine all of the evidence." When you read fiction, you'll be introduced to story characters and settings and told what has happened to whom. In the course of the story, you'll form opinions and re-form them as you read further.

Once you ask and answer basic questions about a story's narrator, you can **draw conclusions** about him or her. Here's how:

Step 1: Review what you've learned about the narrator. *Example: The narrator is a young girl who tells about a special day when fairies visited her.*

Step 2: Make connections between what you've learned and what you know from life. *Example: Fairies don't exist. The narrator is too young to realize her older sister is tricking her.*

Step 3: Draw a conclusion based on the clues in the story and your background knowledge. *Example: The narrator is unreliable; she tells us what she believes to be true but we know is not.*

MO **9.R.1.G.1.c** During reading, utilize strategies: to question the text **9.R.1.H.1.d** Apply post-reading skills to comprehend, interpret, analyze, and evaluate text: draw conclusions **9.R.2.C.1.b** Use details from text(s): to analyze character, plot, setting, point of view

Analyzing Narrator's Perspective

When was the last time you took a photograph? Did you circle your subject as you looked for the best angle? Did you use the zoom feature to focus in on what you found most interesting? Did you stand on a chair or lie on the floor to get an interesting shot? Writers do the same thing when they choose a **narrator** and **perspective,** or viewpoint, from which to tell their tales.

Once you have read a story, identified its narrator, and drawn conclusions about him or her, it's time to dig deeper. Think about the unique way in which the story's narrator views the world.

To begin your analysis, try filling out a chart like this one:

Analyze Narrator's Perspective

Question	My Response
Visualize the narrator. What has he or she seen and told you?	
What, if any, events or ideas are absent from the story? (Write down events that confuse you.)	
How might the story have changed if the writer had chosen a different narrator?	

Your Turn Analyze Point of View

Put your skills to the test by reading the following story passage and using the reading skills of questioning, drawing conclusions, and analyzing a narrator's perspective to answer the questions.

The Tortoise and the Hare

Last week Hare came by my house, and, as usual, he couldn't stop taunting me and saying how slow I am and that I'll never get anywhere in life. That guy just burns me up! Anyway, I decided what the heck and told him I'd race him, and what's more, I'd win. Little did he or I know just how that fateful race would turn out.

The day of the race dawned rainy and chilly, but by ten o'clock the sun peeked through the clouds. Hare and I met under the big elm tree by the schoolhouse. We were to race straight up Meadow Lane, past the Town Hall, and end at the Parkway Oval. . . .

Asking Questions: Who is telling the story? Is the narrator a story character? From what point of view is the story being told?

Drawing Conclusions: What type of person is the narrator? Do you think the narrator of the story is reliable? Why or why not?

Analyzing Narrator's Perspective: This fable is usually told from a different point of view. How does this different perspective change the story?

Now go to the Skills in Action: Reading Model

Learn It Online
Try the *PowerNotes* version of this lesson on:
go.hrw.com
L9-225
Go

SKILLS IN ACTION

Reading Model

SHORT STORY

Build Background

Mirrors are often seen as symbols of truth because they reflect the real world with clarity. However, many writers have also viewed mirrors as a window to the supernatural. Lewis Carroll's Alice walked through a mirror into a world of backward logic in *Alice in Wonderland*. In Bram Stoker's *Dracula,* a notorious count has no reflection at all. As you read the following story, think about what the mirror might symbolize.

Read with a Purpose As you read this story, notice how a mirror helps blur the line between reality and fantasy.

In the Family

by **María Elena Llano**

translated by **Beatriz Teleki**

When my mother found out that the large mirror in the living room was inhabited, we all gradually went from disbelief to astonishment, and from this to a state of contemplation, ending up by accepting it as an everyday thing.

The fact that the old, spotted mirror reflected the dear departed in the family was not enough to upset our life style. Following the old saying of "let the house burn as long as no one sees the smoke," we kept the secret to ourselves since, after all, it was nobody else's business.

Literary Focus

First-Person Narrator The narrator describes something that happened to the family. The pronouns *we* and *ourselves* emphasize that the narrator's ideas about the mirror are shared by others in the family.

At any rate, some time went by before each one of us would feel absolutely comfortable about sitting down in our favorite chair and learning that, in the mirror, that same chair was occupied by somebody else. For example, it could be Aurelia, my grandmother's sister (1939), and even if cousin Natalie would be on my side of the room, across from her would be the almost forgotten Uncle Nicholas (1927). As could have been expected, our departed reflected in the mirror presented the image of a family gathering almost identical to our own, since nothing, absolutely nothing in the living-room—the furniture and its arrangement, the light, etc.—was changed in the mirror. The only difference was that on the other side it was them instead of us.

I don't know about the others, but I sometimes felt that, more than a vision in the mirror, I was watching an old worn-out movie, already clouded. The deceaseds' efforts to copy our gestures were slower, restrained, as if the mirror were not truly showing a direct image but the reflection of some other reflection.

From the very beginning I knew that everything would get more complicated as soon as my cousin Clara got back from vacation. Because of her boldness and determination, Clara had long given me the impression that she had blundered into our family by mistake. This suspicion had been somewhat bolstered by her being one of the first women dentists in the country. However, the idea that she might have been with us by mistake went away as soon as my cousin hung up her diploma and started to embroider sheets beside my grandmother, aunts and other cousins, waiting for a suitor who actually did show up but was found lacking in one respect or another—nobody ever really found out why.

Once she graduated, Clara became the family oracle,[1] even though she never practiced her profession. She would prescribe painkillers and was the arbiter[2] of fashion; she would choose the theater shows and rule on whether the punch had the right amount of liquor at each social gathering. In view of all this, it was fitting that she take one month off every year to go to the beach.

That summer when Clara returned from her vacation and learned about my mother's discovery, she remained pensive for a while, as if weighing the symptoms before issuing a diagnosis. Afterwards, without batting an eye, she leaned over the mirror, saw for herself that it was true, and then tossed her head, seemingly accepting the situation. She immediately sat by the bookcase and craned her neck to see who was sitting in the chair on the other side. "Gosh, look at Gus," was all she said. There in the very same chair the mirror showed us Gus, some sort of godson of Dad, who after a flood in his hometown came to live with us and had remained there in the somewhat ambiguous character of adoptive poor relation. Clara greeted him amiably with a wave of the hand, but he seemed busy, for the moment, with something like a radio tube and did not pay attention to her. Undoubtedly, the mirror people weren't going out of their way to be sociable. This must have wounded Clara's self-esteem, although she did not let it on.

Naturally, the idea of moving the mirror to the dining-room was hers. And so was its sequel: to bring the mirror near the big table, so we could all sit together for meals.

1. **oracle:** person of great knowledge and wisdom; often one who can predict the future.

2. **arbiter:** person who settles disagreements or makes judgments.

Reading Focus

Asking Questions Pause when you come to important story information. When the narrator introduces the idea that everything would change when Clara arrived, you might ask, "How will Clara's coming home affect the family and the mirror?" Keep reading to find the answer.

Literary Focus

Narrator and Voice If you read between the lines, you can detect a note of sarcasm here hinting that the narrator doesn't entirely approve of this cousin.

Reading Focus

Asking Questions Ask yourself questions to clarify story details. You could ask, "Why is moving the mirror to the dining room such a big deal?" When you think about the answer, you might realize that the change brings the family into closer daily contact with the mirror world.

In spite of my mother's fears that the mirror people would run away or get annoyed because of the fuss, everything went fine. I must admit it was comforting to sit every day at the table and see so many familiar faces, although some of those from the other side were distant relatives, and others, due to their lengthy—although unintentional—absence, were almost strangers. There were about twenty of us sitting at the table every day, and even if their gestures and movements seemed more remote than ours and their meals a little washed-out, we generally gave the impression of being a large family that got along well.

At the boundary between the real table and the other one, on this side, sat Clara and her brother Julius. On the other side was Eulalia (1949), the second wife of Uncle Daniel, aloof and indolent in life, and now the most distant of anyone on the other side. Across from her sat my godfather Sylvester (1952), who even though he was not a blood relative was always a soul relation. I was sad to see that Sylvester had lost his ruddiness, for he now looked like a faded mannequin, although his full face seemed to suggest perfect health. This

Literary Focus

Narrator and Voice The narrator's voice is calm, and she speaks with precision and logic. Yet what she has to say is so out of the ordinary that we wonder if she is completely reliable.

The Consultation (1917) by William Sheehan (1894–1923). Oil on canvas (69 cm x 80 cm).

Analyzing Visuals

Viewing and Interpreting Does this painting effectively capture the story's essence? Why or why not?

pallor did not suit the robust Asturian,[3] who undoubtedly felt a bit ridiculous in these circumstances.

For a while we ate all together, without further incidents or problems. We mustn't forget Clara, however, who we had allowed to sit at the frontier between the two tables, the equator separating what was from what was not. Although we paid no attention to the situation, we should have. Compounding our regrettable oversight was the fact that lethargic Eulalia sat across from her so that one night, with the same cordiality with which she had addressed Gus, Clara asked Eulalia to pass the salad. Eulalia affected the haughty disdain of offended royalty as she passed the spectral salad bowl, filled with dull lettuce and grayish semi-transparent tomatoes which Clara gobbled up, smiling mischievously at the novelty of it all. She watched us with the same defiance in her eyes that she had on the day she enrolled in a man's subject. There was no time to act. We just watched her grow pale, then her smile faded away until finally Clara collapsed against the mirror.

Once the funeral business was over and we sat back down at the table again, we saw that Clara had taken a place on the other side. She was between cousin Baltazar (1940) and a great-uncle whom we simply called "Ito."

This *faux pas*[4] dampened our conviviality somewhat. In a way, we felt betrayed; we felt that they had grievously abused our hospitality. However, we ended up divided over the question of who was really whose guest. It was also plain that our carelessness and Clara's irrepressible inquisitiveness had contributed to the mishap. In fact, a short time later we realized that there wasn't a great deal of difference between what Clara did before and what she was doing now, and so we decided to overlook the incident and get on with things. Nevertheless, each day we became less and less sure about which side was life and which its reflection, and as one bad step leads to another, I ended up taking Clara's empty place.

I am now much closer to them. I can almost hear the distant rustle of the folding and unfolding of napkins, the slight clinking of glasses and cutlery, the movement of chairs. The fact is that I can't tell if these sounds come from them or from us. I'm obviously not worried about clearing that up. What really troubles me, though, is that Clara doesn't seem to behave properly, with either the solemnity or with the opacity owed to her new position; I don't know how to put

Reading Focus

Drawing Conclusions The narrator's matter-of-fact recounting of Clara's death may lead you to conclude that either the narrator is half mad and that Clara's death actually occurred in a different way or that the narrator is calm because life goes on after death within the world of the mirror.

Reading Focus

Analyzing Perspective The narrator reveals a new perspective on the situation. He or she no longer thinks that life is very different on the other side of the mirror. The division between the two worlds has become indistinct.

3. **Asturian** (as TUR ee uhn): person from a region of northwestern Spain.

4. ***faux pas:*** French for "false step"; a social blunder.

it. Even worse, the problem is that I—more than anybody else in the family—may become the target of Clara's machinations,[5] since we were always joined by a very special affection, perhaps because we were the same age and had shared the same children's games and the first anxieties of adolescence. . . .

As it happens, she is doing her best to get my attention, and ever since last Monday she has been waiting for me to slip up so she can pass me a pineapple this big, admittedly a little bleached-out, but just right for making juice and also a bit sour, just as she knows I like it.

5. **machinations:** plots or schemes.

Literary Focus

Unreliable Narrator At the story's end, most readers will conclude that the narrator is paranoid and unreliable. Ultimately, however, it's up to individual readers to make that judgment.

Read with a Purpose In your opinion, is the story's narrator telling a true but fantastic story, or might he or she be imagining things? Explain.

Book cover of *Short Stories By Latin American Women: The Magic and the Real*—paperback edition from Arte Público Press.

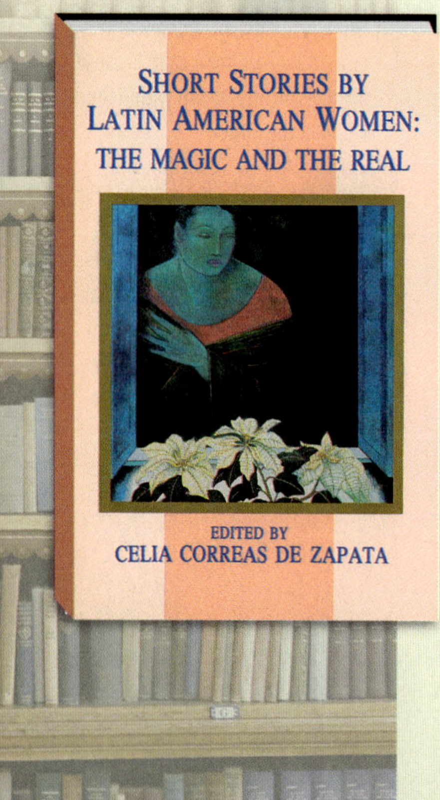

MEET THE WRITER

María Elena Llano

(1936–   )

A Multitalented Writer

María Elena Llano's interests and curiosity have led her to work in a wide variety of writing genres. Born in Cuba, she worked as a journalist for Havana's news agency, Latin Press, where she covered contemporary cultural issues. Llano has written for radio and television in addition to writing fiction, nonfiction, and poetry. In 1966, she published *La Reja* (*The Plow*), a collection of short stories.

A Story Reaches New Audiences

Llano's short story "In the Family" has captured the interest of readers around the world. This short and surprising tale has been included in many collections, including *Short Stories by Latin American Women: The Magic and the Real* and *The Penguin Book of International Women's Stories*. The story was read aloud on Chicago Public Radio as part of the series *Stories on Stage*.

Think About the Writer Why do you think Llano has chosen to write in many genres rather than focus on just one?

SKILLS IN ACTION

Wrap Up

9.R.2.C.1.b Use details from text(s): to analyze character, plot, setting, point of view **9.W.3.A.1.d** Compose a variety of texts: including literary analysis **9.R.1.E.1.c** Develop vocabulary through text: using glossary, dictionary and thesaurus

Into Action: Narrator and Point of View

"In the Family" is a fascinating story, in part because of its narrator. Who is he or she? Is the narrator telling us the truth about what happened, or is he or she interpreting events in an unusual way? Fill in the chart below with story details that will help you understand the story's narrator. Write your responses to those details in the right-hand column. Then, use your findings to draw an overall conclusion about the narrator.

Details About the Narrator	My Response
felt like he or she was watching an old movie	narrator thinks the people on the other side of the mirror look old

My Conclusion:

Talk About . . .

What makes "In the Family" such an interesting story? Get together with a small group of classmates, and discuss your responses to the following questions. Try to use each Academic Vocabulary word listed at right at least once in your discussion.

1. How does the story's narrator portray Clara? Is the narrator's attitude toward Clara understandable, or do you find it unfair? Explain.
2. What overall impression do the story's events create? Would the story have been more effective if the magical elements had been left out? Why or why not?

Write About . . .

Write a comparison of the story's narrator and the narrator's cousin Clara. In what ways are they distinct personalities? In what ways are they similar? What insight about life do their responses to various incidents help reveal?

Writing Focus

Think as a Reader/Writer

Find It in Your Reading Llano's story is fun to read because she uses both realistic and fantastic elements in it. Skim through the story again, and look for examples of both kinds of details. As you read the stories in Collection 3, you will have a chance to analyze the writing styles of other authors and practice using writer's craft in your own writing.

Academic Vocabulary for Collection 3

Talking and Writing About Short Stories

Academic Vocabulary is the language you use to write and talk about literature. Use these words to discuss the short stories you read in this collection. They are underlined throughout the collection.

distinct (dihs TIHNGKT) *adj.:* obviously different; unique. *The narrator's description of Clara conveys a distinct tone.*

impression (ihm PREHSH uhn) *n.:* overall effect. *The story's events leave readers with the impression that life in the narrator's household is unusual.*

insight (IHN syt) *n.:* clear understanding. *With a sudden insight, I realized that the narrator was unreliable.*

portray (pawr TRAY) *v.:* describe with words or other means; show. *If Clara had been the narrator, would she portray the story events differently?*

Your Turn

Copy the words from the list into your *Reader/Writer Notebook*. Then, write sample test questions in which you use each word correctly.

SHORT STORY

Preparing to Read

THE INTERLOPERS

by **Saki**

Face to Face by Jim Dandy. Monoprint / monotype (24" x 17"). Collection of the artist.

What does it take to get two enemies to overcome their differences?

QuickWrite

Think about enemies who have become friends. What happened to help end the fighting? Write down a few examples.

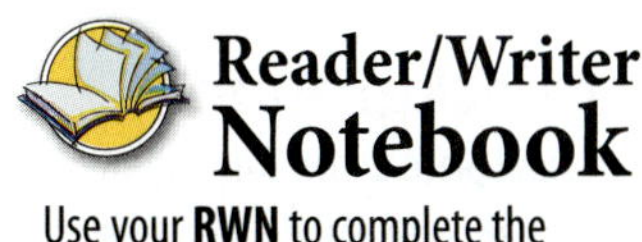

Use your **RWN** to complete the activities for this selection.

9.R.2.C.1.b Use details from text(s): to analyze character, plot, setting, point of view **9.R.1.H.1.d** Apply post-reading skills to comprehend, interpret, analyze, and evaluate text: draw conclusions

Literary Focus

Omniscient Narrator An **omniscient narrator** knows everything about a story's characters. Since this type of narrator is not one of the characters, he or she can move from the mind of one character to the mind of the next, jump from one place to another, or zoom in and out of a scene. Sometimes, an omniscient narrator will save a key piece of information for the very last moment of the story in order to create a surprise ending.

Reading Focus

Drawing Conclusions When you read, you **draw conclusions** based on text clues and your own knowledge of life.

Into Action As you read, look for story elements that you think are strongly significant or meaningful. Put these details together with what you know already to draw conclusions based on the text.

Story Detail	My Knowledge	My Conclusion
Like their families, Ulrich and Georg have been enemies for years.	Some people are enemies because of family history, not because they actually know and dislike each other.	

Writing Focus

Think as a Reader/Writer

Find It in Your Reading As you read, notice how the narrator moves from character to character and gives us details about each one's situations, thoughts, and feelings. In your *Reader/Writer Notebook*, note at least three examples in which the narrator describes what each of the characters thinks or feels.

Vocabulary

disputed (dihs PYOOT ihd) *v.* used as *adj.:* subject of an argument. *The disputed border caused conflict between the neighbors.*

marauders (muh RAW duhrz) *n. pl.:* people who roam in search of loot, or goods to steal; raiders. *The marauders traveled constantly in search of money and valuable items that they could resell.*

exasperation (ehg zas puh RAY shuhn) *n.:* state of great annoyance. *He could not hide his exasperation when he found himself at the mercy of his enemy.*

condolences (kuhn DOH luhns ihz) *n. pl.:* expressions of sympathy. *Georg will send condolences for Ulrich's death.*

reconciliation (rehk uhn sihl ee AY shuhn) *n.:* friendly end to a quarrel. *Ulrich and Georg think about a reconciliation and the changes it will bring.*

Language Coach

Oral Fluency To truly own a word, you need to know more than its meaning; you need to be comfortable pronouncing it so that you can use it in conversation. Study the pronunciation guides above, and answer these questions: How many words have the primary stress on the second syllable? Which words are they? Which word has the most syllables? How many does it have?

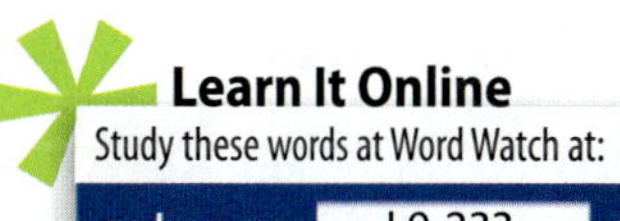
Learn It Online
Study these words at Word Watch at:
go.hrw.com L9-233 Go

MEET THE WRITER

Learn It Online
Learn more about the author at:
go.hrw.com L9-234 Go

Saki

(1870–1916)

A Strict Beginning

Hector Hugh Munro wrote stories with snappy endings that were either wickedly funny or terrifying. Munro was born in Burma (now Myanmar), where his father was a military police officer. When Munro's mother died suddenly, he went to live with his grandmother and two strict aunts in England. The aunts believed in rigid rules and harsh punishments. They thought that children should never show any emotion. The windows were never opened, and Munro was seldom allowed outside to play. The aunts considered him sickly; he played with few children and wasn't sent to school until he was ten. The cruel streak found in many of Munro's stories may be his reaction to his aunts' severe and illogical household.

A New Name for a New Career

When he was twenty-three, Munro became a policeman in Burma. Although he took little interest in his job, he loved the natural setting and even kept a tiger cub as a pet. A year later, he returned to England and set out to become a professional writer. When he began to write political satires, he adopted Saki as his pen name. Saki was the character who served wine to the gods in the then popular poem the *Rubáiyát of Omar Khayyám*. Munro also worked as a newspaper reporter, but he found his strongest voice when writing short, sharp satires as Saki.

Think About the Writer How do you think Saki's aunts might have felt about his dreams of becoming a writer?

Big Ben Westminster
London, UK.

Build Background

In the time and place of this story, animals are hunted as a source of food and pelts. Some hunters also valued animals as trophies. Hunting illegally on someone else's property is called poaching, and arguments over land has sometimes made enemies of close neighbors.

Preview the Selection

Ulrich and **Georg** are bitter enemies. Their families have feuded for generations. Suddenly, they're both stuck in the same situation—one that will have a shocking resolution.

Read with a Purpose Read this story to find out what happens when two enemies come face to face in the forest.

THE INTERLOPERS

by **Saki**

In a forest of mixed growth somewhere on the eastern spurs of the Carpathians,[1] a man stood one winter night watching and listening, as though he waited for some beast of the woods to come within the range of his vision and, later, of his rifle. But the game for whose presence he kept so keen an outlook was none that figured in the sportsman's calendar as lawful and proper for the chase; Ulrich von Gradwitz patrolled the dark forest in quest of a human enemy.

The forest lands of Gradwitz were of wide extent and well stocked with game; the narrow strip of precipitous woodland that lay on its outskirt was not remarkable for the game it harbored or the shooting it afforded, but it was the most jealously guarded of all its owner's territorial possessions. A famous lawsuit, in the days of his grandfather, had wrested it from the illegal possession of a neighboring family of petty landowners; the dispossessed party had never acquiesced[2] in the judgment of the courts, and a long series of poaching affrays and similar scandals had embittered the relationships between the families for three generations. The neighbor feud had grown into a personal one since Ulrich had come to be head of his family; if there was a man in the world whom he detested and wished ill to, it was Georg Znaeym, the inheritor of the quarrel and the tireless game snatcher and raider of the disputed border forest. The feud might, perhaps, have died down or been compromised if the personal ill will of the two men had not stood in the way; as boys they had thirsted for one another's blood, as men each prayed that misfortune might fall on the other, and this wind-scourged winter night Ulrich had banded together his foresters to watch the dark forest, not in quest of four-footed quarry, but to keep a lookout for the prowling thieves whom he suspected of being afoot from across the land boundary. The roebuck,[3] which usually kept in the sheltered hollows during a storm wind, were running like driven things tonight, and there was movement and unrest among the creatures that were wont to sleep through the dark hours. Assuredly there was a disturbing element in the forest, and Ulrich could guess the quarter from whence it came. **A**

1. **Carpathians:** mountain range that starts in Slovakia and extends through Poland, Ukraine, and Romania.
2. **acquiesced** (ak wee EHST) (used with *in*): accepted; complied with.
3. **roebuck** (ROH buhk): male (or males) of the roe deer, small deer that live in Europe and Asia.

A Literary Focus Omniscient Narrator What insight do you get from the omniscient narrator that you probably would not get if one of the two men were telling the story?

Vocabulary disputed (dihs PYOOT ihd) *v.* used as *adj.:* subject of an argument.

He strayed away by himself from the watchers whom he had placed in ambush on the crest of the hill and wandered far down the steep slopes amid the wild tangle of undergrowth, peering through the tree trunks and listening through the whistling and skirling of the wind and the restless beating of the branches for sight or sound of the marauders. If only on this wild night, in this dark, lone spot, he might come across Georg Znaeym, man to man, with none to witness—that was the wish that was uppermost in his thoughts. And as he stepped round the trunk of a huge beech he came face to face with the man he sought.

The two enemies stood glaring at one another for a long silent moment. Each had a rifle in his hand, each had hate in his heart and murder uppermost in his mind. The chance had come to give full play to the passions of a lifetime. But a man who has been brought up under the code of a restraining civilization cannot easily nerve himself to shoot down his neighbor in cold blood and without a word spoken, except for an offense against his hearth and honor. And before the moment of hesitation had given way to action, a deed of Nature's own violence overwhelmed them both. A fierce shriek of the storm had been answered by a splitting crash over their heads, and ere they could leap aside, a mass of falling beech tree had thundered down on them. Ulrich von Gradwitz found himself stretched on the ground, one arm numb beneath him and the other held almost as helplessly in a tight tangle of forked branches, while both legs were pinned beneath the fallen mass. His heavy shooting boots had saved his feet from being crushed to pieces, but if his fractures were not as serious as they might have been, at least it was evident that he could not move from his present position till someone came to release him. The descending twigs had slashed the skin of his face, and he had to wink away some drops of blood from his eyelashes before he could take in a general view of the disaster. At his side, so near that under ordinary circumstances he could almost have touched him, lay Georg Znaeym, alive and struggling, but obviously as helplessly pinioned down as himself. All round them lay a thick-strewn wreckage of splintered branches and broken twigs.

Relief at being alive and exasperation at his captive plight brought a strange medley of pious[4] thank offerings and sharp curses to Ulrich's lips. Georg, who was nearly blinded with the blood which trickled across his eyes, stopped his struggling for a moment to listen, and then gave a short, snarling laugh. **B**

"So you're not killed, as you ought to be, but you're caught, anyway," he cried, "caught fast. Ho, what a jest, Ulrich von Gradwitz snared in his stolen forest. There's real justice for you!"

And he laughed again, mockingly and savagely.

"I'm caught in my own forest land," retorted Ulrich. "When my men come to release us, you will wish, perhaps, that you were in a better plight than caught poaching on a neighbor's land, shame on you."

Georg was silent for a moment; then he answered quietly:

"Are you sure that your men will find much

4. **pious** (PY uhs): showing religious devotion.

B Reading Focus Drawing Conclusions What conclusion can you draw about how seriously the men are taking their situation?

Vocabulary **marauders** (muh RAW duhrz) *n. pl.:* people who roam in search of loot, or goods to steal; raiders.
exasperation (ehg zas puh RAY shuhn) *n.:* state of great annoyance.

The Forest with Red Earth (c. 1891) by Georges Lacombe (1868–1916). Oil on canvas (71 cm x 50 cm).

to release? I have men, too, in the forest tonight, close behind me, and *they* will be here first and do the releasing. When they drag me out from under these branches, it won't need much clumsiness on their part to roll this mass of trunk right over on the top of you. Your men will find you dead under a fallen beech tree. For form's sake I shall send my condolences to your family."

"It is a useful hint," said Ulrich fiercely. "My men had orders to follow in ten minutes' time, seven of which must have gone by already, and when they get me out—I will remember the hint. Only as you will have met your death poaching on my lands, I don't think I can decently send any message of condolence to your family."

"Good," snarled Georg, "good. We fight this quarrel out to the death, you and I and our foresters, with no cursed interlopers to come between us. Death and damnation to you, Ulrich von Gradwitz."

"We fight this quarrel out to the death, you and I and our foresters, with no cursed interlopers to come between us."

"The same to you, Georg Znaeym, forest thief, game snatcher." **C**

Both men spoke with the bitterness of possible defeat before them, for each knew that it might be long before his men would seek him out or find him; it was a bare matter of chance which party would arrive first on the scene.

Both had now given up the useless struggle to free themselves from the mass of wood that held them down; Ulrich limited his endeavors to an effort to bring his one partially free arm near enough to his outer coat pocket to draw out his wine flask. Even when he had accomplished that operation, it was long before he could manage the unscrewing of the stopper or get any of the liquid down his throat. But what a heaven-sent draft[5] it seemed! It was an open winter,[6] and little snow had fallen as yet, hence the captives suffered less from the cold than might have been the case at that season of the year; nevertheless, the wine was warming and reviving to the wounded man, and he looked across with something like a throb of pity to where his enemy lay, just keeping the groans of pain and weariness from crossing his lips.

"Could you reach this flask if I threw it over to you?" asked Ulrich suddenly. "There is good wine in it, and one may as well be as comfortable as one can. Let us drink, even if tonight one of us dies."

"No, I can scarcely see anything; there is so much blood caked round my eyes," said Georg; "and in any case I don't drink wine with an enemy."

Ulrich was silent for a few minutes and lay listening to the weary screeching of the wind. An idea was slowly forming and growing in his brain, an idea that gained strength every time that he looked across at the man who was fighting so grimly against pain and exhaustion. In the pain and languor[7] that Ulrich himself was

5. **draft:** drink.
6. **open winter:** mild winter.
7. **languor** (LANG guhr): weakness; weariness.

C **Literary Focus** **Omniscient Narrator** How does each man predict the situation will be resolved? Does the narrator portray one character more sympathetically than the other—that is, does the narrator make you like one character more than the other? Explain.

Vocabulary **condolences** (kuhn DOH luhns ihz) *n. pl.:* expressions of sympathy.

feeling, the old fierce hatred seemed to be dying down. **D**

"Neighbor," he said presently, "do as you please if your men come first. It was a fair compact. But as for me, I've changed my mind. If my men are the first to come, you shall be the first to be helped, as though you were my guest. We have quarreled like devils all our lives over this stupid strip of forest, where the trees can't even stand upright in a breath of wind. Lying here tonight, thinking, I've come to think we've been rather fools; there are better things in life than getting the better of a boundary dispute. Neighbor, if you will help me to bury the old quarrel, I—I will ask you to be my friend."

Georg Znaeym was silent for so long that Ulrich thought perhaps he had fainted with the pain of his injuries. Then he spoke slowly and in jerks.

"How the whole region would stare and gabble if we rode into the market square together. No one living can remember seeing a Znaeym and a von Gradwitz talking to one another in friendship. And what peace there would be among the forester folk if we ended our feud tonight. And if we choose to make peace among our people, there is none other to interfere, no interlopers from outside. . . . You would come and keep the Sylvester night[8] beneath my roof, and I would come and feast on some high day at your castle. . . . I would never fire a shot on your land, save when you invited me as a guest; and you should come and shoot with me down in the marshes where the wildfowl are. In all the countryside there are none that could hinder if we willed to make peace. I never thought to have wanted to do other than hate you all my life, but I think I have changed my mind about things too, this last half-hour. And you offered me your wine flask. . . . Ulrich von Gradwitz, I will be your friend." **E**

For a space both men were silent, turning over in their minds the wonderful changes that this dramatic **reconciliation** would bring about. In the cold, gloomy forest, with the wind tearing in fitful gusts through the naked branches and whistling round the tree trunks, they lay and waited for the help that would now bring release and succor[9] to both parties. And each prayed a private prayer that his men might be the first to arrive, so that he might be the first to show honorable attention to the enemy that had become a friend.

Presently, as the wind dropped for a moment, Ulrich broke the silence.

"Let's shout for help," he said; "in this lull our voices may carry a little way."

"They won't carry far through the trees and undergrowth," said Georg, "but we can try. Together, then."

The two raised their voices in a prolonged hunting call.

"Together again," said Ulrich a few minutes later, after listening in vain for an answering halloo.

8. **Sylvester night:** feast day honoring Saint Sylvester that is observed on December 31.

9. **succor** (SUHK uhr): help given to someone in distress; relief.

D **Literary Focus** **Omniscient Narrator** How does the omniscient narrator drop a hint about how Ulrich is going to change?

E **Reading Focus** **Drawing Conclusions** What conclusion can you draw about a feud that is ended so quickly?

Vocabulary **reconciliation** (rehk uhn sihl ee AY shuhn) *n.:* friendly end to a quarrel.

Rampaging Wolves Attacking by Mikhail Belomlinsky. Engraving.

Analyzing Visuals **Viewing and Interpreting** Why might seeing wolves like these have terrified Ulrich and Georg?

"I heard something that time, I think," said Ulrich.

"I heard nothing but the pestilential[10] wind," said Georg hoarsely.

There was silence again for some minutes, and then Ulrich gave a joyful cry.

"I can see figures coming through the wood. They are following in the way I came down the hillside."

Both men raised their voices in as loud a shout as they could muster.

"They hear us! They've stopped. Now they see us. They're running down the hill toward us," cried Ulrich.

"How many of them are there?" asked Georg.

"I can't see distinctly," said Ulrich; "nine or ten."

"Then they are yours," said Georg; "I had only seven out with me."

"They are making all the speed they can, brave lads," said Ulrich gladly.

"Are they your men?" asked Georg. "Are they your men?" he repeated impatiently, as Ulrich did not answer.

"No," said Ulrich with a laugh, the idiotic chattering laugh of a man unstrung with hideous fear.

"Who are they?" asked Georg quickly, straining his eyes to see what the other would gladly not have seen.

"*Wolves.*"

---

10. **pestilential** (pehs tuh LEHN shuhl): Strictly speaking, *pestilential* means "deadly; causing disease; harmful." Here, Georg uses the word to mean "cursed."

Applying Your Skills

9.R.2.C.1.b Use details from text(s): to analyze character, plot, setting, point of view **9.R.2.B.2.a** Identify and explain literary techniques in text emphasizing: irony **9.R.2.C.1.d** Use details from text(s): to evaluate the effect of author's style *Also covered* **9.R.1.H.1.d; 9.W.3.A.1.a**

The Interlopers

Respond and Think Critically

Reading Focus

Quick Check

1. How is Ulrich and Georg's reconciliation brought about?
2. What happens when the men end their feud?

Read with a Purpose

3. Were you surprised when Ulrich and Georg became friends? Why or why not?

Reading Skills: Drawing Conclusions

4. What conclusion can you draw about the writer's feelings about family feuds? Complete your chart by listing your conclusion.

Story Detail	My Knowledge	My Conclusion
Like their families, Ulrich and Georg have been enemies for years.	Some people are enemies because of family history, not because they actually know and dislike each other.	

Literary Focus

Literary Analysis

5. **Interpret** What is an interloper? Who are the interlopers in the story? Is there more than one kind of interloper? Explain.
6. **Interpret** What conclusion can you draw about how Saki feels about fate?
7. **Compare and Contrast** There are two distinct conflicts in this story. One is between two men; the other is between humans and nature. Which conflict is harder to resolve? Why?
8. **Analyze** When something turns out to be different from what we expect or think appropriate, that is called **irony.** What is ironic about the ending of the story?
9. **Evaluate** Do you think that stories about family feuds are still relevant today? Why or why not?

Literary Skills: Omniscient Narrator

10. **Analyze** A writer's choice of narrator affects a story's **tone**—the writer's attitude toward a subject or character. What tone does Saki create through the use of an omniscient narrator?
11. **Analyze** How does Saki's choice of narrator help bring about a surprise sending?

Literary Skills Review: Characterization

12. **Compare** The process of revealing the personality of a character is called **characterization.** In what way are Georg's and Ulrich's characters similar? How does this affect the story's plot?

Writing Focus

Think as a Reader/Writer

Use It in Your Writing The narrator of this story doesn't take sides but lets us discover each character by describing his innermost thoughts and feelings. Write a brief scene that takes place between two people in conflict. Like Saki, create an omniscient narrator who lets us see inside the characters' minds.

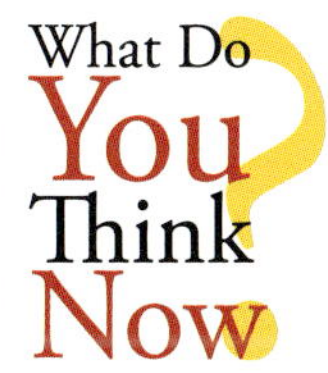

Do you think that Ulrich and Georg would remain friends if they were able to escape? Why or why not?

Applying Your Skills

The Interlopers

Vocabulary Development

Vocabulary Check

Match each Vocabulary word with its definition on the right.

1. disputed	**a.** looters
2. marauders	**b.** annoyance
3. exasperation	**c.** subject of a disagreement
4. condolences	**d.** end to a quarrel
5. reconciliation	**e.** offers of sympathy

Vocabulary Skills: Analogies

Analogies show relationships between words. The second pair of words in an analogy should have the same relationship as the first pair of words. For example:

SURPRISING : PREDICTABLE :: cautious : __________

This formula can be read as "*Surprising* is to *predictable* as *cautious* is to__________." In this example, the first two words are antonyms; they have opposite meanings. To complete the analogy, find a word that is an antonym for *cautious*.

Your Turn

Complete each analogy with a Vocabulary word.

1. FEAR : DREAD :: frustration : __________
2. FRAGILITY : WEAKNESS :: raiders : __________
3. PAIN : COMFORT :: sorrow : __________
4. CLASSIFIED : CATEGORIZED :: agreement : __________
5. OFTEN : FREQUENT :: argued : __________

Language Coach

Oral Fluency Being able to speak clearly and with confidence is a critical skill in school and in the workplace. Get comfortable speaking the Vocabulary words aloud by working with a partner and using each correctly in a sentence. Review the pronunciation guides on page 233 if you need help.

Academic Vocabulary

Write About . . .

1. Why do you think Saki avoided giving Georg and Ulrich distinct personalities?
2. If you were to cast a movie version of "The Interlopers," which actors would you choose to portray Georg and Ulrich? Why?

Learn It Online
Expand your vocabulary with Word Watch online:
go.hrw.com
L9-242
Go

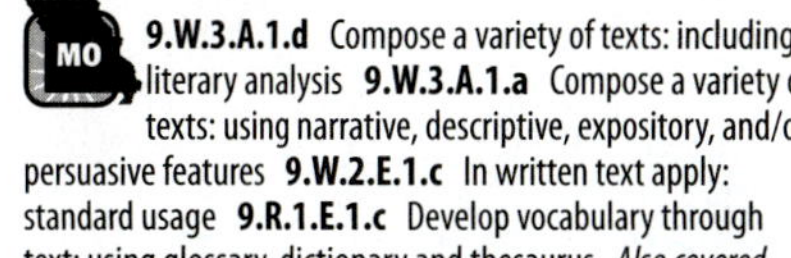

9.W.3.A.1.d Compose a variety of texts: including literary analysis **9.W.3.A.1.a** Compose a variety of texts: using narrative, descriptive, expository, and/or persuasive features **9.W.2.E.1.c** In written text apply: standard usage **9.R.1.E.1.c** Develop vocabulary through text: using glossary, dictionary and thesaurus *Also covered* **9.R.1.E.1.b; 9.R.1.G.1.a**

Grammar Link

Verb Tenses

The tense of a verb indicates the time of the action or the state of being that is expressed by the verb. Different tenses serve different purposes. "The Interlopers" is told in the past tense, although characters use the present and future tenses when they speak.

Tense	Example	Purpose
Past	"Georg *was* silent for a moment; then he *answered* quietly."	• expresses an action that occurred in the past but is not occurring now
Present	"'No, I *can* scarcely *see* anything; there *is* so much blood caked round my eyes.'"	• expresses an action that is occurring now • shows a customary action • expresses a general truth
Future	"'Your men *will find* you dead under a fallen beech tree.'"	• expresses an action that will occur

Your Turn

Writing Applications

1. The narrator of "The Interlopers" uses the past tense to tell the story. Choose a paragraph from the story that has no dialogue. Rewrite the paragraph in the present tense. How does the switch in tense change its feeling?
2. In a sample of your writing, underline the verbs. Label each verb tense. Are your tenses consistent within sentences and paragraphs? Are any switches in verb tense intentional? If not, revise your writing.

CHOICES

As you respond to the Choices, use these **Academic Vocabulary** words as appropriate: distinct, impression, portray, insight.

REVIEW

Write a New Ending

Saki's story has several surprising twists, the most stunning of which is the ending. Choose a point in the last two pages of the story, and create your own plot twist by changing the action and writing a new ending. You might decide not to have Ulrich and Georg reconcile; you might come up with a new twist beyond the final one. In your version, imitate Saki's omniscient narrator by showing what each character is thinking.

CONNECT

Write a Blog

TechFocus Suppose that you are a member of a team of readers deciding whether Saki's story should be included in a textbook. Create a blog that will allow readers to respond to the following: (1) Tell why you think the story will or will not appeal to high school students, (2) give at least two reasons for your opinion, and (3) describe how the story compares with two other stories you have read.

EXTEND

Give Your Opinion

Timed Writing Do you think Saki's story gives insight into the nature of feuds, or do you think the story is told solely for entertainment? Write an essay in which you state your ideas and support them with evidence from the text.

Learn It Online
Take a closer look at this story with these Internet links:
go.hrw.com
L9-243
Go

SHORT STORY

Preparing to Read

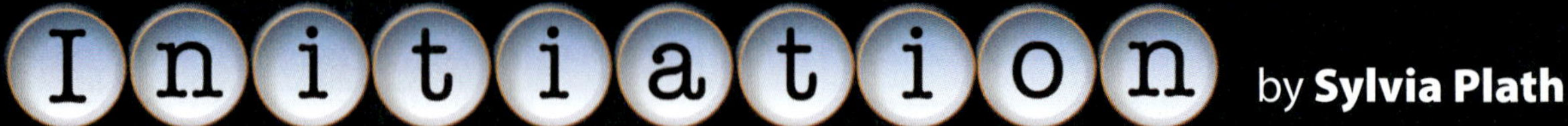

by **Sylvia Plath**

Adolescence (1947) by Milton Avery (1893–1965). Oil and graphite on canvas (30" x 40").
Daniel J. Terra Collection, 1992.3 © 2007 Milton Avery Trust / Artists Rights Society (ARS), New York.

How can our need for popularity and friends affect the way we treat others?

QuickTalk

What is the difference between being popular and having a friend? Which do you prefer? Discuss your ideas with a partner.

Use your **RWN** to complete the activities for this selection.

MO **9.R.2.C.1.b** Use details from text(s): to analyze character, plot, setting, point of view **9.R.1.H.1.d** Apply post-reading skills to comprehend, interpret, analyze, and evaluate text: draw conclusions

Literary Focus

Third-Person-Limited Point of View The story you are about to read is told in the **third-person-limited point of view,** which focuses on the thoughts of a single character—in this case, a teenage girl named Millicent. We learn about Millicent's thoughts, feelings, and actions as she struggles to decide whether or not to accept an invitation to join a sorority.

Reading Focus

Drawing Conclusions As you read this story, think about what the narrator chooses to tell—and not tell—about Millicent. Using that information as well as what you know about people in general, what conclusions can you draw about Millicent?

Into Action Use a graphic organizer like the one below to help you track the clues and evidence that will lead to your conclusions.

Story Details and Clues	My Conclusions
Millicent is going through an initiation.	Millicent wants to join a sorority.
Tracy was blackballed from the sorority.	

Writing Focus

Think as a Reader/Writer

Find It in Your Reading At some points in the story, Plath uses dialogue to show us how Millicent relates with other characters. As you read, find examples of Plath's use of dialogue to characterize some of the other girls in the story. Record those examples in your *Reader/Writer Notebook.*

Vocabulary

vivacious (vy VAY shuhs) *adj.:* spirited; full of life. *Betsy was a young and vivacious teenager.*

anonymity (an uh NIHM uh tee) *n.:* namelessness; lack of individuality. *After being stared at on the crowded bus, Millicent wanted some anonymity.*

vulnerable (VUHL nuhr uh buhl) *adj.:* defenseless; likely to give in to a force or desire. *Millicent felt vulnerable as she performed in front of the strangers at the town square.*

spontaneous (spahn TAY nee uhs) *adj.:* arising naturally; unplanned. *The crowd suddenly broke out in spontaneous laughter.*

exuberant (ehg ZOO buhr uhnt) *adj.:* joyful; high-spirited. *Tracy felt exuberant after receiving the good news.*

Language Coach

Word Origins The Latin word *vulnus* means "wound." Which word on the list above comes from *vulnus*? Look in a dictionary to see if your guess is correct.

Learn It Online
Study these terms with Word Watch at:
go.hrw.com L9-245 Go

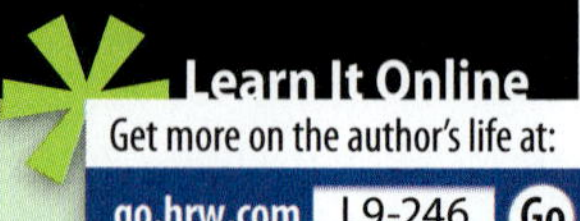

Learn It Online
Get more on the author's life at:
go.hrw.com L9-246 Go

MEET THE WRITER

Sylvia Plath

(1932–1963)

Golden Girl

To the outside world, Sylvia Plath was a golden girl—beautiful, intelligent, and popular. Beneath that shining surface, however, Plath was a troubled soul who struggled with severe episodes of depression. When "Initiation" was accepted for publication by *Seventeen* magazine, the nineteen-year-old Plath wrote, "This news makes me feel that I am maybe not destined to deteriorate, after all."

Early Success and Death

Despite the depression that sometimes plagued her, Plath graduated with the highest honors from Smith College and went to Cambridge University in England on a Fulbright grant. There, she fell in love with and married the brooding, handsome English poet Ted Hughes. Their stormy relationship produced two children and a great deal of poetry, but eventually their marriage fell apart, and Hughes moved out. Overcome by loneliness and despair, Plath took her own life in the winter of 1963, at the age of thirty. Shortly before her death, *The Bell Jar,* an ambitious and haunting novel that Plath based on her earlier experiences of collapse and recovery, was published.

Think About the Writer Do you agree with the notion that artists are their own worst critics? Explain.

Build Background

In "Initiation," a teenager faces an initiation rite for a high school sorority. An initiation rite is a kind of test a person must pass to join a special group. Some initiation rites are tough, mean, or even violent, whereas others are just silly and embarrassing. In many high schools and colleges today, certain types of initiation rites are banned.

Preview the Selection

In this story, you'll meet **Millicent,** a teenager who has been chosen as a pledge for her high school sorority. In addition to meeting the new girls of the sorority, you'll meet Millicent's old friend **Tracy** and witness the test of Millicent's loyalty.

Read with a Purpose Read this story to see how one high school student handles the pressures and challenges of joining a sorority.

Initiation

by **Sylvia Plath**

The basement room was dark and warm, like the inside of a sealed jar, Millicent thought, her eyes getting used to the strange dimness. The silence was soft with cobwebs, and from the small, rectangular window set high in the stone wall there sifted a faint bluish light that must have been coming from the full October moon. She could see now that what she was sitting on was a woodpile next to the furnace.

Millicent brushed back a strand of hair. It was stiff and sticky from the egg that they had broken on her head as she knelt blindfolded at the sorority altar a short while before. There had been a silence, a slight crunching sound, and then she had felt the cold, slimy egg-white flattening and spreading on her head and sliding down her neck. She had heard someone smothering a laugh. It was all part of the ceremony.

Then the girls had led her here, blindfolded still, through the corridors of Betsy Johnson's house and shut her in the cellar. It would be an hour before they came to get her, but then Rat Court would be all over and she would say what she had to say and go home.

For tonight was the grand finale, the trial by fire. There really was no doubt now that she would get in. She could not think of anyone who had ever been invited into the high school sorority and failed to get through initiation time. But even so, her case would be quite different. She would see to that. She could not exactly say what had decided her revolt, but it definitely had something to do with Tracy and something to do with the heather birds. **A**

What girl at Lansing High would not want to be in her place now? Millicent thought, amused. What girl would not want to be one of the elect, no matter if it did mean five days of initiation before and after school, ending in the climax of Rat Court on Friday night when they made the new girls members? Even Tracy had been wistful when she heard that Millicent had been one of the five girls to receive an invitation.

"It won't be any different with us, Tracy," Millicent had told her. "We'll still go around together like we always have, and next year you'll surely get in."

"I know, but even so," Tracy had said quietly, "you'll change, whether you think you will or not. Nothing ever stays the same." **B**

And nothing does, Millicent had thought. How horrible it would be if one never changed . . . if she were condemned to be the plain, shy Millicent of a few years back for the rest of her life. Fortunately there was always the changing, the growing, the going on.

It would come to Tracy, too. She would tell

A Literary Focus Point of View What clues in the first few paragraphs tell you that the point of view is third-person limited?

B Reading Focus Drawing Conclusions What conclusions can you draw from the fact that Millicent was only one of five girls invited to join? How do you think this makes Tracy feel?

Tracy the silly things the girls had said, and Tracy would change also, entering eventually into the magic circle. She would grow to know the special ritual as Millicent had started to last week.

"First of all," Betsy Johnson, the vivacious blonde secretary of the sorority, had told the five new candidates over sandwiches in the school cafeteria last Monday, "first of all, each of you has a big sister. She's the one who bosses you around, and you just do what she tells you."

"Remember the part about talking back and smiling," Louise Fullerton had put in, laughing. She was another celebrity in high school, pretty and dark and Vice-President of the Student Council. "You can't say anything unless your big sister asks you something or tells you to talk to someone. And you can't smile, no matter how you're dying to." The girls had laughed a little nervously, and then the bell had rung for the beginning of afternoon classes.

It would be rather fun for a change, Millicent mused, getting her books out of her locker in the hall, rather exciting to be part of a closely knit group, the exclusive set at Lansing High. Of course, it wasn't a school organization. In fact, the principal, Mr. Cranton, wanted to do away with initiation week altogether, because he thought it was undemocratic and disturbed the routine of school work. But there wasn't really anything he could do about it. Sure, the girls had to come to school for five days without any lipstick on and without curling their hair, and of course everybody noticed them, but what could the teachers do?

Millicent sat down at her desk in the big study hall. Tomorrow she would come to school, proudly, laughingly, without lipstick, with her brown hair straight and shoulder length, and then everybody would know, even the boys would know, that she was one of the elect. Teachers would smile helplessly, thinking perhaps: So now they've picked Millicent Arnold. I never would have guessed it.

Analyzing Visuals **Viewing and Interpreting**
As you read the story, which characters would you say represent the girls shown in this photograph?

A year or two ago, not many people would have guessed it. Millicent had waited a long time for acceptance, longer than most. It was as if she had been sitting for years in a pavilion outside a dance floor, looking in through the windows at the golden interior, with the lights clear and the air like honey, wistfully watching the gay couples waltzing to the never-ending music, laughing in pairs and groups together, no one alone. **C**

C **Literary Focus** **Point of View** What does this insight reveal about the narrator's attitude toward becoming a member of the sorority?

Vocabulary **vivacious** (vy VAY shuhs) *adj.:* spirited; full of life.

But now at last, amid a week of fanfare and merriment, she would answer her invitation to enter the ballroom through the main entrance marked "Initiation." She would gather up her velvet skirts, her silken train, or whatever the disinherited princesses wore in the story books, and come into her rightful kingdom . . . The bell rang to end study hall.

"Millicent, wait up!" It was Louise Fullerton behind her, Louise who had always before been very nice, very polite, friendlier than the rest, even long ago, before the invitation had come.

"Listen," Louise walked down the hall with her to Latin, their next class, "are you busy right after school today? Because I'd like to talk to you about tomorrow."

"Sure. I've got lots of time."

"Well, meet me in the hall after home room then, and we'll go down to the drugstore or something."

Walking beside Louise on the way to the drugstore, Millicent felt a surge of pride. For all anyone could see, she and Louise were the best of friends.

"You know, I was so glad when they voted you in," Louise said.

Millicent smiled. "I was really thrilled to get the invitation," she said frankly, "but kind of sorry that Tracy didn't get in, too."

Tracy, she thought. If there is such a thing as a best friend, Tracy has been just that this last year.

"Yes, Tracy," Louise was saying, "she's a nice girl, and they put her up on the slate, but . . . well, she had three blackballs against her."

"Blackballs? What are they?"

"Well, we're not supposed to tell anybody outside the club, but seeing as you'll be in at the end of the week I don't suppose it hurts." They were at the drugstore now.

"You see," Louise began explaining in a low voice after they were seated in the privacy of the booth, "once a year the sorority puts up all the likely girls that are suggested for membership . . ."

Millicent sipped her cold, sweet drink slowly, saving the ice cream to spoon up last. She listened carefully to Louise, who was going on, ". . . and then there's a big meeting, and all the girls' names are read off and each girl is discussed."

"Oh?" Millicent asked mechanically, her voice sounding strange.

"Oh, I know what you're thinking," Louise laughed. "But it's really not as bad as all that. They keep it down to a minimum of catting.[1]

1. **catting**: making mean, nasty comments.

They just talk over each girl and why or why not they think she'd be good for the club. And then they vote. Three blackballs eliminate a girl."

"Do you mind if I ask you what happened to Tracy?" Millicent said.

Louise laughed a little uneasily. "Well, you know how girls are. They notice little things. I mean, some of them thought Tracy was just a bit *too* different. Maybe you could suggest a few things to her."

"Like what?"

"Oh, like maybe not wearing knee socks to school, or carrying that old bookbag. I know it doesn't sound like much, but well, it's things like that which set someone apart. I mean, you know that no girl at Lansing would be seen dead wearing knee socks, no matter how cold it gets, and it's kiddish and kind of green to carry a bookbag."

"I guess so," Millicent said. **D**

"About tomorrow," Louise went on. "You've drawn Beverly Mitchell for a big sister. I wanted to warn you that she's the toughest, but if you get through all right it'll be all the more credit for you."

"Thanks, Lou," Millicent said gratefully, thinking, this is beginning to sound serious. Worse than a loyalty test, this grilling over the coals. What's it supposed to prove anyway? That I can take orders without flinching? Or does it just make them feel good to see us run around at their beck and call?

"All you have to do really," Louise said, spooning up the last of her sundae, "is be very meek and obedient when you're with Bev and do just what she tells you. Don't laugh or talk back or try to be funny, or she'll just make it harder for you, and believe me, she's a great one for doing that. Be at her house at seven-thirty."

And she was. She rang the bell and sat down on the steps to wait for Bev. After a few minutes the front door opened and Bev was standing there, her face serious.

"Get up, gopher," Bev ordered.

There was something about her tone that annoyed Millicent. It was almost malicious. And there was an unpleasant anonymity about the label "gopher," even if that was what they always called the girls being initiated. It was degrading, like being given a number. It was a denial of individuality.

Rebellion flooded through her.

"I said get up. Are you deaf?"

Millicent got up, standing there.

"Into the house, gopher. There's a bed to be made and a room to be cleaned at the top of the stairs."

Millicent went up the stairs mutely. She found Bev's room and started making the bed. Smiling to herself, she was thinking: How absurdly funny, me taking orders from this girl like a servant. **E**

Bev was suddenly there in the doorway. "Wipe that smile off your face," she commanded.

There seemed something about this relationship that was not all fun. In Bev's eyes, Millicent was sure of it, there was a hard, bright spark of exultation.

On the way to school, Millicent had to walk behind Bev at a distance of ten paces, carrying her books. They came up to the drugstore, where there already was a crowd of boys and

---

D **Reading Focus** **Drawing Conclusions** How does Millicent respond to Louise's comments about Tracy? What conclusion can you draw about what the sorority finds important?

E **Reading Focus** **Drawing Conclusions** Beverly seems to enjoy bossing Millicent around. What conclusion can you draw about Beverly?

Vocabulary **anonymity** (an uh NIHM uh tee) *n.:* namelessness; lack of individuality.

girls from Lansing High waiting for the show.

The other girls being initiated were there, so Millicent felt relieved. It would not be so bad now, being part of the group.

"What'll we have them do?" Betsy Johnson asked Bev. That morning Betsy had made her "gopher" carry an old colored parasol through the square and sing "I'm Always Chasing Rainbows."

"I know," Herb Dalton, the good-looking basketball captain, said.

A remarkable change came over Bev. She was all at once very soft and coquettish.[2]

"You can't tell them what to do," Bev said sweetly. "Men have nothing to say about this little deal."

"All right, all right," Herb laughed, stepping back and pretending to fend off a blow.

"It's getting late." Louise had come up. "Almost eight-thirty. We'd better get them marching on to school."

The "gophers" had to do a Charleston step[3] all the way to school, and each one had her own song to sing, trying to drown out the other four. During school, of course, you couldn't fool around, but even then, there was a rule that you mustn't talk to boys outside of class or at lunch time . . . or any time at all after school. So the sorority girls would get the most popular boys to go up to the "gophers" and ask them out, or try to start them talking, and sometimes a "gopher" was taken by surprise and began to say something before she could catch herself. And then the boy reported her and she got a black mark.

Herb Dalton approached Millicent as she was getting an ice cream at the lunch counter that noon. She saw him coming before he spoke to her, and looked down quickly, thinking: He is too princely, too dark and smiling. And I am much too vulnerable. Why must he be the one I have to be careful of?

I won't say anything, she thought, I'll just smile very sweetly.

She smiled up at Herb very sweetly and mutely. His return grin was rather miraculous. It was surely more than was called for in the line of duty.

"I know you can't talk to me," he said, very low. "But you're doing fine, the girls say. I even like your hair straight and all."

Bev was coming toward them, then, her red mouth set in a bright, calculating smile. She ignored Millicent and sailed up to Herb.

"Why waste your time with gophers?" she caroled gaily. "Their tongues are tied, but completely."

Herb managed a parting shot. "But that one keeps *such* an attractive silence."

Millicent smiled as she ate her sundae at the counter with Tracy. Generally, the girls who were outsiders now, as Millicent had been, scoffed at the initiation antics as childish and absurd to hide their secret envy. But Tracy was understanding, as ever.

The other girls being initiated were there, so Millicent felt relieved. It would not be so bad now, being part of the group.

2. **coquettish** (koh KEHT ihsh): flirtatious.
3. **Charleston** (CHAHRLZ tuhn) **step:** The Charleston is a lively dance from the 1920s.

Vocabulary **vulnerable** (VUHL nuhr uh buhl) *adj.:* defenseless; likely to give in to a force or desire.

"Tonight's the worst, I guess, Tracy," Millicent told her. "I hear that the girls are taking us on a bus over to Lewiston and going to have us performing in the square."

"Just keep a poker face outside," Tracy advised. "But keep laughing like mad inside." **F**

Millicent and Bev took a bus ahead of the rest of the girls; they had to stand up on the way to Lewiston Square. Bev seemed very cross about something. Finally she said, "You were talking with Herb Dalton at lunch today."

"No," said Millicent honestly.

"Well, I saw you smile at him. That's practically as bad as talking. Remember not to do it again."

Millicent kept silent.

"It's fifteen minutes before the bus gets into town," Bev was saying then. "I want you to go up and down the bus asking people what they eat for breakfast. Remember, you can't tell them you're being initiated."

Millicent looked down the aisle of the crowded bus and felt suddenly quite sick. She thought: How will I ever do it, going up to all those stony-faced people who are staring coldly out of the window . . .

"You heard me, gopher."

"Excuse me, madam," Millicent said politely to the lady in the first seat of the bus, "but I'm taking a survey. Could you please tell me what you eat for breakfast?"

"Why . . . er . . . just orange juice, toast and coffee," she said.

"Thank you very much." Millicent went on to the next person, a young businessman. He ate eggs sunny side up, toast and coffee.

By the time Millicent got to the back of the bus, most of the people were smiling at her. They obviously know, she thought, that I'm being initiated into something.

Finally, there was only one man left in the corner of the back seat. He was small and jolly, with a ruddy, wrinkled face that spread into a beaming smile as Millicent approached. In his brown suit with the forest-green tie he looked something like a gnome or a cheerful leprechaun.

"Excuse me, sir," Millicent smiled, "but I'm taking a survey. What do you eat for breakfast?"

"Heather birds' eyebrows on toast," the little man rattled off.

"*What?*" Millicent exclaimed.

"Heather birds' eyebrows," the little man explained. "Heather birds live on the mythological moors[4] and fly about all day long, singing wild and sweet in the sun. They're bright purple and have *very* tasty eyebrows."

Millicent broke out into spontaneous laughter. Why, this was wonderful, the way she felt a sudden comradeship with a stranger.

"Are you mythological, too?"

"Not exactly," he replied, "but I certainly hope to be some day. Being mythological does wonders for one's ego."

The bus was swinging into the station now; Millicent hated to leave the little man. She wanted to ask him more about the birds.

And from that time on, initiations didn't bother Millicent at all. She went gaily about Lewiston Square from store to store asking for broken crackers and mangoes, and she just laughed inside when people stared and then brightened, answering her crazy questions as if she were quite serious and really a person of consequence. So many people were

4. **moors** (murz): open, rolling areas of land, usually covered with heather, a plant with small pinkish-purple flowers.

F **Reading Focus** **Drawing Conclusions** How does Tracy feel about the initiation?

Vocabulary **spontaneous** (spahn TAY nee uhs) *adj.:* arising naturally; unplanned.

shut up tight inside themselves like boxes, yet they would open up, unfolding quite wonderfully, if only you were interested in them. And really, you didn't have to belong to a club to feel related to other human beings.

One afternoon Millicent had started talking with Liane Morris, another of the girls being initiated, about what it would be like when they were finally in the sorority.

"Oh, I know pretty much what it'll be like," Liane had said. "My sister belonged before she graduated from high school two years ago."

"Well, just what *do* they do as a club?" Millicent wanted to know.

"Why, they have a meeting once a week . . . each girl takes turns entertaining at her house . . ."

"You mean it's just a sort of exclusive social group . . ."

"I guess so . . . though that's a funny way of putting it. But it sure gives a girl prestige value. My sister started going steady with the captain of the football team after she got in. Not bad, I say."

No, it wasn't bad, Millicent had thought, lying in bed on the morning of Rat Court and listening to the sparrows chirping in the gutters. She thought of Herb. Would he ever have been so friendly if she were without the sorority label? Would he ask her out (if he ever did) just for herself, no strings attached?

Then there was another thing that bothered her. Leaving Tracy on the outskirts. Because that is the way it would be; Millicent had seen it happen before.

Outside, the sparrows were still chirping, and as she lay in bed Millicent visualized them, pale gray-brown birds in a flock, one like the other, all exactly alike.

CULTURE LINK

Fraternities and Sororities

Fraternities and sororities are part of a continuing tradition on college (and sometimes high school) campuses. These organizations usually provide housing and a social community for their members, who are referred to as brothers and sisters.

There are four types of fraternities and sororities: social, professional, honor, and recognition societies. Social fraternities and sororities encourage both close friendships among members and high academic standards; they also sponsor charitable, educational, and social activities. Professional societies attract members with similar career interests; honor societies are made up of students with exceptional academic success. Recognition societies admit members based on superior work in a particular subject area.

Ask Yourself

What kind of sorority does Millicent want to join? What benefits would she receive by becoming a member?

And then, for some reason, Millicent thought of the heather birds. Swooping carefree over the moors, they would go singing and crying out across the great spaces of air, dipping and darting, strong and proud in their freedom and their sometime loneliness. It was then that she made her decision. **G**

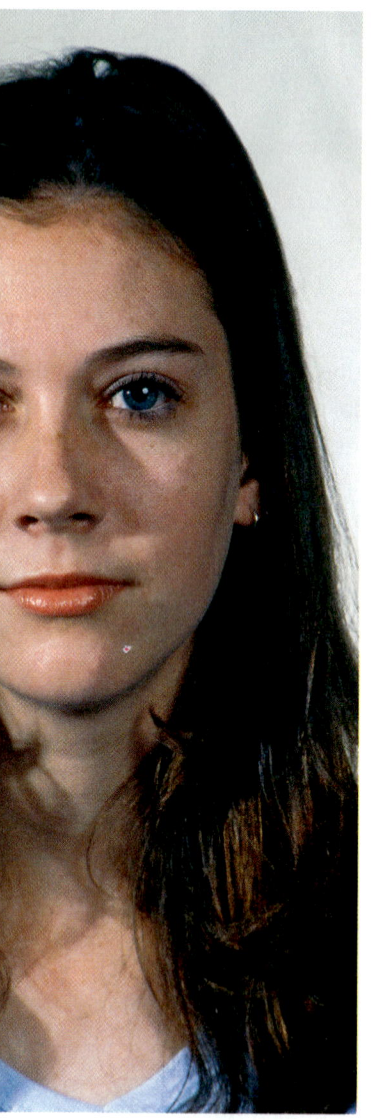

Seated now on the woodpile in Betsy Johnson's cellar, Millicent knew that she had come triumphant through the trial of fire, the searing period of the ego which could end in two kinds of victory for her. The easiest of which would be her coronation as a princess, labeling her conclusively as one of the select flock.

The other victory would be much harder, but she knew it was what she wanted. It was not that she was being noble or anything. It was just that she had learned there were other ways of getting into the great hall, blazing with lights, of people and of life.

It would be hard to explain to the girls tonight, of course, but she could tell Louise later just how it was. How she had proved something to herself by going through everything, even Rat Court, and then deciding not to join the sorority after all. And how she could still be friends with everybody. Sisters with everybody. Tracy, too.

The door behind her opened and a ray of light sliced across the soft gloom of the basement room.

"Hey, Millicent, come on out now. This is it." There were some of the girls outside.

"I'm coming," she said, getting up and moving out of the soft darkness into the glare of light, thinking: This is it, all right. The worst part, the hardest part, the part of initiation that I figured out myself.

But just then, from somewhere far off, Millicent was sure of it, there came a melodic fluting, quite wild and sweet, and she knew that it must be the song of the heather birds as they went wheeling and gliding against wide blue horizons through vast spaces of air, their wings flashing quick and purple in the bright sun.

Within Millicent another melody soared, strong and exuberant, a triumphant answer to the music of the darting heather birds that sang so clear and lilting over the far lands. And she knew that her own private initiation had just begun. **H**

G **Literary Focus** **Point of View** What does the narrator reveal about Millicent's feelings toward the sorority and toward Tracy?

H **Reading Focus** **Drawing Conclusions** Did your conclusions about Millicent prove true? If not, what clues in the story might you have missed?

Vocabulary **exuberant** (ehg ZOO buhr uhnt) *adj.:* joyful; high-spirited.

Applying Your Skills

9.R.2.C.1.b Use details from text(s): to analyze character, plot, setting, point of view **9.R.1.H.1.d** Apply post-reading skills to comprehend, interpret, analyze, and evaluate text: draw conclusions *Also covered* **9.W.3.A.1.a; 9.R.1.G.1.a**

Initiation

Respond and Think Critically

Reading Focus

Quick Check

1. What tests does Beverly put Millicent through? What is the purpose of the tests?
2. Why does Millicent decide not to join the sorority?

Read with a Purpose

3. How well do you think Millicent dealt with the pressures of joining a sorority? Did she do the right thing? Explain.

Reading Skills: Drawing Conclusions

4. While reading, you recorded the evidence and clues that helped you draw conclusions. Look back at your conclusions, and record whether they held true. If your conclusions were faulty, go back through the story and look for any clues that you may have missed.

Story Details and Clues	My Conclusions	Actual Outcome
Millicent is going through an initiation.	Millicent wants to join a sorority.	Millicent chose not to join the sorority.

Vocabulary Check

Match each Vocabulary word with its definition.

5. **vivacious** — a. defenseless
6. **anonymity** — b. lively
7. **vulnerable** — c. joyful
8. **spontaneous** — d. unplanned
9. **exuberant** — e. namelessness

Literary Focus

Literary Analysis

10. **Interpret** Millicent is inspired by the thought of the heather birds. Why does Millicent decide to identify with the heather birds and not with the sparrows?

Literary Skills: Third-Person-Limited Point of View

11. **Analyze** The third-person-limited narrator lets us see the story through the thoughts and actions of Millicent. What pieces of the story *doesn't* the narrator tell us?

Literary Skills Review: Characterization

12. **Analyze** Writers use **direct characterization** to *tell* us what a character is like and **indirect characterization** to *show* us a character's nature through thoughts, actions, and appearances. Find an example of each type of characterization used in depicting Louise Fullerton.

Writing Focus

Think as a Reader/Writer

Use It in Your Writing Write a short scene focusing on an encounter between two friends. Like Plath, use dialogue to reveal the characters' personalities.

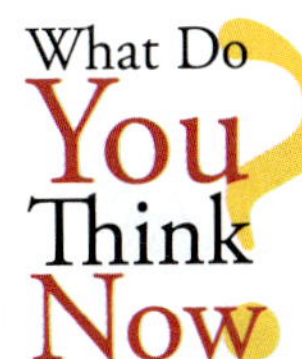

Have your ideas about friendship and popularity changed now that you have read about Millicent and Tracy? Explain why or why not.

SHORT STORY

Preparing to Read

Marigolds

by **Eugenia W. Collier**

Girl in Red (1992) by Tilly Willis. Oil on canvas. Private collection.

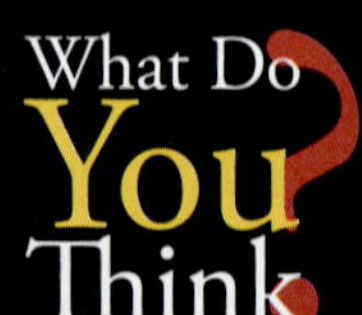

What causes people to feel fear?

QuickWrite

Why might someone or something become the object of fear? Write down at least five reasons.

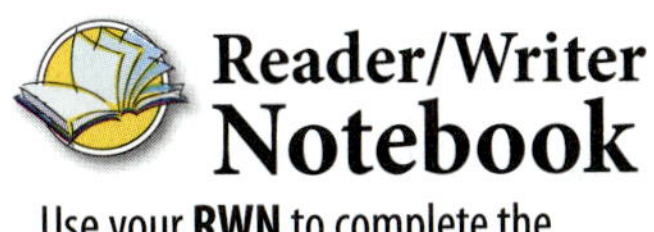

Use your **RWN** to complete the activities for this selection.

MO **9.R.2.C.1.b** Use details from text(s): to analyze character, plot, setting, point of view **9.R.3.C.1.d** Use details from informational text: to analyze and evaluate point of view

Literary Focus

First-Person Narrator A **first-person narrator** is a character in the story who uses the first-person pronoun *I* to tell us about events. We gain a close-up view of the narrator, but our knowledge is limited only to what he or she can or wants to tell us.

Literary Perspectives Apply the literary perspective described on page 259 as you read this story.

Reading Focus

Analyzing Perspectives Writers can reveal the **perspectives,** or viewpoints, of different characters or even the changing perspectives of a single character. It's important to analyze these various perspectives as you read. In "Marigolds," the narrator is an adult looking back on her experiences when she was fourteen years old.

Into Action As you read, note places in the text where the writer presents the perspective of the narrator as an adult and as a teenager. Note your observations about each example.

Page No.	Perspective	My Observations
p. 260	adult's perspective: children isolated; didn't understand their own poverty	adult sees larger picture; appreciates the hardships children faced

Writing Focus

Think as a Reader/Writer

Find It in Your Reading Collier uses striking figures of speech, such as similes and metaphors, to convey the thoughts and feelings of the narrator. A **simile** is a comparison between two unlike things that uses a word such as *like* or *as*. A **metaphor** is a comparison between two unlike things in which one thing becomes another. As you read, record examples of similes and metaphors in your *Reader/Writer Notebook* and note what they tell you about the narrator.

Vocabulary

futile (FYOO tuhl) *adj.:* useless; hopeless; in vain. *Lizabeth's father's attempts to find a job are futile.*

impoverished (ihm PAHV uhr ihsht) *v.* used as *adj.:* poor; poverty-stricken. *Mrs. Ellis gives clothing to Lizabeth's impoverished family.*

inciting (ihn SYT ihng) *v.* used as *n.:* provoking; stirring up. *Lizabeth was mad with the power of inciting rage in Miss Lottie.*

malicious (muh LIHSH uhs) *adj.:* showing a desire to harm another; spiteful. *The children's malicious acts enrage Miss Lottie and her son.*

contrition (kuhn TRIHSH uhn) *n.:* deep feelings of regret and repentance. *The cheerful children feel no contrition for throwing stones at Miss Lottie.*

Language Coach

Word Origins The Latin word *malus* means "bad." Words that come from *malus* include *malice* and *maladjusted.* What word on the Vocabulary list above shares this origin?

Learn It Online
Hear a professional actor read this story online at:
go.hrw.com L9-257 

MEET THE WRITER

Eugenia W. Collier
(1928–   )

"I Must Have Done My Job Well"

"Marigolds" is a story that emerged from a difficult time in the life of its author, Eugenia W. Collier. Collier, who has taught English at Howard University, Baltimore Community College, and Morgan State University, tells how she came to write "Marigolds" and what the story means to her:

"When I talk with people about 'Marigolds,' someone usually asks me whether the story is autobiographical. I am always pleased with the question, because it means that I must have done my job well—convinced the reader that the incidents in the story are actually happening. However, I always end up admitting that Lizabeth and I are two very different people. . . .

I wrote 'Marigolds' at a time of profound unhappiness. One night I had a tremendous urge to write. I wrote nonstop until the story was finished—about twenty-four hours. Later I sent 'Marigolds' (along with a fee I could hardly afford) to a well-advertised literary agency, which returned the story (not the fee) with a note saying that it had no plot, no conflict, and no hope of publication. Discouraged, I put 'Marigolds' away. Five years later, . . . I read stories in *Negro Digest* which were similar in subject matter to 'Marigolds.' I submitted my story, and *Negro Digest* published it. It won the Gwendolyn Brooks Prize for fiction. . . . Of all the fiction I have written, 'Marigolds' remains my favorite."

Think About the Writer What can you infer about Collier's personality from her remarks about "Marigolds"?

Build Background

In the 1930s, a terrible economic depression swept the United States. The booming stock market had collapsed in 1929 and caused businesses to shut down all over America and factories to close their doors. Banks failed, and people lost their life savings. As the narrator of this story says, however, the Great Depression was nothing new to her family. For the African American families of rural Maryland, all times were hard times.

Preview the Selection

Lizabeth, the story's narrator, tells about a time in her youth when her family faced great poverty. **Miss Lottie,** her elderly neighbor, has coped long and hard with her own struggles.

Read with a Purpose Read this story to find out how the narrator's life changes in one confusing, frightening moment.

Marigolds

by **Eugenia W. Collier**

When I think of the hometown of my youth, all that I seem to remember is dust—the brown, crumbly dust of late summer—arid, sterile dust that gets into the eyes and makes them water, gets into the throat and between the toes of bare brown feet. I don't know why I should remember only the dust. Surely there must have been lush green lawns and paved streets under leafy shade trees somewhere in town; but memory is an abstract painting—it does not present things as they are, but rather as they *feel*. And so, when I think of that time and that place, I remember only the dry September of the dirt roads and grassless yards of the shantytown where I lived. And one other thing I remember, another incongruency[1] of memory—a brilliant splash of sunny yellow against the dust—Miss Lottie's marigolds.

Whenever the memory of those marigolds flashes across my mind, a strange nostalgia comes with it and remains long after the picture has faded. I feel again the chaotic emotions of adolescence, illusive as smoke, yet as real as the potted geranium before me now. Joy and rage and wild animal gladness and shame become tangled together in the multicolored skein[2] of fourteen-going-on-fifteen as I recall that devastating moment when I was suddenly more woman than child, years ago in Miss Lottie's yard. I think of those marigolds at the strangest times; I remember them vividly now as I desperately pass away the time. . . . **A**

African Marigolds (1600) by J. J. Walther (Seventeenth century). Watercolor.

1. **incongruency** (ihn kahn GROO uhn see): inconsistency; lack of agreement or harmony.
2. **multicolored skein** (skayn): The writer is comparing her many feelings to a long, coiled piece of multicolored yarn.

A **Reading Focus** **Analyzing Perspectives** How does the memory of marigolds affect the narrator?

Literary Perspectives

Analyzing Archetypes The term *archetype* is used to describe recognizable and recurring patterns in literature. Patterns can be found in genres, situations, character types, symbols, and beliefs. For example, a hero is a type of archetype, an easily recognizable character whose situations and actions follow a predictable pattern. The similarities found in archetypes reflect the universal ways that individuals see the world.

As you read, pay attention to the notes at the bottom of the pages, and think about these questions to help you recognize archetypes:

- What recurring myths, symbols, or character types are present in the story?
- Are there any patterns in this story that I've seen in other stories?

I suppose that futile waiting was the sorrowful background music of our impoverished little community when I was young. The Depression that gripped the nation was no new thing to us, for the black workers of rural Maryland had always been depressed. I don't know what it was that we were waiting for; certainly not for the prosperity that was "just around the corner," for those were white folks' words, which we never believed. Nor did we wait for hard work and thrift to pay off in shining success, as the American Dream promised, for we knew better than that, too. Perhaps we waited for a miracle, amorphous[3] in concept but necessary if one were to have the grit to rise before dawn each day and labor in the white man's vineyard until after dark, or to wander about in the September dust offering one's sweat in return for some meager share of bread. But God was chary[4] with miracles in those days, and so we waited—and waited. **B**

We children, of course, were only vaguely aware of the extent of our poverty. Having no radios, few newspapers, and no magazines, we were somewhat unaware of the world outside our community. Nowadays we would be called culturally deprived and people would write books and hold conferences about us. In those days everybody we knew was just as hungry and ill clad as we were. Poverty was the cage in which we all were trapped, and our hatred of it was still the vague, undirected restlessness of the zoo-bred flamingo who knows that nature created him to fly free.

As I think of those days I feel most poignantly the tag end of summer, the bright, dry times when we began to have a sense of shortening days and the imminence of the cold.

By the time I was fourteen, my brother Joey and I were the only children left at our house, the older ones having left home for early marriage or the lure of the city, and the two babies having been sent to relatives who might care for them better than we. Joey was three years younger than I, and a boy, and therefore vastly inferior. Each morning our mother and father trudged wearily down the dirt road and around the bend, she to her domestic job, he to his daily unsuccessful quest for work. After our few chores around the tumbledown shanty, Joey and I were free to run wild in the sun with other children similarly situated.

For the most part, those days are ill-defined in my memory, running together and combining like a fresh watercolor painting left out in the rain. I remember squatting in the road drawing a picture in the dust, a picture which Joey gleefully erased with one sweep of his dirty foot. I remember fishing for minnows in a muddy creek and watching sadly as they eluded my cupped hands, while Joey laughed uproariously. And I remember, that year, a strange restlessness of body and of spirit, a feeling that something old and familiar was ending, and something unknown and therefore terrifying was beginning.

One day returns to me with special clarity for some reason, perhaps because it was the beginning of the experience that in some inexplicable[5] way marked the end of innocence. I was loafing under the great oak tree in our yard, deep in some reverie which I have now forgotten, except that it involved some secret, secret thoughts of

3. **amorphous** (uh MAWR fuhs): vague; shapeless.
4. **chary** (CHAIR ee): not generous.
5. **inexplicable** (ihn EHK spluh kuh buhl): not explainable or understandable.

B Literary Focus First-Person Narrator Consider not only what the narrator says in this paragraph but also how she says it—her tone, or attitude. What do her statements reveal about her?

Vocabulary **futile** (FYOO tuhl) *adj.:* useless; hopeless; in vain.
impoverished (ihm PAHV uhr ihsht) *v.* used as *adj.:* poor; poverty-stricken.

one of the Harris boys across the yard. Joey and a bunch of kids were bored now with the old tire suspended from an oak limb, which had kept them entertained for a while.

"Hey, Lizabeth," Joey yelled. He never talked when he could yell. "Hey, Lizabeth, let's go somewhere."

I came reluctantly from my private world. "Where you want to go? What you want to do?"

The truth was that we were becoming tired of the formlessness of our summer days. The idleness whose prospect had seemed so beautiful during the busy days of spring now had degenerated to an almost desperate effort to fill up the empty midday hours.

"Let's go see can we find some locusts on the hill," someone suggested.

Joey was scornful. "Ain't no more locusts there. Y'all got 'em all while they was still green."

The argument that followed was brief and not really worth the effort. Hunting locust trees wasn't fun anymore by now.

"Tell you what," said Joey finally, his eyes sparkling. "Let's us go over to Miss Lottie's."

The idea caught on at once, for annoying Miss Lottie was always fun. I was still child enough to scamper along with the group over rickety fences and through bushes that tore our already raggedy clothes, back to where Miss Lottie lived. I think now that we must have made a tragicomic spectacle, five or six kids of different ages, each of us clad in only one garment—the girls in faded dresses that were too long or too short, the boys in patchy pants, their sweaty brown chests gleaming in the hot sun. A little cloud of dust followed our thin legs and bare feet as we tramped over the barren land.

When Miss Lottie's house came into view we stopped, ostensibly to plan our strategy, but actually to reinforce our courage. Miss Lottie's house was the most ramshackle of all our ramshackle homes. The sun and rain had long since faded its rickety frame siding from white to a sullen gray. The boards themselves seemed to remain upright not from being nailed together but rather from leaning together, like a house that a child might have constructed from cards. A brisk wind might have blown it down, and the fact that it was still standing implied a kind of enchantment that was stronger than the elements. There it stood and as far as I know is standing yet—a gray, rotting thing with no porch, no shutters, no steps, set on a cramped lot with no grass, not even any weeds—a monument to decay. C

> For the most part, those days are ill-defined in my memory, running together and combining like a fresh watercolor painting left out in the rain.

In front of the house in a squeaky rocking chair sat Miss Lottie's son, John Burke, completing the impression of decay. John Burke was what was known as queer-headed. Black and ageless, he sat rocking day in and day out in a mindless stupor, lulled by the monotonous squeak-squawk of the chair. A battered hat atop his shaggy head shaded him from the sun. Usually John Burke was totally unaware of everything outside his quiet dream world. But if you disturbed him, if you intruded upon his fantasies, he would become enraged, strike out at you, and curse at you in some strange enchanted language which only he could

---

C **Literary Perspectives** **Analyzing Archetypes** In what way does the description of Miss Lottie's house fit a familiar story pattern?

understand. We children made a game of thinking of ways to disturb John Burke and then to elude his violent retribution.

But our real fun and our real fear lay in Miss Lottie herself. Miss Lottie seemed to be at least a hundred years old. Her big frame still held traces of the tall, powerful woman she must have been in youth, although it was now bent and drawn. Her smooth skin was a dark reddish brown, and her face had Indian-like features and the stern stoicism[6] that one associates with Indian faces. Miss Lottie didn't like intruders either, especially children. She never left her yard, and nobody ever visited her. We never knew how she managed those necessities which depend on human interaction—how she ate, for example, or even whether she ate. When we were tiny children, we thought Miss Lottie was a witch and we made up tales that we half believed ourselves about her exploits. We were far too sophisticated now, of course, to believe the witch nonsense. But old fears have a way of clinging like cobwebs, and so when we sighted the tumbledown shack, we had to stop to reinforce our nerves. D

"Look, there she is," I whispered, forgetting that Miss Lottie could not possibly have heard me from that distance. "She's fooling with them crazy flowers."

"Yeh, look at 'er."

Miss Lottie's marigolds were perhaps the strangest part of the picture. Certainly they did not fit in with the crumbling decay of the rest of her yard. Beyond the dusty brown yard, in front of the sorry gray house, rose suddenly and shockingly a dazzling strip of bright blossoms, clumped together in enormous mounds, warm and passionate and sun-golden. The old black witch-woman worked on them all summer, every summer, down on her creaky knees, weeding and cultivating and arranging, while the house crumbled and John Burke rocked. For some perverse reason, we children hated those marigolds. They interfered with the perfect ugliness of the place; they were too beautiful; they said too much that we could not understand; they did not make sense. There was something in the vigor with which the old woman destroyed the weeds that intimidated us. It should have been a comical sight—the old woman with the man's hat on her cropped white head, leaning over the bright mounds, her big backside in the air—but it wasn't comical, it was something we could not name. We had to annoy her by whizzing a pebble into her flowers or by yelling a dirty word, then dancing away from her rage, reveling in our youth and mocking her age. Actually, I think it was the flowers we wanted to destroy, but nobody had the nerve to try it, not even Joey, who was usually fool enough to try anything.

"Y'all git some stones," commanded Joey now and was met with instant giggling obedience as everyone except me began to gather pebbles from the dusty ground. "Come on, Lizabeth."

I just stood there peering through the bushes, torn between wanting to join the fun and feeling that it was all a bit silly.

"You scared, Lizabeth?"

I cursed and spat on the ground—my favorite gesture of phony bravado. "Y'all children get the stones, I'll show you how to use 'em."

I said before that we children were not

6. **stoicism** (STOH uh sihz uhm): calm indifference to pleasure or pain.

D Literary Focus First-Person Narrator Re-read this description of Miss Lottie. How does the narrator regard Miss Lottie? What characteristics do you think the narrator exaggerates?

We had crouched down out of sight in the bushes, where we stifled the giggles that insisted on coming. Miss Lottie gazed warily across the road for a moment, then cautiously returned to her weeding. *Zing*—Joey sent a pebble into the blooms, and another marigold was beheaded.

Miss Lottie was enraged now. She began struggling to her feet, leaning on a rickety cane and shouting. "Y'all git! Go on home!" Then the rest of the kids let loose with their pebbles,

consciously aware of how thick were the bars of our cage. I wonder now, though, whether we were not more aware of it than I thought. Perhaps we had some dim notion of what we were, and how little chance we had of being anything else. Otherwise, why would we have been so preoccupied with destruction? Anyway, the pebbles were collected quickly, and everybody looked at me to begin the fun. **E**

"Come on, y'all."

We crept to the edge of the bushes that bordered the narrow road in front of Miss Lottie's place. She was working placidly, kneeling over the flowers, her dark hand plunged into the golden mound. Suddenly *zing*—an expertly aimed stone cut the head off one of the blossoms.

"Who out there?" Miss Lottie's backside came down and her head came up as her sharp eyes searched the bushes. "You better git!"

storming the flowers and laughing wildly and senselessly at Miss Lottie's impotent rage. She shook her stick at us and started shakily toward the road crying, "Git 'long! John Burke! John Burke, come help!"

Then I lost my head entirely, mad with the power of inciting such rage, and ran out of the bushes in the storm of pebbles, straight toward Miss Lottie, chanting madly, "Old witch, fell in a ditch, picked up a penny and thought she was rich!" The children screamed with delight, dropped their pebbles, and joined the crazy dance, swarming around Miss Lottie like bees and chanting, "Old lady witch!" while she screamed curses at us. The madness lasted only a moment, for John Burke, startled at last, lurched out of his chair, and we dashed for the bushes just as Miss Lottie's cane went whizzing at my head.

E Reading Focus **Analyzing Perspectives** What is the adult narrator's perspective on the children's actions? What insight does this perspective give us?

Vocabulary **inciting** (ihn SYT ihng) *v.* used as *n.:* stirring up.

I did not join the merriment when the kids gathered again under the oak in our bare yard. Suddenly I was ashamed, and I did not like being ashamed. The child in me sulked and said it was all in fun, but the woman in me flinched at the thought of the malicious attack that I had led. The mood lasted all afternoon. When we ate the beans and rice that was supper that night, I did not notice my father's silence, for he was always silent these days, nor did I notice my mother's absence, for she always worked until well into evening. Joey and I had a particularly bitter argument after supper; his exuberance got on my nerves. Finally I stretched out upon the pallet in the room we shared and fell into a fitful doze. **F**

When I awoke, somewhere in the middle of the night, my mother had returned, and I vaguely listened to the conversation that was audible through the thin walls that separated our rooms. At first I heard no words, only voices. My mother's voice was like a cool, dark room in summer—peaceful, soothing, quiet. I loved to listen to it; it made things seem all right somehow. But my father's voice cut through hers, shattering the peace.

"Twenty-two years, Maybelle, twenty-two years," he was saying, "and I got nothing for you, nothing, nothing."

"It's all right, honey, you'll get something. Everybody out of work now, you know that."

"It ain't right. Ain't no man ought to eat his woman's food year in and year out, and see his children running wild. Ain't nothing right about that."

"Honey, you took good care of us when you had it. Ain't nobody got nothing nowadays."

"I ain't talking about nobody else, I'm talking about *me*. God knows I try." My mother said something I could not hear, and my father cried out louder, "What must a man do, tell me that?"

"Look, we ain't starving. I git paid every week, and Mrs. Ellis is real nice about giving me things. She gonna let me have Mr. Ellis's old coat for you this winter—"

"Damn Mr. Ellis's coat! And damn his money! You think I want white folks' leavings? Damn, Maybelle"—and suddenly he sobbed, loudly and painfully, and cried helplessly and hopelessly in the dark night. I had never heard a man cry before. I did not know men ever cried. I covered my ears with my hands but could not cut off the sound of my father's harsh, painful, despairing sobs. My father was a strong man who could whisk a child upon his shoulders and go singing through the house. My father whittled toys for us, and laughed so loud that the great oak seemed to laugh with him, and taught us how to fish and hunt rabbits. How could it be that my father was crying? But the sobs went on, unstifled, finally quieting until I could hear my mother's voice, deep and rich, humming softly as she used to hum to a frightened child. **G**

The world had lost its boundary lines. My mother, who was small and soft, was now the strength of the family; my father, who was the rock on which the family had been built, was sobbing like the tiniest child. Everything was suddenly out of tune, like a broken accordion. Where did I fit into this crazy picture? I do not now remember my thoughts, only a feeling of great bewilderment and fear.

Long after the sobbing and humming had stopped, I lay on the pallet, still as stone with

---

F **Literary Focus** **First-Person Narrator** What do the feelings that the narrator describes in this paragraph reveal about her?

Vocabulary **malicious** (muh LIHSH uhs) *adj.:* showing a desire to harm another; spiteful.

G **Reading Focus** **Analyzing Perspectives** Describe Lizabeth's perspective in the scene in which she overhears her parents' conversation. Is the perspective one of her as a teenager or as an adult? Explain.

my hands over my ears, wishing that I too could cry and be comforted. The night was silent now except for the sound of the crickets and of Joey's soft breathing. But the room was too crowded with fear to allow me to sleep, and finally, feeling the terrible aloneness of 4 A.M., I decided to awaken Joey.

"Ouch! What's the matter with you? What you want?" he demanded disagreeably when I had pinched and slapped him awake.

"Come on, wake up."

"What for? Go 'way."

I was lost for a reasonable reply. I could not say, "I'm scared and I don't want to be alone," so I merely said, "I'm going out. If you want to come, come on."

The promise of adventure awoke him. "Going out now? Where to, Lizabeth? What you going to do?"

I was pulling my dress over my head. Until now I had not thought of going out. "Just come on," I replied tersely.

I was out the window and halfway down the road before Joey caught up with me.

"Wait, Lizabeth, where you going?"

I was running as if the Furies[7] were after me, as perhaps they were—running silently and furiously until I came to where I had half known I was headed: to Miss Lottie's yard.

The half-dawn light was more eerie than complete darkness, and in it the old house was like the ruin that my world had become—foul and crumbling, a grotesque caricature. It looked haunted, but I was not afraid, because I was haunted too.

"Lizabeth, you lost your mind?" panted Joey.

I had indeed lost my mind, for all the smoldering emotions of that summer swelled in me and burst—the great need for my mother who was never there, the hopelessness of our poverty and degradation, the bewilderment of being neither child nor woman and yet both at once, the fear unleashed by my father's tears. And these feelings combined in one great impulse toward destruction.

"I ain't talking about nobody else, I'm talking about *me.* God knows I try."

"Lizabeth!"

I leaped furiously into the mounds of marigolds and pulled madly, trampling and pulling and destroying the perfect yellow blooms. The fresh smell of early morning and of dew-soaked marigolds spurred me on as I went tearing and mangling and sobbing while Joey tugged my dress or my waist crying, "Lizabeth, stop, please stop!" H

And then I was sitting in the ruined little garden among the uprooted and ruined flowers, crying and crying, and it was too late to undo what I had done. Joey was sitting beside me, silent and frightened, not knowing what to say. Then, "Lizabeth, look."

I opened my swollen eyes and saw in front of me a pair of large, calloused feet; my gaze lifted to the swollen legs, the age-distorted body clad in a tight cotton nightdress, and then the shadowed Indian face surrounded by stubby white hair. And there was no rage in the face now, now that the garden was destroyed and

7. **Furies** (FYOOR eez): in Greek and Roman mythology, spirits that pursue people who have committed crimes, sometimes driving them mad.

H Literary Focus **First-Person Narrator** What feelings of Lizabeth's lead her to want to destroy something?

Solace (1995) by Arnold Rice (Twentieth century). Acrylic on canvas.

Analyzing Visuals

Viewing and Interpreting Which story character—the narrator or Miss Lottie—do you think this painting better portrays? Why?

there was nothing any longer to be protected.

"M-miss Lottie!" I scrambled to my feet and just stood there and stared at her, and that was the moment when childhood faded and womanhood began. That violent, crazy act was the last act of childhood. For as I gazed at the immobile face with the sad, weary eyes, I gazed upon a kind of reality which is hidden to childhood. The witch was no longer a witch but only a broken old woman who had dared to create beauty in the midst of ugliness and sterility. She had been born in squalor and lived in it all her life. Now at the end of that life she had nothing except a falling-down hut, a wrecked body, and John Burke, the mindless son of her passion. Whatever verve there was left in her, whatever was of love and beauty and joy that had not been squeezed out by life, had been there in the marigolds she had so tenderly cared for.

Of course I could not express the things that I knew about Miss Lottie as I stood there awkward and ashamed. The years have put words to the things I knew in that moment, and as I look back upon it, I know that that moment marked the end of innocence. Innocence involves an unseeing acceptance of things at face value, an ignorance of the area below the surface. In that humiliating moment I looked beyond myself and into the depths of another person. This was the beginning of compassion, and one cannot have both compassion and innocence. **I**

The years have taken me worlds away from that time and that place, from the dust and squalor of our lives, and from the bright thing that I destroyed in a blind, childish striking out at God knows what. Miss Lottie died long ago and many years have passed since I last saw her hut, completely barren at last, for despite my wild contrition she never planted marigolds again. Yet, there are times when the image of those passionate yellow mounds returns with a painful poignancy. For one does not have to be ignorant and poor to find that his life is as barren as the dusty yards of our town. And I too have planted marigolds.

I **Literary Perspectives** **Analyzing Archetypes** In what way is the ending of innocence an archetype?

Vocabulary **contrition** (kuhn TRIHSH uhn) *n.:* deep feelings of regret and repentance.

Applying Your Skills

9.R.2.C.1.b Use details from text(s): to analyze character, plot, setting, point of view 9.R.2.B.2.b Identify and explain literary techniques, in text emphasizing: imagery 9.R.3.C.1.d Use details from informational text: to analyze and evaluate point of view *Also covered* 9.W.2.D.1.b; 9.R.1.G.1.a

Marigolds

Respond and Think Critically

Reading Focus

Quick Check

1. What do the children do to Miss Lottie? Why do they do it?
2. Why is Lizabeth's father angry and unhappy? How does she react to his feelings?

Read with a Purpose

3. Lizabeth says that destroying the marigolds was a last act of childhood. Why does she think this?

Reading Skills: Analyzing Perspectives

4. Review your perspectives chart. How would the story be different if it were told solely from the perspective of the narrator at age fourteen?

Vocabulary Check

Tell whether each statement is true (T) or false (F).

5. A **futile** plan will succeed.
6. An **impoverished** family is well off.
7. Speakers inspire an audience by **inciting** interest.
8. A person might feel regret for a **malicious** act.
9. Saying "I'm sorry" helps show **contrition.**

Literary Focus

Literary Analysis

10. **Evaluate** List the internal and external conflicts that characters experience in the story. What actions do the characters take because of them?
11. **Infer** Using details the narrator provides, explain how you think Miss Lottie is affected by the destruction of the marigolds.
12. **Interpret** Why do you think Lizabeth plants her own marigolds at the end of the story?
13. **Literary Perspectives** In what way is the depiction of Miss Lottie a type of archetype?

Literary Skills: First-Person Narrator

14. **Interpret** Through Lizabeth's first-person narration, we learn about her thoughts and feelings as a teenager and as an adult. How would you describe her at each of these stages?
15. **Speculate** How would the story change if Joey or Miss Lottie were the first-person narrator?

Literary Skills Review: Setting and Mood

16. **Analyze** Collier uses vivid **imagery**—language that appeals to our senses—to depict the story's setting. Choose at least three images, and explain how they contribute to the setting. What overall mood does Collier convey?

Images	Setting
1.	
2.	
3.	

Overall Mood:

Writing Focus

Think as a Reader/Writer

Use It in Your Writing Rewrite the scene in which Lizbeth destroys the marigolds, using Joey as the first-person narrator. Use metaphors and similes to convey his thoughts and feelings.

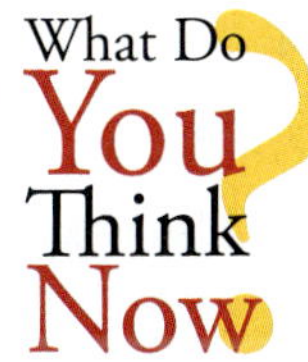

Why does Lizabeth destroy the marigolds? Why do you think she cries as she does so?

SHORT STORY

Preparing to Read

The Wife's Story

by **Ursula K. Le Guin**

What Do You Think?

What's more frightening, the known or the unknown?

QuickTalk

How do we find out what another person is like? What can prevent us from learning about someone's true personality? With a partner, discuss your responses.

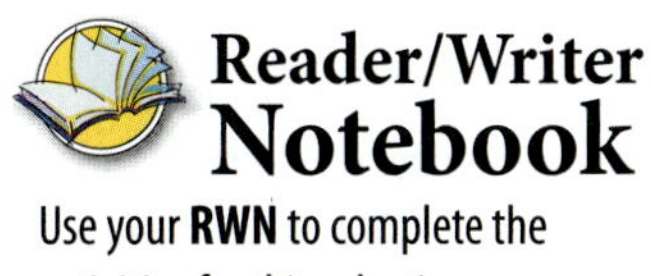

Use your **RWN** to complete the activities for this selection.

MO **9.R.2.C.1.d** Use details from text(s): to evaluate the effect of author's style **9.R.1.H.1.b** Apply post-reading skills to comprehend, interpret, analyze, and evaluate text: question to clarify

Literary Focus

Voice A narrator's **voice** is defined by his or her speaking style, word choice, and **tone** (or attitude). Writers use voice to reveal a narrator's personality and shape our responses to a story. As you read "The Wife's Story," think about how the narrator's voice immediately draws you into her mysterious tale. What makes her story so compelling?

Reading Focus

Asking Questions As you read, ask yourself questions such as *Who? What? When? Where? Why?* and *How?* to help you understand a story's plot, characters, and setting, as well as its meaning. You might also want to ask questions that help you think about the story's larger significance. For example, you might ask yourself if the narrator's feelings are typical of those of a young female.

Into Action As you read, record your questions about the story in the left-hand column of a double-entry journal. As you discover the answers to your questions, record them in the right-hand column. If you can't answer some questions, wait until you finish reading the story and answer them then.

My Questions	Answers
First paragraph: What doesn't the narrator understand?	

Writing Focus

Think as a Reader/Writer

Find It in Your Reading Le Guin's writing style is deceptively simple. She relies on basic details and short sentences to convey her story instead of providing a lot of explanation of ideas. As you read, record in your *Reader/Writer Notebook* examples of the details that help make this story so vivid.

Vocabulary

kin (kihn) *n.:* family members; relatives. *Prior to meeting her husband, the narrator lived with her kin.*

rouse (rowz) *v.:* wake up. *Sometimes her husband's noisy exit would rouse her from sleep.*

mortal (MAWR tuhl) *adj.:* here, very intense; severe. *Suffering from mortal terror, the baby cried and hid.*

brandished (BRAN dihsht) *v.:* waved in a threatening manner. *The man brandished a weapon.*

cowering (KOW uhr ihng) *v.:* drawing back, crouching, or trembling in fear. *Shocked, the narrator was cowering in the passageway.*

Language Coach

Multiple-Meaning Words The adjective *mortal* has multiple meanings. In addition to meaning "very intense," it means "that which will die at some point" (a mortal creature), "relating to humans" (mortal concerns), "causing death" (a mortal injury), and "to the death; not giving in" (mortal enemies). *Mortal* can also be used as a noun, meaning "a human; a being that will die."

Learn It Online
Dig deeper into vocabulary with Word Watch:

go.hrw.com L9-269 Go

MEET THE WRITER

Ursula K. Le Guin

(1929–   )

Newbery
Medal
WINNER

"A Life's Work"

Describing what she was like when she was a young child, Ursula K. Le Guin notes, "I was too shy to speak to anybody in school until fourth grade, and though I did finally make a few dear friends, school was social torture, and I was always glad to be home." Le Guin's father was an anthropologist, and her mother was a writer. Her home in Berkeley, California, was a place in which tales and myths from a variety of cultures were shared with family members and greatly valued.

Noting that her "father wrote every day," Le Guin says, "I grew up knowing writing as both an important thing and an ordinary thing—a life's work." Le Guin herself always wanted to be a writer. By the time she was twelve, she had received her first rejection slip for a story she had submitted to a science fiction magazine.

Literary Partners

Le Guin writes realistic fiction, poetry, and children's picture books, but she is best known for her highly regarded works of fantasy and science fiction. She was one of the first women to achieve acclaim in these genres. For Le Guin, writers and readers, working together, make literature meaningful: "Readers, after all, are making the world with you. You give them the materials, but it's the readers who build that world in their own minds."

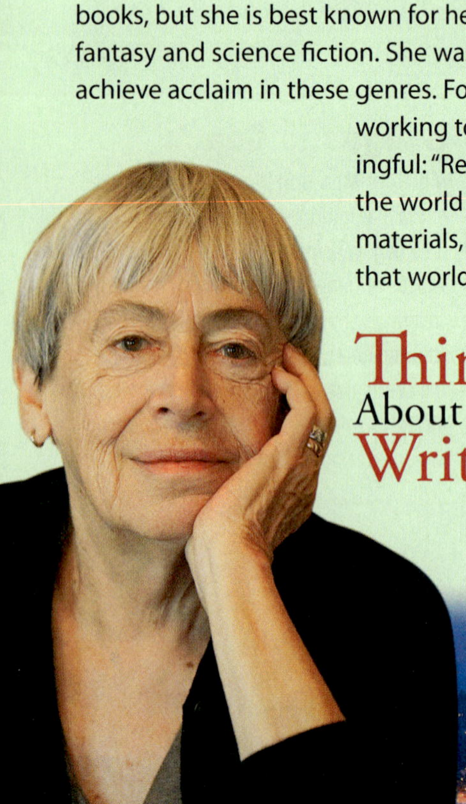

Think About the Writer Do you agree with Le Guin that readers play an essential role in making literature meaningful? Explain.

Preview the Selection

The unnamed narrator of this story has a shocking tale to tell. What has happened, and to whom has it happened? Read on to find out.

Read with a Purpose Read this story to discover what the narrator's experiences reveal about good and evil.

The Wife's Story

by **Ursula K. Le Guin**

He was a good husband, a good father. I don't understand it. I don't believe in it. I don't believe that it happened. I saw it happen but it isn't true. It can't be. He was always gentle. If you'd have seen him playing with the children, anybody who saw him with the children would have known that there wasn't any bad in him, not one mean bone. When I first met him he was still living with his mother over near Spring Lake, and I used to see them together, the mother and the sons, and think that any young fellow that was that nice with his family must be one worth knowing. Then one time when I was walking in the woods I met him by himself coming back from a hunting trip. He hadn't got any game at all, not so much as a field mouse, but he wasn't cast down about it. He was just larking along enjoying the morning air. That's one of the things I first loved about him. He didn't take things hard, he didn't grouch and whine when things didn't go his way. So we got to talking that day. And I guess things moved right along after that, because pretty soon he was over here pretty near all the time. And my sister said—see, my parents had moved out the year before and gone South, leaving us the place—my sister said, kind of teasing but serious, "Well! If he's going to be here every day and half the night, I guess there isn't room for me!" And she moved out—just down the way. We've always been real close, her and me. That's the sort of thing doesn't ever change. I couldn't ever have got through this bad time without my sis. **A**

Well, so he came to live here. And all I can say is, it was the happy year of my life. He was just purely good to me. A hard worker and never lazy, and so big and fine-looking. Everybody looked up to him, you know, young as he was. Lodge Meeting nights, more and

A **Literary Focus** **Voice** How would you describe the word choice of the narrator in this paragraph?

more often they had him to lead the singing. He had such a beautiful voice, and he'd lead off strong, and the others following and joining in, high voices and low. It brings the shivers on me now to think of it, hearing it, nights when I'd stayed home from meeting when the children was babies—the singing coming up through the trees there, and the moonlight, summer nights, the full moon shining. I'll never hear anything so beautiful. I'll never know a joy like that again.

It was the moon, that's what they say. It's the moon's fault, and the blood. It was in his father's blood. I never knew his father, and now I wonder what become of him. He was from up Whitewater way, and had no kin around here. I always thought he went back there, but now I don't know. There was some talk about him, tales, that come out after what happened to my husband. It's something runs in the blood, they say, and it may never come out, but if it does, it's the change of the moon that does it. Always it happens in the dark of the moon. When everybody's home asleep. Something comes over the one that's got the curse in his blood, they say, and he gets up because he can't sleep, and goes out into the glaring sun, and goes off all alone—drawn to find those like him. And it may be so, because my husband would do that. I'd half rouse and say, "Where you going to?" and he'd say, "Oh, hunting, be back this evening," and it wasn't like him, even his voice was different. But I'd be so sleepy, and not wanting to wake the kids, and he was so good and responsible, it was no call of mine to go asking "Why?" and "Where?" and all like that. **B**

So it happened that way maybe three times or four. He'd come back late, and worn out, and pretty near cross for one so sweet-tempered—not wanting to talk about it. I figured everybody got to bust out now and then, and nagging never helped anything. But it did begin to worry me. Not so much that he went, but that he come back so tired and strange. Even, he smelled strange. It made my hair stand up on end. I could not endure it and I said, "What is that—those smells on you? All over you!" And he said, "I don't know," real short, and made like he was sleeping. But he went down when he thought I wasn't noticing, and washed and washed himself. But those smells stayed in his hair, and in our bed, for days.

And then the awful thing. I don't find it easy to tell about this. I want to cry when I have to bring it to my mind. Our youngest, the little one, my baby, she turned from her father. Just overnight. He come in and she got scared-looking, stiff, with her eyes wide, and then she begun to cry and try to hide behind me. She didn't yet talk plain but she was saying over and over, "Make it go away! Make it go away!"

The look in his eyes, just for one moment, when he heard that. That's what I don't want ever to remember. That's what I can't forget. The look in his eyes looking at his own child. **C**

I said to the child, "Shame on you, what's got into you?"—scolding, but keeping her right up close to me at the same time, because I was frightened too. Frightened to shaking.

He looked away then and said something like, "Guess she just waked up dreaming," and passed it off that way. Or tried to. And so did I. And I got real mad with my baby when she kept

---

B **Literary Focus** **Voice** What do you notice about the narrator's phrasing and the types of sentences she uses? How would you describe her speaking style?

C **Reading Focus** **Asking Questions** What questions come to mind as you read this passage?

Vocabulary **kin** (kihn) *n.:* family members; relatives.
rouse (rowz) *v.:* wake up.

on acting crazy scared of her own dad. But she couldn't help it and I couldn't change it.

He kept away that whole day. Because he knew, I guess. It was just beginning dark of the moon.

It was hot and close inside, and dark, and we'd all been asleep some while, when something woke me up. He wasn't there beside me. I heard a little stir in the passage, when I listened. So I got up, because I could bear it no longer. I went out into the passage, and it was light there, hard sunlight coming in from the door. And I saw him standing just outside, in the tall grass by the entrance. His head was hanging. Presently he sat down, like he felt weary, and looked down at his feet. I held still, inside, and watched—I didn't know what for.

And I saw what he saw. I saw the changing. In his feet, it was, first. They got long, each foot got longer, stretching out, the toes stretching out and the foot getting long, and fleshy, and white. And no hair on them.

The hair begun to come away all over his body. It was like his hair fried away in the sunlight and was gone. He was white all over, then, like a worm's skin. And he turned his face. It was changing while I looked. It got flatter and flatter, the mouth flat and wide, and the teeth grinning flat and dull, and the nose just a knob of flesh with nostril holes, and the ears gone, and the eyes gone blue—blue, with white rims around the blue—staring at me out of that flat, soft, white face.

He stood up then on two legs. **D**

I saw him, I had to see him, my own dear love, turned into the hateful one.

The look in his eyes, just for one moment, when he heard that. That's what I don't want ever to remember. That's what I can't forget.

I couldn't move, but as I crouched there in the passage staring out into the day I was trembling and shaking with a growl that burst out into a crazy, awful howling, A grief howl and a terror howl and a calling howl. And the others heard it, even sleeping, and woke up.

It stared and peered, that thing my husband had turned into, and shoved its face up to the entrance of our house. I was still bound by mortal fear, but behind me the children had waked up, and the baby was whimpering. The mother anger come into me then, and I snarled and crept forward.

The man thing looked around. It had no gun, like the ones from the man places do. But it picked up a heavy fallen tree-branch in its long white foot, and shoved the end of that down into our house, at me. I snapped the end of it in my teeth and started to force my way out, because I knew the man would kill our children if it could. But my sister was already coming. I saw her running at the man with her head low and her mane high and her eyes yellow as the winter sun. It turned on her and raised up that

---

D **Reading Focus** **Asking Questions** The husband has just undergone a remarkable transformation. What do you think he has changed into?

Vocabulary **mortal** (MAWR tuhl) *adj.:* here, very intense; severe.

SCIENCE LINK

Howl at the Moon?

Why do wolves howl? Wolves form social units called packs, which generally consist of six to ten animals, and howling is one of the ways the pack members communicate. A pack is usually made up of an alpha male (the dominant male), an alpha female (the dominant female), and their offspring. The territory of a pack can range from thirty-one to twelve hundred miles. Howling is a way for the wolves to keep track of one another. These vocalizations travel over large distances, and each wolf's howl is distinctive, so others can recognize their pack mates. Often a wolf pack engages in chorus howling—pack members howl as a group to ward off intruders.

Ask Yourself

Does the narrator of this story seem more wolf or human? Explain your response.

branch to hit her. But I come out of the doorway, mad with the mother anger, and the others all were coming answering my call, the whole pack gathering, there in that blind glare and heat of the sun at noon. **E**

The man looked round at us and yelled out loud, and brandished the branch it held. Then it broke and ran, heading for the cleared fields and plowlands, down the mountainside. It ran, on two legs, leaping and weaving, and we followed it.

I was last, because love still bound the anger and the fear in me. I was running when I saw them pull it down. My sister's teeth were in its throat. I got there and it was dead. The others were drawing back from the kill, because of the taste of the blood, and the smell. The younger ones were cowering and some crying, and my sister rubbed her mouth against her forelegs over and over to get rid of the taste. I went up close because I thought if the thing was dead the spell, the curse must be done, and my husband could come back—alive, or even dead, if I could only see him, my true love, in his true form, beautiful. But only the dead man lay there white and bloody. We drew back and back from it, and turned and ran, back up into the hills, back to the woods of the shadows and the twilight and the blessed dark. **F**

E **Literary Focus** **Voice** What nouns and pronouns does the narrator use to refer to her husband in the last two paragraphs? What does her choice of words reveal about her attitude toward him?

F **Reading Focus** **Asking Questions** Why do you think the narrator describes the dark as "blessed"?

Vocabulary **brandished** (BRAN dihsht) *v.:* waved in a threatening manner.
cowering (KOW uhr ihng) *v.:* drawing back, crouching, or trembling in fear.

Applying Your Skills

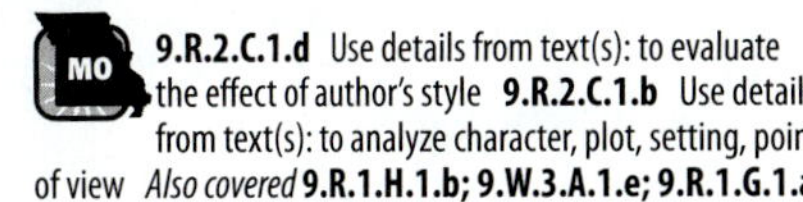

9.R.2.C.1.d Use details from text(s): to evaluate the effect of author's style **9.R.2.C.1.b** Use details from text(s): to analyze character, plot, setting, point of view *Also covered* **9.R.1.H.1.b; 9.W.3.A.1.e; 9.R.1.G.1.a**

The Wife's Story

Respond and Think Critically

Reading Focus

Quick Check

1. Why is the narrator initially happy with her husband? Why does she begin to worry?
2. What has happened to the husband at the end of the story?

Read with a Purpose

3. At first, the narrator describes her husband as "purely good" to her. How does she later regard him?

Reading Skills: Asking Questions

4. Review the double-entry journal you created as you read. Circle any answers you now think should be revised, and note your changes. Then, circle any questions you left unanswered and try to answer them now. Were you surprised by the revelations in the story? Why or why not?

My Questions	Answers
First paragraph: What doesn't the narrator understand?	why her husband lost his temper change: why her husband transforms

Vocabulary Check

Tell whether each statement is true (T) or false (F).

5. Your cousins are considered your **kin.**
6. Most people **rouse** around 3 A.M.
7. **Mortal** dread might prevent you from taking a risk.
8. Some dogs attack when they see weapons **brandished.**
9. A happy boy would be **cowering** in his room.

Literary Focus

Literary Analysis

10. **Interpret** What point is Le Guin making by reversing the typical werewolf tale and telling the story from the wolf's point of view?
11. **Evaluate** Why do you think Le Guin chose to tell the story with a first-person narrator? Was her choice effective? Why or why not?
12. **Extend** Do you think the narrator loves her dead husband? Can one both love and fear someone? Support your ideas.

Literary Skills: Voice

13. **Analyze** Describe the narrator's voice. How does it affect the way you respond to the story?

Literary Skills Review: Suspense

14. **Analyze** Writers use **suspense**—that feeling of uncertainty about what will happen next in a story—to capture a reader's attention. How does Le Guin create suspense in this story?

Writing Focus

Think as a Reader/Writer

Use It in Your Writing Write a description of a transformation in which a person or animal changes into something else. Like Le Guin, use precise details and simple sentences to create suspense.

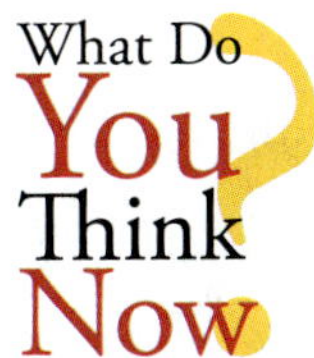

Was the narrator more afraid of the known or the unknown? What made her husband's transformation so frightening?

Author Study: Edgar Allan Poe

CONTENTS

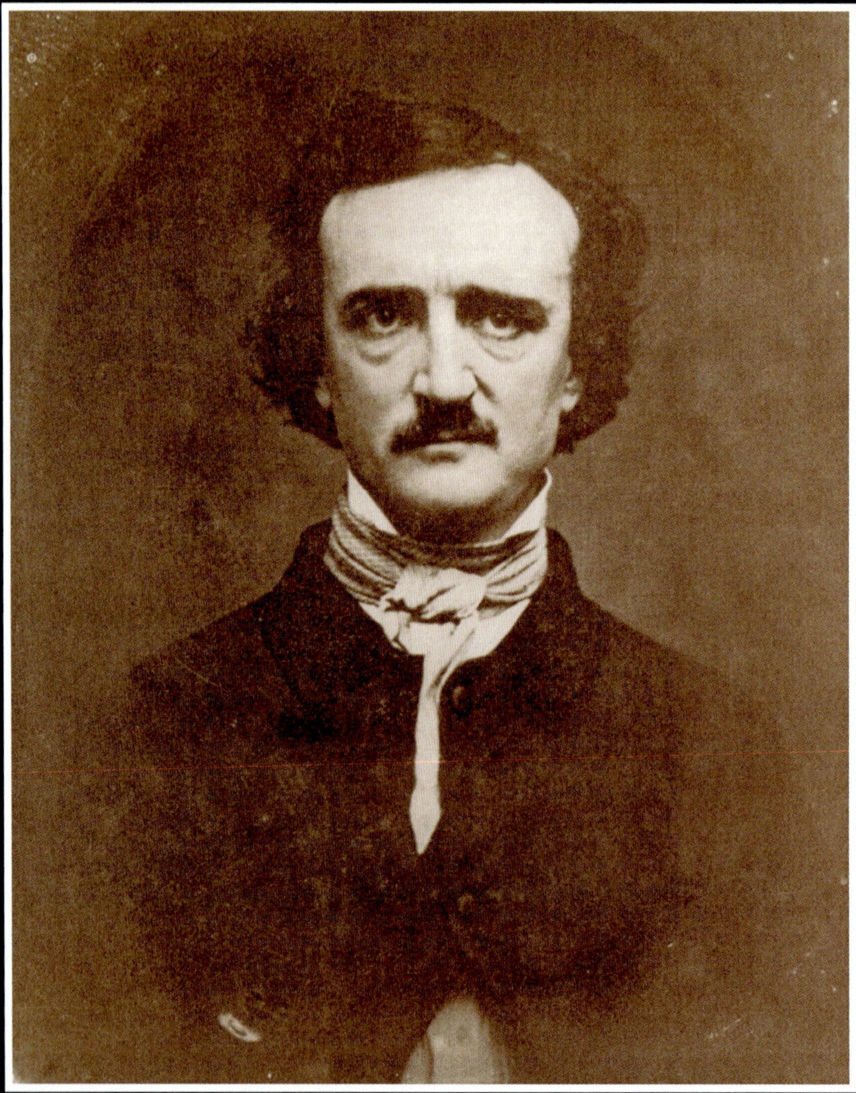

Edgar Allan Poe.

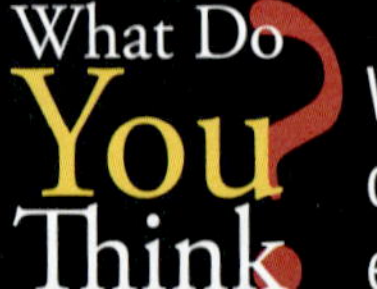

Who has a bigger effect on your life—friends or enemies?

QuickWrite

"No man is an island." That saying conveys the idea that the people around us have a strong influence on our thoughts and actions. Write about a time when your ideas and actions were affected by others.

Preparing to Read

Letter to John Allan / Alone

9.R.1.I.1.c Compare, contrast, analyze and evaluate connections: text to world **9.R.1.H.1.c** Apply post-reading skills to comprehend, interpret, analyze, and evaluate text: reflect *Also covered* **9.R.2.C.1.d; 9.R.3.A.1**

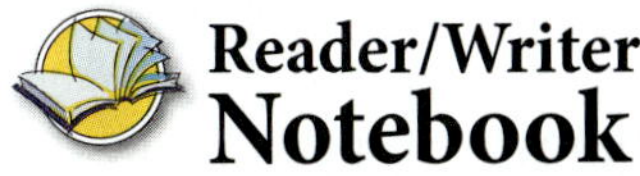

Use your **RWN** to complete the activities for these selections.

Literary Focus

Literary Criticism: Biographical Approach Writers are shaped by the events of their lives as well as the times in which they live. When you make connections between an author's life and works, you are looking at literature from a biographical approach. To understand the works of Edgar Allan Poe, first read his biography on pages 278–279. As you read works by him, think about how his writing reflects the times in which he lived as well as personal events from his life.

Reading Focus

Comparing Works by One Author Reading more than one work by an author helps you gain a deeper understanding of the writer. Each work that you read by the author gives you a greater sense of his of her methods and approach. Look for similarities among works to determine characteristics of the writer's personal style.

Into Action Use a comparison chart to identify key features of the works as you read them.

	Letter to John Allan	Alone
Connections to Poe's Life	Poe feels abandoned by his foster father.	Poe feels he has always been alone, apart.
Traditions of the Time	Fathers are in control of all money matters.	
Author's Attitudes	desperate; emotional	

Writing Focus

Think as a Reader/Writer

Find It in Your Reading As you read Poe's works, look for words and images that evoke an emotional response. List these examples in your *Reader/Writer Notebook* to help you evaluate his use of language.

Vocabulary

Letter to John Allan

unalterable (uhn AWL tuhr uh buhl) *adj.:* not able to be changed. *Poe leaves his foster father's house and says his decision is unalterable.*

aspired (uh SPYRD) *v.:* wanted to achieve something; sought. *Poe aspired to be a great man.*

eminence (EHM uh nuhns) *n.:* rank of distinction; fame. *Poe believed attending a university would help him achieve eminence in his public life.*

caprice (kuh PREES) *n.:* sudden idea or change of mind, often made with little reason. *Poe blames John Allan's caprice for ending Poe's education.*

comply (kuhm PLY) *v.:* act in agreement with something; obey. *Poe asks for a few items but is afraid John Allan won't comply.*

Language Coach

Oral Fluency When you come across unfamiliar words, you might have trouble figuring out how to pronounce them. Read the list of Vocabulary words above and think about how you would pronounce them. Then, check the pronunciations provided to see if you were correct.

Learn It Online
Use Word Watch to explore new words:
go.hrw.com L9-277

MEET THE WRITER

Edgar Allan Poe

(1809–1849)

Medallion of Edgar Allan Poe bust.

From Riches to Rags Edgar Allan Poe was the son of traveling actors. His father deserted the family, and his beautiful young mother died in a theatrical rooming house in Richmond, Virginia, before Edgar was three years old. The little boy was taken in as a foster child by the wealthy and childless Allan family of Richmond.

At first, Edgar's foster parents were pleased with his brilliant scholarship and athletic ability. But later, John Allan became disappointed with his foster son. Allan did not support Poe's literary ambitions and thought his foster son was lazy. Although he was given an allowance by Allan when he enrolled in the University of Virginia, Poe felt the amount was meager. He tried to earn more money by gambling, but when he fell into debt, John Allan refused to support him. Eventually Poe and his foster father lost all contact, and Poe was left penniless.

Major Achievements, Serious Problems After dropping out of college, Poe moved in with his aunt, Maria Poe Clemm, in Baltimore, Maryland. In 1835, Poe married her thirteen-year-old daughter, Virginia Clemm. Two years later, the three of them moved to New York City.

Poe found work as a magazine editor and managed to write his own stories and poems when he

"The want of parental affections has been the heaviest of my trials."

A Poe Time Line

- Poe is born on January 19, **1809**, in Boston, Massachusetts.
- 1810
- On December 8, **1811**, Poe's mother dies. Poe's father has already deserted the family. Later that month, the Allan family takes Poe in as a foster son.
- 1820
- Poe enters the University of Virginia in **1827**. John Allan refuses to give Poe money to repay gambling debts. Poe leaves school in March. In May, he enlists in the U.S. Army. The same year, he publishes his first book of poetry.
- In **1829**, Poe's foster mother dies.
- 1830
- Poe enters West Point in **1830** but is expelled the next year.
- John Allan dies in **1834**. Poe inherits nothing from the estate.
- Poe marries his cousin, Virginia Clemm, in **1835**.
- Poe and Clemm move, along with her mother, to New York in **1837**.
- In **1838**, Poe publishes his only novel, *The Narrative of Arthur Gordon Pym*.

Learn It Online

Get news, secrets, time lines, maps, and more about Edgar Allan Poe's life at:

go.hrw.com L9-279 Go

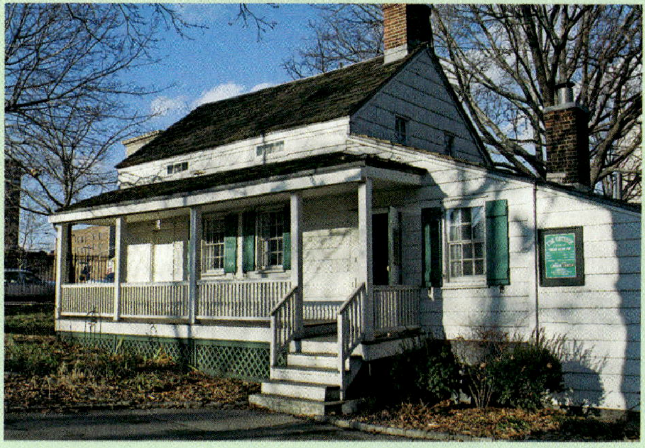

Poe Cottage in Bronx, New York.

found the time. Despite the fact that he drank excessively at times and was always in need of money, he managed to create a significant body of work. He wrote regularly and had increasing success, although his unusual poems and stories were mocked by conservative critics. "The Cask of Amontillado" was published in 1846, during a time when Poe was enduring vicious insults from critics. Some readers objected to his intense psychological tales of horror, which often combined the ghastly and the grotesque. Poe explored these themes not merely to shock or frighten, but to reveal the dark truths that he found within the depths of humanity.

A Mysterious Death Poe's one refuge in life was threatened when Virginia became ill with tuberculosis. When she died, Poe broke down completely. Two years later he was found delirious in a tavern on a rainy election day, wearing clothing that was not his own. The great master of horror died a few days later. Historians do not know the reason for Poe's death. Many assume it was connected directly to his drinking. Others have suggested that he was killed by a disease or was kidnapped by a political gang, forced to drink and vote for their candidate, and then died as a result of the strain to his weak system.

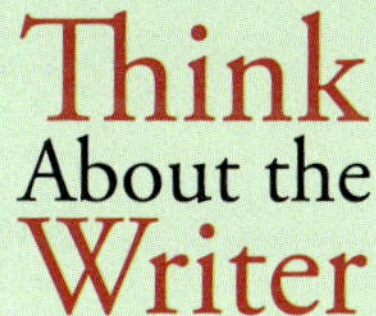

Think About the Writer

What events from his life might have given Poe the urge to write about the dark side of human nature?

Key Elements of Poe's Writing

- An **intense mood,** or atmosphere, that can be highly emotional or purely horrifying
- **Themes** that reflect the dark truths of the irrational inner world of human psychology
- Heightened **language** that emphasizes and exaggerates ideas
- **Repetition** of words that help create a hypnotic and forceful effect

Illustration of Edgar Allan Poe's grave with raven (detail).

1840 — 1850

In **1840**, Poe publishes a two-volume collection of short stories.

In **1841**, Poe writes "The Murders in the Rue Morgue," which is later hailed as the first detective story.

Poe's most famous poem, "The Raven," is published in **1845** and becomes an overnight sensation.

Virginia Poe dies of tuberculosis in **1847**.

After being found delirious on the streets of Baltimore, Poe dies in a hospital on October 7, **1849**.

LETTER

Letter to John Allan

Portrait of John Allan.

Read with a Purpose Read this letter to learn more about Poe's problematic relationship with his foster father.

Build Background

When Edgar Allan Poe entered the University of Virginia in 1827, his foster father, John Allan, gave him an allowance. However, Poe felt that the amount was insultingly small and tried to increase it by gambling. He lost all of his money and ran up a $2,000 debt (worth more than $40,000 in 2005). Poe might have been cheated by gamblers, but he nonetheless felt strongly that his honor was at stake and was determined to repay his debts. When John Allan refused to help, Poe sent his foster father the following letter.

Richmond, Monday [March 19, 1827]

Sir,

After my treatment on yesterday and what passed between us this morning, I can hardly think you will be surprised at the contents of this letter. My determination is at length taken to leave your house and endeavour to find some place in this wide world, where I will be treated—not as you have treated me. This is not a hurried determination, but one on which I have long considered—and having so considered my resolution is unalterable. You may perhaps think that I have flown off in a passion, & that I am already wishing to return; But not so—I will give you the reasons which have actuated me, and then judge—

Since I have been able to think on any subject, my thoughts have aspired, and they have been taught by you to aspire, to eminence in public life—this cannot be attained without a good Education, such a one I cannot obtain at a Primary school—

A collegiate Education therefore was what I most ardently desired, and I had been led to expect that it would at some future time be granted—but in a moment of caprice you have blasted

Vocabulary **unalterable** (uhn AWL tuhr uh buhl) *adj.:* not able to be changed.
aspired (uh SPYRD) *v.:* wanted to achieve something; sought.
eminence (EHM uh nuhns) *n.:* rank of distinction; fame.
caprice (kuh PREES) *n.:* sudden idea or change of mind, often made with little reason.

my hope—because forsooth I disagreed with you in an opinion, which opinion I was forced to express— **A**

Again, I have heard you say (when you little thought I was listening and therefore must have said it in earnest) that you had no affection for me—

You have moreover ordered me to quit your house, and are continually upbraiding[1] me with eating the bread of idleness, when you yourself were the only person to remedy the evil by placing me to some business—

You take delight in exposing me before those whom you think likely to advance my interest in this world—

I request that you will send me my trunk containing my clothes & books—and if you still have the least affection for me, as the last call I shall make on your bounty, to prevent the fulfillment of the Prediction you this morning expressed—send me as much money as will defray the expenses of my passage to some of the Northern cities & then support me for one month, by which time I shall be enabled to place myself in some situation where I may not only obtain a livelihood, but lay by a sum which one day or another will support me at the University. Send my trunk &c. to the Court-House Tavern. Send me I entreat you some money immediately, as I am in the greatest necessity. If you fail to comply with my request—I tremble for the consequence. **B**

Yours, &c.

Edgar A Poe

Edgar. A. Poe

The Old Stone House (1869) is the present-day site of the Poe Museum.

It depends upon yourself if hereafter you see or hear from me.

Edgar. A. Poe

1. **upbraiding:** scolding; criticizing.

A **Literary Focus** **Biographical Approach** According to this letter, what life goals does Poe have?

B **Literary Focus** **Biographical Approach** How would you describe the tone of Poe's letter—the attitude his word choice reveals?

Vocabulary **comply** (kuhm PLY) *v.:* act in agreement with something; obey.

Alone

From childhood's hour I have not been
As others were — I have not seen
As others saw — I could not bring
My passions from a common spring —
From the same source I have not taken
My sorrow — I could not awaken
My heart to joy at the same tone —
And all I lov'd — I lov'd alone —
Thou — in my childhood — in the dawn
Of a most stormy life — was drawn
From ev'ry depth of good & ill
The mystery which binds me still —
From the torrent, or the fountain —
From the red cliff of the mountain —
From the sun that round me roll'd
In its autumn tint of gold —
From the lightning in the sky
As it pass'd me flying by —
From the thunder, & the storm —
And the cloud that took the form
(When the rest of Heaven was blue)
Of a demon in my view —

E. A. Poe

POEM

ALONE

by **Edgar Allan Poe**

Read with a Purpose

Read the following selection to gain insight on how Poe regarded life.

Preparing to Read for this selection is on page 277.

Build Background

Poe wrote this poem by hand in the book of a friend, Lucy Holmes, in 1829. He did not give the poem a title, and it was not published during his lifetime. In 1875, *Scribner's Monthly* published a facsimile of the poem—an exact copy in Poe's original handwriting—but added the title "Alone." The poem has since become known by this title.

From childhood's hour I have not been
As others were—I have not seen
As others saw—I could not bring
My passions from a common spring. **A**
From the same source I have not taken
My sorrow; I could not awaken
My heart to joy at the same tone;
And all I lov'd, *I* lov'd alone.
Then—in my childhood—in the dawn
Of a most stormy life—was drawn
From ev'ry depth of good and ill
The mystery which binds me still—
From the torrent,° or the fountain,
From the red cliff of the mountain,
From the sun that 'round me roll'd
In its autumn tint of gold—
From the lightning in the sky
As it pass'd me flying by—
From the thunder and the storm,
And the cloud that took the form
(When the rest of Heaven was blue)
Of a demon in my view. **B**

13. **torrent:** a fast, powerful rush of liquid.

A Literary Focus **Biographical Approach** What events from Poe's childhood might have made him feel that he was different from other people?

B Reading Focus **Comparing Works by One Author** What "demon" might Poe be referring to here?

Applying Your Skills

MO 9.R.1.I.1.c Compare, contrast, analyze and evaluate connections: text to world 9.R.1.H.1.c Apply post-reading skills to comprehend, interpret, analyze, and evaluate text: reflect 9.R.2.C.1.d Use details from text(s): to evaluate the effect of author's style *Also covered* 9.R.3.A.1; 9.W.3.A.1.a; 9.R.1.G.1.a

Letter to John Allan / Alone

Respond and Think Critically

Reading Focus

Quick Check

1. Why did Poe write his letter of March 19, 1827, to John Allan?
2. How was childhood for the speaker of "Alone"?

Read with a Purpose

3. How would you describe Poe's relationship with his foster father?
4. What idea about life does Poe explore in "Alone"?

Reading Skills: Comparing Works by One Author

5. Add two rows to the chart you began on page 277, and compare and contrast the works you've just read.

	Letter to . . .	Alone
Connections to Poe's life	Poe feels abandoned.	Poe feels alone, apart.
Similarities		
Differences		

Vocabulary Check

Use the boldface Vocabulary word in your answer to each question.

6. What is one thing you have **aspired** to do?
7. What might make you react with **caprice**?
8. Why might someone wish for **eminence**?
9. When is a decision **unalterable**?
10. What is one school rule with which you **comply**?

Literary Focus

Literary Analysis

11. **Speculate** How do you think John Allan responded to Poe's letter? Support your ideas with evidence from the letter and Poe's biography on pages 278–279.
12. **Interpret** What does the speaker of "Alone" mean when he says that "I have not seen / As others saw"?
13. **Evaluate** Poe did not give his poem the title "Alone." It was added by someone else later on. Do you think "Alone" is an effective title? What title would you give this poem? Why?

Literary Skills: Biographical Approach

14. **Synthesize** Poe's relationship with John Allan is described in the biography on pages 278–279. How does reading the letter help you understand Poe's feelings about his foster father?
15. **Interpret** The speaker of a poem is the person addressing the reader and is not always the same person as the poet. However, many critics suggest that "Alone" is one of Poe's most personal poems. What details from his biography and the poem suggest that, in this case, the author and the speaker are the same?

Writing Focus

Think as a Reader/Writer

Use it in Your Writing Skim through the images and other vivid descriptions that you recorded in your *Reader/Writer Notebook*. Then, practice developing images and powerful descriptions in a free-form poem of your own, titled "Alone."

Preparing to Read

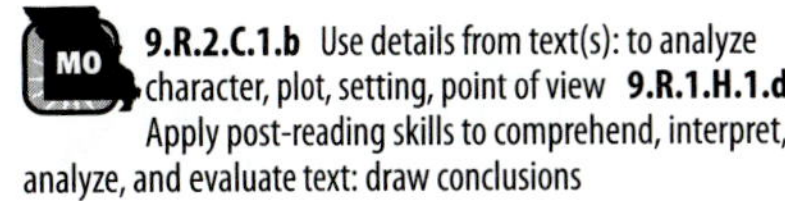

9.R.2.C.1.b Use details from text(s): to analyze character, plot, setting, point of view **9.R.1.H.1.d** Apply post-reading skills to comprehend, interpret, analyze, and evaluate text: draw conclusions

The Cask of Amontillado

Reader/Writer Notebook

Use your **RWN** to complete the activities for this selection.

Literary Focus

Unreliable Narrator When you read a story told by a first-person narrator, you need to ask yourself if you can trust that narrator. Sometimes a writer will purposely use a narrator who does not always tell the truth. An **unreliable narrator** may not know the whole truth or may choose to deceive us. A narrator's actions, statements, and **voice**—his or her style of speaking, **diction** (word choice), and **tone** (attitude)—will provide you with clues about his or her reliability.

Reading Focus

Drawing Conclusions When you read, you act like a detective. You gather evidence and **draw conclusions,** or make judgments, based on that evidence. To decide if the narrator of Poe's story is reliable, look closely at all he says and does. Then, examine what the narrator's enemy, Fortunato, says. What details could support a charge of unreliability—even insanity?

Into Action As you read, keep track of specific details to help you draw conclusions about the narrator of this story.

What the Narrator Says and Does	What Fortunato Says and Does	My Conclusions
Fortunato has injured him a thousand times.	He is surprised Montresor is a Mason.	

Vocabulary

impunity (ihm PYOO nuh tee) *n.:* freedom from punishment or harm. *The narrator has a false sense of impunity.*

retribution (reh truh BYOO shuhn) *n.:* punishment for a wrong; justice; revenge. *Montresor seeks retribution for wrongs done against him.*

impose (ihm POHZ) *v.:* (used with *upon*) take advantage of. *Montresor pretends that he does not want to impose upon Fortunato.*

implore (ihm PLAWR) *v.:* beg. *Montresor says, "Let me implore you to return."*

obstinate (AHB stuh nuht) *adj.:* stubborn. *Fortunato keeps an obstinate silence once he realizes what is happening.*

Language Coach

Denotations/Connotations The dictionary definition of a word is its **denotation;** the feelings and associations connected with a word are its **connotations.** Examine the entry for *obstinate* above. What is that word's denotation? What connotation does the word have? Does the word bring forth positive or negative feelings? Explain.

Writing Focus

Think as a Reader/Writer

Find It in Your Reading Poe uses language to create a portrait of his narrator. As you read, collect examples of words and phrases in your *Reader/Writer Notebook* that reveal the narrator's personality.

TechFocus Jot down titles of stories, artwork, and so on reminding you of Poe's distinct style and think about how to post this online.

Learn It Online

For a story preview, see the video introduction on:

The Cask of Amontillado

by **Edgar Allan Poe**

Read with a Purpose

Read this story to find out how a mysterious narrator seeks revenge on his worst enemy.

Build Background

Centuries ago, Christians in Italy buried their dead in catacombs—long, winding underground tunnels. Later, wealthy families built private catacombs beneath their homes. Dark and cool, these chambers were suitable for both burial and for storing fine wines, such as amontillado (uh mahn tuh LAH doh). Poe's story is set during carnival, which is celebrated before the start of Lent, the season during which Christians give up various pleasures. During the carnival celebration, many people wear costumes and dance in the streets.

The thousand injuries of Fortunato I had borne as best I could; but when he ventured upon insult, I vowed revenge. You, who so well know the nature of my soul, will not suppose, however, that I gave utterance to a threat. At length I would be avenged; this was a point definitively settled—but the very definitiveness with which it was resolved precluded the idea of risk. I must not only punish, but punish with impunity. A wrong is unredressed[1] when retribution overtakes its redresser. It is equally unredressed when the avenger fails to make himself felt as such to him who has done the wrong.

It must be understood that neither by word nor deed had I given Fortunato cause to doubt my goodwill. I continued, as was my wont, to smile in his face, and he did not perceive that my smile *now* was at the thought of his immolation.[2] **A**

He had a weak point—this Fortunato—although in other regards he was a man to be respected and even feared. He prided himself on his connoisseurship in wine. Few Italians have the true virtuoso spirit. For the most part their enthusiasm is adopted to suit the time and opportunity—to practice imposture upon the British and Austrian millionaires. In painting and gemmary, Fortunato, like his countrymen, was a quack—but in the matter of old wines he was sincere. In this respect I did not differ from him materially: I was skillful in the Italian vintages myself and bought largely whenever I could.

It was about dusk, one evening during the supreme madness of the carnival season, that I encountered my friend. He accosted me with excessive warmth, for he had been drinking much. The man wore motley.[3] He had on a tight-fitting parti-striped dress, and his head

1. **unredressed:** not set right; uncorrected.
2. **immolation:** destruction.
3. **motley:** multicolored costume worn by a clown or jester.

A Literary Focus Unreliable Narrator What do you learn about the narrator when he smiles at the thought of Fortunato's death?

Vocabulary impunity (ihm PYOO nuh tee) *n.:* freedom from punishment or harm.
retribution (reh truh BYOO shuhn) *n.:* punishment for a wrong; justice; revenge.

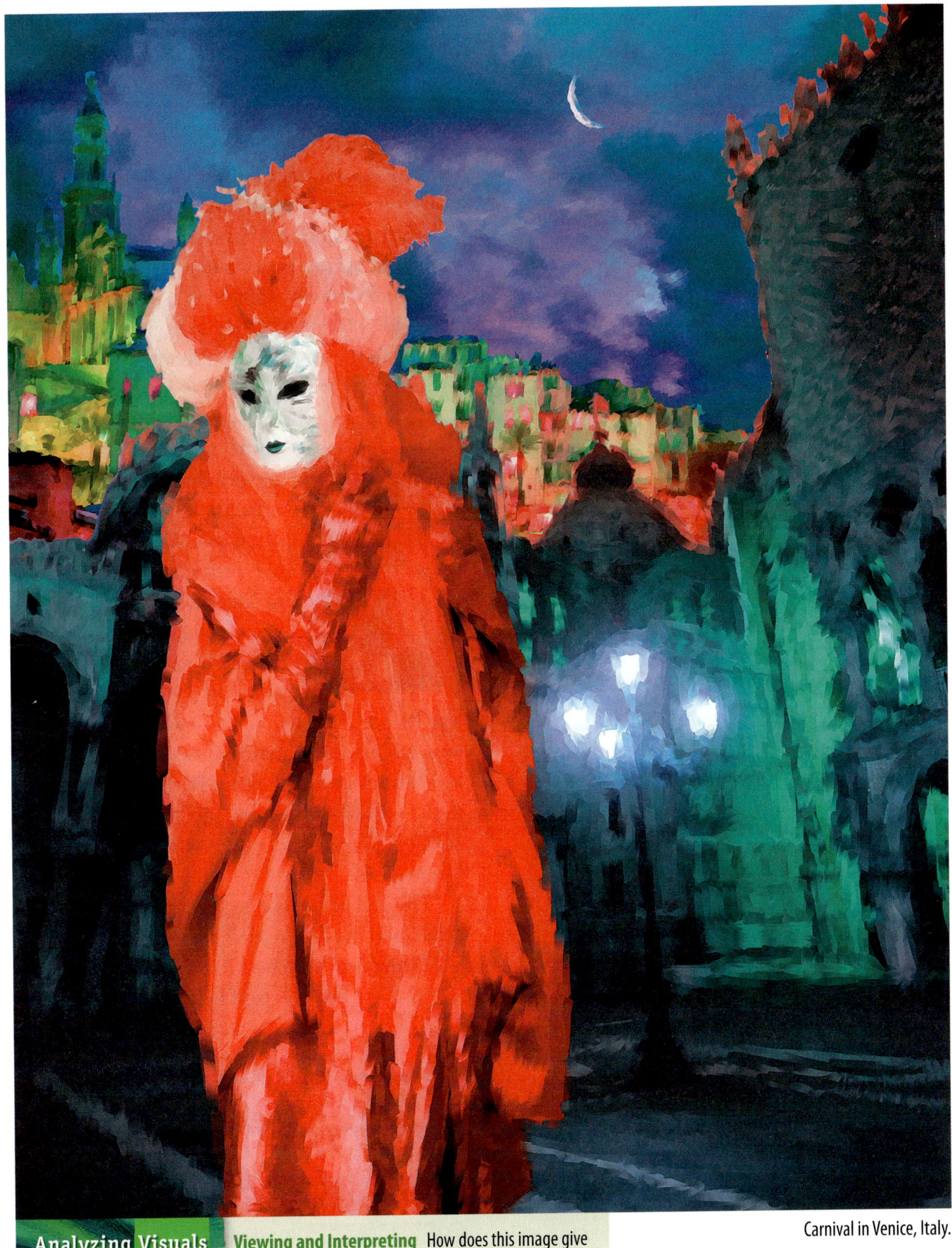

Carnival in Venice, Italy.

Analyzing Visuals **Viewing and Interpreting** How does this image give you the impression of "madness of the carnival season"?

was surmounted by the conical cap and bells. I was so pleased to see him that I thought I should never have done wringing his hand.

I said to him, "My dear Fortunato, you are luckily met. How remarkably well you are looking today! But I have received a pipe[4] of what passes for amontillado, and I have my doubts."

"How?" said he. "Amontillado? A pipe? Impossible! And in the middle of the carnival!"

"I have my doubts," I replied; "and I was silly enough to pay the full amontillado price without consulting you in the matter. You were not to be found, and I was fearful of losing a bargain."

"Amontillado!"

"I have my doubts."

"Amontillado!"

"And I must satisfy them."

"Amontillado!"

"As you are engaged, I am on my way to Luchesi. If anyone has a critical turn, it is he. He will tell me—"

"Luchesi cannot tell amontillado from sherry."

"And yet some fools will have it that his taste is a match for your own."

"Come, let us go."

"Whither?"

"To your vaults."

"My friend, no; I will not impose upon your good nature. I perceive you have an engagement. Luchesi—"

"I have no engagement; come."

"My friend, no. It is not the engagement, but the severe cold with which I perceive you are afflicted. The vaults are insufferably damp. They are encrusted with niter."[5]

"Let us go, nevertheless. The cold is merely nothing. Amontillado! You have been imposed upon. And as for Luchesi, he cannot distinguish sherry from amontillado." **B**

Thus speaking, Fortunato possessed himself of my arm. Putting on a mask of black silk and drawing a roquelaure[6] closely about my person, I suffered him to hurry me to my *palazzo*.[7]

There were no attendants at home; they had absconded to make merry in honor of the time. I had told them that I should not return until the morning and had given them explicit orders not to stir from the house. These orders were sufficient, I well knew, to ensure their immediate disappearance, one and all, as soon as my back was turned.

I took from their sconces two flambeaux[8] and, giving one to Fortunato, bowed him through several suites of rooms to the archway that led into the vaults. I passed down a long and winding staircase, requesting him to be cautious as he followed. We came at length to the foot of the descent and stood together on the damp ground of the catacombs of the Montresors.

The gait of my friend was unsteady, and the bells upon his cap jingled as he strode.

"The pipe," said he.

"It is farther on," said I; "but observe the

4. **pipe:** barrel.

5. **niter:** salt deposits.

6. **roquelaure** (RAHK uh lawr): heavy knee-length cape.

7. ***palazzo*** (pah LAHT soh): Italian for "palace."

8. **sconces:** wall fixtures that hold **flambeaux** (FLAM bohz), candlesticks or flaming pieces of wood.

Vocabulary **impose** (ihm POHZ) *v.:* (used with *upon*) take advantage of.

B **Reading Focus** **Drawing Conclusions** How does the narrator persuade Fortunato to visit his palace? What does the narrator's strategy tell you about him?

white web-work which gleams from these cavern walls."

He turned toward me, and looked into my eyes with two filmy orbs that distilled the rheum[9] of intoxication.

"Niter?" he asked, at length.

"Niter," I replied. "How long have you had that cough?"

"Ugh! ugh! ugh!—ugh! ugh! ugh!—ugh! ugh! ugh!—ugh! ugh! ugh!—ugh! ugh! ugh!"

My poor friend found it impossible to reply for many minutes. **C**

"It is nothing," he said, at last.

"Come," I said, with decision, "we will go back; your health is precious. You are rich, respected, admired, beloved; you are happy, as once I was. You are a man to be missed. For me it is no matter. We will go back; you will be ill, and I cannot be responsible. Besides, there is Luchesi—"

"Enough," he said; "the cough is a mere nothing; it will not kill me. I shall not die of a cough."

"True—true," I replied; "and, indeed, I had no intention of alarming you unnecessarily—but you should use all proper caution. A draft of this Médoc[10] will defend us from the damps."

Here I knocked off the neck of a bottle which I drew from a long row of its fellows that lay upon the mold.

"Drink," I said, presenting him the wine.

He raised it to his lips with a leer. He paused and nodded to me familiarly, while his bells jingled.

"I drink," he said, "to the buried that repose around us."

"And I to your long life."

He again took my arm, and we proceeded.

"These vaults," he said, "are extensive."

"The Montresors," I replied, "were a great and numerous family."

"I forget your arms."[11]

"A huge human foot d'or, in a field azure; the foot crushes a serpent rampant whose fangs are embedded in the heel."[12]

"And the motto?"

"Nemo me impune lacessit."[13]

Here I knocked off the neck of a bottle which I drew from a long row of its fellows that lay upon the mold.

"Good!" he said.

The wine sparkled in his eyes and the bells jingled. My own fancy grew warm with the Médoc. We had passed through walls of piled bones, with casks and puncheons[14] intermingling, into the inmost recesses of the catacombs. I paused again, and this time I made bold to seize Fortunato by an arm above the elbow.

"The niter!" I said. "See, it increases. It hangs like moss upon the vaults. We are below the river's bed. The drops of moisture trickle

9. **rheum** (room): watery discharge.

10. **Médoc** (may DAWK): type of red wine.

11. **arms:** coat of arms, a group of symbols used to represent a family.

12. **foot d'or . . . heel:** The Montresor coat of arms shows a huge golden foot against a blue background, with the foot crushing a snake that is rearing up and biting the heel.

13. ***Nemo me impune lacessit*** (NAY moh may ihm POOH nay lah KAY siht): Latin for "Nobody attacks me without punishment."

14. **puncheons:** large wine casks.

C Literary Focus Unreliable Narrator The narrator refers to Fortunato as "my poor friend." What clues suggest that the narrator means the opposite of what he says?

among the bones. Come, we will go back ere it is too late. Your cough—" **D**

"It is nothing," he said; "let us go on. But first, another draft of the Médoc."

I broke and reached him a flagon of de Grave.[15] He emptied it at a breath. His eyes flashed with a fierce light. He laughed and threw the bottle upward with a gesticulation I did not understand.

I looked at him in surprise. He repeated the movement—a grotesque one.

"You do not comprehend?" he said.

"Not I," I replied.

"Then you are not of the brotherhood."

"How?"

"You are not of the Masons."[16]

"Yes, yes," I said, "yes, yes."

"You? Impossible! A Mason?"

"A Mason," I replied.

"A sign," he said.

"It is this," I answered, producing a trowel[17] from beneath the folds of my roquelaure. **E**

"You jest," he exclaimed, recoiling a few paces. "But let us proceed to the amontillado."

"Be it so," I said, replacing the tool beneath the cloak and again offering him my arm. He leaned upon it heavily. We continued our route in search of the amontillado. We passed through a range of low arches, descended, passed on, and, descending again, arrived at a deep crypt in which the foulness of the air caused our flambeaux rather to glow than flame.

At the most remote end of the crypt there appeared another less spacious. Its walls had been lined with human remains, piled to the vault overhead, in the fashion of the great catacombs of Paris. Three sides of this interior crypt were still ornamented in this manner. From the fourth the bones had been thrown down and lay promiscuously upon the earth, forming at one point a mound of some size. Within the wall thus exposed by the displacing of the bones, we perceived a still interior recess, in depth about four feet, in width three, in height six or seven. It seemed to have been constructed for no especial use within itself, but formed merely the interval between two of the colossal supports of the roof of the catacombs and was backed by one of their circumscribing walls of solid granite.

It was in vain that Fortunato, uplifting his dull torch, endeavored to pry into the depth of the recess. Its termination the feeble light did not enable us to see.

"Proceed," I said; "herein is the amontillado. As for Luchesi—"

"He is an ignoramus," interrupted my friend, as he stepped unsteadily forward, while I followed immediately at his heels. In an instant he had reached the extremity of the niche, and finding his progress arrested by the rock, stood stupidly bewildered. A moment more and I had fettered him to the granite. In its surface were two iron staples, distant from each other about two feet horizontally. From one of these depended a short chain, from the other a pad-

---

15. **flagon of de Grave:** bottle, with a handle and sometimes a lid, containing wine from the Graves region of France.
16. **Masons:** Freemasons, a secret society of people who believe in brotherhood, giving to the poor, and helping one another. Members use secret signs and gestures to recognize one another.
17. **trowel:** flat tool with a pointed blade, especially used by a mason, a person who builds with stone or concrete. The Freemasons probably began as associations of stoneworkers.

D **Literary Focus** **Unreliable Narrator** Does Montresor's concern for Fortunato's health seem genuine? Why or why not?

E **Reading Focus** **Drawing Conclusions** Why might Montresor be carrying a trowel? What can you conclude about his plans?

Analyzing Visuals **Viewing and Interpreting** Compare and contrast these catacombs with the setting that Poe depicts in his story.

Catacomb of SS. Marcellino e Pietro in Rome, Italy.

lock. Throwing the links about his waist, it was but the work of a few seconds to secure it. He was too much astounded to resist. Withdrawing the key, I stepped back from the recess.

"Pass your hand," I said, "over the wall; you cannot help feeling the niter. Indeed it is *very* damp. Once more let me *implore* you to return. No? Then I must positively leave you. But I must first render you all the little attentions in my power."

"The amontillado!" ejaculated my friend, not yet recovered from his astonishment.

"True," I replied; "the amontillado."

As I said these words, I busied myself among the pile of bones of which I have before spoken. Throwing them aside, I soon uncovered a quantity of building stone and mortar. With these materials and with the aid of my trowel, I began vigorously to wall up the entrance of the niche.

I had scarcely laid the first tier of the masonry when I discovered that the intoxication of Fortunato had in a great measure worn off. The earliest indication I had of this was a

Vocabulary **implore** (ihm PLAWR) *v.:* beg.

low moaning cry from the depth of the recess. It was *not* the cry of a drunken man. There was then a long and obstinate silence. I laid the second tier, and the third, and the fourth; and then I heard the furious vibrations of the chain. The noise lasted for several minutes, during which, that I might hearken to it with the more satisfaction, I ceased my labors and sat down upon the bones. When at last the clanking subsided, I resumed the trowel and finished without interruption the fifth, the sixth, and the seventh tier. The wall was now nearly upon a level with my breast. I again paused and, holding the flambeaux over the mason-work, threw a few feeble rays upon the figure within. F

A succession of loud and shrill screams, bursting suddenly from the throat of the chained form, seemed to thrust me violently back. For a brief moment I hesitated—I trembled. Unsheathing my rapier,[18] I began to grope with it about the recess; but the thought of an instant reassured me. I placed my hand upon the solid fabric of the catacombs and felt satisfied. I reapproached the wall; I replied to the yells of him who clamored. I reechoed—I aided—I surpassed them in volume and in strength. I did this, and the clamorer grew still.

It was now midnight, and my task was drawing to a close. I had completed the eighth, the ninth, and the tenth tier. I had finished a portion of the last and the eleventh; there remained but a single stone to be fitted and plastered in. I struggled with its weight; I placed it partially in its destined position. But now there came from out the niche a low laugh that erected the hairs upon my head. It was succeeded by a sad voice, which I had difficulty in recognizing as that of the noble Fortunato. The voice said—

"Ha! ha! ha!—he! he! he!—a very good joke indeed—an excellent jest. We will have many a rich laugh about it at the *palazzo*—he! he! he!—over our wine—he! he! he!"

"The amontillado!" I said.

"He! he! he!—he! he! he!—yes, the amontillado. But is it not getting late? Will not they be awaiting us at the *palazzo*—the Lady Fortunato and the rest? Let us be gone."

"Yes," I said, "let us be gone."

"For the love of God, Montresor!"

"Yes," I said, "for the love of God!"

But to these words I hearkened in vain for a reply. I grew impatient. I called aloud—

"Fortunato!"

No answer. I called again—

"Fortunato!"

No answer still. I thrust a torch through the remaining aperture and let it fall within. There came forth in return only a jingling of the bells. My heart grew sick—on account of the dampness of the catacombs. I hastened to make an end of my labor. I forced the last stone into its position; I plastered it up. Against the new masonry I reerected the old rampart[19] of bones. For the half of a century no mortal has disturbed them. *In pace requiescat.*[20] G

18. **rapier** (RAY pee uhr): long, thin sword with two edges.

19. **rampart:** wall built for protection or defense.

20. ***In pace requiescat*** (ihn PAH chay ray kwee EHS kaht): Latin for "May he rest in peace."

F **Reading Focus** **Drawing Conclusions** What can you conclude about Montresor's state of mind when he stops his work to enjoy Fortunato's cries?

Vocabulary **obstinate** (AHB stuh nuht) *adj.:* stubborn.

G **Literary Focus** **Unreliable Narrator** Do you think Montresor's "heart grew sick" because of the dampness or for some other reason? Explain.

Applying Your Skills

9.R.2.C.1.b Use details from text(s): to analyze character, plot, setting, point of view **9.R.1.I.1.c** Compare, contrast, analyze and evaluate connections: text to world **9.R.1.H.1.c** Apply post-reading skills to comprehend, interpret, analyze, and evaluate text: reflect *Also covered* **9.R.1.H.1.d; 9.W.3.A.1.a**

The Cask of Amontillado

Respond and Think Critically

Reading Focus

Quick Check

1. According to Montresor, what is his motive for this crime?
2. How does Montresor lure Fortunato farther and farther into the catacombs?

Read with a Purpose

3. How does Montresor exact revenge on Fortunato?

Reading Skills: Drawing Conclusions

4. Review the notes in the first two columns of your chart, and then draw conclusions about both Montresor and Fortunato.

What the Narrator Says and Does	What Fortunato Says and Does	My Conclusions
Fortunato has injured him a thousand times.	He is surprised Montresor is a Mason.	Montresor doesn't show what he really feels.

Literary Focus

Literary Analysis

5. **Speculate** To whom could Montresor be telling this story, fifty years after the murder? Why might Montresor have decided to confide in his unidentified listener?
6. **Analyze** What character traits in Fortunato make him fall prey to Montresor?
7. **Identify** Which of Montresor's comments to the unsuspecting Fortunato mean something different from what they seem to mean?
8. **Interpret** What might Montresor be thinking when he says, *"In pace requiescat"*? Explain.

Literary Skills: Unreliable Narrator

9. **Evaluate** Describe the personality that Poe has created for Montresor. Why might Poe have chosen someone like Montresor to tell his story?
10. **Analyze** Think about whether or not Montresor is an unreliable narrator. Do any details suggest that he might have imagined "the thousand injuries" and the insult—or even the whole story? If so, what are those details?

Literary Skills Review: Biographical Approach

11. **Analyze** How might Poe's life (pages 278–279) have informed this story? Could this story have been Poe's way of getting even with his foster father? Consider these facts: Poe's foster father was Scottish, and the Montresor motto is the motto of Scotland. Also, like Fortunato, John Allan was a businessman and a Mason.

Writing Focus

Think as a Reader/Writer

Use It in Your Writing Look back at the list of powerful words and images you collected in your *Reader/Writer Notebok*. Then, choose a simple event from everyday life and give it "the Poe treatment." For example, suppose your event is a home team losing a big game. You might create a narrator who is obsessed with the team and use dark images to create an atmosphere of horror.

Applying Your Skills

The Cask of Amontillado

9.R.1.G.1.a During reading, utilize strategies: to determine meaning of unknown words **9.R.1.E.1.c** Develop vocabulary through text: using glossary, dictionary and thesaurus **9.R.1.E.1.b** Develop vocabulary through text: using context clues

Vocabulary Development

Vocabulary Check

Answer each question using the boldface Vocabulary word in your answer.

1. What tone of voice might you use to **implore** someone to follow your advice?
2. Do you think it is ever possible for someone to commit a crime with complete **impunity**?
3. How might a person **impose** upon your time?
4. What kinds of **retribution** might be demanded by a criminal court?
5. When might being **obstinate** be a positive personality trait?

Vocabulary Skills: Word Maps

A **word map** can supply several different kinds of information about a word's **etymology,** or origin, by listing root words and prefixes. It can also give a definition, a sample sentence, and synonyms. Notice how this word map organizes information for the Vocabulary word *retribution*.

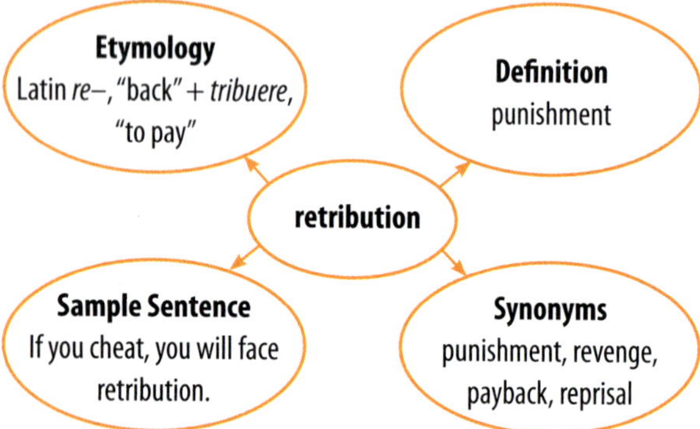

Latin *re*–, "back" + *tribuere*, "to pay"

If you cheat, you will face retribution.

punishment, revenge, payback, reprisal

Your Turn

Use a dictionary to make a word map like the one pictured for the other Vocabulary words: *impunity, impose, implore,* and *obstinate.*

Language Coach

Denotations/Connotations Go back through "The Cask of Amontillado" and find five words (other than the Vocabulary words) that evoke a strong emotional response in you. Write these words down in your *Reader/Writer Notebook.* Look up each word in a dictionary and write down its **denotation,** or definition. Now write down the feelings and associations that you have about the word. These are its **connotations.**

Academic Vocabulary

Talk About . . .

With a partner, discuss your answers to the following questions.

1. In what way are Montresor's and Fortunato's personalities distinct?
2. Which character leaves a stronger impression on you? Why is that so?

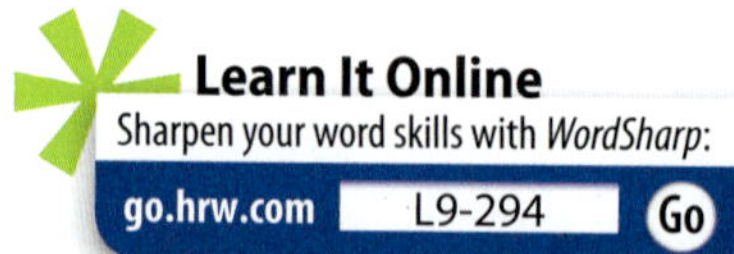

Learn It Online
Sharpen your word skills with *WordSharp*:
go.hrw.com
L9-294
Go

COMPARING TEXTS
Wrap Up

9.W.3.A.1.d Compose a variety of texts: including literary analysis 9.W.3.A.1.b Compose a variety of texts: in various formats, including workplace communication

Author Study: Edgar Allan Poe

Writing Focus

Writing an Analytic Essay

Use It in Your Writing Refer to the details about Poe's writing that you began gathering on page 277. Then, write an essay in which you analyze Poe's letter to John Allan, "Alone," and "The Cask of Amontillado." Begin by choosing one of the following essay topics:

- Examine how Poe's experiences in real life had an impact on his writings.
- Compare Poe's writing style across the selections to find similarities and differences.
- Analyze the themes that run through Poe's works.

Evaluation Criteria for an Essay

- begins with an introduction that introduces your topic and presents a thesis statement
- develops each main idea in well-organized paragraphs
- provides ample support for main ideas
- cites examples from the texts where appropriate
- has transitions that smoothly and clearly connect your ideas
- is free from errors in spelling, grammar, and punctuation

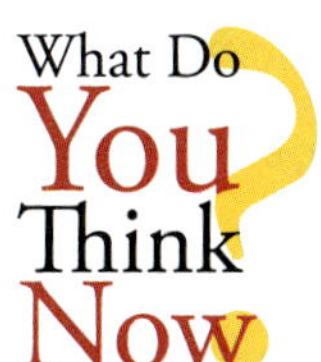

Do you think Poe would have been a different kind of writer if he had more positive support from his friends and family? Explain.

CHOICES

As you respond to the Choices, use these **Academic Vocabulary** words as appropriate: distinct, impression, portray, and insight.

REVIEW
Write a Recommendation

Timed Writing Write a letter to a friend or relative recommending a work by Poe from this collection. Provide enough information about Poe and the work to get your audience interested, but don't give away too many insights.

CONNECT
Analyze Popular Culture

TechFocus What traces of Poe's style can you find in the world today? His influence has left an impression in movies, TV, books, and the Internet. You may find examples that directly refer to Poe, or you might find works that reflect Poe's interest in the dark side of human nature. Organize the resources you find, and post them on a Web page.

EXTEND
Write a Response

Create a response to one of the works you read. Here are a couple of ideas:

- Write a letter from John Allan in response to Poe's letter to him.
- Retell a portion of "The Cask of Amontillado" from Fortunato's point of view.

In your response, create a tone and style that is distinct from Poe's and Montresor's.

Learn It Online
Find more by and about Poe with these Internet links:
go.hrw.com
L9-295
Go

Synthesizing Sources

CONTENTS

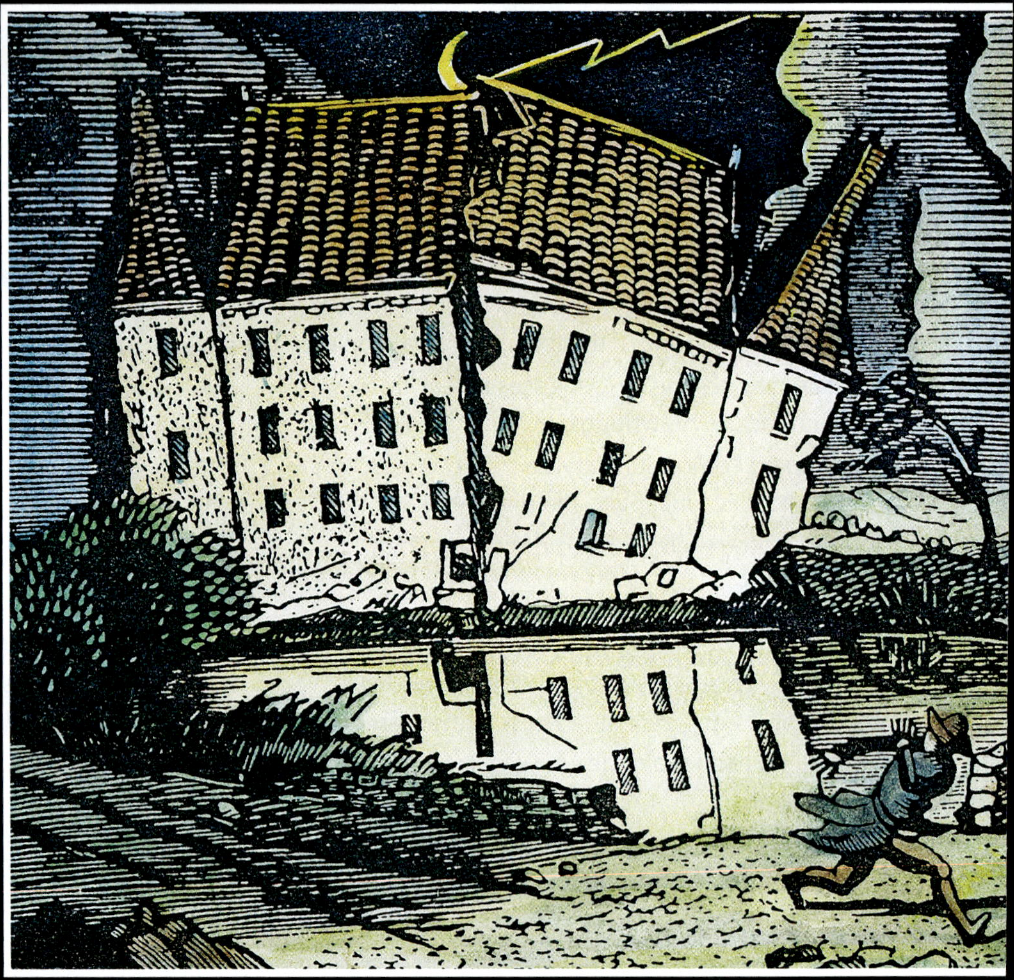

House of Usher (Twentieth century) by Constant le Breton. Woodcut.
The Granger Collection, New York.

What Do You Think?

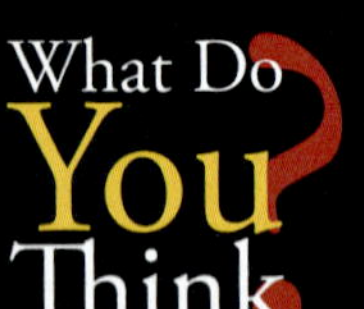

In what ways is it possible to be your own worst enemy?

QuickWrite

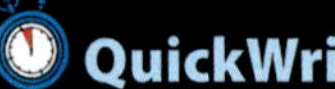

Think of a famous character or public figure who caused his or her own undoing, and write about the behavior that may have played a part in his or her downfall. Could there have been other contributing factors?

BIOGRAPHY, NEWS ARTICLE & LETTERS

Preparing to Read

9.R.1.I.1.a Compare, contrast, analyze and evaluate connections: text to text *Also covered* **9.R.1.H.1.a; 9.R.1.I.1.b; 9.R.1.H.1.d**

Four Readings About Poe's Death

Informational Text Focus

Synthesizing Sources: Drawing Conclusions When you research a subject, you get a balanced view by using several types of sources and examining different points of view. Here are some guidelines to follow:

1. **Find the main idea.** Take notes about each writer's main idea, and if you run into a difficult passage, **paraphrase** it, or restate the passage in your own words.
2. **Look for supporting evidence.** Ask yourself the following questions: "Does the writer support his or her ideas with facts, statistics, examples, anecdotes (brief real-life stories), or quotations?" "Does the writer use logic and reasoning to prove a point?"
3. **Compare and contrast.** After you read, look for similarities and differences between your sources. You might also try **making connections,** or relating what you have just read about to similar ideas you've encountered in the past.
4. **Put it together.** To **synthesize,** or pull together, what you've learned, draw conclusions about the subject.

Into Action As you read, fill in a chart like the one below to help you identify each writer's main idea and support.

Title:				
Main Idea:				
Support:				
Support:				

Writing Focus

Preparing for **Constructed Response**

As you read the selections that follow, note in your *Reader/Writer Notebook* the ways in which the writers present and support their ideas about Poe's death.

Reader/Writer Notebook

Use your **RWN** to complete the activities for these selections.

Vocabulary

Poe's Final Days

insensible (ihn SEHN suh buhl) *adj.:* not fully conscious or aware. *When the doctor arrived, he found Poe insensible.*

imposing (ihm POH zihng) *adj.:* large and impressive looking. *The old stone hospital's appearance is imposing.*

Poe's Death Is Rewritten . . .

conspicuous (kuhn SPIHK yoo uhs) *adj.:* remarkable; notable. *The investigating doctor found the lack of tests conspicuous.*

If Only Poe Had . . .

chronic (KRAHN ihk) *adj.:* frequently occurring. *Poe was known for his chronic drinking.*

Rabies Death Theory

transmitted (trans MIHT ihd) *v.:* passed on. *At the time of Poe's death, doctors were aware of how the disease was transmitted.*

Language Coach

Antonyms An **antonym** is a word that has a meaning that is opposite the meaning of another word. For example, *dark* and *light* are antonyms. Which word on the Vocabulary list above is an antonym of *infrequent*? Which word is an antonym of *aware*?

Learn It Online

Learn how to synthesize sources with the interactive Reading Workshop at:

go.hrw.com L9-297 

BIOGRAPHY

Poe's Final Days

from Edgar A. Poe: Mournful and Never-Ending Remembrance

by **Kenneth Silverman**

Read with a Purpose

What really happened during Poe's last days? Read this selection to learn of one writer's ideas.

Build Background

This biography traces the last few days of Poe's life. Poe had just parted from Elmira Shelton, to whom he was recently engaged. Shelton lived in Richmond, Virginia, and Poe set out from there for Baltimore, Maryland, eventually planning to go to New York City. He never completed his journey.

In the early morning of September 27, a Thursday, Poe began the first leg of his return to the North, setting out from Richmond for Baltimore on the 4 A.M. steamer,[1] with a trunk containing some clothing, books, and manuscripts.

Poe's trunk.

1. **steamer** (STEE muhr): steamship, or ship driven by steam power.

No reliable evidence exists about what happened to or within Poe between that time and October 3, a week later, when a printer named Joseph Walker saw him at Gunner's Hall, a Baltimore tavern, strangely dressed and semiconscious.

It was Election Day for members of Congress, and like other local watering holes[2] the tavern served as a polling place. Poe seemed to Walker "rather the worse for wear" and "in great distress." Apparently flooded with drink, he may also have been ill from exposure. Winds and soaking rains the day before had sent Baltimoreans prematurely hunting up overcoats and seeking charcoal fires for warmth. . . . Poe managed to tell Walker that he knew Joseph Evans Snodgrass, the Baltimore editor and physician with

2. **watering holes:** informal term for bars or taverns.

whom he had often corresponded while living in Philadelphia. As it happened, Walker had worked as a typesetter for Snodgrass's *Saturday Visitor*. He sent Snodgrass a dire note, warning that Poe needed "immediate assistance."

When Snodgrass arrived at Gunner's Hall, he found Poe sitting in an armchair, surrounded by onlookers. Poe had a look of "vacant stupidity." He wore neither vest nor tie, his dingy trousers fit badly, his shirt was crumpled, his cheap hat soiled. Snodgrass thought he must be wearing castoff clothing, having been robbed or cheated of his own. He ordered a room for Poe at the tavern, where he might stay comfortably until his relatives in Baltimore could be notified. Just then, however, one of them arrived—Henry Herring, Poe's uncle by marriage, who somehow had also learned of his condition. A lumber dealer now nearly sixty years old, he had wed Muddy's[3] sister, and spent time with Poe during his early days in Baltimore and later when both families lived in Philadelphia. But he refused now to take over his care, saying that on former occasions, when drunk, Poe had been abusive and ungrateful. Instead, he suggested sending Poe to a hospital. A carriage was called for. Poe had to be carried into it, Snodgrass said—insensible, muttering. **A**

3. **Muddy's:** Muddy was Poe's nickname for Maria Clemm, his aunt and mother-in-law. Poe had married his cousin, Virginia Clemm.

Through the chilly wet streets Poe was driven to the hospital of Washington Medical College, set on the highest ground of Baltimore. An imposing five-story building with vaulted gothic windows, it afforded both public wards and private rooms, advertised as being spacious, well ventilated, and directed by an experienced medical staff. Admitted at five in the afternoon, Poe was given a private room, reportedly in a section reserved for cases involving drunkenness. He was attended by the resident physician, Dr. John J. Moran, who apparently had living quarters in the hospital together with his wife. Moran had received his medical degree from the University of Maryland four years earlier and was now only about twenty-six years old. But he knew the identity of his patient—a "*great* man," he wrote of Poe, to whose "rarely gifted mind are we indebted for many of the brightest thoughts that adorn our literature." He as well as the medical students, nurses, and other physicians—all considered Poe, he said, "an object of unusual regard."

According to Moran and his wife, Poe reached the hospital in a stupor,[4] unaware of who or what had brought him there. He remained thus "unconscious" until three o'clock the next morning, when he developed a tremor[5] of the limbs and

4. **stupor** (STOO puhr): dull, half-conscious state.

5. **tremor** (TREHM uhr): involuntary trembling, especially from a physical illness.

A Informational Focus **Supporting Evidence** Why does Snodgrass think that Poe might have been robbed or cheated out of his clothing?

Vocabulary **insensible** (ihn SEHN suh buhl) *adj.:* not fully conscious or aware.
imposing (ihm POH zihng) *adj.:* large and impressive looking.

Poe's gravestone.

what Moran called "a busy, but not violent or active delirium."[6] His face was pale and he was drenched in sweat. He talked constantly, Moran said, addressing "spectral[7] and imaginary objects on the walls." Apparently during Poe's delirium, his cousin Neilson Poe came to the hospital, having been contacted by Dr. Moran. A lawyer and journalist involved in Whig politics, Neilson was just Poe's age. In happier circumstances Poe would not have welcomed the visit. Not only had Neilson offered Virginia[8] and Muddy a home apart from him; his cousin also, he believed, envied his literary reputation. Years before he had remarked that he considered "the little dog," as he called Neilson, the "bitterest enemy I have in the world." The physicians anyway thought it inadvisable for Neilson to see Poe at the moment, when "very excitable." Neilson sent some changes of linen and called again the next day, to find Poe's condition improved. **B**

Poe being quieted, Moran began questioning him about his family and about where he lived, but found his answers mostly incoherent. Poe did not know what had become of his trunk or when he had left Richmond, but said he had a wife there, as Moran soon learned was untrue. He said that his "degradation," as Moran characterized it, made him feel like sinking into the ground. Trying to rouse Poe's spirits, Moran told him he wished to contribute in every way to his comfort, and hoped Poe would soon be enjoying the company of his friends. . . . **C**

Then Poe seemed to doze, and Moran left him briefly. On returning he found Poe violently delirious, resisting the efforts of two nurses to keep him in bed. From Moran's description, Poe seems to have raved a full day or more, through Saturday evening, October 6, when he began repeatedly calling out someone's name. It may have been that of a Baltimore family named Reynolds or, more likely, the name of his uncle-in-law Henry Herring. Moran later said that he sent for the Herring

6. **delirium** (dih LIHR ee uhm): irrational, raving behavior, often caused by high fever.
7. **spectral** (SPEHK truhl): ghostly; unreal.
8. **Virginia:** Poe's wife, Virginia Clemm. She died of tuberculosis in 1847.

B **Informational Focus** **Main Idea** How would you paraphrase this paragraph? In what way does paraphrasing help you find the main idea?

C **Informational Focus** **Main Idea** How does Poe's behavior at the hospital support the main idea of this selection?

family, but that only one of Herring's two daughters came to the hospital. Poe continued deliriously calling the name until three o'clock on Sunday morning. Then his condition changed. Feeble from his exertions he seemed to rest a short time and then, Moran reported, "quietly moving his head he said *'Lord help my poor Soul'* and expired!"

The cause of Poe's death remains in doubt. Moran's account of his profuse perspiration, trembling, and hallucinations indicates delirium tremens, *mania à potu.*[9] Many others who had known Poe, including the professionally trained Dr. Snodgrass, also attributed his death to a lethal amount of alcohol. Moran later vigorously disputed this explanation, however, and some Baltimore newspapers gave the cause of death as "congestion of the brain" or "cerebral inflammation."[10] Although the terms were sometimes used euphemistically[11] in public announcements of deaths from disgraceful causes, such as alcoholism, they may in this case have come from the hospital staff itself. According to Moran, one of its senior physicians diagnosed Poe's condition as encephalitis, a brain inflammation, brought on by "exposure." This explanation is consistent with the prematurely wintry weather at the time, with Snodgrass's account of Poe's partly clad condition, and with Elmira Shelton's recollection that on leaving Richmond Poe already had a fever. Both explanations may have been correct: Poe may have become too drunk to care about protecting himself against the wind and rain. **D**

9. **delirium tremens, *mania à potu*:** *Delirium tremens* refers to an alcoholic state in which the victim behaves irrationally and sometimes violently, hallucinates (sees imaginary things), and trembles. *Mania à potu* is a Latin phrase meaning "madness from drinking."
10. **"congestion of the brain" or "cerebral inflammation":** These are terms for conditions of the brain caused by injury or infection.
11. **euphemistically** (yoo fuh MIHS tihk lee): in a manner meant to mask or substitute for something unpleasant or offensive.

D Informational Focus Supporting Evidence
Why didn't Dr. Moran believe that Poe died of alcohol poisoning?

Read with a Purpose

What does this writer believe is the real story behind Poe's death?

Illustration of Edgar Allan Poe's grave with raven.

Poe's Death Is Rewritten as Case of Rabies, Not Telltale Alcohol

from **The New York Times, September 15, 1996**

Read with a Purpose

Read the following article for a different account of what might have caused Poe's death.

Preparing to Read for this selection is on page 297.

Build Background

One of the ways doctors keep up with medical advances in their field is by attending medical conferences. While attending such a conference, Dr. R. Michael Benitez from Baltimore presented a new theory about Poe's death.

Edgar Allan Poe did not die drunk in a gutter in Baltimore but rather had rabies, a new study suggests.

The researcher, Dr. R. Michael Benitez, a cardiologist[1] who practices a block from Poe's grave, says it is true that the writer was seen in a bar on Lombard Street in October 1849, delirious and possibly wearing somebody else's soiled clothes.

But Poe was not drunk, said Dr. Benitez, an assistant professor of medicine at the University of Maryland Medical Center. "I think Poe is much maligned[2] in that respect," he added.

The writer entered Washington College Hospital comatose,[3] Dr. Benitez said, but by the next day was perspiring heavily, hallucinating, and shouting at imaginary companions. The next day, he seemed better but could not remember falling ill.

On his fourth day at the hospital, Poe again grew confused and belligerent,[4] then quieted down and died.

That is a classic case of rabies, the doctor said. His study is in the September issue of *The Maryland Medical Journal.*

In the brief period when he was calm and awake, Poe refused alcohol and could drink water only with great difficulty. Rabies victims frequently exhibit hydrophobia, or fear of water, because it is painful to swallow. **A**

There is no evidence that a rabid animal had bitten Poe. About one fourth of rabies victims reportedly cannot remember being bitten. After an infection, the symptoms can take up to a year to appear. But when the symptoms do appear, the disease is a swift and brutal killer. Most patients die in a few days.

1. **cardiologist** (kahr dee AHL uh jihst): doctor who specializes in diseases of the heart.
2. **maligned** (muh LYND): falsely accused of bad conduct; slandered.
3. **comatose** (KOH muh tohs): deeply unconscious and unable to be wakened.
4. **belligerent** (buh LIHJ uhr uhnt): angry and aggressive or ready to start a fight.

A Informational Focus Compare and Contrast What evidence about Poe's condition in this article is similar to that in the biography you just read? What evidence is different?

Poe's house in Baltimore, Maryland.

Poe "had all the features of encephalitic rabies," said Dr. Henry Wilde, who frequently treats rabies at Chulalongkorn University Hospital in Bangkok, Thailand.

Although it has been well established that Poe died in the hospital, legend has it that he succumbed in the gutter, a victim of his debauched[5] ways.

The legend may have been fostered by his doctor, who in later years became a temperance advocate[6] and changed the details to make an object lesson of Poe's death.

5. **debauched** (dih BAWCHT): characterized by extreme indulgence in pleasures.
6. **temperance advocate:** someone who believes that people should not drink alcohol.

The curator of the Edgar Allan Poe House and Museum in Baltimore, Jeff Jerome, said that he had heard dozens of tales but that "almost everyone who has come forth with a theory has offered no proof."

Some versions have Poe unconscious under the steps of the Baltimore Museum before being taken to the hospital. Other accounts place him on planks between two barrels outside a tavern on Lombard Street. In most versions, Poe is wearing someone else's clothes, having been robbed of his suit.

Poe almost surely did not die of alcohol poisoning or withdrawal, Mr. Jerome said. The writer was so sensitive to alcohol that a glass of wine would make him violently ill for days. Poe may have had problems with alcohol as a younger man, Mr. Jerome said, but by the time he died at forty he almost always avoided it. (B)

Dr. Benitez worked on Poe's case as part of a clinical pathologic conference. Doctors are presented with a hypothetical[7] patient and a description of the symptoms and are asked to render a diagnosis.

Dr. Benitez said that at first he did not know that he had been assigned Poe, because his patient was described only as "E. P., a writer from Richmond." But by the time he was scheduled to present his findings a few weeks later, he had figured out the mystery.

"There was a conspicuous lack in this report of things like CT scans and MRI's,"[8] the doctor said. "I started to say to myself, 'This doesn't look like it's from the 1990s.' Then it dawned on me that E. P. was Edgar Poe."

Read with a Purpose

What details make this account of Poe's death plausible?

7. **hypothetical** (hy puh THEHT ih kuhl): in theory; not actual.
8. **CT scans and MRI's:** medical tests that use modern technology. Both tests produce an image of a cross-section of soft tissue such as the brain.

(B) Informational Focus Supporting Evidence What supporting evidence does Jeff Jerome offer for Dr. Benitez's theory?

Vocabulary conspicuous (kuhn SPIHK yoo uhs) *adj.:* remarkable; notable.

Read with a Purpose

Read the following letters to investigate a clash between historic facts and modern medicine.

Preparing to Read for this selection is on page 297.

Build Background

To comment on a publication's article or to challenge it, a reader may opt to write a letter to the editor. Letters to the editor are printed in a later publication and sometimes start a flurry of correspondence. In response to the previous article on page 302, Burton R. Pollin and Robert E. Benedetto wrote a letter disputing Dr. Benitez's theory. Dr. Benitez then replied by writing a letter that defended his ideas.

If Only Poe Had Succeeded When He Said Nevermore to Drink

To the Editor:

Dr. R. Michael Benitez, an assistant professor of medicine at Maryland University Medical Center, is wrong to ascribe[1] the death of Edgar Allan Poe to rabies through animal infection rather than to the traditionally maintained cause of alcoholism (news article, September 15).

Poe was found outside a Baltimore saloon in an alcoholic stupor on October 3, 1849, and died four days later. Dr. John J. Moran's account of his final days is given in a letter to Poe's aunt and mother-in-law, Maria Clemm, a *New York Herald* article in 1875, and a book by Moran in 1885. Supplementary accounts of Poe's alcoholic condition came from Joseph Walker, a Baltimore printer who first found him; Dr. Joseph Snodgrass, an editor well known to Poe; and two of Poe's relatives. None of these confirm Dr. Benitez's statement that "Poe was not drunk." Evidence of Poe's chronic binges is strewn through his letters, in periodic admissions of "recoveries" and promises to his wife, Virginia, and her mother to "reform."

Dr. Benitez admits the primary weakness of his theory—lack of evidence of a bite or scratch. In those days, rabies was well known as to causes and symptoms, including itching and other sensations that could affect an entire limb or side of the body. How could Moran and his staff ignore such symptoms in a patient? **A**

And what of Poe's cat, dearly loved but left behind in the Bronx over three months earlier? Guiltless was the pet Caterina, who, uninfected and showing no sign of rabies, died of starvation when deserted by Clemm after Poe's death.

In short, there is no need to whitewash[2] the self-destructive behavior of this literary genius and major American poet, critic, and teller of tales.

Burton R. Pollin
Robert E. Benedetto
Bronxville, New York
September 20, 1996

The writers are, respectively, professor emeritus of English, City University of New York, and an associate film professor at the University of South Carolina.

from **The New York Times,**
September 23, 1996

1. **ascribe** (uh SKRYB): assign or attribute something to a cause.

2. **whitewash** (HWYT wahsh): cover up the faults or defects of something; give a favorable appearance to something.

A Informational Focus Supporting Evidence What new fact is presented about rabies in this letter?

Vocabulary chronic (KRAHN ihk) *adj.:* frequently occurring.

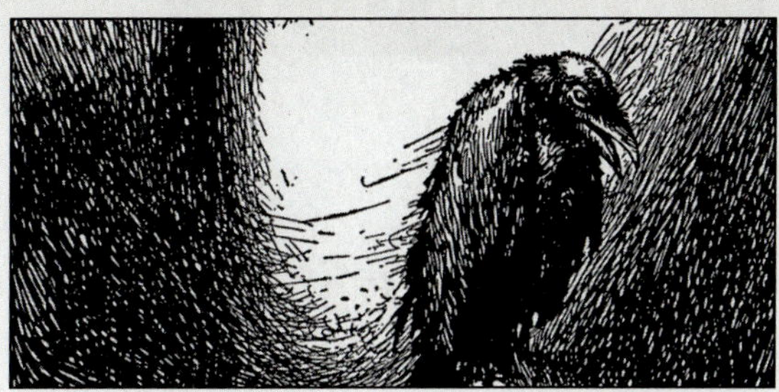

Poe: The Raven (1845) by Edmund Dulac (1882–1953). Illustration. The Granger Collection, New York.

Rabies Death Theory

To the Editor:

Contrary to a September 23 letter, I do not "admit" that the lack of bite or scratch is a weakness in my theory that Edgar Allan Poe may have died of rabies encephalitis.

Data published by the Centers for Disease Control and Prevention indicate that over the past 20 years in the United States there have been 33 reported cases of human rabies, yet only 24 percent of these victims could recall an appropriate history of animal exposure. Bat-related subtypes of rabies have been identified in 15 cases of human rabies since 1980, although patient contact of any sort with bats could be documented in only 7 of these patients.

A diagnosis is not always easy or straightforward. The incubation period[1] in humans may be as long as a year, if the inoculation[2] is small and occurs on the hand or foot. Thus the lack of evidence of a bite or scratch is not inconsistent with the diagnosis. Finally, although physicians knew how rabies was transmitted at the time of Poe's death, even at the time of Louis Pasteur's first use of a rabies "vaccine" in 1885 the causative agent, a rhabdovirus, was unknown.[3]

I was saddened to hear of the fate of Caterina, Poe's cat, yet nowhere have I suggested that Poe contracted rabies from her, although it is worth noting that there was no available vaccine for pets at that time. B

R. Michael Benitez, M.D.
Baltimore, Maryland
September 26, 1996

The writer is an assistant professor of medicine at the University of Maryland Medical Center.

from **The New York Times,**
September 30, 1996

Read with a Purpose

After reading the letters, who do you side with more—Professors Pollin and Benedetto or Dr. Benitez? Why?

1. **incubation period:** amount of time between a person's exposure to a disease and the appearance of symptoms.
2. **inoculation** (ih nahk yooh LAY shuhn): here, skin puncture from an animal bite or scratch through which a disease is passed on.
3. **even at the time of Louis Pasteur's . . . was unknown:** Louis Pasteur (1822–1895) was a French chemist who helped develop the important medical theory linking germs and disease. Pasteur developed a rabies vaccine using tissue from infected animals. Benitez is pointing out, however, that at the time of Poe's death, scientists had not isolated and identified the virus that causes rabies.

B Informational Focus Supporting Evidence Does knowing what happened to Poe's cat Caterina strengthen, weaken, or make no difference to Dr. Benitez's rabies theory? Explain.

Vocabulary **transmitted** (trans MIHT ihd) *v.:* passed on.

Applying Your Skills

Four Readings About Poe's Death

Practicing the Standards

Informational Text and Vocabulary

1. What is the **main idea** of the biography by Kenneth Silverman?
   - **A** The precise cause of Poe's death remains a mystery.
   - **B** Poe died of rabies.
   - **C** Poe died of alcohol poisoning.
   - **D** Poe was neurotic.

2. What is the **main idea** of the letter written by Pollin and Benedetto?
   - **A** Poe has been unjustly accused of being an alcoholic.
   - **B** There is a great deal of evidence that Poe's death was due to alcoholism.
   - **C** Poe's cat could not have bitten him and given him rabies.
   - **D** Poe was a great writer, but he had human faults.

3. What is the *strongest* **evidence** Dr. Benitez presents in his letter to defend his theory?
   - **A** Rabies has a long incubation period, and many victims do not remember being attacked by an animal.
   - **B** There was no available vaccine for pets at the time of Poe's death.
   - **C** During Poe's lifetime, doctors knew how rabies was passed on.
   - **D** Louis Pasteur first used a rabies vaccine in 1885.

4. Which of the following statements contrasting the biography with Pollin and Benedetto's letter is *not* true?
   - **A** The biography states that Dr. Moran eventually claimed Poe didn't die from drinking too much, but the letter states that Dr. Moran provided evidence for this theory.
   - **B** The biography does not refer to Poe's letters as evidence, but Pollin and Benedetto's letter does.
   - **C** The biography does not discuss the rabies death theory, but the letter does.
   - **D** The biography refers to Joseph Walker's description of Poe, but the letter does not.

5. Which statement shows the *most* important **similarity** between the article and Dr. Benitez's letter?
   - **A** Both inform the reader that Dr. Benitez is an assistant professor of medicine.
   - **B** Both use statistics as support.
   - **C** Both point out that lack of a bite or scratch does not weaken the rabies death theory.
   - **D** Both state that only highly skilled doctors can diagnose rabies.

6. What **conclusion** might you draw by synthesizing the information from these four sources?
   - **A** Poe was a tortured genius.
   - **B** Poe's symptoms could point to several different causes of death.
   - **C** All theories should take into account that Poe died drunk.
   - **D** Poe's illness would have been correctly diagnosed by modern doctors.

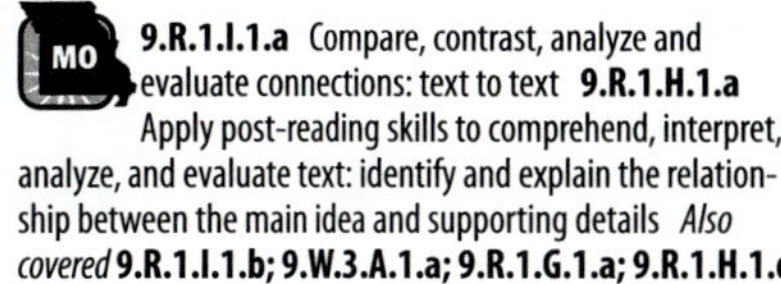

MO
9.R.1.I.1.a Compare, contrast, analyze and evaluate connections: text to text **9.R.1.H.1.a** Apply post-reading skills to comprehend, interpret, analyze, and evaluate text: identify and explain the relationship between the main idea and supporting details *Also covered* **9.R.1.I.1.b; 9.W.3.A.1.a; 9.R.1.G.1.a; 9.R.1.H.1.d**

7. A person who is *insensible* —

A makes good decisions

B is unaware of what he or she is doing

C solves difficult problems

D hurts many people

8. What is the best definition of *imposing*?

A Large and impressive looking

B Commonplace and ordinary

C Small and minuscule

D Showy and dainty

9. Which of the following sentences uses the word *conspicuous* correctly?

A His *conspicuous* running will help the cross-country team at their next meet.

B When the toddler was presented with a gift, she acted very *conspicuous*.

C My grandmother's *conspicuous* absence from the family reunion means she does not approve of it.

D I like to use *conspicuous* paper when writing thank-you notes.

10. What is the best definition of *chronic*?

A Incessantly

B Frequently occurring

C Sporadic

D Hit and miss

11. When an e-mail is *transmitted* to another person, it is —

A decorative

B deleted

C complex

D sent

Writing Focus **Constructed Response**

Which account of Poe's death do you find most convincing? Explain the conclusions you have drawn about Poe's death, and support your conclusion by citing evidence from the texts.

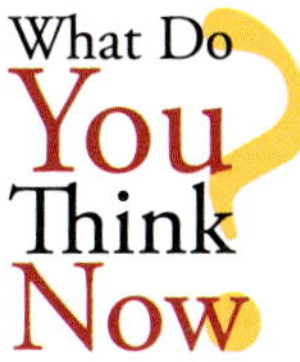

In what ways do you think Poe might have been an enemy to himself? Explain.

FOCUS ON MISSOURI COURSE LEVEL EXPECTATIONS

Literary Skills Review

Narrator and Voice **Directions:** Read the following selection. Then, read and respond to the questions that follow.

Geraldo No Last Name by Sandra Cisneros

She met him at a dance. Pretty too, and young. Said he worked in a restaurant, but she can't remember which one. Geraldo. That's all. Green pants and Saturday shirt. Geraldo. That's what he told her.

And how was she to know she'd be the last one to see him alive. An accident, don't you know. Hit and run. Marin, she goes to all those dances. Uptown. Logan. Embassy. Palmer. Aragon. Fontana. The manor. She likes to dance. She knows how to do cumbias and salsas and rancheras even. And he was just someone she danced with. Somebody she met that night. That's right.

That's the story. That's what she said again and again. Once to the hospital people and twice to the police. No address. No name. Nothing in his pockets. Ain't it a shame.

Only Marin can't explain why it mattered, the hours and hours, for somebody she didn't even know. The hospital emergency room. Nobody but an intern working all alone. And maybe if the surgeon would've come, maybe if he hadn't lost so much blood, if the surgeon had only come, they would know who to notify and where.

But what difference does it make? He wasn't anything to her. He wasn't her boyfriend or anything like that. Just another brazer[1] who didn't speak English. Just another wetback.[2] You know the kind. The ones who always look ashamed. And what was she doing out at 3:00 A.M. anyway? Marin who was sent home with her coat and some aspirin. How does she explain?

She met him at a dance. Geraldo in his shiny shirt and green pants. Geraldo going to a dance.

What does it matter?

They never saw the kitchenettes. They never knew about the two-room flats[3] and sleeping rooms he rented, the weekly money orders sent home, the currency exchange. How could they?

His name was Geraldo. And his home is in another country. The ones he left behind are far away, will wonder, shrug, remember. Geraldo—he went north . . . we never heard from him again.

---

1. **brazer:** Americanization of the Spanish word *bracero,* used in the United States to refer to a Mexican laborer allowed into the United States temporarily to work.
2. **wetback:** offensive term for a Mexican laborer who illegally enters the United States, often by swimming or wading the Rio Grande.
3. **flats:** apartments.

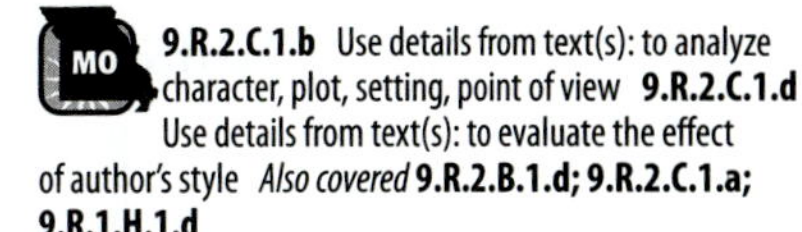
9.R.2.C.1.b Use details from text(s): to analyze character, plot, setting, point of view **9.R.2.C.1.d** Use details from text(s): to evaluate the effect of author's style *Also covered* **9.R.2.B.1.d; 9.R.2.C.1.a; 9.R.1.H.1.d**

1. The story is told by —

A a first-person narrator

B an omniscient narrator

C a third-person-limited narrator

D an unreliable narrator

9.R.2.C.1.a

2. How does the choice of **narrator** affect the telling of the story?

A The reader is presented with only Marin's interpretation of the events.

B The reader is presented with only Geraldo's interpretation of the events.

C The reader is presented with multiple characters in the story.

D The reader sees things from a biased point of view.

9.R.2.B.1.d

3. Which phrase *best* describes the **tone** of the story?

A Sarcastic and superior

B Innocent and playful

C Irritated and frustrated

D Sad and bitter

9.R.2.C.1.a

4. The *best* description of the narrator's **voice** is —

A worried

B hopeful

C informal

D annoyed

9.R.2.B.1.d

5. Which sentence in the story *best* illustrates the narrator's mixed feelings toward Geraldo?

A "Geraldo. That's all."

B "And he was just someone she danced with."

C "He wasn't anything to her."

D "What does it matter?"

9.R.2.C.1.b

6. Near the end of the story, the narrator says "they" never saw certain aspects of Geraldo's life. Who are "they"?

A Other people at the dance

B Other Mexican Americans

C Geraldo's family

D The hospital staff and police

9.R.1.H.1.d

7. At the end of the story, the narrator says "we never heard from him again." Who is "we"?

A The narrator and his or her friends

B Marin

C The doctors at the hospital

D Geraldo's family and friends in his home country

9.R.1.H.1.d

Constructed Response

8. Suppose the story were narrated by Geraldo. What would he be able to tell you that Cisneros's narrator could not? How would the story be different? Support your opinions using specific examples from the story.

9.R.2.C.1.d

Informational Skills Review

Synthesizing Sources **Directions:** Read the following selections. Then, read and respond to the questions that follow.

Coping with Cliques

reviewed by **D'Arcy Lyness**

In many American schools, cliques, or social groups, form and exclude other classmates. In addition, some students become bullies and target unsuspecting classmates. In 2001, it was estimated that about one third of American students in grades six to ten were involved in bullying. Read the articles below to find out what can be done about these problems.

Are you holding back on approaching someone you'd like to be friends with because you think he or she's in a group that's out of your league? Are you concerned about whether you'll still be popular and included this year at school or whether you'll feel like an outcast—or worse, be picked on?

Whether you're on the outside looking in or the inside wanting out, it can help to know what makes cliques tick.

What's the Difference Between a Group of Friends and a Clique?

Usually, friendship groups form around the things people have in common. So skaters, jocks, Goths, preps, punks, and even the math club are naturally drawn together because they share the same values and interests. The people in these groups feel they have a place where they are welcome and supported, and where they can be themselves, quirks and all.

Some groups stick together for a long time. Others drift apart after a while as people develop new interests, make different friends, or just find they have less in common. People can move in and out of different groups and can even be part of several at the same time. Even within a group, people often have one or two friends they feel closest to and enjoy the most.

Some friendship groups seem pretty flexible and welcome people to join in. Others seem much more restricted, though. People in these groups make it clear that not just anyone can be part of their crowd. That type of restricted group is sometimes called a clique.

What's the Deal with Cliques?

Cliques are tight groups that usually have a strict code of membership and ways to act. Instead of being centered on shared values and beliefs, many cliques tend to focus on maintaining their status and popularity. For

MO **9.R.1.I.1.a** Compare, contrast, analyze and evaluate connections: text to text *Also covered* **9.R.1.H.1.a; 9.R.3.C.1.c; 9.R.1.H.1.d**

instance, a certain clique may try to make it seem as if the people in the clique are "better" than those outside, or that their clique is "better" or higher status than another clique.

Unlike regular groups of friends, where members are free to socialize with others outside the group, people in cliques do everything together. They sit together in class, go to the mall together after school—and they only do stuff with other clique members or people they decide are "cool."

Although people might think it's better to belong to a clique than to be excluded, many times people in cliques end up dealing with lots of pressures and rules. They soon start to worry about whether they'll continue to be popular or whether they'll be dropped. After a while, they may begin to realize that true friends wouldn't be so bossy or demanding.

Why Do Cliques Attract People?

Cliques attract people for different reasons: For some people, being popular or cool is the most important thing, and cliques give them a place where they can get this social status. Other people want to be in cliques because they don't like to feel left out. And some people simply feel it's safer to be on the inside than the outside.

Cliques give people who like to take control a chance to be in charge (for good or bad!). And, for people who feel more comfortable following, they offer a place where rules are clearly defined. It's always clear to clique members what they need to do to fit in.

Sometimes clique members decide they want out. They don't like being limited by the rules, and they don't like leaving others out and hurting people's feelings. As people mature, they usually outgrow the need to be part of a clique.

Surviving Cliques

Whether you're on the inside or the outside, cliques can make your life tough. But there are ways to cope:

- Know yourself—and your reputation. Now is a time for getting in touch with your values, interests, and beliefs. If you're encountering cliques, it's a good opportunity to ask yourself what you and your true friends give each other. Do you want to be part of a group because you need to feel accepted or because you actually share their values? Has your group of friends morphed into something you don't like?
- Stay involved in activities that make you feel good about yourself. If you're in a clique, don't let the group pressure you into giving up things you love or spending time and money on things that aren't important to you. If you're on the outside and feeling left out, getting involved in things that interest you is a great way to find a sense of belonging, help you feel valued, and take your mind off a group that's not welcoming.

Informational Skills Review CONTINUED

- Keep your social circles open and diverse. Cliques can be very limiting in the way they control how members look, think, dress, and behave. Don't let them make you miss out on getting to know people who may become close friends. If you're on the outside, it can help to find a close friend or group of friends whose values, goals, and behaviors fit in with yours.
- Speak out. If you feel your group of friends is turning into a clique, take a stand for your beliefs. Be aware that the clique might go on without you (remember those girls who feel threatened by someone else's strength). But there's also a chance that others might follow your lead and stop acting so cliquey. If it's too hard to get up the courage to speak out, you still don't have to participate in things that feel wrong. And if you're on the outside and know that a clique is bullying or intimidating others, let teachers or counselors know about it.

Friendships change. Just as the rising power of one or more cliques can make life miserable, shifting social winds can take their power away. You may encounter cliques as a freshman or sophomore. But the good news is that most cliques have disappeared by the end of high school.

Want to know the real secret to being popular and having friends? Be a good friend yourself. People who enjoy true and lasting popularity are those who have good friendship skills. Being a friend means being respectful, fair, interested, trustworthy, honest, caring, and kind. So if you want to have friends, be just the kind of friend you'd like to have.

---

from And Words Can Hurt Forever

by **James Garbarino** and **Ellen deLara**

"Sticks and stones may break my bones, but words can never hurt me." It's an old rhyme, taught to generations of children as a tactic for deflecting taunts and teasing. Usually it comes with the instruction by a parent or teacher that the child chant it back to those who taunt him or her, like some kind of verbal amulet[1] to ward off the evil spirits of teasing. But the essence of this childhood verse has never really convinced children, not in their hearts. Without denying the importance of physi-

1. **amulet:** object worn as a charm to protect against evil or injury.

9.R.1.I.1.a Compare, contrast, analyze and evaluate connections: text to text *Also covered* **9.R.1.H.1.a; 9.R.3.C.1.c; 9.R.1.H.1.d**

cal pain, they know that what other children think and say about them does matter. Perhaps even more than broken bones, words can hurt forever.

No child is a stranger to teasing, for the roles of victim, perpetrator,[2] and witness can be fluid from day to day and one school year to another. A survey conducted for the National Institute of Child Health and Human Development (NICHHD), published in the *Journal of the American Medical Association* in April 2001, reported that almost a third of American children in grades six through ten are directly involved in serious, frequent bullying (which includes many forms of harassment,[3] intimidation,[4] and emotional violence)—10 percent as bullies, 13 percent as victims, and 6 percent as both. Other national surveys report even higher figures. The U.S. Department of Education reports that 77 percent of middle and high school students in small Midwestern towns have been bullied.

But these numbers tell just a part of the story, because the vast majority of kids at school experience bullying as bystanders. Most acts of bullying occur in front of other children, who rarely come to the aid of their classmates. A very small number of these witnesses may take pleasure in the suffering of others, but most are simply relieved that it is someone else's turn to be the target. Most children watch the bullying of their peers with a sense of helplessness, frozen in fear, with guilt, and ultimately, shame for doing nothing to help.

What is more, the NICHHD survey focuses only on situations in which the bully was more powerful or older than the victim, excluding so-called equals in age, gender, and size. But *damage* is done not just when one child is older or more powerful than the others. We are convinced that emotional damage is done also through bullying by equals or peers.

2. **perpetrator:** person who is guilty of, or commits, a crime.
3. **harassment:** persistent tormenting.
4. **intimidation:** threats.

1. Which statement below *best* describes the **main idea** of "Coping with Cliques"?

A Cliques and friendship groups are the same thing.

B Joining a clique will make you popular.

C A clique is difficult to get out of.

D There are ways to avoid being hurt by cliques.

9.R.1.H.1.a

2. In *And Words Can Hurt Forever,* what **evidence** do the authors provide to support their statement that bullying is a problem?

A They write about their own experiences with bullies.

B They document specific student accounts of bullying.

C They offer statistical information about bullying.

D They do not support their statement.

9.R.3.C.1.c

Informational Skills Review CONTINUED

3. What **conclusion** can you draw from the articles about why bystanders often don't help the victims of bullies?

A They don't think bullies are a problem.

B They think siding with the victim will make them less popular.

C They are relieved that they are not the ones being targeted.

D They don't want to get in trouble.

9.R.1.H.1.d

4. *Both* articles say that students join cliques or become bullies because —

A they don't like the students they hurt

B they feel better about themselves by physically hurting others

C they want to prove they are stronger than others

D they feel powerless and want to keep others from hurting them first

9.R.1.I.1.a

5. How do the selections differ in their approaches to the topics of bullying and cliques?

A One focuses on how to handle hostile students, while the other offers statistical information on the effects of hostile encounters.

B One focuses on personal accounts, while the other is more general.

C One focuses on emotional violence, while the other focuses on physical violence.

D One offers advice for students, while the other offers advice for parents.

9.R.1.I.1.a

6. You could **synthesize** the information in both articles to conclude that —

A physical violence is a more serious problem than emotional violence

B emotional violence is a more serious problem than physical violence

C bullying and cliques are serious problems in schools

D the problems of bullying and cliques are not taken seriously by schools

9.R.1.H.1.d

7. Which of the following statements **comparing** the two selections is *not* true?

A Both selections deal with the difficulties of relationships between people.

B Both selections put forth the idea that children can be mean to one another.

C Both selections use results from scientific studies to support their main ideas.

D Both selections put forth the idea that children care what others think about them.

9.R.1.I.1.a

Constructed Response

8. Think about the information provided in each article. Then, write a few paragraphs about why you think students join cliques or become bullies. What are three pieces of advice that you would offer to a student being harassed by a clique or bully?

9.R.1.I.1.a

FOCUS ON MISSOURI COURSE LEVEL EXPECTATIONS

Vocabulary Skills Review

MO **9.R.1.E.1.b** Develop vocabulary through text: using context clues **9.R.1.E.1.c** Develop vocabulary through text: using glossary, dictionary and thesaurus

Context Clues

Directions: Use the context clues in the following passages to identify the meaning of each italicized Vocabulary word.

1. In "The Interlopers," Georg and Ulrich continue the feud started by their ancestors over the *disputed* border forest.

In this passage, *disputed* means —

A subject of great happiness
B subject of an argument
C subject of a sale
D subject of a newspaper article

9.R.1.E.1.b

2. In "The Interlopers," Ulrich could not hide his *exasperation* at being trapped under the wreckage of the splintered branches.

In this passage, *exasperation* means —

A happiness
B relief
C annoyance
D guilt

9.R.1.E.1.b

3. In "Initiation," Millicent, who liked to be noticed, found the *anonymity* that came with being a "gopher" unpleasant.

In this passage, *anonymity* means —

A joyfulness
B namelessness
C defenselessness
D helplessness

9.R.1.E.1.b

4. In "Initiation," Millicent broke into *spontaneous* laughter after the man on the bus told her that he ate Heather birds' eyebrows for breakfast.

In this passage, *spontaneous* means —

A unplanned
B unwanted
C unpleasant
D unremarkable

9.R.1.E.1.b

5. In "Marigolds," Lizabeth recalls that it was *futile* to wait for prosperity during the Great Depression, a time when most Americans were living in poverty.

In this passage, *futile* means —

A tiresome
B useless
C easy
D irritating

9.R.1.E.1.b

6. In "The Wife's Story," the children were *cowering* and crying after witnessing the frightening attack.

In this passage, *cowering* means —

A shocked
B excited
C trembling in fear
D giddy with laughter

9.R.1.E.1.b

Academic Vocabulary

Directions: Choose the best definition for the following italicized Academic Vocabulary words.

7. When two things are *distinct*, they are —

A different
B memorable
C complex
D unpleasant

9.R.1.E.1.b

8. When you have *insight*, you have —

A special vision
B understanding
C sympathy
D second thoughts

9.R.1.E.1.b

Read On

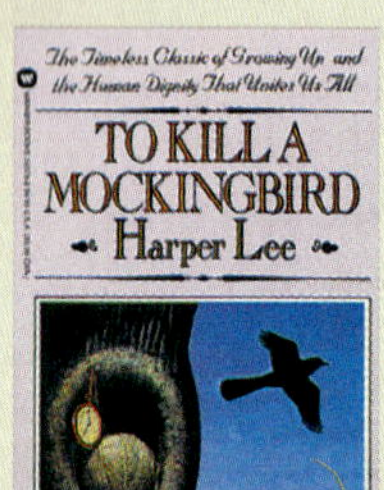

FICTION

To Kill a Mockingbird

Harper Lee's *To Kill a Mockingbird* is a revealing story of race relations as seen by a wise child. Eight-year-old Scout and her brother, Jem, learn an unforgettable lesson about courage, justice, and compassion when their father takes part in a shocking trial that will change their hometown forever. You're not likely to forget this Pulitzer Prize–winning novel.

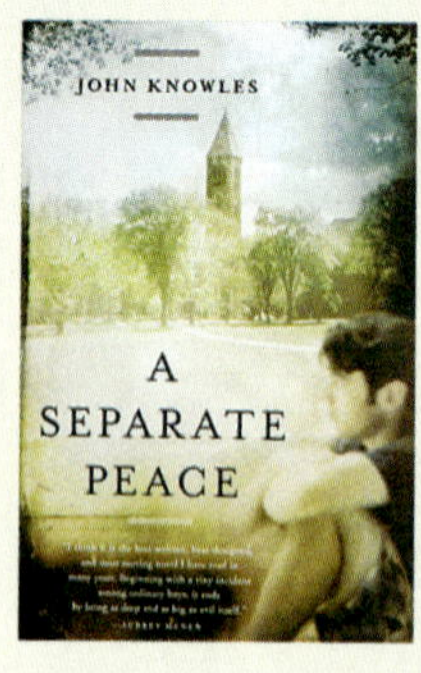

FICTION

A Separate Peace

World War II is about to erupt, and Gene and Phineas are best friends at a New England boarding school in John Knowles's novel *A Separate Peace*. Gene and Phineas are as different as night and day: Gene is an introverted student who must work hard to achieve his goals, while Phineas is a golden boy, a gifted athlete to whom everything comes easily. Then, during one terrible summer, an accident happens that will change the boys' lives forever.

FICTION

The Circuit

When Panchito lived in Mexico, the most excitement he ever had was hunting for chicken eggs and going to church on Sundays. Then Panchito's father moves the family to California, where jobs for migrant workers abound and the promise of an American education awaits. In Francisco Jiménez's *The Circuit,* Panchito describes his family's odyssey from one labor camp to another as they pursue the American dream.

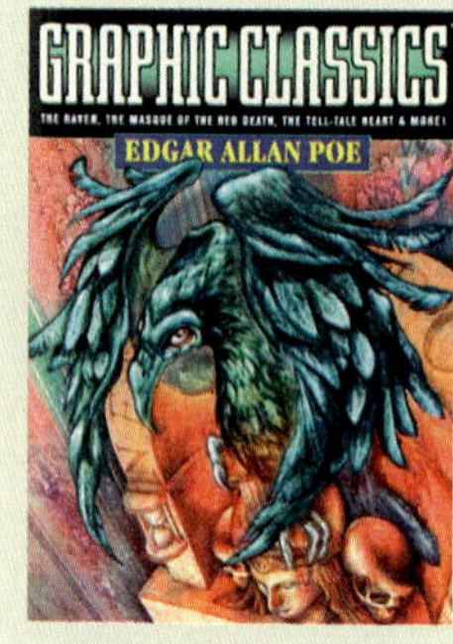

FICTION

Graphic Classics, Volume 1: Edgar Allan Poe

What would Edgar Allan Poe's creepy stories and poems look like if they were illustrated? In *Graphic Classics, Volume 1: Edgar Allan Poe*, thirteen of the writer's works are given the graphic-story treatment. Included are "The Tell-Tale Heart," in which the story's narrator is bothered by an old man's clouded eye and plots to kill him, and "The Fall of the House of Usher," Poe's story of a mysterious brother and sister living in a decrepit castle.

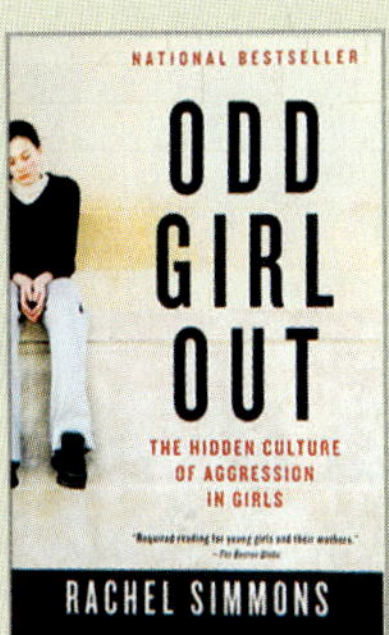

NONFICTION

Odd Girl Out

Dirty looks and taunting notes are just a few examples of bullying by girls. Author Rachel Simmons documented her discussions with girls from around the country about the issues surrounding bullying. *Odd Girl Out* puts the spotlight on this issue, using real-life examples from the perspectives of both the victim and the bully. Simmons looks at the causes of bullying and explains what students can do to deal with this all-too-common problem.

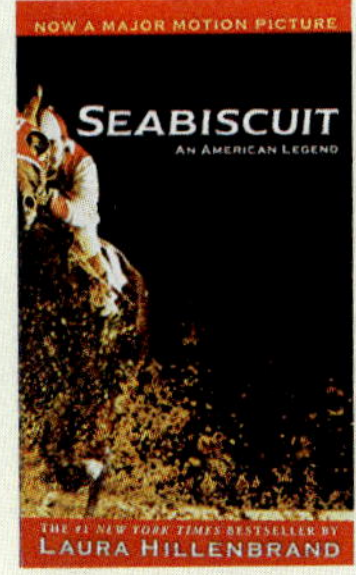

NONFICTION

Seabiscuit: An American Legend

During the Great Depression, an unlikely horse named Seabiscuit became a symbol of hope for down-on-their-luck Americans. When Seabiscuit raced, even President Roosevelt stopped to pay attention. In *Seabiscuit: An American Legend*, sportswriter Laura Hillenbrand tells about the competitive world of horseracing and how one ugly, knock-kneed horse outraced sleek champions to become America's darling.

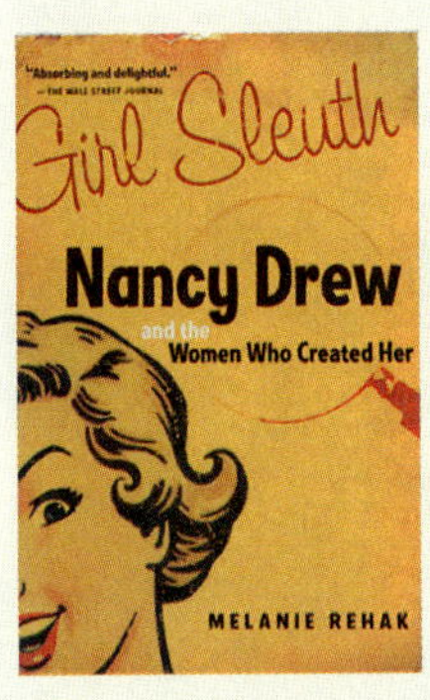

NONFICTION

Girl Sleuth

In 1930, a plucky girl detective named Nancy Drew stepped out of her shiny blue roadster ready to restore a stolen inheritance to its rightful owner. Eighty million books later, Nancy Drew has survived the Depression, World War II, and the 1960s and is as beloved by readers today as she was generations ago. Melanie Rehak's *Girl Sleuth* reveals the behind-the-scenes story of the writers and publishers who developed the Nancy Drew series into a phenomenon, bringing to light a fascinating cast of real-life characters.

NONFICTION

Where the Broken Heart Still Beats

Carolyn Meyer's *Where the Broken Heart Still Beats* is a fictionalized version of the story of Cynthia Ann Parker, who was captured by Comanches when she was about nine years old. Now called Naduah, Cynthia Ann is returned to her white family twenty-five years later. Having lived among the Comanche people for so long, she considers herself an American Indian and must relearn the ways of white society.

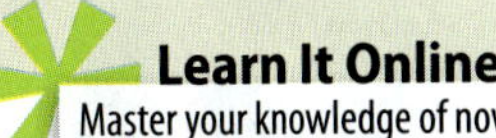

Learn It Online

Master your knowledge of novels. Learn tips for studying them at *NovelWise*:

go.hrw.com L9-317 

Circuitry Man Facing Green Traffic Lights.

COLLECTION 4

Symbolism and Irony

INFORMATIONAL TEXT FOCUS

Synthesizing Sources by One Author

"When you cannot make up your mind which of two evenly balanced courses of action you should take—choose the bolder."

—Ezra Pound

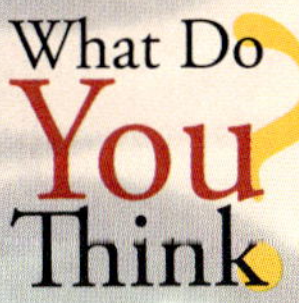

How do we make hard choices?

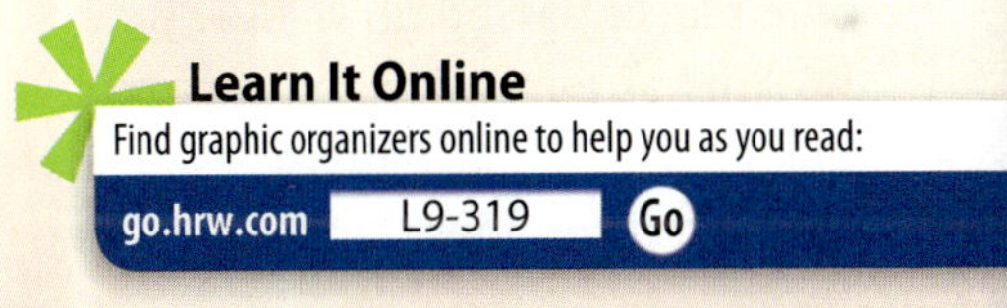

Learn It Online
Find graphic organizers online to help you as you read:
go.hrw.com
L9-319
Go

Literary Focus

by **Carol Jago**

What Do You Need to Know About Symbolism and Irony?

Holding a set of car keys in your hand, you experience a rush of excitement. The keys represent more than the means of operating a vehicle. Those keys are a symbol of freedom. Now imagine that you have the keys to the car, and the car is gassed up, and you suddenly realize you have no place to go! Unexpected outcomes such as this create irony. To learn how symbols and irony are used in literature, read on.

Symbols

A **symbol** is an object, event, person, or animal that stands both for itself and also for something else. Which symbols below are you familiar with? What meaning do you associate with each?

- A red rose
- A skull and crossbones
- A dove

The use of symbols in stories allows writers to suggest layers of meaning—possibilities that a simple, literal statement could never convey.

> On the topmost branch a bird the size of a chicken, with scarlet feathers and long legs, was perched precariously. Its wings hung down loosely, and as we watched, a feather dropped away and floated slowly down through the green leaves.
>
> from "The Scarlet Ibis" by James Hurst

Inherited Symbols Many symbols have been inherited, or passed down over time. For example, the lion has symbolized power and courage for centuries. The lion often serves as a school mascot and appears on countless family crests and flags.

Invented Symbols Some symbols are invented. For example, an advertising agency may create a symbol that conveys the idea of quality, reliability, or superiority. Some invented symbols in literature have become so widely known that they have gained the status of public symbols. J. M. Barrie's Peter Pan, for example, has come to symbolize eternal childhood.

Allegory

A story in which the characters, setting, and action stand for something beyond themselves is called an **allegory.** In some allegories, the characters and setting represent abstract ideas or moral qualities. For example, a character in an allegory named Honesty Brown may be meant to embody the quality of honesty. In other types of allegory, characters and situations stand for historical figures and events.

> Life was full of symbols and omens. Demons lurked everywhere, Death swam in the wetness of an eye, the turn of a gull's wing meant rain, a fan held *so,* the tilt of a roof, and, yes, even a city wall was of immense importance.
>
> from "The Golden Kite, the Silver Wind" by Ray Bradbury

MO **9.R.2.B.2.a** Identify and explain literary techniques in text emphasizing: irony **9.R.2.B.2.d** Identify and explain literary techniques, in text emphasizing: analyze literary techniques previously introduced **9.R.2.B.2.b** Identify and explain literary techniques, in text emphasizing: imagery

Irony

Life is full of surprises. In fact, sometimes things turn out the opposite of what you expect. **Irony** is a term that describes the difference between what we expect or find suitable and what actually happens. Our pleasure in irony comes from our recognition that life rarely turns out the way we would expect.

There are three basic categories of irony: verbal, situational, and dramatic.

Verbal Irony "I just *love* being caught in the rain with no umbrella." "I don't mind doing *all* the cooking and cleaning while you sit around and do nothing." These are examples of verbal irony. **Verbal irony** occurs when someone says one thing but actually means the opposite.

Situational Irony When an event turns out to be completely unexpected—the opposite of what you thought would happen—that's **situational irony.** Here's an example: You race to the store, frantically looking for a perfect costume for a big Halloween party that is taking place that night. After a series of mishaps, you finally find a costume and get to the party—only to find out that you mixed the dates up and the party is the following night.

Dramatic Irony You cringe, waiting for your friend to discover something awful that you knew was going to happen but were unable to warn him or her about. This feeling of suspenseful helplessness is created by **dramatic irony,** in which you know what is going to happen to a character, but he or she doesn't know. Dramatic irony often occurs in plays, which explains how this type of irony got its name.

Ambiguity

Real life is mysterious and ambiguous, or hard to sort out. Some stories and poems, like real life, contain ambiguity. Something is **ambiguous** when we are not certain what has happened and what will happen next. It's up to us to figure the situation out.

Your Turn Analyze Symbolism and Irony

1. This brief poem works on a literal level and a symbolic level. A *fen* is a swampy place. What might it symbolize in the poem?

I May, I Might, I Must

If you will tell me why the fen
appears impassable, I then
will tell you why I think that I
can get across it if I try.

—Marianne Moore

2. Study the cartoon below. What types of irony has the cartoonist used?

Complete Peace

Learn It Online
Use *PowerNotes* to reinforce this lesson at:
go.hrw.com L9-321 Go

Analyzing Visuals

How Can You Recognize Symbols and Irony in Painting?

Very often, artists challenge us to consider the difference between what is shown and what is expected, between what we see and what is meant. By using symbols and irony, painters and other artists add a deeper level of meaning to their work.

Analyzing Symbolism and Irony

Use these guidelines to help you analyze the use of symbolism and irony in a painting.

1. Identify the painting's subject. Look for the elements that attract your attention or show an action taking place on the canvas.
2. Determine what is happening in the painting. Are people represented? If so, what are they doing?
3. Find elements in keeping with the painting's subject. For example, a portrait of a queen might include fancy robes that point to her rank.
4. Look for elements that are unexpected—not in keeping with the subject—or even funny. They may signal irony.
5. Look for common objects or situations and consider the things they bring to mind. Such ideas may point to symbolism.
6. Interpret the painting based on these ironic elements and symbolic content. What do they suggest about the artist's purpose?

Look at the details of the painting to help you answer the questions on page 323.

Details from *La Clairvoyance.*

9.R.2.B.2.b Identify and explain literary techniques, in text emphasizing: imagery
9.R.2.B.2.a Identify and explain literary techniques in text emphasizing: irony

1. What unexpected visual element creates **irony** in this painting?

2. Clairvoyance is the ability to "see" things that can't be detected by the senses. Is there **irony** in the title of this painting? Explain.

3. Surrealistic art makes extensive use of **symbols.** If an egg symbolizes life, what may the artist symbolize?

4. In what way does the style of this painting contrast with the painting's humorous message?

La Clairvoyance (1936) by René Magritte (1898–1967). © 2007 Photo: C. Herscovici, Brussels / Artists Rights Society (ARS), New York.

Your Turn Talk About Symbolism in Art

With a partner, flip through this book and find an image that contains a strong visual symbol. Discuss how the use of that symbol helps the artist convey a message.

Reading Focus

by **Kylene Beers**

What Skills Help You Understand Symbolism and Irony?

It's not difficult to understand the symbols and irony in a story; you just need to ask questions of the text. For example, you could look at the details the author uses and ask yourself, "Why does he or she include these details?" Your observations may lead you to find symbols in the text you otherwise may have overlooked. In the same way, analyzing causes and effects by thinking about *why* a character does something or *why* an event happens can help you understand an author's use of irony. Most important, be an active reader: Make predictions and ask questions. You just may find the answers you seek.

Analyzing Details

One of the first rules of good writing is "Show, don't tell." Through the use of **sensory details** (images that appeal to the senses of sight, taste, smell, hearing, and touch), writers reveal details about elements of the plot and help readers visualize the action in a story. These details can also help you identify symbols in a story and analyze their significance.

As you read, record in a graphic organizer, like the one below, the sensory details you notice in the text. Then, analyze the details and note what they may symbolize. As a last step, describe the importance or significance of that symbol.

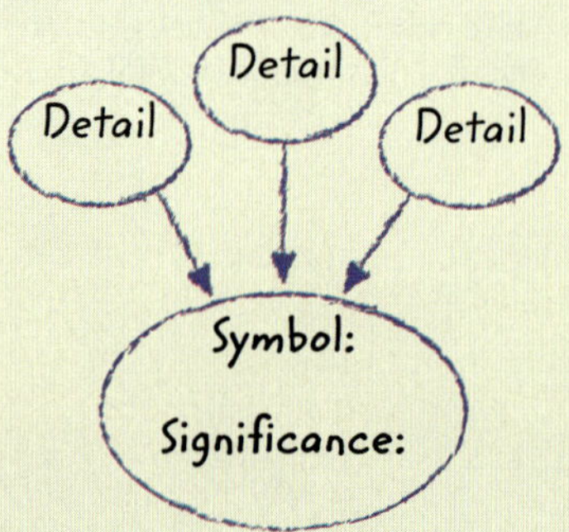

Analyzing Causes and Effects

Ever wonder why things happen? If you're looking for the reason behind a character's actions or a certain turn of events, you're looking for a cause-and-effect relationship. A **cause** is the reason that an action takes place. An **effect** is the result or the consequence of that cause.

A well-crafted story presents a series of events that are logically connected: The events that take place are caused by preceding events. If the outcome of a story is ironic or surprising, retrace the causes of the outcome. What led to this final event?

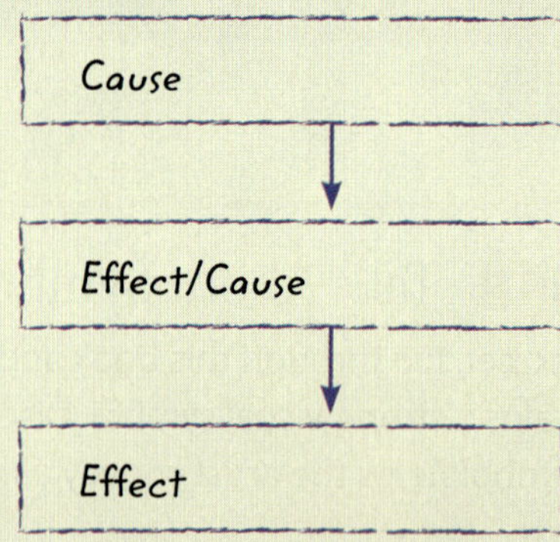

MO **9.R.1.H.1.a** Apply post-reading skills to comprehend, interpret, analyze, and evaluate text: identify and explain the relationship between the main idea and supporting details **9.R.3.C.1.a** Use details from informational text: to identify and explain the organizational pattern **9.R.1.G.1.b** During reading, utilize strategies: to self-monitor comprehension **9.R.1.F.1.c** Apply pre-reading strategies to aid comprehension: predict with text support or rationale **9.R.1.H.1.b** Apply post-reading skills to comprehend, interpret, analyze, and evaluate text: question to clarify **9.R.1.D.1.a** Read grade-level instructional text: with fluency, accuracy, comprehension and appropriate expression

Reading Actively

To get the most out of the stories you read, you must engage yourself with the text, or **read actively.** To read actively, you should—

- **make predictions** and evaluate them as you go along
- **re-read** difficult passages to make sure you fully understand the plot events
- **read aloud** to understand dialogue between two characters
- **ask questions** to understand why things are happening

Another way to read actively is to read with a partner or a small group. As you read, raise questions when you become confused about story events. After you read, compare your reactions to the text with those of your partner or others in your group. Chances are that the places in the text that generate the most comments are the most important.

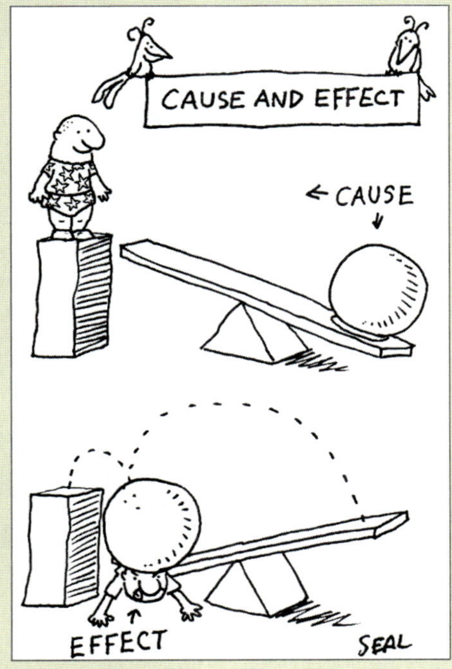

www.bobseal.com

Your Turn

Read this classic tale. Then, answer the questions.

DEATH SPEAKS: There was a merchant in Baghdad who sent his servant to market to buy provisions, and in a little while the servant came back, white and trembling, and said, "Master, just now when I was in the marketplace I was jostled by a woman in the crowd, and when I turned I saw it was Death that jostled me. She looked at me and made a threatening gesture; now, lend me your horse, and I will ride away from this city and avoid my fate. I will go to Samarra, and there Death will not find me." The merchant lent him his horse, and the servant mounted it, and he dug his spurs in its flanks, and as fast as the horse could gallop he went. Then the merchant went down to the marketplace and he saw me standing in the crowd and he came to me and said, "Why did you make a threatening gesture to my servant when you saw him this morning?" "That was not a threatening gesture," I said, "it was only a start of surprise. I was astonished to see him in Baghdad, for I had an appointment with him tonight in Samarra."

"Appointment in Samarra"
by W. Somerset Maugham

1. Why did the servant run away to Samarra?
2. Was the story's ending a surprise? Explain.
3. Death is personified in this story. What idea of life does this depiction of Death convey?

Now go to the Skills in Action: Reading Model

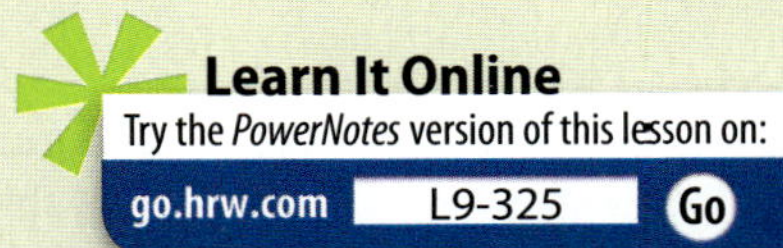

Learn It Online
Try the *PowerNotes* version of this lesson on:
go.hrw.com
L9-325
Go

SKILLS IN ACTION

Reading Model

SHORT STORY

Build Background

This story appeared in Isak Dinesen's second collection of short stories, titled *Winter's Tales,* which she wrote while living in Nazi-occupied Denmark. *Winter's Tales* was published in 1942 after being smuggled out of Denmark. A special edition was printed in America for soldiers fighting in the war.

Literary Focus

Symbol Sometimes writers use symbols to deepen the meaning of their work. A **symbol** is a person, place, thing, or event that stands both for itself and for something beyond itself. In this passage the writer uses the ship's figurehead to symbolize the skipper's wife and his love for her.

Read with a Purpose Read the story to find out what happens when a wife becomes jealous.

Peter and Rosa

by **Isak Dinesen**

There was once a skipper who named his ship after his wife. He had the figurehead[1] of it beautifully carved, just like her, and the hair of it gilt. But his wife was jealous of the ship. "You think more of the figurehead than of me," she said to him. "No," he answered, "I think so highly of her because she is like you, yes, because she is you yourself. Is she not gallant, full-bosomed; does she not dance in the waves, like you at our wedding? In a way she is really even kinder to me than you are. She gallops along where I tell her to go, and she lets her long hair hang down freely, while you put up yours under a cap. But she turns her back to me, so that when I want a kiss I come home to Elsinore." Now once, when this

Figurehead on the *Pommern.*

1. **figurehead:** carved figure on the bow of a ship.

skipper was trading at Trankebar, he chanced to help an old native king to flee traitors in his own country. As they parted, the king gave him two big blue, precious stones, and these he had set into the face of his figurehead, like a pair of eyes to it. When he came home he told his wife of his adventure, and said: "Now she has your blue eyes too." "You had better give me the stones for a pair of earrings," said she. "No," he said again, "I cannot do that, and you would not ask me to if you understood." Still the wife could not stop fretting about the blue stones, and one day, when her husband was with the skippers' corporation, she had a glazier of the town take them out, and put two bits of blue glass into the figurehead instead, and the skipper did not find out, but sailed off to Portugal. But after some time the skipper's wife found that her eyesight was growing bad, and that she could not see to thread a needle. She went to a wisewoman, who gave her ointments and waters, but they did not help her and in the end the old woman shook her

Literary Focus

Symbol The skipper has added blue stones to the figurehead's face to symbolize his wife's eyes. A clue that the stones are a symbol is their appearance throughout the story.

Reading Focus

Analyzing Cause and Effect A **cause** is the reason something happens, and an **effect** is the result of some event or action. Here, the wife's jealousy causes her to take the blue stones.

Analyzing Visuals **Viewing and Interpreting** Just as details in a story provide clues to the text's significance, details in art add to the work's meaning. What might the artist of this figurehead be trying to convey through details of the figure's clothing, body language, and even the look in its eyes?

head, and told her that this was a rare and incurable disease, and that she was going blind. "Oh, God," the wife then cried, "that the ship was back in the harbor of Elsinore. Then I should have the glass taken out, and the jewels put back. For did he not say that they were my eyes?" But the ship did not come back. Instead the skipper's wife had a letter from the Consul of Portugal, who informed her that she had been wrecked, and gone to the bottom with all hands.[2] And it was a very strange thing, the Consul wrote, that in broad daylight she had run straight into a tall rock, rising out of the sea.

Reading Focus

Analyzing Details This final detail emphasizes the idea that the blue stones were more than simply stones. Their loss caused both the woman and her husband to lose their sight—and more.

2. **hands:** ship's crew.

Read with a Purpose What does this story have to say about the effects of jealousy?

The Granger Collection, New York.

MEET THE WRITER

Isak Dinesen

(1885–1962)

Woman of Mystery

Isak (meaning "one who laughs" in Hebrew) Dinesen is the pen name of Baroness Karen Blixen. When she burst onto the literary scene in 1934 with her short-story collection *Seven Gothic Tales,* rumors swirled about the mysterious author: Some thought the author was a man; others thought Isak Dinesen was a brother-and-sister writing team. In fact, Dinesen was a well-to-do Danish woman who spent many years in Africa, which inspired her to write the classic memoir *Out of Africa*.

Dinesen was struck by the African peoples, especially the Somali and the Masai, and said Africa is where she learned to tell tales because she had "the perfect audience." When Ernest Hemingway won the Nobel Prize in Literature in 1954, he claimed that it should have gone to Dinesen. She was nominated for the prize several times but never won.

Think About the Writer How might living in another country have affected the kinds of stories Dinesen wrote?

SKILLS IN ACTION

Wrap Up

MO 9.R.2.B.2.b Identify and explain literary techniques, in text emphasizing: imagery 9.R.2.B.2.d Identify and explain literary techniques, in text emphasizing: analyze literary techniques previously introduced 9.R.1.E.1.c Develop vocabulary through text: using glossary, dictionary and thesaurus

Into Action: Symbolic Meaning

Analyze the meaning of certain symbols from the story by filling in a chart like this one. Then, state why you think Dinesen chose these symbols.

Symbol	→	Symbolic Meaning
figurehead	→	wife
blue stones	→	

My Statement:

Talk About . . .

With a small group, discuss your responses to the following questions, and try to use each Academic Vocabulary word listed at the right at least once.

1. With what do you associate the sea? Could it be a symbol in this story? Explain.
2. What elements in the story are ambiguous—not clearly explained?

Write About . . .

Write a paragraph about the meaning of "Peter and Rosa," using the terms from the Academic Vocabulary list that are underlined below. Consider these points as you write:

- What is the literal meaning of the figurehead? of the blue stones? Is Dinesen's use of these symbols deliberate?
- What truth about human nature is Dinesen trying to imply in her story?

Writing Focus

Think as a Reader/Writer

Find It in Your Reading Dinesen's tales are known for their supernatural themes and feeling of mystery. As you read the selections in Collection 4, you will have an opportunity to analyze the writing styles of other authors and practice using writer's craft in your own writing.

Academic Vocabulary for Collection 4

Talking and Writing About Short Stories

Academic Vocabulary is the language you use to write and talk about literature. Use these words to discuss the stories you read in this collection. The words are underlined throughout the collection.

associate (uh SOH shee ayt) *v.:* mentally make a link. *I associate budding trees with the idea of warmth and promise.*

imply (ihm PLY) *v.:* suggest; hint at. *Did the writer mean to imply that love is always doomed?*

literal (LIHT uhr uhl) *adj.:* based on the ordinary meaning of the actual words. *To get to the truth of a story, you sometimes have to look beyond the story's literal meaning.*

ambiguous (am BIHG yoo uhs) *adj.:* not clearly defined; capable of having two outcomes. *The writer chose to make the ending of the story ambiguous, leaving it up to the reader to determine the outcome.*

Your Turn

Copy the words from the list into your *Reader/Writer Notebook*. Then, write sample test questions, using each word correctly.

SHORT STORY

Preparing to Read

The Scarlet Ibis

by **James Hurst**

What Do You Think?

What might be learned from a relationship or encounter with someone who is different from us?

QuickTalk

Talk with a partner about whether or not it's ever a good idea for one person to try to transform another.

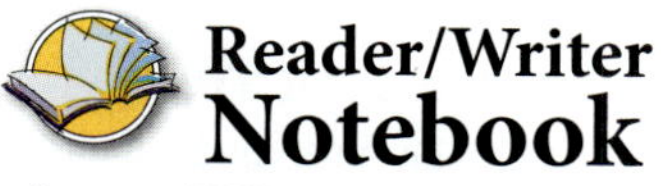

Reader/Writer Notebook

Use your **RWN** to complete the activities for this selection.

MO **9.R.2.B.2.b** Identify and explain literary techniques, in text emphasizing: imagery **9.R.2.C.1.c** Use details from text(s): to analyze the development of a theme across genres **9.R.1.H.1.a** Apply post-reading skills to comprehend, interpret, analyze, and evaluate text: identify and explain the relationship between the main idea and supporting details

Literary Focus

Symbols and Theme A **symbol** is an object, person, animal, or event that we often associate with other concepts, such as peace or freedom. The use of symbols adds deeper levels of meaning to a literary work. Writers also use theme to reveal their ideas about life. **Theme** is a central idea of a work of literature and is not usually stated directly. It is up to the reader to think about all of the elements of a work—including symbol—in order to make an inference, or educated guess, about a work's theme.

TechFocus As you read, think about how you might bring the main theme of this story to life by using graphic design software.

Reading Focus

Analyzing Details In most stories, you will encounter details that describe characters, plot, and setting. Such details may seem insignificant at first, but they can develop more meaning as you read further.

Into Action As you read "The Scarlet Ibis," keep track of the little things—colors, gestures, weather—and see what larger meanings they might point to. Try creating a chart like the following to help you.

Story Details	Larger Meanings
Summer was dead; autumn not yet born.	Nature might mirror human experiences—being born and dying.
Graveyard flowers are blooming.	

Writing Focus

Think as a Reader/Writer

Find It in Your Reading Dialogue not only helps to move a story along, it can also reveal the essence of the story's characters. Note in your *Reader/Writer Notebook* passages of dialogue that reveal character.

Vocabulary

imminent (IHM uh nuhnt) *adj.:* near; about to happen. *After he was born, Doodle's death seemed imminent.*

iridescent (ihr uh DEHS uhnt) *adj.:* rainbowlike; displaying a shifting range of colors. *The water in Old Woman Swamp sometimes looked iridescent.*

infallibility (ihn fal uh BIHL uh tee) *n.:* inability to make a mistake. *After the narrator's first success with Doodle, he believed in his infallibility.*

reiterated (ree IHT uh ray tuhd) *v.:* repeated. *Doodle reiterated what he had already said.*

mar (mahr) *v.:* damage; spoil. *Nothing can mar the bird's beauty.*

Language Coach

Oral Fluency To truly own a word, you need to be able to use it confidently in conversation. Which words on the list above have you never heard spoken aloud? Study the pronunciations of those words and practice pronouncing them with a partner.

Learn It Online
Watch the video introduction to this story at:
go.hrw.com L9-331 Go

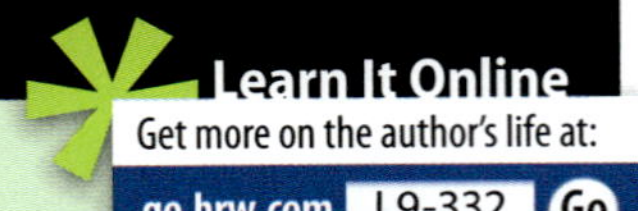

Learn It Online
Get more on the author's life at:
go.hrw.com L9-332 Go

MEET THE WRITER

James Hurst
(1922–)

Jack of All Trades

James Hurst was born on a farm by the sea in North Carolina. Hurst first studied chemical engineering. Later, he studied singing at the Juilliard School of Music in New York City and then tried a career in opera that was short-lived. Hurst eventually turned to working as a bank clerk during the day and writing at night.

Brothers at War

For thirty-four years Hurst worked in the international department of a large bank in New York City. During this time, Hurst also published some short stories, including "The Scarlet Ibis," which was his first story to be published in a national magazine. Hurst reminds readers of "The Scarlet Ibis" to think of how the war raging among "brothers" in Europe is related to the conflict between Doodle and *his* brother. Perhaps Hurst is suggesting that people always suffer when others try to make them over in their own image. Hurst finally retired from banking and returned to North Carolina—to New Bern, a town near his birthplace.

Think About the Writer In what way might Hurst's various skills and interests have inspired him to write?

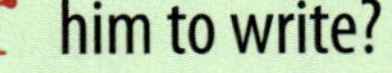

Scarlet Ibis by John James Audubon.

Build Background

This story is set in the American South. Its climax takes place in 1918, the year World War I ended. You'll find references in the story to battles being fought far from its peaceful southern setting. As you read, think about why the author chose such a setting for this story.

Preview the Selection

The brothers in "The Scarlet Ibis" couldn't be more different. In fact, the narrator of this story describes his brother **Doodle** as "just about the craziest brother a boy ever had."

Read with a Purpose Read the following selection to find out what happens when a boy tries to change his younger brother.

The Scarlet Ibis

by **James Hurst**

It was in the clove of seasons, summer was dead but autumn had not yet been born, that the ibis lit in the bleeding tree. The flower garden was stained with rotting brown magnolia petals, and ironweeds grew rank[1] amid the purple phlox. The five o'clocks by the chimney still marked time, but the oriole nest in the elm was untenanted and rocked back and forth like an empty cradle. The last graveyard flowers were blooming, and their smell drifted across the cotton field and through every room of our house, speaking softly the names of our dead.

It's strange that all this is still so clear to me, now that that summer has long since fled and time has had its way. A grindstone stands where the bleeding tree stood, just outside the kitchen door, and now if an oriole sings in the elm, its song seems to die up in the leaves, a silvery dust. The flower garden is prim, the house a gleaming white, and the pale fence across the yard stands straight and spruce. But sometimes (like right now), as I sit in the cool, green-draped parlor, the grindstone begins to turn, and time with all its changes is ground away—and I remember Doodle. **A**

Doodle was just about the craziest brother a boy ever had. Of course, he wasn't a crazy crazy like old Miss Leedie, who was in love with President Wilson and wrote him a letter every day, but was a nice crazy, like someone you meet in your dreams. He was born when I was six and was, from the outset, a disappointment. He seemed all head, with a tiny body which was red and shriveled like an old man's. Everybody thought he was going to die—everybody except Aunt Nicey, who had delivered him. She said he would live because he was born in a caul[2] and cauls were made from Jesus' nightgown. Daddy had Mr. Heath, the carpenter, build a little mahogany coffin for him. But he didn't die, and when he was three months old, Mama and Daddy decided they might as well name him. They named him William Armstrong, which was like tying a big tail on a small kite. Such a name sounds good only on a tombstone.

I thought myself pretty smart at many things, like holding my breath, running, jumping, or climbing the vines in Old Woman Swamp, and I wanted more than anything else someone to race to Horsehead Landing,

1. **rank** (rangk): thick and wild. *Rank* also means "smelly."

2. **caul** (kawl): membrane (thin, skinlike material) that sometimes covers a baby's head at birth.

A **Literary Focus** **Symbols** The adult narrator repeats the words *bleeding tree* to describe a tree whose leaves have turned red. What idea might the bleeding tree symbolize?

Analyzing Visuals **Viewing and Interpreting** In what ways is this swamp like the one described in the story?

Cypress trees and water lilies in Okefenokee Swamp in the state of Georgia.

someone to box with, and someone to perch with in the top fork of the great pine behind the barn, where across the fields and swamps you could see the sea. I wanted a brother. But Mama, crying, told me that even if William Armstrong lived, he would never do these things with me. He might not, she sobbed, even be "all there." He might, as long as he lived, lie on the rubber sheet in the center of the bed in the front bedroom where the white marquisette[3] curtains billowed out in the afternoon sea breeze, rustling like palmetto fronds.[4]

It was bad enough having an invalid brother, but having one who possibly was not all there was unbearable, so I began to make plans to kill him by smothering him with a pillow. However, one afternoon as I watched him, my head poked between the iron posts of the foot of the bed, he looked straight at me and grinned. I skipped through the rooms, down the echoing halls, shouting, "Mama, he smiled. He's all there! He's all there!" and he was.

When he was two, if you laid him on his stomach, he began to try to move himself, straining terribly. The doctor said that with his weak heart this

3. **marquisette** (mahr kuh ZEHT): thin, netlike fabric.
4. **palmetto fronds** (pal MEHT oh frahndz): fanlike leaves of a palm tree.

strain would probably kill him, but it didn't. Trembling, he'd push himself up, turning first red, then a soft purple, and finally collapse back onto the bed like an old worn-out doll. I can still see Mama watching him, her hand pressed tight across her mouth, her eyes wide and unblinking. But he learned to crawl (it was his third winter), and we brought him out of the front bedroom, putting him on the rug before the fireplace. For the first time he became one of us. **B**

As long as he lay all the time in bed, we called him William Armstrong, even though it was formal and sounded as if we were referring to one of our ancestors, but with his creeping around on the deerskin rug and beginning to talk, something had to be done about his name. It was I who renamed him. When he crawled, he crawled backward, as if he were in reverse and couldn't change gears. If you called him, he'd turn around as if he were going in the other direction, then he'd back right up to you to be picked up. Crawling backward made him look like a doodlebug[5] so I began to call him Doodle, and in time even Mama and Daddy thought it was a better name than William Armstrong. Only Aunt Nicey disagreed. She said caul babies should be treated with special respect since they might turn out to be saints. Renaming my brother was perhaps the kindest thing I ever did for him, because nobody expects much from someone called Doodle.

Although Doodle learned to crawl, he showed no signs of walking, but he wasn't idle. He talked so much that we all quit listening to what he said. It was about this time that Daddy built him a go-cart, and I had to pull him around. At first I just paraded him up and down the piazza,[6] but then he started crying to be taken out into the yard and it ended up by my having to lug him wherever I went. If I so much as picked up my cap, he'd start crying to go with me, and Mama would call from wherever she was, "Take Doodle with you."

He was a burden in many ways. The doctor had said that he mustn't get too excited, too hot, too cold, or too tired and that he must always be treated gently. A long list of don'ts went with him, all of which I ignored once we got out of the house. To discourage his coming with me, I'd run with him across the ends of the cotton rows and careen him around corners on two wheels. Sometimes I accidentally turned him over, but he never told Mama. His skin was very sensitive, and he had to wear a big straw hat whenever he went out. When the going got rough and he had to cling to the sides of the go-cart, the hat slipped all the way down over his ears. He was a sight. Finally, I could see I was licked. Doodle was my brother, and he was going to cling to me forever, no matter what I did, so I dragged him across the burning cotton field to share with him the only beauty I knew, Old Woman Swamp. I pulled the go-cart through the sawtooth fern, down into the green dimness where the palmetto fronds whispered by the stream. I lifted him out and set him down in the soft rubber grass beside a tall pine. His eyes were round with wonder as he gazed about him, and his little hands began to stroke the rubber grass. Then he began to cry.

"For heaven's sake, what's the matter?" I asked, annoyed.

"It's so pretty," he said. "So pretty, pretty, pretty."

5. **doodlebug** (DOO duhl buhg): larva of a type of insect that moves backward.

6. **piazza** (pee AHZ uh): large covered porch.

B Reading Focus **Analyzing Details** What does the author imply about the little boy based on the details in this paragraph?

After that day Doodle and I often went down into Old Woman Swamp. I would gather wildflowers, wild violets, honeysuckle, yellow jasmine, snakeflowers, and waterlilies, and with wire grass we'd weave them into necklaces and crowns. We'd bedeck ourselves with our handiwork and loll about thus beautified, beyond the touch of the everyday world. Then when the slanted rays of the sun burned orange in the tops of the pines, we'd drop our jewels into the stream and watch them float away toward the sea.

There is within me (and with sadness I have watched it in others) a knot of cruelty borne by the stream of love, much as our blood sometimes bears the seed of our destruction, and at times I was mean to Doodle. One day I took him up to the barn loft and showed him his casket, telling him how we all had believed he would die. It was covered with a film of Paris green[7] sprinkled to kill the rats, and screech owls had built a nest inside it.

Doodle studied the mahogany box for a long time, then said, "It's not mine."

"It is," I said. "And before I'll help you down from the loft, you're going to have to touch it."

"I won't touch it," he said sullenly.

"Then I'll leave you here by yourself," I threatened, and made as if I were going down.

Doodle was frightened of being left. "Don't go leave me, Brother," he cried, and he leaned toward the coffin. His hand, trembling, reached out, and when he touched the casket, he screamed. A screech owl flapped out of the box into our faces, scaring us and covering us with Paris green. Doodle was paralyzed, so I put him on my shoulder and carried him down the ladder, and even when we were outside in the bright sunshine, he clung to me, crying, "Don't leave me. Don't leave me." **C**

But all of us must have something or someone to be proud of, and Doodle had become mine.

When Doodle was five years old, I was embarrassed at having a brother of that age who couldn't walk, so I set out to teach him. We were down in Old Woman Swamp and it was spring and the sick-sweet smell of bay flowers hung everywhere like a mournful song. "I'm going to teach you to walk, Doodle," I said.

He was sitting comfortably on the soft grass, leaning back against the pine. "Why?" he asked.

I hadn't expected such an answer. "So I won't have to haul you around all the time."

"I can't walk, Brother," he said.

"Who says so?" I demanded.

"Mama, the doctor—everybody."

"Oh, you can walk," I said, and I took him by the arms and stood him up. He collapsed onto the grass like a half-empty flour sack. It was as if he had no bones in his little legs.

"Don't hurt me, Brother," he warned.

"Shut up. I'm not going to hurt you. I'm going to teach you to walk." I heaved him up again, and again he collapsed.

This time he did not lift his face up out of the rubber grass. "I just can't do it. Let's make honeysuckle wreaths."

7. **Paris green:** poisonous green powder used to kill insects.

C **Reading Focus** **Analyzing Details** Based on the details in this paragraph, what do you think Doodle is most afraid of?

"Oh yes you can, Doodle," I said. "All you got to do is try. Now come on," and I hauled him up once more.

It seemed so hopeless from the beginning that it's a miracle I didn't give up. But all of us must have something or someone to be proud of, and Doodle had become mine. I did not know then that pride is a wonderful, terrible thing, a seed that bears two vines, life and death. Every day that summer we went to the pine beside the stream of Old Woman Swamp, and I put him on his feet at least a hundred times each afternoon. Occasionally I too became discouraged because it didn't seem as if he was trying, and I would say, "Doodle, don't you want to learn to walk?"

He'd nod his head, and I'd say, "Well, if you don't keep trying, you'll never learn." Then I'd paint for him a picture of us as old men, white-haired, him with a long white beard and me still pulling him around in the go-cart. This never failed to make him try again.

Finally, one day, after many weeks of practicing, he stood alone for a few seconds. When he fell, I grabbed him in my arms and hugged him, our laughter pealing through the swamp like a ringing bell. Now we knew it could be done. Hope no longer hid in the dark palmetto thicket but perched like a cardinal in the lacy toothbrush tree, brilliantly visible. "Yes, yes," I cried, and he cried it too, and the grass beneath us was soft and the smell of the swamp was sweet. **D**

With success so imminent, we decided not to tell anyone until he could actually walk. Each day, barring rain, we sneaked into Old Woman Swamp, and by cotton-picking time Doodle was ready to show what he could do. He still wasn't able to walk far, but we could wait no longer. Keeping a nice secret is very hard to do, like holding your breath. We chose to reveal all on October eighth, Doodle's sixth birthday, and for weeks ahead we mooned around the house, promising everybody a most spectacular surprise. Aunt Nicey said that, after so much talk, if we produced anything less tremendous than the Resurrection,[8] she was going to be disappointed.

At breakfast on our chosen day, when Mama, Daddy, and Aunt Nicey were in the dining room, I brought Doodle to the door in the go-cart just as usual and had them turn their backs, making them cross their hearts and hope to die if they peeked. I helped Doodle up, and when he was standing alone I let them look. There wasn't a sound as Doodle walked slowly across the room and sat down at his place at the table. Then Mama began to cry and ran over to him, hugging him and kissing him. Daddy hugged him too, so I went to Aunt Nicey, who was thanks-praying in the doorway, and began to waltz her around. We danced together quite well until she came down on my big toe with her brogans,[9] hurting me so badly I thought I was crippled for life.

Doodle told them it was I who had taught him to walk, so everyone wanted to hug me, and I began to cry.

"What are you crying for?" asked Daddy, but I couldn't answer. They did not know that I did it for myself; that pride, whose slave I was, spoke to me louder than all their voices; and that Doodle walked only because I was ashamed of having a crippled brother.

---

8. **Resurrection:** reference to the Christian belief in the rising of Jesus from the dead after his burial.
9. **brogans** (BROH guhnz): heavy, ankle-high shoes.

D **Literary Focus** **Symbols and Theme** What theme is being developed here? What symbols point you to that theme?

Vocabulary **imminent** (IHM uh nuhnt) *adj.:* near; about to happen.

Within a few months Doodle had learned to walk well and his go-cart was put up in the barn loft (it's still there) beside his little mahogany coffin. Now, when we roamed off together, resting often, we never turned back until our destination had been reached, and to help pass the time, we took up lying. From the beginning Doodle was a terrible liar, and he got me in the habit. Had anyone stopped to listen to us, we would have been sent off to Dix Hill.

My lies were scary, involved, and usually pointless, but Doodle's were twice as crazy. People in his stories all had wings and flew wherever they wanted to go. His favorite lie was about a boy named Peter who had a pet peacock with a ten-foot tail. Peter wore a golden robe that glittered so brightly that when he walked through the sunflowers they turned away from the sun to face him. When Peter was ready to go to sleep, the peacock spread his magnificent tail, enfolding the boy gently like a closing go-to-sleep flower, burying him in the gloriously iridescent, rustling vortex.[10] Yes, I must admit it. Doodle could beat me lying. **E**

Doodle and I spent lots of time thinking about our future. We decided that when we were grown, we'd live in Old Woman Swamp and pick dog's-tongue[11] for a living. Beside the stream, he planned, we'd build us a house of whispering leaves and the swamp birds would be our chickens. All day long (when we weren't gathering dog's-tongue) we'd swing through the cypresses on the rope vines, and if it rained we'd huddle beneath an umbrella tree and play stick-frog. Mama and Daddy could come and live with us if they wanted to. He even came up with the idea that he could marry Mama and I could marry Daddy. Of course, I was old enough to know this wouldn't work out, but the picture he painted was so beautiful and serene that all I could do was whisper yes, yes.

Once I had succeeded in teaching Doodle to walk, I began to believe in my own infallibility and I prepared a terrific development program for him, unknown to Mama and Daddy, of course. I would teach him to run, to swim, to climb trees, and to fight. He, too, now believed in my infallibility, so we set the deadline for these accomplishments less than a year away, when, it had been decided, Doodle could start to school.

That winter we didn't make much progress, for I was in school and Doodle suffered from one bad cold after another. But when spring came, rich and warm, we raised our sights again. Success lay at the end of summer like a pot of gold, and our campaign got off to a good start. On hot days, Doodle and I went down to Horsehead Landing, and I gave him swimming lessons or showed him how to row a boat. Sometimes we descended into the cool greenness of Old Woman Swamp and climbed the rope vines or boxed scientifically beneath the pine where he had learned to walk. Promise hung about us like leaves, and wherever we looked, ferns unfurled and birds broke into song.

That summer, the summer of 1918, was blighted.[12] In May and June there was no rain

10. **vortex** (VAWR tehks): something resembling a whirlpool.

11. **dog's-tongue:** wild vanilla.

12. **blighted** (BLYT ihd): suffering from conditions that destroy or prevent growth.

E Reading Focus Analyzing Details Look at the elaborate details of Doodle's "lies." What overall image do the details create?

Vocabulary **iridescent** (ihr uh DEHS uhnt) *adj.:* rainbowlike; displaying a shifting range of colors.
infallibility (ihn fal uh BIHL uh tee) *n.:* inability to make a mistake.

Analyzing Visuals **Viewing and Interpreting** What scene from the story does this painting appear to capture?

The Carefree Days of Childhood (1998) by Kim Koza.

and the crops withered, curled up, then died under the thirsty sun. One morning in July a hurricane came out of the east, tipping over the oaks in the yard and splitting the limbs of the elm trees. That afternoon it roared back out of the west, blew the fallen oaks around, snapping their roots and tearing them out of the earth like a hawk at the entrails[13] of a chicken. Cotton bolls were wrenched from the stalks and lay like green walnuts in the valleys between the rows, while the cornfield leaned over uniformly so that the tassels touched the ground. Doodle and I followed Daddy out into the cotton field, where he stood, shoulders sagging, surveying the ruin. When his chin sank down onto his chest, we were frightened, and Doodle slipped his hand into mine. Suddenly Daddy straightened his shoulders, raised a giant knuckly fist, and with a voice that seemed to rumble out of the earth itself began cursing heaven, hell, the weather, and the Republican party.[14] Doodle and I, prodding each other and giggling, went back to the house, knowing that everything would be all right. **F**

13. **entrails** (EHN traylz): inner organs; guts.

14. **Republican party:** At this time most southern farmers were loyal Democrats.

F **Literary Focus** **Symbols** What might the blighted summer symbolize?

And during that summer, strange names were heard through the house: Château-Thierry, Amiens, Soissons, and in her blessing at the supper table, Mama once said, "And bless the Pearsons, whose boy Joe was lost in Belleau Wood."[15] G

So we came to that clove of seasons. School was only a few weeks away, and Doodle was far behind schedule. He could barely clear the ground when climbing up the rope vines, and his swimming was certainly not passable. We decided to double our efforts, to make that last drive and reach our pot of gold. I made him swim until he turned blue and row until he couldn't lift an oar. Wherever we went, I purposely walked fast, and although he kept up, his face turned red and his eyes became glazed. Once, he could go no further, so he collapsed on the ground and began to cry.

"Aw, come on, Doodle," I urged. "You can do it. Do you want to be different from everybody else when you start school?"

"Does it make any difference?"

"It certainly does," I said. "Now, come on," and I helped him up.

As we slipped through the dog days,[16] Doodle began to look feverish, and Mama felt his forehead, asking him if he felt ill. At night he didn't sleep well, and sometimes he had nightmares, crying out until I touched him and said, "Wake up, Doodle. Wake up."

It was Saturday noon, just a few days before school was to start. I should have already admitted defeat, but my pride wouldn't let me. The excitement of our program had now been gone for weeks, but still we kept on with a tired doggedness. It was too late to turn back, for we had both wandered too far into a net of expectations and had left no crumbs behind.

Daddy, Mama, Doodle, and I were seated at the dining-room table having lunch. It was a hot day, with all the windows and doors open in case a breeze should come. In the kitchen Aunt Nicey was humming softly. After a long silence, Daddy spoke. "It's so calm, I wouldn't be surprised if we had a storm this afternoon."

"I haven't heard a rain frog," said Mama, who believed in signs, as she served the bread around the table.

"I did," declared Doodle. "Down in the swamp."

"He didn't," I said contrarily.

"You did, eh?" said Daddy, ignoring my denial.

"I certainly did," Doodle reiterated, scowling at me over the top of his iced-tea glass, and we were quiet again.

Suddenly, from out in the yard came a strange croaking noise. Doodle stopped eating, with a piece of bread poised ready for his mouth, his eyes popped round like two blue buttons. "What's that?" he whispered.

I jumped up, knocking over my chair, and had reached the door when Mama called, "Pick up the chair, sit down again, and say excuse me."

15. **Château-Thierry** (sha TOH tee EHR ee), **Amiens** (ah MYAN), **Soissons** (swah SAWN), **. . . Belleau** (beh LOH) **Wood:** World War I battle sites in France.

16. **dog days:** hot days in July and August, named after the Dog Star (Sirius), which rises and sets with the sun during this period.

G Reading Focus **Analyzing Details** Which details in the last two paragraphs show that the summer of 1918 was blighted, or suffering from conditions that destroy or prevent growth? What connection can you make between the local blight and events in France?

Vocabulary **reiterated** (ree IHT uh ray tuhd) *v.:* repeated.

By the time I had done this, Doodle had excused himself and had slipped out into the yard. He was looking up into the bleeding tree. "It's a great big red bird!" he called.

The bird croaked loudly again, and Mama and Daddy came out into the yard. We shaded our eyes with our hands against the hazy glare of the sun and peered up through the still leaves. On the topmost branch a bird the size of a chicken, with scarlet feathers and long legs, was perched precariously. Its wings hung down loosely, and as we watched, a feather dropped away and floated slowly down through the green leaves.

It was Saturday noon, just a few days before school was to start. I should have already admitted defeat, but my pride wouldn't let me.

"It's not even frightened of us," Mama said.

"It looks tired," Daddy added. "Or maybe sick."

Doodle's hands were clasped at his throat, and I had never seen him stand still so long. "What is it?" he asked.

Daddy shook his head. "I don't know, maybe it's—"

At that moment the bird began to flutter, but the wings were uncoordinated, and amid much flapping and a spray of flying feathers, it tumbled down, bumping through the limbs of the bleeding tree and landing at our feet with a thud. Its long, graceful neck jerked twice into an S, then straightened out, and the bird was still. A white veil came over the eyes, and the long white beak unhinged. Its legs were crossed and its clawlike feet were delicately curved at rest. Even death did not mar its grace, for it lay on the earth like a broken vase of red flowers, and we stood around it, awed by its exotic beauty. **H**

"It's dead," Mama said.

"What is it?" Doodle repeated.

"Go bring me the bird book," said Daddy.

I ran into the house and brought back the bird book. As we watched, Daddy thumbed through its pages. "It's a scarlet ibis," he said, pointing to a picture. "It lives in the tropics—South America to Florida. A storm must have brought it here."

Sadly, we all looked back at the bird. A scarlet ibis! How many miles it had traveled to die like this, in our yard, beneath the bleeding tree.

"Let's finish lunch," Mama said, nudging us back toward the dining room.

H **Literary Focus** **Symbols and Theme** The description of the bird seems to give it extra meaning. What character in the story does the bird remind you of? Why?

Vocabulary **mar** (mahr) *v.:* damage; spoil.

Portrait of David by Augustus Edwin John (1878–1961). Private collection.

Analyzing Visuals **Viewing and Interpreting** Does this young man remind you more of Doodle or his brother? Explain.

"I'm not hungry," said Doodle, and he knelt down beside the ibis.

"We've got peach cobbler for dessert," Mama tempted from the doorway.

Doodle remained kneeling. "I'm going to bury him."

"Don't you dare touch him," Mama warned. "There's no telling what disease he might have had."

"All right," said Doodle. "I won't."

Daddy, Mama, and I went back to the dining-room table, but we watched Doodle through the open door. He took out a piece of string from his pocket and, without touching the ibis, looped one end around its neck. Slowly, while singing softly "Shall We Gather at the River," he carried the bird around to the front yard and dug a hole in the flower garden, next to the petunia bed. Now we were watching him through the front window, but he didn't know it. His awkwardness at digging the hole with a shovel whose handle was twice as long as he was made us laugh, and we covered our mouths with our hands so he wouldn't hear.

When Doodle came into the dining room, he found us seriously eating our cobbler. He was pale and lingered just inside the screen door. "Did you get the scarlet ibis buried?" asked Daddy.

Doodle didn't speak but nodded his head.

"Go wash your hands, and then you can have some peach cobbler," said Mama.

"I'm not hungry," he said.

"Dead birds is bad luck," said Aunt Nicey, poking her head from the kitchen door. "Specially *red* dead birds!"

As soon as I had finished eating, Doodle and I hurried off to Horsehead Landing. Time was short, and Doodle still had a long way to go if he was going to keep up with the other boys when he started school. The sun, gilded with the yellow cast of autumn, still burned fiercely, but the dark green woods through which we passed were shady and cool. When we reached the landing, Doodle said he was too tired to swim, so we got into a skiff and floated down the creek with the tide. Far off in the marsh a rail was scolding, and over on the beach locusts were singing in the myrtle trees. Doodle did not speak and kept his head turned away, letting one hand trail limply in the water.

After we had drifted a long way, I put the oars in place and made Doodle row back against the tide. Black clouds began to gather in the southwest, and he kept watching them, trying to pull the oars a little faster. When we reached Horsehead Landing, lightning was playing across half the sky and thunder roared out, hiding even the sound of the sea. The sun disappeared and darkness descended, almost like night. Flocks of marsh crows flew by, heading inland to their roosting trees, and two egrets, squawking, arose from the oyster-rock shallows and careened away.

Doodle was both tired and frightened, and when he stepped from the skiff he collapsed onto the mud, sending an armada[17] of fiddler crabs rustling off into the marsh grass. I helped him up, and as he wiped the mud off his trousers, he smiled at me ashamedly. He had failed and we both knew it, so we started back home, racing the storm. We never spoke (what are the words that can solder[18] cracked pride?), but I knew he was watching me, watching for a sign of mercy. The lightning was near now, and from fear he walked so close behind me he kept stepping on my heels. The faster I walked, the faster he walked, so I began to run. The rain was coming, roaring through the pines, and then, like a bursting Roman candle, a gum tree ahead of us was shattered by a bolt of lightning. When the deafening peal of thunder had died, and in the moment before the rain arrived, I heard Doodle, who had fallen behind, cry out, "Brother, Brother, don't leave me! Don't leave me!"

The knowledge that Doodle's and my plans had come to naught was bitter, and that streak of cruelty within me awakened. I ran as fast as I could, leaving him far behind with a wall of rain dividing us. The drops stung my face like nettles, and the wind flared the wet, glistening leaves of the bordering trees. Soon I could hear his voice no more.

I hadn't run too far before I became tired, and the flood of childish spite evanesced[19] as well. I stopped and waited for Doodle. The

17. **armada** (ahr MAH duh): group. *Armada* is generally used to mean "fleet, or group, of warships."

18. **solder** (SAWD uhr): patch or repair. *Solder* is a mixture of melted metals used to repair metal parts.

19. **evanesced** (ehv uh NEHST): faded away; disappeared.

SCIENCE LINK

An Egyptian 13th century B.C. painting depicting Re-Harakhty and Bennu standing on the Tomb of Sennedjem.

The Scarlet Ibis

The scarlet ibis is a medium-sized bird found mostly in South America. Scarlet ibises tend to travel in flocks and nest in large colonies. Except for its black wing tips, the scarlet ibis is entirely red. The bird gets its striking color from the pigment in the crustaceans and small marine animals it eats. The ibis family, of which there are more than twenty species, is an ancient group of birds. The Egyptians, who considered the birds sacred, mummified and buried them in temples with the dead as part of burial rituals. Fossils of the ibis date back more than sixty million years.

Ask Yourself

How are both Doodle and the ibis rare and unique?

Analyzing Visuals **Viewing and Interpreting** Do you think this artwork reflects the way the narrator feels? Explain.

sound of rain was everywhere, but the wind had died and it fell straight down in parallel paths like ropes hanging from the sky. As I waited, I peered through the downpour, but no one came. Finally I went back and found him huddled beneath a red nightshade bush beside the road. He was sitting on the ground, his face buried in his arms, which were resting on his drawn-up knees. "Let's go, Doodle," I said.

He didn't answer, so I placed my hand on his forehead and lifted his head. Limply, he fell backward onto the earth. He had been bleeding from the mouth, and his neck and the front of his shirt were stained a brilliant red. **I**

"Doodle! Doodle!" I cried, shaking him, but there was no answer but the ropy rain. He lay very awkwardly, with his head thrown far back, making his vermilion[20] neck appear unusually long and slim. His little legs, bent sharply at the knees, had never before seemed so fragile, so thin. **J**

I began to weep, and the tear-blurred vision in red before me looked very familiar. "Doodle!" I screamed above the pounding storm, and threw my body to the earth above his. For a long, long time, it seemed forever, I lay there crying, sheltering my fallen scarlet ibis from the heresy[21] of rain.

---

20. **vermilion** (vuhr MIHL yuhn): bright red.
21. **heresy** (HEHR uh see): here, mockery. *Heresy* generally means "denial of what is commonly believed to be true" or "rejection of a church's teaching."

I **Literary Focus** **Symbols** Doodle sits by a red nightshade bush and has blood on his shirt. What do you think the color red might symbolize?

J **Reading Focus** **Analyzing Details** In the last two paragraphs, Doodle is described. What do these description details remind you of? Why do you think the writer makes this association?

Applying Your Skills

MO **9.R.2.B.2.b** Identify and explain literary techniques, in text emphasizing: imagery **9.R.2.C.1.c** Use details from text(s): to analyze the development of a theme across genres *Also covered* **9.R.1.H.1.a; 9.W.2.D.1.b; 9.R.2.C.1.d**

The Scarlet Ibis

Respond and Think Critically

Reading Focus

Quick Check

1. What makes the narrator so persistent in teaching Doodle to walk?
2. Why does Doodle, more than anyone else in the family, feel empathy for the ibis?

Read with a Purpose

3. Why does the narrator want to make his brother into someone different? Do you think this is a common problem among siblings? Explain.

Reading Skills: Analyzing Details

4. Review the entries on your chart, and add your ideas about the story's symbols and theme. You may find this chart helpful as you answer questions 8 and 9.

Story Details	Larger Meanings
Summer was dead; autumn not yet born.	Nature might mirror human experiences—being born and dying.
Symbols: What symbols do the story details create?	
Theme: What overall idea about life do the symbols help to convey?	

Literary Focus

Literary Analysis

5. **Interpret** Explain the narrator's behavior at the end of the story. Is he in some way responsible for Doodle's death? Is his emotion at the very end sorrow, guilt, or something else? Explain.
6. **Connect** By the story's end, whom do you pity more—the narrator or Doodle? Why?
7. **Extend** In what way might this story be a commentary on the events of World War I?

Literary Skills: Symbols and Theme

8. **Analyze** In the story's last sentence the narrator calls his brother his "fallen scarlet ibis." In what ways could the ibis be a symbol for Doodle?
9. **Interpret** In the Meet the Writer (page 332), Hurst hints at what his famous story might signify. How would you state the theme of his story? What truth does the story reveal about choices that people make? Find passages from the story to support your response.

Literary Skills Review: Voice

10. **Analyze** **Voice** refers to a writer's overall use of language and style. This story begins as the narrator, an adult, tells of events that happened long ago. Then, a shift occurs, and the narrator's voice changes as he begins reliving those childhood events. Where does this shift occur? How does the change in voice affect the story?

Writing Focus

Think as a Reader/Writer

Use It in Your Writing Hurst uses dialogue to reveal the story's characters. Choose a passage from the story that contains little or no dialogue, and rewrite it using mostly dialogue. Stay true to the characters and events as you craft your scene.

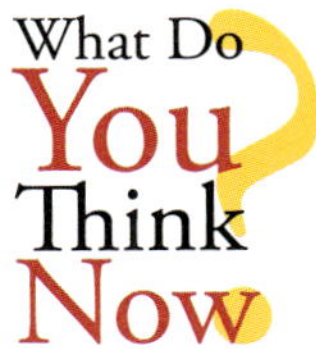

Should the narrator have tried to help his brother lead a "normal" life, or should the narrator have left Doodle alone? Explain.

Applying Your Skills

The Scarlet Ibis

Vocabulary Development

Vocabulary Check

Follow the directions in each item below.

1. Write a headline for a newspaper article using the word **imminent**.
2. Use the word **iridescent** in a sentence for an ad for jewelry.
3. Use the word **infallibility** in a description of a person.
4. Write an instruction from a teacher using the word **reiterated**.
5. Write an apology using the word **mar**.

Vocabulary Skills: Similes

"They named him William Armstrong, which was like tying a big tail on a small kite." How is the name William Armstrong like a big tail? This question is not a riddle. James Hurst is using a simile—the simplest form of figurative language—to help us understand that an impressive name is being given to frail, vulnerable Doodle. A **simile** is a comparison between two dissimilar things using a word such as *like, as,* or *resembles*.

Here are three more sentences with similes from "The Scarlet Ibis":

1. "[The ibis] lay on the earth like a broken vase of red flowers."
2. ". . . The sick-sweet smell of bay flowers hung everywhere like a mournful song."
3. "Success lay at the end of summer like a pot of gold."

Your Turn

1. In each of the example passages at the bottom left, locate the simile and tell what is being compared. What exactly do the two things have in common?
2. Next, reword each passage using a new simile. Can you change the emotional tone of the passage by using a different comparison? Explain.
3. Finally, use a simile in a paragraph describing your own sibling or close friend.

Language Coach

Oral Fluency One step toward owning a word is to become comfortable pronouncing it and using it in conversation. Work with a partner to use each of the Vocabulary words in a discussion about "The Scarlet Ibis."

Academic Vocabulary

Talk About . . .

What is the narrator implying when he says that Doodle's "all there"?

9.R.2.B.2.b Identify and explain literary techniques, in text emphasizing: imagery **9.R.2.C.1.c** Use details from text(s): to analyze the development of a theme across genres **9.W.3.A.1.a** Compose a variety of texts: using narrative, descriptive, expository, and/or persuasive features *Also covered* **9.W.3.A.1.d; 9.W.2.E.1.b; 9.R.1.G.1.a; 9.R.1.E.1.c**

Grammar Link

Dialogue—Who's Talking?

Dialogue—what characters say—can advance the plot, reveal the thoughts of a character, or present important information to a reader. In American usage, dialogue is enclosed in double quotation marks (" "). Usually a new paragraph lets us know when a different person begins to speak, as in this example from "The Scarlet Ibis":

"Let's finish lunch," Mama said, nudging us back toward the dining room.

"I'm not hungry," said Doodle, and he knelt down beside the ibis.

"We've got peach cobbler for dessert," Mama tempted from the doorway.

Doodle remained kneeling. "I'm going to bury him."

Most writers use tag lines (such as *he said* and *I replied*) to identify the speakers in a dialogue. Hurst, however, sometimes includes just a character's words, and it is up to you to figure out who is speaking from the context around the dialogue. Remember that tag lines should not be enclosed in quotation marks.

Your Turn

Writing Applications Rewrite these sentences as dialogue. Add tag lines and check to be sure you punctuate the sentences correctly.

1. Doodle decided he would live in Old Woman Swamp when he grew older.
2. Mama felt Doodle's forehead and asked if he was ill.
3. Because Doodle said that he was too tired to swim, his brother suggested that he ride in the boat instead.

CHOICES

As you respond to the Choices, use these **Academic Vocabulary** words as appropriate: ambiguous, associate, imply, literal.

REVIEW

Design the Cover

TechFocus Using graphic design software, create a cover for "The Scarlet Ibis." In your design include images that reflect the symbols that James Hurst used to tell his tale. Include the story's title and author's name on the cover.

CONNECT

Analyze the Story

Timed Writing Many people find this story memorable. Analyze the story in a short essay. You may want to refer to these points in your essay:

- Was the relationship between the brothers believable? Why or why not?
- Were the narrator's actions toward his brother selfish or noble?
- What idea about life does the story convey?

EXTEND

Research the Flora of the South

There is a distinct feeling of nature in "The Scarlet Ibis"—the seasons, vegetation, and details of the swamp. List the trees, flowers, and grasses mentioned in the story. In an encyclopedia or reference book, research these plants and write entries describing each one.

Learn It Online
Take your understanding of this story further with these Internet links:

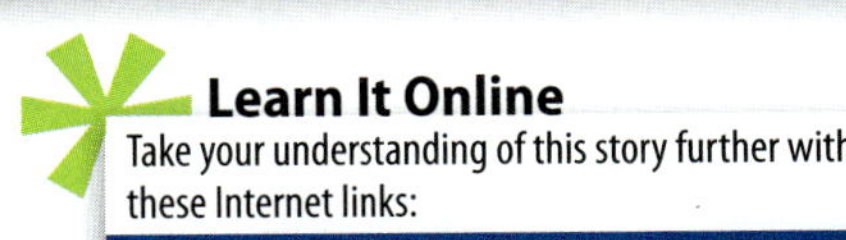

SHORT STORY

Preparing to Read

The Necklace

by **Guy de Maupassant**

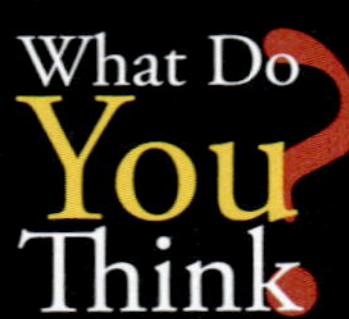

What Do You Think? How might envy cause a person to make an unwise choice?

QuickWrite

Sometimes people think that having what someone else has will make them happy—until they experience the negative results of envy. What would you say to a friend who was unhappy because of his or her envy of someone else? Write down your thoughts.

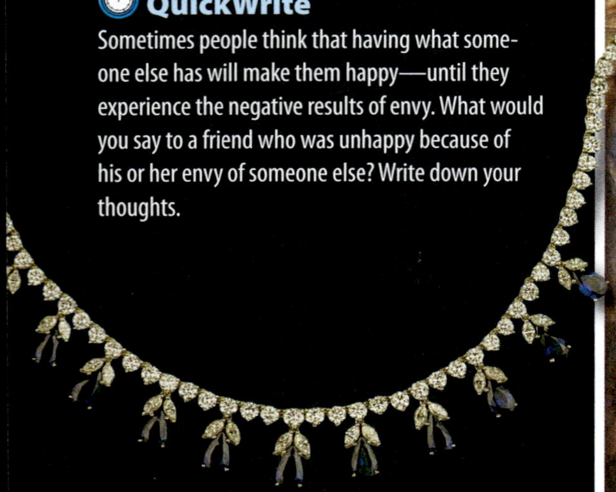

The Necklace (c. 1909) by John William Waterhouse (1849–1917). Oil on canvas.

Reader/Writer Notebook

Use your **RWN** to complete the activities for this selection.

MO **9.R.2.B.2.a** Identify and explain literary techniques in text emphasizing: irony **9.R.1.F.1.c** Apply pre-reading strategies to aid comprehension: predict with text support or rationale **9.R.1.G.1.b** During reading, utilize strategies: to self-monitor comprehension

Literary Focus

Symbols and Irony Stories that contain symbols and irony provide readers with a lot to think about. A **symbol** can be a person, place, thing, or event that stands for something beyond itself—for example, the bald eagle is a symbol of the United States. **Irony** occurs when a situation or a person turns out to be the opposite of what we expect: the fire station burns down or the visionary artist is blind. **Situational irony** occurs when there is a contradiction between what we expect to happen and what really takes place.

Literary Perspectives Apply the literary perspective described on page 351 as you read this story.

Reading Focus

Reading Actively: Making Predictions Part of the pleasure of reading fiction is trying to figure out what lies ahead for the story's characters. Many active readers experience strong feelings as they get involved in the characters' lives. As you read "The Necklace," engage with the story by making predictions about how the lives of the main characters will turn out.

Into Action Keep track of the predictions you make by filling out the left-hand column of a prediction chart like the one below.

My Predictions	What Actually Happens
Mme. Loisel will begin to resent being poor.	

Writing Focus

Think as a Reader/Writer

Find It in Your Reading Throughout the story, Guy de Maupassant describes Mme. Loisel's inner thoughts and feelings. While reading, pay attention to those details and note them in your *Reader/Writer Notebook.*

Vocabulary

disconsolate (dihs KAHN suh liht) *adj.:* causing sadness or depression; also, very unhappy. *The Loisels returned to their home disconsolate when they realized what had been lost.*

pauper (PAW puhr) *n.:* very poor person. *Mathilde is embarrassed to appear in society looking like a pauper.*

adulation (a juh LAY shuhn) *n.:* intense or excessive admiration and praise. *Mathilde feels best when surrounded by others' adulation.*

aghast (uh GAST) *adj.:* horrified; greatly dismayed. *Mathilde's friend is aghast when she runs into a much-changed Mathilde on the street.*

exorbitant (ehg ZAWR buh tuhnt) *adj.:* much greater than is reasonable. *The Loisels pay an exorbitant price for a necklace.*

Language Coach

Word Origins Try to answer the questions below about word origins.

- Which of the words on the list above is formed from the Old English word *gast,* which means "ghost"?
- Which of the words on the list literally means "off track" or "out of orbit"?
- When you console someone, you make him or her feel better. Which word on the list means "unable to be consoled"?

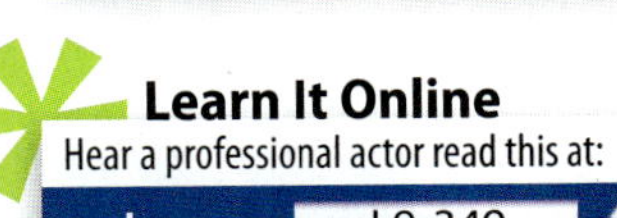

Learn It Online
Hear a professional actor read this at:
go.hrw.com L9-349 Go

MEET THE WRITER

Learn It Online
Get more on the author's life at:
go.hrw.com L9-350 Go

Guy de Maupassant
(1850–1893)

Seeing Things Anew

Guy de Maupassant (GEE duh moh pah SAHN), widely regarded as one of the world's greatest short-story writers, was born in Normandy, the French province that is the setting for much of his fiction. After his parents separated, Maupassant was raised by his mother, a close friend of the great novelist Gustave Flaubert.

Flaubert set out to instruct the young Maupassant in the art of fiction. He explained that good writing depends upon seeing things anew, rather than recording what people before us have thought. Flaubert also gave his student this advice: "Whatever you want to say, there is only one word to express it, only one verb to give it movement, only one adjective to qualify it."

Hard Work and Success

For years, Maupassant sent Flaubert his writing exercises every week, and then they met to discuss his work over lunch. At age thirty, Maupassant quit his job as a clerk with the naval ministry and began to put great energy into writing. He quickly achieved enormous popularity. For eleven years he wrote at a hectic pace and produced nearly three hundred stories and six novels.

Maupassant's story "The Horla" has been called one of the most terrifying stories of madness ever written. It foretold the author's own tragic fate of illness, insanity, and early death. He died in a Paris asylum when he was forty-two years old.

Think About the Writer How did Maupassant's behavior convey his serious intentions about becoming a writer?

The Granger Collection, New York.

Build Background

"The Necklace" takes place in Paris in the late 1880s. At that time and in that place, social classes were all-important; people were born into a certain class, and that was usually where they remained for the rest of their lives.

Preview the Selection

This story revolves around **Mathilde Loisel,** a beautiful woman married to a minor government official. She despises her life and wishes she were part of high society, surrounded by beautiful rooms and furnishings.

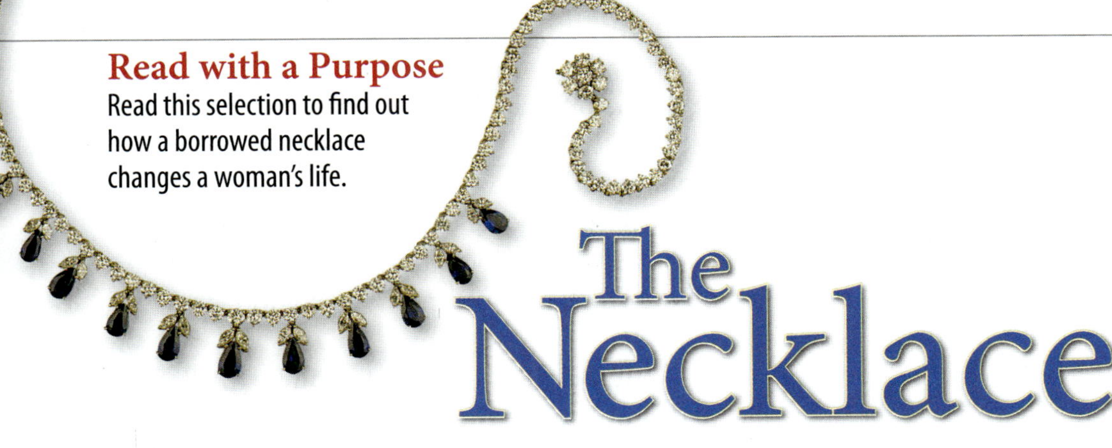

Read with a Purpose

Read this selection to find out how a borrowed necklace changes a woman's life.

The Necklace

by **Guy de Maupassant**

She was one of those pretty and charming girls, born, as if by an accident of fate, into a family of clerks. With no dowry,[1] no prospects, no way of any kind of being met, understood, loved, and married by a man both prosperous and famous, she was finally married to a minor clerk in the Ministry of Education.

She dressed plainly because she could not afford fine clothes, but she was as unhappy as a woman who has come down in the world; for women have no family rank or social class. With them, beauty, grace, and charm take the place of birth and breeding. Their natural poise, their instinctive good taste, and their mental cleverness are the sole guiding principles which make daughters of the common people the equals of ladies in high society.

She grieved incessantly, feeling that she had been born for all the little niceties and luxuries of living. She grieved over the shabbiness of her apartment, the dinginess of the walls, the worn-out appearance of the chairs, the ugliness of the draperies. All these things, which another woman of her class would not even have noticed, gnawed at her and made her furious. The sight of the little Breton girl[2] who did her humble housework roused in her disconsolate regrets and wild daydreams. She would dream of silent chambers, draped with Oriental tapestries and lighted by tall bronze floor lamps, and of two handsome butlers in knee breeches, who, drowsy from the heavy warmth cast by the central stove, dozed in large overstuffed armchairs.

She would dream of great reception halls

1. **dowry** (DOW ree): property that a woman brings to her husband at marriage.

2. **Breton** (BREHT uhn) **girl:** girl from Brittany, a region in northwestern France.

Vocabulary **disconsolate** (dihs KAHN suh liht) *adj.:* causing sadness or depression; also, very unhappy.

Literary Perspectives

Analyzing Credibility in Literature Have you ever read a story and said to yourself, "That's not possible! Nobody would ever do that." With other stories, you might find characters so believable that you are carried away by their thoughts, actions, and events of the story as if it were happening to you. Determining whether characters and their actions are believable is called evaluating credibility. As you read "The Necklace," be sure to read the notes at the bottom of the pages to guide you in using this perspective.

hung with old silks, of fine furniture filled with priceless curios,[3] and of small, stylish, scented sitting rooms just right for the four o'clock chat with intimate friends, with distinguished and sought-after men whose attention every woman envies and longs to attract.

When dining at the round table, covered for the third day with the same cloth, opposite her husband, who would raise the cover of the soup tureen, declaring delightedly, "Ah! a good stew! There's nothing I like better . . . ," she would dream of fashionable dinner parties, of gleaming silverware, of tapestries making the walls alive with characters out of history and strange birds in a fairyland forest; she would dream of delicious dishes served on wonderful china, of gallant compliments whispered and listened to with a sphinxlike smile as one eats the rosy flesh of a trout or nibbles at the wings of a grouse.

She had no evening clothes, no jewels, nothing. But those were the things she wanted; she felt that was the kind of life for her. She so much longed to please, be envied, be fascinating and sought after. **A**

She had a well-to-do friend, a classmate of convent-school days whom she would no longer go to see, simply because she would feel so distressed on returning home. And she would weep for days on end from vexation, regret, despair, and anguish.

Then one evening, her husband came home proudly holding out a large envelope.

"Look," he said, "I've got something for you."

She excitedly tore open the envelope and pulled out a printed card bearing these words:

"The Minister of Education and Mme. Georges Ramponneau beg M. and Mme. Loisel[4] to do them the honor of attending an evening reception at the Ministerial Mansion on Friday, January 18."

Instead of being delighted, as her husband had hoped, she scornfully tossed the invitation on the table, murmuring, "What good is that to me?" **B**

"But, my dear, I thought you'd be thrilled to death. You never get a chance to go out, and this is a real affair, a wonderful one! I had an awful time getting a card. Everybody wants one; it's much sought after, and not many clerks have a chance at one. You'll see all the most important people there."

She gave him an irritated glance and burst out impatiently, "What do you think I have to go in?"

He hadn't given that a thought. He stammered, "Why, the dress you wear when we go to the theater. That looks quite nice, I think."

He stopped talking, dazed and distracted to see his wife burst out weeping. Two large tears slowly rolled from the corners of her eyes to the corners of her mouth; he gasped, "Why, what's the matter? What's the trouble?"

By sheer willpower she overcame her outburst and answered in a calm voice while wiping the tears from her wet cheeks, "Oh, nothing. Only I don't have an evening dress and therefore I can't go to that affair. Give the card to some friend at the office whose wife can dress better than I can." **C**

---

3. **curios** (KYUR ee ohz): unusual items.

4. **Mme. Georges Ramponneau** (mah DAHM zhawrzh rahm puh NOH) . . . **M.** (muh SYUR) . . . **Mme. Loisel** (mah DAHM lwah ZEHL): *M.* and *Mme.* are abbreviations for *Monsieur* and *Madame* and are the French equivalents of *Mr.* and *Mrs.*

A Literary Focus Symbols For Mme. Loisel, what symbolizes high society and wealth?

B Literary Focus Irony In what way is Mme. Loisel's reaction to the invitation unexpected?

C Reading Focus Making Predictions Do you think Mme. Loisel will decide to go to the reception? Why or why not?

He was stunned. He resumed, "Let's see, Mathilde. How much would a suitable outfit cost—one you could wear for other affairs too—something very simple?"

She thought it over for several seconds, going over her allowance and thinking also of the amount she could ask for without bringing an immediate refusal and an exclamation of dismay from the thrifty clerk.

Finally, she answered hesitatingly, "I'm not sure exactly, but I think with four hundred francs I could manage it."

He turned a bit pale, for he had set aside just that amount to buy a rifle so that the following summer, he could join some friends who were getting up a group to shoot larks on the plain near Nanterre.[5]

However, he said, "All right. I'll give you four hundred francs. But try to get a nice dress."

As the day of the party approached, Mme. Loisel seemed sad, moody, ill at ease. Her outfit was ready, however. Her husband said to her one evening, "What's the matter? You've been all out of sorts for three days."

And she answered, "It's embarrassing not to have a jewel or a gem—nothing to wear on my dress. I'll look like a pauper. I'd almost rather not go to the party."

He answered, "Why not wear some flowers? They're very fashionable this season. For ten francs you can get two or three gorgeous roses."

She wasn't at all convinced. "No. . . . There's nothing more humiliating than to look poor among a lot of rich women."

But her husband exclaimed, "My, but you're silly! Go see your friend Mme. Forestier,[6] and ask her to lend you some jewelry. You and she know each other well enough for you to do that."

She gave a cry of joy. "Why, that's so! I hadn't thought of it."

The next day she paid her friend a visit and told her of her predicament.

Mme. Forestier went toward a large closet with mirrored doors, took out a large jewel box, brought it over, opened it, and said to Mme. Loisel, "Pick something out, my dear."

At first her eyes noted some bracelets, then a pearl necklace, then a Venetian cross, gold and gems, of marvelous workmanship. She tried on these adornments in front of the mirror, but

Portrait of Maud Cook (1895) by Thomas Eakins. Mabel Brady Garvan Collection, Yale University Art Gallery, New Haven, Connecticut. Oil on canvas (24" x 20").

5. **Nanterre** (nahn TEHR): town near Paris.

6. **Forestier** (fuh REHS tee ay).

Vocabulary **pauper** (PAW puhr) *n.:* very poor person.

A Soiree (1878) by Jean Beraud (1849–1936), NY. Oil on canvas.

hesitated, unable to decide which to part with and put back. She kept on asking, "Haven't you something else?"

"Oh, yes, keep on looking. I don't know just what you'd like."

All at once she found, in a black satin box, a superb diamond necklace; and her pulse beat faster with longing. Her hands trembled as she took it up. Clasping it around her throat, outside her high-necked dress, she stood in ecstasy looking at her reflection.

Then she asked, hesitatingly, pleading, "Could I borrow that, just that and nothing else?"

"Why, of course."

She threw her arms around her friend, kissed her warmly, and fled with her treasure. **D**

The day of the party arrived. Mme. Loisel was a sensation. She was the prettiest one there, fashionable, gracious, smiling, and wild with joy. All the men turned to look at her, asked who she was, begged to be introduced. All the

D **Literary Focus** **Symbols** Why is wearing the diamond necklace so important to Mme. Loisel? With what does she associate the necklace?

Photo: H. Lewandowski. © 2007 Artists Rights Society (ARS), New York / ADAGP, Paris.

Cabinet officials wanted to waltz with her. The minister took notice of her.

She danced madly, wildly, drunk with pleasure, giving no thought to anything in the triumph of her beauty, the pride of her success, in a kind of happy cloud composed of all the adulation, of all the admiring glances, of all the awakened longings, of a sense of complete victory that is so sweet to a woman's heart. **E**

She left around four o' clock in the morning. Her husband, since midnight, had been dozing in a small, empty sitting room with three other gentlemen whose wives were having too good a time.

He threw over her shoulders the wraps he had brought for going home, modest garments of everyday life whose shabbiness clashed with the stylishness of her evening clothes. She felt this and longed to escape unseen by the other women, who were draped in expensive furs.

Loisel held her back.

"Hold on! You'll catch cold outside. I'll call a cab."

But she wouldn't listen to him and went rapidly down the stairs. When they were on the street, they didn't find a carriage; and they set out to hunt for one, hailing drivers whom they saw going by at a distance.

They walked toward the Seine,[7] disconsolate and shivering. Finally, on the docks, they found one of those carriages that one sees in Paris only after nightfall, as if they were ashamed to show their drabness during daylight hours.

It dropped them at their door in the Rue des Martyrs,[8] and they climbed wearily up to their apartment. For her, it was all over. For him, there was the thought that he would have to be at the Ministry at ten o'clock.

Before the mirror, she let the wraps fall from her shoulders to see herself once again in all her glory. Suddenly she gave a cry. The necklace was gone.

Her husband, already half undressed, said, "What's the trouble?"

7. **Seine** (sehn): river that runs through Paris.
8. **Rue des Martyrs** (roo day mahr TIHR): street in Paris. The name means "Street of the Martyrs." People who suffer for their beliefs or people who suffer for a long time are called martyrs.

E Reading Focus Making Predictions Do you think Mme. Loisel's life will change as a result of her success at the reception? Why or why not?

Vocabulary adulation (a juh LAY shuhn) *n.:* intense or excessive admiration and praise.

She turned toward him despairingly, "I . . . I . . . I don't have Mme. Forestier's necklace."

"What! You can't mean it! It's impossible!"

They hunted everywhere, through the folds of the dress, through the folds of the coat, in the pockets. They found nothing.

He asked, "Are you sure you had it when leaving the dance?"

"Yes, I felt it when I was in the hall of the Ministry."

"But if you had lost it on the street, we'd have heard it drop. It must be in the cab."

"Yes, quite likely. Did you get its number?"

"No. Didn't you notice it either?"

"No."

They looked at each other aghast. Finally Loisel got dressed again.

"I'll retrace our steps on foot," he said, "to see if I can find it."

And he went out. She remained in her evening clothes, without the strength to go to bed, slumped in a chair in the unheated room, her mind a blank.

Her husband came in around seven o'clock. He had had no luck. **F**

He went to the police station, to the newspapers to post a reward, to the cab companies, everywhere the slightest hope drove him.

That evening Loisel returned, pale, his face lined; still he had learned nothing.

"We'll have to write your friend," he said, "to tell her you have broken the catch and are having it repaired. That will give us a little time to turn around."

She wrote to his dictation.

At the end of a week, they had given up all hope.

And Loisel, looking five years older, declared, "We must take steps to replace that piece of jewelry." **G**

The next day they took the case to the jeweler whose name they found inside. He consulted his records. "I didn't sell that necklace, madame," he said. "I only supplied the case."

Then they went from one jeweler to another hunting for a similar necklace, going over their recollections, both sick with despair and anxiety.

> What would have happened if she had not lost that necklace? Who knows? Who can say? How strange and unpredictable life is! How little there is between happiness and misery!

They found, in a shop in Palais Royal,[9] a string of diamonds which seemed exactly like the one they were seeking. It was priced at forty thousand francs. They could get it for thirty-six.

They asked the jeweler to hold it for them for three days. And they reached an agreement that he would take it back for thirty-four thousand if the lost one was found before the end of February.

Loisel had eighteen thousand francs he had inherited from his father. He would borrow the rest.

9. **Palais Royal** (pah LAY roy YAHL): fashionable shopping district in Paris.

F Reading Focus **Making Predictions** What do you think the Loisels will do now that they have lost the necklace?

G Literary Focus **Irony** In what way is Mme. Loisel's change of fortune ironic?

Vocabulary **aghast** (uh GAST) *adj.:* horrified; greatly dismayed.

He went about raising the money, asking a thousand francs from one, four hundred from another, a hundred here, sixty there. He signed notes, made ruinous deals, did business with loan sharks, ran the whole gamut of money-lenders. He compromised the rest of his life, risked his signature without knowing if he'd be able to honor it, and then, terrified by the outlook of the future, by the blackness of despair about to close around him, by the prospect of all the privations[10] of the body and tortures of the spirit, he went to claim the new necklace with the thirty-six thousand francs, which he placed on the counter of the shopkeeper.

When Mme. Loisel took the necklace back, Mme. Forestier said to her frostily, "You should have brought it back sooner; I might have needed it."

She didn't open the case, an action her friend was afraid of. If she had noticed the substitution, what would she have thought? What would she have said? Would she have thought her a thief?

Mme. Loisel experienced the horrible life the needy live. She played her part, however, with sudden heroism. That frightful debt had to be paid. She would pay it. She dismissed her maid; they rented a garret under the eaves.[11]

She learned to do the heavy housework, to perform the hateful duties of cooking. She washed dishes, wearing down her shell-pink nails scouring the grease from pots and pans; she scrubbed dirty linen, shirts, and cleaning rags, which she hung on a line to dry; she took the garbage down to the street each morning and brought up water, stopping on each landing to get her breath. And, clad like a peasant woman, basket on arm, guarding sou[12] by sou her scanty allowance, she bargained with the fruit dealers, the grocer, the butcher, and was insulted by them.

Each month notes had to be paid, and others renewed to give more time.

Her husband labored evenings to balance a tradesman's accounts, and at night, often, he copied documents at five sous a page.

And this went on for ten years.

Finally, all was paid back, everything including the exorbitant rates of the loan sharks and accumulated compound interest.

Mme. Loisel appeared an old woman now. She became heavy, rough, harsh, like one of the poor. Her hair untended, her skirts askew, her hands red, her voice shrill, she even slopped water on her floors and scrubbed them herself. But, sometimes, while her husband was at work, she would sit near the window and think of that long-ago evening when, at the dance, she had been so beautiful and admired. **H**

What would have happened if she had not lost that necklace? Who knows? Who can say? How strange and unpredictable life is! How little there is between happiness and misery!

Then, one Sunday, when she had gone for a walk on the Champs Élysées[13] to relax a bit from the week's labors, she suddenly noticed a woman strolling with a child. It was Mme. Forestier, still

10. **privations** (pry VAY shuhnz): hardships; lack of the things needed for a happy, healthy life.

11. **garret under the eaves:** attic under the overhanging lower edges of a roof.

12. **sou** (soo): old French coin of little value.

13. **Champs Élysées** (chahmp ay lee ZAY): famous avenue in Paris.

H **Literary Perspectives** **Analyzing Credibility in Literature** Do you find the actions of Mme. Loisel and her husband believable? Why or why not?

Vocabulary **exorbitant** (ehg ZAWR buh tuhnt) *adj.:* much greater than is reasonable.

young looking, still beautiful, still charming.

Mme. Loisel felt a rush of emotion. Should she speak to her? Of course. And now that everything was paid off, she would tell her the whole story. Why not?

She went toward her. "Hello, Jeanne."

The other, not recognizing her, showed astonishment at being spoken to so familiarly by this common person. She stammered, "But . . . madame . . . I don't recognize . . . You must be mistaken."

"No, I'm Mathilde Loisel."

Her friend gave a cry, "Oh, my poor Mathilde, how you've changed!"

"Yes, I've had a hard time since last seeing you. And plenty of misfortunes—and all on account of you!"

"Of me . . . How do you mean?"

"Do you remember that diamond necklace you loaned me to wear to the dance at the Ministry?"

"Yes, but what about it?"

"Well, I lost it."

"You lost it! But you returned it."

"I brought you another just like it. And we've been paying for it for ten years now. You can imagine that wasn't easy for us who had nothing. Well, it's over now, and I am glad of it."

Mme. Forestier stopped short. "You mean to say you bought a diamond necklace to replace mine?"

"Yes. You never noticed, then? They were quite alike."

And she smiled with proud and simple joy.

Mme. Forestier, quite overcome, clasped her by the hands. "Oh, my poor Mathilde. But mine was fake. Why, at most it was worth only five hundred francs!" **I**

Woman Ironing by Armand-Desire Gautier (1825–1894). Oil on canvas (31 cm x 24 cm).

Analyzing Visuals **Viewing and Interpreting** How does the subject of the painting represent Mme. Loisel's situation?

I **Literary Focus** **Situational Irony** In what way is the story's ending an example of situational irony?

Applying Your Skills

9.R.2.B.2.a Identify and explain literary techniques in text emphasizing: irony 9.R.2.C.1.b Use details from text(s): to analyze character, plot, setting, point of view 9.R.1.G.1.b During reading, utilize strategies: to self-monitor comprehension *Also covered* 9.R.1.F.1.c; 9.W.3.A.1.a; 9.R.1.G.1.a

The Necklace

Respond and Think Critically

Reading Focus

Quick Check

1. Why is Mme. Loisel unhappy when she receives an invitation to an evening reception?
2. How are Mme. Loisel's dreams realized at the party? How are her dreams destroyed?
3. At the end of the story, what lesson does Mme. Loisel learn about life?

Read with a Purpose

4. In what way is Mme. Loisel's life changed as a result of her borrowing the necklace?

Reading Skills: Reading Actively

5. Review the predictions you made as you read "The Necklace," and record what actually happened in the story. Which story events did you accurately predict? Which story events were unexpected?

My Predictions	What Actually Happens
Mme. Loisel will begin to resent being poor.	Mme. Loisel tells her husband she can't go to a party because she has no fine clothes to wear.

Vocabulary Check

Match each Vocabulary word with its definition.

6. **disconsolate** a. greater than is reasonable
7. **pauper** b. horrified
8. **adulation** c. very unhappy
9. **aghast** d. excessive praise
10. **exorbitant** e. very poor person

Literary Focus

Literary Analysis

11. **Analyze** How would this story change if it were told by Mme. Loisel or her husband?
12. **Literary Perspectives** Are Mme. Loisel and her husband credible characters? Why or why not?
13. **Evaluate** Do you think Maupassant is critical of just Mme. Loisel or of society as a whole? Explain.

Literary Skills: Symbols and Irony

14. **Interpret** After the Loisels lose the necklace, what does it become symbolic of?
15. **Analyze** What irony is revealed in the story's conclusion?

Literary Skills Review: Motivation

16. **Analyze** The fears, conflicts, or needs that drive a character are called **motivation.** What motivates Mme. Loisel to seek out riches and finery?

Writing Focus

Think as a Reader/Writer

Use It in Your Writing Choose a person from fiction or real life. Then, in your *Reader/Writer Notebook,* write a character sketch of him or her. Like Maupassant, develop your character by describing his or her inner thoughts and feelings.

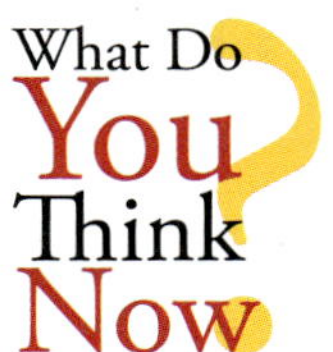

Would Mme. Loisel's life have been happier if she had not been envious of others? Explain.

SHORT STORY

Preparing to Read

The Gift of the Magi

by **O. Henry**

The Present (1845) by Charles Robert Leslie (1794–1859). Oil on canvas (49 cm x 42 cm).

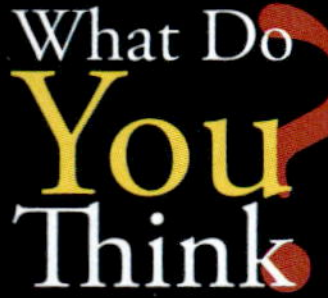

What kinds of sacrifices would you make for a person who mattered to you?

QuickWrite

Think about stories, movies, or real-life events in which people make sacrifices for their family, friends, or even their country. What motivates people to make such sacrifices? Write down your thoughts.

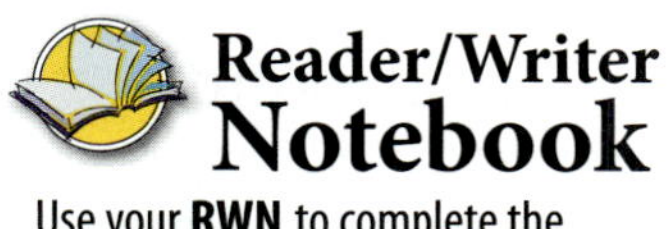

Use your **RWN** to complete the activities for this selection.

9.R.2.B.2.a Identify and explain literary techniques in text emphasizing: irony **9.R.1.H.1.a** Apply post-reading skills to comprehend, interpret, analyze, and evaluate text: identify and explain the relationship between the main idea and supporting details

Literary Focus

Situational Irony **Situational irony** occurs when we expect a certain thing to happen but something entirely different takes place. In "The Gift of the Magi," the ironic situation is essential to the story's meaning.

Literary Perspectives Apply the literary perspective described on page 363 as you read this story.

Reading Focus

Analyzing Details To bring stories to life, writers use details to convey information about characters, settings, and events. When you read, pay attention to such details and determine what the writer is *showing* you, rather than *telling* you, through their use.

Into Action As you read this story, record details and their location in the left-hand column of a two-column chart. In the right-hand column, explain the importance, or significance, of those details.

Story Details	Significance
1st and 6th paragraphs: saved pennies	emphasizes how hard it is for Della to save money because Jim's income is small
6th paragraph: gray cat, fence, and backyard	

Writing Focus

Think as a Reader/Writer

Find It in Your Reading O. Henry's third-person narrator makes his or her presence known in telling this story. As you read, record in your *Reader/Writer Notebook* places in the text where the narrator directly addresses the reader or offers commentary on the story.

Vocabulary

agile (AJ uhl) *adj.:* moving with ease. *Della watched an agile cat walk across a fence.*

prudence (PROO duhns) *n.:* caution; good judgment. *Della showed prudence by saving money for months for Jim's present.*

scrutiny (SKROO tuh nee) *n.:* close inspection. *Della's scrutiny of possible presents finally results in her finding the perfect gift for Jim.*

coveted (KUHV iht ihd) *v.* used as *adj.:* longed for. *The package contained a coveted gift.*

ardent (AHR duhnt) *adj.:* passionate; extremely enthusiastic. *Della and Jim share an ardent love.*

Language Coach

Word Derivations Words take on various forms depending on how they are used in sentences. For example, adding the suffix *–ly* changes the adjective form of a word into an adverb. Scan the list of words above, and take note of their parts of speech. See if you can come up with one derivation, or alternate word form, for each Vocabulary word. Use a dictionary if you need help.

Learn It Online
Meet this story through a video introduction at:
go.hrw.com
L9-361
Go

MEET THE WRITER

Learn It Online
Get more on the author's life at:
go.hrw.com L9-362 Go

O. Henry
(1862–1910)

On the Run

O. Henry, whose real name was William Sydney Porter, grew up in Greensboro, North Carolina, but he moved to Texas when he was twenty. Accused of stealing a thousand dollars from the First National Bank of Austin, where he was a teller, he panicked and fled to Central America. However, news of his wife's illness brought him back to Austin, where he was arrested, tried, and sentenced to five years in prison. Ironically, if he had not run away, Porter might have been acquitted. The bank was poorly run, and the loss of money might have been a case of mismanagement, not a crime.

A Wealth of Stories

Porter served only three years of his sentence. In prison he wrote more than a dozen stories and absorbed the underworld lore that he would use in his fiction. He may also have found his pen name there: One of the prison guards was named Orrin Henry.

Porter left prison in 1901 and went to New York. He loved the city at once, and he wrote about it and its inhabitants for the few remaining years of his life. He wrote more than six hundred stories altogether—sixty-five in 1904 alone. He once remarked:

"There are stories in everything. I've got some of my best yarns from park benches, lampposts, and newspaper stands."

Think About the Writer What do you think O. Henry meant when he said, "There are stories in everything"?

Build Background

The Magi referred to in the title of this story are the "three wise men" who, according to the Bible (Matthew 2:1–13), brought gifts of frankincense and myrrh (substances prized for their fragrance) as well as gold to the infant Jesus. Traditionally the Magi's gifts are regarded as the first Christmas presents.

Preview the Selection

Della and **Jim,** the main characters in this story, have little money, but they do have two prized possessions—and their love for each other.

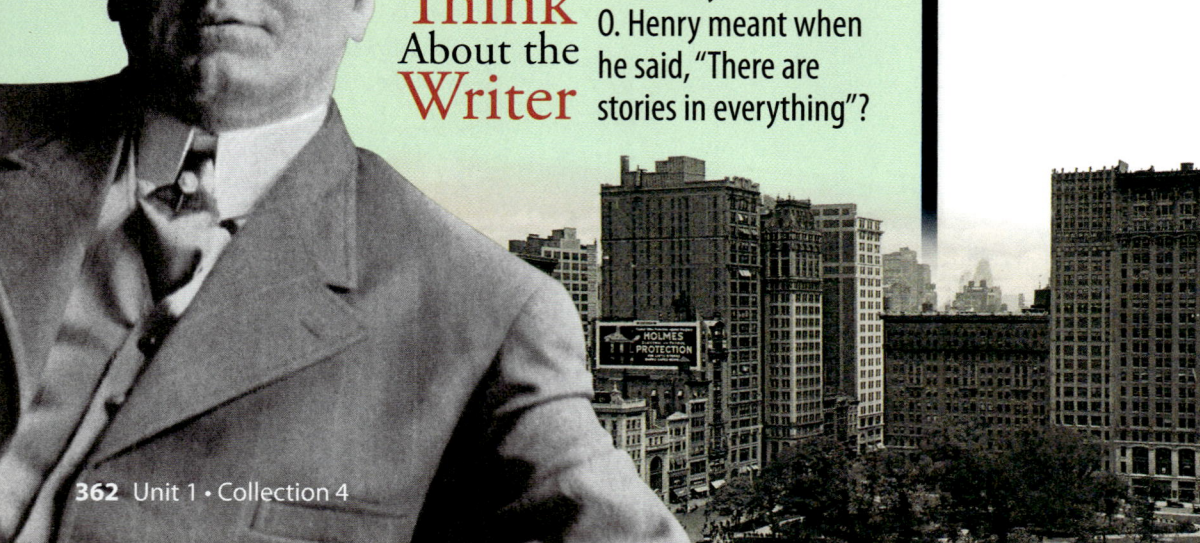

Read with a Purpose Read this story to find out what makes a gift truly valuable.

The Gift of the Magi

by **O. Henry**

One dollar and eighty-seven cents. That was all. And sixty cents of it was in pennies. Pennies saved one and two at a time by bulldozing the grocer and the vegetable man and the butcher until one's cheeks burned with the silent imputation of parsimony[1] that such close dealing implied. Three times Della counted it. One dollar and eighty-seven cents. And the next day would be Christmas.

There was clearly nothing to do but flop down on the shabby little couch and howl. So Della did it. Which instigates the moral reflection that life is made up of sobs, sniffles, and smiles, with sniffles predominating.

While the mistress of the home is gradually subsiding from the first stage to the second, take a look at the home. A furnished flat[2] at $8 per week. It did not exactly beggar description, but it certainly had that word on the lookout for the mendicancy squad.[3]

1. **imputation** (ihm pyoo TAY shuhn) **of parsimony** (PAHR suh moh nee): suggestion of stinginess.
2. **flat:** apartment.
3. **mendicancy** (MEHN duh kuhn see) **squad:** police who arrested beggars and homeless people.

Literary Perspectives

Analyzing an Author's Techniques Authors of fiction are inventors; they make up stories out of thin air. Each author has a toolbox filled with techniques that he or she can use to create interesting stories. As you read "The Gift of the Magi," notice the techniques O. Henry uses to create a one-of-a kind story. Note especially how the story's narrator interacts with readers. Why might O. Henry have chosen to have the story's narrator, who is not a story character, take on such an active role? As you read this story, use the notes at the bottom of the pages to guide you in using this literary perspective.

In the vestibule[4] below was a letter box into which no letter would go, and an electric button from which no mortal finger could coax a ring. Also appertaining[5] thereunto was a card bearing the name "Mr. James Dillingham Young."

The "Dillingham" had been flung to the breeze during a former period of prosperity when its possessor was being paid $30 per week. Now, when the income was shrunk to $20, the letters of "Dillingham" looked blurred, as though they were thinking seriously of contracting to a modest and unassuming *D*. But whenever Mr. James Dillingham Young came home and reached his flat above, he was called Jim and greatly hugged by Mrs. James Dillingham Young, already introduced to you as Della. Which is all very good. **A**

Della finished her cry and attended to her cheeks with the powder rag. She stood by the window and looked out dully at a gray cat walking a gray fence in a gray back yard. Tomorrow would be Christmas Day and she had only $1.87 with which to buy Jim a present. She had been saving every penny she could for months, with this result. Twenty dollars a week doesn't go far. Expenses had been greater than she had calculated. They always are. Only $1.87 to buy a present for Jim. Her Jim. Many a happy hour she had spent planning for something nice for him. Something fine and rare and sterling—something just a little bit near to being worthy of the honor of being owned by Jim.

There was a pier glass[6] between the windows of the room. Perhaps you have seen a pier glass in an $8 flat. A very thin and very agile person may, by observing his reflection in a rapid sequence of longitudinal strips, obtain a fairly accurate conception of his looks. Della, being slender, had mastered the art.

Suddenly she whirled from the window and stood before the glass. Her eyes were shining brilliantly, but her face had lost its color within twenty seconds. Rapidly she pulled down her hair and let it fall to its full length.

Now, there were two possessions of the James Dillingham Youngs in which they both took a mighty pride. One was Jim's gold watch that had been his father's and his grandfather's. The other was Della's hair. Had the Queen of Sheba lived in the flat across the air shaft, Della would have let her hair hang out the window some day to dry just to depreciate Her Majesty's jewels and gifts. Had King Solomon been the janitor, with all his treasures piled up in the basement, Jim would have pulled out his watch every time he passed, just to see him pluck at his beard from envy.

So now Della's beautiful hair fell about her rippling and shining like a cascade of brown waters. It reached below her knee and made itself almost a garment for her. And then she did it up again nervously and quickly. Once she faltered for a minute and stood still while a tear or two splashed on the worn red carpet.

On went her old brown jacket; on went her old brown hat. With a whirl of skirts and with the brilliant sparkle still in her eyes, she fluttered out the door and down the stairs to the street. **B**

Where she stopped, the sign read: "Mme. Sofronie. Hair Goods of All Kinds." One flight up Della ran, and collected herself, panting.

4. **vestibule** (VEHS tuh byool): small entrance hall.
5. **appertaining** (ap uhr TAYN ihng): belonging.
6. **pier glass:** tall mirror hung between two windows.

A Literary Focus Situational Irony Why is it ironic that the name on the card is "Mr. James Dillingham Young"?

Vocabulary agile (AJ uhl) *adj.:* moving with ease.

B Reading Focus Analyzing Details Contrast the description of Della's hair with that of her clothing in the last two paragraphs. What does the narrator imply about Della through this description?

Analyzing Visuals **Viewing and Interpreting** Do you think the setting and details in this painting adequately represent those of the story? Explain.

In Front of the Mirror (1827) by Georg Friedrich Kersting (1785–1847). Oil on wood (46cm x 35cm).

Madame, large, too white, chilly, hardly looked the "Sofronie."

"Will you buy my hair?" asked Della.

"I buy hair," said Madame. "Take yer hat off and let's have a sight at the looks of it." Down rippled the brown cascade.

"Twenty dollars," said Madame, lifting the mass with a practiced hand.

"Give it to me quick," said Della.

Oh, and the next two hours tripped by on rosy wings. Forget the hashed metaphor. She was ransacking the stores for Jim's present.

She found it at last. It surely had been made for Jim and no one else. There was no other like it in any of the stores, and she had turned all of them inside out. It was a platinum fob chain,[7] simple and chaste in design, properly proclaiming its value by substance alone and not by meretricious[8] ornamentation—as all good things should do. It was even worthy of The Watch. As soon as she saw it she knew that it must be Jim's. It was like him. Quietness and value—the description applied to both. Twenty-one dollars they took from her for it, and she hurried home with the 87 cents. With that chain on his watch, Jim might be properly anxious about the time in any company. Grand as the watch was, he sometimes looked at it on the sly on account of the old leather strap that he used in place of a chain. **C**

7. **fob chain:** short chain meant to be attached to a pocket watch.

8. **meretricious** (mehr uh TRIHSH uhs): attractive in a cheap, flashy way.

When Della reached home, her intoxication gave way a little to prudence and reason. She got out her curling irons and lighted the gas and went to work repairing the ravages[9] made by generosity added to love. Which is always a tremendous task, dear friends—a mammoth task.

Within forty minutes her head was covered with tiny, close-lying curls that made her look wonderfully like a truant schoolboy. She looked at her reflection in the mirror long, carefully, and critically.

"If Jim doesn't kill me," she said to herself, "before he takes a second look at me, he'll say I look like a Coney Island chorus girl. But what could I do—oh! what could I do with a dollar and eighty-seven cents?"

At 7 o'clock the coffee was made and the frying pan was on the back of the stove hot and ready to cook the chops.

Jim was never late. Della doubled the fob chain in her hand and sat on the corner of the table near the door that he always entered. Then she heard his step on the stair away down on the first flight, and she turned white for just a moment. She had a habit of saying little silent prayers about the simplest everyday things, and now she whispered: "Please God, make him think I am still pretty." **D**

The door opened and Jim stepped in and closed it. He looked thin and very serious. Poor fellow, he was only twenty-two—and to be burdened with a family! He needed a new overcoat and he was without gloves.

9. **ravages** (RAV ih juhz): terrible damage.

C Reading Focus Analyzing Details The details in this paragraph not only provide information about the fob chain, but they also reveal Della's view of Jim. What do the details reveal about her feelings?

D Reading Focus Analyzing Details What do the details in this paragraph suggest about Della's thoughts and feelings concerning her decision to cut her hair?

Vocabulary **prudence** (PROO duhns) *n.:* caution; good judgment.

Jim stepped inside the door, as immovable as a setter at the scent of quail. His eyes were fixed upon Della, and there was an expression in them that she could not read, and it terrified her. It was not anger, nor surprise, nor disapproval, nor horror, nor any of the sentiments that she had been prepared for. He simply stared at her fixedly with that peculiar expression on his face.

Della wriggled off the table and went for him.

"Jim, darling," she cried, "don't look at me that way. I had my hair cut off and sold it because I couldn't have lived through Christmas without giving you a present. It'll grow out again—you won't mind, will you? I just had to do it. My hair grows awfully fast. Say 'Merry Christmas!' Jim, and let's be happy. You don't know what a nice—what a beautiful, nice gift I've got for you."

Jim was never late. Della doubled the fob chain in her hand and sat on the corner of the table near the door that he always entered.

"You've cut off your hair?" asked Jim, laboriously, as if he had not arrived at that patent fact yet even after the hardest mental labor.

"Cut it off and sold it," said Della. "Don't you like me just as well, anyhow? I'm me without my hair, ain't I?" Jim looked about the room curiously.

"You say your hair is gone?" he said, with an air almost of idiocy.

"You needn't look for it," said Della. "It's sold, I tell you—sold and gone, too. It's Christmas Eve, boy. Be good to me, for it went for you. Maybe the hairs on my head were numbered," she went on with a sudden serious sweetness, "but nobody could ever count my love for you. Shall I put the chops on, Jim?"

Out of his trance Jim seemed quickly to wake. He enfolded his Della. For ten seconds let us regard with discreet scrutiny some inconsequential object in the other direction. Eight dollars a week or a million a year—what is the difference? A mathematician or a wit would give you the wrong answer. The Magi brought valuable gifts, but that was not among them. **E** This dark assertion will be illuminated later on.

Jim drew a package from his overcoat pocket and threw it upon the table.

"Don't make any mistake, Dell," he said, "about me. I don't think there's anything in the way of a haircut or a shave or a shampoo that could make me like my girl any less. But if you'll unwrap that package, you may see why you had me going awhile at first."

White fingers and nimble tore at the string and paper. And then an ecstatic scream of joy; and then, alas! a quick feminine change to hysterical tears and wails, necessitating the immediate employment of all the comforting powers of the lord of the flat.

For there lay The Combs—the set of combs, side and back, that Della had worshiped for long in a Broadway window. Beautiful combs, pure tortoise shell,

---

E **Literary Perspectives** **Analyzing an Author's Techniques** What effect do the narrator's observations about this scene create?

Vocabulary **scrutiny** (SKROO tuh nee) *n.:* close inspection.

with jeweled rims—just the shade to wear in the beautiful vanished hair. They were expensive combs, she knew, and her heart had simply craved and yearned over them without the least hope of possession. And now, they were hers, but the tresses that should have adorned the coveted adornments were gone. **F**

But she hugged them to her bosom, and at length she was able to look up with dim eyes and a smile and say: "My hair grows so fast, Jim!"

And then Della leaped up like a little singed cat and cried, "Oh, oh!"

Jim had not yet seen his beautiful present. She held it out to him eagerly upon her open palm. The dull precious metal seemed to flash with a reflection of her bright and ardent spirit.

"Isn't it a dandy, Jim? I hunted all over town to find it. You'll have to look at the time a hundred times a day now. Give me your watch. I want to see how it looks on it."

Instead of obeying, Jim tumbled down on the couch and put his hands under the back of his head and smiled.

"Dell," said he, "let's put our Christmas presents away and keep 'em a while. They're too nice to use just at present. I sold the watch to get the money to buy your combs. And now suppose you put the chops on."

The Magi, as you know, were wise men—wonderfully wise men—who brought gifts to the Babe in the manger. They invented the art of giving Christmas presents. Being wise, their gifts were no doubt wise ones, possibly bearing the privilege of exchange in case of duplication. And here I have lamely related to you the uneventful chronicle of two foolish children in a flat who most unwisely sacrificed for each other the greatest treasures of their house. But in a last word to the wise of these days, let it be said that of all who give gifts, these two were the wisest. Of all who give and receive gifts, such as they are wisest. Everywhere they are wisest. They are the Magi. **G**

Analyzing Visuals **Viewing and Interpreting** How would you describe the man's expression in this painting? Do you think his emotions might be similar to Jim's at this point in the story? Explain your response.

Man in a Flying Jacket (1916) by Glyn Warren Philpot (1884–1937).

F **Literary Focus** **Situational Irony** How do the events in this passage create situational irony?

G **Literary Perspectives** **Analyzing an Author's Techniques** The narrator again addresses us directly. What idea about life does he share with us?

Vocabulary **coveted** (KUHV iht ihd) *v.* used as *adj.:* longed for.
ardent (AHR duhnt) *adj.:* passionate; extremely enthusiastic.

Applying Your Skills

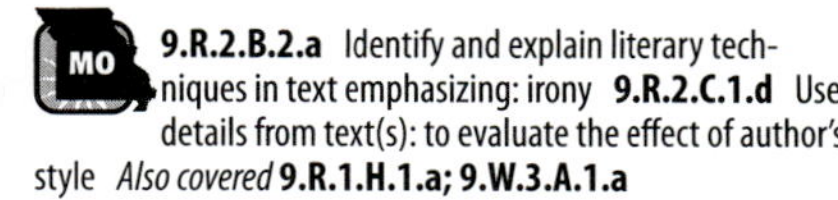

9.R.2.B.2.a Identify and explain literary techniques in text emphasizing: irony **9.R.2.C.1.d** Use details from text(s): to evaluate the effect of author's style *Also covered* **9.R.1.H.1.a; 9.W.3.A.1.a**

The Gift of the Magi

Respond and Think Critically

Reading Focus

Quick Check

1. How do Jim and Della raise the money to buy each other presents?
2. What do Jim's and Della's sacrifices tell you about their feelings for each other?

Read with a Purpose

3. What does the narrator view as the real "gift" in this story, as referred to in the title? (Note that O. Henry uses the word *gift,* not *gifts.*)

Reading Skills: Analyzing Details

4. Review the chart you filled in as you read. How have the details in the story helped you visualize and understand the characters, plot, or setting? Add a row to your chart, and write down your ideas.

Story Details	Significance
1st and 6th paragraphs: saved pennies	emphasizes how hard it is for Della to save money because Jim's income is small
6th paragraph: gray cat, fence, and backyard	

What the Details Add to the Story:

Literary Focus

Literary Analysis

5. **Analyze** Explain Della's **internal conflict,** or struggle, over her decision to cut her hair. Find examples in the text that describe this conflict.
6. **Interpret** A **paradox** is an apparent contradiction that is actually true. Explain the paradox in the story's last paragraph. In what way are Della and Jim both "foolish children" and "the wisest" of all people who give presents?
7. **Literary Perspectives** Describe the story's narrator and his "role" in the story. Do you find the use of this type of narrator effective? Why or why not?

Literary Skills: Situational Irony

8. **Analyze** O. Henry specialized in a particular type of situational irony: the surprise ending. What is your reaction to this ending? Does it seem logical, or contrived? Explain.

Literary Skills Review: Voice

9. **Analyze** A narrator's **voice** is defined by his or her speaking style, word choice, and tone (or attitude). How would you describe the narrator's voice in this story? Support your response with evidence from the text.

Writing Focus

Think as a Reader/Writer

Use It in Your Writing In this story, Jim sells his watch and buys the combs for Della. Rewrite a passage of the story using Jim as the narrator. Like O. Henry's narrator, have your narrator offer his own comments on the situation.

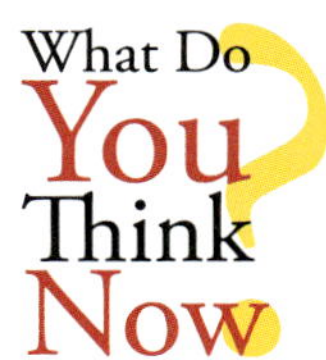

What message about life and love is conveyed by the sacrifices made by Della and Jim?

Applying Your Skills

The Gift of the Magi

Vocabulary Development

Vocabulary Check

agile
prudence
scrutiny
coveted
ardent

Choose the Vocabulary word that *best* completes each sentence.

1. He had always had an _____ desire to be an actor.
2. She displayed _____ by planning her trip well in advance.
3. They could not afford the _____ jewels displayed in the store.
4. The _____ child excelled at gymnastics.
5. The detective's _____ of the documents revealed that they were fake.

Vocabulary Skills: Diction

Diction, or word choice, can make a great difference in a piece of writing. A realistic writer might use slang. A science reporter might use precise, technical language, and a romantic person might want to be poetic.

O. Henry loved flowery and complex diction. In the first paragraph he writes:

> ". . . One's cheeks burned with the silent imputation of parsimony that such close dealing implied."

A writer who preferred a plain style might have said:

> "You blushed to think that bargaining suggested you were stingy."

Your Turn

Find three flowery or ornate sentences in the story, and rewrite each of them using plain, straightforward diction, as if you were modernizing the story for today's readers. Share your rewritten versions with the class.

Language Coach

Word Derivations Derivations of a base word are formed by adding prefixes and suffixes that change its part of speech. For example, adding *–ity* to the adjective *rare* creates the derivation *rarity,* a noun. Apply your new knowledge of the Vocabulary words to write definitions of the following derivations of those words: *agility* (n.), *prudent* (adj.), *scrutinize* (v.), *covetous* (adj.), and *ardor* (n.).

Academic Vocabulary

Talk About . . .

1. What does O. Henry imply about generosity in this story? How does the comparison of Jim and Della to the "wise men" advance the author's ideas?
2. In what way does this story associate the ideas of love and sacrifice?

MO 9.W.3.A.1.e Compose a variety of texts: including reflective writing 9.W.2.D.1.b Compose text using: writing techniques, such as imagery, humor, voice, and figurative language 9.W.2.E.1.c In written text apply: standard usage 9.R.1.G.1.a During reading, utilize strategies: to determine meaning of unknown words *Also covered* 9.R.1.E.1.c

Grammar Link

Pronoun Problems

Some pronouns in English sound exactly like other words: *its* and *it's*; *their* and *they're*; *whose* and *who's*; *your* and *you're*. Words that sound alike are not a problem when you are speaking, but they can be troublesome when you are writing. To avoid making mistakes, you must be aware of the difference between a possessive pronoun and a pronoun contraction:

- A **possessive pronoun** (such as *its*, *their*, *whose*, and *your*) shows ownership or relationship.
- A **pronoun contraction** (such as *it's*, *they're*, *who's*, and *you're*) is a shortened form of a pronoun and a verb (*it is*, *they are*, *who is*, and *you are*). A pronoun contraction *always* contains an apostrophe.

Your Turn

Choose the correct pronoun from each italicized pair in parentheses.

1. "Her eyes were shining brilliantly, but her face had lost (*its/it's*) color within twenty seconds."
2. "'You say (*your/you're*) hair is gone?'"
3. "'(*Its/It's*) Christmas Eve, boy.'"
4. "'(*Their/They're*) too nice to use just at present.'"
5. "Being wise, (*their/they're*) gifts were no doubt wise ones. . . ."

Make sure you pay careful attention when you use these pronouns in your writing.

Writing Applications Review your QuickWrite from page 360. Did you misuse any pronouns? If so, rewrite the passages to make them correct.

CHOICES

As you respond to the Choices, use these **Academic Vocabulary** words as appropriate: ambiguous, associate, imply, literal.

REVIEW

Write a Dialogue

Class Presentation With a partner, brainstorm a list of ironic situations that involve the exchange of gifts. Then, choose your best idea and write a dialogue between the characters that conveys the irony of the situation. Present your dialogue to the rest of the class.

CONNECT

Write an Editorial

Timed Writing Write a short article for your school newspaper in which you express your opinions about the giving of gifts. Why do you think people give gifts? What do you think makes a gift valuable? What associations can be made by giving a certain type of gift? Use your reflections on "The Gift of the Magi" to support your points.

EXTEND

Revisit the Story

"The Gift of the Magi" provides a glimpse of just one brief period in the characters' lives. Choose one of the characters that you met in this story and write a description of him or her ten years after the story. In what ways has the character changed or stayed the same? What is he or she doing? Where does he or she live?

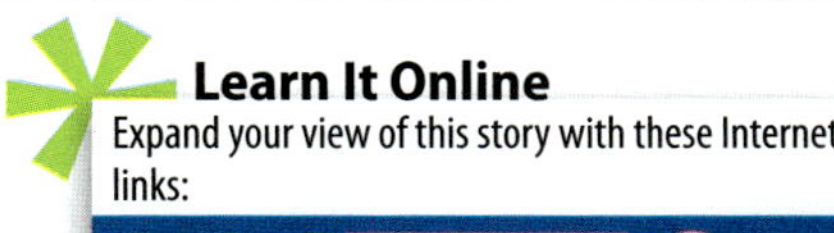

Learn It Online
Expand your view of this story with these Internet links:
go.hrw.com L9-371 Go

SHORT STORY

Preparing to Read

The Golden Kite, the Silver Wind

by **Ray Bradbury**

Great Wall of China (2004) by John Newcomb. Watercolor.

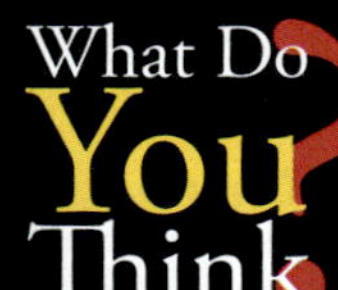

Does it ever make sense to walk away from a competition? Explain.

QuickWrite

We compete in many areas of our lives. Does competition have benefits? disadvantages? Write down your thoughts.

Use your **RWN** to complete the activities for this selection.

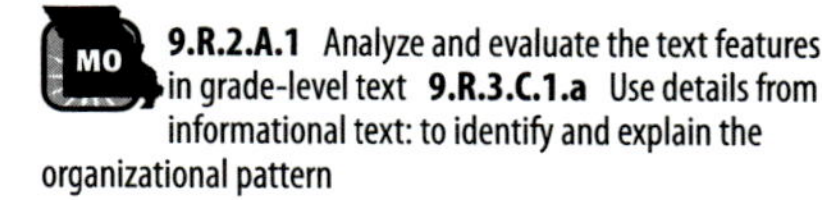

9.R.2.A.1 Analyze and evaluate the text features in grade-level text **9.R.3.C.1.a** Use details from informational text: to identify and explain the organizational pattern

Literary Focus

Allegory An **allegory** is often written to teach a lesson. The events in an allegory can be read on two levels. The events have a straightforward, literal meaning, but they also stand for something larger than themselves.

Ray Bradbury wrote "The Golden Kite, the Silver Wind" during the cold war, a long period of conflict, competition, and suspicion that existed between the United States and the Soviet Union. As you read this allegory, try to figure out the lesson Bradbury wants to teach.

Reading Focus

Identifying Causes and Effects A **cause** explains *why* something happens, and an **effect** is the *result* of something that happens. Well-crafted stories contain events that make sense because one event logically follows another. Use these guidelines to identify cause-and-effect associations in "The Golden Kite, the Silver Wind":

- Watch for words that signal cause-and-effect relationships, such as *because, for, since, so, as a result,* and *therefore.*
- Notice how characters or situations change. Ask yourself, "*Why* do they change?" "*What* event causes the change?"
- Try to predict the effects of events.

Into Action As you read, list story events on a cause-and-effect chain like the one below.

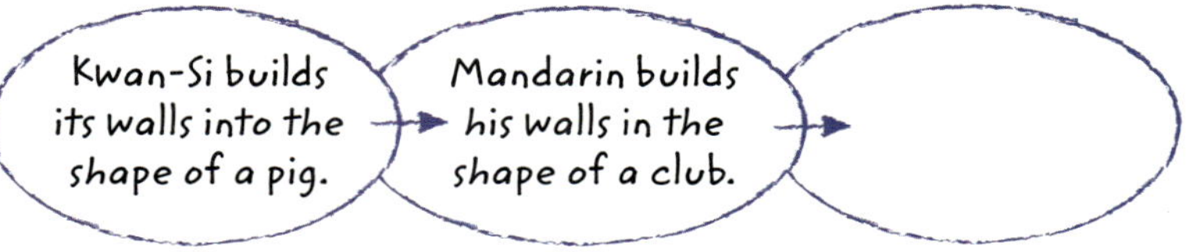

Kwan-Si builds its walls into the shape of a pig.
Mandarin builds his walls in the shape of a club.

Writing Focus

Think as a Reader/Writer

Find It in Your Reading As you read, pay attention to how Bradbury uses symbols to tell his story. Record the symbols and their meanings in your *Reader/Writer Notebook.*

Vocabulary

lurked (luhrkt) *v.:* lay in wait, ready to attack. *Demons lurked in the shadows, waiting for an innocent victim to appear.*

acclaimed (uh KLAYMD) *v.:* greeted with strong approval; applauded. *After restoring peace, the celebrated ruler was acclaimed by the townspeople.*

sustain (suh STAYN) *v.:* support; nourish. *Kites need wind to sustain them in the sky.*

monotony (muh NAHT uh nee) *n.:* lack of variety. *The ruler was bored by the monotony of his daily life.*

enduring (ehn DUR ihng) *adj.:* strong and lasting. *After the feud was ended, the two towns established an enduring relationship.*

Language Coach

Connotations Unlike **denotations,** which are literal definitions of words, **connotations** are based on the emotions and associations a word evokes. For example, the verb *lurked* brings forth feelings of danger. What connotations do the words *acclaimed* and *monotony* evoke? Write your ideas in your *Reader/Writer Notebook.*

Learn It Online
Increase your word knowledge with Word Watch:
go.hrw.com
L9-373
Go

MEET THE WRITER

Learn It Online
Get more on the author's life at:
go.hrw.com L9-374 Go

Ray Bradbury
(1920–)

Preventing the Future

When Ray Bradbury was asked about predicting future events and future technological inventions in his writing, he responded, "That's not my business. My business is to prevent the future." Throughout his career, Bradbury has written to achieve a humane world by warning readers of dangers that accompany technological advances. Whether he is writing about the self-destructive effects of our behavior or the potentially devastating effects of our reliance on science and technology, his stories "are intended as much to instruct how to prevent dooms, as to predict them."

Long After Midnight

At age twelve, Bradbury began writing stories "long after midnight" on a toy typewriter. In his early days as a writer, he wrote about ghosts and dinosaurs, growing up in the Midwest, and going to Mars. Some of these stories ended up as highly respectable "accidental novels," such as *Dandelion Wine* and *The Martian Chronicles*.

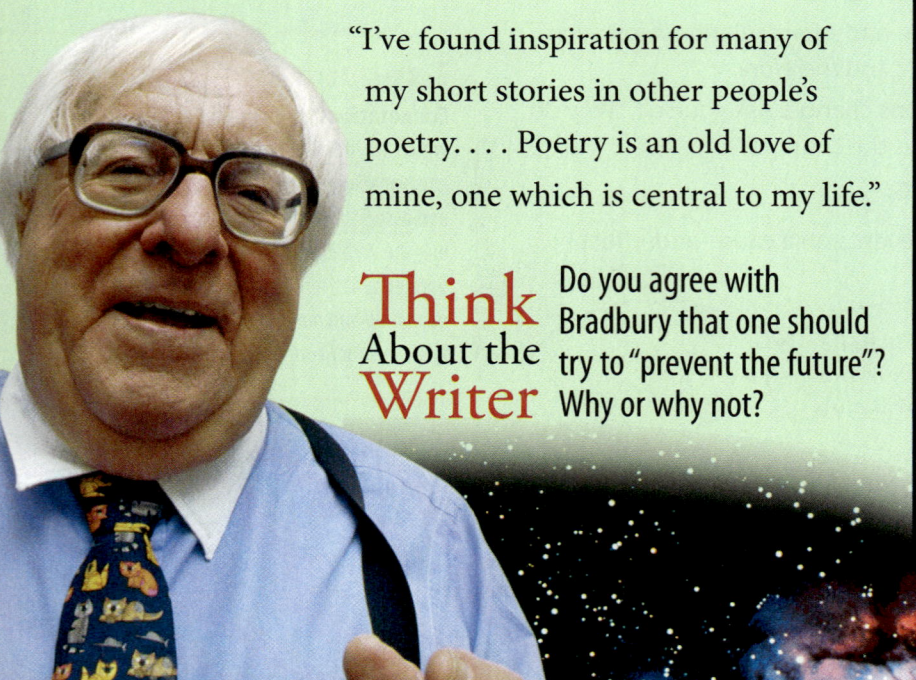

"I've found inspiration for many of my short stories in other people's poetry. . . . Poetry is an old love of mine, one which is central to my life."

Think About the Writer

Do you agree with Bradbury that one should try to "prevent the future"? Why or why not?

Build Background

"The Golden Kite, the Silver Wind" is a comment on the cold war. In 1949, at the beginning of the cold war, the Soviet Union broke the U.S. nuclear monopoly by building an atomic bomb. The United States responded by testing the first hydrogen bomb in 1952. The Soviet Union followed suit one year later. Both countries continued to develop more lethal and expensive weapon systems. Some credit the arms race for bringing about the fall of the Soviet Union's communist system—by bankrupting it.

Preview the Selection

In this story, you'll meet a **Mandarin,** or ruler, who takes extreme steps to combat his rivals in nearby kingdoms. Luckily, the **Mandarin's daughter** steps in and plays a key role in deciding the kingdom's future.

Read with a Purpose Read this story to find out what happens when trouble escalates between rival kingdoms.

Detail of wallpaper depicting funeral procession, 1780.

The Golden Kite, the Silver Wind

by **Ray Bradbury**

"In the shape of a *pig*?" cried the Mandarin.[1]

"In the shape of a pig," said the messenger, and departed.

"Oh, what an evil day in an evil year," cried the Mandarin. "The town of Kwan-Si, beyond the hill, was very small in my childhood. Now it has grown so large that at last they are building a wall."

"But why should a wall two miles away make my good father sad and angry all within the hour?" asked his daughter quietly.

"They build their wall," said the Mandarin, "in the shape of a pig! Do you see? Our own city wall is built in the shape of an orange. That pig will devour us, greedily!"

"Ah."

They both sat thinking.

Life was full of symbols and omens.[2] Demons lurked everywhere, Death swam in the wetness of an eye, the turn of a gull's wing meant rain, a fan held *so*, the tilt of a roof, and,

1. **Mandarin** (MAN duhr ihn): high-ranking government official in the Chinese empire.

2. **omens** (OH muhnz): things or events believed to be signs of future occurrences.

Vocabulary **lurked** (luhrkt) *v.:* lay in wait, ready to attack.

Analyzing Visuals **Viewing and Interpreting** In what way is this ruler similar to the Mandarin described in the story?

Scene at the court of a Chinese Manchu emperor.

yes, even a city wall was of immense importance. Travelers and tourists, caravans, musicians, artists, coming upon these two towns, equally judging the portents,[3] would say, "The city shaped like an orange? No! I will enter the city shaped like a pig and prosper, eating all, growing fat with good luck and prosperity!" **A**

The Mandarin wept. "All is lost! These symbols and signs terrify. Our city will come on evil days."

"Then," said the daughter, "call in your stonemasons[4] and temple builders. I will whisper from behind the silken screen and you will know the words."

3. **portents** (PAWR tehnts): things that warn of events about to occur.

4. **stonemasons** (STOHN may suhnz): people who build with stones.

A **Reading Focus** **Identifying Causes and Effects** What causes the Mandarin to become upset over the new wall's shape?

The old man clapped his hands despairingly. "Ho, stonemasons! Ho, builders of towns and palaces!"

The men who knew marble and granite and onyx and quartz[5] came quickly. The Mandarin faced them most uneasily, himself waiting for a whisper from the silken screen behind his throne. At last the whisper came.

"I have called you here," said the whisper.

"I have called you here," said the Mandarin aloud, "because our city is shaped like an orange, and the vile city of Kwan-Si has this day shaped theirs like a ravenous pig—"

Here the stonemasons groaned and wept. Death rattled his cane in the outer courtyard. Poverty made a sound like a wet cough in the shadows of the room.

"And so," said the whisper, said the Mandarin, "you raisers of walls must go bearing trowels[6] and rocks and change the shape of *our* city!"

The architects and masons gasped. The Mandarin himself gasped at what he had said. The whisper whispered. The Mandarin went on: "And you will change our walls into a club which may beat the pig and drive it off!" **B**

The stonemasons rose up, shouting. Even the Mandarin, delighted at the words from his mouth, applauded, stood down from his throne. "Quick!" he cried. "To work!"

When his men had gone, smiling and bustling, the Mandarin turned with great love to the silken screen. "Daughter," he whispered, "I will embrace you." There was no reply. He stepped around the screen, and she was gone.

Such modesty, he thought. She has slipped away and left me with a triumph, as if it were mine.

The news spread through the city; the Mandarin was acclaimed. Everyone carried stone to the walls. Fireworks were set off and the demons of death and poverty did not linger, as all worked together. At the end of the month the wall had been changed. It was now a mighty bludgeon[7] with which to drive pigs, boars, even lions, far away. The Mandarin slept like a happy fox every night.

"I would like to see the Mandarin of Kwan-Si when the news is learned. Such pandemonium[8] and hysteria; he will likely throw himself from a mountain! A little more of that wine, oh Daughter-who-thinks-like-a-son."

But the pleasure was like a winter flower; it died swiftly. That very afternoon the messenger rushed into the courtroom. "Oh Mandarin, disease, early sorrow, avalanches, grasshopper plagues, and poisoned well water!"

The Mandarin trembled.

"The town of Kwan-Si," said the messenger, "which was built like a pig and which animal we drove away by changing our walls to a mighty stick, has now turned triumph to winter ashes. They have built their city's walls like a great bonfire to burn our stick!"

The Mandarin's heart sickened within him, like an autumn fruit upon the ancient tree. "Oh, gods! Travelers will spurn[9] us. Tradesmen, read-

5. **marble and granite and onyx** (AHN ihks) **and quartz:** high-quality stones.
6. **trowels** (TROW uhlz): tools for laying plaster or mortar.
7. **bludgeon** (BLUHJ uhn): short club.
8. **pandemonium** (pan duh MOH nee uhm): great confusion; chaos.
9. **spurn** (spuhrn): reject someone or something for being unworthy; scorn.

B **Literary Focus Allegory** What plan does the Mandarin reveal? What does his plan reveal about the relationship between the Mandarin and the other kingdom?

Vocabulary **acclaimed** (uh KLAYMD) *v.:* greeted with strong approval; applauded.

ing the symbols, will turn from the stick, so easily destroyed, to the fire, which conquers all!"

"No," said a whisper like a snowflake from behind the silken screen.

"No," said the startled Mandarin.

"Tell my stonemasons," said the whisper that was a falling drop of rain, "to build our walls in the shape of a shining lake."

The Mandarin said this aloud, his heart warmed.

"And with this lake of water," said the whisper and the old man, "we will quench the fire and put it out forever!" **C**

The city turned out in joy to learn that once again they had been saved by the magnificent Emperor of ideas. They ran to the walls and built them nearer to this new vision, singing, not as loudly as before, of course, for they were tired, and not as quickly, for since it had taken a month to rebuild the wall the first time, they had had to neglect business and crops and therefore were somewhat weaker and poorer.

There then followed a succession of horrible and wonderful days, one in another like a nest of frightening boxes.

"Oh, Emperor," cried the messenger, "Kwan-Si has rebuilt their walls to resemble a mouth with which to drink all our lake!"

"Then," said the Emperor, standing very close to his silken screen, "build our walls like a needle to sew up that mouth!"

"Emperor!" screamed the messenger. "They make their walls like a sword to break your needle!"

The Emperor held, trembling, to the silken screen. "Then shift the stones to form a scabbard to sheathe that sword!"[10]

"Mercy," wept the messenger the following morn, "they have worked all night and shaped their walls like lightning which will explode and destroy that sheath!" **D**

Sickness spread in the city like a pack of evil dogs. Shops closed. The population, working now steadily for endless months upon the changing of the walls, resembled Death himself, clattering his white bones like musical instruments in the wind. Funerals began to appear in the streets, though it was the middle of summer, a time when all should be tending and harvesting. The Mandarin fell so ill that he had his bed drawn up by the silken screen and there he lay, miserably giving his architectural orders. The voice behind the screen was weak now, too, and faint, like the wind in the eaves. **E**

"Kwan-Si is an eagle. Then our walls must be a net for that eagle. They are a sun to burn our net. Then we build a moon to eclipse[11] their sun!"

Like a rusted machine, the city ground to a halt.

At last the whisper behind the screen cried out:

"In the name of the gods, send for Kwan-Si!"

Upon the last day of summer the Mandarin Kwan-Si, very ill and withered away, was carried into our Mandarin's courtroom by four starving footmen. The two mandarins were

---

10. **scabbard . . . sword:** a scabbard is a case for a sword's blade. To sheathe a sword means to put it in a case.

11. **eclipse** (ih KLIHPS): here, conceal from view; overshadow.

C **Reading Focus** **Identifying Causes and Effects** What causes the Mandarin of Kwan-Si to literally change the shape of his kingdom's wall? What does the other Mandarin do in response?

D **Reading Focus** **Identifying Causes and Effects** What causes and effects are revealed in the series of exchanges between the messenger and the Mandarin?

E **Literary Focus** **Allegory** Bradbury exaggerates a simple situation in order to make a point. What point is he making about the competition between the two kingdoms?

propped up, facing each other. Their breaths fluttered like winter winds in their mouths. A voice said:

"Let us put an end to this."

The old men nodded.

"This cannot go on," said the faint voice. "Our people do nothing but rebuild our cities to a different shape every day, every hour. They have no time to hunt, to fish, to love, to be good to their ancestors and their ancestors' children."

"This I admit," said the mandarins of the towns of the Cage, the Moon, the Spear, the Fire, the Sword, and this, that, and other things. **F**

"Carry us into the sunlight," said the voice.

The old men were borne out under the sun and up a little hill. In the late summer breeze a few very thin children were flying dragon kites in all the colors of the sun, and frogs and grass, the color of the sea, and the color of coins and wheat.

The first Mandarin's daughter stood by his bed.

"See," she said.

"Those are nothing but kites," said the two old men.

"But what is a kite on the ground?" she said. "It is nothing. What does it need to sustain it and make it beautiful and truly spiritual?"

"The wind, of course!" said the others.

"And what do the sky and the wind need to make *them* beautiful?"

"A kite, of course—many kites, to break the monotony, the sameness of the sky. Colored kites, flying!"

"So," said the Mandarin's daughter. "You, Kwan-Si, will make a last rebuilding of your

---

F **Reading Focus** **Identifying Causes and Effects** Why are the two leaders ready to put an end to their conflict?

Vocabulary **sustain** (suh STAYN) *v.:* support; nourish.
monotony (muh NAHT uh nee) *n.:* lack of variety.

HISTORY LINK

The Great Wall

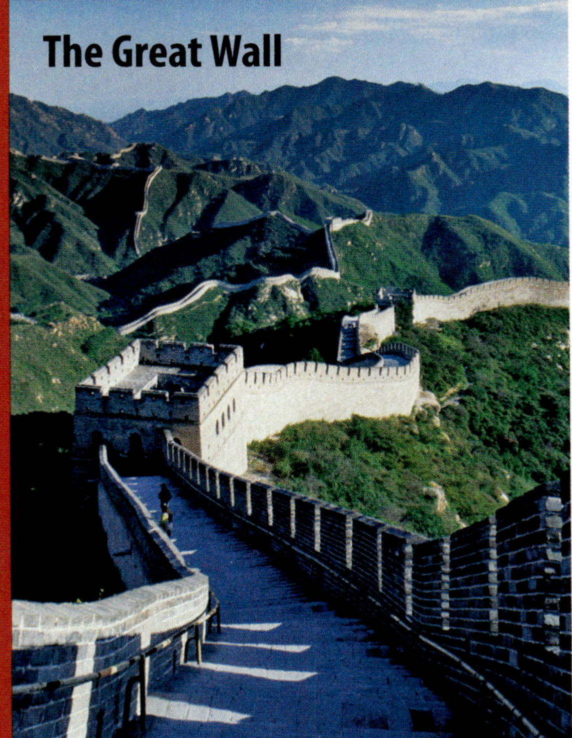

The Great Wall of China is the longest structure ever built, running about 4,500 miles, including loops and branches. The wall was built about two thousand years ago with the intention of protecting China's border from invasions. In the third century B.C., China's first emperor, Shi Huangdi of the Qin dynasty (221–206 B.C.), conceived of the wall. The emperor connected many existing defensive walls into a single protective wall.

Most of what is now called the Great Wall was constructed during the Ming dynasty, which began in 1368. Many of the earlier walls had fallen and the Ming government began building major parts of the wall in response to Mongol attacks in the late 1400s.

Ask Yourself

How are the Mandarin's walls in the story similar to and different from the Great Wall?

Analyzing Visuals **Viewing and Interpreting** In what way does the scene in this painting capture the peace that the formerly warring towns in the story now enjoy?

Illustration of the Great Walls of Beijing (c. 1775) by Antonio Rancati.

town to resemble nothing more nor less than the wind. And we shall build like a golden kite. The wind will beautify the kite and carry it to wondrous heights. And the kite will break the sameness of the wind's existence and give it purpose and meaning. One without the other is nothing. Together, all will be beauty and cooperation and a long and enduring life." **G**

Whereupon the two mandarins were so overjoyed that they took their first nourishment in days, momentarily were given strength, embraced, and lavished praise upon each other, called the Mandarin's daughter a boy, a man, a stone pillar, a warrior, and a true and unforgettable son. Almost immediately they parted and hurried to their towns, calling out and singing, weakly but happily.

And so, in time, the towns became the Town of the Golden Kite and the Town of the Silver Wind. And harvestings were harvested and business tended again, and the flesh returned, and disease ran off like a frightened jackal. And on every night of the year the inhabitants in the Town of the Kite could hear the good clear wind sustaining them. And those in the Town of the Wind could hear the kite singing, whispering, rising, and beautifying them.

"So be it," said the Mandarin in front of his silken screen.

G **Literary Focus** **Allegory** What larger idea about the world might Bradbury be suggesting through the resolution to this conflict?

Vocabulary **enduring** (ehn DUR ihng) *adj.:* strong and lasting.

Applying Your Skills

9.R.2.A.1 Analyze and evaluate the text features in grade-level text 9.R.2.C.1.b Use details from text(s): to analyze character, plot, setting, point of view 9.R.3.C.1.a Use details from informational text: to identify and explain the organizational pattern *Also covered* 9.W.3.A.1.a; 9.R.1.G.1.a

The Golden Kite, the Silver Wind

Respond and Think Critically

Reading Focus

Quick Check

1. What prompts the Mandarin to have the city walls rebuilt? Why does the town of Kwan-Si retaliate?
2. What role does the Mandarin's daughter play in the story?

Read with a Purpose

3. What happens when the two kingdoms continually try to outdo each other? How do they resolve their conflict?

Reading Skills: Identifying Causes and Effects

4. Complete your cause-and-effect chain. Then, write a summary of the story's main events, based on the events you listed.

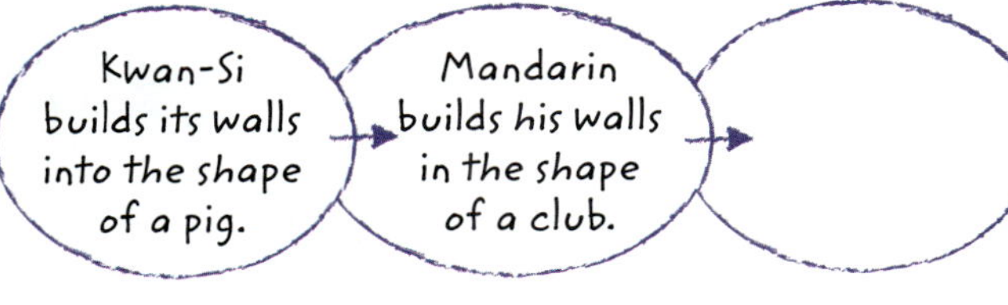
Kwan-Si builds its walls into the shape of a pig.
Mandarin builds his walls in the shape of a club.

Summary:

Vocabulary Check

Match each Vocabulary word with its definition.

5. **lurked**	a. applauded
6. **acclaimed**	b. lasting and strong
7. **sustain**	c. lack of variety
8. **monotony**	d. lay in wait
9. **enduring**	e. nourish; support

Literary Focus

Literary Analysis

10. **Interpret** Referring to the kite in the wind, the Mandarin's daughter says, "One without the other is nothing." Explain her statement, and tell how it helped the kingdoms achieve peace.

Literary Skills: Allegory

11. **Compare** How can this story be seen as an allegory about the cold war? (See Build Background on page 374.) Cite details from the story to support your response.
12. **Extend** Now that the cold war is over, do you think Bradbury's allegory still has something to teach us today? Explain.

Literary Skills Review: Setting

13. **Evaluate** Bradbury's story is set in ancient China. Do you think it would be as effective if it took place in another place and time? Why or why not?

Writing Focus

Think as a Reader/Writer

Use It in Your Writing Read through your notes on the symbols used in the story. Describe the symbols and explain their meaning. Would this story have been as effective without the use of symbols? Tell why or why not.

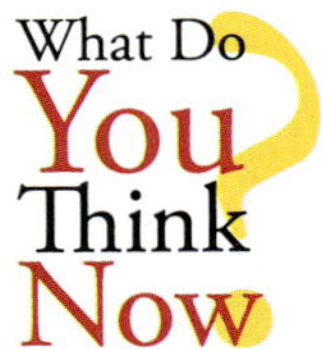
What Do You Think Now

Why is it so difficult for the mandarins to recognize what is happening in their kingdoms and to put an end to the rivalry?

COMPARING TEXTS

Comparing Themes Across Genres

CONTENTS

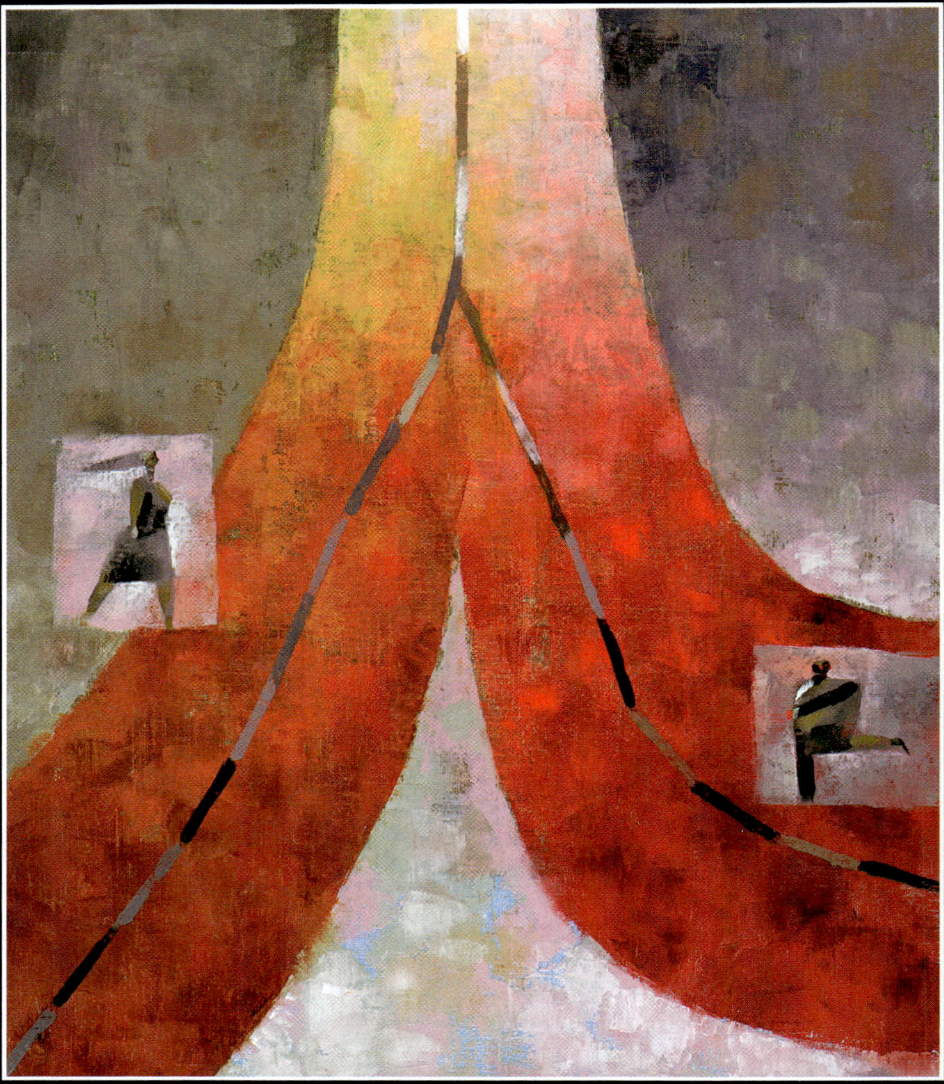

Two Roads Join by Todd Davidson. Oil painting.

Can a single decision change the course of our lives?

QuickWrite

Think of a big decision that high school students might face. What are the possible consequences—either positive or negative—of this decision? Would these consequences have lasting effects?

Preparing to Read

Airport / The Road Not Taken / Untitled Film Still #48

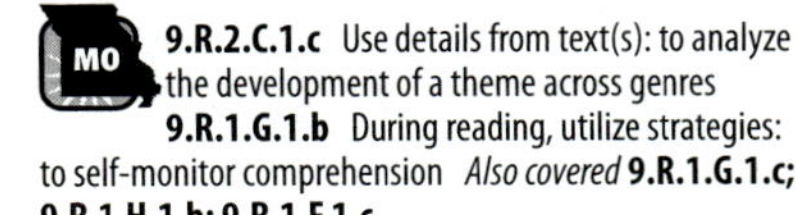

9.R.2.C.1.c Use details from text(s): to analyze the development of a theme across genres **9.R.1.G.1.b** During reading, utilize strategies: to self-monitor comprehension *Also covered* **9.R.1.G.1.c; 9.R.1.H.1.b; 9.R.1.F.1.c**

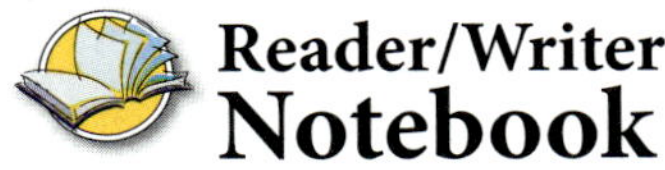

Reader/Writer Notebook

Use your **RWN** to complete the activities for these selections.

Literary Focus

Theme The **theme** of a work is the central idea, or insight, about life that it reveals. Because writers don't usually state a work's theme directly, you must identify it by considering various elements of the work, such as the use of symbols and irony. To analyze symbols, ask yourself, "What do the symbols represent, and why are they important?" To analyze irony, ask, "What does the surprising turn of events lead me to understand?" Keep in mind that there is no single way to state a work's theme, and readers may have different opinions about what the theme of a work is.

Reading Focus

Reading Actively When you **read actively,** you use skills such as making and evaluating predictions, re-reading, reading aloud, and questioning. Try using these skills with the works that follow.

Into Action Note the reading skill you are using, and record your predictions, questions, and observations on a chart like this one.

Airport	*The Road Not Taken*
Questioning: Why would Samir have trouble understanding the menu?	**Questioning:** Why is the wood described as "yellow"?
Making Predictions:	

Writing Focus

Think as a Reader/Writer

Find It in Your Reading Both poets and fiction writers use **imagery**—language that appeals to the five senses—to help convey thoughts, feelings, and experiences as well as to help express their themes. As you read each work, record the images that you find most vivid in your *Reader/Writer Notebook*.

Vocabulary

Airport

agitation (aj uh TAY shuhn) *n.:* state of being troubled or worried; excitement. *Filled with agitation, Hoda could not sleep and had woken up early.*

turmoil (TUR moyl) *n.:* confusion; disturbance. *Hoda's turmoil was the result of the hard choices she faced.*

appease (uh PEEZ) *v.:* make calm or quiet; satisfy. *Samir bought a cup of coffee, not to appease his thirst but to fill the time.*

trepidation (trehp uh DAY shuhn) *n.:* fear; nervous dread. *Concerned that Hoda would never marry, her parents viewed their daughter's future with trepidation.*

articulate (ahr TIHK yuh layt) *v.:* clearly express. *Hoda understood English, and she could articulate her ideas confidently.*

Language Coach

Oral Fluency The word *deliberate* can be pronounced two different ways. When the word is used as a verb, the last syllable is pronounced "ayt." When the word is used as an adjective, the last syllable is pronounced "iht." Which word on the list above follows that same pattern of pronunciation? Find the word in a dictionary to verify your guess.

Learn It Online

Elevate your vocabulary skills with Word Watch:

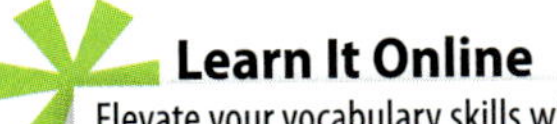

go.hrw.com L9-383

MEET THE WRITERS

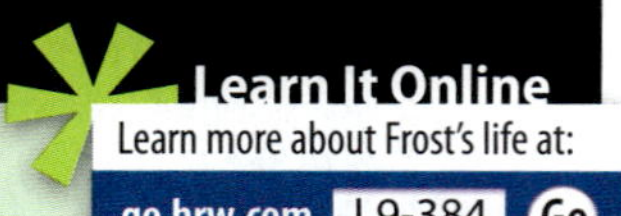

Learn It Online
Learn more about Frost's life at:
go.hrw.com L9-384 Go

Pauline Kaldas

(1961–)

Border Crossings

Born in Egypt, Pauline Kaldas immigrated to the United States when she was eight years old. In her teaching as an assistant professor of English at Hollins University in Virginia, she focuses on multicultural and immigrant literature and Arab women writers. Kaldas has published a poetry collection and a travel memoir, and she has also co-edited an anthology of Arab American fiction. She remarks, "For me the writing comes first and the subject matter comes second. In a sense, by virtue of my immigrant experience, I was handed my subject matter. Where the challenge is for me is in the writing."

Robert Frost

(1874–1963)

A Master Poet

Known in high school as the class poet, Robert Frost attended college on and off, never earning a degree. To make a living, he worked as a teacher, editor, and shoemaker, and also ran a farm, struggling all the while to get his poems published. Ultimately Frost became hugely popular. He accumulated numerous awards and became a beloved American figure. Born in San Francisco, California, Frost eventually settled in New England. In his poems, he conveys the harsh beauty associated with rural New England and creates vivid New England characters. As in "The Road Not Taken," his direct, economical style can be misleading. His poems are often ironic and ambiguous. In Frost's view, "Poetry provides the one permissible way of saying one thing and meaning another."

For more on Frost, see pages 639 and 660.

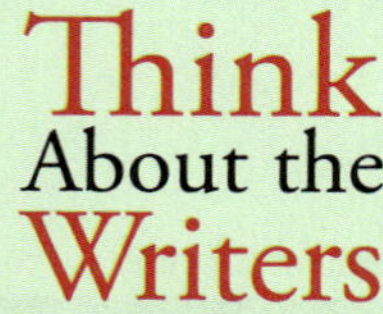

What do the comments by the authors about writing suggest about their attitude toward their work?

Preview the Selections

In alternating passages, "Airport" tells the story of **Samir,** an Egyptian immigrant to the United States, and **Hoda,** an Egyptian woman—two characters who are seeking better lives for themselves.

In "The Road Not Taken," the speaker—coming upon two roads in the woods—faces a difficult choice.

The photograph *Untitled Film Still #48* provides a different way of exploring the themes of choices and journeys.

SHORT STORY

Airport

by **Pauline Kaldas**

Read with a Purpose

Read this story to discover what motivates two strangers to plan a life together.

Build Background

The idea that marriage should be based on romantic love and that people should choose their spouses is a modern notion. In most societies in the past, a person's family arranged his or her marriage based on social and economic factors. In traditional societies today, such as the Egyptian culture depicted in "Airport," arranged marriages are still customary.

He paced the airport waiting room, his steps marking a path in the carpet between the rows of seats. At first those sitting down looked up at this man who could not hold his feet still like the rest of them and curb his agitation. After a while, some returned to their own thoughts or families. A few kept their gaze on his coming and going, perhaps to ease their own turmoil. Even after he left, a few repeated his path with their eyes as if permanently held by the ghost of his movement. **A**

Samir was about five feet seven, with black hair cut short because otherwise it would frizz and wave. His nose was rather large, but his eyes compensated, their brown glimmer and long lashes giving his face an unexpected beauty. He was slender, his physique almost that of a young boy. But around the middle a slight roundness was beginning, probably because for the past year he had been going to a Chinese restaurant and ordering pupu platters for dinner. Once, his coworkers had talked him into going out after work. He was frightened at the prospect of having to understand the menu and perhaps not having enough money. When they ordered something to be shared, he was relieved. The assortment of fried foods soothed him. Although some of the tastes were unfamiliar, he had grown up with the smell of food frying. His mother fried fish, potatoes, cauliflower, so now he could eat with a certain security. He asked a couple of times what this was called, his tongue moving silently in his mouth to repeat the words *pupu platter*. After that, occasionally, he would go to the restaurant alone and order the same thing. He didn't catch the odd twist of the waiter's face, and he ate confidently.

It was eleven o'clock Sunday morning. He had woken early, a little before six, despite having stayed up late cleaning his small apartment thoroughly. Glancing at his watch, he noted there was still another hour before the plane was due. He stretched his pacing out of the waiting area to look at one of the arrival terminals. Flight 822 from Egypt via Switzerland.

A **Reading Focus** **Questioning** Why is this character so nervous?

Vocabulary **agitation** (aj uh TAY shuhn) *n.:* state of being troubled or worried; excitement.
turmoil (TUR moyl) *n.:* confusion; disturbance.

Yes, the arrival time was still twelve o'clock P.M. He turned his gaze around the airport until his eyes fell on some tables and chairs that he hoped were part of a coffee shop. He headed over, lengthening his stride a little. Ordering the coffee, he was tempted to get something to eat but was afraid his stomach would turn, so he settled at a small table with the Styrofoam cup awkwardly balanced in his hand. It was too hot to drink so he could only sit, the sounds of the airport mingling together till they became a steady hum in his head. **B**

She stared at the empty suitcase on her bed. How do you pack for moving to another country? she thought. She circled the room, stopping to sift through open dresser drawers, to flip through clothes hung in the closet, to slightly rearrange items on top of dressers, only to find herself back in front of an empty suitcase.

Her mother appeared at the door. "Hoda, you haven't done anything! The suitcase is empty."

Hoda shifted her eyes to the suitcase as if seeing its open cavity for the first time. "I will. I'm just organizing," Hoda replied to appease her mother.

"You leave early in the morning," her mother said as if ringing a bell.

As her mother stepped out of the room, Hoda sat on the bed, giving her back to the suitcase. She was an attractive woman, but not in the traditional Egyptian sense. Her body was slim without the usual roundness around the hips and legs, probably because she insisted on walking everywhere. Taxis are too expensive and buses are too crowded, she argued. Her black hair was cut straight just above her shoulders. She never put anything in it, didn't use henna,[1] and wore it simply as it was. Her mother had tried to coax her a little, to style it in some way, but after all these years, she knew it was a useless effort. Her face held the energy of youth, and people often found themselves looking at her. It was her mouth that was her most prominent feature. Although it was considered slightly large, there was still something captivating about it, the way her smile pulled you in and made you listen to whatever she was saying.

It was eleven o'clock Saturday morning. She had woken early, a little before six, despite having stayed up late saying good-bye to friends and relatives. The first thing she did was call the airport to check the departure time. Flight 822 to Boston via Switzerland. Yes, it was leaving at two o'clock A.M. in the morning and due to arrive at twelve o'clock P.M. American Eastern time. After she hung up, she made herself a cup of coffee although she rarely drank it. The traffic outside began its erratic rhythm of fitful stops and starts accentuated by the loud honks of impatient drivers. She sat in the kitchen almost in a trance until her ears tuned the noise outside to a steady hum in her head. **C**

Would she be on the plane? It was his brother who had written with the flight information. He had received one letter from her parents, accepting his proposal and giving their blessing. Everything else, signing the church marriage papers, processing the immigration documents, had been done through his brother. And it had taken longer than expected, almost

1. **henna** (HEHN uh): reddish brown dye made from the leaves of the henna plant.

B Reading Focus **Making Predictions** For whom do you think Samir is waiting?

Vocabulary **appease** (uh PEEZ) *v.:* make calm or quiet; satisfy.

C Reading Focus **Re-reading** Re-read this passage and the third paragraph of the story. Then, compare and contrast the details in the two passages. What do these details suggest about Samir and Hoda?

Analyzing Visuals

Viewing and Interpreting
In what ways does the subject of this photograph seem similar to the character of Samir?

two years of filling out forms, presenting proof of this and that, till he felt his life had transformed into a sheaf of papers. He sometimes forgot the purpose behind all this, that it would eventually lead to marrying someone whom he didn't know. At times, fear chimed through Samir's body. Perhaps he should've listened when his brother had urged him to return to Egypt, to choose for himself. But Samir was reluctant to leave his new job. **D**

In the meantime, all he could do was wait and work. He had arrived in this country with little money and little education. The only school that would accept him in Egypt was the agricultural college. For two years, he sat and listened to professors lecturing about crops, soil, irrigation till his mind blurred and he knew if he didn't leave, he would end up another man with a college degree selling cigarettes in a kiosk.[2] He was not a lucky person, but he entered the green card[3] lottery anyway. It was free and they only asked for your name and address. The rumor said fifty thousand each year would be chosen to come to America. And he had heard of people who won and actually went. What a strange country, he thought, to make its immigration decisions through a lottery. He curbed his joy when he received notification that he had been selected. It was clear that the process would be long. Now came the applications to be filled, the requests for documents, the interview which, in halting English, he felt sure would eliminate him, but the end was indeed permission to immigrate, to chance his life in another country. **E**

Would he be there? What was she doing going to another country to marry a man she didn't even know? Her parents had helped convince her that this would be best for her. "He's from a good family and after all he's in America and not many people can get there." "Besides," her father added, "this America is more suited to your independent nature." "Yes," her mother added, in a resigned tone, "and they like educated people there." It was true that in Egypt

2. **kiosk** (KEE ahsk): small structure, used as a newsstand or booth, which is open at one or more sides.
3. **green card:** document granting a foreigner permission to live and work in the United States.

D **Literary Focus** **Theme** This is the first reference in the story to choices. What choices were made on Samir's behalf?

E **Literary Focus** **Theme** How is Samir's immigration to the United States both a result of choice and of chance?

Hoda often felt like a piece of rough wood that needed to be sanded down. No one understood her desire to continue for a master's degree in chemistry. "You have a college degree," her parents argued, "and you're twenty-one now. Look for a husband. It's time to settle down." When a young man approached her parents to propose marriage, she accepted, thinking this would keep people quiet. But she had been naive. The young man was insistent that she quit school and devote her time to setting up their new home. Finally their heated arguments led to a breakup of the engagement, and not surprisingly this only worsened her reputation. She knew her parents feared that now she would never marry.

When the proposal from America came, she hesitated. She had one more year until she completed her degree. But everyone assured her the paperwork would allow her enough time to finish. And they were right. Things dragged out for so long that at times she forgot she was engaged or that she was going to America. So when Samir's brother appeared at their door two weeks ago with the plane tickets and the approved visa,[4] her head spun like a top. **F**

He had arrived with some hope and trepidation. The process had been difficult, but each time he pictured himself standing inside the kiosk, his body trapped and his arms reaching for cigarettes, he was able to push himself and do what was requested. Surely in America there would be more possibilities. But that first year, America kept him dog-paddling and gasping for air. The language confounded him, quick mutterings with hardly any gestures or even a direct look. He took an English class, but the rules of grammar and the purposely slow pronunciation of the teacher did little to improve his understanding. He found a job washing dishes in a restaurant where contact was limited to *Good morning, How are you* and *See you later*. When the radio in the kitchen broke one day, followed by the mumbled swearing of the cook, he offered to fix it. The cook gave him a perplexed look and tossed the radio to him with a *Go ahead*. The dishes piled up a bit as he fiddled with the switches, found a knife to use as a screwdriver, and then managed to make the music reemerge. After that, other radios and sometimes clocks, telephones, or calculators were handed to him. Most of the time he could fix them, and the added conversations made him more confident.

Surely in America there would be more possibilities. But that first year, America kept him dog-paddling and gasping for air.

Fixing things was the one thing he could do. It was like a sixth sense to him. When he was a child, if something broke at home, they couldn't afford to buy another one. Since it was already not working, his family figured there was no harm in letting him fiddle with it, and so he learned how everything was put together, how to take it apart, and how to reconnect the parts so it worked. He was most

4. **visa** (VEE zuh): certificate granting official approval to enter a country.

F **Literary Focus Theme** What choices of Hoda's are revealed in the last two paragraphs? Why does she make those choices?

Vocabulary **trepidation** (trehp uh DAY shuhn) *n.:* fear; nervous dread.

comfortable staring at the inside of a machine with its intricate weaving of wires and knobs. But he had never perceived his ability as a skill; it was simply an instinct. G

When the restaurant manager caught wind of his reputation, he approached him with a request to fix his stereo, adding, *I took it to the shop but they couldn't do anything.*

He spent a day at the manager's house, surrounded by components with wires stretching like a web of animal tails. Every time the manager walked by, Samir saw him shaking his head with a look of doubt clouding his face. By the end of the day, the tails had been untangled, and when Samir pressed the power button, the music spread through the house. *Thank you, thank you,* the manager repeated, and Samir stood puzzled by how a boss could lower himself to thank an employee. The manager sent Samir to the same shop that couldn't fix his stereo. He was hired on a trial basis, but he proved himself quickly. He had found his niche[5] in this country that could make many things, but didn't know how to fix what it broke.

It wasn't that she didn't want to get married. She had always hoped her life would be with a partner, and at some point she expected to have children. But she knew she didn't want the life she saw around her. Women dragging their chores like chains, cleaning house, washing clothes, cooking food, all for others. She had watched friends marry at eighteen and nineteen, sometimes even men of their own choosing whom they loved. Within the first year, their spirits dissipated like sugar crystals in water. It frightened her to envision her life in this way, her days filled with the care of home and family, her body growing heavy with the idleness of her brain.

That is why, against everyone's understanding, she enrolled in the master's program in chemistry. She was one of two women, but the other was there only to pass the time until she found a husband. Her family had determined that it would be more respectable for her to continue her studies than to remain at home waiting. But for Hoda, it was a different matter. Chemistry had caught her fancy and it was the only thing she wanted to do. As a child her mother had to pull her out of the kitchen, where she would find her sitting cross-legged on the floor with a bowl in front of her, mixing starch and water, baking soda and vinegar, or some new combination. "Just to see what would happen," she answered her mother's shouting inquiries. Finally, her mother banished her from the kitchen. The result, aside from Hoda never learning how to cook, was that she began borrowing chemistry books from her friend's older brother who was studying at the university and moved the experiments to more secluded parts of the house. She struggled through the master's program, where the male students laughed directly at her and the professors didn't take her seriously. Still she persisted and gained high marks. It was an act of faith since she knew the only job Egypt would give her would be in a lab analyzing blood and urine samples.

Perhaps that's why she accepted the roll of dice that would lead her to America. There might be a chance there of having a real job, of doing research, of working with someone who would take her seriously, not turn everything back around to her femininity. Her English was strong since all the sciences were taught in

5. **niche** (nihch): position or situation that is especially appropriate for a person.

G **Reading Focus** **Questioning** How might Samir's newfound confidence help him adjust to life in America?

Analyzing Visuals

Viewing and Interpreting Is this woman how you picture Hoda? Why or why not?

English, and she had occasionally had American or British professors with whom she had no trouble communicating. What concerned her was this man who had extended his proposal across the ocean. What kind of man would marry a woman without even seeing her, would choose as if picking a number out of a hat? **H**

After two years in America and turning thirty, Samir knew he had to get married. And he also knew he needed a certain kind of woman, not one who would lean on him, who would expect to be at home while he worked. He needed someone who could stand in this world next to him, perhaps even lead him a little. He sent his request to his brother: a woman who was educated, who knew English well, who wanted to work; a woman who could swim in deep water, he added. His brother argued with him that he was asking for trouble, that such women should remain unmarried. But Samir was insistent and said he would accept nothing else.

Hoda was twenty-five years old. If she didn't marry soon, she would be looked on with either pity or suspicion. And if she remained in Egypt and married the next man who proposed, her life would inevitably fall into the repeated pattern of other women. She couldn't articulate what she wanted, only that it was not here. Hoda caught her breath like the reins of a horse and began to fill the suitcases. She counted the number of dresses, skirts, and pants she had, then divided by half: that's how many she would take. Then she proceeded to do the same with all other items. Within a few hours the two permitted suitcases were filled. **I**

H **Literary Focus** **Theme** What does this paragraph suggest about the choices the two characters make and the risks involved?

Vocabulary **articulate** (ahr TIHK yuh layt) *v.:* clearly express.

I **Literary Focus** **Theme** Why might the author have chosen to end the story by describing how Hoda decides what to pack? What does this detail convey?

Applying Your Skills

Airport

9.R.2.C.1.c Use details from text(s): to analyze the development of a theme across genres 9.R.1.G.1.b During reading, utilize strategies: to self-monitor comprehension 9.W.3.A.1.e Compose a variety of texts: including reflective writing 9.R.1.G.1.a During reading, utilize strategies: to determine meaning of unknown words *Also covered* 9.R.2.C.1.b

Respond and Think Critically

Reading Focus

Quick Check

1. What important decisions do Samir and Hoda face?
2. What are both Samir and Hoda hoping to find in life?

Read with a Purpose

3. Why do Samir and Hoda consent to marry?

Reading Skills: Reading Actively

4. Review the chart you filled in as you read the story. Which skills helped you understand the story? Was one skill more helpful than the others? Add a row to the bottom of the "Airport" column, and record your evaluation.

Vocabulary Check

Tell whether each statement is true (T) or false (F). Vocabulary words appear in boldface.

5. **Turmoil** over a decision might cause a person to feel **agitation**.
6. You can **appease** hunger by eating a healthful meal.
7. When people feel **trepidation,** they are calm and happy.
8. When speakers **articulate** their ideas, they confuse the audience.

Literary Focus

Literary Analysis

9. **Speculate** Do you think Samir and Hoda's marriage will be a happy or unhappy one? Explain.
10. **Compare** What do the qualities Samir seeks in a wife reveal about his attitude toward women and marriage? Compare his views with those of Egyptian society, as presented in the story.
11. **Evaluate** The author tells us about Samir and Hoda in alternating passages. Explain whether you think the story's structure is effective, using details from the text to support your ideas.

Literary Skills: Theme

12. **Interpret** What does this story have to say about the choices we make, the decisions we leave up to others, and the role of chance in our lives? As you respond, consider why the author leaves the story's conclusion ambiguous, or open-ended.
13. **Evaluate** Do you think "Airport" is an effective title for this story? Does that title add to your understanding of the story's theme? Explain.

Literary Skills Review: Conflict

14. **Analyze** Make a list of the **external conflicts,** or outward struggles, that Hoda faces. Then, identify Hoda's main **internal conflict,** or inward struggle. How do her external conflicts contribute to her internal conflict?

Writing Focus

Think as a Reader/Writer

Use It in Your Writing Write a descriptive paragraph about a person waiting in an airport or a train or bus station. Why is the person waiting? What is the person doing, thinking, and feeling? Use vivid imagery to convey your ideas.

POEM

The Road Not Taken

by **Robert Frost**

Read with a Purpose

Read this poem to learn how a simple walk through the woods takes on a larger meaning for the speaker.

Preparing to Read for this selection is on page 383.

Build Background

"The Road Not Taken" is one of Frost's most famous poems. Many critics think it is also widely misinterpreted. Frost himself said, "It's a tricky poem, very tricky," and he remarked, "I bet not one reader in ten knows what 'The Road Not Taken' is about." Contradictory and ambiguous, this poem may leave a lasting impression on you.

Two roads diverged° in a yellow wood,
And sorry I could not travel both
And be one traveler, long I stood
And looked down one as far as I could
To where it bent in the undergrowth;

Then took the other, as just as fair,
And having perhaps the better claim,
Because it was grassy and wanted wear; **A**
Though as for that the passing there
Had worn them really about the same,

And both that morning equally lay
In leaves no step had trodden black. **B**
Oh, I kept the first for another day!
Yet knowing how way leads on to way,
I doubted if I should ever come back.

I shall be telling this with a sigh
Somewhere ages and ages hence:
Two roads diverged in a wood, and I—
I took the one less traveled by,
And that has made all the difference.

1. **diverged** (dy VURJD): branched off in different directions.

A **Reading Focus** **Questioning** What does the phrase "wanted wear" mean?

B **Literary Focus** **Theme** Explain the purpose of the word *equally* in the statement in lines 11–12. What point is the speaker emphasizing about the choice he made?

Applying Your Skills

MO 9.R.2.C.1.c Use details from text(s): to analyze the development of a theme across genres **9.R.2.C.1.d** Use details from text(s): to evaluate the effect of author's style **9.R.2.B.2.a** Identify and explain literary techniques in text emphasizing: irony *Also covered* **9.R.2.B.2.c; 9.R.1.G.1.b; 9.W.3.A.1.a**

The Road Not Taken

Respond and Think Critically

Reading Focus

Quick Check

1. What is the setting described in the poem?
2. What choice does the speaker face?

Read with a Purpose

3. What decision about life has the speaker made?

Reading Skills: Reading Actively

4. Re-reading a poem will help you penetrate the literal words and phrases to understand the work's deeper meaning. Review the chart you filled in when you first read the poem. Then, re-read the entire poem. What new understanding did you gain by re-reading the work? Revise the comments in your chart as you see fit, and write down any new ideas.

The Road Not Taken
Questioning: Why is the wood described as "yellow"?
Re-reading—New Ideas:

Literary Focus

Literary Analysis

5. **Analyze** What do you think the two roads and the woods **symbolize,** or represent? Explain.
6. **Interpret** What do you think the speaker means when he says that he "kept" the first road "for another day" (line 13)? How do we know that he realizes his choice of path is final?
7. **Analyze** In line 19, the speaker says that he took the road "less traveled by." However, given what he says in lines 6–10, is one road really "less traveled" than the other? Explain.

Literary Skills: Theme

8. **Analyze** The ambiguity in this poem—its conflicting meanings—makes it subject to different interpretations. What theme do you think the poem expresses about the choices we make in life? To answer, re-read the last stanza, and then consider the following questions:
   - According to Frost, the most insightful question one could ask about the poem concerns line 16. Why the sigh? How would you describe the **tone,** or attitude, expressed in this line?
   - Is the poem's final line meant as **verbal irony** (in other words, does the speaker say one thing but mean another?), or is it a sincere statement?

Literary Skills Review: Sound Devices

9. **Evaluate** Frost uses several types of sound devices in this poem: rhyme, **alliteration** (the repetition of a consonant sound in several words, usually at the beginnings of the words), and **assonance** (the repetition of vowel sounds in words that are close together). Find examples of each of these devices in the poem. How would you describe the way the poem sounds as a result of Frost's use of these devices?

Writing Focus

Think as a Reader/Writer

Use It in Your Writing Write a road poem of your own (perhaps about a road taken). Like Kaldas and Frost, use vivid images to set the scene and focus on a journey as your theme.

PHOTOGRAPH

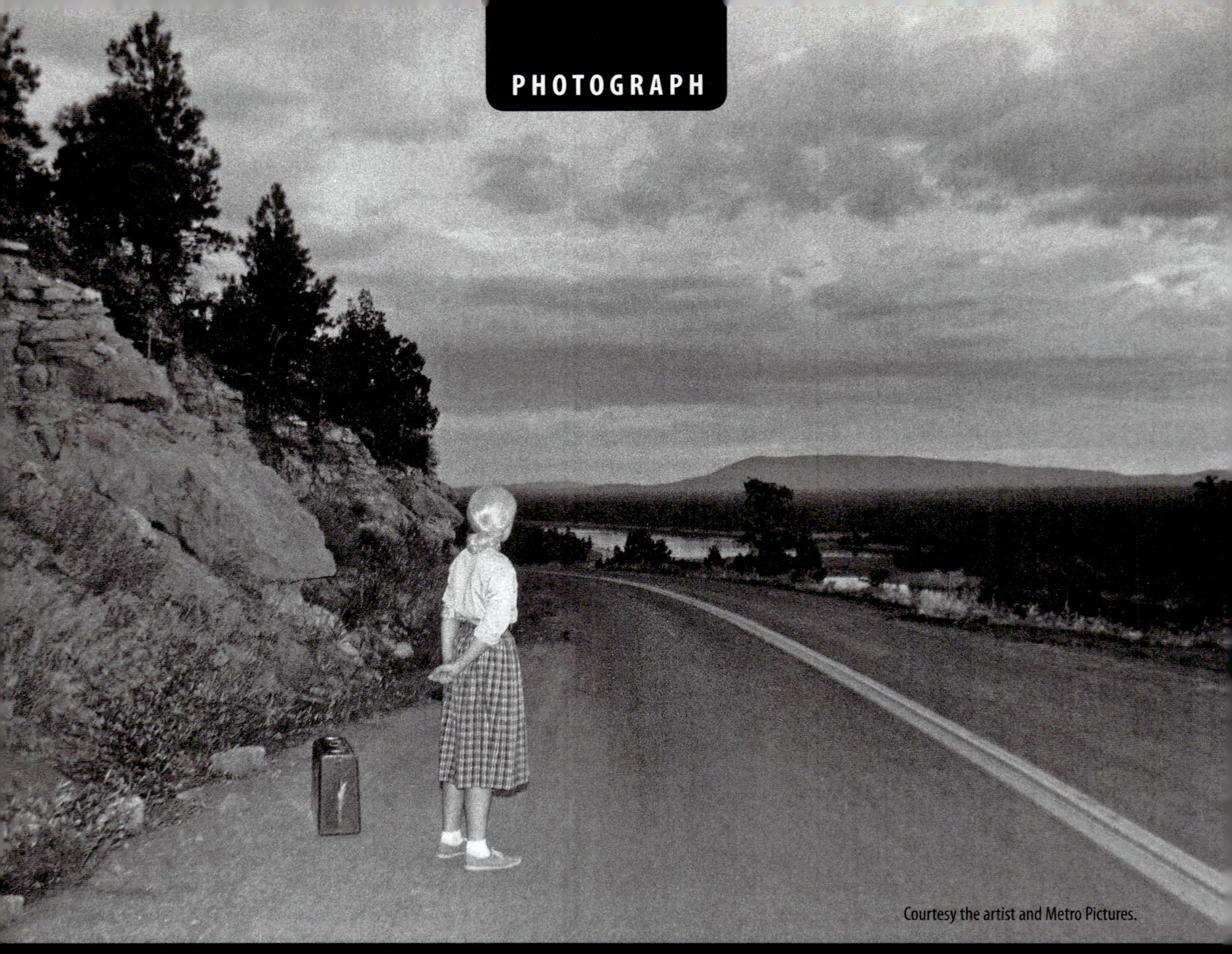

Courtesy the artist and Metro Pictures.

Cindy Sherman Untitled Film Still #48

Analyzing Visuals

Viewing and Interpreting What do you think the woman in the photograph is doing? Whom is she waiting for? Where did she come from? Use your imagination to create the woman's story.

Build Background

Cindy Sherman (1954–) moved to New York in 1977, where she began working on a series of photographs called *Untitled Film Stills.* She created 69 photographs for this series, using herself as a model in the roles of low-budget movie stars. She dressed up in wigs, hats, and costumes and used cinematic techniques like dramatic lighting and scenery to make these 8- by 10-inch photos look like movie scenes.

COMPARING TEXTS

Wrap Up

9.R.2.C.1.c Use details from text(s): to analyze the development of a theme across genres **9.R.1.G.1.b** During reading, utilize strategies: to self-monitor comprehension **9.W.3.A.1.a** Compose a variety of texts: using narrative, descriptive, expository, and/or persuasive features **9.W.3.A.1.d** Compose a variety of texts: including literary analysis

Airport / The Road Not Taken / Untitled Film Still #48

Writing Focus

Writing a Comparison-Contrast Essay

Many works of literature and art focus on journeys. Write an essay in which you compare and contrast the journeys the travelers in these three works take. In your essay, discuss the type of journey in each work, the choices the characters face, and the theme each work expresses.

Gather Details Re-read the story and poem, and study the photograph. Then, list similarities and differences between the works.

Organize Your Details Choose a method of organization for the body of your essay:

- **Block Method:** Organize your essay by subject. First, discuss all your ideas about subject 1. Then, discuss all your ideas about subject 2, and so on.
- **Point-by-Point Method:** Organize your essay by ideas. Discuss your first idea as it relates to subjects 1, 2, and 3. Then, discuss your second idea as it relates to subjects 1, 2, and 3, and so on.

Draft and Revise Your Writing Once you've drafted your essay, re-read it to make sure your ideas are clear and well supported. Proofread to eliminate errors in grammar, spelling, and punctuation.

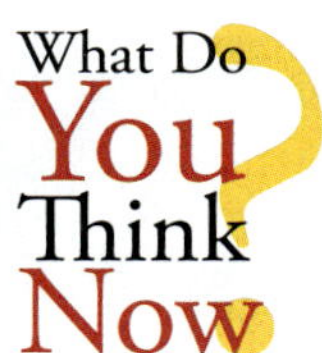

Can our choices in life limit or expand our opportunities? How might Kaldas, Frost, and Sherman respond to that question?

CHOICES

As you respond to the Choices, use these **Academic Vocabulary** words as appropriate: imply, associate, literal, ambiguous.

REVIEW

Evaluate Themes

Create a list of five stories or poems you know that focus on journeys or hard choices. Next to each item in the list, write down your ideas about its theme. Then, identify the work that you feel is most successful in conveying an important idea about life.

CONNECT

Analyze a Photograph

Group Discussion Look back at the photo by Cindy Sherman on page 394. In what way is the photo ambiguous? What does the photo suggest about the concepts of choices and journeys? Form a small group and discuss how the photo evokes a sense of making choices. Then, make a final statement from your group about the photo and share it with the rest of the class.

EXTEND

Write a Letter of Advice

Timed Writing What advice would you give to Hoda or Samir as they wrestle with their decisions? Write a letter to one of the characters in which you persuade him or her to take your advice about what to do. Provide support for your ideas.

INFORMATIONAL TEXT FOCUS

Synthesizing Works by One Author

CONTENTS

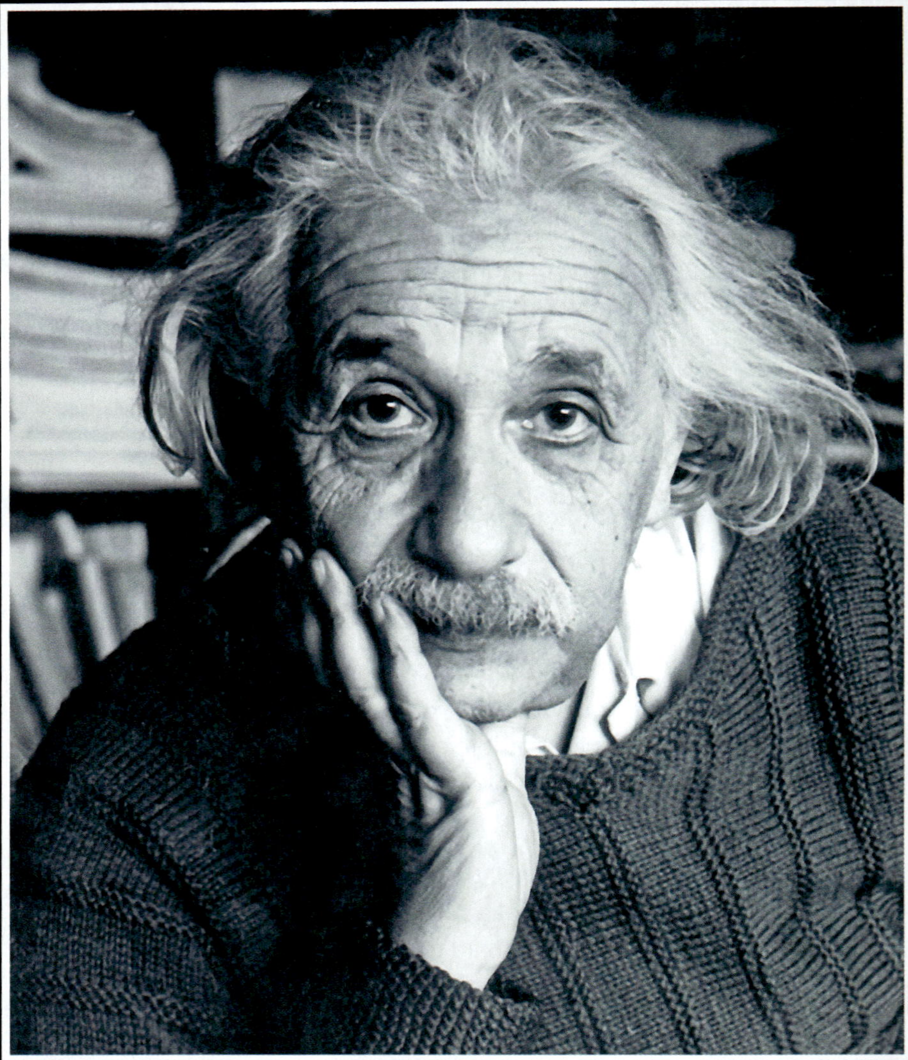

Portrait of German-born U.S. physicist and mathematician Albert Einstein.

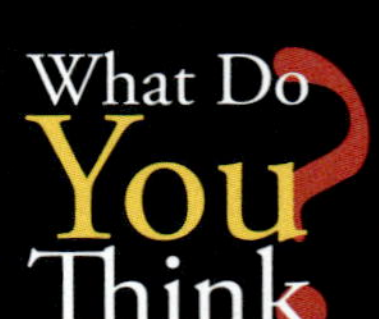

What Do You Think? What issues do people struggle with during times of war?

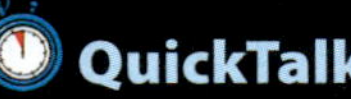

QuickTalk
Recall what you learned about World War II. With a partner, talk about how those events shape our world today.

INTERVIEWS, LETTER & ESSAY

Preparing to Read

Four Readings by Albert Einstein

Use your **RWN** to complete the activities for these selections.

Informational Text Focus

Synthesizing Sources: Works by One Author Some issues are so important to a writer that he or she writes about them again and again. Follow these guidelines to synthesize the content of different works by an author that address the same issues:

- **Paraphrase** To understand complex ideas, paraphrase, or restate them, in your own words. A paraphrase is *not* a literal quotation, which must appear within quotation marks.
- **Compare and Contrast** Relate your sources to one another. Does the author express different opinions about an issue in the sources? If so, how have the author's views changed? What is the author's purpose in writing about the issue each time? Is the audience different? Is the author covering different aspects of the issue in each source?
- **Connect** Relate ideas in your sources to your prior knowledge about the author or the issue.
- **Synthesize** Look at the sources as a group. What do they tell you about the author's views on the issue? By **synthesizing** the content of several works—putting together the information they contain—you will gain a better understanding of the author's ideas.

Into Action Use a problem-solution chart like the one below to keep track of Einstein's ideas.

What is the problem?	What are some solutions?
War wastes energy.	Make heroic sacrifices for peace.

Writing Focus

Preparing for **Constructed Response**

When reading the selections by Einstein, look for ways he presents his ideas and constructs his arguments. Write these details in your *Reader/Writer Notebook.*

Vocabulary

Weapons of the Spirit

eradicate (ih RAD uh kayt) *v.:* eliminate completely; get rid of. *Einstein wants to eradicate humanity's less desirable qualities.*

Letter to President Roosevelt

conceivable (kuhn SEEV uh buhl) *adj.:* capable of being imagined or understood. *Einstein thought new ideas could make a certain technology conceivable.*

On the Abolition of the Threat of War

radical (RAD uh kuhl) *adj.:* extreme. *A ban on war is Einstein's radical solution.*

Language Coach

Word Origins Two of the Vocabulary words above are derived from the Latin word *radix,* which means "root." Which words are they? Use a dictionary to check your guess.

Learn It Online
To read more articles like this, go to the interactive Reading Workshops on:
go.hrw.com L9-397 Go

INTERVIEW

Weapons of the Spirit

by **Albert Einstein**

from an interview with George Sylvester Viereck
from Einstein on Peace

Read with a Purpose

Read the following selections to learn about Einstein's opinion of war.

Build Background

Albert Einstein (1879–1955) is widely regarded as one of the most important scientists of all time. Born and raised in Germany, Einstein studied physics, the science of matter and energy. Einstein, who was Jewish, escaped from Nazi Germany in 1933. He settled in the United States, where he spent the remainder of his life. Einstein was a pacifist who strongly opposed war.

It may not be possible in one generation to eradicate the combative instinct.[1] It is not even desirable to eradicate it entirely. Men should continue to fight, but they should fight for things worthwhile, not for imaginary geographical lines, racial prejudices, and private greed draped in the colors of patriotism. Their arms should be weapons of the spirit, not shrapnel[2] and tanks. A

Think of what a world we could build if the power unleashed in war were applied to constructive tasks! One tenth of the energy that the various belligerents[3] spent in the World War, a fraction of the money they exploded in hand grenades and poison gas, would suffice to raise the standard of living in every country and avert the economic catastrophe of worldwide unemployment.

We must be prepared to make the same heroic sacrifices for the cause of peace that we make ungrudgingly for the cause of war. There is no task that is more important or closer to my heart.

Nothing that I can do or say will change the structure of the universe. But maybe, by raising my voice, I can help the greatest of all causes—goodwill among men and peace on earth. B

—1931

1. **combative instinct:** Einstein views the tendency of human beings to fight with one another as an inborn trait.
2. **shrapnel** (SHRAP nuhl): shells that explode, releasing many small metal balls.
3. **belligerents** (buh LIHJ uhr uhnts): persons engaged in fighting one another.

A Informational Focus Paraphrase According to Einstein, what are the wrong types of battles? Paraphrase this paragraph.

Vocabulary **eradicate** (ih RAD uh kayt) *v.:* eliminate completely; get rid of.

B Informational Focus Author's Purpose What is Einstein's purpose in saying this?

LETTER

Letter to President Roosevelt

by **Albert Einstein**

Preparing to Read for this selection appears on page 397.

President Roosevelt signing the declaration of war against Japan.

Build Background

During the 1930s, the Nazis built up German military power with the aim of dominating Europe. The political situation in Germany convinced Einstein of the importance of researching the possibility of developing nuclear weapons.

At that time, scientists in the United States and Europe were making strides in investigating how to create a nuclear chain reaction, which would release the tremendous amount of energy needed to create bombs. Scientists suspected that the government of Nazi Germany was sponsoring similar experiments.

Shortly before World War II broke out, scientists persuaded Einstein to sign a letter addressed to President Franklin D. Roosevelt warning of the Nazis' research in nuclear weapons. This famous letter led to the establishment of the Manhattan Project, which developed the atomic bombs dropped on Japan in August 1945 that ushered in the nuclear age.

Albert Einstein
Old Grove Rd.
Nassau Point
Peconic, Long Island

August 2nd, 1939

F. D. Roosevelt,
President of the United States,
White House
Washington, D.C.

Sir:

Some recent work by E. Fermi and L. Szilard, which has been communicated to me in manuscript, leads me to expect that the element uranium may be turned into a new and important source of energy in the immediate future. Certain aspects of the situation which has arisen seem to call for watchfulness and, if necessary, quick action on the part of the Administration. I believe therefore that it is my duty to bring to your attention the following facts and recommendations:

In the course of the last four months it has been made probable—through the work of Joliot in France as well as Fermi and Szilard in America—that it may become possible to set up a nuclear chain reaction in a large mass of uranium, by which vast amounts of power and large quantities of new radium-like elements would be generated. Now it appears almost certain that this could be achieved in the immediate future.

This new phenomenon would also lead to the construction of bombs, and it is conceivable—though much less certain—that extremely powerful bombs of a new type may thus be constructed. A single bomb of this type, carried by boat and exploded in a port, might very well destroy the whole port together with some of the surrounding territory. However, such bombs might very well prove to be too heavy for transportation by air. **A**

The United States has only very poor ores of uranium in moderate quantities. There is some good ore in Canada and the former Czechoslovakia while the most important source of uranium is Belgian Congo.

In view of this situation you may think it desirable to have some permanent contact maintained between the Administration and the group of physicists working on chain reactions in America. One possible way of achieving this might be for you to entrust with this task a person who has your confidence and who could perhaps serve in an inofficial capacity. His task might comprise the following:

a) to approach Government Departments, keep them informed of the further development, and put forward recommendations for Government action giving particular attention to the problem of securing a supply of uranium ore for the United States;

b) to speed up the experimental work, which is at present being carried on within the limits of the budgets of University laboratories, by providing funds, if such funds be required, through his contacts with private persons who are willing to make contributions for this cause, and perhaps also by obtaining the co-operation of industrial laboratories which have the necessary equipment. **B**

I understand that Germany has actually stopped the sale of uranium from the Czechoslovakian mines which she has taken over. That she should have taken such early action might perhaps be understood on the ground that the son of the German Under-Secretary of State, von Weizsäcker, is attached to the Kaiser-Wilhelm-Institut in Berlin where some of the American work on uranium is now being repeated.

Yours very truly,

A. Einstein

(Albert Einstein)

A **Informational Focus** **Compare and Contrast** How do the ideas in this letter differ from those in "Weapons of the Spirit"?

B **Informational Focus** **Audience** In what way are these solutions Einstein proposes appropriate for his audience, the president?

Vocabulary

conceivable (kuhn SEEV uh buhl) *adj.:* capable of being imagined or understood.

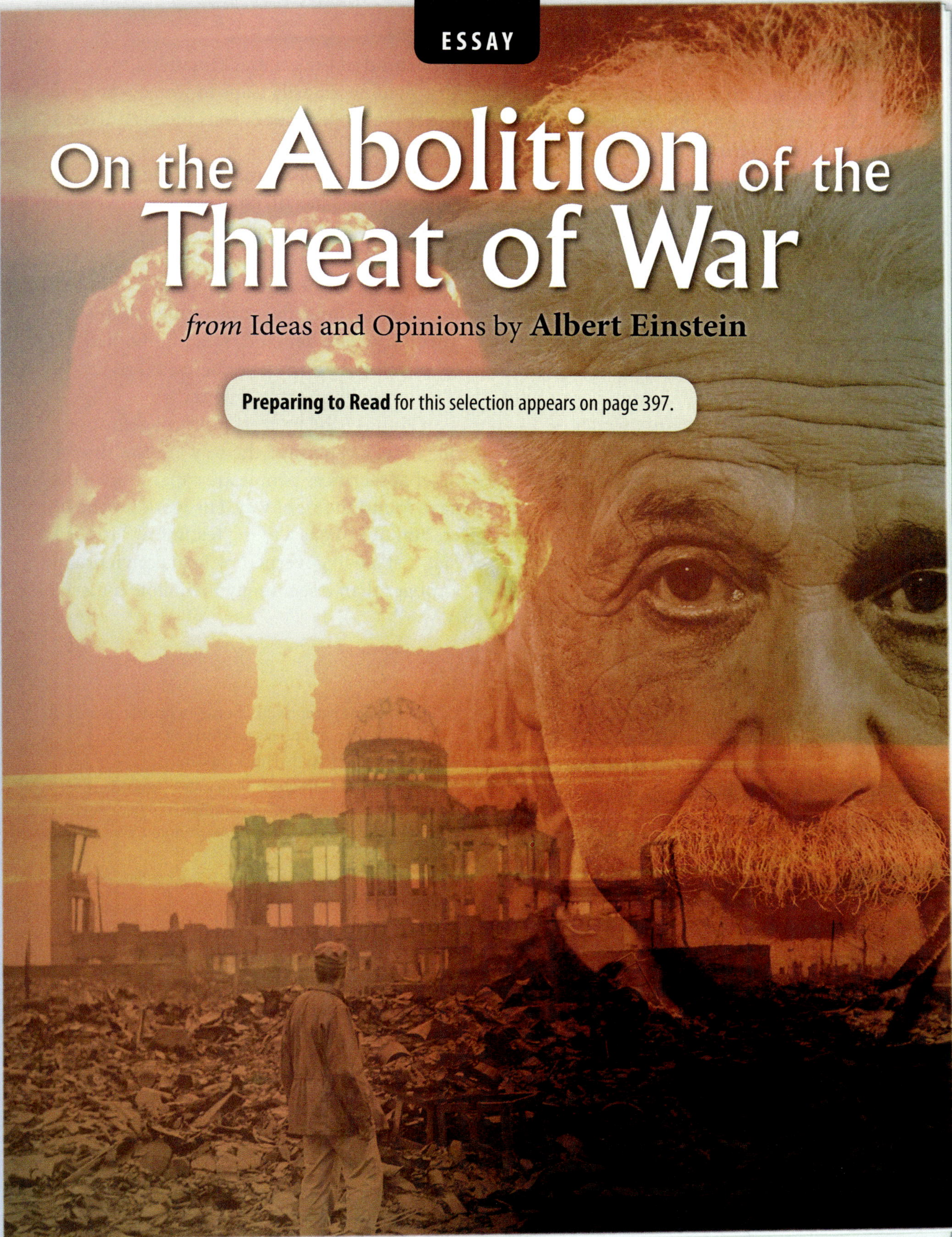

ESSAY

On the Abolition of the Threat of War

from Ideas and Opinions by **Albert Einstein**

Preparing to Read for this selection appears on page 397.

My part in producing the atomic bomb consisted in a single act: I signed a letter to President Roosevelt, pressing the need for experiments on a large scale in order to explore the possibilities for the production of an atomic bomb. **A**

I was fully aware of the terrible danger to mankind in case this attempt succeeded. But the likelihood that the Germans were working on the same problem with a chance of succeeding forced me to this step. I could do nothing else although I have always been a convinced pacifist. To my mind, to kill in war is not a whit better than to commit ordinary murder.

As long, however, as the nations are not resolved to abolish[1] war through common actions and to solve their conflicts and protect their interests by peaceful decisions on a legal basis, they feel compelled to prepare for war. They feel obliged to prepare all possible means, even the most detestable ones, so as not to be left behind in the general armament race.[2] This road necessarily leads to war, a war which under the present conditions means universal destruction.

Under these circumstances the fight against *means* has no chance of success. Only the radical abolition of wars and of the threat of war can help. This is what one has to work for. One has to be resolved not to let himself be forced to actions that run counter to this goal. This is a severe demand on an individual who is conscious[3] of his dependence on society. But it is not an impossible demand.

Gandhi,[4] the greatest political genius of our time, has pointed the way. He has shown of what sacrifices people are capable once they have found the right way. His work for the liberation of India is a living testimony[5] to the fact that a will governed by firm conviction is stronger than a seemingly invincible material power.[6] **B**

—1952

1. **abolish** (uh BAHL ihsh): put an end to. *Abolition* is the noun form of this word.
2. **armament race:** rivalry between hostile nations to build up larger and larger stores of weapons.
3. **conscious** (KAHN shuhs): aware.
4. **Gandhi** (GAHN dee): Mohandas Gandhi (1869–1948) led the struggle for India's independence from Britain. He practiced the use of nonviolent protest to achieve political goals.
5. **testimony** (TEHS tuh moh nee): evidence; proof.
6. **invincible material power:** here, an unconquerable nation.

Watch from the 1945 atomic bomb explosion in Hiroshima, Japan.

A **Informational Focus** **Connect** How does the opening paragraph relate to the previous letter? In the next paragraph, how does Einstein justify writing that letter?

B **Informational Focus** **Paraphrase** Paraphrase this paragraph. Then, explain why Einstein calls Gandhi a political genius.

Vocabulary **radical** (RAD uh kuhl) *adj.:* extreme.

INTERVIEW

Einstein and physicist J. Robert Oppenheimer, who led America's effort to produce an atomic bomb.

THE ARMS RACE

from Einstein on Peace
by **Albert Einstein**

Preparing to Read for this selection appears on page 397.

Build Background

Although the United States and the former Soviet Union were allies during World War II, they later became involved in a power struggle known as the Cold War. The two superpowers engaged in an arms race—a competition to develop more and more powerful nuclear weapons. In 1952, the United States successfully tested the first hydrogen bomb, a weapon much more powerful than the atomic bomb. In 1953, the Soviet Union exploded its own hydrogen bomb.

The arms race between the United States and the Soviet Union, initiated originally as a preventive measure, assumes hysterical proportions. On both sides, means of mass destruction are being perfected with feverish haste and behind walls of secrecy. And now the public has been advised that the production of the hydrogen bomb is the new goal which will probably be accomplished. An accelerated development toward this end has been solemnly proclaimed by the President. If these efforts should prove successful, radioactive poisoning of the atmosphere and, hence, annihilation[1] of all life on earth will have been brought within the range of what is technically possible. The weird aspect of this development lies in its apparently inexorable[2] character. Each step appears as the inevitable consequence of the one that went before. And at the end, looming ever clearer, lies general annihilation. **A**

1. **annihilation** (uh ny uh LAY shuhn): absolute destruction.
2. **inexorable** (ihn EHKS uhr uh buhl): unable to be stopped.

A **Informational Focus** **Paraphrase** Einstein describes a cause-and-effect relationship in the last three sentences of this paragraph. Paraphrase these sentences to clarify the point he makes.

Is there any way out of this impasse[3] created by man himself? All of us, and particularly those who are responsible for the policies of the United States and the Soviet Union, must realize that, although we have vanquished an external enemy,[4] we have proved unable to free ourselves from the war mentality. We shall never achieve real peace as long as every step is taken with a possible future conflict in view, especially since it becomes ever clearer that such a war would spell universal annihilation. The guiding thought in all political action should therefore be: What can we do in the prevailing situation to bring about peaceful coexistence among all nations? The first goal must be to do away with mutual fear and distrust. Solemn renunciation of the policy of violence, not only with respect to weapons of mass destruction, is without doubt necessary. **B**

In the last analysis the peaceful coexistence of peoples is primarily dependent upon mutual trust and, only secondarily, upon institutions such as courts of justice and the police. This holds true for nations as well as for individuals. And the basis of trust is a loyal relationship of give-and-take. —1950

3. **impasse** (IHM pas): difficult situation or problem with no obvious solution.
4. **vanquished** (VAN kwihsht) **an external enemy:** defeated hostile nations. Einstein is referring to Germany, Japan, and their allies in World War II, which were defeated by the United States, Great Britain, and their allies.

B **Informational Focus** **Author's Purpose** Has Einstein's purpose changed over the course of the selection writings? Explain.

Read with a Purpose

What ideas about war did Einstein have?

A fiery mushroom cloud rises into the sky following the test detonation of an 11-megaton nuclear device code-named "Romeo" over Bikini Atoll on March 26, 1954.

INTERVIEWS, LETTER & ESSAY

Applying Your Skills

MO 9.R.1.H.1.e Apply post-reading skills to comprehend, interpret, analyze, and evaluate text: paraphrase 9.R.1.G.1.a During reading, utilize strategies: to determine meaning of unknown words

Four Readings by Albert Einstein

Practicing the Standards

Informational Text and Vocabulary

1. Which idea is included in *both* "On the Abolition of the Threat of War" and "The Arms Race"?

A Gandhi is a political role model.

B The only part Einstein played in creating the bomb was signing a letter to the president.

C The United States is producing a hydrogen bomb.

D The arms race will result in total destruction.

2. In which selections do Einstein's ideas about war and peace differ the *most*?

A "Weapons of the Spirit" and "On the Abolition of the Threat of War"

B "Weapons of the Spirit" and "Letter to President Roosevelt"

C "The Arms Race" and "On the Abolition of the Threat of War"

D "Weapons of the Spirit" and "The Arms Race"

3. If you read *only* "Letter to President Roosevelt," you might draw the *incorrect* conclusion that Einstein —

A felt the United States needed to protect itself

B was aware of new troubling scientific research

C believed nuclear weapons could be dangerous

D was a firm believer in war

4. Which topic below is *most* clearly connected to the content of the selections you just read?

A The breakup of the Soviet Union in the 1990s

B The training of physicists

C The status of nuclear weapons today

D The policies of President Roosevelt

5. What is the best definition of *eradicate*?

A To hinder

B To collect something

C To eliminate completely

D To help along

6. If a person said a *radical* change in weather is coming, what could one expect?

A Another sunny day

B A change from 60 degrees to 55 degrees

C An ice storm during summer

D Fog after rain

7. Which is the *best* synonym for *conceivable*?

A Believable

B Fertile

C Dangerous

D Impossible

Writing Focus Constructed Response

If you had a time machine and could go back to 1939 before Einstein wrote his letter to President Roosevelt, what would you tell Einstein? Considering what you know about Einstein's ideas, do you think he might have acted differently if given different advice? Explain.

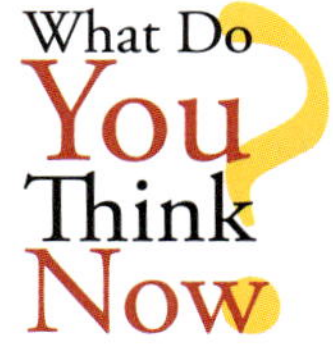

Do you think Einstein would be pleased with the state of the world today? Why or why not?

FOCUS ON MISSOURI COURSE LEVEL EXPECTATIONS

Literary Skills Review

Symbolism and Irony **Directions:** Read the following folk tale. Then, read and respond to the questions that follow.

The Happy Man's Shirt retold by **Italo Calvino**

translated by **George Martin**

A king had an only son that he thought the world of. But this prince was always unhappy. He would spend days on end at his window staring into space.

"What on earth do you lack?" asked the king. "What's wrong with you?"

"I don't even know myself, Father."

"Are you in love? If there's a particular girl you fancy, tell me, and I'll arrange for you to marry her, no matter whether she's the daughter of the most powerful king on earth or the poorest peasant girl alive!"

"No, Father, I'm not in love."

The king tried in every way imaginable to cheer him up, but theaters, balls, concerts, and singing were all useless, and day by day the rosy hue drained from the prince's face.

The king issued a decree,[1] and from every corner of the earth came the most learned philosophers, doctors, and professors. The king showed them the prince and asked for their advice. The wise men withdrew to think, then returned to the king. "Majesty, we have given the matter close thought and we have studied the stars. Here's what you must do. Look for a happy man, a man who's happy through and through, and exchange your son's shirt for his."

That same day the king sent ambassadors to all parts of the world in search of the happy man.

A priest was taken to the king. "Are you happy?" asked the king.

"Yes, indeed, Majesty."

"Fine. How would you like to be my bishop?"

"Oh, Majesty, if only it were so!"

"Away with you! Get out of my sight! I'm seeking a man who's happy just as he is, not one who's trying to better his lot."

Thus the search resumed, and before long the king was told about a neighboring king, who everybody said was a truly happy man. He had a wife as good as she was beautiful and a whole slew of children. He had conquered all his enemies, and his country was at peace. Again hopeful, the king immediately sent ambassadors to him to ask for his shirt.

The neighboring king received the ambassadors and said, "Yes, indeed, I have everything anybody could possibly want. But at the same time I worry because I'll have to die one day and leave it all. I can't sleep at night for worrying about that!" The ambassadors thought it wiser to go home without this man's shirt.

At his wit's end, the king went hunting. He fired at a hare but only wounded it, and the hare scampered away on three legs. The king pursued it, leaving the hunting party far

1. **decree:** official order.

9.R.2.B.2.a Identify and explain literary techniques in text emphasizing: irony **9.R.2.A.1** Analyze and evaluate the text features in grade-level text **9.R.2.C.1.c** Use details from text(s): to analyze the development of a theme across genres *Also covered* **9.R.2.B.1.d; 9.R.2.C.1.b**

behind him. Out in the open field he heard a man singing a refrain. The king stopped in his tracks. "Whoever sings like that is bound to be happy!" The song led him into a vineyard, where he found a young man singing and pruning the vines.

"Good day, Majesty," said the youth. "So early and already out in the country?"

"Bless you! Would you like me to take you to the capital? You will be my friend."

"Much obliged, Majesty, but I wouldn't even consider it. I wouldn't even change places with the Pope."

"Why not? Such a fine young man like you . . ."

"No, no, I tell you. I'm content with just what I have and want nothing more."

"A happy man at last!" thought the king. "Listen, young man. Do me a favor."

"With all my heart, Majesty, if I can."

"Wait just a minute," said the king, who, unable to contain his joy any longer, ran to get his retinue.[2] "Come with me! My son is saved! My son is saved!" And he took them to the young man. "My dear lad," he began, "I'll give you whatever you want! But give me . . . give me . . ."

"What, Majesty?"

"My son is dying! Only you can save him. Come here!"

The king grabbed him and started unbuttoning the youth's jacket. All of a sudden he stopped, and his arms fell to his sides.

The happy man wore no shirt.

2. **retinue:** assistants attending an important person.

1. The unhappy man is a prince. What might his position in life symbolize in this folk tale?

A Respect

B Pride

C Material wealth

D Romance

9.R.2.B.1.d

2. Which pair of words *best* describes the king's feelings for his son?

A Anger and frustration

B Confusion and depression

C Affection and irritation

D Love and concern

9.R.2.C.1.b

Literary Skills Review CONTINUED

MO **9.R.2.B.2.a** Identify and explain literary techniques in text emphasizing: irony **9.R.2.A.1** Analyze and evaluate the text features in grade-level text **9.R.2.C.1.c** Use details from text(s): to analyze the development of a theme across genres *Also covered* **9.R.2.B.1.a; 9.R.2.B.1.d; 9.R.2.C.1.b**

3. The wise men advise the king to —

A find the prince a bride

B have the prince wear a happy man's shirt

C give the prince his freedom

D throw a party for the prince

9.R.2.C.1.b

4. What quality might the character of the priest **symbolize**?

A Flattery

B Modesty

C Ambition

D Hopefulness

9.R.2.B.1.d

5. What is similar about these two **characters:** the prince and the neighboring king?

A Both seem to have everything they could want, but neither is content.

B Both are in love, but they are unhappy.

C Both worry about dying, which makes them unhappy.

D Both are sad, and neither knows why.

9.R.2.C.1.b

6. Why does the king conclude that the young man who sings as he works is truly happy?

A He is polite.

B He is satisfied with his life.

C He is healthy and young.

D He enjoys working outdoors in the country.

9.R.2.C.1.b

7. In what way is the story's ending **ironic**?

A The wise men are proven wrong.

B The shirt represents material wealth.

C The shirt represents what the king and his son cannot have.

D The happy man is working outdoors.

9.R.2.B.1.a

8. The **symbols** in this folk tale might appeal to us in part because they —

A make the setting of the story vivid

B give the narrator a distinct personality

C contribute to the meaning and emotional impact of the story

D provide information about the author's life

9.R.2.B.1.d

9. What statement *best* expresses the **theme** of the story?

A People should not rely on others to help them solve their problems.

B It is difficult to know what other people are truly feeling.

C True happiness must come from within.

D Although you may fail to attain your goals at first, you should not give up.

9.R.2.B.1.d

Constructed Response

10. In what way can this tale be seen as an **allegory**? Support your response by using examples from the text.

9.R.2

Informational Skills Review

Synthesizing Sources: Works by One Author **Directions:** Read the following selections. Then, read and respond to the questions that follow.

Look Who's in the School Kitchen, Dishing Out Advice

by **Sarah Lyall** *from* **The New York Times,** April 23, 2005

LONDON, England—Of all the revolting foods the chef Jamie Oliver has encountered in school cafeterias, from the mysterious feet-shaped meat patties to the fried smiley-faced disks purporting to be potatoes, perhaps the most horrific were the reconstituted so-called pork tenderloins.

"Listen to this reaction," Mr. Oliver said recently, calling out to Pete Begg, a chef on his staff, for a second opinion. They were sitting in his cavernous open-plan office in north London, the nerve center of innumerable Oliver projects, including his latest: a campaign to replace the fatty, salty, greasy, sugary food in Britain's schools with freshly cooked, nutritious meals.

"Pete, what did you think of those pork cutlets that we got in from that company?" Mr. Oliver asked.

Mr. Begg's face fell. "It was the vilest foodstuff I have ever seen," he proclaimed grimly. "Do you remember when we had them out on a bench, and it was in the summer and it kind of warmed up a bit, and you could really see them almost melt?"

Mr. Oliver did remember. "They turned into sludge," he said.

Such is the force of Mr. Oliver's influence that when he says "sludge," people listen. At 29, he is one of Britain's most familiar celebrity chefs, a television star and best-selling cookbook author whose charity, the Fifteen Foundation, runs a popular restaurant in north London staffed by unemployed youths from difficult backgrounds.

Now it is his school-meals project that has captured the imagination of a country growing fatter and unhealthier because of its poor diet and sedentary ways. Even the snippy tabloids, once irritated by Mr. Oliver's un-British chipperness, have taken to calling him, without irony, "Saint Jamie." In *The Daily Telegraph,* a reader from Berkshire recently wrote, "Could Jamie Oliver have a word with the airlines?" . . .

He began the campaign when, on visits to schools as part of his charity work, he found the lunches virtually inedible, made up of dishes like gristly sausage rolls and frozen shapes calling themselves fish, chicken, and pork. Baked beans and French fries were ubiquitous;[1] vegetables were virtually extinct. . . .

For more than a year, he put himself in charge, at least partly. He persuaded a school district in a deprived section of London to let him overhaul its menus. He taught the cooks how to make fresh food and the students

1. **ubiquitous:** everywhere at the same time.

the difference between leeks and zucchini. At lunchtime, increasingly unshaven and exhausted as the months went on, he dished out food in the cafeteria and pleaded with the suspicious children to eat it.

It was not easy, as was made all too clear in "Jamie's School Dinners," a riveting four-part television series broadcast here earlier this year. The budget was a woeful 37 pence, about 70 cents, per child per day. The cooks, used to dealing mainly with frozen nuggets, balked[2] at the extra work involved in preparing things like seven-vegetable pasta sauce from scratch.

The students, deprived of their junk, originally hated the new food. "It looks disgusting and it smells disgusting," said one student, confronted by Mr. Oliver's chicken tagine. Another little boy, tasting what he said was his first-ever vegetable, threw up on the table.

Mr. Oliver resorted to desperate means.

2. **balked:** stopped short; refused to go on.

To win over the primary school, he put on a giant corn-on-the-cob costume, sang a pro-vegetable song written by a friend, and doled out positive-reinforcement stickers. To shock the older children into nutritional awareness, he tossed a chicken carcass into a blender along with bits of skin, fat and bread crumbs, whizzed it around, and showed off the result: stomach-turning mush that, when shaped and cooked, could pass for the nuggets they had been eating.

In a televisual tour de force, he talked his way into a meeting with the chief executive of the company that supplies schools with a notorious dish called turkey twizzlers (ingredients: 30 percent or so turkey, 70 percent other) and scolded him. . . .

Gradually, he won the children over, getting them to try, and even like, his food. At school, the teachers could see improvements in concentration and in academic performance; at home, parents reported that their children were behaving better.

Glorious Food? English Schoolchildren Think Not

by **Sarah Lyall** *from* **The New York Times,** October 18, 2006

ROTHERHAM, England—Five months after the celebrity chef Jamie Oliver succeeded in cajoling, threatening, and shaming the British government into banning junk food from its school cafeterias, many schools are learning that you can lead a child to a healthy lunch, but you can't make him eat.

The fancy new menu at the Rawmarsh School here?

"It's rubbish," said Andreas Petrou, an 11th grader. Instead, en route to school recently, he was enjoying a north of England specialty known as a chip butty: a French-fries-and-butter sandwich doused in vinegar.

"We didn't get a choice," he said of the school food. "They just told us we were having it."

The government's regulations, which took effect in September, have banished from school cafeterias the cheap, instantly gratifying meals that children love by default: the hamburgers, the French fries, the breaded, deep-fried processed meat, the sugary drinks.

Now schools have to provide at least two portions of fresh fruit and vegetables a day for each child, serve fish at least once a week, remove salt from lunchroom tables, limit fried foods to two servings a week and cut out candy, soda and potato chips altogether. . . .

But weaning children who consider French fries a major food group is not easy. There is no nicotine patch equivalent for chicken nuggets.

And many parents object to being lectured by Londoners like Mr. Oliver, whose angry television show "Jamie's School Dinners" first alerted the nation to the horrors of school food like "Turkey Twizzlers"—minuscule bits of meat processed with many nonmeat products, molded into shapes and deep-fried.

"No matter how healthy it is, if kids don't like it they're not going to eat it," said Julie Critchlow, a parent at Rawmarsh, a high school set between a sprawling housing project and the south Yorkshire hills. She mentioned the school's new low-fat pizza and tagliatelle and meatballs as being particularly unappetizing to her children and said the cooks were so overworked that the baked potatoes were being served half-cooked.

The fact that Rawmarsh now bans children who do not go home for lunch from leaving school has made things worse, she said, leading to an overcrowded cafeteria and the elimination of the old fast-food-down-the-road option.

"They shouldn't be allowed to tell the kids what to eat," Mrs. Critchlow said of the school authorities. "They're treating them like criminals."

Mrs. Critchlow has become a notorious figure in Britain. In September she and another mother—alarmed, they said, because their children were going hungry—began selling contraband hamburgers, fries and sandwiches to as many as 50 students a day, passing the food through the school gates.

The mothers closed their business after they were vilified in the national news media as "meat pie mums." Mrs. Critchlow now feeds her children lunch at home.

Shaken by the bad publicity, the school says that the two women represent a small minority and that most children are happy with the healthier menus, which include two hot choices every day—entrees like haddock provençal, beef curry, and navarin of lamb—as well as baked potatoes for the unadventurous.

If the children really hate the food, Rawmarsh argues, they can bring brown-bag lunches.

"It doesn't happen overnight; it takes an effort," said Sonia Sharp, a local government official, speaking of the campaign to win the children over. "We have the responsibility for ensuring the health of our children. We want to teach them how to make the right choices for themselves."

FOCUS ON MISSOURI COURSE LEVEL EXPECTATIONS

Informational Skills Review

MO **9.R.1.H.1.e** Apply post-reading skills to comprehend, interpret, analyze, and evaluate text: paraphrase *Also covered* **9.R.1.H.1.a; 9.R.1.H.1.d; 9.R.1.I.1.a; 9.R.3.C.1.e**

1. Which is the *best* **paraphrase** of the first paragraph of "Look Who's in the School Kitchen, Dishing Out Advice"?

A The most horrible school meal Jamie Oliver encountered was fake pork tenderloin.

B Chef Jamie Oliver thinks school lunches are revolting.

C Pork tenderloins are a horrible food to serve.

D Feet-shaped meat patties and smiley-faced potatoes have no place in school cafeterias.

9.R.1.H.1.e

2. Which statement best expresses the **main idea** of "Glorious Food? English Schoolchildren Think Not"?

A Schoolchildren and parents approve of the changes Oliver has made to school lunch programs.

B Schoolchildren and parents don't like the changes Oliver has made to school lunch programs.

C Britain has not done enough to improve school lunch programs.

D British officials did not take nutrition seriously.

9.R.1.H.1.a

3. If you were to read only "Look Who's in the School Kitchen, Dishing Out Advice," you might draw the **conclusion** that —

A Oliver's school lunch program inspired British students and parents to live healthier lifestyles

B Oliver's new lunch menu was not popular with students

C Oliver was unsuccessful in getting schoolchildren to eat healthfully at lunchtime

D Oliver was successful in changing how children prepare foods

9.R.1.H.1.d

4. **Compare** the two articles. Which idea is found in *both* articles?

A School lunch programs have angered many British parents.

B School lunch programs cost too much money to improve.

C School lunch programs have been successful in getting British students to eat healthfully.

D School lunch programs have not been successful in getting British students to eat healthfully.

9.R.1.I.1.a

5. If you wanted to **connect** the information in both articles to another topic, which topic would be the *most* closely related?

A The latest cookbook from Jamie Oliver

B The physical recreation of British schoolchildren

C The latest article by Sarah Lyall

D Reforms of school lunches in the United States

9.R.1.I.1.a

Constructed Response

6. What do you think of Oliver's program? What advice would you give him to make his program more successful?

9.R.3.C.1.e

FOCUS ON MISSOURI COURSE LEVEL EXPECTATIONS

Vocabulary Skills Review

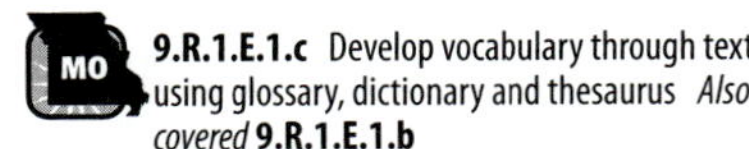

9.R.1.E.1.c Develop vocabulary through text: using glossary, dictionary and thesaurus *Also covered* **9.R.1.E.1.b**

Synonyms

Directions: Choose the *best* synonym for the italicized word in each sentence.

1. In "The Gift of the Magi," Della's *prudence* enabled her to save money.

A caution
B health
C dreams
D courage

9.R.1.E.1.b

2. When Doodle stands up in the woods in "The Scarlet Ibis," his brother knows that Doodle's first steps are *imminent.*

A forever
B forthcoming
C parallel
D distant

9.R.1.E.1.b

3. As Doodle begins walking, the narrator believes in his own *infallibility.*

A deceit
B truthfulness
C magnificence
D perfection

9.R.1.E.1.b

4. At the party in "The Necklace," Mathilde is surrounded by others' *adulation.*

A fine clothes
B good news
C admiration
D coachmen

9.R.1.E.1.b

5. In "The Golden Kite, the Silver Wind," the ruler finds *monotony* a bore.

A sameness
B competition
C agreement
D hatred

9.R.1.E.1.b

6. Samir is in a state of *agitation* as he waits for Hoda in "Airport."

A optimism
B depression
C frustration
D excitement

9.R.1.E.1.b

7. Based on the readings from Einstein, one could say his opinions are *radical.*

A evil
B extreme
C intelligent
D flawed

9.R.1.E.1.b

Academic Vocabulary

Directions: Identify the definition for each italicized Academic Vocabulary word.

8. The poem "The Road Not Taken" has an *ambiguous* ending.

A gloomy
B distinct
C open to interpretation
D surprising or unexpected

9.R.1.E.1.b

9. Poems often have words that contain deeper messages than their *literal* meanings suggest.

A relating to ordinary usage
B unstated or unspecified
C academic
D figurative

9.R.1.E.1.b

Read On

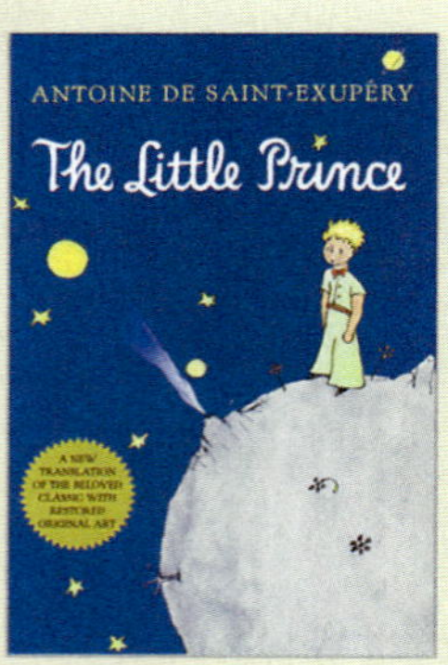

FICTION

The Little Prince

A pilot whose plane has crashed in the African desert is awakened from sleep by a strange, small voice: "Please," a boy says, "draw me a sheep!" So begins Antoine de Saint-Exupéry's timeless book, *The Little Prince*. This story of a lonely, stranded pilot and a gentle prince who has traveled to different planets—meeting a businessman, a king, a lamplighter, and a geographer—can be read as an imaginative allegory about growing up.

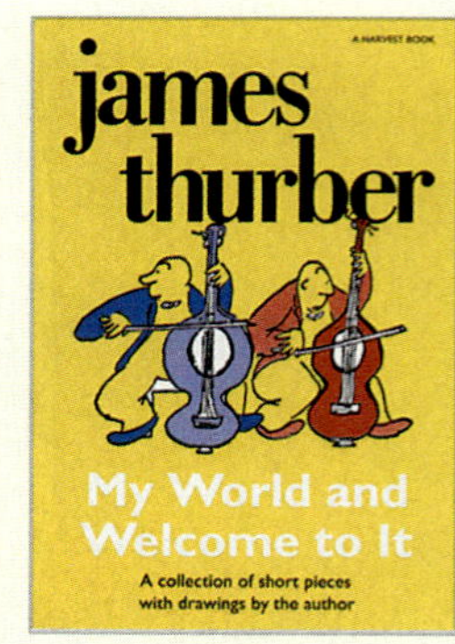

FICTION/NONFICTION

My World and Welcome to It

James Thurber's *My World and Welcome to It* is a collection of essays, sketches, and stories from one of America's great comic writers. Whether recording his funny observations about life abroad or complaining about the phone company, Thurber chooses his targets with gentle good humor. His combination of ironic wit and plain-spoken charm will make you feel as if you're spending the day with a favorite uncle.

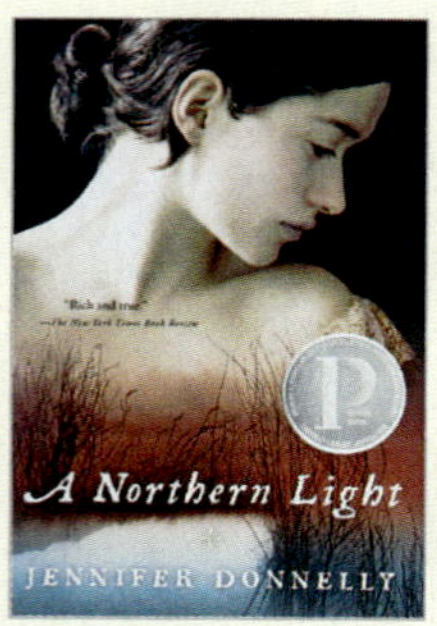

FICTION

A Northern Light

Set in 1906 against the backdrop of a historic murder, *A Northern Light* by Jennifer Donnelly tells the story of Mattie's struggle to overcome the pain of her mother's death while raising her sisters. Mattie's feelings for the handsome Royal Loomis and her dream of becoming a writer are the only things that keep her going. When the drowned body of a young woman turns up at the hotel where Mattie works, all her words are useless. But in the dead woman's symbolic letters, Mattie again finds her voice and a determination to live her own life.

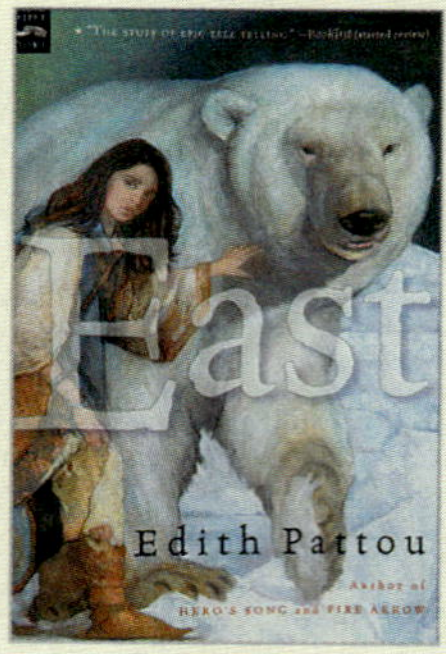

FICTION

East

Rose was given a pair of boots for her first baby gift, and they sealed her fate as an explorer. Now a teenager, Rose feels out of place in her family, and when an enormous white bear enters their house and asks her to go with him—in exchange for health and prosperity for her ailing family—she agrees. The bear takes Rose to a distant castle where each night she is confronted with a mystery that involves a troll queen and the bear's identity. As Edith Pattou's novel progresses, Rose solves the mystery but loses her heart and realizes her travels have just begun.

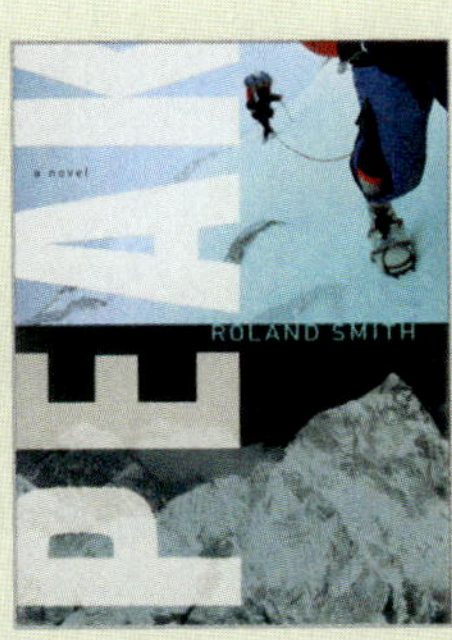

FICTION

Peak

In Roland Smith's novel, Peak Marcello is arrested for scaling a New York City skyscraper and left with two choices: wither away in Juvenile Detention or go live with his long-lost father, who runs a climbing company in Thailand. Peak quickly learns that his father's renewed interest in him is selfish, at best. He wants the publicity from having Peak be the youngest person to reach the summit of Mount Everest, the tallest mountain in the world. For a climbing addict like Peak, tackling Everest is the challenge of a lifetime, but it's also one that could cost him his life.

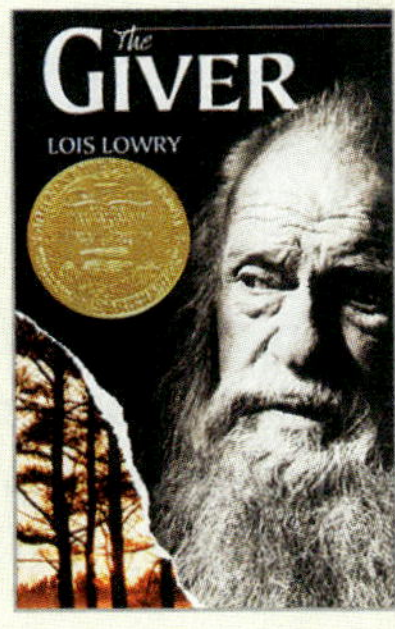

FICTION

The Giver

This Lois Lowry novel is set in an isolated, tightly regulated future society. Pills suppress feelings, and there are no books, music, or colors to arouse emotions. Most people are happy with this arrangement, as they are protected from making wrong choices. At the Ceremony of Twelve, Jonas is chosen to become the society's Receiver of Memory, the one who has books, sees colors, and is burdened with all painful memories. As Jonas gradually learns the truth about his society, he realizes he must accomplish something impossible—escape to Elsewhere.

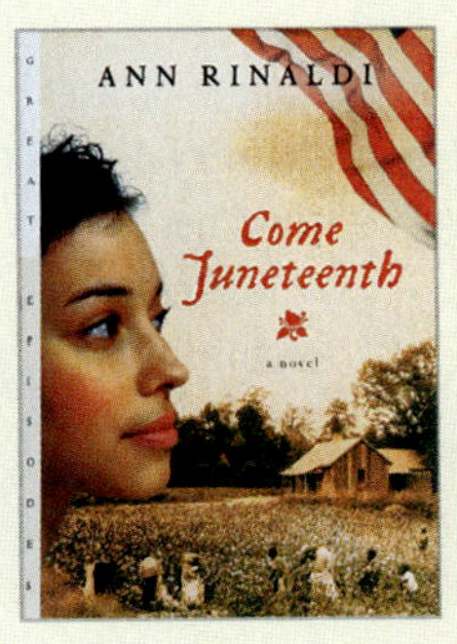

FICTION

Come Juneteenth

Sis Goose is a beloved member of Luli's family, despite the fact that she was born a slave. But the family is keeping a terrible secret, and when Union soldiers arrive on their Texas plantation to announce that slaves were declared free nearly two years before, Sis Goose is horrified to learn that the people she called family have lied to her for so long. She runs away, but her newly found freedom has tragic consequences. In this historical novel, Ann Rinaldi dramatizes events that led to the creation of Juneteenth, a celebration of freedom that continues today.

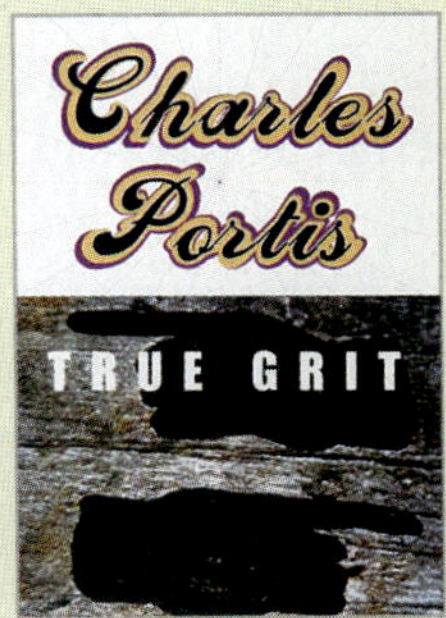

FICTION

True Grit

True Grit is the story of how Mattie Ross, a fourteen-year old-girl, avenges her father's murder. Mattie is mature, single-minded, persuasive, and refuses to take "no" for an answer. (She also carries a huge Colt dragoon pistol in a sack.) Despite their protests, she teams up with Rooster Cogburn, a U.S. marshal, and a Texas Ranger named LaBoeuf. They set out for Indian Territory to hunt down Tom Chaney, Lucky Ned Pepper, and other cutthroats. By the end of this part sad, part comic best-selling novel by Charles Portis, no reader has to guess which characters have "true grit."

Learn It Online
For tips on understanding fiction, use *NovelWise* at:
go.hrw.com L9-415 Go

Writing Workshop

Autobiographical Narrative

Write with a Purpose

Write an autobiographical narrative that reveals the significance of a personal experience. Your **purpose** is to express yourself and to entertain and inspire others. Your **audience** is your classmates and others who can relate to your experience.

A Good Autobiographical Narrative

- focuses on a single experience
- provides essential context or background information
- uses sensory details to describe setting and characters
- reveals thoughts and feelings through interior monologue
- explains why the experience is significant

See page 424 for complete rubric.

Use your **RWN** to complete the activities for this workshop.

Think as a Reader/Writer In this collection, you've seen different techniques writers use to tell stories. Now it is time to write a story based on your own experiences, called an **autobiographical narrative**. Read the following excerpt from Val Plumwood's "Being Prey" (page 90) to see some of the techniques she uses in her autobiographical narrative.

> Yesterday the water lilies and the wonderful bird life had enticed me into a joyous afternoon's idyll as I ventured onto the East Alligator lagoon for the first time in a canoe lent by the park service. "You can play about on the backwaters," the ranger had said, "but don't go onto the main river channel. The current's too swift, and if you get into trouble, there are crocodiles. Lots of them along the river!" I followed his advice and glutted myself on the magical beauty of the lily lagoons, untroubled by crocodiles.
>
> Today, I wanted to repeat that experience despite the drizzle beginning to fall as I neared the canoe launch site. I set off on a day trip in search of an Aboriginal rock art site across the lagoon and up a side channel. The drizzle turned to a warm rain within a few hours, and the magic was lost. The birds were invisible, the water lilies were sparser, and the lagoon seemed even a little menacing. I noticed now how low the 14-foot canoe sat in the water, just a few inches of fiberglass between me and the great saurians, close relatives of the ancient dinosaurs.

← Plumwood sets the **scene** and **context** for the experience.

← **Dialogue** creates suspense by introducing a potential conflict.

← Plumwood uses **sensory details** to show her feelings of excitement, disappointment, and concern.

Think About the Professional Model

With a partner, discuss the following questions about the model.

1. Which details show the change in setting and in Plumwood's mood?
2. How does Plumwood create suspense in this narrative?

MO **9.W.3.A.1.a** Compose a variety of texts: using narrative, descriptive, expository, and/or persuasive features

Prewriting

Search Your Memory for Experiences

In your autobiographical narrative, you will relate and reflect on an experience from your past that is **significant**, or important, to you. What has been your greatest achievement? your biggest failure? your most important lesson learned? Make a list of experiences that are important to you in a chart similar to the one below. Then, make notes: What happened? Where did it happen? Who was there? Why is this event so memorable?

Experience	Where?	Why significant?
Getting my first horse	the farm	I really wanted a horse
Going to my grandmother's house	Rochester	my love for my family

Evaluate Your Memories

How do you choose the best experience for your autobiographical narrative? Ask others which experience is most interesting. Most important, answer these questions about each memory for yourself:

- How important is this experience to me?
- How well do I remember the experience?
- Am I willing to share this experience with others?
- Would others relate to this experience in some way?

A Moment in Time Once you choose an experience to write about, remember that your narrative should focus on a specific **incident** in the experience. In "Being Prey," Plumwood focuses on the moment she encounters the dangerous crocodile and survives—not her entire trip or her notable history as a conservationist. Decide on the most **significant** incident in your experience. What **context** does the reader need in order to understand and appreciate the significant moment in time?

Think About Purpose and Audience

As you plan, keep your purpose and audience in mind. Your **purpose** in writing an autobiographical narrative is to entertain and perhaps inspire your readers. Your **audience** may be your family, friends, fellow students, or readers in a much wider audience. Remember that your audience affects how you convey the experience.

Idea Starters

- the best/worst day of my life
- an experience worth repeating
- one mistake I wish I could correct
- the adventure of my life

Peer Review

Share your chart with another student. Talk about why each memory is significant. Ask your partner which experience would work best for an autobiographical narrative. Repeat this process with your partner's chart. Be sure you both choose an experience for your narratives.

Your Turn

Get Started Freewrite in your **RWN** for ten minutes on the personal experience you've chosen. Be sure your experience is **significant** and that you focus on one specific **incident**. Keep your **purpose** and **audience** in mind as you write.

Learn It Online
To see how one writer composed an autobiographical narrative, use the interactive writer's model:

go.hrw.com L9-417 

Gather Sensory Details

Your audience can better share the experience relayed in your autobiographical narrative if you include **sensory details**. Sensory details appeal to all five senses: sight, sound, taste, smell, and touch. Use your imagination to add details that you can't remember. Sensory details appeal to your audience by bringing the reader into the experience. Notice how one student writer recorded sensory details that she wanted to include in her narrative in the center circle of the graphic organizer.

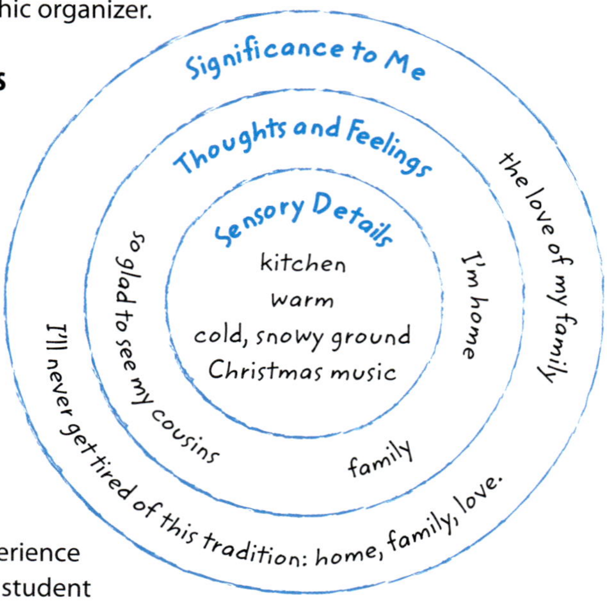

Thoughts and Feelings

Your autobiographical narrative recalls more than just the people, places, and events of your experience. It reveals your **thoughts** and **feelings** through **interior monologue**. An interior monologue expresses in words your thoughts and feelings. Ask yourself, "What did I think and feel as the experience unfolded?" Notice how a student writer shows her feelings about visiting her grandmother's house in the middle circle of the graphic organizer above.

Relate the Significance

Your autobiographical narrative should include broader reflections on the whole experience—your thoughts and feelings on the experience now, after some time has passed. Look back at the details, thoughts, and feelings, and ask the following questions:

- How did the experience change me?
- What did the experience teach me?

Notice how the student writer reflects broadly on the experience of a holiday visit to her grandmother's house in the outer circle of the graphic organizer.

Your Turn

Create a Circle Graph In your **RWN**, draw a circle graph like the one at right. Draw it to fill a page. It will focus your memories of the experience you have chosen for your autobiographical narrative.

- Label the inner circle "Sensory Details," and jot down every detail you can remember.
- Label the middle circle "Thoughts and Feelings," and record there what you thought and how you felt at the time of the event.
- Label the outer circle "Significance to Me." There, write notes about how you feel now that you've had time to think about the significance of the experience.

Drafting

Organize and Draft Your Narrative

Autobiographical narratives usually unfold in **chronological** order—showing the events as they happened over time. You can use the basic structure shown at the right in your autobiographical narrative.

Structure of Autobiographical Narrative

Introduction
- Begin with an engaging opening.
- Supply background information so that readers understand the context of the experience.

Body
- Describe the people, places, and sequence of events.
- Include your thoughts and feelings as the experience unfolds.
- Keep a natural pace in the action, reflecting changes in time or mood.

Conclusion
- Reflect on what the experience means to you now.

Relate Your Experience with Transitions

Because autobiographical narratives relate actions and experiences across time and place, remember to connect ideas and events with transitional words, phrases, and clauses. Transitions keep the events flowing smoothly so that the reader is always aware of time, order, location, and importance of the details in your experience.

Grammar Link Punctuating Introductory Adverb Clauses

One way to connect your ideas in time and place is by using adverbial clauses at the beginning of some sentences. **Adverb clauses** tell readers *why*, *where*, *how*, or *when* something happens. Some common **subordinating conjunctions** begin introductory adverb clauses: *after*, *before*, *because*, *when*, *while*, *as*, *if*, *although*, *since*, *while*, and *until*. They effectively provide transition between events and actions.

Here are two examples of introductory adverb clauses from the student model on pages 421–422.

> When we get off of the plane, we walk through an endless stretch of gates to the baggage claim.
>
> As I look out the window, I see the mushy gray clumps of what used to be snow, now pushed to the side by huge, neon orange snow plows.

Notice that introductory adverbial clauses are set off from the rest of the sentence by **commas**.

Writing Tip

- Use first-person pronouns *I*, *me*, *my*, and *we* when referring to yourself.
- Keep a consistent first-person point of view throughout your autobiographical narrative.

Your Turn

Draft Your Narrative Using the notes on your **circle graph** and the basic structure of an autobiographical narrative, create your first draft. Also think about the following:

- What does my audience need to know to appreciate the experience?
- How can I use transitional devices to connect ideas in time and place?

Autobiographical Narrative

Peer Review

Working with a peer, go over the chart at the right. Then, review your draft. Answer each question in this chart to locate where and how your drafts could be improved. Be sure to take notes on what you and your partner discuss. You can refer to your notes as you revise your draft.

Evaluating and Revising

Read the questions in the left column of the chart, and then use the tips in the middle column to help you make revisions to your autobiographical narrative. The right column suggests techniques you can use to revise your draft.

Autobiographical Narrative: Guidelines for Content and Organization

Evaluation Question	Tip	Revision Technique
1. Does the introduction include engaging opening and background information that creates a context?	**Bracket** the opening statement and details that show where and when the experience happened.	**Replace** weak openers with a quotation, question, or surprising statement to engage the reader. **Add** background information.
2. Does the narrative include sensory details about the events, people, and places?	**Circle** details that describe sights, sounds, smells, textures, and tastes. If you have fewer than three circles in each paragraph, revise to add more.	**Elaborate** with sensory details about events, people, and places.
3. Does the writer include thoughts and feelings in the narrative?	**Highlight** statements of the writer's thoughts and feelings. If there is not at least one piece of interior monologue, add one.	**Add** specific details about thoughts and feelings, including interior monologue.
4. Is the order of the events clear?	**Number** the events as they appear in the paper. Compare the numbered events to the actual sequence of events.	**Rearrange** events in chronological order.
5. Does the writer smoothly connect ideas and events across time and place?	**Put parentheses around** transition words as well as phrases and clauses that connect ideas.	**Add** transition words to connect ideas or combine ideas using introductory phrases and clauses.
6. Does the conclusion indicate why the experience is significant?	**Underline** sentences that reveal the broader meaning of the experience.	**Add** one or two sentences that clearly state the significance of the experience.

Read this student draft, and notice the comments on its strengths and suggestions on how it could be improved.

Student Draft

Traditions

by Lauren Stoker, Harrison High School

Every year in the chill of November, my family and I fly to Rochester, New York, to my grandmother's house. When we get off of the plane, we walk through an endless stretch of gates to baggage claim. My aunt and cousin are there waiting for us, arms open wide, warm and welcoming. My cousin and I embrace in the airport with nothing else in the world bothering us, absorbing the sheer joy we get when we are together. We gather our two-hundred pound suitcases and head for the car, my grandmother's old, teal green Lincoln. As I look out the window, I see the mushy, gray clumps of what used to be snow, now pushed to the side by the huge, neon orange snow plows.

Lauren provides **context** for the experience that she has chosen: the yearly trip to her grandmother's house at Thanksgiving.

Finally, we arrive at my grandmother's house. Inside it is warm, welcoming us with the smell of dinner cooking in the small kitchen. The air is filled with a sweet, flowery perfume, tickling my nose. Then I see her.

Sensory details effectively describe the setting, including the snowy road and the warm interior of the house.

Sweater covered in lint, shoes scuffing across the squeaky hard wood floor, glasses dangling from a chain around her neck, there she is, my grandmother. She greets us with a loving kiss on the forehead, firetruck-red lipstick smearing our tired faces. Soon after the traditional teacakes and hot chocolate, I watch grainy home movies on a forty-year-old projector, seeing my mother and her siblings grow up: birthdays, Thanksgiving, the Fourth of July.

Sensory details describe Lauren's grandmother, providing insight into her personality.

MINI-LESSON How to Use Interior Monologue

Unlike the dialogue between people, **interior monologue** is not spoken aloud or heard by other people. Instead, a person's inner thoughts and feelings are put into words. Lauren's narrative can be improved by adding her thoughts about her experiences. Lauren adds the following interior monologue to her last sentence in the third paragraph above.

Lauren's Revision of Paragraph Three

... seeing my mother and her siblings grow up: birthdays, Thanksgiving, the Fourth of July. ^ *Being at my grandmother's house reminds me that my past and present are made up of laughter and love.*

Your Turn

Use Interior Monologue Read your draft, and then ask yourself:

- What was I feeling and thinking about the experience at this point?
- Where can I best add interior monologue?

Autobiographical Narrative

Student Draft *continues*

Lauren uses **sensory details** to capture the moment when dinner is served and the whole family is together.

Finally it's here, turkey day, Thanksgiving, the day I have been waiting for. The long, hardwood table is surrounded by mismatched chairs and the people sitting in them watching, waiting for the food to arrive. My grandmother says a few words. Then comes the moment we have all been waiting for when the food arrives—steaming, mouth-watering food. Mashed potatoes, homemade rolls, stuffing, green beans, cranberry sauce, creamed onions, the turkey, golden brown in color, flaky outside skin, taunting us. Family from near and far, we pass around the food, chatting, laughing, and loving. We're a modern version of a Norman Rockwell painting.

The conclusion reflects on the **significance** of the experience.

Thinking about that Thanksgiving, I realize the dinner isn't the best part at all. It is my whole family being together. Waiting for the moment makes it so much sweeter, so I dream of when the day will come again. This day, my favorite tradition of them all, is an overlooked holiday that comes once a year in November: Thanksgiving Dinner.

MINI-LESSON How to Create Effective Conclusions

The conclusion of an autobiographical narrative usually leaves the reader with some last thoughts about the **significance** of the experience. Statements that do not add to the significance can be deleted. To improve her conclusion, Lauren decided to delete the last sentence to leave the reader thinking about the significance of the experience. Read the revised version aloud to determine if you think her revision made it more effective.

Lauren's Revision of the Last Paragraph

Thinking about that Thanksgiving, I realize the dinner isn't the best part at all. It is my whole family being together. Waiting for the moment makes it so much sweeter, so I dream of when the day will come again. ~~That day, my favorite tradition of them all, is an overlooked holiday that comes once a year in November: Thanksgiving.~~

Your Turn

Create an Effective Conclusion

- Re-read your final paragraph. Where is your reflection on the significance of the experience?
- What words, phrases, or sentences may divert the reader's attention away from the significance?
- Revise your conclusion to make it more effective.

Proofreading and Publishing

Proofreading

Proofread your paper before you prepare a final copy for publishing. Find and eliminate errors in grammar, mechanics, and usage.

Grammar Link Using Active Voice

When you write about yourself, you often use ***be* verbs**: *am*, *are*, *be*, *been*, *being*, *is*, *was*, and *were*. However, you can unintentionally create passive-voice sentences by using *be* verbs—making the subject of the verb *receive* the action, rather than *perform* the action. Passive voice sentences are not as powerful as ones that use active voice. You can evaluate your use of *be* verbs to determine if you need to change to active voice, keep the *be* verb, or combine sentences to eliminate it.

Lauren found and revised some *be* verbs in her draft.

> Finally, we arrive at my grandmother's house. Inside it is warm, welcoming us with the smell of dinner cooking in the small kitchen. The air ~~is filled~~ fills with a sweet, flowery perfume, tickling my nose. Then I see her.

Why do you think Lauren replaced only the second *be* verb?

Publishing

Readers like to cry, laugh, and learn from others' experiences. Here are some ways you can share your narrative with a wider audience:

- Add photos or drawings; then give it to a loved one as a keepsake.
- Publish your narrative as a blog entry or post it to a Web site dedicated to student writing.

Reflect on the Process

In your **RWN**, write short responses to the following questions:

1. How did writing this narrative help you to understand this experience differently?
2. Which parts of your narrative required the most change? Which required the least? What types of changes did you make?
3. Which step of the writing process was most difficult? What can you do to make it easier next time you write an autobiographical narrative?

Proofreading Tip

Read your autobiographical narrative aloud, taking note of any long introductory phrases or clauses. Remember to use a comma to separate an introductory phrase or clause from the rest of the sentence.

Writing Tip

Not all *be* verbs show passive voice—some express a state of being, such as "I *am* happy" or "She *was* student body president."

Your Turn

Proofread and Publish

Proofread your draft. As you proofread, circle all of the *be* verbs. Revise passive-voice sentences if you think they are awkward or weak. Then, make a final copy of your autobiographical narrative and publish it.

Scoring Rubric

You can use one of the rubrics below to evaluate your autobiographical narrative from the Writing Workshop or from the activity on the next page. Your teacher will tell you which rubric to use.

6-Point Scale

Score 6 *Demonstrates advanced success*

- focuses consistently on a clear, controlling idea
- shows effective organization throughout, with smooth transitions
- offers a thoughtful, creative approach to the narrative
- develops the narrative thoroughly, using incidents, details, and explanation
- exhibits mature control of written language

Score 5 *Demonstrates proficient success*

- focuses on a clear, controlling idea
- shows effective organization, with transitions
- offers a thoughtful approach to the narrative
- develops the narrative competently, using incidents, details, and explanation
- exhibits sufficient control of written language

Score 4 *Demonstrates competent success*

- focuses on a clear, controlling idea, with minor distractions
- shows effective organization, with minor lapses
- offers a mostly thoughtful approach to the narrative
- develops the narrative adequately, using some incidents, details, and explanation
- exhibits general control of written language

Score 3 *Demonstrates limited success*

- includes some loosely related ideas that distract from the controlling idea
- shows some organization, with noticeable gaps in the logical flow of ideas
- offers a routine, predictable approach to the narrative
- develops the narrative with uneven use of incidents, details, and explanation
- exhibits limited control of written language

Score 2 *Demonstrates basic success*

- includes loosely related ideas that seriously distract from the writer's controlling idea
- shows minimal organization, with major gaps in the logical flow of ideas
- offers a narrative that merely skims the surface
- develops the narrative with inadequate use of incidents, details, and explanation
- exhibits significant problems with control of written language

Score 1 *Demonstrates emerging effort*

- shows little awareness of the topic and purpose for writing
- lacks organization
- offers an unclear and confusing narrative
- develops the narrative in only a minimal way, if at all
- exhibits major problems with control of written language

4-Point Scale

Score 4 *Demonstrates advanced success*

- focuses consistently on a clear controlling idea
- shows effective organization throughout, with smooth transitions
- offers a thoughtful, creative approach to the narrative
- develops the narrative thoroughly, using incidents, details, and explanation
- exhibits mature control of written language

Score 3 *Demonstrates competent success*

- focuses on a clear, controlling idea, with minor distractions
- shows effective organization, with minor lapses
- offers a mostly thoughtful approach to the narrative
- develops the narrative adequately, using some incidents, details, and explanation
- exhibits general control of written language

Score 2 *Demonstrates limited success*

- includes some loosely related ideas that distract from the controlling idea
- shows some organization, with noticeable gaps in the logical flow of ideas
- offers a routine, predictable approach to the narrative
- develops the narrative with uneven use of incidents, details, and explanation
- exhibits limited control of written language

Score 1 *Demonstrates emerging effort*

- shows little awareness of the topic and purpose for writing
- lacks organization
- offers an unclear and confusing narrative
- develops the narrative in only a minimal way, if at all
- exhibits major problems with control of written language

Autobiographical Narrative

When responding to a prompt, use what you've learned from your reading, writing your autobiographical narrative, and studying the rubric on page 424. Use the steps below to develop a response to the following prompt.

Writing Prompt

Much has been written and said about the meaning of courage today. Write an autobiographical narrative about an experience that defined courage for you.

Study the Prompt

Begin by reading the prompt carefully. Circle or underline key words: *courage*, *meaning of courage*, *defined*, and *for you*. Re-read the prompt to see if there is additional information that can help you.

Your purpose is to narrate, or tell about, a story from your life that made the meaning of *courage* clear to you. Organize your response around a specific experience set in a context of other events. You will also relate your thoughts and feelings about the experience.

Remember, unless you were **personally** involved, the story you tell will not be autobiographical. **Tip:** Spend about five minutes studying the prompt.

Plan Your Response

Make a list of experiences you have had with courageous actions. Then, using a chart like the one below, record ***how*** the experience defined courage and ***why*** the experience was significant to you.

Experience	How It Defines Courage	Why It Is Significant

Choose the experience from your list that clearly shows what *courage* means to you and that you can describe with specific details. Answer these questions about your chosen experience:

- What background information do my readers need to understand the experience?
- How can I *show* readers, rather than *tell* them, about my experience?
- How will I reveal my thoughts and feelings?
- How will I show a clear connection between the experience and my definition of *courage*?

Tip: Spend about ten minutes planning your response.

Respond to the Prompt

Start writing, even if you are unsure about how to begin. The most important thing is to get your ideas on paper. You can always write an introduction *after* you've told the main part of your story. One way to begin is to create a dialogue that provides background information. **Tip:** Spend about twenty minutes writing your autobiographical narrative.

Improve Your Response

Revising Go back to the key aspects of the prompt. Is your response about your own experience? Have you explained what courage means to you? Do sensory details and narrative actions help convey the story? If not, add these elements.

Proofreading Take a few minutes to edit your response to correct errors in grammar, spelling, punctuation, and capitalization. Make sure that your edits are neat and that the paper is legible.

Checking Your Final Copy Before you turn in your paper, read it one more time to catch any errors you may have missed. You'll be glad you took one more look to present your best writing. **Tip:** Save five or ten minutes to improve your paper.

Presenting an Oral Narrative

Speak with a Purpose

Adapt your written narrative into an oral narrative. Practice your narrative, and then present it to your class.

Reader/Writer Notebook

Use your **RWN** to complete the activities for this workshop.

Think as a Reader/Writer

Like reading and writing, speaking and listening are related processes. Like a reader, a listener takes in and tries to understand someone's ideas. Like a writer, a speaker tries to convey ideas to others. You have probably told many stories aloud, such as what happened when the bus broke down during a blizzard or how your team won the baseball championship. When you tell a story aloud, you are presenting an oral narrative.

Adapt Your Narrative

Try a New Twist

Because people will be listening to your narrative instead of reading it, you'll need to adapt it as you prepare for your presentation. Keep in mind your audience—your classmates—and follow these suggestions to construct your narrative.

- **Word Choice** Use vocabulary that sounds natural. Avoid words that might be unfamiliar to your listeners, who won't be able to stop and look them up in a dictionary.
- **Setting** Locate events in specific places. For instance, say "in the cafeteria line" or "by my locker" rather than "at school." Doing so will help your listeners visualize events.
- **Details** Readers have time to linger over language to form mental images of what a writer describes. Listeners don't. Look carefully at the sensory details you used in your written narrative to describe different sights, sounds, and smells. Read sensory passages aloud, and ask yourself if your language will vividly create images in listeners' minds.
- **Organization of your original narrative** You may need to strengthen the transitional words and phrases you used in your written narrative to help listeners follow the story events. On your own or with a classmate, review your narrative to make sure that one event clearly leads to the next and that important details have not been left out.
- **Conclusion** If you didn't directly state the significance of your experience in the conclusion of your written narrative, do so in the conclusion of your oral narrative. Strongly suggesting or indirectly stating the significance is acceptable in a written narrative that readers can re-read, but not in an oral narrative that listeners have to understand immediately.

MO **9.W.1.A.1.e** Follow a writing process to: share writing **9.R.1.D.1.a** Read grade-level instructional text: with fluency, accuracy, comprehension and appropriate expression

Deliver Your Narrative

When you wrote your narrative, you conveyed the meaning of your experience through words alone. Since you'll deliver your narrative orally, you can also use verbal and nonverbal techniques to show how the experience made you feel and what it meant to you.

Use Verbal Techniques

How you use your voice can give the audience as much information as *what* you say.

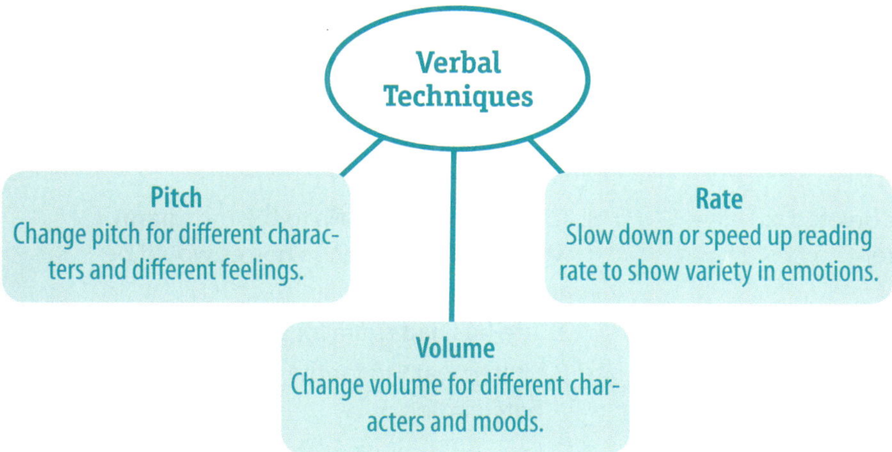

Verbal Techniques
Pitch
Change pitch for different characters and different feelings.
Rate
Slow down or speed up reading rate to show variety in emotions.
Volume
Change volume for different characters and moods.

Use Nonverbal Techniques

Facial expressions and gestures add meaning to your oral narrative. Use gestures to emphasize high points of conflict or humor. Keep in mind that your eyes also convey emotion—involve your listeners by making frequent eye contact with them.

Take Notes

Before your presentation, create notecards with short phrases or single words that remind you of story details, and arrange the notecards in the order in which you will present your ideas. As you give your narrative presentation, refer to your notes to keep you on track.

A Good Oral Narrative

- focuses on the details and significance of a single event
- includes story elements, such as plot, characters, and setting
- presents ideas clearly so listeners can easily follow along
- is delivered using effective verbal and nonverbal speaking techniques

Speaking Tip

To overcome any uneasiness about delivering your narrative, remember to rehearse. By practicing with a friend or in front of a mirror, you can see what you need to do to improve your narrative. Memorizing your presentation will help you feel more comfortable when you speak.

Learn It Online

Learn how to incorporate forms of media in your oral narrative at:

go.hrw.com L9-427 Go

FOCUS ON MISSOURI COURSE LEVEL EXPECTATIONS

Writing Skills Review

Autobiographical Narrative

Directions: Read the following paragraph from a draft of a student's autobiographical narrative. Then, answer the questions below.

(1) Of all the events of my childhood the one I remember best is my first ride on the school bus. (2) It took our bus forty-five minutes to get from my house to the school. (3) As I stepped up the gritty black steps and looked for an empty seat, I saw countless strange faces glaring back at me. (4) I sat near the back of the bus next to a shy-looking kid with glasses that sat crookedly on his nose. (5) As the bus got rolling I soon found myself in the midst of a raging paper war. (6) "Will this ever stop?" I wondered as a thick, wet paper wad struck the back of my neck. (7) "Get under here!" the boy next to me shouted, signaling me to duck under the backpack he had put over his head for protection. (8) As we crouched, we laughed together at the chaos around us. (9) When we arrived, I promised to meet him so we could ride home together.

---

1. Which sentence should be deleted to make the paragraph more coherent?
   A. sentence 2
   B. sentence 4
   C. sentence 7
   D. sentence 8

   9.W.2.B.1.b

2. What is the best revision of this portion of sentence 3?
   A. When I climbed up the gritty black steps of the bus and looked for an empty seat,
   B. As I stepped up the gritty black steps of the school and looked for an empty seat,
   C. Whenever I stepped up the gritty black steps and looked for an empty seat,
   D. The clause is correct.

   9.W.2.E.1.c

3. To add sensory details to the paragraph, which of the following choices would be appropriate?
   A. The bus had room for sixty-four.
   B. I hated waiting for the bus even more than I hated riding it.
   C. I waded through crumpled litter and masses of students to get to my seat.
   D. My friend's mom worked at the school, so she didn't ride the bus.

   9.W.2.D.1.b

4. Where would you place the sentence, "All of the yelling hurt my ears, and wads of paper hurtled through the air like missiles"?
   A. between sentences 1 and 2
   B. between sentences 2 and 3
   C. between sentences 5 and 6
   D. after sentence 9

   9.W.2.C.1.b

9.W.3.A.1.a Compose a variety of texts: using narrative, descriptive, expository, and/or persuasive features *Also covered* **9.W.2.B.1.b; 9.W.2.C.1.b; 9.W.2.D.1.a; 9.W.2.D.1.b; 9.W.2.E.1.b; 9.W.2.E.1.c**

5. Which of the following sentences might the writer add to explain the significance of the experience?
   A. That school bus ride was really awkward.
   B. In the midst of flying trash, I had somehow found a friend.
   C. The bus system was in need of a strict disciplinary program.
   D. The school bus was an efficient mode of transportation.

   9.W.2.B.1.b

6. Which of the following choices shows the correct punctuation for the beginning of sentence 1?
   A. Of all the events, of my childhood the one I remember best
   B. Of all the events, of my childhood, the one I remember best
   C. Of all the events of my childhood, the one I remember best
   D. The sentence is punctuated correctly.

   9.W.2.E.1.b

7. Which of the following choices shows the correct punctuation for this clause from sentence 5?
   A. As the bus got rolling;
   B. As the bus got rolling,
   C. As the bus got rolling—
   D. As the bus got rolling.

   9.W.2.E.1.b

8. What word could be substituted for <u>shouted</u> in sentence 7?
   A. Whispered
   B. Mouthed
   C. Yelled
   D. Panicked

   9.W.2.D.1.a

9. Why did the student put "Will this ever stop?" in quotation marks?
   A. It sets the pace of the story.
   B. It is the title of the story.
   C. It is an important event.
   D. It is interior monologue.

   9.W.2.E.1.b

10. Which revision to sentence 9 shows the best example of adding a prepositional phrase to add detail?
    A. ride home from our last class together.
    B. When we arrived there later,
    C. meet him after the final bell
    D. meet him later on that day

    9.W.2.B.1.b

UNIT 2

Nonfiction

Writers on Writing

Andrew Lam on Nonfiction Andrew Lam was born in Vietnam and came to the United States with his family when he was eleven years old. Today, he is a regular commentator on National Public Radio. His collected essays *Perfume Dreams: Reflections on the Vietnamese Diaspora* was published in 2005.

"I've written short stories, poems, and news analyses. But the personal essay remains my preferred medium. The writer's voice, when honest and frank, provides an emotional intimacy with the reader no other genre can. In my case—a refugee who fled from a war-torn country and became an American writer who travels the world—the

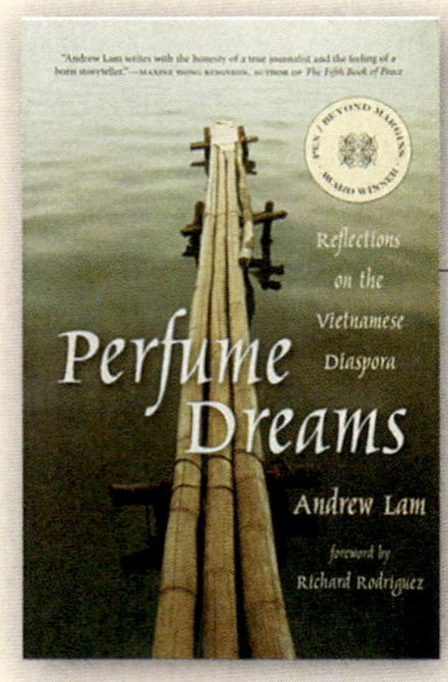

personal often bears witness to the historical, as rivers are to the sea. The essay, indeed, can be all at once familiar, conversational, and reportorial. It can persuade without seemingly trying to. And, arguably, there is as much drama in a personal essay as in any piece of fiction.

Even before I could speak a full English sentence, even before I could distinguish 'bear' from 'bare,' I wanted to tell my story. Fresh from the Guam refugee camp, I tried my best with hand gestures and a few words, and when words and gestures failed, with color chalks and the blackboard during recess. I'd tell my seventh-grade classmates about my childhood in Vietnam—my helicopter rides as an army brat, the Tet celebrations full of relatives and friends, the smell of ripened rice fields at dusk—what I would never experience again.

I was a shy boy. But in America, that was no longer true. I instinctively knew what I could not articulate: That I was not fully part of the New World unless I could bring my full biography—what I lost, what was robbed from me and my family at the end of the Vietnam War—to bear.

It was frustrating at first. I learned to read Vietnamese at four and French at seven. But my first few months in America I didn't understand much. All I could muster were 'No understand!' and 'I don't know!' So I bought a used typewriter and typed out the novel *The Wind in the Willows* and then copied newspaper articles. I learned how to type and read at the same time.

In the morning in the shower, I would practice my English. I would enunciate certain words learned the day before and listen to their vibrations. 'Business,' I would pronounce. 'Stress!' I would shout. 'Necessary!' I could almost see the words with their sharp edges and round arches taking shape in the steamy air. I would try my best to rule over them.

Did I know then that I would grow up to be a writer and essayist? No. But I did find the sound of my American voice intriguing. I was going through puberty when I came to America, and I distinctly heard from my own voice the promises of newness, a future. In college, timidly at first, I began to write down my Vietnamese memories. I began to fancy myself a writer.

Many years passed. . . .

I think of that tongue-tied child at the blackboard in seventh grade drawing pictures of helicopters and rice paddies, trying to tell his story. He's found his medium; but he's still at it."

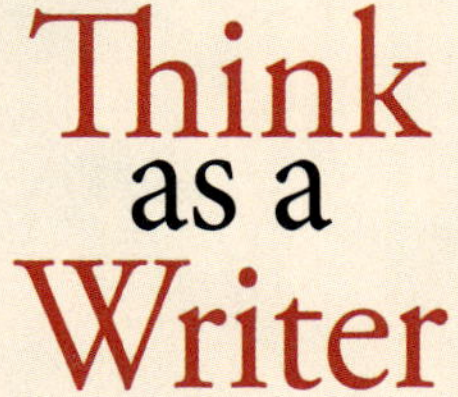

Andrew Lam talks about a lifelong desire to tell his own story. How does writing a personal essay help the writer? What does it do for the reader?

COLLECTION 5

Form and Style

INFORMATIONAL TEXT FOCUS

Structure and Format of Functional Documents

"Memories of our lives, of our works and our deeds will continue in others."

—Rosa Parks

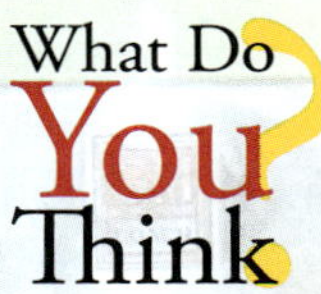

What Do You Think? What do you have to say to the world?

Girl sits in vintage 1950s bus in front of the Metropolitan African Methodist Episcopal Church in Washington D.C. during a 2005 memorial service for Rosa Parks.

Learn It Online

To tell your own nonfiction story, visit the Digital Storytelling site:

go.hrw.com L9-433 

Literary Focus

by **Carol Jago**

What Do You Need to Know About Form and Style?

People with "style" stand out from the crowd. Something about the way they dress, walk, or speak is distinctive. The same is true of writers. Successful essayists use language in a way that is interesting and memorable and that helps convey an aspect of their personalities. While maintaining a coherent form and structure, these authors use style to attract, persuade, entertain, and engage their readers.

Forms of Nonfiction

Nonfiction—true-life stories of people, things, events, and places—comes in many forms. Some writers share a personal story, while others write about someone else's life or reflect on a topic of personal significance. Working within these forms, writers infuse their writing with their own personal style.

Personal Essay A personal essay can be about any topic, serious or humorous. It is usually short and informal and often reveals a great deal about the writer's personality and tastes.

> In my neighborhood, where the smell of somebody's grandmother's cooking could transform a New York corner into Santo Domingo, Kingston or Port-au-Prince, a Panamanian was a sort of fish with feathers—assumed to be a Jamaican who spoke Spanish.
>
> from "The Secret Latina"
> by Veronica Chambers

Expository Essay An expository essay explains something to the reader by giving information or clarifying an idea. Expository essays are usually formal in tone and generally objective.

Autobiography An autobiography is a full-length work that gives an account of the writer's own life.

> When writing about oneself, one must strive to be truthful. Truth is more important than modesty. I must tell you, therefore, that it was I and I alone who had the idea for the great and daring Mouse Plot.
>
> from *Boy*
> by Roald Dahl

Memoir Unlike an autobiography, which is the story of a person's life, a memoir zeroes in on a particular time period in the writer's life.

> The family vacation. Heat, flies, sand and dirt. My mother sweeps and complains, my father forever baits hooks and untangles lines.
>
> from "In the Current"
> by Jo Ann Beard

Biography A biography tells the story of a person's life. It is written or told by someone other than its subject.

9.R.3.C.1.a Use details from informational text: to identify and explain the organizational pattern
9.R.2.C.1.d Use details from text(s): to evaluate the effect of author's style

A Writer's Style

Diction A writer's **style** is revealed through word choice, or **diction,** and through sentence structures. Some authors write in informal English or even in slang. Others prefer to use formal English. Notice how Mark Twain uses language in this excerpt:

> When I was a boy, there was but one permanent ambition among my comrades in our village on the west bank of the Mississippi River. That was, to be a steamboatman.
>
> from "Cub Pilot on the Mississippi" by Mark Twain

Twain could have said the same thing in a simpler way. Instead, he chose to create a humorous contrast by using formal language and complex sentences to convey a very simple idea.

Tone A key element of style is **tone,** a writer's attitude toward a subject, a character, or the audience. Tone isn't only *what* you say but also *how* you say it. Dahl's word choices and an interesting **figure of speech,** or unusual comparison, create a disrespectful yet humorous tone in this passage from his autobiography.

> Her name was Mrs. Pratchett. She was a small skinny old hag with a moustache on her upper lip and a mouth as sour as a green gooseberry.
>
> from *Boy* by Roald Dahl

Mood When you walk into a room full of people, you can often sense the mood—for example, a feeling of celebration or mourning, concern or relaxation. Writers create **mood,** or emotional atmosphere, by choosing their words carefully. The use of **imagery**—words or phrases that appeal to one or more of our senses—also helps establish mood.

As you analyze the selections in this collection, you might find the following words helpful in describing tone and mood.

Words to Describe Tone and Mood
Tone (description of attitude): sarcastic; serious; vengeful; admiring; amused; bitter; forgiving
Mood (description of atmosphere): grim; joyous; ominous; eerie; tense; lighthearted

Your Turn Analyze Style

Here are two paragraphs by two writers. Read the passages, and work with a partner to note each paragraph's different style. Then, describe the diction, tone, and mood of each.

> Restless, shifting, fugacious as time itself is a certain vast bulk of the population of the red brick district of the lower West Side. Homeless, they have a hundred homes. They flit from furnished room to furnished room, transients forever—transients in abode, transients in heart and mind.
>
> from "The Furnished Room" by O. Henry

> But Easter's early morning sun had shown the dress to be a plain ugly cut-down from a white woman's once-was-purple throwaway. It was old-lady-long too, but it didn't hide my skinny legs, which had been greased with Blue Seal Vaseline and powdered with the Arkansas red clay.
>
> from *I Know Why the Caged Bird Sings* by Maya Angelou

Learn It Online
To understand the role of literary elements in novels, visit *NovelWise* at:

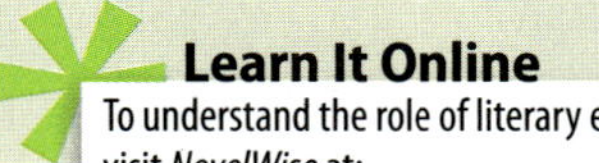

Analyzing Visuals

How Can You Recognize Form and Style in Art?

Visual art has its own forms of nonfiction, but they're classified by different names than in literature. Realism describes art that closely resembles real life. Lifelike portraits painted with great detail fit this category. Photographs are another form of visual nonfiction. The line between fiction and reality blurs as much in art as in literature. Just as a memoirist can stretch the truth to add texture and interest to his or her stories (sometimes causing them to land on the fiction shelf), so too can an artist's use of color, shape, and light inject personal style into his or her realistic work.

Analyzing Realism in Art

Use these guidelines to help you analyze realistic art.

1. Study the subject of the painting and its level of detail.
2. Use your prior knowledge to consider how much the subject and its surroundings appear lifelike.
3. Verify that the artist has included the imperfections you would expect in the subject and setting. If people are pictured, do their faces accurately reflect the action and circumstances of the setting?
4. Assess the level of realism. Does the scene in the artwork portray things as they actually are, or has the artist idealized the subject?

Study the details below to help you answer the questions on page 437.

Details from *Our Washerwoman's Family—New Mexico*.

MO **9.R.3.C.1.a** Use details from informational text: to identify and explain the organizational pattern **9.R.2.C.1.d** Use details from text(s): to evaluate the effect of author's style

1. Look at this painting's title. What **form** of nonfiction does this group portrait most closely resemble? Memoir? Biography? Essay?

2. Which elements of this painting seem true to life? Which elements seem less true to life?

3. Phillips uses color to express ideas. How does the use of color convey the closeness of the family?

4. What **tone,** or attitude, does Phillips convey through his choice of subject matter and his painting **style**?

Our Washerwoman's Family—New Mexico (c. 1918) by Bert Geer Phillips. Oil on canvas (40 ½" x 41 5/8"). Collection of the New Mexico Museum of Art. Gift of Governor and Mrs. Arthur Seligman, 1918.

Your Turn Talk About Form and Style

Choose another portrait in this book, and study it with a group of classmates. Then, discuss ways in which the artist shows the subject in a realistic light yet uses a personal style to convey meaning.

Reading Focus

by **Kylene Beers**

What Skills Help You Understand Form and Style?

Two pop songs—two singers—two styles. Just as experienced singers put their own stamp on standard forms of music, writers inject their style into standard forms of writing. As you read the selections in this collection, use these strategies to analyze forms of nonfiction and writers' styles.

Analyzing Author's Purpose

Suppose you wanted to write about an important person in your life—for instance, a coach or a teacher. How would you present your ideas? Before they begin writing, authors take time to identify their purpose. Often this purpose dictates the form that the author's material takes. For example, a writer who wants to tell the story of a past American president may write a biography. On the other hand, if the writer wants to give an opinion about a past president, he or she may opt to write an essay.

To help you determine an author's purpose for writing a work, ask yourself the following questions:

- What is the author trying to tell me?
- How do I feel as I read this work? Am I entertained? Am I being introduced to a viewpoint I've never considered before?
- What effect does the author's choice of details and overall use of language have on me?

Reading Aloud and Paraphrasing

To get a sense of a writer's style, read aloud passages from the text and listen to the effect of the words. After reading a passage aloud, paraphrase what you have just read. Then, compare your paraphrase with the original. What aspects of the author's style were "lost" in translation?

Original Text	My Paraphrase
Miss Betty said, "You there, girl. Get over here."	Miss Betty called the girl to come over.

Comparison: How does the style of the original differ from the paraphrased version?

Visualizing

No two people look at the same thing in the same way. Pay attention to the way an author describes people, things, or situations. Does he or she use imagery that appeals to the senses, or does he or she prefer to use simple and direct descriptions?

To help you visualize, close your eyes and try to imagine what the underlined details from the excerpt below bring to mind. Then, look for ways in which the writer's language helps you form that mental picture.

> Her apron was gray and greasy. Her blouse had bits of breakfast all over it, toast-crumbs and tea stains and splotches of dried egg-yolk.
>
> from *Boy* by Roald Dahl

MO **9.R.1.H.1.d** Apply post-reading skills to comprehend, interpret, analyze, and evaluate text: draw conclusions **9.R.1.G.1.f** During reading, utilize strategies: to paraphrase **9.R.1.G.1.e** During reading, utilize strategies: to visualize

Making Generalizations

To form a statement about a writer's style, make a **generalization,** or a broad statement. For example, if a story is written in a simple but humorous way, you might make a generalization like this: "This writer's style is engaging and suitable for readers of all ages."

Here's how to make a generalization about style: As you read a selection, take notes about how a writer uses language, and put those notes in a graphic organizer like the one below. Once you have recorded the different details, come up with a statement that conveys a big idea about the author's use of style.

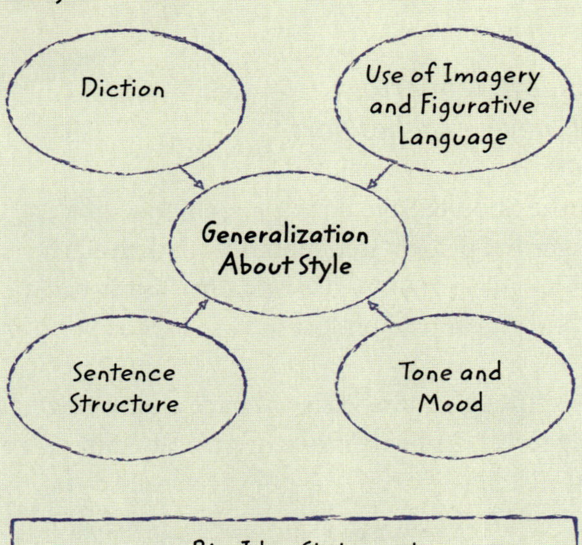

Your Turn Apply Reading Skills

Read this excerpt from T. S. Eliot's poem "Macavity: The Mystery Cat." Use the reading skills you just learned to answer the questions that follow.

from Macavity: The Mystery Cat

by T. S. Eliot

Macavity's a ginger cat, he's very tall and thin;
You would know him if you saw him, for his eyes are sunken in.
His brow is deeply lined with thought, his head is highly domed;
His coat is dusty from neglect, his whiskers are uncombed.
He sways his head from side to side, with movements like a snake;
And when you think he's half asleep, he's always wide awake.

1. **Analyzing Author's Purpose** Why might Eliot have chosen to tell about Macavity in a humorous fashion?
2. **Read Aloud and Paraphrase** With a partner, take turns reading the poem aloud and paraphrasing it. Discuss the differences in wording.
3. **Visualizing** What words help you to visualize Macavity?
4. **Making Generalizations** What broad statement can you make about Eliot's style?

Now go to the Skills in Action: Reading Model

Learn It Online

Use *PowerNotes* to help you learn these skills the multimedia way:

ESSAY

Build Background

The author of "How to Eat a Guava" comes from Puerto Rico, a Caribbean island where guavas and other tropical fruits grow in abundance. Located about one thousand miles southeast of Florida, Puerto Rico is a commonwealth of the United States, and its inhabitants are U.S. citizens. Spanish is the chief language of Puerto Rico, reflecting its long history as a Spanish colony; English is its other official language.

Read with a Purpose Read this essay to find out what triggers a flood of memories for the essay's writer.

How to Eat a Guava

from When I Was Puerto Rican

by **Esmeralda Santiago**

Barco que no anda, no llega a puerto.
A ship that doesn't sail, never reaches port.

Reading Focus

Visualizing The author uses imagery to allow readers to picture her world and experiences.

There are guavas at the Shop & Save. I pick one the size of a tennis ball and finger the prickly stem end. It feels familiarly bumpy and firm. The guava is not quite ripe; the skin is still a dark green. I smell it and imagine a pale pink center, the seeds tightly embedded in the flesh.

A ripe guava is yellow, although some varieties have a pink tinge. The skin is thick, firm, and sweet. Its heart is bright pink and almost solid with seeds. The most delicious part of the guava surrounds the tiny seeds. If you don't know how to eat a guava, the seeds end up in the crevices between your teeth.

When you bite into a ripe guava, your teeth must grip the bumpy surface and sink into the thick edible skin without hitting the center. It takes experience to do this, as it's quite tricky to determine how far beyond the skin the seeds begin.

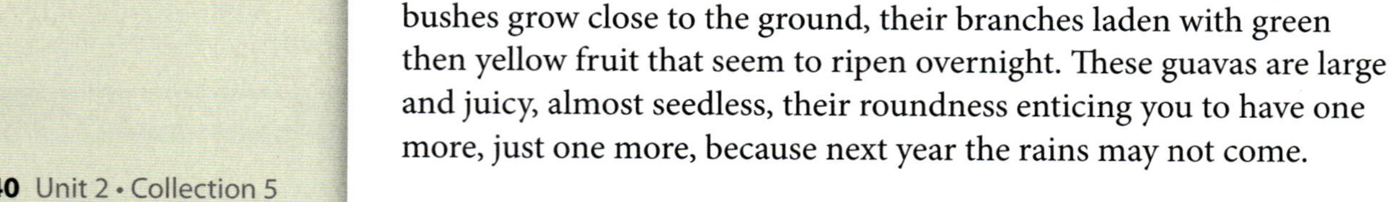

Some years, when the rains have been plentiful and the nights cool, you can bite into a guava and not find many seeds. The guava bushes grow close to the ground, their branches laden with green then yellow fruit that seem to ripen overnight. These guavas are large and juicy, almost seedless, their roundness enticing you to have one more, just one more, because next year the rains may not come.

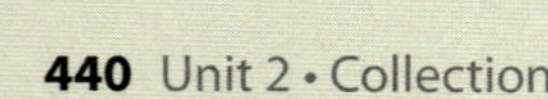

As children, we didn't always wait for the fruit to ripen. We raided the bushes as soon as the guavas were large enough to bend the branch.

Literary Focus

Tone Here, Santiago shares a childhood memory. Her tone suggests she remembers this experience fondly.

A green guava is sour and hard. You bite into it at its widest point, because it's easier to grasp with your teeth. You hear the skin, meat, and seeds crunching inside your head, while the inside of your mouth explodes in little spurts of sour.

You grimace, your eyes water, and your cheeks disappear as your lips purse into a tight O. But you have another and then another, enjoying the crunchy sounds, the acid taste, the gritty texture of the unripe center. At night, your mother makes you drink castor oil,[1] which she says tastes better than a green guava. That's when you know for sure that you're a child and she has stopped being one.

Literary Focus

Diction The author has chosen short, simple, parallel phrases to re-create a sensory memory.

I had my last guava the day we left Puerto Rico. It was large and juicy, almost red in the center, and so fragrant that I didn't want to eat it because I would lose the smell. All the way to the airport I scratched at it with my teeth, making little dents in the skin, chewing small pieces with my front teeth, so that I could feel the texture against my tongue, the tiny pink pellets of sweet.

---

1. **castor oil:** yellow or colorless oil made from castor beans and used as a home remedy for digestive problems.

Today, I stand before a stack of dark green guavas, each perfectly round and hard, each $1.59. The one in my hand is tempting. It smells faintly of late summer afternoons and hopscotch under the mango tree. But this is autumn in New York, and I'm no longer a child.

The guava joins its sisters under the harsh fluorescent lights of the exotic fruit display. I push my cart away, toward the apples and pears of my adulthood, their nearly seedless ripeness predictable and bittersweet.

Literary Focus

Mood The mood of this essay can be described as bittersweet, which sums up not only the taste of the apples and pears, but also the author's feelings toward her new country.

Read with a Purpose How does the author feel about guavas now?

MEET THE WRITER

Esmeralda Santiago

(1948–)

WHEN I WAS PUERTO RICAN

"Touching and revealing . . . takes its unique place in contemporary Latino storytelling." —Los Angeles Times

ESMERALDA SANTIAGO

Author of Almost a Woman

Between Two Worlds

At the age of thirteen, Esmeralda Santiago moved from Puerto Rico to New York City with her mother and ten brothers and sisters. Living in Puerto Rico and in New York, she says, has made her feel that she doesn't quite fit into either culture—a feeling she highlights in her memoir, *When I Was Puerto Rican*. In a note to her readers, she writes:

"When I returned to Puerto Rico after living in New York for seven years, I was told I was no longer Puerto Rican because my Spanish was rusty, my gaze too direct, my personality too assertive. . . . Yet, in the United States, my darkness, my accented speech, my frequent lapses into confused silence between English and Spanish identified me as foreign, non-American. In writing the book I wanted to get back to that feeling of Puertoricanness I had before I came here."

Think About the Writer What purpose does writing serve for Santiago?

SKILLS IN ACTION

Wrap Up

MO **9.R.2.C.1.d** Use details from text(s): to evaluate the effect of author's style **9.R.1.H.1.d** Apply post-reading skills to comprehend, interpret, analyze, and evaluate text: draw conclusions **9.R.1.E.1.c** Develop vocabulary through text: using glossary, dictionary and thesaurus

Into Action: Style Chart

In "How to Eat a Guava," Santiago uses her present experience as well as her childhood memories to reflect on something much more important than a guava. Find examples of elements of her writing style and note them in a chart like the one below.

Element of Style	Example from the Text
Diction and sentence structure	"The skin is thick, firm, and sweet." / simple sentence
Tone, or writer's attitude	
Mood, or atmosphere	

Talk About . . .

Get together with a small group to discuss "How to Eat a Guava," and answer the following questions. Try to use each Academic Vocabulary word listed at right at least once in your discussion.

1. What kind of tone does Santiago establish in her essay?
2. What does Santiago's choice of words reveal about her attitude toward Puerto Rico?
3. Would the addition of more Spanish words throughout the essay enhance your understanding of Santiago's background?
4. How does Santiago's use of vivid images appeal to the reader's senses? Explain.

Write About . . .

What generalization can you make about Santiago's style? Refer to the chart above to guide your response. Also, challenge yourself to use Academic Vocabulary terms, such as those listed to the right, in your response.

Writing Focus

Think as a Reader/Writer

Find It In Your Reading Look for ways in which Santiago's use of imagery helps define her style. As you read the rest of the selections in Collection 5, you will have more opportunities to analyze the writing styles of other nonfiction writers.

Academic Vocabulary for Collection 5

Talking and Writing About Nonfiction

Academic Vocabulary is the language you use to write and talk about literature. Use these words to discuss the prose you read in this collection. The words are underlined throughout the collection.

appeal (uh PEEL) *v.:* attract; interest. *She chose a variety of images to appeal to different senses.*

attitude (AT uh tood) *n.:* way of thinking, acting, or feeling; outlook. *She has a conflicted attitude toward her homeland.*

establish (ehs TAB lihsh) *v.:* set up; create. *Santiago used her childhood memories to help establish her tone.*

enhance (ehn HANS) *v.:* make greater; improve. *Allowing a fruit to fully ripen will enhance its flavor.*

Your Turn

Test your knowledge of the Academic Vocabulary terms by using each in a sentence. Record your sentences in your *Reader/Writer Notebook*.

AUTOBIOGRAPHY

Preparing to Read

Cub Pilot on the Mississippi

by **Mark Twain**

What Do You Think?

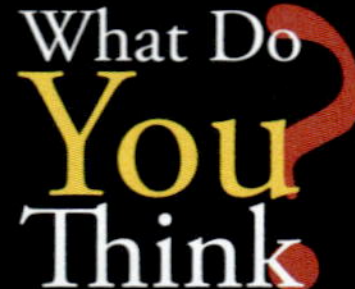

When do actions speak louder than words?

QuickTalk

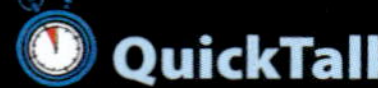

Why is it important to do as you say? Is it ever a good idea to say one thing but secretly do another thing? Talk over your ideas with a partner.

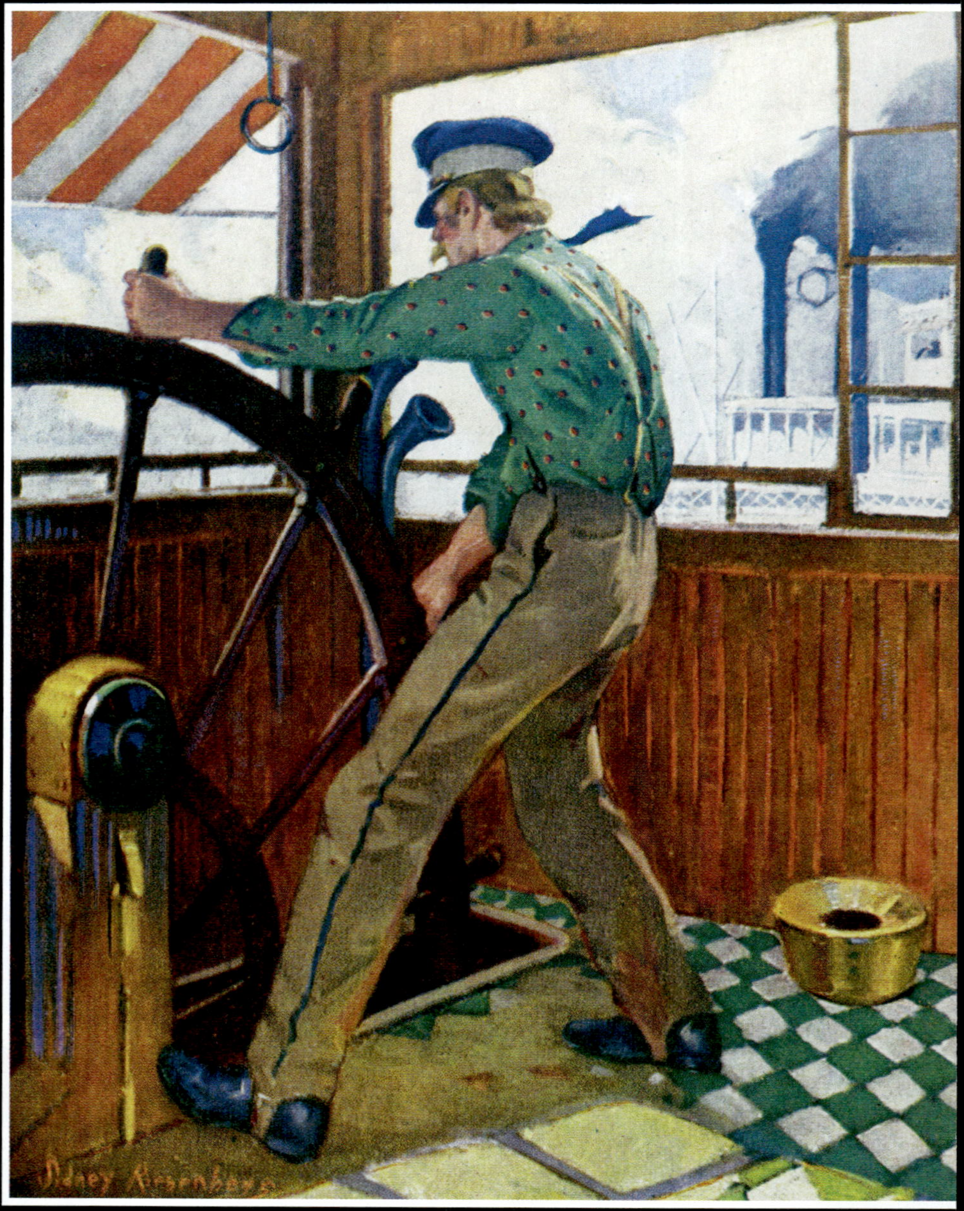

Illustration of Mark Twain (Samuel L. Clemens, 1835–1910) as a river-pilot on the Mississippi by Sidney Riesenberg.

Reader/Writer Notebook

Use your **RWN** to complete the activities for this selection.

MO **9.R.2.C.1.d** Use details from text(s): to evaluate the effect of author's style **9.R.1.G.1.f** During reading, utilize strategies: to paraphrase

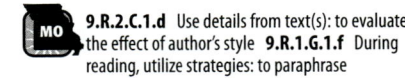

Literary Focus

Style and Tone One key element of Twain's memorable style is his **diction,** or word choice. The words Twain chooses are often direct, but can also be playful or even sarcastic. His style is also marked by a vivid and sometimes comic use of imagery. However, the most striking feature of Twain's writing is the tone that he creates through his use of language. In the following story, for example, Twain's attitude about his subject is made crystal clear.

TechFocus As you read, think about how Twain uses exaggeration to create humor and how you might do the same in a podcast.

Reading Focus

Reading Aloud and Paraphrasing To appreciate a writer's style and tone fully, try these two strategies: (1) **Read aloud** to "hear" the writer's voice. Listen for ways in which the writer's tone is made evident through word choice. (2) **Paraphrase,** or restate, story passages to confirm meaning. Then, compare your paraphrase with the original text to see what elements of style were lost.

Into Action Use a chart like the one below as you paraphrase story passages to clarify meaning.

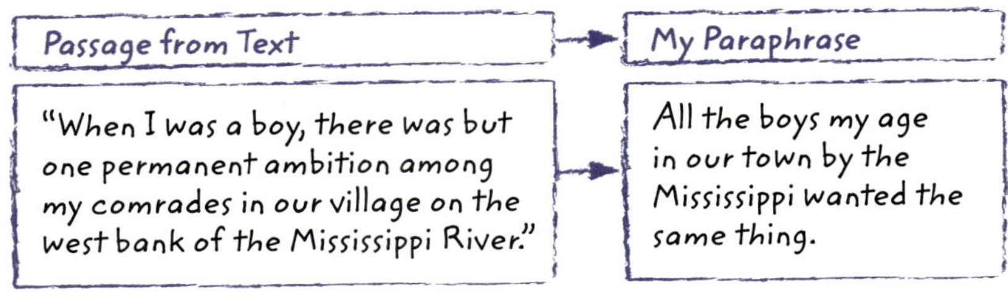

Passage from Text
My Paraphrase
"When I was a boy, there was but one permanent ambition among my comrades in our village on the west bank of the Mississippi River."
All the boys my age in our town by the Mississippi wanted the same thing.

Writing Focus

Think as a Reader/Writer

Find It in Your Reading Mark Twain gave this advice to writers: "Don't say the old lady screamed—bring her on and let her scream." Did Twain follow his own advice? In your *Reader/Writer Notebook,* note when Twain *shows* rather than *tells* what happens.

Vocabulary

transient (TRAN shuhnt) *adj.:* quickly passing; fleeting. *Twain's wish to join the circus was transient, lasting less than a year.*

judicious (joo DIHSH uhs) *adj.:* showing good judgment; wise. *Twain knew it would be judicious to keep quiet.*

inoffensive (ihn uh FEHN sihv) *adj.:* harmless; not objectionable in any way. *Henry was so completely inoffensive that he seemed unable to be rude or angry.*

indulgent (ihn DUHL juhnt) *adj.:* giving in to someone else's wishes. *The indulgent captain never punished the cubs for minor mistakes.*

confronted (kuhn FRUHNT ihd) *v.:* came face to face with someone. *After a serious mistake, the captain confronted Twain.*

Language Coach

Jargon Specialized vocabulary of an occupation or field of knowledge is called **jargon** and is sometimes created by attaching special meanings to familiar words. For example, when Twain describes dangerous *breaks,* he is not talking about rest periods. To a river worker, this word refers to choppy or rough water. Look for other words, such as *wheel* and *tender,* that have special meanings in the context of life on a Mississippi steamboat.

Learn It Online

Preview this autobiography by watching the video introduction at:

go.hrw.com L9-445 

MEET THE WRITER

Learn It Online
Learn more about Twain at:
go.hrw.com L9-446 Go

Mark Twain
(1835–1910)

Life on the River

In many ways, Mark Twain invented himself and became a superstar as a result. He was born Samuel Langhorne Clemens and grew up with six brothers and sisters in Hannibal, Missouri, a small town on the west bank of the Mississippi River. When his father died, Samuel was just eleven years old and had to work to help support the family. He delivered groceries, assisted a blacksmith, and then became a printer's apprentice. Later, he followed his lifelong dream and became a steamboat pilot.

A New Name for a New Life

After an unsuccessful venture trying to find gold in the Nevada Territory, Samuel turned to writing, taking on the pen name Mark Twain. His writing, such as *The Adventures of Tom Sawyer,* reflected a love of adventure and scorn for stuffiness. Twain became one of the most popular writers and lecturers in America, often wearing a striking all-white suit, which he called "a delightful impudence."

"I never write 'metropolis' for seven cents, because I can get the same money for 'city.' I never write 'policeman,' because I can get the same price for 'cop.'"

Think About the Writer What qualities do you think helped make Twain so appealing to his readers?

Build Background

In the nineteenth century, paddle wheel steamboats carried cargo up and down the Mississippi River. Steamboat pilots had to know the river and its obstacles well because boats could be damaged by going into shallow water. When Mark Twain was twenty-two, he joined a steamboat crew as an assistant pilot, or cub pilot. He worked on the river until commercial travel on the Mississippi stopped because of the Civil War. Twain recalls his early days in this selection from his autobiography *Life on the Mississippi* (1883).

Preview the Selection

Mark Twain has finally achieved his big goal—he's the assistant to a steamboat pilot. Unfortunately, the pilot is a man named **Brown,** who makes life tough for the young cub pilot.

Home of Mark Twain in Hartford, Connecticut.

Read with a Purpose Read the following selection to find out how Mark Twain handled a bad-tempered boss named Brown.

Cub Pilot on the Mississippi

by **Mark Twain**

When I was a boy, there was but one permanent ambition among my comrades in our village on the west bank of the Mississippi River. That was, to be a steamboatman. We had transient ambitions of other sorts, but they were only transient. When a circus came and went, it left us all burning to become clowns; the first minstrel show that came to our section left us all suffering to try that kind of life; now and then we had a hope that if we lived and were good, God would permit us to be pirates. These ambitions faded out, each in its turn; but the ambition to be a steamboatman always remained. . . . **A**

I first wanted to be a cabin-boy, so that I could come out with a white apron on and shake a tablecloth over the side, where all my old comrades could see me; later I thought I would rather be the deckhand who stood on the end of the stage-plank with the coil of rope in his hand, because he was particularly conspicuous. . . .

Boy after boy managed to get on the river. The minister's son became an engineer. The doctor's and the post-master's sons became "mud clerks";[1] the wholesale liquor dealer's son became a barkeeper on a boat; four sons of the chief merchant, and two sons of the county judge, became pilots. Pilot was the grandest position of all. The pilot, even in those days of trivial wages, had a princely salary—from a hundred and fifty to two hundred and fifty dollars a month, and no board to pay. Two months of his wages would pay a preacher's salary for a year. Now some of us were left disconsolate. We could not get on the river—at least our parents would not let us.

So by and by I ran away. I said I never would come home again till I was a pilot and could come in glory. . . . **B**

1. **"mud clerks":** the lowest of several clerks who assisted the financial officer.

A **Literary Focus** **Tone** What tone does Twain establish in the first paragraph? Which words and images create this tone?

Vocabulary **transient** (TRAN shuhnt) *adj.:* quickly passing; fleeting.

B **Reading Focus** **Paraphrasing** Restate this passage in your own words. Were your word choices more formal or informal than Twain's?

During the two or two and a half years of my apprenticeship, I served under many pilots, and had experience of many kinds of steamboatmen and many varieties of steamboats. . . . I am to this day profiting somewhat by that experience; for in that brief, sharp schooling, I got personally and familiarly acquainted with about all the different types of human nature that are to be found in fiction, biography, or history. . . .

The figure that comes before me oftenest, out of the shadows of that vanished time, is that of Brown, of the steamer "Pennsylvania"—the man referred to in a former chapter, whose memory was so good and tiresome. He was a middle-aged, long, slim, bony, smooth-shaven, horse-faced, ignorant, stingy, malicious, snarling, fault hunting, mote-magnifying tyrant. I early got the habit of coming on watch with dread at my heart. No matter how good a time I might have been having with the off-watch below, and no matter how high my spirits might be when I started aloft, my soul became lead in my body the moment I approached the pilot-house. **C**

I still remember the first time I ever entered the presence of that man. The boat had backed

C **Literary Focus** **Style** What effect does the string of adjectives that Twain uses to describe Brown have?

Analyzing Visuals **Viewing and Interpreting**
How does the artist establish the setting of the Mississippi River in this painting?

View on the Mississippi River (1857) by Ferdinand Reichardt.

out from St. Louis and was "straightening down"; I ascended to the pilot-house in high feather, and very proud to be semi-officially a member of the executive family of so fast and famous a boat. Brown was at the wheel. I paused in the middle of the room, all fixed to make my bow, but Brown did not look around. I thought he took a furtive glance at me out of the corner of his eye, but as not even this notice was repeated, I judged I had been mistaken. By this time he was picking his way among some dangerous "breaks" abreast the woodyards; therefore it would not be proper to interrupt him; so I stepped softly to the high bench and took a seat.

There was silence for ten minutes; then my new boss turned and inspected me deliberately and painstakingly from head to heel for about—as it seemed to me—a quarter of an hour. After which he removed his countenance[2] and I saw it no more for some seconds; then it came around once more, and this question greeted me— **D**

"Are you Horace Bixby's[3] cub?"

"Yes, sir."

After this there was a pause and another inspection. Then—

"What's your name?"

I told him. He repeated it after me. It was probably the only thing he ever forgot; for although I was with him many months he never addressed himself to me in any other way than "Here!" and then his command followed. **E**

"Where was you born?"

"In Florida, Missouri."

A pause. Then—

"Dern sight better stayed there!"

2. **countenance:** face.
3. **Horace Bixby's:** Twain met steamboat pilot Horace Bixby in 1857. When Bixby agreed to take him on as an apprentice, Twain happily quit his job writing comic letters for a local newspaper.

D **Literary Focus** **Tone** How does Twain's exaggeration of time enhance the humorous tone of the essay?

E **Literary Focus** **Style** How does this anecdote about Brown forgetting Twain's name contribute to the author's style?

By means of a dozen or so of pretty direct questions, he pumped my family history out of me.

The leads[4] were going now, in the first crossing. This interrupted the inquest. . . .

It must have been all of fifteen minutes—fifteen minutes of dull, homesick silence—before that long horse-face swung round upon me again—and then, what a change! It was as red as fire, and every muscle in it was working. Now came this shriek—

"Here!—You going to set there all day?"

I lit in the middle of the floor, shot there by the electric suddenness of the surprise. As soon as I could get my voice I said, apologetically:—"I have had no orders, sir."

"You've had no ORDERS! My, what a fine bird we are! We must have ORDERS! Our father was a GENTLEMAN—owned slaves—and we've been to SCHOOL. Yes, WE are a gentleman, TOO, and got to have ORDERS! ORDERS, is it? ORDERS is what you want! Dod dern my skin, I'LL learn you to swell yourself up and blow around here about your dod-derned ORDERS! G'way from the wheel! (I had approached it without knowing it.) F

I moved back a step or two, and stood as in a dream, all my senses stupefied by this frantic assault.

"What you standing there for? Take that ice-pitcher down to the texas-tender![5] Come, move along, and don't you be all day about it!"

The moment I got back to the pilot-house, Brown said—

"Here! What was you doing down there all this time?"

"I couldn't find the texas-tender; I had to go all the way to the pantry."

"Derned likely story! Fill up the stove."

I proceeded to do so. He watched me like a cat. Presently he shouted—

"Put down that shovel? Deadest numskull I ever saw—ain't even got sense enough to load up a stove."

All through the watch this sort of thing went on. Yes, and the subsequent watches were much like it, during a stretch of months. As I have said, I soon got the habit of coming on duty with dread. The moment I was in the presence, even in the darkest night, I could feel those yellow eyes upon me, and knew their owner was watching for a pretext to spit out some venom on me. Preliminarily he would say—

"Here! Take the wheel."

Two minutes later—

"WHERE in the nation you going to? Pull her down! pull her down!"

After another moment—

"Say! You going to hold her all day? Let her go—meet her! meet her!"

Then he would jump from the bench, snatch the wheel from me, and meet her himself, pouring out wrath upon me all the time.

George Ritchie was the other pilot's cub. He was having good times now; for his boss, George Ealer, was as kindhearted as Brown wasn't. Ritchie had steeled for Brown the season before; consequently he knew exactly how to entertain himself and plague me, all by the

4. **leads** (lehdz): weights lowered to test the depth of the river.

5. **texas-tender:** a tray in the officers' quarters. The rooms on Mississippi steamboats were named after the states. Since the officers' area was the largest, it was named after Texas, the largest state at the time.

F Reading Focus Reading Aloud Read this paragraph aloud. What effect does the use of capital letters create in this passage?

one operation. Whenever I took the wheel for a moment on Ealer's watch, Ritchie would sit back on the bench and play Brown, with continual ejaculations of "Snatch her! snatch her! Derndest mud-cat I ever saw!" "Here! Where you going NOW? Going to run over that snag?" "Pull her DOWN! Don't you hear me? Pull her DOWN!" "There she goes! JUST as I expected! I TOLD you not to cramp that reef! G'way from the wheel!" G

So I always had a rough time of it, no matter whose watch it was; and sometimes it seemed to me that Ritchie's good-natured badgering was pretty nearly as aggravating as Brown's dead-earnest nagging.

I often wanted to kill Brown, but this would not answer. A cub had to take everything his boss gave, in the way of vigorous comment and criticism; and we all believed that there was a United States law making it a penitentiary offense[6] to strike or threaten a pilot who was on duty. . . .

Two trips later, I got into serious trouble. Brown was steering; I was "pulling down." My younger brother appeared on the hurricane deck, and shouted to Brown to stop at some landing or other a mile or so below. Brown gave no intimation that he had heard anything. But that was his way: he never condescended to take notice of an under clerk. The wind was blowing; Brown was deaf (although he always pretended he wasn't), and I very much doubted if he had heard the order. If I had two heads, I would have spoken; but as I had

6. **penitentiary offense:** an action for which one would be sent to jail.

G **Literary Focus Style** Describe the image that Twain creates of George Ritchie. To which senses does this image appeal?

GEOGRAPHY LINK

The Mississippi River

The largest river in North America, the Mississippi, is a vital navigation route. Flowing south from Minnesota to the Gulf of Mexico, it is one of the busiest waterways in the world, despite the fact that navigating its twisting path can be a challenge. Geographers classify the Mississippi as a meandering alluvial river. A meander is a sharp twist or bend, and an alluvial river carries and deposits sediments. The resulting turns, cutoffs, and swampy areas posed constant threats for heavy steamboats. While working as a cub pilot and pilot, Mark Twain became deeply familiar with the Mississippi's unique geography, explaining that "the face of the water, in time, became a wonderful book—a book that was a dead language to the uneducated passenger, but which told its mind to me without reserve, delivering its most cherished secrets as clearly as if it uttered them with a voice."

Ask Yourself

Could the constant dangers of the Mississippi partly explain Brown's bad temper? Why or why not?

only one, it seemed judicious to take care of it; so I kept still.

Presently, sure enough, we went sailing by that plantation. Captain Klinefelter appeared on the deck, and said—

"Let her come around, sir, let her come around. Didn't Henry tell you to land here?"

"NO, sir!"

"I sent him up to do it."

"He did come up; and that's all the good it done, the dod-derned fool. He never said anything."

"Didn't YOU hear him?" asked the captain of me.

Of course I didn't want to be mixed up in this business, but there was no way to avoid it; so I said—

"Yes, sir."

I knew what Brown's next remark would be, before he uttered it; it was—

"Shut your mouth! you never heard anything of the kind."

I closed my mouth according to instructions. An hour later, Henry entered the pilot-house, unaware of what had been going on. He was a thoroughly inoffensive boy, and I was sorry to see him come, for I knew Brown would have no pity on him. Brown began, straightway—

"Here! why didn't you tell me we'd got to land at that plantation?"

"I did tell you, Mr. Brown."

"It's a lie!"

I said—

"You lie, yourself. He did tell you."

Brown glared at me in unaffected surprise; and for as much as a moment he was entirely speechless; then he shouted to me—

"I'll attend to your case in half a minute!" then to Henry, "And you leave the pilot-house; out with you!"

It was pilot law, and must be obeyed. The boy started out, and even had his foot on the upper step outside the door, when Brown, with a sudden access of fury, picked up a ten-pound lump of coal and sprang after him; but I was between, with a heavy stool, and I hit Brown a good honest blow which stretched him out.

I had committed the crime of crimes—I had lifted my hand against a pilot on duty! I supposed I was booked for the penitentiary sure, and couldn't be booked any surer if I went on and squared my long account with this person while I had the chance; consequently I stuck to him and pounded him with my fists a considerable time—I do not know how long, the pleasure of it probably made it seem longer than it really was;—but in the end he struggled free and jumped up and sprang to the wheel: a very natural solicitude, for, all this time, here was this steamboat tearing down the river at the rate of fifteen miles an hour and nobody at the helm! However, Eagle Bend was two miles wide at this bank-full stage, and correspondingly long and deep; and the boat was steering herself straight down the middle and taking no chances. Still, that was only luck—a body MIGHT have found her charging into the woods. **H**

Perceiving, at a glance, that the "Pennsylvania" was in no danger, Brown gathered up the big spy-glass, war-club fashion, and ordered me out of the pilot-house with more than bluster. But I was not afraid of him now; so, instead of going, I tarried, and criticized his grammar; I reformed his ferocious speeches for him, and

---

Vocabulary **judicious** (joo DIHSH uhs) *adj.:* showing good judgment; wise.
inoffensive (ihn uh FEHN sihv) *adj.:* harmless; not objectionable in any way.

H **Literary Focus** **Tone** How does the tone shift when Brown and Twain come to blows?

put them into good English, calling his attention to the advantage of pure English over the dialect of the Pennsylvanian collieries[7] whence he was extracted. He could have done his part to admiration in a cross-fire of mere vituperation,[8] of course; but he was not equipped for this species of controversy; so he presently laid aside his glass and took the wheel, muttering and shaking his head; and I retired to the bench. The racket had brought everybody to the hurricane deck, and I trembled when I saw the old captain looking up from the midst of the crowd. I said to myself, "Now I AM done for!"—For although, as a rule, he was so fatherly and **indulgent** toward the boat's family, and so patient of minor shortcomings, he could be stern enough when the fault was worth it. **I**

7. **collieries** (KAHL yuhr eez): coal mines.
8. **vituperation** (vy too puhr AY shuhn): abusive language.

I **Reading Focus** **Paraphrasing** Paraphrase this passage. What is Twain doing here?

Vocabulary **indulgent** (ihn DUHL juhnt) *adj.:* giving in to someone else's wishes.

I tried to imagine what he WOULD do to a cub pilot who had been guilty of such a crime as mine, committed on a boat guard-deep[9] with costly freight and alive with passengers. Our watch was nearly ended. I thought I would go and hide somewhere till I got a chance to slide ashore. So I slipped out of the pilot-house, and down the steps, and around to the texas door—and was in the act of gliding within, when the captain confronted me! I dropped my head, and he stood over me in silence a moment or two, then said impressively—

"Follow me."

I dropped into his wake; he led the way to his parlor in the forward end of the texas. We were alone, now. He closed the after door; then moved slowly to the forward one and closed that. He sat down; I stood before him. He looked at me some little time, then said—

"So you have been fighting Mr. Brown?

I answered meekly—

"Yes, sir."

"Do you know that that is a very serious matter?"

"Yes, sir."

"Are you aware that this boat was plowing down the river fully five minutes with no one at the wheel?"

"Yes, sir."

"Did you strike him first?"

"Yes, sir."

"What with?"

"A stool, sir."

"Hard?"

"Middling, sir."

"Did it knock him down?"

"He—he fell, sir."

"Did you follow it up? Did you do anything further?"

"Yes, sir."

"What did you do?"

"Pounded him, sir."

"Pounded him?"

"Yes, sir."

"Did you pound him much?—that is, severely?"

"One might call it that, sir, maybe." **J**

"I'm deuced glad of it! Hark ye, never mention that I said that. You have been guilty of a great crime; and don't you ever be guilty of it again, on this boat. BUT—lay for him ashore! Give him a good sound thrashing, do you hear? I'll pay the expenses. Now go—and mind you, not a word of this to anybody. Clear out with you!—you've been guilty of a great crime, you whelp!"[10]

I slid out, happy with the sense of a close shave and a mighty deliverance; and I heard him laughing to himself and slapping his fat thighs after I had closed his door.

When Brown came off watch he went straight to the captain, who was talking with some passengers on the boiler deck, and demanded that I be put ashore in New Orleans—and added—

"I'll never turn a wheel on this boat again while that cub stays."

The captain said—

"But he needn't come round when you are on watch, Mr. Brown."

"I won't even stay on the same boat with him. One of us has got to go ashore."

"Very well," said the captain, "let it be yourself"; and resumed his talk with the passengers.

9. **guard-deep:** loaded to the guard, an extension of the deck.

10. **whelp:** a puppy or cub; here, a disrespectful young man.

Vocabulary **confronted** (kuhn FRUHNT ihd) *v.:* came face to face with someone.

J **Literary Focus** **Tone** How do Twain's short responses to the captain affect the story's humorous tone?

Applying Your Skills

9.R.2.C.1.d Use details from text(s): to evaluate the effect of author's style 9.R.2.C.1.b Use details from text(s): to analyze character, plot, setting, point of view 9.R.1.G.1.f During reading, utilize strategies: to paraphrase *Also covered* 9.W.3.A.1.a; 9.W.2.D.1.b

Cub Pilot on the Mississippi

Respond and Think Critically

Reading Focus

Quick Check

1. How is Twain's desire to be a steamboat pilot different from his other childhood dreams?
2. What advice does the captain offer Twain, and why?

Read with a Purpose

3. Brown seemed to be furious with Twain the first time they met. Why do you think the old pilot disliked the young cub so much?

Reading Skills: Reading Aloud and Paraphrasing

4. Review your paraphrases of the text. Which of the following elements do you think contributes the most to Twain's tone: exaggeration, playful diction, or humorous situations? Support your answer with examples from the text.

Literary Focus

Literary Analysis

5. **Interpret** How does Twain handle Brown's treatment of him? What do Twain's actions reveal about his personality?
6. **Make a Judgment** Does Twain's tone suggest that he took being a cub pilot seriously or that he was careless and idle? Explain.
7. **Evaluate** Do you think the captain made a wise decision when resolving the conflict between Twain and Brown? Why or why not?

Literary Skills: Style and Tone

8. **Evaluate** How would you describe Twain's style to someone who has never read any of his work? What kind of reader do you think would enjoy this style?
9. **Analyze** Find a sentence in the story that you think could only have been written by Mark Twain. Explain your selection.
10. **Extend** How does Twain's diction differ from the way people speak today? Find specific examples from the story.

Literary Skills Review: Characterization

11. **Interpret** Twain describes people in his story, but he also shows what they say and do. Describe the picture of Brown that emerges from these forms of characterization.

Writing Focus

Think as a Reader/Writer

Use It in Your Writing Twain shows us how the captain handles the situation at the end of the story by quoting his exact words. Write about a time when you or someone you know faced an authority figure. Use dialogue to show what happened.

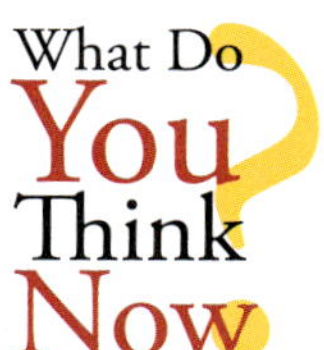

Do Twain's actions speak louder than his words? Was he right to attack Brown? Explain.

Applying Your Skills

Cub Pilot on the Mississippi

Vocabulary Development

Vocabulary Check

Match each Vocabulary word on the left with its synonym.

1. transient	**a.** sensible
2. judicious	**b.** faced
3. inoffensive	**c.** permissive
4. indulgent	**d.** harmless
5. confronted	**e.** momentary

Vocabulary Skills: Idioms

An **idiom** is an expression peculiar to a particular language that means something different from the literal meanings of its words. Common idioms include *a fish out of water* (out of one's element) and *cry wolf* (raise a false alarm).

Your Turn

Identify the idiom in each of these story passages.

1. ". . . I ascended to the pilot-house in high feather, and very proud to be semi-officially a member of the executive family of so fast and famous a boat."
2. "I had committed the crime of crimes—I had lifted my hand against a pilot on duty!"
3. "I said to myself, 'Now I AM done for!'—For although, as a rule, he was so fatherly and indulgent . . . he could be stern enough when the fault was worth it."

Language Coach

Jargon Twain uses words and phrases that steamboat workers used in their daily work to describe his life as a cub pilot. The terms *cub* and *pilot-house* are examples of **jargon,** the specialized vocabulary of an occupation or field of knowledge. You can often use context clues to infer the general significance of jargon, even when you cannot guess the exact meaning.

Text Passage	Term and Inferred Meaning
"The figure that comes before me oftenest . . . is that of Brown, of the steamer '*Pennsylvania*.'"	*steamer*: "another word for steamboat or paddle boat."
"My younger brother appeared on the *hurricane deck*. . . ."	*hurricane deck*: "a level of the boat, possibly one that is safer during a hurricane."

Find several more examples of jargon throughout the story, and try to guess the words' meanings. Check your guesses with a dictionary or online.

Academic Vocabulary

Talk About...

Judging from his tone in "Cub Pilot on the Mississippi," what do you think Twain's attitude was toward his childhood experiences? Discuss your opinions with a classmate.

MO **9.W.2.E.1.b** In written text apply: conventions of punctuation **9.W.2.E.1.c** In written text apply: standard usage **9.R.1.E.1.c** Develop vocabulary through text: using glossary, dictionary and thesaurus **9.R.1.G.1.a** During reading, utilize strategies: to determine meaning of unknown words *Also covered* **9.R.1.E.1.b; 9.W.3.A.1.a**

Grammar Link

Complex Sentences

Twain's style is created in part by his use of many complex sentences that follow the logic of his thoughts and his analysis of a situation. Notice how the semicolon in the following example connects two ideas. The first part of the sentence introduces the main idea; the second part expands upon the idea:

> "I am to this day profiting somewhat by that experience; for in that brief, sharp schooling, I got personally and familiarly acquainted with about all the different types of human nature that are to be found in fiction, biography, or history."

Twain's use of semicolons helps him avoid **run-on sentences,** two or more sentences that run together as if they were one complete sentence.

Your Turn

Correct each run-on sentence by adding semicolons in their proper places.

1. For a short time, Twain wanted to be a clown later he decided he would rather be a pirate his dream of working on a steamboat was more lasting.
2. Some young men became clerks others became assistants to pilots.
3. Brown is a strict boss and a mean bully George Ealer is a kindhearted manager the captain is an understanding leader.
4. Twain was a popular speaker in the United States and Europe his fame was based both on his writings and his entertaining presentations.

CHOICES

As you respond to the Choices, use these **Academic Vocabulary** words as appropriate: establish, attitude, enhance, appeal.

REVIEW

Exaggerate an Anecdote

TechFocus Exaggeration is a key trait of Twain's humorous style. Look back at how Twain exaggerates some details in his story for comic effect. Then, write your own anecdote, a short account of an event in your life, and turn it into a podcast to which others can listen. Use exaggeration to establish a comical tone.

CONNECT

Write a Persuasive Essay

TimedWriting Mr. Brown, the pilot, abused his position of power and terrorized young Mark Twain. Write a persuasive essay in which you convince your audience of the importance of balanced and fair treatment of employees. Support your argument with examples.

EXTEND

Create a Checklist Challenge

Can you help other readers figure out whether or not Mark Twain wrote a passage? Create a checklist that tells readers the key marks of Twain's writing style. Then, collect four sample passages: two by Mark Twain and two by other writers. Ask readers to use your checklist to test each of the passages. Can they identify which ones are by Twain?

PERSONAL ESSAY

Preparing to Read

The Secret Latina

by **Veronica Chambers**

Panamanian woman dances while wearing a *pollera*, the traditional Panamanian dress.

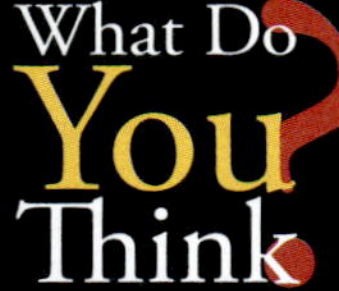

What do our different identities say about us and the world in which we live?

QuickTalk

Discuss with a partner what it means to be "from" somewhere. Can you be from a country? a culture? a region? a ZIP Code?

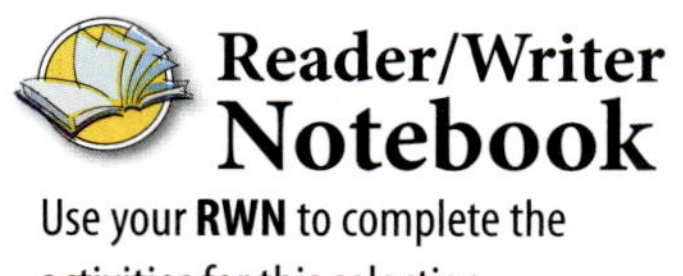

Use your **RWN** to complete the activities for this selection.

9.R.2.C.1.d Use details from text(s): to evaluate the effect of author's style **9.R.1.H.1.d** Apply post-reading skills to comprehend, interpret, analyze, and evaluate text: draw conclusions

Literary Focus

Style: Figurative Language One element of a writer's style is the use of **figurative language**—language that is intentionally used in an unusual way. By appealing to the imagination, figurative language provides new ways of looking at the world. Figurative language consists of **figures of speech** such as the following:

- **Similes** make creative comparisons between unlike things using a connecting word such as *like, as,* or *seems.* Example: "I am as happy as a bird in flight."
- A **metaphor** makes comparisons between unlike things by saying one thing *is* another thing. Example: "Happiness is a bird in flight."
- **Personification** occurs when a writer gives human qualities to nonhuman objects, as in "The bird danced with happiness."

Reading Focus

Analyzing Author's Purpose Writers usually have at least one of three main purposes: to inform, to persuade, or to entertain. To identify an author's purpose, look for details in the story that directly express opinions or ideas. Also look for words that reveal the author's **tone,** or attitude toward his or her topic.

Into Action As you read, use a graphic organizer like the one below to help you analyze Chambers's purpose for writing:

Detail from Text	Opinion or Idea
"my Latin identity is murkier"	Identity is complex.

Writing Focus

Think as a Reader/Writer

Find It in Your Reading Look for figures of speech in Chambers's essay. In your *Reader/Writer Notebook,* record examples you find.

Vocabulary

intact (ihn TAKT) *adj.:* with no missing parts; whole. *Although Mom moved to the United States, her Panamanian identity was still intact.*

isolated (Y suh layt ihd) *v.* used as *adj.:* alone; separated. *Chambers felt isolated from others in the community.*

forging (FAWRJ ihng) *v.:* making; forming. *By speaking Spanish together, I realized that my mother and I were forging an important bond.*

enlisted (ehn LIHS tihd) *v.:* secured the services of. *I enlisted my cousin to help me prepare for the trip.*

Language Coach

Word Origins Did you know that the Latin word *insula* means "island" or that the Latin word *tact* means "touch"? Look at the Vocabulary words on the list above and see if you can identify the two words that spring from these Latin words. For an extra challenge, see if you can figure out how the meanings of the Latin words relate to the modern meanings of these words.

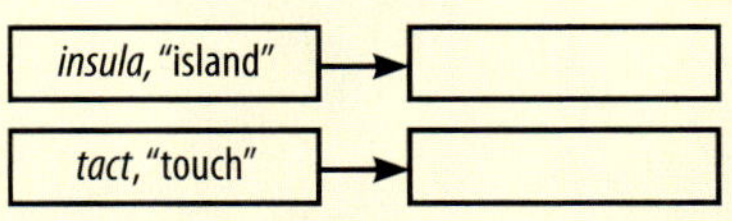

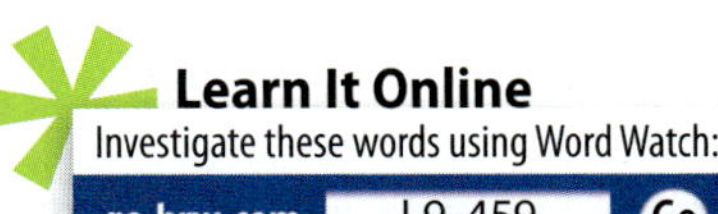

Learn It Online

Investigate these words using Word Watch:

go.hrw.com L9-459 Go

MEET THE WRITER

Veronica Chambers

(1971–)

From Brooklyn to Japan

Veronica Chambers grew up in Brooklyn, New York, the daughter of a Panamanian mother and an African American father. Chambers's work often explores her bicultural identity. She has written several books, including a popular memoir, *Mama's Girl;* a book for children titled *Double Dutch: A Celebration of Jump Rope;* and *Rhyme and Sisterhood,* about growing up in New York and Los Angeles in the 1970s and 1980s. In 2000, Chambers received a fellowship to travel and do research in Japan. While there, she fell in love with the country and wrote a book about the changing roles of women in Japanese society.

A Disciplined Writer

Chambers began her career as a magazine writer and editor. She has written for *Newsweek, Esquire, The New York Times,* the *Los Angeles Times Book Review, Travel and Leisure, Vogue, Essence, Glamour,* and other magazines. Chambers says being a magazine writer taught her discipline. "Many novelists wait for inspiration, but if you're a journalist who's used to deadlines, you know eventually you have to just start writing. I'm more disciplined because of my journalism background, but it's an ongoing process, trusting that your imagination can be as compelling as facts."

Think About the Writer How does Chambers use writing to explore her sense of self?

Build Background

The term *Latina* refers to a woman or girl of Hispanic or Latin American descent. Chambers grew up in Brooklyn, New York, but her mother was born and raised in Panama, a small country in Central America.

Preview the Selection

In this personal essay, we are introduced to **Veronica Chambers** and her fun-loving **mother.**

Brooklyn Bridge in New York City, New York.

Read with a Purpose Read this personal essay to learn why Chambers refers to herself as a "secret Latina."

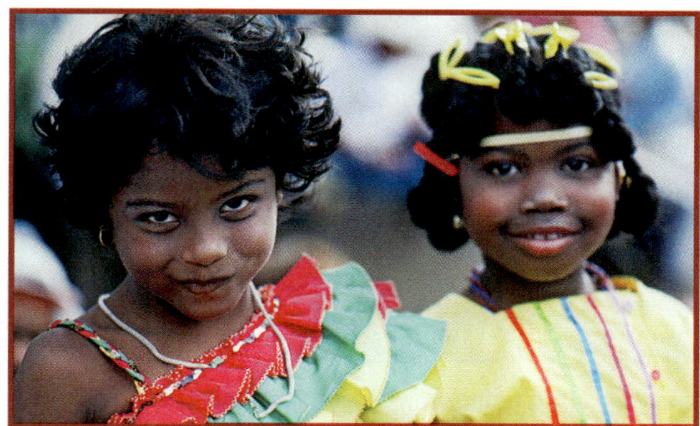

The Secret Latina

by **Veronica Chambers**

from Essence, July 2000

She's a platanos-frying, malta Dukesa–drinking, salsa-dancing Mamacita[1]—my dark-skinned Panamanian mother. She came to this country when she was 21, her sense of culture intact, her Spanish flawless. Even today, more than 20 years since she left her home country to become an American citizen, my mother still considers herself Panamanian and checks "Hispanic" on census forms.

As a Black woman in America, my Latin identity is murkier than my mother's, despite the fact that I, too, was born in Panama, and call that country "home." My father's parents came from Costa Rica and Jamaica, my mother's from Martinique.[2] I left Panama when I was 2 years old. My family lived in England for three years, then came to the States when I was 5. Having dark skin and growing up in Brooklyn in the 1970's meant I was Black, period. You could meet me and not know I was of Latin heritage. Without a Spanish last name or my mother's fluent Spanish at my disposal, I often felt isolated from the Latin community. . . . **A**

I found it almost impossible to explain to my elementary-school friends why my mother would speak Spanish at home. They would ask if I was Puerto Rican and look bewildered when I told them I was not. To them, Panama was a kind of nowhere. There weren't enough Panamanians in Brooklyn to be a force.

1. **platanos-frying, malta Dukesa–drinking, salsa-dancing Mamacita:** Chambers uses these hyphenated words to describe her mother as a woman who fries *platanos* (or plantains), a type of banana; who drinks Dukesa, an alcoholic beverage similar to beer; and who dances to salsa, a type of Latin American dance music. *Mamacita* means "little mama" in Spanish.

2. **Martinique:** an island in the eastern Caribbean Sea.

A **Reading Focus** **Analyzing Author's Purpose** What purpose do the first two paragraphs of this essay serve?

Vocabulary **intact** (ihn TAKT) *adj.:* with no missing parts; whole.
isolated (Y suh layt ihd) *v.* used as *adj.:* alone; separated.

Analyzing Visuals **Viewing and Interpreting** Why do you think Chambers's mother has such fond memories of carnival celebrations such as this?

Carnival in Panama City, Panama, 2007.

Everybody knew where Jamaicans were from because of famous singers like Bob Marley. Panamanians had Ruben Blades,[3] but most of my friends thought he was Puerto Rican, too.

In my neighborhood, where the smell of somebody's grandmother's cooking could transform a New York corner into Santo Domingo, Kingston or Port-au-Prince, a Panamanian was a sort of fish with feathers—assumed to be a Jamaican who spoke Spanish. The analogy was not without historical basis: A century ago, Panama's Black community was largely drawn to the country from all over the Caribbean as cheap labor to build the Panama Canal. **B**

My father didn't mind that we considered ourselves Black rather than Latino. He named my brother Malcolm X, and if my mother hadn't put her foot down, I would have been called Angela Davis Chambers. It's not that my mother didn't admire Angela Davis,[4] but you have only to hear how "Veronica Victoria" flows off her Spanish lips to know that she was homesick for Panama and for those names that sang like timbales[5] on carnival day. So between my father and my mother was a Black-Latin divide. Because of my father, we read and discussed books about Black history and civil rights. Because of my mother, we ate Panamanian food, listened to salsa and heard Spanish at home.

Still, it wasn't until my parents divorced when I was 10 that my mother tried to teach Malcolm and me Spanish. She was a terrible language teacher. She had no sense of how to explain structure, and her answer to every question was "That's just the way it is." A few short weeks after our Spanish lessons began, my mother gave up and we were all relieved. But I remained intent on learning my mother's language. When she spoke Spanish, her words were a fast current, a stream of language that was colorful, passionate, fiery. I wanted to speak Spanish because I wanted to swim in the river of her words, her history, my history, too. **C**

3. **Ruben Blades** (1948–   ): a popular singer-songwriter from Panama.
4. **Angela Davis** (1944–   ): Davis was born in Birmingham, Alabama, and was part of the Black Panther Party, an African American activist group.
5. **timbales** (tihm BAH lays): a type of Latin American drum.

B **Literary Focus** **Figurative Language** Identify the metaphor used in this paragraph. What two things are being compared?

C **Literary Focus** **Figurative Language** What effect does Chambers's use of figurative language have on you?

SOCIAL STUDIES LINK

The Panama Canal

Panama fieldworkers drilling at Panama Canal site.

Harsh working conditions and shortages of labor and materials hampered construction efforts on the Panama Canal in 1904. The situation worsened when an outbreak of yellow fever hit, but malaria was an even bigger threat. Unlike yellow fever, malaria could strike people again and again. During the first month of U.S. construction, nearly the entire workforce was stricken with malaria. To eliminate the mosquitoes that spread malaria, sanitation workers drained swamps; cleared vegetation; spread oil on pools of standing water; and bred spiders, ants, and lizards to feed on the adult mosquitoes.

Ask Yourself

Why was it important to control malaria and yellow fever in Panama?

At school I dove into the language, matching what little I knew from home with all that I learned. One day, when I was in the ninth grade, I finally felt confident enough to start speaking Spanish with my mother. I soon realized that by speaking Spanish with her, I was forging an important bond. When I'd spoken only English, I was the daughter, the little girl. But when I began speaking Spanish, I became something more—a *hermanita,* a sisterfriend, a Panamanian homegirl who could hang with the rest of them. Eventually this bond would lead me home.

Two years ago, at age 27, I decided it was finally time. I couldn't wait any longer to see Panama, the place my mother and my aunts had told me stories about. I enlisted my cousin Digna as a traveling companion and we made arrangements to stay with my godparents, whom I had never met. We planned our trip for the last week in February—carnival time.

Panama, in Central America, is a narrow sliver of a country: You can swim in the Caribbean Sea in the morning and backstroke across the Pacific in the afternoon. As our plane touched down, bringing me home for the first time since I was 2, I felt curiously comfortable and secure. In the days that followed, there was none of the culture shock that I'd expected—I had my mother and aunts to thank for that. My godmother Olga reminded me of them. The first thing she did was book appointments for Digna and me to get our eyebrows plucked and our nails and feet done with Panamanian-style manicures and pedicures. "It's carnival," Aunt Olga said, "and you girls have to look your best." We just laughed.

Vocabulary **forging** (FAWRJ ihng) *v.:* making; forming.
enlisted (ehn LIHS tihd) *v.:* secured the services of.

Woman in traditional Panamanian costume.

In Panama, I went from being a lone Black girl with a curious Latin heritage to being part of the Latinegro tribe or the *Afro-Antillanos,* as we were officially called. I was thrilled to learn there was actually a society for people like me. Everyone was Black, everyone spoke Spanish and everyone danced the way they danced at fiesta time back in Brooklyn, stopping only to chow down on a smorgasbord of souse,[6] rice with black-eyed peas, beef patties, empanadas[7] and codfish fritters. The carnival itself was an all-night bacchanal[8] with elaborate floats, brilliantly colored costumes and live musicians. In the midst of all this, my godmother took my cousin and me to a photo studio to have our pictures taken in *polleras,* the traditional dress. After spending an hour on makeup and hair and donning a rented costume, I looked like Scarlett in *Gone with the Wind.* **D**

Back in New York, I gave the photo to my mother. She almost cried. She says she was so moved to see me in a *pollera* because it was "such a patriotic thing to do." Her appreciation made me ridiculously happy; ever since I was a little girl, I'd wanted to be like my mother. In one of my most vivid memories, I am 7 or 8 and my parents are having a party. Salsa music is blaring and my mother is dancing and laughing. She sees me standing off in a corner, so she pulls me into the circle of grown-ups and tries to teach me how to dance to the music. Her hips are electric. She puts her hands on my sides and says, "Move these," and I start shaking my hip bones as if my life depends on it.

Now I am a grown woman, with hips to spare. I can salsa. My Spanish isn't shabby. You may look at me and not know that I am Panamanian, that I am an immigrant, that I am both Black and Latin. But I am my mother's daughter, a secret Latina, and that's enough for me.

6. **souse:** pickled meat, usually pork.
7. **empanadas** (ehm puh NAH duhs): meat, seafood, or cheese-filled pastries.
8. **bacchanal** (bak uh NAHL): a noisy, often drunken celebration. In classical mythology, Bacchus is the Greek god of wine.

D Reading Focus Analyzing Author's Purpose Why do you think Chambers chose to share these particular details?

Applying Your Skills

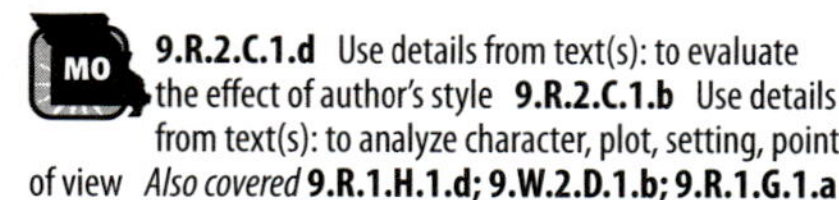

9.R.2.C.1.d Use details from text(s): to evaluate the effect of author's style **9.R.2.C.1.b** Use details from text(s): to analyze character, plot, setting, point of view *Also covered* **9.R.1.H.1.d; 9.W.2.D.1.b; 9.R.1.G.1.a**

The Secret Latina

Respond and Think Critically

Reading Focus

Quick Check

1. Why does Chambers feel isolated from others in her Brooklyn community?
2. Why does Chambers's mother cry when she sees a photo of her daughter in traditional Panamanian dress?

Read with a Purpose

3. Why does Chambers refer to her Latina identity as a "secret"?

Reading Skills: Analyzing Author's Purpose

4. Look back at the details you put in your graphic organizer. What was Chambers's tone? What do you think was her overall purpose for writing this essay?

Detail from Text	Opinion or Idea
"my Latin identity is murkier"	Identity is complex.
Author's Tone:	
Overall Purpose:	

Vocabulary Check

Match each Vocabulary word with its definition.

5. forging	**a.** whole
6. enlisted	**b.** got the support of
7. isolated	**c.** forming
8. intact	**d.** alone or separated

Literary Focus

Literary Analysis

9. **Interpret** What does Chambers mean when she says her mother's words "were a fast current, a stream of language that was colorful, passionate, fiery"?
10. **Analyze** Does Chambers's relationship with her mother change after her Panama trip? Explain.

Literary Skills: Figurative Language

11. **Analyze** Re-read the essay, and identify at least three examples of figurative language. How do these instances affect the style of the essay?
12. **Extend** How do you think Chambers's use of figurative language might be influenced by her ability to speak Spanish?

Literary Skills Review: Setting

13. **Evaluate** Which setting does Chambers bring to life more vividly, that of Brooklyn or Panama? Use examples from the text in your response.

Writing Focus

Think as a Reader/Writer

Use It in Your Writing Develop your own style by using figurative language to describe some aspect of your background or childhood.

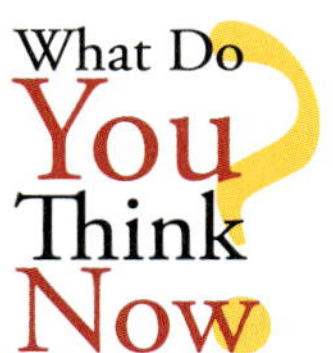

What does Chambers's essay have to say about the different identities within each of us?

PERSONAL ESSAY

Preparing to Read

The Grandfather

by **Gary Soto**

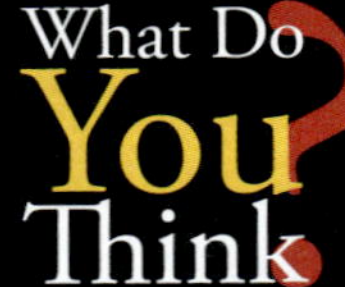

What things in life are worth waiting for?

QuickTalk

Some things in life are not easy to achieve. With a group, talk about why having patience is a positive quality. In what ways is having to work for something more rewarding than getting instant results?

Avocado Plant (1965) by Joan Warburton (1920–1996). Private collection. Gouache (73 cm x 53 cm).

Reader/Writer Notebook

Use your **RWN** to complete the activities for this selection.

MO **9.R.2.C.1.d** Use details from text(s): to evaluate the effect of author's style **9.R.2.B.2.b** Identify and explain literary techniques, in text emphasizing: imagery **9.R.1.H.1.d** Apply post-reading skills to comprehend, interpret, analyze, and evaluate text: draw conclusions

Literary Focus

Style and Imagery The selection you are about to read is a personal essay. Personal essays are usually written in the first person and present the writer's unique thoughts, feelings, and experiences. A writer's style and use of imagery help personalize his or her writing.

Style refers to the many ways writers use language. For example, writers can create a distinctive style though their word choice (formal or informal) and sentence structure (simple or complex). The way writers use **imagery**—words or phrases that appeal to one or more of our senses—can also shape a writer's style.

TechFocus As you read the essay, look for ways Soto brings his grandfather to life for readers.

Reading Focus

Making Generalizations A **generalization** is a broad statement supported by specific details. To make a generalization, you—

- examine details in the text
- consider the overall effect those details create
- formulate a broad statement that sums up these details

Into Action As you read "The Grandfather", gather details that strike you as significant. Later, you will use these details to make a generalization about Soto's tone in this essay.

Details from Essay

"scream my fool head off"
"ate the smile from an ice cold watermelon"

Writing Focus

Think as a Reader/Writer

Find It in Your Reading As you read this essay, think about how Soto's use of imagery contributes to his writing style. Write down examples of his images in your *Reader/Writer Notebook.*

Vocabulary

gurgle (GUR guhl) *v.:* flow or run with a bubbling sound. *I saw the water gurgle out of the hose and onto the rosebush.*

hovered (HUHV uhrd) *v.:* stayed suspended over something. *The lemon tree's branches hovered over the clothesline.*

sulked (suhlkt) *v.:* showed resentment and ill humor. *Grandfather sulked because his allergies were bothering him.*

meager (MEE guhr) *adj.:* thin; small; inadequate. *The meager tree provided little shade.*

Language Coach

Onomatopoeia A word whose sounds imitate or suggest the word's meaning is called an **onomatopoeia** (ahn uh mat uh PEE uh). *Moo,* for example, describes the sound a cow makes. Note that onomatopoeic words differ from language to language. Here are examples.

English	Spanish
cock-a-doodle-doo	quiquiriqui
meow	miau
ka-boom	pataplum

What Vocabulary word above is also an example of onomatopoeia?

Learn It Online
Check out the *PowerNotes* introduction to this story on:

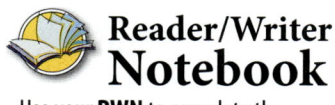

MEET THE WRITER

Learn It Online
Learn more about Soto's life at:
go.hrw.com L9-468 Go

Gary Soto
(1952–)

A California Boy

Gary Soto grew up in a Mexican American family in Fresno, a city in California's San Joaquin Valley. He went to college, planning to major in geography. Then a poem—"Unwanted" by Edward Field—changed his life. The poem helped him discover the power of language. He began to see how he could reach other people by writing about his own experiences, and that's exactly what he did—and is still doing.

Remembering San Joaquin

Soto titled his first book *The Elements of San Joaquin* (1977), after his birthplace. Much of his award-winning fiction and poetry draws on childhood memories and the everyday details of Mexican American life. As Soto put it, "I tried to remain faithful to the common things of my childhood—dogs, alleys, my baseball mitt, curbs, and the fruit of the valley. . . . I wanted to give these things life."

Think About the Writer How do you think Soto's vivid memories from childhood might influence his writing style?

Build Background

Soto's grandfather immigrated to the United States from Mexico. Like many immigrants, his grandfather worked hard and earned little money. The fruit he grew in his backyard helped feed him, allowing him to save more of his hard-earned money.

Preview the Selection

In this personal essay, you will read about Soto's **grandfather,** a hardworking man who never lost hope and who inspired his family with his dedication.

Read with a Purpose Read this personal essay to find out how an immigrant establishes his roots in America.

The Grandfather

by **Gary Soto**

Grandfather believed a well-rooted tree was the color of money. His money he kept hidden behind portraits of sons and daughters or taped behind the calendar of an Aztec[1] warrior. He tucked it into the sofa, his shoes and slippers, and into the tight-lipped pockets of his suits. He kept it in his soft brown wallet that was machine tooled with "MEXICO" and a campesino[2] and donkey climbing a hill. He had climbed, too, out of Mexico, settled in Fresno and worked thirty years at Sun Maid Raisin, first as a packer and later, when he was old, as a watchman with a large clock on his belt. (A)

After work, he sat in the backyard under the arbor,[3] watching the water gurgle in the rosebushes that ran along the fence. A lemon tree hovered over the clothesline. Two orange trees stood near the alley. His favorite tree, the avocado, which had started in a jam jar from a seed and three toothpicks lanced in its sides, rarely bore fruit. He said it was the wind's fault, and the mayor's, who allowed office buildings so high that the haze of pollen from the countryside could never find its way into the city. He sulked about this. He said that in Mexico buildings only grew so tall. You could see the moon at night, and the stars were clear points all the way to the horizon. And wind reached all the way from the sea, which was blue and clean, unlike the oily water sloshing against a San Francisco pier.

During its early years, I could leap over that tree, kick my bicycling legs over the top branch and scream my fool head off because I thought for sure I was flying. I ate fruit to keep my strength up, fuzzy peaches and branch-scuffed plums cooled in the refrigerator. From the kitchen chair he brought out in the evening, Grandpa would scold, "Hijo,[4] what's the matta

1. **Aztec:** culture existing in Mexico before the Spanish conquest of the early 1500s.
2. **campesino** (kahm pay SEE noh): Spanish for "peasant" or "farmworker."
3. **arbor:** shelter made of branches or covered with vines.
4. **Hijo** (EE hoh): Spanish for "child" or "son."

(A) **Literary Focus** **Style** How would you describe Soto's word choice? Clear and direct? Poetic and imaginative? Explain.

Vocabulary **gurgle** (GUR guhl) *v.:* flow or run with a bubbling sound.
hovered (HUHV uhrd) *v.:* stayed suspended over something.
sulked (suhlkt) *v.:* showed resentment and ill humor.

with you? You gonna break it."

By the third year, the tree was as tall as I, its branches casting a meager shadow on the ground. I sat beneath the shade, scratching words in the hard dirt with a stick. I had learned "Nile"[5] in summer school and a dirty word from my brother who wore granny sunglasses. The red ants tumbled into my letters, and I buried them, knowing that they would dig themselves back into fresh air.

A tree was money. If a lemon cost seven cents at Hanoian's Market, then Grandfather saved fistfuls of change and more because in winter the branches of his lemon tree hung heavy yellow fruit. And winter brought oranges, juicy and large as softballs. Apricots he got by the bagfuls from a son, who himself was wise for planting young. Peaches he got from a neighbor, who worked the night shift at Sun Maid Raisin. The chile plants, which also saved him from giving up his hot, sweaty quarters, were propped up with sticks to support an abundance of red fruit.

But his favorite tree was the avocado because it offered hope and the promise of more years. After work, Grandpa sat in the backyard, shirtless, tired of flagging trucks loaded with crates of raisins, and sipped glasses of ice water. His yard was neat: five trees, seven rosebushes, whose fruit were the red and white flowers he floated in bowls, and a statue of St. Francis that stood in a circle of crushed rocks, arms spread out to welcome hungry sparrows.

5. **Nile:** very long river in Africa, flowing through Egypt into the Mediterranean Sea.

After ten years, the first avocado hung on a branch, but the meat was flecked with black, an omen, Grandfather thought, a warning to keep an eye on the living. Five years later, another avocado hung on a branch, larger than the first and edible when crushed with a fork into a heated tortilla. Grandfather sprinkled it with salt and laced it with a river of chile.

"It's good," he said, and let me taste.

I took a big bite, waved a hand over my tongue, and ran for the garden hose gurgling in the rosebushes. I drank long and deep, and later ate the smile from an ice cold watermelon. **B**

Birds nested in the tree, quarreling jays with liquid eyes and cool, pulsating throats. Wasps wove a horn-shaped hive one year, but we smoked them away with swords of rolled up newspapers lit with matches. By then, the tree was tall enough for me to climb to look into the neighbor's yard. But by then I was too old for that kind of thing and went about with my brother, hair slicked back and our shades dark as oil.

After twenty years, the tree began to bear. Although Grandfather complained about how much he lost because pollen never reached the poor part of town, because at the market he had to haggle over the price of avocados, he loved that tree. It grew, as did his family, and when he died, all his sons standing on each other's shoulders, oldest to youngest, could not reach the highest branches. The wind could move the branches, but the trunk, thicker than any waist, hugged the ground. **C**

B **Literary Focus** **Imagery** To what senses do these details appeal?

C **Reading Focus** **Making Generalizations** Review the personal essay and take note of Soto's word choice and use of imagery. What generalizations can you make about Soto's writing style?

Vocabulary **meager** (MEE guhr) *adj.:* thin; small; inadequate.

Applying Your Skills

MO 9.R.2.C.1.d Use details from text(s): to evaluate the effect of author's style 9.R.2.B.2.b Identify and explain literary techniques, in text emphasizing: imagery 9.R.1.H.1.d Apply post-reading skills to comprehend, interpret, analyze, and evaluate text: draw conclusions *Also covered* 9.W.3.A.1.e

The Grandfather

Respond and Think Critically

Reading Focus

Quick Check

1. Why did Soto's grandfather believe that "a tree was money"?

Read with a Purpose

2. How does the grandfather's garden help establish his family's roots?

Reading Skills: Making Generalizations

3. Review the details you recorded while reading. Then, add a column to your chart, as shown below. Finally, make a generalization about Soto's tone in this essay.

Details from Essay	Tone of Details
"scream my fool head off"	humorous
"ate the smile from an ice cold watermelon"	joyful
Generalization about Soto's tone:	

Literary Focus

Literary Analysis

4. **Analyze** How would you describe Soto's grandfather? Consider his move to California and his attitude toward the avocado tree.
5. **Infer** What differences did Soto's grandfather see between Mexico and California? How did he feel about these differences?
6. **Reflect** How does Soto describe his relationship with the avocado tree? What images does Soto use to make this connection clear?

Literary Skills: Style and Imagery

7. **Analyze** Soto's essay is filled with **imagery**—language that appeals to our senses of sight, sound, touch, taste, and smell. Choose two or three images that you find interesting. Explain to which sense each image appeals. Is Soto's use of imagery effective? Why or why not?
8. **Evaluate** Other than imagery, what elements of style does Soto use? How do these elements help establish tone? How do they reveal Soto's attitude toward his subject?

Literary Skills Review: Symbolism

9. **Interpret** In this essay, the avocado tree is a **symbol** that has multiple meanings. Use examples from the text to explain how the tree might symbolize the grandfather, Soto, and the grandfather's family.

Writing Focus

Think as a Reader/Writer

Use It in Your Writing Write a personal essay about a person or experience that has made an impression on you. Like Soto, use images that appeal to the senses.

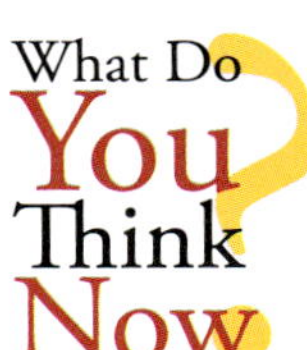

What does the grandfather's refusal to get rid of the slowly growing avocado tree reveal about him and about life?

Applying Your Skills

The Grandfather

Vocabulary Development

Vocabulary Check

gurgle
hovered
sulked
meager

Fill in each blank using the correct Vocabulary word.

1. The farmer got a __________ amount of money for his small crop.
2. The helicopter __________ over the landing site.
3. After hearing that his application had been denied, the man ___________ for several hours.
4. I listened to the river __________ as it flowed over the rocks.

Vocabulary Skills: Connotations and Denotations

The power of a word begins with its dictionary definition, or its **denotation.** In addition, a word can set off ripples of feelings and associations—these are its **connotations.**

Your Turn

For each Vocabulary word, find the sentence from the story in which the word is used and check the word's denotation. Then, write down any connotations the word has for you. Finally, rewrite the sentence, substituting a word that has a different connotation than the Vocabulary word. Describe how the meaning of the sentence has changed.

Language Coach

Onomatopoeia The word *onomatopoeia* is from the Greek language and means "name making." The word *gurgle* is onomatopoeic because its sound reflects its meaning. See if you can locate the onomatopoeic words in these sentences.

1. The tinkle of the wind chimes sounded beautiful.
2. With a clank, the heavy chain fell to the ground.
3. In the distance they could hear the boom of thunder.
4. It was difficult to hear anything but the machine's whir.
5. Full of food and content with life, the cat purred.

Academic Vocabulary

Talk About . . .

1. In a group of two or three classmates, talk about the description of food in the story. How does Soto's writing appeal to your sense of taste? What words does he use to bring these foods to life?
2. How would you describe the grandfather's attitude toward life? toward money? toward his family?

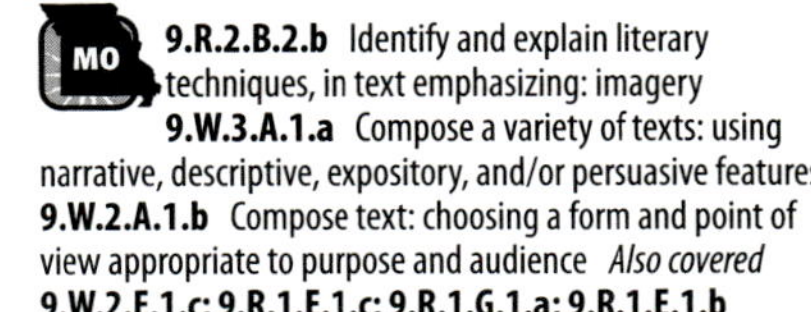

MO
9.R.2.B.2.b Identify and explain literary techniques, in text emphasizing: imagery
9.W.3.A.1.a Compose a variety of texts: using narrative, descriptive, expository, and/or persuasive features
9.W.2.A.1.b Compose text: choosing a form and point of view appropriate to purpose and audience *Also covered* 9.W.2.E.1.c; 9.R.1.E.1.c; 9.R.1.G.1.a; 9.R.1.E.1.b

Grammar Link

Parallel Structure

"I took a big bite, waved a hand over my tongue, and ran for the garden hose gurgling in the rosebushes." This sentence uses a series of verbs to re-create Soto's actions when he bites into an avocado. This is an example of **parallel structure,** in which related ideas or actions are expressed in similar ways. To create grammatically parallel sentences, match a noun with a noun, an adjective with an adjective, a phrase with a phrase, and so on.

Not Parallel

My favorite activities are playing baseball and to read.

Parallel

My favorite activities are *playing baseball* and *reading books.*

Your Turn

Complete the following sentences so they have parallel structure.

1. The grandfather's backyard was neat, colorful, and ______________.
2. The grandfather's daily routine was divided between working at Sun Maid Raisin and ______________.
3. The grandfather grew heavy lemons, juicy oranges, and ______________.
4. The grandfather planted the avocado tree, took care of it for many years, and ______________.
5. At first, Soto could leap over the avocado tree; then he could sit in its shade; and finally ______________.

CHOICES

As you respond to the Choices, use these **Academic Vocabulary** words as appropriate: establish, attitude, enhance, appeal.

REVIEW

Annotate a Passage

Soto creates a vivid portrait of his grandfather, using sensory details to bring the memory to life. Copy a passage from the story, and use different colored highlighters to indicate to which senses the imagery appeals. For example, use pink for imagery that appeals to the sense of sight, yellow for sound, and so on.

CONNECT

Write an Essay

Timed Writing The avocado tree in "The Grandfather" symbolizes many things for Gary Soto. In an essay, explain the significance of the avocado tree. Also, discuss ways in which the use of the tree as a symbol reveals Soto's insights about life. Support your ideas by citing examples from the text.

EXTEND

Interview a Friend or Relative

TechFocus Soto learned about his grandfather by spending time with him in his garden. Spend some time with a person in your life to find out what makes him or her special. Prepare questions that will reveal your subject's ideas about life. Videotape the interview in an appropriate setting, and then share the interview with your class.

Learn It Online
Expand your view of this story with these Internet links:
go.hrw.com
L9-473
Go

AUTOBIOGRAPHY

Preparing to Read

from BOY

by **Roald Dahl**

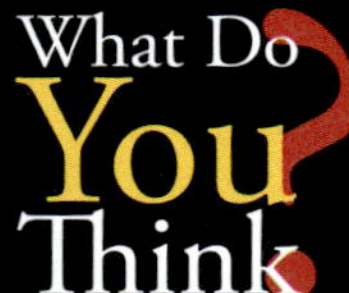

What could happen if a practical joke or prank goes too far?

QuickTalk Talk with your class about pranks that you have read or heard about. Did any of the pranks backfire? What happened as a result?

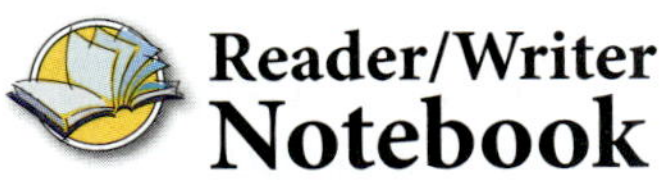

Use your **RWN** to complete the activities for this selection.

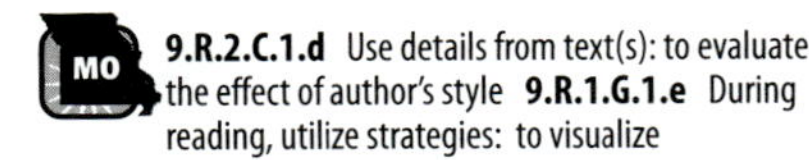

MO
9.R.2.C.1.d Use details from text(s): to evaluate the effect of author's style **9.R.1.G.1.e** During reading, utilize strategies: to visualize

Literary Focus

Style: Tone An **autobiography** is the story of a person's life written by that person. The narrative tells about the events in the author's life; the **style,** or writer's way of using words, helps reveal the author's personality. For example, if a writer uses formal, serious language, probably he or she has a serious outlook on life.

Another dimension to a writer's style is **tone,** or the attitude that a writer takes toward a subject, a character, or the audience. Tone, like style, is shown through the writer's choice of words and details.

Literary Perspectives Apply the literary perspective described on page 477 as you read this autobiography.

Reading Focus

Visualizing Though the incident Dahl tells about took place a long time ago in another country, his vivid descriptions enable you to **visualize**—or picture in your mind—the unfamiliar setting and unusual characters in this story.

Into Action As you read, fill in this chart to see how Dahl brings the character of Mrs. Pratchett to life. You can use this method to visualize other characters, events, or settings.

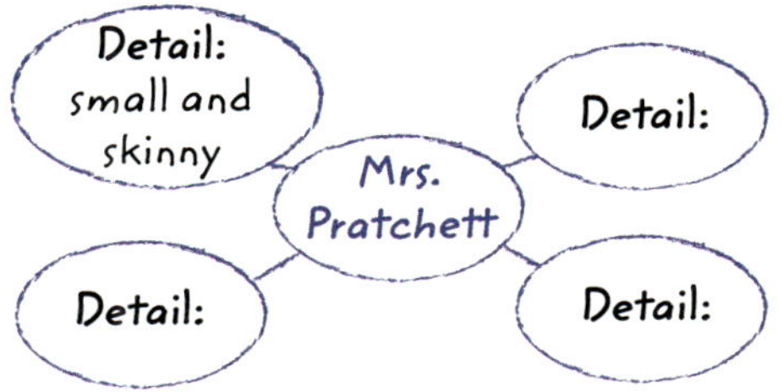

Writing Focus

Think as a Reader/Writer

Find It in Your Reading Dahl relies on exaggeration to make his autobiography humorous. Instead of just saying that he and his friends liked a certain candy store, he says, "Without it, there would have been little to live for." Pay attention to the way Dahl enhances or exaggerates people and situations. Write down these details in your *Reader/Writer Notebook*.

Vocabulary

loathsome (LOHTH suhm) *adj.:* hateful; disgusting. *The most loathsome thing about the woman was the dirt that clung to her.*

tramp (tramp) *n.:* person who goes about on foot, sometimes doing odd jobs or begging for a living. *The sweet-shop owner's appearance was so filthy that even a tramp wouldn't have asked her for candy.*

desperados (dehs puh RAH dohz) *n.:* reckless criminals. *When the boys came up with their top-secret plan, they felt like desperados.*

malignant (muh LIHG nuhnt) *adj.:* evil; cruel. *Roald and his friends thought Mrs. Pratchett had a malignant presence.*

cross (kraws) *adj.:* angry. *The headmaster always had a cross expression on his face.*

Language Coach

Multiple-Meaning Words Many words in the English language have more than one meaning. For instance, the word *tramp* can also be used as a verb, meaning "to walk heavily." Look again at the list, and see if there are any other words that might have another meaning besides the one listed. Use a dictionary to check your guesses.

Learn It Online
Develop your vocabulary with Word Watch:
go.hrw.com L9-475 Go

MEET THE WRITER

Learn It Online
Learn more about Dahl's life at:
go.hrw.com L9-476 Go

Roald Dahl

(1916–1990)

"Children Love to Be Spooked"

The British writer Roald Dahl has the unusual distinction of being famous as the author of works for both adults and children. Among his best-known children's books are *James and the Giant Peach* and *Charlie and the Chocolate Factory,* both of which have been made into movies. In most of Dahl's fiction for children, young heroes win over fearsome enemies. Responding to criticism of the violence in his children's books, Dahl said, "Children love to be spooked. . . . They like a touch of the macabre as long as it's funny too. . . . And my nastiness is never gratuitous. It's retribution. Beastly people must be punished."

School of Hard Knocks

Readers of Dahl's autobiography *Boy* understand his concern about "beastly people." During the years he spent attending British boarding schools, Dahl endured harsh discipline, including beatings, by cruel headmasters. But school wasn't all misery. The Cadbury chocolate company sent the boys boxes of candy bars, asking them to rate the taste. Dahl was very serious about his job. "Too subtle for the common palate" was his rating for one candy bar he tasted.

Think About the Writer

Given his boarding school experience, what kind of boyhood story do you think Dahl might write?

Build Background

At the English prep school that Dahl attended, a grade level is called a form. For example, a student in the first form is a first-grader. Also, in the English school system, a principal is referred to as a headmaster (if male) or a headmistress (if female). When Dahl attended classes, many schools were either all male or all female. Some schools still maintain this tradition.

Preview the Selection

In this autobiography, you will meet **Mrs. Pratchett,** a candy-store owner, and **Mr. Coombes,** the school's headmaster, both of whom have something to say to the young, joke-loving **Roald Dahl.**

Read with a Purpose Read this story to see how the author and his friends use a mouse to get revenge.

by **Roald Dahl**

The Bicycle and the Sweet-Shop

The sweet-shop in Llandaff in the year 1923 was the very center of our lives. To us, it was what a bar is to a drunk, or a church is to a Bishop. Without it, there would have been little to live for. But it had one terrible drawback, this sweet-shop. The woman who owned it was a horror. We hated her and we had good reason for doing so.

Her name was Mrs. Pratchett. She was a small skinny old hag with a moustache on her upper lip and a mouth as sour as a green gooseberry. She never smiled. She never welcomed us when we went in, and the only times she spoke were when she said things like, "I'm watchin' you so keep yer thievin' fingers off them chocolates!" Or "I don't want you in 'ere just to look around! Either you *forks* out or you *gets* out!"

But by far the most loathsome thing about Mrs. Pratchett was the filth that clung around her. Her apron was gray and greasy. Her blouse had bits of breakfast all over it, toast-crumbs and tea stains and splotches of dried egg-yolk. It was her hands, however, that disturbed us most. They were disgusting. They were black with dirt and grime. They looked as though they had been putting lumps of coal on the fire all day long. And do not forget please that it was these very hands and fingers that she plunged into the sweet-jars when we asked for a pennyworth of Treacle Toffee or Wine Gums or Nut Clusters or whatever. There were precious few health laws in those days, and nobody, least of all Mrs. Pratchett, ever thought of using a little shovel for getting out the sweets as they do today. The mere sight of her grimy right hand with its black fingernails digging an ounce of Chocolate

Literary Perspectives

Analyzing Philosophical Context Philosophy is a conscious search for truth. This perspective asks us to uncover and consider the philosophical arguments of the author when we read literature. Philosophical context refers to an author's underlying assumptions about larger questions about life and its meaning. An author's philosophy influences literary texts in a variety of ways: through the credibility of the characters, the form in which the text is written, and the overarching themes or messages the author seems to convey. As you read this selection, use the notes and questions at the bottom of the pages to guide you in using this perspective.

Vocabulary **loathsome** (LOHTH suhm) *adj.:* hateful; disgusting.

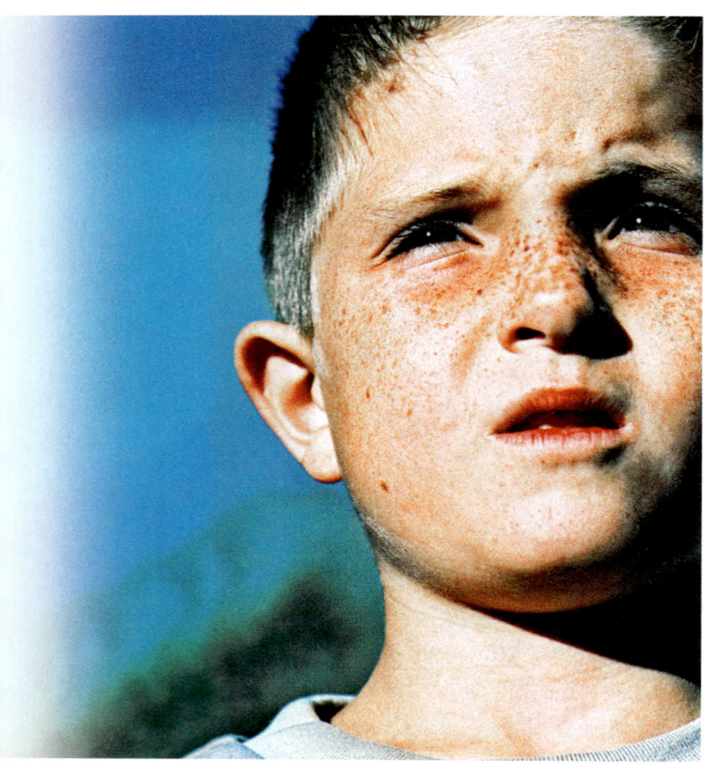

Fudge out of a jar would have caused a starving tramp to go running from the shop. But not us. Sweets were our life-blood. We would have put up with far worse than that to get them. So we simply stood and watched in sullen silence while this disgusting old woman stirred around inside the jars with her foul fingers. **A**

The other thing we hated Mrs. Pratchett for was her meanness. Unless you spent a whole sixpence[1] all in one go, she wouldn't give you a bag. Instead you got your sweets twisted up in a small piece of newspaper which she tore off a pile of old *Daily Mirrors* lying on the counter.

So you can well understand that we had it in for Mrs. Pratchett in a big way, but we didn't quite know what to do about it. Many schemes were put forward but none of them was any good. None of them, that is, until suddenly, one memorable afternoon, we found the dead mouse.

The Great Mouse Plot

My four friends and I had come across a loose floor-board at the back of the classroom, and when we prized it up with the blade of a pocket-knife, we discovered a big hollow space underneath. This, we decided, would be our secret hiding place for sweets and other small treasures such as conkers[2] and monkey-nuts[3] and birds' eggs. Every afternoon, when the last lesson was over, the five of us would wait until the classroom had emptied, then we would lift up the floor-board and examine our secret hoard, perhaps adding to it or taking something away.

One day, when we lifted it up, we found a dead mouse lying among our treasures. It was an exciting discovery. Thwaites took it out by its tail and waved it in front of our faces. "What shall we do with it?" he cried.

"It stinks!" someone shouted. "Throw it out of the window quick!"

"Hold on a tick," I said. "Don't throw it away."

Thwaites hesitated. They all looked at me.

When writing about oneself, one must strive to be truthful. Truth is more important than modesty. I must tell you, therefore, that it was I and I alone who had the idea for the

1. **sixpence:** an old British coin worth about six pennies.

2. **conkers:** A conker is a seed from a horse chestnut tree and is used in a British children's game called conkers.

3. **monkey-nuts:** peanuts.

A **Reading Focus** **Visualizing** What details help you visualize Mrs. Pratchett?

Vocabulary **tramp** (tramp) *n.:* person who goes about on foot, sometimes doing odd jobs or begging for a living.

great and daring Mouse Plot. We all have our moments of brilliance and glory, and this was mine. **B**

"Why don't we," I said, "slip it into one of Mrs. Pratchett's jars of sweets? Then when she puts her dirty hand in to grab a handful, she'll grab a stinky dead mouse instead."

The other four stared at me in wonder. Then, as the sheer genius of the plot began to sink in, they all started grinning. They slapped me on the back. They cheered me and danced around the classroom. "We'll do it today!" they cried. "We'll do it on the way home! *You* had the idea," they said to me, "so *you* can be the one to put the mouse in the jar."

Thwaites handed me the mouse. I put it into my trouser pocket. Then the five of us left the school, crossed the village green, and headed for the sweet-shop. We were tremendously jazzed up. We felt like a gang of desperados setting out to rob a train or blow up the sheriff's office.

"Make sure you put it into a jar which is used often," somebody said.

"I'm putting it in Gobstoppers," I said. "The Gobstopper jar is never behind the counter."

"I've got a penny," Thwaites said, "so I'll ask for one Sherbet Sucker and one Bootlace. And while she turns away to get them, you slip the mouse in quickly with the Gobstoppers."

Thus everything was arranged. We were strutting a little as we entered the shop. We were the victors now and Mrs. Pratchett was the victim. She stood behind the counter, and her small malignant pig-eyes watched us suspiciously as we came forward.

"One Sherbet Sucker, please," Thwaites said

to her, holding out his penny.

I kept to the rear of the group, and when I saw Mrs. Pratchett turn her head away for a couple of seconds to fish a Sherbet Sucker out of the box, I lifted the heavy glass lid of the Gobstopper jar and dropped the mouse in. Then I replaced the lid as silently as possible. My heart was thumping like mad and my hands had gone all sweaty. **C**

"And one Bootlace, please," I heard Thwaites saying. When I turned round, I saw Mrs. Pratchett holding out the Bootlace in her filthy fingers.

"I don't want all the lot of you troopin' in 'ere if only one of you is buyin'," she screamed at us. "Now beat it! Go on, get out!"

B **Literary Focus** **Tone** After reading this paragraph, how would you describe its tone? Which words led you to this conclusion?

C **Reading Focus** **Visualizing** What details bring this scene to life?

Vocabulary **desperados** (dehs puh RAH dohz) *n.:* reckless criminals.
malignant (muh LIHG nuhnt) *adj.:* evil; cruel.

As soon as we were outside, we broke into a run. "Did you do it?" they shouted at me.

"Of course I did!" I said.

"Well done you!" they cried. "What a super show!"

I felt like a hero. I *was* a hero. It was marvelous to be so popular. D

Mr. Coombes

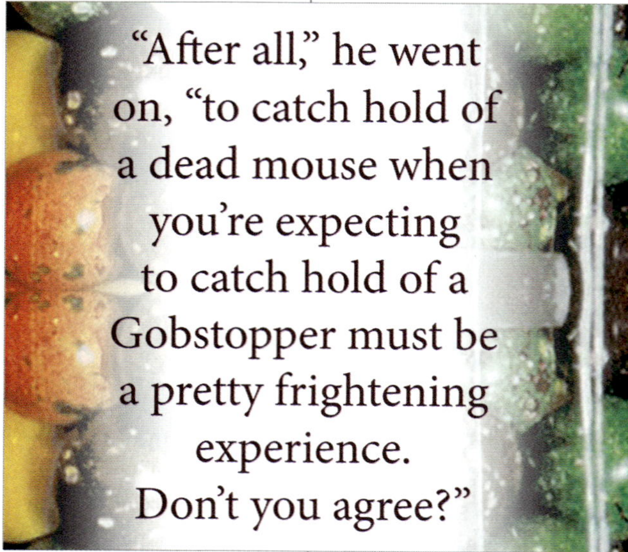
"After all," he went
on, "to catch hold of
a dead mouse when
you're expecting
to catch hold of a
Gobstopper must be
a pretty frightening
experience.
Don't you agree?"

The flush of triumph over the dead mouse was carried forward to the next morning as we all met again to walk to school.

"Let's go in and see if it's still in the jar," somebody said as we approached the sweet-shop.

"Don't," Thwaites said firmly. "It's too dangerous. Walk past as though nothing has happened."

As we came level with the shop we saw a cardboard notice hanging on the door.

We stopped and stared. We had never known the sweet-shop to be closed at this time in the morning, even on Sundays.

"What's happened?" we asked each other. "What's going on?"

We pressed our faces against the window and looked inside. Mrs. Pratchett was nowhere to be seen.

"Look!" I cried. "The Gobstopper jar's gone! It's not on the shelf! There's a gap where it used to be!"

"It's on the floor!" someone said. "It's smashed to bits and there's Gobstoppers everywhere!"

"There's the mouse!" someone else shouted.

We could see it all, the huge glass jar smashed to smithereens with the dead mouse lying in the wreckage and hundreds of many-colored Gobstoppers littering the floor.

"She got such a shock when she grabbed hold of the mouse that she dropped everything," somebody was saying.

"But why didn't she sweep it all up and open the shop?" I asked.

Nobody answered me.

We turned away and walked towards the school. All of a sudden we had begun to feel slightly uncomfortable. There was something not quite right about the shop being closed. Even Thwaites was unable to offer a reasonable explanation. We became silent. There was a faint scent of danger in the air now. Each one of us had caught a whiff of it. Alarm bells were beginning to ring faintly in our ears. E

After a while, Thwaites broke the silence. "She must have got one heck of a shock," he said. He paused. We all looked at him, wondering what wisdom the great medical authority was going to come out with next.

"After all," he went on, "to catch hold of a dead mouse when you're expecting to catch hold of a Gobstopper must be a pretty frightening experience. Don't you agree?"

Nobody answered him.

D **Literary Perspectives** **Philosophical Context** What idea about power and heroism does Dahl convey in this message?

E **Reading Focus** **Visualizing** What are the boys doing now?

"Well now," Thwaites went on, "when an old person like Mrs. Pratchett suddenly gets a very big shock, I suppose you know what happens next?"

"What?" we said. "What happens?"

"You ask my father," Thwaites said. "He'll tell you."

"You tell us," we said.

"It gives her a heart attack," Thwaites announced. "Her heart stops beating and she's dead in five seconds."

For a moment or two my own heart stopped beating. Thwaites pointed a finger at me and said darkly, "I'm afraid you've killed her."

"*Me*?" I cried. "Why just *me*?"

"It was *your* idea," he said. "And what's more, you put the mouse in."

All of a sudden, I was a murderer. **F**

At exactly that point, we heard the school bell ringing in the distance and we had to gallop the rest of the way so as not to be late for prayers.

Prayers were held in the Assembly Hall. We all perched in rows on wooden benches while the teachers sat up on the platform in armchairs, facing us. The five of us scrambled into our places just as the Headmaster marched in, followed by the rest of the staff.

The Headmaster is the only teacher at Llandaff Cathedral School that I can remember, and for a reason you will soon discover, I can remember him very clearly indeed. His name was Mr. Coombes and I have a picture in my mind of a giant of a man with a face like a ham and a mass of rusty-colored hair that sprouted in a tangle all over the top of his head. All grown-ups appear as giants to small children. But Headmasters (and policemen) are the biggest giants of all and acquire a marvelously exaggerated stature. It is possible that Mr. Coombes was a perfectly normal being, but in my memory he was a giant, a tweed-suited giant who always wore a black gown over his tweeds and a waistcoat under his jacket. **G**

Mr. Coombes now proceeded to mumble through the same old prayers we had every day, but this morning, when the last amen had been spoken, he did not turn and lead his group rapidly out of the Hall as usual. He remained standing before us, and it was clear he had an announcement to make.

"The whole school is to go out and line up around the playground immediately," he said. "Leave your books behind. And no talking."

Mr. Coombes was looking grim. His hammy pink face had taken on that dangerous scowl which only appeared when he was extremely cross and somebody was for the high-jump. I sat there small and frightened among the rows and rows of other boys, and to me at that moment the Headmaster, with his black gown draped over his shoulders, was like a judge at a murder trial.

"He's after the killer," Thwaites whispered to me.

I began to shiver.

"I'll bet the police are here already," Thwaites went on. "And the Black Maria's[4] waiting outside."

As we made our way out to the playground, my whole stomach began to feel as though it was slowly filling up with swirling

---

4. **Black Maria's:** slang for a British police wagon for prisoners.

F **Literary Perspectives** **Philosophical Context** Instead of being a hero, how is Dahl now regarded?

G **Literary Focus** **Style** Notice how Dahl describes Mr. Coombes. How would you describe Dahl's use of language?

Vocabulary **cross** (kraws) *adj.:* angry.

Analyzing Visuals **Viewing and Interpreting** How does the photograph capture the time and setting of the story?

water. *I am only eight years old,* I told myself. *No little boy of eight has ever murdered anyone. It's not possible.*

Out in the playground on this warm cloudy September morning, the Deputy Headmaster was shouting, "Line up in forms! Sixth Form over there! Fifth Form next to them! Spread out! Spread out! Get on with it! Stop talking all of you!"

Thwaites and I and my other three friends were in the Second Form, the lowest but one, and we lined up against the red-brick wall of the playground shoulder to shoulder. I can remember that when every boy in the school was in his place, the line stretched right round the four sides of the playground—about one hundred small boys altogether, aged between six and twelve, all of us wearing identical gray shorts and gray blazers and gray stockings and black shoes. **H**

"Stop that *talking*!" shouted the Deputy Head. "I want absolute silence!"

But why for heaven's sake were we in the playground at all? I wondered. And why were we lined up like this? It had never happened before.

I half-expected to see two policemen come bounding out of the school to grab me by the arms and put handcuffs on my wrists.

A single door led out from the school on to the playground. Suddenly it swung open and through it, like the angel of death, strode Mr. Coombes, huge and bulky in his tweed suit and black gown, and beside him, believe it or not, right beside him trotted the tiny figure of Mrs. Pratchett herself!

Mrs. Pratchett was alive!

The relief was tremendous.

"She's alive!" I whispered to Thwaites stand-

H **Reading Focus** **Visualizing** What do you see happening here? Which details create the most vivid pictures in this scene?

ing next to me. "I didn't kill her!" Thwaites ignored me.

"We'll start over here," Mr. Coombes was saying to Mrs. Pratchett. He grasped her by one of her skinny arms and led her over to where the Sixth Form was standing. Then, still keeping hold of her arm, he proceeded to lead her at a brisk walk down the line of boys. It was like someone inspecting the troops.

"What on earth are they doing?" I whispered.

Thwaites didn't answer me. I glanced at him. He had gone rather pale.

"Too big," I heard Mrs. Pratchett saying. "Much too big. It's none of this lot. Let's 'ave a look at some of them titchy[5] ones."

5. **titchy:** slang for "tiny."

Mr. Coombes increased his pace. "We'd better go all the way round," he said. He seemed in a hurry to get it over with now and I could see Mrs. Pratchett's skinny goat's legs trotting to keep up with him. They had already inspected one side of the playground where the Sixth Form and half the Fifth Form were standing. We watched them moving down the second side . . . then the third side.

"Still too big," I heard Mrs. Pratchett croaking. "Much too big! Smaller than these! Much smaller! Where's them nasty little ones?"

They were coming closer to us now . . . closer and closer.

They were starting on the fourth side . . .

Every boy in our form was watching Mr. Coombes and Mrs. Pratchett as they came walking down the line towards us.

"Nasty cheeky lot, these little 'uns!" I heard Mrs. Pratchett muttering. "They comes into my shop and they thinks they can do what they damn well likes!"

Mr. Coombes made no reply to this.

"They nick things when I ain't looking," she went on. "They put their grubby 'ands all over everything and they've got no manners. I don't mind girls. I never 'ave no trouble with girls, but boys is 'ideous and 'orrible! I don't 'ave to tell *you* that, 'Eadmaster, do I?"

"These are the smaller ones," Mr. Coombes said.

I could see Mrs. Pratchett's piggy little eyes staring hard at the face of each boy she passed.

Suddenly she let out a high-pitched yell and pointed a dirty finger straight at Thwaites. "That's 'im!" she yelled. "That's one of 'em! I'd know 'im a mile away, the scummy little bounder!" **I**

The entire school turned to look at Thwaites. "W-what have *I* done?" he stuttered, appealing to Mr. Coombes.

"Shut up," Mr. Coombes said.

Mrs. Pratchett's eyes flicked over and settled on my own face. I looked down and studied the black asphalt surface of the playground.

"'Ere's another of 'em!" I heard her yelling. "That one there!" She was pointing at me now.

"You're quite sure?" Mr. Coombes said.

"Of course I'm sure!" she cried. "I never forgets a face, least of all when it's as sly as that! 'Ee's one of 'em all right! There was five altogether! Now where's them other three?"

The other three, as I knew very well, were coming up next.

Mrs. Pratchett's face was glimmering with venom as her eyes traveled beyond me down the line.

"There they are!" she cried out, stabbing the air with her finger. "'*Im* . . . and '*im* . . . and '*im*! That's the five of 'em all right! We don't need to look no farther than this, 'Eadmaster! They're all 'ere, the nasty dirty little pigs! You've got their names, 'ave you?"

"I've got their names, Mrs. Pratchett," Mr. Coombes told her. "I'm much obliged to you."

"And I'm much obliged to *you*, 'Eadmaster," she answered.

As Mr. Coombes led her away across the playground, we heard her saying, "Right in the jar of Gobstoppers it was! A stinkin' dead mouse which I will never forget as long as I live!"

"You have my deepest sympathy," Mr. Coombes was muttering.

"Talk about shocks!" she went on. "When my fingers caught 'old of that nasty soggy stinkin' dead mouse . . ." Her voice trailed away as Mr. Coombes led her quickly through the door into the school building.

I **Literary Focus** **Tone** In the preceding paragraphs, which details reveal Dahl's feelings about Mrs. Pratchett?

Applying Your Skills

9.R.2.C.1.d Use details from text(s): to evaluate the effect of author's style **9.R.2.C.1.b** Use details from text(s): to analyze character, plot, setting, point of view **9.R.1.G.1.e** During reading, utilize strategies: to visualize *Also covered* **9.W.3.A.1.a; 9.R.1.G.1.a**

from **Boy**

Respond and Think Critically

Reading Focus

Quick Check

1. What is the great Mouse Plot? Who came up with the plot?

Read with a Purpose

2. What happens when the boys try to get the best of Mrs. Pratchett with their prank?

Reading Skills: Visualizing

3. Review the details in your visualizing chart. What kinds of words and images does Dahl use to portray Mrs. Pratchett?

Vocabulary Check

Match each Vocabulary word to the correct definition.

loathsome
tramp
desperados
malignant
cross

4. angry
5. reckless criminals
6. person on foot who does odd jobs
7. disgusting
8. evil

Literary Focus

Literary Analysis

9. **Hypothesize** What do you think draws the mouse to the boys' hiding spot? Why aren't the boys scared of it?
10. **Analyze** How do you think Mr. Coombes feels about Mrs. Pratchett? Find details to support your answer.
11. **Literary Perspectives** On page 476, Dahl says, "Beastly people must be punished." Who do you think the "beastly people" are in his autobiography? What philosophy of life do the statement and story reveal?

Literary Skills: Tone

12. **Analyze** What tone does Dahl use to describe the prank he played on Mrs. Pratchett? When does the tone of the story change? Why do you think Dahl chose to make this shift?

Literary Skills Review: Static and Dynamic Characters

13. **Analyze** A **static character** does not change in the course of a story. A **dynamic character** grows and changes as a result of story events. Which kind of character is this story's main character? How can you tell?

Writing Focus

Think as a Reader/Writer

Use It in Your Writing Dahl is known for making the adult characters of his stories as awful as possible—like the unclean Mrs. Patchett and Mr. Coombes, who has a "face like a ham." Think of a funny episode from your childhood. Write down what happened and try to use Dahl's technique of exaggeration to make your story humorous.

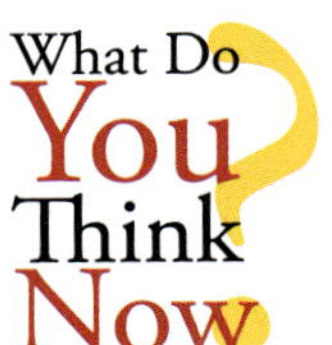

At what point did the joke the boys played go too far? What can we all learn from Dahl's experiences?

COMPARING TEXTS

Author Study: Maya Angelou

CONTENTS

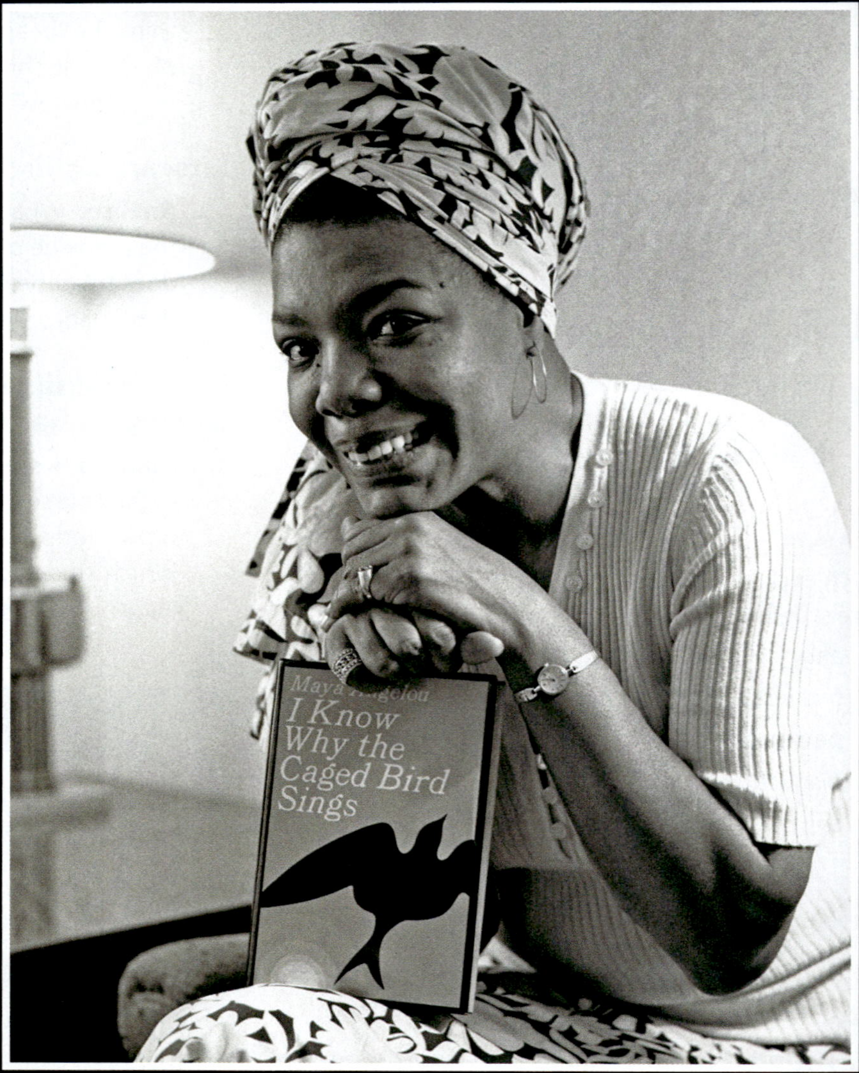

Maya Angelou, 1971.

How do you define *freedom* and *liberty?*

QuickWrite

Think about historical and current events and perhaps your own family history. What does it mean to be truly free? Write about how some types of freedom lead to other forms of liberty.

Preparing to Read

from I Know Why the Caged Bird Sings / Caged Bird / New Directions / Woman Work

MO **9.R.1.I.1.c** Compare, contrast, analyze and evaluate connections: text to world **9.R.1.H.1.c** Apply post-reading skills to comprehend, interpret, analyze, and evaluate text: reflect *Also covered* **9.R.3.A.1; 9.R.1.H.1.d**

Use your **RWN** to complete the activities for these selections.

Literary Focus

Literary Criticism: Biographical Approach When you use a **biographical approach** to analyze literature, you explore how texts reflect the heritage, attitudes, and beliefs of the author. In **autobiographies,** authors write about their life experiences. Other genres, such as essays and poems, may also reflect certain themes, or ideas about an author's beliefs and heritage. Use the biographical information about Maya Angelou (pages 488–489) to help you analyze the selections you are about to read.

Reading Focus

Comparing Works by One Author When comparing an author's works, look for similarities and differences among the texts. Then, **synthesize** (or combine) your observations with your knowledge about the author, and draw conclusions about the author's work as a whole.

Into Action Use a chart, like the one below, to record your observations about Angelou's work. Create a new row for each work.

Title	Main Idea(s) or Theme(s)	Connection to Author's Life	Style (Diction and Tone)
from I Know Why the Caged Bird Sings	People faced hardships growing up in the segregated South.	This story is Angelou's true account of growing up.	Use of dialect brings characters to life.

Writing Focus

Think as a Reader/Writer

Find It in Your Reading Angelou's use of imagery makes the experiences and people she writes about real for the reader. As you read these four works, record in your *Reader/Writer Notebook* the images that you find most effective.

Vocabulary

from I Know Why the Caged Bird Sings

affluent (AF loo ehnt) *adj.:* wealthy. *The cotton pickers were not affluent and had trouble paying off their debts.*

sparse (spahrs) *adj.:* growing or spaced wide apart; small in quantity and thinly spread. *When the crops were sparse, the workers could not earn enough money to support their families.*

New Directions

meticulously (muh TIHK yoo luhs lee) *adv.:* carefully; with great attention to detail. *Annie prepared her meat pies meticulously, and the workers eagerly bought them.*

ominous (AHM ih nuhs) *adj.:* unfavorable. *Since it was difficult for an African American woman to get a job in 1903, Annie Johnson's future looked ominous.*

resolve (rih ZAHLV) *n.:* determination; fixed purpose. *Annie Johnson's careful planning was a sign of her resolve.*

Language Coach

Multiple-Meaning Words The Vocabulary word *resolve* has multiple meanings. You might be familiar with its definitions as a verb: "reach a decision" and "solve." What does this word mean when used as a noun?

Learn It Online

Hear a professional actor read these selections at:

go.hrw.com L9-487 

MEET THE WRITER

Maya Angelou

(1928–)

A Harsh Beginning

"Courage," Maya Angelou believes, "is the most important of all the virtues, because without courage you can't practice any other virtues consistently." Courage has been an underlying theme and a hallmark of Angelou's extraordinary life and work.

Maya Angelou's youth was filled with both great hardship and love. In 1931, Marguerite Annie Johnson (Angelou's given name) was three years old and her brother, Bailey, was four when their parents divorced. The children were sent from their home in California to Stamps, Arkansas, to live with their paternal grandmother. Feeling abandoned by her mother and subjected to the racism that raged in the segregated South, Angelou found unflagging support in the home of her grandmother, who gave Angelou the "confidence" that she "was loved." On a visit to her mother, then living in St. Louis, Missouri, when she was eight years old, Angelou was abused and subsequently stopped speaking for a number of years. While others thought that the silent child must be unintelligent, Angelou's grandmother knew that when Maya was ready, she would have something important to say to the world—and her grandmother was right.

"New Directions"

After ten years, Angelou returned to California where she graduated from high school at the age of sixteen. Multitalented and resilient, Angelou never shied away from taking risks and pursuing "new directions." In the course of her life, she has been a dancer, singer, actress, playwright, screenwriter, director, and journalist.

In her life and her work, Angelou has also promoted civil rights. A friend of Dr. Martin Luther King, Jr., and his wife, Coretta Scott King, she served as the northern coordinator for the Southern Christian Leadership Conference, established by King to further the activities of the civil rights movement. Angelou firmly believes that "human beings are more alike" than they "are unalike," and she continually promotes the need for people to respect and understand each other: "Equal rights, fair play, justice, are all like the air," she notes. "We all have it or none of us has it. That is the truth of it."

The Human Spirit

Although Angelou has traveled down many roads in her life, she sees herself primarily as a teacher and a writer. A frequent lecturer, she received a lifetime

A Maya Angelou Time Line

1928 Angelou is born on April 4, in St. Louis, Missouri.

1931 Angelou is sent to live with her grandmother in Stamps, Arkansas.

1936 Angelou stops talking after a brutal attack.

1944 Angelou graduates from high school in San Francisco, California.

1959–1960 Angelou serves as the northern coordinator for the Southern Christian Leadership Conference.

1930 · 1940 · 1950 · 1960

Angelou speaks before delegates of the 2004 Democratic National Convention in Boston, Massachusetts.

appointment as the Reynolds Professor of American Studies at Wake Forest University in North Carolina in 1981. Her appreciation for the written word began in her youth. During the years when she did not talk, she submerged herself in reading and memorized poetry—sixty sonnets by Shakespeare, seventy-five poems by Paul Laurence Dunbar, all the works she could find by Edgar Allan Poe.

In 1970, Angelou published *I Know Why the Caged Bird Sings*, the first of six autobiographies. The book was hailed for bringing to light the struggles faced by an African American girl growing up in the South and for depicting the dignity and fortitude of her community. Critics view the works as a reflection of the social history of the African American community as well as a sober telling of Angelou's own life.

Praised for the power of her prose, Angelou has also devoted herself to writing poetry, which she defines as "music written for the human voice." In 1993, she received the honor of being invited by President Clinton to read one of her poems at his inauguration.

Angelou's life and work are a testament to the strength of the human spirit. She notes, "All my work is meant to say, 'You may encounter many defeats but you must not be defeated.'"

Think About the Writer

Now that you have read this biography, what words would you use to describe Maya Angelou?

Key Characteristics of Angelou's Writing

Concrete details, vivid images, and **imaginative figures of speech** help convey the truth of people's experiences.

The use of **dialect** and **everyday language** brings people and characters to life.

Rhythm and other **sound devices** give works a musical quality.

Main ideas and **themes** often focus on hope, freedom, equality, the human spirit, and the strength of the African American community.

1977 Angelou is nominated for an Emmy award for her performance in the trailblazing television series *Roots*.

1981 Angelou receives a lifetime appointment as a professor at Wake Forest University in Winston-Salem, North Carolina.

2000 Angelou receives the National Medal of Arts, the highest possible honor given to an artist by the U.S. government.

1970 — 1980 — 1990 — 2000

1970 *I Know Why the Caged Bird Sings*, Angelou's first autobiography, is published. **1971** *Just Give Me a Cool Drink of Water 'Fore I Die*, her first book of poetry, is published.

1993 Angelou reads "On the Pulse of the Morning" at President Bill Clinton's inauguration.

2002 Angelou's sixth autobiography, *A Song Flung Up to Heaven*, is published.

AUTOBIOGRAPHY

from I Know Why the Caged Bird Sings

by **Maya Angelou**

Read with a Purpose

Read these two selections to explore what a caged bird represents for the author.

Build Background

Maya Angelou begins the following section of her autobiography *I Know Why the Caged Bird Sings* by describing the trip she and her brother, Bailey, made to Stamps, Arkansas, to live with their grandmother. The African American community in the small rural town of Stamps suffered from both poverty and racism. In the 1930s, when the events in this selection take place, people all over the country were suffering from the effects of the Great Depression, a severe economic decline. The poor were made even poorer, and farmers were particularly hurt. During this time, Jim Crow laws throughout the South maintained racial segregation in public transportation, schools, parks, theaters, and restaurants. These laws remained in effect until the 1960s.

When I was three and Bailey four, we had arrived in the musty little town, wearing tags on our wrists which instructed—"To Whom It May Concern"—that we were Marguerite and Bailey Johnson Jr., from Long Beach, California, en route to Stamps, Arkansas, c/o Mrs. Annie Henderson.

Our parents had decided to put an end to their calamitous marriage, and Father shipped us home to his mother. A porter had been charged with our welfare—he got off the train the next day in Arizona—and our tickets were pinned to my brother's inside coat pocket.

I don't remember much of the trip but after we reached the segregated southern part of the journey, things must have looked up. Negro passengers, who always traveled with loaded lunch boxes, felt sorry for "the poor little motherless darlings" and plied us with cold fried chicken and potato salad.

Years later I discovered that the United States had been crossed thousands of times by frightened Black children traveling alone to their newly affluent parents in Northern cities, or back to grandmothers in Southern towns when the urban North reneged[1] on its economic promises. **A**

The town reacted to us as its inhabitants had reacted to all things new before our coming. It regarded us a while without curiosity but with caution, and after we were seen to be harmless (and children) it closed in around us, as a real mother embraces a stranger's child. Warmly, but not too familiarly.

1. **reneged** (rih NIHGD): backed out of a promise or an agreement.

A **Reading Focus** **Main Idea** Why do you think Angelou makes a connection between her trip to her grandmother's home and the experiences of other African American children during this time period?

Vocabulary **affluent** (AF loo ehnt) *adj.:* wealthy.

We lived with our grandmother and uncle in the rear of the Store (it was always spoken of with a capital *s*), which she had owned some twenty-five years.

Early in the century, Momma (we soon stopped calling her Grandmother) sold lunches to the sawmen in the lumberyard (east Stamps) and the seedmen at the cotton gin[2] (west Stamps). Her crisp meat pies and cool lemonade, when joined to her miraculous ability to be in two places at the same time, assured her business success. From being a mobile lunch counter, she set up a stand between the two points of fiscal[3] interest and supplied the workers' needs for a few years. Then she had the Store built in the heart of the Negro area. Over the years it became the lay[4] center of activities in town. On Saturdays, barbers sat their customers in the shade on the porch of the Store, and troubadours[5] on their ceaseless crawlings through the South leaned across its benches and sang their sad songs of The Brazos[6] while they played juice harps[7] and cigar-box guitars.

The formal name of the Store was the Wm. Johnson General Merchandise Store. Customers could find food staples, a good variety of colored thread, mash for hogs, corn for chickens, coal oil for lamps, light bulbs for the wealthy, shoestrings, hair dressing, balloons, and flower seeds. Anything not visible had only to be ordered.

Until we became familiar enough to belong to the Store and it to us, we were locked up in a Fun House of Things where the attendant had gone home for life. **B**

Each year I watched the field across from the Store turn caterpillar green, then gradually frosty white. I knew exactly how long it would be before the big wagons would pull into the front yard and load on the cotton pickers at daybreak to carry them to the remains of slavery's plantations.

During the picking season my grandmother would get out of bed at four o'clock (she never used an alarm clock) and creak down to her knees and chant in a sleep-filled voice, "Our

2. **cotton gin:** factory in which machines are used to separate the seeds from the fibers of cotton.
3. **fiscal** (FIHS kuhl): relating to money; financial.
4. **lay:** not related to the church.
5. **troubadours** (TROO buh dawrz): traveling singers and musicians.
6. **The Brazos:** river in central and southeast Texas.
7. **juice harps:** children's name for Jew's harps, stringed instruments held between the teeth and played by plucking the strings with the fingers.

B **Literary Focus** **Biographical Approach** Explain the metaphor in this paragraph. What does it suggest about Angelou's and Bailey's initial experience of living with their grandmother?

Father, thank you for letting me see this New Day. Thank you that you didn't allow the bed I lay on last night to be my cooling board, nor my blanket my winding sheet.[8] Guide my feet this day along the straight and narrow, and help me to put a bridle on my tongue. Bless this house, and everybody in it. Thank you, in the name of your Son, Jesus Christ, Amen."

Before she had quite arisen, she called our names and issued orders, and pushed her large feet into homemade slippers and across the bare lye-washed wooden floor to light the coal-oil lamp.

The lamplight in the Store gave a soft make-believe feeling to our world which made me want to whisper and walk about on tiptoe. The odors of onions and oranges and kerosene had been mixing all night and wouldn't be disturbed until the wooded slat was removed from the door and the early morning air forced its way in with the bodies of people who had walked miles to reach the pickup place.

"Sister, I'll have two cans of sardines."

"I'm gonna work so fast today I'm gonna make you look like you standing still."

"Lemme have a hunk uh cheese and some sody crackers."

"Just gimme a coupla them fat peanut paddies." That would be from a picker who was taking his lunch. The greasy brown paper sack was stuck behind the bib of his overalls. He'd use the candy as a snack before the noon sun called the workers to rest. **C**

In those tender mornings the Store was full of laughing, joking, boasting, and bragging. One man was going to pick two hundred pounds of cotton, and another three hundred. Even the children were promising to bring home fo' bits and six bits.[9]

The champion picker of the day before was the hero of the dawn. If he prophesied[10] that the cotton in today's field was going to be sparse and stick to the bolls[11] like glue, every listener would grunt a hearty agreement.

The sound of the empty cotton sacks dragging over the floor and the murmurs of waking people were sliced by the cash register as we rang up the five-cent sales.

If the morning sounds and smells were touched with the supernatural, the late afternoon had all the features of the normal Arkansas life. In the dying sunlight the people dragged, rather than their empty cotton sacks.

Brought back to the Store, the pickers would step out of the backs of trucks and fold down, dirt-disappointed, to the ground. No matter how much they had picked, it wasn't enough. Their wages wouldn't even get them out of debt to my grandmother, not to mention the staggering bill that waited on them at the white commissary[12] downtown.

The sounds of the new morning had been replaced with grumbles about cheating houses, weighted scales, snakes, skimpy cotton, and dusty rows. In later years I was to confront the

8. **winding sheet:** cloth used to wrap a person for burial; shroud.

9. **fo' bits and six bits:** *Two bits* is slang for 25 cents, so four and six bits are 50 cents and 75 cents respectively.

10. **prophesied** (PRAHF uh syd): predicted, as if granted knowledge by God or gods.

11. **bolls** (bohlz): seed pods of plants.

12. **commissary** (KAHM uh sehr ee): store selling food and supplies.

C **Reading Focus** **Style** Angelou's use of dialect is a hallmark of her style. What do these few short lines of dialogue contribute to the selection?

Vocabulary **sparse** (spahrs) *adj.:* growing or spaced wide apart; small in quantity and thinly spread.

Cotton pickers waiting for the workday to start on the Alexander Plantation in Arkansas in 1935.

Analyzing Visuals **Viewing and Interpreting** How does this photograph reflect the place and the setting of the selection? Explain.

stereotyped picture of gay song-singing cotton pickers with such inordinate rage that I was told even by fellow Blacks that my paranoia was embarrassing. But I had seen the fingers cut by the mean little cotton bolls, and I had witnessed the backs and shoulders and arms and legs resisting any further demands. **D**

Some of the workers would leave their sacks at the Store to be picked up the following morning, but a few had to take them home for repairs. I winced to picture them sewing the coarse material under a coal-oil lamp with fingers stiffening from the day's work. In too few hours they would have to walk back to Sister Henderson's Store, get vittles, and load, again, onto the trucks. Then they would face another day of trying to earn enough for the whole year with the heavy knowledge that they were going to end the season as they started it. Without the money or credit necessary to sustain a family for three months. In cotton-picking time the late afternoons revealed the harshness of Black Southern life, which in the early morning had been softened by nature's blessing of grogginess, forgetfulness, and the soft lamplight.

D **Reading Focus** **Main Idea** Why do you think Angelou, as an adult, describes her reactions to the stereotypical view that the cotton pickers were happy? What point is she making?

POEM

CAGED BIRD

by **Maya Angelou**

Preparing to Read for this selection is on page 487.

Bird Cage Among Mountains (1996) by Vivien Rothwell (1945–). Oil on canvas.

A free bird leaps
on the back of the wind
and floats downstream
till the current ends
and dips his wing
in the orange sun rays
and dares to claim the sky.

But a bird that stalks
down his narrow cage
can seldom see through
his bars of rage
his wings are clipped° and
his feet are tied
so he opens his throat to sing. **A**

The caged bird sings
with a fearful trill°
of things unknown
but longed for still
and his tune is heard
on the distant hill
for the caged bird
sings of freedom.

12. **his wings are clipped:** birds with clipped wings cannot fly.

16. **trill:** fluttering, wavering sound.

The free bird thinks of another breeze
and the trade winds° soft through the
sighing trees
and the fat worms waiting on a
dawn-bright lawn
and he names the sky his own.

But a caged bird stands on the grave of
dreams
his shadow shouts on a nightmare scream
his wings are clipped and his feet are tied
so he opens his throat to sing.

The caged bird sings
with a fearful trill
of things unknown
but longed for still
and his tune is heard
on the distant hill
for the caged bird
sings of freedom. **B**

24. **trade winds:** strong, regular tropical winds.

A Reading Focus **Making Connections** Why do you think the metaphor of a caged bird holds so much meaning for Angelou? Do you think the metaphor applies to her life? Explain.

B Literary Focus **Biographical Approach** What belief do you think the song of the caged bird represents for Angelou? How is it related to the plight of African Americans?

Applying Your Skills

MO 9.R.1.I.1.c Compare, contrast, analyze and evaluate connections: text to world 9.R.1.H.1.c Apply post-reading skills to comprehend, interpret, analyze, and evaluate text: reflect 9.R.2.B.2.c Identify and explain literary techniques, in text emphasizing: repeated sound, line or phrase and *Also covered* 9.R.2.C.1.b; 9.R.3.A.1; 9.W.3.A.1.e; 9.R.1.G.1.a

from I Know Why the Caged Bird Sings / Caged Bird

Respond and Think Critically

Reading Focus

Quick Check

1. What observations about the Store's customers does Angelou make?
2. What does the caged bird sing for in Angelou's poem?

Read with a Purpose

3. How are the cotton pickers in the autobiography similar to the caged bird described in the poem?

Reading Skills: Comparing Works by One Author

4. Review the chart you filled in as you read these two selections. Do you see any similarities between the works? Add another row, labeled "Comparisons," to the bottom of the chart, and record your observations.

Title	Main Idea(s) or Theme(s)	Connection to Author's Life	Style (Diction and Tone)
from I Know Why the Caged Bird Sings			
Caged Bird			
Comparisons:			

Vocabulary Check

Tell whether each statement is true (T) or false (F).

5. An **affluent** person might own more than one home.
6. When trees are **sparse,** there is little shade.

Literary Focus

Literary Analysis

7. **Analyze** According to the autobiography, what role does the Store play in the African American community?
8. **Contrast** In the poem, how do the lives of the caged bird and the free bird differ? What part of humanity does each bird represent?
9. **Analyze** How does Angelou's style contribute to the expression of her ideas?

Literary Skills: Literary Criticism

10. **Analyze** Identify the **refrain** (repeated lines in a poem or song) in "Caged Bird." How does Angelou's use of this device contribute to the poem's theme and sound? In what ways does the refrain reflect Angelou's belief that poetry is "music written for the human voice"?

Literary Skills Review: Indirect Characterization

11. **Interpret** Instead of making direct statements about her grandmother, Angelou relies on indirect characterization to show, rather than tell, what she is like. What do her grandmother's actions suggest about her? Explain.

Writing Focus

Think as a Reader/Writer

Use It in Your Writing Describe what a particular place is like in the morning. Then, describe the same place in the evening. Be sure to use imagery to help you create two distinct depictions of this place.

ESSAY

NEW DIRECTIONS

by **Maya Angelou**

Read with a Purpose

Read this selection to find out how work transforms the life of Maya Angelou's grandmother.

Preparing to Read for this selection is on page 487.

Build Background

Mrs. Annie Johnson, whom the author calls Annie Henderson in the excerpt from *I Know Why the Caged Bird Sings,* was Maya Angelou's grandmother. As a woman and an African American living at the turn of the twentieth century, Annie Johnson faced discrimination and limited opportunities, yet she overcame great obstacles to create a successful life for herself. Angelou has described her grandmother as "one of the greatest human beings" she has ever known.

Cooking Rice (2001) by Tilly Willis.

In 1903 the late Mrs. Annie Johnson of Arkansas found herself with two toddling sons, very little money, a slight ability to read and add simple numbers. To this picture add a disastrous marriage and the burdensome fact that Mrs. Johnson was a Negro. **A**

When she told her husband, Mr. William Johnson, of her dissatisfaction with their marriage, he conceded that he too found it to be less than he expected, and had been secretly hoping to leave and study religion. He added that he thought God was calling him not only to preach but to do so in Enid, Oklahoma. He did not tell her that he knew a minister in Enid with whom he could study and who had a friendly, unmarried daughter. They parted amicably, Annie keeping the one-room house and William taking most of the cash to carry himself to Oklahoma.

Annie, over six feet tall, big-boned, decided that she would not go to work as a domestic[1] and leave her "precious babes" to anyone else's care. There was no possibility of being hired at the town's cotton gin[2] or lumber mill, but maybe there was a way to make the two factories work for her. In her words, "I looked up the road I was going and back the way I come, and since I wasn't satisfied, I decided to step off the road and cut me a new path." She told herself that she wasn't a fancy cook but that she could "mix groceries well enough to scare hungry away and keep from starving a man."

She made her plans meticulously and in secret. One early evening to see if she was ready, she placed stones in two five-gallon pails and carried them three miles to the cotton gin. She rested a little, and then, discarding some rocks, she walked in the darkness to the saw mill five miles farther along the dirt road. On her way back to her little house and her babies, she dumped the remaining rocks along the path.

That same night she worked into the early hours boiling chicken and frying ham. She made dough and filled the rolled-out pastry with meat. At last she went to sleep.

The next morning she left her house carrying the meat pies, lard, an iron brazier,[3] and coals for a fire. Just before lunch she appeared in an empty lot behind the cotton gin. As the dinner noon bell rang, she dropped the savors into boiling fat and the aroma rose and floated over to the workers who spilled out of the gin, covered with white lint, looking like specters.[4]

Most workers had brought their lunches of pinto beans and biscuits or crackers, onions and cans of sardines, but they were tempted by the hot meat pies which Annie ladled out of the fat. She wrapped them in newspapers, which soaked up the grease, and offered them for sale at a nickel each. Although business was slow, those first days Annie was determined. She balanced her appearances between the two hours of activity.

So, on Monday if she offered hot fresh pies at the cotton gin and sold the remaining

1. **domestic** (duh MEHS tihk): household servant, such as a maid or cook.
2. **cotton gin:** factory in which machines are used to separate the seeds from the fibers of cotton.
3. **brazier** (BRAY zhuhr): cooking device used to grill food over burning coals.
4. **specters** (SPEHK tuhrz): ghosts.

A Reading Focus Main Idea Why might Angelou have chosen to begin the essay by presenting these particular details?

Vocabulary meticulously (muh TIHK yoo luhs lee) *adv.:* carefully; with great attention to detail.

cooled-down pies at the lumber mill for three cents, then on Tuesday she went first to the lumber mill presenting fresh, just-cooked pies as the lumbermen covered in sawdust emerged from the mill.

For the next few years, on balmy spring days, blistering summer noons, and cold, wet, and wintry middays, Annie never disappointed her customers, who could count on seeing the tall, brown-skin woman bent over her brazier, carefully turning the meat pies. When she felt certain that the workers had become dependent on her, she built a stall between the two hives of industry and let the men run to her for their lunchtime provisions.

She had indeed stepped from the road which seemed to have been chosen for her and cut herself a brand-new path. In years that stall became a store where customers could buy cheese, meal, syrup, cookies, candy, writing tablets, pickles, canned goods, fresh fruit, soft drinks, coal, oil, and leather soles for worn-out shoes.

Each of us has the right and the responsibility to assess the roads which lie ahead, and those over which we have traveled, and if the future road looms ominous or unpromising, and the roads back uninviting, then we need to gather our resolve and, carrying only the necessary baggage, step off that road into another direction. If the new choice is also unpalatable,[5] without embarrassment, we must be ready to change that as well. **B**

5. **unpalatable** (uhn PAL uh tuh buhl): unpleasant; unacceptable.

B **Reading Focus** **Main Idea** What idea about life does Angelou reveal in this passage?

Vocabulary **ominous** (AHM ih nuhs) *adj.:* unfavorable. **resolve** (rih ZAHLV) *n.:* determination; fixed purpose.

POEM

WOMAN WORK

by **Maya Angelou**

Read with a Purpose

Read this poem to explore how work shapes the speaker's life.

Preparing to Read for this selection is on page 487.

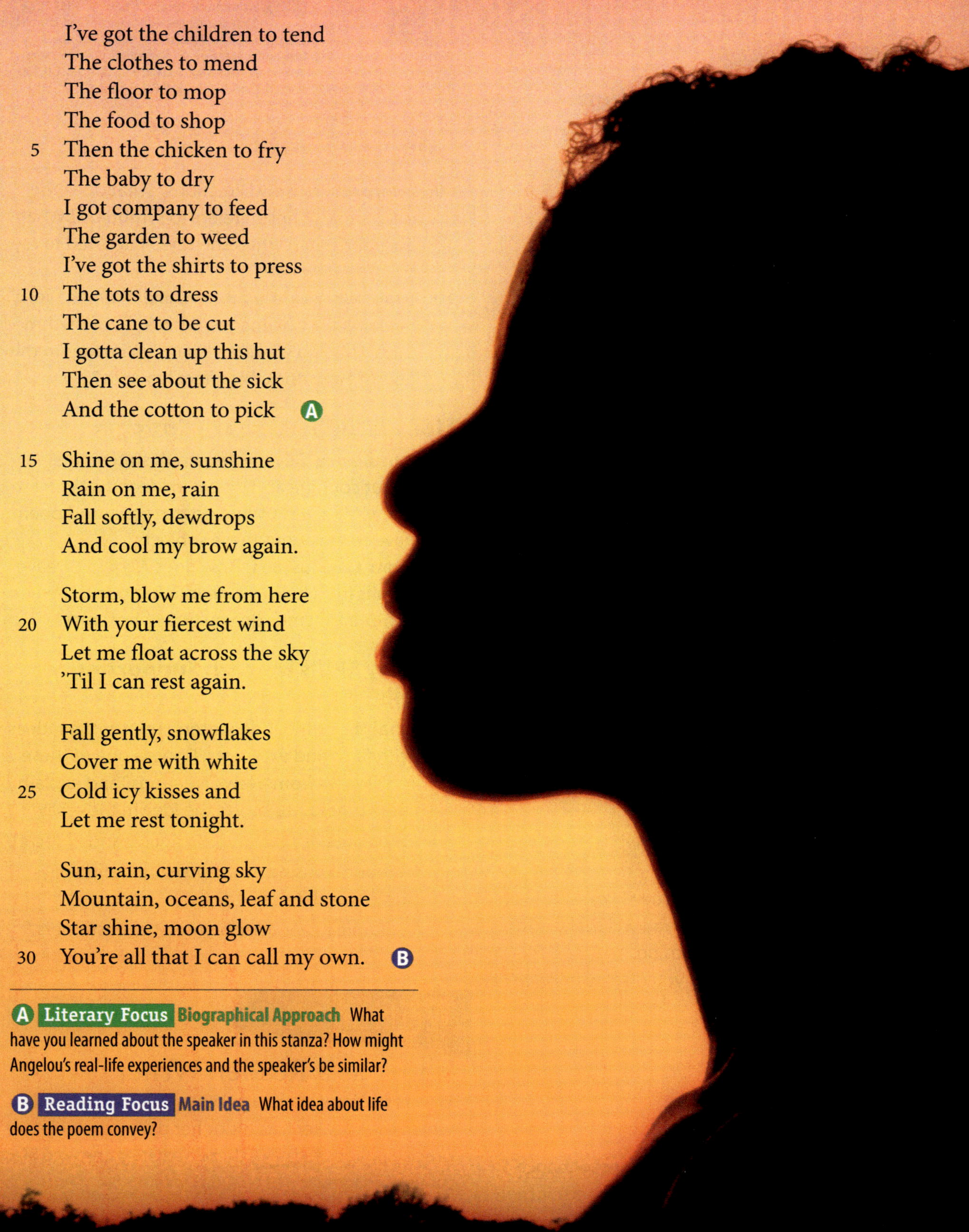

I've got the children to tend
The clothes to mend
The floor to mop
The food to shop
Then the chicken to fry
The baby to dry
I got company to feed
The garden to weed
I've got the shirts to press
The tots to dress
The cane to be cut
I gotta clean up this hut
Then see about the sick
And the cotton to pick **A**

Shine on me, sunshine
Rain on me, rain
Fall softly, dewdrops
And cool my brow again.

Storm, blow me from here
With your fiercest wind
Let me float across the sky
'Til I can rest again.

Fall gently, snowflakes
Cover me with white
Cold icy kisses and
Let me rest tonight.

Sun, rain, curving sky
Mountain, oceans, leaf and stone
Star shine, moon glow
You're all that I can call my own. **B**

A **Literary Focus** **Biographical Approach** What have you learned about the speaker in this stanza? How might Angelou's real-life experiences and the speaker's be similar?

B **Reading Focus** **Main Idea** What idea about life does the poem convey?

Applying Your Skills

New Directions / Woman Work

9.R.1.I.1.c Compare, contrast, analyze and evaluate connections: text to world 9.R.1.H.1.c Apply post-reading skills to comprehend, interpret, analyze, and evaluate text: reflect 9.R.2.C.1.c Use details from text(s): to analyze the development of a theme across genres *Also covered* 9.R.2.C.1.d; 9.R.3.A.1; 9.R.1.H.1.d; 9.R.1.H.1.a; 9.W.3.A.1.a; 9.R.1.G.1.a

Respond and Think Critically

Reading Focus

Quick Check

1. In "New Directions," why does Annie Johnson decide to sell meat pies?
2. In "Woman Work," what is the speaker trying to convey by listing certain types of activities?

Read with a Purpose

3. Compare the role of work in the lives of Annie Johnson in the essay and the speaker in the poem. How do the attitudes toward their work differ between the two people? How does this attitude shape their respective lives?

Reading Skills: Comparing Works by One Author

4. Review your comparison chart. In the row labeled "Comparisons," record any similarities and differences you note between all the selections. Add another row, labeled "Conclusions," and record your conclusions about Angelou's work as a whole.

Vocabulary Check

Tell whether each statement is true (T) or false (F).

5. By working **meticulously,** you will make errors.
6. An **ominous** sound is soothing.
7. When you show **resolve,** you display uncertainty.

Literary Focus

Literary Analysis

8. **Reflect** How does "New Directions" enhance your understanding of Angelou's grandmother?
9. **Interpret** In "New Directions," what does the road Annie Johnson refers to symbolize? What does she mean when she says, "I decided to . . . cut me a new path"?
10. **Evaluate** A **catalog poem,** like "Woman Work," presents a list of images. What kind of rhythm does Angelou create by piling up images in this poem? How does this affect her style?

Literary Skills: Literary Criticism

11. **Synthesize** Review Angelou's statements about courage and defeat in Meet the Writer (pages 488–489). What do this essay and poem have to say about these subjects?
12. **Draw Conclusions** How does Angelou weave details from her own life into her poems? What common themes do you find in her work?

Literary Skills Review: Supporting Details

13. **Analyze** Nonfiction writers support their ideas with facts and examples. Choose one of these statements from "New Directions," and explain how Angelou supports the idea in the essay:
- "She made her plans meticulously and in secret."
- "Although business was slow, those first days Annie was determined."
- ". . . Annie never disappointed her customers."

Writing Focus

Think as a Reader/Writer

Use It in Your Writing Write a catalog poem in which the speaker lists his or her daily activities. Use precise images to make these activities come to life for your reader.

COMPARING TEXTS

Wrap Up

Author Study: Maya Angelou

MO **9.R.1.I.1.c** Compare, contrast, analyze and evaluate connections: text to world **9.R.1.H.1.c** Apply post-reading skills to comprehend, interpret, analyze, and evaluate text: reflect **9.R.2.C.1.d** Use details from text(s): to evaluate the effect of author's style **9.R.3.A.1** Explain, analyze and evaluate the author's use of text features to clarify meaning *Also covered* **9.W.3.A.1.a; 9.W.3.A.1.d**

Writing Focus

Writing a Response to Literature: Biographical Approach

Maya Angelou has remarked, "I'm always inspired by men and women who rise. . . . That ability to rise is nobleness of the human spirit."

Write an essay in which you analyze Angelou's beliefs about the human spirit, as reflected in the four works you just read. Before you begin, consider what Angelou has to say about her work: "I speak to the black experience, but I am always talking about the human condition—about what we can endure, dream, fail at, and still survive."

Writing Your Essay As you plan, draft, and revise your essay, keep the following tips in mind:

- In the **introduction,** or beginning of your essay, include a specific **thesis statement** that presents the key point you will prove in your essay.
- Support your ideas with **evidence** from the four selections. Be sure to analyze how Angelou's tone and use of stylistic devices contribute to the expression of her themes or main ideas.
- Make sure that every paragraph has **unity** and **coherence.** All the sentences in the paragraph should relate to one main idea and help develop that idea.
- End your essay with a **conclusion** in which you summarize your main points. Include a new, but related, closing insight or reflection.

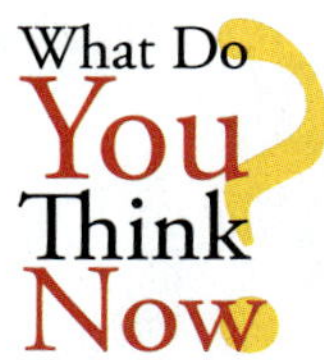

What ideas about freedom does Maya Angelou express in these four selections?

CHOICES

As you respond to the Choices, use these **Academic Vocabulary** words as appropriate: establish, attitude, enhance, appeal.

REVIEW

Write a Press Release

Think of a short story, novel, poem, or work of nonfiction that you like, and use the Internet or library resources to learn about the author. Then, write a press release that encourages people to read the work. Include a brief, catchy description of the work and an explanation of how the work reflects the author's life, beliefs, or attitudes.

CONNECT

Write a Letter

Timed Writing Choose one of Maya Angelou's statements quoted in Meet the Writer (pages 488–489) that you find particularly striking—perhaps her comment about courage, the similarity of all people, or equal rights. Do you agree or disagree with the statement? Does Angelou's belief relate to your life or the lives of people around you in some way? Write a letter to Angelou in which you explain your response to her remark.

EXTEND

Write a Poem

Write a poem titled either "Caged Bird" or "Woman Work" in which Angelou's grandmother is the speaker. Make sure that the thoughts and feelings expressed in the poem are consistent with what you have learned about her character by reading the excerpt from *I Know Why the Caged Bird Sings* and "New Directions."

INFORMATIONAL TEXT FOCUS

Structure and Format

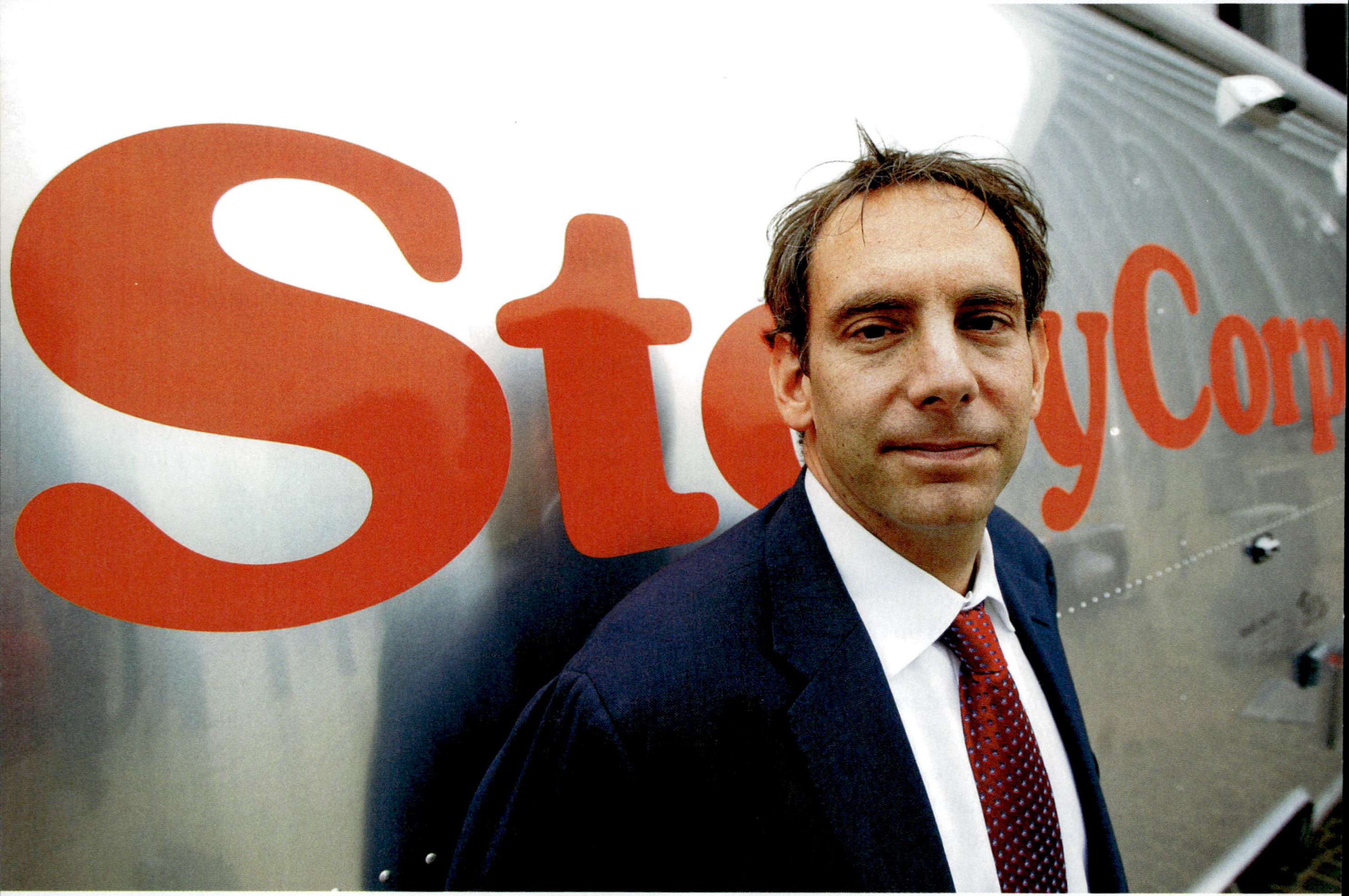

Radio documentarian Dave Isay—creating founder of StoryCorps—stands near a StoryCorps trailer (2005).

CONTENTS

What Do You Think?

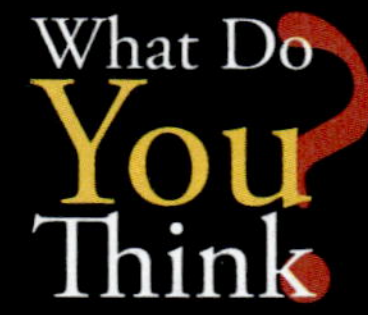

How can hearing a person's life story change you?

QuickTalk

Everybody has a story to tell, and you can learn a lot from hearing about others' experiences. Think of an anecdote that a parent or guardian or perhaps a friend told you. With a partner, share stories.

FUNCTIONAL DOCUMENTS

Preparing to Read

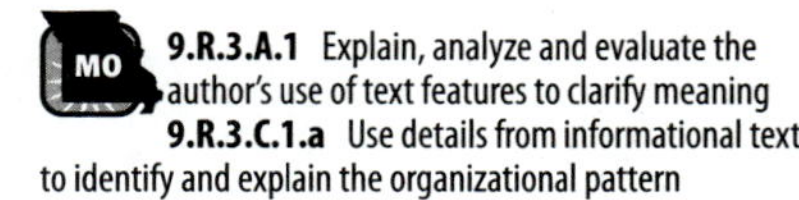

9.R.3.A.1 Explain, analyze and evaluate the author's use of text features to clarify meaning **9.R.3.C.1.a** Use details from informational text: to identify and explain the organizational pattern

About StoryCorps / Do-It-Yourself Interview

Reader/Writer Notebook

Use your **RWN** to complete the activities for these selections.

Informational Text Focus

Structure and Format of Functional Documents

At school, at work, and in other areas of your life, you will encounter **functional documents**—sets of instructions, memos, or other texts that show you how to accomplish a task. Here are a few of their features:

Structure Many documents are divided into sections. A section of a document might be as long as a paragraph or as short as a single sentence. Each section usually has a heading, which summarizes its content and helps readers locate the information they need.

Format A document's **format,** or design, helps readers focus on key words, sections, and important ideas. Functional documents may contain the following elements:

- **Formatting elements**, including boldface and italic type, margin widths, indentations, and line spacing
- **Graphic elements**, including drawings, photos, charts, and art
- **Design elements**, including placement of text and graphic elements on the page, use of white space, and choice of colors

Into Action As you read, take notes on the structure and format of the documents that follow.

	About StoryCorps	Do-It-Yourself Interview
Formatting Elements		
Graphic Elements		
Design Elements		

Writing Focus

Preparing for **Constructed Response**

When you write for tests, it is important to organize your ideas carefully and present them clearly. As you read these selections, look for ways in which their structure and format help the writers present ideas. Make a list of these techniques in your *Reader/Writer Notebook.*

Vocabulary

About StoryCorps

facilitator (fuh SIHL uh tay tuhr) *n.:* person who assists. *If you need help recording your interview for StoryCorps, a facilitator will help you.*

collective (kuh LEHK tihv) *adj.:* of or as a group. *StoryCorps' mission is to make a record of our nation's collective identity.*

Do-It-Yourself Interview

sacred (SAY krihd) *adj.:* here, set aside for or dedicated to one person or use. *StoryCorps recommends making the room where you conduct your interview a sacred space.*

constrain (kuhn STRAYN) *v.:* confine; restrict. *A list of questions can help prompt you during an interview but shouldn't constrain you from asking others.*

Language Coach

Derivations One of the words above is related to the adjective *facile,* which means "easy." A related word is the noun *facility,* a business or place that provides services for its customers—making it easy for them to get what they want. Which word on the list above is also a derivation of *facile?*

Learn It Online

Learn about functional documents through a *PowerNotes* interactive lesson online:

go.hrw.com L9-503 

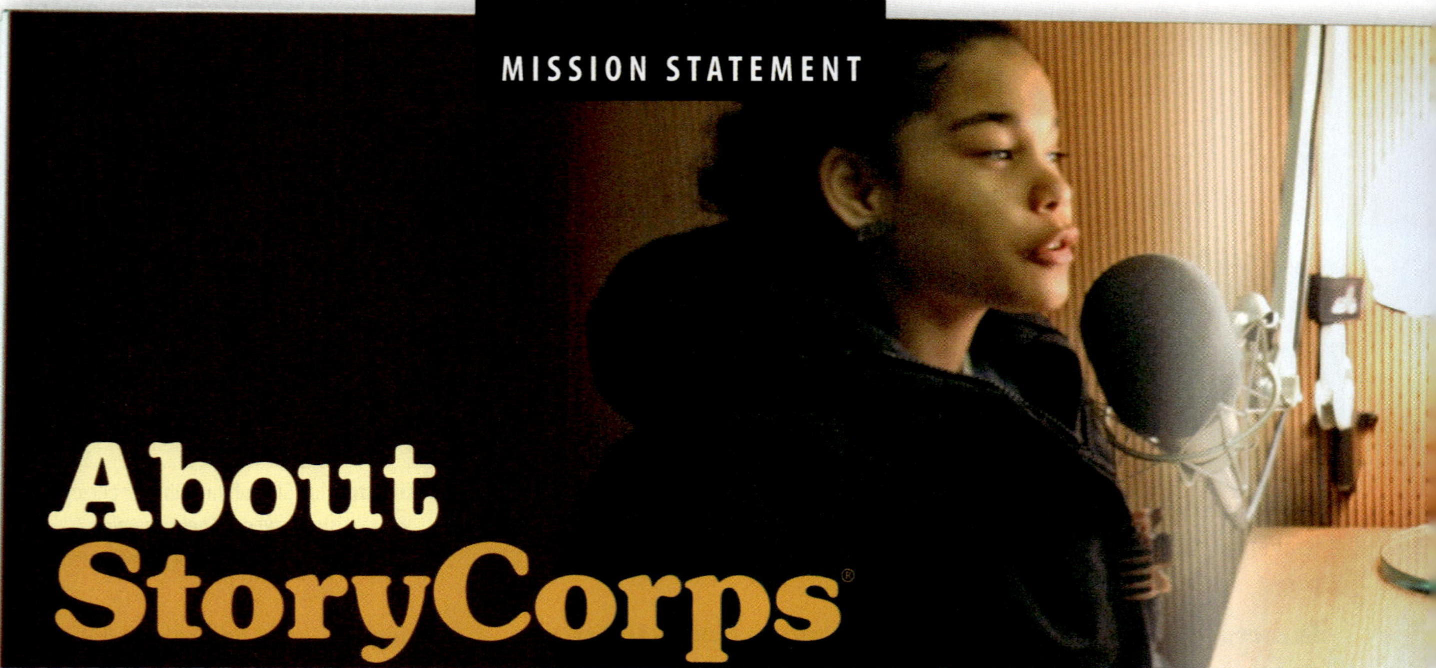

About StoryCorps®

Read with a Purpose

Read the following selection to find out about the StoryCorps organization and its mission.

Build Background

StoryCorps patterns itself after the Works Project Administration (WPA), which was created by President Franklin Delano Roosevelt in 1935. This program was intended to give work to the unemployed. Many arts projects were created under this program, giving work to destitute authors, actors, and artists.

StoryCorps is a national project to instruct and inspire people to record one another's stories in sound.

We're here to help you interview your grandmother, your uncle, the lady who has worked at the luncheonette down the block for as long as you can remember—anyone whose story you want to hear and preserve.

To start, we're building soundproof recording studios across the country, called StoryBooths. You can use these StoryBooths to record broadcast-quality interviews with the help of a trained facilitator. Our first StoryBooth opened in New York City's Grand Central Terminal on October 23, 2003. StoryCorps opened its second StoryBooth in New York City in Lower Manhattan on July 12, 2005. We also have two traveling recording studios, called MobileBooths, which embarked on cross-country tours on May 19, 2005.

We've tried to make the experience as simple as possible: We help you figure out what questions to ask. We handle all the technical aspects of the recording. At the end of the hour-long session, you get a copy of your interview on CD.

Vocabulary **facilitator** (fuh SIHL uh tay tuhr) *n.:* person who assists.

Teens interview each other in the StoryCorps booth at Grand Central Station in New York City.

Since we want to make sure your story lives on for generations to come, we'll also add your interview to the StoryCorps Archive, housed at the American Folklife Center at the Library of Congress, which we hope will become nothing less than an oral history of America.

Our Vision (A)

StoryCorps is modeled—in spirit and in scope—after the Works Progress Administration (WPA) of the 1930s, through which oral history interviews with everyday Americans across the country were recorded. These recordings remain the single most important collection of American voices gathered to date. We hope that StoryCorps will build and expand on that work, becoming a WPA for the 21st Century.

StoryCorps celebrates our shared humanity and collective identity. It captures and defines the stories that bond us. The process of interviewing a friend, neighbor, or family member can have a profound impact on both the interviewer and storyteller. People change, friendships grow, families walk away feeling closer and understand each other better. Listening, after all, is an act of love.

A StoryCorps interview is an opportunity to ask the questions that never get asked because the occasion never arises. *How did you come to this country? How did you and mom meet? How did Uncle Harry get the nickname "Twinkles?"* (B)

Read with a Purpose

What is the mission of the StoryCorps organization?

(A) **Informational Focus** **Structure** What does this heading signify?

(B) **Informational Focus** **Format** Why do you think italic type is used here?

Vocabulary **collective** (kuh LEHK tihv) *adj.:* of or as a group.

FUNCTIONAL DOCUMENT

Do-It-Yourself Interview

A StoryCorps trailer parked outside the Missouri History Museum in St. Louis, Missouri (2005).

Read with a Purpose

Read this article to learn what steps need to be followed to conduct a StoryCorps-style interview.

Preparing to Read for this selection is on page 503.

Build Background

One of the most important information-gathering tools is the interview. People are storehouses of information, and you can share in their knowledge by asking them a few questions about what they know. Many newspaper and magazine articles are based on quotations and information gathered through reporters' interviews.

StoryCorps®

At StoryCorps, we have big dreams. (A)

We want StoryCorps to spark a revolution in this country—of thoughtful communication, of gathering the wisdom of older Americans, of appreciating the importance and beauty in the stories of loved ones and friends. We believe that the stories of everyday Americans have value. We believe that recording loved ones' stories reminds them that they matter, and that they won't be forgotten. We believe that listening is an act of love.

If you want to participate in StoryCorps but can't find a time at one of our StoryBooths, we encourage you to **Do-It-Yourself.** Conduct your own interview at home; ask the questions you've always wanted to ask; listen closely to a loved one. Although your recording won't be archived at the Library of Congress, it can stand as a family heirloom[1] for years to come. (B)

1. Pick a storyteller.

Start your own interview by figuring out whom you want to interview. A grandparent? An old friend? A former teacher? The person you invite might be hesitant. "I don't have much to say," he'll say, or, "You already know everything about my life." Remind your friend, your cousin—whoever it is—that his life story is important and that you will create a recording that will last for years. Let that person know you would be honored to record his story.

2. Create a question list.

No matter how well you know your storyteller, a little preparation will improve the quality of your interview enormously. What are the important aspects of your storyteller's life? What would you like to learn from that person?

Here are some questions that have yielded great responses:

- What have you learned in life?
- What does your future hold?
- What are you most proud of?
- Do you have any regrets?
- What was the happiest moment of your life? The saddest?
- Is there something about yourself that you think no one knows?
- How would you like to be remembered? (C)

1. **heirloom** (AIR loom): something handed down from generation to generation.

(A) **Informational Focus** **Structure** Why do you think this boldface header is used?

(B) **Informational Focus** **Format** Which words in this paragraph are key words? How can you tell?

(C) **Informational Focus** **Format** What do the bullets (•) signify?

We've also found that at the end of a session it can be powerful to turn the tables and tell the person you're interviewing the most important lessons you've learned from her.

3. Purchase or borrow recording equipment (and get comfortable with it).

To record a StoryCorps-style interview, you need three pieces of equipment: a recording device, a microphone, and headphones. The recording equipment can be as simple as a cassette recorder, a pair of headphones, and an inexpensive microphone (handheld, not clip-on). Whatever option you choose, we strongly suggest that you practice using your equipment before you sit down for your interview.

A few things to remember:

* Always wear headphones when recording. Your headphones are your "ears" for the interview; they tell you exactly what you'll hear on your finished recording. Use them to adjust the microphone position so the sound is as clear as possible.
* Hold the mic[2] close, about seven inches from your storyteller's mouth. Always hold the mic in your hand, moving it between you and your storyteller.
* Be careful of mic noise. The low rumbling sound you hear when you move the mic in your hands is known as "mic handling noise." You can avoid it by using a light touch and not shifting around too much. If you need to move the mic, make sure to wait until your storyteller has finished speaking.

Start a StoryCorps group. You may want to get together a group of friends and purchase recording equipment together. Someone from the group can act as the "engineer" during your interview and handle the equipment so you can focus on asking the questions. Share and discuss the stories you've recorded with the group.

2. **mic** (MYK): abbreviated form of *microphone*.

4. Choose an interview location.

D

Pick the quietest place possible. A carpeted living room or bedroom is best. Avoid large empty rooms and kitchens, which are filled with reflective surfaces and appliance noise. We try to make the inside of each StoryCorps booth something of a sacred space, as peaceful and serene as possible. You may want to do the same: turn the lights low, light a candle. Do whatever you can to make you and your subject most comfortable.

Prevent noisy distractions. Close the door; unplug the phone; turn off your cell phone. Turn off anything that is making noise: buzzing fluorescent lights, air conditioners, fans, etc. Listen for noise during the interview as well. If your storyteller fiddles with her necklace, for example, feel free to let her know it's making noise. Never record interviews with a radio or television on in the background.

5. Set up and test the equipment.

Set up your equipment as early as possible and make sure you're comfortable with it. This way you'll be able to focus on the person you are interviewing and not the equipment. Before you begin your interview, record your storyteller answering a few warm-up questions like, "Can you describe what this room looks like?" or "Tell me what you had for breakfast." Stop, rewind, and listen to the recording you just made to make sure everything is working. Remember to press "record" again when you start the interview for real.

6. Begin the conversation.

Start your interview by stating your name, your age, the date, and the location of the interview. For example, "My name is Frank. I'm forty-one years old. The date is August 3, 2005, and I'm sitting with my grandma Lucy Johnson in her living room in Port Jackson, Iowa." Now ask your storyteller to state the same information.

Use your question list. Remember, the questions you write in advance are just suggestions. Trust your instincts. If something interests you or merits exploring, ask more questions. Sometimes your

---

D Informational Focus Structure What do the numbered headers help you understand about the interviewing process?

Vocabulary **sacred** (SAY krihd) *adj.:* here, set aside for or dedicated to one person or use.

storyteller will need "permission" to explore a certain topic. Granting that permission might be as easy as saying, "Tell me more." Think of the question list as a crutch. If you get tongue-tied or need a place to start, use it, but don't let it constrain you. Feel free to ask questions in whatever order feels right. Take breaks if your storyteller needs them.

Don't make noise when your storyteller is talking.
Don't say, "uh huh," or interrupt when something interesting or important is being said. Instead, use visual cues like nodding your head.

7. Get great stories.

Here are some tips for helping the conversation flow:

Listen closely. Look at your storyteller's eyes, not the mic. Stay interested and engaged.

Be yourself. You can laugh with the person you are interviewing or even cry with him. Real moments are the best moments.

Stick with the good stuff. When you hear something that moves you, feel free to talk about it more. If the current topic isn't what you wanted to put on tape, gently steer the conversation back on course.

Ask emotional questions. Questions like "How does this make you feel?" often elicit thoughtful responses. Don't be afraid to ask.

Take notes during the interview. Write down any questions or stories you might want to return to later in your interview. E

Be curious and honest and keep an open heart. Great things will happen.

8. Wrap it up.

Before you turn off your recorder, do two things: Ask the storyteller if there is anything else that she wants to talk about, and thank her. Sharing a story can be difficult for some people. It's a privilege to have someone share her story with you. Express your gratitude.

Congratulations.

You have just joined the StoryCorps revolution.

Read with a Purpose Whom do you think you would like to interview? What might that person have to teach you?

E **Informational Focus** **Format** Why do some sentences in this section appear in bold blue type?

Vocabulary **constrain** (kuhn STRAYN) *v.:* confine; restrict.

9.R.3.C.1.a Use details from informational text: to identify and explain the organizational pattern
9.W.2.C.1.b Compose text with: a logical order
9.R.1.G.1.a During reading, utilize strategies: to determine meaning of unknown words

About StoryCorps / Do-It-Yourself Interview

Practicing the Standards

Informational Text and Vocabulary

1. If you were going to improve the **format** of "About StoryCorps," which of the following would be the *best* choice?
   - **A** Add a map showing StoryCorps locations.
   - **B** Add a graphic that shows a time line of the WPA projects.
   - **C** Run all the sections in together.
   - **D** Use different colored type for each paragraph.

2. Section headings in the "Do-It-Yourself Interview" are —
   - **A** in bold type
   - **B** set off by white space
   - **C** numbered
   - **D** all of the above

3. The functional documents use *all* of the following elements of **structure** and **format** *except* —
   - **A** bold and italic print
   - **B** headers
   - **C** charts
   - **D** key words

4. If your teacher asks you to be a *facilitator*, he or she wants you to —
   - **A** participate in the discussion
   - **B** do your homework thoroughly
   - **C** pay close attention to someone
   - **D** help with something

5. A *collective* effort is a —
   - **A** significant effort
   - **B** group effort
   - **C** wholehearted effort
   - **D** unnecessary effort

6. If a person said, "My bedroom is my *sacred* space," you would expect that room to be —
   - **A** private
   - **B** cramped
   - **C** shared
   - **D** windowless

7. Which is the *best* definition of *constrain*?
   - **A** Enable
   - **B** Injure
   - **C** Tidy up
   - **D** Confine

Writing Focus Constructed Response

The "Do-It-Yourself Interview" explains the process of conducting an interview by using point-by-point sequence (first, one should . . .; do this second; and so on). Think of a step-by-step process you know well, such as fixing a flat tire on your bicycle or recovering lost data on your computer. Break the process down into steps, and write about each step.

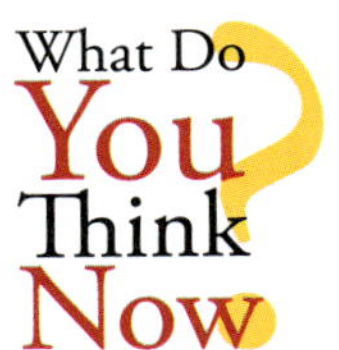

Do you believe that hearing about another person's experiences can change the way you think? Explain.

Literary Skills Review

Form and Style **Directions:** Read the following autobiographical essay. Then, read and respond to the questions that follow.

In the Current by **Jo Ann Beard**

The family vacation. Heat, flies, sand and dirt. My mother sweeps and complains, my father forever baits hooks and untangles lines. My younger brother has brought along his imaginary friend, Charcoal, and my older sister has brought along a real-life majorette[1] by the name of Nan. My brother continually practices allstar wrestling moves on poor Charcoal. "I got him in a figure-four leglock!" he will call from the ground, propped up on one elbow, his legs twisted together. My sister and Nan wear leg makeup, white lipstick, and say things about me in French. A river runs in front of our cabin, the color of bourbon, foamy at the banks, full of water moccasins and doomed fish. I am ten. The only thing to do is sit on the dock and read, drink watered-down Pepsi, and squint. No swimming allowed.

One afternoon three teenagers get caught in the current while I watch. They come sweeping downstream, hollering and gurgling while I stand on the bank, forbidden to step into the water, and stare at them. They are waving their arms.

I am embarrassed because teenagers are yelling at me. Within five seconds men are throwing off their shoes and diving from the dock; my own dad gets hold of one girl and swims her back in. Black hair plastered to her neck, she throws up on the mud about eight times before they carry her back to wherever she came from. One teenager is unconscious when they drag him out and a guy pushes on his chest until a low fountain of water springs up out of his mouth and nose. That kid eventually walks away on his own, but he's crying. The third teenager lands a ways down the bank and comes walking by fifteen minutes later, a grownup on either side of him and a towel around his waist. His skin looks like Silly Putty.

"Oh man," he says when he sees me. "I saw her go by about ninety miles an hour!" He stops and points at me. I just stand there, embarrassed to be noticed by a teenager. I hope my shorts aren't bagging out again. I put one hand in my pocket and slouch sideways a little. "Man, I thought she was gonna be the last thing I ever seen!" he says, shaking his head.

The girl teenager had had on a swimming suit top with a built-in bra. I cross my arms nonchalantly[2] across my chest and smile at the teenage boy. He keeps walking and talking, the grownups supporting him and giving each other looks over the top of his head. His legs are shaking like crazy. "I thought, man-oh-man, that skinny little chick is gonna be the last thing *ever,*" he exclaims.

I look down. My shorts are bagging out.

1. **majorette** (may juh REHT): a girl or woman who twirls a baton while accompanying a marching band.

2. **nonchalantly** (nahn shuh LAHNT lee): in an unconcerned manner.

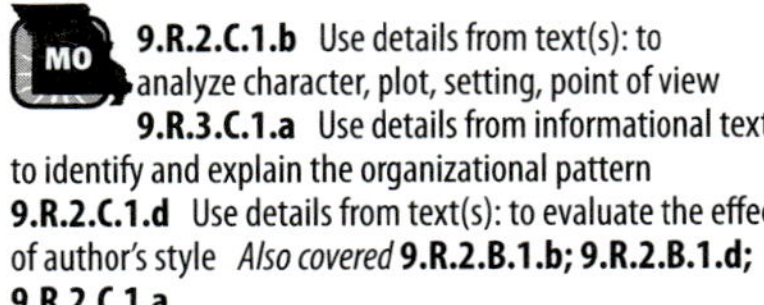

9.R.2.C.1.b Use details from text(s): to analyze character, plot, setting, point of view **9.R.3.C.1.a** Use details from informational text: to identify and explain the organizational pattern **9.R.2.C.1.d** Use details from text(s): to evaluate the effect of author's style *Also covered* **9.R.2.B.1.b; 9.R.2.B.1.d; 9.R.2.C.1.a**

1. Which of the following sentences contains the *best* example of imagery?

A "I am ten."

B "A river runs in front of our cabin, the color of bourbon, foamy at the banks, full of water moccasins and doomed fish."

C "'Oh man,' he says when he sees me."

D "I put one hand in my pocket and slouch sideways a little."

9.R.2.B.1

2. The sentence, "I saw her go by about ninety miles an hour!" is an example of —

A symbolism

B figure of speech

C exaggeration

D flowery language

9.R.2.B.1.d

3. How would you describe the **mood,** or emotional atmosphere, of "In the Current"?

A Nostalgic

B Fanciful

C Gloomy

D Tense

9.R.2.B.1.d

4. The author's **style** in this selection can be characterized as —

A ornate

B wordy

C simple

D precise

9.R.2.C.1.d

5. Beard's **style** in this selection is characterized by her use of —

A dialogue and symbolism

B imagery and humor

C repetition and irony

D ambiguity and contradiction

9.R.2.C.1.d

6. The overall **tone** of this piece is —

A sarcastic

B educational

C comedic

D casual

9.R.2.C.1.a

7. Which of the following items would turn this personal essay into a biography?

A If the author told about her school

B If the author wrote about her brother's experiences

C If the author imagined that one of the teenagers drowned and wrote about that

D If the author wrote a paragraph describing her feelings after seeing the teenagers saved

9.R.3

Constructed Response

8. This essay depicts a vivid episode from the author's childhood. List at least three examples of imagery from the story. Explain whether or not you found the use of imagery effective.

9.R.2.B.1.b

Informational Skills Review

Structure and Format of Functional Documents

Directions: Read the following selection. Then, read and respond to the questions that follow.

Hurricanes . . .

Unleashing Nature's Fury

Are You Ready? A Preparedness Guide

U.S. Department of Commerce
National Oceanic and Atmospheric Administration
National Weather Service
September 2006

Before the Hurricane Season

- ✔ Determine safe evacuation routes inland.
- ✔ Learn location of official shelters.
- ✔ Make emergency plans for pets.
- ✔ Check emergency equipment, such as flashlights, generators, battery-powered radios and cell phones.
- ✔ Buy food that will keep and store drinking water.
- ✔ Buy plywood or other material to protect your home.
- ✔ Clear loose and clogged rain gutters and downspouts.
- ✔ Trim trees and shrubbery.
- ✔ Review your insurance policy.

Terms to Know

Hurricane Watch: Hurricane conditions are *possible* in the specified area of the watch, usually within 36 hours.

Hurricane Warning: Hurricane conditions are *expected* in the specified area of the warning, usually within 24 hours.

Tropical Storm Watches and Warnings: Take these alerts seriously. Although Tropical Storms have lower wind speeds than hurricanes, they often bring life-threatening flooding and dangerous winds. Take precautions!

MO 9.R.3.A.1 Explain, analyze and evaluate the author's use of text features to clarify meaning
9.R.3.C.1.a Use details from informational text: to identify and explain the organizational pattern

During the Storm

When in a Watch Area . . .

- ✔ Frequently listen to radio or TV for official bulletins of the storm's progress.
- ✔ Fuel and service family vehicles.
- ✔ Have extra cash on hand.
- ✔ Prepare to cover all windows and doors with shutters or other shielding materials.
- ✔ Check batteries and stock up on canned food, first-aid supplies, drinking water and medications.
- ✔ Bring in lightweight objects such as garbage cans, garden tools, toys and lawn furniture.

Plan to Leave If You . . .

- ✔ Live in a mobile home. They are unsafe in high winds no matter how well fastened to the ground.
- ✔ Live on the coastline, an offshore island, or near a river or a flood plain.
- ✔ Live in a high-rise building. Hurricane winds are stronger at higher elevations.

What to Bring to a Shelter

- First-aid kit
- Medicine, prescriptions
- Baby food and diapers
- Games, books, music players with headphones
- Toiletries
- Battery-powered radio and cell phone
- Flashlights
- Extra batteries
- A blanket or sleeping bag for each person
- Identification
- Copies of key papers such as insurance policies
- Cash, credit card

REMINDER: If you are told to leave, do so immediately!

Informational Skills Review CONTINUED

When in a Warning Area . . .

- ✔ Closely monitor radio and TV for official bulletins.
- ✔ Close storm shutters.
- ✔ Follow instructions issued by local officials. **Leave immediately if ordered!**
- ✔ If evacuating, leave as soon as possible. Stay with friends or relatives, at a low-rise inland motel or at a designated public shelter outside the flood zone.
- ✔ **DO NOT** stay in a mobile or manufactured home.
- ✔ Notify neighbors and a family member outside of the warned area of your evacuation plans.
- ✔ Take pets with you if possible, but remember, most public shelters do not allow pets other than those used by people with disabilities. Identify pet-friendly motels along your evacuation route.

If Staying in a Home . . .

- ✔ Turn refrigerator to maximum cold and keep closed.
- ✔ Turn off utilities if told to do so by authorities.
- ✔ Turn off propane tanks.
- ✔ Unplug small appliances.
- ✔ Fill bathtub and large containers with water in case tap water is unavailable. Use water in bathtubs for cleaning and flushing only. Do NOT drink it.

If Winds Become Strong . . .

- ✔ Stay away from windows and doors, even if they are covered. Take refuge in a small interior room, closet or hallway.
- ✔ Close all interior doors. Secure and brace external doors.
- ✔ If you are in a two-story house, go to an interior first-floor room.
- ✔ If you are in a multi-story building and away from water, go to the first or second floor and stay in the halls or other interior rooms away from windows.
- ✔ Lie on the floor under a table or other sturdy object.

9.R.3.A.1 Explain, analyze and evaluate the author's use of text features to clarify meaning **9.R.3.C.1.a** Use details from informational text: to identify and explain the organizational pattern

Be Alert For . . .

- ✔ Tornadoes. They are often spawned by hurricanes.
- ✔ The calm "eye" of the storm. It may seem like the storm is over but after the eye passes, the winds will change direction and quickly return to hurricane force.
- ✔ Storm surge flooding. These high waves can be more deadly than hurricane winds. Leave the coast and stay away from low lying areas, creeks, streams and other inland waterways.

After the Storm

- ✔ Keep listening to radio or TV.
- ✔ Wait until an area is declared safe before entering.
- ✔ Watch for closed roads. If you come upon a barricade or a flooded road, turn around.
- ✔ Avoid weakened bridges and washed out roads.
- ✔ Stay on firm ground. Moving water only 6 inches deep can sweep you off your feet. Standing water may be electrically charged from power lines.
- ✔ Once home, check gas, water and electrical lines and appliances for damage.
- ✔ Use a flashlight to inspect for damage. Never use candles and other open flames indoors.
- ✔ Do not drink or prepare food with tap water until officials say it is safe.
- ✔ If using a generator, avoid carbon monoxide poisoning by following the manufacturer instructions.
- ✔ Avoid electrocution by not walking in flooded areas with downed power lines.

Informational Skills Review

MO **9.R.3.A.1** Explain, analyze and evaluate the author's use of text features to clarify meaning **9.R.3.C.1.a** Use details from informational text: to identify and explain the organizational pattern *Also covered* **9.R.3.C.1.c; 9.R.3.C.1.e; 9.R.3.D.1**

1. The **purpose** of this guide is to tell people —
   A what to do in the event of a hurricane
   B what a hurricane is
   C what they should know about shelters
   D terms they should know when talking about hurricanes

   9.R.3

2. Which of the following *best* describes the **organizational pattern** of the preparedness guide?
   A Chronological order
   B Outline
   C Checklist
   D Step-by-step

   9.R.3.C.1.c

3. The guide uses *all* of the following **text features** *except* —
   A underlining
   B italics
   C boldface
   D bullets

   9.R.3.A.1

4. If you were in your home during a hurricane, you should do all of the following *except* —
   A fill the bathtub with water
   B turn the refrigerator to maximum cold
   C stand away from the doors and windows
   D move to the garage

   9.R.3.D.1

5. If your community is ordered to evacuate, you should —
   A stay in your house and board up the windows and doors
   B monitor the radio and TV for updates
   C gather family mementos
   D leave the area immediately

   9.R.3.D.1

6. Where does information on weather warnings appear?
   A In inset box titled "Terms to Know"
   B In section titled "After the Storm"
   C In the document's footnotes
   D In the document's subtitle

   9.R.3.D.1

Constructed Response

7. How well do you think the hurricane guide prepares readers for a disaster? If you were to write a similar document, what information would you add? What information would you leave out? Is there anything you might change about the way the document is structured? Explain why or why not.

   9.R.3.C.1.e

FOCUS ON MISSOURI COURSE LEVEL EXPECTATIONS

Vocabulary Skills Review

MO **9.R.1.E.1.b** Develop vocabulary through text: using context clues **9.R.1.E.1.c** Develop vocabulary through text: using glossary, dictionary and thesaurus

Context Clues

Directions: Use the context clues in the following passages to help you identify the meaning of the italicized Vocabulary words.

1. In "Cub Pilot on the Mississippi," Twain says his desire to work in the circus was *transient* and he had many other ambitions during that time.

In this passage, *transient* means —

A important

B strong

C quickly passing

D slow to come about

9.R.1.E.1.b

2. In "Cub Pilot on the Mississippi," poor Henry conducted himself in an entirely *inoffensive* manner, but Brown felt threatened by him.

In this passage, *inoffensive* means —

A harmless

B intelligent

C unreliable

D successful

9.R.1.E.1.b

3. In "The Secret Latina," Chambers says that although her mother has lived in the United States for more than twenty years, her mother's Panamanian identity remains *intact*.

In this passage, *intact* means —

A whole

B shaken

C ruined

D exposed

9.R.1.E.1.b

4. The writer of "The Grandfather" remembers that the avocado tree was *meager* in size, so he could jump over it.

In this passage, *meager* means —

A frightening

B enormous

C robust

D small

9.R.1.E.1.b

5. In *Boy,* Roald Dahl and his friends think that the most *loathsome* thing about Mrs. Pratchett is the filth that clings to her.

In this passage, *loathsome* means —

A disgusting

B interesting

C remarkable

D important

9.R.1.E.1.b

Academic Vocabulary

Directions: Choose the *best* definition for each italicized Academic Vocabulary word below.

6. Mark Twain's stories were often written with a playful *attitude*.

A outlook

B anger

C response

D respect

9.R.1.E.1.b

7. Photographs can *enhance* the experience of reading a biography.

A ruin

B change

C improve

D lessen

9.R.1.E.1.b

Read On

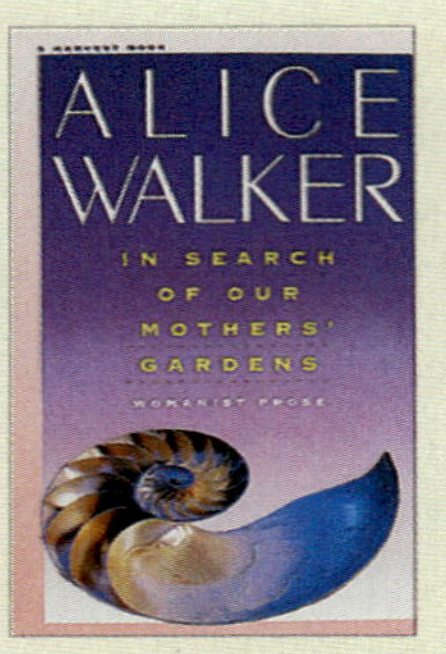

NONFICTION

In Search of Our Mothers' Gardens

In Alice Walker's *In Search of Our Mothers' Gardens,* you'll meet the writer—up close and personal. This collection of essays, articles, reviews, and speeches covers a wide range of topics. You'll read moving tributes to famous African American writers such as Langston Hughes and Zora Neale Hurston, and you'll also learn about Walker's own writing process. The collection also contains autobiographical pieces including her experiences as a civil rights activist during the 1960s.

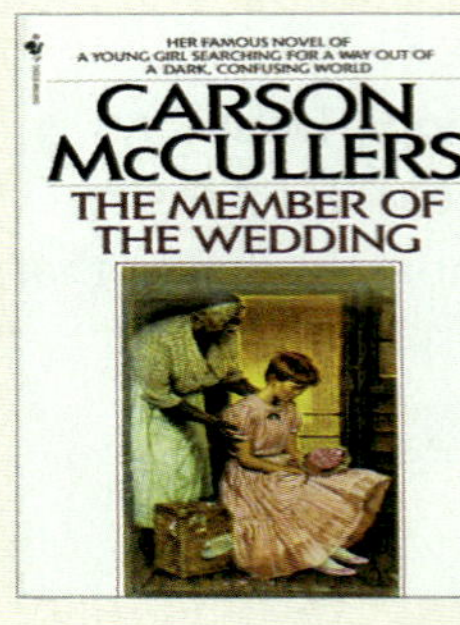

FICTION

The Member of the Wedding

Twelve-year-old Frankie Addams is filled with contradictions. She wants to be accepted for who she is—and she wants to change into somebody different. She wants to be treated as a grown-up—and she wants to remain a child forever. Most of all, she wants a sense of belonging. When Frankie's older brother announces his engagement, Frankie senses the town coming together through its excitement. You can find out what happens to Frankie by reading *The Member of the Wedding* by Carson McCullers.

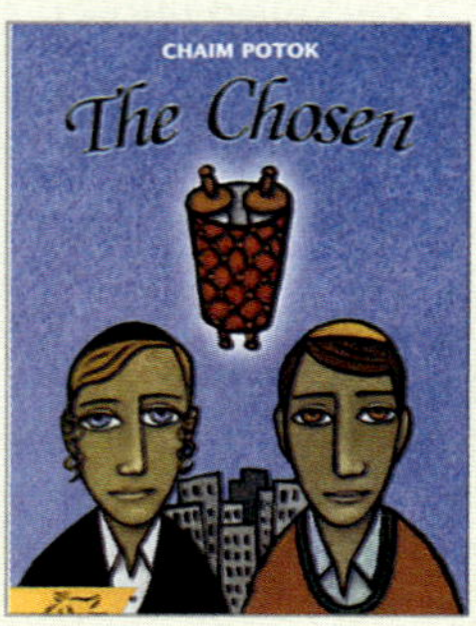

FICTION

The Chosen

A baseball game goes afoul for Reuven Malter when a wildly thrown ball hits him square in the eye. The pitcher is Danny Saunders—an opponent who unexpectedly becomes a friend. Reuven and Danny have much in common—their Brooklyn upbringing and their interest in their studies—but they are divided by their faiths. Danny is part of a Hasidic sect of Judaism, while Reuven belongs to a more liberal Orthodox sect. Chaim Potok's *The Chosen* is a compassionate story about tradition, tolerance, and understanding.

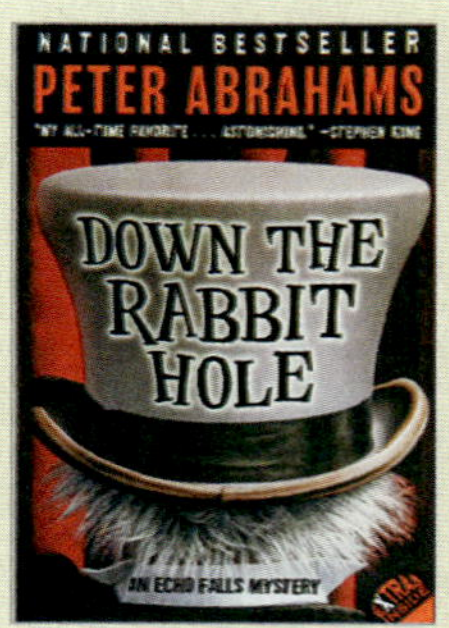

FICTION

Down the Rabbit Hole

Teenager Ingrid Levin-Hill gets lost in an unfamiliar part of Echo Falls, her hometown. She meets Cracked-Up Katie, the village eccentric, who calls a cab for her. A few minutes after Ingrid leaves, however, Katie is mysteriously murdered. In Peter Abrahams's suspenseful *Down the Rabbit Hole,* Ingrid tries to balance young love, pass a difficult algebra course, keep the lead role in a play adaptation of *Alice in Wonderland,* all while trying to figure out who Katie's killer is.

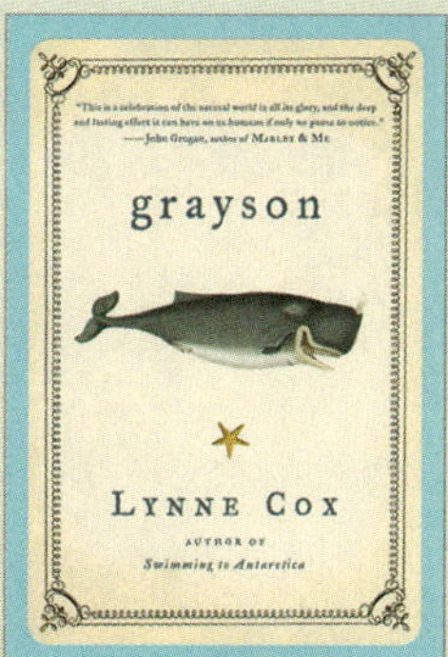

NONFICTION

Grayson

Author Lynne Cox was swimming her last half mile back to the pier after a long ocean workout when she became aware that a baby gray whale was following alongside her. Lynn quickly realized that if she swam back to the pier, the young calf would follow her onto shore and die from collapsed lungs. She had to find the mother whale before the baby starved to death. How could Lynne possibly find her? *Grayson* is the story—part mystery, part magical tale—of what happened.

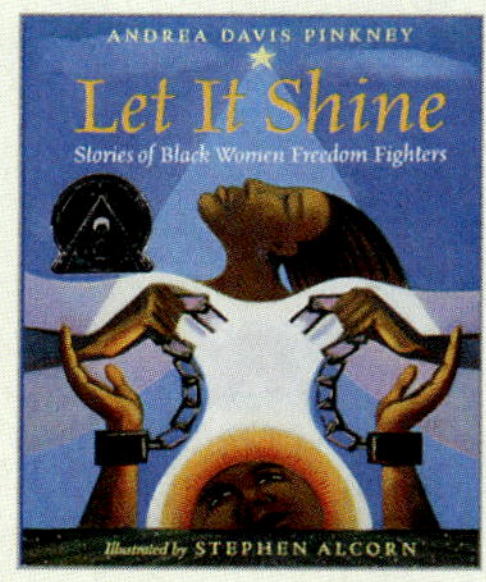

NONFICTION

Let It Shine: Stories of Black Women Freedom Fighters

Rosa Parks refused to give up her seat on a bus and sparked a boycott that changed America. Fannie Lou Hamer fought for years to secure voting rights for blacks in Mississippi. In *Let It Shine: Stories of Black Women Freedom Fighters,* Andrea Davis Pinkney documents the lives of these women and many others who showed remarkable courage in the face of oppression.

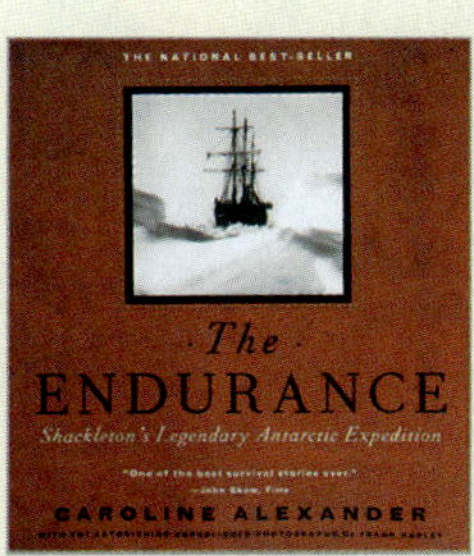

NONFICTION

The Endurance

In August 1914, Ernest Shackleton and a crew of twenty-seven men sailed on the *Endurance* from England to Antarctica where they hoped to travel by dog sled across the frozen continent. Instead, their ship became trapped in the icepack and was crushed. Shackleton and his crew then faced the horrible prospect of trying to travel more than a thousand miles in lifeboats over shifting ice floes and through seas with seventy-foot-high waves to South Georgia Island. Caroline Alexander recounts their legendary journey in *The Endurance.*

NONFICTION

Pilgrim at Tinker Creek

"I am no scientist," author Annie Dillard says of herself. "I am a wanderer with a background in theology and a penchant for quirky facts." In *Pilgrim at Tinker Creek,* Dillard draws on her yearlong experiences in an isolated Virginia valley. The collection of essays creates a memorable reflection on life, death, and the mysteries of nature.

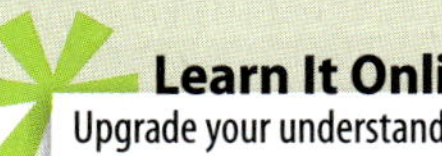

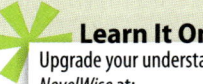

Learn It Online

Upgrade your understanding of novels. Visit *NovelWise* at:

go.hrw.com L9-521 

Wakako Tsuchida of Japan (right) passes Switzerland's Edith Hunkerler in the 5,000-meter Paralympic wheelchair race final at Athens's Olympic complex in 2004.

COLLECTION 6

Persuasion

INFORMATIONAL TEXT FOCUS

Evaluating Arguments

"First we have to believe, and then we believe."

—Martha Graham

What Do You Think? What do you believe in, and why?

Learn It Online

Explore multimedia forms of persuasion at the MediaScope mini-site at:

go.hrw.com L9-523 

Literary Focus

by **Carol Jago**

How Do Writers Persuade You?

Do you know people who are able to get everyone around them to do exactly what they want? These people are skilled in the art of persuasion. The more you know about the tools that persuasive speakers and writers use, the less vulnerable you will be to their wiles and the more persuasive you will be.

Author's Purpose

An **author's purpose** is his or her reason for writing. If an author's purpose is to persuade, for example, the writer wants to convince you to think or do something. Other purposes for writing might be to entertain, to inform, or to pay tribute.

Sometimes an author's purpose will be obvious. For example, when Marjane Satrapi titles an article "Why I Wrote *Persepolis,*" you can be pretty sure that her purpose will be to explain why she wrote that book. Keep in mind that a writer can have more than one purpose for writing. Persuasion can be a secondary goal for writers, even when they are writing stories or poems.

> I could work as much and eat as much as a man—when I could get it—and bear the lash as well! And ain't I a woman?
>
> from "Ain't I a Woman?"
> by Sojourner Truth

The purpose of Sojourner Truth's speech is twofold: She wants to share her experiences with the audience, and she hopes to persuade her listeners to respect women and value their contributions.

Author's Argument: Structure and Tone

A writer tries to persuade you to accept his or her **argument,** or main point of view. An argument can be as quick as the headline of an ad or as complex as an hour-long presidential speech. You can analyze the structure and tone of an argument.

Structure Arguments are structured carefully in order to present the evidence most effectively. The Q-and-A organization, for example, provides immediate answers to direct questions. Ideas can also be organized in order of importance or by time order.

Tone A writer's attitude toward a topic is reflected in his or her **tone.** Tone is created by a writer's word choice. In this example, Satrapi's informal word choice and conversational sentences make her tone friendly and direct:

> People always ask me, "Why didn't you write a book?" But that's what *Persepolis* is. To me, a book is pages related to something that has a cover. Graphic novels are not traditional literature, but that does not mean they are second-rate.
>
> from "Why I Wrote *Persepolis*"
> by Marjane Satrapi

MO **9.R.3.C.1.c** Use details from informational text: to analyze and evaluate the accuracy and adequacy of evidence

Argument: Pro and Con

There are almost always two or more points of view about anything. A **pro argument** is in favor of or supports something, whereas a **con argument** is against the same thing. In this example, Robin Brenner refutes the argument that comics are just for kids:

> **Q: What are some common misconceptions about graphic novels?**
> **A: *Comics and graphic novels are for kids.*** In reality, comics never were just for kids.
>
> from "Graphic Novels 101: FAQ"
> by Robin Brenner

Persuasion: Appeals to Logic and Emotion

Writers might try to convince you that their argument is correct by using **appeals to logic,** careful reasoning that leads to a supported conclusion.

However, logic alone might not grab your attention. That's why authors often use **appeals to emotion,** which elicit personal reactions, such as anger, laughter, or tears.

> I am alarmed by the willingness of women to enslave other women. I am alarmed by a growing absence of decency on the killing floor of professional women's worlds.
>
> from "Cinderella's Stepsisters"
> by Toni Morrison

Emotional appeals are not less valid because they work on your feelings. However, watch out for writers who use loaded language to cover up a weak argument.

Credibility and Evidence

Persuasive writers want you to believe what they are saying, but you are the final judge of an argument's **credibility,** or believability. Make your evaluation based on the **evidence** a writer presents, such as facts, experiences, and logical or emotional appeals. For some arguments a single strong statistic will be enough to persuade you. More complicated arguments might require several sources of information.

Your Turn Analyze Persuasion

1. Working with a partner, read this proposal. What is your first response?

   Resolution: *High school students should be required to do at least three hours of community service per month.*

2. Choose a strong position, either pro or con. Think for five minutes of ways to support your argument.
3. Organize a plan to persuade others. Consider the following:
   - How will you structure your argument?
   - What tone will you use?
   - How will you respond to opposing opinions?

Learn It Online
Organize your thoughts! Use one of the interactive graphic organizers at:
go.hrw.com
L9-525
Go

Analyzing Visuals

How Can You Recognize Persuasion in Graphic Art?

An image of a happy family strolling on the beach . . . a photograph of a beautiful tropical sunset . . . and a headline urging you to buy a certain brand of sunscreen! Those are the components of a typical advertisement in a magazine. People who create ads use persuasive techniques much as writers do. They often use color, images, and interesting text structures to create mood and to appeal to their audiences' logic and emotion.

Analyzing Graphic Art

Use these guidelines to analyze persuasive techniques in graphic art:

1. Identify the product, service, or idea being promoted.
2. Study the image, and ask yourself, "What makes this image interesting or appealing?"
3. Examine the artist's use of color, contrast, and shadow. What mood has been created?
4. Look for visual elements meant to please and catch the eye. Pay particular attention to imagery, color, and type fonts and sizes.
5. Consider the effect of the work as a whole. What overall message does the work convey?

Study the details below to help you answer the questions on page 527.

Details from 1944 Women's Land Army poster.

9.R.3.C.1.c Use details from informational text: to analyze and evaluate the accuracy and adequacy of evidence **9.W.3.A.1.b** Compose a variety of texts: in various formats, including workplace communication

1944 Women's Land Army poster.
Courtesy Northwestern University Library/www.library.northwestern.edu.

1. What is the overall **mood** of this image? How has the artist created that effect?

2. During World War II, women worked jobs left empty by the call for soldiers. What elements of the poster evoke feelings of patriotism?

3. Since women were key to the war effort, women of the 1940s advanced gender equality. How does the poster use those ideas persuasively?

Your Turn Analyze Persuasion in Art

An image doesn't have to be part of an advertisement to be persuasive. Many works of fine art also convey persuasive messages. Flip through this book to find an image you consider persuasive, and describe the elements that make it so.

Reading Focus

by **Kylene Beers**

What Skills Help You Respond to Persuasion?

You're flipping through a magazine and pass an ad for a new soda. Two pages later, you're heading to the fridge for a cool drink. Were you already thirsty, or did the ad persuade you to drink something? Sometimes it can be hard to tell when you've been influenced. Passive reading leaves you vulnerable to persuasion. When you read actively, you pay attention to the ways that writers try to shape your opinions. Strong reading skills help make you a strong thinker.

Questioning

Asking yourself questions as you read helps you make sure that you fully understand what a writer is saying. It can also help you challenge a writer's claims.

Questions can be as simple as "What does *that* mean?" You can find answers by re-reading, reading on, or using another reference source, such as a dictionary. Don't be afraid to ask questions that seem obvious—the answers may surprise you.

Questioning also helps you respond to an author's claims. Evaluate an argument by asking, "What evidence proves that point?" and "Do I agree?"

Some questions will lead you directly to other questions or conclusions. You can use a three-part chart to record key questions, answers, and any ideas or questions that follow from your answer.

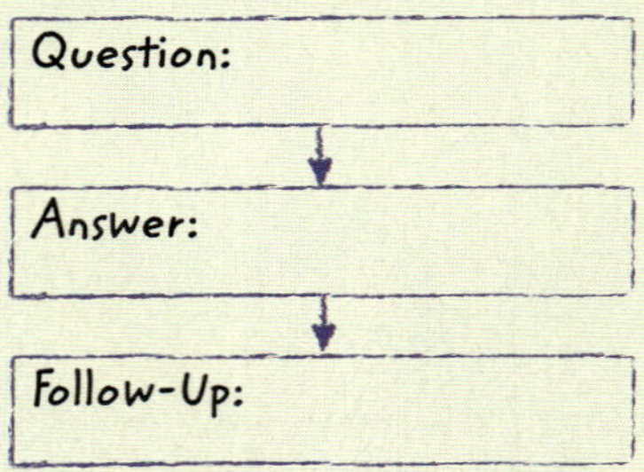

Summarizing

When you **summarize,** you tell the main ideas and leave out the details. This strategy can help you make sure that you understand the key parts of an argument. You can also summarize a text to evaluate the essential elements of an argument without getting distracted by emotional language or a writer's personal style.

To create an effective summary, begin by looking at the structure of the writing. Break the work into smaller parts. Depending on the length of the writing, you might first summarize each paragraph, page, section, or chapter. Use your own words to state the main ideas.

Part	Summary
1.	
2.	
3.	

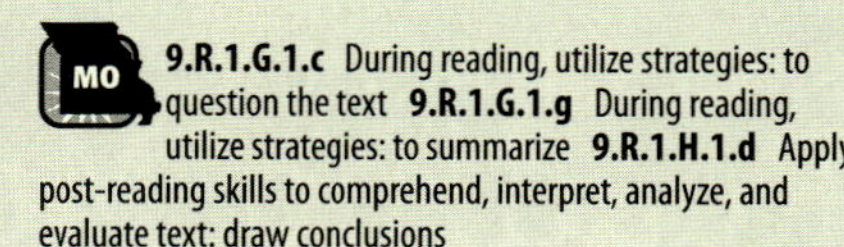

MO
9.R.1.G.1.c During reading, utilize strategies: to question the text 9.R.1.G.1.g During reading, utilize strategies: to summarize 9.R.1.H.1.d Apply post-reading skills to comprehend, interpret, analyze, and evaluate text: draw conclusions

After you summarize each section of a work, it can be helpful to write a summary of the entire work. This summary will emphasize the ideas that are most important overall.

Overall Summary:

Drawing Conclusions

When you read persuasive writing, you need to decide for yourself whether or not the author's argument is convincing. You can **draw conclusions,** or make judgments based on evidence and reasoning, about the argument presented.

Drawing conclusions about persuasive writing involves weighing arguments and deciding which ones are credible. You will collect two different kinds of information:

- Look for the most important facts and details in the text. These are the author's most important pieces of evidence.
- Consider your own knowledge of the topic as well as your experiences. Your ideas will help you draw a conclusion that reflects your insights and values.

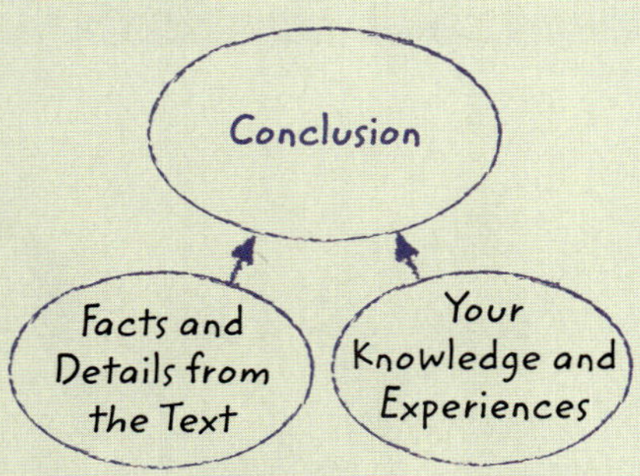

Your Turn Apply Reading Skills

Practice your thinking and reading skills by reading this question and answer from an advice column. Then, complete the activities that follow.

Dear Miss Manners:

I have an unlisted telephone number because I live alone and hate being bothered by calls when I am apt to be in the bathtub or watching a television program. If it's someone I really want to hear from, I do give out the number. But I resent it when people expect me to tell them my telephone number as a matter of course. Can I just make up a number and give it to them?

Gentle Reader:

At the other end of that made-up number lives a person who is lying in the bathtub or watching television, and not anxious to hear from your acquaintances. When people ask you for your telephone number, write down your email or street address.

from *Miss Manners' Guide to Excruciatingly Correct Behavior*
by Judith Martin

1. Summarize the reader's original question. Then, summarize Miss Manners' response.
2. Draw a conclusion about the advice that is given. Is the advice sensible? Explain.

Now go to the Skills in Action: Reading Model

SKILLS IN ACTION

Reading Model

SPEECH

Build Background

In 1863, a warrior who was not a Nez Percé chief signed a treaty with the United States giving up Nez Percé lands in Oregon. Chief Joseph did not accept the treaty but reluctantly agreed to move his people to Idaho. While preparing for the move, four white settlers were killed. Fearing retaliation, the chief led about 250 Nez Percé more than a thousand miles toward Canada. About forty miles from the border, they were surrounded. U.S. General Miles promised that the people could return to Idaho. Chief Joseph surrendered, but General Miles broke his promise.

Read with a Purpose Read this speech to find out what plea Chief Joseph is making.

from An Indian's Views of Indian Affairs

by **Chief Joseph**

I have heard talk and talk, but nothing is done. Good words do not last long unless they amount to something. Words do not pay for my dead people. They do not pay for my country, now overrun by white men. They do not protect my father's grave. They do not pay for all my horses and cattle. Good words will not give me back my children. Good words will not make good the promise of your war chief General Miles. Good words will not give my people good health and stop them from dying. Good words will not get my people a home where they can live in peace and take care of themselves.

Literary Focus

Argument: Tone The excerpt begins by explaining Chief Joseph's attitude toward empty negotiations. His tone is direct and passionate.

I am tired of talk that comes to nothing. It makes my heart sick when I remember all the good words and all the broken promises. There has been too much talking by men who had no right to talk. Too many misrepresentations have been made, too many misunderstandings have come up between the white men about the Indians.

Nez Percé and Yakima Indians stand in front of tepees near Astoria, Oregon, in 1911.

Analyzing Visuals

Viewing and Interpreting Do you think displaying a photograph such as this one of the Nez Percé Indians would have added to the persuasiveness of Chief Joseph's speech? Explain.

If the white man wants to live in peace with the Indian, he can live in peace. There need be no trouble. Treat all men alike. Give them the same law. Give them an even chance to live and grow. All men were made by the same Great Spirit Chief. They are all brothers. The earth is the mother of all people, and all people should have equal rights upon it.

You might as well expect the rivers to run backward as that any man who was born a free man should be contented when penned up and denied liberty to go where he pleases. If you tie a horse to a stake, do you expect he will grow fat? If you pen an Indian up on a small spot of earth and compel him to stay there, he will not be contented, nor will he grow and prosper. I have asked some of the great white chiefs where they get their authority to say to the Indian that he shall stay in one place while he sees white men going where they please. They cannot tell me.

I only ask of the government to be treated as all other men are treated. If I cannot go to my own home, let me have a home in some country where my people will not die so fast. . . .

When I think of our condition, my heart is heavy. I see men of my race treated as outlaws and driven from country to country or shot down like animals.

I know that my race must change. We cannot hold our own with white men as we are. We ask only an even chance to live as other men live. We ask to be recognized as men. We ask that the same law shall work alike on all men. If the Indian breaks the law, punish him by the law. If the white man breaks the law, punish him also.

Reading Focus

Summarizing You can summarize this passage with a statement such as "Chief Joseph wants all people to be treated alike."

Literary Focus

Appeal to Emotion The blunt metaphor "shot down like animals" appeals to an audience's sense of humanity.

Let me be a free man—free to travel, free to stop, free to work, free to trade where I choose, free to choose my own teachers, free to follow the religion of my fathers, free to think and talk and act for myself—and I will obey every law or submit to the penalty.

Whenever white men treat Indians as they treat each other, then we will have no more wars. We shall all be alike—brothers of one father and one mother, with one sky above us and one country around us, and one government for all. Then the Great Spirit Chief who rules above will smile upon this land and send rain to wash out the bloody spots made by brothers' hands from the face of the earth.

For this time the Indian race is waiting and praying. I hope that no more groans of wounded men and women will ever go to the ear of the Great Spirit Chief above and that all people may be one people.

Reading Focus

Drawing Conclusions Use your knowledge of U.S. history to draw a conclusion about how Chief Joseph's speech might have contributed to social change.

Read with a Purpose How does Chief Joseph want American Indians to be treated?

MEET THE WRITER

Chief Joseph

(1840–1904)

A Humane and Eloquent Leader

His name, In-mut-too-yah-lat-lat, means "Thunder Rolling in the Mountains." At the age of about thirty-one, he became Chief Joseph, the leader of the Nez Percé, and would become a strong voice of support for American Indian rights. In 1877, Chief Joseph was forced to lead his people on a lengthy and harrowing retreat across Oregon, Washington, Idaho, and Montana. Along the way, many white settlers came to respect him because of his kind treatment of all people, including women, children, the aged, and prisoners. He never stole from ranchers, preferring to buy the supplies his people needed. When he surrendered, he made a speech that is remembered to this day: "Hear me, my chiefs; my heart is sick and sad. . . . I will fight no more forever."

Think About the Writer What did Chief Joseph teach through his kind words and actions toward others?

SKILLS IN ACTION

Wrap Up

MO **9.R.3.C.1.c** Use details from informational text: to analyze and evaluate the accuracy and adequacy of evidence **9.R.1.E.1.c** Develop vocabulary through text: using glossary, dictionary and thesaurus

Into Action: Persuasion Chart

Complete a chart like this one to analyze the elements Chief Joseph uses to put forth his argument:

Element of Persuasion	How Chief Joseph Uses This Element
Clear Structure	First, he explains his frustration; then, he tells how to improve the situation.
Tone	
Response to Opposing Arguments	
Appeals to Logic	
Appeals to Emotion	

Talk About . . .

Get together with a small group and discuss "An Indian's Views of Indian Affairs" by answering these questions. Try to use each Academic Vocabulary word listed at right at least once in your discussion.

1. Which paragraph do you think can best influence the audience's reaction to the chief? Explain why this section is effective.
2. Why were the "white chiefs" unable to counter Chief Joseph's arguments?
3. Is Chief Joseph's angry tone valid? Why or why not?
4. Which of Chief Joseph's statements could you verify using outside sources?

Write About . . .

Suppose you were there when this speech was delivered. Write a letter to a friend or relative in which you describe the ideas Chief Joseph presented and the impact the speech had on you.

Writing Focus

Think as a Reader/Writer

Find It in Your Reading As you read Collection 6, you will analyze how different writers use persuasion. The Writing Focus activities will help you identify the tools each writer uses to influence an audience and give you ways to use these persuasive techniques in your own writing.

Academic Vocabulary for Collection 6

Talking and Writing About Persuasive Texts

Academic Vocabulary is the language you use to write and talk about literature. Use these words to discuss the persuasive texts you read in this collection. The words are underlined throughout the collection.

influence (IHN floo uhns) *v.:* persuade or affect someone. *A strong speech can influence people to take action.*

counter (KOWN tuhr) *v.:* oppose or take issue with. *His writings effectively counter the argument that American Indians should not receive equal rights.*

valid (VAL ihd) *adj.:* supported by facts; true. *I know the statement is valid because it is based on the facts.*

verify (VEHR uh fy) *v.:* prove something to be true. *You can verify the fact by looking it up in a trustworthy source.*

Your Turn

Write a sentence using each Academic Vocabulary word. Then, read your sentences to a partner, leaving out the Vocabulary word. Can your partner guess the missing word?

SPEECH

Preparing to Read

Ain't I a Woman?

by **Sojourner Truth**

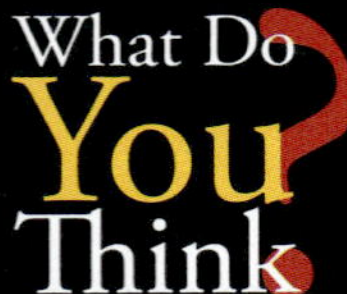

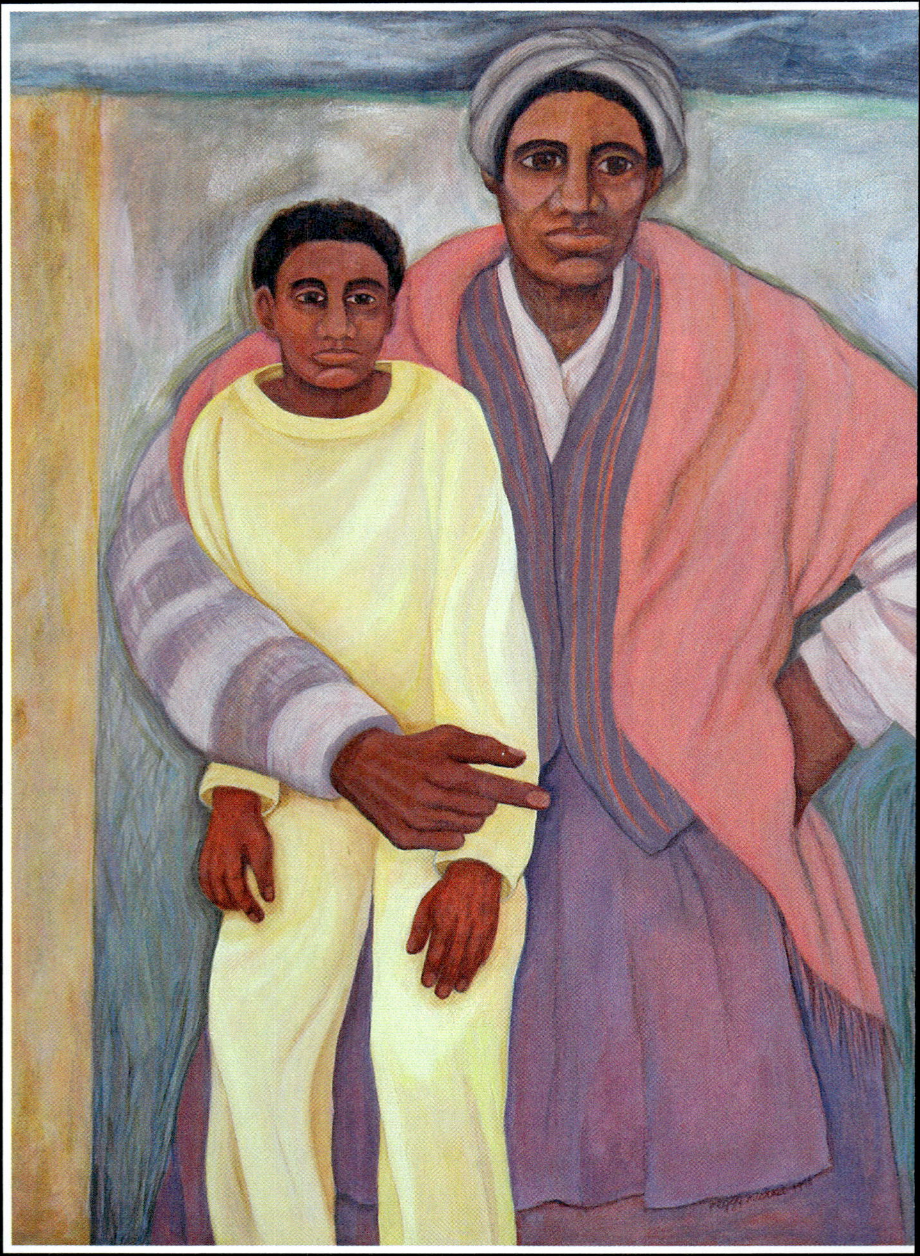

Soujourner Truth Reclaiming Her Son by Peggy Michael. Oil painting.

What Do You Think? How do our life experiences shape our beliefs?

QuickWrite

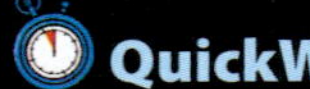

Think of a leader who fought for a cause, such as equal rights. How did the person's own experiences influence his or her beliefs and actions? Write down your ideas.

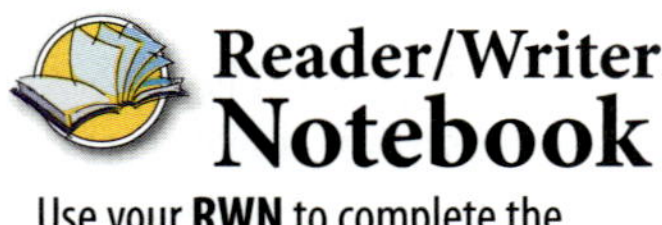

Use your **RWN** to complete the activities for this selection.

MO **9.R.3.C.1.c** Use details from informational text: to analyze and evaluate the accuracy and adequacy of evidence **9.R.1.G.1.g** During reading, utilize strategies: to summarize **9.R.1.H.1.a** Apply post-reading skills to comprehend, interpret, analyze, and evaluate text: identify and explain the relationship between the main idea and supporting details

Literary Focus

Argument: Logical and Emotional Appeals To be persuasive, a speaker or writer tries to appeal to both head and heart—to logic and emotion—to win over an audience. **Logical appeals** are supported by evidence, such as facts, statistics, quotations, and examples. To create **emotional appeals,** writers may use loaded words, repetition of ideas, and **rhetorical questions—**questions asked purely for effect, with no answer expected. As you read this speech, note the powerful use of a rhetorical question.

Reading Focus

Summarizing When you **summarize** a text, you reinforce your understanding of it. You should begin a summary by stating the author's name and the title of the text. Then, restate the main ideas in the order in which they appear in the text, and include key supporting details.

Into Action As you read this speech and prepare to summarize it, record its main ideas and key supporting details in a two-column chart like the one below.

Main Ideas	Supporting Details
Although men say women should be treated gently, Truth says they aren't.	She is not helped into carriages or over mud puddles. She plows and plants.

Writing Focus

Think as a Reader/Writer

Find It in Your Reading Writers of speeches pay close attention not only to the meaning of words and phrases, but also to the way they sound. By making a text sound a certain way, a writer can influence the way we react emotionally to it. As you read, record in your *Reader/Writer Notebook* your observations about the way the rhythm and sound of the speech affect you.

Language Coach

Dialect The way of speaking that is particular to a region or group of people is called **dialect.** Sojourner Truth's speech "Ain't I a Woman?" contains dialect—phrases, contractions, and idioms that were particular to her world. Here are some examples:

Passage with Dialect	Meaning
out of kilter	phrase meaning "not right"
'twixt	contraction for *betwixt*, meaning "between two things"
in a fix	idiom meaning "having problems or difficulty"
ain't	contraction meaning "aren't"
they is asking	nonstandard subject-verb combination

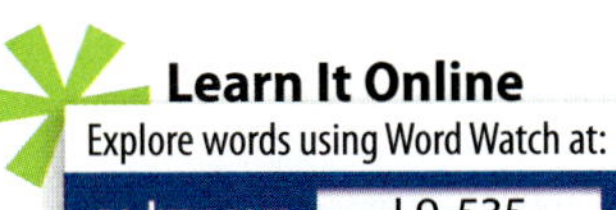

Learn It Online
Explore words using Word Watch at:
go.hrw.com
L9-535
Go

MEET THE WRITER

Sojourner Truth

(c. 1797–1883)

Free at Last

Born in Ulster County, New York, Sojourner Truth was the daughter of slaves. Named Isabella, she was taken from her parents when she was young and was sold to several different masters over the years. Just before New York State abolished slavery in 1827, she was sold to a man named Isaac van Wagener, who gave Isabella her freedom.

"Up and Down the Land"

In 1829, Isabella and her two youngest children moved to New York City, where she worked as a servant until 1843. Then she had a vision that changed her life. According to her own testimony, God instructed her to take the name Sojourner Truth (*sojourner* means "one who travels from place to place") and to "travel up and down the land" spreading a message about the importance of love and fellowship. She began to speak out against slavery and in support of women's rights. Traveling throughout the Midwest and New England, she became famous for her passionate speeches.

During the Civil War, Truth, who then lived in Battle Creek, Michigan, continued her work for civil rights. Invited to meet President Abraham Lincoln in 1864, she became an adviser to him on ways to aid freed slaves. Although Sojourner Truth never learned to read and write, she made society more just through her powerful use of words.

Think About the Writer

Do you think Sojourner Truth's name is appropriate for her? Why or why not?

A Bird's Eye View Down the Battle Creek River, Battle Creek, Mich.

Postcard of Battle Creek River in Battle Creek, Michigan.

Build Background

In 1851, a women's rights convention was held in Akron, Ohio. Various speakers, many of them members of the clergy, used the Bible to argue that the rights and principles of men were superior to those of women. Sojourner Truth, who had not been invited to the convention, walked up to the platform and attacked those arguments. Unfortunately, there is no exact copy of her speech in existence today. The version that follows captures the essence of what she said.

Preview the Selection

After a man at a convention argues against women's rights, **Sojourner Truth** speaks her mind—and speaks from her heart.

Read with a Purpose Read this speech to explore Sojourner Truth's attitude toward being a woman in an age when women were not viewed as equals of men.

Ain't I a Woman?

by **Sojourner Truth**

Well, children, where there is so much racket there must be something out of kilter. I think that 'twixt the negroes of the South and the women at the North, all talking about rights, the white men will be in a fix pretty soon. But what's all this here talking about?

That man over there says that women need to be helped into carriages, and lifted over ditches, and to have the best place everywhere. Nobody ever helps me into carriages, or over mud-puddles, or gives me any best place! And ain't I a woman? Look at me! Look at my arm! I have plowed and planted, and gathered into barns, and no man could head[1] me! And ain't I a woman? I could work as much and eat as much as a man—when I could get it—and bear the lash as well! And ain't I a woman? I have borne thirteen children, and seen most all sold off to slavery, and when I cried out with my mother's grief, none but Jesus heard me! And ain't I a woman? **A**

Then they talk about this thing in the head; what's this they call it? ["Intellect," someone whispers.] That's it, honey. What's that got to do with women's rights or negroes' rights? If my cup won't hold but a pint, and yours holds a quart, wouldn't you be mean not to let me have my little half-measure full?

Then that little man in black there, he says women can't have as much rights as men, 'cause Christ wasn't a woman! Where did your Christ come from? Where did your Christ come from? From God and a woman![2] Man had nothing to do with Him.

If the first woman God ever made[3] was strong enough to turn the world upside down all alone, these women together ought to be able to turn it back, and get it right side up again! And now they is asking to do it, the men better let them. **B**

Obliged to you for hearing me, and now old Sojourner ain't got nothing more to say.

---

1. **head:** outdo; take the lead over.
2. **woman:** a reference to Mary, who, according to the New Testament, was the mother of Jesus.
3. **the first woman God ever made:** reference to Eve. According to the book of Genesis in the Bible, Eve brought sorrow and death into the world by eating the forbidden fruit and encouraging Adam to do likewise. For their disobedience to God's law, they were banished from Eden.

A **Reading Focus** **Summarizing** What idea is the speaker expressing in this passage?

B **Literary Focus** **Logical and Emotional Appeals** Does this paragraph present a logical or emotional appeal? How can you tell?

HISTORY LINK

Women's Rights (1870s). A meeting of the National Woman's Suffrage Association in the 1870s with Susan B. Anthony and Elizabeth Cady Stanton on the platform. Contemporary colored engraving. The Granger Collection, New York.

Seneca Falls

On July 19 and 20, 1848, people gathered in Seneca Falls, New York, to discuss the issue of women's rights. The organizers were Elizabeth Cady Stanton, later the president of the National American Woman Suffrage Association (NAWSA), and Lucretia Mott, an abolitionist and women's advocate. Stanton and Mott had "resolved to host a convention and form a society to advance the rights of women."

In Seneca Falls the organizers put forth the Declaration of Sentiments, which was signed by one hundred people. In the declaration it was resolved "that woman is man's equal—was intended to be so by the Creator, and the highest good of the race demands that she be recognized as such." The declaration helped shape the women's rights movement.

It would take nearly three quarters of a century for women to win the right to vote. By 1919, there were twenty-six state legislatures willing to pass a congressional amendment to allow women suffrage, or the right to vote. Finally, in 1920, the Nineteenth Amendment was passed with the help of the NAWSA and the National Woman's Party (NWP).

Ask Yourself

It was a small, determined group of people who initiated change for women in the United States. Do you think such a group could be effective today? Explain your opinion.

Applying Your Skills

9.R.3.C.1.c Use details from informational text: to analyze and evaluate the accuracy and adequacy of evidence 9.R.2.C.1.d Use details from text(s): to evaluate the effect of author's style
Also covered 9.R.2.B.2.c; 9.R.1.G.1.g; 9.W.3.A.1.a

Ain't I a Woman?

Respond and Think Critically

Reading Focus

Quick Check

1. Who is the "little man in black" that Truth addresses in the speech? What point has the man made?
2. What does Truth want her audience to understand?

Read with a Purpose

3. What is Sojourner Truth's attitude toward being a woman? Support your answer with evidence from the text.

Reading Skills: Summarizing

4. Review the chart you filled in as you read. Then, use the ideas and details you recorded to write a summary of the speech. Compare your summary with a partner's. Did you include the same ideas and details? Do your opinions differ about which information is important to include?

Main Ideas	Supporting Details
Although men say . . .	She is not helped into . . .

My Summary:

Literary Focus

Literary Analysis

5. **Draw Conclusions** What have you learned about Sojourner Truth's life from this speech?
6. **Evaluate** Do you think "Ain't I a Woman?" is of interest purely as a historical document, or does it have something to say to readers today? Explain your opinion.

Literary Skills: Argument—Logical and Emotional Appeals

7. **Identify** Sojourner Truth presents **counter-arguments** in which she opposes the claims of the "man over there." What are his claims, and what logical appeals does she present to counter them?
8. **Analyze** Sojourner Truth uses the rhetorical question "Ain't I a woman?" as a **refrain**—a line that is repeated in a poem or song. Why do you think she repeats this question?

Literary Skills Review: Diction

9. **Analyze** A writer's **diction,** or word choice, helps shape our reactions to a work. Describe the diction used in this speech. How does it contribute to Sojourner Truth's argument and your response to it?

Writing Focus

Think as a Reader/Writer

Use It in Your Writing Write a short speech in which you present an argument. Like Truth, use the rhythm and sound of your words to appeal to your audience's emotions.

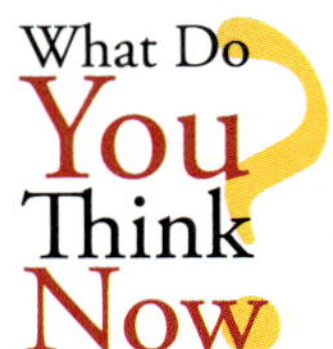

How did Sojourner Truth's personal experiences drive her to support women's rights?

SPEECH

Preparing to Read

Cinderella's Stepsisters

by **Toni Morrison**

Toni Morrison gives a speech in 2000.

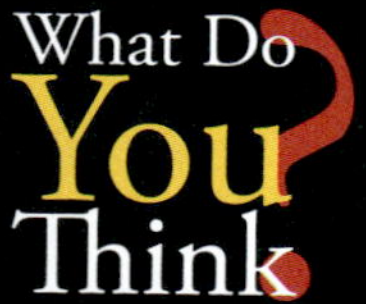

How important is it to treat others well?

QuickTalk

With a partner, brainstorm a list of movies or television shows in which a person is hurt by someone who is busy pursuing his or her own goals.

Reader/Writer Notebook

Use your **RWN** to complete the activities for this selection.

MO **9.R.2.C.1.d** Use details from text(s): to evaluate the effect of author's style **9.R.3.C.1.d** Use details from informational text: to analyze and evaluate point of view **9.R.1.H.1.b** Apply post-reading skills to comprehend, interpret, analyze, and evaluate text: question to clarify

Literary Focus

Argument: Intent and Tone A writer's **intent** (purpose) affects not only the content of an argument, but also its **tone**—the attitude expressed toward the subject or the audience. As you read this speech, note Morrison's intent and tone, and consider how she achieves her purpose by using an **analogy**—a comparison used to explain something complex or unfamiliar by relating it to something familiar.

Reading Focus

Questioning When you read any type of persuasive writing, think of yourself as participating in a debate. Challenge and counter the author and his or her points by asking questions as you read. Doing so will help you evaluate the author's argument.

Into Action As you read this speech, record your questions in a two-column chart. Record the answers to your questions as well.

Questions	Answers
Why is Morrison beginning a speech by talking about "Cinderella"?	

Writing Focus

Think as a Reader/Writer

Find It in Your Reading Writers of speeches often use repetition to emphasize ideas, to help the audience remember their points, and to create rhythm. As you read, record in your *Reader/Writer Notebook* examples of repetition that you find in the speech. Why do you think Morrison uses repetition?

TechFocus Reading repetition in a speech is not as powerful as hearing the effect of repetition when a speaker delivers a speech. As you read, mark off passages with repetition that you could record on an electronic device.

Vocabulary

deflect (dih FLEHKT) *v.:* turn aside. *The stepsisters do not take action to deflect their mother's abuse of Cinderella.*

expendable (ehk SPEHN duh buhl) *adj.:* not worth saving; unnecessary. *In pursuing our goals, we should not view other people's careers as expendable.*

indispensable (ihn dih SPEHN suh buhl) *adj.:* absolutely necessary; essential. *Powerful people have the authority to decide what or who is indispensable.*

sensibilities (sehn suh BIHL uh teez) *n.:* ability to respond emotionally. *We should not let our ambition overwhelm our better sensibilities.*

diminish (duh MIHN ihsh) *v.:* lessen; reduce. *Our actions should not diminish the success of our colleagues.*

Language Coach

Synonyms and Antonyms A **synonym** is a word that has the same or almost the same meaning as another word. Look at the Vocabulary list above, and find the word that could be a synonym for *reduce.* An **antonym** is a word that has the opposite meaning of another word. Which two Vocabulary words above are antonyms?

Learn It Online

For a preview of this speech, see the video introduction on:

go.hrw.com L9-541 

MEET THE WRITER

Toni Morrison

(1931–   )

A Valuable Lesson

One day, Toni Morrison's father, a ship welder, told her, "I welded a perfect seam and I signed my name to it." When Morrison exclaimed, "But, Daddy, no one's going to see it," he responded, "Yeah, but I know it's there."

Morrison carried this lesson about pride and dignity with her when she began to help support her family by doing housework for others at about age thirteen. Her family faced not only economic hardship, but also racism and segregation. Growing up during the Great Depression in Lorain, Ohio, Morrison overcame all this. She had been raised to succeed.

Nobel Winner

When she published her first novel in 1970, Morrison was a divorced mother of two young sons and a full-time editor who "stole" time to write. She went on to become one of the country's most acclaimed writers, publishing eight novels and holding a professorship at Princeton University. In 1993, she was the first African American to win the Nobel Prize for literature. Her novel *Beloved*, published in 1987, was later singled out by the *New York Times Book Review* as the best work of American fiction published in the last twenty-five years. She is lauded for exploring the experiences of African Americans, particularly women, in rich, poetic prose.

Think About the Writer

Do you think the lesson Morrison's father taught her is a valuable one? Why or why not?

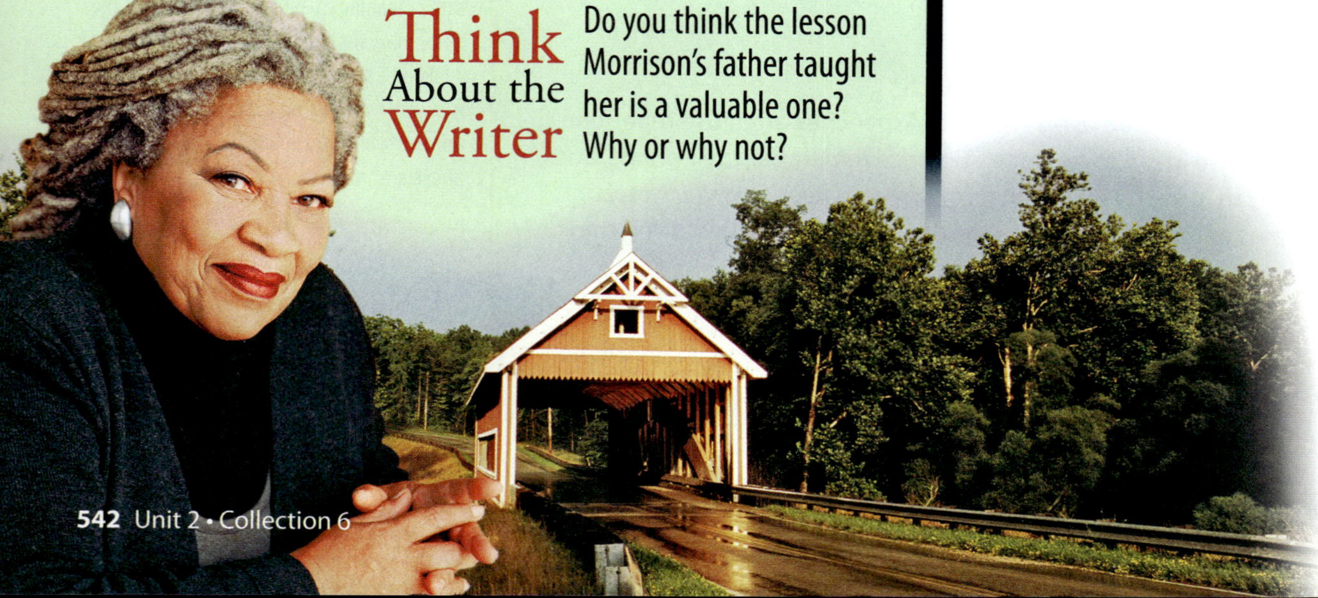

Build Background

During the women's rights movement in the 1960s and 1970s, women passionately fought to gain the same rights and opportunities as men had. The 1979 graduates of Barnard College, an all-women's college in New York City, grew up during this era. In this speech, which was delivered at the Barnard graduation that year, Toni Morrison discusses the power these graduates will soon wield.

Preview the Selection

In this speech, **Toni Morrison** has some strong words of advice for college graduates who are about to take their place in the world.

Read with a Purpose
Read this speech to explore Toni Morrison's beliefs about the abuse of power.

Cinderella's Stepsisters

by **Toni Morrison**

Let me begin by taking you back a little. Back before the days at college. To nursery school, probably, to a once-upon-a-time time when you first heard, or read, or, I suspect, even saw "Cinderella." Because it is Cinderella that I want to talk to you about; because it is Cinderella who causes me a feeling of urgency. What is unsettling about that fairy tale is that it is essentially the story of a household—a world, if you please—of women gathered together and held together in order to abuse another woman. There is, of course, a rather vague absent father and a nick-of-time prince with a foot fetish.[1] But neither has much personality. And there are the surrogate "mothers" of course (god- and step-) who contribute both to Cinderella's grief and to her release and happiness. But it is her stepsisters who interest me. How crippling it must have been for those young girls to grow up with a mother, to watch and imitate that mother, enslaving another girl. **A**

I am curious about their fortunes after the story ends. For contrary to recent adaptations, the stepsisters were not ugly, clumsy, stupid girls with outsize feet. The Grimm collection[2] describes them as "beautiful and fair in appearance." When we are introduced to them they are beautiful, elegant, women of status, and clearly women of power. Having watched and participated in the violent dominion[3] of another woman, will they be any less cruel when it comes their turn to enslave other children, or even when they are required to take care of their own mother?

It is not a wholly medieval[4] problem. It is quite a contemporary one: feminine power when directed at other women has historically been wielded in what has been described as a "masculine" manner. Soon you will be in a position to do the very same thing. Whatever your background—rich or poor—whatever the history of education in your family—five generations or one—you have taken advantage of what has been available to you at Barnard and you will therefore have both the economic and social status of the stepsisters and you will have their power. **B**

I want not to *ask* you but to *tell* you not to participate in the oppression of your sisters. Mothers who abuse their children are women, and another woman, not an agency, has to be

1. **fetish** (FEHT ihsh): irrational devotion.
2. **Grimm collection:** reference to the famous collection of fairy tales compiled by Jacob and Wilhelm Grimm in the early nineteenth century.
3. **dominion** (duh MIHN yuhn): rule; control.
4. **medieval** (mehd EE vuhl): relating to the Middle Ages, a period in European history from about the fifth to about the fifteenth centuries.

A **Reading Focus** **Questioning** Why does Morrison begin her speech by discussing "Cinderella"?

B **Literary Focus** **Intent** What is Morrison's purpose in addressing the graduates?

willing to stay their hands. Mothers who set fire to school buses are women, and another woman, not an agency, has to tell them to stay their hands. Women who stop the promotion of other women in careers are women, and another woman must come to the victim's aid. Social and welfare workers who humiliate their clients may be women, and other women colleagues have to deflect their anger.

I am alarmed by the violence that women do to each other: professional violence, competitive violence, emotional violence. I am alarmed by the willingness of women to enslave other women. I am alarmed by a growing absence of decency on the killing floor of professional women's worlds. You are the women who will take your place in the world where you can decide who shall flourish and who shall wither; you will make distinctions between the deserving poor and the undeserving poor; where you can yourself determine which life is expendable and which is indispensable. Since you will have the power to do it, you may also be persuaded that you have the right to do it. As educated women the distinction between the two is first-order business. C

I am suggesting that we pay as much attention to our nurturing[5] sensibilities as to our ambition. You are moving in the direction of freedom and the function of freedom is to free somebody else. You are moving toward self-fulfillment, and the consequences of that fulfillment should be to discover that there is something just as important as you are and that just-as-important thing may be Cinderella—or your stepsister.

In your rainbow journey toward the realization of personal goals don't make choices based only on your security and your safety. Nothing is safe. That is not to say that anything ever was, or that anything worth achieving ever should be. Things of value seldom are. It is not safe to have a child. It is not safe to challenge the status quo.[6] It is not safe to choose work that has not been done before. Or to do old work in a new way. There will always be someone there to stop you. But in pursuing your highest ambitions, don't let your personal safety diminish the safety of your stepsister. In wielding the power that is deservedly yours, don't permit it to enslave your stepsisters. Let your might and your power emanate[7] from that place in you that is nurturing and caring. D

Women's rights is not only an abstraction, a cause; it is also a personal affair. It is not only about "us"; it is also about me and you. Just the two of us. E

5. **nurturing** (NUR chuhr ihng): promoting growth or development.

6. **status quo** (STAT uhs KWOH): existing state of affairs.

7. **emanate** (EHM uh nayt): come from.

C **Reading Focus** **Questioning** What does the word *violence* mean in the first sentence of this paragraph?

D **Reading Focus** **Questioning** What does the phrase "personal safety" mean? What kind of safety is Morrison talking about?

E **Literary Focus** **Tone** What is the tone of this paragraph? Explain whether you think this paragraph is an effective ending for the speech.

Vocabulary **deflect** (dih FLEHKT) *v.:* turn aside.
expendable (ehk SPEHN duh buhl) *adj.:* not worth saving; unnecessary.
indispensable (ihn dih SPEHN suh buhl) *adj.:* absolutely necessary; essential.
sensibilities (sehn suh BIHL uh teez) *n.:* ability to respond emotionally.
diminish (duh MIHN ihsh) *v.:* lessen; reduce.

Applying Your Skills

MO **9.R.2.C.1.d** Use details from text(s): to evaluate the effect of author's style **9.R.3.C.1.d** Use details from informational text: to analyze and evaluate point of view **9.R.1.H.1.b** Apply post-reading skills to comprehend, interpret, analyze, and evaluate text: question to clarify

Cinderella's Stepsisters

Respond and Think Critically

Reading Focus

Quick Check

1. Why does the story of Cinderella's stepsisters interest Morrison?
2. According to Morrison, what have the Barnard graduates gained from their education?

Read with a Purpose

3. Explain Morrison's distinction between having the *power* to do something and having the *right* to do it. Why does she make this distinction?

Reading Skills: Questioning

4. Review the chart you filled in as you read. If you left any questions unanswered, try to answer them now. Then, add a row labeled "My Evaluation" to the bottom of the chart, and record your evaluation of the speech.

Questions	Answers
Why is Morrison beginning a speech by talking about "Cinderella"?	
My Evaluation:	

Literary Focus

Literary Analysis

5. **Interpret** What does Morrison mean when she says that "the function of freedom is to free somebody else"?
6. **Extend** Is Morrison's argument valid for men? How might her speech be adapted for a coed audience?

Literary Skills: Argument—Intent and Tone

7. **Analyze** What is Morrison's purpose in this speech? In your own words, express the point she is making.
8. **Evaluate** Explain the **analogy,** or comparison, Morrison presents in her speech. Do you think this analogy suits her intent and her audience? Why or why not?
9. **Evaluate** Describe the tone of Morrison's speech. In your opinion, does this tone contribute to or detract from the effectiveness of Morrison's argument? Explain.

Literary Skills Review: Style

10. **Analyze** Writers' use of language—their diction and sentence patterns—defines their **style.** Describe Morrison's style in this speech.

Writing Focus

Think as a Reader/Writer

Use It in Your Writing What advice do you have for students entering ninth grade next year? Write a short speech in which you offer guidance. Be sure to use repetition to help you express your ideas effectively.

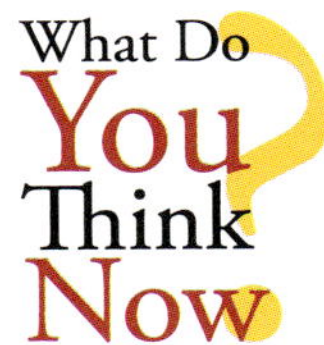

In what way is Morrison urging her audience to break a traditional pattern? Do you agree with her ideas? Explain.

Applying Your Skills

Cinderella's Stepsisters

Vocabulary Development

Vocabulary Check

deflect
expendable
indispensable
sensibilities
diminish

Write the Vocabulary word that best completes the meaning of each sentence.

1. The company eliminated the jobs that were ___________.
2. Spending too much money will ___________ your savings.
3. The superb doctor played a(n) ___________ role at the hospital.
4. Sara was able to ___________ her mother's anger with a sincere apology.
5. The heartwarming movie appealed to our ___________.

Vocabulary Skills: Word Origins

Many English words are derived from Latin and Greek words. You could say that these English words have their roots in another language. Learning the meanings of root words and prefixes can help you determine the meanings of many English words.

For example, let's say you know that the Latin root word *dominus* means "a master." When you encounter the word *dominion* in "Cinderella's Stepsisters," you will then be able to make an educated guess that the word's meaning relates in some way to authority and power.

Your Turn

Use a dictionary to look up the origin of each Vocabulary word. Include prefixes, when appropriate, along with root words. Then, think of other English words that are derived from the same root words or that share the same prefixes. Put your information in a chart like the one below for *dominion*.

dominion
Meaning: rule; control
Word Origin: Latin dominus, "a master"
Related Words: dominate, dominant, domineering

Language Coach

Synonyms and Antonyms A **synonym** is a word that has the same meaning as another word; for example, *kind* is a synonym for *type*. An **antonym** is a word that has the opposite meaning of another word. *Increase*, for example, is an antonym for the word *reduce*. Go through Toni Morrison's speech, and find five words for which you can find synonyms. Write those words and synonyms down in your *Reader/Writer Notebook*. To challenge yourself, see if you can come up with antonyms for the words you took from Morrison's speech. Remember, some words do not have antonyms.

Academic Vocabulary

Talk About . . .

With a small group of classmates, discuss whether or not you find Morrison's argument valid. Support your ideas using details from the text.

MO **9.W.3.A.1.a** Compose a variety of texts: using narrative, descriptive, expository, and/or persuasive features **9.W.2.E.1.c** In written text apply: standard usage **9.R.1.G.1.a** During reading, utilize strategies: to determine meaning of unknown words **9.R.1.E.1.c** Develop vocabulary through text: using glossary, dictionary and thesaurus

Grammar Link

Active and Passive Voice

Like people, action verbs have voices. A verb in the **active voice** expresses an action performed *by* its subject.

"[A]nother woman *must come* to the victim's aid."

". . . You *will make* distinctions between the deserving poor and the undeserving poor."

A verb in the **passive voice** expresses an action done *to* its subject. (Hint: A passive-voice verb always includes a form of *be* and the past participle of a verb.)

"When we *are introduced* to them . . ."

". . . You may also *be persuaded* that you have the right to do it."

The active voice sounds strong and direct. A verb in the passive voice is not as strong. However, the passive voice is useful when a writer does not know who or what performed an action *(My bicycle was stolen)* or when a writer does not want readers to know who performed an action *(The TV was left on)*.

Your Turn

Writing Applications Rewrite each sentence, changing the verb from the passive voice to the active voice. Notice that the active voice results in shorter, more vigorous sentences.

1. A comparison is made by Morrison in her speech.
2. Cinderella is abused by her stepmother.
3. The stepsisters are described as beautiful by the Grimm brothers.
4. Her promotion was challenged by her colleague.
5. Important goals will soon be achieved by the graduates.

CHOICES

As you respond to the Choices, use these **Academic Vocabulary** words as appropriate: influence, counter, valid, verify.

REVIEW

Outline an Argument

Re-read Morrison's speech, and make an outline of her argument. Include in your outline the details she gives to support her argument. Circle any details that you find especially effective. Here is a sample outline format to help you get started:

I. Main Topic
  A. Idea
    1. Supporting Detail
    2. Supporting Detail

CONNECT

Write an Editorial

Timed Writing Which ideas in Morrison's speech might be relevant to life in high school? Consider, for example, how her ideas can be applied to the way students treat each other while pursuing their goals. Write an editorial in which you respond to Morrison's speech by explaining what high school students can learn from her message.

EXTEND

Record a Speech

TechFocus Choose a passage from "Cinderella's Stepsister" that contains repetition. Re-read the passage, and note how repetition creates rhythm and emphasizes key points. Now, record your passage, and ask a friend to evaluate your performance. Did the repetition have an influence on how you delivered the speech? Why or why not?

ESSAY

Preparing to Read

The Next Green Revolution

by **Alex Nikolai Steffen**

Santiago, Chile, 1999.

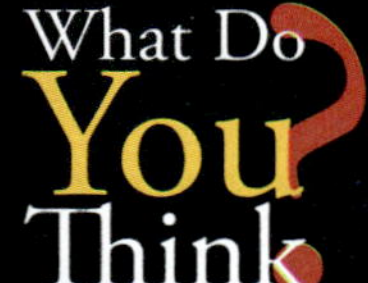

What do you believe the world will be like in fifty years?

QuickWrite

What changes do you expect to see in the world fifty years from now? How do you think your actions today will influence the future? Explain.

Reader/Writer Notebook

Use your **RWN** to complete the activities for this selection.

MO **9.R.3.C.1.c** Use details from informational text: to analyze and evaluate the accuracy and adequacy of evidence **9.R.1.H.1.d** Apply post-reading skills to comprehend, interpret, analyze, and evaluate text: draw conclusions

Literary Focus

Argument and Support Persuasive essays present an **argument**—a point of view, or opinion, on a topic. For an argument to be effective, writers need to provide **support,** specific evidence that backs up their ideas. It's your job as a reader to analyze and evaluate the support that is provided. Types of support might include facts, statistics, examples, and quotes from experts in the field.

Literary Perspectives Apply the literary perspective described on page 551 as you read this essay.

Reading Focus

Drawing Conclusions As you react to a writer's argument, you will draw your own conclusions. When you **draw conclusions,** you make judgments based on evidence and reasoning as well as on what you already know about the topic.

Into Action Use a chart like the one below to combine your own knowledge and experience with facts and details from the text. Then, draw a conclusion based on both kinds of information.

Details from the Text	My Knowledge and Experiences
Political parties who focus on environmental issues have not gained a lot of support.	None of the candidates running for mayor last year made a big deal about environmental issues.

My Conclusion The writer's statement is probably valid.

Writing Focus

Think as a Reader/Writer

Find It in Your Reading Essay writers often present lists of parallel ideas to make their points. As you read, record in your *Reader/Writer Notebook* examples of parallel lists in the essay. How do the lists affect your response?

Vocabulary

abundance (uh BUHN duhns) *n.:* full supply; plenty. *New technology has brought us an abundance of opportunities.*

innovative (IHN uh vay tihv) *adj.:* new and original; groundbreaking. *We need innovative ideas to solve problems that have resisted traditional solutions.*

sustainable (suh STAY nuh buhl) *adj.:* able to be maintained. *We must find sustainable solutions that provide lasting results, not just quick fixes.*

unmitigated (uhn MIHT uh gay tihd) *adj.:* absolute; not lessened in any way. *The result was an unmitigated disaster for the environment.*

ingenuity (ihn juh NOO uh tee) *n.:* cleverness. *Human ingenuity has led to a wide range of remarkable inventions.*

Language Coach

Word Endings Word endings often signal whether a word is a noun, verb, or adjective. Which Vocabulary words on the list above are nouns? Identify their endings, and try to name other nouns with the same endings. Then, look at the adjectives on the list. What endings do you find? What other adjectives do you know with these endings?

Learn It Online

Strengthen your vocabulary with Word Watch:

MEET THE WRITER

Alex Nikolai Steffen

(1969–)

Working for a Bright, Green Future

Alex Nikolai Steffen believes that "we find ourselves facing two futures, one unthinkable and the other currently unimaginable." He works passionately to help people bring the unimaginable future to life. As a reporter and environmental advocate, his mission is "looking for ways to create a future which is sustainable, dynamic, prosperous and fair."

Steffen has traveled four continents in search of environmental news. His essays have appeared in newspapers and magazines across the country and have been translated into German, Japanese, Portuguese, and Spanish. He has consulted with more than fifty environmental groups, advising them on topics from protecting endangered species to preventing the use of nuclear weapons.

Connecting People and Technology

Steffen believes that we have the technology we need to solve many of our resource problems. However, people don't always have access to that information. That's why he runs the Web site Worldchanging.com. The site provides links, models, and ideas that connect people with the newest data and technology. Tapping the Internet's capability to share information is a perfect example of Steffen's vision: using technology to create powerful, positive change.

Think About the Writer

Why might it be important to Steffen to have his writing translated?

Build Background

The adjective *green* took on a new political meaning with the development of the green movement toward the end of the twentieth century. Green parties and politicians focus on protecting the environment from destructive technology. To be "green-minded" is to make careful choices that will have limited negative impact on the environment.

Preview the Selection

In this essay, **Alex Nikolai Steffen** says that green parties have been sending the wrong message. He outlines the message he thinks they *should* be promoting, and he tells us why.

Read with a Purpose Read this essay to find out how the writer envisions the future.

The Next Green Revolution

How technology is leading environmentalism out of the anti-business, anti-consumer wilderness.

by **Alex Nikolai Steffen**

For decades, environmentalists have warned of a coming climate crisis. Their alarms went unheeded, and last year[1] we reaped an early harvest: a singularly ferocious hurricane season, record snowfall in New England, the worst-ever wildfires in Alaska, arctic glaciers at their lowest ebb in millennia, catastrophic drought in Brazil, devastating floods in India—portents[2] of global warming's destructive potential. **A**

Green-minded activists failed to move the broader public not because they were wrong about the problems, but because the solutions they offered were unappealing to most people. They called for tightening belts and curbing appetites, turning down the thermostat and living lower on the food chain. They rejected technology, business, and prosperity in favor of returning to a simpler way of life. No wonder the movement got so little traction. Asking people in the world's wealthiest, most advanced

---

1. **last year:** 2005.
2. **portents** (PAWHR tehnts): indications that something will happen; signs.

Literary Perspectives

Analyzing Responses Sometimes readers find that relating their own experiences or ideas to what they read helps them discover meaning. For example, as you read Steffen's argument, you might be thinking about other arguments you've heard on the topic of global warming. Your past experiences have helped you form opinions on the subject, and your evaluation of Steffen's ideas will be uniquely influenced by your own perspectives.

As you continue reading this article, think about what assumptions you had before reading Steffen's argument. Ask yourself, "Have any of those assumptions or ideas influenced my opinion of his argument?" As you read, be sure to notice the notes and questions at the bottom of the pages, which will guide you in using each perspective.

A **Literary Focus** **Argument and Support** What support does Steffen offer for the argument that we are already seeing signs of global warming's negative impact?

societies to turn their backs on the very forces that drove such abundance is naive[3] at best.

With climate change hard upon us, a new green movement is taking shape, one that embraces environmentalism's concerns but rejects its worn-out answers. Technology can be a font[4] of endlessly creative solutions. Business can be a vehicle for change. Prosperity can help us build the kind of world we want. Scientific exploration, innovative design, and cultural evolution are the most powerful tools we have. Entrepreneurial zeal[5] and market forces, guided by sustainable policies, can propel the world into a bright green future.

Americans trash the planet not because we're evil, but because the industrial systems we've devised leave no other choice. Our ranch houses and high-rises, factories and farms, freeways and power plants were conceived before we had a clue how the planet works. They're primitive inventions designed by people who didn't fully grasp the consequences of their actions. **B**

Consider the unmitigated ecological disaster that is the automobile. Every time you turn on the ignition, you're enmeshed in a system whose known outcomes include a polluted atmosphere, oil-slicked seas, and desert wars. As comprehension of the stakes has grown, though, a market has emerged for a more sensible alternative. Today you can drive a hybrid car that burns far less gasoline than a conventional car. Tomorrow we might see vehicles that consume no fossil fuels and emit no greenhouse gases. Combine cars like that with smarter urban growth and we're well on our way to sustainable transportation. **C**

You don't change the world by hiding in the woods, wearing a hair shirt, or buying indulgences in the form of save the earth bumper stickers. You do it by articulating a vision for the future and pursuing it with all the ingenuity humanity can muster. Indeed, being green at the start of the 21st century requires a wholehearted commitment to upgrading civilization. Four key principles can guide the way: **D**

Renewable energy is plentiful energy. Burning fossil fuels is a filthy habit, and the supply won't last forever. Fortunately, a growing number of renewable alternatives promise clean, inexhaustible power: wind turbines, solar arrays, wave-power flotillas, small hydroelectric generators, geothermal systems, even bioengineered algae that turn waste into hydrogen. The challenge is to scale up these technologies to deliver power in industrial quantities—exactly the kind of challenge brilliant businesspeople love.

Efficiency creates value. The number one U.S. industrial product is waste. Waste is worse than stupid; it's costly, which is why we're seeing businesspeople in every sector getting a jump on the competition by consuming less water,

---

3. **naive** (ny EEV): overly simple; artless.
4. **font** (fahnt): inexhaustible source.
5. **entrepreneurial zeal** (ahn truh pruh NUR ee uhl ZEEL): enthusiastic pursuit of self-made business opportunities.

B Literary Focus Argument and Support Why does Steffen include these details?

C Reading Focus Drawing Conclusions What do you conclude about how willing people will be to follow the author's advice about cars?

D Literary Perspectives Analyzing Responses So far, how have your own perspectives helped you analyze Steffen's ideas?

Vocabulary **abundance** (uh BUHN duhns) *n.:* full supply; plenty.
innovative (IHN uh vay tihv) *adj.:* new and original; groundbreaking.
sustainable (suh STAY nuh buhl) *adj.:* able to be maintained.
unmitigated (uhn MIHT uh gay tihd) *adj.:* absolute; not lessened in any way.
ingenuity (ihn juh NOO uh tee) *n.:* cleverness.

Polar bear in Svalbard, Norway. Global warming is melting the Arctic region's ice floes, where polar bears hunt for food.

power, and materials. What's true for industry is true at home, too: Think well-insulated houses full of natural light, cars that sip instead of guzzle, appliances that pay for themselves in energy savings.

Cities beat suburbs. Manhattanites[6] use less energy than most people in North America. Sprawl eats land and snarls traffic. Building homes close together is a more efficient use of space and infrastructure. It also encourages walking, promotes public transit, and fosters community.

Quality is wealth. More is not better. Better is better. You don't need a bigger house; you need a different floor plan. You don't need more stuff; you need stuff you'll actually use. **E**

Ecofriendly designs and nontoxic materials already exist, and there's plenty of room for innovation. You may pay more for things like long-lasting, energy-efficient LED lightbulbs,

6. **Manhattanites:** people who live in Manhattan, one of the five boroughs of New York City.

E **Reading Focus** **Drawing Conclusions** What conclusion can you draw about the difference between what people think they want and what might improve their lives?

but they'll save real money over the long term.

Redesigning civilization along these lines would bring a quality of life few of us can imagine. That's because a fully functioning ecology is tantamount to tangible wealth.[7] Clean air and water, a diversity of animal and plant species, soil and mineral resources, and predictable weather are annuities[8] that will pay dividends for as long as the human race survives—and may even extend our stay on Earth.

It may seem impossibly far away, but on days when the smog blows off, you can already see it: a society built on radically green design, sustainable energy, and closed-loop[9] cities; a civilization afloat on a cloud of efficient, nontoxic, recyclable technology. That's a future we can live with.

---

7. **tantamount** (TAN tuh mownt) **to tangible** (TAN juh buhl) **wealth:** the same as actual wealth or value.
8. **annuities** (uh NOO uh teez): amounts of money paid in regular installments.
9. **closed-loop:** self-sufficient; not relying on outside materials.

Analyzing Visuals **Viewing and Interpreting**

Why does Steffen approve of alternative energy sources such as these wind turbines?

Applying Your Skills

MO 9.R.3.C.1.c Use details from informational text: to analyze and evaluate the accuracy and adequacy of evidence 9.R.1.H.1.d Apply post-reading skills to comprehend, interpret, analyze, and evaluate text: draw conclusions *Also covered* 9.W.3.A.1.a; 9.R.1.G.1.a

The Next Green Revolution

Respond and Think Critically

Reading Focus

Quick Check

1. According to Steffen, what do environmental activists traditionally ask people to do?
2. According to Steffen, why do people "trash the planet"?

Read with a Purpose

3. What aspects of our lives does Steffen think must change in order to avoid a disastrous future?

Reading Skills: Drawing Conclusions

4. Expand your chart to review your conclusions. Does your conclusion still make sense to you? Note why or why not in a box titled "Confirm." Then, add a box labeled "Adjust or Extend." If you rejected your conclusion, adjust the conclusion to reflect your new thoughts. If you accepted it, extend your conclusion by making a stronger statement.

My Conclusion The writer's statement is probably valid.	
Confirm	Adjust or Extend

Vocabulary Check

Match each Vocabulary word with its definition.

5. **abundance** a. able to be maintained
6. **ingenuity** b. groundbreaking
7. **innovative** c. absolute or complete
8. **sustainable** d. full supply
9. **unmitigated** e. cleverness

Literary Focus

Literary Analysis

10. **Literary Perspectives** How did your own ideas influence your response to Steffen's argument? Did he change your mind or reinforce any pre-existing opinions? Explain.
11. **Classify** Is Steffen's attitude about the future optimistic or pessimistic? Explain your answer.

Literary Skills: Argument and Support

12. **Identify** What is the author's main argument?
13. **Analyze** Which element of support do you find most convincing? Why?
14. **Evaluate** Does Steffen supply enough support to persuade you to accept his argument? Point to specific examples to show why or why not.

Literary Skills Review: Author's Purpose

15. **Identify** Steffen's purpose for writing is to persuade readers to take action. Name three specific actions that Steffen hopes readers will take.

Writing Focus

Think as a Reader/Writer

Use It in Your Writing Imagine that a neighbor is not participating in your community's recycling program. Write a persuasive letter encouraging him or her to recycle. Follow Steffen's model of using lists to make your support clear and persuasive.

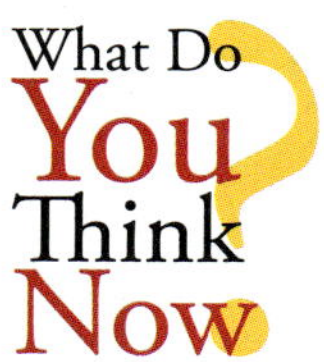

Did reading this essay change your vision of what the world will be like in fifty years? Why or why not?

COMPARING TEXTS

Comparing Forms of Persuasion

CONTENTS

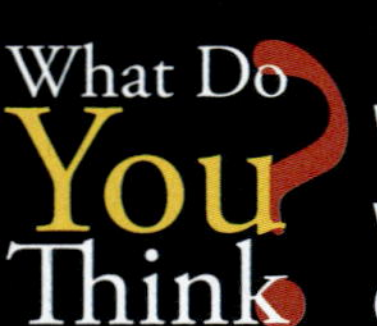

Which has more power—words or images—to influence our beliefs and opinions?

QuickWrite

When you want to persuade someone about an idea that's important to you, how do you do it? List a few ways you use persuasion in your day-to-day life.

Preparing to Read

Why I Wrote *Persepolis*

9.R.1.H.1.d Apply post-reading skills to comprehend, interpret, analyze, and evaluate text: draw conclusions 9.R.1.G.1.c During reading, utilize strategies: to question the text

Literary Focus

Author's Purpose Authors usually have a primary **purpose** in mind when they write or speak. To achieve their purposes, they make use of several techniques. They use **exposition** to explain or inform, **narration** to tell about a series of events, and **persuasion** to convince their audience to think or act in a certain way. Notice how Satrapi uses several techniques to achieve her primary purpose in the interview that follows.

Reading Focus

Questioning the Text Asking a variety of questions as you read will help you become involved in a text, aid your comprehension, and sharpen your critical-thinking skills. To evaluate persuasive writing, think about what kinds of information are being offered. In an essay such as this one, you might expect to find **anecdotes** (which tell about real-life incidents), **examples,** and statements of **fact** and **opinion.**

Into Action As you read, take note of the statements the writer makes, and ask yourself what type of statement each one is.

Text Passage	What Kind of Statement Is This?
"From the time I came to France in 1994, I was always telling stories about life in Iran to my friends."	Anecdote—this is a detail from real life.

Writing Focus

Think as a Reader/Writer

Find It in Your Reading Speakers and nonfiction writers often use question-and-answer statements to organize and explain their main points. As you read, record in your *Reader/Writer Notebook* the questions and answers that Satrapi uses. What effect does the use of questions and answers create?

Reader/Writer Notebook

Use your **RWN** to complete the activities for this selection.

Vocabulary

justifying (JUHS tuh fy ihng) *v.:* proving that something is correct or valid. *Satrapi has been justifying her decision to tell her story in the form of a graphic novel.*

evolved (ee VAHLVD) *v.:* developed or changed gradually. *Some people's views of Iran evolved after they read* Persepolis.

pacifist (PAS uh fihst) *n.:* person who believes that conflicts should be resolved by peaceful means and not by war or violence. *Satrapi, a pacifist, does not believe the world will solve its problems by engaging in war.*

stark (stahrk) *adj.:* complete; absolute. *Satrapi felt that depictions of Iranians on TV contained stark misunderstandings.*

Language Coach

Word Origins The word *evolve* comes from the Latin prefix *e–*, meaning "out," and the Latin root word *volvere*, meaning "to roll." List at least two other words that come from the root word *volvere*. Use a dictionary if you need help.

Learn It Online

There's more to words than just definitions. Get the whole story on:

go.hrw.com L9-557 

MEET THE WRITER

Marjane Satrapi

(1969–)

A Young Artist

Born in Rasht, Iran, Marjane Satrapi, the award-winning graphic novelist, was not exposed to many comic books in her youth, but she loved to draw. While a student in Vienna, Austria, she was assigned to write a book report in French, a language she had not studied in three years. Satrapi decided to use drawings to express her ideas and received "the best grade." Satrapi says of her teacher: "She made me become a writer because what she told me was, 'You have understood everything; now you have to learn how to write it.' "

An International Story

Satrapi's graphic novels *Persepolis* and *Persepolis 2* describe her youth—her childhood in Tehran, Iran; the years she spent at school in Vienna; her return to Iran—and the political upheaval there in the 1970s and 1980s, including the Islamic Revolution, the overthrow of the ruler (called the shah), and the Iran-Iraq War.

For Satrapi, who now lives in Paris and speaks four languages, "image is an international language." Translated into over twenty languages and taught in numerous U.S. high schools and colleges, *Persepolis* and *Persepolis 2* have not only illuminated life in Iran for people around the world but have also taken on universal significance as the story of life under a dictatorship.

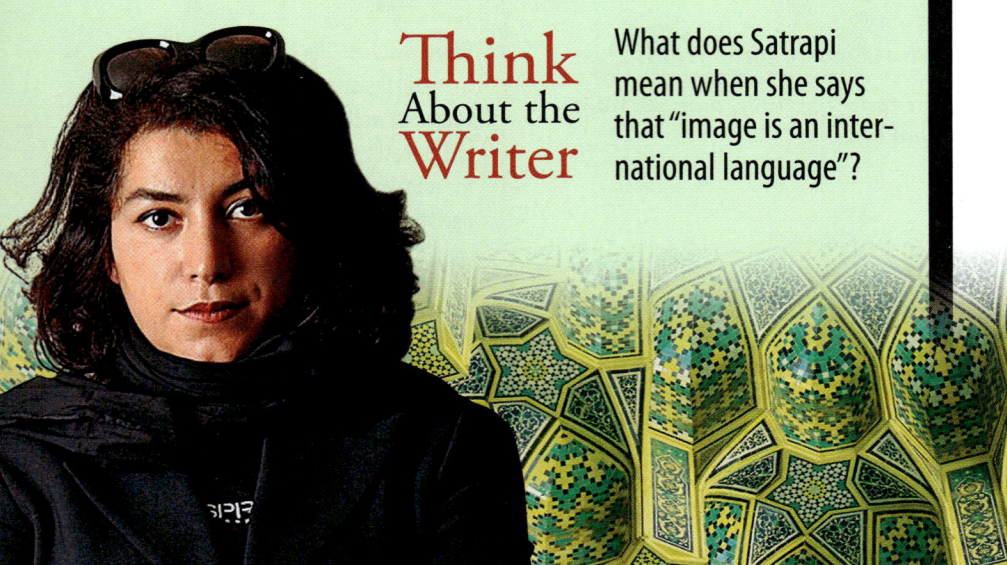

Think About the Writer

What does Satrapi mean when she says that "image is an international language"?

Build Background

Persepolis and *Persepolis 2* cover years of turmoil in twentieth-century Iran. Led by the Ayatollah Khomeini, the Islamic Revolution of 1978–1979 resulted in the exile of the shah, or ruler, of Iran in 1979. The shah, an oppressive, corrupt ruler, had modernized and westernized the country. Executing his opponents, Khomeini headed a repressive government guided by Islamic teachings that rejected the West. From 1980 to 1988, the country fought a brutal war against Iraq during which both sides used chemical weapons.

The selection that you are about to read is a portion of an interview about Satrapi's graphic novel, *Persepolis*.

Preview the Selection

In this interview, **Marjane Satrapi** discusses what can be gained if we take the time to understand other people.

INTERVIEW

Why I Wrote *Persepolis*

by **Marjane Satrapi**

Read with a Purpose
Read this interview to learn what one writer wanted to say about her nation.

From the time I came to France in 1994, I was always telling stories about life in Iran to my friends. We'd see pieces about Iran on television, but they didn't represent my experience at all. I had to keep saying, "No, it's not like that there." I've been justifying why it isn't negative to be Iranian for almost twenty years. How strange when it isn't something I did or chose to be?

After I finished university, there were nine of us, all artists and friends, working in a studio together. That group finally said, "Do something with your stories." They introduced me to graphic novelists. Spiegelman[1] was first. And when I read him, I thought, "It's possible to tell a story and make a point this way." It was amazing. **A**

Writing a Graphic Novel Is Like Making a Movie

People always ask me, "Why didn't you write a book?" But that's what *Persepolis* is. To me, a book is pages related to something that has a cover. Graphic novels are not traditional literature, but that does not mean they are second-rate. Images are a way of writing. When you have the talent to be able to write and to draw it seems a shame to choose one. I think it's better to do both.

We learn about the world through images all the time. In the cinema we do it, but to make a film you need sponsors and money and 10,000 people to work with you. With a graphic novel, all you need is yourself and your editor.

Of course, you have to have a very visual vision of the world. You have to perceive life with images; otherwise it doesn't work. Some artists are more into sound; they make music. The point is that you have to know what you want to say, and find the best way of saying it. It's hard to say how *Persepolis* evolved once I started writing. I had to learn how to write it as a graphic novel by doing.

1. **Spiegelman:** A highly influential graphic novelist, Art Spiegelman (1948–) won the Pulitzer Prize in 1992 for *Maus,* a Holocaust narrative in which the Jews are depicted as mice and the Nazis as cats.

A Reading Focus Questioning the Text What types of information is Satrapi presenting here: examples, anecdotes, or facts?

Vocabulary **justifying** (JUHS tuh fy ihng) *v.:* proving that something is correct or valid.
evolved (ee VAHLVD) *v.:* developed or changed gradually.

THINGS GOT WORSE FROM ONE DAY TO THE NEXT. IN SEPTEMBER 1980, MY PARENTS ABRUPTLY PLANNED A VACATION. I THINK THEY REALIZED THAT SOON SUCH THINGS WOULD NO LONGER BE POSSIBLE. AS IT HAPPENED, THEY WERE RIGHT. AND SO WE WENT TO ITALY AND SPAIN FOR THREE WEEKS...
...IT WAS WONDERFUL.

Analyzing Visuals **Viewing and Interpreting** What purpose do you think Satrapi is trying to achieve with this panel from *Persepolis*?

What I Wanted to Say

I'm a pacifist. I believe there are ways to solve the world's problems. Instead of putting all this money to create arms, I think countries should invest in scholarships for kids to study abroad. Perhaps they could become good and knowledgeable professors in their own countries. You need time for that kind of change, though.

I have been brought up open-minded. If I didn't know any people from other countries, I'd think everyone was evil based on news stories. But I know a lot of people, and know that there is no such thing as stark good and evil. Isn't it possible there is the same amount of evil everywhere?

If people are given the chance to experience life in more than one country, they will hate a little less. It's not a miracle potion, but little by little you can solve problems in the basement of a country, not on the surface. That is why I wanted people in other countries to read *Persepolis*, to see that I grew up just like other children.

It's so rewarding to see people at my book signings who never read graphic novels. They say that when they read mine they became more interested. If it opens these people's eyes not to believe what they hear, I feel successful. **B**

B **Reading Focus** **Questioning the Text** Which detail offers an opinion based on Satrapi's real-life experiences as a graphic novelist?

Vocabulary **pacifist** (PAS uh fihst) *n.:* person who believes that conflicts should be resolved by peaceful means and not by war or violence.
stark (stahrk) *adj.:* complete; absolute.

HISTORY LINK

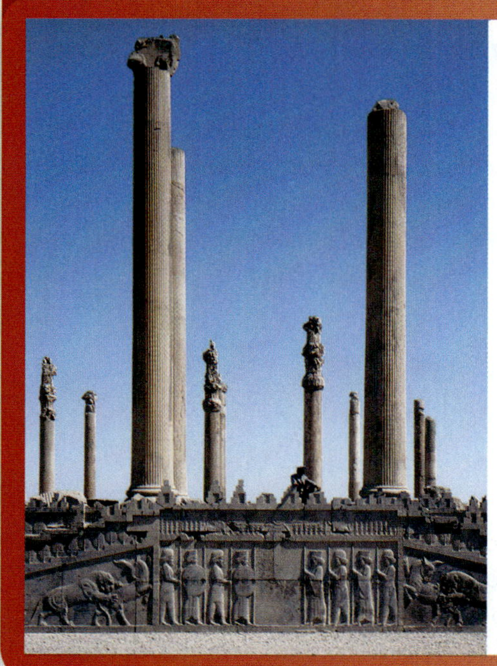

Persepolis

In a mountainous region of southwest Iran lie the ruins of Persepolis, the ancient capital of Persia (the former name of Iran). Walls, stairs, and enormous columns mark the spot where King Darius I built the city as the glorious, ceremonial capital of the Persian Empire in approximately 500 B.C. Receptions, festivals, and New Year's celebrations were held there, while other cities served as administrative centers. In 330 B.C., Alexander the Great, king of Macedonia, seized Persepolis, burning one of the palaces and looting the city. By naming her memoir *Persepolis*, Marjane Satrapi points to the thousands of years of history that preceded the political events she describes in her book.

Ask Yourself **Given the goals Satrapi describes in "Why I Wrote *Persepolis*," do you think *Persepolis* is an appropriate title for her book? Explain.**

Applying Your Skills

MO 9.R.1.H.1.d Apply post-reading skills to comprehend, interpret, analyze, and evaluate text: draw conclusions 9.R.3.C.1.a Use details from informational text: to identify and explain the organizational pattern 9.R.1.G.1.c During reading, utilize strategies: to question the text *Also covered* 9.W.3.A.1.a; 9.R.1.G.1.a

Why I Wrote *Persepolis*

Respond and Think Critically

Reading Focus

Quick Check

1. How did Satrapi first learn about graphic novels? What effect did that discovery have on her?
2. Why does Satrapi find book signings rewarding?

Read with a Purpose

3. Why does Satrapi want people to read her graphic novel *Persepolis*?

Reading Skills: Questioning the Text

4. Add a row to the chart you filled in as you read. In that row, provide your responses to the following questions: What did you learn about Satrapi from the information in the essay? What details did you want to learn more about?

Text Passage	What Kind of Statement Is This?
"From the time I came to France in 1994 . . ."	Anecdote—this is a detail from real life.

My Responses:

Vocabulary Check

justifying
evolved
pacifist
stark

Choose the Vocabulary word that *best* completes each sentence.

5. The _____ protested against the war.
6. Yesterday Jenny was _____ her decision to stop playing basketball, but today she showed up for the game.
7. He created _____ contrasts by using red and black paint.
8. The plans for the new park _____ over the year.

Literary Focus

Literary Analysis

9. **Identify** Whom does Satrapi cite as an inspiration in her career as a graphic novelist?
10. **Evaluate** Satrapi defines a book as "pages related to something that has a cover." Do you think this is a good definition? Explain.
11. **Evaluate** How does Satrapi think we can best solve the world's problems? Explain whether you think she presents an effective argument.

Literary Skills: Author's Purpose

12. **Analyze** Consider the title of the interview. What is Satrapi's primary purpose in this piece? What persuasive techniques does Satrapi use to achieve her purpose?

Literary Skills Review: Text Structures

13. **Analyze** In nonfiction, such as magazine articles and textbooks, information is often divided into sections, each introduced by a **subheading.** In this interview, what purpose does each subheading serve? Explain whether you think the subheadings are effective.

Writing Focus

Think as a Reader/Writer

Use It in Your Writing Satrapi has strong beliefs about what can be done to create tolerance between populations. Write an essay in which you explain your own ideas about how to promote tolerance. Like Satrapi, use a combination of questions and statements to help you explain your ideas. Be sure to address any arguments that counter yours.

Preparing to Read

Setting the Record Straight / Graphic Novels 101: FAQ

Literary Focus

Persuasion and Form When you want to persuade people, consider what form your **argument** will take. For example, an author might choose to write an essay, give an interview, deliver a speech, and so on. Choosing a form dictates how an argument will be delivered and what types of details might influence an audience's thinking. The persuasive works you are about to read are in the forms of a **graphic essay** and an **FAQ** (Frequently Asked Questions). As you read, look for ways these forms of persuasion deliver information.

TechFocus Keep track of questions as you read, and think about a topic to research and how you would post your findings online.

Reading Focus

Drawing Conclusions When you read persuasion, it's important to draw conclusions about the effectiveness of the argument. Take note of the details given by the author and of how they are presented.

Into Action As you read the two persuasive pieces that follow, note persuasive details that support the writers' arguments. Identify each type of detail (fact, opinion, illustration, quotation, or statistic).

Text Details from "Setting the Record Straight"	Type of Detail
"Comics is a vessel which can hold any number of ideas and images."	Fact

Writing Focus

Think as a Reader/Writer

Find It in Your Reading Comic book artists use many elements in their stories: words, illustrations, background, sound effects, and points of view. In your *Reader/Writer Notebook,* note the elements that McCloud uses in his graphic essay.

MO **9.R.3.C.1.c** Use details from informational text: to analyze and evaluate the accuracy and adequacy of evidence **9.R.1.H.1.d** Apply post-reading skills to comprehend, interpret, analyze, and evaluate text: draw conclusions

Reader/Writer Notebook

Use your **RWN** to complete the activities for the selections.

Vocabulary

Setting the Record Straight

encompass (ehn KUHM puhs) *v.:* include; contain. *According to McCloud, comics now encompass many genres.*

arbitrary (AHR buh trehr ee) *adj.:* based on one's preferences; capricious. *McCloud has to revise his definition of comics so it does not appear arbitrary.*

Graphic Novels 101: FAQ

tenuous (TEHN yoo uhs) *adj.:* slight; flimsy. *The evidence presented in the 1950s linking youth crimes to comics was tenuous.*

compelling (kuhm PEHL ihng) *adj.:* interesting; engaging. *A graphic novel can have just as compelling a story as a conventional book.*

Language Coach

Word Parts Two of the words on the list above contain *–com–*, a word part derived from Latin that means "together." Which words are they? Try to list at least three other words that use the word part *–com–*.

MEET THE WRITERS

Scott McCloud

(1960–)

A Comic Obsession

When Scott McCloud was given his first comic book at age fourteen, he reluctantly read it, thinking he was too old for comics. Soon he became obsessed with comics, and while he was in high school, he decided to become a comic book artist. McCloud realized in college that he would need to know more than just drawing in order to fulfill his dream. "I needed to be a writer, I needed to be a set designer, a costumer, an actor—I had to be all these things to make these stories come true," said McCloud.

After graduating from college, McCloud landed a production job at DC Comics in New York, one of the largest American publishers of comic books. He learned more about the business there and eventually left the company to work on his own comic series, titled *Zot!*

Robin Brenner

(1977–)

Late Bloomer

Robin Brenner is a writer and librarian for young adults for the Brookline Public Library in Massachusetts. Early in her career, she was asked to research graphic novels because the books were so popular that high school librarians couldn't keep them on the shelves. Once Brenner figured out how to read this new format, she was surprised that no one had ever told her about the art form before. The graphic novel format was a perfect fit for her interests as a young writer and artist. Now Brenner makes sure graphic novel information and recommendations are available to teens with her Web site *No Flying, No Tights.*

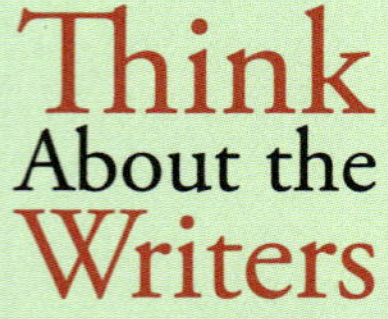

How does each of these writers share his or her passion for graphic novels with others?

Preview the Selections

In *Understanding Comics,* the book in which "Setting the Record Straight" first appeared, **Scott McCloud** uses visuals and words to teach about the comics art form.

Robin Brenner presents her ideas about the value of graphic stories and essays in "Graphic Novels 101: FAQ."

Build Background

As you read McCloud's graphic essay, you may encounter some unfamiliar terms that he uses in his discussion about graphic pieces. For example, *aesthetic* means "artistic," and *juxtaposed* means "placed side by side." Another term with which you may not be familiar is *static,* which means "not moving."

GRAPHIC ESSAY

Read with a Purpose

Read "Setting the Record Straight" and "Graphic Novels 101: FAQ" to find out what the writers think about comics and graphic novels.

Setting the Record Straight

by **Scott McCloud**

from Understanding Comics

A **Literary Focus** **Persuasion and Form** What first impression does this format—a graphic essay—create?

B **Reading Focus** **Drawing Conclusions** Look at the panels on this page. How does McCloud introduce himself to readers?

C

C Literary Focus Persuasion and Form Are the humorous details shown on this page in the middle panels what you might expect to see in this form of persuasion? Why or why not?

D E

D Literary Focus Persuasion and Form Where on this page does McCloud reveal his purpose for writing?

E Literary Focus Persuasion and Form How does this format enable McCloud to take us on a "journey"?

Vocabulary **encompass** (ehn KUHM puhs) *v.:* include; contain.

F

F **Literary Focus** **Persuasion and Form** In what way does this form allow McCloud to give the history of comics in a brief and interesting way?

THE ARTFORM--THE *MEDIUM*--KNOWN AS COMICS IS A *VESSEL* WHICH CAN HOLD ANY *NUMBER* OF *IDEAS* AND *IMAGES*.

COMICS
Writers
ARTISTS
Trends
GENRES
STYLES
Subject matter
THEMES

*EISNER'S OWN *COMICS AND SEQUENTIAL ART* BEING A HAPPY EXCEPTION.

G H

G Reading Focus Drawing Conclusions What type of information is given in the illustrations on this page?

H Reading Focus Drawing Conclusions According to the author, what do comics *rarely* receive? Do you agree with the author?

I

I **Literary Focus** **Persuasion and Form** Is dialogue typically found in persuasive essays and speeches? What purpose does dialogue serve here?

J **Reading Focus** **Drawing Conclusions** Look at the vertical sequence of images on the left and the border that McCloud uses. What point does this panel help McCloud make?

Vocabulary **arbitrary** (AHR buh trehr ee) *adj.:* based on one's preferences; capricious.

K **Literary Focus** **Persuasion and Form** What contrast between persuasive forms can be found on this page?

GRAPHIC NOVELS 101: FAQ

by **Robin Brenner**

Read with a Purpose

Read Brenner's FAQ to compare her ideas about graphic novels to the ideas of McCloud.

Preparing to Read for this selection is on page 563.

Build Background

Many instructional documents, magazines, and Web sites include FAQ sections. FAQ stands for Frequently Asked Questions; in this section, the most commonly asked questions about a subject are answered and posted. Reading an FAQ is a good place to start for an overview of a subject.

Q: What are some common misconceptions about graphic novels?

A: ***Comics and graphic novels are for kids.*** In reality, comics never were just for kids. Even in the 1940s–1950s Golden Age of superhero comics, there were crime, fantasy, and science fiction comics intended for teens and adults rather than children. However, due to the hullabaloo started by psychologist Fredric Wertham's *Seduction of the Innocent* (1954), which drew a tenuous connection between juvenile delinquency and comics, comics' content became watered down. Many adults are still under the impression that the format automatically means juvenile content—but as the average age of a comics reader is thirty, this is certainly not true.

Graphic novels are all full of violence. An almost opposite tack to the idea that graphic novels are for kids, many adults fear that they are full of violence. Like many previous formats, graphic novels are painted with the extremes of what's available. There are comics with R- or X-rated content, but they are not the bulk of what's available, nor are those titles intended for younger audiences. (A)

Comics and graphic novels are only superheroes. Yes, superheroes are still the bread and butter of the big companies, but genre diversity is increasing every day with more and more independent companies publishing a range of genres, from memoir to fantasy to historical fiction. This is partly what has allowed graphic novels to truly break into the book market. On the other hand, this distinction could also lead to the mistaken conclusion that there is nothing of value in superhero comics. A few years ago, many dismissed fantasy as a lesser genre, but the success and popularity of *Harry Potter* has reminded the reading public that genre does not define quality.

Graphic novels are for reluctant readers. One of the biggest benefits of graphic novels is that they often attract kids who are considered "reluctant" readers. This is not just hype—the combination of less text, narrative support from images, and a feeling of reading outside the expected canon[1] often relieves the tension of reading expectations for kids who are not natural readers, and lets them learn to be confident and engaged consumers of great

1. **canon:** works of literature that are considered to be essential reading.

(A) Literary Focus **Persuasion and Form** Scan this page and look at the format. Where is each question or issue presented? Where does the writer present her arguments and support them?

Vocabulary **tenuous** (TEHN yoo uhs) *adj.:* slight; flimsy.

stories. That being said, graphic novels are not *only* for reluctant readers—they're for everyone! It's a disservice to the format to dismiss it as only for those who don't read otherwise, and relegating graphic novels to a lower rung of the reading scale is not only snobbish, but wrong. **B**

Graphic novels aren't "real" books. This one's a zinger and contains a bit of truth and a lot of prejudice. The key to categorizing graphic novels is to remember that they're a format, akin to audiobooks, videos, and television, all media that have struggled for acceptance. Graphic novels are not and were never intended to be a replacement for prose. Sequential art is just another way to tell a story, with different demands on the reader. So, yes, graphic novels don't work exactly the same way that traditional novels do, but they can be as demanding, creative, intelligent, compelling, and full of story as any book.

Q Why should kids read comics and graphic novels?

A Graphic novels are simply another way to get a story. They represent an *alternative* to other formats, not a replacement. They are as varied as any other medium and have their fair share of every kind of title, from fluff to literary masterpieces. What

B **Reading Focus** **Drawing Conclusions** Here the author gives information on reluctant readers. What audience does she appear to be addressing? Explain.

Vocabulary **compelling** (kuhm PEHL ihng) *adj.:* interesting; engaging.

Jai Nitz, a comic book creator from Lawrence, Kansas, browses through the comic book *The Wretch* at his local comics shop.

they always involve, though, is reading—just as books, from Newbery winners to the latest installment in the Animorphs series, do. Stephen Krashen, who examines voluntary reading in his book *The Power of Reading,* discovered that comics are an unrecognized influence on reading. He found that not only were kids more likely to pick up comics voluntarily, but the average comic book has twice the vocabulary as the average children's book and three times the vocabulary of a conversation between an adult and child. And the very fact that a child chooses to read them gives them a greater impact on that child's confidence in reading.

Not only do graphic novels entail reading in the traditional sense, they also require reading in a new way. To read a comic requires an active participation in the text that is quite different from reading prose: the reader must make the connections between the images and the text and create the links between each panel and the page as a whole. This is generally referred to as "reading between the panels," and this kind of literacy is not only new but vital in interacting with and succeeding in our multimedia world. If you've ever struggled to make the connections in reading a graphic novel while a teen reader whizzes through it, you've experienced how different this type of literacy is. **C**

C Reading Focus **Drawing Conclusions**
What types of evidence does Brenner include in her answer?

Applying Your Skills

9.R.3.C.1.c Use details from informational text: to analyze and evaluate the accuracy and adequacy of evidence 9.R.1.H.1.d Apply post-reading skills to comprehend, interpret, analyze, and evaluate text: draw conclusions 9.W.3.A.1.a Compose a variety of texts: using narrative, descriptive, expository, and/or persuasive features *Also covered* 9.R.1.G.1.a

Setting the Record Straight / Graphic Novels 101: FAQ

Respond and Think Critically

Reading Focus

Quick Check

1. When McCloud was a "little kid," what did he think comics were? What does he say comics are now?
2. According to "Graphic Novels 101: FAQ," why did comics get a bad reputation in the 1950s?

Read with a Purpose

3. What idea about graphic stories do the authors share?

Reading Skills: Drawing Conclusions

4. Review the information you recorded on your chart. Then, add a row and state your conclusion about how the form of each piece—graphic essay or FAQ—governs the shape and tone of its argument. Use your conclusions to help you answer questions 11 and 12.

Text Details from "Setting the . . ."	Type of Detail	My Conclusions About Form
"Comics is a vessel which can hold any number of ideas and images."	Fact	

Vocabulary Check

Match each boldface Vocabulary word with the correct definition.

5. **arbitrary** a. contain
6. **compelling** b. interesting
7. **tenuous** c. capricious
8. **encompass** d. flimsy

Literary Focus

Literary Analysis

9. **Interpret** According to McCloud, what kinds of ideas and images can be found in comics? (Hint: Look at the full pitcher on page 569.)
10. **Compare and Contrast** Both McCloud and Brenner say that comics are about more than just superheroes. How does each writer convey this message a different way?

Literary Skills: Persuasion and Form

11. **Analyze** What main idea does McCloud want you to understand? Why do you think he chose to present his ideas in a graphic-essay format?
12. **Identify** Where does Brenner present opposing arguments in "Graphic Novels 101: FAQ"? Is the format that she uses effective? Explain why or why not.

Literary Skills Review: Style

13. **Analyze** An author's **style** is created by his or her distinctive use of words and—in the case of graphic stories—images. How are McCloud's and Brenner's styles similar and different?

Writing Focus

Think as a Reader/Writer

Use It in Your Writing McCloud juggles many elements—dialogue, main illustration, point of view, sound effects, and background—to create just one panel. Use the graphic story format and some of the elements McCloud uses to create your own story.

COMPARING TEXTS
Wrap Up

9.W.3.A.1.a Compose a variety of texts: using narrative, descriptive, expository, and/or persuasive features

Why I Wrote *Persepolis* / Setting the Record Straight / Graphic Novels 101: FAQ

Writing Focus

Comparison-Contrast Essay

The three pieces in this section all deal with the topic of graphic stories, but the writers present their arguments in different forms. Write a comparison-contrast essay in which you analyze the authors' arguments and discuss their persuasiveness. Consider how the form of each piece helped the writers express their views.

Prewriting Review the selections and your notes about the details used to present each argument. Then, choose an overall structure for your essay.

Point-by-Point Organization	Block Organization
Point 1	Selection A
Selections A, B, and C	Points 1 & 2
Point 2	Selection B
Selections A, B, and C	Points 1 & 2
	Selection C
	Points 1 & 2

Drafting Write a draft of your essay. Begin with your thesis statement, and then develop your ideas in the body paragraphs.

Revising Re-read your essay, adding important details and deleting unimportant ones. Add transitional words to help readers follow your ideas.

Proofread and Publish Re-read your draft and correct errors in spelling, grammar, and punctuation.

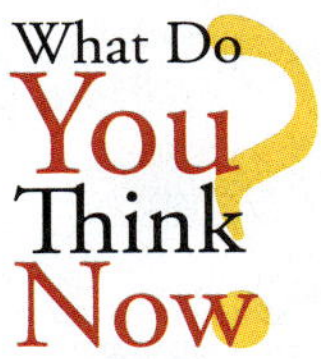

How might you use an image to persuade a person?

CHOICES

As you respond to the Choices, use these **Academic Vocabulary** words as appropriate: influence, counter, valid, verify.

REVIEW

Analyze Persuasive Forms

Think of an argument you might develop—for example, why comics are better than books. Then explore what form (essay, graphic story, ad, speech, and so on) your argument might take. Write down your ideas about what goal each form might help you accomplish. You may want to use a chart like this to explore your ideas:

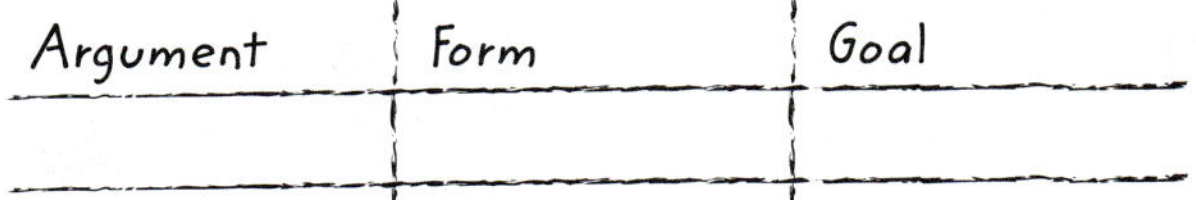

CONNECT

Write an Essay

Timed Writing Choose a controversial issue about which you have strong opinions. Write a three-paragraph persuasive essay in which you present the issue and your ideas about it. Support your argument where appropriate with anecdotes, facts, examples, and quotations.

EXTEND

Conduct Research

TechFocus Now that you have read these pieces, what would you like to learn more about? With a partner, select a narrow topic to research, such as the history of graphic stories or how to illustrate a comic. Use Internet or library resources to research your topic, making sure you verify each source you use. Then, use words and images to present your findings in an online post.

INFORMATIONAL TEXT FOCUS

Evaluating Arguments

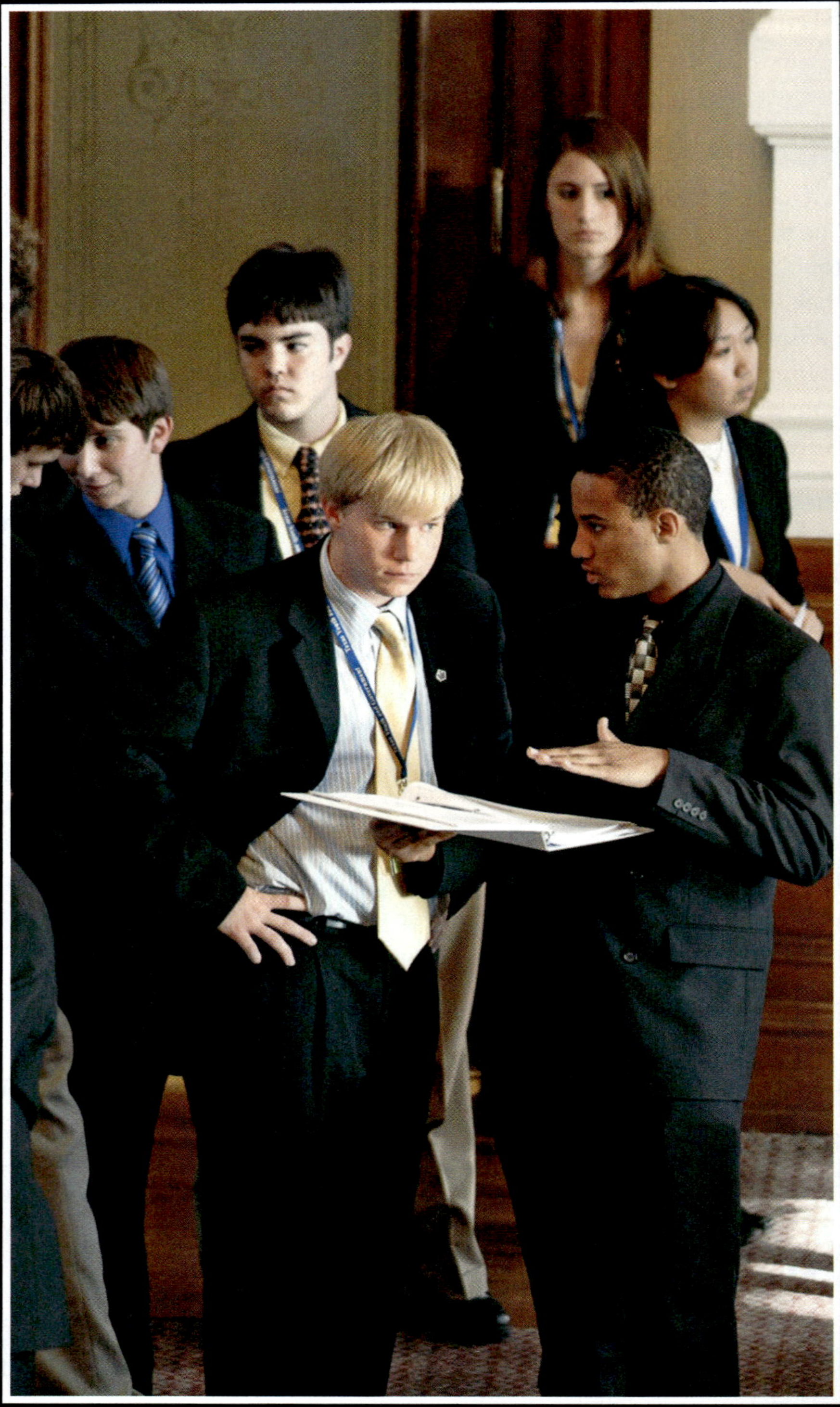

CONTENTS

How do you decide which side to take on an issue?

QuickTalk

Have you ever had to decide whether or not someone was telling the truth? What clues helped you decide? Share your experiences with a small group of classmates.

Texas high school students participate in YMCA Youth in Government sessions in the Texas House where they learn to draft, refine, and debate legislation with peers from around the state.

BLOG & WEB ARTICLE

Preparing to Read

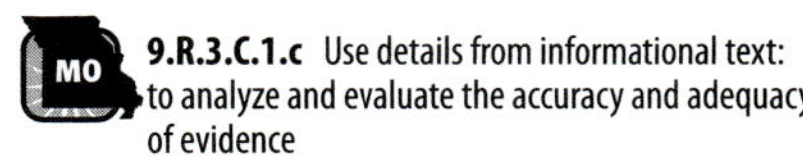

9.R.3.C.1.c Use details from informational text: to analyze and evaluate the accuracy and adequacy of evidence

Kaavya Viswanathan: Unconscious Copycat or Plagiarist? / Kaavya Syndrome

Informational Text Focus

Evaluating Arguments When presented with opposing views on an issue, how do you decide which to agree with? To evaluate **pro and con arguments,** considering the following questions:

1. **What is the claim, and how is it supported?** Check that facts, statistics, examples, and quotes from experts have been used.
2. **Is the argument logical?** Check that the author's reasons make sense and are relevant. Look for **logical fallacies,** errors in logical thinking, which fall into the following categories:
    - **Circular reasoning.** Making statements that look like reasons or conclusions but simply restate the author's opinion.
    - **False cause and effect.** Stating that one event caused another when the two events are not truly related.
    - **Hasty generalizations.** Presenting broad statements as facts when they are actually based on only one or two cases.
    - **Personal attacks.** Focusing on an opponent's character or judgment rather than the issue.
3. **How comprehensive is the support?** Check that the writer provides reasons and sufficient evidence to support generalizations, and evaluate how well the writer deals with opposing evidence.

Into Action Use the chart below to record information from the blog and Web article to help you evaluate each author's argument.

	Blog	Web Article
Claim and Support		
Logic of Argument		
Comprehensiveness		

Writing Focus

Preparing for **Constructed Response**

As you read, keep track of the details you find most persuasive in your *Reader/Writer Notebook.*

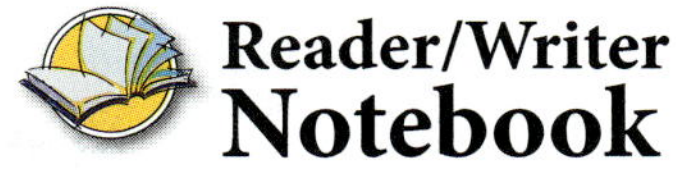

Reader/Writer Notebook

Use your **RWN** to complete the activities for these selections.

Vocabulary

Kaavya Viswanathan: Unconscious Copycat or Plagiarist?

internalized (ihn TUR nuh lyzd) *v.:* adopted as one's own. *Kaavya internalized the writer's words and made them her own.*

Kaavya Syndrome

perseverance (pur suh VIHR uhns) *n.:* sticking to a purpose; never giving up. *The scholar exhibited great perseverance in committing every page of the book to memory.*

inadvertent (ihn ad VUR tuhnt) *adj.:* unintentional, accidental; not done on purpose. *Kaavya claimed her actions were inadvertent because she did not realize she was copying someone else's words.*

Language Coach

Word Parts Look carefully at the list of Vocabulary words. Do you recognize any word parts? Write the list of words in your *Reader/Writer Notebook,* and circle the word parts. How do those word parts help you understand the meanings of the words?

Learn It Online

Practice evaluating arguments with the interactive Reading Workshop online:

go.hrw.com L9-579 

BLOG

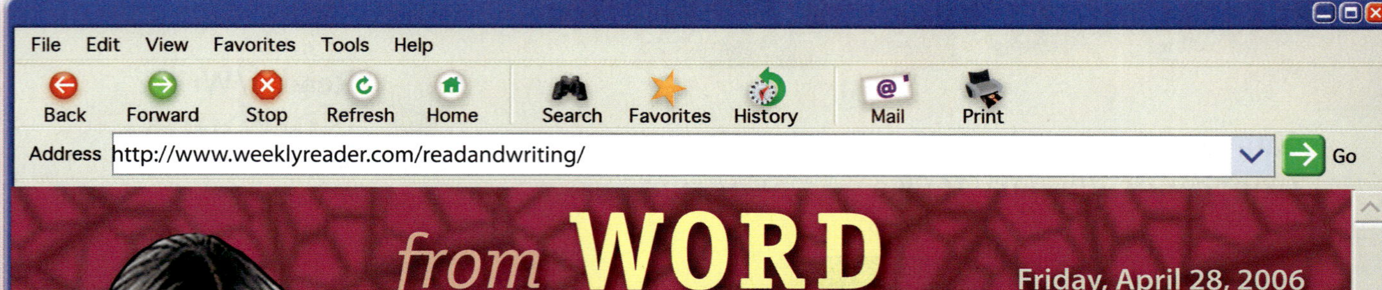

Caricature of Sandhya Nankani.

Kaavya Viswanathan: Unconscious Copycat or Plagiarist?

by Sandhya Nankani

Plagiarism is no laughing matter. If you are found guilty of doing it, you can fail a class or be expelled from school. In the real world, the penalties are much stiffer. In 2003, a 27-year-old *New York Times* reporter, Jayson Blair, lost his job after he admitted to copying other journalists' writing and faking reports. **A**

In 2006, the person in the spotlight was Kaavya Viswanathan.

The Harvard student was given a $500,000 advance by the publishing giant Little, Brown to write a novel about an overachieving high school senior's attempts to get popular and gain admission to Harvard University. The book: *How Opal Mehta Got Kissed, Got Wild, and Got a Life.*

In February, I read an advance copy of the book with much interest. It's not every day that a new "young literary genius" is discovered and publicized by a major publishing company. Kaavya was 17 when she got her book deal; she was the youngest author signed by Little, Brown in decades.

My friend and colleague Pooja read *How Opal Mehta* . . . too. The following week, we got together for lunch and talked about it, dissecting it bit by bit. Literary tastes aside (there were a few things about the book that bothered us), we decided that any 19-year-old who could write a 250+ page novel deserved to be credited for her accomplishments. After reaching this conclusion, we sat back and waited for the book to come out—we were curious to know what others would think, whether our concerns would be mirrored by critics and readers, and whether the book would be as big a hit as the publisher had hoped for. **B**

Read with a Purpose

Read the following pro and con arguments to help you decide if Kaavya Viswanathan, a Harvard student, intentionally plagiarized another writer's work.

Build Background

The first selection you are about to read is from a blog, an online journal. In addition to teaching, its writer, Sandhya Nankani, has written for WORD, *Weekly Reader*'s literary blog. The second selection is by Joshua Foer, a freelance writer who specializes in science writing.

A **Informational Focus** **Evaluating Arguments** What claim about plagiarism does the writer make? What example does she provide to support her assertion?

B **Informational Focus** **Evaluating Arguments** For what purpose does the writer offer her first impressions of Viswanathan?

On April 1, Kaavya Viswanathan's much-anticipated book came to life in bookstores. A flurry of reviews followed in all major newspapers and literary outfits. Then, things took an unexpected turn. The downward spiral began.

Neither Pooja nor I had expected this.

Last Sunday, the *Harvard Crimson* newspaper published a story alleging that Kaavya had plagiarized over 40 sections from two young adult novels by Megan McCafferty, *Sloppy Firsts* and *Second Helpings*.

In an email she sent on Monday, Kaavya said that she had "internalized" McCafferty's work without realizing. That is, she had been such a fan of McCafferty's books since high school and had read them 3 or 4 times and had copied her style without realizing. "Any phrasing similarities between her works and mine," Kaavya wrote, "were completely unintentional and unconscious."

Many were not convinced. . . .

I read one document at Publisher's Weekly that cited 49 different examples. Some seemed a stretch and others were pretty compelling. . . . C

The plot thickens.

Tuesday: Kaavya's publisher issued a statement saying that they would reprint the book with revisions and an acknowledgement to McCafferty.

Wednesday: Kaavya appeared on NBC's *Today* Show. "When I was writing, I genuinely believed each word was my own," she said.

Later Wednesday: At an interview at her publisher's office, she also added that some of the plagiarism may have happened because she "had a photographic memory." She also admitted that she had help developing the plot from 17th Street Media Productions, a "book packager."

Thursday: Publisher Little, Brown essentially pulled the book off the shelves. They "sent a notice to retail and wholesale accounts asking them to stop selling copies of the book and to return unsold inventory to the publisher for full credit," said Michael Pietsch, senior vice president and publisher of Little, Brown.

Is this the end of Kaavya's story? Has she had her 15 minutes of fame, and will everyone forget about her by next Friday at this time? I'm not sure.

This controversy does not seem so black and white to me. Is Kaavya an intentional plagiarist or an unconscious copycat? What role did her editor(s) and the marketing company play in this story? And if she did sit down and cut and paste the alleged 49 sections, did she think it was OK because she was paraphrasing—*i.e.,* rewriting another writer's words in her own words and changing the nouns, names, places, and things around?

C **Informational Focus** **Evaluating Arguments** What evidence supports the claim that Viswanathan plagiarized another writer's work?

Vocabulary **internalized** (ihn TUR nuh lyzd) *v.:* adopted as one's own.

As writers—whether we are writing for fun, for school, or for money—we all bear a mighty responsibility to our readers and to ourselves. That responsibility is to select each word we use with precision and to do our utmost best to offer original thoughts and words to the world. **D**

That task is not always easy—and in this respect, I empathize with Kaavya. There have been many occasions when I have written something and thought, "Hmmm, that sounds familiar. Did someone else say that?" As a writer, I need to be responsible for looking it up, investigating, poking around to see whether that is the case. If I find that yes, my words do sound a great deal like someone else's, I need to go back and delete and rewrite.

Of course, there are some things that there just aren't too many ways of saying:

> Her name was Lucy. She lived in a house
>
> She was named Lucy. In a house she lived.
>
> Lucy was her name. She resided in a house.

If you rewrite something like that or state a fact that's widely known—"There are 12 months in a year"—that's not plagiarism. Plagiarism is copying someone else's writing without noting the source. That's very different from being inspired by another writer and learning from his or her style. **E**

You see why this is so complicated? I'm still trying to wrap my brain around it. What I think we should take away from this is not a sense of glee ("Aha! Kaavya got caught. Serves her right!" I've been hearing a lot of that out there.) Rather, we should step away from this situation and use Kaavya's experience to remind us of the importance of consciously choosing our words. We should use it to remind ourselves that when it comes to writing, there's nothing better than writing in our own voices. **F**

At the end of the day, when Kaavya's book has disappeared from bookshelves and her life has returned to a sense of normalcy, I hope that she will pick up a pen again and ask herself: What is my original writing voice? I wish her good luck in finding it. From what I've seen so far, it is a voice that glimmers with wit.

D **Informational Focus** **Evaluating Arguments** In this portion of the blog, what new idea is the writer presenting? Is her idea a fact or an opinion? How can you tell?

E **Informational Focus** **Evaluating Arguments** Do you find this type of evidence convincing? Why or why not?

F **Informational Focus** **Evaluating Arguments** What final idea does the writer present? Has her overall argument been logical and comprehensive? Explain.

Internet

WEB ARTICLE

Kaavya Syndrome

by **Joshua Foer**

April 27, 2006

Kaavya Viswanathan has an excuse. In this morning's *New York Times*, the author of *How Opal Mehta Got Kissed, Got Wild, and Got a Life* explained how she "unintentionally and unconsciously" plagiarized upward of 29 passages from the books of another young-adult novelist, Megan McCafferty. Viswanathan said she has a photographic memory. "I never take notes."

Kaavya Viswanathan.

This seems like as good an opportunity as any to clear up the greatest enduring myth about human memory. Lots of people claim to have a photographic memory, but nobody actually does. Nobody. **A**

Well, maybe one person.

In 1970, a Harvard vision scientist named Charles Stromeyer III published a landmark paper in *Nature* about a Harvard student named Elizabeth, who could perform an astonishing feat. Stromeyer showed Elizabeth's right eye a pattern of 10,000 random dots, and a day later, he showed her left eye another dot pattern. She mentally fused the two images to form a random-dot stereogram and then saw a three-dimensional image floating above the surface. Elizabeth seemed to offer the first conclusive proof that photographic memory is possible. But then in a soap-opera twist, Stromeyer married her, and she was never tested again.

In 1979, a researcher named John Merritt published the results of a photographic memory test he had placed in magazines and newspapers around the country. Merritt hoped someone might come forward with abilities similar to Elizabeth's, and he figures that roughly 1 million people tried their hand at the test. Of that

A **Informational Focus** **Evaluating Arguments** What claim has the author made in this passage?

number, 30 wrote in with the right answer, and he visited 15 of them at their homes. However, with the scientist looking over their shoulders, not one of them could pull off Elizabeth's trick. **B**

There are so many unlikely circumstances surrounding the Elizabeth case—the marriage between subject and scientist, the lack of further testing, the inability to find anyone else with her abilities—that some psychologists have concluded that there's something fishy about Stromeyer's findings. He denies it. "We don't have any doubt about our data," he told me recently. Still, his one-woman study, he says, "is not strong evidence for other people having photographic memory."

That's not to say there aren't people with extraordinarily good memories—there are. They just can't take mental snapshots and recall them with perfect fidelity. Kim Peek, the 53-year-old savant[1] who was the basis for Dustin Hoffman's character in *Rain Man,* is said to have memorized every page of the 9,000-plus books he has read at 8 to 12 seconds per page (each eye reads its own page independently), though that claim has never been rigorously tested. Another savant, Stephen Wiltshire, has been called the "human camera" for his ability to create sketches of a scene after looking at it for just a few seconds. But even he doesn't have a truly photographic memory. His mind doesn't work like a Xerox. He takes liberties. . . .

In every case except Elizabeth's where someone has claimed to possess a photographic memory, there has always been another explanation. A group of Talmudic scholars[2] known as the Shass Pollaks supposedly stored mental snapshots of all 5,422 pages of the Babylonian Talmud. According to a paper published in 1917 in the journal *Psychological Review,* psychologist George Stratton tested the Shass Pollaks by sticking a pin through various tractates of the Talmud. They responded by telling him exactly which words the pin passed through on every page. In fact, the Shass Pollaks probably didn't possess photographic memory so much as heroic perseverance. If the average person decided he was going to dedicate his entire life to memorizing 5,422 pages of text, he'd probably also be pretty good at it. It's an impressive feat of single-mindedness, not of memory.

Truman Capote famously claimed to have nearly absolute recall of dialogue and used his prodigious memory as an excuse never to take notes or use a tape

---

1. **savant** (suh VAHNT): person with a mental disability who displays exceptional skill in a specialized field.
2. **Talmudic** (tahl MUD ihk) **scholars:** people who study the Talmud, a collection of writings on Jewish civil and religious law.

B **Informational Focus** **Evaluating Arguments** What evidence does the author give to support his claim? What effect does the use of the word *trick* to describe Elizabeth's accomplishments create?

Vocabulary **perseverance** (pur suh VIHR uhns) *n.:* sticking to a purpose; never giving up.

RELATED
The image at right is an MRI scan of the human brain.

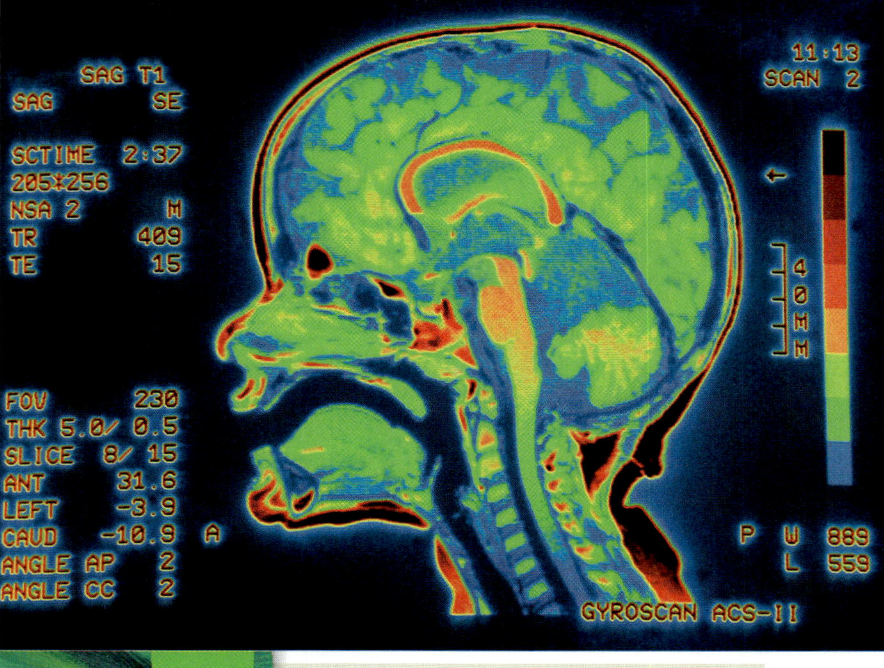

Analyzing Visuals **Viewing and Interpreting** How might scientists today utilize technology to help them better understand people like Elizabeth?

recorder, but I suspect his memory claims were just a useful cover to invent dialogue whole cloth. Not even S, the Russian journalist and professional mnemonist[3] who was studied for three decades by psychologist A. R. Luria, had a photographic memory. Rather, he seemed to have implicitly mastered a set of mnemonic[4] techniques that allowed him to memorize certain kinds of information. C

Viswanathan is hardly the first plagiarist to claim unconscious influence from memory's depths. George Harrison said he never intended to rip off the melody of the Chiffons' "He's So Fine" when he wrote "My Sweet Lord." He had just forgotten he'd ever heard it. And when a young Helen Keller cribbed from Margaret Canby's "The Frost Fairies" in her story "The Frost King," Canby herself said, "Under the circumstances, I do not see how any one can be so unkind as to call it a plagiarism; it is a wonderful feat of memory." Keller claimed she was forever after terrified. "I have ever since been tortured by the fear that what I write is not my own. For a long time, when I wrote a letter, even to my mother, I was seized with a sudden feeling, and I would spell the sentences over and over,

3. **mnemonist** (nih MAHN ihst): someone who is able to recall large amounts of information.
4. **mnemonic** (nih MAHN ihk): aiding or intended to aid the memory.

C **Informational Focus** **Evaluating Arguments** How does the writer explain opposing arguments about photographic memories?

to make sure that I had not read them in a book," she wrote. "It is certain that I cannot always distinguish my own thoughts from those I read, because what I read becomes the very substance and texture of my mind."

Psychologists label this kind of inadvertent appropriation cryptomnesia, and have captured the phenomenon in the laboratory. In one study, researchers had subjects play Boggle against a computer and then afterward try to recreate a list of the words they themselves found. Far more often then expected, the researchers found that their subjects would claim words found by the computer opponent as their own. Even if cryptomnesia is a real memory glitch that happens to all of us from time to time, however, it's hard to figure how it could lead to the involuntary swiping of 29 different passages. D

Then again, who knows, maybe Viswanathan really does have a photographic memory. She could be the first (or second). Earlier this year, a group of memory researchers at the University of California-Irvine published an astonishing article about a woman called AJ who can apparently remember every day of her life since childhood. Such people weren't supposed to exist. Her case totally upends everything we thought we knew about the limits of human memory. The scientists even had to coin a new name for her disorder, hyperthymestic syndrome. If Viswanathan really wants to stick to her story, I know a few scientists who'd probably like to meet her. She might even be able to get a syndrome named after her. E

Read with a Purpose What is your verdict? Did Viswanathan intentionally plagiarize another writer's work? Why do you think as you do?

D **Informational Focus** **Evaluating Arguments** Given the evidence about cryptomnesia, do you find the writer's conclusions about Viswanathan convincing? Why or why not?

E **Informational Focus** **Evaluating Arguments** Does the writer's tone, or attitude toward his subject, strengthen or weaken his argument? Explain.

Vocabulary **inadvertent** (ihn uhd VUR tuhnt) *adj.:* unintentional; accidental; not done on purpose.

Internet

BLOG & WEB ARTICLE
Applying Your Skills

MO 9.R.3.C.1.c Use details from informational text: to analyze and evaluate the accuracy and adequacy of evidence 9.R.1.G.1.a During reading, utilize strategies: to determine meaning of unknown words

Kaavya Viswanathan: Unconscious Copycat or Plagiarist? / Kaavya Syndrome

Practicing the Standards

Informational Text and Vocabulary

1. The two writers have opposing views about —
   - **A** the seriousness of plagiarism
   - **B** whether a person can unintentionally plagiarize another's work
   - **C** young writers' ability to publish original works
   - **D** the fairness of plagiarism codes

2. Most of Nankani's **argument** is supported by —
   - **A** examples and anecdotes
   - **B** expert quotations
   - **C** statistics
   - **D** scientific studies

3. Foer addresses an opposing **argument** by —
   - **A** attacking the people making it
   - **B** using circular reasoning
   - **C** providing expert testimony
   - **D** providing real-life examples and scientific data

4. Which statement *most* accurately describes a key difference between the two pieces?
   - **A** Nankani provides mostly statistics, and Foer provides mostly examples.
   - **B** Nankani condemns Viswanathan's actions, and Foer defends them.
   - **C** Nankani provides mostly anecdotes and opinions, and Foer provides mostly facts.
   - **D** Foer provides quotations from Viswanathan herself, and Nankani does not.

5. What definition below best defines the word *internalized?*
   - **A** Hidden
   - **B** Made evident
   - **C** Made one's own
   - **D** Consumed

6. Something that is *inadvertent* happens —
   - **A** by accident
   - **B** quickly
   - **C** deliberately
   - **D** once a year

7. Which is the best antonym for *perseverance*?
   - **A** Sloppiness
   - **B** Indecisiveness
   - **C** Brightness
   - **D** Operation

Writing Focus — Constructed Response

Whose argument, Nankani's or Foer's, did you find more effective? List at least three reasons for your choice. Be careful to cite specific passages from the texts to support your ideas.

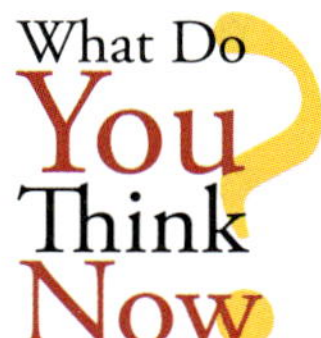

What do you think about the Kaavya Viswanathan case? Is it possible for both Nankani's and Foer's arguments to be valid? Explain.

Literary Skills Review

Persuasion **Directions:** Read the following essay. Then, read and respond to the questions that follow.

Homeless by **Anna Quindlen**

Her name was Ann, and we met in the Port Authority Bus Terminal several Januaries ago. I was doing a story on homeless people. She said I was wasting my time talking to her; she was just passing through, although she'd been passing through for more than two weeks. To prove to me that this was true, she rummaged through a tote bag and a manila envelope and finally unfolded a sheet of typing paper and brought out her photographs.

They were not pictures of family, or friends, or even a dog or cat, its eyes brown-red in the flashbulb's light. They were pictures of a house. It was like a thousand houses in a hundred towns, not suburb, not city, but somewhere in between, with aluminum siding and a chain-link fence, a narrow driveway running up to a one-car garage, and a patch of back yard. The house was yellow. I looked on the back for a date or a name, but neither was there. There was no need for discussion. I knew what she was trying to tell me, for it was something I had often felt. She was not adrift, alone, anonymous, although her bags and her raincoat with the grime shadowing its creases had made me believe she was. She had a house, or at least once upon a time had had one. Inside were curtains, a couch, a stove, potholders. You are where you live. She was somebody.

I've never been very good at looking at the big picture, taking the global view, and I've always been a person with an overactive sense of place, the legacy of an Irish grandfather. So it is natural that the thing that seems most wrong with the world to me right now is that there are so many people with no homes. I'm not simply talking about shelter from the elements or three square meals a day or a mailing address to which the welfare people can send the check—although I know that all these are important for survival. I'm talking about a home, about precisely those kinds of feelings that have wound up in cross-stitch and French knots on samplers[1] over the years.

Home is where the heart is. There's no place like it. I love my home with a ferocity[2] totally out of proportion to its appearance or location. I love dumb things about it: the hot-water heater, the plastic rack you drain dishes in, the roof over my head, which occasionally leaks. And yet it is precisely those dumb things that make it what it is—a place of certainty, stability, predictability, privacy, for me and for my family. It is where I live. What more can you say about a place than that? That is everything.

1. **cross-stitch and French knots on samplers:** decorative designs embroidered on cloth with sayings like "Home Sweet Home."
2. **ferocity:** extreme intensity.

9.R.3.C.1.c Use details from informational text: to analyze and evaluate the accuracy and adequacy of evidence

Yet it is something that we have been edging away from gradually during my lifetime and the lifetimes of my parents and grandparents. There was a time when where you lived often was where you worked and where you grew the food you ate and even where you were buried. When that era passed, where you lived at least was where your parents had lived and where you would live with your children when you became enfeebled.[3] Then, suddenly, where you lived was where you lived for three years, until you could move on to something else and something else again.

And so we have come to something else again, to children who do not understand what it means to go to their rooms because they have never had a room, to men and women whose fantasy is a wall they can paint a color of their own choosing, to old people reduced to sitting on molded-plastic chairs, their skin blue-white in the lights of a bus station, who pull pictures of houses out of their bags. Homes have stopped being homes. Now they are real estate.

People find it curious that those without homes would rather sleep sitting up on benches or huddled in doorways than go to shelters. Certainly some prefer to do so because they are emotionally ill, because they have been locked in before and they are damned if they will be locked in again. Others are afraid of the violence and trouble they may find there. But some seem to want something that is not available in shelters, and they will not compromise, not for a cot, or oatmeal, or a shower with special soap that kills the bugs. "One room," a woman with a baby who was sleeping on her sister's floor once told me, "painted blue." That was the crux[4] of it: not size or location, but pride of ownership. Painted blue.

This is a difficult problem, and some wise and compassionate people are working hard at it. But in the main I think we work around it, just as we walk around it when it is lying on the sidewalk or sitting in the bus terminal—the problem, that is. It has been customary to take people's pain and lessen our own participation in it by turning it into an issue, not a collection of human beings. We turn an adjective into a noun: the poor, not poor people; the homeless, not Ann or the man who lives in the box or the woman who sleeps on the subway grate.

Sometimes I think we would be better off if we forgot about the broad strokes and concentrated on the details. Here is a woman without a bureau. There is a man with no mirror, no wall to hang it on. They are not the homeless. They are people who have no homes. No drawer that holds the spoons. No window to look out upon the world. My God. That is everything.

3. **enfeebled:** weakened, usually by old age or illness.

4. **crux:** basic or deciding point.

Literary Skills Review CONTINUED

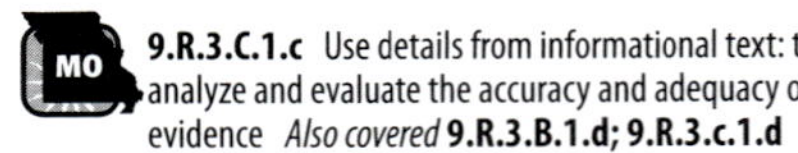

9.R.3.C.1.c Use details from informational text: to analyze and evaluate the accuracy and adequacy of evidence *Also covered* **9.R.3.B.1.d; 9.R.3.c.1.d**

1. Quindlen's **purpose** for writing is to —

A convince others that a sense of home is important

B offer alternatives to homelessness

C tell Ann's story

D demand homes for everyone

9.R.3.C.1.d

2. What type of **evidence** does Quindlen use to support her argument?

A Statistics

B Examples

C Scientific experiments

D Expert opinions

9.R.3.C.1.c

3. Which of the following ideas from the essay is an **emotional appeal**?

A Homes are nothing more than real estate.

B Ann had no family photos.

C Quindlen has a strong sense of place.

D Everyone needs one room to call their own.

9.R.3.C.1.c

4. Which of the following ideas from the essay is a **logical appeal**?

A "Home is where the heart is."

B Home is something different for everyone.

C Home offers a sense of stability that should be afforded to everyone.

D Home is no longer a fixed place.

9.R.3.C.1.c

5. Quindlen's argument would have more **credibility** if she —

A made judgments

B offered opinions

C provided historical context

D added statistics

9.R.3.C.1.c

6. Which of the following ideas revealed in the essay is a **fact**?

A What makes a person is where he or she lives.

B Shelters can be violent places.

C Ann intends to return home.

D A home is everything.

9.R.3.C.1.c

7. Which of the following statements from the essay is an **opinion**?

A "You are where you live."

B Ann was just "passing through."

C A woman wants one room "painted blue."

D Quindlen's roof leaks occasionally.

9.R.3.C.1.c

8. What would you say is the **tone** of Quindlen's argument?

A Mocking

B Preaching

C Scolding

D Earnest

9.R.3.B.1.d

Constructed Response

9. What persuasive techniques does Quindlen use to try to convince you of her views? Do you think her essay would be more persuasive if she presented her ideas in a different way? Explain.

9.R.3.C.1.c

FOCUS ON MISSOURI COURSE LEVEL EXPECTATIONS

Informational Skills Review

Argument **Directions:** Read the following selection. Then, read and respond to the questions that follow.

Jackie Robinson by **Henry Aaron**

I was fourteen years old when I first saw Jackie Robinson. It was the spring of 1948, the year after Jackie changed my life by breaking baseball's color line. His team, the Brooklyn Dodgers, made a stop in my hometown of Mobile, Alabama, while barnstorming its way north to start the season, and while he was there, Jackie spoke to a big crowd of black folks over on Davis Avenue. I think he talked about segregation, but I didn't hear a word that came out of his mouth. Jackie Robinson was such a hero to me that I couldn't do anything but gawk at him.

They say certain people are bigger than life, but Jackie Robinson is the only man I've known who truly was. In 1947 life in America—at least my America, and Jackie's—was segregation. It was two worlds that were afraid of each other. There were separate schools for blacks and whites, separate restaurants, separate hotels, separate drinking fountains, and separate baseball leagues. Life was unkind to black people who tried to bring those worlds together. It could be hateful. But Jackie Robinson, God bless him, was bigger than all of that.

Jackie Robinson had to be bigger than life. He had to be bigger than the Brooklyn teammates who got up a petition to keep him off the ball club, bigger than the pitchers who threw at him or the base runners who dug their spikes into his shin, bigger than the bench jockeys who hollered for him to carry their bags and shine their shoes, bigger than the so-called fans who wrote him death threats.

When Branch Rickey first met with Jackie about joining the Dodgers, he told him that for three years he would have to turn the other cheek and silently suffer all the vile things that would come his way. Believe me, it wasn't Jackie's nature to do that. He was a fighter, the proudest and most competitive person I've ever seen. This was a man who, as a lieutenant in the army, risked a court-martial[1] by refusing to sit in the back of a military bus. . . .

To this day, I don't know how he withstood the things he did without lashing back. I've been through a lot in my time, and I consider myself to be a patient man, but I know I couldn't have done what Jackie did. I don't think anybody else could have done it. Somehow, though, Jackie had the strength to suppress his instincts, to sacrifice his pride for his people's. It was an incredible act of selflessness that brought the races closer together than ever before and shaped the dreams of an entire generation.

1. **court-martial:** military trial.

Informational Skills Review CONTINUED

Before Jackie Robinson broke the color line, I wasn't permitted even to think about being a professional baseball player. I once mentioned something to my father about it, and he said, "Ain't no colored ballplayers." There were the Negro Leagues, of course, where the Dodgers discovered Jackie, but my mother, like most, would rather her son be a schoolteacher than a Negro Leaguer. All that changed when Jackie started stealing bases in a Brooklyn uniform.

Jackie's character was much more important than his batting average, but it certainly helped that he was a great ballplayer, a .311 career hitter whose trademark was rattling pitchers and fielders with his daring base running. He wasn't the best Negro League talent at the time he was chosen, and baseball wasn't really his best sport—he had been a football and track star at UCLA—but he played the game with a ferocious creativity that gave the country a good idea of what it had been missing all those years. With Jackie in the infield, the Dodgers won six National League pennants.

I believe every black person in America had a piece of those pennants. There's never been another ballplayer who touched people as Jackie did. The only comparable athlete, in my experience, was Joe Louis.[2] The difference was that Louis competed against white men; Jackie competed with them as well. He was taking us over segregation's threshold[3] into a new land whose scenery made every black person stop and stare in reverence.[4] We were all with Jackie. We slid into every base that he swiped, ducked at every fastball that hurtled toward his head. The circulation of the Pittsburgh *Courier,* the leading black newspaper, increased by 100,000 when it began reporting on him regularly. All over the country, black preachers would call together their congregations just to pray for Jackie and urge them to demonstrate the same forbearance that he did.

Later in his career, when the "Great Experiment"[5] had proved to be successful, Jackie allowed his instincts to take over in issues of race. He began striking back and speaking out. And when Jackie Robinson spoke, every black player got the message. He made it clear to us that we weren't playing just for ourselves or for our teams; we were playing for our people. I don't think it's a coincidence that the black players of the late '50s and '60s—me, Roy Campanella, Monte Irvin, Willie Mays, Ernie Banks, Frank Robinson, Bob Gibson, and others—dominated the National League. If we played as if

2. **Joe Louis:** Nicknamed "the Brown Bomber," Joe Louis (1914–1981) was world heavyweight champion from 1937 to 1949.

3. **threshold** (THREHSH ohld): doorsill; here, a boundary marking the end of one thing and the start of something new.

4. **reverence** (REHV uhr uhns): tremendous respect.

5. **"Great Experiment":** term used to describe the breaking of the color barrier in major-league baseball.

9.R.3.C.1.c Use details from informational text: to analyze and evaluate the accuracy and adequacy of evidence

we were on a mission, it was because Jackie Robinson had sent us out on one.

Even after he retired in 1956 and was inducted into the Hall of Fame in 1962, Jackie continued to chop along the path that was still a long way from being cleared. He campaigned for baseball to hire a black third-base coach, then a black manager. In 1969 he refused an invitation to play in an old-timers' game at Yankee Stadium to protest the lack of progress along those lines.

A great star from my generation, Frank Robinson (who was related to Jackie only in spirit), finally became the first black manager, in 1975. Jackie was gone by then. His last public appearance was at the 1972 World Series; he showed up with white hair, carrying a cane and going blind from diabetes. He died nine days later.

Most of the black players from Jackie's day were at the funeral, but I was appalled by how few of the younger players showed up to pay him tribute. At the time, I was 41 home runs short of Babe Ruth's[6] career record, and I felt that it was up to me to keep Jackie's dream alive. I was inspired to dedicate my home-run record to the same great cause to which he dedicated his life. I'm still inspired by Jackie Robinson. Hardly a day goes by that I don't think of him.

—*from* American Legends: From the Time 100

6. **Babe Ruth's:** George Herman Ruth (1895–1948), nicknamed "the Babe," was one of the most successful and popular baseball players in history. In 1974, Ruth's home-run record was finally beaten by Henry ("Hank") Aaron.

1. What **claim** does Henry Aaron make about Jackie Robinson?

A Robinson was the greatest baseball player to ever live.

B It was Robinson who was responsible for getting audiences interested in baseball.

C Robinson never got the credit he deserved.

D It was Robinson's selflessness that broke the color line.

9.R.3.C.1.c

2. Which of the statements from the essay reveals **logic**?

A "They say certain people are bigger than life, but Jackie Robinson is the only man I've known who truly was."

B "We were all with Jackie. . . . The circulation of the Pittsburgh *Courier,* the leading black newspaper, increased by 100,000 when it began reporting on him regularly."

C "I believe every black person in America has a piece of those pennants."

D "Jackie Robinson had to be bigger than life . . . bigger than the so-called fans who wrote him death threats."

9.R.3.C.1.c

Informational Skills Review

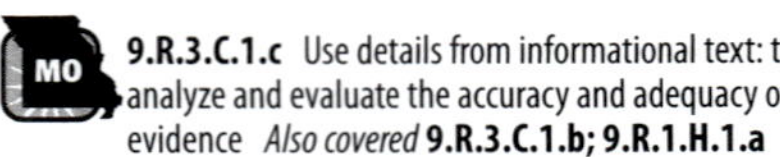

9.R.3.C.1.c Use details from informational text: to analyze and evaluate the accuracy and adequacy of evidence *Also covered* **9.R.3.C.1.b; 9.R.1.H.1.a**

3. Which statement supports this **generalization:** "And when Jackie Robinson spoke, every black player got the message."

A "Most of the black players from Jackie's day were at the funeral."

B "He campaigned for baseball to hire a black third-base coach."

C "There's never been another ballplayer who touched people as Jackie did."

D "Jackie's character was much more important than his batting average. "

9.R.1.H.1.a

4. Which of the following statements uses **loaded words**?

A "I was fourteen years old when I first saw Jackie Robinson."

B "I didn't hear a word that came out of his mouth."

C "For three years he would have to turn the other cheek and silently suffer all the vile things that would come his way."

D "Jackie's character was much more important than his batting average."

9.R.3.C.1.b

5. All of the following statements are **facts** *except*—

A "He campaigned for baseball to hire a black third-base coach."

B "With Jackie in the infield, the Dodgers won six National League pennants."

C "I believe every black person in America had a piece of those pennants."

D "He retired in 1956 and was inducted into the Hall of Fame in 1962."

9.R.3.C.1.c

6. Aaron uses the **anecdote** about Robinson risking a court-martial to show that Robinson —

A did not respect laws

B was a proud person who fought for respect

C could not control his temper

D did not like being a soldier

9.R.3.C.1.c

7. Which of the following statements is the *most* accurate **evaluation** of Aaron's argument?

A It relies almost entirely on emotional appeals.

B Facts, statistics, and other objective evidence make up the argument's main support.

C It uses a mix of facts and emotional appeals to convince the reader.

D Aaron includes little support in his argument.

9.R.3.C.1.c

Constructed Response

8. According to Aaron, why did Jackie Robinson have to be "bigger than life"? Support your answer by citing details from the text.

9.R.3.C.1.c

FOCUS ON MISSOURI COURSE LEVEL EXPECTATIONS

Vocabulary Skills Review

MO **9.R.1.E.1.c** Develop vocabulary through text: using glossary, dictionary and thesaurus *Also covered* **9.R.1.E.1.b**

Synonyms

Directions: Choose the *best* synonym for the italicized word in each sentence.

1. In "Cinderella's Stepsisters," Morrison argues that women must *deflect* other women colleagues' anger.

A translate
B end
C turn aside
D emphasize

9.R.1.E.1.b

2. According to Morrison in "Cinderella's Stepsisters," a woman should not allow her drive for success to *diminish* the lives or feelings of other females.

A reduce
B outdo
C wound
D discontinue

9.R.1.E.1.b

3. In "Setting the Record Straight," McCloud explains that comics *encompass* many different genres.

A judge
B disturb
C list
D contain

9.R.1.E.1.b

4. In "Graphic Novels 101: FAQ," Brenner states that *tenuous* evidence presented in a 1950s study tarnished comics' reputation.

A scandalous
B indifferent
C flimsy
D solid

9.R.1.E.1.b

5. In her interview, Satrapi reports that her graphic memoir *evolved* as she wrote it.

A gained meaning
B developed gradually
C became sophisticated
D lessened in difficulty

9.R.1.E.1.b

6. In her interview, Satrapi says she believes there is no such thing as *stark* good and evil.

A real
B decent
C definable
D absolute

9.R.1.E.1.b

Academic Vocabulary

Directions: Choose the *best* definition for the italicized word in each sentence.

7. The argument that was presented to the committee was not *valid*.

A convincing
B appropriate
C substantial
D true

9.R.1.E.1.b

8. It is important to *verify* all facts.

A include
B accept unconditionally
C prove true
D dissect one by one

9.R.1.E.1.b

Read On

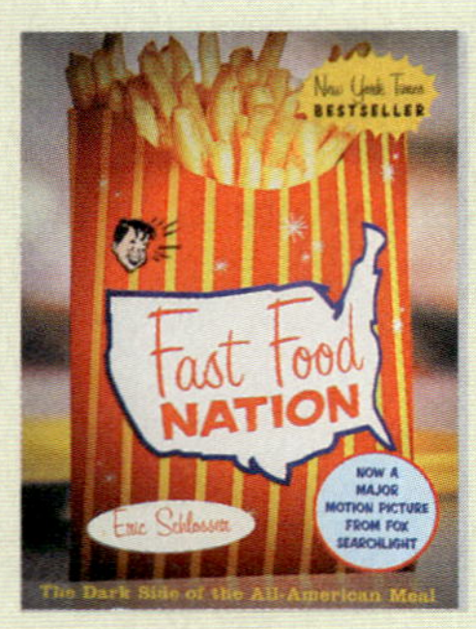

NONFICTION

Fast Food Nation

It's hard to get through a day now without seeing a fast-food ad or restaurant, but it didn't always used to be that way. In *Fast Food Nation,* author Eric Schlosser provides a history of the American fast-food market, starting with Harlan Sanders and the McDonald brothers, who brought factory techniques into the kitchen. Schlosser brings readers full circle by showing how fast food operates in our lives today, where most Americans eat three fast-food hamburgers a week and four orders of fries.

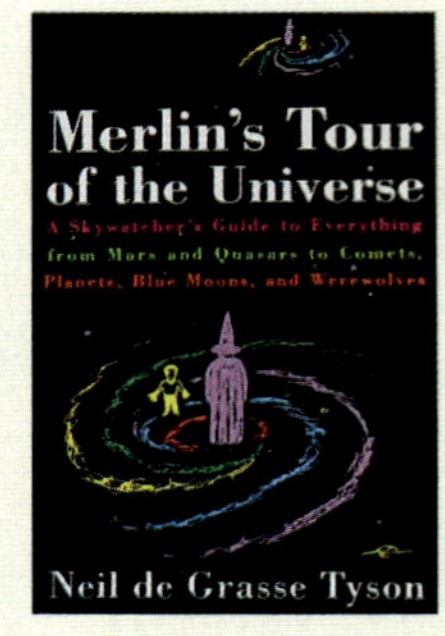

NONFICTION

Merlin's Tour of the Universe

Merlin is a fictional character created by Neil de Grasse Tyson for his column in *StarDate* magazine. In his column, Tyson answers questions about the solar system, galaxies, and universe. Here are a few of the questions: Why are solar eclipses so dangerous to look at? What is a light-year? Does the full moon affect people's behavior? How many galaxies are there in the universe? In *Merlin's Tour of the Universe,* Tyson has collected hundreds of the questions he has been asked. His answers are clear, concise, and scientifically accurate.

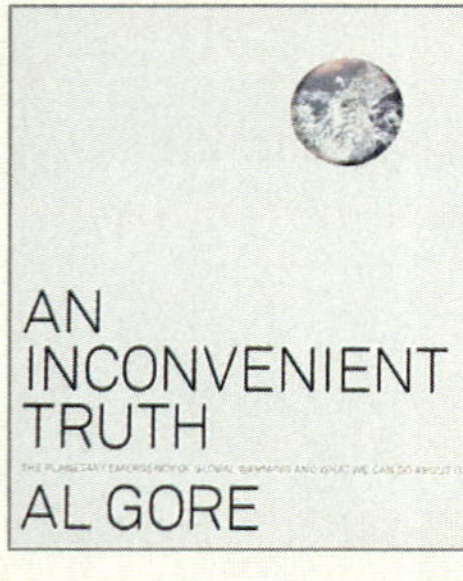

NONFICTION

An Inconvenient Truth

Al Gore argues in *An Inconvenient Truth* that global warming is a truth that cannot be ignored. We humans have produced so much carbon dioxide that we are steadily warming the atmosphere and causing the polar ice caps and glaciers to melt and gradually raise sea levels. Summers are getting hotter, oceans warmer, and storms stronger. Using stunning aerial photographs and graphics, Gore shows readers how our planet is changing. He also tells us what we can do to help.

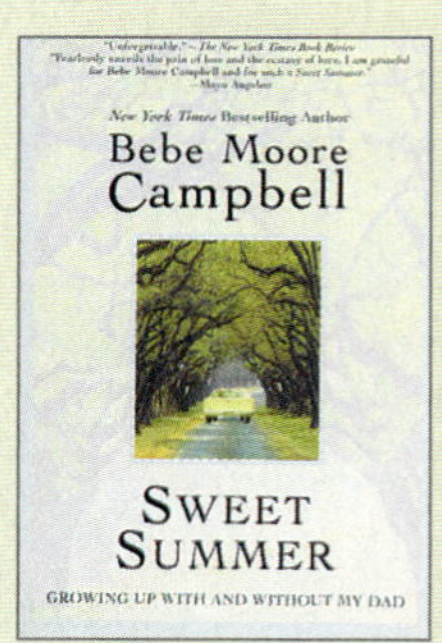

NONFICTION

Sweet Summer

The absence of her father was always painful to Bebe Moore Campbell while she was growing up. She saw him during the summers, but she desperately wished they could have more time together. In *Sweet Summer: Growing Up with and Without My Dad,* the story of her youth, Campbell tells how she learned to deal with the pain of missing him. Read this memoir and find out how her father came to be a constant presence in her life in spite of their separation.

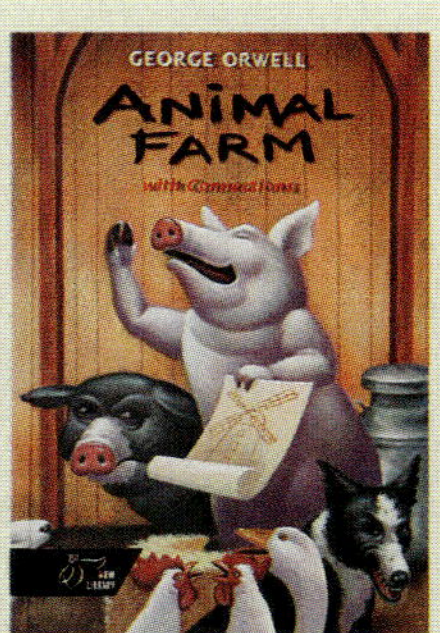

FICTION

Animal Farm

George Orwell reveals the absurdities of human nature with his cast of animals in the classic novel *Animal Farm.* The animals of Manor Farm rebel against their incompetent owner. After overthrowing the farmer, the animals come up with their own form of government, which the sheep sum up as "four legs good, two legs bad." Two pigs, Napoleon and Snowball, fight for control of the farm's future, and a battle of wills ensues.

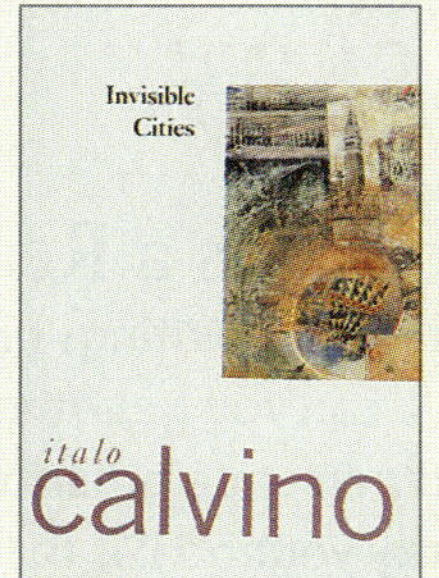

FICTION

Invisible Cities

In this fantastical novel, Italo Calvino's fictional Marco Polo sits with the emperor Kublai Khan in a garden. Marco Polo entertains the old man with tales of all the cities he has visited in his travels around the world. Khan realizes his empire is coming to an end as he listens to Polo's stories about cities made up of roller coasters and circuses, mirror cities, and cities filled with only the dead. Eventually the emperor comes to recognize that all of these cities are really one place in *Invisible Cities.*

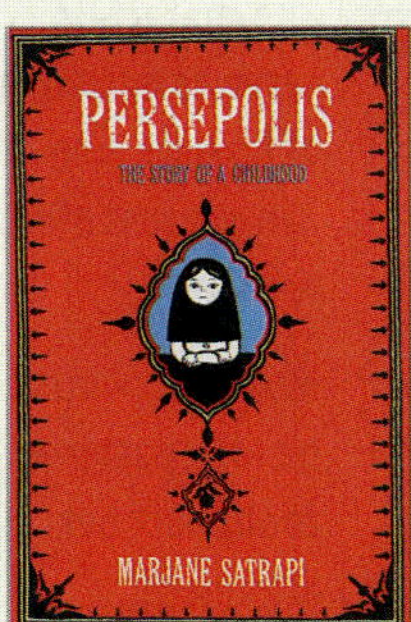

NONFICTION

Persepolis

Marjane Satrapi recalls her childhood in Tehran, Iran, from ages six to fourteen in her graphic-story memoir *Persepolis.* During that time, Iran went through the Islamic Revolution and a war with Iraq. Young Marjane suddenly had to start wearing a veil, quit going to the French school she attended, and began to keep her private life secret from authorities. Using the form of black-and-white comics, Satrapi describes what it felt like to grow up during a painful chapter of her country's history.

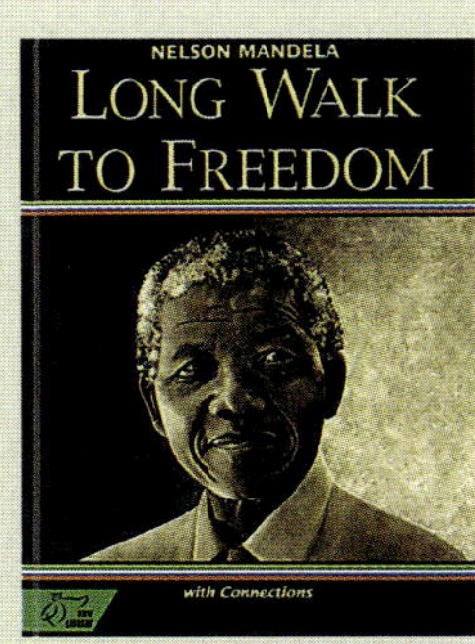

NONFICTION

Long Walk to Freedom

Nelson Mandela's *Long Walk to Freedom* is an inspiring chronicle of a man who fought to put an end to apartheid, the official policy of racial segregation and discrimination against blacks in South Africa. Mandela, whose humanitarian activism resulted in a twenty-seven-year imprisonment, wrote much of this autobiography while behind bars. His story is an epic journey that begins with Mandela's country childhood and ends with his winning the presidency in South Africa's first multiracial election.

Learn It Online
Explore more novels online at *NovelWise*:
go.hrw.com
L9-597
Go

Writing Workshop

Persuasive Essay

Write with a Purpose

Write a persuasive essay on a topic that is important to you and about which you have a strong opinion. Your **purpose** is to persuade, or convince, your **audience** to accept your views. Your audience is your classmates or other readers who are also interested in your topic.

A Good Persuasive Essay

- includes an introduction that states your argument
- provides at least three reasons to back up your argument
- supports each reason with at least two pieces of evidence
- has a logical and effective organization
- addresses possible counterarguments made by your reader
- ends with a restatement of your thesis

See page 606 for complete rubric.

Reader/Writer Notebook

Use your **RWN** to complete the activities for this workshop.

Think as a Reader/Writer

In this collection, you have read persuasive writings on a variety of topics. What issue do you care about? How can you get others to care about it, too? One way to share your views and persuade others to accept them is to write persuasively. In a **persuasive essay** your goal is to state your opinion clearly and support it with evidence.

Read the following excerpt from Toni Morrison's "Cinderella's Stepsisters" (page 543) to see how Morrison uses evidence and reasoning to persuade her readers.

> Let me begin by taking you back a little . . . to a once-upon-a-time when you first heard, or read, or, I suspect, even saw "Cinderella." But it is her stepsisters who interest me. . . . How crippling it must have been for those young girls to grow up with a mother, to watch and imitate that mother, enslaving another girl.

← Morrison uses a popular fairy tale as a springboard into her argument.

> I am curious about their fortunes after the story ends. . . . Having watched and participated in the violent dominion of another woman, will they be any less cruel when it comes their turn to enslave other children, or even when they are required to take care of their own mother?

← The characters serve as **examples** of how women can oppress other women.

> . . . feminine power when directed at other women has historically been wielded in what has been described as a "masculine" manner. Soon you will be in a position to do the very same thing. . . .

← Morrison points to historic patterns to support her argument.

> I want not to *ask* you but to *tell* you not to participate in the oppression of your sisters.

← In this **call to action**, Morrison tells the reader what to do.

Think About the Professional Model

With a partner, discuss the following questions about the model.

1. What is Morrison's purpose for writing this article?
2. After reading the passage, do you support Morrison's call to action? Why or why not?

9.W.3.A.1.a Compose a variety of texts: using narrative, descriptive, expository, and/or persuasive features 9.W.2.C.1.b Compose text with: a logical order 9.W.2.B.1.b Compose text with: relevant specific details

Prewriting

Choose an Issue

For your persuasive essay, consider **issues,** or topics of concern, that stir your emotions. List a few of them. Then, use the following questions to help you decide which issue to write about.

- Which issue do you care about the most?
- About what issue can you gather enough evidence to support your position?
- Which issue is interesting enough to hold a reader's interest in an essay of about 1,500 words?

Think About Your Topic

An important next step is to probe your topic more deeply. Ask yourself the following questions about your topic.

1. Is my topic one about which people have opposing opinions?
2. Can I think of three good reasons to convince others of my ideas?
3. Are there any counterarguments that I can address in my essay? (A counterargument is one that supports an opposing view on the topic.)

If you answer *no* to any of the above, you should select another topic.

Write an Opinion, or Thesis, Statement

What is your position on the issue? To guide your writing, state your opinion in an **opinion, or thesis, statement.** This statement should indicate both the issue and your position on it. For example, one student wrote this thesis statement: School begins too early in the day. The issue—when school starts—and his position—that it starts too early—are both clearly stated.

Gather Support for Your Argument

To be convincing, you'll need to give at least three strong **reasons** that support your argument. Using a chart like the one below, write your opinion statement and three or more reasons that support it.

Opinion Statement: School begins too early in the day.

Reasons

1. Teenagers need more sleep.
2. Walking to the bus stop in the dark is dangerous.
3.

Idea Starters

- Recycling should be mandatory worldwide.
- Cell phones should be allowed in school.
- Bicycles should not be banned from sidewalks.
- Students should volunteer.
- Pets should have rights, too.

Peer Review

Before you decide on a topic for your persuasive essay, ask a group of peers if they can find reasons for *not* agreeing with your opinion on your topic. If no one disagrees with your opinion, consider finding another topic. Persuasion always deals with opposing views, not agreement.

Your Turn

Get Started In your **RWN,** state the **issue** and your **opinion, or thesis, statement** about the issue. Draw a chart like the one at the left, and list **reasons** that support your opinion. Be sure to state your position clearly and to support it with at least three strong reasons.

Learn It Online

To see how one writer met all the assignment criteria, visit

Collect Evidence

Reasons get their strength from the **evidence** that supports them. Effective evidence is **relevant,** or clearly related to your issue; evidence will help convince readers to accept your position.

EVIDENCE FOR PERSUASIVE ESSAYS	
Types of Evidence	**Examples**
1. **Analogies:** comparisons that show similarities between otherwise unrelated ideas	*We should be as concerned about disturbing students' natural sleep patterns as we are about skipping school.*
2. **Anecdotes:** personal examples or stories that illustrate a point	*My grandfather says that when he was in school, students went to school later and were better rested.*
3. **Commonly accepted beliefs:** ideas that most people share	*Most people know that walking to school in the dark poses dangers.*
4. **Examples:** specific instances or illustrations of a general idea	*For example, motorists might not see pedestrians in the pre-dawn darkness.*
5. **Expert opinion:** statement made by an authority on the subject	*Our school principal said, "Students in first-period classes tend to score lower on standardized math tests than their peers who take the same classes later in the day."*
6. **Facts:** statements that can be proven true. Some facts are in the form of statistics, or numerical information.	*Eighty-five percent of teens in America aren't getting the sleep they need.*

Think About Audience and Purpose

Keeping **purpose** and **audience** in mind, evaluate your reasons and evidence. Remember that the purpose of a persuasive essay is to convince the audience to accept your opinion or to take action. Ask yourself,

- **"Will the reasons and evidence make my audience think about this issue?"** Identify how your persuasive support addresses your readers' interest in the issue.
- **"What concerns might my audience have?"** Consider how your issue looks from their **bias,** or point of view. For example, some readers may think that recycling is too expensive. Take this objection, or **counterargument,** into account as you write your essay.
- **"What will my audience expect from my essay?"** What aspects of the issues might readers want to know more about? Readers will expect your essay to provide solid information to help them make a decision about their position on the issue.

Your Turn

Gather Evidence Gather **evidence** to support each **reason** you have developed for your persuasive essay.

- Search encyclopedias, books, or magazine articles for facts to back up your argument.
- Use reliable and trustworthy Web sites to locate articles that support or counter your position on the issue.
- Write down any personal experiences that relate to your topic.
- Consider your audience for this essay. What evidence will be most convincing to them?

Drafting

Follow the Writer's Framework

The **Writer's Framework** to the right outlines how to plan your draft to create an effective persuasive essay.

Framework for a Persuasive Essay

Introduction

- Grab your readers' interest with an attention-getter. Give background information to help readers understand the issue. Present an opinion statement that identifies the issue and your opinion on the issue.

Body

- Provide at least three reasons that support your opinion statement. Give at least two pieces of evidence to support each reason. Make sure to organize the reasons and evidence logically. Show any cause-and-effect relationships by using **transitions** such as *therefore, as a result, consequently,* and so on.

Conclusion

- Once you've finished making your points, restate your opinion. Then, summarize your reasons, or include a **call to action**—a sentence that urges your readers to do what you want them to do about the issue.

Organize Your Support

Organize the reasons that support your opinion statement by **order of importance.** To draw readers in, begin with your second most important reason. To leave them with a strong impression, end with your most important reason.

Use Appeals

To effectively persuade your readers, use a combination of these appeals.

- A **logical appeal** speaks to a reader's common sense.
- An **emotional appeal** is aimed at a reader's heart, addressing emotions such as fear, love, sympathy, and pride.
- An **ethical appeal** addresses a reader's sense of right and wrong.

Writer's Tip

As you draft, double-space your essay on the computer or skip lines if you are writing by hand. This space will allow room for peer review comments and suggested edits when you revise your essay.

Grammar Link Parallel Structures

The use of parallel structures can help you to emphasize key ideas and stir the audience's emotions. **Parallel structure** refers to words, phrases, or sentences that have the same grammatical form. Repeating the form creates evenness and rhythm that emphasize your ideas. As you draft, see if you can use parallel structure to enhance your persuasive argument. Here are some examples:

Type of Structure	Example
parallel words	Sleep **refreshes, energizes,** and **soothes** . . .
parallel phrases	**Playing sports, completing homework,** and **doing chores** can drain you of energy.
parallel sentences	Isn't it important to do well in school? Isn't it important to perform at your best?

Reference Note For more on parallel structure, see the Language Handbook.

Your Turn

Write Your Draft Organize your essay with an **introduction,** a **body,** and a **conclusion.** Be sure to organize your **reasons** effectively and to consider what type of **appeal** is best suited to your **audience.** Consider using **parallel structures** to present your ideas.

Peer Review

Work with a partner to review each evaluation question in the chart at the right. Then, determine where you and your peer need to improve your drafts. You can use the tips and revision techniques to guide your revisions.

Remember to look at each other's essays in terms of their logic and organization—not for whether you agree with the author's opinion. Be sure to discuss whether you've convinced each other.

Evaluating and Revising

Exchange your persuasive essays with a peer. Use the chart below to help you evaluate and revise each other's drafts.

Persuasive Essay: Guidelines for Content and Organization

Evaluation Questions	Tips	Revision Techniques
1. Does the introduction express a clear opinion, or thesis, statement?	**Bracket** the opinion statement.	**Add** an opinion statement that identifies the issue and states an opinion on it.
2. Do at least three reasons support the opinion statement?	**Underline** each reason. **Label** logical appeals with an *L*, emotional appeals with an *E*, and ethical appeals with an *H*.	**Add** reasons. **Elaborate** on existing reasons so that they appeal to readers' logic, emotions, or ethics. Make sure the appeals are balanced.
3. Are there at least two pieces of evidence to support each reason?	**Circle** each piece of evidence, and **draw an arrow** to the reason it supports.	**Add** evidence for each reason. **Rearrange** evidence so that it is in the paragraph with the reason it supports.
4. Is the organization logical and effective?	**Number** each reason with a rank (1 for strongest, and so on).	**Rearrange** paragraphs to put the strongest reason last.
5. Are possible reader counterarguments addressed?	**Put a plus sign** by any sentence that addresses a reader's counterargument.	**Add** sentences that identify and respond to readers' counterarguments.
6. Does the conclusion restate the writer's opinion? Does it include a summary of reasons or a call to action?	**Put a box** around the restatement of your opinion. **Highlight** the summary of the reasons or the call to action.	**Add** a sentence that restates the position. **Add** a summary of reasons or a call to action.

Read this student draft, and notice the comments on its strengths as well as suggestions on how the draft could be improved.

Student Draft

Should School Start Later?

by Jon Attridge, Quincy Junior High School

Beep! Beep! Beep! Beep! You sit up in bed and shut off the alarm. It's 6:00 a.m.—time to get ready for school, but you don't have near enough energy. You, like 85 percent of teens in America, aren't getting the sleep you need. Is this the morning you want to experience for the rest of your school career? If not, then you must agree that schools should start later.

← Jon grabs his readers' attention with his introduction. Both his topic and his **opinion statement** are clear.

Getting up too early, has serious consequences. Studies show that the frontal lobe (the section of the brain in charge of learning ability and memory) is still developing in many adolescents. Disturbing REM (rapid eye movement) sleep can slow the development of this vital portion of the brain. This can result in much lower test scores. Starting school later ensures that students get plenty of uninterrupted sleep. Doing this allows students to concentrate more on school and less on getting enough sleep.

← Here, Jon uses **cause-and-effect reasoning** to present his information.

Grades aren't the only thing to improve. An additional hour of sleep can affect a student's mood and attitude. A later schedule doesn't just help students to be more positive and productive; teachers will be in a better mood, providing more skilled teaching. With students' moods boosted, teachers and students will get along in a stress-free learning environment.

← Although this is a good set of reasons, this paragraph could use more **support**.

MINI-LESSON How to Use Anecdotes to Persuade Your Readers

In his third paragraph, Jon states that one hour of sleep can improve a student's mood. He might be more persuasive if he relates this to his own experience. **Anecdotes,** or short personal stories, add emotional appeal to writing. Readers can connect on a personal level to real human experiences. Jon inserted an anecdote, shown in blue.

Jon's Revision to Paragraph Three

Grades aren't the only thing to improve. An additional hour of sleep can affect a student's mood and attitude. ^ *Last Saturday, for example, I slept until 7:30, and I felt rested and energized the whole day. I eagerly did my homework and my chores around the house.* A later schedule doesn't just help students; teachers will be in a better mood, providing more skilled teaching.

Your Turn

Use Anecdotes to Persuade Your Readers Read through your draft, and take note of areas you'd like to improve. Ask yourself,

- "What details would help make the material more persuasive?"

Student Draft *continues*

Jon uses a strong **emotional appeal** by focusing on the safety of the students.

Many students have to walk a lengthy distance to the bus stop or to school. It is dark between 6:45 and 7:20 a.m. To be outside and walking in this minute amount of light can pose a danger to pedestrians. It's quite possible that a car won't be able to see a student walking in the road. With school starting around 8:30 a.m., this risk is much less likely to occur.

Although Jon addresses a **counterargument**, the **cause-and-effect** relationship is unclear.

"What about the extra hour of school?" you ask. It is, in fact, a good thing that students will be in school for another hour at the end of the day.

Jon creates a strong **conclusion** by restating and reframing his opening argument.

Now imagine that morning again. It's 7:00 a.m. You say to yourself, "Wow, I feel great, and I've got plenty of time to get ready." Just one hour can make a huge difference in your mood and your day.

MINI-LESSON How to Add Cause-Effect Reasoning

When addressing a counterargument, you try to address the reader's questions and concerns. In his draft, Jon does address a counterargument in the statement, "What about the extra hour in school?"

To further address the concerns of those who oppose his ideas, Jon added cause-effect reasoning to his argument. Cause-effect reasoning is particularly effective in persuasion because the writer can argue: If this occurs—the **cause** (kids are in school later)—then this will be the **effect** (students will be safer). That's a strong reason that supports Jon's argument.

Jon's Draft of Paragraph Five

"What about the extra hour of school?" you ask. It is, in fact, a good thing that students will be in school for another hour at the end of the day.

Jon's Revision of Paragraph Five

"What about the extra hour of school?" you ask. It is, in fact, a good thing that students will be in school for another hour at the end of the day.

Many parents have to work until 5:00 p.m. or later. For them, that one additional hour of school is one less hour that their child is home alone. Instead, their child is safe at school for one more hour.

Your Turn

Evaluate and Revise Your Essay Use the input you received from your partner to revise your work. Determine where you can add cause-and-effect reasoning to strengthen your argument.

Proofreading and Publishing

Proofreading

Now that you have looked at the content, organization, and style of your essay, **proofread,** or **edit,** the essay to be sure that it is free of grammar, spelling, and punctuation errors.

Good persuasive ideas can lose their impact if the reader gets bored by monotonous writing. To add variety and interest to your essay, add **gerunds** and **gerund phrases** to your sentences.

Proofreading Tip

Reading your text aloud may help you to catch errors that you do not see when scanning the page. If you stumble over phrases when reading aloud, there may be punctuation errors that you need to correct.

Grammar Link **Use Gerunds**

A **gerund** is a verb form ending in *–ing* that is used as a **noun.** Writers sometimes confuse gerunds with **present participles,** verb forms that also end in *–ing,* but are used as **adjectives.**

> **Sleeping later** allows students to wake up mentally prepared for the day. [The gerund phrase is the subject of the verb *allows.*]
>
> **Sleeping later,** students score better on tests. [The present participial phrase modifies the subject *students.*]

Notice that a comma follows an introductory participial phrase, but not a gerund or gerund phrase. Jon corrected the following mistake in his use of gerunds.

> Getting up too early, has serious consequences. [*Getting up too early* is the subject of the verb *has.*]

Reference Note For more on **gerunds,** see the Language Handbook.

Publish Your Writing

Persuasive writing is meant to be shared. Here are some ways you might share your persuasive essay with an audience.

- Send your essay to an organization with an interest in your issue or with the power to make the change you want.
- Publish your essay on a school or community Web site or on a Web site devoted to the issue you addressed. Be sure to include graphics.

Reflect on the Process

In your **RWN,** write short responses to the following questions.

1. How did addressing your readers' counterarguments or concerns help you to strengthen your persuasive argument?
2. What did you learn about your audience and the other side of the issue by writing persuasively?

Your Turn

Proofread and Publish Correct any errors in your essay. Add variety to your sentence beginnings by using gerunds. Be sure not to separate gerunds from the rest of the sentence with commas. Publish your final essay using one of the suggestions on this page.

Scoring Rubric

Use one of the rubrics below to evaluate your persuasive essay from the Writing Workshop or your response to the on-demand prompt on the next page. Your teacher will tell you to use either the six- or the four-point rubric.

6-Point Scale

Score 6 *Demonstrates advanced success*

- focuses consistently on a clear and reasonable position
- shows effective organization throughout, with smooth transitions
- offers thoughtful, creative ideas and reasons
- supports a position thoroughly, using convincing, fully elaborated reasons and evidence
- exhibits mature control of written language

Score 5 *Demonstrates proficient success*

- focuses on a clear and reasonable position
- shows effective organization, with transitions
- offers thoughtful ideas and reasons
- supports a position competently, using convincing, well-elaborated reasons and evidence
- exhibits sufficient control of written language

Score 4 *Demonstrates competent success*

- focuses on a reasonable position, with minor distractions
- shows effective organization, with minor lapses
- offers mostly thoughtful ideas and reasons
- elaborates reasons and evidence with a mixture of the general and the specific
- exhibits general control of written language

Score 3 *Demonstrates limited success*

- includes some loosely related ideas that distract from the writer's position
- shows some organization, with noticeable gaps in the logical flow of ideas
- offers routine, predictable ideas and reasons
- supports ideas with uneven reasoning and elaboration
- exhibits limited control of written language

Score 2 *Demonstrates basic success*

- includes loosely related ideas that seriously distract from the writer's persuasive purpose
- shows minimal organization, with major gaps in the logical flow of ideas
- offers ideas and reasons that merely skim the surface
- supports ideas with inadequate reasoning and elaboration
- exhibits significant problems with control of written language

Score 1 *Demonstrates emerging effort*

- shows little awareness of the topic and purpose for writing
- lacks organization
- offers unclear and confusing ideas
- demonstrates minimal persuasive reasoning or elaboration
- exhibits major problems with control of written language

4-Point Scale

Score 4 *Demonstrates advanced success*

- focuses consistently on a clear and reasonable position
- shows effective organization throughout, with smooth transitions
- offers thoughtful, creative ideas and reasons
- supports a position thoroughly, using convincing, fully elaborated reasons and evidence
- exhibits mature control of written language

Score 3 *Demonstrates competent success*

- focuses on a reasonable position, with minor distractions
- shows effective organization, with minor lapses
- offers mostly thoughtful ideas and reasons
- elaborates reasons and evidence with a mixture of the general and the specific
- exhibits general control of written language

Score 2 *Demonstrates limited success*

- includes some loosely related ideas that distract from the writer's position
- shows some organization, with noticeable gaps in the logical flow of ideas
- offers routine, predictable ideas and reasons
- supports ideas with uneven reasoning and elaboration
- exhibits limited control of written language

Score 1 *Demonstrates emerging effort*

- shows little awareness of the topic and purpose for writing
- lacks organization
- offers unclear and confusing ideas
- demonstrates minimal persuasive reasoning or elaboration
- exhibits major problems with control of written language

Persuasive Essay

When responding to an on-demand writing task in a persuasive prompt, use what you've learned from your reading, writing the persuasive essay, and the rubric on page 606. Use the steps below to develop a persuasive essay.

Writing Prompt

Imagine that your school board is planning to implement coed physical education classes—classes with boys *and* girls instead of single-gender classes. Write a persuasive essay convincing parents to support or oppose this plan.

Study the Prompt

Read the prompt carefully. Then, read it again, underlining the words that tell the type of writing, the topic, and the purpose. The *school board* is your audience; *coed physical education classes* is the topic. You must take one position or another: *for it* or *against it*. Those words signal *persuasion*. **Tip:** Spend about five minutes studying the prompt.

Plan Your Response

Think about the reasons for each side of the argument. Make a list of pros and cons for coed physical education classes. Which side can you defend more effectively with examples and reasoning? Which side will appeal more to parents—your audience? Take a position, and narrow your reasons down to your top three. Use the organizer below to help you gather support. List your reasons in the first column. In the second, list specific evidence (facts, statistics, anecdotes, expert testimony, examples) for each reason. **Tip:** Spend about ten minutes planning your response.

Reasons	Evidence

Respond to the Prompt

Begin drafting your essay. You may want to start by simply stating your thesis, your opinion on the topic. As you write, keep the following points in mind.

- In the introduction, grab your readers' attention and state your position, including the reasons that support your opinion.
- In each body paragraph, give one reason for your position, with valid support and specific examples for that reason. You can always use examples from your experience or someone else's. Using specific names, dates, and places adds convincing detail.
- Conclude your essay with a statement of strong conviction and a call to action.

Tip: Spend about twenty minutes writing your draft.

Improve Your Response

Revising Review your draft to compare it with the prompt. Does your draft state a position on the classes? Does it provide evidence to back up your position? Do you conclude with a call to action?

Proofreading Now spend a few minutes finding and correcting any errors in grammar, usage, and mechanics. Make sure that your paper and any edits are neatly written and legible.

Checking Your Final Copy Before you turn in your paper, examine it once more to make sure that you have done your best work. Pay careful attention to the words on the page to make sure they are grammatically correct and accurately convey your meaning. **Tip:** Save five to ten minutes to improve your paper.

Giving a Persuasive Speech

Speak with a Purpose

Adapt your persuasive essay into a persuasive speech. Practice your speech, and then present it to your class.

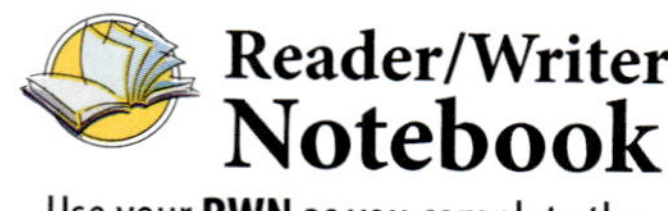

Reader/Writer Notebook

Use your **RWN** as you complete the activities for this workshop.

Think as a Reader/Writer Remember that speaking and listening are related processes, similar to reading and writing. Like a reader, a listener takes in and tries to understand someone's ideas. Like a writer, a speaker tries to convey ideas to others.

You have probably made persuasive speeches before, such as pleas to your parents to allow you a freedom or appeals to your friends to adopt an idea or to lend their help. When you try to convince others aloud, you are giving a persuasive speech.

Adapt Your Essay

Because people will be listening to your argument instead of reading it, you'll need to adapt your essay as you prepare for your presentation. Keep in mind that your classmates are your audience, and follow these suggestions to construct your speech.

- **Audience** Use vocabulary that suits your audience. Avoid words that may be unfamiliar to your listeners. For a formal speech, however, maintain the formal tone you used in your essay.
- **Introduction** Adapt the introduction of your essay to make a dramatic impact from the very beginning. For example, use an intriguing quotation, an interesting anecdote, or a reference to an authority on the subject of your speech.
- **Your Case** Evaluate your explanation of the issue's causes and effects and assess the strength of your supporting evidence. Present only the information that will be most compelling to your audience. The evidence and logical reasoning that you use should be relevant to your explanation of the issue and its effects.
- **Anticipation of Counterclaims** One of the most effective strategies for persuasion is to anticipate and address the concerns and counterclaims of audience members who might disagree with you.
- **Additional Evidence** If you think you need additional evidence, consider interviewing an authority on your subject.
- **Conclusion** End your speech by summarizing effects of the issue. Restate your opinion in memorable fashion. Then make an impression by speaking your last sentence slowly so your listeners feel its impact. A great last line often earns sincere applause.

9.R.1.D.1.a Read grade-level instructional text: with fluency, accuracy, comprehension and appropriate expression 9.W.2.C.1.b Compose text with: a logical order 9.R.1.D.1.a Read grade-level instructional text: with fluency, accuracy, comprehension and appropriate expression

Deliver Your Speech

Use Verbal Techniques

Oratory is the art of the eloquent public speaker. How you use your voice can be as persuasive as what you say. Before you deliver your persuasive speech, practice your delivery techniques. Look at the chart below for tips:

Using Your Voice To Create Effects

EFFECTS	Volume	Enunciation	Pace	Rhythm
Oratorical	Forceful; not loud	Clear, precise, formal	Steady, slow for key ideas	Stress syllables to form a rhythm
Dramatic	Medium-loud; lower for key points	Clear but not forced	Pause before a key point	Steady; poetic for key points
Comic	Normal, conversational	Informal; casual but clear	Quick and light	Bouncy, singsong
Authoritative	Forceful; loud for key ideas	Clear, precise, formal	Steady to slow	Natural; emphatic for key points

Use Nonverbal Techniques

Facial expressions and gestures can make your speech more persuasive.

- Use hand gestures to emphasize key points in your argument and to underscore a particular rhythm.
- Slightly adjust your facial expressions to match the content of your speech.
- Turn your head to address all sections of the audience during your speech.
- Consider using props, charts, or other visual aids to clarify your case and make it more convincing.

Use an Outline

Just as you outlined your essay, you'll want to outline the main points of your speech. Doing so will keep you on track, especially if you get nervous when speaking in front of a crowd. Use numbers to organize your main points and bullets to keep track of the supporting details.

A Good Persuasive Speech

- focuses on the central opinion of your thesis
- delivers logical reasoning with clarity and force
- offers supportive proof
- anticipates and addresses possible counterclaims
- uses effective verbal and nonverbal speaking techniques

Speaking Tip

Deliver your speech to a friend. Ask your friend to evaluate both your argument and your speaking techniques. Use his or her feedback to make any necessary adjustments to your argument and to improve your speaking skills.

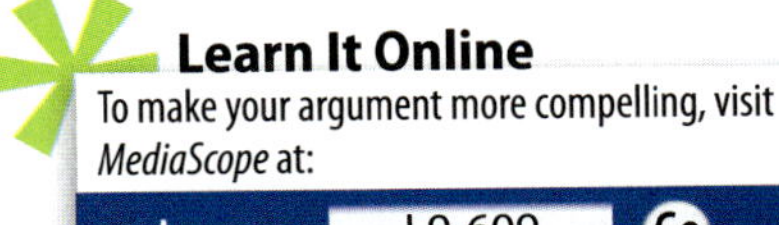

Learn It Online

To make your argument more compelling, visit *MediaScope* at:

go.hrw.com L9-609 Go

FOCUS ON MISSOURI COURSE LEVEL EXPECTATIONS

Writing Skills Review

Persuasive Essay **Directions:** Read the following persuasive essay by a student. Then read and respond to the questions that follow.

Go Ride a Bike

(1) More people should ride bicycles. (2) Using a bicycle as a means of transportation helps you to exercise every day. (3) Riding a bicycle, according to health experts, provides an excellent cardiovascular work-out. (4) That means it is good for your heart and circulatory system. (5) It is also good for the environment.

(6) Bicycle riding is not only good for the health of the rider. (7) The planet benefits because exhaust from motor vehicles contributes to air, ground, and water pollution. (8) The world is in danger as it is, so we must find ways to protect our fragile planet.

(9) If you ride a bike as quick as a flash, you can burn 240 calories an hour. (10) That is not bad if you want to lose weight or just improve your health in general. (11) So instead of paying to work out at a gym, as many adults and even teenagers do, go ride a bike!

(12) Using a bicycle as transportation is one of those activities that has very little downside. (13) The dangers are overrated, and the benefits far outweigh any drawbacks that bicycle riding poses. (14) So it's time to get a move on for your health and the environment: Dust off that old ten-speed, pump up the tires, and ride to school tomorrow!

---

1. To better grab the reader's attention, the writer could rewrite the first sentence to read:

A More people should ride bicycles; if they did, the world would be a better place.

B The best thing about riding a bicycle is the breeze running through your hair.

C Riding a bicycle can help the planet.

D People should ride bicycles so that they will be more like Lance Armstrong.

9.W.2.C.1.a

2. To better convey an important point, the writer could expand the first paragraph with a second sentence that reads:

A Bicycling can be good for both you and the environment.

B I have two bicycles—a mountain bike and a road bike.

C Repairing a flat bicycle tire is easy when you know how.

D Many families enjoy bicycling as a hobby they can do together.

9.W.2.C.1.f

9.W.3.A.1.a Compose a variety of texts: using narrative, descriptive, expository, and/or persuasive features *Also covered* **9.W.2.B.1.b; 9.W.2.C.1.a; 9.W.2.C.1.b; 9.W.2.C.1.f; 9.W.2.D.1.b**

3. To improve the organization of the essay, which of these revisions would be *most* effective?

A Move sentence 9 up to after sentence 1.

B Switch the order of the second and third paragraphs.

C Combine the second and fourth paragraphs.

D Switch the order of sentences 8 and 9.

9.W.2.C.1.b

4. Which of the following sentences could be added to support the argument that biking is good exercise?

A Ride slowly when you begin.

B I prefer riding a bike to jogging.

C Two-mile trips are quicker by bike.

D Bike riding tones the leg muscles.

9.W.2.B.1.b

5. How could the writer revise sentence 9 so that it conveys a more serious **tone?**

A If you ride as quick as a flash, you can burn major calories.

B If you want to burn 240 calories in an hour, go as fast as you can for as long as you can stand it.

C If you ride at a vigorous 6 miles per hour, you can burn 240 calories in an hour.

D If you do 6 miles per hour, you can burn a lot of calories.

9.W.2.D.1.b

6. How might the writer better address the concern that bicycle riding is dangerous?

A by citing weight-loss statistics of people who ride bicycles twice a week

B by comparing bicycles to pedestrians

C by showing how helmets and bike lanes have improved bicycle safety

D by listing average bicycle prices

9.W.2.B.1.b

7. How could the writer make the third paragraph more persuasive?

A by offering statistics on car emissions

B by offering facts about global warming

C by citing a reputable source

D all of the above

9.W.2.B.1.b

UNIT 3

Poetry

Writers on Writing

Judith Ortiz Cofer on Poetry

Judith Ortiz Cofer was born in Puerto Rico and immigrated to New Jersey as a child, where she learned English. She is now an English professor and writes award-winning poems, essays, and stories. Her writing often explores the power of heritage, family, and memory.

"Poems take me to what my grandmother called *la pura verdad.* When she was about to tell us a *cuento,* my abuela would begin by declaring, *Es la pura verdad,* or, 'the whole

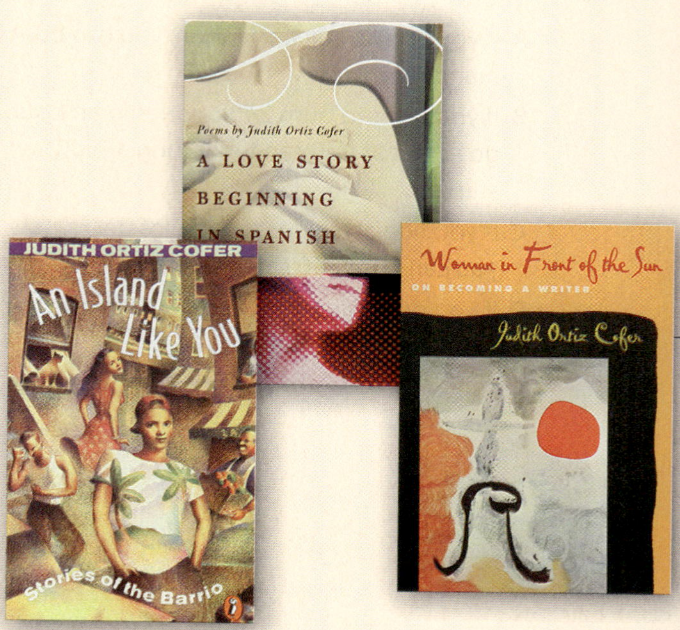

truth.' This meant that even if it was a tale of fairies, witches, talking animals, or whatever she chose to invent for us on a particular day, we were to listen closely for the truth the story contained, a lesson for our life to be found within the thrilling, scary, or funny story.

The real truth of a poem or story may not be strictly factual, that is, based only on what actually happened on a particular day to a specific person. Instead it shows us what it can possibly mean to have imagined an event or stepped into someone else's heart or mind. This is why most people will not ask, is this poem true? The poem is always true. And it is always about us because it reveals the truth about being human.

To me, writing a poem is like boarding a time machine. By harnessing the energy of language, with its tremendous powers of association, connotation, symbolism and metaphor-making, the poet may travel to any location in the past, present, or future, and discover new ways to look at her world and her life. Poems can show us what we know and also, on occasions, what we don't but should know. This is why the best poems often pose revelation in the form of a question: Who am I? What does it mean?

Poetry, if it's good, is the ultimate connection between minds. It gives us a common ground. The poem is a territory that is open to all; no passports are necessary. I do not have to be British to be struck with awe again and again by Shakespeare's genius, nor Irish to be carried away by W. B. Yeats's beautiful and wise words, nor do I need to be African-American to be able to meld minds with Langston Hughes or with Rita Dove. Nor do you need to be a Latina to understand the messages in my poems. I am there with every poet whose work I read, and you are here with me in the poems I write because no matter what the subject is, they are always about us sharing this world as human beings who experience joy and pain in similar ways. *Es la pura verdad.*"

Think as a Writer

In this essay, Judith Ortiz Cofer says, "The poem is always true." What do you think she means?

Song of Songs IV (1958) by Marc Chagall (1887–1985). Oil on paper.

COLLECTION 7

Poetry

INFORMATIONAL TEXT FOCUS

Generating Research Questions

"The man who has no imagination has no wings."

—Muhammad Ali

What Do You Think? What are the limits of the imagination?

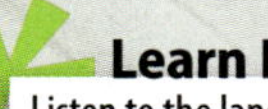

Learn It Online

Listen to the language of poetry through the audio recordings online:

go.hrw.com L9-615 Go

Literary Focus

by **Carol Jago**

What Is the Language of Poetry?

Like soccer and ballet, poetry employs specialized vocabulary to describe particular techniques. Understanding the terms described below will help you be more articulate as you talk and write about the poems you read in this collection.

Forms of Poetry

Every poem has a **speaker,** the voice that speaks to us, but not every poem has the same form. Here are some poetic forms included in this collection:

Lyric Poem A **lyric poem** expresses a speaker's emotions or thoughts. It does not tell a story. Most lyric poems are short, like "A Blessing" by James Wright (page 654). Lyric poems usually convey a single strong emotion.

Free Verse Poetry that does not have a regular meter or rhyme scheme is called **free verse.** Poets writing in free verse try to capture the natural rhythms of ordinary speech. Notice how E. E. Cummings arranges words on the page to create rhythm in his free verse poem "in Just-" on page 632.

Haiku A **haiku** is a three-line poem with seventeen syllables—five each in lines 1 and 3 and seven in line 2. Haiku (like those on page 636) usually contrast two images from nature or daily life. They may also include a seasonal word and a moment of discovery.

Sonnet A **sonnet** is a fourteen-line lyric poem. Like "Once by the Pacific" by Robert Frost (page 640), most sonnets are written in iambic pentameter (see page 618) and have a regular rhyme scheme.

Catalog Poem A **catalog poem** presents a list of many different images. Look at "The Car" by Raymond Carver (page 648) for an example of how a catalog of images can create depth and intensity.

Ballad A **ballad** is a song that tells a story. Ballads use a steady rhythm, strong rhymes, and repetition. Read "Ballad of Birmingham" (page 714) by Dudley Randall, and listen for the refrain that repeats with slight changes.

Imagery

Imagery is one of a poet's most powerful tools. An **image** is a word or phrase that appeals to one or more of our five senses. An image can help us picture color or motion. Sometimes it helps us imagine that we hear a sound, smell an odor, feel a texture, or even taste something.

Notice how these two poets create images using **sensory details,** elements that help you imagine how something looks, sounds, smells, feels, or tastes:

These tortillas we slice and fry to crisp strips
This rich egg scrambled in a gray clay bowl

from "Daily" by Naomi Shihab Nye

. . . a shepherd's horn echoing in the valley,
fishnets stretched to dry on sandy flats.

from "Country Scene"
by Hồ Xuân Hương

MO 9.R.2.A.1 Analyze and evaluate the text features in grade-level text 9.R.2.B.2.b Identify and explain literary techniques, in text emphasizing: imagery 9.R.2.B.2.c Identify and explain literary techniques, in text emphasizing: repeated sound, line or phrase

Figures of Speech

One way that poets play with words is by using **figurative language**—expressions that put aside literal meanings in favor of imaginative connections. A figure of speech is based on a comparison that is not literally true. If your brother says to you, "I'm going to give you a piece of my mind," you understand that he is using a figure of speech to make a point.

Figurative language can be a kind of shorthand. While it can take a lot of words to express an idea in literal terms, the same idea can be communicated instantly by a figure of speech.

Similes: *X* Is Like *Y* In a **simile** (SIHM uh lee), two unlike things are compared using a word such as *like, as, than,* or *resembles*. Here, Robert Frost uses the word *like* to compare clouds to hair getting blown in front of one's face:

> The clouds were low and hairy in the skies,
> Like locks blown forward in the gleam of eyes.
> from "Once by the Pacific"
> by Robert Frost

In this poem, William Wordsworth creates a different simile about clouds:

> I wandered lonely as a cloud
> That floats on high o' er vales and hills,
> from "I Wandered Lonely as a Cloud"
> by William Wordsworth

Metaphors: *X* Is *Y* A **metaphor** (MEHT uh fawr) is a comparison of two unlike things in which one thing is said to *be* another. Unlike similes, metaphors do not contain a word such as *like* or *as*. For example: "You eat like a pig!" is a simile, and "You are a pig!" is a metaphor.

A metaphor can be direct or implied. A **direct metaphor** directly compares two things by using a verb such as *is.*

> The days are nouns: touch them
> The hands are churches that worship the world
> from "Daily" by Naomi Shihab Nye

An **implied metaphor** implies or suggests a comparison between two things, rather than stating the comparison directly. The speaker in "Starfish," by Lorna Dee Cervantes, looks at a colony of these animals and calls them "hundreds; no— / Thousands of baby stars." The metaphor is indirect because she does not state that the starfish *are* baby stars; she just suggests that idea.

Personification In **personification,** which is a type of metaphor, human qualities are given to something that is not human, such as an object, an animal, a force of nature, or even an idea. In this poem, the sea is personified as someone holding a person protectively:

> lie gently and wide to the light-year
> stars, lie back, and the sea will hold you.
> from "First Lesson"
> by Philip Booth

Here a poet personifies twilight as someone springing quietly into a grassy field:

> Off the highway to Rochester, Minnesota,
> Twilight bounds softly forth on the grass,
> from "A Blessing" by James Wright

(*continued*)

Literary Focus

The Sounds of Poetry: Rhyme and Rhythm

In poetry, words communicate more than just their meanings. They are full of beats and sounds that can create musical sensations and emotional effects.

Rhyme A **rhyme** is the repetition of a stressed vowel sound and any sounds that follow it in words that are close together in a poem: *nails* and *whales, material* and *cereal, icicle* and *bicycle*.

Rhyme Scheme Rhymes in poetry occurring at the ends of lines are called **end rhymes.** A **rhyme scheme** is a regular pattern of end rhymes. In this stanza, lines 1 and 3 rhyme; so do lines 2 and 4. You can use letters to describe this rhyme scheme, such as *abab:*

> The golden brooch my mother wore
> She left behind for me to wear;
> I have no thing I treasure more:
> Yet, it is something I could spare.
>
> from "The Courage That My Mother Had" by Edna St. Vincent Millay

Internal Rhyme Not all rhymes come at the ends of lines. **Internal rhymes** occur when at least one of the rhymed words falls within a line. These rhymes can be much less obvious than end rhymes. This stanza follows an *abba* rhyme scheme:

> The man of snow is, nonetheless, content,
> Having no wish to go inside and die.
> Still, he is moved to see the youngster cry.
> Though frozen water is his element . . .
>
> from "Boy at the Window" by Richard Wilbur

When you listen again, you will hear the internal rhymes *snow, no,* and *go* in the first two lines.

Approximate Rhyme **Approximate rhymes** repeat some sounds but are not exact echoes. Approximate rhymes are also called *half rhymes, near rhymes,* and *slant rhymes*. Instead of being an exact echo like *moon* and *June*, approximate rhyme is a partial echo, like *moon* and *morn*.

Rhythm **Rhythm** is a musical quality based on repetition. When you talk about the beat you hear when you read a poem, you are describing its rhythm.

Meter One common form of rhythm is **meter,** a regular pattern of stressed and unstressed syllables in the lines of a poem. You can **scan** a poem to identify its meter. Stressed syllables are marked ´; unstressed syllables are marked ˘.

A **foot** usually consists of one stressed syllable and one or more unstressed syllables. An **iamb** is a foot that has an unstressed syllable followed by a stressed syllable (da DAH). This line is written in iambic pentameter: it has five iambs:

> ˘ ´ ˘ ´ ˘ ´ ˘
> "But soft! / What light / through yon / der
> ´ ˘ ´
> win / dow breaks?"
>
> from *The Tragedy of Romeo and Juliet* by William Shakespeare

You will also find these common feet in poems:

- A **trochee** (TROH kee) has a stressed syllable followed by an unstressed syllable (DAH dah).
- An **anapest** (AN uh pehst) has two unstressed syllables, then a stressed syllable (dah dah DAH), as in the word *underneath.*
- A **dactyl** (DAK tuhl) has one stressed syllable, then two unstressed syllables (DAH dah dah), as in the word *hickory.*
- A **spondee** (SPAHN dee) is two stressed syllables (DAH DAH).

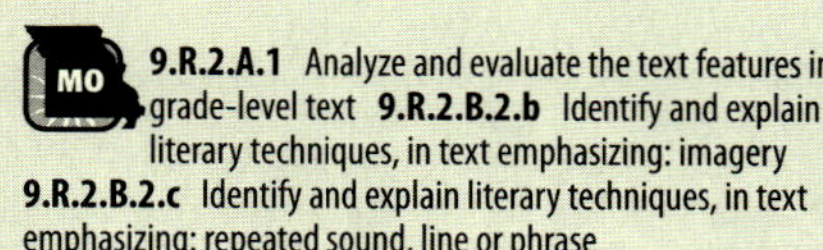
9.R.2.A.1 Analyze and evaluate the text features in grade-level text **9.R.2.B.2.b** Identify and explain literary techniques, in text emphasizing: imagery **9.R.2.B.2.c** Identify and explain literary techniques, in text emphasizing: repeated sound, line or phrase

This poet mixes spondees, trochees, and iambs to create a complex, driving rhythm:

Sun, rain, / curving sky
Mountain, / Oceans, / Leaf and / stone
Star shine, / moon glow
You're all / that I / can call / my own.

from "Woman Work"
by Maya Angelou

Sound Devices

Poets also create sound effects by listening to the sounds the words make when you say them aloud.

Onomatopoeia Using words that sound like what they mean is **onomatopoeia** (ahn uh mat uh PEE uh). The words can echo a natural sound (*buzz, hiss*) or a mechanical noise (*clickety-clack, toot*).

Alliteration Repeating the same consonant sound in several words is **alliteration** (uh liht uh RAY shuhn): *fragrant flowers, dog days, cool as a cucumber*. The *w, m,* and *st* sounds are repeated in these lines.

They were women then
My mama's generation
Husky of voice—stout of
Step

from "Women" by Alice Walker

Assonance The repetition of vowel sounds in several words is **assonance** (AS uh nuhns). You hear the same sounds in *quick fix* and *around town*.

Your Turn Analyze Poetry

Read these poems. Then, complete the activities.

Dust of Snow

The way a crow
Shook down on me
The dust of snow
From a hemlock tree

Has given my heart
A change of mood
And saved some part
Of a day I had rued.

—Robert Frost

Lost

Desolate and lone
All night long on the lake
Where fog trails and mist creeps,
The whistle of a boat
Calls and cries unendingly,
Like some lost child
In tears and trouble
Hunting the harbor's breast
And the harbor's eyes.

—Carl Sandburg

1. How would you describe the form of each poem?
2. Name one image in each poem. Identify the sensory details that create each image.
3. Which poem makes greater use of figurative language? How does this poem use metaphor, simile, and/or personification?

Learn It Online
Learn how to read the language of poetry. Try *PowerNotes* at:
go.hrw.com L9-619 Go

Analyzing Visuals

How Can You Recognize Poetic Elements in Art?

Try to visualize the night sky ripping open and leaking liquid moonlight in buttery falls. Or the sun plummeting into the ocean in a huge steamy splash. Poetic images such as these happily ignore reality. Instead, they speak to our imagination. Similarly, artists use imagery, repetition, form, color, and contrasts to create visual poetry—images that reinvigorate or alter our take on a common subject.

Analyzing an Artwork

Use these guidelines to help you identify poetic elements in an artwork.

1. Study the artwork. What image provides the focus of the work?
2. Take note of contrasts in color, light, and shadow. What effect does the use of contrast create?
3. Evaluate the artist's representation of the subject. Is it realistic or fantastic? What idea is the artist trying to convey?
4. Analyze the mood that is suggested by the artist's use of color, line, and imagery.
5. Look for repeated shapes, lines, and colors. What effect does the use of repetition create?

Look at the details of the artwork below to help you answer the questions on page 621.

MO **9.R.2.B.2.b** Identify and explain literary techniques, in text emphasizing: imagery **9.R.2.C.1.b** Use details from text(s): to analyze character, plot, setting, point of view

1. What **image** dominates this artwork? What has the artist done to make this image appear powerful?

2. Where has the artist used **repetition** of color and shapes? What effect has the use of **repetition** created?

3. Is this depiction of the sun and waves realistic or imaginative? Explain.

4. What **mood** is created by the artist's use of color, contrast, and form?

Japanese lacquer screen with sun and sea design (detail) (17th–18th century). Private collection.

Your Turn Talk About an Artwork

Spend some time analyzing this artwork. Next, discuss with a partner ways in which this artwork is like a poem. Finally, page through your book to find another artwork that contains poetic elements. What are they?

Reading Focus

by **Kylene Beers**

What Skills Help You Understand and Enjoy Poetry?

Reading a poem is just like reading a story. Not so! Compared to prose, poetry looks different on the page. Poets use fewer words than prose writers do, so their word choice is critical. Often, the words poets use have both a literal meaning (denotation) and an implied meaning (connotation). Poets may also use far more figurative language, imagery, and sound devices than most prose writers do. The reading skills that follow will help you understand and appreciate the poems in this collection.

Reading a Poem

Use these tips when you read a poem:

- Look for punctuation telling you where sentences begin and end.
- If lines of a poem are difficult to understand, look for the subject, verb, and object (if there is one) of each sentence.
- You may wish to paraphrase lines of poetry as you read. Remember that when you paraphrase, you restate the writer's ideas in your own words.

	My Paraphrase
Sentence 1 (or Stanza 1)	
Sentence 2 (or Stanza 2)	

Read Aloud

You will better understand the meaning of a poem if you read it aloud. Read slowly and clearly. Remember not to stop at the ends of lines unless a punctuation mark tells you to. Finally, re-read the poem. Each time you read a poem, you'll get more meaning—and probably more pleasure—from it.

Visualizing

The ability to **visualize,** or see in your mind what you are reading, is important for understanding and responding to poetry. To visualize a poem, pay attention to the descriptive words and phrases that the poet uses. Note which descriptive words appeal to the senses of sight, hearing, smell, taste, and touch. Then, do your best to create that sensory experience in your mind. A chart like the one below will help you analyze how the use of sensory details helps poets to create fully realized images and ideas.

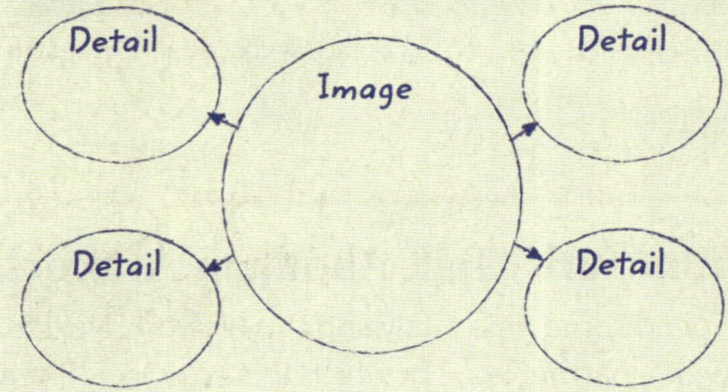

Analyzing Word Choice

Every word in a poem is important. Poets choose words carefully in order to create the right impression. As you read, pay close attention to the words' shades of meaning.

Denotation and Connotation The **denotation** of a word is its literal dictionary definition. The **connotations** of a word are all the meanings, associations, or emotions that have come to be attached to it. For example, *large* and *bulky* have similar denotations but different connotations. The connotation of *large* is fairly neutral; the connotation of *bulky* is more negative. Describing something as bulky suggests that it is awkward or *too* big.

Use a denotation and connotation chart like the one below to identify meanings and associations for key words in a poem.

Word	Denotation	Connotations

Syntax When you consider a poet's word choices, you can also examine the poem's **syntax,** or word order and grammar. For example, some poems include inverted, or reversed, word order. Instead of saying "The night is cold," a poet might emphasize the adjective by writing "Cold is the night."

Your Turn Apply Reading Skills

Practice your reading skills by reading this poem. Then, complete the activities that follow.

Fork

This strange thing must have crept
Right out of hell.
It resembles a bird's foot
Worn around the cannibal's neck.
As you hold it in your hand,
As you stab with it into a piece of meat,
It is possible to imagine the rest of the bird:
Its head which like your fist
Is large, bald, beakless, and blind.

—Charles Simic

1. How many sentences are in this poem? Paraphrase each one.
2. Read the poem aloud. What sound devices and rhythms are more apparent when you hear the poem? Read the poem a second time. How did your reading change when you were familiar with the poem?
3. Visualize the bird that the speaker describes. What sensory details help you create a strong mental image?
4. Consider the poet's use of the verb *stab* in line 6. He might also have used *poke*. What other verbs might he have selected? What connotations do you associate with *stab?*
5. Choose three key words in the poem and explain their denotations and connotations.

Now go to the Skills in Action: Reading Model

Learn It Online
Practice these skills with *PowerNotes* online:
go.hrw.com
L9-619
Go

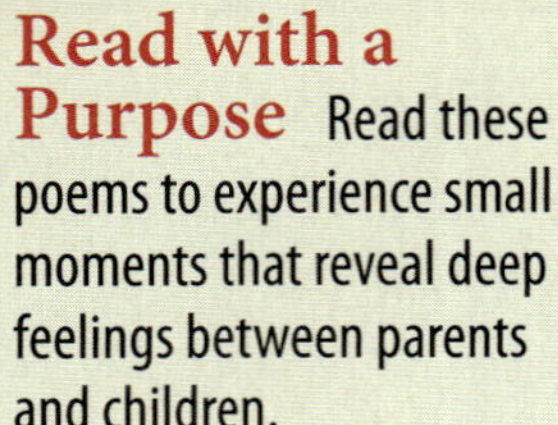

SKILLS IN ACTION

Reading Model

POETRY

My Father's Song

by **Simon J. Ortiz**

Read with a Purpose Read these poems to experience small moments that reveal deep feelings between parents and children.

Wanting to say things,
I miss my father tonight.
His voice, the slight catch,
the depth from his thin chest,
the tremble of emotion
in something he has just said
to his son, his song:

We planted corn one Spring at Acu°—
we planted several times
but this one particular time
I remember the soft damp sand
in my hand.

My father had stopped at one point
to show me an overturned furrow;
the plowshare had unearthed
the burrow nest of a mouse
in the soft moist sand.

Very gently, he scooped tiny pink animals
into the palm of his hand
and told me to touch them.
We took them to the edge
of the field and put them in the shade
of a sand moist clod.

I remember the very softness
of cool and warm sand and tiny alive mice
and my father saying things.

Literary Focus

Metaphor The implied metaphor compares the father's words to a song.

Literary Focus

Rhyme These lines contain the internal rhyme of *furrow* and *burrow*.

Literary Focus

Alliteration The repeated *t* sounds emphasize the father's delicate handling of the mice.

Reading Focus

Visualizing Sensory details help you experience the final image.

---

8. Acu: The Acoma Pueblo community in which Ortiz and his family lived.

First Lesson

by **Philip Booth**

Lie back daughter, let your head
be tipped back in the cup of my hand.
Gently, and I will hold you. Spread
your arms wide, lie out on the stream
and look high at the gulls. A dead-
man's float is face down. You will dive
and swim soon enough where this tidewater
ebbs to the sea. Daughter, believe
me, when you tire on the long thrash
to your island, lie up, and survive.
As you float now, where I held you
and let go, remember when fear
cramps your heart what I told you:
lie gently and wide to the light-year
stars, lie back, and the sea will hold you.

Reading Focus

Reading Aloud The first time you read the poem aloud, listen to its natural rhythms. Notice how the commas in lines 1 and 3 guide your reading.

Literary Focus

Rhyme Line endings include some exact rhymes, as in lines 1 and 3 (*head/Spread*), as well as some approximate rhymes (*believe/survive*).

Literary Focus

Personification The poem opens with the image of a father holding his child. At the end of the poem, the sea takes over and performs this human action.

MEET THE WRITERS

Simon J. Ortiz
(1941–   )

A Storyteller Poet from New Mexico

Simon J. Ortiz grew up in a village with two names. In English it was called McCarty's. But his family called it Deetseyamah. They lived in the Acoma Pueblo community in Albuquerque, New Mexico. For the first six years of his life, Ortiz spoke only the Acoma language, an experience he says "was the basis and source of all I would do later in poetry." He began to learn English when he attended day school. With English came an understanding of the divided world in which many Native Americans live.

Ortiz's father gave him the nickname "the Reporter" because of his habit of listening to and telling stories. As a writer, Ortiz translated this natural curiosity into a strong commitment to preserving the ancient heritage of Pueblo storytellers who share songs, stories, and chants.

Philip Booth
(1925–2007)

A Teacher Poet from New England

Philip Booth felt a strong connection with the landscape of his childhood. He was born in Hanover, New Hampshire, but spent many years in Maine, living in a house that had been owned by his family for generations. His poetry often focuses on the geography of New England as well as the daily lives of New Englanders.

In his first year at Dartmouth College, Booth took a poetry class with the famous poet Robert Frost. In addition to encouraging Booth to become a poet, the experience increased his desire to become a teacher. He taught at several universities and founded the creative writing program at Syracuse University.

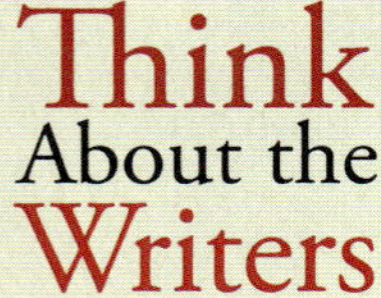

Think About the Writers

What impact might you expect the poets' feelings about their heritage to have on their writing?

SKILLS IN ACTION
Wrap Up

9.R.2 Develop and apply skills and strategies to comprehend, analyze and evaluate fiction, poetry and drama from a variety of cultures and times
9.R.1.E.1.c Develop vocabulary through text: using glossary, dictionary and thesaurus

Into Action: Elements of Poetry Checklist

Complete this chart to analyze the poetic elements used in these poems.

Elements of Poetry	"My Father's Song"	"First Lesson"
Form		
Imagery		
Figurative Language		
Rhyme/ Rhythm		
Sound Devices		

Talk About . . .

Get together with a small group, and discuss "My Father's Song" and "First Lesson" by answering the following questions. Try to use each Academic Vocabulary word listed at the right at least once in your discussion.

1. What are the nuances of the final image in "My Father's Song"?
2. What life lessons does the speaker of "First Lesson" associate with learning to swim?
3. How do memories of childhood evoke deep feelings in these poems?
4. How does each poet elaborate on a single clear event or memory?

Write About . . .

5. Which of these poems had a greater impact on you? Identify the poetic elements and techniques you think evoke strong responses in readers.

Writing Focus

Think as a Reader/Writer

Find It in Your Reading You will read a wide variety of poetry in Collection 7. The Writing Focus activities on the Preparing to Read pages help you identify key elements of each writer's craft. You will have an opportunity to practice your writing skills in the Applying Your Skills pages.

Academic Vocabulary for Collection 7

Talking and Writing About Poetry

Academic Vocabulary is the language you use to write and talk about literature. Use these words to discuss the poetry you read in this collection. The words are underlined throughout the collection.

nuances (NOO ahns ihz) *n.:* shades of difference in meaning or feeling. *The meaning of the poem is obvious, but the small nuances make it special.*

associate (uh SOH shee ayt) *v.:* connect in thought. *Poets might associate the moon with love.*

evoke (ih VOHK) *v.:* bring a memory or feeling to mind. *Pine trees might evoke memories of winter.*

elaborate (ih LAB uh rayt) *v.:* go into greater detail about something. *The second and third sections of the poem elaborate on the ideas in the opening section.*

Your Turn

Copy the words from the Academic Vocabulary list into your *Reader/Writer Notebook*. Then, write a sentence in which you use each word correctly.

Imagery and Form

CONTENTS

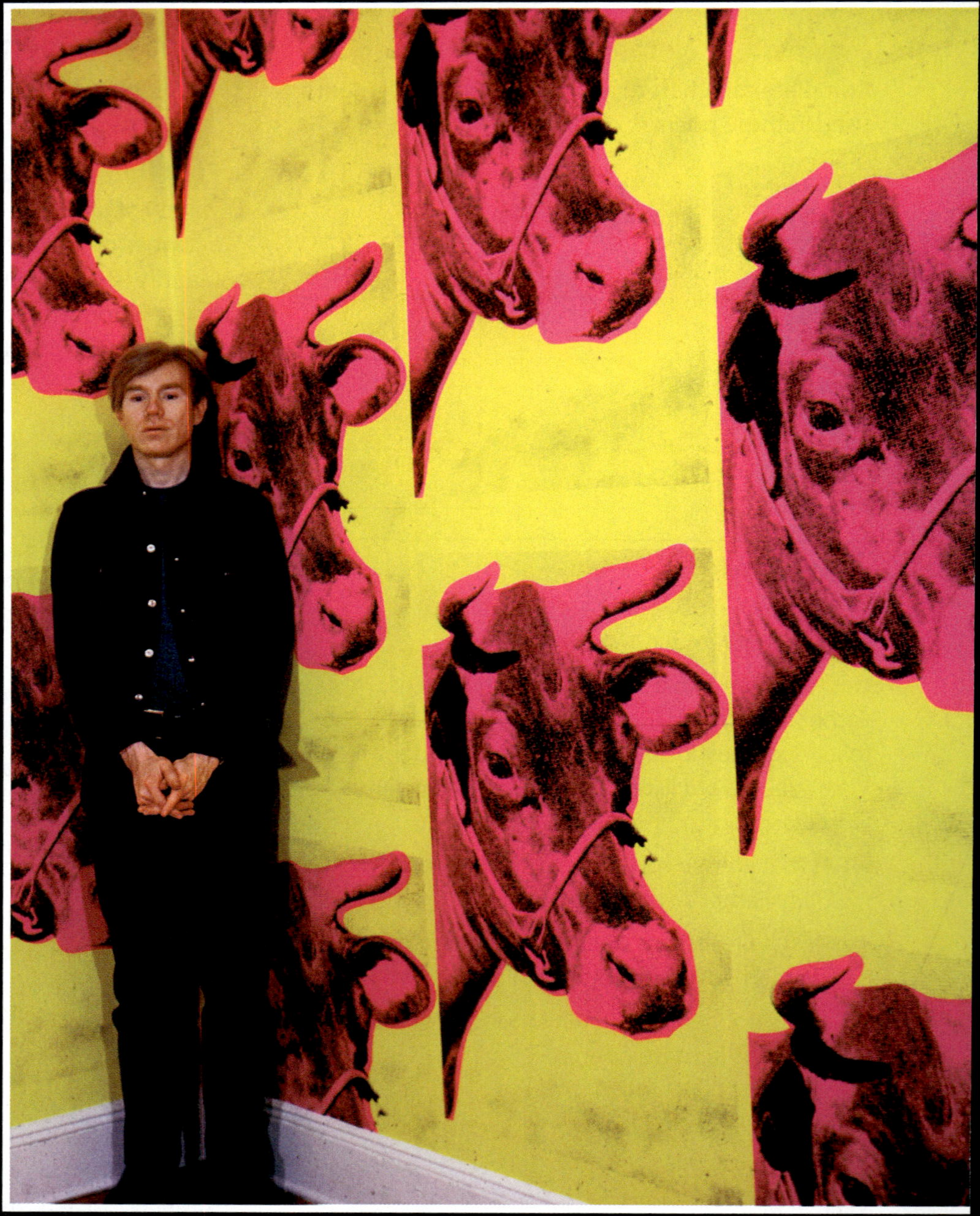

Andy Warhol with Cow Wallpaper, 1966. Image: © Steve Schapiro/Corbis Artwork: © The Andy Warhol Foundation for the Visual Arts/Corbis.

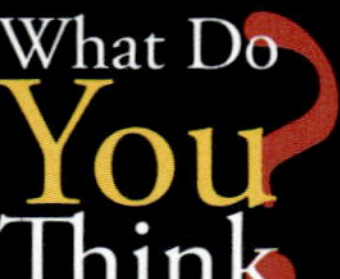

How do poets help us view ordinary aspects of life in new ways?

QuickWrite

Look around you and choose an ordinary object you see. What could you say about this object that would make a friend regard it in a new way? Write down your thoughts.

POETRY

Preparing to Read

Starfish / in Just-

9.R.2.B.2.b Identify and explain literary techniques, in text emphasizing: imagery
9.R.2 Develop and apply skills and strategies to comprehend, analyze and evaluate fiction, poetry and drama from a variety of cultures and times

Literary Focus

Imagery An **image** is a word or phrase that appeals to one or more of our senses: hearing, sight, touch, smell, and taste. Poets use imagery to help us share their sensory experiences. As you read "Starfish" and "in Just-," notice how the poets use images to help us experience the world in an unusual or original way.

TechFocus As you read the poems in this section, think about the way images are used to create advertisements and commercials.

Reading Focus

Reading a Poem To determine where one thought begins and ends in a poem, look at the poet's use of punctuation, line breaks, and spacing. The poems you are about to read contain **run-on lines,** which do not have punctuation at the end. To follow the speaker's train of thought, look carefully at the way words and phrases run together—and then apart—in a playful way.

Into Action As you read, fill in a chart to indicate where you think each thought begins and ends in each poem.

Complete Thoughts in "Starfish"	Complete Thoughts in "in Just-"
1. "They [line 5]. . . . fish jaw."	1.
2.	2.

Writing Focus

Think as a Reader/Writer

Find It in Your Reading Cervantes and Cummings use parallel structure to create balanced images. **Parallel structure** refers to the use of the same grammatical form—two nouns, adjectives, or phrases, for example—to express ideas. As you read the poems, record examples of parallel structure in your *Reader/Writer Notebook*. How does the poets' use of it enhance the images in each work?

Reader/Writer Notebook

Use your **RWN** to complete the activities for these selections.

Vocabulary

Starfish

pliant (PLY uhnt) *adj.:* easily bendable. *When they are alive, starfish are pliant.*

sprawled (sprawld) *v.:* lying down with limbs spread out awkwardly. *The speaker collected some of the starfish sprawled in the sand.*

martyrs (MAHR tuhrz) *n.:* people who choose to die rather than give up their beliefs. *The speaker compares the starfish washed up on the beach to martyrs.*

artless (AHRT lihs) *adj.:* simple; innocent. *The soft, beautiful starfish look like artless creatures.*

splayed (splayd) *v.* used as *adj.:* spread out. *With their splayed legs, the starfish looked like hands.*

Language Coach

Suffixes **Suffixes,** or word parts added to the ends of words, can change words' meanings. For example, the word *art* can mean "skill in trickery or deception." Look what happens when you add the suffix *–less,* meaning "without" or "lacking," to *art: art* + *–less* = "lacking skill in trickery." In other words, *artless* means "innocent." What do you think *artful* means?

Learn It Online
Take an in-depth look at vocabulary with Word Watch at:

go.hrw.com L9-629 

Learn It Online
Learn more about Cummings at:
go.hrw.com L9-630 Go

MEET THE WRITERS

Lorna Dee Cervantes

(1954–)

The Freedom of Words

Growing up in San Jose, California, Lorna Dee Cervantes discovered literature by reading the books in the houses that her mother cleaned for a living. Cervantes was writing poetry by the age of eight and completed her first collection of poems when she was fifteen. Writing gave Cervantes, who is of Mexican and American Indian ancestry, a sense of freedom: "When you grow up as I did, a Chican-India in a barrio in a Mexican neighborhood in California . . . you're ignored. . . . And you're not expected to speak, much less write."

Cervantes explores the Mexican American experience in her award-winning poetry. She also plays an important role in furthering the work of other Chicana and Chicano writers.

E. E. Cummings

(1894–1962)

Nobody-but-Himself

A highly innovative and experimental poet—and an extremely popular one—E. E. Cummings played with punctuation, language, and typography in his works. Here is what he had to say about being a poet: "A poet is somebody who feels, and who expresses his feeling through words. This may sound easy. It isn't . . . [because] the moment you feel, you're nobody-but-yourself. To be nobody-but-yourself—in a world which is doing its best, night and day, to make you everybody else—means to fight the hardest battle which any human being can fight." Cummings viewed a poet's life of "fighting and working and feeling" as "the most wonderful . . . on earth."

Think About the Writers

For Cervantes and Cummings, how does poetry serve as a form of self-expression?

Build Background

The word *starfish* is misleading. Starfish are not actually fish but echinoderms, animals with spiny skeletons. Although starfish come in a wide range of sizes, most species are between eight and twelve inches in diameter and have five arms. Their colors range from brown to various shades of yellow, orange, and pink. Starfish are flexible and move by using the tube feet on the undersides of their arms.

"in Just-" contains an allusion, or reference, to the Greek god Pan. Known for his ugliness, Pan was part animal, with a goat's horns, legs, and hooves. A god of the woodlands and merrymaking, he is usually shown playing a flute and leading shepherds in a dance. Like many other Greek gods, Pan was rather tricky. The word *panic* stems from his name because he was considered the source of scary noises that came from the forest at night.

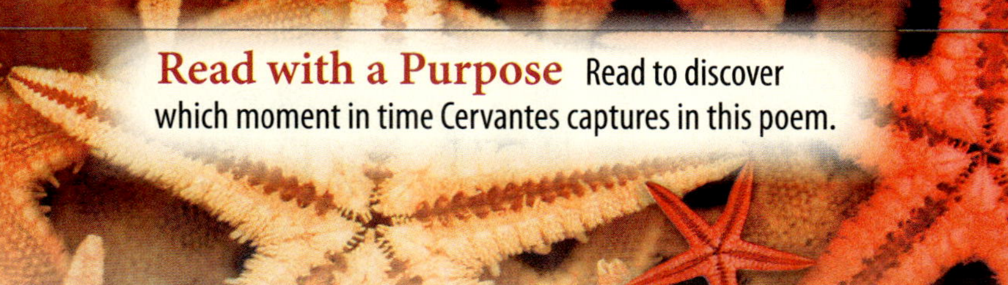

Read with a Purpose Read to discover which moment in time Cervantes captures in this poem.

Starfish

by **Lorna Dee Cervantes**

They were lovely in the quartz and jasper° sand
As if they had created terrariums° with their bodies
On purpose; adding sprigs of seaweed, seashells,
White feathers, eel bones, miniature
Mussels, a fish jaw. Hundreds; no— (A)
Thousands of baby stars. We touched them,
Surprised to find them soft, pliant, almost
Living in their attitudes. We would dry them, arrange them,
Form seascapes, geodesics . . .° We gathered what we could
In the approaching darkness. Then we left hundreds of (B)
Thousands of flawless five-fingered specimens sprawled
Along the beach as far as we could see, all massed
Together: little martyrs, soldiers, artless suicides
In lifelong liberation from the sea. So many
Splayed hands, the tide shoveled in. (C)

1. **quartz** (kwawrts) **and jasper** (JAS puhr): Quartz, a hard mineral, is the most common element in sand. Jasper is a reddish, yellow, or brown type of quartz.

2. **terrariums** (tuh RAIR ee uhmz): small enclosures or containers that house plants or animals.

9. **geodesics** (jee uh DEHS ihks): interlocking, repeating patterns.

(A) **Reading Focus** **Reading a Poem** What effect does Cervantes create by ending line 5 in the middle of a thought, as indicated by the dash?

(B) **Literary Focus** **Imagery** What does the image of the approaching darkness contribute to the feeling of the poem?

(C) **Reading Focus** **Reading a Poem** Find the subject, verb, and object of the sentence in lines 14–15. What effect does Cervantes create by placing the words of the last sentence in nontraditional order?

Vocabulary **pliant** (PLY uhnt) *adj.:* easily bendable.
sprawled (sprawld) *v.:* lying down with limbs spread out awkwardly.
martyrs (MAHR tuhrz) *n.:* people who choose to die rather than give up their beliefs.
artless (AHRT lihs) *adj.:* simple; innocent.
splayed (splayd) *v.* used as *adj.:* spread out.

Read with a Purpose
Read this poem to find out why the boys and girls are celebrating.

in Just-

by **E. E. Cummings**

in Just-
spring   when the world is mud-
luscious the little
lame balloonman

whistles   far   and wee **A**

and eddieandbill come
running from marbles and
piracies and it's
spring

when the world is puddle-wonderful

the queer
old balloonman whistles
far   and   wee
and bettyandisbel come dancing

from hop-scotch and jump-rope and **B**

it's
spring
and
    the

            goat-footed

balloonMan   whistles
far
and
wee

A **Reading Focus** **Reading a Poem** How does the spacing of the words in line 5 reflect the meaning of the line?

B **Literary Focus** **Imagery** To which sense does the image in lines 14–15 appeal? What mood does Cummings evoke through the use of this image?

Applying Your Skills

MO **9.R.2.B.2.b** Identify and explain literary techniques, in text emphasizing: imagery **9.R.2.B.2.c** Identify and explain literary techniques, in text emphasizing: repeated sound, line or phrase *Also covered* **9.R.2; 9.W.3.A.1.a; 9.R.1.G.1.a**

Starfish / in Just-

Respond and Think Critically

Reading Focus

Read with a Purpose

1. What event does Cervantes explore in her poem?
2. What is the reason for celebration in "in Just-"?

Reading Skills: Reading a Poem

3. Compare the ideas you recorded in your chart to the original poems. What main ideas does Cervantes convey in her poem? How does Cummings's use of spacing and punctuation add nuance to his ideas about spring?

Complete Thoughts in "Starfish"	Complete Thoughts in "in Just-"
1. "They [line 1]. . . . fish jaw [line 5]"	1. "in Just- [line 1] . . . far and wee [line 5]"
2.	2.

Vocabulary Check

Tell whether each statement is true (T) or false (F).

4. **Pliant** metals cannot be twisted easily.
5. People **sprawled** on a couch might look relaxed.
6. **Martyrs** are people who lack strong beliefs.
7. An **artless** person might be easily tricked.
8. One uses **splayed** fingers to form a fist.

Literary Focus

Literary Analysis

9. **Interpret** Why do you think the speaker in "Starfish" compares the starfish to martyrs, soldiers, and suicides? What do these comparisons tell you about the speaker's view of the starfish?
10. **Analyze** Could "Starfish" be about something more than just starfish? What might the poem have to say about humans?
11. **Interpret** What two meanings might the word *just* have in "in Just-"? What activities and emotions does the speaker associate with spring?
12. **Hypothesize** Why might Cummings have made single words out of the names *Eddie* and *Bill* and *Betty* and *Isbel*?

Literary Skills: Imagery

13. **Identify** List images in "Starfish" that appeal to the senses of sight and touch. In "in Just-," to what senses do the images "mud-luscious" and "puddle-wonderful" appeal? Which images do you find most effective? Why?

Literary Skills Review: Refrain

14. **Identify** A **refrain** is a repeated word, phrase, line, or group of lines that writers use to create rhythm and emphasize points. Find the refrains used in "in Just-." What does Cummings's use of refrain contribute to the poem?

Writing Focus

Think as a Reader/Writer

Use It in Your Writing Write a poem in which you use vivid imagery to convey the feelings you associate with a season. Be sure to use parallel structure when you express your ideas.

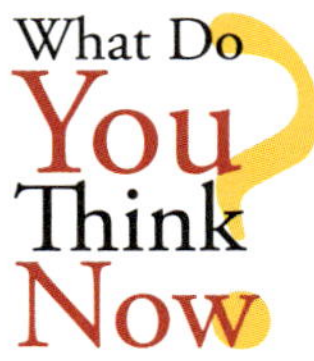

How have the poets transformed fleeting moments into lasting memories?

POETRY

Preparing to Read

Haiku

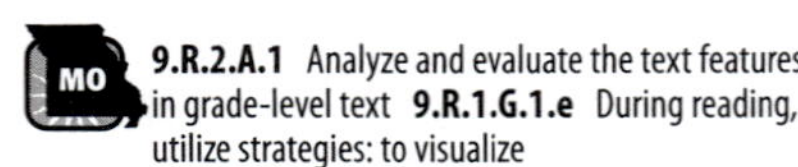

9.R.2.A.1 Analyze and evaluate the text features in grade-level text **9.R.1.G.1.e** During reading, utilize strategies: to visualize

Reader/Writer Notebook

Use your **RWN** to complete the activities for these selections.

Literary Focus

Haiku The most famous form of Japanese poetry, haiku can capture moments of life with the speed and precision of a snapshot. In the Japanese language, a **haiku**

- has seventeen syllables—five each in lines 1 and 3, seven in line 2
- presents images from nature and everyday life—usually two contrasting images
- often contains a seasonal word or symbol (*kigo*)
- presents a moment of discovery or enlightenment (*satori*)

Language Coach

Translations Below, in the original Japanese with the English translation, is Bashō's haiku, which also appears on page 636. *Ya* is a word frequently used in haiku to mean something like *Lo!* in English, which means "Look!" or "See!" Some translators indicate it with a colon, since it suggests a kind of equation.

Furu *ike* *ya*
old pond :

Kawazu *tobikomu*
frog jump in

Mizu *no* *oto*
water of sound

Reading Focus

Visualizing Since haiku work by suggestion, **visualizing** the scene described in a haiku—forming impressions in your mind—will enhance your appreciation of the poem. Visualizing will help you enter the moment of insight captured in the haiku.

Into Action For each haiku, use a cluster diagram to record the sensory impressions that come to mind as you read the poem.

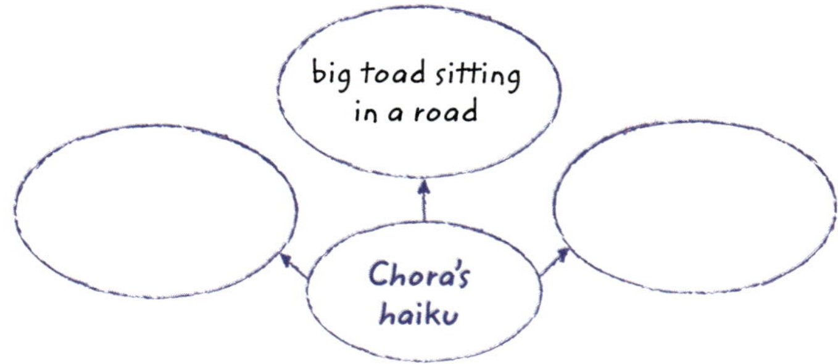

Writing Focus

Think as a Reader/Writer

Find It in Your Reading The power of haiku lies in the appeal to our senses. As you read each haiku, record in your *Reader/Writer Notebook* the sense or senses to which each poem appeals.

Learn It Online

Improve your comprehension of these poems by listening online at:

go.hrw.com L9-634 

MEET THE WRITERS

Miura Chora

(1729–1780)

In the eighteenth century, members of the "Back to Bashō" movement believed that the quality of *haikai,* a form of linked verse, had declined. They sought to restore the form to the ideals established by Matsuo Bashō in his works. Miura Chora, a member of the movement, was a *haikai* master with many students.

Chiyo

(1703–1775)

Chiyo is the most celebrated of the women writers of haiku. Some critics, preferring haiku that are more subtle, indirect, and suggestive, believe her poems too explicit and lacking the mystery of true haiku. However, Chiyo's admirers think that such critics mistake haziness in haiku for profound thought.

Matsuo Bashō

(1644–1694)

Matsuo Bashō is considered to be both the creator and greatest master of the haiku form. Bashō was a deeply spiritual man who became a Zen monk in his later years. His haiku show a zest for every speck of life—a sense that nothing in this world is unimportant.

Kobayashi Issa

(1763–1827)

Kobayashi Issa had a very sad life. Despite his poverty and the fact that he saw all his beloved children die, he wrote extraordinarily simple poems that are full of human tenderness and wry humor.

Think About the Writers

What did Bashō represent for Chora?

Build Background

Haiku evolved in seventeenth-century Japan from long multiverse poems called *haikai no renga*. Poets detached the first three lines from these longer poems—the opening stanza (*hokku*)—and transformed them into independent structures. Today, writing haiku remains extremely popular in Japan.

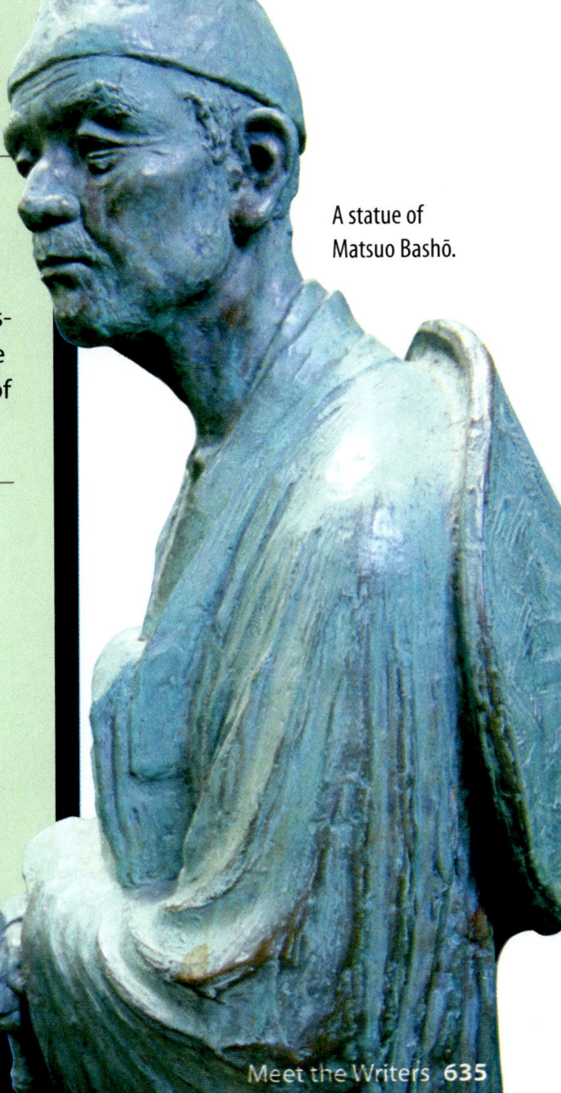

A statue of Matsuo Bashō.

Read with a Purpose As you read these haiku, identify the aspect of nature described in each.

Analyzing Visuals

Viewing and Interpreting How does this scene evoke the feeling, or tone, of the haiku on this page?

Lotus Collage (c. 1965–1970) by Robert McIntosh.

Haiku

Get out of my road
and allow me to plant these
bamboos, Mr. Toad.
—Miura Chora

A morning glory
Twined round the bucket:
I will ask my neighbor for water. **A**
—Chiyo

The old pond;
A frog jumps in:
Sound of water. **B**
—Matsuo Bashō

A dragonfly!
The distant hills
Reflected in his eyes.
—Kobayashi Issa

A Literary Focus Haiku Colons, dashes, and exclamation points in a haiku indicate a shift in subject or mood. Note the colon in this haiku. Why might the speaker decide to get water from a neighbor?

B Reading Focus Visualizing What do you visualize happening when the frog jumps in?

Applying Your Skills

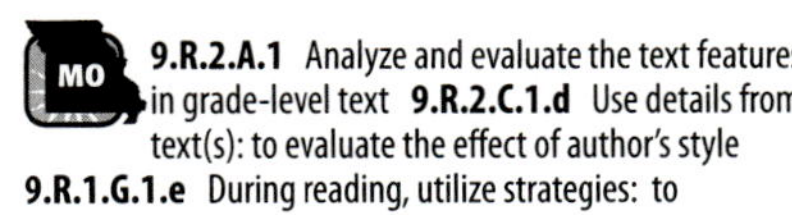

9.R.2.A.1 Analyze and evaluate the text features in grade-level text **9.R.2.C.1.d** Use details from text(s): to evaluate the effect of author's style **9.R.1.G.1.e** During reading, utilize strategies: to visualize *Also covered* **9.W.3.A.1.a**

Haiku

Respond and Think Critically

Reading Focus

Read with a Purpose

1. What aspect of nature is explored in each poem?

Reading Skills: Visualizing

2. Review the cluster diagrams you filled in as you read, and answer the following questions:
   - Which haiku created the most vivid pictures in your mind? Why?
   - Bashō viewed haiku's restricted length as an advantage, not a drawback, asking, "Is there any good in saying everything?" How would you respond to this question? Support your answer with evidence from your cluster diagrams.

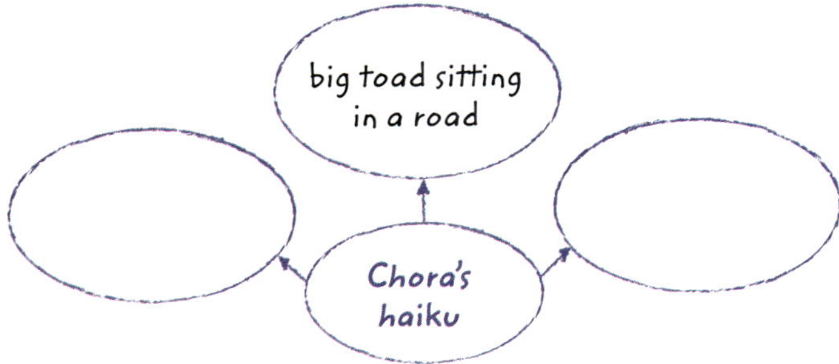

Literary Focus

Literary Analysis

3. **Hypothesize** Think about the person speaking in each haiku. Where do you think the speaker is, and what might he or she be doing?
4. **Interpret** Consider the name of the plant in Chiyo's haiku. In what way could the words *morning glory* also be used to describe what the speaker experiences?
5. **Interpret** Critics have made the following observation about the sound of water in Bashō's haiku: It is there, and it is not there. What do you think this statement means?
6. **Analyze** In Issa's haiku, what is the larger meaning of the speaker's discovery—what insight about nature does the poem convey?

Literary Skills: Haiku

7. **Identify** These haiku are translated from Japanese. Which of the four haiku contains the traditional number of syllables in each line?
8. **Analyze** Haiku often balance two contrasting images. For example, in Chora's poem the toad in the road, probably resting, contrasts with the human, busy planting bamboo. What contrasting images can you find in the other haiku?

Literary Skills Review: Tone

9. **Analyze** The imagery, word choice, and punctuation in haiku help convey the **tone,** or attitude, of the speaker. How would you describe the speaker's tone in Chora's and Issa's haiku?

Writing Focus

Think as a Reader/Writer

Use It in Your Writing Write a haiku presenting images from nature or everyday life. Limit your haiku to three lines, but it is not necessary to use just seventeen syllables—unless you want a challenge!

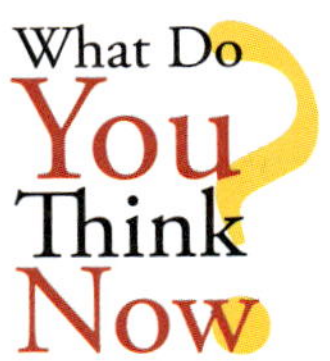

In what way do the haiku poets show the wonders of nature in a new light?

POETRY

Preparing to Read

Once by the Pacific

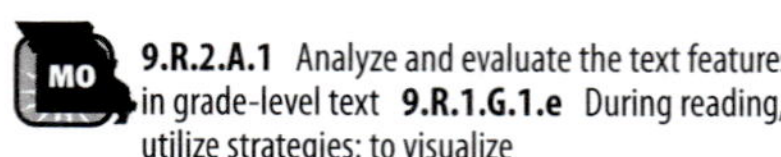

9.R.2.A.1 Analyze and evaluate the text features in grade-level text **9.R.1.G.1.e** During reading, utilize strategies: to visualize

Reader/Writer Notebook

Use your **RWN** to complete the activities for this selection.

Literary Focus

Sonnet A **sonnet** is a centuries-old poetic form with a strict structure. It has fourteen lines, follows a regular rhyme pattern, and is usually written in **iambic pentameter.** An **iamb** is an unstressed syllable followed by a stressed one (dah DAH), as in the word *before*. **Pentameter** means there are five stressed syllables, or beats, in each line.

There are two traditional types of sonnets. In an **Italian sonnet,** also called a **Petrarchan sonnet,** the first eight lines (the **octave**) pose a problem, which is responded to in the last six lines (the **sestet**). In an **English sonnet,** also known as a **Shakespearean sonnet,** three four-line units—each usually presenting an idea—are followed by a **couplet,** a two-line unit. Some modern poets create their own types of sonnets. As you read "Once by the Pacific," consider the characteristics it shares with traditional sonnets.

Reading Focus

Visualizing By allowing images to fill your mind as you read, or **visualizing,** you can step inside a scene described in a poem. Doing so will help improve your understanding of the poem.

Into Action As you read, list images in the left-hand column of a chart. In the right-hand column, sketch the scene that you visualize.

Images	What I Visualize
great waves low clouds	

Writing Focus

Think as a Reader/Writer

Find It in Your Reading This sonnet contains powerful images. As you read, record in your *Reader/Writer Notebook* the emotions evoked by these images.

Vocabulary

din (dihn) *n.:* loud, continuous noise. *The crashing waves created a din.*

gleam (gleem) *n.:* shining; glow; flash of light. *There was a gleam of light before the sky clouded over.*

intent (ihn TEHNT) *n.:* purpose; goal. *The violent waves were signs of a destructive intent.*

Language Coach

Multiple-Meaning Words The word *intent* has multiple meanings. *Intent* can be used as an adjective that means "determined" (*we were intent on winning the election*); "intense" (*the child's intent stare made me uncomfortable*); "having the attention fixed" (*intent on her work, she was not distracted by the noise*). How is the word *intent* defined on the list above? Write a sentence using *intent* as an adjective and as a noun.

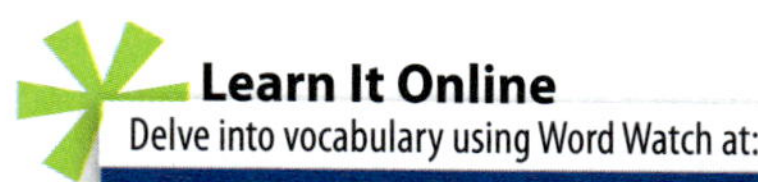

Learn It Online

Delve into vocabulary using Word Watch at:

go.hrw.com L9-638

Applying Your Skills

MO **9.R.2.A.1** Analyze and evaluate the text features in grade-level text **9.R.2.C.1.d** Use details from text(s): to evaluate the effect of author's style **9.R.1.G.1.e** During reading, utilize strategies: to visualize *Also covered* **9.W.3.A.1.a**

Haiku

Respond and Think Critically

Reading Focus

Read with a Purpose

1. What aspect of nature is explored in each poem?

Reading Skills: Visualizing

2. Review the cluster diagrams you filled in as you read, and answer the following questions:
   - Which haiku created the most vivid pictures in your mind? Why?
   - Bashō viewed haiku's restricted length as an advantage, not a drawback, asking, "Is there any good in saying everything?" How would you respond to this question? Support your answer with evidence from your cluster diagrams.

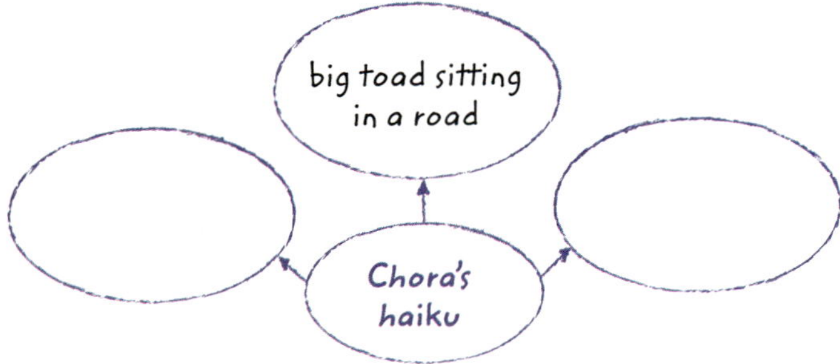

Literary Focus

Literary Analysis

3. **Hypothesize** Think about the person speaking in each haiku. Where do you think the speaker is, and what might he or she be doing?
4. **Interpret** Consider the name of the plant in Chiyo's haiku. In what way could the words *morning glory* also be used to describe what the speaker experiences?
5. **Interpret** Critics have made the following observation about the sound of water in Bashō's haiku: It is there, and it is not there. What do you think this statement means?
6. **Analyze** In Issa's haiku, what is the larger meaning of the speaker's discovery—what insight about nature does the poem convey?

Literary Skills: Haiku

7. **Identify** These haiku are translated from Japanese. Which of the four haiku contains the traditional number of syllables in each line?
8. **Analyze** Haiku often balance two contrasting images. For example, in Chora's poem the toad in the road, probably resting, contrasts with the human, busy planting bamboo. What contrasting images can you find in the other haiku?

Literary Skills Review: Tone

9. **Analyze** The imagery, word choice, and punctuation in haiku help convey the **tone,** or attitude, of the speaker. How would you describe the speaker's tone in Chora's and Issa's haiku?

Writing Focus

Think as a Reader/Writer

Use It in Your Writing Write a haiku presenting images from nature or everyday life. Limit your haiku to three lines, but it is not necessary to use just seventeen syllables—unless you want a challenge!

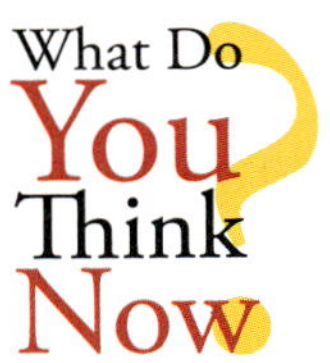

In what way do the haiku poets show the wonders of nature in a new light?

POETRY

Preparing to Read

Once by the Pacific

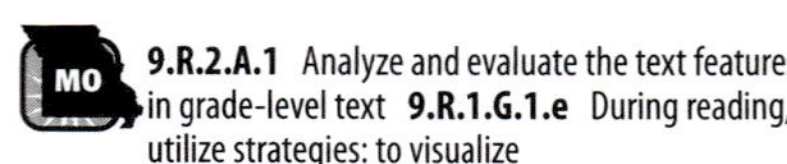

9.R.2.A.1 Analyze and evaluate the text features in grade-level text **9.R.1.G.1.e** During reading, utilize strategies: to visualize

Reader/Writer Notebook

Use your **RWN** to complete the activities for this selection.

Literary Focus

Sonnet A **sonnet** is a centuries-old poetic form with a strict structure. It has fourteen lines, follows a regular rhyme pattern, and is usually written in **iambic pentameter.** An **iamb** is an unstressed syllable followed by a stressed one (dah DAH), as in the word *before*. **Pentameter** means there are five stressed syllables, or beats, in each line.

There are two traditional types of sonnets. In an **Italian sonnet,** also called a **Petrarchan sonnet,** the first eight lines (the **octave**) pose a problem, which is responded to in the last six lines (the **sestet**). In an **English sonnet,** also known as a **Shakespearean sonnet,** three four-line units—each usually presenting an idea—are followed by a **couplet,** a two-line unit. Some modern poets create their own types of sonnets. As you read "Once by the Pacific," consider the characteristics it shares with traditional sonnets.

Reading Focus

Visualizing By allowing images to fill your mind as you read, or **visualizing,** you can step inside a scene described in a poem. Doing so will help improve your understanding of the poem.

Into Action As you read, list images in the left-hand column of a chart. In the right-hand column, sketch the scene that you visualize.

Images	What I Visualize
great waves low clouds	

Writing Focus

Think as a Reader/Writer

Find It in Your Reading This sonnet contains powerful images. As you read, record in your *Reader/Writer Notebook* the emotions evoked by these images.

Vocabulary

din (dihn) *n.:* loud, continuous noise. *The crashing waves created a din.*

gleam (gleem) *n.:* shining; glow; flash of light. *There was a gleam of light before the sky clouded over.*

intent (ihn TEHNT) *n.:* purpose; goal. *The violent waves were signs of a destructive intent.*

Language Coach

Multiple-Meaning Words The word *intent* has multiple meanings. *Intent* can be used as an adjective that means "determined" (*we were intent on winning the election*); "intense" (*the child's intent stare made me uncomfortable*); "having the attention fixed" (*intent on her work, she was not distracted by the noise*). How is the word *intent* defined on the list above? Write a sentence using *intent* as an adjective and as a noun.

Learn It Online

Delve into vocabulary using Word Watch at:

go.hrw.com L9-638 Go

MEET THE WRITER

Learn It Online
Learn more about Robert Frost at:
go.hrw.com L9-639 Go

Robert Frost

(1874–1963)

"A Terrifying Poet"

It should not be surprising to learn that the poet who wrote "Once by the Pacific" had been afraid of the dark since he was a child. Robert Frost is often viewed as a "gentleman farmer" whose poetry about the New England countryside and the rural lives of ordinary people is characterized by simplicity, innocence, and cheerfulness. However, Frost experienced deep sadness and fear in his life, and his poetry also explores the harshness of the world. The critic Lionel Trilling called Frost "a terrifying poet."

A Presidential Honor

Frost once said, "I look at a poem as a performance. I look on the poet as a man of prowess, just like an athlete. He's a performer. And the things you can do in a poem are very various. You speak of figures, tones of voice varying all the time." Highly regarded by both the general public and critics, Frost gave his own hugely popular public performances in which he would read—or "say"—his poems and offer his reflections. Two years before his death, he received the great honor of being invited to read his poem "The Gift Outright" at the inauguration of President John F. Kennedy in 1961. Frost was the first poet ever to read a poem at a presidential inauguration.

For another biography of Frost, see page 660.

Think About the Writer In what ways do you think a poem can sometimes be considered a "performance"?

Build Background

In "Once by the Pacific," Robert Frost makes an allusion, or reference, to the Bible. In the biblical account of the creation of the universe, God says, "Let there be light" (Genesis 1:3). After each stage of creation, the Bible says, "And God saw that it was good." Keep these words in mind as you read Frost's vision of an event that is the opposite of creation.

Read with a Purpose Read this poem to find out what the speaker is observing.

Once by the Pacific

by **Robert Frost**

The shattered water made a misty din.
Great waves looked over others coming in,
And thought of doing something to the shore
That water never did to land before.
The clouds were low and hairy in the skies, A
Like locks blown forward in the gleam of eyes.
You could not tell, and yet it looked as if
The shore was lucky in being backed by cliff,
The cliff in being backed by continent;
It looked as if a night of dark intent
Was coming, and not only a night, an age. B
Someone had better be prepared for rage.
There would be more than ocean-water broken
Before God's last *Put out the Light* was spoken.

A **Literary Focus** **Sonnet** Is this line written in iambic pentameter? Count out the unstressed and stressed syllables.

B **Reading Focus** **Visualizing** What do you visualize when you think about the image "a night of dark intent / Was coming"?

Vocabulary **din** (dihn) *n.:* loud, continuous noise.
gleam (gleem) *n.:* shining; glow; flash of light.
intent (ihn TEHNT) *n.:* purpose; goal.

Applying Your Skills

9.R.2.A.1 Analyze and evaluate the text features in grade-level text **9.R.2.C.1.d** Use details from text(s): to evaluate the effect of author's style **9.R.1.G.1.e** During reading, utilize strategies: to visualize **9.R.1.G.1.a** During reading, utilize strategies: to determine meaning of unknown words

Once by the Pacific

Respond and Think Critically

Reading Focus

Read with a Purpose

1. Where is the speaker while observing the ocean? What are the waves doing?

Reading Skills: Visualizing

2. Compare the sketches you made as you read the poem with those of a partner. What do the similarities and differences in your sketches suggest about the poet's use of imagery?

Vocabulary Check

Tell whether each statement is true (T) or false (F).

3. The **din** in a crowded restaurant can make it difficult to hear what someone is saying.
4. You polish silver to give it a **gleam**.
5. An **intent** is sometimes hostile.

Literary Focus

Literary Analysis

6. **Analyze** What images in lines 1–4 help you hear and see the waves?
7. **Analyze** What images in lines 5–6 help you picture the clouds?
8. **Interpret** Whose "rage" is described in line 12? What could cause that rage?
9. **Interpret** Review the Build Background (on page 639). How does the last line of the sonnet differ from God's words of creation in the Bible? How do you interpret the meaning of the sonnet's last two lines? What is going to happen?
10. **Analyze** What do you think is the **theme,** or insight about life, of Frost's sonnet?

Literary Skills: Sonnet

11. **Classify** Look at how "Once by the Pacific" is structured. What characteristics of a sonnet does it have? Is it an Italian sonnet or an English sonnet, or is it a modern variation of the sonnet form? Give examples to support your ideas.

Literary Skills Review: Tone and Mood

12. **Interpret** A writer's **tone** is his or her attitude toward the topic, and **mood** is the atmosphere that the writer's word choice creates. Re-read Frost's poem, and describe its tone and mood. What details help to create each? You may want to use a chart like this one to help you.

Details Creating Tone	Details Creating Mood

Writing Focus

Think as a Reader/Writer

Use It in Your Writing Look through the notes you took in your *Reader/Writer Notebook* about the images that Frost uses in this poem. Which image do you find the most powerful? Write a short response to this poem, describing the image and why you find it so moving.

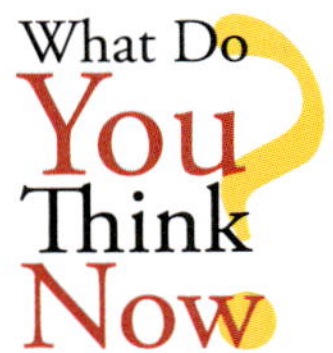

Has this poem helped you to see the ocean differently? Why or why not?

POETRY

Preparing to Read

Country Scene

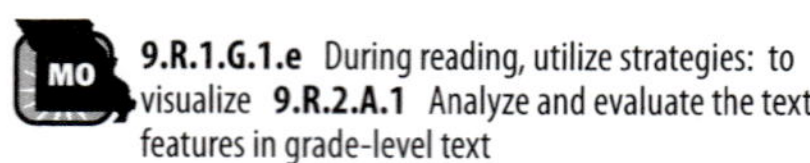

Literary Focus

Lyric Poem A **lyric poem** is a short poem that expresses a speaker's thoughts or feelings. Lyric poems come in many forms, such as sonnets like Robert Frost's "Once by the Pacific" (page 640). In ancient Greece, lyric poems were sung to the music of a stringed instrument called a lyre, so today we call the words to all types of songs lyrics. In "Country Scene" the speaker expresses her thoughts about what lasts—and what does not.

Reading Focus

Visualizing Poets appeal to our imaginations, and by **visualizing,** or creating mental images, you can set your imagination to work. Visualizing will help you grasp not only what poets state directly but also what their words suggest indirectly.

Into Action As you read, list images in the left-hand column of a chart. In the right-hand column, sketch the scene that you visualize.

Images	What I Visualize
waterfall plunges in mist	

Writing Focus

Think as a Reader/Writer

Find It in Your Reading This lyric poem is filled with unstated emotion. As you read, record in your *Reader/Writer Notebook* the images that appeal to your senses of sight and hearing. What emotions do those images evoke?

Use your **RWN** to complete the activities for this selection.

Vocabulary

desolate (DEHS uh liht) *adj.:* not lived in; gloomy; producing a feeling of loneliness and sadness. *There are no people in this desolate scene.*

canopy (KAN uh pee) *n.:* in a forest, the leafy layer formed by the tops of trees. *The canopy cast shadows on the ground.*

tolling (TOHL ihng) *v.:* ringing slowly at regular intervals. *In the distance, a bell is tolling.*

Language Coach

Multiple-Meaning Words Re-read the definition of *canopy* in the list above. Did you know that the word *canopy* can also refer to an awning or rooflike covering? You have probably seen a canopy at the entrance to a building or perhaps over a bed. What other uses of *canopy* do you know?

Learn It Online
Expand your vocabulary with Word Watch online:
go.hrw.com L9-642 Go

MEET THE WRITER

Hồ Xuân Hu'o'ng

(c. 1770s–1820s)

The Mysterious Spring Essence

During the Vietnam War, an American named John Balaban brought medical care to wounded Vietnamese children. Along with supplies, he brought a tape recorder to capture the classic poems he heard the villagers recite. Many of their favorites, they told him, had been written by the great poet Hồ Xuân Hu'o'ng, whose name means "spring essence."

Little is known about Hồ. She is thought to have been born to the "second wife," or concubine, of a scholar in north central Vietnam. She became a concubine as well, to an official she ridiculed in a poem as Mr. Toad. At that time, Vietnamese women had little status. Yet Hồ earned fame and admiration for her writing. Her poetry was so popular with Vietnamese readers that her attacks on male authority figures went unpunished.

Rescuing a Language

Today only a few dozen people know how to read Nom, the traditional Vietnamese writing system Hồ used. Balaban, her translator, has worked to change that. His collection of Hồ's poetry, *Spring Essence,* includes her poems in both the modern Vietnamese and the Nom scripts next to his English translations. It is the first time the ancient script, which was originally reproduced by woodblock, has ever come off a printing press.

Think About the Writer

What can you infer about Hồ from her nickname?

Build Background

In its original Vietnamese, "Country Scene" is an example of a poetic form called *lu-shih*. The English translation cannot begin to show how challenging *lu-shih* poems are to write. Vietnamese is a tonal language, and the tones in a poem must fall at certain places in each seven-syllable line. Every *lu-shih* poem has eight lines, with rhymes usually at the end of the first, second, fourth, sixth, and eighth lines. While we may not be able to appreciate the complexity of this *lu-shih* poem in its English translation, we can certainly think about its message and share the beauty of its imagery.

Sisters in Spirit by Vu Thu Hien. Watercolor on handmade paper, 23" x 31".

Courtesy of Raquelle Azran Vietnamese Contemporary Fine Art, www.artnet.com/razran.html.

Read with a Purpose Read this poem to find out what the poem's speaker is looking at and thinking about.

Country Scene

by **Hô` Xuân Hu'o'ng**
translated by **John Balaban**

The waterfall plunges in mist.
Who can describe this desolate scene:

the long white river sliding through
the emerald shadows of the ancient canopy (A)

. . . a shepherd's horn echoing in the valley,
fishnets stretched to dry on sandy flats.

A bell is tolling, fading, fading
just like love. Only poetry lasts. (B)

(A) **Reading Focus** **Visualizing** What do you visualize when you think about the image "the ancient canopy"?

(B) **Literary Focus** **Lyric Poem** Explain the comparison that the speaker makes between love and a tolling bell.

Vocabulary **desolate** (DEHS uh liht) *adj.:* not lived in; gloomy; producing a feeling of loneliness and sadness.
canopy (KAN uh pee) *n.:* in a forest, the leafy layer formed by the tops of trees.
tolling (TOHL ihng) *v.:* ringing slowly at regular intervals.

The Drai Sap waterfalls on part of the Ho Chi Minh Trail in Vietnam.

Applying Your Skills

9.R.2.A.1 Analyze and evaluate the text features in grade-level text **9.R.2.C.1.d** Use details from text(s): to evaluate the effect of author's style **9.R.1.G.1.e** During reading, utilize strategies: to visualize **9.R.1.G.1.a** During reading, utilize strategies: to determine meaning of unknown words

Country Scene

Respond and Think Critically

Reading Focus

Read with a Purpose

1. What is this poem's speaker looking at? What does she or he hear?

Reading Skills: Visualizing

2. Review your sketch of the poem's images. Do you think your sketch fully captures the imagery in the poem's text? Explain why or why not.

Vocabulary Check

Tell whether each statement is true (T) or false (F).

3. People who like company seek out **desolate** places.
4. In the woods, a dense **canopy** provides shade.
5. When a bell is **tolling**, it can be heard.

Literary Focus

Literary Analysis

6. **Analyze** What is missing from the description in lines 5–6? Why is it significant that the speaker mentions a shepherd's horn, but not the shepherd, and fishnets, but not the fisher?
7. **Analyze** To what does the speaker compare and contrast love in lines 7–8?
8. **Make Judgments** According to this speaker, what outlasts both nature and love? In your opinion, which is more lasting—love or poetry? Explain your response.

Literary Skills: Lyric Poem

9. **Analyze** A lyric poem is generally short and expresses a speaker's thoughts and feelings. What thoughts does this poem's speaker express? How would you describe the speaker's feelings?

Literary Skills Review: Tone and Mood

10. **Evaluate** How would you describe the speaker's **tone,** or attitude? Is this a pessimistic, negative poem? Or is it a positive poem? Explain.
11. **Interpret** What **mood,** or atmosphere, does this poem evoke? What words and phrases help to create this mood?

Writing Focus

Think as a Reader/Writer

Use It in Your Writing Write a lyric poem about a place you know well. Use imagery to convey the emotions you associate with this place. Use a chart like this one to help you think of images that appeal to many senses.

Imagery

Sight	Hearing	Smell	Taste	Touch

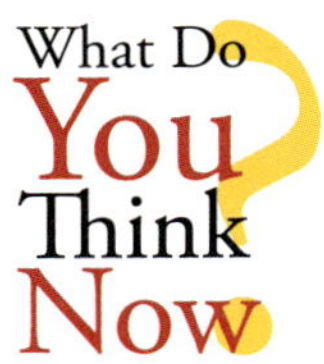

How might a scene from nature spark thoughts about life and its meaning?

POETRY

Preparing to Read

The Car / Daily

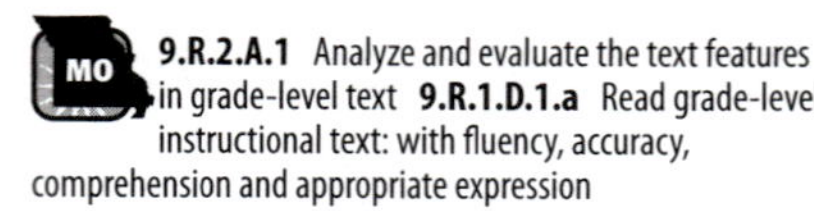

9.R.2.A.1 Analyze and evaluate the text features in grade-level text **9.R.1.D.1.a** Read grade-level instructional text: with fluency, accuracy, comprehension and appropriate expression

Literary Focus

Catalog Poem Like the catalogs that come from stores, catalog poems bring together many different images and present them for your attention. A **catalog poem** takes the form of a list of images, united by the poet's use of repetition and an underlying message, as you will see when you read "The Car" and "Daily."

Reading Focus

Reading Aloud Poems are meant to be heard. Since a poem's sound is essential to its meaning, it is important to read a poem aloud. When you read a poem aloud, pay attention to line breaks and punctuation. They can indicate when a thought ends and when you should pause or come to a full stop. Capitalization may also indicate a new thought or sentence.

Into Action As you read each poem aloud, record your ideas about its meaning.

"The Car"	"Daily"
1. Lines 1 through 5 describe an old car. 2.	

Writing Focus

Think as a Reader/Writer

Find It in Your Reading Raymond Carver and Naomi Shihab Nye use repetition very differently in their catalog poems. As you read, record in your *Reader/Writer Notebook* examples of repetition in each poem. What are the effects of each poet's use of repetition?

Reader/Writer Notebook

Use your **RWN** to complete the activities for these selections.

Vocabulary

The Car

alignment (uh LYN muhnt) *n.:* arranged in a straight line; condition of having the parts of something coordinated or in the proper relationship. *Parts of the damaged car were out of alignment.*

corroded (kuh ROH dihd) *v.* used as *adj.:* slowly worn away or decayed, especially by rust or chemicals. *The car had broken and corroded parts.*

Daily

shriveled (SHRIHV uhld) *v.* used as *adj.:* shrunken and wrinkled, often as a result of being dried out. *The speaker covers the shriveled bean seeds with soil.*

Language Coach

Word Origins *Ligne* is a French word meaning "line." It is pronounced LIHN yuh—the *g* is silent. Which word on the list above is derived from *ligne*? Is the *g* silent? How can you tell?

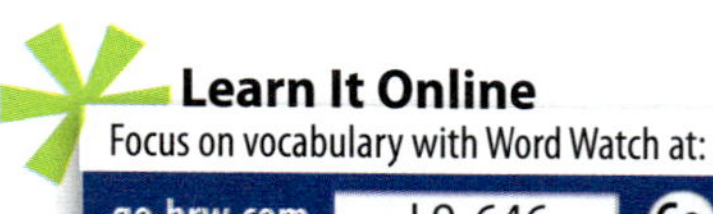

Learn It Online

Focus on vocabulary with Word Watch at:

go.hrw.com L9-646 

MEET THE WRITERS

Raymond Carver
(1938–1988)

In Short

The characters in Raymond Carver's stories are working-class people who struggle with financial and personal problems—problems that Carver himself experienced. In the early days of his career, he and his first wife endured "years of hard work with nothing to show for it except an old car . . . and new creditors on our backs."

An extremely influential, master short-story writer, Carver was also a poet. He once commented, "My stories are better known, but, myself, I love my poetry." Explaining the relationship between his stories and poems, Carver noted, "I write them the same way, and I'd say the effects are similar. There's a compression of language, of emotion, that isn't to be found in the novel."

Naomi Shihab Nye
(1952–)

Noticing the World

Many of Naomi Shihab Nye's poems are inspired by her childhood memories and by her travels, including visits to her Palestinian grandmother in Jerusalem. Her work draws on her Palestinian American background as well as on the lives of people in her ethnically diverse neighborhood. Born and raised in St. Louis, Missouri, Nye currently lives in San Antonio, Texas. A short-story writer and songwriter as well as a poet, she runs workshops to help students find the poetry hidden in their own imaginations. She says, "Being alive is a common road. It's what we notice [that] makes us different."

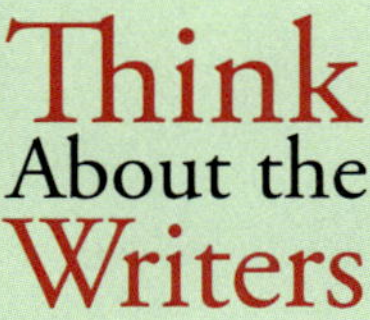

Both poets have written short stories. What kinds of stories would you expect them to write?

Build Background

If you know a lot about cars, you will understand the **jargon**—the specialized words or technical vocabulary—in "The Car." However, even if you do not know what a head gasket, a carburetor, or a muffler is, you will get a clear picture of the speaker's car from the imagery in this poem.

Read with a Purpose As you read this poem, think about what positive and negative feelings the speaker associates with cars.

THE CAR

by **Raymond Carver**

The car with a cracked windshield.
The car that threw a rod.
The car without brakes.
The car with a faulty U-joint.
The car with a hole in its radiator.
The car I picked peaches for.
The car with a cracked block.
The car with no reverse gear.
The car I traded for a bicycle. **A**
The car with steering problems.
The car with generator trouble.
The car with no back seat.
The car with the torn front seat.
The car that burned oil.
The car with rotten hoses.
The car that left the restaurant without paying.
The car with bald tires.
The car with no heater or defroster.

A Literary Focus Catalog Poem Why might Carver have included in the catalog this detail about trading the car? What does it suggest about the speaker's view of the car?

The car with its front end out of alignment.
The car the child threw up in.
The car *I* threw up in.
The car with the broken water pump.
The car whose timing gear was shot.
The car with a blown head-gasket.
The car I left on the side of the road.
The car that leaked carbon monoxide.
The car with a sticky carburetor.
The car that hit the dog and kept going.
The car with a hole in its muffler.
The car with no muffler.
The car my daughter wrecked.
The car with the twice-rebuilt engine.
The car with corroded battery cables.
The car bought with a bad check.
Car of my sleepless nights. **B**
The car with a stuck thermostat.
The car whose engine caught fire.
The car with no headlights.
The car with a broken fan belt.
The car with wipers that wouldn't work. **C**
The car I gave away.
The car with transmission trouble.
The car I washed my hands of.
The car I struck with a hammer.
The car with payments that couldn't be met.
The repossessed car.
The car whose clutch-pin broke.
The car waiting on the back lot.
Car of my dreams.
My car.

B **Literary Focus** **Catalog Poem** What changes here? Why do you think Carver chooses to interrupt the pattern he has set up?

C **Reading Focus** **Reading Aloud** Read this line aloud. What sounds does Carver use to emphasize the meaning of this line?

Vocabulary **alignment** (uh LYN muhnt) *n.:* arranged in a straight line; condition of having the parts of something coordinated or in the proper relationship.
corroded (kuh ROH dihd) *v.* used as *adj.:* slowly worn away or decayed, especially by rust or chemicals.

Read with a Purpose What day-to-day chores does the speaker list in this poem?

Daily

by **Naomi Shihab Nye**

These shriveled seeds we plant,
corn kernel, dried bean,
poke into loosened soil,
cover over with measured fingertips
These T-shirts we fold
into perfect white
squares (A)
These tortillas we slice and fry to crisp strips
This rich egg scrambled in a gray clay bowl
This bed whose covers I straighten
smoothing edges till blue quilt fits brown blanket
and nothing hangs out
This envelope I address
so the name balances like a cloud
in the center of the sky
This page I type and retype
This table I dust till the scarred wood shines
This bundle of clothes I wash and hang and wash again
like flags we share, a country so close
no one needs to name it
The days are nouns: touch them
The hands are churches that worship the world (B)

(A) **Literary Focus** **Catalog Poem** What does the image "perfect white / squares" suggest about the way the speaker and others approach the task of folding the shirts?

(B) **Reading Focus** **Reading Aloud** What do you notice as you read aloud the final two lines of this poem?

Vocabulary **shriveled** (SHRIHV uhld) *v.* used as *adj.:* shrunken and wrinkled, often as a result of being dried out.

Applying Your Skills

MO **9.R.2.A.1** Analyze and evaluate the text features in grade-level text **9.R.2.C.1.d** Use details from text(s): to evaluate the effect of author's style **9.R.1.D.1.a** Read grade-level instructional text: with fluency, accuracy, comprehension and appropriate expression *Also covered* **9.R.1.G.1.a**

The Car / Daily

Respond and Think Critically

Reading Focus

Read with a Purpose

1. In "The Car," what positive and negative things does the speaker associate with cars?
2. What chores does Nye list in her poem?

Reading Skills: Reading Aloud

3. Review the chart you filled in as you read. How did reading aloud bring out the humor and despair in "The Car"? How did reading aloud help you understand the main point Nye makes in her poem?

Vocabulary Check

Tell whether each statement is true (T) or false (F).

4. Raisins look **shriveled**.
5. Chairs in messy rows are in **alignment**.
6. **Corroded** hinges might prevent a door from opening properly.

Literary Focus

Literary Analysis

7. **Analyze** In "The Car" the speaker uses **personification**—a figure of speech in which human qualities are given to a nonhuman thing. How does the use of personification affect the meaning of lines 16 and 28?
8. **Analyze** What **theme,** or insight about life, is revealed in "The Car"? What details in the poem help reveal its theme?
9. **Interpret** In lines 1–8 of "Daily," the speaker uses the plural pronoun *we*. In line 10, she switches to the pronoun *I*. To whom might *we* refer? Explain.
10. **Analyze** Why might Nye have chose to title the poem "Daily"?

Literary Skills: Catalog Poem

11. **Interpret** In lines 35 and 49 of "The Car," the speaker breaks the pattern of his lines. What might the speaker mean when he calls the vehicle "car of my sleepless nights"? How might the vehicle be the "car" of his "dreams"?
12. **Analyze** The last two lines of "Daily" aren't part of the catalog of images; rather, they sum up the speaker's message. Explain the **metaphors,** or comparisons between unlike things, in these lines. What is the speaker saying about daily work?

Literary Skills Review: Diction

13. **Analyze** How would you describe Carver's **diction,** or word choice, in "The Car"? Does his diction suit the poem's subject matter? Why or why not?

Writing Focus

Think as a Reader/Writer

Use It in Your Writing Write a catalog poem about a day in your own life. Use repetition to enhance the meaning and the sound of your poem.

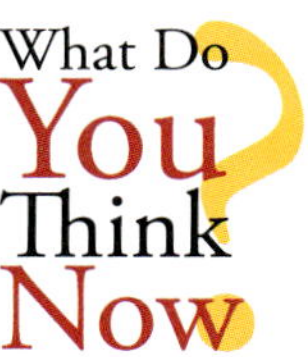

What new light do these poets shed on everyday chores and objects?

POETRY

Preparing to Read

A Blessing

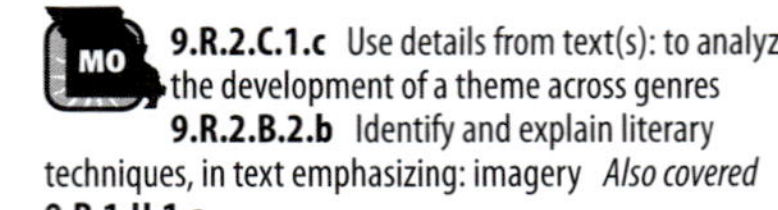

9.R.2.C.1.c Use details from text(s): to analyze the development of a theme across genres **9.R.2.B.2.b** Identify and explain literary techniques, in text emphasizing: imagery *Also covered* **9.R.1.H.1.a**

Reader/Writer Notebook

Use your **RWN** to complete the activities for this selection.

Literary Focus

Imagery and Theme Poets want their words to excite our emotions and our imaginations. To achieve that effect, poets use **imagery**—language that appeals to the senses. As you read this poem, pay close attention to the meanings and emotions suggested by its imagery. Then, consider how the imagery contributes to the **theme,** or central idea, of the poem.

Reading Focus

Analyzing Details Poets face a variety of choices when determining how to turn their thoughts into verse. They might choose simple words or complex words; they might choose words that create rhythm and rhyme or words that convey a specific mood when used together.

Into Action As you read, use a chart like this one to record key descriptive words from the poem. Then, when you finish reading, fill in the other two columns with each word's definition (denotation) as well as the feelings the word evokes (connotations).

Words from Poem	Denotation	Connotations
"bounds"	leaps forward	
"darken"		

Writing Focus

Think as a Reader/Writer

Find It in Your Reading Writers use imagery not only to appeal to our emotions but also to contribute to the meaning of a work. As you read, record in your *Reader/Writer Notebook* examples of images and the ideas they convey.

Vocabulary

twilight (TWY lyt) *n.:* soft light just after sunset; period between sunset and night. *The ponies grazed in the twilight.*

bounds (bowndz) *v.:* leaps or springs forward. *As night falls, the growing darkness bounds over the pasture.*

nuzzled (NUHZ uhld) *v.:* rubbed gently with the nose. *The affectionate pony nuzzled the speaker.*

caress (kuh REHS) *v.:* touch gently in an affectionate manner. *The speaker wants to caress the pony's ear.*

Language Coach

Word Origins The prefix *twi–* is from Middle English and means "two." Read the definition of the word *twilight* in the list above. In what way can twilight be regarded as a "second light"?

Learn It Online
Watch the video introduction to learn more at:
go.hrw.com
L9-652
Go

MEET THE WRITER

James Wright
(1927–1980)

"We Know What He's Talking About"

Travelers who pull off I-90 at the High Forest Rest Area in Stewartville, Minnesota, may not find two ponies in a pasture, like the ones that inspired James Wright. Thanks to the radio host Garrison Keillor, however, they will find a plaque engraved with the poem "A Blessing."

Keillor dedicated the plaque in 1998. A pair of horses was on hand, as were more than two hundred students. One sophomore said he liked Wright's poem because it spoke "about the beauty of Minnesota. And it's so close to us; we know what he's talking about."

"A Love Poem"

The Pulitzer Prize–winner James Wright often wrote about the places in his life—Minnesota, where he taught college for eight years (Keillor was his student there); New York City, his home in later life; and especially Martin's Ferry, the mill town in Ohio, where he grew up in a poor family during the Great Depression.

Much of Wright's poetry is dark and explores themes of loneliness and alienation. "A Blessing" escapes this darkness—perhaps that is the reason for its popularity. Keillor has said of the poem, "I've seen it done in needlework, and in rye seeds glued to particle board and entered in the crop show at the state fair. I've heard it read at weddings in meadows, weddings attended by horses. . . . It is a love poem."

Think About the Writer What does the reaction to "A Blessing" suggest about the power of Wright's poem?

Build Background

You may have heard of horses like the ones in "A Blessing." Mustangs, pintos, and cayuses are also known as Indian ponies. Found in the western United States, Indian ponies are strong, small horses of various colors. Their ancestors roamed the Arabian Desert and Spain before eventually being brought to the Americas several centuries ago.

Read with a Purpose What event does this poem describe?

A Blessing

by **James Wright**

Just off the highway to Rochester, Minnesota,
Twilight bounds softly forth on the grass,
And the eyes of those two Indian ponies
Darken with kindness.
They have come gladly out of the willows
To welcome my friend and me.
We step over the barbed wire into the pasture
Where they have been grazing all day, alone.
They ripple tensely, they can hardly contain their happiness
That we have come.
They bow shyly as wet swans. They love each other. **A**
There is no loneliness like theirs.
At home once more,
They begin munching the young tufts of spring in the darkness.
I would like to hold the slenderer one in my arms,
For she has walked over to me
And nuzzled my left hand.
She is black and white,
Her mane falls wild on her forehead,
And the light breeze moves me to caress her long ear
That is delicate as the skin over a girl's wrist. **B**
Suddenly I realize
That if I stepped out of my body I would break
Into blossom.

A **Reading Focus** **Analyzing Details** What effect does this description of the horses create?

B **Literary Focus** **Imagery and Theme** To what senses does the image in lines 20–21 appeal?

Vocabulary **twilight** (TWY lyt) *n.:* soft light just after sunset; period between sunset and night.
bounds (bowndz) *v.:* leaps or springs forward.
nuzzled (NUHZ uhld) *v.:* rubbed gently with the nose.
caress (kuh REHS) *v.:* touch gently in an affectionate manner.

Applying Your Skills

9.R.2.B.2.b Identify and explain literary techniques, in text emphasizing: imagery **9.R.2.C.1.c** Use details from text(s): to analyze the development of a theme across genres **9.R.2.C.1.b** Use details from text(s): to analyze character, plot, setting, point of view *Also covered* **9.R.1.H.1.a; 9.R.1.G.1.a**

A Blessing

Respond and Think Critically

Reading Focus

Read with a Purpose

1. What event does the poem's speaker describe?

Reading Skills: Analyzing Details

2. Complete the word choices chart you began on page 652. Describe three strong images that Wright created through his word choices. Now, review the connotations of the words. How does Wright's word choice contribute to the mood of the poem?

Words from Poem	Denotation	Connotations
"bounds"	leaps forward	positive; moving with youthful energy

Vocabulary Check

Tell whether each statement is true (T) or false (F).

3. **Twilight** falls in the middle of the day.
4. When an animal **bounds,** it crawls.
5. A puppy that **nuzzled** you was being affectionate.
6. You might **caress** a sweet-looking kitten.

Literary Focus

Literary Analysis

7. **Analyze** In describing the ponies, Wright uses **personification,** a figure of speech in which human characteristics are given to a nonhuman thing. What human qualities and feelings does Wright attribute to the things he personifies?
8. **Interpret** You may have read myths in which a character undergoes a metamorphosis, a change from one form to another. Explain the metamorphosis referred to in the final lines of the poem. What is the figurative meaning of the phrase "I would break / Into blossom"? What emotion is the speaker expressing?

Literary Skills: Imagery and Theme

9. **Evaluate** Most of the images in this poem appeal to the senses of sight and touch. Make a chart like this one, and list images in the appropriate columns. Some images may be listed in both columns.

Sight	Touch

10. **Analyze** What do you think is the theme of the poem? Which images helped you identify this theme?

Literary Skills Review: Setting and Mood

11. **Evaluate** Wright sets "A Blessing" in a particular time and place. List all the details you know about this setting. What **mood,** or feeling, is created by the setting? How does this mood contribute to the meaning of the poem?

Writing Focus

Think as a Reader/Writer

Use It in Your Writing Write a letter to Wright in which you tell him what you feel about this poem. Focus especially on how you reacted to his imagery.

IMAGERY AND FORM

Wrap Up

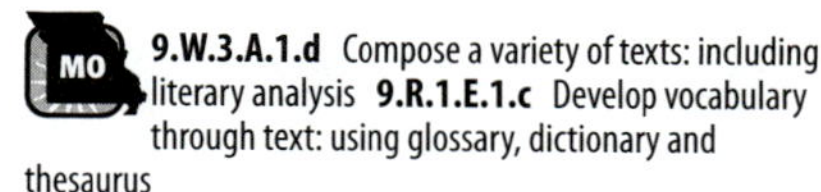
9.W.3.A.1.d Compose a variety of texts: including literary analysis **9.R.1.E.1.c** Develop vocabulary through text: using glossary, dictionary and thesaurus

Starfish / in Just- / Haiku / Once by the Pacific / Country Scene / The Car / Daily / A Blessing

Vocabulary Development

Vocabulary Skills: Synonyms

Every word counts in a poem. When poets decide whether to use a particular word or a **synonym,** a word that has a similar meaning as another word, they make sure that the chosen word contributes to the intended effect of the poem. To determine which word to use, poets consider some or all of the following factors:

- the word's **denotation(s),** or dictionary definition(s)
- the word's **connotations,** or the emotions, nuances, and associations the word evokes
- the type of word. For example, is the word informal or formal? Is it **jargon**—a technical term?
- the word's sound
- the number of syllables in the word

Your Turn

For each item below, list two synonyms for the boldface word. Then, explain how substituting each synonym for the boldface word would affect the line(s). To complete this activity, you might want to use a dictionary and a thesaurus.

1. "We touched them, / Surprised to find them soft, **pliant,** almost / Living in their attitudes." ("Starfish," lines 6–8)
2. "The shattered water made a misty **din.** / Great waves looked over others coming in." ("Once by the Pacific," lines 1–2)
3. "Who can describe this **desolate** scene:" ("Country Scene," line 2)
4. "The car with **corroded** battery cables." ("The Car," line 33)

CHOICES

As you respond to the Choices, use these **Academic Vocabulary** words as appropriate: nuances, evoke, associate, elaborate.

REVIEW

Create a Commercial

TechFocus Use video software to create a commercial for an everyday product. Create a voice-over script in which you use imagery to make the product sound appealing. Include visuals and sound effects that enhance the product's appeal.

CONNECT

Respond to a Poem

Timed Writing Which of the poems in this collection appealed to you the most in terms of form and style? Write a brief essay in which you discuss the poem and explain its appeal for you. Be sure to support your ideas with details from the poem.

EXTEND

Adapt a Poem

Robert Frost loved writing sonnets because he enjoyed the challenge of fitting his thoughts into a very strict form. Try one of these challenges:

- Think about the subject and theme of "A Blessing," and write a haiku version.
- Turn "The Car" into a sonnet.
- Expand Bashō's haiku to create a lyric poem.
- Turn "Starfish" into a catalog poem.

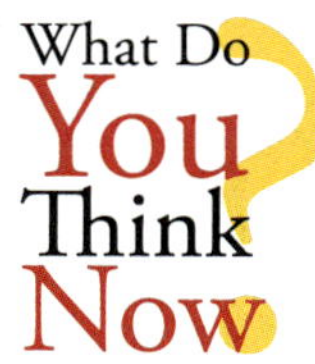

Which poem or poems in this section caused you to see something ordinary in a new light? Explain.

Figures of Speech

CONTENTS

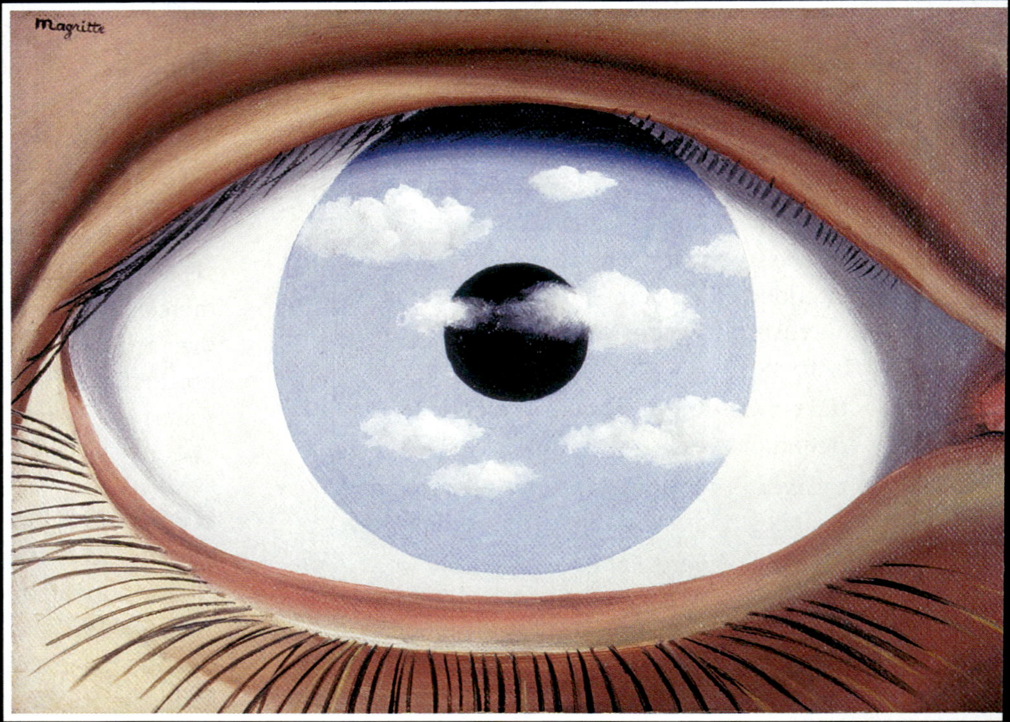

The False Mirror (*Le faux miroir*) (1929) by René Magritte (1898–1967). © C. Herscovici, Brussels / Artists Rights Society (ARS), New York.

What Do You Think?

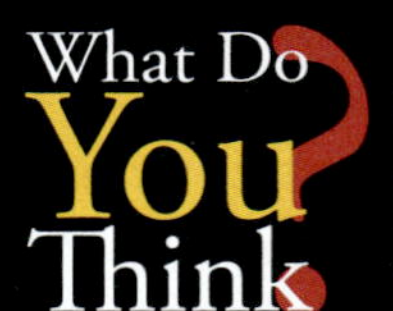

What scenes in life spark your imagination?

QuickWrite

Create a short list of ordinary things you see at school, such as lockers, lunch trays, and book bags. Then, choose one item on your list and think of three different ways to describe it.

POETRY

Preparing to Read

Fog / Fire and Ice

9.R.2.B.2.d Identify and explain literary techniques, in text emphasizing: analyze literary techniques previously introduced
Also covered **9.R.1.H.1.a**

Reader/Writer Notebook

Use your **RWN** to complete the activities for these selections.

Literary Focus

Implied Metaphor A **metaphor** is a comparison between two unlike things in which one thing becomes another. There are different types of metaphors. A **direct metaphor** tells us directly that one thing *is* something else:

The moon is a balloon.

An **implied metaphor,** however, does not tell us directly that one thing is something else. Instead, it suggests the comparison:

Without a string, the moon drifts across the sky.

The following poems are two of the shortest that Sandburg and Frost ever wrote, but both contain strong examples of implied metaphors.

TechFocus Think about how you might use metaphors in a newscast.

Reading Focus

Analyzing Details Poets choose words for precise effects, to create moods, sensations, and associations. Word choice also affects the meaning of a poem and the impression it leaves with the reader.

Into Action Before you read, fill out the chart below with the feelings and ideas you associate with key words from these poems. When you have finished reading the poems, look back at your word associations to see if they have changed based on the poets' word choices.

	fog	fire	ice
My associations	cold and gray		

Writing Focus

Think as a Reader/Writer

Find It in Your Reading As you read "Fire and Ice," look for the contrasting ideas that Frost describes. Write in your *Reader/Writer Notebook* words that are opposites from the poem.

Vocabulary

Fog

haunches (HAWN chuhz) *n.:* the hindquarters of an animal; the part of the body around the hips. *The cat sat silently on his haunches.*

Fire and Ice

perish (PEHR ihsh) *v.:* die. *To perish in a fire is a tragic way to die.*

suffice (suh FYS) *v.:* be enough; be adequate. *Either outcome would suffice.*

Language Coach

Connotations Often, poets use language in unusual, nonliteral ways. For example, in "Fire and Ice," the speaker tells us he "tasted of desire." How does describing desire as something you can taste emphasize the idea that desire is sometimes so strong, it seems as if you can hold it, smell it, and taste it? Explain your response.

Learn It Online
Explore vocabulary terms with Word Watch at:
go.hrw.com L9-659 Go

MEET THE WRITERS

Learn It Online
Learn more about Frost's life at:
go.hrw.com L9-660 Go

Carl Sandburg

(1878–1967)

The Poet of Chicago

Carl Sandburg, the son of Swedish immigrants, was born in Galesburg, Illinois. Between the ages of thirteen and nineteen, he worked on a milk wagon, in a barbershop, at a theater, in a brickyard, and as a hotel dishwasher and a harvest hand. He became known as the poet of Chicago in the days when the city was becoming a center for the steel mills, stockyards, and railroads. Though he was unknown to the poetry world until he was thirty-six, Sandburg's name was a household word by the time he died. His sometimes tough, often tender poems about nature and the American people—especially those in the working-class—were loved by millions.

Robert Frost

(1874–1963)

The New England Poet

Robert Frost lived and wrote in New England for most of his life and was well-liked by the American public. New England still bears the scars of the Ice Age glacier that stripped the land bare and buried everything in its path. Indeed, Frost had only to look out his farmhouse window to see the destructive effects of ice—and he had only to take a short walk to find the charred clearings left by lightning fires. Like all human beings, he had only to look inside himself to discover the destructive forces of desire and hate.

For another biography of Frost, see page 639.

Think About the Writers Why do you think Sandburg and Frost were so revered by the communities in which they lived?

Build Background

In addition to writing poetry, Carl Sandburg worked as a newspaper reporter. This experience influenced his poetry. On the day Sandburg wrote "Fog," he had an appointment to interview a juvenile court judge. As he walked to his appointment, Sandburg watched the fog settle over the Chicago harbor. While he was waiting to meet with the judge, Sandburg took out a pencil and wrote "Fog" on a piece of newsprint.

In Robert Frost's poem, simple things take on deep significance. Describing his writing, the poet remarked, "Poetry begins in trivial metaphors and goes on to the profoundest thinking we have."

Read with a Purpose Read these poems to find out how the poets regard three elements in nature—fog, fire, and ice.

FOG

by **Carl Sandburg**

The fog comes
on little cat feet. **A**

It sits looking
over harbor and city
on silent haunches
and then moves on.

A **Reading Focus** **Analyzing Details** What impression does the choice of the word *little* create? How would the poem be different if Sandburg had chosen the word *small* or *tiny*?

Vocabulary **haunches** (HAWN chuhz) *n.:* the hindquarters of an animal; the part of the body around the hips.

FIRE AND ICE

by **Robert Frost**

Some say the world will end in fire,
Some say in ice.
From what I've tasted of desire
I hold with those who favor fire.
But if it had to perish twice,
I think I know enough of hate
To say that for destruction ice
Is also great A
And would suffice.

A Literary Focus **Implied Metaphor** With what two emotions does the speaker indirectly compare fire and ice?

Vocabulary **perish** (PEHR ihsh) *v.:* die.
suffice (suh FYS) *v.:* be enough; be adequate.

Applying Your Skills

MO **9.R.2.B.2.d** Identify and explain literary techniques, in text emphasizing: analyze literary techniques previously introduced **9.R.2.B.2.b** Identify and explain literary techniques, in text emphasizing: imagery *Also covered* **9.R.1.H.1.a; 9.W.2.D.1.a; 9.R.1.G.1.a**

Fog / Fire and Ice

Respond and Think Critically

Reading Focus

Read with a Purpose

1. What elements of nature do these poets explore?

Reading Skills: Analyzing Details

2. Add two more rows to the chart you began on page 659. In the first row, describe the poets' metaphors for fog, fire, and ice. Then, in the bottom row, write down any new <u>associations</u> you may have relating to fog, fire, and ice.

	fog	fire	ice
My associations	cold and gray		
Poets' metaphors			
My new associations			

Vocabulary Check

Fill in each of the sentences with the correct Vocabulary word.

haunches
perish
suffice

3. Hamsters may _________ if they get too hot or cold.
4. One blanket will _________ to keep us warm.
5. The rabbit's powerful _________ allow it to scamper quickly through the tall grass.

Literary Focus

Literary Analysis

6. **Infer** What is the setting of the poem "Fog"? How can you tell?
7. **Interpret** According to the speaker in "Fire and Ice," what disagreement do some people have about how the world will end?
8. **Connect** Why might the speaker in "Fire and Ice" think that hate and ice have something in common? How could hate cause the destruction of the world? How could desire?

Literary Skills: Implied Metaphor

9. **Analyze** According to the speaker in "Fog," how is fog like a cat?
10. **Interpret** In "Fire and Ice," to what is fire compared? To what is ice compared?

Literary Skills Review: Imagery

11. **Evaluate** An **image** is a word or phrase that appeals to the senses. What images are in each poem? To what senses do these images appeal?

Writing Focus

Think as a Reader/Writer

Use It in Your Writing In "Fire and Ice," Frost explores fascinating opposites. Think about opposite ideas—such as youth and age, for example—that you'd like to explore in your writing. Then, write a description of each concept, using imagery to reinforce your ideas.

What Do You Think Now?

Do you think the unpredictability of nature can spark our imaginations? Why or why not?

POETRY

Preparing to Read

9.R.2.B.2.d Identify and explain literary techniques, in text emphasizing: analyze literary techniques previously introduced 9.R.1.G.1.f During reading, utilize strategies: to paraphrase

"Hope" is the thing with feathers / Fame is a fickle food

Literary Focus

Extended Metaphor An **extended metaphor** is a comparison between two unlike things that is developed over several lines or even an entire poem. In "'Hope' is the thing with feathers," Emily Dickinson states her metaphor in the first line: "Hope," she says, is like a bird ("the thing with feathers"); she builds the comparison over three stanzas. "Fame is a fickle food" requires the reader to read the entire poem in order to understand the metaphor.

Reading Focus

Paraphrasing One way to find a poem's meaning is to paraphrase it, stanza by stanza. Once you find basic meaning, re-read the poem to find deeper meanings created by the poet's word choices, imagery, and use of figurative language.

Into Action Fill in this chart by paraphrasing each stanza of Dickinson's poems.

	My Paraphrase
"'Hope' is the thing with feathers"	Stanza 1: "Hope" is like a bird that sings no matter what happens. Stanza 2: Stanza 3:
"Fame is a fickle food"	Stanza 1: Stanza 2:

Writing Focus

Think as a Reader/Writer

Find It in Your Reading As you read these poems, think about the metaphors that help define hope and fame. In your *Reader/Writer Notebook,* note what hope and fame mean to you.

Reader/Writer Notebook

Use your **RWN** to complete the activities for these selections.

Language Coach

Connotations Poets choose words for many reasons—they consider the sounds of the words as well as which syllables of the words are stressed. Poets also consider a word's **connotations**—the associations most people have with the word.

- *Fickle* is an adjective meaning "likely to change loyalties or switch affections." Why do you think Dickinson chose to use the word *fickle* in the title of "Fame is a fickle food," when she could have chosen a synonym such as *capricious* or *changeable*?
- *Abash*, in line 7 of "'Hope' is the thing with feathers," is a word that is not often used as a verb. It means "embarrass." Read aloud line 7 of "'Hope' is the thing with feathers." Why do you think Dickinson chose to use the word *abash* rather than *embarrass* or *humiliate*?

Learn It Online

Listen to these poems online:

Learn It Online
Learn more about the author's life at:
go.hrw.com L9-665 Go

Emily Dickinson

(1830–1886)

The Woman of Mystery

Unlike most people today, Emily Dickinson was born, lived most of her life, and died in the same house. From the time she was twenty-six, she rarely left her house in Amherst, Massachusetts. Yet for the next thirty years she traveled to the ends of the universe—in her imagination. She jotted down poems in the margins of newspapers, on paper bags, and even on the insides of envelopes.

Dickinson had an ordinary childhood, but in her early twenties she began to retreat from social circles. Eventually, she withdrew from the outside world. Dickinson dressed in all white, stayed indoors, and devoted herself to her family and her writing—some eighteen hundred poems in all. Of those, however, only seven were published in her lifetime, and all anonymously. She once wrote about her own poetry, "This is my letter to the World / That never wrote to Me."

A World Apart

Dickinson's poems often deal with the relationship between her inner self and the outside world, a world she abandoned. After Dickinson's death her sister, Lavinia, found the poems locked away and folded and sewn into neat packets. Dickinson was known for giving her poems as gifts for Valentine's Day or tucking them into packages to her family.

Dickinson developed a new and uniquely American style of poetry, abandoning the traditional rhyme and rhythm of her counterparts. Her bold ideas and creative use of words have resonated around the globe, creating her legacy as one of the greatest American poets.

"If I read a book and it makes my whole body so cold no fire can ever warm me, I know it is poetry. If I feel physically as if the top of my head were taken off, I know that it's poetry. These are the only ways I know it."

Think About the Writer

How do you think Dickinson, with little or no contact with the outside world, had such great poetic insight into her surroundings?

Read with a Purpose Read the following poems to find out how Emily Dickinson defines *hope* and *fame.*

"Hope" is the thing with feathers

by **Emily Dickinson**

"Hope" is the thing with feathers—
That perches in the soul— **A**
And sings the tune without the words—
And never stops—at all—

And sweetest—in the Gale—is heard—
And sore must be the storm—
That could abash the little Bird
That kept so many warm—

I've heard it in the chillest land—
And on the strangest Sea—
Yet, never, in Extremity,
It asked a crumb—of Me. **B**

A **Literary Focus** **Extended Metaphor** What does the speaker mean by describing hope as "the thing with feathers"?

B **Reading Focus** **Reading a Poem** What observation about the bird does the speaker make in the final stanza?

Fame is a fickle food

by **Emily Dickinson**

Fame is a fickle food
Upon a shifting plate
Whose table once a
Guest but not
The second time is set. 

Whose crumbs the crows inspect
And with ironic caw
Flap past it to the Farmer's Corn—
Men eat of it and die. B

A Literary Focus Extended Metaphor In what way is fame like a fickle food?

B Reading Focus Reading a Poem What point about fame does Dickinson make in the poem's final line?

Applying Your Skills

9.R.2.B.2.d Identify and explain literary techniques, in text emphasizing: analyze literary techniques previously introduced 9.R.2.B.2.b Identify and explain literary techniques, in text emphasizing: imagery *Also covered* 9.R.2; 9.W.3.A.1.a

"Hope" is the thing with feathers / Fame is a fickle food

Respond and Think Critically

Reading Focus

Read with a Purpose

1. How does Dickinson define *hope*? How does she regard the desire for fame?

Reading Skills: Paraphrasing

2. If you haven't already done so, complete the chart you began on page 664. Then, add a row and describe how Dickinson's use of word choice and punctuation adds meaning to her poems.

	My Paraphrase
"'Hope' is the thing with feathers"	Stanza 1: "Hope" is like a bird that sings no matter what happens. Stanza 2: Stanza 3:
"Fame is a fickle food"	Stanza 1: Stanza 2:

Dickinson's language and punctuation . . .

Literary Focus

Literary Analysis

3. **Analyze** In writing, giving human qualities to a nonhuman object is called **personification.** What is being personified in the second stanza of "'Hope' is the thing with feathers"?
4. **Analyze** Why do you think Dickinson chose to capitalize the word *extremity* in line 11 of "'Hope' is the thing with feathers"?
5. **Interpret** The speaker in "'Hope' is the thing with feathers" says the bird never asked for a "crumb." What might that statement mean?
6. **Analyze** What point is Dickinson making when she describes crows flying past fame to eat the farmer's food instead?

Literary Skills: Extended Metaphor

7. **Interpret** Think of all the ways Dickinson extends the metaphor of the bird in "'Hope' is the thing with feathers." How is hope's song endless? How might a bird keep you warm?
8. **Draw Conclusions** In what way is fame a "fickle food"? What does Dickinson mean when she says men who covet fame "eat of it and die"?

Literary Skills Review: Symbols

9. **Analyze** A **symbol** is something that stands for itself and for something else. The word *gale* means "a strong wind." What might "the Gale" symbolize in "'Hope' is the thing with feathers"?

Writing Focus

Think as a Reader/Writer

Use It in Your Writing Dickinson uses metaphors to describe hope and fame. In a few sentences (or a poem, if you prefer), define what hope or fame means to you. Challenge yourself to use a metaphor as part of your definition.

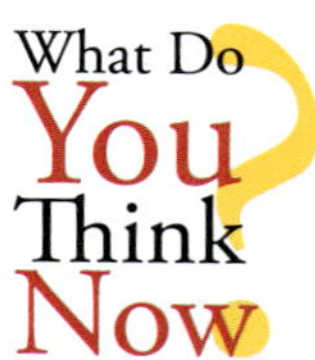

What new ideas about hope and fame do these poems reveal? Do you agree with these ideas? Why or why not?

POETRY

Preparing to Read

Tiburón / Fifteen

MO **9.R.2.B.2.d** Identify and explain literary techniques, in text emphasizing: analyze literary techniques previously introduced **9.R.1.G.1.e** During reading, utilize strategies: to visualize

Literary Focus

Simile and Personification The poems that follow contain similes and personification. A **simile** is a comparison between two unlike things that uses a connecting word such as *like* or *as*. **Personification** is a type of figurative language in which the writer speaks of something nonhuman as if it had human qualities. If you say, for example, "The sun smiled down on us," you are personifying the sun, which, of course, can't smile at all.

Reading Focus

Visualizing The poems you are about to read contain vivid and striking images. Taking time to visualize the images can help you better understand the ideas the poets are conveying.

Into Action Create an image map like the one below for each poem. In the center circle, draw the image you mentally envision as you read. Then, in the circles around the picture, write the details that helped you to visualize the image.

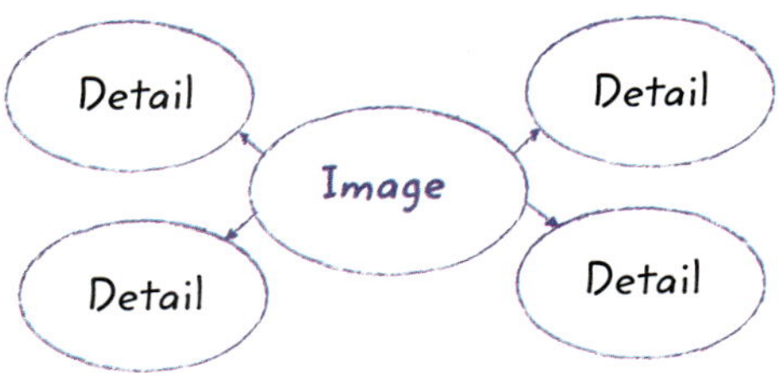

Writing Focus

Think as a Reader/Writer

Find It in Your Reading As you read the poems that follow, jot down in your *Reader/Writer Notebook* any unusual or surprising adjectives that the poets use to describe the car and the motorcycle.

Reader/Writer Notebook

Use your **RWN** to complete the activities for these selections.

Vocabulary

Fifteen

demure (dih MYUR) *adj.:* modest and proper. *Despite its large size, the bike seemed demure to the boy.*

indulged (ihn DUHLJD) *v.:* gave way to one's desires. *The boy indulged in his dream of riding a motorcycle.*

Language Coach

Connotations A **denotation** is the dictionary definition of a word, and a **connotation** is the feeling or association attached to that word. When you read the word *demure* in William Stafford's poem "Fifteen," ask yourself why the poet chose this word to describe the headlights of a growling motorcycle. What are the connotations of *demure*?

Learn It Online

Master these words. Visit Word Watch at:

go.hrw.com L9-669 Go

MEET THE WRITERS

Martín Espada

(1957–   )

A Fearless Voice

Martín Espada was born in Brooklyn, New York, the son of Puerto Rican parents. He dropped out of college, discouraged by literature classes that taught only works by white male authors. Then a friend introduced him to Latin American revolutionary poetry, and he realized that his kind of writing—politically charged and deeply personal—did have its own tradition. He completed college and went on to law school. As both a lawyer and a poet, Espada tries to speak for those who cannot speak for themselves. Espada's poetry often causes controversy, but he says, "The worst thing you can say to a poet is 'Don't say that.' You can't tell a poet to shut up. That just makes us want to say it all the more."

William Stafford

(1914–1993)

The Edge of Exploration

Born in Hutchinson, Kansas, William Stafford moved frequently while he was growing up. The people, animals, and varying landscapes were the backdrop of his life—and his writing. He wrote that the houses of his youth were always on the outside of town, on the cusp of "adventure fields forever, or rivers that wended off over the horizon, forever." In the center of these small villages was always a library, "another kind of edge out there forever, to explore." His work has been praised for its skillful evocation of the natural splendor of the western plains.

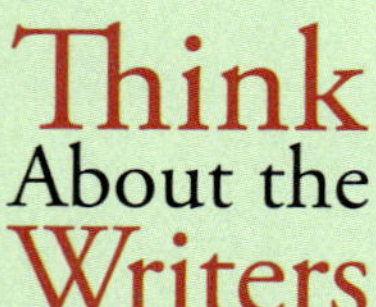

Think About the Writers In what way have both poets succeeded in overcoming their initial feelings of being outsiders?

Build Background

Martín Espada writes primarily in English, but he often laces his poetry with a few Spanish words. He says, "I do that a lot so you will find Spanish words and phrases sprinkled throughout my poems." This poem's title, "Tiburón," means "shark" in Spanish.

Read with a Purpose Read this poem to find out what surprising comparison the speaker makes.

by **Martín Espada**

East 116th
and a long red car
stalled with the hood up
roaring salsa
like a prize shark (A)
mouth yanked open
and down in the stomach
the radio
of the last fisherman
still tuned
to his lucky station

(A) **Literary Focus** **Simile and Personification**
What words serve to personify the red car?

Read with a Purpose Read this poem to find out about a memorable event in the speaker's life.

Fifteen

by **William Stafford**

South of the Bridge on Seventeenth
I found back of the willows one summer
day a motorcycle with engine running
as it lay on its side, ticking over
slowly in the high grass. I was fifteen.

I admired all that pulsing gleam, the
shiny flanks, the demure headlights
fringed where it lay; I led it gently
to the road and stood with that
companion, ready and friendly. I was fifteen. (A)

We could find the end of a road, meet
the sky on out Seventeenth. I thought about
hills, and patting the handle got back a
confident opinion. On the bridge we indulged
a forward feeling, a tremble. I was fifteen.

Thinking, back farther in the grass I found
the owner, just coming to, where he had flipped
over the rail. He had blood on his hand, was pale—
I helped him walk to his machine. He ran his hand
over it, called me a good man, roared away. (B)

I stood there, fifteen.

(A) **Literary Focus** **Personification** How does the writer use personification to bring the motorcycle to life?

(B) **Reading Focus** **Visualizing** What details in this stanza help you visualize the motorcycle's owner?

Vocabulary **demure** (dih MYUR) *adj.:* seeming more modest and proper than one really is.
indulged (ihn DUHLJD) *v.:* gave way to one's desires.

Applying Your Skills

MO 9.R.2.B.2.d Identify and explain literary techniques, in text emphasizing: analyze literary techniques previously introduced 9.R.2.B.2.b Identify and explain literary techniques, in text emphasizing: imagery *Also covered* 9.R.1.G.1.e; 9.W.3.A.1.a; 9.R.1.G.1.a

Tiburón / Fifteen

Respond and Think Critically

Reading Focus

Read with a Purpose

1. To what does the speaker in "Tiburón" compare the red car?
2. What has happened to the speaker in "Fifteen"?

Reading Skills: Visualizing

3. Look at the image maps you created for the poems. How did visualizing these images help you understand the ideas that the poets wanted to convey? Use your image maps to help you answer questions 6 and 8.

Vocabulary Check

Tell whether each statement is true (T) or false (F).

4. Rude people often behave in a **demure** manner.
5. As a reward for completing his research paper, Bernard **indulged** in seeing an afternoon movie with his friends.

Literary Focus

Literary Analysis

6. **Analyze** To what senses—sight, hearing, taste, touch, or smell—do the images in "Tiburón" appeal?
7. **Interpret** In "Tiburón," what do you think happened to the "last fisherman"? Why is his station "lucky"?
8. **Analyze** To what senses do the images in "Fifteen" appeal?
9. **Evaluate** What internal conflict does the speaker in "Fifteen" experience? Is the conflict resolved? Explain.
10. **Infer** In "Fifteen," how does the speaker feel when the owner of the motorcycle rides off? Why does he feel this way?
11. **Interpret** What **theme,** or insight about life, does "Fifteen" reveal?
12. **Compare and Contrast** In what ways are the two poems alike and different?

Literary Skills: Simile and Personification

13. **Evaluate** In "Tiburón" a simile compares a car to a shark. In what way is this car like a shark?
14. **Analyze** In which stanzas is the motorcycle in "Fifteen" personified? Why does the speaker seem to want the motorcycle as a companion?

Literary Skills Review: Symbols

15. **Connect** A **symbol** stands for itself and for something else. Look back at the poems, and make a list of all the symbols you can find. How do the car, motorcycle, and other images symbolize boyhood and growing older?

Writing Focus

Think as a Reader/Writer

Use It in Your Writing Write a poem about one of the items you described in your QuickWrite. Use interesting and powerful adjectives to help bring the subject of your poem to life.

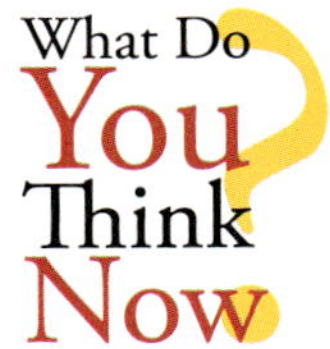

After reading these poems, will you regard cars and motorcycles the same way you did before? Why or why not?

POETRY

Preparing to Read

9.R.2.C.1.d Use details from text(s): to evaluate the effect of author's style 9.R.2.B.2.d Identify and explain literary techniques, in text emphasizing: analyze literary techniques previously introduced
Also covered 9.R.3.C.1.b

Internment / Sanctuary

Reader/Writer Notebook

Use your **RWN** to complete the activities for these selections.

Literary Focus

Figurative Language and Mood Poets often use **figures of speech** to make comparisons that add depths of meaning to their poems. Figures of speech include **metaphors,** comparisons between two unlike things without the use of a specific word of comparison; **similes,** comparisons using words such as *like* or *as;* and **personification,** the attribution of human qualities to nonhuman things. For example, lines 1–2 of the poem "Sanctuary" contain personifications in which New York is compared to a beast on a rampage:

New York came, rampaging, . . .

The use of this particular figure of speech to describe the city evokes a **mood,** or feeling, of rage or anger.

Literary Perspectives Apply the literary perspective described on page 677 as you read these poems.

Reading Focus

Analyzing Details Words on a page are not as simple as they look. Words often have many meanings and represent complex ideas.

Into Action To appreciate the full meaning of a poem, track the writer's word choices in a chart like this one. Record key words, their dictionary definitions, and your own associations about the words.

Word from Poem	Definition	My Associations
barracks	large, simple building	cold, bare, lonely

Writing Focus

Think as a Reader/Writer

Find It in Your Reading These two poems contain many precise adjectives. As you read, record in your *Reader/Writer Notebook* any adjectives that you find interesting or unusual.

Vocabulary

Internment

indignation (ihn dihg NAY shuhn) *n.:* anger at something unworthy, unjust, unfair, or mean. *The prisoner's feelings of indignation were hard for her to overcome.*

impaled (ihm PAYLD) *v.* used as *adj.:* pierced with something pointed. *Impaled, the plastic bag hung on the sharp points of the fence.*

Sanctuary

rampaging (RAM pay jihng) *v.* used as *adj.:* rushing wildly about. *Panicked, rampaging people filled the city streets.*

enveloped (ehn VEHL uhpt) *v.:* wrapped around; surrounded. *The fog enveloped the city.*

Language Coach

Synonyms Reinforce your ownership of a word by comparing the word to its **synonyms,** other words that have the same or similar meanings. Identify a synonym for at least two of the Vocabulary words above.

Learn It Online

There's more to words than just definitions. Get the whole story on:

go.hrw.com L9-674 

MEET THE WRITERS

Juliet S. Kono
(1943–)

"They Just Love It When I Misspell Something"

Juliet S. Kono was born and raised in Hilo, on Hawaii's Big Island. When Kono was a child, her Japanese American family survived a thirty-foot-high tsunami, a tidal wave that swept away their house and car and killed 159 people. The extraordinary experience of fleeing from the disaster turns up in many of her poems.

Now, as a poet and college professor, Kono says that she writes when her students write. She says, "They like to listen and see these first drafts because they can see how raw and 'chicken scratch' even my work can be. They just love it when I misspell something or if the ideas do not flow."

©2003 Stella Kalaw.

Luis H. Francia
(1945–)

One Must Already Be on a Journey of Self-Discovery

Luis H. Francia was born and raised in Manila, the Philippines. In his poems he depicts the human spirit and self-discovery. He often tries to challenge the reader's intellect, using words with double- and even triple-entendre (that is, words with two or three meanings). "Sanctuary," from his book *Museum of Absences,* memorializes the events that occurred in New York City on September 11, 2001. At the time of that tragedy, he was living in New York and working as a professor at New York University.

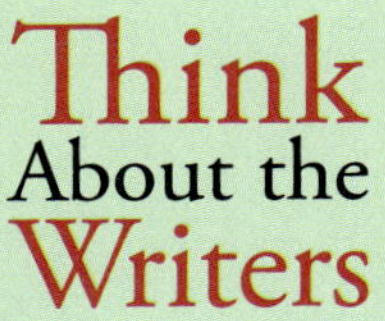

Think About the Writers

Why do you think these poets write about the tragedies they have witnessed?

Build Background

On December 8, 1941, the day after Japan attacked Pearl Harbor, the United States entered World War II. Early in 1942, the U.S. government sent notices to thousands of Japanese Americans living on the West Coast, requiring them to report to relocation centers. There they were assigned to internment camps in inland areas. More than 110,000 people—many of them American citizens—were confined behind barbed wire until 1946, after the war had ended. When the families returned to their homes, many of them found that their property had been stolen. Some forty years later, the U.S. government formally apologized and paid a small compensation to the Americans who had been interned in the camps. "Internment" describes what it was like for a young girl living in a camp.

On September 11, 2001, the United States was attacked by nineteen men associated with al Qaeda, an Islamic militant group. The terrorists hijacked four planes, two of which they flew into the towers of the World Trade Center in New York City, setting the massive buildings on fire until they crumbled to the ground. The third plane was flown into the southwest side of the Pentagon in Washington, D.C. The fourth crashed into an empty field in the Pennsylvania countryside when heroic passengers challenged their hijackers. That day was like no other in American history. "Sanctuary" reflects on what it was like to be in New York City on September 11. The poet has dedicated the poem to his wife, Midori.

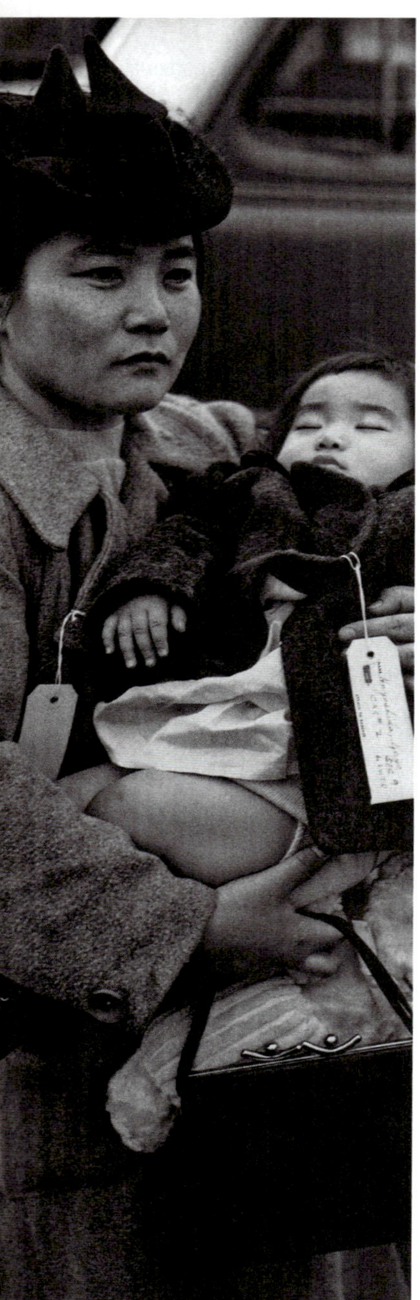

A Japanese American mother carries her sleeping daughter during the relocation from Bainbridge Island to internment camps.

Read with a Purpose Read the following poems to see how two writers use poetry to reflect on frightening experiences.

Internment

by **Juliet S. Kono**

Corralled, they are herded inland
From Santa Rosa.
After the long train ride
on the Santa Fe,
the physical exam,
the delousing with DDT,°
the branding of her indignation,
she falls asleep. **A**

Days later, she awakens
in an unfamiliar barracks—
Crystal City, Texas—
on land once a pasture.
Not wanting to,
not meaning to see beauty
in this stark landscape,
she sees, nonetheless,
through her tears—
on the double row
of barbed wire fencing
which holds them in
like stolid° cattle—
dewdrops, impaled
and golden. **B**

6. **DDT:** An abbreviation for a highly effective pesticide introduced in the 1940s. Its use was banned in the United States in 1972 because it was extremely harmful to the environment and humans.

21. **stolid** (STAHL ihd): placid; not easily excitable.

A **Literary Perspectives** **Historical Context** What period in history is captured in this poem? How do you know?

B **Literary Focus** **Figurative Language** What comparison does Kono make in this passage?

Vocabulary **indignation** (ihn dihg NAY shuhn) *n.:* anger at something unworthy, unjust, unfair, or mean.
impaled (ihm PAYLD) *v.* used as *adj.:* pierced with something pointed.

Sanctuary

for Midori
by **Luis H. Francia**

New York came, rampaging.
Broadway approached, barking. **A**
The mad heavens roared down,
Clouds enveloped me. **B**
All was motion, darkness, the
Ground rushing up.
Mountains leveled themselves
And my feet, faithful dogs, brought me
Home to you, my anchor, my light. **C**

A **Literary Perspectives** **Historical Context**
How do these lines reflect events on September 11, 2001?

B **Literary Focus** **Figurative Language** What things are personified in lines 1–4?

C **Reading Focus** **Analyzing Details** What is the denotation of the word *anchor*? What is its connotation?

Vocabulary **rampaging** (RAM pay jihng) *v.* used as *adj.:* rushing wildly about.
enveloped (ehn VEHL uhpt) *v.:* wrapped around; surrounded.

Literary Perspectives

Analyzing Historical Context When you apply this perspective, you think about ways in which history affected an author's writing. For example, when you read these poems, you'll consider the time period in which the authors wrote and the historical events that are reflected in the poems. You will also consider the social, political, economic, and cultural climate of the times. Doing so will help you better understand what the poet is trying to achieve through his or her writing. For help applying this literary perspective, be sure to read the background information provided on page 675.

Applying Your Skills

9.R.2.C.1.d Use details from text(s): to evaluate the effect of author's style 9.R.2.B.2.d Identify and explain literary techniques, in text emphasizing: analyze literary techniques previously introduced *Also covered* 9.R.1.H.1.a; 9.R.3.C.1.b; 9.W.3.A.1.a; 9.R.1.G.1.a

Internment / Sanctuary

Respond and Think Critically

Reading Focus

Read with a Purpose

1. What real-life experiences do Kono and Francia explore in these poems?

Reading Skills: Analyzing Details

2. Complete the chart you began as you read the poems. Then, add a column to show how the writers' word choices contribute to the overall mood of their poems.

Word from Poem	Definition	My Associations	Mood
barracks	large, simple building	cold, bare, lonely	gloomy

Vocabulary Check

Use the Vocabulary words to correctly complete each sentence.

indignation
impaled
rampaging
enveloped

3. The angry bull came _________ down the street.
4. The smoke quickly _________ the building.
5. Feelings of _________ welled up in the girl because of the unfair treatment she received.
6. The sharp object was thrown so hard it _________ the wooden board.

Literary Focus

Literary Analysis

7. **Interpret** In Kono's poem, what does the girl see that she considers beautiful? Why is she reluctant to find beauty in her situation?
8. **Literary Perspectives** What is the historical context of "Sanctuary"? What do the words and sounds used in the poem convey about the time and place in which the poem is set?

Literary Skills: Figurative Language and Mood

9. **Analyze** What words in the first stanza of "Internment" suggest that Kono is comparing the treatment of the imprisoned travelers to that of cattle? Identify another simile that restates this comparison. How do these words help you to understand the girl's feelings?
10. **Analyze** At the end of "Sanctuary," there is a shift in mood. What metaphors does the writer use to create that shift?

Literary Skills Review: Tone

11. **Evaluate** A writer's attitude toward a subject is **tone.** Describe the tone of each poem. What does the tone tell you about the speaker's attitude toward the subject of each poem?

Writing Focus

Think as a Reader/Writer

Use It in Your Writing When you **reformulate** a text, you rewrite it using a different format. Reformulate "Internment" or "Sanctuary" as a news article or an interview. Be sure to incorporate the subtle nuances of the original poem into your piece.

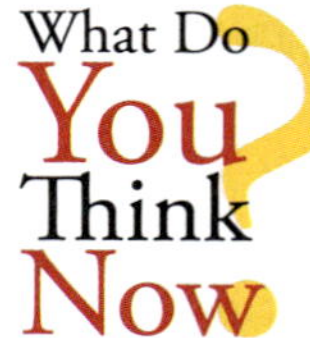

Which aspects of these poems are grounded in frightening realities? Which aspects have grown out of the writers' imaginations?

POETRY

Preparing to Read

Women

Literary Focus

Speaker and Tone The voice that talks to us in a poem is called the **speaker.** Sometimes the speaker is identical with the poet, but often the speaker and poet are not the same. The speaker may be a child, a woman, a man, an animal, or even an object.

Tone is a writer's or speaker's attitude toward a subject or toward an audience. A speaker's tone may be playful, serious, or warning, for example. To create tone, a poet carefully chooses words and details and sometimes creates similes and metaphors.

Reading Focus

Analyzing Details Poets choose their words carefully. When describing a person, for example, they may choose words that are short and blunt, or they may create figures of speech that are imaginative and fanciful.

Into Action As you read "Women," take note of the words and phrases that Alice Walker chooses to bring her ideas to life. Then, write down how those words affect you.

Words/Phrases from Poem	My Responses
"My mama's generation"	The speaker seems fond of her mom; she uses the word "mama."

Writing Focus

Think as a Reader/Writer

Find It in Your Reading As you read this poem, write down in your *Reader/Writer Notebook* vivid adjectives that help Walker describe women of her mother's generation.

MO **9.R.2.C.1.d** Use details from text(s): to evaluate the effect of author's style **9.R.1.H.1.a** Apply post-reading skills to comprehend, interpret, analyze, and evaluate text: identify and explain the relationship between the main idea and supporting details **9.R.2.C.1.b** Use details from text(s): to analyze character, plot, setting, point of view

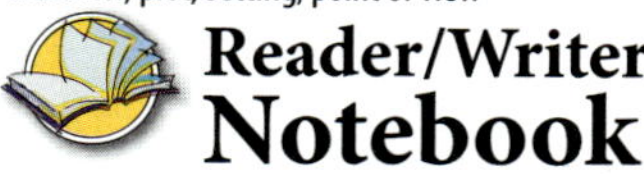

Reader/Writer Notebook

Use your **RWN** to complete the activities for this selection.

Language Coach

Word Roots Two words from "Women" appear to spring from the same word root, but in actuality they do not. *Generation* (line 2) comes from the Latin *generatio*, meaning "to be born." *Generals* (line 14) is from the Latin root *generis*, meaning "type" or "kind." Here are some word families that come from those two Latin roots.

generatio	*generis*
gentleman	generic
genius	generous
genesis	genealogy

Use a word from each word family in a sentence of your own.

Learn It Online

Use *PowerNotes* to enhance your learning at:

go.hrw.com L9-679 Go

MEET THE WRITER

Learn It Online
Learn more about Walker's life at:
go.hrw.com L9-680 Go

Alice Walker
(1944–)

Small-Town Roots

Alice Walker is a poet, novelist, short-story writer, and essayist. She is best known for her novel *The Color Purple*, which won a Pulitzer Prize in 1983 and was adapted into a movie and a Broadway musical in later years. Walker was born in Eatonton, a small town in Georgia. She was the youngest of eight children. Her father was a sharecropper, and her mother was a maid.

Teachers Inspired Her

Walker says that "Women" is for her mother, one of several important people in her life. Other important people were her teachers. "When I was four and my mother had to go to work in the fields, my first-grade teacher let me start in her class. Right on through grammar school and high school and college, there was one—sometimes even two—teachers who saved me from feeling alone, from worrying that the world I was stretching to find might not even exist."

Think About the Writer

What do Walker's words about her teachers suggest about her as a student?

Read with a Purpose Read this poem to find out how the speaker remembers women of her mother's era.

Women

by **Alice Walker**

They were women then
My mama's generation (A)
Husky of voice—stout of
Step
With fists as well as
Hands
How they battered down
Doors (B)
And ironed
Starched white
Shirts
How they led
Armies
Headragged generals
Across mined
Fields
Booby-trapped
Ditches
To discover books
Desks
A place for us
How they knew what we
Must know
Without knowing a page
Of it
Themselves.

Analyzing Visuals **Viewing and Interpreting** What details in this portrait remind you of the women described in the poem?

(A) **Literary Focus** **Speaker** What do you learn about the speaker in these lines?

(B) **Reading Focus** **Analyzing Details** What effect does the phrase "battered down / Doors" create?

Applying Your Skills

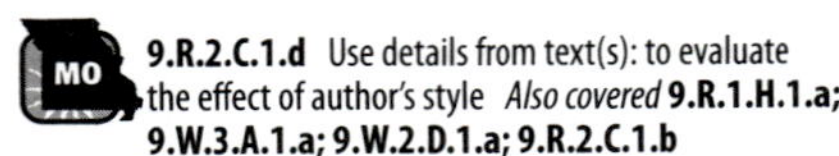

9.R.2.C.1.d Use details from text(s): to evaluate the effect of author's style *Also covered* **9.R.1.H.1.a; 9.W.3.A.1.a; 9.W.2.D.1.a; 9.R.2.C.1.b**

Women

Respond and Think Critically

Reading Focus

Read with a Purpose

1. What does the poem's speaker remember about the women from her mother's generation?

Reading Skills: Analyzing Details

2. Complete the chart you began on page 679. Review the words and phrases you wrote down as well as your responses. Then, add a row to the bottom of your chart, and describe the speaker's **tone,** or attitude toward the subject of the poem. Use your chart to help you answer question 7.

Words/Phrases from Poem	*My Responses*
"My mama's generation"	*The speaker seems fond of her mom; she uses the word "mama."*
Speaker's tone:	

Literary Focus

Literary Analysis

3. **Interpret** In lines 12–18, Walker uses an **implied metaphor,** which suggests a comparison rather than states one. To what does she compare the women?
4. **Analyze** Think about the historical context of this poem. What "doors" did these women have to batter down? What do you think the "mined fields" and "booby-trapped ditches" stand for?
5. **Infer** What do you think these women *knew* that their children had to know?

Literary Skills: Speaker and Tone

6. **Evaluate** What can you tell about the speaker of this poem? What clues help you to identify the speaker?
7. **Analyze** What is the speaker's **tone,** her attitude toward the women? What words or phrases in this poem help you to identify the speaker's tone? Refer to the chart you began on page 679 to help you with your response.

Literary Skills Review: Character

8. **Analyze** Writers reveal character by giving us clues about how they look, speak, act, and think. Find at least three details in this poem that help you understand the characters that Walker describes in this poem.

Writing Focus

Think as a Reader/Writer

Use It in Your Writing Refer to the adjectives you wrote down in your *Reader/Write Notebook.* Notice the vivid adjectives Alice Walker chooses to describe the women in her poem. Now, write a character description of someone you remember fondly. In your description, use vivid adjectives to bring that person to life for readers.

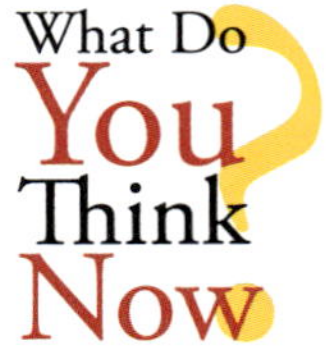

In what way are the women in this poem ordinary? In what way are they extraordinary?

FIGURES OF SPEECH

Wrap Up

9.R.2.B.2.d Identify and explain literary techniques, in text emphasizing: analyze literary techniques previously introduced 9.W.3.A.1.d Compose a variety of texts: including literary analysis 9.W.1.A.1.e Follow a writing process to: share writing *Also covered* 9.W.3.A.1.a; 9.R.1.E.1.b; 9.R.1.E.1.c

Fog / Fire and Ice / "Hope" is the thing with feathers / Fame is a fickle food / Tiburón / Fifteen / Internment / Sanctuary / Women

Vocabulary Development

Vocabulary Skills: Idioms

An **idiom** is an expression that is peculiar to a particular language and that means something different from the literal meaning of its words. The idiom *clay feet* refers to a hero who is found to have hidden faults. The expression comes from the idea that a statue with clay feet will topple, since clay can easily crack and crumble.

Other common idioms include *fish out of water* ("out of one's element"), *cry wolf* ("give a false alarm," based on a fable by Aesop), and *long in the tooth* ("somewhat old," based on judging a horse's age by the length of its teeth).

Your Turn

Identify the idiom in each sentence below. Then, explain the meaning of the idiom, using context clues within the sentence to help you figure out the idiom's meaning.

1. "Hold your horses," the teacher said. "The class hasn't been dismissed yet."
2. Sally is a couch potato who does nothing but watch television.
3. "Step on it!" called her mother. "You're going to be late for school!"
4. Natasha sent her letter to the editor both by e-mail and snail mail.
5. Pavel was star-struck after meeting the best surfer on the beach.

CHOICES

As you respond to the Choices, use these **Academic Vocabulary** words as appropriate: associate, elaborate, evoke, nuances.

REVIEW

Analyze a Poem

Timed Writing Choose one of the poems you read in this collection. Then, perform a line-by-line analysis of the poem. Point out the use of any figures of speech and discuss the meaning of each stanza. To conclude, evaluate the poet's overall execution of the work and explain why you think the poem is or is not successful.

CONNECT

Write a Newscast

TechFocus In a group, write an evening newscast using as many figures of speech as possible. Take turns writing and acting out the newscast. Your newscast should last about five minutes. Then, make an audio or a video recording of your newscast and present it to your class. Ask your classmates to identify the figures of speech in your newscast.

EXTEND

Compare Poems

Look on the Internet or in the library for other poems by Espada and Stafford. Choose a poem and write a brief essay comparing and contrasting that poem with the author's poem in this collection. Discuss the poet's use of figures of speech in the two poems and explain what elements of the new poem appeal to you.

Sounds of Poetry

CONTENTS

"Rippled surface" (1950) by M. C. Escher. Linoleum cut in black and gray-brown, printed from two blocks.

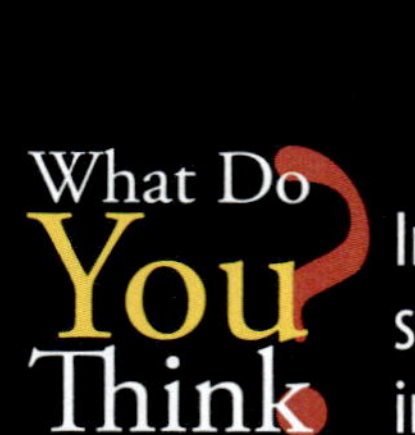

In what ways can sounds inspire the imagination?

Recall a sound that made a strong impression on you, such as lapping waves, the calls of migrating birds, or a jackhammer. Make notes about what you heard and what feelings those sounds evoked in your *Reader/Writer Notebook*.

POETRY

Preparing to Read

I Wandered Lonely as a Cloud

MO **9.R.2.B.2.c** Identify and explain literary techniques, in text emphasizing: repeated sound, line or phrase and **9.R.1.D.1.a** Read grade-level instructional text: with fluency, accuracy, comprehension and appropriate expression **9.R.1.G.1.b** During reading, utilize strategies: to self-monitor comprehension

Reader/Writer Notebook

Use your **RWN** to complete the activities for this selection.

Literary Focus

Rhythm and Meter **Rhythm,** or the repetition of sound patterns, is one of the elements that gives poems their musical quality. Wordsworth created rhythm by arranging words so that the lines repeat a regular pattern of stressed and unstressed syllables. This pattern is called **meter.** When you **scan** a poem for meter, you mark the stressed syllables with the symbol ʹ and the unstressed syllables with the symbol ˘.

TechFocus As you read the poems in this section, think about which one you would like to use for a presentation on sound effects.

Reading Focus

Reading Aloud Reading a poem aloud can help you understand its basic meaning as well as analyze its rhythm and meter.

Into Action Scan the lines of Wordsworth's poem. Mark each stressed syllable ʹ and each unstressed syllable ˘.

Text of Poem and Scan Marks

˘ ʹ ˘ ʹ ˘ ʹ ˘ ʹ
I wandered lonely as a cloud
˘ ʹ ˘ ʹ ˘ ʹ ˘ ʹ
That floats on high o'er vales and hills,
˘ ʹ ˘ ʹ ˘ ʹ ˘ ʹ
When all at once I saw a crowd,
˘ ʹ ˘ ʹ ˘ ʹ ˘ ʹ
A host, of golden daffodils, . . .

Writing Focus

Think as a Reader/Writer

Find It in Your Reading Some poets use **inverted word order**—where a verb comes before the subject, or the object of a verb comes before the verb—to create rhyme or rhythm. As you read the poem, record examples of inverted word order.

Vocabulary

sprightly (SPRYT lee) *adj.:* lively; full of spirit. *The speaker of the poem remembers the daffodils' sprightly movements in the breeze.*

glee (glee) *n.:* great delight; merriment. *The poem's speaker thinks that if daffodils could feel, they would be filled with glee.*

pensive (PEHN sihv) *adj.:* thoughtful in a serious manner; reflective. *When the speaker is in a pensive mood, he likes to lie down on his couch.*

solitude (SAHL uh tood) *n.:* being alone; isolation. *In solitude, the speaker likes to think back on the field of daffodils that he once passed.*

Language Coach

Connotation and Denotation A word's **connotations** are the feelings and associations that the word suggests, which are quite different from a word's **denotation,** or its strict dictionary definition. In Wordsworth's poem "I Wandered Lonely as a Cloud," he describes two different moods—one of joy and excitement and one that is more serious and somber. Which two words from the list above connote feelings of happiness? Which words have connotations of a serious nature?

Learn It Online

Use the video introduction online to get a preview of this poem:

go.hrw.com L9-685 

MEET THE WRITER

Learn It Online
Learn more about the author at:
go.hrw.com L9-686 Go

William Wordsworth
(1770–1850)

Early Tragedy and Early Success

The English Romantic poet William Wordsworth suffered a tragic childhood. Wordsworth's mother died when he was just seven, and six years later his father also passed away. He and his four orphaned siblings were then sent away to school by an uncle. Wordsworth started writing poems by the age of fifteen. When he was twenty-eight, he and his close friend Samuel Taylor Coleridge published a collection of poems called *Lyrical Ballads*. This slim book contained only twenty-four poems, all very different from the fancy, aristocratic poetry of their contemporaries. Wordsworth and Coleridge used simple people and ordinary experiences as their subjects and described them with common speech.

A Reflective Soul

According to Wordsworth, poetry begins when we get in touch with a memory and relive the experience: "Poetry is the spontaneous overflow of powerful feelings: It takes its origin from emotion recollected in tranquility." In other words, Wordsworth believed that it's better to write about an experience later rather than when you're right in the middle of it. He also believed that nature is the best teacher and that the human mind is intimately related to the workings of the natural world, a subject that is prevalent in much of his work.

Think About the Writer Do you agree that experiences can best be described long after they occur?

Build Background

This poem captures with enormous precision a special moment that occurred two hundred years ago—on April 15, 1802, to be precise. We can be precise because there was another witness to that special moment—the poet's sister, Dorothy—who captured the very same scene in her journal. On that day, she wrote: "I never saw daffodils so beautiful. They grew along the mossy stones; some rested their heads upon those stones as on a pillow for weariness; and the rest tossed and reeled and danced. . . ."

Portrait of William Wordsworth at age twenty-eight by William Shuter.

Read with a Purpose Read this poem to find out what sight inspired Wordsworth for years to come.

I Wandered Lonely as a Cloud

by **William Wordsworth**

I wandered lonely as a cloud
That floats on high o'er vales° and hills,
When all at once I saw a crowd,
A host, of golden daffodils,
Beside the lake, beneath the trees,
Fluttering and dancing in the breeze. **A**

Continuous as the stars that shine
And twinkle on the Milky Way,
They stretched in never-ending line
Along the margin of a bay;
Ten thousand saw I at a glance,
Tossing their heads in sprightly dance.

The waves beside them danced, but they
Outdid the sparkling waves in glee;
A poet could not but be gay,
In such a jocund° company;
I gazed—and gazed—but little thought
What wealth the show to me had brought:

For oft,° when on my couch I lie
In vacant or in pensive mood,
They flash upon that inward eye
Which is the bliss of solitude;
And then my heart with pleasure fills,
And dances with the daffodils. **B**

2. **vales** (vaylz): valleys.

16. **jocund** (JAHK uhnd): merry.

19. **oft** (awft): shortened form of *often*.

A Literary Focus Rhythm Do these lines have a rhythmic pattern? How can you tell?

B Reading Focus Reading Aloud Read this final stanza aloud. What causes the speaker's heart to fill with pleasure?

Vocabulary **sprightly** (SPRYT lee) *adj.*: lively; full of spirit.
glee (glee) *n.*: great delight; merriment.
pensive (PEHN sihv) *adj.*: thoughtful in a serious manner; reflective.
solitude (SAHL uh tood) *n.*: being alone; isolation.

Applying Your Skills

MO **9.R.2.B.2.c** Identify and explain literary techniques, in text emphasizing: repeated sound, line or phrase **9.R.2.B.2.d** Identify and explain literary techniques, in text emphasizing: analyze literary techniques previously introduced *Also covered* **9.R.1.D.1.a; 9.R.1.G.1.b; 9.W.3.A.1.a; 9.R.1.G.1.a**

I Wandered Lonely as a Cloud

Respond and Think Critically

Reading Focus

Read with a Purpose

1. As the speaker wanders, what does he see "all at once"? How does the memory of what he saw affect him?

Reading Skills: Reading Aloud

2. Complete the scan of the poem you began on page 685. Then, compare it with a peer's to see if they match up. Refer to your work to help you answer question 10.

Text of Poem and Scan Marks

˘ ´ ˘ ´ ˘ ´ ˘ ´
I wandered lonely as a cloud
˘ ´ ˘ ´ ˘ ´ ˘ ´
That floats on high o'er vales and hills,
˘ ´ ˘ ´ ˘ ´ ˘ ´
When all at once I saw a crowd,
˘ ´ ˘ ´ ˘ ´ ˘ ´
A host, of golden daffodils, . . .

Vocabulary Check

For each of the sentences below, mark a *C* where the boldface Vocabulary word has been used correctly. Mark an *I* where it has been used incorrectly, and then rewrite the sentence to make it correct.

3. Following hip surgery, Grandma walked about her room in a **sprightly** fashion.
4. José is only able to complete his homework in **solitude.**
5. I feel a sense of **glee** whenever I've had a bad day.
6. My friend tends to get in a **pensive** state of mind when he thinks about the future.

Literary Focus

Literary Analysis

7. **Identify** What simile does the speaker use to describe his loneliness?
8. **Analyze** What is the speaker's mood at the beginning of the poem? How does the speaker's mood change by the end of the poem?
9. **Interpret** What is the "inward eye" in line 21 of the poem? Explain its meaning.

Literary Skills: Rhythm and Meter

10. **Analyze** "I Wandered Lonely as a Cloud" has a distinct rhythm. What pattern of stressed and unstressed syllables is used in the poem? How does the pattern help to move the poem along?

Literary Skills Review: Personification

11. **Identify** **Personification** is a figure of speech in which a nonhuman thing or quality is talked about as if it were human. Which words in the poem personify the daffodils?

Writing Focus

Think as a Reader/Writer

Use It in Your Writing Write a paragraph in which you discuss your opinion of Wordsworth's use of inverted word order. Do you think it adds to or detracts from the poem? Use examples to explain.

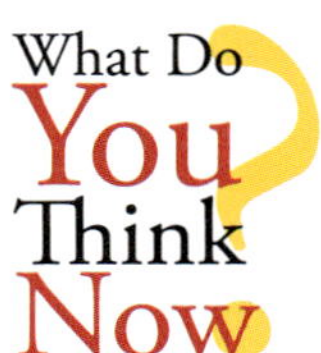

Why does the memory of the daffodils comfort Wordsworth? How might the sights and sounds of nature create lifelong memories?

POETRY

Preparing to Read

9.R.2.B.2.c Identify and explain literary techniques, in text emphasizing: repeated sound, line or phrase 9.R.1.H.1.a Apply post-reading skills to comprehend, interpret, analyze, and evaluate text: identify and explain the relationship between the main idea and supporting details

The Courage That My Mother Had / Advice for a Stegosaurus

Reader/Writer Notebook

Use your **RWN** to complete the activities for these selections.

Literary Focus

Rhyme **Rhyme** is the repetition of accented vowel sounds, and all sounds following them, in words that are close together. There are different types of rhyme. **Exact rhyme** occurs where the words echo each other exactly, like *moon* and *June*. **Approximate rhyme** occurs where words repeat some, but not all sounds, like *hollow* and *mellow*.

When the rhyme occurs in the middle of a line, it is called **internal rhyme,** but when the rhyme occurs at the end of a line, it is called **end rhyme.** A regular pattern of end rhyme is a **rhyme scheme.** Rhyme scheme is indicated by using different letters of the alphabet, beginning with *a,* for each new rhyme. Here is an example:

Little Miss Muffet *a*
Sat on a tuffet *a*
Eating her curds and whey. *b*
Along came a spider *c*
Who sat down beside her *c*
And frightened Miss Muffet away. *b*

Reading Focus

Analyzing Details To track the rhymes in Millay's and Goodheart's poems, fill in a chart like this as you read.

	The Courage . . .	Advice . . .
Rhyme Scheme	had/still/quarried/hill (abcb)	
Exact Rhymes	still/hill	
Approximate Rhymes		

Writing Focus

Think as a Reader/Writer

Find It in Your Reading As you read, note instances of repetition in your *Reader/Writer Notebook* and how they evoke meaning.

Vocabulary

The Courage That My Mother Had

spare (spair) *v.:* give up the use or possession of; part with. *She could not spare the time to speak with me.*

Advice for a Stegosaurus

deliberate (dih LIHB uhr iht) *adj.:* done with careful thought or method in mind. *The dinosaur walked with deliberate steps.*

armored (AHR muhrd) *adj.:* covered with defensive or protective covering, as on animals or plants. *The stegosaurus is said to have had armored eyelids.*

Language Coach

Word Origins Millay's poem focuses on her mother's courage. The word *courage* derives from the Old French *corage,* meaning "heart" or "spirit." In what way does a person who has courage display heart or spirit?

Learn It Online
Broaden your word power with Word Watch:
go.hrw.com L9-689 Go

MEET THE WRITERS

Edna St. Vincent Millay

(1892–1950)

The Granger Collection, New York.

Family Ties

Edna St. Vincent Millay was born and raised in Rockland, Maine. She started writing poetry as a child. Millay wrote "Renascence" (rih NAS uhns), one of her most famous poems, when she was only nineteen. Millay published her first book of poetry in 1917, the year she graduated from Vassar College. After graduation, Millay moved to New York City's Greenwich Village and quickly found a place in the writing community that flourished there. In 1923, Millay was awarded the Pulitzer Prize for *The Harp Weaver and Other Poems.*

Jessica Goodheart

(1967–)

"Don't Eat Me, Dinosaur"

Jessica Goodheart was born in Boston, Massachusetts. According to Goodheart, "'Advice for a Stegosaurus' emerged from a resonant phrase. . . . I could not have set out to write a poem about our threatened species and produced anything readable. Rather, I had a simple childish phrase stuck in my head, one that was ultimately dropped from the poem. During a summer trip to Mexico, our host used to entertain my three-year-old son at mealtime by saying, 'Don't eat me, dinosaur.'"

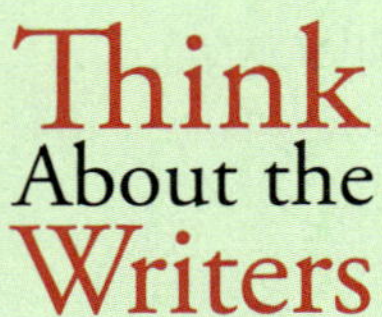

What do these two poets seem to have in common?

Build Background

Jessica Goodheart's poem, "Advice for a Stegosaurus," refers to a type of dinosaur characterized by the two rows of bony plates that ran along its back and tail. An herbivore, or plant-eater, the stegosaurus was quite large: as much as thirty feet long and eleven feet tall, weighing around three tons. Despite its impressive size, its brain was the size of a golf ball.

Read with a Purpose Read the following poems to see how two different speakers approach the subject of courage.

The Courage That My Mother Had

by **Edna St. Vincent Millay**

The courage that my mother had
Went with her, and is with her still:
Rock from New England quarried;
Now granite° in a granite hill. **A**

The golden brooch° my mother wore
She left behind for me to wear;
I have no thing I treasure more:
Yet, it is something I could spare.

Oh, if instead she'd left to me
The thing she took into the grave!—
That courage like a rock, which she
Has no more need of, and I have. **B**

---

4. **granite** (GRAN iht): hard igneous rock.
5. **brooch** (brohch): ornamental pin that fastens with a clasp.

A Literary Focus Rhyme Where do rhymes occur in this stanza?

B Literary Focus Rhyme What rhyme scheme occurs in this stanza?

Vocabulary **spare** (spair) *v.*: give up the use or possession of; part with.

Analyzing Visuals **Viewing and Interpreting** What makes the woman in this photograph appear courageous?

ADVICE FOR A STEGOSAURUS

by **Jessica Goodheart**

Never mind the asteroid,
the hot throat of the volcano,
a sun that daily drops into the void.

Comb the drying riverbed for drink.
Strut your bird-hipped body.
Practice a lizard grin. Don't think. **A**

Stretch out your tail. Walk, as you must,
in a slow deliberate gait.
Don't look back, Dinosaur. Dust is dust.

You'll leave your bones, your fossil feet
and armored eye-lids.
Put your chin to the wind. Eat what you eat. **B**

A **Literary Focus** **Rhyme** What is the rhyme scheme of this stanza?

B **Literary Focus** **Rhyme** What type of rhyme do the words *chin* and *wind* create?

Vocabulary **deliberate** (dih LIHB uhr iht) *adj.*: done with careful thought or method in mind.
armored (AHR muhrd) *adj.*: covered with defensive or protective covering, as on animals or plants.

Applying Your Skills

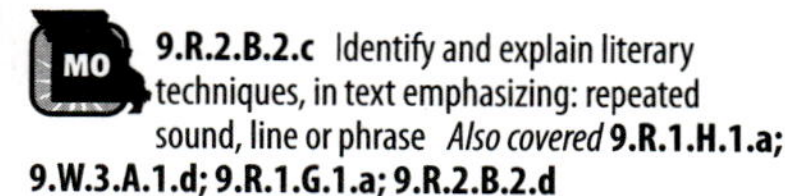

9.R.2.B.2.c Identify and explain literary techniques, in text emphasizing: repeated sound, line or phrase *Also covered* **9.R.1.H.1.a; 9.W.3.A.1.d; 9.R.1.G.1.a; 9.R.2.B.2.d**

The Courage That My Mother Had / Advice for a Stegosaurus

Respond and Think Critically

Reading Focus

Read with a Purpose

1. In what way is each poem about courage? What general statement can you make about the subject of courage based on the poems?

Reading Skills: Analyzing Details

2. Complete the chart you began on page 689. Use the chart to answer question 9.

	The Courage . . .	Advice . . .
Rhyme Scheme	had/still/ quarried/hill (abcb)	
Exact Rhymes	still/hill	
Approximate Rhymes		

Vocabulary Check

Use the Vocabulary words to complete each sentence.

spare
deliberate
armored

3. The cactus has needles to give it an ________ appearance.
4. The tightrope walker used very ________ steps.
5. Could you ________ a cup of sugar?

Literary Focus

Literary Analysis

6. **Interpret** What effect does Goodheart's use of repeated sentence types create?
7. **Analyze** Like all lyric poems, these two evoke strong feelings. What emotion does each speaker display?
8. **Analyze** Find an example of **alliteration** (repeated consonant sounds in words close together) in both poems.

Literary Skills: Rhyme

9. **Analyze** Describe the rhyme scheme in each poem by using letters to indicate each end rhyme. Then, list which pairs of words are approximate rhyme and which are exact rhyme.

Literary Skills Review: Implied Metaphor

10. **Evaluate** An **implied metaphor** suggests a comparison between two things without stating it directly. Some readers interpret "Advice for a Stegosaurus," as being about uncaring humans. Do you agree with that interpretation? Explain.

Writing Focus

Think as a Reader/Writer

Use It in Your Writing Write a short essay analyzing how each poet addresses the subject of courage. Then, comment on how the use of repetition helps each poet convey her ideas.

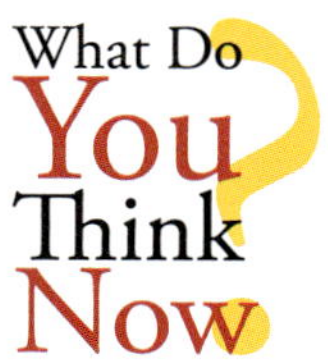

Have your thoughts about courage changed since you read these poems? Explain.

POETRY

Preparing to Read

The Gift / Possum Crossing

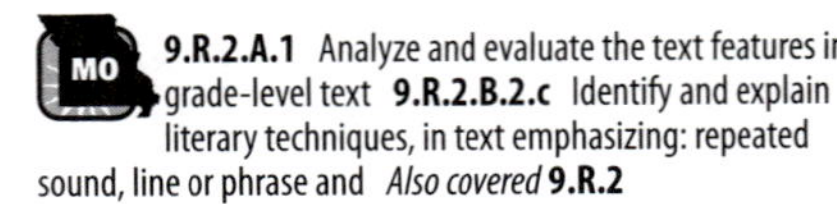

9.R.2.A.1 Analyze and evaluate the text features in grade-level text **9.R.2.B.2.c** Identify and explain literary techniques, in text emphasizing: repeated sound, line or phrase and *Also covered* **9.R.2**

Literary Focus

Alliteration and Assonance Poetry that does not adhere to strict patterns of rhythm and meter is called **free verse.** Free-verse poems are written to imitate ordinary conversation. Free verse has rhythm, but it is not written to meter. Free verse makes use of various poetic elements to create its music, including alliteration and assonance.

- **Alliteration** is the repetition of consonant sounds in words that appear close together. Many tongue-twisters contain alliteration. For example, "**S**he **s**ells **s**ea **s**hells by the **s**ea**s**hore."
- **Assonance** is the repetition of vowel sounds in words that appear close together. Listen for the short *e* sound in this example: "S**e**t the br**ea**d n**e**xt to the v**e**getables."

Reading Focus

Reading a Poem When you read a poem, punctuation can be just as important as word choice. If a line has no end punctuation such as a period or question mark, pause briefly at the end of the line but do not make a full stop; instead, read on until you encounter punctuation indicating a stop. If a poem has no end punctuation, look for other clues for how to read the poem, such as subjects and verbs that require emphasis.

Into Action Keep track of clues that indicate pauses in the poems.

"The Gift"	"Possum Crossing"
Lines 1–3 state a complete thought.	

Writing Focus

Think as a Reader/Writer

Find It in Your Reading The poems that follow move from the past to the present and back again. As you read, take notes in your *Reader/Writer Notebook* about how the poets indicate time shifts.

Reader/Writer Notebook

Use your **RWN** to complete the activities for these selections.

Vocabulary

The Gift

shard (shahrd) *n.:* a small bit or broken piece of something. *The speaker's father plucked a shard from his son's hand.*

Possum Crossing

eerie (IHR ee) *adj.:* causing fear; strange. *In the fog, the car's headlights appeared as an eerie glow.*

anticipate (an TIHS uh payt) *v.:* expect; look forward to. *Careful drivers should anticipate possible dangers.*

exasperated (ehg ZAS puh ray tuhd) *adj.:* irritated and angry. *The driver became exasperated after spilling coffee.*

Language Coach

Synonyms When bringing an idea to life, a poet may consider several **synonyms**—words that mean the same thing or almost the same thing—before deciding on the best word. For example, if a poet is describing how an anxious person feels, he or she might choose from words such as *fret, agonize,* and *worry*. Pick two words from the Vocabulary list. Create a list of synonyms for each word and try using them in sentences.

Learn It Online

Go beyond the definitions with Word Watch at:

go.hrw.com L9-694 

Li-Young Lee

(1957–)

A Political History

The great-grandfather of Li-Young Lee was the first president of the Republic of China. His father, on whom the character in "The Gift" is based, was the personal physician to the revolutionary leader Mao Tse-tung. The family fled China not long after the Communist People's Republic was established in 1949. They went first to Indonesia, and Li-Young Lee was born in Jakarta. There, his father was thrown into jail by the corrupt dictator Sukarno. His father spent nineteen months in prison, seventeen of them in a leper colony. When the family fled again, they went to Hong Kong. When Lee was six, they arrived in the United States, where his father became a Presbyterian minister.

Nikki Giovanni

(1943–)

An Observer

Born in Tennessee and raised in Cincinnati, Ohio, Nikki Giovanni has worked hard to become one of the greatest living American poets. She has written more than twenty-six books, been nominated for a Grammy award for Best Spoken Word, and even had a bat species named after her by a scientist who was impressed with her work. Giovanni expresses her own ideas, however unpopular they might be, and her body of work includes everything from calls for revolution to children's poetry. In observing her surroundings, Giovanni comments, "I'm not trying to tell people what to do or what to think or none of that. I'm not a leader. I'm not a guru. I'm just a poet looking at the world."

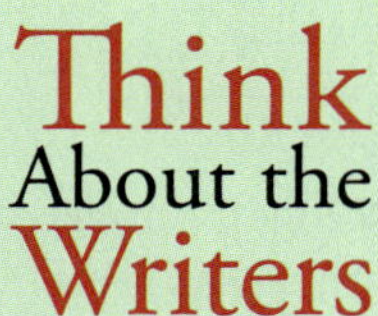

Based on the information above, how do you think Li-Young Lee and Nikki Giovanni look at the world?

Build Background

Nikki Giovanni's poem "Possum Crossing" takes its title from the small American mammal, the opossum. Opossums are about the size of a hefty house cat and have short, dense fur, long noses, and beady eyes. Their outstanding feature is the long prehensile tail that enables them to climb and hang upside down from tree branches. As nocturnal animals, opossums search for food at night and enjoy a varied diet, from insects to fruit to chicken to garbage. When in danger, opossums enter a state that makes them appear to be dead—hence the expression "playing possum."

Read with a Purpose Read this poem to learn what "gift" a father gives his son.

THE GIFT

by **Li-Young Lee**

To pull the metal splinter from my palm
my father recited a story in a low voice. **A**
I watched his lovely face and not the blade.
Before the story ended he'd removed
the iron sliver I thought I'd die from. **B**

I can't remember the tale
but hear his voice still, a well
of dark water, a prayer.
And I recall his hands,
two measures of tenderness
he laid against my face,
the flames of discipline
he raised above my head.

Had you entered that afternoon
you would have thought you saw a man
planting something in a boy's palm,
a silver tear, a tiny flame.
Had you followed that boy
you would have arrived here,
where I bend over my wife's right hand.

Look how I shave her thumbnail down
so carefully she feels no pain.
Watch as I lift the splinter out.
I was seven when my father
took my hand like this,
and I did not hold that shard
between my fingers and think,
Metal that will bury me,
christen it Little Assassin,
Ore° Going Deep for My Heart.
And I did not lift up my wound and cry,
Death visited here!
I did what a child does
when he's given something to keep.
I kissed my father. **C**

30. **ore** (ohr): mineral or rock, especially one from which metals might be profitably extracted.

A Literary Focus Alliteration Read the first two lines aloud, softly. What consonant sound is repeated in these lines?

B Literary Focus Assonance What instances of assonance can you find in line 5?

C Reading Focus Reading a Poem What is the poet trying to indicate to the reader by using italics in the last stanza? How might you read those lines differently than you would the rest of the poem?

Vocabulary **shard** (shahrd) *n.*: a small bit or broken piece of something.

Read with a Purpose Read this poem to find out what the speaker wants to warn her neighbors about.

Possum Crossing

by **Nikki Giovanni**

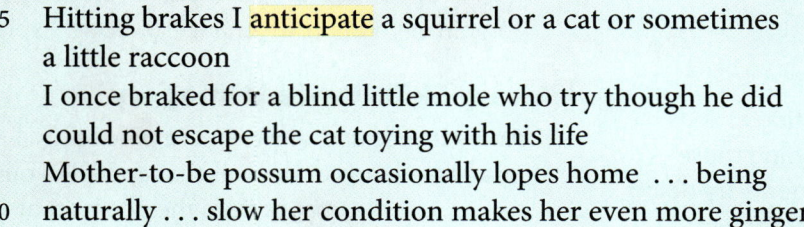

Backing out the driveway
the car lights cast an eerie glow
in the morning fog centering
on movement in the rain slick street

Hitting brakes I anticipate a squirrel or a cat or sometimes
a little raccoon
I once braked for a blind little mole who try though he did
could not escape the cat toying with his life
Mother-to-be possum occasionally lopes home . . . being
naturally . . . slow her condition makes her even more ginger

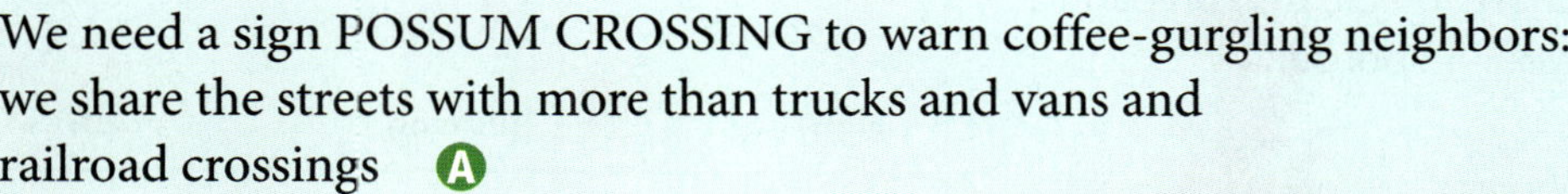

We need a sign POSSUM CROSSING to warn coffee-gurgling neighbors:
we share the streets with more than trucks and vans and
railroad crossings **A**

All birds being the living kin of dinosaurs
think themselves invincible and pay no heed
to the rolling wheels while they dine
on an unlucky rabbit

I hit brakes for the flutter of the lights hoping it's not a deer
or a skunk or a groundhog
coffee splashes over the cup which I quickly put away from me
and into the empty passenger seat
I look . . .
relieved and exasperated . . .
to discover I have just missed a big wet leaf
struggling . . . to lift itself into the wind
and live **B**

A **Literary Focus** **Alliteration** What instances of alliteration can you find in this stanza?

B **Reading Focus** **Reading a Poem** What effect is produced by the punctuation in the last five lines of this stanza?

Vocabulary **eerie** (IHR ee) *adj.*: causing fear; strange.
anticipate (an TIHS uh payt) *v.*: expect; look forward to.
exasperated (ehg ZAS puh ray tuhd) *adj.*: irritated and angry.

Applying Your Skills

MO 9.R.2.B.2.c Identify and explain literary techniques, in text emphasizing: repeated sound, line or phrase 9.R.2.B.2.b Identify and explain literary techniques, in text emphasizing: imagery *Also covered* 9.R.2; 9.W.3.A.1.a; 9.R.1.G.1.a

The Gift / Possum Crossing

Respond and Think Critically

Reading Focus

Read with a Purpose

1. What does the father do that the son always remembers as a "gift"?
2. What warning does Giovanni express in "Possum Crossing"?

Reading Skills: Reading a Poem

3. Imagine that there is no punctuation in lines 24–32 of "The Gift." How does reading those lines with no stops change the poem? Try doing the same thing with lines 9–10 of "Possum Crossing." Use the chart you created on page 694 to help you in your response.

Vocabulary Check

Match each Vocabulary word with its definition.

4. **shard** — a. strange
5. **eerie** — b. expect
6. **anticipate** — c. a broken piece
7. **exasperated** — d. caused irritation

Literary Focus

Literary Analysis

8. **Infer** Why do you think the speaker's father recites a story to his son (stanza 1) in "The Gift"?
9. **Analyze** What metaphors describe the father's voice and hands in stanza 2 of "The Gift"?
10. **Analyze** Giovanni uses **onomatopoeia**—words whose sound suggest or imitate their meaning—to add sound effects to her poem. What example of onomatopoeia can you find?

Literary Skills: Alliteration and Assonance

11. **Analyze** Copy the second stanza of "The Gift" and read it aloud softly. Circle instances of alliteration. Underline instances of assonance.
12. **Analyze** Does the line "All birds being the living kin of dinosaurs" from "Possum Crossing" contain alliteration, assonance, or both? Explain.

Literary Skills Review: Imagery

13. **Analyze** Lee and Giovanni use precise **images**—words or phrases that appeal to our senses. List the images from the poems that appeal to the senses of sight, hearing, and touch.

Sight	Hearing	Touch

Writing Focus

Think as a Reader/Writer

Use It in Your Writing Both poets narrate events, past and present. Verb tenses help guide us to understand when those events took place. Think of an experience you had recently that reminded you of a past event. Write a paragraph describing both the recent and the past experience. Use correct verb tenses to help your reader understand.

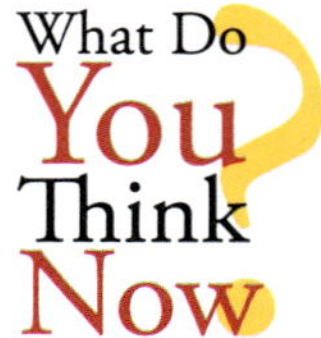

What small acts of caring do both poems describe? How are those small acts deeply meaningful for the poems' speakers?

POETRY

Preparing to Read

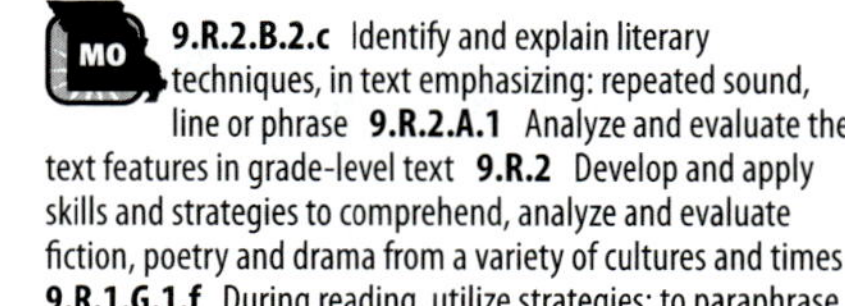

9.R.2.B.2.c Identify and explain literary techniques, in text emphasizing: repeated sound, line or phrase **9.R.2.A.1** Analyze and evaluate the text features in grade-level text **9.R.2** Develop and apply skills and strategies to comprehend, analyze and evaluate fiction, poetry and drama from a variety of cultures and times **9.R.1.G.1.f** During reading, utilize strategies: to paraphrase

from Song of Myself, Number 32 / I Hear America Singing

Reader/Writer Notebook

Use your **RWN** to complete the activities for these selections.

Literary Focus

Rhythm The musical quality in language that is produced by repetition is called **rhythm.** Rhythm occurs in all forms of spoken and written language and often evokes strong feelings. Whitman created rhythm by repeating sentence structures, words, and sounds. The most obvious kind of rhythm is produced by **meter,** a regular repetition of stressed and unstressed syllables. Writers can also create rhythm by using rhymes, repeated words, and repeated phrases.

Parallelism The repetition of words, phrases, or sentences that have the same grammatical structure or that state a similar idea is called **parallelism.** Parallelism, or parallel structure, helps make lines rhythmic and memorable, and it heightens their emotional effect.

Reading Focus

Reading Poetry When you read a poem, it's a good idea to **paraphrase** it—restate it in your own words—to help you understand the poem's basic meaning. Then, compare your paraphrase with the original to better appreciate the poet's diction and word choice.

Into Action Use a chart like this as you paraphrase the poems.

	Original Text	My Paraphrase
"I Hear America Singing"		
"Song of Myself"		

Writing Focus

Think as a Reader/Writer

Find It in Your Reading As you read Whitman's poems, look for repeated words and images. Write examples of this repetition in your *Reader/Writer Notebook*. What nuances, or variations, can you find within the repetition?

Vocabulary

***from* Song of Myself**

placid (PLAS ihd) *adj.:* quiet; still and peaceful. *The animals in the field were placid.*

I Hear America Singing

blithe (blyth) *adj.:* cheerful; happy. *The speaker of the poem hears the mechanics' blithe songs.*

intermission (IHN tuhr MIHSH uhn) *n.:* a pause between periods of activity. *The speaker hears the plowboy singing during his intermission from work.*

robust (roh BUHST) *adj.:* sturdy; healthy and strong. *The young mechanics are robust.*

Language Coach

Multiple-Meaning Words Whitman uses many words that can mean different things, depending on their context. For example, in "I Hear America Singing," Whitman describes the singing as *strong,* meaning "powerful." But in a different context, such as "I am not a strong speller," the word means something different. As you read, list the multiple-meaning words you encounter in your *Reader/Writer Notebook.*

Learn It Online
Listen to the rhythm of these poems online:
go.hrw.com
L9-699
Go

MEET THE WRITER

Learn It Online
Learn more about Whitman's life at:
go.hrw.com L9-700 Go

Walt Whitman

(1819–1892)

A Poet with Confidence

Walt Whitman, born on Long Island, New York, was one of the first world-class poets America produced. He transformed the language of poetry—by writing it in free verse and using common speech and slang. Nobody would publish his radical book *Leaves of Grass,* so he published it himself in 1855. He even wrote his own glowing reviews. In one review he said: "Very devilish to some, and very divine to some, will appear the poet of these new poems. . . ."

A Memorable Personality

Whitman left school at the age of eleven and went to work. But on weekends he read Sir Walter Scott, the Bible, Shakespeare, Homer, Dante, and "the ancient Hindoo poems." In his thirties, he described himself as "a Fine Brute." He dressed differently from most people and is said, on one occasion, to have driven a horse-drawn carriage up and down Broadway reciting passages of Shakespeare at the top of his lungs.

An American Treasure

The great naturalist John Burroughs, who often saw Whitman on the street, wrote: "The first and last impression which his personal presence always made upon one was of a nature wonderfully gentle, tender, and benignant. . . . He always had the look of a man who had just taken a bath." Whitman gave old-fashioned poetry a good, hard scrubbing, but at first not many people thanked him for it. As a poor old man, he was reduced to selling his book out of a basket on the streets of Philadelphia, but he never stopped revising and adding to it until his death. Today, *Leaves of Grass* is one of the treasures of American literature.

"Behold, I do not give lectures or a little charity. When I give I give myself."

Think About the Writer Do you think Whitman's eccentric ways contributed to or detracted from his greatness as a poet?

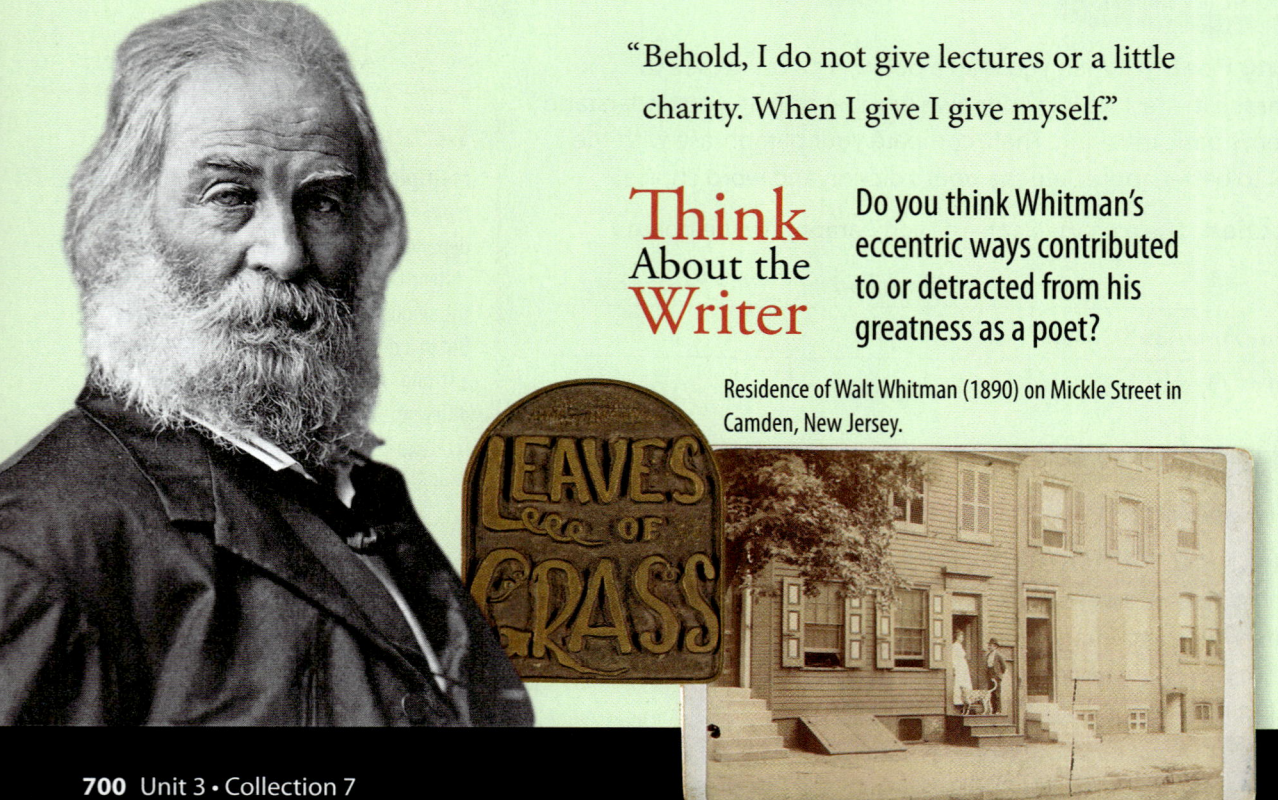

Residence of Walt Whitman (1890) on Mickle Street in Camden, New Jersey.

Read with a Purpose Read this selection to find out how the speaker regards animals and people.

from

Song of Myself
Number 32

by **Walt Whitman**

I think I could turn and live with animals, they are so placid
and self-contain'd;
I stand and look at them long and long.
They do not sweat and whine about their condition;
They do not lie awake in the dark and weep for their sins;
They do not make me sick discussing their duty to God; (A)
Not one is dissatisfied—not one is demented with the mania
of owning things;
Not one kneels to another, nor to his kind that lived thou-
sands of years ago;
Not one is respectable or industrious over the whole
earth. (B)

(A) **Literary Focus** **Rhythm** In lines 3–5, how does Whitman create rhythm?

(B) **Reading Focus** **Paraphrasing** Restate lines 6–8 in your own words. What point is Whitman making?

Vocabulary **placid** (PLAS ihd) *adj.*: quiet; still and peaceful.

Construction of the Dam (c. 1937) by William Gropper (1897–1977). Mural study, Department of the Interior, National Park Service. Oil on canvas (27¼" x 87¼").

Read with a Purpose Read this poem to find out why America is singing.

I HEAR AMERICA SINGING

by **Walt Whitman**

I hear America singing, the varied carols I hear,
Those of mechanics, each one singing his as it should be blithe and strong,
The carpenter singing his as he measures his plank or beam,
The mason singing his as he makes ready for work, or leaves off work,
The boatman singing what belongs to him in his boat, the deckhand singing
    on the steamboat deck, (A)

(A) **Literary Focus** **Rhythm** How does Whitman create rhythm in lines 3–5?

Vocabulary **blithe** (blyth) *adj.*: cheerful; happy.

Analyzing Visuals **Viewing and Interpreting** In what ways does this painting reflect the America that Whitman writes about?

The shoemaker singing as he sits on his bench, the hatter singing as
    he stands,
The wood-cutter's song, the plowboy's on his way in the morning,
    or at noon intermission or at sundown,
The delicious singing of the mother, or of the young wife at work,
    or of the girl sewing or washing,
Each singing what belongs to him or her and to none else,
The day what belongs to the day—at night the party of young fellows, robust,
    friendly,
Singing with open mouths their strong melodious songs. **B**

B **Reading Focus** **Paraphrasing** What does Whitman seem to be saying about the workers of America?

Vocabulary **intermission** (IHN tuhr MIHSH uhn) *n.:* a pause between periods of activity.
robust (roh BUHST) *adj.:* sturdy; healthy and strong.

Applying Your Skills

from Song of Myself / I Hear America Singing

MO **9.R.2.B.2.c** Identify and explain literary techniques, in text emphasizing: repeated sound, line or phrase **9.R.1.G.1.f** During reading, utilize strategies: to paraphrase **9.W.3.A.1.e** Compose a variety of texts: including reflective writing *Also covered* **9.R.1.G.1.a; 9.R.2.B.2.d; 9.R.1.H.1.a**

Respond and Think Critically

Reading Focus

Read with a Purpose

1. According to the speaker of "I Hear America Singing," how does America sing?
2. Why does the speaker in "Song of Myself" prefer animals to humans?

Reading Skills: Reading Poetry

3. Complete your paraphrases of Whitman's poems. Then, add a row to your chart, and describe how the original texts compare with your paraphrases. Did your paraphrase contain rhythm or other sound effects? What aspects of the poems were lost by translating them?

	Original Text	My Paraphrase
"I Hear America Singing"		
"Song of Myself"		

Comparison of Paraphrases to Originals:

Vocabulary Check

Match the Vocabulary words with their definitions.

4. **blithe** — a. strong
5. **intermission** — b. happy and carefree
6. **robust** — c. calm
7. **placid** — d. break or rest period

Literary Focus

Literary Analysis

8. **Interpret** What does Whitman mean when he uses the word *singing* to describe America?
9. **Speculate** In "I Hear America Singing," Whitman appears to celebrate the industrious nature of people, yet in "Song of Myself" the opposite seems to be true. Why do you think Whitman's point of view toward humanity changes?

Literary Skills: Rhythm and Parallelism

10. **Analyze** How does Whitman use rhythm in "I Hear America Singing"?
11. **Identify** In "Song of Myself," Whitman uses parallelism. Identify each instance.

Literary Skills Review: Implied Metaphor

12. **Analyze** An **implied metaphor** suggests a comparison between two things without stating it directly. In "Song of Myself," Whitman describes animals by saying what "they do not" do. To whom or what is Whitman comparing animals? Why do you think he chose not to directly state the object of his displeasure?

Writing Focus

Think as a Reader/Writer

Use It in Your Writing Would "I Hear America Singing" be different if it were written today? In an essay, suggest words and phrases Whitman might use to evoke the songs America is now singing.

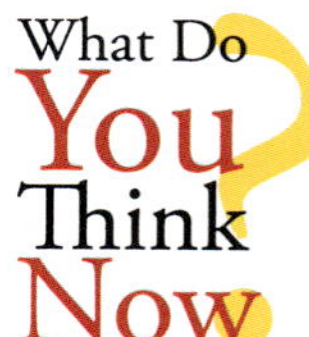

How does Whitman regard the world, judging from these poems? How are his eccentric ways reflected in his poetry?

POETRY

Preparing to Read

Legal Alien / Extranjera legal

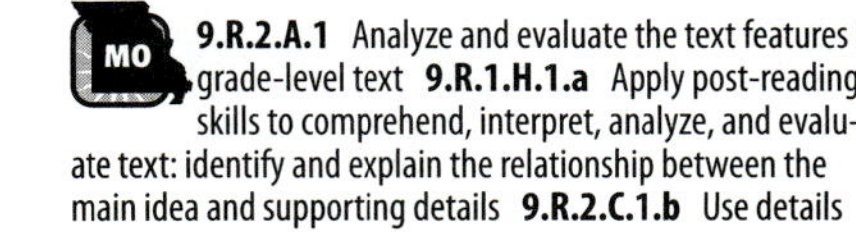

9.R.2.A.1 Analyze and evaluate the text features in grade-level text **9.R.1.H.1.a** Apply post-reading skills to comprehend, interpret, analyze, and evaluate text: identify and explain the relationship between the main idea and supporting details **9.R.2.C.1.b** Use details from text(s): to analyze character, plot, setting, point of view

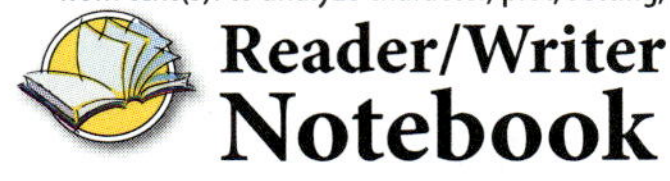

Reader/Writer Notebook

Use your **RWN** to complete the activities for this selection.

Literary Focus

Speaker Poets can imagine anyone or anything as their **speaker,** the voice talking to us in a poem. The speaker is often the poet—but not always. The poet may assume a **persona,** or mask, and speak as someone other than himself or herself.

Wordplay and Parallel Structures Poems convey ideas through language. As they craft their poems, poets might play with meaning, experiment with sound effects, and pair unlikely words. They also pay close attention to structure. As you read this poem, look for ways in which Mora uses parallel structures to reinforce her ideas.

Language Coach

Prefixes A **prefix** is a word part placed at the beginning of a word. The prefix *bi–*, meaning "two," is in the words *bilingual* and *bicultural*. Although these two words are not usually hyphenated, Mora separates the word parts to emphasize the feeling of living in two different worlds. What other prefixes in the poem does Mora choose to hyphenate? Why do you think she does so?

Reading Focus

Analyzing Details To fully appreciate a poem, you should read it several times: for enjoyment, for comprehension, and for analysis, in which you look for deeper meanings and elements of style.

Into Action Read "Legal Alien" at least three times. After each reading, fill in a chart with your ideas about the poem.

"Legal Alien"

First Reading (enjoyment)	Second Reading (comprehension)	Third Reading (analysis)
On first reading, the poem seemed part happy and part sad to me.		

Writing Focus

Think as a Reader/Writer

Find It in Your Reading As you read, notice how Mora weaves Spanish words into the English version of her poem. Would the poem be as meaningful without them? Write down your thoughts in your *Reader/Writer Notebook.*

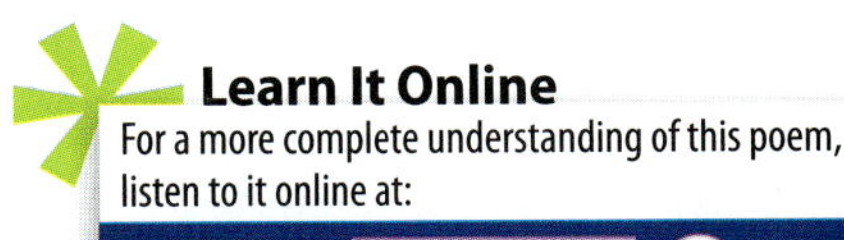

Learn It Online

For a more complete understanding of this poem, listen to it online at:

go.hrw.com L9-705 Go

MEET THE WRITER

Pat Mora
(1942–)

The Magic of Poetry

Pat Mora was born on the border of Mexico and El Paso, Texas. Raised in a Mexican American household, she grew up learning to speak and read in English and Spanish. Her unique poetry is reflective of her own life, blending Hispanic culture into American society. She once commented about her work, "I write because I believe that Hispanics need to take their rightful place in American culture."

Beyond Borders

Mora stresses the harmonic ties between cultures, the results of centuries of shared living. She finds the differences between people less important than the core idea of culture—living, loving, marrying, raising children, working, growing old, and dying. Culture and identity play a vital role in her work, as she maintains that one's identity grows and evolves both from what is inherited and what is encountered in daily life.

Passing the Torch

Poetry entered Mora's life at an early age: "It came in all the poems teachers had me memorize in school," she commented. "I couldn't resist the magic of poetry. I still can't." Aside from being a writer, Pat Mora is the founder and a tour-de-force behind the El día de los niños / El día de los libros (Children's Day / Book Day), which is celebrated each year on April 30.

Think About the Writer How did growing up in a bicultural home influence the poet that Mora grew up to be?

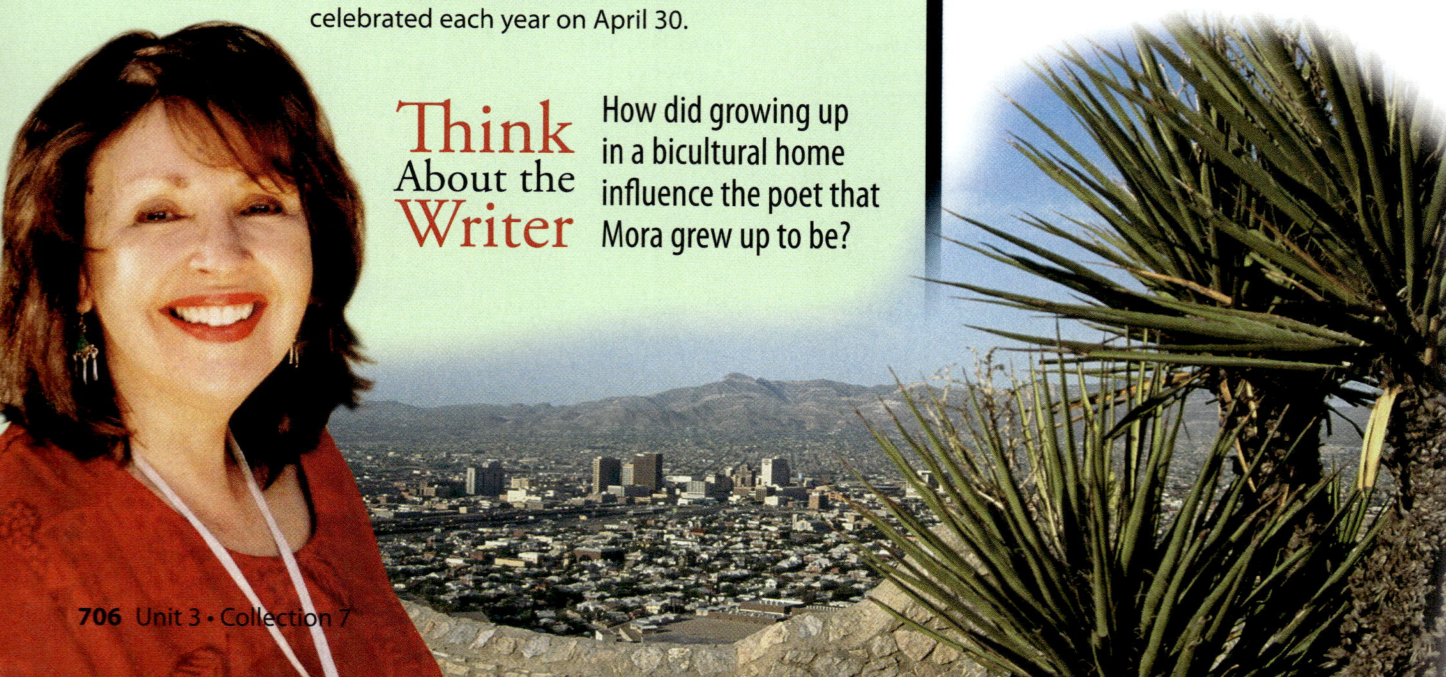

Build Background

The poem "Legal Alien" is from *Chants* (1984), Mora's first book of poems. A legal alien is an immigrant who enters a country through approved channels, though this term is fading out of use.

Read with a Purpose Read this poem to discover the two worlds in which the speaker lives.

Legal Alien

by **Pat Mora**

Bi-lingual, Bi-cultural,
able to slip from "How's life?"
to *"Me'stan volviendo loca,"*° **A**
able to sit in a paneled office
drafting memos in smooth English,
able to order in fluent Spanish
at a Mexican restaurant,
American but hyphenated,
viewed by Anglos as perhaps exotic,
perhaps inferior, definitely different,
viewed by Mexicans as alien
(their eyes say, "You may speak
Spanish but you're not like me"),
an American to Mexicans
a Mexican to Americans **B**
a handy token
sliding back and forth
between the fringes of both worlds
by smiling
by masking the discomfort
of being pre-judged
Bi-laterally.°

3. ***Me'stan ... loca*** (meh STAHN vohl vee EHN doh LOH kah): Spanish for "They're driving me crazy."

22. **Bi-laterally** (by LAT uhr uhl lee): by both sides. (Mora has added a hyphen to this word.)

A **Literary Focus** **Speaker** What does it mean "to slip from 'How's life?' to *'Me'stan volviendo loca'* "? What ability does the speaker have?

B **Literary Focus** **Parallelism** What type of parallel structure does the poet employ in lines 14–15?

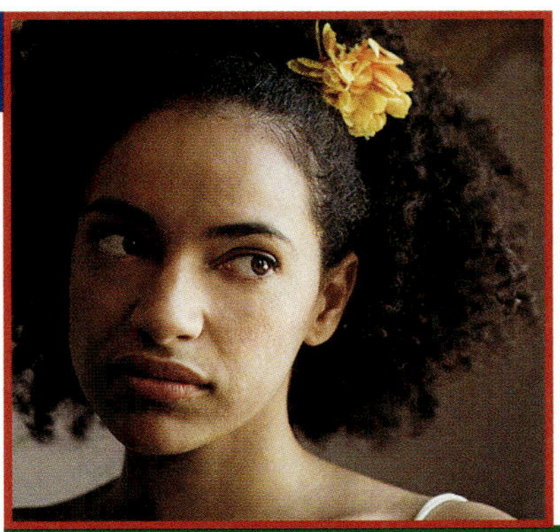

Extranjera Legal

por **Pat Mora**

Bi-lingüe, bi-cultural,
capaz de deslizarse de "*How's life?*"
a "Me'stan volviendo loca,"
capaz de ocupar un despacho bien apun-
tado,
redactando memorandums en inglés liso,
capaz de ordenar la cena en español
fluido
en restaurante mexicano,
americana pero con guión,
vista por los anglos como exótica,
quizás inferior, obviamente distinta,
vista por mexicanos como extranjera
(sus ojos dicen "Hablas español
pero no eres como yo"),
americana para mexicanos
mexicana para americanos
una ficha servible
pasando de un lado al otro
de los márgenes de dos mundos
sonriéndome
disfrazando la incomodidad
del pre-juicio
bi-lateralmente.

Applying Your Skills

MO 9.R.2.C.1.b Use details from text(s): to analyze character, plot, setting, point of view 9.R.2.B.2.c Identify and explain literary techniques, in text emphasizing: repeated sound, line or phrase and 9.R.1.G.1.b During reading, utilize strategies: to self-monitor comprehension *Also covered* 9.R.3.C.1.b

Legal Alien / Extranjera legal

Respond and Think Critically

Reading Focus

Read with a Purpose

1. How would you describe the two different worlds where the poem's speaker lives?

Reading Skills: Analyze Details

2. English and Spanish may have more in common than you think. Take a look at "Extranjera legal," the Spanish version of "Legal Alien." List the words you recognize as similar to English words.
3. Complete the chart you began on page 705. How did your analysis of the poem change with each reading?

"Legal Alien"

First Reading (enjoyment)	Second Reading (comprehension)	Third Reading (analysis)
On 1st reading, the poem seemed part happy and part sad to me.	The speaker can speak both English and Spanish.	

Literary Focus

Literary Analysis

4. **Interpret** What does the speaker mean when she says, "American but hyphenated"? In the great "melting pot" of cultures that is America, why might "hyphenated Americans" feel proud of their two heritages?
5. **Identify** What does the speaker mask, or hide (lines 20–21)?

Literary Skills: Speaker, Wordplay, and Parallel Structures

6. **Analyze** Who do you think is the speaker of "Legal Alien"? How do you know?
7. **Infer** Why do you think Mora hyphenates *bilingual, bicultural,* and *bilaterally,* given that these words usually don't have a hyphen?
8. **Interpret** In line 16, the speaker uses a metaphor in which she compares herself to a token. *Token* is a word with multiple meanings. What different meaning of *token* is the poet suggesting? In what way is the phrase "handy token" (line 16) an example of word play?
9. **Analyze** What parallel structures can you find in this poem? What effect does the use of this type of repetition create?

Literary Skills Review: Theme

10. **Analyze** A **theme** is the observation about life a writer conveys. What idea about life is Mora sharing in "Legal Alien"? What details help you identify this theme?

Writing Focus

Think as a Reader/Writer

Use It in Your Writing Mora uses a Spanish phrase in the English version of her poem. In a short paragraph, explain whether or not you find her use of Spanish in the poem effective.

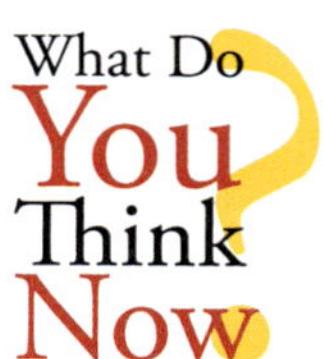

What effect can growing up in two cultures have on your own sense of self? Explain.

Wrap Up

MO 9.R.1.E.1.c Develop vocabulary through text: using glossary, dictionary and thesaurus 9.R.1.E.1.b Develop vocabulary through text: using context clues 9.W.3.A.1.e Compose a variety of texts: including reflective writing *Also covered* 9.R.1.D.1.a

I Wandered Lonely as a Cloud / The Courage That My Mother Had / Advice for a Stegosaurus / The Gift / Possum Crossing / Song of Myself / I Hear America Singing / Legal Alien / Extranjera legal

Vocabulary Development

Vocabulary Skills: Multiple-Meaning Words

In line 16 of "Legal Alien," the speaker compares herself to a *token,* a word that has multiple meanings. In the sense of "symbol," *token* suggests that the speaker has no individual identity or value. The literal definition of the word, "something used in place of money," suggests that the speaker is a medium of exchange between cultures.

Your Turn

The common words in the list below have multiple meanings. Each word is used at least once in Mora's poem. Find where each word is used, examine its context, and then create a word map like the one here to help you explore other meanings of each word.

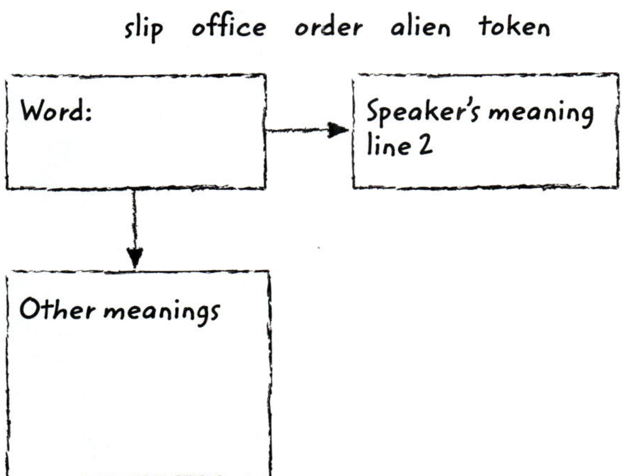

CHOICES

As you respond to the Choices, use these **Academic Vocabulary** words as appropriate: associate, elaborate, evoke, nuances.

REVIEW

Create Audio Effects

TechFocus Find sound effects to go along with one of the poems from this section. Search the Internet, and download appropriate sound effects, such as weather, sirens, animals, or people, to use as background while reading a poem aloud. You might want to create a classroom anthology CD where you and your peers record your poetry readings with sound effects.

CONNECT

Write a Response

Timed Writing Choose one of the poems from this section, and write a one-page letter to the poet in response to the poem. In your letter, describe the feelings and reactions evoked by the poet's use of sound devices such as rhythm, rhyme, or alliteration.

EXTEND

Hold a Poetry Reading

With a partner, choose your favorite poet from this section of the collection. Research other poems written by that person. Choose your favorite poems, and hold a poetry reading for the class in which you and your partner take turns reading the poems aloud.

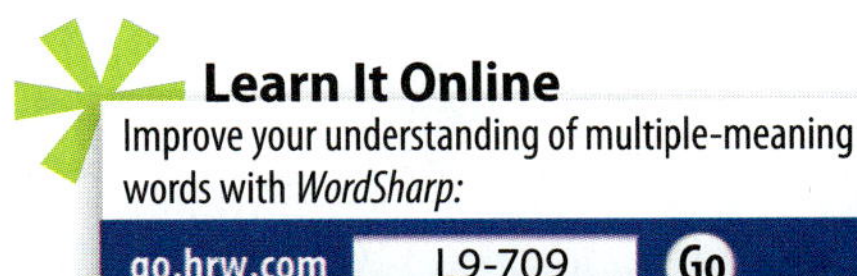

Learn It Online
Improve your understanding of multiple-meaning words with WordSharp:
go.hrw.com L9-709 Go

COMPARING TEXTS

Historical Accounts Across Genres

CONTENTS

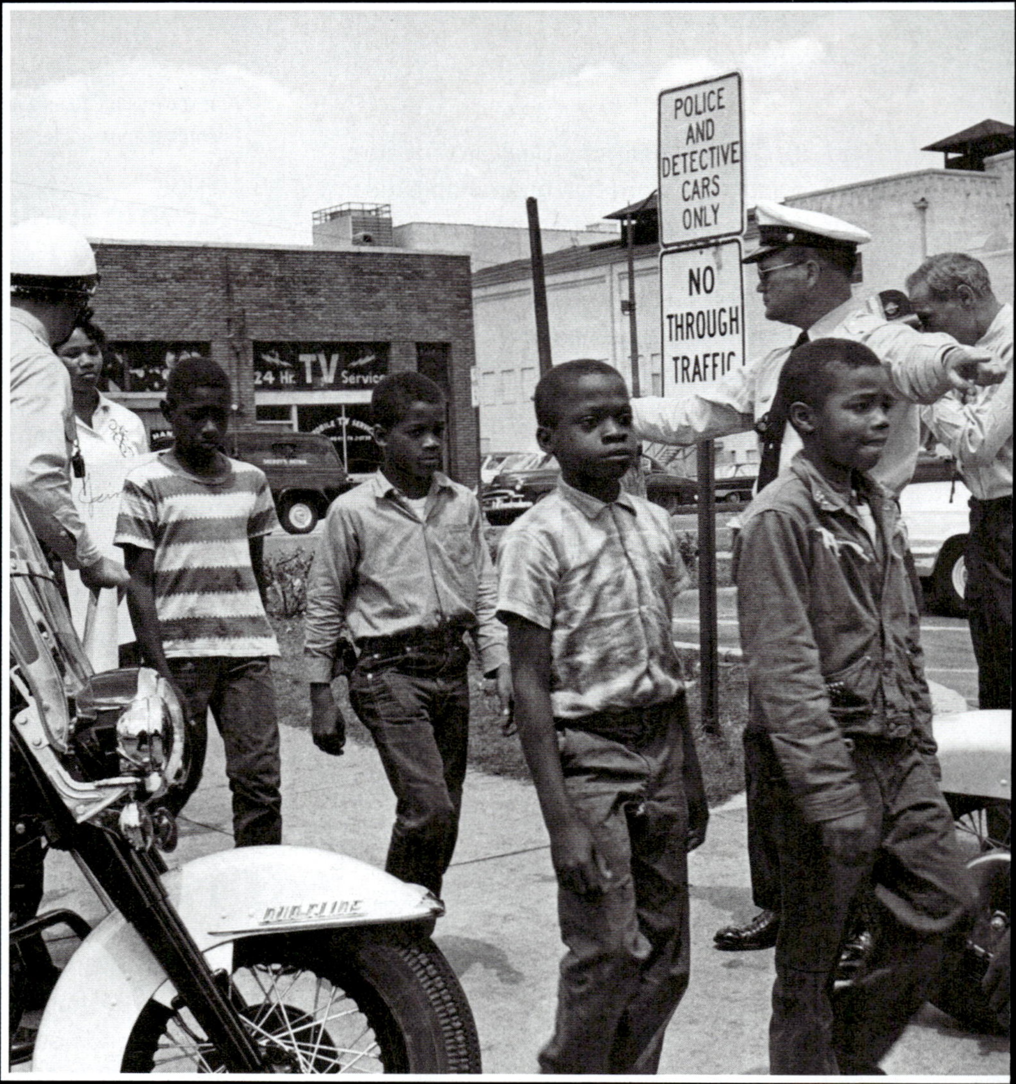

Police officers leading a group of black schoolchildren into jail, following their arrest for protesting against racial discrimination near the city hall of Birmingham, Alabama, on May 4, 1963.

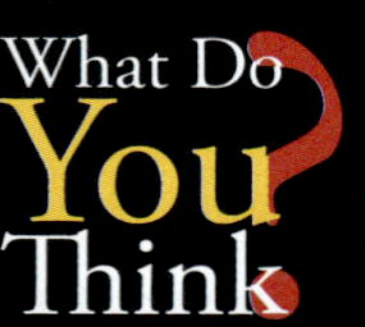

How can imagination help you understand things that really happened?

QuickWrite

Name a specific historic event, such as the stock market crash of 1929. Jot down factual details you know about the event. Then, use your imagination to think about how people felt during the event. How does your imagination affect your perception of history?

Preparing to Read

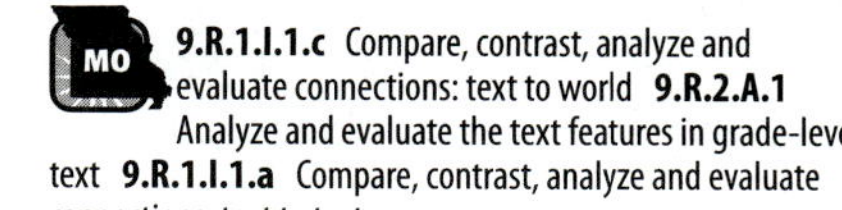

9.R.1.I.1.c Compare, contrast, analyze and evaluate connections: text to world **9.R.2.A.1** Analyze and evaluate the text features in grade-level text **9.R.1.I.1.a** Compare, contrast, analyze and evaluate connections: text to text

The History Behind the Ballad / Ballad of Birmingham / 4 Little Girls

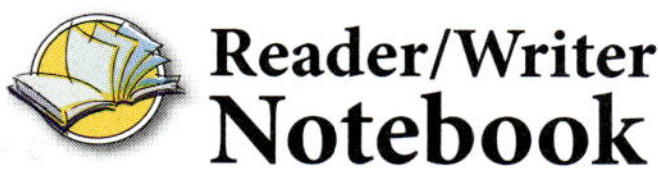

Reader/Writer Notebook

Use your **RWN** to complete the activities for these selections.

Literary Focus

Historical Accounts Across Genres Writers can choose many different ways to respond to a historical event. The form they choose reflects their purpose for writing. For example, a writer who wants to elaborate upon the details of an event might write a nonfiction account. A writer who wants to emphasize an event's emotional impact might write a **ballad**—a poem that tells a story, using steady rhythm, simple rhymes, and a repeated refrain. Still another writer might offer personal commentary in a review of a documentary film.

Reading Focus

Comparing Messages in Different Forms To compare different works inspired by the same historical event, ask yourself, "Why did the writer choose this form?" Consider how the form shaped the writer's style. For example, the writer of a ballad will shape ideas by using rhythm and rhyme; a historian probably won't use those tools.

Into Action You will be reading three works, in different genres, inspired by the same event. As you read, think about the strengths and limitations of each form. Use a chart to gather your ideas.

Form	Strengths	Limitations
historical account	factual; quotes from people who were there	
ballad		

Writing Focus

Think as a Reader/Writer

Find It in Your Reading A film review offers an opinion about a film, often commenting on the movie's themes and meaning. When you read Roger Ebert's review, take notes in your *Reader/Writer Notebook* about his personal reflections.

Vocabulary

The History Behind the Ballad

literally (LIHT uhr uh lee) *adv.:* taking words at their exact meaning. *After the explosion, the bodies had literally disappeared.*

4 Little Girls

infamous (IHN fuh muhs) *adj.:* having a bad reputation; notorious. *The infamous crime took the lives of four innocent children.*

charisma (kuh RIHZ muh) *n.:* personal charm. *Even in home movies, her powerful charisma shines through.*

rationalizations (rash uh nuh luh ZAY shuhnz) *n.:* excuses made for behavior. *They gave many rationalizations for the crime, but none were acceptable.*

Language Coach

Word Origins You are probably familiar with the word *famous,* meaning "well known." Which word on the list above comes from the same word family? How is that word's pronunciation different from what you might expect? How is the word's meaning different from what you might expect?

Learn It Online

Find graphic organizers online to help you compare texts:

go.hrw.com  L9-711  Go

MEET THE WRITERS

Taylor Branch

(1947–)

A Passionate Historian

Parting the Waters is the Pulitzer Prize–winning first book in Taylor Branch's monumental trilogy about Dr. Martin Luther King, Jr., and the civil rights movement. In addition to writing nonfiction and a novel, Branch took part in nearly eighty late-night conversations with Bill Clinton during his presidency.

Dudley Randall

(1914–2000)

Helping People Speak

Dudley Randall grew up in a house filled with books. As an adult, he built on his love of literature by founding a publishing company "so black people could speak to and for their people." The first poem Broadside Press published was "Ballad of Birmingham." It was an actual broadside—a large poster with the poem printed on it. Many outstanding poets of the time sent their work to Broadside. Randall encouraged and supported African American writers, and they, in turn, saw Broadside Press as their own.

Roger Ebert

(1942–)

Thumbs Up for the Movies

In 1975, Roger Ebert became the first film critic to win a Pulitzer Prize. He also hosts a TV show in which he offers his opinions on current movies. Ebert has written more than fifteen books about film.

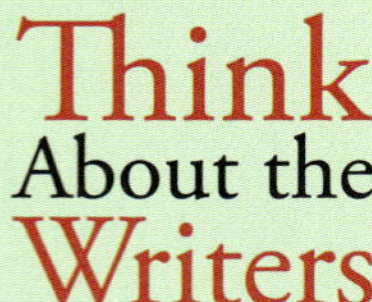

How might the age of each of these writers have affected his perspective on the events of 1963?

Preview the Selections

Taylor Branch presents a historic account of what really happened on that Sunday in 1963.

In "Ballad of Birmingham," **Dudley Randall** uses poetry to shine light on the dark feelings raised by the tragedy in Birmingham.

While reviewing a documentary about the bombing, **Roger Ebert** takes time to reflect on the event's lasting effects.

HISTORICAL ACCOUNT

The History Behind the Ballad

by **Taylor Branch**

Read with a Purpose Read these works to see how three writers responded to a horrifying historical event.

Build Background
The following account is from *Parting the Waters,* a book that won the Pulitzer Prize in history in 1989. Branch continued his history of the civil rights movement and Dr. Martin Luther King, Jr., in his books *Pillar of Fire* and *At Canaan's Edge*.

That Sunday was the annual Youth Day at the Sixteenth Street Baptist Church. Mamie H. Grier, superintendent of the Sunday school, stopped in at the basement ladies' room to find four young girls who had left Bible classes early and were talking excitedly about the beginning of the school year. All four were dressed in white from head to toe, as this was their day to run the main service for the adults at eleven o'clock. Grier urged them to hurry along and then went upstairs to sit in on her own women's Sunday-school class. They were engaged in a lively debate on the lesson topic, "The Love That Forgives," when a loud earthquake shook the entire church and showered the classroom with plaster and debris. Grier's first thought was that it was like a ticker-tape parade. Maxine McNair, a schoolteacher sitting next to her, reflexively went stiff and was the one to speak. "Oh, my goodness!" she said. She escaped with Grier, but the stairs down to the basement were blocked and the large stone staircase on the outside literally had vanished. They stumbled through the church to the front door and then made their way around outside through the gathering noise of moans and sirens. A hysterical church member shouted to Grier that her husband had already gone to the hospital in the first ambulance. McNair searched desperately for her only child until finally she came upon a sobbing old man and screamed, "Daddy, I can't find Denise!" The man helplessly replied, "She's dead, baby. I've got one of her shoes." He held a girl's white dress shoe, and the look on his daughter's face made him scream out, "I'd like to blow the whole town up!" **A**

A Reading Focus Comparing Messages What message is conveyed in this historical account?

Vocabulary **literally** (LIHT uhr uh lee) *adv.:* taking words at their exact meaning.

POEM

Ballad of Birmingham

(On the bombing of a church in Birmingham, Alabama, 1963) A

by **Dudley Randall**

Preparing to Read for this selection is on page 711.

Build Background

Tragic events made the headlines on September 15, 1963. In the midst of the struggle for civil rights for African Americans, a bomb exploded in a church in Birmingham, Alabama. Four young African American girls were killed.

"Mother dear, may I go downtown
Instead of out to play,
And march the streets of Birmingham
In a Freedom March today?"

"No, baby, no, you may not go,
For the dogs are fierce and wild,
And clubs and hoses, guns and jails
Aren't good for a little child."

A **Reading Focus** **Comparing Messages** Why do you think the poet included a subtitle? What information does the subtitle give that might have been difficult to convey in a poem?

Bombed interior of the church.

"But, mother, I won't be alone.
Other children will go with me,
And march the streets of Birmingham
To make our country free."

"No, baby, no, you may not go,
For I fear those guns will fire.
But you may go to church instead
And sing in the children's choir." **B**

She has combed and brushed her night-dark hair,
And bathed rose-petal sweet,
And drawn white gloves on her small brown hands,
And white shoes on her feet.

The mother smiled to know her child
Was in the sacred place,
But that smile was the last smile
To come upon her face.

For when she heard the explosion,
Her eyes grew wet and wild.
She raced through the streets of Birmingham
Calling for her child.

She clawed through bits of glass and brick,
Then lifted out a shoe.
"O, here's the shoe my baby wore,
But, baby, where are you?"

B **Literary Focus** **Historical Accounts** What elements of poetry does Randall use to tell a story?

Analyzing Visuals

Viewing and Interpreting
In what way does this photograph affect the way you feel about this historical event?

MOVIE REVIEW

4 Little Girls

by **Roger Ebert**

Preparing to Read for this selection is on page 711.

Build Background

The director Spike Lee observed that there are "a lot of young people, both black and white, that really don't know about the civil rights struggle and civil rights movement." In 1997, he helped raise awareness of that struggle by making *4 Little Girls,* a documentary about the bombing in Birmingham in 1963. His film was nominated for an Academy Award for Best Documentary. In this essay the critic Roger Ebert reviews the film and offers his own reflections on the event.

Spike Lee's "4 Little Girls" tells the story of the infamous Birmingham, Ala., church bombing of Sept. 15, 1963, when the lives of an 11-year-old and three 14-year-olds, members of the choir, were ended by an explosion. More than any other event, that was the catalyst for the civil rights movement, the moment when all of America could look away no longer from the face of racism. "It was the awakening," says Walter Cronkite[1] in the film.

The little girls had gone to church early for choir practice, and we can imagine them, dressed in their Sunday best, meeting their friends in the room destroyed by the bomb. We can fashion the picture in our minds because Lee has, in a way, brought them back to life, through photographs, through old home movies and especially through the memories of their families and friends.

By coincidence, I was listening to the radio not long after seeing "4 Little Girls," and I heard a report from Charlayne Hunter-Gault. In 1961, when she was 19, she was the first black woman to desegregate the University of Georgia. Today she is an NPR correspondent. That is what happened to her. In 1963, Carole Robertson was 14, and her Girl Scout sash was covered with merit badges. Because she was killed that day, we will never know what would have happened in her life. **A**

That thought keeps returning: The four little girls never got to grow up. Not only were their lives stolen, but so were their contributions to ours. I have a hunch that Denise McNair, who was 11 when she died, would have made

1. **Walter Cronkite:** Walter Cronkite (1916–) is a well-known broadcast journalist. His voice became a trusted source of news on both radio and television.

Vocabulary **infamous** (IHN fuh muhs) *adj.:* having a bad reputation; notorious.

A **Literary Focus** **Historical Accounts** What factual information is given in this film review? What information is more personal?

her mark. In home movies, she comes across as poised and observant, filled with charisma. Among the many participants in the film, two of the most striking are her parents, Chris and Maxine McNair, who remember a special child.

Chris McNair talks of a day when he took Denise to downtown Birmingham, and the smell of onions frying at a store's lunch counter made her hungry. "That night I knew I had to tell her she couldn't have that sandwich because she was black," he recalls. "That couldn't have been any less painful than seeing her with a rock smashed into her head."

Lee's film re-creates the day of the bombing through newsreel footage, photographs and eyewitness reports. He places it within a larger context of the Southern civil rights movement, and sit-ins and the arrests, the marches, the songs and the killings.

Birmingham was a tough case. Police commissioner Bull Connor is seen directing the resistance to marchers and traveling in an armored vehicle—painted white, of course. Gov. George Wallace makes his famous vow to stand in the schoolhouse door and personally bar any black students from entering. Though they could not know it, their resistance was futile after Sept. 15, 1963, because the hatred exposed by the bomb pulled all of their rhetoric and rationalizations out from under them.

Spike Lee says he has wanted to make this film since 1983, when he read a *New York Times Magazine* article by Howell Raines about the bombing. "He wrote me asking permission back then," Chris McNair told me in an interview. "That was before he had made any of his films." It is perhaps good that Lee waited, because he is more of a filmmaker now, and events have supplied him a denouement in the conviction of a man named Robert Chambliss ("Dynamite Bob") as the bomber. He was, said Raines, who met quite a few, "the most pathological racist I've ever encountered." The other victims were Addie Mae Collins and Cynthia Wesley, both 14. In shots that are almost unbearable, we see the victims' bodies in the morgue. Why does Lee show them? To look full into the face of what was done, I think. To show racism its handiwork. There is a memory in the film of a burly white Birmingham policeman who after the bombing tells a black minister, "I really didn't believe they would go this far." The man was a Klansman, the movie says, but in using the word "they" he unconsciously separates himself from his fellows. He wants to disassociate himself from the crime. So did others. Before long even Wallace was apologizing for his behavior and trying to define himself in a different light. There is a scene in the film where the former governor, now old and infirm, describes his black personal assistant, Eddie Holcey, as his best friend. "I couldn't live without him," Wallace says, dragging Holcey in front of the camera, insensitive to the feelings of the man he is tugging over for display.

Why is that scene there? It's sort of associated with the morgue photos, I think. There is mostly sadness and regret at the surface in "4 Little Girls," but there is anger in the depths, as there should be. **B**

B **Reading Focus** **Comparing Messages** How does Ebert's final judgment on the film also reflect his personal message?

Vocabulary **charisma** (kuh RIHZ muh) *n.:* personal charm. **rationalizations** (rash uh nuh luh ZAY shuhnz) *n.:* excuses made for behavior.

Applying Your Skills

9.R.1.I.1.c Compare, contrast, analyze and evaluate connections: text to world 9.R.2.A.1 Analyze and evaluate the text features in grade-level text 9.R.2.B.2.a Identify and explain literary techniques in text emphasizing: irony 9.R.1.I.1.a Compare, contrast, analyze and evaluate connections: text to text *Also covered* 9.W.3.A.1.a; 9.W.3.A.1.e; 9.R.1.G.1.a

The History Behind the Ballad / Ballad of Birmingham / 4 Little Girls

Respond and Think Critically

Reading Focus

Quick Check

1. According to Taylor Branch, what were the girls doing when the bomb exploded?
2. What story about a mother and daughter does "Ballad of Birmingham" tell?

Read with a Purpose

3. What idea were these three writers trying to convey about the Birmingham bombing?

Reading Skills: Comparing Messages

4. Add a column to your chart. In it, comment on the effect each work had on you. What feelings did the work evoke? How did it give you a deeper understanding of history?

Form	Strengths	Limitations	Effect
historical account	factual; quotes from people who were there		

Vocabulary Check

Use the boldface Vocabulary word in your answers to the following questions:

5. What is one **infamous** historic date?
6. When might a student rely on **rationalizations**?
7. How can having **charisma** help a person succeed in life?
8. What might leave you **literally** speechless?

Literary Focus

Literary Analysis

9. **Analyze** How do most people respond to tragedy? Do these emotions change over time? As you respond, consider the attitudes of the different characters in the texts.
10. **Evaluate** Which of these works pays the most effective tribute to the girls killed in the bombing? Use details to support your opinion.

Literary Skills: Historical Accounts Across Genres

11. **Analyze** How do rhyme, rhythm, and repetition help "Ballad of Birmingham" communicate a message?
12. **Compare and Contrast** Both Taylor Branch and Roger Ebert wrote prose works about the bombing. In what ways are the two pieces similar or different?

Literary Skills Review: Dramatic Irony

13. **Analyze** **Dramatic irony** occurs when the reader knows something that a character does not know. How does "Ballad of Birmingham" use this technique in a powerful way?

Writing Focus

Think as a Reader/Writer

Use It in Your Writing Following Ebert's model, write a review that includes your response to a film or television documentary you have seen recently. First, summarize and evaluate the work. Then, share your perspective on the film and its subject.

COMPARING TEXTS

Wrap Up

MO **9.W.3.A.1.a** Compose a variety of texts: using narrative, descriptive, expository, and/or persuasive features

The History Behind the Ballad / Ballad of Birmingham / 4 Little Girls

Writing Focus

Writing a Comparison-Contrast Essay

You have evaluated three works that address the Birmingham church bombing of 1963. Choose two of these to compare and contrast in an essay. You might choose the two works that had the greatest impact on you, or you might want to explore the works that left you with the most questions. Elaborating on your responses in a comparison-contrast essay can help you reach a deeper understanding.

Prewriting

Select a Topic Select a focus for your essay. You might use one of the following prompts:

- How does each writer take advantage of the chosen form? What are the strengths and limitations of each form? How does each work use elements of form to achieve a specific purpose?
- Which of these works would you give a higher recommendation? Compare and contrast the works to emphasize which one you find more effective in its purpose.

Review the Elements of the Writing Form As you plan, remember that an effective comparison-contrast essay

- states what is being compared in the opening paragraph
- follows a logical and consistent order
- identifies both similarities and differences between the works being analyzed
- uses details from the works to support ideas

Gather Details Create a chart to identify similarities and differences between the works you have selected.

	Similarities	Differences
Work 1		
Work 2		

Drafting

Choose an organizational method for your essay. Most comparison-contrast essays begin with an introduction and then follow one of the two following patterns:

Point by Point	Block by Block
Body paragraph • subject 1 detail • subject 2 detail	Body paragraph • all subject 1 details
Body paragraph • subject 1 detail • subject 2 detail	Body paragraph • all subject 2 details

Revising and Proofreading

- Check to be sure your introduction clearly states what you are comparing.
- Connect unclear ideas by adding transitional words and phrases.
- Review your draft, making sure you have fully discussed each work. If necessary, add details.
- Proofread your essay for grammar and spelling.

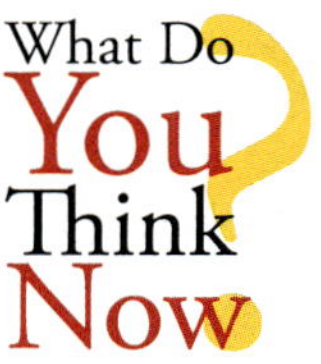

Why is it important for writers to spark our imaginations concerning tragic or horrifying events?

INFORMATIONAL TEXT FOCUS

Generating Research Questions

CONTENTS

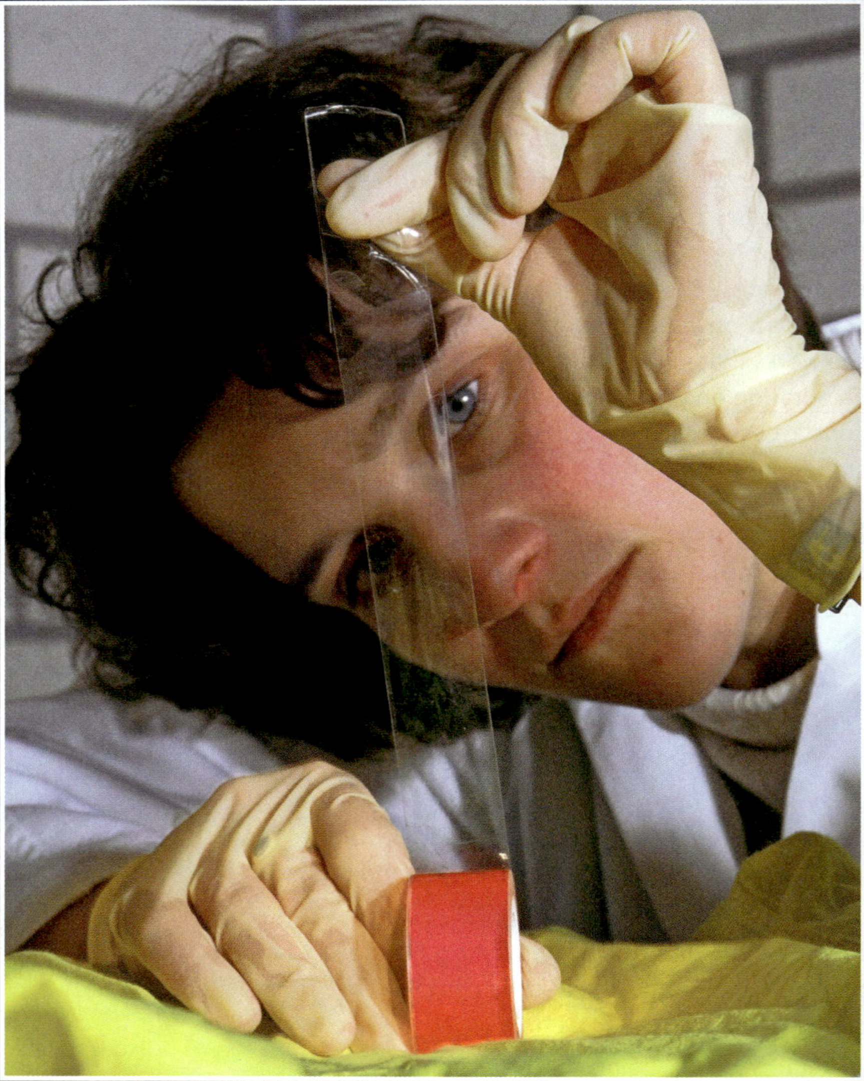

Forensic scientist lifts fiber sample evidence using cellophane tape.

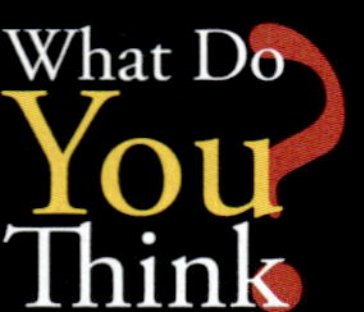

In what ways can imagination help recover a stolen work of art?

QuickWrite

Art heists are the subjects of many movies and books. Can you think of a famous work of art? What do you think would happen if it were stolen? Write a brief scenario discussing this heist.

WEB PAGE & NEWSPAPER ARTICLE

Preparing to Read

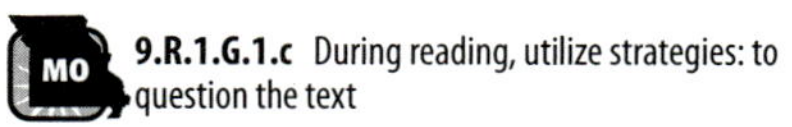

FBI Art Crime Team / Collection Is Found to Contain Stolen Rockwell Art

Informational Text Focus

Generating Research Questions When you research a topic, you aim to build your general understanding of the subject into a more specific knowledge. You will find that doing research is largely a question-and-answer process. You begin by looking at a subject and assessing what you already know about it. Then, you ask questions on more specific details and do research to answer these questions. Asking good questions is the key to doing research that will lead to an interesting, informative report.

Into Action A good method for generating research questions is to ask the ***5W-How?* questions:** *Who* was involved? *What* happened? *When* and *where* did it happen? *Why* and *how* did it happen? Fill out the following *5W-How?* chart as you read these articles about art crime.

Who?	What?	When?	Where?	Why?	How?
FBI Art Crime Team					

Writing Focus

Preparing for **Constructed Response**

As you read these selections, list your questions in your *Reader/Writer Notebook.* You may find that one question leads to another. Think about where you might find answers for your questions.

Reader/Writer Notebook

Use your **RWN** to complete the activities for these selections.

Vocabulary

FBI Art Crime Team

inception (ihn SEHP shuhn) *n.:* start of something; beginning. *Since the team's inception, it has recovered stolen art worth more than $65 million.*

ceremonial (sehr uh MOH nee uhl) *adj.:* having to do with a rite or ceremony. *The team found some American Indian ceremonial garments.*

Collection Is Found to Contain Stolen Rockwell Art

legitimate (luh JIHT uh miht) *adj.:* complying with the law. *Spielberg bought a stolen painting through a legitimate art dealer.*

client (KLY uhnt) *n.:* person or group for which a professional person or service works. *The client lost the art when the gallery was burglarized.*

Language Coach

Word Origins The Latin word *legitimus* means "lawful." Which word on the list above is the English word meaning the same thing? What other words do you know that are derived from *leg,* meaning "law"?

Learn It Online
Supplement your learning with *PowerNotes* at:
go.hrw.com L9-721 Go

WEB PAGE

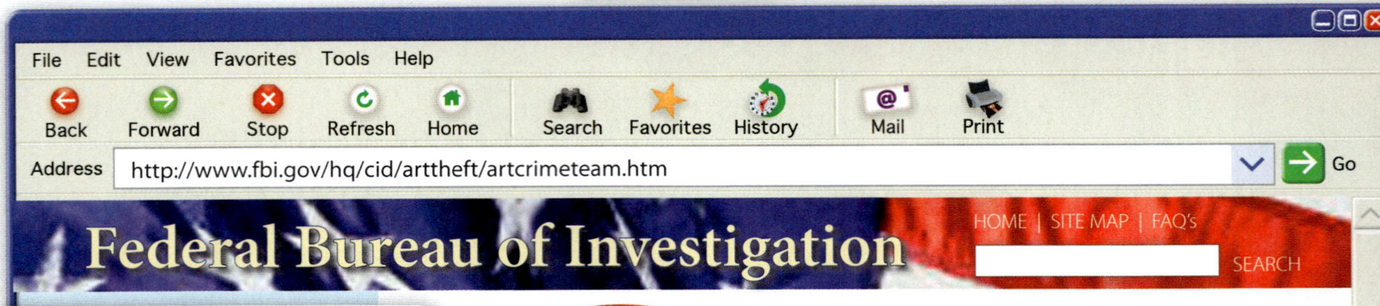

Read with a Purpose
Read these two selections to learn what the FBI Art Crime Team does.

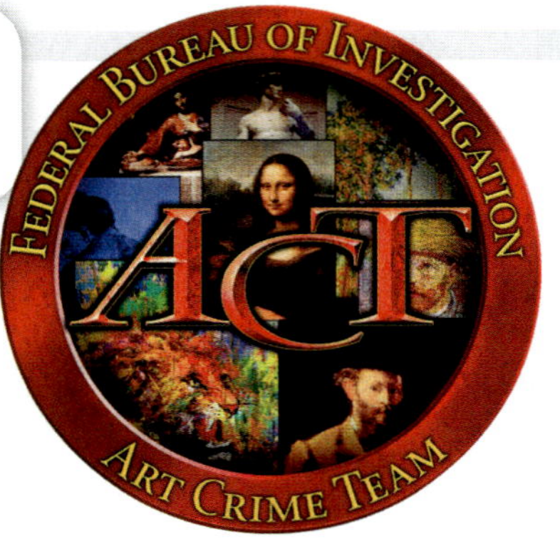

About Us

Art Theft Program Home

Criminal Investigative Division

America's Criminal Enterprise

Major Theft Unit

Contact Us
- Your Local FBI Office
- Overseas Offices
- Submit a Crime Tip
- Report Internet Crime
- More Contacts

Learn About Us
- Quick Facts
- What We Investigate
- Natl. Security Branch
- Information Technology
- Fingerprints & Training
- Laboratory Services
- Reports & Publications
- History
- More About Us

Get Our News
- Press Room
- E-mail Updates
- News Feeds

Be Crime Smart
- Wanted by the FBI
- More Protections

Use Our Resources
- For Law Enforcement
- For Communities
- For Researchers
- More Services

Visit Our Kids' Page

Apply for a Job

Art Crime Team

The FBI established a rapid deployment Art Crime Team in 2004. The team is composed of twelve Special Agents, each responsible for addressing art and cultural property crime cases in an assigned geographic region. The Art Crime Team is coordinated through the FBI's Art Theft Program, located at FBI Headquarters in Washington, D.C. Art Crime Team agents receive specialized training in art and cultural property investigations and assist in art-related investigations worldwide in cooperation with foreign law enforcement officials and FBI Legal Attaché offices. The U.S. Department of Justice has assigned three Special Trial Attorneys to the Art Crime Team for prosecutive[1] support. **A**

Since its inception, the Art Crime Team has recovered over 850 items of cultural property with a value exceeding $65 million. These include:

- Approximately 700 pre-Columbian artifacts.[2] The objects recovered in Miami were the result of a sting operation in coordination with the Ecuadorian authorities.

1. **prosecutive** (PRAH suh kyoo tihv): relating to legal proceedings in court against someone.
2. **pre-Columbian artifacts:** tools and objects dating from the time period before Columbus arrived in the Americas.

A **Informational Focus** **Generating Research Questions** Which of the *5W-How?* questions are answered by this paragraph?

Vocabulary **inception** (ihn SEHP shuhn) *n.:* start of something; beginning.

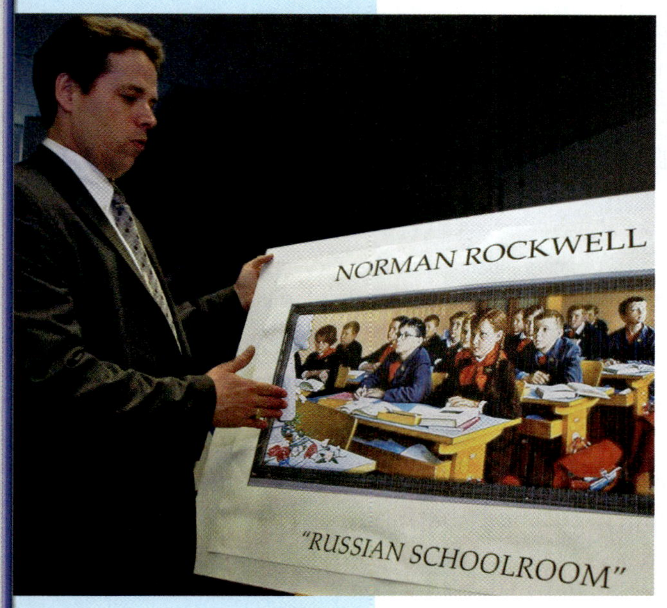

- Three paintings by the German painter Heinrich Buerkel (1802–1869), stolen at the conclusion of World War II and consigned[3] for sale at an auction house near Philadelphia in 2005.
- Rembrandt's *Self Portrait* (1630) in a sting operation in Copenhagen carried out in cooperation with ICE[4] and law enforcement agencies in Sweden and Denmark. The FBI had previously recovered Renoir's *The Young Parisian*. Both paintings had been stolen from the Swedish National Museum in Stockholm in 2000. 
- Approximately 100 paintings that had been stolen from a Florida family's art collection in a fine art storage facility. This collection included works by Picasso, Rothko, Matisse, and others that were recovered from Chicago, New York, and Tokyo.
- An extremely rare, experimental Springfield "Trapdoor" rifle to the Armory Museum in Springfield, Massachusetts. It had been stolen from the Armory Museum in the 1970s.
- Native American ceremonial material and eagle feathers belonging to the Taos Pueblo. The items included a war bonnet and a "Butterfly Bustle." With the assistance of the Bureau of Indian Affairs, the items were returned to the Taos Pueblo.
- Four rare books stolen from Transylvania University in Lexington, Kentucky. Among the items recovered were rare pencil sketches by John James Audubon and a first edition of Charles Darwin's *On the Origin of the Species*.
- Eight cylinder seals taken from archaeological sites in Iraq. C

---

3. **consigned** (kuhn SYND): sent or delivered, as goods to be sold.
4. **ICE:** acronym for U.S. Immigration and Customs Enforcement.

B Informational Focus **Generating Research Questions** If you wanted to narrow your topic and just focus on this particular art crime, what questions could you ask to help generate research questions?

C Informational Focus **Generating Research Questions** Were all the *5W-How?* questions answered by the end of the article? Explain.

Vocabulary **ceremonial** (sehr uh MOH nee uhl) *adj.:* having to do with a rite or ceremony.

 Internet

Collection Is Found to Contain Stolen Rockwell Art (A)

from The New York Times, March 4, 2007

Build Background

Norman Rockwell (1894–1978) was a famous American painter who for forty-seven years illustrated covers for the magazine *The Saturday Evening Post*. Rockwell's work is known for its humorous tone and focus on American families and small-town life. The American public had always embraced Rockwell's work, but some art critics were dismissive of his efforts. Despite the critics, President Gerald Ford awarded Rockwell the Presidential Medal of Freedom.

LOS ANGELES, March 3 (AP) — A Norman Rockwell painting stolen from a gallery in Clayton, Mo., more than three decades ago was found in Steven Spielberg's art collection, the F.B.I. said Friday.

Mr. Spielberg bought the painting, *Russian Schoolroom,* in 1989 from a legitimate dealer and did not know it was stolen until his staff spotted its image last week on a Federal Bureau of Investigation Web site listing stolen works of art, the bureau said in a statement.

After Mr. Spielberg's staff brought it to the attention of the authorities, experts inspected the painting at one of Mr. Spielberg's offices and confirmed its authenticity on Friday. Early F.B.I. estimates put the painting's value at $700,000, officials said.

Mr. Spielberg is cooperating and will retain possession of the painting until its "disposition can be determined," the bureau said.

The painting, an oil on canvas, shows children in a classroom with a bust of Lenin.[1] Mary Ellen Shortland, who worked at the Clayton Art Gallery, recalled that someone from Missouri paid $25,000 for the painting after seeing it during a Rockwell exhibition.

The client agreed to keep it on display, she said, but a few nights later someone smashed the gallery's glass door and escaped with the painting. (B)

"That was all they took," Ms. Shortland said. "That's what they wanted, that painting."

There was no sign of the work for years. Then in 1988, it was auctioned in New Orleans.

In 2004, the F.B.I.'s newly formed Art Crime Team initiated an investigation to recover the work after determining it had been advertised for sale at a Rockwell exhibit in New York in 1989.

It was not immediately known whether Mr. Spielberg bought the painting at that New York exhibit.

Russian Schoolroom appeared in *Look* magazine, but Rockwell is best known for more than 300 covers he did for *The Saturday Evening Post.*

1. **Lenin:** Vladimir Ilich Lenin (1870–1924), founder of the former Soviet Union, of which Russia was a part.

Read with a Purpose What is the primary duty of the FBI Art Crime Team?

(A) **Informational Focus** **Generating Research Questions**
What *5W-How?* questions does the title answer?

(B) **Informational Focus** **Generating Research Questions**
If you wanted to focus on the original theft, what other questions might you ask to get more information about the topic?

Vocabulary **legitimate** (luh JIHT uh miht) *adj.:* complying with the law.
client (KLY uhnt) *n.:* person or group for which a professional person or service works.

WEB PAGE & NEWSPAPER ARTICLE

Applying Your Skills

MO 9.R.1.G.1.c During reading, utilize strategies: to question the text 9.W.3.A.1.a Compose a variety of texts: using narrative, descriptive, expository, and/or persuasive features 9.R.1.G.1.a During reading, utilize strategies: to determine meaning of unknown words

FBI Art Crime Team / Collection Is Found to Contain Stolen Rockwell Art

Practicing the Standards

Informational Text and Vocabulary

1. What is the **main idea** of these two informational pieces?

A Stealing FBI art is a crime.

B Norman Rockwell paintings are targeted by thieves.

C A new FBI team recovers stolen art.

D The FBI is taking job applications.

2. If you wanted to do more research on the FBI Art Crime Team, which of the following would be the *best* question to ask?

A When was the FBI Art Crime Team founded?

B Why was the FBI Art Crime Team created?

C Is the FBI Art Crime Team in charge of stolen art in other countries?

D What does FBI stand for?

3. If you wanted to do more research on the stolen Rockwell painting, which of the following sources would be the *best* to consult?

A An art database listing Rockwell's paintings

B An encyclopedia article about the FBI

C An Internet message board about art crimes

D A Steven Spielberg movie

4. When you read a news story discussing a group's *inception*, you know the story is talking about the group's —

A beginning

B organization

C ideas regarding the community

D distinguishing characteristics

5. A *ceremonial* robe is used for a —

A baseball game

B business meeting

C special occasion

D costume party

6. An antonym for the word *legitimate* is —

A judge

B illegal

C lawful

D lawyer

7. A *client* is a(n) —

A investigator

B consumer

C owner

D customer

Writing Focus — Constructed Response

Review your completed *5W-How?* questions chart. Then, consider what questions were *not* answered on the Web page or in the article. If you were to do your own investigation of the stolen Rockwell painting, what other questions might you ask? List specific examples from the texts in your response.

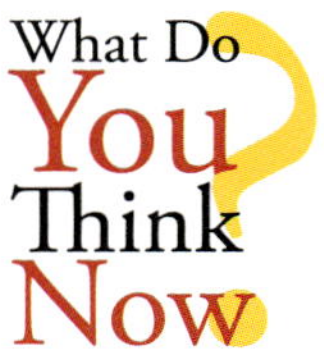

How does imagination play an important role in the recovery of stolen art?

FOCUS ON MISSOURI COURSE LEVEL EXPECTATIONS

Literary Skills Review

Poetry **Directions:** Read the following poem. Then, read and respond to the questions that follow.

The Girl Who Loved the Sky

by **Anita Endrezze**

Outside the second-grade room,
the jacaranda tree blossomed
into purple lanterns, the papery petals
drifted, darkening the windows.
Inside, the room smelled like glue.
The desks were made of yellowed wood,
the tops littered with eraser rubbings,
rulers, and big fat pencils.
Colored chalk meant special days.
The walls were covered with precise
bright tulips and charts with shiny stars
by certain names. There, I learned
how to make butter by shaking a jar
until the pale cream clotted
into one sweet mass. There, I learned
that numbers were fractious° beasts
with dens like dim zeros. And there,
I met a blind girl who thought the sky
tasted like cold metal when it rained
and whose eyes were always covered
with the bruised petals of her lids.
She loved the formless sky, defined
only by sounds, or the cool umbrellas
of clouds. On hot, still days
we listened to the sky falling
like chalk dust. We heard the noon
whistle of the pig-mash factory,
smelled the sourness of homebound men.
I had no father; she had no eyes;
we were best friends. The other girls
drew shaky hopscotch squares
on the dusty asphalt, talked about
pajama parties, weekend cookouts,
and parents who bought sleek-finned cars.
Alone, we sat in the canvas swings,
our shoes digging into the sand, then pushing,
until we flew high over their heads,
our hands streaked with red rust
from the chains that kept us safe.
I was born blind, she said, an act of nature.
Sure, I thought, like birds born
without wings, trees without roots.
I didn't understand. The day she moved
I saw the world clearly; the sky
backed away from me like a departing father.
I sat under the jacaranda, catching
the petals in my palm, enclosing them
until my fist was another lantern
hiding a small and bitter flame.

16. **fractious** (FRAK shuhs): hard to manage; rebellious.

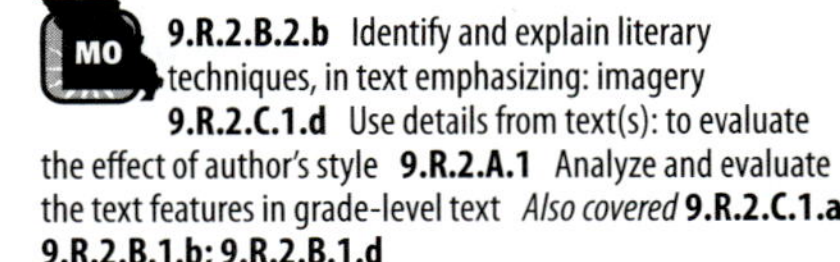

9.R.2.B.2.b Identify and explain literary techniques, in text emphasizing: imagery **9.R.2.C.1.d** Use details from text(s): to evaluate the effect of author's style **9.R.2.A.1** Analyze and evaluate the text features in grade-level text *Also covered* **9.R.2.C.1.a; 9.R.2.B.1.b; 9.R.2.B.1.d**

1. This poem is a —

A sonnet

B haiku

C ballad

D free-verse poem

9.R.2

2. The **speaker** in this poem is a —

A blind woman looking back at her lonely childhood

B popular girl in second grade

C girl who felt like an outsider

D child who felt uneasy in the natural world

9.R.2.C.1.a

3. In line 35, "Alone, we sat in the canvas swings," the poet uses the word *alone* to convey that the speaker and the blind girl —

A have lost their parents

B are separated from their classmates

C are not supervised by their teacher

D are independent, self-confident children

9.R.2.C.1.d

4. The poet uses the word *papery* in the **image** "the papery petals / drifted" (lines 3–4) to show that the petals are —

A white

B stiff

C lightweight

D heavy

9.R.2.B.1.b

5. An example of **metaphor** in this poem is —

A "The walls were covered with precise / bright tulips" (lines 10–11)

B "the pale cream clotted" (line 14)

C "I saw the world clearly" (line 44)

D "my fist was another lantern" (line 48)

9.R.2.B.1.d

6. An example of **implied metaphor** is —

A "The desks were made of yellowed wood, / the tops littered with eraser rubbings" (lines 6–7)

B "and whose eyes were always covered / with the bruised petals of her lids" (lines 20–21)

C "dens like dim zeros" (line 17)

D "the jacaranda tree blossomed" (line 2)

9.R.2.B.1.d

7. Which phrase does *not* include **alliteration**?

A "our hands streaked with red rust" (line 38)

B "the cool umbrellas / of clouds" (lines 23–24)

C "whistle of the pig-mash factory" (line 27)

D "birds born / without wings" (lines 41–42)

9.R.2.B.1.d

8. "The sky / backed away from me like a departing father" (lines 44–45) is an example of **simile** and —

A rhyme

B metaphor

C onomatopoeia

D personification

9.R.2.B.1.d

Constructed Response

9. How would you describe the speaker's **tone** in this poem? Did you find the tone effective? Cite specific lines or words to support your opinion.

9.R.2.B.1.d

Informational Skills Review

Generating Research Questions

Directions: Read the following selection. Then, read and respond to the questions that follow.

Internment History from **PBS.org**

The selection you are about to read is from PBS.org. It gives background information for a documentary titled Children of the Camps. *The documentary features the stories of six Japanese Americans who were placed in internment camps when they were children.*

Following the Japanese attack on Pearl Harbor on December 7, 1941, President Franklin D. Roosevelt issued Executive Order 9066, which permitted the military to circumvent the constitutional safeguards of American citizens in the name of national defense.

The order set into motion the exclusion from certain areas, and the evacuation and mass incarceration of 120,000 persons of Japanese ancestry living on the West Coast, most of whom were U.S. citizens or legal permanent resident aliens.

These Japanese Americans, half of whom were children, were incarcerated for up to 4 years, without due process of law or any factual basis, in bleak, remote camps surrounded by barbed wire and armed guards.

They were forced to evacuate their homes and leave their jobs; in some cases family members were separated and put into different camps. President Roosevelt himself called the 10 facilities "concentration camps."

Some Japanese Americans died in the camps due to inadequate medical care and the emotional stresses they encountered. Several were killed by military guards posted for allegedly resisting orders.

At the time, Executive Order 9066 was justified as a "military necessity" to protect against domestic espionage[1] and sabotage. However, it was later documented that "our government had in its possession proof that not one Japanese American, citizen or not, had engaged in espionage, not one had committed any act of sabotage." (Michi Weglyn, 1976).

Rather, the causes for this unprecedented action in American history, according to the Commission on Wartime Relocation and Internment of Civilians, "were motivated largely by racial prejudice, wartime hysteria, and a failure of political leadership."

Almost 50 years later, through the efforts of leaders and advocates of the Japanese American community, Congress passed the Civil Liberties Act of 1988. Popularly known

1. **espionage** (EHS pee uh nahzh): spying.

9.R.1.G.1.c During reading, utilize strategies: to question the text *Also covered* **9.R.1.H.1.b; 9.IL.1.A.1**

as the Japanese American Redress Bill, this act acknowledged that "a grave injustice was done" and mandated Congress to pay each victim of internment $20,000 in reparations.[2]

The reparations were sent with a signed apology from the President of the United States on behalf of the American people. The period for reparations ended in August of 1998.

2. **reparations** (rehp uh RAY shuhnz): something given, such as money, to correct an injustice.

1. Which of the following questions is *not* answered in the article?

A What reason did President Roosevelt give for placing Japanese Americans in internment camps?

B How did the American public react to Executive Order 9066?

C What percentage of prisoners held in the camps were children?

D What efforts did the government make to offer amends for the suffering of the interned prisoners?

9.R.1.H.1.b

2. Which of the following research questions about the internment is the *most* narrow and focused?

A Why would such imprisonment take place?

B What politicians, if any, fought to free the prisoners?

C What other countries have ordered similar imprisonments?

D What actions led to Executive Order 9066, and what did it mean for Japanese Americans?

9.IL.1.A.1

Informational Skills Review CONTINUED

MO **9.R.1.G.1.c** During reading, utilize strategies: to question the text *Also covered* **9.IL.1.A.1; 9.R.3.C.1.e**

3. Assume your initial research question is *What actions prompted President Roosevelt to issue Executive Order 9066?* Which follow-up question will *best* help narrow your research?

A What were the internment camps like?

B Why did Japan attack Pearl Harbor?

C What tactics did the United States employ during the war?

D Other than the president, who was responsible for issuing the evacuation order?

9.IL.1.A.1

4. If you wanted to do further research on the effects of imprisonment on the Japanese American children who were held in the camps, which questions would give you the *most* relevant information?

A What medical problems did the interned prisoners face?

B What emotional issues did the children experience while in the camps?

C What lasting effects have the children experienced as a result of being interned?

D What happened to the children's homes while they were in the camps?

9.IL.1.A.1

5. Which research question about the effects of the internment on the prisoners follows *most* directly from the information in the article?

A After they were released, how well did the children of the camps perform in school?

B What were the psychological and medical implications of imprisonment?

C How many people died in the camps?

D Did any of the prisoners escape the camps?

9.IL.1.A.1

6. If you wanted to use an Internet search engine to learn more about what happened to the individuals who were placed in the internment camps, which would be the *most* helpful search terms?

A reparations for internment of Japanese Americans

B survivors of the Japanese American internment

C Commission on Wartime Relocation and Internment of Civilians

D Executive Order 9066

9.IL.1.A.1

Constructed Response

7. According to the article, Congress paid each interned prisoner $20,000 in reparations and the president sent notices of apology. Do you think this was a sufficient way to make amends? Explain why or why not.

9.R.3.C.1.e

FOCUS ON MISSOURI COURSE LEVEL EXPECTATIONS

Vocabulary Skills Review

MO **9.R.1.E.1.b** Develop vocabulary through text: using context clues **9.R.1.G.1.a** During reading, utilize strategies: to determine meaning of unknown words

Multiple-Meaning Words

Directions: Choose the answer in which the italicized word is used in the same way it is used in the quoted item.

1. "And sings the *tune* without the words—"

A Let's tune in to our favorite radio program!

B That piano is severely out of tune.

C To clear my head, I tune out the city's noises.

D The birds sang a tune that was simple, yet profound.

9.R.1.E.1.b

2. "The clouds were low and hairy in the skies, / Like *locks* blown forward in the gleam of eyes."

A These security locks need special keys.

B The jailer locks the prisoners inside a cell.

C Her locks were so curly that they looked like spaghetti.

D The treasure chest's locks gleamed in the moonlight.

9.R.1.E.1.b

3. "It looked as if a night of dark intent / Was coming, and not only a night, an *age*."

A Once you reach a certain age, you can drive a car.

B The old couch is showing some signs of age.

C Mozart wrote his first composition at a very young age.

D The 1930s was the golden age of jazz swing music.

9.R.1.E.1.b

4. "These shriveled seeds we *plant*"

A The manufacturing plant created many new jobs.

B In the springtime I always plant annual flowers.

C Her favorite plant is the tulip.

D After hours at sea, it felt good to *plant* my feet on solid ground.

9.R.1.E.1.b

5. "The courage that my mother had / Went with her, and is with her *still*"

A Certain beverages are made in a still.

B There's a bee on you; stand very still.

C He still has the gift I gave him years ago.

D The still photograph brought back many memories.

9.R.1.E.1.b

6. "The thing she took into the grave!— / That courage like a *rock*"

A His performance was as steady as a rock.

B The band's music is totally rock-and-roll!

C The mother likes to rock her baby to sleep.

D I felt ill when the boat started to *rock* back and forth.

9.R.1.E.1.b

Academic Vocabulary

Directions: Choose the best definition for the italicized Academic Vocabulary words.

7. If a food has a *nuanced* flavor, its taste is —

A spicy

B bold

C subtle

D unpleasant

9.R.1.E.1.b

8. An *elaborate* answer would generally be —

A very long

B very short

C direct and simple

D dishonest and sneaky

9.R.1.E.1.b

Read On

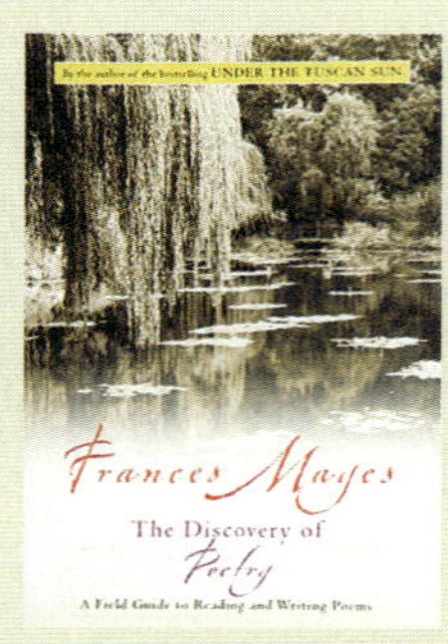

NONFICTION

The Discovery of Poetry

In her book *The Discovery of Poetry,* an accessible "field guide" to reading and writing poetry, Frances Mayes shares her passion with readers. Mayes shows how focusing on one aspect of a poem can help you better understand, appreciate, and enjoy the reading and writing experience. With its wonderful anthology, which includes such diverse authors as Shakespeare and Jamaica Kinkaid, *The Discovery of Poetry* is an invaluable guide to what Mayes calls "the natural pleasures of language—a happiness we were born to have."

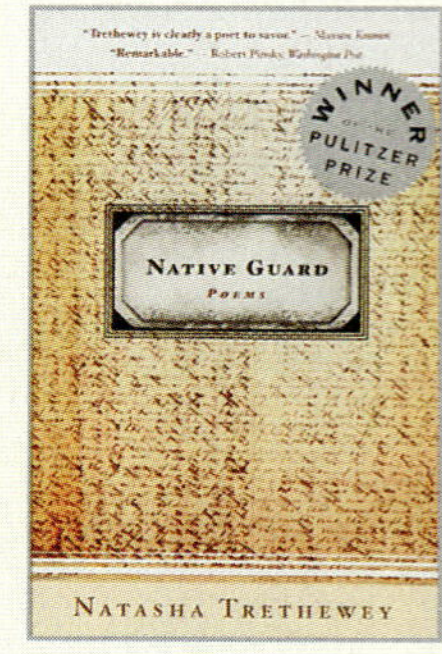

POETRY

Native Guard

In the title poem of her collection *Native Guard,* Natasha Trethewey honors the memory of one of the first regiments of black soldiers in the Union army. Despite their loyalty, these soldiers were mistreated by Union officers, and one Union general even refused to bury dead Native Guard soldiers. Trethewey's poems often explore how the Civil War past influences the present. In several poems she tells of the hardships her black mother and her white father faced in Mississippi and how they broke the law by marrying. The collection won the 2007 Pulitzer Prize for Poetry.

POETRY

Talking to the Sun

Have you ever read any African chants, European lullabies, or American Indian myths set to verse? *Talking to the Sun* is a good place to start. The poems in this collection cover many aspects of life and nature—such as the sky, sand, animals, and love. Works by such poets as Langston Hughes, Edna St. Vincent Millay, and William Shakespeare appear alongside tribal hymns and American folk songs. This beautiful collection is enhanced by artwork from New York's Metropolitan Museum of Art.

POETRY

You Come Too

Discover some of the best of Robert Frost's poetry in *You Come Too.* In this collection for readers of all ages, you'll encounter poems like "Christmas Tree," "Hayla Brook," and Frost's famous, inviting title poem. Frost brings to life the trees, mountains, cliffs, dirt roads, old fences, grassy fields, and abandoned houses of his beloved New England. Reading his work, you'll have the sense that you are there—deep in the woods or at the edge of a babbling brook.

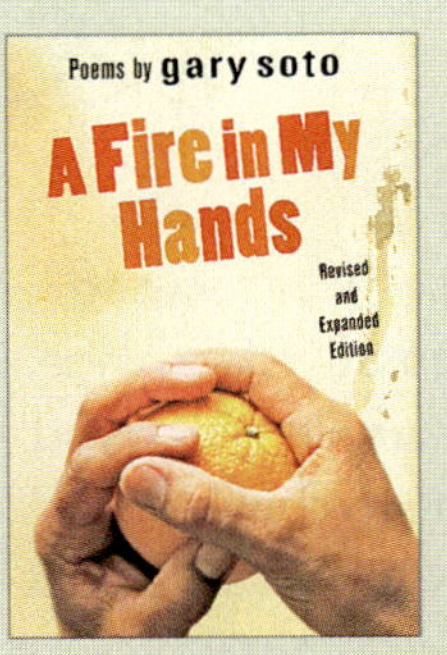

POETRY

A Fire in My Hands

Few writers capture the everyday moments of life like Gary Soto does. In direct and vivid poems, he draws on experiences from his own youth in California's San Joaquin Valley to portray the joys and sorrows of young people. His writing focuses on Latino characters yet speaks to readers of all ethnicities. *A Fire in My Hands* has been one of Soto's most popular books of poetry. This new edition contains an interview in which he discusses how he writes poems, where his ideas come from, and why he decided to become a poet.

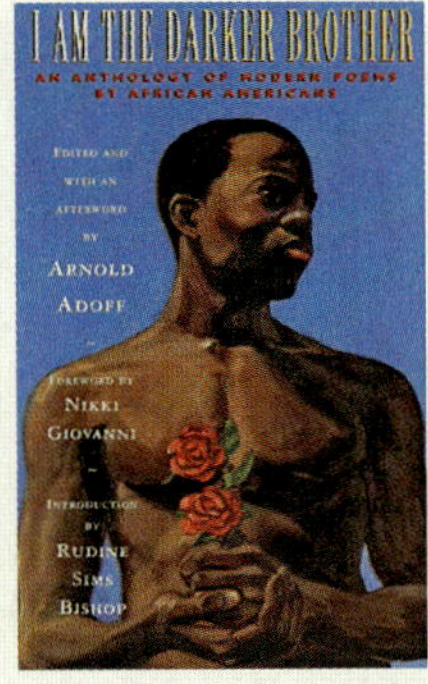

POETRY

I Am the Darker Brother

I Am the Darker Brother: An Anthology of Modern Poems by African Americans, edited by Arnold Adoff, celebrates the African American experience. Poems range from the tearful to the joyous, from bleak realism to bitter irony. Poets include Lucille Clifton, Mari Evans, Ishmael Reed, Langston Hughes, and Rita Dove. In the anthology's forward the poet Nikki Giovanni sums up the book, saying, "Poems shouted the truth; mumbled the pain; threatened with anger; soothed with love."

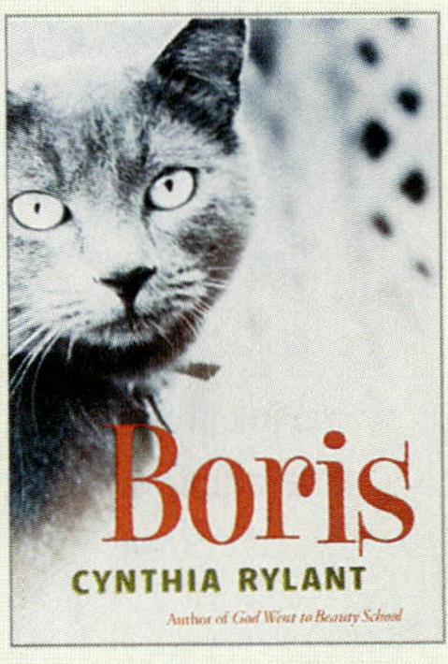

POETRY

Boris

Boris is a big gray cat who loves sleeping and playing and exploring and hunting. And his owner loves him for all of his simple cat ways. But Boris, typical as he may be, is part of a much larger story in this moving exploration of love, longing, compassion, and most of all, the continuous give-and-take of companionship. *Boris,* a powerful collection of poems by Newbery medalist Cynthia Rylant, is sure to find its place in the hearts of readers of all ages, especially those who have been lucky enough to experience the many joys and hardships that come with true friendship.

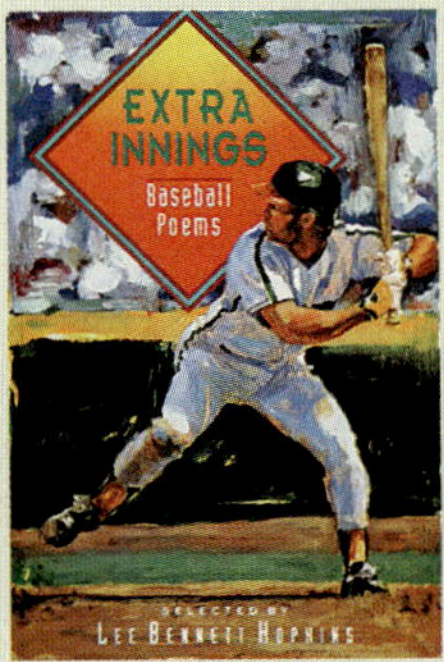

POETRY

Extra Innings

This entertaining collection of nineteen poems includes the famous "Casey at the Bat," May Swenson's classic "Analysis of Baseball," and Robert Francis's "Base Stealer" as well as newer, lesser-known pieces that will be embraced by all who play, dream about, or watch the game of baseball. *Extra Innings* was edited by Lee Bennett Hopkins and illustrated by Scott Medlock.

Writing Workshop

Response to Literature

Write with a Purpose

Write a response to a poem that supports important ideas and viewpoints by using accurate references to the text. Your **purpose** is to share your analysis of a poem with others. Your **audience** is your classmates and others who have read the poem.

A Good Response to Literature

- includes the work's title and author
- has a clear thesis, using the key elements and theme
- analyzes each key literary element
- supports analysis with evidence from the work
- organizes literary elements logically
- restates the thesis in the conclusion
- shows how the work relates to broader themes in life

See page 742 for complete rubric.

Reader/Writer Notebook

Use your **RWN** to complete the activities for this workshop.

Think as a Reader/Writer

In this collection, you've focused on important elements of poetry, such as imagery and figurative language. In this Writing Workshop you'll write a **response to literature** in which you examine a poem's elements to discover how they combine to convey the poem's theme and overall effect. This excerpt from David Pink's essay about James Wright's poem, "A Blessing" (see page 654) shows an author writing a response to a poem, using detailed and accurate references from the poem to support his ideas.

> "A Blessing" is perhaps James Wright's best known poem. . . . Although the speaker of the poem is wistfully serious, the poem is touched by situational irony. The . . . communion between human and horse occurs "just off the highway," a manmade avenue of high-speed commerce. The encounter between the poet and nature must take place "just off" the highway to amplify the gulf between man and nature. Furthermore, the horses are enclosed in "barbed wire"; the poet and his friend must transgress an unnatural boundary to enter into the natural setting. The artificial boundary of the fence, but more important, the limits of being—of otherness—between the horses, . . . and the poet who wants to transcend himself almost dissolve. It is a credit to Wright's poetic sensibility that they do not.

← Pink identifies the title and author of the poem.

← Text excerpts from the poem support the critic's ideas.

← Pink provides an evaluation of the poet's craft.

Think About the Professional Model

With a partner, discuss the following questions about the model.

1. According to Pink, in what way is the setting of the poem important?
2. How does Pink's use of quotations from the poem support his interpretation of the poem?
3. What idea about boundaries does Pink share in his response to the poem?

MO **9.W.1.A.1.c** Follow a writing process to: revise in response to feedback **9.W.3.A.1.d** Compose a variety of texts: including literary analysis

Prewriting

Choose a Poem

The poem you select for analysis should not be so short that it contains too little to examine nor so long that you can't cover it in detail in an essay of several paragraphs. Poems of ten to twenty lines that are rich in meaning are well suited to analyses of such length.

Gather Details

To respond to a poem, first read it several times, paying attention to the poem's **literary elements.** Consider how they create meaning and certain effects. The following chart lists common elements found in poetry and gives questions to help you analyze those elements.

Literary Element	Analysis Questions
Speaker: the voice talking in the poem (not necessarily the poet)	Who is the speaker in the poem? Is the speaker the poet or a character created by the poet?
Theme: the meaning, or main idea, of the poem, usually involving a significant insight	Does the poem examine some common life experience or problem? Does it suggest solutions or answers?
Tone: the poet's attitude toward the subject, the audience, or a character	What is the poet's attitude toward the subject (sarcastic, respectful)? the audience (friendly, hostile)? the characters (sympathetic, cruel)?
Stylistic Devices: the techniques the poet uses to create certain effects	How does **diction**, the poet's choice of key words, influence the poem's meaning? Does the poet use **figurative language**, such as **metaphors** and **similes**, to make comparisons? What **sound devices**, such as **rhythm, rhyme,** and **repetition**, does the poet use? What are their effects?

Think About Purpose and Audience

As you plan your response, consider your purpose and audience. Your **purpose** is to share your analysis of the poem, so be sure you have a clear understanding of the poem. Your **audience** includes people who have read the poem. You can't read the poem for them, but you can share your ideas about what the poem means.

Idea Starters

- Re-read poems you have enjoyed.
- Ask your teacher, a librarian, family member, or friend for recommendations.
- Look for collections of poems in the library or on the Internet.

Peer Review

Use the questions in the chart to interview a partner about the poem he or she has selected. Use follow-up questions to dig deeper and get more complete answers. Then answer your partner's questions about the poem you have decided to analyze.

Your Turn

Get Started Write the name of the poem and its author in your **RWN**. Jot down notes that explain **why** you chose this poem and what you think it means. Make a chart like the one to the left. Answer each analysis question about the poem's most important **literary elements.** Keep your **purpose** and **audience** in mind as you write.

Learn It Online

To see how one writer met all the assignment criteria, visit

go.hrw.com L9-735 

Writing Tip

To focus your thesis, identify one or more **key literary elements** that are essential to understanding the poem's theme.

Your Turn

Support Your Thesis; Organize Text Evidence In your **RWN,** write your **thesis statement.** Be sure it clearly states your main idea about the poem.

- After your thesis statement, draw a chart like the one to the right to show the literary elements, details or quotations, and elaboration you'll include in your essay.
- Next, number each literary element you have identified by order of importance in supporting your thesis.
- Finally, use your rankings of importance to decide how to organize the elements and text evidence in your essay.

Write and Support Your Thesis

After answering and thinking about the analysis questions, formulate a **thesis statement**—one or two sentences that make the focus of your analysis clear to your audience. Your thesis statement should coherently and concisely summarize the main idea of your analysis of the poem. For example, in the excerpt from Pink's essay about "A Blessing," the following sentence is Pink's thesis: "Although the speaker of the poem is wistfully serious, the poem is touched by situational irony." Pink signals to us, his readers, that he plans to discuss the poem's situational irony.

Next, gather evidence to support your thesis. Remember that a response to a poem should include specific **references** to the poem. These references—quotations from the poem and other details that are restated in your own words—will support your thesis. Each piece of text evidence should be followed by **elaboration:** an explanation of how the quotation or detail supports your thesis. Notice how Pink uses both text evidence and elaboration on page 734. Elaboration shows that you have a good grasp of the poem's **significant ideas** and enables you to address the poem's **ambiguities, nuances,** and **complexities.**

- **Ambiguities** are lines or words that lend themselves to more than one interpretation.
- **Nuances** are changes in tone or meaning. For example, a poem might start with a light tone and then turn more serious.
- **Complexities** result when a poem is rich in meaning but difficult to interpret.

Jot down your ideas for support in a chart like the following.

Literary Element	Detail or Quotation	Elaboration
(for example, speaker, theme, figurative language, or tone)	(a line or group of lines)	(an analysis of the element as it's used in these lines)

Organize Your Response

Before you begin drafting, put your ideas in order. You need to organize your text evidence and elaboration to support your thesis clearly and effectively. You can arrange your ideas in two ways: (a) by **order of importance** or (b) by the **order in which the elements appear** in the poem. You might want to try both structures to see which method will better support your ideas.

Drafting

As you write, keep in mind the essentials of a good response to literature (page 734). Be sure to review the chart you created, and then try structuring your response according to the **Framework** to the right.

Framework for a Response to Literature

Introduction

- Grab the readers' attention by relating the poem's meaning to experiences that people share. Be sure to introduce the poem's title and author and to clearly state your thesis.

Body

- Note each key literary element, and use quotations and other references to support your discussion for each element. Remember to elaborate on these literary elements.
- Organize the key literary elements by order of importance or in order in which they appear in the poem.

Conclusion

- Summarize your main points, and restate your thesis. Finally, show how the poem is connected to broader themes.

Respond in Style

Critics have a certain style that they use when they analyze a poem. For this kind of academic writing, you should also follow this style.

- Write in the third person:

  The poem is a beautiful description of a moment of communion between animals and humans.

  Notice that the writer discusses "the poem."
- Avoid writing in the first person. Starting sentences with "I think" or "in my opinion" can make you sound unsure of yourself. Also avoid writing in the second person. Do not address your readers as "you," telling them how they will react to a poem.
- Use the **literary present tense** to describe what is happening in the poem. Although the poet wrote the poem in the past, critics discuss the literary work with present-tense verbs: *The speaker **sees** the horses and **is awed** by their beauty.*
- Attribute, or give credit to, the poet, using the correct possessive form.

Grammar Link **Singular and Plural Possessives**

Part of critical style is attributing a poem correctly to the writer. Treat the name of an author as a singular noun.

- To form the possessive of a singular noun, add an apostrophe and an *s*.

  James Wright's poem *Jorge Luis Borges's story*
- To form the possessive case of a plural noun ending in *s*, add only the apostrophe. To form the possessive case of a plural noun that does not end in *s*, add an apostrophe and an *s*.

  the ponies' tails *the women's response*
- To choose the correct possessive, decide if the noun is singular or plural.

  the horse's beauty (one horse) *the horses' beauty* (more than one)

Reference Note For more on possessives, see the Language Handbook.

Your Turn

Draft Your Response Using the notes in your chart, your organizational plan, and the Framework for a Response to Literature, create your first draft. Also think about these questions:

- How can you show your audience that your interpretation of the poem is accurate?
- How will you convey the more formal tone expected in this kind of writing?

Peer Review

Work with a partner to review the chart at the right. For each other's drafts, ask and answer each question in the chart. Be sure your classmate reads your response and the poem you analyzed. He or she may offer you more ideas about how the key literary elements you identified influence the poem.

Evaluating and Revising

To make your response to a poem as clear, precise, and effective as it can be, review your paper carefully before you revise. Use the following guidelines, tips, and revision techniques to evaluate and revise the content and organization of your analysis.

Response to Literature: Guidelines for Content and Organization

Evaluation Questions	Tips	Revision Techniques
1. Does the introduction mention the poem's title and author? Does it include a clear thesis statement that states your main idea about the poem's key literary elements?	**Circle** the poet, title, and thesis statement. **Put a check mark** next to the key literary elements in the thesis statement.	**Add** a sentence that names the poem's title and author. **Add** a clear thesis statement that states your main idea about the key literary elements.
2. Does each body paragraph discuss a key literary element that supports the thesis?	**Bracket** the key literary element in each body paragraph.	**Replace** body paragraphs that don't address key elements.
3. Is each key literary element supported with references to the poem? Is each reference explained, or elaborated?	**Highlight** quotations or restated details from the poem, and **draw an arrow** to their explanations, or elaborations.	**Add** quotations or restated details. **Elaborate** on how the quotations and details support the thesis.
4. Is the analysis organized by order of importance or in the order that key elements appear?	**Number** the key details. If the numbers do not reflect an effective sequence, revise.	**Rearrange** details in order of importance or in the order the key elements appear in the poem.
5. Does the conclusion effectively remind readers of the thesis and summarize its main points? Does it show how the poem relates to broader themes in life?	**Underline** the sentence that restates the thesis. **Put a star** beside the sentences that summarize the main points. **Put two stars** by the sentence(s) that relates the poem to broader themes.	If necessary, **add** a sentence restating the thesis. **Add** sentences that summarize the main points and relate the poem to broader themes.

Read this student draft, and notice the comments on its strengths and suggestions on how it could be improved.

Student Draft

Nature's Blessing

by Adrienne Seiler, Parkland High School

James Wright's poem "A Blessing" captures a moment in time that is both beautiful and poignant. The narrative structure recounts a brief encounter. Friends driving through the Minnesota countryside stop to admire two Indian ponies in a field.

To the travelers, the ponies behave as the friendliest of neighbors. Personified by the poet, the ponies' eyes "Darken with kindness." The poem's speaker describes them as coming out of the willows "gladly," emphasizing their spirit of welcome. The ponies, who "can hardly contain their happiness/ That we have come," greet the strangers then turn to "munching the young tufts of spring." The interruption in there peaceful meadow is not intrusive because the ponies go back to their eating in the Minnesota twilight.

← Adrienne clearly identifies the **poem, its context,** and its **author.** However, her writing lacks a strong thesis.

← In this paragraph, Adrienne explains one key **literary element** used by the poet: personification. "She uses quotations from the poem. . ." to support her analysis.

MINI-LESSON How to Write a Thesis Statement

An effective **thesis statement** guides your writing and your reader's understanding of your response to a piece of literature. A thesis statement for an analysis of a literary work expresses how the author uses literary elements to express a theme or observation about life. In her first paragraph, Adrienne created a good context for the reader to understand the poem and also included the title and author, but she did not include a thesis statement that made clear what approach she would take in her response. Since she analyzed Wright's use of figurative language and determined he is praising the beauty of the natural world, she revised her opening paragraph to include a thesis statement.

Adrienne's Revision of Paragraph One

James Wright's poem "A Blessing" captures a moment in time that is both beautiful and poignant. The narrative structure recounts a brief encounter. ^ *Through detail and figurative language, Wright captures the beauty of the moment and the mystery of the natural world in a poem that reflects its name, "A Blessing."* Friends driving through the Minnesota countryside stop to admire two Indian ponies in a field.

Your Turn

Write a Thesis Statement Ask yourself these questions:

- What is the main idea of my response?
- How can I make my thesis statement clearly reflect that idea?

Make any changes that will strengthen your thesis.

Adrienne organizes her response by discussing elements in the **order in which they appear** in the poem.

She elaborates on the text evidence.

In the conclusion, Adrienne restates her thesis and makes a connection between the **theme** of the poem and the world.

Student Draft *continues*

Using a simile, Wright describes the graceful ponies, saying "they bow shyly as wet swans," and captures their unity with nature and regal beauty. Wright also comments on their obvious affection and companionship for each other. "They love each other. There is no loneliness like theirs." This interesting and ironic commentary observes that they really aren't alone at all in the big field because they have each other's companionship.

The poem's speaker is particularly enchanted by the black-and-white pony who nuzzles his hand. As he pets its ear, he compares it's delicate texture with that of girl's skin. This simile emphasizes the pony's beauty and innocence in nature.

So moved is the speaker that he concludes with an image that captures both his amazement and joy at the unexpected experience. He says, "if I stepped out of my body I would break/Into blossom." His sense of wonder at their beauty will stay with him long after the moment is gone. Perhaps Wright is reminding us that beauty and peace can be found along every path, if we just stop long enough to appreciate it.

MINI-LESSON How to Add Evidence from the Text

As she reviewed her draft, Adrienne decided that she had not supported her ideas in the fourth paragraph (the description of the black-and-white pony) with adequate textual evidence. She decided to use her favorite short quotations and interweave them into her own sentences as proof. Notice the quotations she chose to add. All three fit well into her own sentence structure.

Adrienne's Draft of Paragraph Four

The poem's speaker is particularly enchanted by the black-and-white pony who nuzzles his hand. As he pets its ear, he compares its delicate texture with that of a girl's skin. This simile emphasizes the pony's beauty and innocence in nature.

Adrienne's Revision of Paragraph Four

The poem's speaker is particularly enchanted by the black-and-white pony, "the slenderer one" who nuzzles his hand. As he ~~pets her ear~~ caresses "her long ear", he compares its delicate texture with that of ~~a girl's skin~~ "the skin over a girl's wrist." This simile emphasizes the pony's beauty and innocence in nature.

Your Turn

Add Evidence from the Text

With a partner, review your draft for ideas that are stated without evidence from the text to support them. Add quotations or references from the poem wherever needed. Be sure to elaborate on the text evidence.

Proofreading and Publishing

Proofreading

Don't let minor mistakes in your final draft distract readers or discredit your ideas. **Proofread,** or **edit** your paper carefully to eliminate any errors in grammar, usage, and mechanics. Even a few errors in your response can damage its effectiveness.

While spell-checking software is a helpful tool, it often cannot identify instances where you have used homonyms incorrectly.

Grammar Link **Homonyms**

Homonyms are words that sound the same but are spelled differently. Often, some possessive pronouns have common homonyms.

Possessive Pronouns	Contractions
its	it's (it is)
whose	who's (who is)
their	they're (they are)
theirs	there's (there is)

Adrienne found and revised some misused homonyms in her draft.

The interruption in ~~there~~ their peaceful meadow . . .

. . . he compares ~~it's~~ its delicate texture . . .

Publishing

Here are some suggestions on how you might share your response to literature with a larger audience.

- Submit your work to your school's literary magazine.
- Post your work on a teen literary Web site.
- Organize a poetry night at your school. Read aloud the poems you and your classmates analyzed as well as your responses.

Reflect on the Process

In your **RWN**, write short responses to the following questions:

1. How did writing a response to the poem change or deepen your understanding of it?
2. How did searching for effective text evidence increase your understanding of the poem?
3. Which of your revision changes had the greatest effect? Explain.

Proofreading Tip

Make sure you don't add any new errors when you make editing changes. Look over new text carefully, checking your spelling, punctuation, and grammar. Ask a partner to review any material you added or changed. Discuss any changes before you make them in your draft.

Your Turn

Proofread and Publish

Proofread your draft. As you proofread, circle homonyms such as *their, they're,* and *there.* Check that you used the correct word. Then, make a final copy of your response to literature and publish it.

Scoring Rubric

Use one of the rubrics below to evaluate your response to literature from the Writing Workshop or your response to the on-demand prompt on the next page. Your teacher will tell you to use either the six- or the four-point rubric.

6-Point Scale

Score 6 ***Demonstrates advanced success***

- focuses consistently on a clear thesis
- shows effective organization throughout, with smooth transitions
- offers thoughtful, creative ideas
- develops ideas thoroughly, using examples, details, and fully elaborated explanation
- exhibits mature control of written language

Score 5 ***Demonstrates proficient success***

- focuses on a clear thesis
- shows effective organization, with transitions
- offers thoughtful ideas
- develops ideas competently, using examples, details, and well-elaborated explanation
- exhibits sufficient control of written language

Score 4 ***Demonstrates competent success***

- focuses on a clear thesis, with minor distractions
- shows effective organization, with minor lapses
- offers mostly thoughtful ideas
- develops ideas adequately, using a mixture of general and specific elaboration
- exhibits general control of written language

Score 3 ***Demonstrates limited success***

- includes some loosely related ideas that distract from the writer's focus
- shows some organization, with noticeable gaps in the logical flow of ideas
- offers routine, predictable ideas
- develops ideas with uneven elaboration
- exhibits limited control of written language

Score 2 ***Demonstrates basic success***

- includes loosely related ideas that seriously distract from the writer's focus
- shows minimal organization, with major gaps in the logical flow of ideas
- offers ideas that merely skim the surface
- develops ideas with inadequate elaboration
- exhibits significant problems with control of written language

Score 1 ***Demonstrates emerging effort***

- shows little awareness of the topic and purpose for writing
- lacks organization
- offers unclear and confusing ideas
- develops ideas in only a minimal way, if at all
- exhibits major problems with control of written language

4-Point Scale

Score 4 ***Demonstrates advanced success***

- focuses consistently on a clear thesis
- shows effective organization throughout, with smooth transitions
- offers thoughtful, creative ideas
- develops ideas thoroughly, using examples, details, and fully elaborated explanation
- exhibits mature control of written language

Score 3 ***Demonstrates competent success***

- focuses on a clear thesis, with minor distractions
- shows effective organization, with minor lapses
- offers mostly thoughtful ideas
- develops ideas adequately, using a mixture of general and specific elaboration
- exhibits general control of written language

Score 2 ***Demonstrates limited success***

- includes some loosely related ideas that distract from the writer's focus
- shows some organization, with noticeable gaps in the logical flow of ideas
- offers routine, predictable ideas
- develops ideas with uneven elaboration
- exhibits limited control of written language

Score 1 ***Demonstrates emerging effort***

- shows little awareness of the topic and purpose for writing
- lacks organization
- offers unclear and confusing ideas
- develops ideas in only a minimal way, if at all
- exhibits major problems with control of written language

Preparing for Timed Writing

Response to Literature

When responding to a prompt that asks you to respond to a literary element, topic, or a quote from a piece of literature, use what you've learned from your reading, writing your response-to-literature essay, and the rubric on page 742. Use the steps below to develop a response to the following prompt.

Writing Prompt

Conflict between characters often forms the basis of a piece of literature. Think of a selection that you have read in which the central character's conflict is resolved so that he or she learns an important lesson about life. In your response, explain the conflict and how its resolution affects the character.

Study the Prompt

Read the prompt carefully. Then read it again, circling important words and phrases: *conflict between characters, resolved, lesson about life, explains, how,* and *affects the character.* Re-read the prompt and make sure you understand every aspect of it.

Tip: Spend about five minutes studying the prompt.

Plan Your Response

Choose a piece of literature that includes a character who is in conflict with another character, resolves the conflict, and then learns something in the process. Specific details from the text should support your analysis. The prompt requires that you explain how these parts work together.

Use this **framework** to organize ideas in your essay:

- Introduce the **characters** and **conflict.**
- Include any **complications** that lead to the resolution.
- Explain how the **conflict** is resolved and how the central character learns a lesson.

Next, draft a **thesis statement** that states what the central character learns as a result of the conflict.

Tip: Spend about ten minutes planning your response.

Respond to the Prompt

Begin drafting your essay. Since you are writing about a piece of literature, include the author and title of the selection in the first paragraph.

Your thesis is a statement about how the conflict is resolved and how the character learns an important lesson. The essay answers the question *how?* by offering evidence from the text and elaborating on it. As you write, keep the following points in mind:

- Your reader may not be familiar with the literary work. Be specific and provide a context.
- Your organization should mirror the piece of literature. The last scene is probably important to explain at the conclusion of your own essay.
- Your evidence should include summaries, paraphrases, or direct quotations from the text (if you can recall them correctly).

  Tip: Spend about twenty minutes writing your draft.

Improve Your Response

Revising Review your draft to compare it with the prompt. Does your draft have a thesis that states the conflict, resolution, and lesson learned? Does it provide evidence to support your thesis?

Proofreading Spend a few minutes finding and correcting any errors in grammar, usage, and mechanics. Make sure that your paper and any edits are neatly written and legible.

Checking Your Final Copy Before you turn in your paper, examine it once more to make sure that you have done your best work. **Tip:** Save five to ten minutes to improve your paper.

Listening & Speaking Workshop

Presenting a Response to a Poem

Speak with a Purpose

Adapt your response to a poem into an oral presentation. Practice your oral response, and then present it to your class.

Think as a Reader/Writer Presenting a response to a poem to a group of listeners is similar in ways to writing an analysis of a poem for readers. Like readers, listeners take in and try to comprehend someone's ideas. Unlike readers, though, listeners do not have the luxury of taking in another's ideas at their own pace. Clarity, therefore, is crucial in speaking.

Adapt Your Response to Literature

Try a New Twist

Because people will be listening to your response to a poem instead of reading it, you'll need to adapt it as you prepare for your presentation. Keep in mind that your classmates are your audience, and follow these suggestions to construct your presentation.

- **Word Choice** Apart from literary terms, such as *simile* and *diction*, try to keep your vocabulary from being too showy. Use vivid verbs that describe actions, rather than overusing verbs like *is* and *has*. Repeat or define words that your audience may find difficult.
- **Introduction** Adapt the introduction of your essay to capture your audience's attention quickly. Discussing a poet's use of stylistic devices is not riveting for everyone. Opening with a candid statement of personal response or a colorful detail from the poet's life might be a better approach. Then you can move on to your thesis statement.
- **Organization** Review the body of your response, and add transition words and phrases, where necessary, to help your audience follow the organization of your response and progression of your thoughts.
- **Analysis** Try to relate themes in the work you analyzed to your classmates' lives. If you chose a poem that you relate to, doing so should not be too difficult. Suppose, for example, you are responding to "Dream Deferred" by Langston Hughes. You might relate Hughes's subject—the thwarted dreams of African Americans—to the work of a rapper or other popular artist who has examined that same subject.
- **Conclusion** Close your presentation with a crisp restatement of your thesis. Quoting a line from the poem to reinforce a thesis is often effective. As in all presentations, a great last line leaves a strong impression and can make earlier statements resonate.

Reader/Writer Notebook

Use your **RWN** to complete the activities for this workshop.

9.R.1.D.1.a Read grade-level instructional text: with fluency, accuracy, comprehension and appropriate expression **9.R.2.C.1.b** Use details from text(s): to analyze character, plot, setting, point of view *Also covered* **9.W.2.C.1.b; 9.W.2.C.1.a; 9.R.1.D.1.a**

Deliver Your Response to Literature

Show and Tell

When you deliver your response orally, you can use verbal and nonverbal techniques to reinforce your analysis. These techniques work best when you know your material, so try to memorize at least a section of the poem and rehearse your presentation.

Use Verbal Techniques

Your attitude can have a great impact on your audience. How will you use your voice to convey tone? Will you sound academic? serious? breezy? How will you make your points clear and interesting? Here are a few ideas:

Verbal Techniques

- **Diction:** Diction can refer to the clarity of your pronunciation. Speak clearly and carefully.
- **Emphasis:** Stress key words by saying them in a different voice, volume, or tone from that of the overall presentation.
- **Pauses:** Use pauses to help listeners follow your ideas.

Use Nonverbal Techniques

You can make your presentation clearer and more interesting by using gestures and facial expressions. Review the tips in the table below.

Improve Your Delivery: Nonverbal Techniques	
Eye Contact	Look into the eyes of audience members. Eye contact conveys confidence and sincerity.
Facial Expression	Be relaxed and natural, using a smile, a grimace, or a raised eyebrow to convey meaning.
Gestures	Make natural gestures with your head and hands. Move around a bit; try writing poetry lines on the board.

Take Note

While presenting your response, you may want to use concise notes to keep you on track. Make notecards with short reminder phrases, and arrange the cards in the correct order.

A Good Oral Response to Literature

- engages attention from the start by relating the thesis to relevant aspects of your listeners' lives
- focuses on the main points in your thesis
- relates the literary devices used in the text to the theme(s) in the work
- offers evidence from the text to illustrate any literary devices you address
- delivers a conclusion that restates your thesis and wraps up the response with a noteworthy comment

Speaking Tip

To quell anxiety, rehearse your speech in front of an observant friend or family member. You will know your presentation better and will get valuable feedback.

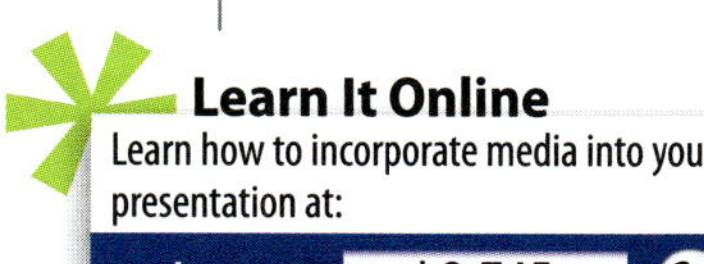

Learn It Online
Learn how to incorporate media into your presentation at:
go.hrw.com
L9-745
Go

Writing Skills Review

Response to Literature **Directions:** First, read the poem. Next, read a student's analysis log and draft for a response to the poem, and then answer the questions that follow.

Dream Deferred

by **Langston Hughes**

What happens to a dream deferred?

Does it dry up
like a raisin in the sun?
Or fester like a sore—
And then run?
Does it stink like rotten meat?
Or crust and sugar over—
like a syrupy sweet?

Maybe it just sags
like a heavy load.

Or does it explode?

(1) What happens when the pursuit of a dream is postponed or denied—again and again? (2) "Dream Deferred" asks this rhetorical question and then gives several answers. (3) The answers offered by the poem's speaker have Hughes's stylistic devices, including blunt diction and simple figurative language. (4) Hughes poses answers to this basic question with similes, most of which are questions in themselves. (5) The first simile for example, asks if a dream deferred dries up like a raisin in the sun.

(6) The poem's title is important: the word *dream* here means "hope for a better future." (7) Hughes starts with the rhetorical question, and his diction in line 1 is important. (8) He chooses the word *deferred* for its two meanings: "to put something off until sometime in the future" and "to give in to what someone else wants." (9) Hughes could be suggesting that someone else postpones the dream. (10) But the dreamer gives in to the delay. (11) The title helps convey the poem's theme: that blocking people from the pursuit of their dreams can end up causing destruction.

MO **9.W.3.A.1.d** Compose a variety of texts: including literary analysis *Also covered* **9.W.2.B.1.b; 9.W.2.C.1.b; 9.W.2.D.1.a; 9.W.2.E.1.b**

1. What information would be the *best* addition to sentence 2?

A A definition of *rhetorical*

B The specific number of "answers"

C The name of the poet

D Background information on the poem

9.W.2.B.1.b

2. Which of these words or phrases would improve sentence 3 if substituted for the word *have*?

A are

B are formed from

C are negated by

D seem dulled by

9.W.2.D.1.a

3. Which of the following sentences *best* supports the ideas in sentence 4?

A For instance, Hughes avoids the use of rhyme.

B The metaphor in line 11, for example, is italicized to make this point.

C By using strong verbs such as *fester* and *stink*, Hughes's similes become vivid and memorable.

D All of the above

9.W.2.B.1.b

4. Which of the following shows the *best* revision to sentence 5?

A The first simile for example; asks if a dream deferred dries up like a raisin in the sun.

B The first simile, for example, asks if a dream deferred dries up like a raisin in the sun.

C The first simile—for example—asks if a dream deferred dries up like a raisin in the sun.

D The first simile for example asks if a Dream Deferred dries up like a raisin in the sun.

9.W.2.E.1.b

5. What is the *best* revision to sentence 10?

A Combine it with sentence 9.

B Delete the first word.

C Add an adjective describing the "dreamer."

D Insert an exclamation point in place of the period.

9.W.2.E.1

6. To improve the coherence of the response, which sentence should be deleted?

A Sentence 1

B Sentence 4

C Sentence 7

D Sentence 9

9.W.2.C.1.b

UNIT 4

Drama

Writers on Writing

Anna Deavere Smith on Drama

Actor, playwright, and teacher Anna Deavere Smith was born in Baltimore, Maryland. In her plays, Smith often combines interviews, research, and her own impressions, a style that has been called "a new form of theater." Like much of her work, her award-winning play *Fires in the Mirror* explores racial prejudice and the possibility of achieving understanding. She was awarded a MacArthur Fellowship in 1996.

"Drama, as an art form, is exactly what helps us understand and grapple with the more powerful parts of our human experience. Drama is often, though not always, the most 'lifelike' of the art forms, even when they include dancing, singing, and abstract visual design. Dramas mirror our existence. They seek to illuminate aspects of the human condition.

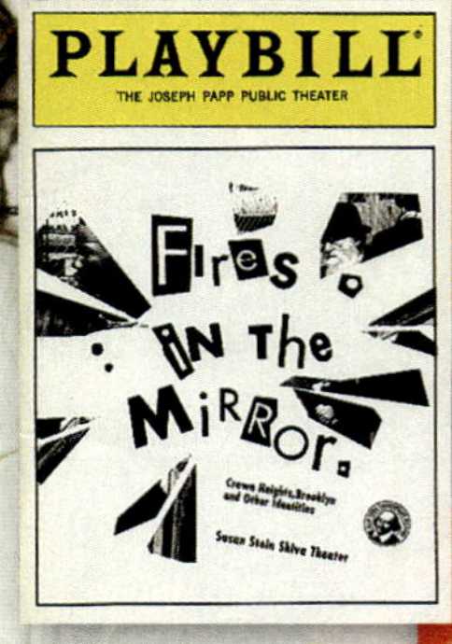

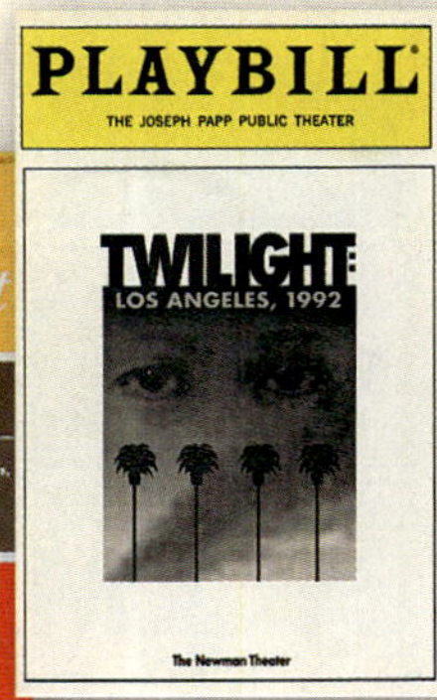

They are sometimes grand, sometimes tragic, sometimes joyous, sometimes wickedly funny. We leave the theaters humming new tunes, walking to the rhythm of dance steps we seek to repeat, or wishing to own a dress or vest we have seen on stage, film, or digital format. Some of us sit in the theater long after the audience has left, stunned and moved emotionally by what we've seen, unable to move physically—suspended, gripped by the magic of the myth that descended, enchanted, enraged, engulfed, and just as quickly, evaporated.

An actor's gift is empathy—the ability to imagine that you could be someone else, to the point that it takes over every muscle in your body, even if that person's existence is something far different from yours. The gift of those who write drama is the gift of being able to imagine other worlds, other people, other living things. The author for drama has the gift of the story—he or she can align events into a comprehendible story. The writer anticipates the actor, director, and designers, and so provides a blueprint.

And then there is the audience. Regardless of the gifts of the artist, the greatest gift given to the drama maker is the audience. Drama, as I stated earlier, 'mirrors our existence.' The audience, by its very presence, brings and adds another level of richness to the mirror of humanity. When the work is successful, the audience is gripped by that which it watches: sometimes gripped in joy, sometimes gripped in terror, sometimes gripped in tragedy, sometimes gripped by the truth wrapped and unwound by the fiction. Without those gripping moments, where audience and artist are deeply connected, there is no drama. For me, the greatest drama is *the drama of connection*—the connection which allows both artist and audience to transcend reality, even if for a second.

How lucky you are, in your time, whoever you are, wherever you are, whenever you are, reading this. Your world will be both larger and smaller than mine. When I was your age, I was exposed, in school, to dramas written from a European background. At church, and in my community, I was exposed to dramas written from an African American perspective. I had to learn how to *reach* in order to appreciate and learn from both perspectives. I thought my reach was pretty long! Yet in the world today and, I suspect, in the world of the future, your reach will need to be long enough to put together exponentially more perspectives than I did. Your reach is exactly—your *imagination*. ”

Think as a Writer

Do you agree that drama helps us better understand the human experience? Explain why or why not.

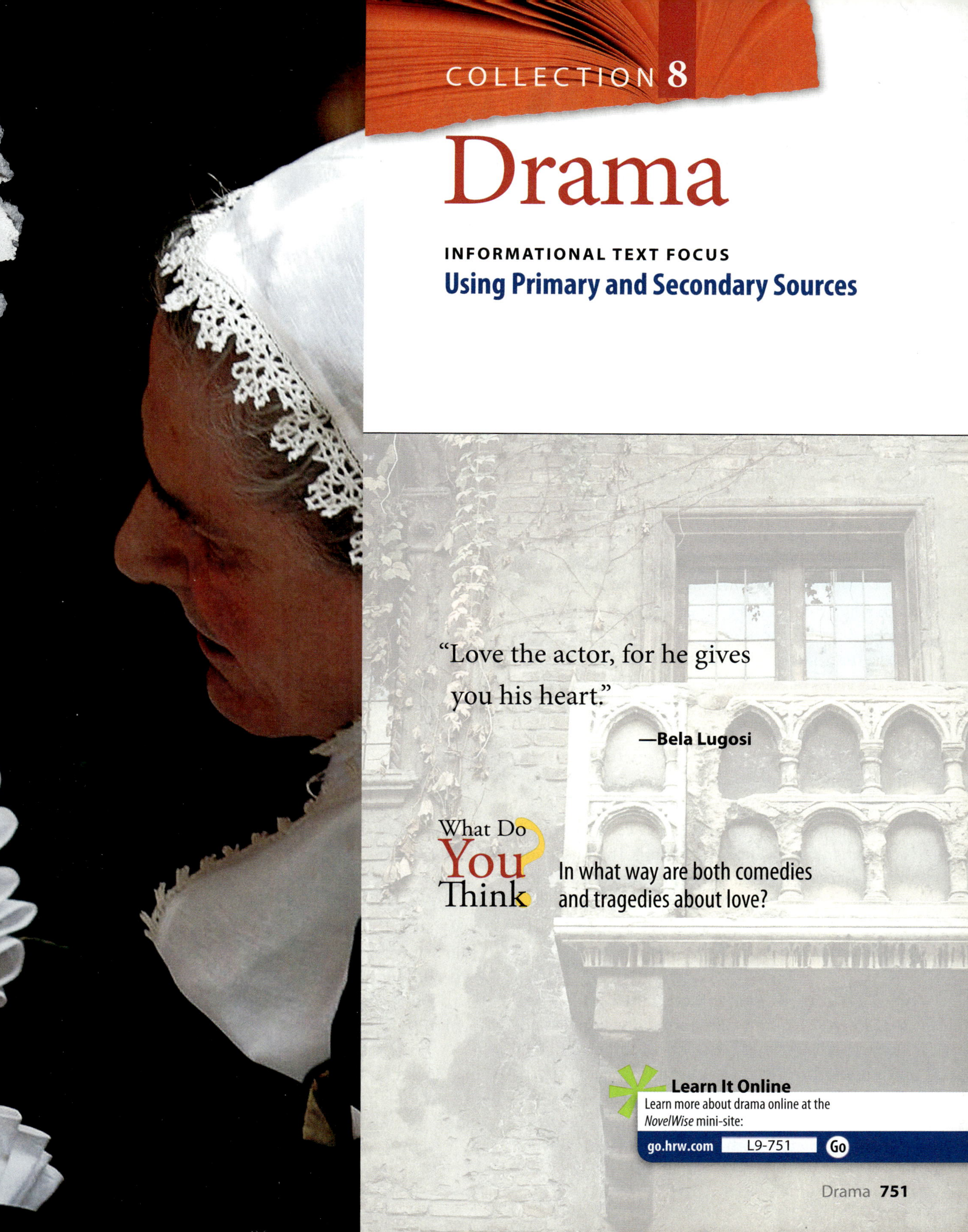

COLLECTION 8

Drama

INFORMATIONAL TEXT FOCUS

Using Primary and Secondary Sources

"Love the actor, for he gives you his heart."

—Bela Lugosi

What Do You Think?

In what way are both comedies and tragedies about love?

Learn It Online

Learn more about drama online at the *NovelWise* mini-site:

go.hrw.com L9-751 Go

Literary Focus

by **Carol Jago**

What Elements Create Drama?

The script for a play is just its beginning, like the blueprint for a house. You can imagine what a house will look like by studying the blueprint, but only when it's built can you walk around and really feel what the house is like. It takes a team of theatrical artists to bring a play to life. Directors guide actors as they learn their parts. Technical workers design and create costumes, scenery, lighting, and makeup. Learning to recognize the elements in a play will help you imagine how the words on the page can become an exciting live work of art.

Dramatic Structure

A **play** is a story acted out live and onstage. It presents characters performed by real people in a physical setting, interacting before our eyes. Like stories, plays consist of characters carrying out a series of actions and driven by a conflict. However, stories and plays have different formats.

A story is a prose narrative—a narrator in a short story describes the characters, action, and settings, and the characters' words are usually marked by quotation marks. In contrast, a play consists entirely of the characters' words and actions. The playwright may describe the setting and the characters' actions, but the audience never hears these stage directions. The audience sees and hears only the actors' interpretations of the stage directions.

Plot Structure You can expect the **plot** of a play to follow a rising-and-falling structure, much as a story does. The plot is based on a **conflict,** whether an age-old family battle, as in Shakespeare's *The Tragedy of Romeo and Juliet,* or a man ashamed to confess his love, as in Rostand's *Cyrano de Bergerac.* Various conflicts—both internal and external—create tension that increases as the play progresses. Finally, the tension reaches a **climax,** the emotional high point of the story. Then the conflict is resolved, the action winds down, and the play ends.

Dramatic Elements

The **script** is the text of a play. It includes all of the words that actors will speak and some instructions for the actors, designers, and director.

The Words Characters Speak The conversation between characters in a play is called **dialogue.** A long speech by one character to one or more other characters onstage is a **monologue,** and a speech by a character alone onstage, who is speaking to himself or herself or to the audience, is a **soliloquy.** Playwrights often use monologues and soliloquies to develop ideas or have characters express complex emotions.

Sometimes a character speaks in an **aside,** a comment that only the audience is supposed to hear. In this aside, Romeo wonders whether or not to interrupt Juliet:

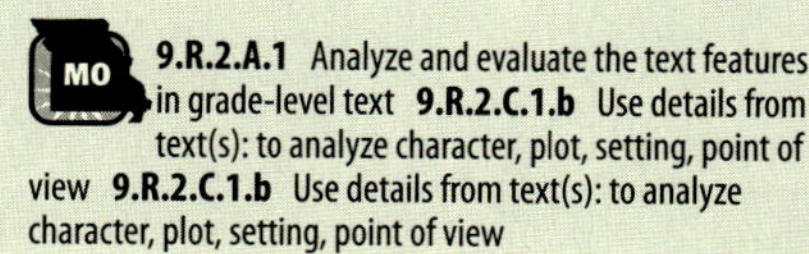

> **Juliet.**
> O Romeo, Romeo! Wherefore art thou
> Romeo?
> Deny thy father and refuse thy name;
> Or, if thou wilt not, be but sworn my love,
> And I'll no longer be a Capulet.
> **Romeo** *(aside).*
> Shall I hear more, or shall I speak at this?
>
> from *The Tragedy of Romeo and Juliet,* Act II, Scene 2, lines 33–37, by William Shakespeare

Stage Directions Scripts also include **stage directions,** which describe the appearance of the stage, as well as how the characters move and speak. This stage direction tells what an audience sees at the beginning of a scene:

> *Winter. The* SERVINGMAN *(in rags) and the* PRINCE *(as a frog) sitting around a campfire. The* PRINCE *reading a newspaper . . .*
>
> from *The Frog Prince* by David Mamet

Actors, directors, and designers usually regard stage directions as suggestions rather than rigid demands. The actor and director decide how to interpret the lines of a play—what the words mean, why the character says them, and how the character feels while saying them. If you were to see two productions of the same play, the words would be the same, but the actors' actions and interpretations would certainly differ. Think about how different actors might interpret these simple stage directions:

> **Milkmaid.** I love another.
> **Prince.** Oh. (*Pause*) Oh. (*Pause*) Oh. (*Pause*) Fine. That's fine. . . .
>
> from *The Frog Prince* by David Mamet

Elements of Staging

Staging includes everything that is part of a play, but is not part of the written script. Thinking about these elements will help you imagine what the play will be like when it is presented for an audience.

Stage A **stage** can be grand or small in size. It can be positioned in front of the audience, or it can be in the middle of a theater, surrounded by the audience. A stage is like a small world unto itself, with its own coordinates: not north, south, east, and west, but upstage (away from audience), downstage (toward audience), and stage right and stage left (an actor's right and left when facing the audience).

Set Every play takes place somewhere and at some time, and a **set** transforms a bare stage into that place and time. A set might be realistic and detailed, looking just like a cozy living room, a bustling office, or an autumn forest. It might be abstract or minimal, meeting the needs of the action with just a few movable boxes and screens.

Lighting Until the last few centuries most plays (including those of Shakespeare) were performed outdoors in natural light. Today most plays are performed indoors and so require artificial lighting. Lights can wash the entire stage with golden sunlight or cast blue twilight shadows, depending on their brightness, placement, and filter colors.

Costumes and Props Like sets, costumes and props can be elaborate or minimal. In one production of a play, for example, a king might wear velvet robes and a crown, but in another production the same king might wear a T-shirt and a cardboard crown. All the elements of the scene design—sets, lights, costumes, and props—work together to support the action and create the appropriate mood.

(*continued*)

Literary Focus

Tragedy

A **tragedy** is the presentation of serious and important actions that end unhappily. The oldest plays were performed in ancient Greece as part of religious festivals and included tragedies and comedies. The tragedies dealt with heroic characters and subjects such as fate, life, and death.

Tragic Heroes Some plays, like *The Tragedy of Romeo and Juliet,* portray the suffering of innocent characters, but in most tragedies the central character is a noble figure, known as the **tragic hero,** who has a personal failing that leads to his or her downfall. This **tragic flaw** might be excessive pride, ambition, or passion—they are imperfections that lead the otherwise noble hero to make choices that doom him or her to a tragic end.

Even the innocent victims in *The Tragedy of Romeo and Juliet* have flaws that contribute to their downfall. Their youthful passion makes them act urgently when patience might have saved their lives.

Character Foil A **foil** is a character who is used to contrast another character. Playwrights often use foils to accentuate and clarify the distinct qualities of the two characters. In a tragedy, foils can highlight a hero's tragic flaw by showing an opposite virtue.

In this dialogue, Romeo speaks in sweeping, romantic terms about his feelings. The character of the Friar is a foil whose down-to-earth language contrasts with Romeo's emotional speech:

Romeo.
I bear no hatred, blessèd man, for, lo,
My intercession likewise steads my foe.
Friar.
Be plain, good son, and homely in thy drift.

from *The Tragedy of Romeo and Juliet,* Act II, Scene 3, lines 53–55, by William Shakespeare

Tragic Plots Tragedies contain the same plot elements that you find in a story: a basic situation, or **exposition,** and a **conflict.** The plot develops in scenes, each of which contains one or more events that are important to the plot. The drama heightens when a scene includes a **turning point,** or moment at which the conflict shifts in an important way for one or more characters. **Complications** are events that make it harder for the main characters to achieve their goals. Romeo and Juliet face many complications after they fall in love. Some are obvious, like the firm objections of their parents. However, even a complication that seems trivial, like a missed message, can have grave effects in a tragedy.

Suspense is the uncertainty or anxiety that the audience feels about what will happen next. Often in a tragedy, the outcome is already known. The audience knows that Romeo and Juliet will not survive. Yet the playwright can still create great suspense because the audience will feel increasingly anxious as the tragic end approaches.

Dramatic Irony The contrast between appearance and reality is often a key element in tragedy. **Dramatic irony** occurs when the audience or the reader knows something important that a character does not know. In this scene, the audience knows that Juliet is drugged, while her father thinks she is dead. The result is heartbreaking dramatic irony:

Capulet.
Despised, distressèd, hated, martyred, killed!
Uncomfortable time, why cam'st thou now
To murder, murder our solemnity?
O child, O child! My soul, and not my child!
Dead art thou—alack, my child is dead,
And with my child my joys are burièd!

from *The Tragedy of Romeo and Juliet,* Act IV, Scene 5, lines 59–64

9.R.2.A.1 Analyze and evaluate the text features in grade-level text **9.R.2.C.1.b** Use details from text(s): to analyze character, plot, setting, point of view **9.R.2.C.1.b** Use details from text(s): to analyze character, plot, setting, point of view

Comedy

A **comedy** is simply a play that ends happily. Many people would define a comedy as a funny play, and in fact most comedies are meant to make us laugh. Comedies can have other, more important purposes as well, including making us think about issues and question things that we take for granted.

Characters in Comedy While the principal characters in classical tragedies are noble, the central characters in comedies can be from any class—they can be princes, townspeople, or servants. Like tragic heroes, characters in comedies almost always have flaws. Instead of marching to their doom, however, these flawed characters usually discover the error of their ways, and order is restored.

Conflicts in Comedy Like tragedy, comedy is rooted in conflict, but the conflict in a comedy is often romantic: Someone wants to marry someone else but faces an obstacle, such as an opposing parent, a rival suitor, or a witch's spell. In comedy the obstacle is always overcome, but not before complications—often ridiculous but sometimes serious—heighten the suspense. The complications can involve misunderstandings, mistaken identities, disguises, and other transformations.

Peasant. Are they for me?
Prince. No. I've *told* you.
Peasant (*pause*). Who are they for?
Prince. A friend of mine, what's it to you?
Peasant. I want them.
Prince. Tough.
Peasant. Give them to me.
[*Pause*]
Prince (*to* SERVINGMAN). She's a rare old bird—

from *The Frog Prince*
by David Mamet

Your Turn Analyze Drama

Choose a play or movie you remember seeing. Follow these steps to analyze its dramatic elements.

1. Describe the set (or sets) where the scenes took place. Were they realistic? How did they contribute to the presentation?
2. List at least two costumes worn by the actors. What did the costumes tell you about the characters?
3. Tell what you remember about the dialogue. Was it convincing? clever? emotional? Do you recall any monologues or asides?
4. Would you classify the work as a tragedy, a comedy, or a mixture of the two? Why?
5. Could you describe the main character as a tragic hero? Why or why not?
6. What characters acted as foils to provide contrast with the main characters?
7. Describe one turning point in the work. What complications developed as a result?
8. How did the work build suspense? What happened in the climax?

Learn It Online
Jump into drama with *PowerNotes* online:
go.hrw.com
L9-755
Go

Analyzing Visuals

What Elements of Drama Can Be Captured in Photographs?

Photographers often try to capture the magic of theater in photographs. Very often, they attend dress rehearsals, when every element needed to stage a play for an audience is in place: actors are costumed, sets are constructed; stage lights are illuminated; props are organized, and sound effects are cued. The most successful photographs convey all the stagecraft as well as capture a memorable moment of the story that is unfolding onstage.

Analyzing a Photograph

Use these guidelines to help you find elements of drama in a photograph.

1. Study the photograph. What do the actors' costumes suggest about the plot or the time period of the play?
2. Examine the set, which includes the backdrop, floor, fixtures, and any furnishings. What environment or images does the set create?
3. What mood does the lighting help create?
4. Consider the perspective of the photograph. Would the audience see the action from the same angle?
5. What aspects of the photo communicate the excitement of a live performance?

Look at the details of the photograph. How do they help you answer the questions on page 757?

9.R.2.A.1 Analyze and evaluate the text features in grade-level text

1. Shakespeare's *Henry V* dramatizes the life of that English king. How can you tell which actor is playing Henry V in this photograph?

2. In this scene, Henry prepares his men for battle. Are they ready to fight? What do their facial expressions and body language suggest?

3. Henry V ruled from 1413 to 1422, yet the king in this production is wearing a modern shirt and tie. What does this tell you about the director's interpretation?

4. Take a moment to study the **set** in the photograph. Would you describe the setting for this play as realistic or based in fantasy? Explain.

Liev Schreiber and the ensemble of *Henry V* during rehearsal on June 27, 2003.

Your Turn Talk About a Photograph

Flip through the photographs that accompany *The Tragedy of Romeo and Juliet,* which appears later in this collection. Choose one photograph you find interesting. What aspects of drama does the photograph capture?

Reading Focus

by **Kylene Beers**

What Skills Help You Analyze Drama?

Even if you have not seen a play at a professional theater, chances are you've seen a school play. When you watch a play, the sets, actors, lighting, music, and costumes bring the play to life. When you *read* a play, you create the scenes in your mind by visualizing the action. By reading aloud, you hear the words and can paraphrase them to understand what is going on. Making inferences is also important; stage directions telling characters to "whisper" lead you to different inferences than directions suggesting they "yell." Finally, analyzing causes and effects can help you understand why characters act as they do.

Visualizing Drama

When you **visualize drama,** you try to get a clear, specific image of what's happening onstage. Think about how many characters are present, and remember, characters who aren't talking can still be part of the action.

To visualize what the sets, costumes, lights, and props will be like in a particular production, fill out a graphic organizer like the one below. Add in any important scenery elements, and take notes to describe the scene that you envision.

Play	*The Tragedy of Romeo and Juliet*
Scene	*The balcony scene*
Notes	*Very spare. The characters wear regular street clothes. No big scenery. Juliet stands on a ladder. Romeo climbs up the ladder to kiss her. The lighting is soft and romantic; dark.*

Making Inferences

You will need to **make inferences** to understand what is not stated directly in the dialogue. Very few plays have a narrator to tell you what a character is like. You will need to make inferences to understand a character's overall personality (friendly, stubborn, cynical?) as well as his or her moods at specific points in the play (angry, confused, playful).

Begin with a line of dialogue that seems meaningful. Then, think about the connections you can discover, and make an inference about the unstated meaning.

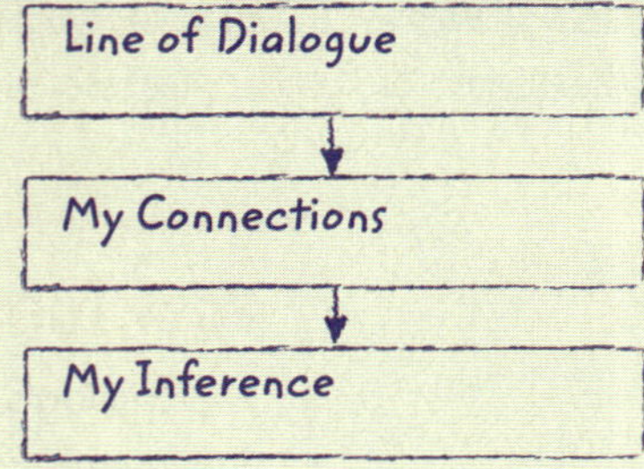

MO **9.R.1.G.1.e** During reading, utilize strategies: to visualize **9.R.1.G.1.d** During reading, utilize strategies: to infer **9.R.3.C.1.a** Use details from informational text: to identify and explain the organizational pattern **9.R.1.G.1.f** During reading, utilize strategies: to paraphrase

Analyzing Cause and Effect

Plays are filled with actions, but you may need to slow down while you are reading to understand why something happens. You can **analyze causes and effects** to understand character motivations.

If you want to know why a character did something, look for the *cause* of his or her actions. Think about the earlier events and actions that led to this action. If you want to know what happens as a *result* of a character's action, look for the effect it creates. You can use a cause-and-effect chart to identify relationships between key events in the play.

Causes	Effects
1.	1.
2.	2.
3.	3.

Remember that many events have more than one cause or lead to more than one effect. Many effects also become the causes of other events, creating a chain of events. You may wish to extend your chart to note more complex relationships.

Reading Aloud and Paraphrasing

Reading a script aloud (by yourself or with a partner) will help you understand the action and identify conflicts between characters. Here are some tips:

- Try reading a scene twice. The first time, don't try to act. Begin by reading the scene to find out what's happening. If you don't at first understand the meaning of the lines, **paraphrase** them in your own words, and then read the original lines again.
- Let the punctuation and stage directions guide your reading choices. If the play is in verse, don't pause at line endings unless there is punctuation.

Your Turn Apply Reading Skills

Practice your reading skills by reading this scene opening. Then, complete the activities that follow.

Shipwrecked and alone in an unfamiliar city, Viola disguises herself as a young man. She finds a job working for Count Orsino, who is in love with Olivia. Orsino sends Viola to try to persuade Olivia to speak with him.

Olivia.
Give me my veil; come, throw it o'er my face.
We'll once more hear Orsino's embassy.
[*Enter* VIOLA.]

Viola.
The honorable lady of the house, which is she?

Olivia.
Speak to me; I shall answer for her. Your will?

Viola.
Most radiant, exquisite, and unmatchable beauty
—I pray you tell me if this be the lady of the house,
for I never saw her. I would be loath to cast away
my speech; for, besides that it is excellently well
penned, I have taken great pains to con it. . . .

from *Twelfth Night,* Act I, Scene 5, lines 164–172, by William Shakespeare

1. What clue in the dialogue hints at how Olivia is dressed?
2. Read the scene aloud with a partner. How does hearing the language help you understand what is happening?

Now go to the Skills in Action: Reading Model

Learn It Online
Try the *PowerNotes* version of this lesson on:
go.hrw.com
L9-759
Go

SKILLS IN ACTION

Reading Model

DRAMA

Build Background

This comic romance begins in France in 1640, when the French are fighting the Spanish. Christian is a strikingly handsome soldier, but he lacks the gift of eloquent, poetic language needed to win Roxane's love. Cyrano, who has a huge nose, is too ashamed of his appearance to reveal his love for Roxane. He has the heart and soul of a poet, however, and he offers to write love letters to Roxane for Christian. The scheme works so well that Roxane marries Christian in secret. In the scene from Act IV that follows, Roxane has placed herself in great danger by traveling to Christian and Cyrano's military camp to see her beloved Christian.

Read with a Purpose Read this scene to find out what happens when two men finally admit that they are both in love with the same woman.

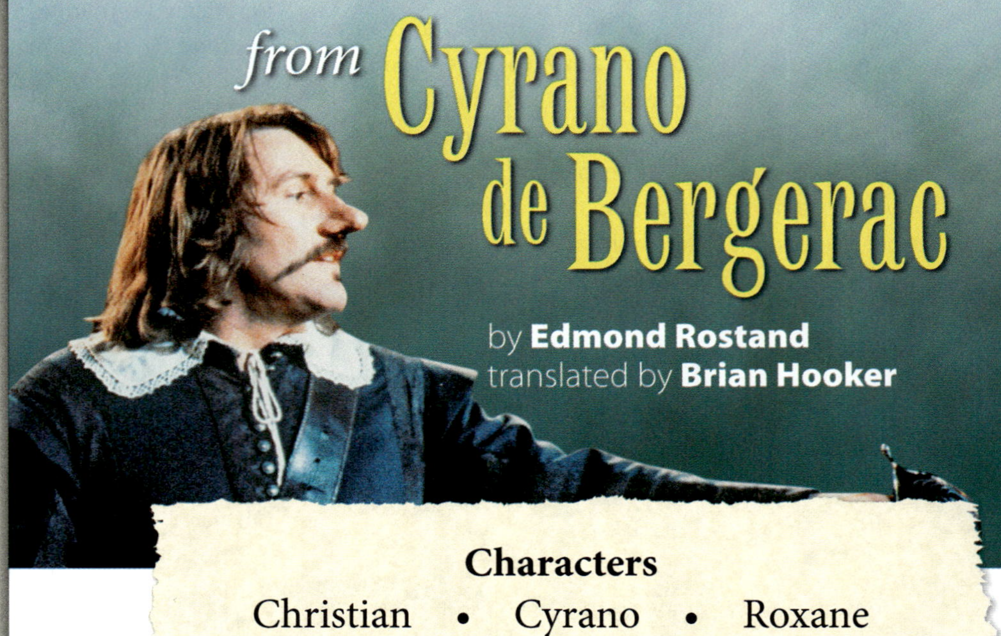

from Cyrano de Bergerac

by **Edmond Rostand**
translated by **Brian Hooker**

Characters
Christian • Cyrano • Roxane

Literary Focus

Sets This brief stage direction indicates what the stage might look like. A set designer would decide how to present this image to an audience. It might be realistic, impressionistic, or somewhere in between.

Scene: *A military camp outside of Arras, France.*

Christian.
What is it?[1]

Cyrano.
If Roxane . . .

Christian.
Well?

Cyrano.
Speaks about your letters . . .

Christian.
Yes—I know!

Cyrano.
Do not make the mistake of showing . . .

1. The line spacing in this scene reflects the fact that the play was originally written in French verse.

Christian.

What?

Cyrano.
Showing surprise.
Christian.

Surprise—why?

Cyrano.

I must tell you! . . .

It is quite simple—I had forgotten it
Until just now. You have . . .
Christian.

Speak quickly!—

Cyrano.

You

Have written oftener than you think.
Christian.

Oh—have I!

Cyrano.
I took upon me to interpret you;
And wrote—sometimes . . . without . . .
Christian.

My knowing. Well?

Cyrano.
Perfectly simple!
Christian.

Oh yes, perfectly!
For a month, we have been blockaded[2] here!—
How did you send all these letters?
Cyrano.

Before

Daylight, I managed—
Christian.

I see. That was also

Perfectly simple!

—So I wrote to her,
How many times a week? Twice? Three times?
Four?

2. **blockaded** (blah KAY duhd): cut off by enemy troops and prevented from passing in or out.

The photographs throughout the play are from the 1990 film *Cyrano de Bergerac* directed by Jean-Paul Rappeneau, starring Gérard Depardieu as Cyrano, Vincent Perez as Christian, and Anne Brochet as Roxane. A modern retelling of the play is the 1987 film *Roxanne.*

Literary Focus

Dialogue The short lines of dialogue create a rapid rhythm between these two characters, building suspense about what is to come.

Reading Focus

Reading Aloud Do not pause at the ends of lines if there is no punctuation. Read this line as "Before daylight, I managed—"

Cyrano.
Oftener.
Christian.
Every day?
Cyrano.
Yes—every day . . .
Every single day . . .
Christian.
(Violently)
And that wrought[3] you up
Into such a flame that you faced death—
Cyrano.
(Sees Roxane *returning.)*
Hush—
Not before her!
(He goes quickly into the tent. Roxane *comes up to* Christian.*)*
Roxane.
Now—Christian!
Christian.
(Takes her hands.)
Tell me now
Why you came here—over these ruined roads—

Literary Focus

Stage Directions Rostand writes that Christian reacts "violently." He wants to make sure that the actors maintain energy in this scene.

3. **wrought** (rawt): alternate past-tense form of *work*.

Why you made your way among mosstroopers[4]
And ruffians[5]—you—to join me here?
Roxane.
Because—
Your letters . . .
Christian.
Meaning?
Roxane.
It was your own fault
If I ran into danger! I went mad—
Mad with you! Think what you have written me,
How many times, each one more wonderful
Than the last!
Christian.
All this for a few absurd
Love-letters—
Roxane.
Hush—absurd! How can you know?
I thought I loved you, ever since one night
When a voice that I never would have known
Under my window breathed your soul to me . . .[6]
But—all this time, your letters—every one
Was like hearing your voice there in the dark,
All around me, like your arms around me . . .
(More lightly)
At last,
I came. Anyone would! Do you suppose
The prim Penelope had stayed at home
Embroidering,—if Ulysses wrote like you?
She would have fallen like another Helen—
Tucked up those linen petticoats of hers
And followed him to Troy![7]

Reading Focus

Making Inferences By comparing Roxane's and Christian's speeches, you can infer that she has a much more romantic view of love than he does.

Literary Focus

Monologue Roxane speaks fluently, in long poetic speeches, which Christian merely interrupts with brief statements.

---

4. **mosstroopers** (MAWS troop uhrz): raiders.
5. **ruffians** (RUHF ee uhnz): tough, violent, lawless people.
6. **ever since . . . soul to me:** Christian addressed Roxane one night as she stood on a balcony. She was frustrated by his inability to express his love eloquently until Cyrano, who was hiding in the bushes, stepped in. Under cover of darkness, Cyrano spoke so poetically that Roxane was deeply moved.
7. **Do you suppose . . . to Troy:** A reference to the great Greek hero Ulysses, or Odysseus. While she waits for her husband to return home from the Trojan War, Penelope weaves and unweaves a shroud for her father-in-law as a trick to put off her suitors. Helen, the wife of King Menelaus of Sparta, runs off to Troy with Paris, a Trojan prince, thus sparking the Trojan War.

Christian.

But you—

Roxane.

I read them
Over and over. I grew faint reading them.
I belonged to you. Every page of them
Was like a petal fallen from your soul—
Like the light and the fire of a great love,
Sweet and strong and true—

Christian.

Sweet . . . and strong . . . and true . . .
You felt that, Roxane?—

Roxane.

You know how I feel! . . .

Christian.

So—you came . . .

Roxane.

Oh, my Christian, oh my king,—
Lift me up if I fall upon my knees—
It is the heart of me that kneels to you,
And will remain forever at your feet—
You cannot lift that!—

I came here to say
"Forgive me"—(It is time to be forgiven
Now, when we may die presently)—forgive me
For being light and vain and loving you
Only because you were beautiful.

Christian.

(Astonished)

Roxane! . . .

Roxane.

Afterwards I knew better. Afterwards
(I had to learn to use my wings) I loved you
For yourself too—knowing you more, and loving
More of you. And now—

Christian.

Now? . . .

Roxane.

It is yourself
I love now: your own self.

Reading Focus

Visualizing Drama You can make your own decisions about what the actors might do. You might imagine that Roxane literally falls to her knees in this scene, or you might decide that she fights her temptation to do so.

Christian.

(Taken aback)

Roxane!

Roxane.

(Gravely)

Be happy!—

You must have suffered; for you must have seen
How frivolous[8] I was; and to be loved
For the mere costume, the poor casual body
You went about in—to a soul like yours,
That must have been torture! Therefore with words
You revealed your heart. Now that image of you
Which filled my eyes first—I see better now,
And I see it no more!

Literary Focus

Dramatic Structure Christian reaches a dramatic **turning point:** He realizes that Roxane truly loves not himself, but the man who wrote the letters—Cyrano.

8. **frivolous** (FRIHV uh luhs): silly; not serious or sensible.

Reading Focus

Analyzing Cause and Effect Roxane misinterprets Christian's misery as being her own fault. This causes her to make apologies for herself.

Christian.
Oh!—
Roxane.
You still doubt
Your victory?
Christian.
(Miserably)
Roxane!—
Roxane.
I understand:
You cannot perfectly believe in me—
A love like this—
Christian.
I want no love like this!
I want love only for—
Roxane.
Only for what
Every woman sees in you? I can do
Better than that!
Christian.
No—it was best before!

Roxane.
You do not altogether know me . . . Dear,
There is more of me than there was—with this,
I can love more of you—more of what makes
You your own self—Truly! . . . If you were less
Lovable—
Christian.
No!
Roxane.
—Less charming—ugly even—
I should love you still.
Christian.
You mean that?
Roxane.
I do
Mean that!
Christian.
Ugly? . . .
Roxane.
Yes. Even then!
Christian.
(Agonized)
Oh . . . God! . . .
Roxane.
Now are you happy?
Christian.
(Choking)
Yes . . .
Roxane.
What is it?
Christian.
(Pushes her away gently.)
Only . . .
Nothing . . . one moment . . .
Roxane.
But—
Christian.
(Gesture toward the Cadets)
I am keeping you
From those poor fellows—Go and smile at them;
They are going to die!

Literary Focus

Dialogue The short lines of dialogue emphasize the quick exchange of emotions between Roxane and Christian, who are experiencing very different feelings.

Roxane.

(Softly)

Dear Christian!

Christian.

Go—

(She goes up among the Gascons[9] who gather round her respectfully.)

Cyrano!

Cyrano.

(Comes out of the tent, armed for the battle.)

What is wrong? You look—

Christian.

She does not

Love me any more.

Cyrano.

(Smiles)

You think not?

Christian.

She loves

You.

Cyrano.

No!—

Christian.

(Bitterly)

She loves only my soul.

Cyrano.

No!

Christian.

Yes—

That means you. And you love her.

Cyrano.

I?

Christian.

I see—

I know!

Cyrano.

That is true . . .

Christian.

More than—

Literary Focus

Costumes Cyrano's battle gear would send two messages to the audience. One is literal; he is preparing for war. The other is metaphoric; he will soon be fighting for Roxane's love.

9. **Gascons** (GAS kuhnz): people from Gascony, in southwestern France.

Cyrano.

(Quietly)

More than that.

Christian.

Tell her so!

Cyrano.

No.

Christian.

Why not?

Cyrano.

Why—look at me!

Christian.

She would love me if I were ugly.

Cyrano.

(Startled)

She—

Said that?

Christian.

Yes. Now then!

Cyrano.

(Half to himself)

It was good of her

To tell you that . . .

(Change of tone)

Nonsense! Do you believe

Any such madness—

It was good of her

To tell you. . . .

Do not take her at her word!

Go on—you never will be ugly—Go!

She would never forgive me.

Christian.

That is what

We shall see.

Cyrano.

No, no—

Christian.

Let her choose between us!—

Tell her everything!

Reading Focus

Making Inferences From Christian's words, you can infer that he is becoming an honest man who does not want to take advantage of his friend.

Literary Focus

Aside This line, spoken "half to himself," is an aside. The audience hears Cyrano's thoughts, but Christian does not.

Reading Focus

Visualizing Drama The confrontation scene between Christian and Cyrano might be staged to emphasize the growing physical tension between the two friends as they realize they are now rivals.

Cyrano.
No—you torture me—
Christian.
Shall I ruin your happiness, because
I have a cursed pretty face? That seems
Too unfair!
Cyrano.
And am I to ruin yours
Because I happen to be born with power
To say what you—perhaps—feel?
Christian.
Tell her!
Cyrano.
Man—
Do not try me too far!
Christian.
I am tired of being
My own rival!
Cyrano.
Christian!—
Christian.
Our secret marriage—
No witnesses—fraudulent[10]—that can be
Annulled[11]—
Cyrano.
Do not try me—
Christian.
I want her love
For the poor fool I am—or not at all!
Oh, I am going through with this! I'll know,
One way or the other. Now I shall walk down
To the end of the post. Go tell her. Let her choose
One of us.
Cyrano.
It will be you.
Christian.
God—I hope so!

---

10. **fraudulent** (FRAW juh luhnt): deceitful; deliberately unlawful.
11. **annulled** (uh NUHLD): declared invalid.

Analyzing Visuals **Viewing and Interpreting** Based upon what you have read in this scene, what do you think Cyrano and Christian are doing in this photograph?

Just as Cyrano is ready to tell Roxane the truth about the letters, Christian is killed. Cyrano feels he can't tell Roxane that he is the author of the letters. The grief-stricken Roxane does not learn the truth until fifteen years later, when Cyrano is dying.

Read with a Purpose What does each character want most in this scene?

MEET THE WRITER

Edmond Rostand

(1868–1918)

Young Poet Pens Hit Play

Edmond Rostand was born into a wealthy family in Marseille, France. Rostand's father hoped his son would pursue a career in law, but Rostand was drawn to the theater instead. In his youth he liked nothing better than to create costumes and stage sets for his puppet theater.

Rostand attended college in Paris, where he spent most of his time writing plays and poetry rather than concentrating on his studies. In 1890, he published his first book of poetry and married the poet Rosemonde Gérard. After his marriage he concentrated on writing plays and often wrote special parts for the famous actors of the time.

Rostand based his most famous play, *Cyrano de Bergerac,* on the life of a real French writer and soldier. Performed in 1897, when Rostand was only twenty-nine years old, the play was greeted with great acclaim. During the first performance every seat in the theater was taken. After each act the audience got to its feet, cheering and applauding, sometimes for up to ten minutes. Rostand's later plays never quite matched this early success.

Think About the Writer How do you think Rostand felt about his later plays? Could his early success have made him resentful? Explain.

SKILLS IN ACTION

Wrap Up

9.R.2.A.1 Analyze and evaluate the text features in grade-level text 9.R.1.G.1.d During reading, utilize strategies: to infer 9.R.3.C.1.a Use details from informational text: to identify and explain the organizational pattern *Also covered* 9.R.1.E.1.c

Into Action: Elements of Drama

Complete this chart by listing one example from *Cyrano de Bergerac* of each dramatic element.

Element of Drama	Example from the Play
Characters/ Character Foils	
Dialogue	
Soliloquy	
Stage Directions	
Conflict	

Talk About . . .

Get together with a small group and discuss *Cyrano de Bergerac* by answering the following questions. Try to use each Academic Vocabulary word listed at the right at least once in your discussion.

1. What conventions of the stage can you find in this scene?
2. What ideas about love and life does each character embody?
3. How might two actors give different interpretations of the title role?
4. What actors would you cast in a production of this play?

Write About . . .

Based on this scene, do you think that *Cyrano de Bergerac* is a comedy, a tragedy, or a modern mixture of the two forms? Write a brief essay in which you explain your answer, and identify the dramatic elements that contribute to your classification. Try to use at least two of the Academic Vocabulary words in your essay.

Writing Focus

Think as a Reader/Writer

Find It In Your Reading You will read a tragedy and a comedy in Collection 8. The Writing Focus activities on the Preparing to Read pages will help you identify the dramatic tools that each writer uses. The Applying Your Skills pages will help you use these tools in your own writing.

Academic Vocabulary for Collection 8

Talking and Writing About Drama

Academic Vocabulary is the language you use to write and talk about literature. Use these words to discuss the plays you read in this collection. The words are underlined throughout the collection.

convention (kuhn VEHN shuhn) *n.:* standard technique. *The aside is a theatrical convention—we know the other characters are not supposed to hear it.*

embody (ehm BAHD ee) *v.:* give form to something abstract. *Cyrano's nose embodies feelings many have about being ugly.*

interpretation (ihn tur pruh TAY shuhn) *n.:* portrayal that conveys a particular understanding of a work. *From the actor's interpretation, it is clear he thinks that Christian is not very smart.*

production (pruh DUHK shuhn) *n.:* presentation of a play; performance. *The production is updated to take place in Los Angeles.*

Your Turn

Write a review of a play, movie, or TV show in your *Reader/Writer Notebook*. Use each Academic Vocabulary word at least once.

COMEDY

Preparing to Read

The Frog Prince

by **David Mamet**

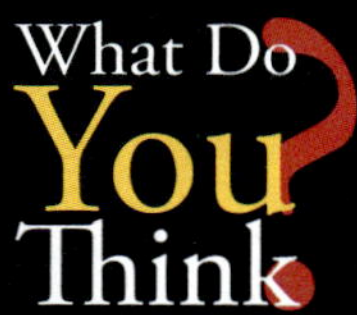

What are the characteristics of true love?

QuickTalk

Think about movies, television shows, or stories in which characters face conflicts over love. What distinguishes true love from false love in these works? Discuss your observations with the class.

Reader/Writer Notebook

Use your **RWN** to complete the activities for this selection.

9.R.2.C.1.d Use details from text(s): to evaluate the effect of author's style **9.R.1.G.1.e** During reading, utilize strategies: to visualize **9.R.1.G.1.d** During reading, utilize strategies: to infer

Literary Focus

Comedy A **comedy** is a play that ends happily and makes us laugh along the way. However, a good comedy shows us something true about life—something that may not be funny at all. **Conflict** is at the heart of comedies; the characters confront obstacles and often a series of complications as well. In traditional comedies, the flawed central characters learn from their mistakes, and order is restored in the end.

Literary Perspectives Use the literary perspective described on page 777 as you read this play.

Reading Focus

Reading a Play When you read a short story, you usually rely on the narrator to provide information about the plot. When you read a play, plot information is provided by the dialogue and stage directions. The dialogue and stage directions will help you to **visualize** the action and **make inferences,** or educated guesses, about the play.

Into Action Use a chart to record details from the dialogue or stage directions. Then, record your inferences and visualizations.

Details from the Play	My Inferences / Visualizations
Prince: walking in woods, holding bouquet; Servingman: picking flowers	I can infer that the prince is a romantic because he is holding flowers.

Writing Focus

Think as a Reader/Writer

Find It in Your Reading Dialogue is a convention that playwrights use to move the plot forward and to tell the audience about their characters. What characters say—and don't say—as well as how they say it can provide clues about the characters. In your *Reader/Writer Notebook,* record your observations about what the dialogue suggests about each character.

Vocabulary

zeal (zeel) *n.:* great enthusiasm or devotion to an ideal or goal. *The servingman carries out his duties with zeal.*

susceptible (suh SEHP tuh buhl) *adj.:* easily affected or influenced. *The peasant woman is not susceptible to threats.*

malevolent (muh LEHV uh luhnt) *adj.:* evil; harmful. *The new king and queen issue malevolent rules.*

vile (vyl) *adj.:* disgusting; offensive. *The prince accuses the milkmaid of thinking he is vile.*

exuberance (ehg ZOO buhr uhns) *n.:* overflowing joy or enthusiasm. *The prince is filled with exuberance when he speaks of marrying the Fair Patricia.*

Language Coach

Denotations and Connotations A word has two kinds of meanings: The **denotation** is the definition; the **connotation** is the associations or feelings a word evokes, either positive or negative. Read the definitions of the words above and sort the words into two lists: one list of words with positive connotations and one list of words with negative connotations.

Positive Connotations	or	Negative Connotations
zeal		

Learn It Online
Develop your vocabulary with Word Watch:
go.hrw.com L9-775 Go

MEET THE WRITER

David Mamet

(1947–   )

A Comic Flair

David Mamet, who grew up in Chicago, Illinois, and his best friend from college had a running gag. Whenever one of them was picking up the other at the airport, he would dress in disguise to see if his friend could spot him in the crowd. A "master of disguises," Mamet is known for playing practical jokes.

An Essential Art

Mamet has written novels, essays, and children's books, but his greatest achievements have been as a playwright and screenwriter. The themes that run through Mamet's works include loyalty and betrayal, the success and failure of the American dream, and the need to speak the truth. His works are characterized by the distinct style of his dialogue—created by rhythmic, clipped, overlapping lines—which some call "Mamet-speak."

"In our interaction in our daily lives we tell stories to each other, we gossip, we complain. . . . These are means of defining what our life is. The theater is a way of doing it continually, of sharing that experience, and it's absolutely essential."

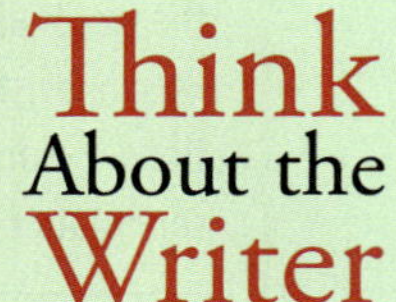

How do you think drama can serve as a way of "defining what our life is"?

Build Background

Across cultures and across the centuries, people have told stories about frogs that turn into princes and princes that turn into frogs. In the early 1800s in Germany, the Grimm brothers published two versions of such a tale, "The Frog King" and "The Frog Prince." Folk tales from Vietnam, China, and Sri Lanka feature enchanted frogs as well. Contemporary writers, such as David Mamet, have created their own interpretations of these age-old stories.

Preview the Selection

The main character in this play is a **prince** with a problem of royal proportions. His trusty **servingman** stays by his side. Will the **milkmaid** provide the solution to his problem?

Read with a Purpose Read this play to explore the extraordinary changes the prince undergoes.

The Frog Prince

by **David Mamet**

CHARACTERS	
The Prince	**The Witch**
A Servingman	**A Milkmaid**

Scene 1

Summer. The PRINCE, *gaily attired in a Court Uniform, and his* SERVINGMAN *are walking through the Wood gathering flowers. The* PRINCE *holds a bouquet. The* SERVINGMAN *hurries about engaged in the actual picking of the flowers.*

Prince. Huh. I don't think I've ever been in this part of the Forest before. (*Pause*) It's nice . . .

Servingman. Yes, it is, Sire.

Prince. And what a *day,* huh . . . ?

Servingman. Absolutely, Sire.

Prince. A *day* . . . a *day* . . .

Servingman. . . . an exceptional day.

Prince. Yes. An exceptional day. And a *portentous* day. Enough said about that! You know what I want? A blue flower. Something blue. A touch of blue. I want to tell you something, Bill: what we *need,* what we *need* in life (and *art* is a part of life—and flower arrangement is a part of art—the Japanese have a word for it. Which I've forgotten. It's a two-syllable word. Something like "Kamooka"[1]—a long discipline intended, no doubt, to get you in touch with yourself . . .) What you need in *art,* and what you need in a *bouquet,* in short, is what you need in *life.*

Servingman. And what is that, Sire . . . ?

Prince. Thank you. *Contrast.* Eh? Contrast and balance. Call it Fire and Water. Call it, I don't know, call it *thrust* and equilibrium . . . whatever you call it. You need both of 'em. You need 'em both.

1. **"Kamooka":** The Japanese art of flower arrangement is called *ikebana.*

Literary Perspectives

Analyzing Archetypes In literature, **archetypes** are recurring patterns found in works from different cultures and time periods. They can be plots or events (the heroic journey), settings (the dark forest), characters (the trickster), themes (love at first sight), or objects or things (a magic potion). Archetypes point to the universal nature of people's desires, concerns, and beliefs throughout the ages. As you read this play, note how the playwright puts a twist on some common archetypes. As you read, be sure to notice the notes and questions at the bottom of the pages, which will guide you in using this perspective.

The prince and the servingman in the forest.

Servingman (*Handing him his blue flower*): Your blue flower, Sire.
Prince. . . . who knew this stuff just grew wild . . .
Servingman. . . . for the Fair Patricia . . .
Prince. . . . I mean of course we all know they grow wild. How *else* would they grow . . . ? It's just, you know, you get them at the *florist's,* it's *one* thing. It's a mercantile transaction. You pick 'em out *here* and it's so *personal.*

[*Pause*]

Servingman. It is, Sire.
Prince. And you know what *else*? I want to tell you something, Bill: It has an element of *fear* in it. Don't you feel that?
Servingman. I do.
Prince. Hey, you're a cheap date. You know that? But it *does* nonetheless . . . snuffing out a *life* . . . I mean, these things are *breeding* out here. Who knows *why* . . . ? It's awesome. (*Pause*) Huh? They're so *promiscuous* . . . all the time . . . *who* knows why? Who knows to what purpose they're put here, all the time, feast and famine, liberal, conservative, *they* don't care. They don't care. You know why they don't?
Servingman. Why, Sire?
Prince. 'Cause they're in tune with *Nature.*

[*An* OLD PEASANT WOMAN *walks through the forest near them.*]

Ah! An Old Peasant Woman! Gathering . . . who knows what, huh? Some . . . some *plants* for some herbal *remedy* . . . some, some long lost wisdom, I don't know . . . to cure an aching *tooth,* who knows, some *daffodils* to grace her grandson's *nuptial* bed . . . huh?

Servingman. Yes, Sire.

Prince. . . . for the upcoming day of his Happy Marriage. Just as in *whose* case . . . ? *Exactly.* So you see what's on *my* mind. (*He expatiates*[2] *on the bouquet he holds.*) A bouquet for my sweet Patricia. Flowers. Picked by Hand. Out of love. For you, My Fair Patricia. (*Pause*) May we . . . may we in our Married State be closely bound as the *buds* are in this bouquet: Individual, separate, each having its *own* life, and its own destiny . . . but each *united* into something *larger* than itself. By God, I *like* that. I'm going to tell her that when I give her these flowers. You got a pencil . . . ? I swear, walking outside brings out the best in you. **A**

[*The* SERVINGMAN *hands the* PRINCE *a pencil. The* PRINCE *starts writing down his encomium.*[3]]

I think it's something like a carburetor: You got to get the air in you to burn the fuel correctly.

Servingman. Sire—

Prince. What?

Servingman. Would Your Highness like someone to gather daffodils to grace Your Highness' Nuptial Sheets?

Prince. Yes, I would, Bill. I would. But it would have either to be a spontaneous *gesture,* eh? Arising out of an *impulse,* eh? *Unheralded* on someone's part . . . an, let's say, an *artistic impulse,* a spontaneous impulse on the part—excuse me here—but it would of necessity need be someone of my own *class,* don't you think? Or it would be puhrutty pre*sump*tive, don't you think? *Or, or* . . . see what I'm saying, if someone in my own class, through an excess of *zeal* got thrown back to some, some atavistic *thing. Or, or* it would have to be, say, if it were a *ritual* the *peasants* had. Do you know what I mean—which ones are the daffodils?

[BILL *shows him.*]

They're nice. I like them. Yes. If it were an old *ritual,* and, gosh, I don't know . . . if the *peasants,* out of *joy* at the Plighting of my Troth[4] (whatever *that* may mean . . .) eh? To The Fair Patricia, out of jubilation at the uniting of our Kingdoms, and the implied *peace,* good *humor* and *prosperity,* so on, that that may bring; if they dug deep into their past and came up with this custom *just for us.* To make us feel a *part* of things . . . what do you think? Or out of raptures at her beauty. They could do that. That could happen.

Servingman. Sire; The Fair Patricia is possessed of beauty bordering on the Ideal . . . the more so for that it shines from within.

Prince. Yeah. And she's a good kid, too. Don't you think?

Servingman. Yes. I do, Sire.

Prince. No. Tell me seriously.

Servingman. No, I do.

Prince. You aren't just *saying* that . . . ? I mean, *you're* gonna have to live with her, too. (*Pause*) Bill . . . ? Well, *I* think she's exceptional. What do the *People* think?

2. **expatiates** (ehk SPAY shee ayts): speaks about in detail.
3. **encomium** (ehn KOH mee uhm): formal expression of praise.
4. **plighting of my troth:** promising to marry; becoming engaged.

A Literary Perspectives Analyzing Archetypes Does this prince seem like the archetypal royalty you have encountered before in other tales? Explain.

Vocabulary **zeal** (zeel) *n.:* great enthusiasm or devotion to an ideal or goal.

Servingman. They love her as yourself.

Prince. They love her as myself, they do?

Servingman. They've taken her *completely* to their hearts.

Prince. Yeah? I couldn't get an honest opinion out of you with a Smith and Wesson . . . just kidding. You're a pal, and I appreciate it. (*The* PEASANT WOMAN *walks near to them.*) Madam! (What do they say . . . ?) Mother! Good Mother . . . (*To* BILL) Oh! Oh! Oh! I got it! I got it! You don't know me. You don't know me. Okay . . . ? (*To* PEASANT WOMAN) Hola, Good Mother! And how doth the day find you? And what a *lovely* day it is! (*Pause*) I'm but a traveler from Across the Forest who's come here seeking to ply his trade and better his lot. What news is hereabouts? (*Pause*) What occurrences of note? (*Pause*) What's in the air, if you get my drift? Uh . . . rumors of the *Court* . . . ? (*Pause*) Royal *Marriages* . . . That sort of thing . . . didn't I hear the *Prince* was getting married? Which, as we all know, must needs affect us all . . . What sort of a guy is he? And how do the countryfolk take to his fiancée, who I have heard is called the Fair Patricia . . . ? **B**

Peasant. Are those flowers for me?

Prince. Um, *no.*

Peasant. But you have picked them in my field.

Prince. I have?

Peasant. Yes.

Prince. Well. Okay. It's actually not *your* field. It's part of the boundary of the Royal Wood, but if you feel I've trespassed on some *land* you, by "usage," have come to view as *yours,* I understand.

Peasant. Are they for me?

Prince. No. I've *told* you.

Peasant (*pause*). Who are they for?

Prince. A friend of mine, what's it to you?

Peasant. I want them.

Prince. Tough.

Peasant. Give them to me.

[*Pause*]

Prince (*to* SERVINGMAN). *She's* a rare old bird— (*To* PEASANT) Well, you know, I *would* give 'em to you, I would, but I made a *promise* over them. I, I made a sort of, they're for someone *close* to me. I made a sort of a little *prayer* over them. Now, if you like, my friend will *pick* you some? Would you like that? Bill . . . ? (*To* PEASANT) How is that?

Peasant. Those flowers must be an offering.

Prince. Well, they are, sort of.

Peasant. For me.

Prince. No, I can't do that. I've told you that. Bill! Give the Good Woman a coin. (*To* PEASANT) Go buy something nice.

Peasant. Those flowers you must offer me, or you will dwell in misery.

Servingman. See here: You have just broken the law. You have Threatened and Insulted . . .

Prince. It's okay. Bill, Bill . . . Alright. (*To* PEASANT) Look. Look here: I've been kind of joking around. *Actually* I'm the Prince. It's alright. I'm not mad at you. I picked the flowers for my Betrothed. The Fair Patricia. Alright? And I said a sort of silly little *prayer* over them that the F.P. and I would be happy. (*Pause*) Now would you *really* want me to go and give these flowers to

---

B **Reading Focus** **Reading a Play** The stage directions indicate that the prince directs the lines "I got it! You don't know me. You don't know me. Okay . . . ?" to Bill. Explain these lines. What is the prince planning to do?

someone else? Now? Knowing who they're for? (*To* SERVINGMAN) Give her the money . . .

Peasant. Those flowers you must offer me, or you will dwell in misery.

Prince. Okay, now that's not funny anymore. I'm understandably all *full* of things these days and I'm very *suggestible* and susceptible. Alright? To all sorts of malevolent *influences* and *suggestions* so you just take back what you said. Okay? I'm not *giving* you the flowers, and unless you retract your curse I'm going to throw your tush in jail. Can I make it more clear than that? (*Pause*) Eh? (*Pause*) Alright! Well, that's fine! No? (*Pause*) Bill? I think that I've had enough fresh *air* today . . . when we get back I want her taken *care* of. Get it? In fact, you hurry back and tell the Captain of the Guard I got an *errand* for him. He'll know what I mean. (*The* PRINCE *starts off with the* SERVINGMAN. *Sotto*[5]) Just kidding. Thought I'd throw a little *scare* into her. (*To* PEASANT) And one last thought I'd like to leave you with: *Monarchy* . . . **C**

Those Flowers you must offer me, or you will dwell in Misery.

Peasant. Those Flowers you must offer me, or you will dwell in Misery.

Prince. You're pushing your luck, Babe. (*Pause*) You really are, and you just wait 'til these big *brawny* types get down here with their *pickaxes,* you're gonna be whistlin' a different *tune.* You see there's such a thing as *civility* . . .

Peasant. Those flowers . . .

Prince. I'm not going to *give* you the flowers . . .

5. **sotto:** shortened form of *sotto voce,* meaning "to speak in soft or low tones, in order to avoid being overheard."

[*A big flash; the* PRINCE *is changed into a frog.*]

Peasant. You shall remain in this vile form until a pure and honest woman of her own free will shall plant a selfless kiss upon your lips. At that time you shall be restored, but should you tell her of your former state you shall remain a frog forever. Sic Transit Gloria Mundi.[6] You should never have come into my part of the forest.

Scene 2

Fall. The PRINCE (*now a frog*) *and a* MILKMAID.

Prince. I really appreciate your spending this time with me.

Milkmaid. I like you.

Prince. Well, I like you, too, as a matter of fact I like you a lot. I like you more the more I *see* you and you tend to *grow* on me. I think you're smart. I think you're smart and pretty, now what do you think about that—are you susceptible to flattery? (*Pause*) I know, we all are, everybody likes to be told nice things about themselves, you know what *else* I like about you. You're *generous.* That's something in today's world. Isn't it? It's a *lot:* I think it's rather a *lot.* Not to be . . . *judgmental,* not to be "stuck-*up*". . . to say, "however 'lowly' someone is, I'm going to see the *good* in them." *You* do that, and I think it's admirable. (*Pause*) I do. **D**

6. **Sic transit gloria mundi.:** Latin for "Thus passes away the glory of the world," meaning that worldly things are not lasting.

C **Literary Perspectives** **Analyzing Archetypes** What familiar literary pattern does the peasant fit?

D **Reading Focus** **Reading a Play** What do you infer has happened between the end of Scene 1 and the beginning of Scene 2? Why has the prince been spending time with the milkmaid?

Vocabulary **susceptible** (suh SEHP tuh buhl) *adj.:* easily affected or influenced.
malevolent (muh LEHV uh luhnt) *adj.:* evil; harmful.
vile (vyl) *adj.:* disgusting; offensive.

Milkmaid. You're funny.
Prince. Ah, gedouddahere . . .
Milkmaid. No, you *are.*
Prince. Well, *thank* you.
Milkmaid. You say funny things.
Prince (*pause*). Gee, you're swell.
Milkmaid. You always *flatter* me . . .
Prince. It's just the truth. It's nothing but the *truth,* here you are, *working* every day, working so *hard,* carrying *milk* the whole time . . . uh, carrying *hay,* you look so *pretty* working in the Sun . . . I see you walking *by* . . . you *do* something to me, and Grace . . . can I call you Grace?
Milkmaid. Yes.
Prince. *Grace,* you *do* something to me. Every day I see you going past a *feeling* has grown in my breast, and, Grace, I want to ask you something . . .
Milkmaid. What?
Prince (*sotto*). Okay, here it goes. I choose and elect this woman. And if she will give me all her selfless Love as evidenced by the physical evidence of her giving me a kiss I will be Free. And I choose her. (*To the* MILKMAID) Grace: I'd like to give you a kiss. Would you give me a kiss? (*Pause*) Grace . . . ? Would you do that?

[*Mourning bells sound.*]

Milkmaid. Aren't those bells sad . . . ?
Prince. Did you hear what I said . . . ?
Milkmaid. What? I'm sorry? Wait, I, when I hear those bells, I'm so . . . I suppose that we all have to die. (*Pause*) And I suppose it's good to be reminded of it. But it makes me sad. They say he was a good man. (*Pause*) Who's to know? It's hard to know what Great people are, if they're real at all. What qualities they have. I'll tell you what I know. It's sad he died when he was going to wed. (*Pause*) Life is such a mystery. What do you think happened to him? **E**

[*Pause*]

Prince. I don't know what you mean.
Milkmaid. The *Prince.* Our Prince who disappeared on his *Wedding* day.
Prince. What happened to him?
Milkmaid. Yes.
Prince. I'm sure that I don't know.
Milkmaid. Maybe it's better. (*Pause*) Maybe it is. Gone two months and his fiancée is marrying his cousin. (*Pause*) Life is so strange. I'm sure we love the trials of the Great in that they save us from experiencing them ourselves. (*Pause*) I suppose that we think they're *more* than, us. They can *bear* them. (*Pause*) That they are *stronger,* or *better* (*pause*) or *worse* . . . (*Sighs*) I'll tell you what I think, though.

[*Pause*]

Prince. And what is that?
Milkmaid. It's *wrong* to hold a funeral for him today and for his fiancée to wed tomorrow. (*Pause*) I don't think that that's right.
Prince. You don't?
Milkmaid. Even if she did not love him. (*Pause*) She could be true to his memory. (*Pause*) Or she could show respect by being true to the appearance. (*Pause*) That's what I think. My father says she's doing it to keep the fortune. His cousin inherits today and tomorrow she will wed. I pity the new prince. I do. Life is so tenuous.

E **Reading Focus** **Reading a Play** What can you infer about the relationship between the milkmaid and the prince?

You can't buy loyalty. It's so good to be loved for yourself. That's something that cannot fade. F

Prince. I, look, look, look, I want you to . . . Will you give me a kiss, I really want to kiss you, would you do that?

Milkmaid. Oh, I couldn't.

[*Pause*]

Prince. You're disgusted, fine. I disgusted you. All you are is fine talk, when it comes down to *cases* you only care what's on the outside.

[*Pause*]

Milkmaid. I hurt you.

Prince. Huh . . .

Milkmaid. I'm sorry. No. Please understand.

Prince. I understand *completely,* you're like all the rest.

Milkmaid. I could only kiss a man I was pledged to marry.

Prince. Will you marry me?

Milkmaid. You're speaking so hastily.

Prince. No, I'm not. I mean it. I will *marry* you. I mean it. I've . . . from my soul . . . now. We'll get married today. I'll take care of you. You won't regret it, I promise you. Someday you're going to look back and remember I said this to you. Will you be mine?

[*Pause*]

Milkmaid. I am deeply touched.

Prince. Yeah. You aren't touched. I *know* this preamble. You're *hurt.* You're *appalled,* that I would *presume* on our *acquaintance* . . . a mere . . .

Milkmaid. I am *touched.* I never will forget this moment. (*Pause*) I never will forget it.

[*Pause*]

Prince. You could learn to love me.

Milkmaid. I love another.

Prince. . . . I have many qualities, and you bring them out *in* me, that *no* one has seen. I could *learn* from you, and you could learn to love *me* . . .

Milkmaid. I love another. G

[*Pause*]

Prince. I'm sorry . . . ?

[*Pause*]

Milkmaid. I love another.

Prince. Oh. (*Pause*) Oh. (*Pause*) Oh. (*Pause*) Fine. That's fine. Getting there a little after the barn *door* was open, all the *horses* left, I'm shutting up to close the *door.* Ha. Ha.

[*Pause*]

Milkmaid. . . . you're hurt.

Prince. "You love another . . ." never mentioned *that* . . . some *other* guy . . . well, why don't you go marry *him,* then, if you're so "in love" the whole time. Why don't you do *that* . . . ?

Milkmaid. We have no money. (*Pause*) I'm going to go. I want to see the Prince's Funeral.

Prince. Oh, whattaya going to see his "body"? They don't even *have* a body . . . they don't have anything, just a bunch of cheap sentiment,

---

F **Literary Focus** **Comedy** What have you learned from the milkmaid's speech about the conflict the prince faces?

G **Literary Focus** **Comedy** What new complication has been introduced?

cheap, tawdry, false emotions. Well, maybe that's where you belong . . .

Milkmaid. You're hurt.

Prince. No, I'm not hurt.

Milkmaid. We'll still be friends.

Prince. Oh. We will.

Milkmaid. This was hard for you. I'll always remember that you asked.

Prince. Swell. Tell your boyfriend, too. I'm sure that he'll be touched.

Milkmaid. I'll see you tomorrow.

Prince. Wait. Wait a second. Wait. Hold on. You can't get married 'cause, you have no money.

[*Pause*]

Milkmaid. No.

Prince. If you *had,* if you could *find* the money you'd get married.

Milkmaid. Yes.

Prince. Okay now, okay now, okay, now, *great.* If someone could—what is it you need, a *dowry,*[7] something like that . . . ? How much do you need?

Milkmaid. Twenty-five Gold Coins.

Prince. Twenty-five Gold Coins, great . . .

Milkmaid. . . . to buy my fiancé out of his apprenticeship.[8]

Prince. Yeah. Yeah. Fine. If someone could *help* you to marry, if someone could *find* you that money, I don't mean to sound *crass,* but if someone *got* you that money, what would you *do* for that guy?

Milkmaid. I'd be eternally in his debt.

Prince. That's good enough for me. Okay! Go on, I'm not going to hold you up, you run along. I don't want you to worry about a thing.

Milkmaid. Oh, I'm not worried.

Prince. You aren't?

Milkmaid. No. I think that Love will find a Way. (*Pause*) See you tomorrow!

Prince. You bet your boots you will.

[PRINCE *whistles;* SERVINGMAN *appears; pause*]

Servingman. Sire? (*Pause*) Sire . . . ? Did she . . .

[*Pause*]

Prince. What? Oh. No. No go. Not at all. She won't go for it.

Servingman. But did Your Highness elect her the one who must bestow the kiss?

Prince. Yes. Yes. I did. (*Pause*) We're committed. (*Pause*) We're in it, now . . . We're in a little bit of a *quandary*[9] (*pause*), but I think I can pull it out.

Servingman. Sire: if we don't pull it out by tomorrow you will be pronounced dead, your fortune will devolve on your Cousin Charles, he will marry the Fair Patricia . . .

Prince. . . . and I'll be Broke and Friendless the rest of my life, yeah, I'm *talking* about fixing it before tomorrow, I'm talking about fixing it right *now,* can you believe the gall of this broad, dead two months, dead two months, dead two months, not *even* dead, what am I *talking* about, I'm right *here* . . . and she's marrying someone else.

[*Pause*]

Servingman. It must be very difficult for you.

[*Pause*]

Prince. Yeah. Yeah. (*Pause*) We're going to pull this one off yet. Here's what I want you to do.

7. **dowry** (DOW ree): money or property a woman brings to her husband when they marry.

8. **apprenticeship** (uh PREHN tihs shihp): legal agreement dictating that a person will work for a given amount of time in exchange for being trained in a craft or trade.

9. **quandary** (KWAHN dree): confusing, difficult situation.

Go to the Palace. Alright? In the *library* of my *study* on the top *shelf* facing the *windows* there's a Big Blue Book. Alright? It's hollow. Now. We got a little *getaway* money in there, so be careful bringing it back. That was needless. I'm sorry. I know that you'd be careful. (*Pause*) Bring it back, *tonight* we'll go to the *milkmaid's* house, we'll give her a dowry she'll never forget, she'll kiss me out of gratitude, we hop on back to the Castle, put the kibosh on[10] this whole affair, I save my *fortune,* put the Fair Patricia on a *bus* (you best believe it) and it's *business* as *usual* back at the Old Stand. *Okay.* Let's *do* it. **H**

Servingman. I'm on my way, Sire.

Prince. And, hey, and how would you like to be the *Earl* of somewhere . . .

[*Pause*]

Servingman. I . . .

Prince. Let's not count our chickens, all I want to tell you, it hasn't gone unnoticed what you've done for me.

Servingman. I . . .

Prince. We'll celebrate later. Okay, you better hit the bricks.

Servingman (*exiting*). Your Servant, Sire . . .

Prince. . . . I mean, you can't go around feeling *sorry* for yourself the whole time. The Going Gets Tough, The Tough Get Going. (*Pause*) Now I've stopped *moping* and we're gonna set a couple of things *straight* around this place.

10. **put the kibosh on:** slang for "put an end to."

> Dead two months, not *even* dead, what am I *talking* about, I'm right *here* . . . and she's marrying someone else.

Scene 3

Winter. The SERVINGMAN (*in rags*) *and the* PRINCE (*as a frog*) *sitting around a campfire.* The PRINCE *reading a newspaper . . .* **I**

Prince. Here's a good one. Woman about five miles from here arrested for not paying the Milk Tax. Five years in prison. " 'What will Happen to my Babes' Mom says." Well, that's the Fair Patricia for you . . .

Servingman. Yes, Sire . . .

Prince. Anything for a laugh. You warm enough?

Servingman. Yes. Thank you, Sire.

Prince. "Worst winter in 200 years" well, these things always seem to coincide. Don't you think? Hard times and Hard Weather? (*Pause*) You know what I think? I think it's sunspots. That's what I think it is. (*Pause*) You doing okay? Bill . . . ? You okay? I know it's easier for me. I don't eat much. I have cold blood. You got to keep *warm,* and you need a little *protein* once in a while.

Servingman. I'm okay, Sire.

Prince. Here's a good one, "Her Radiance the Fair Patricia and Prince Charles off for extended Foreign Tour. Thousands Cheer." And I don't blame them. Good Riddance to Bad Rubbish. Oh. Here's a happy note! "Parliament endorses emergency Discretionary Powers for Bailiffs." (*Sighs*) Whaddaya know about that . . . (*The* PRINCE *looks up from his paper.*) Yep. Looks like they're

H **Reading Focus** **Reading a Play** What do you visualize the prince doing as he makes his plans?

I **Reading Focus** **Reading a Play** Note what the stage directions tell you about the prince and servingman as well as the passage of time. What can you infer has happened between the end of Scene 2 and the beginning of Scene 3?

gonna make the *trains* run on time. You okay, Bill . . . ?

Servingman. Yes, Sire.

Prince. You don't look well.

Servingman. I'm fine, Sire.

Prince. You got a fever?

Servingman. No, Sire. Not at all.

Prince. Hey, look, Bill, I've been thinking, you don't have to call me "Sire" anymore. (*Pause*) Okay? (*Pause*) I mean, these are new times, we have to change with them.

Servingman. The old times will return, Sire.

Prince. Somehow I don't think so.

Servingman. I've never ceased to hope.

Prince. Well, Hope is a wonderful thing, but *reasonably* they've changed the locks on us at the Palace, Fair Patricia's issued a dictum[11] anyone *resembling* The Late Prince was to be shot on sight for defamation[12] of my sainted memory—*she* don't fool around—it's a crime to be seen wearing my *emblem,* and she's got the whole place pretty well cowtied. It looks like Under New Management. That's what *I'd* say. J

[*Pause*]

Servingman. I've never ceased to hope.

Prince. Well, you hope, but keep it silent, cause if you hope out *loud* it's El Biggo Sleepo, if you follow me, and I'd rather have you around.

Servingman. Thank you, Sire.

Prince. No, it is I who thank *you,* Bill. (*Pause*) It's I who am in your debt constantly and I am never not mindful of that. You've cared for and protected me with everything at your disposal, and the only coin with which I can repay you is my constant thanks. (*Pause*) Thank you.

[*Pause*]

Servingman. Sire! Here she comes!

Prince. And *someday,* I'm gonna get that broad to *kiss* me, and then we're going to saddle up and *blow* this joint, and go down somewhere

11. **dictum** (DIHK tuhm): formal, authoritative statement.
12. **defamation** (dehf uh MAY shuhn): damaging the honor of.

J **Literary Perspectives** **Analyzing Archetypes** At this point in the play, is the plot following an archetypal pattern? Explain.

The prince, as a frog, reading the news of the kingdom.

warm! (MILKMAID *enters.*) . . . and we're gonna start a *shoe store* or something. (*To* MILKMAID) Hi! (*Pause; to* SERVINGMAN) She doesn't look so good today. (*To* MILKMAID) Hi! Kiddo! Hi! How are you, why don't you sit *down* a spell. Hey, Grace . . . (*To* SERVINGMAN) Get her a *log* or something . . . (SERVINGMAN *does so. She sits.*) *That's* better! (*To* SERVINGMAN) What have we got to eat? (*To* MILKMAID) You look pale as a sheet . . . (SERVINGMAN *brings broth.*) Some *broth* . . . ? You want some nice *broth* . . . ? (*They feed her.*) Yeesssss. *That's* better . . . ! *That's* better . . . ! Yesssssss. Now: what's the *matter* with you, letting yourself get so run *down* and all . . . ! And how come we don't *see* you anymore . . . you alright? You okay . . . ?

Milkmaid. They took everything.

Prince. Who took everything?

Milkmaid. The Bailiff.

Prince. What did they take? What?

Milkmaid. My fiancé . . .

Prince. . . . yes?

Milkmaid. Could I have some more broth . . . ?

Servingman (*serving her*). My pleasure.

Milkmaid. Thank you. (*Pause*) Thank you. My fiancé made a remark against The Fair Patricia. (*Pause*) He was turned in. They took his farm. They came to my farm and they took my cow.

Prince. They took your cow?

Milkmaid. And, yes, and they, he's gone. They put a price on his head. Fifty Golden Coins. Dead or Alive.

Prince. Where is he gone?

Milkmaid. Gone away. He left the country in the night. He left me a note. (*Hands note to the* PRINCE)

Prince (*reads*). "Don't worry."

Milkmaid. . . . and they took my cow.

Prince. Who took your cow . . . ?

Milkmaid. I'm basically not a political person . . . I'm going to town to plead my case before The Fair Patricia . . .

Prince. . . . she's out of town . . .

Servingman. Why did they take your cow?

Milkmaid. They said that I was an Accessory.[13]

Prince. What is it that your boyfriend said that got them so ticked off?

13. **accessory** (ak SEHS uhr ee): person who helps a criminal, but who is not present when the crime is committed.

Milkmaid. Someone was talking about The Fair Patricia and he said "Handsome is as Handsome Does." I'm going to ask them for my cow back. Do you think that's disloyal to him . . . ?

Prince. No. And I don't think it's gonna get you your *cow* back, either. As a matter of fact, I wouldn't go in there at all.

Milkmaid. . . . I have to eat . . .

Prince. They're going to ask you where he is.

Milkmaid. I won't tell them.

Prince. You won't tell them . . . you *know* where he is?

Milkmaid. No.

[*Pause*]

Prince. Somehow I don't believe you.

Milkmaid. I won't *tell* them, though. I'll say I don't know where he is. How will they know?

Prince. You've got a face like a transparent book, for starters. This is no good.

Milkmaid. It wasn't right of them to take my cow.

Prince. It certainly was not.

Milkmaid. What *right* do they have?

Prince. Only force.

Milkmaid. Isn't there any *law* anymore . . . ? K

[SERVINGMAN *produces a golden sword from under his ragged cloak.*]

Prince. What's that?

[*Pause*]

Milkmaid. Is that *gold* . . . ?

Prince. Yeah. It's gold. But what is it *doing* here, if you get my meaning, when everything *like* it should have been buried *months* ago . . .

Servingman. This is my sword.

Prince. Now, Bill, don't be silly, how could that be *your* sword? When it's festooned all over with the blazonments[14] of Our Late Prince, the ownership of which emblem is *Death*? I'm sure you must have *found* it somewhere, and are going to *bury* it. Immediately . . .

Milkmaid. . . . how did you get that sword?

Well, these are hard times, and I think he feels that we all have to stick together.

Servingman. I'm taking it to town.

Prince. Now, that's the dumbest thing I ever heard . . . why would someone unless he didn't want to live anymore *do* a thing like that?

Servingman. I'm taking it to the Goldsmith to be melted down, and with the proceeds[15] I am buying this Young Lady food. In fact I'm buying her a *cow* . . . and some new *clothes* . . .

Milkmaid. No, you can't do that, if they catch you on the *road* with it . . .

Prince. . . . have you been carrying that thing the whole time?

Servingman. It has been my Great honor to.

Milkmaid. No, you can't do that. Thank you, no. It's much too dangerous . . .

Servingman. Farewell.

Prince. I forbid you to go.

Servingman. In what capacity?

14. **festooned . . . blazonments:** decorated with emblems or coats of arms.

15. **proceeds** (PROH seedz): money gained from a business transaction.

K **Literary Focus Comedy** How has the mood, or the overall feeling, of the play changed in this scene?

[*Pause*]

Prince. As your *friend* . . .
Servingman. And as your friend I beg your understanding for my so precipitous departure. Farewell. [*He exits; pause*]
Milkmaid. I can't believe he's doing that for me. (*Pause*) I can't believe he's doing this.
Prince. Well, these are hard times, and I think he feels that we all have to stick together.
Milkmaid. Your friend is a very good man.
Prince. Yes. He is.
Milkmaid. What will we do if he doesn't come back?
Prince. I don't know.
Milkmaid. He's got a lot of Pride, hasn't he?
Prince. Yes. He has.
Milkmaid. Is that a good thing?
Prince. I don't know. (*Pause*)

Scene 4

Spring. The PRINCE (*as a frog*) *is gathering flowers. He holds a bouquet.*

Prince.
A Blue Flower's best for Spring.
A Blue Flower's best for Spring,
When Ground is raw. (*Pause*)
Red is the Color of Lust . . .
(*To himself*) Well, that's true. Can blue be the Color of Lust? No, I don't think so. Perhaps some perverted blue, some *violet* midnight blue . . . some *midnight* blue, perhaps, it probably depends a great deal on what *surrounds* it. (*Pause*) Bill—I wish you were around to hear this. 'Cause I think you would appreciate it. (*He goes over to his journal and writes in it.*)
"A Blue Flower's Best for Spring,
When Ground is raw . . .
Red is the Color of Lust . . ."

[*The* MILKMAID *appears, watches him*]

"Red is the Color of Lust . . . of Saline life, of blood . . ." well, we know red is the color of blood . . . that's not very good . . . What other flowers do we have around here? (*He turns; sees* MILKMAID) **L**
Milkmaid. Hello.
Prince. Oh, Hi! Oh, wait a minute, will you . . . "Red is the Color of Lust, of Saline Life . . . of Arrogance and Sloth; but *Blue* . . ."
Milkmaid. . . . are you writing a poem . . . ?
Prince. . . . hold on a second . . . "*Red* is the color of pride, and *blue* of loyalty." (*Pause*) Um . . .

[*Pause*]

Milkmaid. . . . did I break your train of thought?
Prince. It's alright. (*Pause*) It's alright. How are you? I'm sorry. My mind was somewhere else for a second. How are you? I haven't seen you in a while.
Milkmaid. No.
Prince. What have you been doing?
Milkmaid. I've been trying to farm.
Prince. You have.
Milkmaid. Yes. I was getting the farm ready for planting.
Prince. But they took your horse.
Milkmaid. I laid out a small patch behind the hut. (*Pause*) How have you been?
Prince. I been okay. I was, you know, I was unwell for a time there . . .
Milkmaid. Yes, I know . . .
Prince. . . . since my . . .

L **Reading Focus** **Reading a Play** What can you infer has happened to Bill?

Analyzing Visuals **Viewing and Interpreting** Do you think the set and costume design in this production are what Mamet may have envisioned? Explain why or why not.

Milkmaid. Yes, I know . . .
Prince. . . . since my *friend* died . . . (*Pause*) but I'm alright now, I think. Ⓜ

[*Pause*]

Milkmaid. What were you doing just now? You were writing a poem.
Prince. Just now. Yes.
Milkmaid. I didn't know that you could write.
Prince. Well, I've been working at it.
Milkmaid. You were writing it for *him*?
Prince. Yes. (*Pause*) Yes. I was. (*Pause*) I was picking some *flowers* to take over to his grave,

---

Ⓜ **Reading Focus** **Reading a Play** Review the prince and milkmaid's dialogue, starting with the prince's line "It's alright." What plot events does Mamet convey through this passage of dialogue?

and some thoughts came to me. (*Pause*) Well!
Milkmaid (*hands him a package*). I brought you this.
Prince. Thank you. What is it?
Milkmaid. My heavy shawl.
Prince. You brought me your shawl?
Milkmaid. Yes. I thought that you could make a little, you could make a *nest* for yourself.
Prince. But *you'll* need it. Next winter . . . You'll surely need it.
Milkmaid. I'm going away.

[*Pause*]

Prince. You're going away.
Milkmaid. Yes.

[*Pause*]

Prince. Where?
Milkmaid. I'm going South. I got a letter from my fiancé. He wants me to *join* him.

[*Pause*]

Prince. Then you must go.
Milkmaid. I (*pause*) I wanted to *ask* you if you would like to *come* with us. N

[*Pause*]

Prince. To come with you to the South.
Milkmaid. Yes.
Prince (*pause*). That's very good of you.
Milkmaid. We would be glad to have you. There would be a place for you.
Prince. That's very good of you. That's very good of you, indeed.
Milkmaid. Will you come?
Prince (*pause*). You want me to come with you and live with you.
Milkmaid. Yes.
Prince. You know, you're a good woman. (*Pause*) I've wanted to tell you that for a long time. (*Pause*) And your fiancé's a lucky man. A very lucky man to have someone as loyal as you. (*Pause*) And as good as you. (*Pause*) And there's something else, there's something that I'd like to say. I owe you an apology.
Milkmaid. You don't owe me.
Prince. Yes. I do, though. I've, uh, you know, when I *met* you . . . when I *met* you . . .
Milkmaid. That's, that's long ago . . .
Prince. Yes, I think that it is, and do you remember . . .
Milkmaid. You don't have to talk about that if . . .
Prince. No, I want to.
Milkmaid. I know that you were *hurt* that I *refused* you . . .
Prince. Yes, I was . . .
Milkmaid. If I were *free* . . .
Prince. I was hurt. More im*por*tantly . . .
Milkmaid. If I were *free* your offer would not have been *refused.* (*Pause*)

Prince (*pause*). Thank you. (*Pause*) Thank you very much. I . . . thank you very much. I . . . (*Pause*) You would have married me? (*Pause*)

Milkmaid. Yes.
Prince. I'm honored.

[*Pause*]

Milkmaid (*starting to go*) Well . . .
Prince. Wait, please, I wanted to *say* . . . I

N **Literary Perspectives** **Analyzing Archeytpes** Does the milkmaid's behavior and attitude seem to fit or break a literary pattern? Explain.

wanted to *say* when I first *knew* you I, I think, I wanted, there was something I *wanted*, I *wanted* to take advan . . .

Milkmaid. Shhh.

Prince. To, no, to take . . .

Milkmaid. . . . it's alright.

Prince. . . . to take *advantage* of you. (*Pause*) There. (*Pause*) There. And *further*more, however I've *changed* has in large part been because of you, and Bill, of course, but because of you. Okay. I'm through. Enough. Okay. I've said it. There. I apologize. It came out a bit creepy but I mean it. (*Pause*) O

Milkmaid. Will you come with me?

Prince. I . . .

Milkmaid. Will you come with me to the South? And live with us?

Prince. I . . . (*Pause*) I . . . *Thank* you. But I don't think that I can. (*Pause*) I think I'll stay here.

[Pause]

Milkmaid. It will be cold here.

Prince. Yes. (*Pause*) I . . . Yes, it will, but . . .

Milkmaid. . . . you have *ties* here.

Prince. Yes. (*Pause*) But thank you for asking me.

Milkmaid. I have to go. I want to cross the border before it gets dark. They close it down.

Prince. You have a safe trip.

Milkmaid. I'll think of you.

Prince. I'll think of you, too. I wish, I wish there was something I could *give* you . . . to *think* of me.

Milkmaid. Oh, I won't forget you.

Prince. I . . . isn't it funny; I was looking for a "jewel" or something to give you. Hah. Haha. I don't even have a *pocket!* Hah! Isn't it funny how some things take us back.

Milkmaid. What do you mean?

Prince. I was thinking of my Old Friend. I must have been thinking of him, and it took me back to another time. (*Pause*) Do you think we never know the good things 'til they've passed?

Milkmaid. I don't know.

Prince. I've been thinking that.

[*Pause*]

Milkmaid. You have a good heart.

Prince. Do I? Thank you . . . You do, too. Thank you. Oh. Oh. (*He starts writing.*) "Red for Pride, Blue for Loyalty . . . a good heart's *red* . . . a good heart's red . . ."

Milkmaid (*softly*). Goodbye . . . (*She kisses him and slips quietly away.*)

Prince. "A Good Heart's red . . ." Now we need *yellow,* we need some *contrast* . . . *yellow* . . . Blue . . . (*He changes back into a prince.*) Blue for Spring, red for Saline Lust . . . P

[*The* OLD PEASANT WOMAN *appears.*]

Peasant. Hello. (*The* PRINCE *looks up; pause*) Hello.

Prince. What are you doing here?

[*Pause*]

Peasant. Hello.

Prince. Yes. Hello. It's been a long time.

Peasant. Look at yourself.

Prince. I know what I look like.

Peasant. Look at yourself. (*The* PRINCE *does so; pause*)

Prince. I seem to have changed. (*Pause*) Well. (*Pause*) Yes. (*Pause*) It's been a long time. Hasn't it? (*Pause*) Yes. And here you are again. (*Pause*) And now I have changed back. (*Pause*) How

---

O Literary Focus Comedy What flaw has the prince recognized in himself, as indicated by his apology?

P Reading Focus Reading a Play What do you visualize happening here?

about that. (*Pause*) How about that. (*Pause*) How about that. (*Pause*) May I ask you something? I'd like to understand. There's something that I've wanted to ask you for so long. The last time that we met . . . may I ask you . . . the last time that we met. I was about to get married. I ruled the kingdom. I refused a request that you made, at that time I thought that I was within my rights . . . I was on Royal Land . . . I was, let us say, on land I *knew* as Royal Land. Even if we were to say that possession of that land was in some form a usurpation.[16] I picked *flowers*. In a moment of exuberance. I felt no ill will toward you. None at all. And I was punished. My love proved false. My kingdom was taken from me. My friends were ruined. My comrade lost his life . . . (*Pause*) Don't you think I was unduly[17] punished? (*Pause*) Or was it punishment for some . . . for some general *arrogance*? For my acceptance of the perquisites[18] of *rank*?

Peasant. Are those for me?

Prince. I'm sorry?

Peasant. Those flowers that you hold, are they for me?

Prince. No. (*Pause*) They're for my friend. (*Pause*) Who has died. I'm taking them to his grave.

Do you think we never know the good things 'til they've passed?

Peasant. You must offer them to me.

Prince. They're for my friend's grave.

Peasant. Those flowers you must offer me, or you will dwell in Misery.

[*Pause*]

Prince. They're somewhat *sacred.* (*Pause*) They're for my friend. (*Pause*) Here. Here they are. (*He gives her the bouquet.*) Take them. (*Pause*)

Peasant. Thank you. (*Pause*) They're lovely.

Prince. Yes. They are.

Peasant. I think that they're the loveliest thing in this part of the Wood.

Prince. Yes. I do, too.

Peasant. Thank you for offering them to me.

[*Pause*]

Prince. That's perfectly alright.

[*She exits. He puts the* MILKMAID*'s shawl over his uniform and starts out of the Wood.*] Q

16. **usurpation** (yoo suhr PAY shuhn): unlawful taking of power, property, or rights.
17. **unduly** (uhn DOO lee): excessively; to an extreme or unreasonable degree.
18. **perquisites** (PUR kwuh zihts): privileges; benefits.

Q **Literary Focus** **Comedy** What similarities and differences do you notice between Scenes 1 and 4?

Vocabulary **exuberance** (ehg ZOO buhr uhns) *n.:* overflowing joy or enthusiasm.

Applying Your Skills

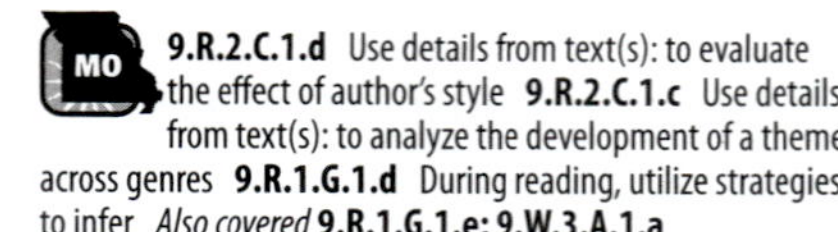

9.R.2.C.1.d Use details from text(s): to evaluate the effect of author's style **9.R.2.C.1.c** Use details from text(s): to analyze the development of a theme across genres **9.R.1.G.1.d** During reading, utilize strategies: to infer *Also covered* **9.R.1.G.1.e; 9.W.3.A.1.a**

The Frog Prince

Respond and Think Critically

Reading Focus

Quick Check

1. In Scene 1, why does the prince refuse to give the flowers to the peasant woman?
2. What offer does the milkmaid make to the prince? Does he take the offer?

Read with a Purpose

3. Characters in myths and folk tales often undergo a metamorphosis—a fantastic transformation, or change, from one form to another. How does the prince change during the course of the play?

Reading Skills: Reading a Play

4. Review the chart you filled in as you read. Then, add a row, labeled "My Comparison/Evaluation," and record your observations of how the story would be different if it were told in the form of a tale instead of a play. Explain.

Details from the Play	My Inferences/Visualizations

My Comparison/Evaluation:

Literary Focus

Literary Analysis

5. **Analyze** In what ways is the prince a **round character**—one who grows and changes in the course of the play?
6. **Literary Perspectives** What archetypal plot elements, themes, or characters does the play contain? How does Mamet defy our expectations of these archetypes?
7. **Analyze** At the end of the play, the prince asks the peasant woman, "Don't you think I was unduly punished?" Do you agree? What point is Mamet making by having the prince suffer harsh consequences for his action?

Literary Skills: Comedy

8. **Compare and Contrast** In what ways is this play similar to and different from a traditional comedy?
9. **Connect** Does the play have a "happy ending"? What effect does the play's resolution have on you?

Literary Skills Review: Theme

10. **Analyze Theme** is the insight about life that a literary work conveys. What theme does Mamet explore? What does the prince learn, and what do *we* learn about life from his experiences?

Writing Focus

Think as a Reader/Writer

Use It in Your Writing Write a dialogue in which the prince confronts the Fair Patricia. Convey the characters' personalities through what they say and how they say it.

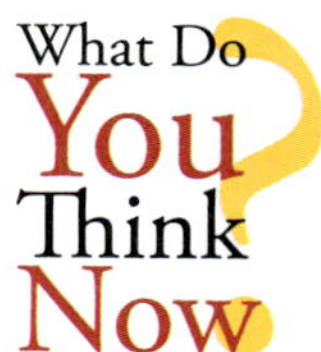

Is the milkmaid's belief that "love will find a way" supported by events in the play? Explain.

MO 9.R.1.G.1.a During reading, utilize strategies: to determine meaning of unknown words 9.R.1.E.1.c Develop vocabulary through text: using glossary, dictionary and thesaurus 9.W.3.A.1.a Compose a variety of texts: using narrative, descriptive, expository, and/or persuasive features

Vocabulary Development

Vocabulary Check

Tell whether each statement is true (T) or false (F).

1. Politicians who speak with **zeal** can be persuasive.
2. Sickly people are **susceptible** to illness.
3. **Malevolent** people are kindhearted.
4. Flowers with a **vile** smell can make a home inviting.
5. At graduation ceremonies, people often display **exuberance.**

Vocabulary Skills: Using Resources

Identifying **synonyms** (words with similar meanings) and **antonyms** (words with opposite meanings) can enhance your understanding of new words and help you expand your vocabulary. In dictionaries, synonyms and antonyms may appear at the end of entries for words. You can also find synonyms (and sometimes antonyms as well) in a thesaurus. In thesauruses that group words in categories, use the index to guide you in finding synonyms. Other thesauruses present words in alphabetical order, as in a dictionary.

Your Turn

For each Vocabulary word—*zeal, susceptible, malevolent, vile,* and *exuberance*—create a chart, like the sample one below for *spontaneous*. Use a thesaurus or a dictionary for help identifying synonyms and antonyms.

spontaneous		
Definition: resulting from a natural feeling; without prior thought	Synonyms: impulsive, instinctive, automatic	Antonyms: premeditated, calculated, deliberate

CHOICES

As you respond to the Choices, use these **Academic Vocabulary** words as appropriate: interpretation, convention, production, embody.

REVIEW

Write a Critique

Choose a comic movie or an episode of a TV situation comedy that you particularly like. Which characteristics of a traditional comedy does it share? How does it differ from a traditional comedy? Write your analysis in the form of a critique to be included in the arts section of your local newspaper.

CONNECT

Create Director's Notes

Imagine that you are directing a production of *The Frog Prince*. Who is your target audience—young children or young adults? What vision of the play do you want to convey to the audience? For example, will you emphasize the serious or the lighthearted elements of the play? What is your interpretation of the characters—how do you want the actors to play their roles? Create a log of the notes you will use to direct the performance.

EXTEND

Write an Essay

Timed Writing Was the prince's decision to give the flowers to the peasant at the end of the play a good one? Why do you think Mamet chose to end the play as he did? Defend your opinion in a brief persuasive essay. Support your argument with examples from life and the play.

The Tragedy of Romeo and Juliet

by **William Shakespeare**

Romeo and Juliet touch hands at their first meeting.

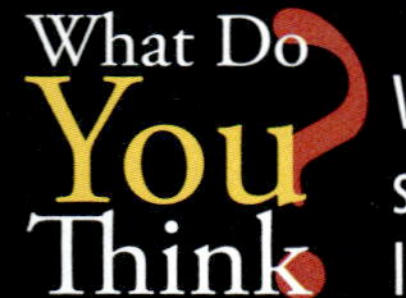

Why is the quest for love such a popular aspect of literature and film?

 **QuickWrite**

What movies or TV shows have you seen in which a young character falls in love for the first time? Was the show a comedy or tragedy? In other words, did the character find true love, or was he or she disappointed? Jot down your responses.

An Introduction to
Romeo and Juliet

It's not hard for playgoers to say what makes *Romeo and Juliet* one of Shakespeare's most popular plays. Most of the audience can easily identify with the main characters: a young couple who fall madly, hopelessly in love and then are doomed because of their passion. Even though most playgoers know how the play will end, they enjoy watching it again and again.

In fact, Shakespeare's audiences already knew the story behind *Romeo and Juliet*. It is based on a long narrative poem by Arthur Brooke, which was published in 1562 as *The Tragicall Historye of Romeus and Juliet*. Brooke's popular poem was itself based on older Italian stories.

Romeo and Juliet, a very young man and a nearly fourteen-year-old girl, fall in love at first sight. They are caught up in an idealized, almost unreal, passionate love. They are in love with love. In his prologue, Brooke preaches a moral, which people of his time expected. He says that Romeo and Juliet had to die because they broke the laws and married unwisely, against their parents' wishes. Shakespeare avoids this moralizing. He presents the couple as "star-crossed lovers," doomed to disaster by fate.

To understand what *star-crossed* means, you have to realize that most people of Shakespeare's time believed in astrology. They believed that the course of their lives was partly determined by the hour, day, month, and year of their birth—hence "the stars" under which they were born. Shakespeare himself may not have shared this belief. In a later play, *Julius Caesar*, he has a character question the age-old idea about astrology and the influence of the stars:

The fault, dear Brutus, is not in our stars,
But in ourselves, that we are underlings.

Although Shakespeare says in his prologue that Romeo and Juliet are star-crossed, he does not make them mere victims of fate. Romeo and Juliet make decisions that lead to their disaster. More important, other characters have a hand in the play's tragic ending.

How important do *you* think fate is in affecting what happens to us? How much do you think we control our own destinies?

Romeo and Juliet (1977) by Milton Hebald, at the Delacorte Theater in Central Park, New York City.

William Shakespeare's Life: A Genius from Stratford

by **Robert Anderson**

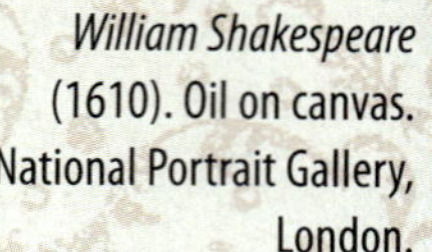

William Shakespeare (1610). Oil on canvas. National Portrait Gallery, London.

He is the most famous writer in the world, but he left us no journals or letters—he left us only his poems and his plays. What we know about William Shakespeare's personal life comes mostly from church and legal documents—a baptismal registration, a marriage license, and records of real estate transactions. We also have a few remarks that others wrote about him during his lifetime.

We know that William was born the third of eight children around April 23, 1564, in Stratford, a market town about one hundred miles northwest of London. His father, John, was a shopkeeper and a man of some importance in Stratford, serving at various times as justice of the peace and high bailiff (mayor).

William attended grammar school, where he studied Latin grammar, Latin literature, and rhetoric (the uses of language). As far as we know, he had no further formal education.

At the age of eighteen, he married Anne Hathaway, who was eight years older than he was. Sometime after the birth of their second and third children (twins), Shakespeare moved to London, apparently leaving his family in Stratford.

We know that several years later, by 1592, Shakespeare had already become an actor and a playwright. By 1594, he was a charter member of the theatrical company called the Lord Chamberlain's Men, which was later to become the King's Men. (As the names of these acting companies indicate, theatrical groups depended on the support of a wealthy patron—the King's Men were supported by King James himself.) Shakespeare worked with this company for the rest of his writing life. Year after year he provided it with plays. Shakespeare was the ultimate professional writer. He had a theater that needed plays, actors who needed parts, and a family that needed to be fed.

Romeo and Juliet was probably among the early plays that Shakespeare wrote, between 1594 and 1596. By 1612, when he returned to Stratford to live the life of a prosperous retired gentleman, Shakespeare had written thirty-seven plays, including such masterpieces as *Julius Caesar, Hamlet, Othello, King Lear,* and *Macbeth.*

Shakespeare's plays are still produced all over the world. During a Broadway season in the 1980s, one critic estimated that if Shakespeare were alive, he would be receiving $25,000 a week in royalties for a production of *Othello* alone. The play was attracting larger audiences than any other nonmusical production in town.

Shakespeare died on April 23, 1616, at the age of fifty-two. He is buried under the old stone floor in the chancel of Holy Trinity Church in Stratford. Carved over his grave is the following verse (the spelling has been modernized):

Good friend, for Jesus' sake forbear
To dig the dust enclosèd here!
Blessed be the man that spares these stones
And cursed be he that moves my bones.

These are hardly the best of Shakespeare's lines (if indeed they are his at all), but like his other lines, they seem to have worked. His bones have lain undisturbed to this day.

Birthplace of William Shakespeare at Stratford-upon-Avon in England, UK.

Learn It Online
Explore Shakespeare with AuthorSpace:
go.hrw.com L9-799 Go

Shakespeare and His Theater: A Perfect Match

by **Robert Anderson**

Model of Globe Theatre.

Sometimes playwrights influence the shape and form of a theater, but more often existing theaters seem to influence the shape and form of plays. It is important that we understand Shakespeare's theater because it influenced how he wrote his plays. Shakespeare took the theater of his time, and he used it brilliantly.

The "Wooden O"

In 1576, outside the city walls of London, an actor-manager named James Burbage built the first permanent theater in England. He called it the Theatre. Up to that time, touring acting companies had played wherever they could rent space. Usually this would be in the courtyards of inns. There the actors would erect a temporary platform stage at one end of the yard and play to an audience that stood around the stage or sat in the tiers of balconies that surrounded the courtyard. It was natural, then, that the first theater built by Burbage should derive its shape and form from the inns. In 1599, Burbage's theater was torn down and its timbers were used by Shakespeare and his company to build the Globe Theatre.

In his play *Henry V,* Shakespeare called his theater a "wooden O." It was a large, round (or polygonal) building, three stories high, with a large platform stage that projected from one end into a yard open to the sky. In the back wall of this stage was a curtained-off inner stage. Flanking the inner stage were two doors for entrances and exits. Above this inner stage was a small balcony or upper stage, which could be used to suggest Juliet's balcony or the high walls of a castle or the bridge of a ship. Trapdoors were placed in the floor of the main stage for the entrances and exits of ghosts and for descents into hell.

The plays were performed in the afternoon. Since the stage was open to the sky, there was no need for stage lighting. There were very few sets (scenery, furniture, and so on). The stage was "set" by the language. A whole forest scene was created in one play when a character announced, "Well, this is the Forest of Arden." But costumes were often elaborate, and the stage might have been hung with colorful banners and trappings. (The groundlings, those eight hundred or more people who stood shoulder to shoulder around the stage for the price of a penny, loved a good show. Most people still do.)

We can see that this stage, with its few sets and many acting areas—forestage, inner stage, and upper stage—made for a theater of great fluidity. That is, scene could follow scene with almost cinematic ease.

In one interesting aspect the theater in Shakespeare's day was very different from the theater we know today. Plays were originally performed by the all-male medieval trade guilds, so all women's parts were played by boys. It would be many years before women appeared onstage in the professional English theater. In Shakespeare's day, Juliet would have been played by a trained boy actor.

The Modern Stage: Back to Shakespeare's Theater

It has been said that all you need for a theater is "two planks and a passion." Since Shakespeare's time "the planks" (the stage) have undergone various changes. First, the part of the stage that projected into the yard grew narrower, and the small curtained inner stage grew larger, until there developed what is called the **proscenium stage.** Here there is no outer stage; there is only the inner stage, and a large curtain that separates it from the audience. The effect is like looking inside a window or inside a picture frame. This is the stage most of us know today. It has been standard for well over a hundred years.

But recently we have seen a reversal of this design. Now more and more theaters (especially university and regional theaters) are building "thrust" stages, or arena stages. The audience once again sits on three or even four sides of the stage.

The Movies and the Theater: Words Versus Action

Theater and movies are different media. People who go to plays often prefer to spend a long time watching the subtle development of conflicts among a small group of people, all in one setting. For example, all of the action in Lorraine Hansberry's play *A Raisin in the Sun* takes place inside one small apartment on Chicago's South Side.

Movies are basically a *visual* medium that can whisk us from place to place. Movies must chiefly engage and delight the eye rather than the ear. (One movie director once referred to a dialogue in a movie as "foreground *noise*"!) The theater is much more a medium of *words.* When we go to see a play, it is the movement of the words rather than the movement of the scenery that delights us.

Reading Shakespeare Aloud

The Poetry

Whatever Shakespeare learned of rhetoric, or the art of using words, in school, he parades with relish in *Romeo and Juliet*. He is obviously having a fine time here with puns and wordplay and all the other variations he can ring on the English language.

Romeo and Juliet is written in both prose and poetry. Prose is for the most part spoken by the common people and, occasionally, by Mercutio when he is joking. Most of the other characters speak in poetry.

Blank Verse The poetry is largely written in unrhymed iambic pentameter. In **iambic meter** each unstressed syllable is followed by a stressed syllable, as in the word *prĕfér.* In **iambic pentameter** there are five of these iambic units in each line. Unrhymed iambic pentameter is called **blank verse.** The word *blank* just means that there is no rhyme at the ends of lines.

Read aloud this perfect example of iambic pentameter, spoken by Romeo. The syllables marked with a stress (′) should be stressed.

> ˘ ′ ˘ ′ ˘ ′ ˘
> But soft! What light through yonder
> ′ ˘ ′
> window breaks?

Couplets When Shakespeare uses rhymes, he generally uses **couplets**, two consecutive lines of

Students rehearse a scene from a play.

poetry that rhyme. The couplets often punctuate a character's exit or signal the end of a scene. Read aloud Juliet's exit line from the balcony:

> Good night, good night! Parting is such
>   sweet sorrow
> That I shall say good night till it be morrow.

Reading the Lines We have all heard people ruin a good poem by mechanically pausing at the end of each line, whether or not the meaning of the line calls for a pause. (Maxwell Anderson, who wrote verse plays, had his plays typed as though they were prose, so that actors would not be tempted to pause at the end of each line. Consider using this technique when you stage a scene.)

Lines of poetry are either end-stopped or run-on. An **end-stopped line** has some punctuation at its end. A **run-on line** has no punctuation at its end. In a run-on line the meaning is always completed in the line or lines that follow.

Try reading aloud this passage from Act II, Scene 2, where Juliet speaks in end-stopped lines—lines ending with punctuation that requires her to pause:

> O, Romeo, Romeo! Wherefore art thou
>   Romeo?
> Deny thy father and refuse thy name;
> Or, if thou wilt not, be but sworn my love,
> And I'll no longer be a Capulet.

Romeo's speech in the same scene has many run-on lines. Read these lines aloud; where does Romeo pause?

> The brightness of her cheek would shame
>   those stars
> As daylight doth a lamp; her eyes in heaven
> Would through the airy region stream so
>   bright
> That birds would sing and think it were not
>   night.

The glory of *Romeo and Juliet* is its poetry and its theatricality. The play is fast moving, and the poetry suits the story of young people dealing with a matter very important to them—passionate, once-in-a-lifetime love.

The Words

Shakespeare wrote this play about four hundred years ago. It's not surprising, then, that many words are by now **archaic,** which means that they (or their particular meanings) have disappeared from common use. The sidenotes in the play will help you with these archaic words and with other words and expressions that might be unfamiliar to you. Here are some of the archaic words that are repeatedly used in the play:

'a: he.
a': on.
an' or **and:** if.
anon: soon; right away; coming.
but: if; except; only.
Good-den or **go-den** or **God-den:** Good evening (said in the late afternoon).
hap: luck.
happy: lucky.
humor: mood; moisture.
Jack: common fellow; ordinary guy.
maid: unmarried girl.
mark: listen to.
Marry: mild oath, shortened from "by the Virgin Mary."
nice: trivial; foolish.
owes: owns.
shrift: confession or forgiveness for sins that have been confessed to a priest. After confession a person was said to be **shriven.**
soft: quiet; hush; slow up.
stay: wait.
still: always.
withal: with that; with.
wot: know.

DRAMA
Preparing to Read

9.R.2.C.1.b Use details from text(s): to analyze character, plot, setting, point of view 9.R.2.A.1 Analyze and evaluate the text features in grade-level text *Also covered* 9.R.2; 9.R.1.G.1.f; 9.R.1.G.1.d; 9.R.3.C.1.a

The Tragedy of Romeo and Juliet

Literary Focus

Tragedy A **tragedy** is a narrative about serious and important actions that ends unhappily. In some tragedies, disaster hits innocent characters; in others, the main characters are responsible for their downfall. Tragedies usually follow this **dramatic structure:** The setting, main characters, and main conflict are introduced in the **exposition.** During the **rising action,** the conflict escalates. The **turning point** occurs when the main characters decide on a course of action that determines the conflict's outcome. The **climax** is the moment of greatest emotional intensity and often occurs with the death of the main characters. In the **resolution,** loose plot ends are tied up.

Reading Focus

Reading a Play When you read a full-length play it helps to use a variety of strategies. **Read aloud** dialogue to bring it to life. **Paraphrase,** or restate in your own words, complex passages to be sure you understand them. **Make inferences,** guesses based on text clues, to figure out why characters act as they do. **Analyze causes and effects** to clarify the action and **predict** what might happen next.

Into Action As you read, fill in a chart like this one to help you understand and enjoy the play.

Reading Strategy	My Notes
Read Aloud/Paraphrase	
Make Inferences	
Analyze Causes and Effects	

Writing Focus

Think as a Reader/Writer

Find It in Your Reading As you read, write down in your *Reader/Writer Notebook* key plot events that will help you write a summary of each act and analyze the pattern of the play.

Use your **RWN** to complete the activities for this selection.

Language Coach

Shakespeare's Language Shakespeare's characters use images and figures of speech so rich and varied that the play, which has existed now for more than four hundred years, will probably be performed many centuries from now.

As you read *The Tragedy of Romeo and Juliet,* you will explore:

- archaic meanings of words that are still in use today
- archaic words that are no longer in common use
- origins of names from the play
- how to paraphrase inverted phrases
- Shakespeare's use of figurative language

Elements of Drama Sidenotes and questions appear throughout the play to aid your understanding of key elements of drama.

Staging the Play Sidenotes and questions are provided to help you envision the action of the play.

Learn It Online
Check out the *PowerNotes* introduction to this play on:

Characters

The Montagues

Lord Montague
Lady Montague
Romeo, son of Montague
Benvolio, nephew of Montague and friend of Romeo
Balthasar, servant of Romeo
Abram, servant of Montague

The Capulets

Lord Capulet
Lady Capulet
Juliet, daughter of Capulet
Tybalt, nephew of Lady Capulet
Nurse to Juliet
Peter, servant to the Nurse
Sampson, **Gregory** } servants of Capulet
An Old Man of the Capulet family

The Others

Prince Escalus, ruler of Verona
Mercutio, a relative of the Prince and friend of Romeo
Friar Laurence, a Franciscan priest
Friar John, another Franciscan priest
Count Paris, a young nobleman, a relative of the Prince
An Apothecary (a druggist)
Page to Paris
Chief Watchman
Three Musicians
An Officer
Citizens of Verona, Relatives of both families, **Maskers, Guards, Watchmen,** and **Attendants**

Scene: Verona and Mantua, cities in northern Italy

ACT I

Romeo + Juliet movie still with Leonardo DiCaprio and Claire Danes released in 1996.

Read with a Purpose As you read, think about how the actions of Romeo and Juliet help set the play in motion.

The Tragedy of Romeo and Juliet

by **William Shakespeare**

The Prologue

Enter CHORUS.

Chorus.

Two households, both alike in dignity,°
  In fair Verona, where we lay our scene,
From ancient grudge break to new mutiny,
  Where civil blood makes civil hands unclean.°
From forth the fatal loins of these two foes
  A pair of star-crossed lovers take their life;
Whose misadventured piteous overthrows
  Do with their death bury their parents' strife.
The fearful passage of their death-marked love,
  And the continuance of their parents' rage,
Which, but° their children's end, naught could remove,
  Is now the two hours' traffic° of our stage;
The which if you with patient ears attend,
What here shall miss, our toil shall strive to mend. Ⓐ

[*Exit.*]

1. **dignity:** status.

4. **Where . . . unclean:** That is, where civilians' passions ("civil blood") make their hands unclean (because they have been used for killing).

11. **but:** except for.

12. **traffic:** business.

Elements of Drama
14. *This prologue is spoken by a single actor called the Chorus. The Chorus welcomes the audience and gives them a taste of the story. What will the "two hours' traffic" of this stage be about? What will happen to the two lovers?*

Ⓐ **Literary Focus** **Exposition** Who do you think will be the main characters of this play?

ACT I

SCENE 1. *Verona. A public place.*

Enter SAMPSON *and* GREGORY, *of the house of Capulet, with swords and bucklers (shields).*

Sampson. Gregory, on my word, we'll not carry coals.°

Gregory. No, for then we should be colliers.°

Sampson. I mean, and° we be in choler,° we'll draw.°

Gregory. Ay, while you live, draw your neck out of collar.°

Sampson. I strike quickly, being moved.

Gregory. But thou art not quickly moved to strike.

Sampson. A dog of the house of Montague moves me.

Gregory. To move is to stir, and to be valiant is to stand. Therefore, if thou art moved, thou run'st away.

Sampson. A dog of that house shall move me to stand. I will take the wall° of any man or maid of Montague's.

Gregory. That shows thee a weak slave; for the weakest goes to the wall.°

Sampson. 'Tis true; and therefore women, being the weaker vessels, are ever thrust to the wall. Therefore I will push Montague's men from the wall and thrust his maids to the wall.

Gregory. The quarrel is between our masters and us their men.

Sampson. 'Tis all one. I will show myself a tyrant. When I have fought with the men, I will be civil with the maids—I will cut off their heads.

Gregory. The heads of the maids?

Sampson. Ay, the heads of the maids or their maidenheads. Take it in what sense thou wilt.

Gregory. They must take it in sense that feel it.

Sampson. Me they shall feel while I am able to stand; and 'tis known I am a pretty piece of flesh.

Gregory. 'Tis well thou art not fish; if thou hadst, thou hadst been Poor John.° Draw thy tool!° Here comes two of the house of Montagues. **A**

? **Elements of Drama**
Stage direction: *In this stage direction, two servants enter, bragging and teasing each other. What actions do you imagine they are engaged in as they cross the city square?*

1. carry coals: do dirty work (put up with insults). People often made jokes about men who carted coal.

2. colliers: coal dealers (men with dirty jobs). Notice how the servants start making jokes based on words that sound similar (*colliers, choler,* and *collar*).

3. and: if. **choler:** anger. **draw:** pull out swords.

4. collar: hangman's noose.

11. take the wall: take the best place on the path (which is closest to the wall).

12–13. goes to the wall: is defeated.

30. Poor John: kind of salted fish, a poor person's food. **tool:** sword.

A **Reading Focus** **Analyzing Cause and Effect** What causes the Capulet servants Sampson and Gregory to draw their weapons?

[*Enter two other servingmen,* ABRAM *and* BALTHASAR.]

Sampson. My naked weapon is out. Quarrel! I will back thee.

Gregory. How? Turn thy back and run?

Sampson. Fear me not.°

Gregory. No, marry. I fear thee!

Sampson. Let us take the law of our sides;° let them begin.

Gregory. I will frown as I pass by, and let them take it as they list. **B**

Sampson. Nay, as they dare. I will bite my thumb° at them, which is disgrace to them if they bear it.

Abram. Do you bite your thumb at us, sir?

Sampson. I do bite my thumb, sir.

Abram. Do you bite your thumb at us, sir?

Sampson (*aside to* GREGORY). Is the law of our side if I say ay?

Gregory (*aside to* SAMPSON). No.

Sampson. No, sir, I do not bite my thumb at you, sir; but I bite my thumb, sir.

Gregory. Do you quarrel, sir?

Abram. Quarrel, sir? No, sir.

Sampson. But if you do, sir, I am for you. I serve as good a man as you.

Abram. No better.

Sampson. Well, sir.

[*Enter* BENVOLIO.]

Gregory. Say "better." Here comes one of my master's kinsmen. **C**

Sampson. Yes, better, sir.

Abram. You lie.

Sampson. Draw, if you be men. Gregory, remember thy swashing° blow.

[*They fight.*]

? Elements of Drama
Stage direction: *In this stage direction, Sampson and Gregory's swaggering stops when they spy their enemies. What's Sampson doing when he says, "Quarrel! I will back thee"?*

34. Fear me not: Do not distrust me.

36. Let . . . sides: Let us stay on the right side of the law.

39. bite my thumb: insulting gesture.

? Staging the Play
41. *It takes the Montague servants some time to speak. How might their actions show that these four servants are very wary of one another?*

? Elements of Drama
44. *An* ***aside*** *is dialogue spoken by a character to the audience or to another character that others are not supposed to hear. Sampson and Gregory speak to each other in asides. Who is not supposed to overhear them?*

60. swashing: slashing with great force.

B **Reading Focus** **Making Inferences** What can you infer about Sampson's and Gregory's characters based on these speeches?

C **Reading Focus** **Analyzing Cause and Effect** What causes Gregory's behavior toward the Montague servants to change?

The opening skirmish between Abram and Gregory.

Benvolio.
Part, fools!
Put up your swords. You know not what you do. **D**

[*Enter* TYBALT.]

Tybalt.
What, art thou drawn among these heartless hinds?°
Turn thee, Benvolio; look upon thy death. **E**

Benvolio.
I do but keep the peace. Put up thy sword,
Or manage it to part these men with me.

Tybalt.
What, drawn, and talk of peace? I hate the word
As I hate hell, all Montagues, and thee.
Have at thee, coward! **F**

[*They fight.*]

[*Enter an* OFFICER, *and three or four* CITIZENS *with clubs, bills, and partisans, or spears.*]

63. **heartless hinds:** cowardly hicks.

D **Reading Focus** **Making Inferences** What action is Benvolio involved in here?

E **Reading Focus** **Reading Aloud** In some productions, Tybalt's second line is spoken after a dramatic silence. Why should this line demand our attention?

F **Reading Focus** **Making Inferences** This is a key speech. What is Tybalt's mood? How is he shown to be opposite in nature to Benvolio?

Officer. Clubs, bills, and partisans! Strike! Beat them down!
Down with the Capulets! Down with the Montagues!

[*Enter old* CAPULET, *in his gown, and his wife,* LADY CAPULET.]

Capulet.
What noise is this? Give me my long sword, ho!

Lady Capulet.
A crutch, a crutch! Why call you for a sword?

Capulet.
My sword, I say! Old Montague is come
And flourishes his blade in spite of° me.

[*Enter old* MONTAGUE *and his wife,* LADY MONTAGUE.]

Montague.
Thou villain Capulet!—Hold me not; let me go. **G**

Lady Montague.
Thou shalt not stir one foot to seek a foe.

[*Enter* PRINCE ESCALUS, *with his* TRAIN.]

Prince.
Rebellious subjects, enemies to peace,
Profaners of this neighbor-stainèd steel—
Will they not hear? What, ho! You men, you beasts,
That quench the fire of your pernicious rage
With purple fountains issuing from your veins!
On pain of torture, from those bloody hands
Throw your mistempered° weapons to the ground
And hear the sentence of your movèd prince. **H**
Three civil brawls, bred of an airy° word
By thee, old Capulet, and Montague,
Have thrice disturbed the quiet of our streets
And made Verona's ancient citizens
Cast by their grave beseeming° ornaments
To wield old partisans, in hands as old,
Cankered° with peace, to part your cankered° hate.
If ever you disturb our streets again,

? **Elements of Drama**
73. *In the midst of the tension over Tybalt, we have a* ***comic touch.*** *Why is Lady Capulet talking about a crutch?*

75. in spite of: in defiance of.

? **Elements of Drama**
Stage direction: *Based on this stage direction, how would you stage the entrance of the prince if you were directing the play? His dignified procession must contrast with the bloody rioting. How do you know from his speech that the prince is at first ignored by the brawlers?*

84. mistempered: used with bad temper.

86. airy: light or harmless.

90. grave beseeming: dignified, as they should be.

92. cankered: The first *cankered* means "rusted" (from lack of use in peaceful times); the second means "diseased," like a canker, a running sore.

G **Reading Focus** **Making Inferences** Who is holding Montague back?

H **Reading Focus** **Reading Aloud/Making Inferences** There is a dramatic pause before the next line is spoken. What are the brawlers doing now?

Your lives shall pay the forfeit of the peace.
For this time all the rest depart away.
You, Capulet, shall go along with me;
And, Montague, come you this afternoon,
To know our farther pleasure in this case,
To old Freetown, our common judgment place.
Once more, on pain of death, all men depart. **I**

[*Exeunt all but* MONTAGUE, LADY MONTAGUE, *and* BENVOLIO.]

Montague.
Who set this ancient quarrel new abroach?°
Speak, nephew, were you by when it began?

Benvolio.
Here were the servants of your adversary
And yours, close fighting ere I did approach.
I drew to part them. In the instant came
The fiery Tybalt, with his sword prepared,
Which, as he breathed defiance to my ears,
He swung about his head and cut the winds,
Who, nothing hurt withal, hissed him in scorn.
While we were interchanging thrusts and blows,
Came more and more, and fought on part and part,°
Till the prince came, who parted either part.

Lady Montague.
O, where is Romeo? Saw you him today?
Right glad I am he was not at this fray.

Benvolio.
Madam, an hour before the worshiped sun
Peered forth the golden window of the East,
A troubled mind drave me to walk abroad;
Where, underneath the grove of sycamore
That westward rooteth from this city side,
So early walking did I see your son.
Towards him I made, but he was ware° of me
And stole into the covert of the wood.
I, measuring his affections by my own,
Which then most sought where most might not be found,°

101. new abroach: newly opened.

111. on part and part: some on one side, some on the other.

? **Elements of Drama**
114. *For the first time, Romeo is mentioned—by his mother, whose parental concern is accented by a* ***rhyme.*** *Lady Montague does not say anything else in this scene. What do you imagine she is doing while her husband and Benvolio discuss her son?*

121. ware: aware.

124. sought . . . found: He sought a place where no one could be found. (He wanted to be alone.)

I **Literary Focus** **Exposition** What has been happening in Verona? What is the prince's warning?

Being one too many by my weary self,
Pursued my humor° not pursuing his,
And gladly shunned who gladly fled from me.

Montague.
Many a morning hath he there been seen,
With tears augmenting the fresh morning's dew,
Adding to clouds more clouds with his deep sighs;
But all so soon as the all-cheering sun
Should in the farthest East begin to draw
The shady curtains from Aurora's° bed,
Away from light steals home my heavy° son
And private in his chamber pens himself,
Shuts up his windows, locks fair daylight out,
And makes himself an artificial night.
Black and portentous must this humor prove
Unless good counsel may the cause remove. **J**

Benvolio.
My noble uncle, do you know the cause?

Montague.
I neither know it nor can learn of him.

Benvolio.
Have you importuned° him by any means?

Montague.
Both by myself and many other friends;
But he, his own affections' counselor,
Is to himself—I will not say how true—
But to himself so secret and so close,
So far from sounding° and discovery,
As is the bud bit with an envious° worm
Ere he can spread his sweet leaves to the air
Or dedicate his beauty to the sun.
Could we but learn from whence his sorrows grow,
We would as willingly give cure as know.

[*Enter* ROMEO.]

Benvolio.
See, where he comes. So please you step aside;
I'll know his grievance, or be much denied.

126. humor: mood.

133. Aurora's: In Roman mythology, Aurora (uh RAWR uh) is goddess of the dawn.

134. heavy: heavy-hearted.

142. importuned: questioned.

147. So far from sounding: so far from being sounded out for his mood (as a river is sounded for its depth).

148. envious: evil.

? Elements of Drama
Stage direction: *When Romeo makes his entrance, he doesn't initally see his parents or Benvolio. How do you think he would be acting as he enters?*

J Reading Focus Paraphrasing What do we know of Romeo so far? Paraphrase what Romeo's father and friend have said about him.

Montague.
I would thou wert so happy° by the stay
To hear true shrift.° Come, madam, let's away.

[*Exeunt* MONTAGUE *and* LADY MONTAGUE.]

Benvolio.
Good morrow, cousin. (K)
Romeo. Is the day so young?
Benvolio.
But new struck nine.
Romeo. Ay me! Sad hours seem long.
Was that my father that went hence so fast?
Benvolio.
It was. What sadness lengthens Romeo's hours?
Romeo.
Not having that which having makes them short.
Benvolio. In love?
Romeo. Out—
Benvolio. Of love?
Romeo.
Out of her favor where I am in love. (L)
Benvolio.
Alas that love, so gentle in his view,°
Should be so tyrannous and rough in proof!°
Romeo.
Alas that love, whose view is muffled still,°
Should without eyes see pathways to his will!
Where shall we dine? O me! What fray was here?
Yet tell me not, for I have heard it all.
Here's much to do with hate, but more with love.° (M)
Why then, O brawling love, O loving hate,
O anything, of nothing first created!
O heavy lightness, serious vanity,
Misshapen chaos of well-seeming forms,

155. happy: lucky.

156. shrift: confession.

166. view: appearance.

167. in proof: in reality.

168. muffled still: always blindfolded. Romeo is talking about Cupid (the god of love in Roman mythology), who was often depicted as blindfolded.

172. more with love: They enjoyed fighting.

? Elements of Drama
175–178. *All of these are **contradictions,** things that are really the opposite of the way they are described. How does Romeo bitterly relate these to the love he feels?*

(K) **Reading Focus** **Reading Aloud** Benvolio is trying to be casual. What attitude should Romeo convey in his answer to Benvolio's cheery greeting?

(L) **Reading Focus** **Analyzing Cause and Effect** Romeo blurts out the truth. What is the cause of his strange behavior?

(M) **Reading Focus** **Paraphrasing** Romeo wants to change the subject and then notices the signs of the street fighting. What does he say about the rivalry between the two families?

Love is a smoke made with
the fume of sighs;
Being purged, a fire
sparkling in lovers' eyes.

Feather of lead, bright smoke, cold fire, sick health,
Still-waking sleep, that is not what it is!
This love feel I, that feel no love in this.
Dost thou not laugh?

Benvolio. No, coz,° I rather weep.

Romeo.
Good heart, at what?

Benvolio. At thy good heart's oppression.

Romeo.
Why, such is love's transgression.
Griefs of mine own lie heavy in my breast,
Which thou wilt propagate,° to have it prest°
With more of thine. This love that thou hast shown
Doth add more grief to too much of mine own.
Love is a smoke made with the fume of sighs;
Being purged, a fire sparkling in lovers' eyes;
Being vexed, a sea nourished with loving tears.
What is it else? A madness most discreet,°
A choking gall, and a preserving sweet. **N**
Farewell, my coz.

Benvolio. Soft!° I will go along.
And if you leave me so, you do me wrong.

Romeo.
Tut! I have lost myself; I am not here;
This is not Romeo, he's some other where.

Benvolio.
Tell me in sadness,° who is that you love?

Romeo.
What, shall I groan and tell thee?

Benvolio. Groan? Why, no;
But sadly tell me who.

180. coz: cousin (or other relative).

184. propagate: increase. **prest:** pressed; burdened.

190. discreet: discriminating.

192. Soft: Wait.

196. sadness: seriousness.

N Reading Focus Paraphrasing Romeo refuses to reveal more about his troubles and suggests to Benvolio that he is driven mad by love. What things does he compare love to before he tries to get away from Benvolio?

Romeo.

Bid a sick man in sadness make his will.
Ah, word ill urged to one that is so ill!
In sadness, cousin, I do love a woman.

Benvolio.

I aimed so near when I supposed you loved.

Romeo.

A right good markman. And she's fair I love.

Benvolio.

A right fair mark, fair coz, is soonest hit.

Romeo.

Well, in that hit you miss. She'll not be hit
With Cupid's arrow. She hath Dian's wit,°
And, in strong proof° of chastity well armed,
From Love's weak childish bow she lives uncharmed.
She will not stay° the siege of loving terms,
Nor bide th' encounter of assailing eyes,
Nor ope her lap to saint-seducing gold.°
O, she is rich in beauty; only poor
That, when she dies, with beauty dies her store.°

Benvolio.

Then she hath sworn that she will still° live chaste?

Romeo.

She hath, and in that sparing makes huge waste;
For beauty, starved with her severity,
Cuts beauty off from all posterity.
She is too fair, too wise, wisely too fair,
To merit bliss° by making me despair.
She hath forsworn° to love, and in that vow
Do I live dead that live to tell it now. **O**

Benvolio.

Be ruled by me; forget to think of her.

Romeo.

O, teach me how I should forget to think!

Benvolio.

By giving liberty unto thine eyes.
Examine other beauties.

206. Dian's wit: the cunning of Diana, the Roman goddess of chastity, the moon, and hunting, who was not interested in men.

207. proof: armor.

209. stay: submit to.

211. Nor ope … gold: In Greek mythology, the god Zeus visited Danae in the form of a shower of gold, and Danae bore Zeus a son.

213. when she dies … her store: Her store of beauty dies with her, since she'll have no children.

214. still: always.

219. bliss: heaven.

220. forsworn: renounced an oath; promised to give up.

O Reading Focus Paraphrasing What vow has the young woman made?

Romeo. 'Tis the way
To call hers, exquisite, in question° more.
These happy masks° that kiss fair ladies' brows,
Being black, put us in mind they hide the fair.
He that is strucken blind cannot forget
The precious treasure of his eyesight lost.
Show me a mistress that is passing fair:
What doth her beauty serve but as a note
Where I may read who passed that passing fair? **P**
Farewell. Thou canst not teach me to forget.

Benvolio.
I'll pay that doctrine, or else die in debt.°

[*Exeunt.*]

226. call ... in question: bring her beauty to mind.

227. masks: Women often wore masks to protect their faces from the sun.

235. or else die in debt: or die trying.

? Staging the Play
235: *Benvolio can exit here as if running after Romeo. The pair will reenter later, Romeo still being pursued. How would the audience feel about Benvolio?*

SCENE 2. *A street.*

Enter CAPULET, COUNT PARIS, *and the clown, his* SERVANT.

Capulet.
But Montague is bound° as well as I,
In penalty alike; and 'tis not hard, I think,
For men so old as we to keep the peace.

Paris.
Of honorable reckoning° are you both,
And pity 'tis you lived at odds so long.
But now, my lord, what say you to my suit?

Capulet.
But saying o'er what I have said before:
My child is yet a stranger in the world,
She hath not seen the change of fourteen years;
Let two more summers wither in their pride
Ere we may think her ripe to be a bride.

Paris.
Younger than she are happy mothers made.

1. is bound: is pledged to keep the peace.

4. reckoning: reputation.

? 12. *Paris is very much at ease with old Capulet and more composed than the lovesick Romeo we just saw. What does Paris want?*

P Reading Focus Paraphrasing Why won't looking at other women help Romeo?

Capulet.

And too soon marred are those so early made.
Earth hath swallowed all my hopes but she;
She is the hopeful lady of my earth.
But woo her, gentle Paris, get her heart;
My will to her consent is but a part.
And she agreed, within her scope of choice°
Lies my consent and fair according° voice.
This night I hold an old accustomed° feast,
Whereto I have invited many a guest,
Such as I love; and you among the store,
One more, most welcome, makes my number more.
At my poor house look to behold this night
Earth-treading stars° that make dark heaven light.
Such comfort as do lusty young men feel
When well-appareled April on the heel
Of limping winter treads, even such delight
Among fresh fennel° buds shall you this night
Inherit° at my house. Hear all, all see,
And like her most whose merit most shall be;
Which, on more view of many, mine, being one,
May stand in number,° though in reck'ning none.°
Come, go with me.

[*To* SERVANT, *giving him a paper.*]

Go, sirrah, trudge about
Through fair Verona; find those persons out
Whose names are written there, and to them say
My house and welcome on their pleasure stay.° **A**

[*Exit with* PARIS.]

? **15.** *Why doesn't Capulet want his daughter to marry right away? How is Capulet now different from the man who drew his sword in Scene 1?*

18. within her scope of choice: among all she can choose from.

19. according: agreeing.

20. accustomed: traditional.

25. Earth-treading stars: that is, young girls.

29. fennel: an herb. Capulet compares the young girls to fennel flowers.

30. Inherit: have.

33. stand in number: be one of the crowd (of girls). **though in reck'ning none:** though none will be worth more than Juliet is.

37. stay: wait.

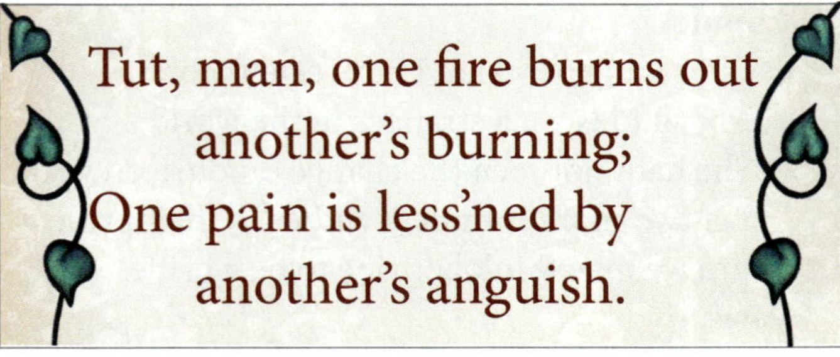
Tut, man, one fire burns out
another's burning;
One pain is less'ned by
another's anguish.

A **Reading Focus** **Reading Aloud** Capulet can be played many ways by actors. Some play him here as a loving, considerate father. Other actors interpret him as a man who chiefly wants a socially advantageous marriage for his daughter. Read this scene aloud and decide how you would play him.

Servant. Find them out whose names are written here? It is written that the shoemaker should meddle with his yard and the tailor with his last, the fisher with his pencil and the painter with his nets;° but I am sent to find those persons whose names are here writ, and can never find° what names the writing person hath here writ. I must to the learned. In good time!°

[*Enter* BENVOLIO *and* ROMEO.]

Benvolio.
Tut, man, one fire burns out another's burning;
One pain is less'ned by another's anguish;
Turn giddy, and be holp by backward turning;°
One desperate grief cures with another's languish.
Take thou some new infection to thy eye,
And the rank poison of the old will die.

Romeo.
Your plantain leaf is excellent for that.

Benvolio.
For what, I pray thee?

Romeo. For your broken° shin.

Benvolio.
Why, Romeo, art thou mad?

Romeo.
Not mad, but bound more than a madman is;
Shut up in prison, kept without my food,
Whipped and tormented and—God-den,° good fellow.

Servant. God gi' go-den. I pray, sir, can you read?

Romeo.
Ay, mine own fortune in my misery.

Servant. Perhaps you have learned it without book. But, I pray, can you read anything you see?

Romeo.
Ay, if I know the letters and the language.

Servant. Ye say honestly. Rest you merry.

Staging the Play

38. *Like the other servants, this one plays for comedy. He can't read or write. How should he show his bewilderment?*

39–41. shoemaker ... nets: The servant is quoting mixed-up proverbs. He's trying to say that people should attend to what they do best.

42. find: understand.

44. In good time: Just in time.

Staging the Play

44. *The servant looks up from the note to see the young gentlemen enter. He now tries to get them to read the note, while Benvolio chases Romeo across the stage. How do Romeo's comments in the following conversation show that he is trying to change the subject?*

47. be holp by backward turning: be helped by turning in the opposite direction.

52. broken: scratched.

56. God-den: good evening.

Staging the Play

56. *Romeo turns to get away and runs into the servant, who has been listening to them in stupefied silence. How should the two gentlemen treat the servant in this brief encounter?*

Romeo and Benvolio talk.

Romeo. Stay, fellow; I can read.

[*He reads the letter.*]

"Signior Martino and his wife and daughters;
County Anselm and his beauteous sisters;
The lady widow of Vitruvio;
Signior Placentio and his lovely nieces;
Mercutio and his brother Valentine;
Mine uncle Capulet, his wife and daughters;
My fair niece Rosaline; Livia;
Signior Valentio and his cousin Tybalt;
Lucio and the lively Helena."
A fair assembly. Whither should they come?

Servant. Up.

Romeo. Whither? To supper?

Servant. To our house.

Romeo. Whose house?

Servant. My master's.

Romeo.
Indeed I should have asked you that before.

Staging the Play
70. *Rosaline, Capulet's niece, is the young woman Romeo is in love with. Some actors read this line to reveal Romeo's secret to the audience. How would you have Romeo read this line? How would he ask his question in line 73?*

Servant. Now I'll tell you without asking. My master is the great rich Capulet; and if you be not of the house of Montagues, I pray come and crush a cup of wine. Rest you merry.

[*Exit.*]

Benvolio.
At this same ancient° feast of Capulet's
Sups the fair Rosaline whom thou so loves;
With all the admirèd beauties of Verona.
Go thither, and with unattainted° eye
Compare her face with some that I shall show,
And I will make thee think thy swan a crow.

Romeo.
When the devout religion of mine eye
   Maintains such falsehood, then turn tears to fires;
And these, who, often drowned, could never die,
   Transparent heretics,° be burnt for liars!
One fairer than my love? The all-seeing sun
Ne'er saw her match since first the world begun.

Benvolio.
Tut! you saw her fair, none else being by,
Herself poised° with herself in either eye;
But in that crystal scales° let there be weighed
Your lady's love against some other maid
That I will show you shining at this feast,
And she shall scant° show well that now seems best.

Romeo.
I'll go along, no such sight to be shown,
But to rejoice in splendor of mine own. **B**

[*Exeunt.*]

84. ancient: old; established by an old custom.

87. unattainted: untainted; unspoiled (by prejudice).

? **89.** *What does Benvolio say to lure Romeo to the party?*

93. Transparent heretics: His eyes would be easily "seen through"—they would betray the truth.

97. poised: balanced (for comparison).

98. crystal scales: Romeo's eyes.

101. scant: scarcely.

? **Staging the Play**
103. *If we know from the letter that Rosaline is to be at the party and that she is the one Romeo loves, we know why Romeo decides to go to Capulet's. Actors usually say these lines to indicate that the decision to go is crucial and fateful. What mood is Romeo in?*

B **Reading Focus** **Making Inferences** What do you learn of Romeo in this scene's concluding lines?

Scene 3. A room in Capulet's house.

Enter Capulet's wife, LADY CAPULET, *and* NURSE.

Lady Capulet.
Nurse, where's my daughter? Call her forth to me.

Nurse.
Now, by my maidenhead at twelve year old,
I bade her come. What,° lamb! What, ladybird!
God forbid, where's this girl? What, Juliet!

[*Enter* JULIET.]

Juliet.
How now? Who calls?

Nurse. Your mother.

Juliet. Madam, I am here.
What is your will?

Lady Capulet.
This is the matter.—Nurse, give leave awhile;
We must talk in secret. Nurse, come back again.
I have rememb'red me; thou's° hear our counsel.
Thou knowest my daughter's of a pretty age.

Nurse.
Faith, I can tell her age unto an hour.

Lady Capulet.
She's not fourteen.

Nurse. I'll lay fourteen of my teeth—
And yet, to my teen° be it spoken, I have but four—
She's not fourteen. How long is it now
To Lammastide?°

Lady Capulet. A fortnight and odd days.

Nurse.
Even or odd, of all days in the year,
Come Lammas Eve at night shall she be fourteen.
Susan and she (God rest all Christian souls!)
Were of an age.° Well, Susan is with God;

3. What: impatient call, like "Hey!" or "Where are you?"

9. thou's: thou shalt.

Staging the Play
10. *The nurse and Lady Capulet are opposites in nature. Lady Capulet sends the nurse off and then calls her back. Some actresses use this impulsive move to indicate Lady Capulet's reluctance to speak to her daughter about marriage. In contrast, how does the nurse react in this scene?*

13. teen: sorrow.

15. Lammastide: Christian church feast, held in England on August 1.

19. Were of an age: were the same age.

She was too good for me. But, as I said,
On Lammas Eve at night shall she be fourteen;
That shall she, marry; I remember it well.
'Tis since the earthquake now eleven years;
And she was weaned (I never shall forget it),
Of all the days of the year, upon that day;
For I had then laid wormwood to my dug,°
Sitting in the sun under the dovehouse wall.
My lord and you were then at Mantua.
Nay, I do bear a brain. But, as I said,
When it° did taste the wormwood on the nipple
Of my dug and felt it bitter, pretty fool,
To see it tetchy° and fall out with the dug!
Shake, quoth the dovehouse!° 'Twas no need, I trow,
To bid me trudge.
And since that time it is eleven years,
For then she could stand high-lone;° nay, by th' rood,°
She could have run and waddled all about;
For even the day before, she broke her brow;
And then my husband (God be with his soul!
'A was a merry man) took up the child.
"Yea," quoth he, "dost thou fall upon thy face?
Thou wilt fall backward when thou hast more wit;°
Wilt thou not, Jule?" and, by my holidam,°
The pretty wretch left° crying and said, "Ay."
To see now how a jest shall come about!
I warrant, and I should live a thousand years,
I never should forget it. "Wilt thou not, Jule?" quoth he,
And, pretty fool, it stinted° and said, "Ay."

Lady Capulet.
Enough of this. I pray thee hold thy peace.

Nurse.
Yes, madam. Yet I cannot choose but laugh
To think it should leave crying and say, "Ay."
And yet, I warrant, it had upon its brow
A bump as big as a young cock'rel's stone;
A perilous knock; and it cried bitterly.
"Yea," quoth my husband, "fall'st upon thy face?
Thou wilt fall backward when thou comest to age,
Wilt thou not, Jule?" It stinted and said, "Ay."

26. laid wormwood to my dug: applied a bitter substance (wormwood) to her breast to wean the baby.

30. it: she, the young Juliet.

32. tetchy: angry.

33. Shake, quoth the dovehouse: The dovehouse shook (from the earthquake).

36. high-lone: alone. **by th' rood:** by the cross (a mild oath).

42. wit: understanding.

43. by my holidam: by my holy relic (object associated with a saint).

44. left: stopped.

48. stinted: stopped.

? Staging the Play

48. *Shakespeare often includes* ***comic scenes*** *and speeches in his tragedies. The nurse laughs heartily at her husband's joke. How would Lady Capulet react?*

Juliet.
And stint thou too, I pray thee, nurse, say I. **A**

Nurse.
Peace, I have done. God mark thee to his grace!
Thou wast the prettiest babe that e'er I nursed.
And I might live to see thee married once,
I have my wish.

Lady Capulet.
Marry, that "marry" is the very theme
I came to talk of. Tell me, daughter Juliet,
How stands your disposition to be married?

Juliet.
It is an honor that I dream not of.

Nurse.
An honor? Were not I thine only nurse,
I would say thou hadst sucked wisdom from thy teat.

Lady Capulet.
Well, think of marriage now. Younger than you,
Here in Verona, ladies of esteem,
Are made already mothers. By my count,
I was your mother much upon these years
That you are now a maid. Thus then in brief:
The valiant Paris seeks you for his love.

Nurse.
A man, young lady! Lady, such a man
As all the world.—Why, he's a man of wax.°

Lady Capulet.
Verona's summer hath not such a flower.

Nurse.
Nay, he's a flower, in faith—a very flower.

Lady Capulet.
What say you? Can you love the gentleman? **B**
This night you shall behold him at our feast.
Read o'er the volume of young Paris' face,
And find delight writ there with beauty's pen;

Staging the Play
62. *Line 62 suggests another dramatic pause. Often a director will have Juliet rush to the nurse and kiss her. Her fondness for and gaiety with the nurse must contrast with her reserve toward her mother. How should Juliet react when she speaks in line 66?*

76. man of wax: man like a wax statue, with a perfect figure.

A Reading Focus Making Inferences How would Juliet react to her nurse's chatter? Do you think she finds the story funny?

B Reading Focus Making Inferences Notice that Juliet isn't answering. How do you suppose she is feeling during the conversation between the nurse and her mother about this man they want her to marry?

Examine every married lineament,°
And see how one another lends content;°
And what obscured in this fair volume lies
Find written in the margent of his eyes.
This precious book of love, this unbound lover,
To beautify him only lacks a cover.
The fish lives in the sea, and 'tis much pride
For fair without the fair within to hide.°
That book in many's eyes doth share the glory,
That in gold clasps locks in the golden story;
So shall you share all that he doth possess,
By having him, making yourself no less.

Nurse.
No less? Nay, bigger! Women grow by men.

Lady Capulet.
Speak briefly, can you like of Paris' love?

Juliet.
I'll look to like, if looking liking move;
But no more deep will I endart mine eye
Than your consent gives strength to make it fly.

[*Enter* SERVINGMAN.]

Servingman. Madam, the guests are come, supper served up, you called, my young lady asked for, the nurse cursed in the pantry, and everything in extremity. I must hence to wait. I beseech you follow straight.

[*Exit.*]

Lady Capulet.
We follow thee. Juliet, the county stays.°

Nurse.
Go, girl, seek happy nights to happy days.

[*Exeunt.*]

That book in many's eyes
doth share the glory,
That in gold clasps locks in
the golden story.

83. married lineament: harmonious feature.

84. how one another lends content: how one feature makes another look good.

90. For fair without the fair within to hide: for those who are handsome outwardly also to be handsome inwardly.

? **94.** *Lady Capulet has made an elegant appeal to Juliet, to persuade her to consider marrying Paris. Which images in this speech compare Paris to a fine book?*

? **Elements of Drama**
96. *A **character foil** is a character who sets off another character by contrast so that each will stand out vividly. How does the nurse serve as a foil to Lady Capulet?*

? **99.** *Juliet says she'll look at Paris to see if she likes him (if liking is brought about by looking). How does she show that she is a dutiful daughter?*

? **Staging the Play**
100. *Another comical servant enters, speaking breathlessly, but our attention still must be on Juliet. In some productions we now hear the sounds of music coming from offstage, and Juliet exits excitedly, with little dancing motions. Do we really know much about Juliet yet?*

104. the county stays: the count waits.

? **105.** *We meet Juliet for the first time in this scene. What is your first impression of her?*

Analyzing Visuals **Viewing and Interpreting**

What facial expressions might be hidden by these masks?

At the Capulets' party, the guests are costumed in face masks.

Scene 4. *A street.*

Enter ROMEO, MERCUTIO, BENVOLIO, *with five or six other* MASKERS; TORCHBEARERS.

Romeo.
What, shall this speech be spoke for our excuse?°
Or shall we on without apology?

Benvolio.
The date is out of such prolixity.°
We'll have no Cupid hoodwinked° with a scarf,
Bearing a Tartar's painted bow of lath,
Scaring the ladies like a crowkeeper;°
Nor no without-book prologue,° faintly spoke
After the prompter, for our entrance;
But, let them measure° us by what they will,
We'll measure them a measure° and be gone.

Romeo.
Give me a torch. I am not for this ambling.
Being but heavy, I will bear the light.

Mercutio.
Nay, gentle Romeo, we must have you dance.

Romeo.
Not I, believe me. You have dancing shoes
With nimble soles; I have a soul of lead
So stakes me to the ground I cannot move.

Mercutio.
You are a lover. Borrow Cupid's wings
And soar with them above a common bound.

Romeo.
I am too sore enpiercèd with his shaft
To soar with his light feathers; and so bound
I cannot bound a pitch° above dull woe.
Under love's heavy burden do I sink.

Mercutio.
And, to sink in it, should you burden love—
Too great oppression for a tender thing.

Romeo.
Is love a tender thing? It is too rough,
Too rude, too boist'rous, and it pricks like thorn.

? Elements of Drama
Stage direction: *For this stage direction, it's night. The stage is lit with torches and filled with masked young men. The mood is one of excitement—but we are watching Romeo. What does he say in the next speeches to indicate that he is still heavy-hearted?*

1. shall . . . excuse?: Shall we introduce ourselves with the usual speeches? (Uninvited maskers were usually announced by a messenger.)

3. The date . . . prolixity: Such long-winded speeches are out of fashion now.

4. hoodwinked: blindfolded.

6. crowkeeper: scarecrow.

7. without-book prologue: memorized speech.

9. measure: examine; appraise.

10. measure them a measure: dance a dance.

? Staging the Play
13. *Mercutio is a key character. Here he comes out of the crowd and speaks to Romeo. They engage in a verbal duel about love. In the following dialogue, how do Mercutio and Romeo differ in their attitudes toward love?*

21. bound a pitch: fly as high as a falcon.

? **23.** *In what ways does Mercutio show that he is a good friend to Romeo? Would you want to be Mercutio's friend?*

Mercutio.
If love be rough with you, be rough with love;
Prick love for pricking, and you beat love down.
Give me a case to put my visage in.
A visor° for a visor! What care I
What curious eye doth quote deformities?°
Here are the beetle brows shall blush° for me.

Benvolio.
Come, knock and enter; and no sooner in
But every man betake him to his legs.°

Romeo.
A torch for me! Let wantons light of heart
Tickle the senseless rushes° with their heels;
For I am proverbed with a grandsire phrase,°
I'll be a candleholder and look on;
The game was ne'er so fair, and I am done.° **A**

Mercutio.
Tut! Dun's the mouse, the constable's own word!
If thou art Dun,° we'll draw thee from the mire
Of this sir-reverence love,° wherein thou stickest
Upon to the ears. Come, we burn daylight, ho!

Romeo.
Nay, that's not so.

Mercutio. I mean, sir, in delay
We waste our lights° in vain, like lights by day.
Take our good meaning, for our judgment sits
Five times in that° ere once in our five wits.

Romeo.
And we mean well in going to this masque,
But 'tis no wit° to go.

Mercutio. Why, may one ask?

Romeo.
I dreamt a dream tonight.

Mercutio. And so did I.

Romeo.
Well, what was yours?

Mercutio. That dreamers often lie.

? Staging the Play
29. *Mercutio pauses and asks for a mask. What activity would he be engaged in here?*

30. visor: mask.

31. quote deformities: see imperfections (in the way he looks).

32. Here . . . blush: The mask's heavy eyebrows will blush for him.

34. betake . . . legs: begin dancing.

36. rushes: The dance floor is covered with rushes, plants with small green flowers.

37. grandsire phrase: old man's saying.

39. The game . . . I am done: The game (dancing) was never very good, and I'm exhausted.

41. Dun: pun on Romeo's "done"; Dun was the common name used for a horse in an old game called "Dun is in the mire."

42. sir-reverence love: "Save your reverence" is an apologetic expression. Mercutio means "We'll save you from—pardon me for saying so—love."

45. lights: torches.

47. in that: in our good meaning.

49. no wit: not a good idea.

A Reading Focus Making Inferences Despite Mercutio's teasing and Benvolio's urging, what is Romeo determined to do at the dance? What do his intentions suggest about him?

Romeo.
In bed asleep, while they do dream things true.
Mercutio.
O, then I see Queen Mab hath been with you.
She is the fairies' midwife, and she comes
In shape no bigger than an agate stone
On the forefinger of an alderman,
Drawn with a team of little atomies°
Over men's noses as they lie asleep;
Her wagon spokes made of long spinners'° legs,
The cover, of the wings of grasshoppers;
Her traces,° of the smallest spider web;
Her collars, of the moonshine's wat'ry beams;
Her whip, of cricket's bone; the lash, of film;°
Her wagoner, a small gray-coated gnat,
Not half so big as a round little worm
Pricked from the lazy finger of a maid;°
Her chariot is an empty hazelnut,
Made by the joiner squirrel or old grub,
Time out o' mind the fairies' coachmakers.
And in this state she gallops night by night
Through lovers' brains, and then they dream of love;
On courtiers' knees, that dream on curtsies straight;
O'er lawyers' fingers, who straight dream on fees;
O'er ladies' lips, who straight on kisses dream,
Which oft the angry Mab with blisters plagues,
Because their breaths with sweetmeats tainted are.
Sometime she gallops o'er a courtier's nose,
And then dreams he of smelling out a suit;°
And sometime comes she with a tithe pig's° tail
Tickling a parson's nose as 'a lies asleep,
Then dreams he of another benefice.°
Sometime she driveth o'er a soldier's neck,
And then dreams he of cutting foreign throats,
Of breaches, ambuscadoes, Spanish blades,
Of healths° five fathom deep; and then anon
Drums in his ear, at which he starts and wakes,
And being thus frighted, swears a prayer or two
And sleeps again. This is that very Mab
That plaits the manes of horses in the night
And bakes the elflocks° in foul sluttish hairs,
Which once untangled much misfortune bodes.

? Elements of Drama
53. *Mercutio, as a ringleader and a born entertainer, serves as a* ***character foil*** *for the more serious and emotional Romeo. Mercutio grabs everyone's attention with this famous* ***monologue****—a long speech directed at other characters onstage. What point is Mercutio making about dreams and their significance? What does he claim Queen Mab has to do with Romeo?*

57. atomies: tiny creatures.

59. spinners': spiders'.

61. traces: reins and harnesses for a wagon.

63. film: filament, or thread.

66. lazy finger of a maid: Lazy maids were said to have worms breeding in their fingers.

78. suit: person who might want to buy his influence at court.

79. tithe pig's: A tithe is a tenth of one's income, given to the church. Farmers often gave the parson one pig as a tithe.

81. benefice: church office that enabled a minister to make a living.

85. healths: toasts to his health.

90. elflocks: locks of hair that were tangled by mischievous elves.

This is the hag,° when maids lie on their backs,
That presses them and learns them first to bear,
Making them women of good carriage.°
This is she— **B**

Romeo. Peace, peace, Mercutio, peace!
Thou talk'st of nothing.

Mercutio. True, I talk of dreams;
Which are the children of an idle brain,
Begot of nothing but vain fantasy;
Which is as thin of substance as the air,
And more inconstant than the wind, who woos
Even now the frozen bosom of the North
And, being angered, puffs away from thence,
Turning his side to the dewdropping South.

Benvolio.
This wind you talk of blows us from ourselves.
Supper is done, and we shall come too late.

Romeo.
I fear, too early; for my mind misgives **C**
Some consequence yet hanging in the stars
Shall bitterly begin his fearful date
With this night's revels and expire the term
Of a despisèd life, closed in my breast,
By some vile forfeit of untimely death.
But he that hath the steerage of my course
Direct my sail! On, lusty gentlemen!

Benvolio. Strike, drum.

[*They march about the stage and retire to one side.*]

92. hag: nightmare. Nightmares were thought to be spirits who molested women at night.

94. women of good carriage: women who can bear children well.

? **94.** *Mercutio's tone changes here. How are these last details getting into subjects that are more shocking and cynical? Romeo doesn't like this turn of events and cuts Mercutio off.*

? **103.** *Mercutio could be comparing Romeo to the frozen north. If he is, what warning does he give his friend about remaining cold too long?*

But he that hath
the steerage
of my course
Direct my sail!
On, lusty
gentlemen!

B Reading Focus Reading Aloud/Paraphrasing Why does Mercutio say this to Romeo? Clarify your understanding of this monologue by reading it aloud. Paraphrase any passages that seem confusing.

C Literary Focus Tragedy Romeo here expresses his feeling that something will happen. Does he give reasons for his fear? Which words in this speech suggest that he is going to the party because he is in the hands of fate?

Juliet at the party.

Analyzing Visuals **Viewing and Interpreting** Does this image of Juliet match up with how you envisioned the character? What do you think Juliet should look like?

Scene 5. *A hall in Capulet's house.*

SERVINGMEN *come forth with napkins.*

First Servingman. Where's Potpan, that he helps not to take away? He shift a trencher!° He scrape a trencher!

Second Servingman. When good manners shall lie all in one or two men's hands, and they unwashed too, 'tis a foul thing.

First Servingman. Away with the join-stools,° remove the court cupboard, look to the plate. Good thou, save me a piece of marchpane,° and as thou loves me, let the porter let in Susan Grindstone and Nell, Anthony, and Potpan!

Second Servingman. Ay, boy, ready.

First Servingman. You are looked for and called for, asked for and sought for, in the great chamber.

Third Servingman. We cannot be here and there too. Cheerly, boys! Be brisk awhile, and the longer liver take all.

[*Exeunt.*]

[*Enter* CAPULET, LADY CAPULET, JULIET, TYBALT, NURSE, *and all the* GUESTS *and* GENTLEWOMEN, *meeting the* MASKERS.]

Capulet.

Welcome, gentlemen! Ladies that have their toes
Unplagued with corns will walk a bout° with you.
Ah, my mistresses, which of you all
Will now deny to dance? She that makes dainty,°
She I'll swear hath corns. Am I come near ye now?
Welcome, gentlemen! I have seen the day
That I have worn a visor and could tell
A whispering tale in a fair lady's ear,
Such as would please. 'Tis gone, 'tis gone, 'tis gone.
You are welcome, gentlemen! Come, musicians, play.

[*Music plays, and they dance.*]

? Staging the Play

Stage direction: *As you read these servants' speeches, note that one speaks in short emphatic phrases and bosses everyone else around. Which one is this? What mood do you think is suggested in this short scene?*

2. trencher: wooden plate.

6. join-stools: wooden stools made by a carpenter (a joiner).

8. marchpane: marzipan.

17. bout: dance.

19. makes dainty: pretends to be shy.

? Elements of Drama

Stage direction: *The dance, slow and stately, takes place at center stage. Old Capulet and his relative reminisce at one side, but our attention is focused on Romeo (in a mask) and Juliet, who is dancing with someone else. How does the following conversation contrast the two old men with Romeo and Juliet?*

A hall,° a hall! Give room! And foot it, girls.
More light, you knaves, and turn the tables up,
And quench the fire; the room is grown too hot.
Ah, sirrah, this unlooked-for sport° comes well.
Nay, sit; nay, sit, good cousin Capulet;
For you and I are past our dancing days.
How long is't now since last yourself and I
Were in a mask?

Second Capulet. By'r Lady, thirty years.

Capulet.
What, man? 'Tis not so much, 'tis not so much;
'Tis since the nuptial of Lucentio,
Come Pentecost as quickly as it will,
Some five-and-twenty years, and then we masked.

Second Capulet.
'Tis more, 'tis more. His son is elder, sir;
His son is thirty.

Capulet. Will you tell me that?
His son was but a ward° two years ago.

Romeo (*to a* SERVINGMAN).
What lady's that which doth enrich the hand
Of yonder knight?

Servingman. I know not, sir.

Romeo.
O, she doth teach the torches to burn bright!
It seems she hangs upon the cheek of night
As a rich jewel in an Ethiop's ear—
Beauty too rich for use, for earth too dear!
So shows a snowy dove trooping with crows
As yonder lady o'er her fellows shows.
The measure° done, I'll watch her place of stand
And, touching hers, make blessèd my rude° hand.
Did my heart love till now? Forswear it, sight!
For I ne'er saw true beauty till this night. **A**

Tybalt.
This, by his voice, should be a Montague.
Fetch me my rapier, boy. What! Dares the slave
Come hither, covered with an antic face,°
To fleer° and scorn at our solemnity?

26. A hall: clear the floor (for dancing).

29. unlooked-for sport: He hadn't expected to find some of the dancers masked.

40. ward: minor.

? Staging the Play
41. *In some productions, Romeo puts his torch down here, to draw our attention to his urgent question. Where would Juliet be onstage at this point?*

50. measure: dance.

51. rude: rough or simple.

? Staging the Play
54. *Why would we feel a sense of fear when we see Tybalt stepping onto center stage again?*

56. antic face: hideous mask.

57. fleer: jeer.

A Reading Focus **Making Inferences** What has happened to Romeo?

Romeo removes his mask at the party.

Analyzing Visuals **Viewing and Interpreting** Does this image of Romeo match up with how you pictured the character? What do you think Romeo should look like?

Now, by the stock and honor of my kin,
To strike him dead I hold it not a sin.

Capulet.
Why, how now, kinsman? Wherefore storm you so?

Tybalt.
Uncle, this is a Montague, our foe,
A villain, that is hither come in spite
To scorn at our solemnity this night.

Capulet.
Young Romeo is it?

Tybalt. 'Tis he, that villain Romeo.

Capulet.
Content thee, gentle coz, let him alone.
'A bears him like a portly° gentleman,
And, to say truth, Verona brags of him
To be a virtuous and well-governed youth.
I would not for the wealth of all this town
Here in my house do him disparagement.
Therefore be patient; take no note of him.
It is my will, the which if thou respect,
Show a fair presence and put off these frowns,
An ill-beseeming semblance for a feast.

Tybalt.
It fits when such a villain is a guest.
I'll not endure him.

Capulet. He shall be endured.
What, goodman boy!° I say he shall. Go to!°
Am I the master here, or you? Go to!
You'll not endure him, God shall mend my soul!
You'll make a mutiny among my guests!
You will set cock-a-hoop.° You'll be the man!

Tybalt.
Why, uncle, 'tis a shame.

Capulet. Go to, go to!
You are a saucy boy. Is't so, indeed?
This trick may chance to scathe° you. I know what.
You must contrary me! Marry, 'tis time—
Well said, my hearts!—You are a princox°—go!
Be quiet, or—More light, more light!—For shame!
I'll make you quiet. What!—Cheerly, my hearts!

Tybalt.
Patience perforce° with willful choler° meeting

66. portly: well-mannered.

? **74.** *What is Capulet's sensible reply to Tybalt's hostility? What feelings is Capulet revealing in his next speeches? Have Capulet's feelings about the Montagues changed since Scene 1?*

77. goodman boy: a scornful phrase. *Goodman* is below the rank of gentleman; *boy* is insulting. **Go to:** similar to "Go on" or "Cut it out."

81. set cock-a-hoop: start trouble.

84. scathe: hurt.

86. princox: rude youngster.

89. Patience perforce: enforced patience. **choler:** anger.

Makes my flesh tremble in their different greeting.
I will withdraw; but this intrusion shall,
Now seeming sweet, convert to bitt'rest gall. **B**

[*Exit.*]

Romeo.
If I profane with my unworthiest hand
This holy shrine, the gentle sin is this:°
My lips, two blushing pilgrims, ready stand
To smooth that rough touch with a tender kiss.

Juliet.
Good pilgrim, you do wrong your hand too much,
Which mannerly devotion shows in this;
For saints have hands that pilgrims' hands do touch,
And palm to palm is holy palmers'° kiss.

Romeo.
Have not saints lips, and holy palmers too?

Juliet.
Ay, pilgrim, lips that they must use in prayer.

Romeo.
O, then, dear saint, let lips do what hands do!
They pray; grant thou, lest faith turn to despair.

Juliet.
Saints do not move,° though grant for prayers' sake.

Romeo.
Then move not while my prayer's effect I take.
Thus from my lips, by thine my sin is purged.

[*Kisses her.*]

Juliet.
Then have my lips the sin that they have took.

Romeo.
Sin from my lips? O trespass sweetly urged!
Give me my sin again. [*Kisses her.*]

Juliet. You kiss by th' book.°

? Staging the Play
93. *In contrast to the raging Tybalt, Romeo is now at center stage with Juliet. Romeo takes Juliet's hand, and in their next fourteen lines (lines 93–106), the two young speakers' words form a* ***sonnet.*** *Romeo pretends to be a pilgrim going to a saint's shrine. What religious images do the two young lovers use to talk of their feelings for each other?*

94. the gentle sin is this: this is the sin of a gentleman.

100. palmers': pilgrims'. Pilgrims often carried palm leaves to show they had been to the Holy Land.

? Staging the Play
100. *Romeo and Juliet bring the palms of their hands together here. What in their words suggests that this is what they are doing?*

105. do not move: do not make the first move.

? Staging the Play
107. *In the midst of the swirling dancers, Romeo and Juliet kiss. All of the audience's attention must be on this kiss. What do you fear as you watch, remembering that Tybalt is nearby?*

110. You kiss by th' book: You take my words literally (to get more kisses).

B Reading Focus Paraphrasing Paraphrase lines 54–92, putting the exchange between Capulet and Tybalt in modern-day language.

Nurse.
Madam, your mother craves a word with you. **C**

Romeo.
What is her mother?

Nurse. Marry, bachelor,
Her mother is the lady of the house,
And a good lady, and a wise and virtuous.
I nursed her daughter that you talked withal.°
I tell you, he that can lay hold of her
Shall have the chinks.°

Romeo. Is she a Capulet?
O dear account! My life is my foe's debt.°

Benvolio.
Away, be gone; the sport is at the best.

Romeo.
Ay, so I fear; the more is my unrest.

Capulet.
Nay, gentlemen, prepare not to be gone;
We have a trifling foolish banquet towards.°
Is it e'en so? Why then, I thank you all.
I thank you, honest gentlemen. Good night.
More torches here! Come on then; let's to bed.
Ah, sirrah, by my fay,° it waxes late;
I'll to my rest.

[*Exeunt all but* JULIET *and* NURSE.]

Juliet.
Come hither, nurse. What is yond gentleman?

115. withal: with.

117. chinks: money.

118. My life is my foe's debt: My foe now owns my life.

? Staging the Play
120: *Romeo stands alone here, horrified. What activity goes on around him?*

122. towards: in preparation.

126. fay: faith.

? Staging the Play
128: *Juliet has moved to the side of the stage. What feelings must she convey in this question? (She is not pointing to Romeo.)*

C Literary Focus Conflict As the nurse interrupts, the dance ends. Juliet runs off, and Romeo is left alone with the nurse. What do we know about the Capulets' plans for Juliet that Romeo does not know?

Nurse.
The son and heir of old Tiberio.

Juliet.
What's he that now is going out of door?

Nurse.
Marry, that, I think, be young Petruchio.

Juliet.
What's he that follows there, that would not dance? **D**

Nurse.
I know not.

Juliet.
Go ask his name.—If he be marrièd,
My grave is like to be my wedding bed.

Nurse.
His name is Romeo, and a Montague,
The only son of your great enemy.

Juliet.
My only love, sprung from my only hate!
Too early seen unknown, and known too late!
Prodigious° birth of love it is to me
That I must love a loathèd enemy.

Nurse.
What's this? What's this?

Juliet. A rhyme I learnt even now
Of one I danced withal.

[*One calls within,* "Juliet."]

Nurse. Anon, anon!°
Come, let's away; the strangers all are gone.

[*Exeunt.*]

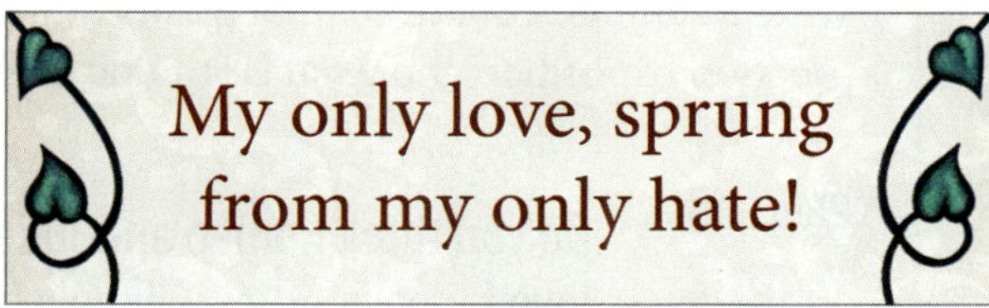
My only love, sprung
from my only hate!

140. Prodigious (pruh DIHJ uhs): huge and monstrous.

143. anon: at once.

Staging the Play
143. *What tone of voice would Juliet use here? What has she just realized?*

D Reading Focus **Making Inferences** Juliet has asked her nurse the names of several men at the dance. Why do you think she asks about Romeo last?

Applying Your Skills

The Tragedy of Romeo and Juliet, Act I

Respond and Think Critically

Reading Focus

Quick Check

1. What does the prologue say ends the rage between two families of Verona?
2. Who is Tybalt? What does he do that is unsafe?
3. Where do Romeo and Juliet first meet?

Read with a Purpose

4. In Act I, have Romeo and Juliet merely been victims of fate, or have they made conscious decisions about their actions? Explain your answer.

Reading Skills: Reading a Play

5. You recorded the causes that led Romeo to the party where he meets Juliet. What is the effect of their meeting? What do you predict will happen: Will they marry, run off together, break up?

Analyze Causes and Effects	My Notes
What happens when Romeo meets Juliet?	

Literary Focus

Literary Analysis

6. **Analyze** Mercutio is a character foil to Romeo. In drama, a **character foil** is a character who sets off another character by strong contrast. In what way is Mercutio a foil to Romeo?
7. **Interpret** Romeo and Juliet first speak to each other in a sonnet in which Romeo sees himself as a pilgrim and Juliet as the saint he worships. How does the language and imagery embody their feelings for each other?
8. **Evaluate** Romeo and Juliet fall deeply in love at first sight. Does Shakespeare succeed in making this scene convincing? Explain.

Literary Skills: Tragedy

9. **Analyze** What problem, or **complication,** is presented in Scenes 2 and 3 that may limit Juliet's freedom?
10. **Analyze** The title of the play tells us it is a **tragedy**—a play in which the main characters come to an unhappy end. How do Romeo's and Juliet's reactions in Scene 5 (when they learn each other's identity) **foreshadow,** or give clues to, what trouble may lie ahead?

Literary Skills Review: Characterization

11. **Analyze** The process of revealing the personality of a character is called **characterization.** In Scene 3, what do you learn about Juliet's relationship with her mother and her feelings about marriage?

Writing Focus

Think as a Reader/Writer

Use It in Your Writing Using your notes on Act I, write a summary of the act that points out various aspects of exposition and what is left unexplained.

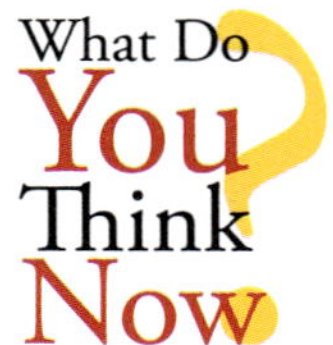

Do you think Romeo and Juliet's love for each other will help them overcome the difficulties surrounding them? Why or why not?

9.R.2.C.1.b Use details from text(s): to analyze character, plot, setting, point of view *Also covered* 9.R.2; 9.R.3.C.1.a; 9.R.1.F.1.c; 9.W.3.A.1.c; 9.R.1.E.1.c; 9.R.1.E.1.b

Vocabulary Development

Vocabulary Skills: Shakespeare's Words—Then and Now

Many words in Shakespeare's plays have different meanings today. *Humor,* for example, comes from a Latin word for "moisture; fluid." In Shakespeare's time, people believed there were four fluids, or humors, in the body, which regulated a person's temperament, or mood. *Humorous* eventually came to refer to a person who can see comedy in situations.

Your Turn

The following words are used frequently in modern English, but in Shakespeare's day the words had different meanings. Use a good dictionary to research their **derivations,** or origins. (Which words are very old English words, rooted in Anglo-Saxon or Old English?) Make a diagram like the one below, showing their origins, what each word meant in Shakespeare's day, and what it means today.

	Word Origin	Archaic Meaning	Modern Meaning
maid (Scene 1, line 11)			
stay (Scene 1, line 155)			
still (Scene 1, line 168)			
soft (Scene 1, line 192)			
wit (Scene 3, line 42)			

Language Coach

Context Clues When you come across a familiar word that has an archaic meaning, it can be confusing at first. To overcome your confusion, re-read the passage that contains the word and identify the word that doesn't seem to make sense in the context. Use the context clues to try to figure out what other meaning that familiar word may have.

Example: His *view* is pleasing but his soul is rotten.

Strategy: The word *view* in this sentence may not seem to make sense at first. In modern English, it means "something one sees." The context clues can help you to see that a contrast is being made between a man's view and his soul. Therefore, *view,* in this context, means "appearance."

Academic Vocabulary

Talk About . . .

Look back through Act I of *The Tragedy of Romeo and Juliet*, and re-read some of the Staging the Play sidenotes. Discuss with a partner how you would stage a production of the play. What costume decisions would you make? What would you do for sets, casting, or props? Use Academic Vocabulary words in your discussion.

ACT II

2004 production of *Romeo and Juliet* performed at the Globe Theatre, London.

Read with a Purpose As you read, think about the decisions that Romeo and Juliet make in this act and how those decisions might affect their lives.

ACT II

Enter CHORUS.

Chorus.

Now old desire doth in his deathbed lie,
And young affection gapes to be his heir;
That fair° for which love groaned for and would die,
With tender Juliet matched, is now not fair.
Now Romeo is beloved and loves again,
Alike° bewitchèd by the charm of looks;
But to his foe supposed he must complain,°
And she steal love's sweet bait from fearful hooks.
Being held a foe, he may not have access
To breathe such vows as lovers use to swear,°
And she as much in love, her means much less
To meet her new belovèd anywhere;
But passion lends them power, time means, to meet,
Temp'ring extremities° with extreme sweet.° [*Exit.*] **A**

3. That fair: Rosaline.

6. Alike: both (both Romeo and Juliet).

7. complain: ask Juliet's father, his foe, for her hand in marriage.

10. use to swear: are used to promising.

14. extremities: difficulties. **extreme sweet:** very sweet delights.

SCENE 1. *Near Capulet's orchard.*

Enter ROMEO *alone.*

Romeo.

Can I go forward when my heart is here?
Turn back, dull earth, and find thy center° out.

[*Enter* BENVOLIO *with* MERCUTIO. ROMEO *retires.*]

2. center: Juliet. The "dull earth" is Romeo, and Juliet is his soul.

? **Elements of Drama**
Stage direction: *Although the stage direction says that Romeo "retires," a few lines later Benvolio says that Romeo ran and leapt over the wall. Since leaping a wall is difficult, most actors simply move behind it. How might the stage be designed so that we see Romeo hiding in Capulet's orchard and Benvolio and Mercutio on the other side of the wall?*

A **Literary Skills** **Rising Action** According to the Chorus, what has happened to Romeo's old love? What is his new problem? What line suggests that these young people fell in love at first sight?

Benvolio.
Romeo! My cousin Romeo! Romeo!
Mercutio. He is wise
And, on my life, hath stol'n him home to bed.
Benvolio.
He ran this way and leapt this orchard wall.
Call, good Mercutio.
Mercutio. Nay, I'll conjure too.
Romeo! Humors! Madman! Passion! Lover!
Appear thou in the likeness of a sigh;
Speak but one rhyme, and I am satisfied!
Cry but "Ay me!" pronounce but "love" and "dove";
Speak to my gossip° Venus one fair word,
One nickname for her purblind° son and heir,
Young Abraham Cupid,° he that shot so true
When King Cophetua loved the beggar maid!°
He heareth not, he stirreth not, he moveth not;
The ape is dead,° and I must conjure him.
I conjure thee by Rosaline's bright eyes,
By her high forehead and her scarlet lip,
By her fine foot, straight leg, and quivering thigh,
And the demesnes° that there adjacent lie,
That in thy likeness thou appear to us!
Benvolio.
And if he hear thee, thou wilt anger him. **B**
Mercutio.
This cannot anger him. 'Twould anger him
To raise a spirit in his mistress' circle°
Of some strange nature, letting it there stand
Till she had laid it and conjured it down.
That were some spite;° my invocation
Is fair and honest: in his mistress' name,
I conjure only but to raise up him.
Benvolio.
Come, he hath hid himself among these trees
To be consorted° with the humorous° night.
Blind is his love and best befits the dark.
Mercutio.
If love be blind, love cannot hit the mark.

11. gossip: good friend. In Roman mythology, Venus is the goddess of love.

12. purblind (PUR blynd): blind.

13. Young Abraham Cupid: To Mercutio, Romeo seems the very figure of love—old like Abraham in the Bible and young like Cupid, the god of love in Roman mythology.

14. When . . . maid: from a popular ballad.

16. The ape is dead: Romeo is "playing" dead.

20. demesnes (dih MAYNZ): domains; regions.

24. circle: magical place.

27. spite: cause to be angry.

31. consorted: familiar. **humorous:** damp.

B **Reading Focus** **Making Inferences** What is Benvolio's tone here? Why would Romeo be angry at Mercutio's remarks?

And wish his mistress were that kind of fruit
As maids call medlars when they laugh alone.
O, Romeo, that she were, O that she were
An open et cetera, thou a pop'rin pear!
Romeo, good night. I'll to my truckle bed;
This field bed is too cold for me to sleep.
Come, shall we go?

Benvolio. Go then, for 'tis in vain
To seek him here that means not to be found.

[*Exit with others.*]

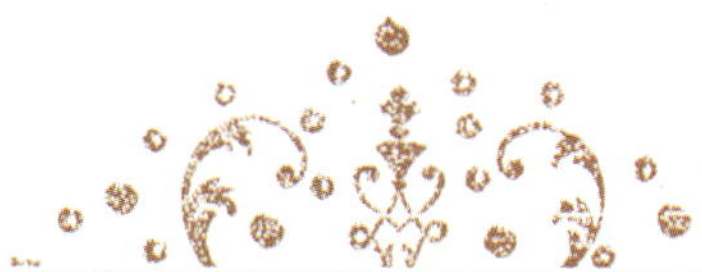

SCENE 2. *Capulet's orchard.*

Romeo (*coming forward*).
He jests at scars that never felt a wound.

[*Enter* JULIET *at a window.*]

But soft! What light through yonder window breaks?
It is the East, and Juliet is the sun!
Arise, fair sun, and kill the envious moon,
Who is already sick and pale with grief
That thou her maid° art far more fair than she.
Be not her maid, since she is envious.
Her vestal livery° is but sick and green,°
And none but fools do wear it. Cast it off.
It is my lady! O, it is my love!
O, that she knew she were!
She speaks, yet she says nothing. What of that?
Her eye discourses;° I will answer it.
I am too bold; 'tis not to me she speaks.
Two of the fairest stars in all the heaven,
Having some business, do entreat her eyes
To twinkle in their spheres till they return.
What if her eyes were there, they in her head?
The brightness of her cheek would shame those stars
As daylight doth a lamp; her eyes in heaven
Would through the airy region stream so bright

? **1.** *Romeo has heard all the joking. Whom is he referring to here, and what kind of "wound" is he talking about?*

? **Elements of Drama**
2. *Romeo's* ***soliloquy*** *begins the balcony scene. This is one of the most famous scenes in all dramatic literature—in which the two lovers woo and win each other. (In the Elizabethan theater [see page 800], a balcony was already built into the stage, so the* ***scene design*** *was not a problem. In modern theaters, however, it is often difficult to have a balcony high enough and yet still visible to people sitting in the back of the theater.) What is Juliet doing while Romeo is speaking aloud to himself?*

6. thou her maid: Juliet, whom Romeo sees as the servant of the virgin goddess of the moon, Diana in Roman mythology.

8. vestal livery: maidenly clothing. **sick and green:** Unmarried girls supposedly had "greensickness," or anemia.

13. discourses: speaks.

That birds would sing and think it were not night.
See how she leans her cheek upon her hand!
O, that I were a glove upon that hand,
That I might touch that cheek!

Juliet. Ay me!

Romeo. She speaks.
O, speak again, bright angel, for thou art
As glorious to this night, being o'er my head,
As is a wingèd messenger of heaven
Unto the white-upturnèd wond'ring eyes
Of mortals that fall back to gaze on him
When he bestrides the lazy puffing clouds
And sails upon the bosom of the air.

Juliet.
O Romeo, Romeo! Wherefore° art thou Romeo?
Deny thy father and refuse thy name;
Or, if thou wilt not, be but sworn my love,
And I'll no longer be a Capulet.

Romeo (*aside*).
Shall I hear more, or shall I speak at this? **A**

Juliet.
'Tis but thy name that is my enemy.
Thou art thyself, though not° a Montague.
What's Montague? It is nor hand, nor foot,
Nor arm, nor face. O, be some other name
Belonging to a man.
What's in a name? That which we call a rose
By any other word would smell as sweet.
So Romeo would, were he not Romeo called,
Retain that dear perfection which he owes°
Without that title. Romeo, doff thy name;
And for thy name, which is no part of thee,
Take all myself.

Romeo. I take thee at thy word.
Call me but love, and I'll be new baptized;
Henceforth I never will be Romeo.

Juliet.
What man art thou, that, thus bescreened in night,
So stumblest on my counsel?°

? **Elements of Drama**
25. *Romeo and Juliet rarely talk of each other in straightforward prose. What are some of the* ***figures of speech*** *and images that Romeo uses to express his love here?*

33. Wherefore: why. *In other words, "Why is your name Romeo?" (It is the name of her enemy.)*

? **Elements of Drama**
Stage direction: *Here Romeo is speaking an* ***aside****—a remark made to the audience or to another character that others onstage are not meant to hear. Why do you think Romeo would not want Juliet to hear his thoughts?*

39. though not: even if you were not.

? **Elements of Drama**
42. *Short lines like this one usually indicate an interruption or pause. Here Juliet pauses to think about a question. What does she say in answer to this question about the true significance of a name?*

46. owes: owns.

? **Elements of Drama**
49. *All of Romeo's and Juliet's speeches in this scene so far have been soliloquies. A* ***soliloquy*** *is a speech in which a character, who is usually alone onstage, expresses private thoughts or feelings that the audience hears. (A soliloquy is different from a* ***monologue,*** *which is directed to other characters onstage.) Here the lovers speak their thoughts out loud, but not to each other. Which of the lines that follow tell us that Romeo is now speaking to Juliet?*

53. counsel: private thoughts.

A **Reading Focus** **Paraphrasing** Juliet does not know that Romeo is standing beneath her balcony. What has Romeo now learned about her feelings for him?

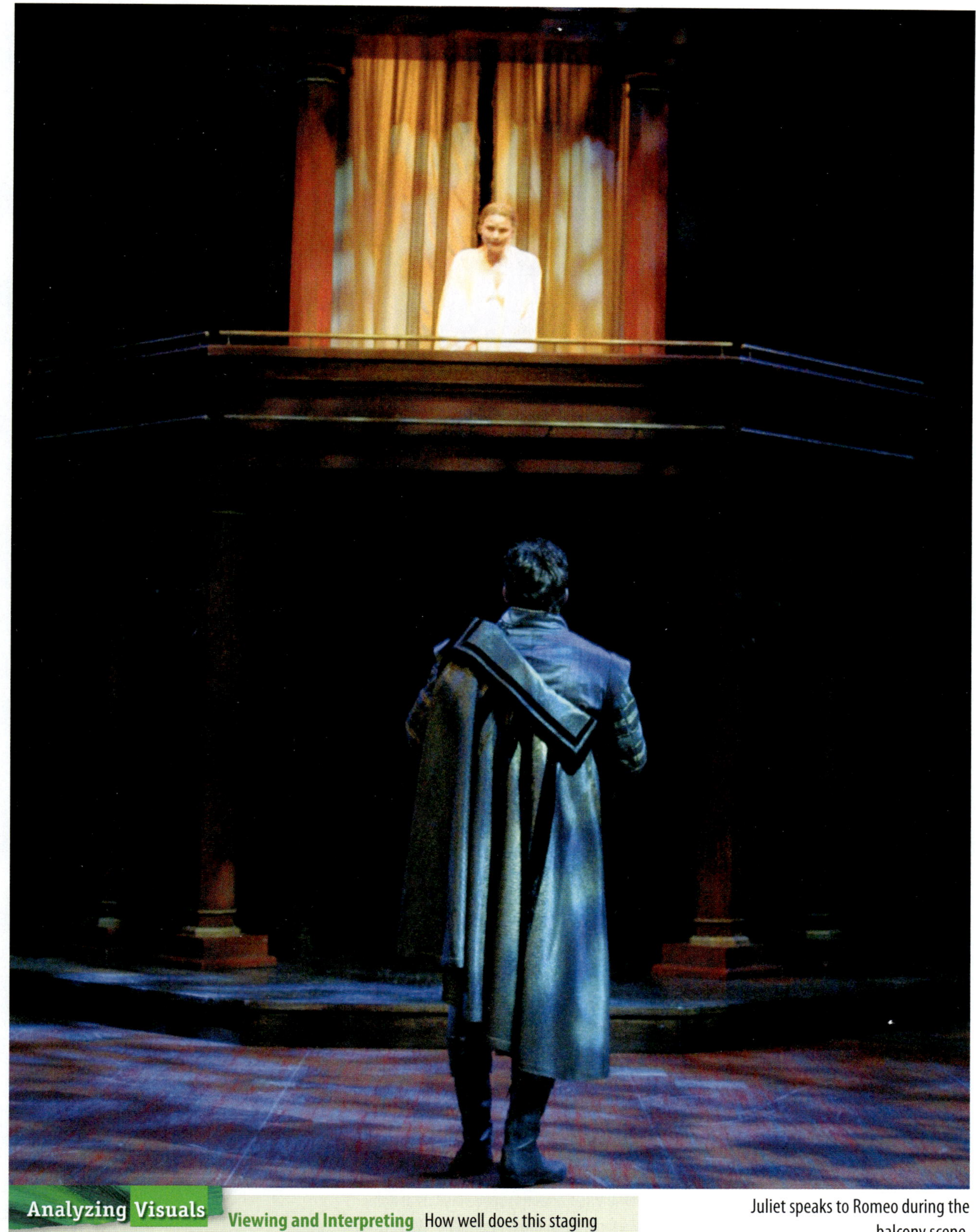

Analyzing Visuals **Viewing and Interpreting** How well does this staging reflect Scene 2? Do you think this is what Shakespeare envisioned when he wrote the scene?

Juliet speaks to Romeo during the balcony scene.

Romeo. By a name
I know not how to tell thee who I am.
My name, dear saint, is hateful to myself
Because it is an enemy to thee.
Had I it written, I would tear the word.

Juliet.
My ears have yet not drunk a hundred words
Of thy tongue's uttering, yet I know the sound.
Art thou not Romeo, and a Montague?

Romeo.
Neither, fair maid, if either thee dislike.

Juliet.
How camest thou hither, tell me, and wherefore?
The orchard walls are high and hard to climb,
And the place death, considering who thou art,
If any of my kinsmen find thee here.

Romeo.
With love's light wings did I o'erperch° these walls;
For stony limits cannot hold love out,
And what love can do, that dares love attempt.
Therefore thy kinsmen are no stop to me.

Juliet.
If they do see thee, they will murder thee.

Romeo.
Alack, there lies more peril in thine eye
Than twenty of their swords! Look thou but sweet,
And I am proof° against their enmity.

Juliet.
I would not for the world they saw thee here. **B**

Romeo.
I have night's cloak to hide me from their eyes;
And but° thou love me, let them find me here.
My life were better ended by their hate
Than death proroguèd,° wanting of thy love. **C**

66. o'erperch: fly over.

73. proof: armored.

76. but: if only.

78. proroguèd: postponed.

B **Reading Focus** **Making Inferences** Juliet is practical. She fears Romeo will be murdered. What is Romeo's tone—is he also fearful, or is he reckless and elated?

C **Reading Focus** **Analyzing Cause and Effect** The two lovers will repeatedly remind us that they prefer death to separation. What does this speech tell us of Romeo's intentions? What might happen if he follows through on those intentions? What would happen if he doesn't?

Juliet.
By whose direction found'st thou out this place?
Romeo.
By Love, that first did prompt me to inquire.
He lent me counsel, and I lent him eyes.
I am no pilot; yet, wert thou as far
As that vast shore washed with the farthest sea,
I should adventure for such merchandise.

My ears have yet not drunk
a hundred words
Of thy tongue's uttering,
yet I know the sound.

Juliet.
Thou knowest the mask of night is on my face;
Else would a maiden blush bepaint my cheek
For that which thou hast heard me speak tonight.
Fain would I dwell on form—fain, fain deny
What I have spoke; but farewell compliment.°
Dost thou love me? I know thou wilt say "Ay";
And I will take thy word. Yet, if thou swear'st,
Thou mayst prove false. At lovers' perjuries,
They say Jove laughs. O gentle Romeo,
If thou dost love, pronounce it faithfully.
Or if thou think'st I am too quickly won,
I'll frown and be perverse and say thee nay,
So thou wilt woo; but else, not for the world.
In truth, fair Montague, I am too fond,°
And therefore thou mayst think my havior° light;
But trust me, gentleman, I'll prove more true
Than those that have more cunning to be strange.°
I should have been more strange, I must confess,
But that thou overheard'st, ere I was ware,
My truelove passion. Therefore pardon me,
And not impute this yielding to light love,
Which the dark night hath so discoverèd.°
Romeo.
Lady, by yonder blessèd moon I vow,
That tips with silver all these fruit-tree tops—
Juliet.
O, swear not by the moon, the inconstant moon,
That monthly changes in her circle orb,
Lest that thy love prove likewise variable.

? Elements of Drama
85. *Juliet's thoughts race now, and she probably speaks rapidly here. Read this* **monologue** *aloud. Where does Juliet shift from embarrassment to frankness, to pleading, to anxiety, to doubt? Why is she worried that Romeo will think poorly of her?*

89. compliment: good manners.

98. fond: affectionate, tender.

99. havior: behavior.

101. strange: aloof or cold.

106. discoverèd: revealed.

? Staging the Play
109. *Why is Juliet afraid of having Romeo swear by the moon? If you were speaking these lines, would you make them comic, or would you make Juliet sound genuinely frightened?*

Romeo.
What shall I swear by?

Juliet. Do not swear at all;
Or if thou wilt, swear by thy gracious self,
Which is the god of my idolatry,
And I'll believe thee.

Romeo. If my heart's dear love—

Juliet.
Well, do not swear. Although I joy in thee,
I have no joy of this contract tonight.
It is too rash, too unadvised, too sudden;
Too like the lightning, which doth cease to be
Ere one can say it lightens. Sweet, good night!
This bud of love, by summer's ripening breath,
May prove a beauteous flower when next we meet.
Good night, good night! As sweet repose and rest
Come to thy heart as that within my breast!

Romeo.
O, wilt thou leave me so unsatisfied?

Juliet.
What satisfaction canst thou have tonight?

Romeo.
The exchange of thy love's faithful vow for mine.

Juliet.
I gave thee mine before thou didst request it;
And yet I would it were to give again.

Romeo.
Wouldst thou withdraw it? For what purpose, love?

Juliet.
But to be frank° and give it thee again.
And yet I wish but for the thing I have.
My bounty° is as boundless as the sea,
My love as deep; the more I give to thee,
The more I have, for both are infinite.
I hear some noise within. Dear love, adieu!

[NURSE *calls within.*]

Anon, good nurse! Sweet Montague, be true.
Stay but a little, I will come again.

[*Exit.*]

? **120.** *Romeo is quick with vows and promises. Why has Juliet become fearful and cautious?*

131. frank: generous.

133. bounty: capacity for giving.

Romeo.
O blessèd, blessèd night! I am afeard,
Being in night, all this is but a dream,
Too flattering-sweet to be substantial.

[*Enter* JULIET *again.*]

Juliet.
Three words, dear Romeo, and good night indeed.
If that thy bent° of love be honorable,
Thy purpose marriage, send me word tomorrow,
By one that I'll procure to come to thee,
Where and what time thou wilt perform the rite;
And all my fortunes at thy foot I'll lay
And follow thee my lord throughout the world. Ⓓ
Nurse (*within*). Madam!
Juliet.
I come anon.—But if thou meanest not well,
I do beseech thee—
Nurse (*within*). Madam!
Juliet. By and by I come.—
To cease thy strife° and leave me to my grief.
Tomorrow will I send.
Romeo. So thrive my soul—
Juliet.
A thousand times good night!

[*Exit.*]

Romeo.
A thousand times the worse, to want thy light!
Love goes toward love as schoolboys from their books;
But love from love, toward school with heavy looks.

[*Enter* JULIET *again.*]

Juliet.
Hist! Romeo, hist! O for a falc'ner's voice
To lure this tassel gentle° back again!
Bondage is hoarse° and may not speak aloud,
Else would I tear the cave where

143. bent: intention.

153. strife: efforts to win her.

? **Staging the Play**
154. *With this fervent vow, Romeo swears by his immortal soul. What lines that follow indicate that Romeo turns around and heads away from Juliet's balcony?*

160. tassel gentle: male falcon.

161. Bondage is hoarse: Juliet is in "bondage" to her parents and must whisper.

Ⓓ **Reading Focus Paraphrasing** What is Juliet making clear to Romeo here? Where does she show that she still fears he may be false with her?

Echo° lies
And make her airy tongue more hoarse than mine
With repetition of "My Romeo!"

Romeo.
It is my soul that calls upon my name.
How silver-sweet sound lovers' tongues by night,
Like softest music to attending ears!

Juliet.
Romeo!

Romeo.
My sweet?

Juliet. What o'clock tomorrow
Shall I send to thee?

Romeo. By the hour of nine.

Juliet.
I will not fail. 'Tis twenty years till then.
I have forgot why I did call thee back.

Romeo.
Let me stand here till thou remember it.

Juliet.
I shall forget, to have thee still stand there,
Rememb'ring how I love thy company.

Romeo.
And I'll still stay, to have thee still forget,
Forgetting any other home but this.

Juliet.
'Tis almost morning. I would have thee gone—
And yet no farther than a wanton's° bird,
That lets it hop a little from his hand,
Like a poor prisoner in his twisted gyves,°
And with a silken thread plucks it back again,
So loving-jealous of his liberty.

Romeo.
I would I were thy bird.

Juliet. Sweet, so would I.
Yet I should kill thee with much cherishing. 

Parting is such sweet sorrow
That I shall say good night
till it be morrow.

162. Echo: In Greek mythology, a girl who could only repeat others' final words.

174. *When Juliet first discovers that Romeo is in the garden, she urges him to leave for his own safety. Why does she now want him to stay?*

178. wanton's: careless child's.

180. gyves (jyvz): chains, like the threads that hold the bird captive.

E Literary Focus Rising Action What terrible event might Juliet's words foreshadow?

Good night, good night! Parting is such sweet sorrow
That I shall say good night till it be morrow. [*Exit.*]

185. *Why is parting "sweet" to Juliet? (Is she enjoying this prolonged farewell?)*

Romeo.
Sleep dwell upon thine eyes, peace in thy breast!
Would I were sleep and peace, so sweet to rest!
Hence will I to my ghostly friar's° close cell,
His help to crave and my dear hap° to tell. [*Exit.*]

189. ghostly friar's: spiritual father's.

190. hap: luck.

SCENE 3. *Friar Laurence's cell.*

Enter FRIAR LAURENCE *alone, with a basket.*

Friar.
The gray-eyed morn smiles on the frowning night,
Check'ring the eastern clouds with streaks of light;
And fleckèd darkness like a drunkard reels
From forth day's path and Titan's burning wheels.°
Now, ere the sun advance his burning eye
The day to cheer and night's dank dew to dry,
I must upfill this osier cage° of ours
With baleful° weeds and precious-juicèd flowers.
The earth that's Nature's mother is her tomb.
What is her burying grave, that is her womb;
And from her womb children of divers kind
We sucking on her natural bosom find,
Many for many virtues excellent,
None but for some, and yet all different.
O, mickle° is the powerful grace that lies
In plants, herbs, stones, and their true qualities;
For naught so vile that on the earth doth live
But to the earth some special good doth give;
Nor aught so good but, strained° from that fair use,
Revolts from true birth,° stumbling on abuse.
Virtue itself turns vice, being misapplied,
And vice sometime by action dignified.

Elements of Drama
1. *In the absence of lighting, Shakespeare had his characters "set the stage" in their speeches. What "scene" does the friar set in this* ***soliloquy?*** *How are his images of night different from Romeo's images in his "O blessèd, blessèd night" speech in the last scene?*

4. Titan's burning wheels: wheels of the sun god's chariot.

7. osier (OH zhuhr) **cage:** cage woven of willow branches.

8. baleful: evil or poisonous.

15. mickle: great.

19. strained: turned aside.

20. true birth: true purpose.

22. *How, according to the friar, can good turn to evil and evil turn to good?*

Romeo talks with Friar Laurence.

Analyzing Visuals **Viewing and Interpreting** Look closely at the actors' facial expressions and body language. How well does each actor embody his character (Romeo and Friar Laurence)? Explain.

[*Enter* ROMEO.] 

Within the infant rind° of this weak flower
Poison hath residence and medicine° power;
For this, being smelt, with that part cheers each part;°
Being tasted, stays all senses with the heart.
Two such opposèd kings encamp them still°
In man as well as herbs—grace and rude will;
And where the worser is predominant,
Full soon the canker° death eats up that plant.

Romeo.
Good morrow, father.

Friar. Benedicite!°
What early tongue so sweet saluteth me?
Young son, it argues a distemperèd head°
So soon to bid good morrow to thy bed.
Care keeps his watch in every old man's eye,
And where care lodges, sleep will never lie;
But where unbruisèd° youth with unstuffed° brain
Doth couch his limbs, there golden sleep doth reign.
Therefore thy earliness doth me assure
Thou art uproused with some distemp'rature;
Or if not so, then here I hit it right—
Our Romeo hath not been in bed tonight.

Romeo.
That last is true. The sweeter rest was mine.

Friar.
God pardon sin! Wast thou with Rosaline?

Romeo.
With Rosaline, my ghostly father? No.
I have forgot that name and that name's woe.

Friar.
That's my good son! But where hast thou been then?

Romeo.
I'll tell thee ere thou ask it me again.
I have been feasting with mine enemy,
Where on a sudden one hath wounded me
That's by me wounded. Both our remedies
Within thy help and holy physic° lies.

A **Literary Focus** **Rising Action** Romeo enters quietly, unseen by the friar. As the friar explains that his flower contains the power to heal as well as kill, why might the audience fear for Romeo and Juliet?

23. rind: outer covering.

24. medicine: medicinal.

25. For . . . part: When the flower is smelled, each part of the body is stimulated.

27. still: always.

30. canker: cankerworm, a larva that feeds on leaves.

31. Benedicite (behn uh DIHS uh tee): Latin for "bless you."

33. distemperèd head: troubled mind.

37. unbruisèd: innocent. **unstuffed:** untroubled.

? Staging the Play
44. *Does the friar approve? If you were playing the friar, how would you speak to Romeo?*

52. holy physic: the friar's healing power (physic) to make Romeo and Juliet husband and wife.

I bear no hatred, blessèd man, for, lo,
My intercession° likewise steads° my foe.

Friar.

Be plain, good son, and homely° in thy drift.
Riddling confession finds but riddling shrift.°

Romeo.

Then plainly know my heart's dear love is set
On the fair daughter of rich Capulet;
As mine on hers, so hers is set on mine,
And all combined,° save what thou must combine
By holy marriage. When and where and how
We met, we wooed, and made exchange of vow,
I'll tell thee as we pass; but this I pray,
That thou consent to marry us today.

Friar.

Holy Saint Francis! What a change is here!
Is Rosaline, that thou didst love so dear,
So soon forsaken? Young men's love then lies
Not truly in their hearts, but in their eyes.
Jesu Maria! What a deal of brine
Hath washed thy sallow cheeks for Rosaline!
How much salt water thrown away in waste
To season° love, that of it doth not taste!
The sun not yet thy signs from heaven clears,
Thy old groans ring yet in mine ancient ears.
Lo, here upon thy cheek the stain doth sit
Of an old tear that is not washed off yet.
If e'er thou wast thyself, and these woes thine,
Thou and these woes were all for Rosaline.
And art thou changed? Pronounce this sentence then:
Women may fall when there's no strength in men.

Romeo.

Thou chid'st me oft for loving Rosaline.

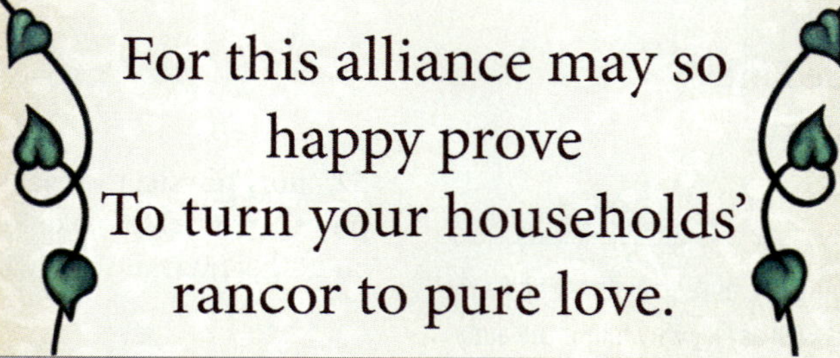
For this alliance may so
happy prove
To turn your households'
rancor to pure love.

54. intercession: request.
steads: helps.

55. homely: simple and straightforward.

Elements of Drama

56. *As we have seen, the play is mostly written in* ***blank verse,*** *but Shakespeare varies his verse forms from time to time. The prologues are written in* ***sonnet form.*** *The endings of scenes are marked by* ***rhymed couplets.*** *What is the* ***rhyme scheme*** *of this dialogue?*

56. shrift: forgiveness (in the religious rite of confession).

60. combined: agreed.

Elements of Drama

65. *In the* ***exposition*** *of the play, Shakespeare keeps Romeo's intense love in perspective by letting us see how others regard him. We have heard Mercutio's sarcastic "The ape is dead." How does Friar Laurence continue with this scolding and ridicule? What actions do you imagine Romeo is engaged in as he listens to the priest?*

72. season: preserve; keep fresh. (In Shakespeare's day, food was seasoned with salt to keep it from spoiling.)

Friar.
For doting, not for loving, pupil mine.

Romeo.
And bad'st me bury love.

Friar. Not in a grave
To lay one in, another out to have.

Romeo.
I pray thee chide me not. Her I love now
Doth grace° for grace and love for love allow.
The other did not so.

Friar. O she knew well
Thy love did read by rote, that could not spell.°
But come, young waverer, come go with me.
In one respect I'll thy assistant be;
For this alliance may so happy prove
To turn your households' rancor to pure love.

Romeo.
O, let us hence! I stand on° sudden haste.

Friar.
Wisely and slow. They stumble that run fast. [*Exeunt.*] **B**

86. grace: favor.

88. Thy love . . . spell: Romeo recited words of love without understanding them.

? **92.** *In Shakespeare's time it was not at all unusual to form alliances and settle disputes by arranging marriages. How does this explain Friar Laurence's decision to help the young couple?*

93. I stand on: I am firm about.

SCENE 4. *A street.*

Enter BENVOLIO *and* MERCUTIO.

Mercutio.
Where the devil should this Romeo be?
Came he not home tonight?

Benvolio.
Not to his father's. I spoke with his man.

Mercutio.
Why, that same pale hardhearted wench, that Rosaline,
Torments him so that he will sure run mad.

Benvolio.
Tybalt, the kinsman to old Capulet,

B **Reading Focus** **Analyzing Cause and Effect** Romeo has gotten what he wants, and he dashes offstage. Nonetheless, why do the friar's last words leave us with a sense that danger lies ahead?

Hath sent a letter to his father's house. (A)

Mercutio. A challenge, on my life.

Benvolio. Romeo will answer it.

Mercutio. Any man that can write may answer a letter.

Benvolio. Nay, he will answer the letter's master, how he dares, being dared.

Mercutio. Alas, poor Romeo, he is already dead: stabbed with a white wench's black eye; run through the ear with a love song; the very pin° of his heart cleft with the blind bow-boy's butt-shaft; and is he a man to encounter Tybalt?

Benvolio. Why, what is Tybalt?

Mercutio. More than Prince of Cats.° O, he's the courageous captain of compliments. He fights as you sing pricksong°—keeps time, distance, and proportion; he rests his minim rests,° one, two and the third in your bosom! The very butcher of a silk button, a duelist, a duelist! A gentleman of the very first house,° of the first and second cause.° Ah, the immortal passado!° The punto reverso!° The hay!°

Benvolio. The what?

Mercutio. The pox of° such antic, lisping, affecting fantasticoes°—these new tuners of accent! "By Jesu, a very good blade! A very tall° man! A very good whore!" Why, is not this a lamentable thing, grand sir, that we should be thus afflicted with these strange flies, these fashionmongers, these pardon-me's, who stand so much on the new form° that they cannot sit at ease on the old bench? O, their bones,° their bones!

[*Enter* ROMEO.]

Benvolio. Here comes Romeo! Here comes Romeo!

Mercutio. Without his roe,° like a dried herring. O flesh, flesh, how art thou fishified! Now is he for the numbers° that Petrarch flowed in. Laura, to his lady, was a kitchen wench (marry, she had a better love to berhyme her), Dido° a dowdy, Cleopatra a gypsy, Helen and Hero hildings° and harlots, Thisbe a gray eye° or so, but not to

15. pin: center (of a target).

19. Prince of Cats: Tybalt is the name of a cat in a fable who is known for his slyness.

20–21. sing pricksong: sing with attention to every note on a printed sheet of music.

22. minim rests: shortest pauses in a bar of music.

24. first house: first rank.

25. first and second cause: dueling terms ("first," offense is taken; "second," a challenge is given). **passado:** lunge.

26. punto reverso: backhand stroke. **hay:** home thrust.

? Staging the Play
26. *Mercutio mocks Tybalt's dueling style. What do you picture Mercutio doing as he talks of duels?*

28. pox of: plague on (curse on).

29. fantasticoes: dandies; men who copy French fashions.

30. tall: brave.

34. new form: new fashions.

35. bones: pun on their use of the French *bon* ("good").

37. roe: pun on *roe,* female deer. *Roe* also means "fish eggs," so Mercutio is also suggesting that love has made Romeo gutless.

38. numbers: verses. Petrarch was an Italian poet who wrote verses to a woman named Laura.

41. Dido: queen of Carthage in the *Aeneid,* who loved Aeneas. (The women who follow also were famous lovers in history, legend, and literature: Cleopatra was the queen of Egypt, loved by Antony; Helen of Troy was loved by Paris; Hero was loved by Leander; Thisbe was loved by Pyramus.)

42. hildings: good-for-nothings. **gray eye:** gleam in the eye.

(A) **Reading Focus** **Analyzing Cause and Effect** Now that the play's love story seems to be heading toward a marriage, Shakespeare turns again to the feuding families. Why is Tybalt looking for Romeo?

the purpose. Signior Romeo, bonjour! There's a French salutation to your French slop.° You gave us the counterfeit° fairly last night.

Romeo. Good morrow to you both. What counterfeit did I give you?

Mercutio. The slip, sir, the slip. Can you not conceive?°

Romeo. Pardon, good Mercutio. My business was great, and in such a case as mine a man may strain courtesy.

Mercutio. That's as much as to say, such a case° as yours constrains a man to bow in the hams.

Romeo. Meaning, to curtsy.

Mercutio. Thou hast most kindly hit it.

44. slop: loose trousers then popular in France.

45. counterfeit: slip.

48. conceive: understand.

51. case: set of clothes.

Elements of Drama

52. *Romeo is being lured by Mercutio to match wits. How can you tell that Romeo soon gets into the spirit of the game and for the moment forgets his romantic problems? In the following verbal duel the two friends use **puns**.*

HISTORY LINK

No Female Actors

On a visit to Venice in 1608, the English traveler Thomas Coryate recorded his astonishment: "For I saw women act, a thing I never saw before, though I have heard that it hath been sometimes used in London." Coryate was surprised because at the time in London, boy actors between the ages of about ten and eighteen regularly took the parts of women onstage. For a part such as Juliet—who is not yet fouteen—makeup, a costume, and the higher voice of a boy actor could easily sustain the illusion.

The roots of this custom were bound up with the origins of medieval drama. Centuries earlier in English cathedrals, stories from the Bible were acted in brief plays. The performers—all male—came from the clergy, and they were assisted by choirboys. It wasn't until 1660 that women were permitted on the English stage—by the express order of King Charles II, whose fondness for the theater was to become a mark of his reign.

Shakespeare's Globe Theatre. Photo by John Tramper.

Boy actors were divided into two categories: members of all-boy companies, like the Children of St. Paul's Cathedral, and the Children of the Chapel Royal. Other boy actors were apprentices to actors in the adult companies. These boys were preparing for a professional career. They took women's parts onstage until their late teens, when they switched to men's roles.

Casting boys as women had another unexpected twist. Plays with women in male disguise were highly popular at the time. Shakespeare wrote five such dramas, including *The Merchant of Venice* and *Twelfth Night*. In these cases, boys played women who disguised themselves as young men.

Ask Yourself

What does the exclusion of women from the Shakespearean stage suggest about their place in Elizabethan society?

Romeo. A most courteous exposition.

Mercutio. Nay, I am the very pink of courtesy.

Romeo. Pink for flower.

Mercutio. Right.

Romeo. Why, then is my pump° well-flowered.°

Mercutio. Sure wit, follow me this jest now till thou hast worn out thy pump, that, when the single sole of it is worn, the jest may remain, after the wearing, solely singular.

Romeo. O single-soled jest, solely singular for the singleness!°

Mercutio. Come between us, good Benvolio! My wits faint.

Romeo. Swits° and spurs, swits and spurs; or I'll cry a match.

Mercutio. Nay, if our wits run the wild-goose chase, I am done; for thou hast more of the wild goose in one of thy wits than, I am sure, I have in my whole five. Was I with you there for the goose?°

Romeo. Thou wast never with me for anything when thou wast not there for the goose.°

Mercutio. I will bite thee by the ear for that jest.

Romeo. Nay, good goose, bite not!

Mercutio. Thy wit is a very bitter sweeting;° it is a most sharp sauce.

Romeo. And is it not, then, well served in to a sweet goose?°

Mercutio. O, here's a wit of cheveril,° that stretches from an inch narrow to an ell broad!°

Romeo. I stretch it out for that word "broad," which, added to the goose, proves thee far and wide a broad° goose.

Mercutio. Why, is not this better now than groaning for love? Now art thou sociable, now art thou Romeo; now art thou what thou art, by art as well as by nature. For this driveling love is like a great natural° that runs lolling up and down to hide his bauble° in a hole. **B**

Benvolio. Stop there, stop there!

Mercutio. Thou desirest me to stop in my tale against the hair.°

Benvolio. Thou wouldst else have made thy tale large.°

Mercutio. O, thou art deceived! I would have made it short; for I was come to the whole depth of my tale, and meant

59. pump: shoe. **well-flowered:** pun on well floored. Men's shoes were "pinked," or cut with decorations.

64. singleness: pun on "silliness."

? **Staging the Play**
65. *What exaggerated action might Mercutio perform here?*

66. swits: switches (a pun on "wits").

70–71. Was . . . goose?: Was I right in calling you a goose?

73. goose: here, woman.

76. bitter sweeting: kind of apple.

78. sweet goose: sour sauce was considered best for sweet meat.

79. cheveril: kid leather (another reference to fashion).

80. ell broad: forty-five inches across.

82. broad: indecent.

86. natural: idiot.

87. bauble: cheap jewel.

89–90. against the hair: against my inclination.

91. large: indecent.

B **Reading Focus** **Making Inferences** What does the loyal Mercutio think he has accomplished for Romeo by this game of wits?

indeed to occupy the argument no longer.

Romeo. Here's goodly gear!°

[*Enter* NURSE *and her man* PETER.]

A sail, a sail!

Mercutio. Two, two! A shirt and a smock.°

Nurse. Peter!

Peter. Anon.

Nurse. My fan, Peter.

Mercutio. Good Peter, to hide her face; for her fan's the fairer face.

Nurse. God ye good morrow, gentlemen.

Mercutio. God ye good-den,° fair gentlewoman.

Nurse. Is it good-den?

Mercutio. 'Tis no less, I tell ye; for the bawdy hand of the dial is now upon the prick of noon.

Nurse. Out upon you! What a man are you!

Romeo. One, gentlewoman, that God hath made, himself to mar.

Nurse. By my troth, it is well said. "For himself to mar," quoth 'a? Gentlemen, can any of you tell me where I may find the young Romeo?

Romeo. I can tell you; but young Romeo will be older when you have found him than he was when you sought him. I am the youngest of that name, for fault of a worse.°

Nurse. You say well.

Mercutio. Yea, is the worst well? Very well took, i' faith! Wisely, wisely.

Nurse. If you be he, sir, I desire some confidence with you.

Benvolio. She will endite° him to some supper.

Mercutio. A bawd, a bawd, a bawd! So ho!

Romeo. What hast thou found?

Mercutio. No hare,° sir; unless a hare, sir, in a Lenten pie,° that is something stale and hoar° ere it be spent.

[*He walks by them and sings.*]

An old hare hoar,
And an old hare hoar,
Is very good meat in Lent;
But a hare that is hoar
Is too much for a score
When it hoars ere it be spent.

95. gear: matter for teasing.

Elements of Drama

96. *After establishing the bad news that Tybalt is looking for Romeo, this scene turns into a playful duel of wits between Romeo and Mercutio. Wordplay of this sort was very popular with Elizabethan audiences but can be difficult for modern audiences to follow due to the many changes in word usage in four hundred years. The scene moves into a third phase as the nurse and her servant "sail" on-stage. What does Romeo's comment suggest about the nurse's size?*

97. A shirt and a smock: a man (shirt) and a woman (smock).

104. God ye good-den: God grant you a good evening.

116. for fault of a worse: for want of a better.

121. endite (ehn DYT): invite. Benvolio mocks the nurse, for she said "confidence" but meant "conference."

Staging the Play

122. *Mercutio, who knows nothing of Romeo's plan to marry Juliet, thinks the nurse has come to arrange a secret date between Romeo and her mistress. He mocks and insults the nurse by suggesting that she is a bawd, or "procurer," for Juliet. Mercutio dominates the stage when he's on it. What do you imagine he's doing here?*

124. hare: slang for "morally loose woman." **Lenten pie:** rabbit pie, eaten sparingly during Lent, so that it is around for a long time and gets stale.

125. hoar (hawr): gray with mold (the old nurse has gray hair).

131. *Mercutio teases the nurse about being a flirt by singing the chorus of an old song about a "chaste" lady. The nurse is outraged and struggles to keep her fine airs. How does Romeo try to calm her?*

Romeo, will you come to your father's? We'll to dinner thither.

Romeo. I will follow you.

Mercutio. Farewell, ancient lady. Farewell (*singing*) "Lady, lady, lady." [*Exeunt* MERCUTIO, BENVOLIO.]

Nurse. I pray you, sir, what saucy merchant was this that was so full of his ropery?°

138. ropery: roguery; vulgar ways.

Romeo. A gentleman, nurse, that loves to hear himself talk and will speak more in a minute than he will stand to in a month.

Nurse. And 'a speak anything against me, I'll take him down, and 'a were lustier than he is, and twenty such Jacks; and if I cannot, I'll find those that shall. Scurvy knave! I am none of his flirt-gills;° I am none of his skainsmates.° And thou must stand by too, and suffer every knave to use me at his pleasure!

145. flirt-gills: flirty girls.

146. skainsmates: loose women.

147. *Whom is the nurse talking to here?*

Peter. I saw no man use you at his pleasure. If I had, my weapon should quickly have been out, I warrant you. I dare draw as soon as another man, if I see occasion in a good quarrel, and the law on my side.

Nurse. Now, afore God, I am so vexed that every part about me quivers. Scurvy knave! Pray you, sir, a word; and, as I told you, my young lady bid me inquire you out. What she bid me say, I will keep to myself; but first let me tell ye, if ye should lead her in a fool's paradise, as they say, it were a very gross kind of behavior, as they say; for the gentlewoman is young; and therefore, if you should deal double with her, truly it were an ill thing to be offered to any gentlewoman, and very weak dealing. **C**

? **Elements of Drama**
152. *In which part of this passage of* ***dialogue*** *does the nurse refer to Mercutio? When does the nurse turn to Romeo? How might her manner change?*

Romeo. Nurse, commend me to thy lady and mistress. I protest unto thee—

Nurse. Good heart, and i' faith I will tell her as much. Lord, Lord, she will be a joyful woman.

Romeo. What wilt thou tell her, nurse? Thou dost not mark° me.

166. mark: listen to.

Nurse. I will tell her, sir, that you do protest, which, as I take it, is a gentlemanlike offer.

Romeo.
Bid her devise

C **Reading Focus** **Making Inferences** What warning does the nurse give Romeo, and why do you think she does this?

Some means to come to shrift this afternoon;
And there she shall at Friar Laurence' cell
Be shrived° and married. Here is for thy pains.

Nurse. No, truly, sir; not a penny.

Romeo. Go to! I say you shall.

Nurse. This afternoon, sir? Well, she shall be there.

Romeo.
And stay, good nurse, behind the abbey wall.
Within this hour my man shall be with thee
And bring thee cords made like a tackled stair,°
Which to the high topgallant° of my joy
Must be my convoy° in the secret night.
Farewell. Be trusty, and I'll quit° thy pains.
Farewell. Commend me to thy mistress.

Nurse.
Now God in heaven bless thee! Hark you, sir.

Romeo.
What say'st thou, my dear nurse?

Nurse.
Is your man secret? Did you ne'er hear say,
Two may keep counsel, putting one away?

Romeo.
Warrant thee my man's as true as steel.

Nurse. Well, sir, my mistress is the sweetest lady. Lord, Lord! When 'twas a little prating thing—O, there is a nobleman in town, one Paris, that would fain lay knife aboard;° but she, good soul, had as lieve see a toad, a very toad, as see him. I anger her sometimes, and tell her that Paris is the properer man; but I'll warrant you, when I say so, she looks as pale as any clout° in the versal° world. Doth not rosemary and Romeo begin both with a letter? **D**

Romeo. Aye, nurse; what of that? Both with an R.

Nurse. Ah, mocker! That's the dog's name.° R is for the—no; I know it begins with some other letter; and she hath the prettiest sententious° of it, of you and rosemary, that it would do you good to hear it.

Romeo. Commend me to thy lady.

Nurse. Ay, a thousand times. [*Exit* ROMEO.] Peter!

Peter. Anon.

Nurse. Before, and apace. [*Exit after* PETER.]

D **Literary Focus** **Rising Action** The nurse becomes confiding as she rattles on and on. What trouble for Romeo and Juliet does she talk about? What is Juliet's feeling for Paris now?

172. shrived (shryvd): forgiven of her sins.

178. tackled stair: rope ladder.

179. topgallant: highest platform on a sailing ship's mast.

180. convoy: means of conveyance.

181. quit: repay.

190–191. lay knife aboard: take a slice (lay claim to Juliet).

194. clout: rag cloth. **versal:** universal.

197. That's the dog's name.: In other words, a dog's growl has an *r* sound (*r-r-r-r*).

199. sententious: The nurse means "sentence."

? Elements of Drama
204. *Romeo abruptly rushes offstage, leaving the nurse with Peter. She bossily pushes Peter ahead of her as she exits, to show that she still has authority over someone. How has this scene advanced the love story? What action has been set in motion?*

SCENE 5. *Capulet's orchard.*

Enter JULIET.

Juliet.
The clock struck nine when I did send the nurse;
In half an hour she promised to return.
Perchance she cannot meet him. That's not so.
O, she is lame! Love's heralds should be thoughts,
Which ten times faster glide than the sun's beams
Driving back shadows over low'ring hills.
Therefore do nimble-pinioned doves° draw Love,
And therefore hath the wind-swift Cupid wings.
Now is the sun upon the highmost hill
Of this day's journey, and from nine till twelve
Is three long hours; yet she is not come.
Had she affections and warm youthful blood,
She would be as swift in motion as a ball;
My words would bandy her° to my sweet love,
And his to me.
But old folks, many feign as they were dead—
Unwieldy, slow, heavy, and pale as lead.

[*Enter* NURSE *and* PETER.]

O God, she comes! O honey nurse, what news?
Hast thou met with him? Send thy man away.

Nurse.
Peter, stay at the gate. [*Exit* PETER.]

Juliet.
Now, good sweet nurse—O Lord, why look'st thou sad?
Though news be sad, yet tell them merrily;
If good, thou sham'st the music of sweet news
By playing it to me with so sour a face.

Nurse.
I am aweary, give me leave awhile.
Fie, how my bones ache! What a jaunce° have I!

Juliet.
I would thou hadst my bones, and I thy news.
Nay, come, I pray thee speak. Good, good nurse, speak.

7. nimble-pinioned doves: Nimble-winged doves were said to pull the chariot of Venus, the Roman goddess of love.

14. bandy her: send her back and forth, like a tennis ball.

? Elements of Drama
17. *Juliet either has run onstage or is standing on the balcony. What is her mood in this* ***soliloquy*** *as she waits for the nurse to return?*

26. jaunce: tiring journey.

Juliet with her nurse.

Analyzing Visuals **Viewing and Interpreting** Judging by Juliet's face, what do you think the nurse has just told her?

Nurse.
Jesu, what haste! Can you not stay° awhile?
Do you not see that I am out of breath?

Juliet.
How art thou out of breath when thou hast breath
To say to me that thou art out of breath?
The excuse that thou dost make in this delay
Is longer than the tale thou dost excuse.
Is thy news good or bad? Answer to that.
Say either, and I'll stay the circumstance.°
Let me be satisfied, is't good or bad?

Nurse. Well, you have made a simple° choice; you know not how to choose a man. Romeo? No, not he. Though his face be better than any man's, yet his leg excels all men's; and for a hand and a foot, and a body, though they be not to be talked on, yet they are past compare. He is not the flower of courtesy, but, I'll warrant him, as gentle as a lamb. Go thy ways, wench; serve God. What, have you dined at home?

Juliet.
No, no. But all this did I know before.
What says he of our marriage? What of that?

Nurse.
Lord, how my head aches! What a head have I!
It beats as it would fall in twenty pieces.
My back a'° t' other side—ah, my back, my back!
Beshrew° your heart for sending me about
To catch my death with jauncing up and down!

Juliet.
I' faith, I am sorry that thou art not well.
Sweet, sweet, sweet nurse, tell me, what says my love?

Nurse. Your love says, like an honest gentleman, and a courteous, and a kind, and a handsome, and, I warrant, a virtuous—where is your mother?

Juliet.
Where is my mother? Why, she is within.
Where should she be? How oddly thou repliest!
"Your love says, like an honest gentleman,
'Where is your mother?'"

Nurse. O God's Lady dear!
Are you so hot?° Marry come up, I trow.°
Is this the poultice for my aching bones?

29. stay: wait.

? Staging the Play
30. *The actor playing the nurse can interpret her actions here in several ways. She could be genuinely weary; she could be teasing Juliet; or she could be fearful about the part she has agreed to play in the elopement. How do you think the nurse should play this scene?*

36. stay the circumstance: wait for the details.

38. simple: foolish.

? Elements of Drama
38. *In* ***comedy*** *a character sometimes has one peculiarity that can always be counted on for a laugh. You push a button, and you get the same response. Such a character is sometimes called a jack-in-the-box. What is the nurse's almost inevitable way of responding when she is asked for information?*

50. a': on.

51. Beshrew: shame on.

? **52.** *What line in this speech indicates that Juliet has tried to humor the nurse by rubbing her back?*

? Staging the Play
61. *Juliet can play this scene in several ways. Do you imagine she is angry here? Is she bewildered? impatient? Is she mocking the old nurse?*

62. hot: angry. **Marry come up, I trow.:** something like "By the Virgin Mary, come off it, I swear."

Henceforward do your messages yourself.

Juliet.
Here's such a coil!° Come, what says Romeo?

Nurse.
Have you got leave to go to shrift today?

Juliet.
I have.

Nurse.
Then hie° you hence to Friar Laurence' cell;
There stays a husband to make you a wife. **A**
Now comes the wanton blood up in your cheeks.
They'll be in scarlet straight at any news.
Hie you to church; I must another way,
To fetch a ladder, by the which your love
Must climb a bird's nest soon when it is dark.
I am the drudge, and toil in your delight;
But you shall bear the burden soon at night.
Go; I'll to dinner; hie you to the cell.

Juliet.
Hie to high fortune! Honest nurse, farewell. [*Exeunt.*]

65. coil: fuss.

68. hie (hy)**:** hurry.

? **Elements of Drama**
78. *Even Juliet* ***puns****—or makes jokes based on words. What pun does she exit on? What is her mood?*

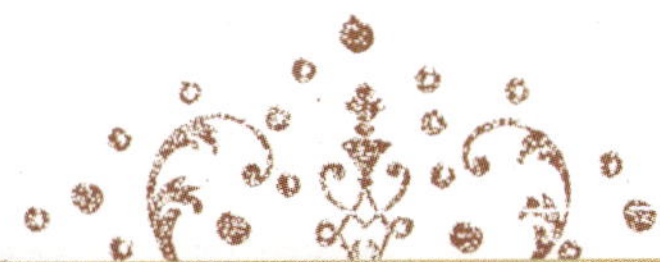

Scene 6. Friar Laurence's cell.

Enter FRIAR LAURENCE *and* ROMEO.

Friar.
So smile the heavens upon this holy act
That afterhours with sorrow chide us not!

Romeo.
Amen, amen! But come what sorrow can,
It cannot countervail° the exchange of joy
That one short minute gives me in her sight.
Do thou but close our hands with holy words,
Then love-devouring death do what he dare—
It is enough I may but call her mine. **B**

4. countervail: match or equal.

A **Literary Focus** **Turning Point** At last the nurse tells Juliet what she has been waiting to hear. What do you think will happen now that Romeo and Juliet have decided to marry? In what way might their marriage be a turning point?

B **Reading Focus** **Paraphrasing** What does Romeo say here to remind us again of how desperate his and Juliet's love is, and what might happen if they are separated?

Friar Laurence marries Romeo and Juliet.

Friar.
These violent delights have violent ends
And in their triumph die, like fire and powder,°
Which, as they kiss, consume. The sweetest honey
Is loathsome in his own deliciousness
And in the taste confounds° the appetite.
Therefore love moderately: long love doth so;
Too swift arrives as tardy as too slow. **C**

[*Enter* JULIET.]

Here comes the lady. O, so light a foot
Will ne'er wear out the everlasting flint.°
A lover may bestride the gossamers°
That idle in the wanton summer air,
And yet not fall; so light is vanity.°

Juliet.
Good even to my ghostly confessor.

Friar.
Romeo shall thank thee, daughter, for us both.

Juliet.
As much to him,° else is his thanks too much.

Romeo.
Ah, Juliet, if the measure of thy joy
Be heaped like mine, and that thy skill be more
To blazon° it, then sweeten with thy breath
This neighbor air, and let rich music's tongue
Unfold the imagined happiness that both
Receive in either by this dear encounter.

Juliet.
Conceit,° more rich in matter than in words,
Brags of his substance, not of ornament.°
They are but beggars that can count their worth;
But my true love is grown to such excess
I cannot sum up sum of half my wealth.

Friar.
Come, come with me, and we will make short work;
For, by your leaves, you shall not stay alone
Till holy church incorporate two in one. [*Exeunt.*]

10. powder: gunpowder.

13. confounds: destroys.

17. flint: stone.

18. gossamers: finest spider threads.

20. vanity: fleeting human love.

23. As much to him: the same to him.

26. blazon: describe.

? **29.** *What is Romeo asking Juliet to do?*

30. Conceit: genuine understanding.

31. ornament: fancy language.

? **34.** *What is Juliet's response to Romeo's request?*

? **Elements of Drama**
37. *What do you think is friar's tone in this section? Is there a slightly humorous or teasing note here?*

C **Reading Focus** **Analyzing Cause and Effect** What warning does the friar give about passionate love? What effect do you think the warning will have?

Applying Your Skills

The Tragedy of Romeo and Juliet, Act II

Respond and Think Critically

Reading Focus

Quick Check

1. What plans do the two lovers make in Scene 2?
2. What fault does Friar Laurence find in Romeo in Scene 3?
3. In Scene 4, why is Tybalt looking for Romeo?
4. How does Mercutio feel about Tybalt?
5. What purpose does the Nurse serve in Act II?

Read with a Purpose

6. Have Romeo and Juliet made rational decisions about their lives, or has fate directed them? Explain.

Reading Skills: Reading a Play

7. In a chart, take notes on your inferences about the play's characters. For example, what inference can you make about why the friar agrees to marry Romeo and Juliet?

Make Inferences	My Notes
What can I infer about the friar?	

Literary Focus

Literary Analysis

8. **Analyze** This play, particularly the balcony scene, is greatly admired for the beauty of the poetry. Pick one passage in Act II that especially appeals to you and explain the poetic and literary devices involved. Is there rhyme, rhythm, or alliteration? How do you interpret the figures of speech? To what senses do the images appeal?
9. **Evaluate** In Scene 2, line 37, Romeo talks in an **aside,** a short speech usually delivered to the audience but sometimes to another character, that others onstage are not supposed to hear. Whom is Romeo talking to in his aside? What is the purpose of this convention here?

Literary Skills: Tragedy

10. **Identify** Act II is fairly happy, a kind of calm before the storm. But Shakespeare does remind us that this is a tragedy and will end unhappily. Find lines that **foreshadow** trouble ahead.
11. **Evaluate** In terms of **dramatic structure** (exposition, rising action, turning point, climax, resolution), where are we when this act ends?

Literary Skills Review: Dramatic Irony

12. **Analyze** **Dramatic Irony** occurs when the audience knows something that a character does not know. Since the prologue told us how the play will end, we sense the irony when we hear the friar's motive for marrying the lovers. Find another moment of dramatic irony in this act, when you know something the characters don't.

Writing Focus

Think as a Reader/Writer

Use It in Your Writing Using your notes on Act II, write a summary of the act. What complications occurred in this section of the play?

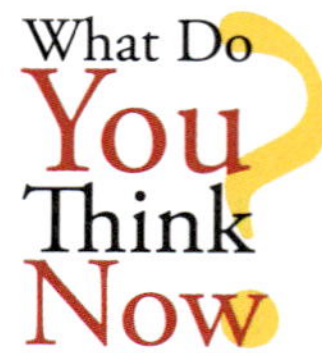

Do you think Romeo and Juliet are taking a reasonable risk in deciding to get married without getting their parents' permission?

MO **9.R.2.C.1.b** Use details from text(s): to analyze character, plot, setting, point of view **9.R.2** Develop and apply skills and strategies to comprehend, analyze and evaluate fiction, poetry and drama from a variety of cultures and times *Also covered* **9.R.1.G.1.d; 9.W.3.A.1.c; 9.R.1.E.1.c; 9.R.1.E.1.b**

Vocabulary Development

Vocabulary Skills: Archaic Words and Meanings

Shakespeare's language is different from the English we use today. Many of Shakespeare's words and expressions are now *archaic,* or out of use, or their meaning has changed. Also, Shakespeare often omits words. In the Prologue the speaker says:

> If you with patient ears attend,
> What here shall miss, our toil shall strive to mend.

Shakespeare depends on your instinct and your ear to fill in the missing words. He has also used the word *attend* in a way not commonly used today. Here's how we might say the same thing:

> If you listen patiently, we'll try to make clear whatever you've missed from the speech by our work onstage.

Your Turn

Juliet's nurse speaks the passages below using expressions that are no longer in use today. Rewrite each passage in modern English. Use context clues, the sidenotes to the play, and a dictionary for help.

1. I pray you, sir, what *saucy* merchant was this that was so full of his *ropery*? (II.4.137–138)
2. Is your man secret? Did you ne'er hear say, Two may keep counsel, *putting one away?* (II.4.185–186)
3. But she, good soul, had as *lieve* see a toad, a very toad, as see him. (II.4.191–192)
4. I am aweary, give me leave awhile. *Fie,* how my bones ache! What a *jaunce* have I! (II.5.25–26)
5. Then *hie* you *hence* to Friar Laurence' cell; There stays a husband to make you a wife. (II.5.68–69)

Language Coach

Archaic Slang You've probably noticed that slang words that were extremely popular with one generation fall into disuse, become obsolete, and archaic. For example, in the 1920s, terms such as *23-skidoo, flapper, cat's pajamas,* and *bee's knees* were in everyday use.

What slang terms in use today might become archaic in five years' time? Try to name three.

Academic Vocabulary

Talk About . . .

Choose a character from Act II. Make a list of all the characteristics that the character embodies, including his or her personality type, manner of speaking, thoughts, and appearance. If you played this character onstage, how would you make the audience believe you were the character? Share your ideas with the class, using Academic Vocabulary words.

ACT III

2004 production of *Romeo and Juliet* performed at the Royal Shakespeare Theatre.

Read with a Purpose As you read, consider whether fate plays a role in Romeo's actions.

ACT III

SCENE 1. *A public place.*

Enter MERCUTIO, BENVOLIO, *and* MEN.

Benvolio.
I pray thee, good Mercutio, let's retire.
The day is hot, the Capels° are abroad,
And, if we meet, we shall not 'scape a brawl,
For now, these hot days, is the mad blood stirring. **A**

Mercutio. Thou art like one of these fellows that, when he enters the confines of a tavern, claps me his sword upon the table and says, "God send me no need of thee!" and by the operation of the second cup draws him on the drawer,° when indeed there is no need.

Benvolio. Am I like such a fellow?

Mercutio. Come, come, thou art as hot a Jack in thy mood as any in Italy; and as soon moved to be moody, and as soon moody to be moved.

Benvolio. And what to?

Mercutio. Nay, and there were two such, we should have none shortly, for one would kill the other. Thou! Why, thou wilt quarrel with a man that hath a hair more or a hair less in his beard than thou hast. Thou wilt quarrel with a man for cracking nuts, having no other reason but because thou hast hazel eyes. What eye but such an eye would spy out such a quarrel? Thy head is as full of quarrels as an egg is full of meat; and yet thy head hath been beaten as addle° as an egg for quarreling. Thou hast quarreled with a man for coughing in the street, because he hath wakened thy dog that hath lain asleep in the sun. Didst thou not fall out with a tailor for wearing his new doublet° before Easter? With another for tying his new shoes with old riband? And yet thou wilt tutor me from

2. Capels: Capulets.

8–9. draws him on the drawer: draws his sword on the waiter (who "draws" the drink).

? Staging the Play

16. *Mercutio mocks Benvolio, who is anything but a troublemaker. (Mercutio is the one who can't seem to resist a quarrel.) If you were playing Benvolio, what would you be doing as Mercutio goes on and on? If you were playing Mercutio, how would you behave as your comments become more and more exaggerated?*

23. addle: rotten.

27. doublet: jacket.

A Reading Focus Making Inferences Romeo's friends enter the stage. Again Shakespeare "sets the stage" by having the characters tell us what the weather is like. Why does this weather seem to breed trouble?

quarreling!

Benvolio. And I were so apt to quarrel as thou art, any man should buy the fee simple of° my life for an hour and a quarter.

Mercutio. The fee simple? O simple!°

[*Enter* TYBALT *and others.*]

Benvolio. By my head, here come the Capulets.

Mercutio. By my heel, I care not.

Tybalt.
Follow me close, for I will speak to them.
Gentlemen, good-den. A word with one of you.

Mercutio.
And but one word with one of us?
Couple it with something; make it a word and a blow.

Tybalt. You shall find me apt enough to that, sir, and you will give me occasion.

Mercutio. Could you not take some occasion without giving?

Tybalt. Mercutio, thou consortest with Romeo.

Mercutio. Consort?° What, dost thou make us minstrels? And thou make minstrels of us, look to hear nothing but discords. Here's my fiddlestick;° here's that shall make you dance. Zounds,° consort!

Benvolio.
We talk here in the public haunt of men.
Either withdraw unto some private place,
Or reason coldly of your grievances,
Or else depart. Here all eyes gaze on us.

Mercutio.
Men's eyes were made to look, and let them gaze.
I will not budge for no man's pleasure, I.

[*Enter* ROMEO.]

Tybalt.
Well, peace be with you, sir. Here comes my man.

Mercutio.
But I'll be hanged, sir, if he wear your livery.°
Marry, go before to field,° he'll be your follower!
Your worship in that sense may call him man.

Tybalt.
Romeo, the love I bear thee can afford

31. buy the fee simple of: buy insurance on.

33. O simple: Oh stupid.

44. Consort: Mercutio pretends to think that Tybalt means a *consort,* or group of musicians.

46. fiddlestick: bow for playing a fiddle or violin (Mercutio is referring to his sword).

47. Zounds: an exclamation; from the phrase "by God's wounds."

? Elements of Drama
Stage direction: *Romeo is returning from his secret marriage—he has no thoughts of hatred or killing. What would he be doing as he enters? How would he react to the tense situation?*

55. livery: servant's uniform. By *man,* Tybalt meant "target," but Mercutio uses the word to mean "servant."

56. field: dueling field.

No better term than this: thou art a villain.°

Romeo.
Tybalt, the reason that I have to love thee
Doth much excuse the appertaining° rage
To such a greeting. Villain am I none.
Therefore farewell. I see thou knowest me not.

Tybalt.
Boy, this shall not excuse the injuries
That thou hast done me; therefore turn and draw.

Romeo.
I do protest I never injured thee,
But love thee better than thou canst devise°
Till thou shalt know the reason of my love;
And so, good Capulet, which name I tender°
As dearly as mine own, be satisfied.

Mercutio.
O calm, dishonorable, vile submission!
Alla stoccata° carries it away.

[*Draws.*]

Tybalt, you ratcatcher, will you walk?°

Tybalt.
What wouldst thou have with me?

Mercutio. Good King of Cats, nothing but one of your nine lives. That I mean to make bold withal,° and, as you shall use me hereafter, dry-beat° the rest of the eight. Will you pluck your sword out of his pilcher° by the ears? Make haste, lest mine be about your ears ere it be out.

Tybalt. I am for you.

[*Draws.*]

Romeo.
Gentle Mercutio, put thy rapier up.

Mercutio. Come, sir, your passado!

[*They fight.*]

Romeo.
Draw, Benvolio; beat down their weapons.
Gentlemen, for shame! Forbear this outrage!
Tybalt, Mercutio, the prince expressly hath

? **58–65.** *What insult does Tybalt use to try to make Romeo draw his sword?*

59. villain: boor; clumsy, stupid fellow.

61. appertaining: appropriate.

67. devise: imagine.

69. tender: value.

? **70.** *Why does Romeo refuse to duel with Tybalt?*

? **Staging the Play**
71. *Mercutio doesn't know about Romeo's marriage to Juliet (a Capulet). Why is Mercutio so outraged? What feeling should the actor playing Tybalt express as he asks Mercutio what he wants?*

72. Alla stoccata (AH lah stuh KAH tah): Italian for "at the thrust"; a fencing term.

73. walk: make a move.

76. make bold withal: make free with (take away).

77. dry-beat: thrash.

78. pilcher: scabbard (sword holder).

? **Elements of Drama**
Stage Direction: *The stage direction simply says "They fight," but how would you—as director—choreograph the action? The sword fight can range all over the stage, but where must the three characters be placed when Tybalt stabs Mercutio?*

Analyzing Visuals **Viewing and Interpreting** How can you tell that Romeo considers the fight an "outrage"?

A sword fight between Mercutio and Tybalt, with Benvolio and Romeo in the background.

Forbid this bandying° in Verona streets.
Hold, Tybalt! Good Mercutio!

[TYBALT *under Romeo's arm thrusts* MERCUTIO *in, and flies.*]

Mercutio. I am hurt.
A plague a' both houses! I am sped.°
Is he gone and hath nothing?
Benvolio. What, art thou hurt?
Mercutio.
Ay, ay, a scratch, a scratch. Marry, 'tis enough.
Where is my page? Go, villain, fetch a surgeon.

[*Exit* PAGE.]

Romeo.
Courage, man. The hurt cannot be much.
Mercutio. No, 'tis not so deep as a well, nor so wide as a church door; but 'tis enough, 'twill serve. Ask for me

86. bandying: brawling.

88. sped: wounded.

tomorrow, and you shall find me a grave man. I am peppered,° I warrant, for this world. A plague a' both your houses! Zounds, a dog, a rat, a mouse, a cat, to scratch a man to death! A braggart, a rogue, a villain, that fights by the book of arithmetic!° Why the devil came you between us? I was hurt under your arm.

Romeo.
I thought all for the best. **B**

Mercutio.
Help me into some house, Benvolio,
Or I shall faint. A plague a' both your houses!
They have made worms' meat of me. I have it,
And soundly too. Your houses!

[*Exeunt* MERCUTIO *and* BENVOLIO.]

Romeo.
This gentleman, the prince's near ally,°
My very friend, hath got this mortal hurt
In my behalf—my reputation stained
With Tybalt's slander—Tybalt, that an hour
Hath been my cousin. O sweet Juliet,
Thy beauty hath made me effeminate
And in my temper soft'ned valor's steel!

[*Enter* BENVOLIO.]

Benvolio.
O Romeo, Romeo, brave Mercutio is dead!
That gallant spirit hath aspired° the clouds,
Which too untimely here did scorn the earth.

Romeo.
This day's black fate on more days doth depend;°
This but begins the woe others must end.

[*Enter* TYBALT.]

Benvolio.
Here comes the furious Tybalt back again.

Romeo.
Alive in triumph, and Mercutio slain?

96. peppered: given a deadly wound (peppered food is ready to eat; Mercutio is "ready" to die).

99. fights by the book of arithmetic: fights according to the formal rules of fencing.

? Staging the Play
105. *What curse has Mercutio pronounced four times? Some actors playing Mercutio make him seem bitter about his approaching death and hostile to Romeo. Other Mercutios are gallant to the end and extend a hand to Romeo in friendship. How would you play this death speech?*

106. ally: relative. Mercutio is related to Verona's Prince Escalus.

114. aspired: climbed to.

116. depend: hang over.

? Elements of Drama
Stage direction: *Does it seem unlikely that Tybalt would return so soon? He must return, of course, so that Romeo can avenge Mercutio. An alternative would have been to have Romeo attack Tybalt as soon as he stabbed Mercutio, but then Shakespeare would have lost Mercutio's great dying speech. How would you stage Tybalt's return so that it seems believable?*

B **Reading Focus** **Reading Aloud** How would Romeo say this pathetic line?

Away to heaven respective lenity,
And fire-eyed fury be my conduct now!
Now, Tybalt, take the "villain" back again
That late thou gavest me; for Mercutio's soul
Is but a little way above our heads,
Staying for thine to keep him company.
Either thou or I, or both, must go with him.

Tybalt.
Thou, wretched boy, that didst consort him here,
Shalt with him hence.

Romeo. This shall determine that.

[*They fight.* TYBALT *falls.*] **C**

Benvolio.
Romeo, away, be gone!
The citizens are up, and Tybalt slain.
Stand not amazed. The prince will doom thee death
If thou art taken. Hence, be gone, away!

Romeo.
O, I am fortune's fool! **D**

Benvolio. Why dost thou stay?

[*Exit* ROMEO.]

[*Enter* CITIZENS.]

Citizen.
Which way ran he that killed Mercutio?
Tybalt, that murderer, which way ran he?

Benvolio.
There lies that Tybalt.

Citizen. Up, sir, go with me.
I charge thee in the prince's name obey.

[*Enter* PRINCE, *old* MONTAGUE, CAPULET, *their* WIVES, *and all.*]

? **132.** *What details in Benvolio's speech tell us what Romeo is doing and how he is feeling after this second death?*

? **Elements of Drama**
Stage Direction: *What do you imagine the stage looks like as the prince and two families enter?*

C **Literary Focus** **Turning Point** In what way might the death of Tybalt be a turning point in the play?

D **Literary Focus** **Tragedy** What do you think Romeo means by calling himself "fortune's fool"? What does he realize will now happen to him and Juliet?

“Hold, friends! Friends, part!” and swifter than his tongue, His agile arm beats down their fatal points.

Prince.
Where are the vile beginners of this fray?

Benvolio.
O noble prince, I can discover° all
The unlucky manage° of this fatal brawl.
There lies the man, slain by young Romeo,
That slew thy kinsman, brave Mercutio.

139. discover: reveal.
140. manage: course.

Lady Capulet.
Tybalt, my cousin! O my brother's child!
O prince! O cousin! Husband! O, the blood is spilled
Of my dear kinsman! Prince, as thou art true,
For blood of ours shed blood of Montague.
O cousin, cousin!

Prince.
Benvolio, who began this bloody fray?

Benvolio.
Tybalt, here slain, whom Romeo's hand did slay.
Romeo, that spoke him fair, bid him bethink
How nice° the quarrel was, and urged° withal
Your high displeasure. All this—utterèd
With gentle breath, calm look, knees humbly bowed—
Could not take truce with the unruly spleen°
Of Tybalt deaf to peace, but that he tilts°
With piercing steel at bold Mercutio's breast;
Who, all as hot, turns deadly point to point,
And, with a martial scorn, with one hand beats
Cold death aside and with the other sends
It back to Tybalt, whose dexterity
Retorts it. Romeo he cries aloud,
“Hold, friends! Friends, part!” and swifter than his tongue,
His agile arm beats down their fatal points,
And 'twixt them rushes; underneath whose arm
An envious° thrust from Tybalt hit the life
Of stout Mercutio, and then Tybalt fled;
But by and by comes back to Romeo,
Who had but newly entertained° revenge,

151. nice: trivial. **urged:** mentioned.
154. spleen: anger.
155. tilts: thrusts.
165. envious: full of enmity or hatred.
168. entertained: thought of.

The death scene of Tybalt and Mercutio.

Analyzing Visuals **Viewing and Interpreting** Using clues in the photo, identify the different characters in this production's staging of Act III, Scene 1.

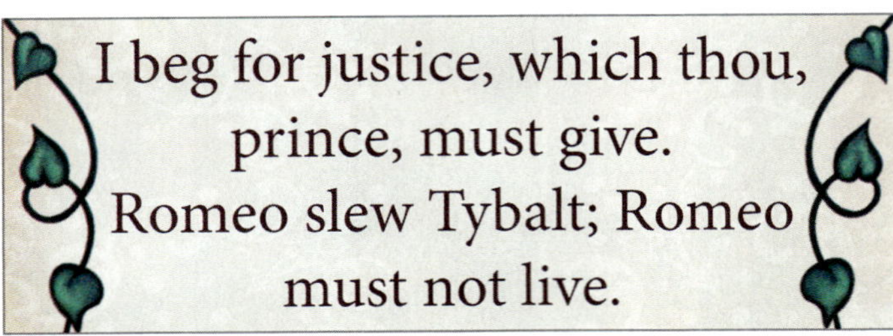
I beg for justice, which thou, prince, must give. Romeo slew Tybalt; Romeo must not live.

And to't they go like lightning; for, ere I
Could draw to part them, was stout Tybalt slain;
And, as he fell, did Romeo turn and fly.
This is the truth, or let Benvolio die.

Lady Capulet.
He is a kinsman to the Montague;
Affection makes him false, he speaks not true.
Some twenty of them fought in this black strife,
And all those twenty could but kill one life.
I beg for justice, which thou, prince, must give.
Romeo slew Tybalt; Romeo must not live.

Prince.
Romeo slew him; he slew Mercutio.
Who now the price of his dear blood doth owe?

Montague.
Not Romeo, prince; he was Mercutio's friend;
His fault concludes but what the law should end,
The life of Tybalt.

Prince. And for that offense
Immediately we do exile him hence.
I have an interest in your hate's proceeding,
My blood° for your rude brawls doth lie a-bleeding;
But I'll amerce° you with so strong a fine
That you shall all repent the loss of mine.
I will be deaf to pleading and excuses;
Nor tears nor prayers shall purchase out abuses.
Therefore use none. Let Romeo hence in haste,
Else, when he is found, that hour is his last.
Bear hence this body and attend our will.
Mercy but murders, pardoning those that kill. **E**

[*Exit with others.*]

? **172.** *Is Benvolio's testimony about events fully accurate?*

? **176.** *How does Lady Capulet think Tybalt was killed? Why does she think Benvolio is lying?*

186. My blood: that is, Mercutio, his blood relative.

187. amerce: punish.

? **Elements of Drama**
Stage direction: *The families exit in separate processions, carrying their dead. How does this scene contrast with the fighting that has just taken place?*

E Reading Focus Analyzing Cause and Effect The prince has heard arguments from both families and has given judgment in the case. What is Romeo's punishment? Why won't the prince show Romeo greater mercy?

Scene 2. *Capulet's orchard.*

Enter JULIET *alone.*

Juliet.

Gallop apace, you fiery-footed steeds,°
Towards Phoebus' lodging! Such a wagoner
As Phaethon° would whip you to the west
And bring in cloudy night immediately.
Spread thy close curtain, love-performing night,
That runaways' eyes may wink,° and Romeo
Leap to these arms untalked of and unseen.
Lovers can see to do their amorous rites,
And by their own beauties; or, if love be blind,
It best agrees with night. Come, civil° night,
Thou sober-suited matron all in black,
And learn me how to lose a winning match,
Played for a pair of stainless maidenhoods.
Hood° my unmanned° blood, bating° in my cheeks,
With thy black mantle till strange° love grow bold,
Think true love acted simple modesty.
Come, night; come, Romeo; come, thou day in night;
For thou wilt lie upon the wings of night
Whiter than new snow upon a raven's back.
Come, gentle night; come, loving, black-browed night;
Give me my Romeo; and, when he shall die,
Take him and cut him out in little stars,
And he will make the face of heaven so fine
That all the world will be in love with night
And pay no worship to the garish sun. **A**
O, I have bought the mansion of a love,
But not possessed it; and though I am sold,
Not yet enjoyed. So tedious is this day
As is the night before some festival
To an impatient child that hath new robes
And may not wear them. O, here comes my nurse, **B**

? Elements of Drama
1. *In this famous* ***soliloquy,*** *Juliet yearns for the night, when she and Romeo will be together. What do we in the audience know that Juliet does not yet know?*

1. steeds: horses. (In Greek mythology, horses pull the sun god Phoebus's chariot across the sky each day.)

3. Phaethon: (FAY uh thahn): Phoebus's reckless son, who couldn't hold the horses' reins.

6. That runaways' eyes may wink: so that the eyes of the sun god's horses may shut.

10. civil: well-behaved.

14. Hood: cover. **unmanned:** unmated. **bating:** fluttering.

15. strange: unfamiliar.

? 24. *What associations, images, and synonyms can you come up with for the word* night? *How do they compare with Juliet's view of night?*

? 26. *What is the "mansion of a love" that Juliet has bought?*

A Literary Focus Rising Action In which lines does Juliet unconsciously foreshadow Romeo's death?

B Literary Focus Dramatic Irony What dramatic irony is created in this scene?

[*Enter* NURSE, *with a ladder of cords.*]

And she brings news; and every tongue that speaks
But Romeo's name speaks heavenly eloquence.
Now, nurse, what news? What hast thou there, the cords
That Romeo bid thee fetch?

Nurse. Ay, ay, the cords.

Juliet.
Ay me! What news? Why dost thou wring thy hands?

Nurse.
Ah, weraday!° He's dead, he's dead, he's dead!
We are undone, lady, we are undone!
Alack the day! He's gone, he's killed, he's dead!

Juliet.
Can heaven be so envious?

Nurse. Romeo can,
Though heaven cannot. O Romeo, Romeo!
Who ever would have thought it? Romeo!

Juliet.
What devil art thou that dost torment me thus?
This torture should be roared in dismal hell.
Hath Romeo slain himself? Say thou but "Ay,"
And that bare vowel "I" shall poison more
Than the death-darting eye of cockatrice.°
I am not I, if there be such an "Ay,"
Or those eyes' shot that make thee answer "Ay."
If he be slain, say "Ay"; or if not, "No."
Brief sounds determine of my weal or woe.

Nurse.
I saw the wound, I saw it with mine eyes,
(God save the mark!)° here on his manly breast.
A piteous corse,° a bloody piteous corse;
Pale, pale as ashes, all bedaubed in blood,
All in gore-blood. I swounded° at the sight.

Juliet.
O, break, my heart! Poor bankrout,° break at once!
To prison, eyes; ne'er look on liberty!
Vile earth,° to earth resign; end motion here,
And thou and Romeo press one heavy bier! **C**

? Staging the Play
35. *How might the nurse speak this line?*

37. weraday: well-a-day (or alas).

? 39. *The nurse rattles on again—but this time, how does she seem to give the wrong news even as she delays it?*

47. cockatrice: legendary serpent that could kill by a glance.

53. God save the mark!: God forbid!

54. corse: corpse.

56. swounded: swooned (fainted).

57. bankrout: bankrupt.

59. Vile earth: Juliet is referring to her own body.

C Literary Focus Dramatic Irony This is another example of dramatic irony in this scene, in which we cannot share a character's feelings because we know something that the character does not know. What does Juliet think has happened? What has really happened?

Nurse.

O Tybalt, Tybalt, the best friend I had!
O courteous Tybalt! Honest gentleman!
That ever I should live to see thee dead!

Juliet.

What storm is this that blows so contrary?
Is Romeo slaught'red, and is Tybalt dead?
My dearest cousin, and my dearer lord?
Then, dreadful trumpet, sound the general doom!
For who is living, if those two are gone?

Nurse.

Tybalt is gone, and Romeo banishèd;
Romeo that killed him, he is banishèd. **D**

Juliet.

O God! Did Romeo's hand shed Tybalt's blood?

Nurse.

It did, it did! Alas the day, it did!

Juliet.

O serpent heart, hid with a flow'ring face!
Did ever dragon keep so fair a cave?
Beautiful tyrant! Fiend angelical!
Dove-feathered raven! Wolvish-ravening lamb!
Despisèd substance of divinest show!
Just opposite to what thou justly seem'st—
A damnèd saint, an honorable villain!
O nature, what hadst thou to do in hell
When thou didst bower the spirit of a fiend
In mortal paradise of such sweet flesh?
Was ever book containing such vile matter
So fairly bound? O, that deceit should dwell
In such a gorgeous palace!

Nurse. There's no trust,
No faith, no honesty in men; all perjured,
All forsworn, all naught, all dissemblers.°
Ah, where's my man? Give me some aqua vitae.°
These griefs, these woes, these sorrows make me old.
Shame come to Romeo!

? Elements of Drama
***73.** The news that Romeo has killed Tybalt is terrible for Juliet. Try writing stage directions that will help an actor express her horror.*

? ***85.** A moment ago Juliet thought of Romeo as her "day in night." Now what does she think of him?*

87. dissemblers: liars.

88. aqua vitae (AK wuh VY tee): brandy (Latin for "water of life").

D Reading Focus Making Inferences Why do you think the nurse waits so long to give Juliet the correct news? Is she being self-centered here, or is she truly overwhelmed by the news she bears?

Juliet. Blistered be thy tongue
For such a wish! He was not born to shame.
Upon his brow shame is ashamed to sit;
For 'tis a throne where honor may be crowned
Sole monarch of the universal earth.
O, what a beast was I to chide at him!

Nurse.
Will you speak well of him that killed your cousin?

Juliet.
Shall I speak ill of him that is my husband?
Ah, poor my lord, what tongue shall smooth thy name
When I, thy three-hours wife, have mangled it?
But wherefore, villain, didst thou kill my cousin?
That villain cousin would have killed my husband.
Back, foolish tears, back to your native spring!
Your tributary drops° belong to woe,
Which you, mistaking, offer up to joy.
My husband lives, that Tybalt would have slain;
And Tybalt's dead, that would have slain my husband.
All this is comfort; wherefore weep I then?
Some word there was, worser than Tybalt's death,
That murd'red me. I would forget it fain;°
But O, it presses to my memory
Like damnèd guilty deeds to sinners' minds!
"Tybalt is dead, and Romeo—banishèd."
That "banishèd," that one word "banishèd,"
Hath slain ten thousand Tybalts. Tybalt's death
Was woe enough, if it had ended there;
Or, if sour woe delights in fellowship
And needly will be ranked with° other griefs,
Why followed not, when she said "Tybalt's dead,"
Thy father, or thy mother, nay, or both,
Which modern° lamentation might have moved?°
But with a rearward° following Tybalt's death,
"Romeo is banishèd"—to speak that word
Is father, mother, Tybalt, Romeo, Juliet,
All slain, all dead. "Romeo is banishèd"—
There is no end, no limit, measure, bound,
In that word's death; no words can that woe sound.
Where is my father and my mother, nurse?

? **97.** *Why does Juliet turn against her nurse here?*

103. tributary drops: tears poured out in tribute.

109. fain: willingly.

117. ranked with: accompanied by.

120. modern: ordinary. **moved:** provoked.

121. rearward: soldiers at the rear of a troop; here, an additional source of injury and pain after the bad news about Tybalt.

? **124.** *Juliet comprehends what has happened. Why does she fix on the word* banished?

? **Staging the Play**
127. *Juliet pauses before she speaks her last line here. How would she change her tone as she asks the nurse about her father and mother?*

Nurse.

Weeping and wailing over Tybalt's corse.
Will you go to them? I will bring you thither.

Juliet.

Wash they his wounds with tears? Mine shall be spent,
When theirs are dry, for Romeo's banishment.
Take up those cords. Poor ropes, you are beguiled,
Both you and I, for Romeo is exiled.
He made you for a highway to my bed;
But I, a maid, die maiden-widowèd.
Come, cords; come, nurse. I'll to my wedding bed;
And death, not Romeo, take my maidenhead! **E**

Nurse.

Hie to your chamber. I'll find Romeo
To comfort you. I wot° well where he is.
Hark ye, your Romeo will be here at night.
I'll to him; he is hid at Laurence' cell.

Juliet.

O, find him! Give this ring to my true knight
And bid him come to take his last farewell.

[*Exit with* NURSE.]

139. wot: know.

E **Reading Focus** **Analyzing Cause and Effect** Juliet addresses the rope ladder in this speech. What has she decided to do with the ropes?

Juliet is distraught after the nurse brings her terrible news.

Analyzing Visuals **Viewing and Interpreting** During what speech from Act III, Scene 2, might an actor playing Juliet give this interpretation?

Scene 3. *Friar Laurence's cell.*

Enter FRIAR LAURENCE.

Friar.
Romeo, come forth; come forth, thou fearful man.
Affliction is enamored of thy parts,
And thou art wedded to calamity. **A**

[*Enter* ROMEO.]

Romeo.
Father, what news? What is the prince's doom?
What sorrow craves acquaintance at my hand
That I yet know not?

Friar. Too familiar
Is my dear son with such sour company.
I bring thee tidings of the prince's doom.

Romeo.
What less than doomsday° is the prince's doom?

Friar.
A gentler judgment vanished° from his lips—
Not body's death, but body's banishment.

Romeo.
Ha, banishment? Be merciful, say "death";
For exile hath more terror in his look,
Much more than death. Do not say "banishment."

Friar.
Here from Verona art thou banishèd.
Be patient, for the world is broad and wide.

Romeo.
There is no world without Verona walls,
But purgatory, torture, hell itself.
Hence banishèd is banished from the world,
And world's exile is death. Then "banishèd"
Is death mistermed. Calling death "banishèd,"

9. doomsday: my death.

10. vanished: escaped.

A Literary Focus Tragedy When we last saw Romeo, he was speaking of himself as "fortune's fool" (Act III, Scene 1, line 133). Now, in the first lines of this scene, how does the friar remind us again that Romeo seems fated for ill fortune?

Thou cut'st my head off with a golden ax
And smilest upon the stroke that murders me.

Friar.
O deadly sin! O rude unthankfulness!
Thy fault our law calls death; but the kind prince,
Taking thy part, hath rushed aside the law,
And turned that black word "death" to "banishment."
This is dear mercy, and thou see'st it not.

Romeo.
'Tis torture, and not mercy. Heaven is here,
Where Juliet lives; and every cat and dog
And little mouse, every unworthy thing,
Live here in heaven and may look on her;
But Romeo may not. More validity,°
More honorable state, more courtship lives
In carrion flies than Romeo. They may seize
On the white wonder of dear Juliet's hand
And steal immortal blessing from her lips,
Who, even in pure and vestal modesty,
Still blush, as thinking their own kisses sin;
But Romeo may not, he is banishèd.
Flies may do this but I from this must fly;
They are freemen, but I am banishèd.
And sayest thou yet that exile is not death?
Hadst thou no poison mixed, no sharp-ground knife,
No sudden mean of death, though ne'er so mean,
But "banishèd" to kill me—"banishèd"?
O friar, the damnèd use that word in hell;
Howling attends it! How hast thou the heart,
Being a divine, a ghostly confessor,
A sin-absolver, and my friend professed,
To mangle me with that word "banishèd"?

Elements of Drama

23. *Romeo and Friar Laurence have just had a* ***dialogue****—the talk between or among characters in a play—about the words* banished *and* banishment. *What do these words mean to Romeo? What do they mean to Friar Laurence?*

28. *Why is the friar angry at Romeo?*

33. validity: value

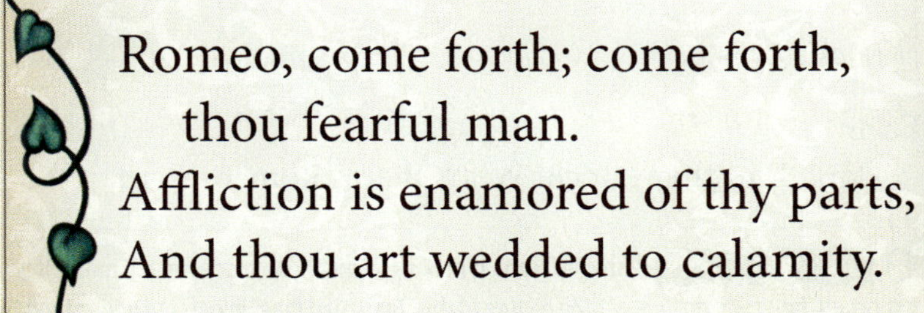
Romeo, come forth; come forth,
thou fearful man.
Affliction is enamored of thy parts,
And thou art wedded to calamity.

Friar.
Thou fond° mad man, hear me a little speak.

Romeo.
O, thou wilt speak again of banishment.

Friar.
I'll give thee armor to keep off that word;
Adversity's sweet milk, philosophy,
To comfort thee, though thou art banishèd.

Romeo.
Yet "banishèd"? Hang up philosophy!
Unless philosophy can make a Juliet,
Displant a town, reverse a prince's doom,
It helps not, it prevails not. Talk no more. **B**

Friar.
O, then I see that madmen have no ears.

Romeo.
How should they, when that wise men have no eyes?

Friar.
Let me dispute with thee of thy estate.°

Romeo.
Thou canst not speak of that thou dost not feel.
Wert thou as young as I, Juliet thy love,
An hour but married, Tybalt murderèd,
Doting like me, and like me banishèd,
Then mightst thou speak, then mightst thou tear thy hair,
And fall upon the ground, as I do now,
Taking the measure of an unmade grave.

[*The* NURSE *knocks.*]

Friar.
Arise, one knocks. Good Romeo, hide thyself.

Romeo.
Not I; unless the breath of heartsick groans
Mistlike infold me from the search of eyes.

[*Knock.*]

Friar.
Hark, how they knock! Who's there? Romeo, arise;

52. fond: foolish

? **62.** *Whom is Romeo talking about?*

63. estate: situation.

? **Staging the Play**
70. *How do you think the friar responds to these harsh words?*

B Literary Focus Rising Action It may seem that Romeo goes on too much. It is important, however, that we get the picture of this "fond mad man" in order to understand the action of the play. None of the other characters can understand Romeo's love. Are they more levelheaded, or simply less lucky in love? How is Romeo's response to banishment like Juliet's?

O holy friar, O, tell me, holy friar,
Where is my lady's lord,
where's Romeo?

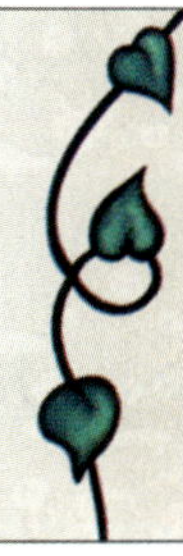

Thou wilt be taken.—Stay awhile!—Stand up;

[*Knock.*]

Run to my study.—By and by!—God's will,
What simpleness is this.—I come, I come!

[*Knock.*]

Who knocks so hard? Whence come you? What's your
  will?

[*Enter* NURSE.]

Nurse.
Let me come in, and you shall know my errand.
I come from Lady Juliet.

Friar. Welcome then.

Nurse.
O holy friar, O, tell me, holy friar,
Where is my lady's lord, where's Romeo?

Friar.
There on the ground, with his own tears made drunk.

Nurse.
O, he is even in my mistress' case,°
Just in her case! O woeful sympathy!
Piteous predicament! Even so lies she,
Blubb'ring and weeping, weeping and blubb'ring.
Stand up, stand up! Stand, and you be a man.
For Juliet's sake, for her sake, rise and stand!
Why should you fall into so deep an O?°

Romeo (*rises*). Nurse—

Nurse.
Ah sir, ah sir! Death's the end of all.

Romeo.
Spakest thou of Juliet? How is it with her?
Doth not she think me an old murderer,

Staging the Play
78. *There is a great deal of action in this scene while the knocks are heard at the door. What action is the friar engaged in, and what is Romeo doing?*

84. case: condition.

90. O: fit of moaning ("oh, oh, oh").

Now I have stained the childhood of our joy
With blood removed but little from her own?
Where is she? And how doth she? And what says
My concealed lady to our canceled love?

Nurse.
O, she says nothing, sir, but weeps and weeps;
And now falls on her bed, and then starts up,
And Tybalt calls; and then on Romeo cries,
And then down falls again.

Romeo. As if that name,
Shot from the deadly level° of a gun,
Did murder her; as that name's cursèd hand
Murdered her kinsman. O, tell me, friar, tell me,
In what vile part of this anatomy
Doth my name lodge? Tell me, that I may sack°
The hateful mansion.

[*He offers to stab himself, and* NURSE *snatches the dagger away.*]

Friar. Hold thy desperate hand.
Art thou a man? Thy form cries out thou art;
Thy tears are womanish, thy wild acts denote
The unreasonable fury of a beast.
Unseemly woman in a seeming man!
And ill-beseeming beast in seeming both!
Thou hast amazed me. By my holy order,
I thought thy disposition better tempered.
Hast thou slain Tybalt? Wilt thou slay thyself?
And slay thy lady that in thy life lives,
By doing damnèd hate upon thyself?
Why rail'st thou on thy birth, the heaven, and earth?
Since birth and heaven and earth,° all three do meet
In thee at once; which thou at once wouldst lose.
Fie, fie, thou sham'st thy shape, thy love, thy wit,
Which,° like a usurer, abound'st in all,
And usest none in that true use indeed
Which should bedeck° thy shape, thy love, thy wit.
Thy noble shape is but a form of wax,
Digressing from the valor of a man;
Thy dear love sworn but hollow perjury,
Killing that love which thou hast vowed to cherish;

103. level: aim.

107. sack: plunder and destroy.

? Staging the Play
108. *Romeo is disarmed without a struggle. He probably stands broken as the friar, in this long speech, gradually reestablishes control. It is important to remember that to the people in this play, suicide was a mortal sin, which damned one to hell forever. Where does the friar angrily remind Romeo of this?*

120. birth and heaven and earth: family origin, soul, and body.

123. Which: who (speaking of Romeo).

125. bedeck: do honor to.

Thy wit, that ornament to shape and love,
Misshapen in the conduct° of them both,
Like powder in a skill-less soldier's flask,
Is set afire by thine own ignorance,
And thou dismembered with thine own defense.°
What, rouse thee, man! Thy Juliet is alive,
For whose dear sake thou wast but lately dead.
There art thou happy.° Tybalt would kill thee,
But thou slewest Tybalt. There art thou happy.
The law, that threatened death, becomes thy friend
And turns it to exile. There art thou happy.
A pack of blessings light upon thy back;
Happiness courts thee in her best array;
But, like a misbehaved and sullen wench,
Thou pouts upon thy fortune and thy love.
Take heed, take heed, for such die miserable.
Go get thee to thy love, as was decreed,
Ascend her chamber, hence and comfort her.
But look thou stay not till the watch be set,
For then thou canst not pass to Mantua,
Where thou shalt live till we can find a time
To blaze° your marriage, reconcile your friends,
Beg pardon of the prince, and call thee back
With twenty hundred thousand times more joy
Than thou went'st forth in lamentation.
Go before, nurse. Commend me to thy lady,
And bid her hasten all the house to bed,
Which heavy sorrow makes them apt unto.
Romeo is coming. C

Nurse.

O Lord, I could have stayed here all the night
To hear good counsel. O, what learning is!
My lord, I'll tell my lady you will come.

Romeo.

Do so, and bid my sweet prepare to chide.

[NURSE *offers to go in and turns again.*]

131. conduct: management.

134. And . . . defense: Romeo's own mind (wit), which should protect him, is destroying him.

137. happy: lucky.

151. blaze: announce.

? **155.** *The friar turns to the nurse. What are his instructions?*

? **Staging the Play**
161. *The nurse's amazement at what she calls the friar's "learning" often brings a laugh from the audience and breaks the tension. Romeo thus far has said nothing. How do you imagine he shows that the friar's speech has brought him back to life?*

C **Reading Focus** **Paraphrasing** The friar's speech is long and complex. Paraphrase the speech to make the essential points clear.

Nurse.
Here, sir, a ring she bid me give you, sir.
Hie you, make haste, for it grows very late. [*Exit.*]

Romeo.
How well my comfort is revived by this!

Friar.
Go hence; good night; and here stands all your state:°
Either be gone before the watch be set,
Or by the break of day disguised from hence.
Sojourn in Mantua. I'll find out your man,
And he shall signify from time to time
Every good hap to you that chances here.
Give me thy hand. 'Tis late. Farewell; good night. **D**

Romeo.
But that a joy past joy calls out on me,
It were a grief so brief to part with thee.
Farewell. [*Exeunt.*]

166. state: situation.

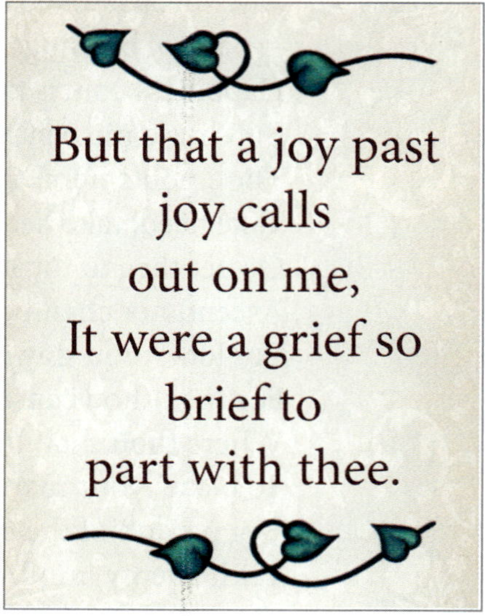
But that a joy past
joy calls
out on me,
It were a grief so
brief to
part with thee.

Scene 4. A room in Capulet's house.

Enter old CAPULET, *his wife,* LADY CAPULET, *and* PARIS.

Capulet.
Things have fallen out, sir, so unluckily
That we have had no time to move° our daughter.
Look you, she loved her kinsman Tybalt dearly,
And so did I. Well, we were born to die.
'Tis very late; she'll not come down tonight.
I promise you, but for your company,
I would have been abed an hour ago. **A**

Paris.
These times of woe afford no times to woo.

2. move: persuade (to marry Paris).

D **Reading Focus** **Analyzing Cause and Effect** In spite of Romeo and Juliet's anguish, the problem at this point seems to have a simple solution. What plans have been made to resolve the young people's difficulties?

A **Literary Focus** **Dramatic Irony** What intense dramatic irony does the audience feel as this scene unfolds? What do we know that the Capulets and Paris don't know?

Madam, good night. Commend me to your daughter.

Lady Capulet.

I will, and know her mind early tomorrow;
Tonight she's mewed up to her heaviness.° **B**

Capulet.

Sir Paris, I will make a desperate tender°
Of my child's love. I think she will be ruled
In all respects by me; nay more, I doubt it not.
Wife, go you to her ere you go to bed;
Acquaint her here of my son Paris' love
And bid her (mark you me?) on Wednesday next—
But soft! What day is this?

Paris. Monday, my lord.

Capulet.

Monday! Ha, ha! Well, Wednesday is too soon.
A' Thursday let it be—a' Thursday, tell her,
She shall be married to this noble earl.
Will you be ready? Do you like this haste?
We'll keep no great ado—a friend or two;
For hark you, Tybalt being slain so late,
It may be thought we held him carelessly,
Being our kinsman, if we revel much.
Therefore we'll have some half a dozen friends,
And there an end. But what say you to Thursday?

Paris.

My lord, I would that Thursday were tomorrow.

Capulet.

Well, get you gone. A' Thursday be it then.
Go you to Juliet ere you go to bed;
Prepare her, wife, against this wedding day.
Farewell, my lord.—Light to my chamber, ho!
Afore me,° it is so very late
That we may call it early by and by.
Good night. **C** [*Exeunt.*]

11. mewed up to her heaviness: shut away because of her great grief.

12. desperate tender: bold offer.

? Staging the Play
19. *In some productions, Capulet is played as a foolish old man. Why might he want to get Juliet married as soon as possible? What do you think his* ***mood*** *is here?*

? Staging the Play
32. *Capulet speaks this line to his wife. In some productions, Lady Capulet seems uneasy about her husband's plans here. Why would she be uneasy?*

34. Afore me: indeed.

B Reading Focus **Analyzing Cause and Effect** Why has Paris come to see the Capulets at such a late hour? Why has Paris's courtship of Juliet been delayed?

C Literary Focus **Rising Action** Just as we feel that Romeo and Juliet's situation can be rescued, Shakespeare raises the stakes with this short scene. How does this development increase the tension?

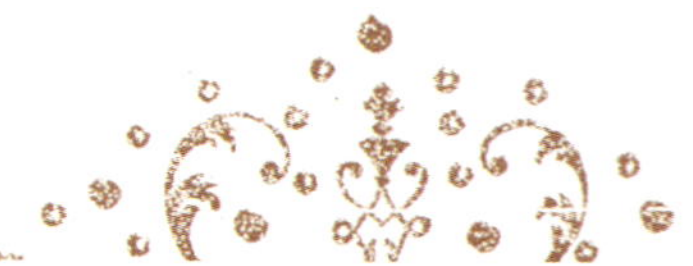

Scene 5. **Capulet's orchard**

Enter ROMEO *and* JULIET *aloft.*

Juliet.

Wilt thou be gone? It is not yet near day.
It was the nightingale, and not the lark,
That pierced the fearful hollow of thine ear.
Nightly she sings on yond pomegranate tree.
Believe me, love, it was the nightingale.

Romeo.

It was the lark, the herald of the morn;
No nightingale. Look, love, what envious streaks
Do lace the severing clouds in yonder east.
Night's candles are burnt out, and jocund day
Stands tiptoe on the misty mountaintops.
I must be gone and live, or stay and die.

Juliet.

Yond light is not daylight; I know it, I.
It is some meteor that the sun exhales°
To be to thee this night a torchbearer
And light thee on thy way to Mantua.
Therefore stay yet; thou need'st not to be gone.

Romeo.

Let me be taken, let me be put to death.
I am content, so thou wilt have it so.
I'll say yon gray is not the morning's eye,
'Tis but the pale reflex° of Cynthia's brow;°
Nor that is not the lark whose notes do beat
The vaulty heaven so high above our heads.
I have more care to stay than will to go.
Come, death, and welcome! Juliet wills it so.
How is't, my soul? Let's talk; it is not day.

Juliet.

It is, it is! Hie hence, be gone, away!
It is the lark that sings so out of tune,
Straining harsh discords and unpleasing sharps.
Some say the lark makes sweet division;°
This doth not so, for she divideth us.
Some say the lark and loathèd toad change eyes;°

? Staging the Play

Stage direction: *Given the design of Elizabethan theaters, this scene was probably played on the upper stage in Shakespeare's time. Modern directors often place this scene in Juliet's bedroom (with varying degrees of frankness). How would you design the scene for a movie or modern stage production?*

? **1.** *Juliet's first words here alert us to the time: It must be near morning, when Romeo must go to Mantua. We hear the song of a lark, which sings at daybreak. The nightingale, on the other hand, sings at night. Why does Juliet insist she hears the nightingale?*

13. exhales: gives off. (It was believed that the sun drew up vapors and ignited them as meteors.)

20. reflex: reflection. **Cynthia's brow:** In Greek mythology, Cynthia is the goddess of the moon.

? **26.** *What has Romeo said that makes Juliet suddenly practical and aware of danger?*

29. division: literally, a rapid run of notes, but Juliet is punning on the word's other meaning ("separation").

31. the lark . . . change eyes: a fable that explains why the lark, which sings beautifully, has ugly eyes and why the toad, which croaks harshly, has beautiful ones.

Romeo embraces Juliet.

Analyzing Visuals **Viewing and Interpreting** Read the Staging the Play sidenote on page 896, and then decide where this scene is staged in the above photo. How can you tell?

O, now I would they had changed voices too,
Since arm from arm that voice doth us affray,°
Hunting thee hence with hunt's-up° to the day.
O, now be gone! More light and light it grows.

Romeo.
More light and light—more dark and dark our woes. 

33. affray: frighten.

34. hunt's-up: morning song for hunters.

A **Reading Focus** **Reading Aloud/Paraphrasing** To fully appreciate the power and beauty of this scene, read it aloud—softly, if you are in class. Paraphrase any passages you have trouble understanding.

[*Enter* NURSE.]

Nurse. Madam!

Juliet. Nurse?

Nurse.
Your lady mother is coming to your chamber.
The day is broke; be wary, look about. [*Exit.*]

Juliet.
Then, window, let day in, and let life out.

Romeo.
Farewell, farewell! One kiss, and I'll descend.

[*He goes down.*]

Juliet.
Art thou gone so, love-lord, ay husband-friend?
I must hear from thee every day in the hour,
For in a minute there are many days.
O, for this count I shall be much in years
Ere I again behold my Romeo!

Romeo.
Farewell!
I will omit no opportunity
That may convey my greetings, love, to thee.

Juliet.
O, think'st thou we shall ever meet again?

Romeo.
I doubt it not; and all these woes shall serve
For sweet discourses in our times to come.

Juliet.
O God, I have an ill-divining soul!
Methinks I see thee, now thou art so low,
As one dead in the bottom of a tomb.
Either my eyesight fails, or thou look'st pale. B

Romeo.
And trust me, love, in my eye so do you.
Dry° sorrow drinks our blood. Adieu, adieu! [*Exit.*]

Juliet.
O Fortune, Fortune! All men call thee fickle.
If thou art fickle, what dost thou with him

Staging the Play
41. *What is Juliet doing as she speaks these lines?*

Staging the Play
43. *Where is Romeo now, as Juliet asks him to communicate with her?*

Staging the Play
51. *Remember what the Chorus has told you in the Prologue about what will happen to Romeo and Juliet. How do you feel when you hear Juliet speak this line?*

59. Dry: thirsty (sorrow was thought to drain color from the cheeks).

B Literary Focus Tragedy At this point in the story, Friar Laurence thinks the situation can be resolved happily. As the lovers part now, where does Juliet foresee Romeo's doom?

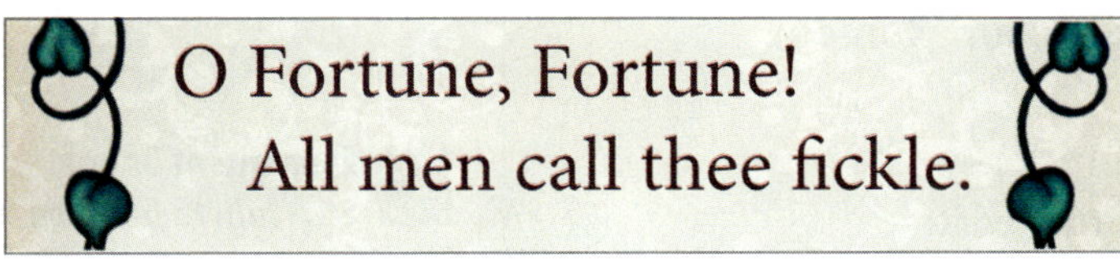
O Fortune, Fortune!
All men call thee fickle.

That is renowned for faith? Be fickle, Fortune,
For then I hope thou wilt not keep him long
But send him back.

[*Enter Juliet's mother,* LADY CAPULET.]

Lady Capulet.
Ho, daughter! Are you up?

Juliet.
Who is't that calls? It is my lady mother.
Is she not down so late,° or up so early?
What unaccustomed cause procures her hither?

Lady Capulet.
Why, how now, Juliet?

Juliet. Madam, I am not well.

Lady Capulet.
Evermore weeping for your cousin's death?
What, wilt thou wash him from his grave with tears?
And if thou couldst, thou couldst not make him live.
Therefore have done. Some grief shows much of love;
But much of grief shows still some want of wit.

Juliet.
Yet let me weep for such a feeling loss.°

Lady Capulet.
So shall you feel the loss, but not the friend
Which you weep for.

Juliet. Feeling so the loss,
I cannot choose but ever weep the friend.

Lady Capulet.
Well, girl, thou weep'st not so much for his death
As that the villain lives which slaughtered him.

Juliet.
What villain, madam?

67. down so late: so late getting to bed.

Staging the Play
74. *Actors playing Lady Capulet have interpreted her character in different ways. Some portray her as loving toward Juliet. Others find in her speeches a signal to play her as distant and strong-willed, to contrast with Juliet's helplessness. What do you think Lady Capulet's **tone** is here?*

75. feeling loss: loss so deeply felt.

78. *All Juliet's lines in this scene have double meanings. Whom is she really grieving for?*

Lady Capulet. That same villain Romeo.

Juliet (*aside*).

Villain and he be many miles asunder—
God pardon him! I do, with all my heart;
And yet no man like he doth grieve my heart.

Lady Capulet.

That is because the traitor murderer lives.

Juliet.

Ay, madam, from the reach of these my hands.
Would none but I might venge my cousin's death!

Lady Capulet.

We will have vengeance for it, fear thou not.
Then weep no more. I'll send to one in Mantua,
Where that same banished runagate° doth live,
Shall give him such an unaccustomed dram°
That he shall soon keep Tybalt company;
And then I hope thou wilt be satisfied.

Juliet.

Indeed I never shall be satisfied
With Romeo till I behold him—dead—
Is my poor heart so for a kinsman vexed.
Madam, if you could find out but a man
To bear a poison, I would temper° it—
That Romeo should, upon receipt thereof,
Soon sleep in quiet. O, how my heart abhors
To hear him named and cannot come to him,
To wreak° the love I bore my cousin
Upon his body that hath slaughtered him!

Lady Capulet.

Find thou the means, and I'll find such a man.
But now I'll tell thee joyful tidings, girl.

Juliet.

And joy comes well in such a needy time.
What are they, I beseech your ladyship?

Lady Capulet.

Well, well, thou hast a careful° father, child;
One who, to put thee from thy heaviness,
Hath sorted out° a sudden day of joy
That thou expects not nor I looked not for.

Juliet.

Madam, in happy time!° What day is that?

Elements of Drama
82. *Juliet's first line here is an* ***aside,*** *or words that her mother does not hear. In her next lines, how does Juliet convince her mother that she hates Romeo?*

90. runagate (RUHN uh gayt): fugitive.

91. unaccustomed dram: unexpected drink (of poison).

Staging the Play
93. *This is a fearful threat. How does Juliet reply, and with what hidden emotions does she speak her next words? How does she continue to speak with double meanings?*

Staging the Play
95. *How should lines 95–96 be said to indicate that Juliet intends* dead *to refer to her heart?*

98. temper: mix (she really means "weaken").

102. wreak: avenge (she really means "express").

105. *Has Juliet convinced her mother that she wants Romeo dead?*

Staging the Play
106. *We know what the "tidings" are, but Juliet doesn't. How would she speak these lines?*

108. careful: full of caring (for Juliet).

110. sorted out: selected.

112. in happy time: at an appropriate time.

Lady Capulet.
Marry, my child, early next Thursday morn
The gallant, young, and noble gentleman,
The County Paris, at Saint Peter's Church,
Shall happily make thee there a joyful bride.

Juliet.
Now by Saint Peter's Church, and Peter too,
He shall not make me there a joyful bride!
I wonder at this haste, that I must wed
Ere he that should be husband comes to woo.
I pray you tell my lord and father, madam,
I will not marry yet; and when I do, I swear
It shall be Romeo, whom you know I hate,
Rather than Paris. These are news indeed!

Lady Capulet.
Here comes your father. Tell him so yourself,
And see how he will take it at your hands.

[*Enter* CAPULET *and* NURSE.]

Capulet.
When the sun sets the earth doth drizzle dew,
But for the sunset of my brother's son
It rains downright.
How now? A conduit,° girl? What, still in tears?
Evermore showering? In one little body
Thou counterfeits a bark,° a sea, a wind:
For still thy eyes, which I may call the sea,
Do ebb and flow with tears; the bark thy body is,
Sailing in this salt flood; the winds, thy sighs,
Who, raging with thy tears and they with them,
Without a sudden calm will overset
Thy tempest-tossèd body. How now, wife?
Have you delivered to her our decree?

Lady Capulet.
Ay, sir; but she will none, she gives you thanks.
I would the fool were married to her grave!

Capulet.
Soft! Take me with you,° take me with you, wife.
How? Will she none? Doth she not give us thanks?
Is she not proud? Doth she not count her blest,
Unworthy as she is, that we have wrought°
So worthy a gentleman to be her bride?

? **120.** *Juliet becomes sarcastic as she repeats her mother's words. Despite this shocking news, how does Juliet manage to make a reasonable protest to her mother?*

130. conduit (KAHN doo iht): water pipe (Juliet is weeping).

132. counterfeits a bark: imitates a boat.

? **Staging the Play**
139. *Lord Capulet, self-satisfied and certain of his plan, tries to humor and tease the weeping Juliet. Again, what sense of* ***irony*** *is created in this scene?*

142. Soft! Take me with you: Wait! Let me understand you.

145. wrought: arranged.

Juliet.
Not proud you have, but thankful that you have.
Proud can I never be of what I hate,
But thankful even for hate that is meant love.

Capulet.
How, how, how, how, chopped-logic?° What is this?
"Proud"—and "I thank you"—and "I thank you not"—
And yet "not proud"? Mistress minion° you,
Thank me no thankings, nor proud me no prouds,
But fettle° your fine joints 'gainst Thursday next
To go with Paris to Saint Peter's Church,
Or I will drag thee on a hurdle thither.
Out, you greensickness carrion! Out, you baggage!
You tallow-face!

Lady Capulet. Fie, fie! What, are you mad?

Juliet.
Good father, I beseech you on my knees,
Hear me with patience but to speak a word.

Capulet.
Hang thee, young baggage! Disobedient wretch!
I tell thee what—get thee to church a' Thursday
Or never after look me in the face.
Speak not, reply not, do not answer me!
My fingers itch. Wife, we scarce thought us blest
That God had lent us but this only child;
But now I see this one is one too much,
And that we have a curse in having her.
Out on her, hilding!°

Nurse. God in heaven bless her!
You are to blame, my lord, to rate° her so.

Capulet.
And why, my Lady Wisdom? Hold your tongue,
Good Prudence. Smatter with your gossips,° go!

Nurse.
I speak no treason.

Capulet. O, God-i-god-en!°

Nurse.
May not one speak?

Capulet. Peace, you mumbling fool!
Utter your gravity o'er a gossip's bowl,

? **149.** *How does Juliet show that she knows her father loves her even though she hates what he has done for her?*

150. chopped-logic: hair-splitting.

152. minion (MIHN yuhn): badly behaved girl.

154. fettle: make ready.

? **Staging the Play**
158. *What insulting names does Capulet call Juliet? What would Capulet's actions be, as he speaks these vicious words to his only daughter? Whom is Juliet's mother talking to in her next line?*

169. hilding: low, contemptible person.

170. rate: berate; scold.

172. Smatter with your gossips: Chatter with your gossipy friends.

173. God-i-god-en: Get on with you ("God give you good evening").

A close-up of Lady Capulet.

Analyzing Visuals

Viewing and Interpreting
Lady Capulet does not speak much in this scene, but based on this photo, how do you think she feels about her daughter Juliet?

For here we need it not.
Lady Capulet. You are too hot.
Capulet.
God's bread!° It makes me mad.
Day, night; hour, tide, time; work, play;
Alone, in company; still my care hath been
To have her matched; and having now provided
A gentleman of noble parentage,
Of fair demesnes, youthful, and nobly trained,
Stuffed, as they say, with honorable parts,
Proportioned as one's thought would wish a man—
And then to have a wretched puling° fool,
A whining mammet,° in her fortune's tender,°
To answer "I'll not wed, I cannot love;
I am too young, I pray you pardon me"!
But, and you will not wed, I'll pardon you!°
Graze where you will, you shall not house with me.
Look to't, think on't; I do not use to jest.

177. God's bread: oath on the sacrament of Communion (in the traditional Christian church service).

185. puling (PYOO lihng): whining.

186. mammet: puppet. **in her fortune's tender:** with all her good fortunes.

? **188.** *What does Lord Capulet think are Juliet's reasons for not wanting to marry Paris?*

189. I'll pardon you: I'll give you permission to go.

Thursday is near; lay hand on heart, advise.°
And you be mine, I'll give you to my friend;
And you be not, hang, beg, starve, die in the streets,
For, by my soul, I'll ne'er acknowledge thee,
Nor what is mine shall never do thee good.
Trust to't. Bethink you. I'll not be forsworn.° [*Exit.*]

Juliet.
Is there no pity sitting in the clouds
That sees into the bottom of my grief?
O sweet my mother, cast me not away!
Delay this marriage for a month, a week;
Or if you do not, make the bridal bed
In that dim monument where Tybalt lies.

Lady Capulet.
Talk not to me, for I'll not speak a word.
Do as thou wilt, for I have done with thee. C D [*Exit.*]

Juliet.
O God!—O nurse, how shall this be prevented?
My husband is on earth, my faith in heaven.°
How shall that faith return again to earth
Unless that husband send it me from heaven
By leaving earth? Comfort me, counsel me.
Alack, alack, that heaven should practice stratagems
Upon so soft a subject as myself!
What say'st thou? Hast thou not a word of joy?
Some comfort, nurse.

Nurse. Faith, here it is.
Romeo is banishèd; and all the world to nothing°
That he dares ne'er come back to challenge you;
Or if he do, it needs must be by stealth.
Then, since the case so stands as now it doth,
I think it best you married with the county.
O, he's a lovely gentleman!
Romeo's a dishclout° to him. An eagle, madam,
Hath not so green, so quick, so fair an eye

192. advise: consider.

197. forsworn: guilty of breaking my vow.

Staging the Play
197. *In most productions there is a moment of stunned silence onstage after Capulet leaves. What exactly will Lord Capulet do if Juliet refuses to marry Paris? In the next speech, how does Juliet appeal to her mother for help?*

207. my faith in heaven: my wedding vow is recorded in heaven.

210. *Romeo and Juliet constantly remind us that they take their marriage vows seriously. According to Juliet here, how can these vows be broken?*

215. all the world to nothing: it is a safe bet.

221. dishclout: dishcloth; something limp and weak.

C Reading Focus Reading Aloud To get a clearer picture of the family's conflict, read aloud the dialogue from lines 127 to 205 with two other classmates.

D Reading Focus Analyzing Cause and Effect What does Juliet do following her father's departure? What does her mother do?

As Paris hath. Beshrew° my very heart,
I think you are happy in this second match,
For it excels your first; or if it did not,
Your first is dead—or 'twere as good he were
As living here and you no use of him.

Juliet.
Speak'st thou from thy heart?

Nurse.
And from my soul too; else beshrew them both.

Juliet. Amen!

Nurse. What?

Juliet.
Well, thou hast comforted me marvelous much.
Go in; and tell my lady I am gone,
Having displeased my father, to Laurence' cell,
To make confession and to be absolved.

Nurse.
Marry, I will; and this is wisely done. [*Exit.*]

Juliet.
Ancient damnation!° O most wicked fiend!
Is it more sin to wish me thus forsworn,
Or to dispraise my lord with that same tongue
Which she hath praised him with above compare
So many thousand times? Go, counselor!
Thou and my bosom henceforth shall be twain.°
I'll to the friar to know his remedy.
If all else fail, myself have power to die. **E** [*Exit.*]

223. Beshrew: curse.

? Elements of Drama
227. *What is the nurse's "comfort" and advice for Juliet? Which line in this passage of dialogue suggests that Juliet has reacted with shock and that the nurse must pause? Did you expect such advice from the nurse?*

? Staging the Play
235. *In most productions the nurse embraces Juliet to comfort her. Now Juliet has made a decision. What do you see Juliet doing as she speaks?*

237. Ancient damnation: damned old woman.

242. twain: two (thus, separate).

E Reading Focus Making Inferences Why doesn't Juliet just tell her parents why she cannot marry Paris? Why do you think she does not tell the truth?

Applying Your Skills

The Tragedy of Romeo and Juliet, Act III

Respond and Think Critically

Reading Focus

Quick Check

1. What causes the fatal sword fight between Mercutio and Tybalt in Scene 1? How is Mercutio killed? Why does Romeo kill Tybalt?
2. What does Juliet threaten in Scene 2 after hearing of Romeo's banishment?
3. What is the friar's plan in Scene 3?
4. By the end of Scene 4, what plans have Juliet's parents made for her?

Read with a Purpose

5. Is Romeo's decision to fight Tybalt an act of fate or an act of free will? Explain.

Reading Skills: Reading a Play

6. As each scene unfolds, every cause and its effect seems to make things worse. The friar has a plan that may help the lovers, but Capulet wants Juliet to marry Paris. In your chart, predict how Capulet's plan may affect the friar's plan. Continue to record causes and effects in Act IV.

Analyze Causes and Effects	My Notes
Capulet wants Juliet to marry Paris.	I think the friar will . . .

Literary Focus

Literary Analysis

7. **Draw Conclusions** Shakespeare didn't write a prologue to Act III. What does that signify? How might it affect the audience response to events in Act III?
8. **Explain** How does the nurse offend Juliet in Scene 5 and cease to be her ally? How does this development add to the tragedy of events?
9. **Analyze** In drama, **suspense** causes us to wonder, "What will happen next?" How is suspense created in Act III?

Literary Skills: Tragedy

10. **Analyze** Romeo's killing of Tybalt is the **turning point** of the play—the point when something happens that turns the action toward either a happy ending (a **comedy**) or an unhappy ending (a **tragedy**). What actions does the killing set in motion? What are the possible tragic consequences?

Literary Skills Review: Dynamic Characters

11. **Evaluate** Romeo and Juliet are **dynamic characters;** they learn and grow during the course of the play. Describe how the lovers have changed in Act III. What hard lessons have they learned about love?

Writing Focus

Think as a Reader/Writer

Use It in Your Writing Using your notes on Act III, write a summary of the act that points out various aspects of the turning point. What direction does the play now take?

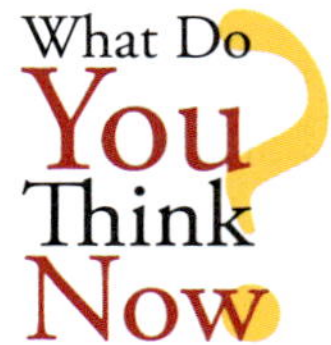

How can Romeo and Juliet reduce the damage from the various risks they have taken?

MO **9.R.2.C.1.b** Use details from text(s): to analyze character, plot, setting, point of view **9.R.2** Develop and apply skills and strategies to comprehend, analyze and evaluate fiction, poetry and drama from a variety of cultures and times *Also covered* **9.R.3.C.1.a; 9.W.3.A.1.c; 9.R.1.E.1.c; 9.R.1.E.1.a**

Vocabulary Development

Vocabulary Skills: Word Origins

In Act II, Scene 2, Juliet, upset to discover that the handsome young man she has just met is named Montague, speaks these famous lines about the insignificance of a name:

> What's in a name? That which we call a rose
> By any other word would smell as sweet.

Names, however *are* significant in Shakespeare's plays. They are often used to suggest something about a person's character or temperament.

Your Turn

Finding the Meanings of Names Use a dictionary and the sidenotes for help as you answer the following questions about the names of four characters in *The Tragedy of Romeo and Juliet.*

1. Mercutio is named for the chemical element *mercury,* which itself is named for the Roman god Mercury, the messenger of the gods. Which characteristics of both the element and the god match Mercutio's character? What does it mean to say that someone's temperament is *mercurial*?
2. Benvolio's name comes from the same Latin words as the adjective *benevolent*. What are these Latin words, and what do they mean? How does Benvolio's name match his character?
3. Tybalt is named for a cat that is known for its slyness in the fable "Reynard the Fox." How is Tybalt like the cat he is named for?
4. Paris has the same name as the Trojan prince in Homer's epic the *Iliad*, who persuades Helen to leave her husband and marry him. Although Count Paris never marries Juliet, what does he do in the play that is similar to what the Greek prince does in the epic?
5. If you were renaming these four characters for an updated version of the tragedy, what names would you give them?

Language Coach

Word Origins Names sometimes have their origin in a trade. For example, last names such as Cooper (barrel maker), Baker, Miller (a mill worker), or Sawyer (one who saws wood) explained what sort of job a person had.

Nicknames often describe a physical attribute, such as Red for a redhead, or a playful opposite such as Shorty for someone who is six and a half feet tall.

Think about names of people you know or have heard of and explain the meanings of their names.

Academic Vocabulary

Write About . . .

How would you update *The Tragedy of Romeo and Juliet*? Look back at the Staging the Play sidenotes in Act III and the Language Coach and question 5 from the Your Turn activity on this page. Now, write a brief description of your modern interpretation. Include Academic Vocabulary words in your description.

ACT IV

2004 production of *Romeo and Juliet* by the Guthrie Theater.

Read with a Purpose As you read, identify the terrible risk Juliet takes in order to be with Romeo.

ACT IV

SCENE 1. *Friar Laurence's cell.*

Enter FRIAR LAURENCE *and* COUNT PARIS.

Friar.
On Thursday, sir? The time is very short.

Paris.
My father Capulet will have it so,
And I am nothing slow to slack his haste.

Friar.
You say you do not know the lady's mind.
Uneven° is the course; I like it not.

Paris.
Immoderately she weeps for Tybalt's death,
And therefore have I little talked of love;
For Venus smiles not in a house of tears.
Now, sir, her father counts it dangerous
That she do give her sorrow so much sway,
And in his wisdom hastes our marriage
To stop the inundation of her tears,
Which, too much minded° by herself alone,
May be put from her by society.
Now do you know the reason of this haste.

Friar (*aside*).
I would I knew not why it should be slowed,—
Look, sir, here comes the lady toward my cell.

[*Enter* JULIET.]

Paris.
Happily met, my lady and my wife!

Juliet.
That may be, sir, when I may be a wife.

Paris.
That "may be" must be, love, on Thursday next.

Juliet.
What must be shall be.

Friar. That's a certain text.

5. Uneven: irregular or unusual.

13. minded: thought about.

? **15.** *According to Paris, why is Capulet pushing his daughter to marry so quickly?*

Paris.
Come you to make confession to this father?
Juliet.
To answer that, I should confess to you.
Paris.
Do not deny to him that you love me.
Juliet.
I will confess to you that I love him.
Paris.
So will ye, I am sure, that you love me.
Juliet.
If I do so, it will be of more price,
Being spoke behind your back, than to your face.
Paris.
Poor soul, thy face is much abused with tears.
Juliet.
The tears have got small victory by that,
For it was bad enough before their spite.°
Paris.
Thou wrong'st it more than tears with that report.
Juliet.
That is no slander, sir, which is a truth;
And what I spake, I spake it to my face.
Paris.
Thy face is mine, and thou hast slandered it.
Juliet.
It may be so, for it is not mine own.
Are you at leisure, holy father, now,
Or shall I come to you at evening mass?
Friar.
My leisure serves me, pensive daughter, now.
My lord, we must entreat the time alone.
Paris.
God shield° I should disturb devotion!
Juliet, on Thursday early will I rouse ye.
Till then, adieu, and keep this holy kiss. [*Exit.*]
Juliet.
O, shut the door, and when thou hast done so,

? Elements of Drama
26. *In this scene, Juliet's action is to keep up appearances and ward off Paris, who presses his attentions on her. She does this by wittily playing with words. We are fascinated by two things here: what is being done and how it is being done. What double meanings does Juliet intend in the* ***dialogue*** *with Paris that follows?*

31. spite: injury or damage (to her face).

? Staging the Play
38. *Juliet must show here that the tension of keeping up this pretense is unbearable. Where do you think she pauses and changes her tone?*

41. God shield: God forbid.

Come weep with me—past hope, past care, past help! **A**

Friar.

O Juliet, I already know thy grief;
It strains me past the compass of my wits.
I hear thou must, and nothing may prorogue° it,
On Thursday next be married to this county.

Juliet.

Tell me not, friar, that thou hearest of this,
Unless thou tell me how I may prevent it.
If in thy wisdom thou canst give no help,
Do thou but call my resolution wise
And with this knife I'll help it presently.
God joined my heart and Romeo's, thou our hands;
And ere this hand, by thee to Romeo's sealed,
Shall be the label° to another deed,°
Or my true heart with treacherous revolt
Turn to another, this shall slay them both.
Therefore, out of thy long-experienced time,
Give me some present counsel; or, behold,
'Twixt my extremes and me this bloody knife
Shall play the umpire, arbitrating that
Which the commission° of thy years and art
Could to no issue of true honor bring.
Be not so long to speak. I long to die
If what thou speak'st speak not of remedy.

Friar.

Hold, daughter. I do spy a kind of hope,
Which craves as desperate an execution
As that is desperate which we would prevent.
If, rather than to marry County Paris,
Thou hast the strength of will to slay thyself,
Then is it likely thou wilt undertake
A thing like death to chide away this shame,
That cop'st° with death himself to scape from it;
And, if thou darest, I'll give thee remedy.

Juliet.

O, bid me leap, rather than marry Paris,
From off the battlements of any tower,
Or walk in thievish ways, or bid me lurk

48. prorogue (proh ROHG): postpone.

? **54.** *What is Juliet holding in her hand? What is she threatening to do?*

57. label: seal. **deed:** contract (of marriage).

? **Elements of Drama**
62. *The friar has to put up with a good deal of brandishing of knives and daggers from Romeo and Juliet. Now that the nurse is no longer Juliet's ally, the friar has to be the confidant of both Juliet and Romeo. He must listen with patience to their threats of suicide if they cannot be together. What line in Juliet's speech indicates that she has paused and that the friar for a time is silent?*

64. commission: authority.

75. cop'st: negotiates.

? **Staging the Play**
77. *What would Juliet's mood be as she delivers this speech? What is she willing to do rather than marry Paris?*

A Literary Focus Conflict Paris has gone, and Juliet has endured his "holy kiss." How has the conflict escalated? What does she now ask Friar Laurence to do?

Analyzing Visuals **Viewing and Interpreting** How does the actress convey to the audience the seriousness of the friar's words to her?

Where serpents are; chain me with roaring bears,
Or hide me nightly in a charnel house,°
O'ercovered quite with dead men's rattling bones,
With reeky° shanks and yellow chapless° skulls;
Or bid me go into a new-made grave
And hide me with a dead man in his shroud—
Things that, to hear them told, have made me tremble—
And I will do it without fear or doubt,
To live an unstained wife to my sweet love.

Friar.

Hold, then. Go home, be merry, give consent
To marry Paris. Wednesday is tomorrow.
Tomorrow night look that thou lie alone;
Let not the nurse lie with thee in thy chamber.
Take thou this vial, being then in bed,
And this distilling° liquor drink thou off;
When presently through all thy veins shall run
A cold and drowsy humor;° for no pulse
Shall keep his native° progress, but surcease;°
No warmth, no breath, shall testify thou livest;
The roses in thy lips and cheeks shall fade
To wanny° ashes, thy eyes' windows fall
Like death when he shuts up the day of life;
Each part, deprived of supple government,°
Shall, stiff and stark and cold, appear like death;
And in this borrowed likeness of shrunk death
Thou shalt continue two-and-forty hours,
And then awake as from a pleasant sleep. **B**
Now, when the bridegroom in the morning comes
To rouse thee from thy bed, there art thou dead.
Then, as the manner of our country is,
In thy best robes uncovered on the bier
Thou shalt be borne to that same ancient vault
Where all the kindred of the Capulets lie.
In the meantime, against° thou shalt awake,
Shall Romeo by my letters know our drift;°
And hither shall he come; and he and I

81. charnel house: building where bones from old graves are kept.

83. reeky: damp; stinking. **chapless:** jawless.

? **89.** *Juliet must pay strict attention to the friar's plan, as must the audience. On what day does the friar tell Juliet to take the potion?*

94. distilling: penetrating.

96. humor: fluid.

97. native: natural. **surcease:** stop.

100. wanny: pale.

102. government: control.

113. against: before.

114. drift: intentions.

B **Reading Focus** **Analyzing Cause and Effect** Where have we seen the friar taking care of his herbs and heard him talk of magical potions before? What will happen to Juliet when she takes the drug? What complications do you think might occur as a result?

Will watch thy waking, and that very night
Shall Romeo bear thee hence to Mantua.
And this shall free thee from this present shame,
If no inconstant toy° nor womanish fear
Abate thy valor in the acting it. Ⓒ

Juliet.
Give me, give me! O, tell not me of fear!

Friar.
Hold! Get you gone, be strong and prosperous
In this resolve. I'll send a friar with speed
To Mantua, with my letters to thy lord.

Juliet.
Love give me strength, and strength shall help afford.
Farewell, dear father.

[*Exit with* FRIAR.]

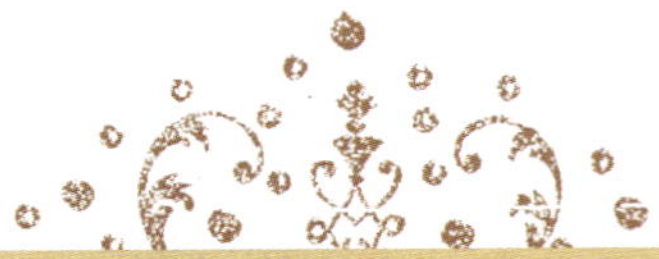

SCENE 2. *A hall in Capulet's house.*

Enter father CAPULET, LADY CAPULET, NURSE, *and* SERVINGMEN, *two or three.*

Capulet.
So many guests invite as here are writ.

[*Exit a* SERVINGMAN.]

Sirrah, go hire me twenty cunning° cooks.

Servingman. You shall have none ill, sir; for I'll try if they can lick their fingers.

Capulet.
How canst thou try them so?

Servingman. Marry, sir, 'tis an ill cook that cannot lick his own fingers. Therefore he that cannot lick his fingers goes not with me.

Capulet. Go, be gone.

[*Exit* SERVINGMAN.]

? ***117.*** *How is Romeo to be told of this plan? When is he to watch Juliet wake and take her to Mantua?*

119. toy: whim.

? **Staging the Play**
126. *In some productions the friar holds Juliet back for just a moment and silently blesses her. Why would this action make us more anxious about what might happen to her?*

? **Elements of Drama**
1. *Capulet is sending his servant off to invite guests to Juliet's wedding. How does this comic and busy domestic scene contrast with the previous one?*

2. cunning: skillful.

Ⓒ **Literary Focus** **Turning Point** What is the friar's plan? What do you think will be the outcome of this turning point in the play?

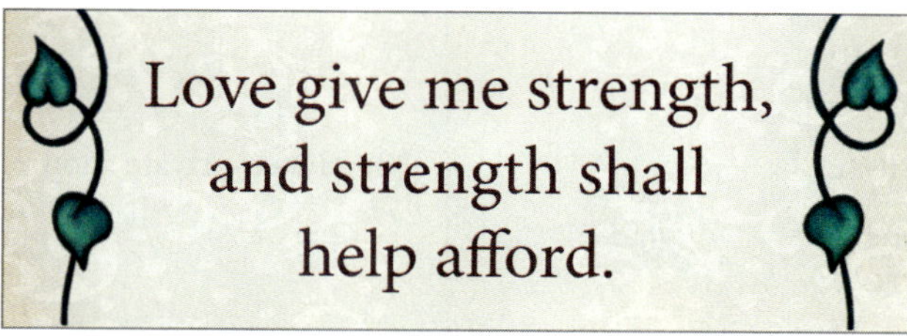
Love give me strength,
and strength shall
help afford.

We shall be much unfurnished° for this time.
What, is my daughter gone to Friar Laurence?

Nurse. Ay, forsooth.

Capulet.
Well, he may chance to do some good on her.
A peevish self-willed harlotry it is.

10. unfurnished: unsupplied (without food).

[*Enter* JULIET.]

Nurse.
See where she comes from shrift with merry look.

Capulet.
How now, my headstrong? Where have you been gadding?

14. *Harlotry means a "good-for-nothing," a prostitute. Whom is Capulet referring to as "it"?*

15. *Do you think Juliet really has a "merry look," or is the nurse trying to cover up?*

Juliet.
Where I have learnt me to repent the sin
Of disobedient opposition
To you and your behests, and am enjoined
By holy Laurence to fall prostrate here
To beg your pardon. Pardon, I beseech you!
Henceforward I am ever ruled by you.

Capulet.
Send for the county. Go tell him of this.
I'll have this knot knit up tomorrow morning. **A**

Juliet.
I met the youthful lord at Laurence' cell
And gave him what becomèd° love I might,
Not stepping o'er the bounds of modesty.

Capulet.
Why, I am glad on't. This is well. Stand up.
This is as't should be. Let me see the county.
Ay, marry, go, I say, and fetch him hither.

26. becomèd: proper or becoming.

28. *According to this speech, what has Juliet been doing since she first addressed her father?*

A **Reading Focus** **Making Inferences** Why do you think Capulet pushes the marriage up to Wednesday?

Now, afore God, this reverend holy friar,
All our whole city is much bound to him.

Juliet.
Nurse, will you go with me into my closet,°
To help me sort such needful ornaments
As you think fit to furnish me tomorrow?

Lady Capulet.
No, not till Thursday. There is time enough.

Capulet.
Go, nurse, go with her. We'll to church tomorrow. **B**
[*Exeunt* JULIET *and* NURSE.]

Lady Capulet.
We shall be short in our provision.
'Tis now near night.

Capulet. Tush, I will stir about,
And all things shall be well, I warrant thee, wife.
Go thou to Juliet, help to deck up her.
I'll not to bed tonight; let me alone.
I'll play the housewife for this once. What, ho!
They are all forth; well, I will walk myself
To County Paris, to prepare up him
Against tomorrow. My heart is wondrous light,
Since this same wayward girl is so reclaimed.
[*Exit with* LADY CAPULET.]

33. **closet:** private room.

Staging the Play
47. *Lord Capulet realizes all the servants are gone. What action is he involved in during this speech? What is his new mood?*

Scene 3. Juliet's chamber.

Enter JULIET *and* NURSE.

Juliet.
Ay, those attires are best; but, gentle nurse,
I pray thee leave me to myself tonight;
For I have need of many orisons°
To move the heavens to smile upon my state,
Which, well thou knowest, is cross and full of sin.

3. **orisons** (AWR uh zuhnz): prayers.

B **Literary Focus** **Rising Action** The wedding has been moved to Wednesday. How will this affect the timing of the friar's plans? What plot complications might it create?

Lady Capulet and Juliet discuss Juliet's impending marriage to Paris. The nurse listens in the background.

[*Enter* LADY CAPULET.]

Lady Capulet.
What, are you busy, ho? Need you my help?

Juliet.
No, madam; we have culled such necessaries
As are behoveful° for our state° tomorrow.
So please you, let me now be left alone,
And let the nurse this night sit up with you;
For I am sure you have your hands full all
In this so sudden business.

Lady Capulet. Good night.
Get thee to bed, and rest; for thou hast need.

[*Exeunt* LADY CAPULET *and* NURSE.]

Staging the Play

6. *In some productions, Lady Capulet is played here as loving and gentle with Juliet, perhaps suggesting that she is uneasy about her daughter's change of heart. What emotions should her next speech show?*

8. behoveful: suitable. **state:** ceremonies.

Juliet.

Farewell! God knows when we shall meet again.
I have a faint cold fear thrills through my veins
That almost freezes up the heat of life.
I'll call them back again to comfort me.
Nurse!—What should she do here?
My dismal scene I needs must act alone.
Come, vial.
What if this mixture do not work at all?
Shall I be married then tomorrow morning?
No, no! This shall forbid it. Lie thou there.

[*Lays down a dagger.*]

What if it be a poison which the friar
Subtly hath ministered to have me dead,
Lest in this marriage he should be dishonored
Because he married me before to Romeo?
I fear it is; and yet methinks it should not,
For he hath still been tried° a holy man. **A**
How if, when I am laid into the tomb,
I wake before the time that Romeo
Come to redeem me? There's a fearful point!
Shall I not then be stifled in the vault,
To whose foul mouth no healthsome air breathes in,
And there die strangled ere my Romeo comes?
Or, if I live, is it not very like
The horrible conceit of death and night,
Together with the terror of the place—
As in a vault, an ancient receptacle
Where for this many hundred years the bones
Of all my buried ancestors are packed;
Where bloody Tybalt, yet but green in earth,°
Lies fest'ring in his shroud; where, as they say,
At some hours in the night spirits resort—
Alack, alack, is it not like that I,
So early waking—what with loathsome smells,
And shrieks like mandrakes° torn out of the earth,
That living mortals, hearing them, run mad—

? Elements of Drama
14. *Here is an example of a conventional Shakespearean* ***soliloquy,*** *where a character who is poised on the edge of action thinks over its pros and cons. What are the fears and doubts that Juliet must consider before taking the potion?*

29. still been tried: always been proved.

42. green in earth: newly buried.

47. mandrakes: plants resembling the human body, which were said to grow beneath the gallows and to scream when torn up.

A Reading Focus Paraphrasing Audiences always wonder why the friar has not simply told the families of Romeo and Juliet's secret wedding rather than involve them in such a dangerous plan. How does Juliet explain the friar's actions?

I, if I wake, shall I not be distraught,
Environèd with all these hideous fears,
And madly play with my forefathers' joints,
And pluck the mangled Tybalt from his shroud,
And, in this rage, with some great kinsman's bone
As with a club dash out my desp'rate brains?
O, look! Methinks I see my cousin's ghost
Seeking out Romeo, that did spit his body
Upon a rapier's point. Stay, Tybalt, stay!
Romeo, Romeo, Romeo, I drink to thee. **B**

[*She falls upon her bed within the curtains.*]

? **54.** *Draw the mental picture you have of the tomb from Juliet's description of it.*

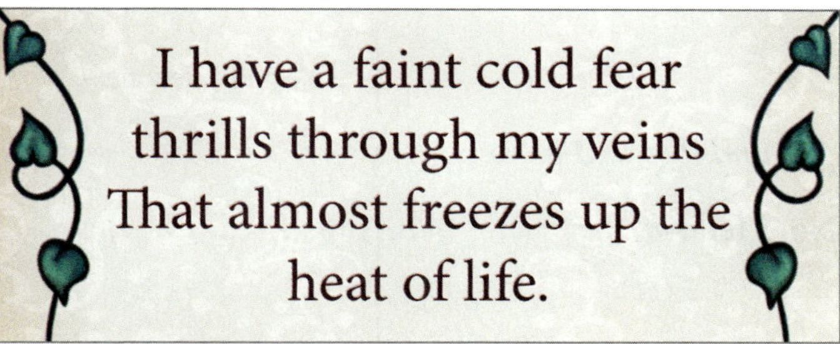
I have a faint cold fear
thrills through my veins
That almost freezes up the
heat of life.

Scene 4. A hall in Capulet's house.

Enter LADY CAPULET *and* NURSE.

? **1.** *How does this peaceful domestic scene contrast with what has just happened? What is everyone preparing for?*

Lady Capulet.
Hold, take these keys and fetch more spices, nurse.

Nurse.
They call for dates and quinces in the pastry.

[*Enter old* CAPULET.]

Capulet.
Come, stir, stir, stir! The second cock hath crowed,

B Literary Focus Turning Point What does Juliet's uneasiness about the decided course of action tell you about the weaknesses in the friar's plan? How might those weaknesses complicate the plan?

The curfew bell hath rung, 'tis three o'clock.
Look to the baked meats, good Angelica;
Spare not for cost.

Nurse. Go, you cotquean,° go,
Get you to bed! Faith, you'll be sick tomorrow
For this night's watching.

Capulet.
No, not a whit. What, I have watched ere now
All night for lesser cause, and ne'er been sick.

Lady Capulet.
Ay, you have been a mouse hunt° in your time;
But I will watch you from such watching now.
[*Exeunt* LADY CAPULET *and* NURSE.]

Capulet.
A jealous hood,° a jealous hood!

[*Enter three or four* FELLOWS *with spits and logs and baskets.*]

Now, fellow,
What is there?

First Fellow.
Things for the cook, sir; but I know not what.

Capulet.
Make haste, make haste. [*Exit* FIRST FELLOW.]

Sirrah, fetch drier logs.
Call Peter; he will show thee where they are.

Second Fellow.
I have a head, sir, that will find out logs°
And never trouble Peter for the matter.

Capulet.
Mass,° and well said; a merry whoreson, ha!
Thou shalt be loggerhead.°
[*Exit* SECOND FELLOW, *with the others.*]

Good faith, 'tis day.
The county will be here with music straight,
For so he said he would. (*Play music offstage.*)
I hear him near.
Nurse! Wife! What, ho! What, nurse, I say!

Staging the Play
5. *Angelica is the nurse's name. How does Lord Capulet treat her now, as opposed to how he treated her in Act III, Scene 5? What humor does the nurse add to this scene?*

6. cotquean (KAHT kween): old woman (a man who acts like an old woman).

11. mouse hunt: woman chaser or night prowler.

12. *What is Lady Capulet's tone here?*

13. hood: female.

18. I . . . logs: in other words, "I have a wooden head."

20. Mass: mild oath, "by the Mass."

21. loggerhead: blockhead.

Staging the Play
21. *Capulet fusses around and has his nose in everything. What actions do you imagine the old man is involved in, in this scene?*

Elements of Drama
23. *The music is bridal music, for the wedding. What* ***irony*** *would the audience sense on hearing this music and knowing what has happened to Juliet?*

[*Enter* NURSE.]

Go waken Juliet; go and trim her up.
I'll go and chat with Paris. Hie, make haste,
Make haste! The bridegroom he is come already:
Make haste, I say. [*Exit.*] **A**

A **Reading Focus** **Analyzing Cause and Effect** Why do you think Capulet is so happy to see his daughter marry Paris? What effect will the marriage have on his family and the feud between the Capulets and Montagues?

FILM LINK

Shakespeare on the Screen

Film and television have introduced the magic of William Shakespeare to millions of viewers. Filmmakers and screenwriters, inspired by Shakespeare's characters and poetry, have adapted his plays for more than a century. Between 1978 and 1985, all of Shakespeare's plays were filmed for television.

In 1996, Director Baz Luhrmann reenvisioned *Romeo and Juliet*, transporting Shakespeare's Elizabethan masterpiece into the present. *Romeo + Juliet,* starring Leonardo DiCaprio and Claire Danes, is set in a fictionalized modern-day city called Verona Beach. The director retained Shakespeare's original dialogue but swapped swords and castles for guns and skyscrapers.

Shakespeare, himself, has been fictionalized for film. The award-winning 1998 film *Shakespeare in Love* follows the writer as he struggles to create his play *Romeo and Ethel the Pirate's Daughter.* With the help of Viola, an aspiring actress, he completes his great tragedy, *Romeo and Juliet.*

Critics have pointed out drawbacks in the performance of Shakespeare's plays on screen. Some argue that film controls our perception of the play and deprives us of the thrill of seeing a live performance.

Today Shakespeare is accessible as never before. A performance of one of his plays is as close as your local library or video store.

Ask Yourself **Is it a good idea for filmmakers to edit and alter Shakespeare's plays to create their films? Explain why or why not.**

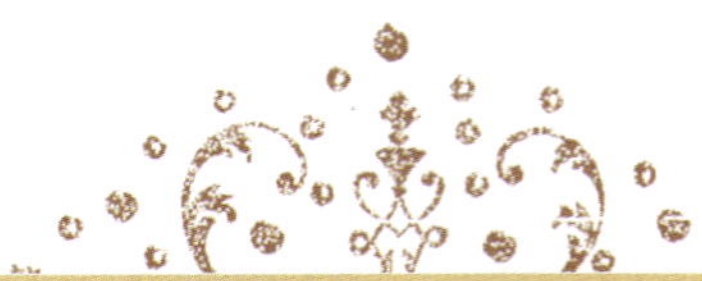

Scene 5. Juliet's chamber.

Nurse.
Mistress! What, mistress! Juliet! Fast,° I warrant her, she.
Why, lamb! Why, lady! Fie, you slugabed.
Why, love, I say! Madam; sweetheart! Why, bride!
What, not a word? You take your pennyworths° now;
Sleep for a week; for the next night, I warrant,
The County Paris hath set up his rest°
That you shall rest but little. God forgive me!
Marry, and amen. How sound is she asleep!
I needs must wake her. Madam, madam, madam!
Ay, let the county take you in your bed;
He'll fright you up, i' faith. Will it not be?

[*Draws aside the curtains.*]

What, dressed, and in your clothes, and down again?
I must needs wake you. Lady! Lady! Lady!
Alas, alas! Help, help! My lady's dead!
O weraday that ever I was born!
Some aqua vitae, ho! My lord! My lady!

[*Enter* LADY CAPULET.]

Lady Capulet.
What noise is here?

Nurse. O lamentable day!

Lady Capulet.
What is the matter?

Nurse. Look, look! O heavy day!

Lady Capulet.
O me, O me! My child, my only life!
Revive, look up, or I will die with thee!
Help, help! Call help.

[*Enter* CAPULET.]

Capulet.
For shame, bring Juliet forth; her lord is come.

1. Fast: fast asleep.

Staging the Play
1. *As the nurse speaks to Juliet and to herself, she is busy arranging clothes, opening windows, and doing things around the room. In what line here does she touch Juliet and discover she is cold?*

4. pennyworths: short naps.

6. set up his rest: become firmly resolved.

Nurse.
She's dead, deceased; she's dead, alack the day!
Lady Capulet.
Alack the day, she's dead, she's dead, she's dead!
Capulet.
Ha! Let me see her. Out alas! She's cold,
Her blood is settled, and her joints are stiff;
Life and these lips have long been separated.
Death lies on her like an untimely frost
Upon the sweetest flower of all the field.
Nurse.
O lamentable day!
Lady Capulet. O woeful time!
Capulet.
Death, that hath ta'en her hence to make me wail,
Ties up my tongue and will not let me speak.

[*Enter* FRIAR LAURENCE *and* PARIS, *with* MUSICIANS.]

Friar.
Come, is the bride ready to go to church?
Capulet.
Ready to go, but never to return.
O son, the night before thy wedding day
Hath Death lain with thy wife. There she lies,
Flower as she was, deflowerèd by him.
Death is my son-in-law, Death is my heir;
My daughter he hath wedded. I will die
And leave him all. Life, living, all is Death's.
Paris.
Have I thought, love, to see this morning's face,
And doth it give me such a sight as this?
Lady Capulet.
Accursed, unhappy, wretched, hateful day!
Most miserable hour that e'er time saw
In lasting labor of his pilgrimage!
But one, poor one, one poor and loving child,
But one thing to rejoice and solace in,
And cruel Death hath catched it from my sight. 

Staging the Play
29. *What actions are taking place onstage as the three actors now find Juliet "dead"?*

Elements of Drama
48. *Here again, as with Juliet's bemoaning Romeo's supposed death in an earlier scene, we have Lord and Lady Capulet and the nurse expressing anguish when we, the audience, know that Juliet is not dead. We listen to them, but we are not moved in the way they are.*

A Reading Focus Paraphrasing What words here suggest that the Capulets have a loving concern for Juliet that seemed to be missing from earlier scenes? Restate those lines in your own words.

Nurse.
O woe! O woeful, woeful, woeful day!
Most lamentable day, most woeful day
That ever ever I did yet behold!
O day, O day, O day! O hateful day!
Never was seen so black a day as this.
O woeful day! O woeful day!

Paris.
Beguiled, divorcèd, wrongèd, spited, slain!
Most detestable Death, by thee beguiled,
By cruel, cruel thee quite overthrown.
O love! O life!—not life, but love in death! **B**

Capulet.
Despised, distressèd, hated, martyred, killed!
Uncomfortable time, why cam'st thou now
To murder, murder our solemnity?
O child, O child! My soul, and not my child!
Dead art thou—alack, my child is dead,
And with my child my joys are burièd!

Friar.
Peace, ho, for shame! Confusion's cure lives not
In these confusions. Heaven and yourself
Had part in this fair maid—now heaven hath all,
And all the better is it for the maid.
Your part in her you could not keep from death,
But heaven keeps his part in eternal life.
The most you sought was her promotion,
For 'twas your heaven she should be advanced;
And weep ye now, seeing she is advanced
Above the clouds, as high as heaven itself?
O, in this love, you love your child so ill
That you run mad, seeing that she is well.°
She's not well married that lives married long,
But she's best married that dies married young. **C**
Dry up your tears and stick your rosemary°
On this fair corse, and, as the custom is,
And in her best array bear her to church;

? **64.** *These expressions of grief are by now sounding mechanical and repetitive. Shakespeare might have written them this way to prevent grief at a false death from gaining our sympathy. How could these lines of the parents, of the nurse, and of Paris also suggest that the speakers' feelings might not be very deep?*

76. she is well: that is, she is in heaven.

79. rosemary: herb that stands for remembrance.

B Reading Focus Making Inferences What might the nurse, Paris, and the Capulets think caused Juliet's death?

C Reading Focus Paraphrasing The friar, of course, knows that Juliet is drugged, not dead. What consolation does he offer, and what sharp rebuke does he give the adults?

For though fond nature° bids us all lament,
Yet nature's tears are reason's merriment.

Capulet.
All things that we ordainèd festival
Turn from their office to black funeral—
Our instruments to melancholy bells,
Our wedding cheer to a sad burial feast;
Our solemn hymns to sullen dirges change;
Our bridal flowers serve for a buried corse;
And all things change them to the contrary.

Friar.
Sir, go you in; and, madam, go with him;
And go, Sir Paris. Everyone prepare
To follow this fair corse unto her grave.
The heavens do lower° upon you for some ill;
Move them no more by crossing their high will.

[*Exeunt, casting rosemary on her and shutting the curtains. The* NURSE *and* MUSICIANS *remain.*]

First Musician.
Faith, we may put up our pipes and be gone.

Nurse.
Honest good fellows, ah, put up, put up!
For well you know this is a pitiful case. [*Exit.*]

First Musician.
Ay, by my troth, the case may be amended.

[*Enter* PETER.]

Peter. Musicians, O, musicians, "Heart's ease," "Heart's ease"! O, and you will have me live, play "Heart's ease."

First Musician. Why "Heart's ease"?

Peter. O, musicians, because my heart itself plays "My heart is full." O, play me some merry dump° to comfort me.

First Musician. Not a dump we! 'Tis no time to play now.

Peter. You will not then?

First Musician. No.

Peter. I will then give it you soundly.

First Musician. What will you give us?

Peter. No money, on my faith, but the gleek.° I will give you° the minstrel.

First Musician. Then will I give you the serving-creature.

82. fond nature: foolish human nature.

83. *Why does the friar say that reason tells us to be merry about death?*

94. lower: frown.

98. *These are the nurse's last lines in the play. True to her character, she jokes as she leaves, though she might do this to cover her grief. The musicians are talking about the cases for their instruments. What "case" is the nurse referring to?*

104. dump: sad tune.

110. gleek: jeer or insult.

110–111. give you: call you. (To be called a minstrel was an insult to a musician.)

Analyzing Visuals **Viewing and Interpreting** How well do the actors embody the grief Shakespeare tried to portray?

Peter. Then will I lay the serving-creature's dagger on your pate. I will carry° no crotchets. I'll re you, I'll fa° you. Do you note me?

First Musician. And you re us and fa us, you note us.

Second Musician. Pray you put up your dagger, and put out your wit. Then have at you with my wit!

Peter. I will dry-beat° you with an iron wit, and put up my iron dagger. Answer me like men.

"When griping grief the heart doth wound,
And doleful dumps the mind oppress,
Then music with her silver sound"—
Why "silver sound"? Why "music with her silver sound"?
What say you, Simon Catling?°

First Musician. Marry, sir, because silver hath a sweet sound.

114. carry: endure. **re . . . fa:** notes on the musical scale.

119. dry-beat: beat soundly.

125. Catling: lute string.

The Capulets grieve for their daughter whom they believe dead.

Peter. Pretty! What say you, Hugh Rebeck?°

Second Musician. I say "silver sound" because musicians sound for silver.

Peter. Pretty too! What say you, James Soundpost?°

Third Musician. Faith, I know not what to say.

Peter. O, I cry you mercy, you are the singer. I will say for you. It is "music with her silver sound" because musicians have no gold for sounding.°
"Then music with her silver sound
With speedy help doth lend redress." [*Exit.*]

First Musician. What a pestilent knave is this same!

Second Musician. Hang him, Jack! Come, we'll in here, tarry for the mourners, and stay dinner.

[*Exit with others.*]

127. Rebeck: fiddle.

130. Soundpost: supporting post inside a violin.

134. no gold for sounding: no money to jingle in their pockets.

Elements of Drama

139. *Peter, who was always bossed about by the nurse, here has grabbed at the chance to boss the musicians, who are a step below him socially. What actions do you imagine during this exchange of insults? (Note that they all want to stay for dinner.) How does this scene provide relief for us and remind us that ordinary life goes on amid tragedy?*

Applying Your Skills

The Tragedy of Romeo and Juliet, Act IV

Respond and Think Critically

Reading Focus

Quick Check

1. What is the friar's plan for Romeo and Juliet?
2. What is the situation in the Capulet house at the end of Act IV?

Read with a Purpose

3. What risk does Juliet take to be with Romeo?

Reading Skills: Reading a Play

4. Capulet's rush to have Paris marry Juliet forces the friar to make a new plan. Add to the chart you started on page 804 and record your predictions for what could go wrong now that Juliet appears to be dead and Romeo is waiting to hear from the friar.

Analyze Causes and Effects	My Notes
Cause: Juliet has taken the potion and appears to be dead.	Effect: Now, . . .

Literary Focus

Literary Analysis

5. **Infer** Why is Juliet so willing to trust the friar? Do you think she is wise to follow his advice?
6. **Synthesize** What challenges does Juliet face in this act? What do her responses to these challenges reveal about her character?
7. **Evaluate** Knowing something that a character onstage does not know creates **dramatic irony.** Find dramatic irony in Scenes 2, 3 and 4. What audience reaction is Shakespeare trying to arouse by using this technique?

Literary Skills: Tragedy

8. **Analyze** The falling action in Act IV moves the play toward its inevitable end. Curiously though, Romeo is absent from the act. Now all of the stress and pressure to decide what to do is on Juliet. Why do you think Shakespeare decided to keep Romeo away during this act?

Literary Skills Review: Characterization

9. **Evaluate** Juliet's parents have plans for her that make it seem impossible for the lovers to unite. Does Shakespeare present the Capulets as villains or as complex human beings? Explain how Shakespeare characterizes these characters, using details from the play to make your points.

Writing Focus

Think as a Reader/Writer

Use It in Your Writing Using your notes on Act IV, write a summary of the act that points out critical decisions that Juliet makes. What does her faked death prepare us for?

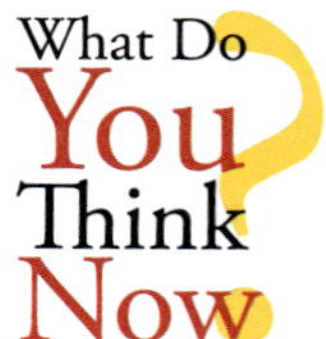

Is Juliet taking too many risks for her love of Romeo? At this point in the play, what other choice does she have?

MO **9.R.2.C.1.b** Use details from text(s): to analyze character, plot, setting, point of view **9.R.2** Develop and apply skills and strategies to comprehend, analyze and evaluate fiction, poetry and drama from a variety of cultures and times *Also covered* **9.R.3.C.1.a; 9.W.3.A.1.a; 9.R.1.E.1.b; 9.R.1.E.1.c**

Vocabulary Development

Vocabulary Skills: Inverted Word Order

Shakespeare's plays are written in verse. In order to create the rhythmic pattern of the verse, Shakespeare sometimes uses inverted word order. For example, we are accustomed to adverbs following the verbs they modify. In this example, however, notice how the adverb *immoderately* precedes the subject (*she*) in order to create iambic pentameter.

Paris (*speaking about Juliet*).

> **Immoderately she weeps** for Tybalt's death,
> And therefore have I little talked of love;
> For Venus smiles not in a house of tears. (IV.1.6–8)

Here is that same passage, rewritten in standard order. Note that two other inversions from the original passage have been re-ordered in this version.

> She weeps immoderately for Tybalt's death, and I have therefore talked little of love; for Venus does not smile in a house of tears.

Your Turn

Locate the instances of inverted word order in these passages. Then write a paraphrase of each passage, in which you present the words in standard order.

1. Juliet, on Thursday early will I rouse ye.
   Till then, adieu, and keep this holy kiss.
   (Act IV, Scene 1, Lines 42–43)
2. Shall Romeo by my letters know our drift;
   And hither shall he come; and he and I
   Will watch thy waking, and that very night
   Shall Romeo bear thee hence to Mantua.
   (Act IV, Scene 1, Lines 114–117)
3. What, are you busy, ho? Need you my help?
   (Act IV, Scene 3, Lines 6)

Language Coach

Word Roots Look at the chart below that shows words derived from the Latin verb *vertere*. In what way is "verse" or poetry something that is "turned"?

Latin ***vertere***—meaning "to turn"
Latin ***versus***—meaning "verse"
inverted—meaning "switched" or "turned"

Academic Vocabulary

Write About . . .

Pick one scene from Act IV. Then, write a plan for a modern production of that scene. Before writing, think about the following questions, and use Academic Vocabulary words to describe your plan.

1. How can I embody the friar's personality in a modern setting?
2. Which conventions should be kept?
3. In what way will my interpretation appeal to a modern audience?

ACT V

Movie still from director Franco Zeffirelli's 1968 adaptation of *Romeo and Juliet*.

Read with a Purpose As you read this final act, think about which aspects of their destiny Romeo and Juliet can control and which aspects are out of their control.

ACT V

SCENE 1. *Mantua. A street.*

Enter ROMEO.

Romeo.
If I may trust the flattering truth of sleep,
My dreams presage° some joyful news at hand.
My bosom's lord° sits lightly in his throne,
And all this day an unaccustomed spirit
Lifts me above the ground with cheerful thoughts.
I dreamt my lady came and found me dead
(Strange dream that gives a dead man leave to think!)
And breathed such life with kisses in my lips
That I revived and was an emperor.
Ah me! How sweet is love itself possessed,
When but love's shadows° are so rich in joy!

[*Enter Romeo's man* BALTHASAR, *booted from riding.*]

News from Verona! How now, Balthasar?
Dost thou not bring me letters from the friar?
How doth my lady? Is my father well?
How fares my Juliet? That I ask again,
For nothing can be ill if she be well.

Balthasar.
Then she is well, and nothing can be ill.
Her body sleeps in Capel's monument,
And her immortal part with angels lives.
I saw her laid low in her kindred's vault
And presently took post° to tell it you.
O, pardon me for bringing these ill news,
Since you did leave it for my office,° sir.

Romeo.
Is it e'en so? Then I defy you, stars!
Thou knowest my lodging. Get me ink and paper

2. presage: foretell.

3. bosom's lord: heart.

11. shadows: dreams.

Staging the Play
16. *Some actors playing Romeo reveal in this line that they suspect bad news. What, meanwhile, would Balthasar be doing?*

21. post: post horse (horse kept at an inn and rented by travelers).

23. office: duty.

Staging the Play
23. *Balthasar must show that he dreads giving his master the tragic news. What do we know that Balthasar does not know?*

And hire post horses. I will hence tonight. **A**

Balthasar.
I do beseech you, sir, have patience.
Your looks are pale and wild and do import
Some misadventure.

Romeo. Tush, thou art deceived.
Leave me and do the thing I bid thee do.
Hast thou no letters to me from the friar?

Balthasar.
No, my good lord.

Romeo. No matter. Get thee gone.
And hire those horses. I'll be with thee straight.
[*Exit* BALTHASAR.]
Well, Juliet, I will lie with thee tonight.
Let's see for means. O mischief, thou art swift
To enter in the thoughts of desperate men!
I do remember an apothecary,
And hereabouts 'a dwells, which late I noted
In tattered weeds,° with overwhelming° brows,
Culling of simples.° Meager were his looks,
Sharp misery had worn him to the bones;
And in his needy shop a tortoise hung,
An alligator stuffed, and other skins
Of ill-shaped fishes; and about his shelves
A beggarly account° of empty boxes,
Green earthen pots, bladders, and musty seeds,
Remnants of packthread, and old cakes of roses
Were thinly scatterèd, to make up a show.
Noting this penury,° to myself I said,
"And if a man did need a poison now
Whose sale is present death in Mantua,
Here lives a caitiff° wretch would sell it him."
O, this same thought did but forerun my need,
And this same needy man must sell it me.
As I remember, this should be the house.
Being holiday, the beggar's shop is shut.
What, ho! Apothecary! **B**

? Staging the Play
26. *In some productions, actors move away here or hide their faces in their hands. Romeo could address the stars or fate defiantly or tonelessly, to suggest defeat. What would you say is Romeo's tone here?*

? **28.** *What does Balthasar suggest Romeo looks like, even though Romeo pretends to be calm?*

? **31.** *What letter is Romeo waiting for?*

? **34.** *This line is spoken in a still, quiet moment. After a pause, what does Romeo immediately set out to do? Does he hesitate at all to consider his course of action, or does he plunge into it?*

39. weeds: clothes. **overwhelming:** overhanging.

40. simples: herbs.

45. account: number.

49. penury (PEHN yuhr ee): poverty.

52. caitiff (KAYT ihf): miserable.

? Staging the Play
57. *What actions do you imagine Romeo is engaged in as he speaks these lines about the apothecary?*

A Reading Focus Analyzing Cause and Effect What do you think Romeo is planning to do?

B Reading Focus Making Inferences Why has Romeo chosen this particular apothecary? How does he think his request might be treated by other apothecaries?

[*Enter* APOTHECARY.]

Apothecary. Who calls so loud?

Romeo.

Come hither, man. I see that thou art poor.
Hold, there is forty ducats. Let me have
A dram of poison, such soon-speeding gear°
As will disperse itself through all the veins
That the life-weary taker may fall dead,
And that the trunk° may be discharged of breath
As violently as hasty powder fired
Doth hurry from the fatal cannon's womb.

Apothecary.

Such mortal drugs I have; but Mantua's law
Is death to any he that utters° them.

Romeo.

Art thou so bare and full of wretchedness
And fear'st to die? Famine is in thy cheeks,
Need and oppression starveth in thy eyes,
Contempt and beggary hangs upon thy back:
The world is not thy friend, nor the world's law;
The world affords no law to make thee rich;
Then be not poor, but break it and take this.

Apothecary.

My poverty but not my will consents.

Romeo.

I pay thy poverty and not thy will.

Apothecary.

Put this in any liquid thing you will
And drink it off, and if you had the strength
Of twenty men, it would dispatch you straight.

Romeo.

There is thy gold—worse poison to men's souls,
Doing more murder in this loathsome world,
Than these poor compounds that thou mayst not sell.
I sell thee poison; thou has sold me none.
Farewell. Buy food and get thyself in flesh.
Come, cordial and not poison, go with me
To Juliet's grave; for there must I use thee. [*Exeunt.*] **C**

60. gear: stuff.

63. trunk: body.

67. utters: sells.

? **74.** *What argument does Romeo use to persuade the apothecary to break the law?*

? **Staging the Play**
79. *What actions do you think have taken place before the apothecary gives Romeo instructions for taking the poison?*

? **85.** *Why does Romeo call the poison a cordial, which is a kind of medicine that restores the heartbeat?*

C **Reading Focus** **Reading Aloud** Softly read Scene 1 aloud. After each character speaks, pause and ask yourself if you understand what is taking place. How does reading the scene aloud help you appreciate Romeo's intense emotions?

SCENE 2. *Friar Laurence's cell.*

Enter FRIAR JOHN.

John.
Holy Franciscan friar, brother, ho!

[*Enter* FRIAR LAURENCE.]

Laurence.
This same should be the voice of Friar John.
Welcome from Mantua. What says Romeo?
Or, if his mind be writ, give me his letter.

John.
Going to find a barefoot brother out,
One of our order, to associate° me
Here in this city visiting the sick,
And finding him, the searchers° of the town,
Suspecting that we both were in a house
Where the infectious pestilence did reign,
Sealed up the doors, and would not let us forth,
So that my speed to Mantua there was stayed.

Laurence.
Who bare my letter, then, to Romeo?

John.
I could not send it—here it is again—
Nor get a messenger to bring it thee,
So fearful were they of infection. **A**

Laurence.
Unhappy fortune! By my brotherhood,
The letter was not nice,° but full of charge,°
Of dear import; and the neglecting it
May do much danger. Friar John, go hence,
Get me an iron crow and bring it straight
Unto my cell.

John. Brother, I'll go and bring it thee. [*Exit.*]

Laurence.
Now must I to the monument alone.

? **3.** *In the previous scene we learned that Romeo had received no letters from the friar. How would the friar's question immediately put questions in the minds of the audience?*

6. associate: accompany.

8. searchers: health officers.

18. nice: trivial. **charge:** importance.

A **Reading Focus** **Analyzing Cause and Effect** Why wasn't the friar's letter delivered to Romeo?

Within this three hours will fair Juliet wake.
She will beshrew me much that Romeo
Hath had no notice of these accidents;°
But I will write again to Mantua,
And keep her at my cell till Romeo come—
Poor living corse, closed in a dead man's tomb! [*Exit.*]

26. accidents: happenings.

? **29.** *If we can accept the "accidents" of fate, we have here something like a chase scene. We know, but the friar does not, that Romeo also is on his way to the tomb. Why is it essential that the friar get there first?*

SCENE 3. *A churchyard; in it, a monument belonging to the Capulets.*

Enter PARIS *and his* PAGE *with flowers and scented water.*

Paris.
Give me thy torch, boy. Hence, and stand aloof.
Yet put it out, for I would not be seen.
Under yond yew trees lay thee all along,°
Holding the ear close to the hollow ground.
So shall no foot upon the churchyard tread
(Being loose, unfirm, with digging up of graves)
But thou shalt hear it. Whistle then to me,
As signal that thou hear'st something approach.
Give me those flowers. Do as I bid thee, go.

Page (*aside*).
I am almost afraid to stand alone
Here in the churchyard; yet I will adventure.°

[*Retires.*]

Paris.
Sweet flower, with flowers thy bridal bed I strew
(O woe! thy canopy is dust and stones)
Which with sweet water nightly I will dew;
Or, wanting that, with tears distilled by moans.
The obsequies° that I for thee will keep
Nightly shall be to strew thy grave and weep.

[BOY *whistles.*]

The boy gives warning something doth approach.
What cursèd foot wanders this way tonight

3. all along: at full length (on the ground).

? **9.** *Paris's presence is a surprise. He adds an interesting* ***complication,*** *as well as some action, to this scene. Why is Paris here?*

? **Elements of Drama**
Stage direction: *Paris and his page are alone onstage. To whom does the page speak his* ***aside?*** *Whom does he not want to hear it?*

11. adventure: risk it.

? **Staging the Play**
13. *In Shakespeare's theater we would see a tomb at the rear of the stage. Juliet's body, in its burial gown, would be placed in this tomb, on top of a raised structure. Tybalt's body would lie nearby. What* ***atmosphere*** *must be suggested in this scene? How would lighting be used on a modern stage to create such an atmosphere?*

16. obsequies (AHB suh kweez): observances or rituals.

By heaven, I love thee better than myself,
For I come hither armed against myself.

To cross° my obsequies and true love's rite?
What, with a torch? Muffle° me, night, awhile.

[*Retires.*]

[*Enter* ROMEO *and* BALTHASAR *with a torch, a mattock, and a crowbar of iron.*]

Romeo.
Give me that mattock and the wrenching iron.
Hold, take this letter. Early in the morning
See thou deliver it to my lord and father.
Give me the light. Upon thy life I charge thee,
Whate'er thou hearest or see'st, stand all aloof
And do not interrupt me in my course.
Why I descend into this bed of death
Is partly to behold my lady's face,
But chiefly to take thence from her dead finger
A precious ring—a ring that I must use
In dear employment.° Therefore hence, be gone.
But if thou, jealous,° dost return to pry
In what I farther shall intend to do,
By heaven, I will tear thee joint by joint
And strew this hungry churchyard with thy limbs.
The time and my intents are savage-wild,
More fierce and more inexorable far
Than empty tigers or the roaring sea.

Balthasar.
I will be gone, sir, and not trouble ye.

Romeo.
So shalt thou show me friendship. Take thou that.
Live, and be prosperous; and farewell, good fellow.

Balthasar (*aside*).
For all this same, I'll hide me hereabout.

20. cross: interrupt.

21. Muffle: hide.

? Staging the Play
32. *Paris enters with flowers and perfumed water, but Romeo enters with iron tools—a mattock, which is something like a hoe, and a crowbar. Like Paris, Romeo and his servant enter at the upper level. What strange excuse does Romeo give his servant for wanting to descend into the tomb alone?*

32. dear employment: important business.

33. jealous: curious.

? **39.** *Romeo makes sure his servant will not interrupt him. What do the last three lines reveal about his state of mind?*

His looks I fear, and his intents I doubt. [*Retires.*]

Romeo.

Thou detestable maw,° thou womb of death,
Gorged with the dearest morsel of the earth,
Thus I enforce thy rotten jaws to open,
And in despite° I'll cram thee with more food. **A**

[ROMEO *opens the tomb.*]

Paris.

This is that banished haughty Montague
That murd'red my love's cousin—with which grief
It is supposed the fair creature died—
And here is come to do some villainous shame
To the dead bodies. I will apprehend him.
Stop thy unhallowèd toil, vile Montague!
Can vengeance be pursued further than death?
Condemnèd villain, I do apprehend thee.
Obey, and go with me; for thou must die.

Romeo.

I must indeed; and therefore came I hither.
Good gentle youth, tempt not a desp'rate man.
Fly hence and leave me. Think upon these gone;
Let them affright thee. I beseech thee, youth,
Put not another sin upon my head
By urging me to fury. O, be gone!
By heaven, I love thee better than myself,
For I come hither armed against myself.
Stay not, be gone. Live, and hereafter say
A madman's mercy bid thee run away.

Paris.

I do defy thy conjurations°
And apprehend thee for a felon here.

Romeo.

Wilt thou provoke me? Then have at thee, boy!

[*They fight.*]

Page.

O Lord, they fight! I will go call the watch.
[*Exit.* PARIS *falls.*]

45. maw: mouth.

48. in despite: to spite you.

? **51.** *What was believed to be the cause of Juliet's sudden "death"?*

? **Staging the Play**
54. *What does Paris do as he speaks this line?*

? **67.** *Romeo doesn't attempt even to fight Paris. How do his words here show calmness and maturity?*

68. conjurations: solemn orders.

? **70.** *What has Paris done to provoke Romeo?*

A **Reading Focus** **Making Inferences** To whom or what is Romeo talking here? What is he doing? What "food" is he going to feed this "maw"?

Analyzing Visuals **Viewing and Interpreting** Here, Romeo believes that Juliet is dead, though the effects of the potion have begun to wear off. How could Juliet give signs that she is waking up?

Romeo finds Juliet after she has taken the sleeping potion.

Paris.
O, I am slain! If thou be merciful,
Open the tomb, lay me with Juliet. [*Dies.*]

Romeo.
In faith, I will. Let me peruse this face.
Mercutio's kinsman, noble County Paris!
What said my man when my betossèd soul
Did not attend° him as we rode? I think
He told me Paris should have married Juliet.
Said he not so, or did I dream it so?
Or am I mad, hearing him talk of Juliet,
To think it was so? O, give me thy hand,
One writ with me in sour misfortune's book! **B**
I'll bury thee in a triumphant grave.
A grave? O, no, a lanthorn,° slaught'red youth,
For here lies Juliet, and her beauty makes
This vault a feasting presence full of light.
Death, lie thou there, by a dead man interred.

[*Lays him in the tomb.*]

How oft when men are at the point of death
Have they been merry! Which their keepers° call
A lightning before death. O, how may I
Call this a lightning? O my love, my wife!
Death, that hath sucked the honey of thy breath,
Hath had no power yet upon thy beauty.
Thou art not conquered. Beauty's ensign° yet
Is crimson in thy lips and in thy cheeks,
And death's pale flag is not advancèd there.
Tybalt, liest thou there in the bloody sheet?
O, what more favor can I do to thee
Than with that hand that cut thy youth in twain
To sunder his that was thine enemy?
Forgive me, cousin! Ah, dear Juliet,
Why art thou yet so fair? Shall I believe
That unsubstantial Death is amorous,
And that the lean abhorrèd monster keeps
Thee here in dark to be his paramour?
For fear of that I still will stay with thee

? Staging the Play
74. *Whatever we thought of Paris before, we understand now that he loved Juliet. What does Romeo do here?*

77. attend: pay attention to.

84. lanthorn: lantern; here, a room with glass walls.

? **85.** *Romeo, dragging Paris's body across the stage, now sees Juliet. What words indicate that he sees the tomb transformed? Who is the "dead man" in line 87?*

89. keepers: jailers.

94. ensign (EHN syn): flag (signal).

? Staging the Play
97. *Romeo turns to see Tybalt's body. Is he angry at his enemy, or does he ask forgiveness?*

? **102.** *Where in this speech does Romeo see life in Juliet, reminding us that she is not dead?*

B Literary Focus Tragedy Remember that Romeo has spoken of himself as "fortune's fool." Why does he see Paris as another victim?

And never from this pallet of dim night
Depart again. Here, here will I remain
With worms that are thy chambermaids. O, here
Will I set up my everlasting rest
And shake the yoke of inauspicious stars
From this world-wearied flesh. Eyes, look your last!
Arms, take your last embrace! And, lips, O you
The doors of breath, seal with a righteous kiss
A dateless° bargain to engrossing° death!
Come, bitter conduct;° come, unsavory guide!
Thou desperate pilot,° now at once run on
The dashing rocks thy seasick weary bark!
Here's to my love! (*Drinks.*) O true apothecary!
Thy drugs are quick. Thus with a kiss I die. **C**

[*Falls.*]

[*Enter* FRIAR LAURENCE, *with lanthorn, crowbar, and spade.*]

Friar.
Saint Francis be my speed! How oft tonight
Have my old feet stumbled at graves! Who's there?

Balthasar.
Here's one, a friend, and one that knows you well.

Friar.
Bliss be upon you! Tell me, good my friend,
What torch is yond that vainly lends his light
To grubs and eyeless skulls? As I discern,
It burneth in the Capels' monument.

Balthasar.
It doth so, holy sir; and there's my master,
One that you love.

Friar. Who is it?

Balthasar. Romeo.

Friar.
How long hath he been there?

Balthasar. Full half an hour.

C Reading Focus Reading Aloud/Paraphrasing Softly read Romeo's final speech aloud beginning with line 74. As you read, use punctuation clues to help you identify complete thoughts. After you have read Romeo's speech aloud, write a paraphrased version.

? Staging the Play
108. *Romeo lies down beside Juliet. What other actions do you see him performing here?*

115. dateless: timeless. **engrossing:** all-encompassing.

116. conduct: guide (the poison).

117. desperate pilot: Romeo himself.

? Elements of Drama
120. *Actors playing Romeo interpret this last speech in different ways: Some play him as if he is in a dream; others as if he is mad; others as if he is in full control of himself; others as if he is desperate and out of his mind with grief, desire, and fear. What clues would direct the way you'd interpret Romeo's feelings as he delivers his final* ***soliloquy?***

? Staging the Play
130. *What feelings must the friar reveal when he hears that Romeo has gotten to the tomb before he has heard of the plan to drug Juliet?*

Friar.
Go with me to the vault.

Balthasar. I dare not, sir.
My master knows not but I am gone hence,
And fearfully did menace me with death
If I did stay to look on his intents.

Friar.
Stay then; I'll go alone. Fear comes upon me.
O, much I fear some ill unthrifty° thing.

Balthasar.
As I did sleep under this yew tree here,
I dreamt my master and another fought,
And that my master slew him.

Friar. Romeo!
Alack, alack, what blood is this which stains
The stony entrance of this sepulcher?
What mean these masterless and gory swords
To lie discolored by this place of peace?

[*Enters the tomb.*]

Romeo! O, pale! Who else? What, Paris too?
And steeped in blood? Ah, what an unkind° hour
Is guilty of this lamentable chance!
The lady stirs.

[JULIET *rises.*]

Juliet.
O comfortable° friar! Where is my lord?
I do remember well where I should be,
And there I am. Where is my Romeo?

Friar.
I hear some noise. Lady, come from that nest
Of death, contagion, and unnatural sleep.

What's here? A cup, closed in my truelove's hand? Poison, I see, hath been his timeless end.

136. unthrifty: unlucky.

? **141.** *Where is the friar as he discovers the bloodstains?*

145. unkind: unnatural.

? **Staging the Play**
147. *This short line suggests that the friar rushes to Juliet and waits for her to speak. What must he be feeling?*

148. comfortable: comforting.

? **152.** *For the friar this is a terrible moment. What is his reaction to the noise he hears?*

A greater power than we can contradict
Hath thwarted our intents. Come, come away.
Thy husband in thy bosom there lies dead;
And Paris too. Come, I'll dispose of thee
Among a sisterhood of holy nuns.
Stay not to question, for the watch is coming.
Come, go, good Juliet. I dare no longer stay.

Juliet.
Go, get thee hence, for I will not away.

[*Exit* FRIAR.]

What's here? A cup, closed in my truelove's hand?
Poison, I see, hath been his timeless° end.
O churl!° Drunk all, and left no friendly drop
To help me after? I will kiss thy lips.
Haply some poison yet doth hang on them
To make me die with a restorative.

[*Kisses him.*]

Thy lips are warm!

Chief Watchman (*within*). Lead, boy. Which way?

Juliet.
Yea, noise? Then I'll be brief. O happy° dagger! **D**

[*Snatches Romeo's dagger.*]

This is thy sheath; there rust, and let me die. **E**

[*She stabs herself and falls.*]

[*Enter Paris's* BOY *and* WATCH.]

Boy.
This is the place. There, where the torch doth burn.

Chief Watchman.
The ground is bloody. Search about the churchyard.
Go, some of you; whoe'er you find attach.

159. *What plan does the friar propose to Juliet? What is Juliet doing or refusing to do as the friar repeatedly tries to move her?*

? Staging the Play
160. *It is hard to believe that after all his concern for these two young lovers, the friar would become a coward at this moment and leave Juliet to harm herself. How must the friar act here to convince us that he is frantic and not very sensible?*

162. timeless: untimely.

163. churl: selfish person.

169. happy: appropriate or suitable for the occasion.

? Elements of Drama
Stage direction: *Do you see Juliet in her last moments as half-crazed? calm and purposeful? something else? Do you think this scene can be played only one way? Can it be played several ways? How would you play the scene?*

D Literary Focus Climax Do you think the lovers' deaths were fated to occur, as Romeo hinted earlier? Might either Romeo or Juliet have survived?

E Reading Focus Reading Aloud Beginning with line 121, the dialogue reveals important information about the plot, ending with the climax of the play. Read these lines softly to yourself. Pause after reading the dialogue between the friar and Balthasar, and after the dialogue with Juliet, asking yourself after each section if the action is clear.

The bodies of Romeo and Juliet are found.

[*Exeunt some of the* WATCH.]

Pitiful sight! Here lies the county slain;
And Juliet bleeding, warm, and newly dead,
Who here hath lain this two days burièd.
Go, tell the prince; run to the Capulets;
Raise up the Montagues; some others search.

[*Exeunt others of the* WATCH.]

We see the ground whereon these woes do lie,
But the true ground° of all these piteous woes
We cannot without circumstance° descry.

[*Enter some of the* WATCH, *with Romeo's man* BALTHASAR.]

Second Watchman.
Here's Romeo's man. We found him in the churchyard.

Chief Watchman.
Hold him in safety till the prince come hither.

[*Enter* FRIAR LAURENCE *and another* WATCHMAN.]

Third Watchman.
Here is a friar that trembles, sighs, and weeps.
We took this mattock and this spade from him
As he was coming from this churchyard's side.

Chief Watchman.
A great suspicion! Stay the friar too.

180. ground: cause.

181. circumstance: details.

? **184.** *How do the watchman's words help us picture the state the friar is in?*

[*Enter the* PRINCE *and* ATTENDANTS.]

Prince.
What misadventure is so early up,
That calls our person from our morning rest?

[*Enter* CAPULET *and his wife,* LADY CAPULET, *with others.*]

Capulet.
What should it be, that is so shrieked abroad?

Lady Capulet.
O, the people in the street cry "Romeo,"
Some "Juliet," and some "Paris"; and all run
With open outcry toward our monument.

Prince.
What fear is this which startles in your ears?

Chief Watchman.
Sovereign, here lies the County Paris slain;
And Romeo dead; and Juliet, dead before,
Warm and new killed.

Prince.
Search, seek, and know how this foul murder comes.

Chief Watchman.
Here is a friar, and slaughtered Romeo's man,
With instruments upon them fit to open
These dead men's tombs.

Capulet.
O heavens! O wife, look how our daughter bleeds!
This dagger hath mista'en, for, lo, his house°
Is empty on the back of Montague,
And it missheathèd in my daughter's bosom!

Lady Capulet.
O me, this sight of death is as a bell
That warns° my old age to a sepulcher.

[*Enter* MONTAGUE *and others.*]

Prince.
Come, Montague; for thou art early up
To see thy son and heir more early down.

Montague.
Alas, my liege, my wife is dead tonight!
Grief of my son's exile hath stopped her breath.
What further woe conspires against mine age?

Staging the Play
193. *As the tomb begins to fill with people, noises and cries are heard offstage. What does Lady Capulet suggest is being "shrieked abroad" in Verona?*

203. house: sheath.

207. warns: summons.

Prince.
Look, and thou shalt see.

Montague.
O thou untaught! What manners is in this,
To press before thy father to a grave?

Prince.
Seal up the mouth of outrage for a while,
Till we can clear these ambiguities
And know their spring, their head, their true descent;
And then will I be general of your woes°
And lead you even to death. Meantime forbear,
And let mischance be slave to patience.
Bring forth the parties of suspicion.

Friar.
I am the greatest, able to do least,
Yet most suspected, as the time and place
Doth make against me, of this direful murder;
And here I stand, both to impeach and purge°
Myself condemnèd and myself excused.

Prince.
Then say at once what thou dost know in this.

Friar.
I will be brief, for my short date of breath°
Is not so long as is a tedious tale.
Romeo, there dead, was husband to that Juliet;
And she, there dead, that Romeo's faithful wife.
I married them; and their stolen marriage day
Was Tybalt's doomsday, whose untimely death
Banished the new-made bridegroom from this city;
For whom, and not for Tybalt, Juliet pined.
You, to remove that siege of grief from her,
Betrothed and would have married her perforce
To County Paris. Then comes she to me
And with wild looks bid me devise some mean
To rid her from this second marriage,
Or in my cell there would she kill herself.
Then gave I her (so tutored by my art)
A sleeping potion; which so took effect
As I intended, for it wrought on her
The form of death. Meantime I writ to Romeo
That he should hither come as° this dire night
To help to take her from her borrowed grave,

? **215.** *Whom is Montague talking to here?*

219. general of your woes: leader of your mourning.

226. impeach and purge: charge and acquit.

229. date of breath: term of life.

? **Elements of Drama**
230. *All of what the friar says here is known by the audience. In some productions this long* **monologue** *is cut entirely, but it is important for us to imagine the effect the speech has on the Montagues, the Capulets, and the prince. This is the moment when they discover what we've known all along. Where do you think the friar must pause as the families cry out and weep?*

? **237.** *Whom does the friar mean by "you"?*

247. as: on.

Being the time the potion's force should cease.
But he which bore my letter, Friar John,
Was stayed by accident, and yesternight
Returned my letter back. Then all alone
At the prefixèd hour of her waking
Came I to take her from her kindred's vault,
Meaning to keep her closely at my cell
Till I conveniently could send to Romeo.
But when I came, some minute ere the time
Of her awakening, here untimely lay
The noble Paris and true Romeo dead.
She wakes; and I entreated her come forth
And bear this work of heaven with patience; **F**
But then a noise did scare me from the tomb,
And she, too desperate, would not go with me,
But, as it seems, did violence on herself.
All this I know, and to the marriage
Her nurse is privy;° and if aught in this
Miscarried by my fault, let my old life
Be sacrificed some hour before his time
Unto the rigor of severest law. **G**

Prince.
We still° have known thee for a holy man.
Where's Romeo's man? What can he say to this?

Balthasar.
I brought my master news of Juliet's death;
And then in post he came from Mantua
To this same place, to this same monument.
This letter he early bid me give his father,
And threat'ned me with death, going in the vault,
If I departed not and left him there.

Prince.
Give me the letter. I will look on it.
Where is the county's page that raised the watch?
Sirrah, what made your master in this place?

Boy.
He came with flowers to strew his lady's grave;

265–266. to the marriage . . . privy: Juliet's nurse knows about the marriage.

270. still: always.

F **Reading Focus** **Analyzing Cause and Effect** This line expresses the friar's view of life. How would the play have been different if both Romeo and Juliet had been able from the start to bear their trials "with patience"? How does this also apply to the adults in the play?

G **Literary Focus** **Resolution** Does the friar accept full responsibility for his part in the tragedy? What does he say?

And bid me stand aloof, and so I did.
Anon comes one with light to ope the tomb;
And by and by my master drew on him;
And then I ran away to call the watch.

Prince.
This letter doth make good the friar's words,
Their course of love, the tidings of her death;
And here he writes that he did buy a poison
Of a poor pothecary and therewithal
Came to this vault to die and lie with Juliet.
Where be these enemies? Capulet, Montague,
See what a scourge is laid upon your hate,
That heaven finds means to kill your joys with love,
And I, for winking at° your discords too,
Have lost a brace° of kinsmen. All are punished. **H**

Capulet.
O brother Montague, give me thy hand.
This is my daughter's jointure,° for no more
Can I demand.

Montague. But I can give thee more;
For I will raise her statue in pure gold,
That whiles Verona by that name is known,
There shall no figure at such rate° be set
As that of true and faithful Juliet.

Capulet.
As rich shall Romeo's by his lady's lie—
Poor sacrifices of our enmity! **I**

Prince.
A glooming peace this morning with it brings.
The sun for sorrow will not show his head.
Go hence, to have more talk of these sad things;
Some shall be pardoned, and some punishèd;
For never was a story of more woe
Than this of Juliet and her Romeo. [*Exeunt omnes.*]

? **Staging the Play**
286. *What would the families be doing as the prince now pauses to read the letter?*

294. winking at: closing his eyes to.

295. brace: pair (Mercutio and Paris).

297. jointure: property passed on to a woman after her husband's death.

301. rate: value.

? **Staging the Play**
310. *As the actors solemnly file out, the friar is usually the last to exit. In some productions the fathers leave last. In others the nurse reappears and makes the final exit. What different effects would be produced by having different characters be the last to leave the stage? Which one would you have exit last?*

Finally only the bodies are left onstage. How might lighting be used as the action closes?

H **Literary Focus** **Resolution** We have been repeatedly reminded of the role of fate in this tragedy, but the human characters also admit their responsibility. What does the prince admit? Do you think that some people have been punished too harshly and some not severely enough? Explain.

I **Literary Focus** **Resolution** The central focus onstage now is not the families but the bodies of Romeo and Juliet. Over the bodies of their children, the families join hands. What words of Capulet's admit his part in the tragedy?

Applying Your Skills

MO 9.R.2.C.1.b Use details from text(s): to analyze character, plot, setting, point of view 9.R.2.C.1.c Use details from text(s): to analyze the development of a theme across genres *Also covered* 9.R.2; 9.R.3.C.1.a; 9.W.3.A.1.d

The Tragedy of Romeo and Juliet, Act V

Respond and Think Critically

Reading Focus

Quick Check

1. What news does Romeo learn in Scene 1?
2. Why doesn't Romeo receive the friar's letter explaining the latest plans?
3. What finally happens to Romeo and then to Juliet?

Read with a Purpose

4. What do you think caused the tragedy of Romeo and Juliet? Was it fate or a series of human errors? Draw a web showing the people or forces that might be responsible.

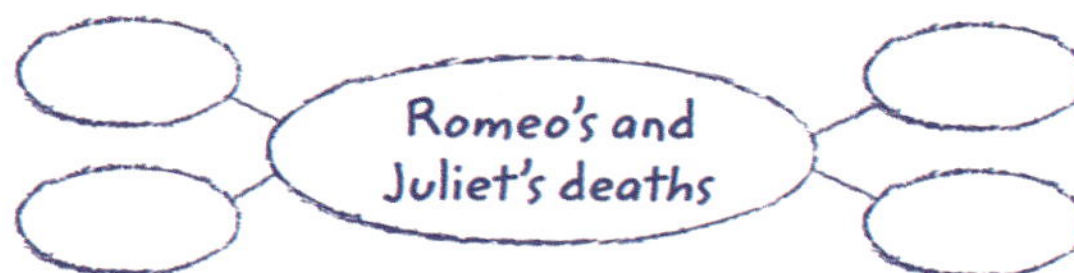

Reading Skills: Reading a Play

5. Now that you have finished reading the play, look at the causes and effects you listed earlier. Did any relationships or events seem improbable, or did they all seem logical? Explain.

Literary Focus

Literary Analysis

6. **Infer** In Scene 3, the friar claims to hear a noise that panics him, and he leaves Juliet. What is Shakespeare's purpose in having him leave?
7. **Analyze** In what scene of this act do you think the dramatic irony peaks? Explain.
8. **Interpret** Explain the significance of the prince's line when he says, "That heaven finds means to kill your joys with love" (Act V, Scene 3, line 293).
9. **Analyze** This act includes examples of **soliloquies** (long speeches in which a character alone onstage expresses thoughts aloud) and **monologues** (long speeches that a character delivers to other characters onstage). Find an example of each, and explain what it adds to the play.

Literary Skills: Tragedy

10. **Analyze** The **climax** of a play is its most intense moment, when we know how the conflict will end. In a tragedy, it is a moment when we are overcome by sadness, fear, or regret. At what point do you think the climax occurs?

Literary Skills Review: Theme

11. **Interpret** A **theme** is an observation about life that writers convey when they write. In a long work, such as this play, there can be several themes. What point about life do you think Shakespeare is conveying in this play?

Writing Focus

Think as a Reader/Writer

Use It in Your Writing Use your summaries of the five acts of the play to help you write an essay in which you analyze the play's structure to determine whether it follows the conventional five-part pattern of tragedy.

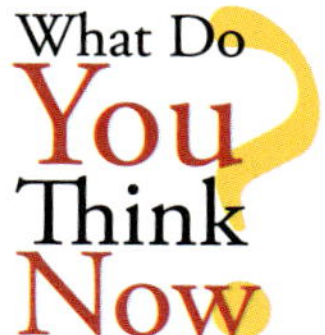

In what ways do the various characters in this drama act out of love?

Applying Your Skills

The Tragedy of Romeo and Juliet, Act V

Vocabulary Development

Vocabulary Skills: Figures of Speech

Shakespeare's characters use images and figures of speech so rich and so varied that the play, which has lived now for over four hundred years, will probably live as long as English continues to be spoken. Shakespeare's characters use figures of speech, such as similes, metaphors, personification, and puns, and the audience delights in hearing such clever use of language.

Language Coach

Figures of Speech Use these definitions to help you answer the questions in Your Turn.
Similes are comparisons between two different things using a connecting word such as *like, as,* or *than.*
Metaphors omit connecting words and make a direct comparison between things.
Personification is a kind of metaphor in which something nonhuman is given human characteristics.
Puns play with the fact that words can have double meanings.

Your Turn

Explaining Figurative Language

1. In the following lines, identify the simile and tell what two things are compared.

    Lord Capulet.
    Death lies on her like an untimely frost
    Upon the sweetest flower of all the field.
    (Act IV, Scene 5, lines 28–29)

2. Here are two passages containing metaphors. Find each metaphor, and identify the two things that it compares.

    Romeo *(under Juliet's balcony).*
    But soft! What light through yonder window breaks?
    It is the East, and Juliet is the sun!
    (Act II, Scene 2, lines 2–3)

    Juliet *(to Romeo).*
    This bud of love, by summer's ripening breath,
    May prove a beauteous flower when next we meet.
    (Act II, Scene 2, lines 121–122)

3. In this passage, what nonhuman things are personified?

    Capulet.
    When well-appareled April on the heel
    Of limping winter treads . . .
    (Act I, Scene 2, lines 27–28)

4. What pun is made in these lines?

    Mercutio *(after he is stabbed).*
    Ask for me tomorrow, and you shall
    find me a grave man.
    (Act III, Scene 1, lines 94–95)

Academic Vocabulary

Talk About . . .
With a partner, use the Academic Vocabulary words to discuss the qualities (youth, foolishness, and so on) that Romeo and Juliet embody. How do these qualities contribute to their fateful end?

MO **9.W.2.B.1.b** Compose text with: relevant specific details **9.W.3.A.1.d** Compose a variety of texts: including literary analysis **9.W.1.A.1.e** Follow a writing process to: share writing **9.R.1.D.1.a** Read grade-level instructional text: with fluency, accuracy, comprehension and appropriate expression *Also covered* **9.R.1.E.1.b; 9.R.1.E.1.c**

CHOICES

As you respond to the Choices, use these **Academic Vocabulary** words as appropriate: convention, embody, interpretation, production.

REVIEW

Prevent the Tragedy

Group Discussion Shakespeare doesn't idealize Romeo and Juliet. He is careful to remind us that their love is destructive partly because they fail to see life as it really is. Romeo and Juliet do not act with caution, patience, or wisdom. They act on impulse and in haste. They also get bad advice. Form a discussion group to address these questions:

- What should Romeo and Juliet have done, instead of what they actually did, at three or more points in the play?
- Could Romeo and Juliet have triumphed—if they had received good advice? Explain.

CONNECT

Respond to a Critical Comment

Timed Writing Read the following critical comment by the scholar G. B. Harrison. Then, write a paragraph or two in which you agree or disagree with the comment. Include quotations and evidence from the play to support your opinion.

> Juliet begins as a demure [modest] girl who is prepared to listen respectfully to the advice of her mother. When she has fallen in love, she becomes suddenly a woman of great courage and resource, who will face even death and fantastic horror to regain her husband.

EXTEND

Review the Movie

Get a movie production of *Romeo and Juliet* from your library or video store. Watch the movie, and then write a short essay in which you compare one scene of the play with that scene in the film. Which was more effective? Why?

Find the Characters Today

TechFocus Prepare an oral report for the class in which you tell how the character types in *Romeo and Juliet* are found in movies, novels, TV sitcoms, and dramas today. Focus on these types: beautiful girl; handsome boy; loyal best friend; hotheaded bully. Videotape your presentations.

Update the Tragedy

Prepare a plan for an updated *Romeo and Juliet*. Use the chart below as a guide. It shows how the play was changed into the musical *West Side Story* (1957). After you finish your rough plan, try mapping your scenes.

Romeo and Juliet	***West Side Story***
Verona, 1300s	New York, 1950s
Feuding families: Montagues and Capulets	Gang war: Jets versus Sharks
Authority: Prince	New York City police
Friend/confidant: Benvolio (Romeo's); nurse (Juliet's)	Friend/confidant: Riff (Tony's); Anita (Maria's)
Leaders: Mercutio (Montagues); Tybalt (Capulets)	Leaders: Riff (Jets); Bernardo (Sharks)

COMPARING TEXTS

Comparing Narratives Across Genres

CONTENTS

Bird of Portent
by Francois-Louis Schmied.

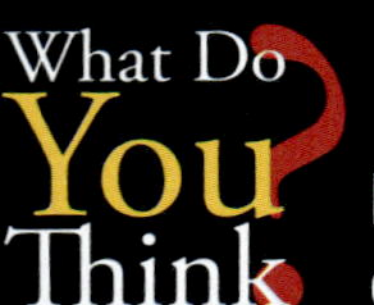

How can love stories restore our faith in troubled times?

QuickWrite

What books, movies, or television shows cheer you up? Make a list of titles you might read or watch when you're feeling blue. Then, review your list. Which items involve love of some type (romantic love, love between family members and friends, and so on)?

Preparing to Read

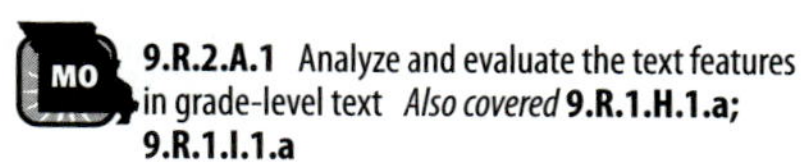
9.R.2.A.1 Analyze and evaluate the text features in grade-level text *Also covered* 9.R.1.H.1.a; 9.R.1.I.1.a

Lost at Sea: The Story of Ceyx and Alcyone / Alcyone and Ceyx *from* Metamorphoses

Literary Focus

Narratives Across Genres A **myth** and a **play** are both **narratives;** they share the same basic elements of plot, setting, theme, and character. Myths and plays, however, tell their tales very differently. A myth is usually told in prose, with a **narrator** who describes what happens. The **dialogue** in a myth presents a character's words, but it does not carry the action. A play, however, tells a story mainly with dialogue. Plays may use a narrator to explain key information, but the plot moves forward because of what characters say and what they do, as described in the stage directions.

Reading Focus

Analyzing Details In prose, writers can describe characters directly. They can also present their thoughts, dialogue, and actions. Playwrights reveal character mainly through dialogue and action.

Into Action As you read these two versions of the same story, take notes on *how* the different writers bring the characters to life.

Character	Myth	Play
Alcyone	Thoughts: Fears for Ceyx Words: "Oh, poor sailor" Actions: Weeps and prays	Thoughts: Words: Actions:

Writing Focus

Think as a Reader/Writer

Find It in Your Reading This story describes a surprising change. As you read, note in your *Reader/Writer Notebook* how each writer presents this climactic moment.

Reader/Writer Notebook

Use your **RWN** to complete the activities for these selections.

Vocabulary

Lost at Sea

consoled (kuhn SOHLD) *v.:* comforted; calmed; cheered up. *Her fear was so great that she could not be consoled by any jokes or songs.*

Alcyone and Ceyx

endure (ehn DUR) *v.:* put up with something difficult; suffer. *The sailor had no choice but to endure the terrible storm at sea.*

mourning (MAWR nihng) *n.* used as *adj.:* indicating sorrow. *After her husband's death, she wore only mourning clothes.*

transforming (trans FAWRM ihng) *v.* used as *adj.:* changing from one thing into another. *We see spring trees transforming from lifeless skeletons into green bursts.*

Language Coach

Etymology The Latin noun *durus* means "hard." The Latin verb *indurare* means "to harden the heart." The Middle English word *duren*, meaning "last" or "continue," is a later form of those words. Which Vocabulary word on the list is part of this word history? Try to identify two other words that belong to this word family.

Learn It Online

Use Word Watch to build your knowledge of terms at:

go.hrw.com L9-953 Go

MEET THE WRITERS

Mary Pope Osborne
(1949–)

Sharing Classic Adventures

Mary Pope Osborne traveled the world in search of adventure. She lived for a while in a cave on the island of Crete. Then she and some friends traveled through Asia. The trip wasn't always easy: "We nearly lost our lives," she explains, "first in an earthquake in northern Afghanistan and then in a riot in Kabul."

When she later turned to writing, Osborne wanted to share her love of adventure and classic stories. She has retold the myths and legends of many cultures, including ancient Greek and Norse myths, American tall tales, and mermaid stories from around the world. Her popular Magic Tree House series for children involves exciting time-traveling adventures.

Mary Zimmerman
(1960–)

Translating from the Page to the Stage

A lifelong reader, Mary Zimmerman found a unique way to share the books she loves: She writes and directs plays inspired by classical literature. Her theatrical flair helps her create dramatic, memorable plays and productions. In *Metamorphoses,* she adapts a collection of classical Greek tales that focus on supernatural changes. Zimmerman finds the human element that makes these tales universal. As she points out, facing a sudden change can be "excruciating but then it can produce something new."

Zimmerman has also adapted tales from *The Arabian Nights* as well as Homer's *Odyssey.* She even created a play based on the notebooks of the Renaissance artist Leonardo da Vinci.

Think About the Writers

Why do you think each of these writers decided to retell a story that is thousands of years old?

Preview the Selections

In "Lost at Sea," Mary Pope Osborne retells a classic Greek myth about **Alcyone** and **Ceyx,** whose love story has inspired many writers and poets.

Mary Zimmerman's "Alcyone and Ceyx" brings the same story to dramatic life in her theatrical adaptation.

MYTH

Lost at Sea: The Story of Ceyx and Alcyone

retold by **Mary Pope Osborne**

Read with a Purpose

Read these two works to see how two writers retell and interpret a classic tale of true love lost and regained.

Build Background

Ovid (43 B.C.–A.D. 18) was a Latin poet whose most famous work is *Metamorphoses*, a collection of poems retelling classical legends. As the title suggests, each tale describes a metamorphosis, or complete change. In these stories, people transform into animals, plants, and even stars.

Mary Pope Osborne retells Ovid's version of the myth of Ceyx (SEE ihks) and Alcyone (al SY uh nee). This story is an example of an origin myth. **Origin myths** explain how something in the world began. The ancient Greeks noticed that the short breeding season of a seabird called a kingfisher took place near the winter solstice each year. The sea during this period is often unusually calm. The myth of Ceyx and Alcyone explains why this peaceful period, known as halcyon days, happens each year. One key to understanding is knowing that another name for the kingfisher is the halcyon.

King Ceyx, son of the morning star, walked along the shore with his wife, Alcyone, daughter of the king of the winds.

"I must leave in a few days on a long sea voyage and travel to the Oracle of Delphi,"[1] King Ceyx told his wife. "But I promise I will be gone for no more than two months."

Alcyone turned pale. She knew the rough winds in the open seas were very dangerous. "My father, Aeolus, rules the winds—I know what force he can unleash in a bad storm. I beg you, if you love me, don't go!"

King Ceyx assured Alcyone of his love for her and promised to return soon, but she would not be consoled. A few days later, when he stood in the stern of his ship and waved good-bye, she flung herself down on the sands and wept bitterly. Then she dragged herself home and began her long wait for her husband's return. **A**

1. **Oracle of Delphi** (AWR uh kuhl uhv DEHL fy): An oracle in ancient Greece and Rome was a shrine where people would go to pay tribute to a god. The Oracle of Delphi, a shrine to the god Apollo, was the best-known and most powerful oracle in ancient Greece.

A **Reading Focus** **Analyzing Details** What do you learn about Ceyx and Alcyone in the opening paragraphs?

Vocabulary **consoled** (kuhn SOHLD) *v.:* comforted; calmed; cheered up.

Analyzing Visuals **Viewing and Interpreting** Which event in the myth does this painting represent?

Ceyx and Alcyone (1768) by Richard Wilson (1714–1782). Oil on canvas.

One night, as King Ceyx's ship sailed upon the open sea, the waves began rising. "Pull in your oars! Lower the sails!" the captain shouted.

But the men could not hear him, for the winds had begun to howl, and thunder rumbled in the sky. Ocean spray leapt for the stars, as lightning lit the night. Then the sea turned yellow, and the heavens poured water in great torrents, as waves crashed in on the king's ship.

Ceyx's last thoughts were of Alcyone. He cried to the gods, "Wash my body to my wife over the sea!" And he called her name again and again, until a great arc of water took him down to the dark depths of the ocean. And then there was no more lightning and no more starlight; everything was pitch-black.

The morning star did not shine the next day, but hid behind the clouds, grieving for his drowned son. **B**

Alcyone was counting the days until Ceyx returned. She wove a beautiful robe for him and a dress for herself to wear when he came home. Every day she burned incense and prayed to Juno, the goddess who protects married women, asking her to bring her husband home safely.

Hearing Alcyone's prayers, Juno[2] felt pity. Finally she summoned her messenger, Iris, the rainbow goddess. She instructed Iris to travel to the god Sleep and ask Sleep to send Alcyone a dream, telling her that her husband had drowned at sea. **C**

2. **Juno** (JOO noh): Roman name for the Greek goddess Hera.

B **Literary Focus** **Narratives Across Genres** Are the main events told through narration or dialogue? Explain your answer.

C **Reading Focus** **Analyzing Details** Why does the narrator describe Juno's feelings of pity? Why is Juno's reaction important to the story?

Iris took off at once, trailing her thousand colors across the sky, until she touched down upon the twilight lands of the Cimmerian country. There the god Sleep lived in the hollow of a mountain. When Iris arrived at Sleep's cave, she heard no birds singing or dogs barking or geese cackling. Only the river, Lethe,[3] whispered sleepily in the twilight as Iris stepped past poppy beds and entered Sleep's cave.

The rainbow goddess pushed aside the empty dreams in her way, then came upon Sleep, snoring in a great ebony bed. Iris awakened the slumbering god and bid him send a dream to Alcyone. After Sleep agreed, Iris soared back to Mount Olympus,[4] trailing her rainbow colors across the sky.

Sleep roused Morpheus,[5] one of his thousand sons, the one who could best imitate humans. He instructed Morpheus to fly to Alcyone. Then the god returned to his bed, letting his drowsy head sink down again into the land of dreams. **D**

On silent wings, Morpheus took off through the twilight. When he finally came to the home of Alcyone, he assumed the face and body of King Ceyx. He slipped into Alcyone's chamber and stood before her bed.

Ceyx's ghostly beard dripped with sea water, and tears ran down his face as he bent over his sleeping wife and whispered, "Oh, my love, do you see me? Have I changed in death? Cherish no hope for my return. My ship went down in a storm far out at sea, and I died, calling your name. Arise now and weep for me."

3. **Lethe** (LEE thee): Lethe was one of five rivers in Hades, the Greek underworld of mythology. The river was associated with forgetfulness.
4. **Mount Olympus:** home of the gods.
5. **Morpheus** (MAWR fee uhs): often referred to as the Greek god of dreams.

In her sleep, Alcyone wept and tried to take her husband into her arms, but it was no use. She clutched the air and cried out for him, until her own voice woke her. Alcyone realized she'd been dreaming, but fearing her dream might have been the truth, she wept until dawn.

When light crept into her bedroom chamber, Alcyone rose and slipped down to the shore, to the place where she had last seen Ceyx, standing in the stern of his boat, waving to her.

As she stared at the sea, Alcyone spotted something floating on the water. She stepped closer and saw a man's body on top of the waves. "Oh, poor sailor," she said, "and poor wife, if you're married."

When the waves washed the body closer to shore, Alcyone saw it was her husband. She cried out, "Oh, my love! Why have you come back to me this way?"

Then she rushed into the sea. And though the waves broke against her, she did not go under. Instead, she began beating the water with giant wings. Then, crying out like a bird, she rose into the air and flew over the sea to Ceyx's lifeless body. When she touched her husband's cold lips with her beak, he also became a bird, and the two of them were together again. **E**

Since that time, every year, for seven days before the winter solstice, the waves are quiet, and the water is perfectly calm. These days are called *halcyon days,* for during them, the king of the winds keeps the wind at home—because his daughter, Alcyone, is brooding[6] on her nest upon the sea.

6. **brooding**: taking care of newly born offspring.

D **Literary Focus** **Narratives Across Genres** How would you describe the narrator's tone in this passage?

E **Reading Focus** **Analyzing Details** How does the writer use imagery to describe what happens when the characters change from one form to another?

PLAY

Alcyone and Ceyx

from Metamorphoses

by **Mary Zimmerman**

Build Background

The New York production of *Metamorphoses* had a most unusual set—all of the action took place in and around a large, shallow pool. Actors could float, splash, and submerge in the water as they acted out Ovid's ancient tales.

Zimmerman and her cast were rehearsing in New York on September 11, 2001, when a terrorist attack destroyed the twin towers of the World Trade Center and killed thousands of people. The play went on as planned, and its first performance took place one week later. Many observers felt that these ancient stories had taken on a new level of meaning and relevance. Zimmerman noted that "the play suddenly had all of these very profound resonances." As she points out, "Alcyone and Ceyx" is a story in which "someone goes away, off to work basically, and is suddenly taken from the earth—just destroyed."

[*Music. Transition. The* SECOND LAUNDRESS *becomes the* NARRATOR *of the following story.*[1] ALCYONE *and* CEYX *enter variously.*]

NARRATOR:
There once was a king named Ceyx who had as his queen Alcyone,
daughter of Aeolus, master of the winds. These two
adored each other and lived in a monotony of happiness.
But nothing in this world is safe. **A**

ALCYONE:
It isn't true.

1. This tale is one of a series of stories told during the course of the play. The play's lines are reproduced as they appear in the published script.

A Reading Focus **Analyzing Details** What information does the narrator tell us directly about Ceyx and Alcyone?

CEYX:
It is.

NARRATOR:
One day Alcyone had heard that Ceyx had ordered his ship to be made ready for a sea voyage, to visit a far-off oracle.[2]

2. **oracle:** shrine in tribute to a god.

ALCYONE:
How can you leave me alone? I'll pine in your absence.
Overland, it's a long and arduous trip, but I'd still prefer that
to a voyage by sea—which I fear, for my father's winds are wild and savage.
You think as his son-in-law you may get some special treatment. Not so!
Once they've escaped my father's cave, those winds are wild
and beyond anyone's control. As a girl I watched them come home
exhausted and spent, and I learned to fear them then.
Now I am petrified, surely— **B**

NARRATOR:
she said,

ALCYONE:
if you die my life is over
and I shall be cursed with every reluctant breath I draw.

CEYX:
My love, I hate to choose between my journey and you
but how can I live this way? Stranded on shore, afraid,
domesticated, diminished, a kind of lap dog?

ALCYONE:
Take me with you at least, and we'll meet the storms together,
which I fear much less than to be left a widow.

CEYX:
In two months' time, I'll be back.

ALCYONE:
No. I fear you won't. I know you won't.

B **Literary Focus** **Narratives Across Genres** How does Alcyone's personality come through as she speaks? What clues reveal her character?

CEYX:
In two months' time. For that short time, you can be brave
and endure the trial of waiting.

NARRATOR:
She was hardly consoled, but she saw she could not hold out any longer
in the face of his resolve. She allowed herself to be soothed
and consented to his going.

[*Music begins and continues through the next long sequence.*
SAILORS *enter with oars.*]

There were no more details left to be checked,
no last-minute changes to make, and the men, arranged on their benches,
were ready to row and go. He boarded and gave the sign.
And then he turned to wave at her.
She waved at him while the ribbon of black water widened between the ship
and shore. She gazed at him until he was no longer distinguishable
but still she could see the ship. And she narrowed her eyes to the horizon
and watched it as it receded to a smaller and smaller object. And then
the whole hull was gone, and only the sails remained,
and then they, too, disappeared.
She gazed still at the empty and desolate blue
and then went to her empty bedroom to lie on the huge
and vacant bed and give herself over to weeping.

CEYX:
The vessel cleared the harbor and caught the freshening wind,
which set the rigging to singing and slapping against the spars.[3]
I ordered the rowers to ship their oars and the sailors
to set the yards and make sail. Our ship ran before the wind.
We made satisfactory progress all that day and had reached
a point of no return, with as much blue water astern
as remained ahead. **C**

3. **spars:** poles, such as masts, that support or extend the sail of a ship.

C **Literary Focus** **Narratives Across Genres** Why might Zimmerman have decided to use Ceyx as a second narrator? What information does Ceyx give the audience?

Vocabulary **endure** (ehn DUR) *v.:* put up with something difficult; suffer.

NARRATOR:
But as the sun was sinking in the West, the water,
everywhere blue until now, began to be flecked
with the whitecapped waves sailors dislike.

[*Enter* POSEIDON[4] *and his* HENCHMAN.]

The weather was worse with every moment
for the winds were on the loose.

[*The storm begins.* POSEIDON *and his* HENCHMAN *attack* CEYX, *the boat, the* SAILORS.]

The weather was worse with every moment
for the winds were on the loose.

CEYX:
Reef the sails! Bail the water! Secure the spars!

NARRATOR:
But Poseidon and his Henchman had arrived. The rest
was one enormous green catastrophe.

[*The storm escalates. The chandelier flashes as though it were lightning or as if it were a lamp shorting out. The men wrestle in the pool.*] **D**

CEYX:
He thinks in an oddly abstracted way that the waves are lions
crazed with hunters' wounds, or that the ship
is a besieged town attacked by a horde of madmen.

4. **Poseidon** (puh SY duhn): Greek god of the sea and of earthquakes.

D **Literary Focus** **Narratives Across Genres** What actions do the stage directions describe? What elements from a prose narrative do stage directions replace?

HENCHMAN AND CEYX:
One would think that the heavens were crazed with lust

CEYX:
to join the turbulent sea

HENCHMAN AND CEYX:
which returned their bizarre passion
and tried to rise up and embrace the air.

NARRATOR:
The men have lost their belief in their captain, their courage,
their nautical skill, and even their will to live as they wait for the end. One weeps
and groans aloud. Another, no braver, is silent, dumbstruck.
One calls on the gods for mercy. Another curses his fate.
And one says one word,

CEYX:
Alcyone,

NARRATOR:
again and again,

CEYX:
Alcyone, my treasure, Alcyone.

NARRATOR:
And this is the end of the world.

[APHRODITE[5] *enters above the sky.*]

CEYX:
O gods, hear my modest prayer: that my body may wash ashore at her feet
where she may with gentle hands prepare it to be buried.

[CEYX *sinks below the water.*]

NARRATOR:
Nothing left but the slow parade led by Hermes[6] to the Underworld.

5. Aphrodite (af ruh DY tee): Greek goddess of love and beauty.

6. Hermes: in Greek mythology, the god of dreams, a messenger of the gods, and the protector of travelers.

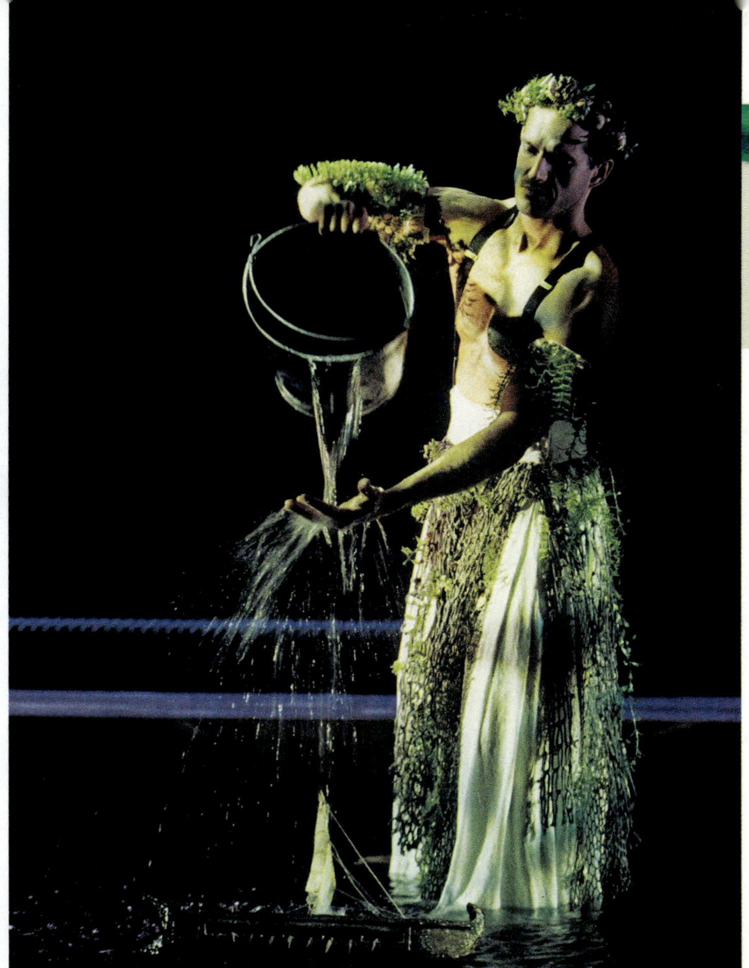
© Joan Marcus.

Analyzing Visuals

Viewing and Interpreting What does the bucket of water in the photograph represent? Whom do you think the actor represents?

[*Music ends. Everyone but* ALCYONE *exits.* ALCYONE *stirs in her sleep and begins to count, covering her eyes, like a child who counts to a certain number, hoping that when she reaches it her wish will be granted.*]

ALCYONE:
One two three four, fifteen sixteen seventeen eighteen, ninety-eight ninety-nine, one hundred . . .

[*She uncovers her eyes and looks toward the horizon, then covers her eyes and begins again.* APHRODITE *enters and watches from the sky. She summons* IRIS[7] *to watch.*]

One two three four, fifteen sixteen seventeen eighteen, ninety-eight ninety-nine, one hundred.

7. **Iris:** messenger of the gods, personified as a rainbow.

[*She uncovers her eyes and looks toward the horizon. She then begins again and continues under the following lines.*]

APHRODITE:
Look at her, Iris, she's moved her vigil down to the shore
and now she's sleeping there.

ALCYONE:
. . . ninety-eight, ninety-nine, one hundred. Ceyx? Come home.
I'm nearer now, I'm sleeping on the shore. It's not so far until
you see me.

[*She begins to count again, quietly.*]

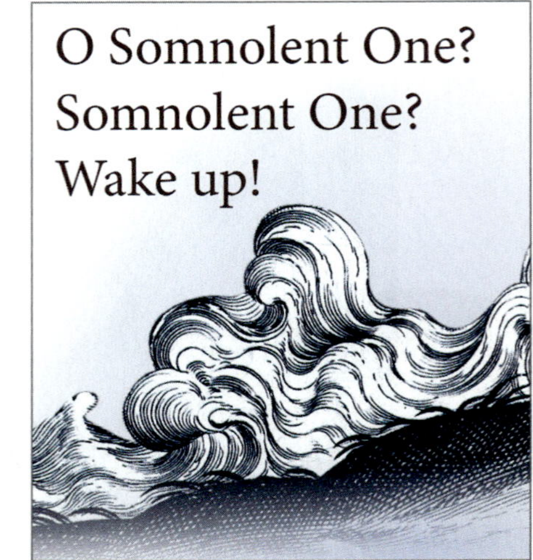
O Somnolent One?
Somnolent One?
Wake up!

APHRODITE:
This can't go on forever. Go to the house of Sleep and ask him to
arrange a nighttime visitation, a dream that might show our
Alcyone
the sorry truth. **E**

[IRIS *departs.* ALCYONE *falls asleep in the shallow waters of the pool. A* SECOND NARRATOR *appears. As he speaks,* SLEEP *enters, wrapped in a black velvet blanket, with eyeshades.* APHRODITE *slowly drops white letter Z's from the sky.*]

SECOND NARRATOR:
Far off in remotest Campania,[8] beyond where the Cimmerians[9]
live in their gloomy caves, is a deeper and even darker grotto,
the home of Sleep. In this place the sun never can, even at midday,
penetrate with the faintest beams. In that cloudy twilight
no rooster dares disturb the silence with his rude crowing,
no dog or nervous goose gives voice to challenge the passing
stranger. Not even branches sigh in occasional passing breezes,
but an almost total silence fills the air.

8. Campania: region in southern Italy, formerly a Greek colony.

9. Cimmerians: ancient people living in southern Russia, north of the Black Sea.

[SLEEP *snores.* IRIS *creeps in, wearing an illuminated rainbow-colored skirt and carrying an alarm clock.*]

At the heart of an almost painted stillness,

E **Reading Focus** **Analyzing Details** What can you infer about Aphrodite's character based on her words and actions? What human qualities does she embody?

in a huge, darkened chamber, the god himself relaxes, drifting in languor.[10] Around him the fragments of ill-assorted dreams hover over the floor in grand profusion like leaves the trees have let go to float through the currents of air and fall in their gorgeous billows below.

IRIS:
Hello?

SECOND NARRATOR:
Into this strange and breathless place, Iris the rainbow intrudes.

IRIS:
O Somnolent[11] One? Somnolent One? Wake up!

SLEEP:
Wha—?

IRIS:
Mildest of all the gods, soother of souls, and healer of wearied and pain-wracked bodies and minds.

SLEEP:
Iris! Let me rest a moment.

[*He sleeps a bit. Wakes up.*]

Iris! What do you want? **F**

IRIS:
Devise, if you can, some form to resemble King Ceyx
and send it down in a dream to his wife, the Queen Alcyone.
Let her know the news of the wreck of his ship and the death
of the husband she loves so well. Sleep [*she yawns*] do this for us—
can you?

[*She yawns and falls asleep with him for a moment, but luckily her alarm goes off, startling them both. She runs away.*]

10. languor (LANG guhr): tiredness of the body or mind.

11. somnolent: sleepy; drowsy.

F **Reading Focus** **Analyzing Details** How does the playwright use humor to characterize Sleep? Why might she have decided to lighten the tone here?

Farewell!

SLEEP [*calling*]:
Morpheus![12] Mor-phe-us! Come and change your shape
to that of King Ceyx. Go to his wife and tell her [*yawning*]
. . . tell her he is dead.

12. **Morpheus:** one of the sons of the god of sleep, who sends human shapes to dreamers.

[MORPHEUS *enters as* CEYX. SLEEP *sees him.*]

That's good. That's very good. Now go!

[SLEEP *stumbles away.* CEYX, *shrouded, approaches* ALCYONE. *She stirs.*]

ALCYONE:
Sir, you seem like a seafaring man, can you tell me,
Where is my husband, Ceyx? Have you seen him on the sea?
When is he coming home? His ship is strong and unmistakable.
Have you seen him? [*Pause.*] Sir?

CEYX [*dropping his shroud*]:
Do you not know me? Has death undone me so?

ALCYONE:
No!

CEYX:
Look at me, I charge you—look at me.

ALCYONE:
No! I won't. I won't!

CEYX:
Look at me, and know your husband's ghost.
Your prayers have done no good,
for I am gone, beyond all help or hope forever.

ALCYONE:
Go away! G

G Reading Focus **Analyzing Details** How does Alcyone initially react to the appearance of Morpheus as Ceyx?

CEYX:
I am not some bearer of tales, but the man himself
to whom it happened. Look at me, my little bird.

ALCYONE:
I told you. I knew it would happen and I begged you
not to go. I knew the day you sailed I had lost you forever.
The ship, my hopes, and my life grew smaller
all at the same time. You should have allowed me to come—

CEYX:
Little bird—

ALCYONE:
This is no good, no good—that I should be living
and you be elsewhere or nowhere? I'm drowning now
in the air, I'm wrecked here on the land
where the currents are just as cold and cruel.

CEYX:
Get up from your bed and put on your mourning clothes.

[*He begins to go.*]

ALCYONE:
Wait for me! Come back! Where are you going?
Wait and I'll go with you
as wives are supposed to go with their husbands.

[*But he is gone.*]

[*Calling*] Lucina! Lucina! Give me your lantern.

[LUCINA *enters and gives her lantern to* ALCYONE, *who searches the pool with it, stumbling and frantic.*]

Ceyx! Come back! Where are you?
Come back! He was here. Where is he? Where is he?

LUCINA:
All that night she searched along the shore for her drowned,
dreamed husband. But she found nothing, not even footprints,
only wave after wave of black water. When morning came

[*Music begins.*]

she narrowed her eyes to the horizon, and remembered
how she had looked on that other day.

[HERMES *enters carrying* CEYX *and places him in the water.*]

She remembered
his last kiss, the way he turned to the ship, could not bear it,
and turned again to her.

ALCYONE:
What is that out there? Oh, it is a man. Alas, poor sailor, for
your wife and . . .

Vocabulary **mourning** (MAWR nihng) *n.* used as *adj.:* indicating sorrow.

[*She sees that it is* CEYX. *Music ends.*]

Together they still fly, just over
the water's surface.

LUCINA:
The gods are not altogether unkind. Some prayers are answered.

ALCYONE:
Ceyx, is this how you return to me?

LUCINA:
She began to run to him; but as she ran, crying, a strange thing happened.

[ALCYONE *moves slowly toward* CEYX, *transforming. The sound of waves and seabirds crying comes up.*]

By the time she reached him, she was a bird.
She tried to kiss him with her bill, and by some trick
of the ocean's heaving, it seemed that his head reached up to hers
in response. You ask, How could he have felt her kiss? H

APHRODITE:
But better ask, How could the gods not have felt it?
Seen this, and not had compassion?

LUCINA:
For the dead body was changing, restored to life,
and renewed as another seabird.
Together they still fly, just over the water's surface,
and mate and rear their young, and for seven days each winter
Alcyone broods on her nest that floats on the gentled water—
for Aeolus, her father, then keeps the winds short reined
and every year gives seven days of calm upon the ocean—
the days we call the halcyon[13] days.

13. halcyon: bird identified with the kingfisher, which, according to legend, has a peaceful, calming influence on the sea during the time of the winter solstice.

H **Literary Focus** **Narratives Across Genres** How do the stage directions and dialogue work together to help you witness Alcyone's transformation?

Vocabulary **transforming** (trans FAWRM ihng) *v.* used as *adj.:* changing from one thing into another.

Applying Your Skills

9.R.2.A.1 Analyze and evaluate the text features in grade-level text 9.R.1.H.1.a Apply post-reading skills to comprehend, interpret, analyze, and evaluate text: identify and explain the relationship between the main idea and supporting details 9.W.2.B.1.c Compose text with: complex ideas *Also covered* 9.R.1.E.1.c; 9.R.1.I.1.a

Lost at Sea: The Story of Ceyx and Alcyone / Alcyone and Ceyx *from* Metamorphoses

Respond and Think Critically

Reading Focus

Quick Check

1. How does Alcyone find out about Ceyx's death?
2. What natural event do the myth and play explain?

Read with a Purpose

3. Do both of these versions of the myth suggest that true love can last? Explain.

Reading Skills: Analyzing Details

4. Now that you have read both versions of this myth, add a column to your chart, and identify similarities and differences in the ways the characters are presented.

Myth	Play	Similarities/ Differences
Thoughts: Fears for Ceyx Words: "Oh, poor sailor" Actions: Weeps and prays	Thoughts: Fears for Ceyx Words: "One two three . . ." Actions: Weeps and prays	Similar: Worries, becomes bird Differences: Play: Counts numbers to bring him back

Vocabulary Check

Identify the Vocabulary word that matches each synonym or antonym.

consoled
endure
mourning
transforming

5. synonym for *tolerate*
6. antonym for *rejoicing*
7. synonym for *soothed*
8. synonym for *converting*

Literary Focus

Literary Analysis

9. **Analyze** Identify the three instances of personification used in the myth. What effect does the use of personification create?
10. **Interpret** The narrator of Zimmerman's play says that Alcyone and Ceyx "lived in a monotony of happiness." What does the narrator mean?
11. **Analyze** How might staging *Metamorphoses* in a pool have affected its impact? Explain.

Literary Skills: Narratives Across Genres

12. **Compare** What plot elements do the myth and play have in common?
13. **Analyze** How does each version of the story use narration? Does narration in a play have the same effect it has in prose? Why or why not?
14. **Evaluate** How does Zimmerman change the story in her adaptation? Do you think these changes were necessary? Why or why not?

Writing Focus

Think as a Reader/Writer

Use It in Your Writing Review your notes about the moment when Alcyone and Ceyx are transformed into birds. Then, describe the scene in another genre, such as poetry or nonfiction.

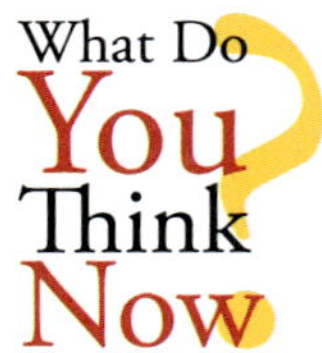

How might this story provide someone with comfort in a time of grief? Explain.

COMPARING TEXTS
Wrap Up

MO **9.R.2.C.1.b** Use details from text(s): to analyze character, plot, setting, point of view **9.W.3.A.1.a** Compose a variety of texts: using narrative, descriptive, expository, and/or persuasive features **9.W.3.A.1.d** Compose a variety of texts: including literary analysis

Lost at Sea: The Story of Ceyx and Alcyone / Alcyone and Ceyx *from* Metamorphoses

Writing Focus

Comparison-Contrast Essay

You have read two versions of the same story. You can now write a comparison-contrast essay to share your thoughts on the works. Choose one of these topics as the focus for your essay:

- Which version do you prefer? Focus on the reasons you think that version is more effective.
- Why was each version written? Focus on each author's purpose for writing. Tell how well you think each goal was achieved.

Prewriting Re-read the selections, and review the notes you took during and after reading. Be sure to identify the most important similarities and differences between the two versions. Then, choose an overall structure for your essay. Use one of these comparison structures:

Point-by-Point Organization	Block Organization
Point 1 Myth, Play	Myth Points 1, 2, and 3
Point 2 Myth, Play	Play Points 1, 2, and 3

Drafting Write a draft of your essay, beginning with your thesis statement. Then, develop your ideas in the body paragraphs.

Revising As you review your essay, look for ideas that need more support. Add quotations from the text to strengthen your points. Be sure that you have provided enough information about both the myth and the play.

Proofreading and Publishing Read your draft carefully, and correct errors in spelling, grammar, and punctuation.

CHOICES

As you respond to the Choices, use these **Academic Vocabulary** words as appropriate: interpretation, convention, production, embody.

REVIEW

Compare Plots

Timed Writing Write a brief essay describing the plot structure of the myth of Alcyone and Ceyx. What critical elements did both the myth and the play include? Did both the myth and the play tell the same story? Why or why not?

CONNECT

Stage the Play

Listening and Speaking Work with a team to create a staged reading of "Alcyone and Ceyx" by Mary Zimmerman. Of course, you probably won't be able to stage it in a large pool of water. What kind of set design could take the place of the pool? Rehearse your presentation, looking for opportunities to make characterizations clear.

EXTEND

Adapt a Classic

Find another story that you would like to adapt or retell by looking through collections of classical myths or legends. Your retelling might be traditional, or you could update the myth to modern times. If you create a dramatic adaptation, imagine how you might use the conventions of theater, including sets, costumes, lights, and props, to bring the story to life.

INFORMATIONAL TEXT FOCUS

Using Primary and Secondary Sources

CONTENTS

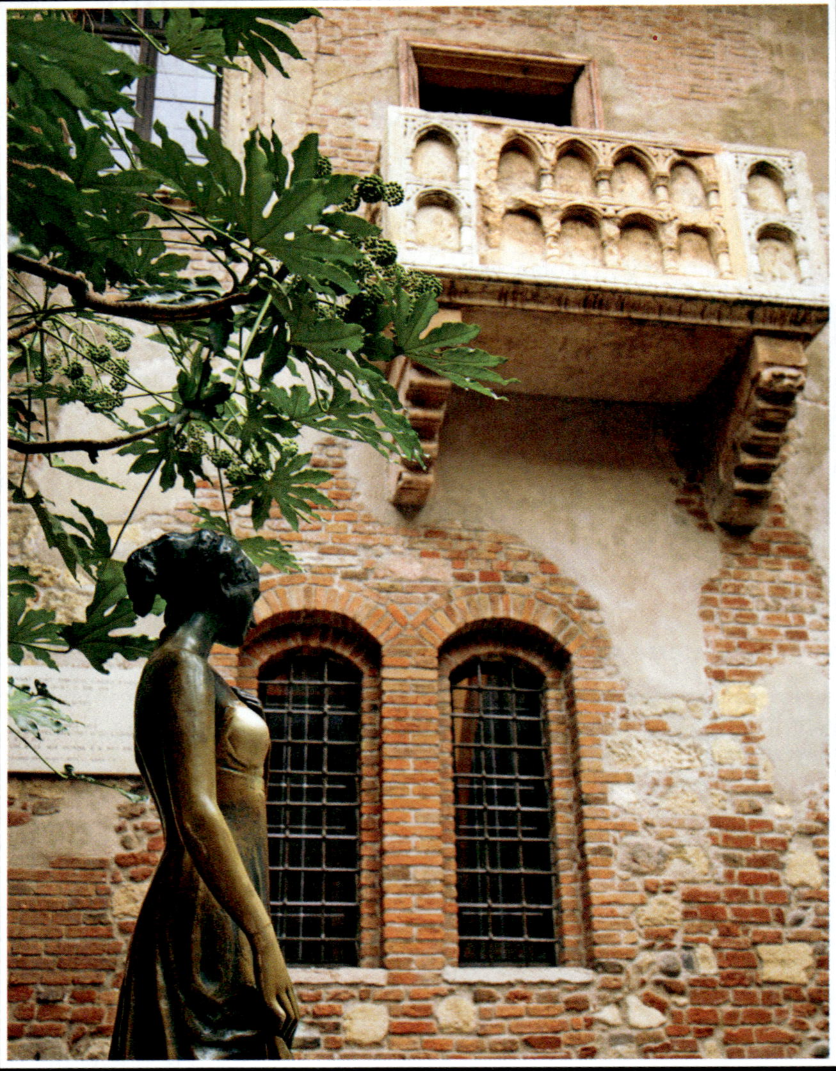

Balcony and statue in the courtyard of Juliet's house in Verona, Italy.

What Do You Think?

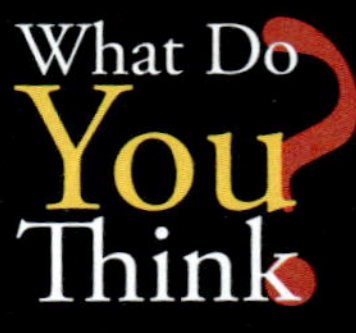

How can literary characters help us solve the problems in our own lives?

QuickTalk

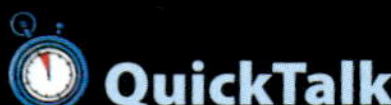

If you could ask any literary character for advice, whom would you ask, and why? Discuss your thoughts with a partner.

NEWSPAPER ARTICLE & LETTER

Preparing to Read

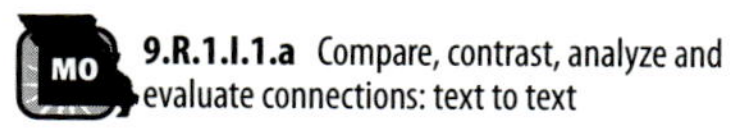

9.R.1.I.1.a Compare, contrast, analyze and evaluate connections: text to text

"Dear Juliet": Seeking Succor from a Veteran of Love / *from* The Juliet Club

Informational Text Focus

Primary and Secondary Sources When you do research, you use sources that fall into two main categories: primary sources and secondary sources.

A **primary source** is a firsthand account, such as a speech, an autobiography, or a letter. This kind of source directly expresses the thoughts and feelings of a writer, who in some cases may be biased or have limited knowledge. A **secondary source** is a secondhand account, often based on more than one viewpoint. Examples include encyclopedias, textbooks, biographies, many magazine articles, and most newspaper articles. Writers of secondary sources summarize, interpret, or analyze events in which they did not participate.

Into Action As you read the newspaper article, note where the writer has consulted primary and secondary sources. Write examples of these sources in a chart like the one below.

"Dear Juliet": Seeking Succor from a Veteran of Love

Primary Sources in the Text	Secondary Sources in the Text
phone interview with Elena Marchi	

Writing Focus

Preparing for **Constructed Response**

When you read nonfiction, you should think about the source of the material being communicated and whether the information you are getting is firsthand or secondhand. As you read these selections, note in your *Reader/Writer Notebook* the reactions you have to the types of information presented.

Reader/Writer Notebook

Use your **RWN** to complete the activities for these selections.

Vocabulary

"Dear Juliet": Seeking Succor from a Veteran of Love

precipice (PREHS uh pihs) *n.:* rock face that projects out, such as a cliff; the brink of a dangerous or disastrous situation. *Some lovelorn writers feel as if they are hanging over the edge of an emotional precipice.*

vital (VY tuhl) *adj.:* very important. *The club members provide a vital service.*

missives (MIHS ihvz) *n.:* written messages, such as letters. *Most of the missives are addressed to Juliet, not to Romeo.*

collaborate (kuh LAB uh rayt) *v.:* work together. *The authors decided to collaborate on a book about the letters.*

Language Coach

Etymology The Latin word *mittere* means "to send." Which Vocabulary word on the list above comes from the word *mittere*? What other words can you think of that might come from *mittere*?

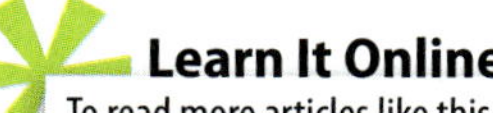

Learn It Online

To read more articles like this, go to the interactive Reading Workshops at:

go.hrw.com L9-973 Go

NEWSPAPER ARTICLE

"Dear Juliet": Seeking Succor[1] from a Veteran of Love by DINITIA SMITH

from **The New York Times,** March 27, 2006

Read with a Purpose

Read this newspaper article to discover what the Juliet Club (Club di Giulietta) is and what it does.

Build Background

Verona, Italy, is a popular destination for tourists, many of whom come to visit Juliet's tomb. Verona is also the home of the Club di Giulietta.[2] The club's "secretaries" have been responding to the letters addressed to Juliet since the 1930s. Every year, the club awards the annual Cara Giulietta prize for the best letter of the thousands sent from around the world.

"Dear Juliet," the letters all begin.

"Dear Juliet . . . You are my last hope. The woman I love more than anything in the world has left me. . . ."

"Dear Juliet, I live on the third floor. My parents don't allow my boyfriend to come to my house."

"Dear Juliet, my name is Riccardo. I am 10 years old." Riccardo is in love with an older woman, 14. He saw her in Verona the summer before. Does Juliet have news of her? **A**

Every week, hundreds of letters pour into the office of the Club di Giulietta, in Verona, Italy, the city that is the setting for Shakespeare's "Romeo and Juliet." Some are addressed simply "To Juliet, Verona," but the postman always knows to deliver them to the club's Via Galilei headquarters. Every letter is answered by the club's group of volunteers, no matter what the language, sometimes with the assistance of outside translators. (In the past, the owner of a local Chinese restaurant helped.)

"Help me! Save me!" wrote an Italian woman whose husband had left her. "I feel suspended on a precipice. I am afraid of going mad."

Her answer came from Ettore Solimani who was the custodian of Juliet's tomb for nearly 20 years, beginning in the 1930's.

"Have faith . . . ," Mr. Solimani wrote in the letter, "The day of humiliation will come for the intruder, and your husband will come back to you."

Now two American sisters, Lise and Ceil Friedman, have put some of the letters and a few of the responses into a book, "Letters to Juliet," along with the story of the club and the play's historical background. It is being published in November by Stewart, Tabori & Chang. But on Wednesday, Lise Friedman, an adjunct professor at New York University,

1. **succor** (SUHK uhr): assistance in a difficult time; relief.

2. **Club di Giulietta** (kluhb dee jyoo lee EHT uh): Italian for "Juliet Club."

A **Informational Focus** **Primary and Secondary Sources** What primary sources appear in this passage so far?

Vocabulary **precipice** (PREHS uh pihs) *n.:* rock face that projects out, such as a cliff; the brink of a dangerous or disastrous situation.

Club di Giulietta mailbox full of letters from all around the world.

Analyzing Visuals **Viewing and Interpreting** What does this photograph tell you about the Club di Giulietta?

will read from it at the university's Bronfman Center for Jewish Student Life.

And what is the real history of the play? The theme of tragic love between two young people from feuding families goes back at least to Ovid. Luigi da Porto, in "Newly Discovered Story of Two Noble Lovers" (1530), set the tale in Verona with rival families, the Montecchis and Cappellettis. There is no evidence that Shakespeare ever visited Italy, and some scholars think he based "Romeo and Juliet" on a poem by Arthur Brooke published some three decades before. But the myth of Romeo and Juliet—and it is something of a myth—has become vital to the tourism industry in Verona, where Juliet's house and tomb are supposedly located. Giulio Tamassia, president of the Club di Giulietta, has said that the house on Via Cappello has been called "Juliet's" only since the 19th century. And the balcony on its front dates from the first half of the 20th century. (Shakespeare mentions no balcony in the play. For her famous Act II, Scene 2 speech, Juliet comes from "above.") B

For years, tourists stuck notes to Juliet on the walls of the house with bubblegum. Last year the gum was removed, and white plasterboard put up for those who feel they must write. There is also a letterbox at the house, and its missives are collected and answered by the club. These days you can even send an e-mail to Juliet at info@julietclub.com. Very few letters, oddly enough, are sent to Romeo.

"There are hundreds of letters from U.S. teenagers," said Elena Marchi, the assistant to Mr. Tamassia, in a telephone interview from Verona. One reason is that "Romeo and Juliet" is part of many American high school curriculums.

"It's easier to talk to someone you don't know," said Ms. Marchi, a professional translator when she is not answering letters. "There are things you wouldn't say to your mother."

Ms. Marchi goes to the club every day, she said. "Once you start," she said, "you never give up, it's so interesting."

At least since the turn of the last century, messages have been left at Juliet's tomb in a former monastery on the Via del Pontiere, about a 15-minute walk from Juliet's house. But the letters really began flowing in 1937, the year after George Cukor's film "Romeo and Juliet" was released. That same year, Mr. Solimani was hired as the custodian of the tomb, which was probably originally an animal trough. (There are no bones there. Although the two lovers are supposedly buried together, over the years Romeo seems to have vanished from the picture, and it is now usually called just Juliet's tomb.)

Mr. Solimani planted rose bushes and a willow tree, trained two dozen turtledoves to fly around the cloister and to land on the shoulders of female visitors, and took it upon himself to answer the letters.

In the late 1980's, the club began to answer them. It receives money from the city for stationery and postage, but is otherwise run by volunteers.

About two years ago, when the Friedman sisters—who, according to Lise, "tend to finish each other's sentences"—were looking for a project on which to collaborate, Ceil was given some of the letters to translate. She sent copies to her sister, who immediately thought they might make a book.

The club has about 50,000 letters stored in boxes. The Friedman sisters went through about 5,000, choosing representative examples from different times. A few choice letters were remembered by the volunteers. The Friedmans have included about 75 in their book, changing the writers' names to protect their privacy.

B Informational Focus Primary and Secondary Sources What source might the author have used to find the information in this paragraph?

Vocabulary **vital** (VY tuhl) *adj.:* very important.
missives (MIHS ihvz) *n.:* written messages, such as letters.
collaborate (kuh LAB uh rayt) *v.:* work together.

The sisters found that during the nearly 70 years the letters have been arriving, they have become a reflection of the changing times. In 1970, a girl from Montana wrote, "Five years ago I met a Negro boy, William, at Bible camp." They had fallen in love, she explained, but added: "My parents and friends are against us getting married. William and I have separated many times, trying to get over each other."

In 1967 a Louisiana woman wrote that her husband was in Vietnam, and that she had fallen in love with his best friend. And in 1972, a soldier wrote from Vietnam itself: "I am in a bunker. Outside I hear missiles exploding, bullets being fired. I am 22 years old and I'm scared."

And then there are those who have yet to find love, who write to Juliet the way children write to Santa Claus, hoping he can bring them the gift they most desire. A woman from Ukraine asks: "I have a daughter, 27, who has never been married, but is looking for a fiancé." Can Juliet help?

"It's about suspending disbelief," Lise Friedman said, trying to explain why so many people would write to Juliet, unseen, perhaps only a chimera.[3] "It's about having a life of the imagination." **C**

"It's one of those ineffable[4] things."

Read with a Purpose

What is the Juliet Club? Why do you think it's so popular?

3. **chimera** (ky MIHR uh): in Greek mythology, a grotesque creature formed from a lion, a goat, and a serpent; here, a strange product of the imagination.
4. **ineffable** (ihn EHF uh buhl): indescribable.

C **Informational Focus** **Primary and Secondary Sources** What primary sources does the author use in these two paragraphs?

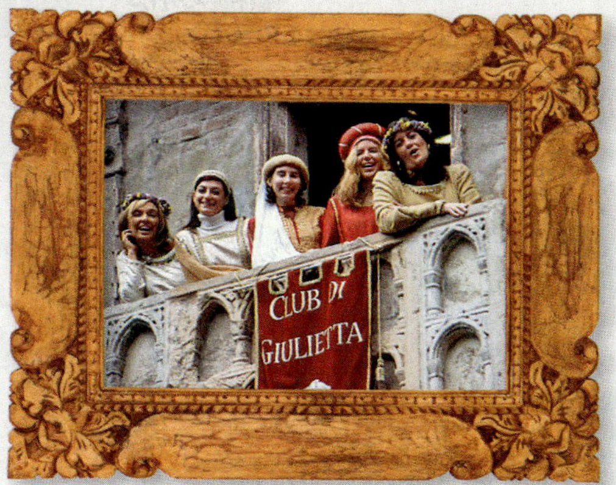

Club di Giulietta secretaries on balcony, dressed in period costumes.

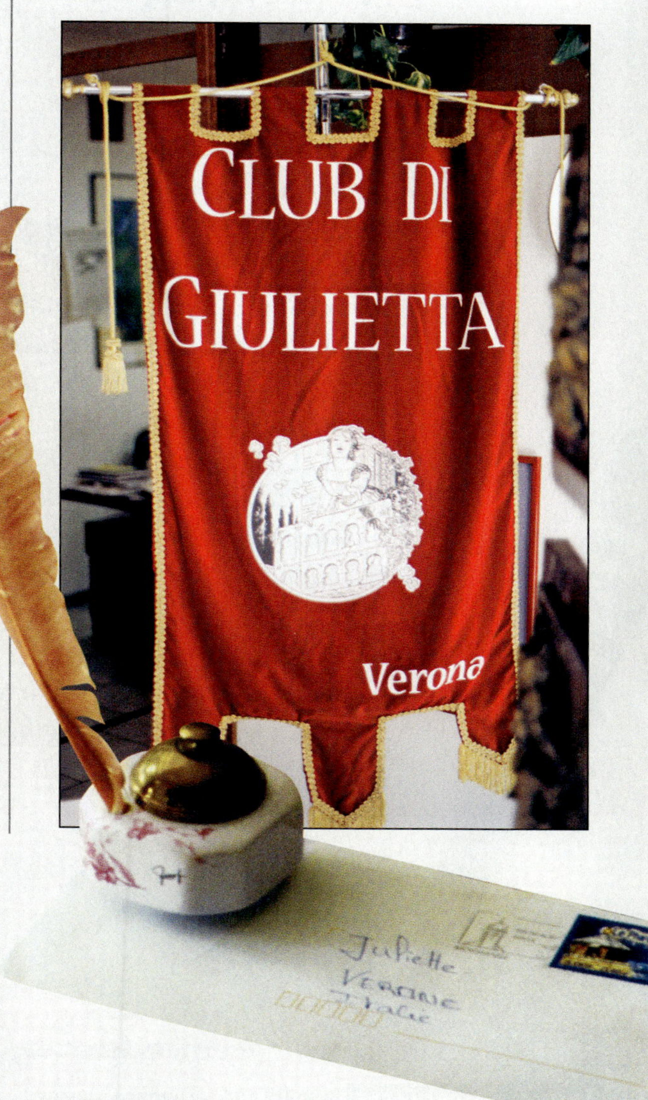

LETTER

from The Juliet Club

Read with a Purpose

Read the following letter to explore an example of "Juliet's" assistance. **Preparing to Read** for this selection is on page 973.

Build Background

Every week, "Juliet" receives hundreds of letters from writers asking for her help or advice. Each year on Valentine's Day, Club di Giulietta (The Juliet Club) in Verona, Italy, awards the Dear Juliet Prize for "the most beautiful letter sent to Juliet." Charlotte Schein is one of these winners.

Dear Juliet,

My dear friend, I dream of being on your balcony, which guarded your secret love, under which Romeo declared his passion, on which you proved to him that same dangerous passion.

As I write you this letter, I'm not desperate, just a little melancholy and romantic, but still fascinated by the great power of love.

Yes, Juliet, you are the hurricane and the calm, salt and sugar, tenderness and strength. But wherever did you get this strength?

I, too, listen to the song of the nightingale and the lark. I look for the dawn's light and await the tender night.

My thoughts are both timid and bold, sensible and foolish or imaginary because we are the stuff that dreams are made of.

But must we really believe that our destiny is rarely to be with our beloved? **A**

Yes, I dream of being part of this tragedy, if only for a moment, of entering the legend of love.

Charlotte

Read with a Purpose What does Charlotte want "Juliet's" advice about?

A Informational Focus **Primary and Secondary Sources**
What do you learn about Charlotte from this letter?

NEWSPAPER ARTICLE & LETTER

Applying Your Skills

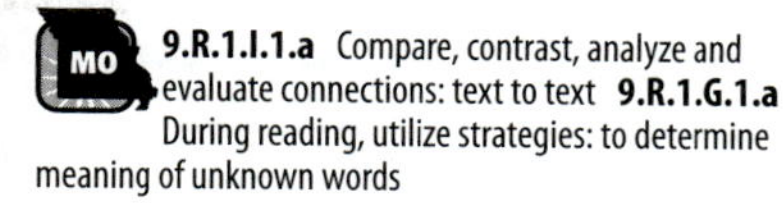

9.R.1.I.1.a Compare, contrast, analyze and evaluate connections: text to text **9.R.1.G.1.a** During reading, utilize strategies: to determine meaning of unknown words

"Dear Juliet": Seeking Succor from a Veteran of Love / *from* The Juliet Club

Practicing the Standards

Informational Text and Vocabulary

1. Which of the following is a **primary source** that might tell you more about the Club di Giulietta?
   - **A** A history book about Italy
   - **B** A copy of *Romeo and Juliet*
   - **C** A biography of Shakespeare
   - **D** A journal kept by the club's founder

2. Of the following, which is the *only* **primary source**?
   - **A** A textbook
   - **B** An interview
   - **C** A magazine article
   - **D** A newspaper article

3. What **secondary source** might give Dinitia Smith more useful information for her article?
   - **A** A textbook
   - **B** A literary essay
   - **C** An encyclopedia
   - **D** A guidebook of Verona

4. **Primary sources** are sometimes unreliable because they —
   - **A** may describe facts rather than opinions
   - **B** express the viewpoint of only one person
   - **C** give a broad view of the subject
   - **D** are objective

5. What is the *best* definition of *collaborate*?
   - **A** Alter
   - **B** Challenge
   - **C** Assist
   - **D** Cooperate

6. When something is *vital*, it is —
   - **A** interesting
   - **B** varied
   - **C** crucial
   - **D** expensive

7. Someone standing on a *precipice* is —
   - **A** in a line
   - **B** curious
   - **C** in danger
   - **D** sick

8. Which is the *best* synonym for *missives*?
   - **A** Letters
   - **B** Offices
   - **C** Tourists
   - **D** Requests

Writing Focus Constructed Response

What information do you learn in the article, the secondary source, that you don't learn in the letter, the primary source? Why do you think Dinitia Smith chose to include primary sources in her article? Explain, and give details to support your ideas.

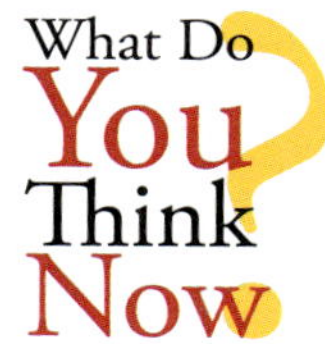

In what way does the character of Juliet help the people who write to her at the Juliet Club?

Literary Skills Review

Drama **Directions:** Read the following passage. Then, read and respond to the questions that follow.

from Barefoot in the Park by **Neil Simon**

Here's the climactic scene, Act II, Scene 2, of Neil Simon's comedy Barefoot in the Park. *As the scene opens, a young couple—Corie and Paul—have just returned from a late evening with Corie's widowed mother and their colorful next-door neighbor. This neighbor is a gourmet, and he has taken Paul, Corie, and her mother to an unusual restaurant on Staten Island, in New York City. Now he is accompanying Corie's mother home to New Jersey. Corie has had a wonderful evening; Paul has not had a good time at all.*

Corie. What are you so angry about, Paul?

Paul (*crossing to the closet*). I just told you. I felt terrible for your mother. (*He gets the wallet out of his jacket pocket.*)

Corie (*following after him to the front of the couch*). Why? Where is she at this very minute? Alone with probably the most attractive man she's ever met. Don't tell me *that* doesn't beat . . . hair curlers and *The Late Late Show*.

Paul (*crossing onto bedroom landing*). Oh, I can just hear it now. What sparkling conversation. He's probably telling her about a chicken cacciatore he once cooked for the High Lama of Tibet, and she's sitting there shoving pink pills in her mouth.

Corie (*taking her coat from the couch and putting it on the armchair at right*). You can never tell what people talk about when they're alone.

Paul. I don't understand how you can be so unconcerned about this. (*He goes into the bedroom.*)

Corie (*moving to the stairs*). Unconcerned . . . I'm plenty concerned. Do you think I'm going to get one wink of sleep until that phone rings tomorrow? I'm scared to death for my mother. But I'm grateful there's finally the opportunity for something to be scared about . . . (*She moves right, then turns back.*) What I'm really concerned about is you!

Paul (*bursts out of the bedroom, nearly slamming through the door*). Me? Me?

Corie. I'm beginning to wonder if you're capable of *having* a good time.

Paul. Why? Because I like to wear my gloves in the winter?

Corie. No. Because there isn't the least bit of adventure in you. Do you know what you are? You're a Watcher. There are Watchers in this world and there are Do-ers. And the Watchers sit around watching the Do-ers do. Well, tonight you watched and I did.

Paul (*moves down the stairs to* CORIE). Yeah . . . Well, it was harder to watch what you did than it was for you to *do* what I was watching. (*He goes back up the stairs to the landing.*)

Corie. You won't let your hair down for a minute? You couldn't even relax for one night. Boy, Paul, sometimes you act like a . . . a . . .

(*She gets her shoes from under the couch.*)

Paul (*stopping on the landing*). What . . . ? A stuffed shirt?

Corie (*drops the shoes on the couch*). I didn't say that.

Paul. That's what you're implying.

Corie (*moves to the right armchair and begins to take off her jewelry*). That's what you're anticipating. I didn't say you're a stuffed shirt. But you are extremely proper and dignified.

Paul. I'm proper and dignified? (*He moves to* CORIE.) When . . . ? When was I proper and dignified? . . .

Corie. Always. You're always dressed right, you always look right, you always say the right things. You're very close to being perfect.

Paul (*hurt to the quick*). That's . . . that's a *rotten* thing to say.

Corie (*moves to* PAUL). I have never seen you without a jacket. I always feel like such a slob compared to you. Before we were married, I was sure you slept with a tie.

Paul. No, no. Just for very *formal* sleeps.

Corie. You can't even walk into a candy store and ask the lady for a Tootsie Roll. (*Playing the scene out, she moves down to right side of the couch.*) You've got to walk up to the counter and point at it and say, "I'll have that thing in the brown-and-white wrapper."

Paul (*moving to the bedroom door*). That's ridiculous.

Corie. And you're not. That's just the trouble. (*She crosses to the foot of the stairs.*) Like Thursday night. You wouldn't walk barefoot with me in Washington Square Park. Why not?

Paul (*moving to the head of the stairs*). Very simple answer. It was seventeen degrees.

Corie (*moves back to the chair and continues taking down her hair*). Exactly. That's very sensible and logical. Except it isn't any fun.

Paul (*moves down the stairs to the couch*). You know, maybe I *am* too proper and dignified for you. Maybe you would have been happier with someone a little more colorful and flamboyant . . . like the Greek! (*He starts back to the bedroom.*)

Corie. Well, he'd be a lot more laughs than a stuffed shirt.

Paul (*turns back on the landing*). Oh, oh . . . I thought you said I wasn't.

Corie. Well, you are now.

Paul (*reflectively*). I'm not going to listen to this . . . I'm not going to listen . . . (*He starts for the bedroom.*) I've got a case in court in the morning.

Corie (*moves left*). Where are you going?

Paul. To sleep.

Corie. *Now?* How can you sleep now?

Paul (*steps up on the bed and turns back, leaning on the door jamb*). I'm going to close my eyes and count knichis.° Good night!

Corie. You can't go to sleep now. We're having a fight.

° **knichis** (NEE cheez): unusual appetizer they had eaten with dinner.

Paul. *You* have the fight. When you're through, turn off the lights. *(He turns back into the bedroom.)*

Corie. Ooh, that gets me insane. You can even control your emotions.

Paul (*storms out to the head of the stairs*). Look, I'm just as upset as you are. . . . (*He controls himself.*) But when I get hungry, I eat. And when I get tired, I sleep. You eat and sleep, too. Don't deny it, I've seen you . . .

Corie (*moves right with a grand gesture*). Not in the middle of a crisis.

Paul. What crisis? We're just yelling a little.

Corie. You don't consider this a crisis? Our whole marriage hangs in the balance.

Paul (*sits on the steps*). It does? When did that happen?

Corie. Just now. It's suddenly very clear that you and I have absolutely *nothing* in common.

Paul. Why? Because I won't walk barefoot in the park in winter? . . .

Corie (*seething*). Don't oversimplify this. I'm angry. Can't you see that?

Paul (*brings his hands to his eyes, peers at her through imaginary binoculars, and then looks at his watch*). Corie, it's two-fifteen. If I can fall asleep in about half an hour, I can get about five hours' sleep. I'll call you from court tomorrow, and we can fight over the phone. (*He gets up and moves to the bedroom.*)

Corie. You will *not* go to sleep. You will stay here and fight to save our marriage.

Paul (*in the doorway*). If our marriage hinges on breathing fish balls and pooflapoo pie, it's not worth saving. . . . I am now going to crawl into our tiny little single bed. If you care to join me, we will be sleeping from left to right tonight. (*He goes into the bedroom and slams the door.*)

Corie. You won't discuss it . . . You're *afraid* to discuss it . . . I married a coward!! . . . (*She takes a shoe from the couch and throws it at the bedroom door.*)

Paul (*opens the door*). Corie, would you bring in a pail? The closet's dripping.

Corie. Ohh, I hate you! I really, really hate you!

Paul (*storms to the head of the stairs*). Corie, there is one thing I learned in court. Be careful when you're tired and angry. You might say something you will soon regret. I-am-now-tired-and-angry.

Corie. And a coward.

Paul (*comes down the stairs to her at right of the couch*). And I will now say something I will soon regret . . . OK, Corie, maybe you're right. Maybe we have nothing in common. Maybe we rushed into this marriage a little too fast. Maybe Love isn't enough. Maybe two people should have to take more than a blood test. Maybe they should be checked for common sense, understanding, and emotional maturity.

Corie (*that hurt*). All right . . . Why don't you get it passed in the Supreme Court? Only those couples bearing a letter from their psychiatrists proving they're well adjusted will be permitted to be married.

Paul. You're impossible.

9.R.2.A.1 Analyze and evaluate the text features in grade-level text **9.R.2.C.1.d** Use details from text(s): to evaluate the effect of author's style *Also covered* **9.R.2.C.1.b; 9.R.1.F.1.c; 9.R.1.G.1.g; 9.R.1.H.1.a**

Corie. You're unbearable.

Paul. You belong in a nursery school.

Corie. It's a lot more fun than the Home for the Fuddy Duddies.

Paul (*reaches out his hand to her*). All right, Corie, let's not get . . .

Corie. Don't you touch me . . . Don't you touch me . . .

---

1. Corie is mad at Paul because he —

A insulted her mother

B didn't like the restaurant

C has a court case in the morning

D doesn't know how to have fun

9.R.1.G.1.g

2. Paul describes Corie's character as —

A impossible

B charming

C mature

D serious

9.R.2.C.1.b

3. Because *Barefoot in the Park* is a **comedy,** you can predict that by the end of the play —

A Paul and Corie will resolve their differences

B Paul and Corie will get divorced

C there will be a funny scene with the neighbor

D Corie's mother will move in with them

9.R.1.F.1.c

4. If the play were a **tragedy** instead of a comedy, it might end with —

A Corie's mother getting married

B the death of Paul and Corie

C Paul and Corie moving to another apartment

D Paul's winning his case in court

9.R.1.F.1.c

5. This excerpt from the play consists of —

A monologues

B narration

C dialogue

D asides

9.R.2.A.1

6. Which of the following stage directions tells you something about the **scene design**?

A *"hurt to the quick"*

B *"crossing onto bedroom landing"*

C *"He controls himself."*

D *"reaches out his hand to her"*

9.R.2.A.1

7. If this scene were followed by a **soliloquy,** it might be delivered by —

A Paul, telling Corie how he really feels about her

B Paul and Corie, apologizing to each other for getting so angry

C Corie alone, talking about how much she loves Paul

D Corie's mother, telling Paul and Corie what a good time she had

9.R.2.A.1

Constructed Response

8. Although the playwright presents a comical argument in this excerpt, what serious topic does he also want the audience to think about? Use evidence from the play excerpt to support your opinion.

9.R.1.H.1.a

Informational Skills Review

Primary and Secondary Sources **Directions:** Read the following encyclopedia article and personal recollection. Then, read and respond to the questions that follow.

Kennedy's Assassination by Eric Sevareid

John F. Kennedy was shot to death by an assassin on November 22, 1963, as he rode through the streets of Dallas, Texas. His death continued the unhappy coincidence that, since William H. Harrison, every American president elected in a year ending in "0" had died while in office. These presidents and the years of election were Harrison (1840), Abraham Lincoln (1860), James A. Garfield (1880), William McKinley (1900), Warren G. Harding (1920), and Franklin D. Roosevelt (1940). Only one president elected in a year ending in "0" has not died in office. That president was Ronald Reagan, who was elected in 1980. Kennedy was succeeded by Lyndon B. Johnson, the first Southerner to become president since Andrew Johnson succeeded Lincoln when Lincoln was assassinated in 1865.

The new president. Television and radio flashed the news of the shooting to a shocked world. Vice President Johnson raced to the hospital and remained until Kennedy died. Then, he went to the airport where the presidential plane waited. Mrs. Kennedy and the coffin holding her husband's body arrived later. At 2:39 P.M., U.S. District Judge Sarah T. Hughes administered the oath of office to Johnson, who became the 36th president of the United States. As Johnson took the oath in the airplane, he was flanked by his wife and by Mrs. Kennedy.

Then the plane carrying the new chief executive and his wife, the body of the dead president, and the late president's widow returned to Washington. When the plane arrived, Johnson told the nation: "This is a sad time for all people. We have suffered a loss that cannot be weighed. . . ."

The world mourns. The sudden death of the young and vigorous American president shocked the world. Kennedy's body was brought back to the White House and placed in the East Room for 24 hours. On the Sunday after the assassination, the president's flag-draped coffin was carried to the Capitol Rotunda to lie in state.° Throughout the day and night, hundreds of thousands of people filed past the guarded casket. Representatives from over 90 countries attended the funeral on November 25.

Kennedy was buried with full military honors at Arlington National cemetery across the Potomac River from Washington, D.C. At the close of the funeral service, Mrs. Kennedy lighted an "eternal flame" to burn over the president's grave. In one of his first acts, President Johnson named the National Aeronautics and

° **Capitol Rotunda to lie in state:** The Capitol Rotunda is the round room beneath the dome of the Capitol, the building in which the U.S. Congress meets in Washington, D.C. *Lie in state* means "be displayed to the public before burial."

Space Administration installation in Florida the John F. Kennedy Space Center.

Other public buildings and geographical sites throughout the world were named for President Kennedy. Congress voted funds for the John F. Kennedy Center for the Performing Arts in Washington, D.C. Great Britain made one acre of ground permanent United States territory as part of a Kennedy memorial at Runnymede. In 1979, the John F. Kennedy Library opened in Boston.

—from "John Fitzgerald Kennedy," *The World Book Encyclopedia* (2001)

For Me, It Was a Dramatic Day

by **Pierre Salinger**

Pierre Salinger, President Kennedy's press secretary, remembers where he was and how he felt when he heard the news of Kennedy's assassination.

For me, it was a dramatic day. I had left the White House on November 19 to accompany six members of JFK's cabinet[1] to an economic conference in Tokyo. President Kennedy had asked me to join the trip to organize his visit to Tokyo, planned for February 1964. This would have been the first visit by an American president to Japan since the end of World War II.

We stopped in Honolulu[2] for three days for an important meeting on the Vietnam crisis. Early in the morning of November 22, the White House plane headed for Tokyo. I was in the back of the plane reading the economic papers when suddenly somebody came and told me the six cabinet secretaries had to see me. They were in the office in the front of the plane. When I walked in, it was grim. They handed me a wire bulletin[3] saying Kennedy had been shot.

The plane turned around and headed back to Honolulu, and I was instructed to take over the communications system to the White House and find out what had happened. When I connected with the White House, there was

1. **cabinet:** The president's cabinet includes the heads of the various departments of the executive branch, such as the departments of State, Treasury, and Defense.
2. **Honolulu** (hahn uh LOO loo): capital of Hawaii.
3. **wire bulletin:** news bulletin from a wire service, an organization that transmits news stories to newspapers and radio and television stations by telegraph or electronic means.

Informational Skills Review CONTINUED

total confusion. For many minutes nothing was coming through clearly. About a half hour after the plane had turned around, I heard in my ear: "Wayside. Standby." Wayside was my code name. About every thirty seconds for the next five minutes, I heard the same thing. Then suddenly came a new message. "Wayside. Lancer is dead." Lancer was the code name for President Kennedy.

I was destroyed. I so admired and liked JFK. I had a feeling that not only was he lost, but that my life was lost.

When we reached Washington, a car took me to the White House. JFK's body had just arrived in the East Room and there was a short prayer service. Jackie Kennedy came up to me after the prayer and said I had had a terrible day and should sleep in the White House.

I went upstairs where I talked with colleagues like Ken O'Donnell and Larry O'Brien until five in the morning. Finally, I went to sleep.

At 7 A.M. the phone rang. I heard the operator say: "Mr. Salinger, the president wants to talk to you." For an instant, I thought I'd had a nightmare. Then, on the phone I heard: "Pierre, this is Lyndon."[4] It was over. It was now clear to me that Kennedy was dead.

—from *Where Were You When President Kennedy Was Shot?*

4. **Lyndon:** Lyndon B. Johnson, Kennedy's vice president, who became president after Kennedy was killed.

1. Why is "Kennedy's Assassination" a valuable source for research?

A It is written for an audience made up of experts.

B Its purpose is to show why Kennedy was a great president.

C It reveals Lyndon B. Johnson's opinion of the assassination.

D It presents a factual, historical perspective on the assassination and its aftermath.

9.IL.1.B.1.a

2. What is the tone of "Kennedy's Assassination"?

A Dramatic

B Objective

C Sorrowful

D Enraged

9.R.3.B.1.d

3. Which statement is the *most* accurate evaluation of "Kennedy's Assassination"?

A It is a primary source because it is a firsthand account of one person's experiences.

B It is a secondary source because the author did not actually witness the assassination.

C It is a secondary source because it is a strictly factual description of an event.

D It is a primary source because it includes only opinions and no facts.

9.IL.1.B.1

9.R.1.I.1.a Compare, contrast, analyze and evaluate connections: text to text *Also covered* **9.R.1.H.1.d; 9.R.3.B.1.a; 9.R.3.B.1.d; 9.R.3.C.1.c; 9.R.3.C.1.d; 9.IL.1.B.1**

4. The intended audience for "Kennedy's Assassination" is *most* likely —

A Kennedy's family

B a kindergarten class

C a close friend of the author

D the general public

9.R.1.H.1.d

5. What is the tone of "For Me, It Was a Dramatic Day"?

A Instructional

B Somber

C Objective

D Frantic

9.R.3.B.1.d

6. Which statement is the *most* accurate evaluation of "For Me, It Was a Dramatic Day"?

A It is a primary source because it is a firsthand account of one person's experiences.

B It is a secondary source because the author did not actually witness the assassination.

C It is a secondary source because it is a strictly factual description of an event.

D It is a primary source because it includes only opinions and no facts.

9.IL.1.B.1

7. Which point in "For Me, It Was a Dramatic Day" can be verified by reading "Kennedy's Assassination"?

A Kennedy's code name was Lancer.

B Kennedy had planned to visit Japan.

C Kennedy's body was placed in the East Room in the White House.

D Pierre Salinger communicated with the White House about Kennedy's death.

9.R.1.I.1.a

8. Which of the following sentences from "For Me, It Was a Dramatic Day" is a **factual statement**?

A "This would have been the first visit by an American president to Japan since the end of World War II."

B "For me, it was a dramatic day."

C "When I walked in, it was grim."

D "I had a feeling that not only was he lost, but that my life was lost."

9.R.3.C.1.c

9. The *main* **purpose** of "For Me, It Was a Dramatic Day" is to —

A reveal the author's sense of shock and loss at the news of Kennedy's death

B show that Lyndon B. Johnson effectively took control of the country

C warn that the government could easily be thrown into confusion

D emphasize the author's personal relationship with Kennedy and his family

9.R.3.C.1.d

Constructed Response

10. Examine the two sources, "Kennedy's Assassination" and "For Me, It Was a Dramatic Day," and explain how they differ. How might each source be used in a research paper about John F. Kennedy's assassination?

9.R.1.I.1.a *9.IL.1.B.1*

Vocabulary Skills Review

Multiple-Meaning Words

Directions: Choose the answer in which the italicized word is used in the same way it is used in the sentence from *The Frog Prince*.

1. "I mean of course we all know they grow *wild*."

A The cheering audience was *wild* about the film.

B "Green hair? What a *wild* idea!"

C A *wild* wind rattled the windows.

D The gardener warned us not to eat *wild* mushrooms.

9.R.1.E.1.b

2. "You *pick* 'em out here and it's so personal."

A "Don't *pick* that scab!"

B The farmer took a *pick* to the dry, packed earth.

C The princess had her *pick* of suitors.

D The guitarist plucked the strings with a *pick*.

9.R.1.E.1.b

3. "I understand completely, you're like all the *rest*."

A Bill graduated in the spring with the *rest* of the class.

B *Rest* assured that I will finish the project by noon.

C *Rest* the glass on the table.

D She felt better after a day of *rest*.

9.R.1.E.1.b

4. "What's in the air, if you get my *drift*?"

A The blizzard caused snow to *drift* against the front door.

B A *drift* of barbecue smoke excited the hungry hikers.

C Paulo couldn't speak German, but he got the *drift* of what the guide said.

D "Stay on the trail; don't *drift* away from the group!"

9.R.1.E.1.b

5. "I think that I've had enough *fresh* air today."

A The author waited a month so he could read his story with *fresh* eyes.

B The baby sitter was *fresh* out of patience with the children.

C "I could not believe how *fresh* that salesperson was!"

D The vegetables at the farmer's market are always *fresh*.

9.R.1.E.1.b

6. "For You, My *Fair* Patricia."

A The weather was cool and *fair*.

B "I won that race *fair* and square!"

C The next antique *fair* is in July.

D *My Fair Lady* is a popular musical.

9.R.1.E.1.b

7. "A *Blue* Flower's best for Spring."

A "Do you feel sad and *blue*?"

B Her father, Lord Higgelly, is a *blue* blood.

C He got a phone call from out of the *blue*.

D Jeans are often made from *blue* denim.

9.R.1.E.1.b

8. "Well, these are *hard* times, and I think he feels that we all have to stick together."

A Working in the coal mines is *hard* work.

B The wood was too *hard* to be drilled.

C A *hard* rain fell during the storm.

D The test questions were not too *hard*.

9.R.1.E.1.b

9. "How are you, why don't you sit down a *spell*."

A The wizard cast a *spell* on the town.

B "Must I *spell* the answer out for you?"

C After the storm we had a *spell* of good weather.

D You can *spell* that word two ways.

9.R.1.E.1.b

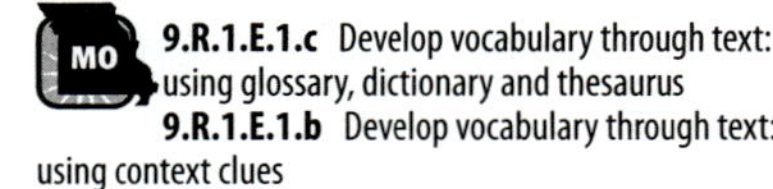
9.R.1.E.1.c Develop vocabulary through text: using glossary, dictionary and thesaurus
9.R.1.E.1.b Develop vocabulary through text: using context clues

10. "We're in a little *bit* of a quandary, but I think I can pull it out."

A The family went through a *bit* of trouble.

B Tyrone *bit* hungrily into the sandwich.

C He was angry, and his words *bit.*

D The comedian did his famous impression *bit.*

9.R.1.E.1.b

11. "I laid out a small *patch* behind the hut."

A My grandfather sewed a *patch* on my jeans.

B "*Patch* the tire before we drive."

C Every cook should have a *patch* of herbs.

D The pirate wore a *patch* over his left eye.

9.R.1.E.1.b

12. "You have *ties* here."

A She *ties* a bow around the present.

B Traffic *ties* up cars at this intersection.

C Kisha loves California, but her *ties* to Michigan are strong.

D His slide into home plate *ties* the score.

9.R.1.E.1.b

13. "I want to cross the *border* before it gets dark."

A I crocheted a lace *border* on her sweater.

B His outbursts in the court *border* on insanity.

C The *border* between the countries is guarded.

D A *border* of pansies grows along the driveway.

9.R.1.E.1.b

14. "I refused a request that you made, at that time I thought that I was within my *rights.*"

A To get to the bank, make two *rights* and a left.

B The hero *rights* wrongs.

C Prisoners have *rights* and must be treated fairly.

D The boxer threw a few *rights* and knocked out his opponent.

9.R.1.E.1.b

Academic Vocabulary

Directions: Test your knowledge of the italicized Academic Vocabulary words by choosing the correct answer.

15. When you follow *conventions* for writing a script, you —

A create a new format

B avoid formatting

C repeat important formats

D follow a traditional format

9.R.1.E.1.b

16. When you *embody* a character, you —

A embrace it

B draw it

C portray it

D study it

9.R.1.E.1.b

Read On

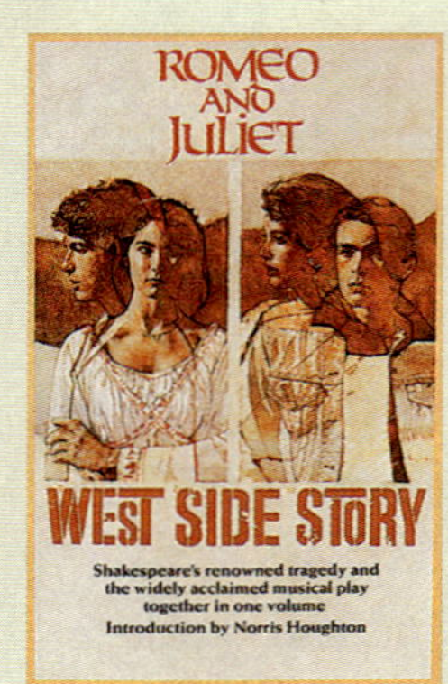

PLAY

West Side Story

Tony and Maria are in love, but they come from different social worlds—Tony is Italian American, and Maria is Puerto Rican. Add to their problems the fact that Tony is the former ringleader of the Jets—a tough street-fighting gang—and that Maria's brother, Bernardo, is the leader of the equally fearsome Sharks. If the story line sounds familiar, it should: This musical takes its cue from *Romeo and Juliet*. This updated spin on Shakespeare's tale of star-crossed lovers is set in New York City in the 1950s.

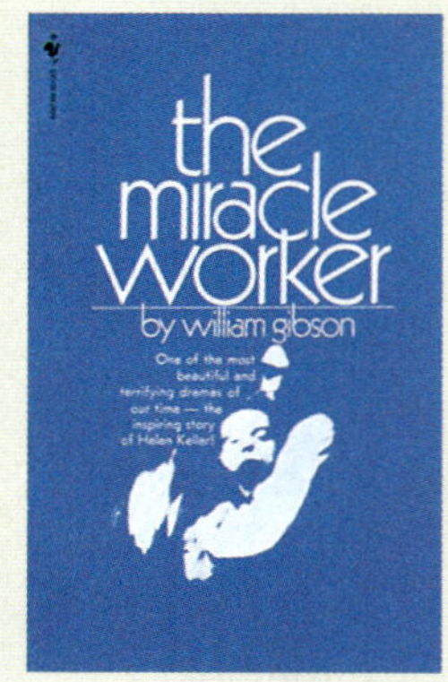

PLAY

The Miracle Worker

Blind, hearing impaired, and unable to speak, six-year-old Helen was an angry prisoner of her own body. A teacher, Annie Sullivan, was asked to help—if help was possible. Slowly but surely the patient instructor taught Helen to "see" with her hands, to learn sign language, and to open herself to a world beyond darkness and silence. William Gibson's play stands as a classic story of two amazing women—one a student, the other a teacher.

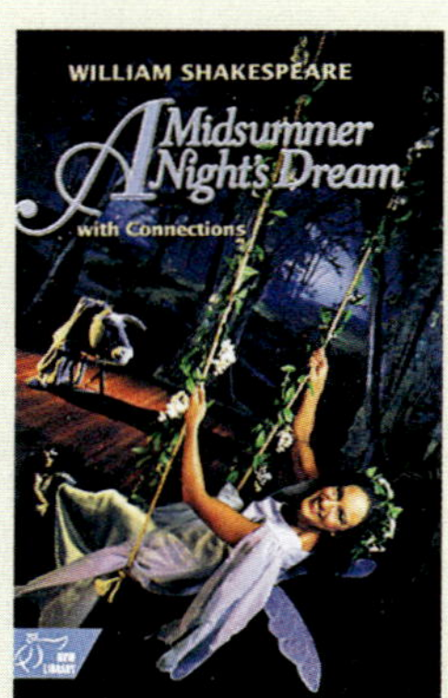

PLAY

A Midsummer Night's Dream

A wedding, an argument, a series of bungling rehearsals, and misfortunes in love—these four plot elements are woven together in this William Shakespeare comedy. This play, which some critics consider Shakespeare's funniest and most imaginative, features characters ranging from fairies and fools to a king and a queen—all of whose paths intersect in surprising ways.

PLAYS

Famous Stories for Performance

This work includes stage plays and teleplays as well as some famous tales adapted for performance with a new dramatic spin. Here you'll find comedy (*Pyramus and Thisby* by William Shakespeare), a tragic true story (*Brian's Song* by William Blinn), and a legend to make the hair on the back of your neck stand up (*The Legend of Sleepy Hollow* by Washington Irving).

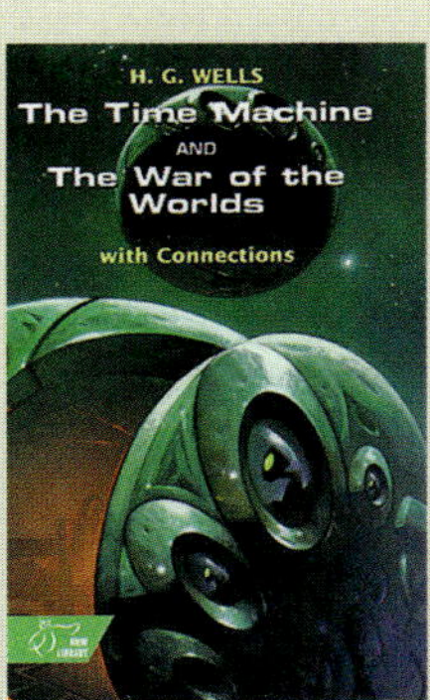

FICTION

The Time Machine and the War of the Worlds

In 1938, thousands of panic-stricken Americans took to the streets to flee a Martian invasion that they had heard about on the radio. What they actually were hearing was *Invasion from Mars,* a radio drama based on *The War of the Worlds,* a novel by H. G. Wells. Now, in one book you can read the novel and the radio script. Also included is a CD of the original radio broadcast read by the famous actor Orson Welles and of his press conference the next day.

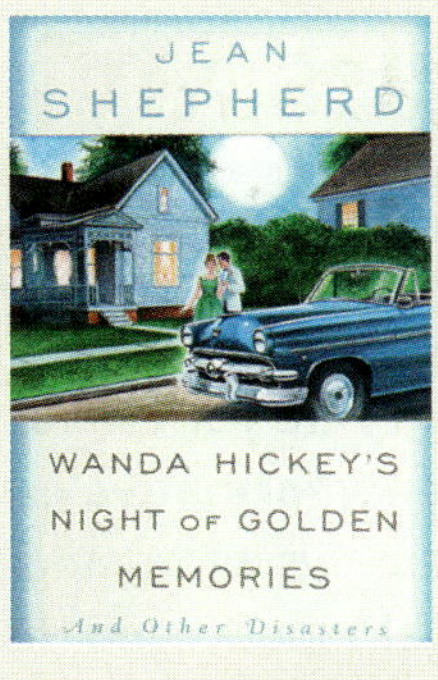

FICTION

Wanda Hickey's Night of Golden Memories

It's prom night, and Wanda Hickey is aglow—with sweat, according to the humorist Jean Shepherd. The short stories in Shepherd's collection *Wanda Hickey's Night of Golden Memories and Other Disasters* uncover what's awkward, weird, even disastrous about growing up—and all for laughs. Join Wanda and friends—like Ollie Hopnoodle, Josephine Cosnowski, and Daphne Bigelow—as Shepherd leads them through romance and murder and, of course, to the Junior Prom.

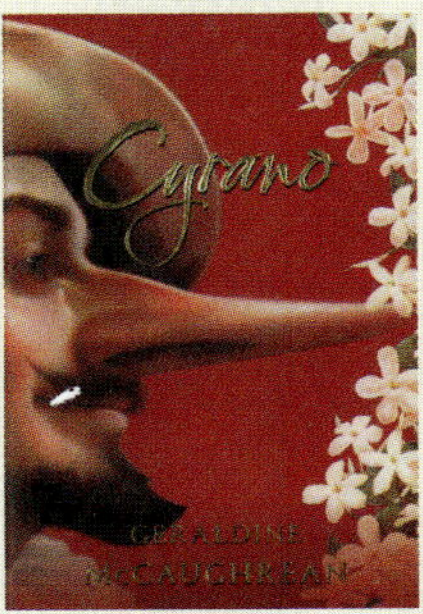

FICTION

Cyrano

Cyrano de Bergerac is a sharp-witted soldier and a hopeless romantic. He has just one flaw, an unmistakably large nose. Having romanticized the lovely, but taken Roxane from afar, he writes her love letters on behalf of the handsome Christian. What will happen when Roxane finds out that it is not Christian but Cyrano whose words she has fallen in love with? Geraldine McCaughrean transforms Edmond Rostand's beloved play, *Cyrano de Bergerac,* into a funny, romantic, and action packed novel, titled *Cyrano*.

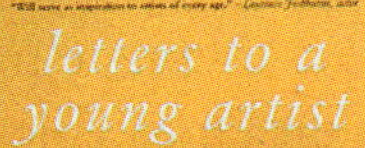

NONFICTION

Letters to a Young Artist

If you dream of one day pursuing a career in the arts, you will want to read Anna Deavere Smith's *Letters to a Young Artist*. Smith is a successful writer, actor, and director, who shares the knowledge she has gained along the way. The book is a series of letters written to BZ, a fictional teenager in need of a mentor. Smith offers BZ ideas on artistic growth; tips for negotiating with agents; and advice on overcoming procrastination, jealousy, and low self-esteem.

Learn It Online
Visit NovelWise for tips on studying fiction:
go.hrw.com
L9-991
Go

Writing Workshop

Informative Essay

Write with a Purpose

Write an informative essay about a topic that interests you. Your **purpose** is to inform your readers about a topic. Your **audience** is your classmates, teacher, and anyone else who might like to know more about your topic.

A Good Informative Essay

- presents a main idea, or thesis
- presents accurate and complete information
- supports ideas with evidence, including facts and details
- follows a clear organizational structure
- presents information in an objective fashion, without giving the writer's opinions

See page 1000 for complete rubric.

Think as a Reader/Writer

In this unit, you've read informative essays by writers who use evidence to support their assertions. What topics are you interested in, and what would you like to explain to others? In an **informative essay,** you develop your understanding of a topic and share this information with others. As shown in the following excerpt from "Shakespeare and His Theater: A Perfect Match" (p. 800) by Robert Anderson, informative essays use clear writing and evidence to engage and inform readers.

It has been said that all you need for a theater is "two planks and a passion." Since Shakespeare's time "the planks" (the stage) have undergone various changes. First, the part of the stage that projected into the yard grew narrower, and the small curtained inner stage grew larger, until there developed what is called the **proscenium stage.** Here there is no outer stage; there is only the inner stage, and a large curtain separates it from the audience. As a result, watching a play on a proscenium stage is like looking inside a window or inside a picture frame. This is the stage most of us know today. It has been standard for well over a hundred years.

But recently we have seen a reversal of this design. Now more and more theaters (especially university and regional theaters) are building "thrust" stages, or arena stages. In this kind of theater, the audience once again sits on three or even four sides of the stage.

A quote attracts the reader's attention. The next sentence introduces the **main idea.**

Anderson **defines** the theatrical term—***proscenium***.

The phrase "as a result" introduces the **effect** of the new stage shape.

Facts appear in **chronological order.**

Think About the Professional Model

With a partner, discuss the following questions about the model:

1. What information does Anderson provide to explain what "'the planks'" means?
2. How does the writer use both chronological order and cause and effect to organize these paragraphs? Why does he use both?

Reader/Writer Notebook

Use your **RWN** to complete the activities for this workshop.

MO 9.W.1.A.1.a Follow a writing process to: appropriate prewriting strategies as needed 9.W.2.C.1.d Compose text with: cohesive devices 9.W.2.B.1.a Compose text with: strong controlling idea 9.W.3.A.1.a Compose a variety of texts: using narrative, descriptive, expository, and/or persuasive features

Prewriting

Choose a Topic

Interview yourself to discover topics for your essay. Think about subjects that interest you. Do you have a favorite hobby or sport? Perhaps there are skills you would like to learn or a person or current event that interests you. Ask yourself these questions to focus your search:

- What are some topics about which I already know something?
- About what topic would I enjoy learning more?
- What topics might interest my audience?
- What information can I present in an objective fashion, without giving my own opinion?

Explore Your Topic

Once you have decided on a topic that interests you, create a chart like the one below. This chart will help you determine what you already know and what you need to learn about your topic.

Subject	Research
What do I already know about the topic?	[Jot down what you already know here—include where you learned your information.]
What do I want to learn?	[Note your questions here.]
What does my audience need to know?	[Think about basic facts your audience needs to have in order to understand your information. Write questions that target that information here.]
What might my audience want to know?	[Think about the kinds of questions your audience might have after learning the basic facts. Write those questions here.]

Think About Purpose and Audience

Remember your purpose and audience as you plan. Your **purpose** is to share what you already know and will learn about your topic. Your **audience** might be students or adults. Think about what they might already know about your topic, what you need to tell them, and what will interest them the most.

Idea Starters

- today's musical styles
- a career choice
- the cause and effect of a local environmental problem
- the evolution of a specific piece of technology or software
- the history of a sport or a game

Peer Review Tip

Ask a classmate or two to look at your ideas and give you feedback on which topics they would like to learn more about.

Your Turn

Choose and Explore Your Topic List three or four **topic ideas** in your **RWN** and choose one for your essay. Then, create a chart like the one on this page to explore your topic. Make your answers as specific as possible; they will help you stay on target. They will also help you decide when you have enough information to begin writing. Keep your **purpose** and **audience** in mind too.

Learn It Online

Check out the interactive writer's model online for another look at an informative essay:

go.hrw.com L9-993 

Informative Essay

Writing Tip

If you find something especially amusing or intriguing about your topic, use a red pen when you write it down in your notes. You might want to use this fact to make the opening or closing of your essay especially interesting.

Write Your Thesis

To focus your ideas about your topic and your search for information about it, write a thesis statement. This **thesis statement** should indicate your main idea about your topic. One student, for example, was very interested in poverty in the United States. She developed the following thesis statement to guide the development of her paper. She can revise this thesis statement later as she drafts and revises her essay.

> Thesis Statement: Federal programs have changed how the United States combats poverty and its effects.

Gather Information to Support Your Thesis

To make your explanation credible, or believable, to your readers, you'll need to support your thesis statement with examples, anecdotes, facts, and statistics. Ask yourself the following questions as you gather information to support your thesis:

- *What kinds of sources are best for my topic?* If you're writing about a current event, select up-to-date sources.
- *What sources specifically relate to my topic?* Many specialized sources provide helpful information about a specific topic, such as books on environmental issues.
- *What Internet sources can I trust for accurate, reliable information about my topic?* Use Web sites that are recognized as being authoritative, such as online encyclopedias and reputable news organizations.
- *What expert can I interview about my topic?* You may know someone who is knowledgeable about your topic and can provide helpful first-hand information.

Study the following chart. Once you have gathered your information, organize it using one of the following structures:

Structures for Organizing Support

Chronological Order	Cause and Effect Structure	Topical Structure
Thesis 1. First event 2. Second event 3. Third event, and so on	1. Focus on causes: Thesis → cause 1, cause 2, cause 3 2. Focus on effects: Thesis → effect 1, effect 2, effect 3 3. Cause-effect chain: Thesis → cause → cause/effect → cause/effect → final effect. [Notice how each effect then becomes a cause.]	1. Supporting idea for thesis with example, fact, or detail 1 2. Supporting idea for thesis with example, fact, or detail 2 3. Supporting idea for thesis with example, fact, or detail 3

Your Turn

Write and Support Your Thesis Write your thesis statement, and then gather information to support it. Collect notes in your **RWN** or on individual note cards. Using note cards can help you try different arrangements of facts as you begin to organize your thoughts. Keep your purpose and audience in mind as you collect information.

Drafting

Follow the Framework

Keep your thesis, supporting information, and organizational structure in mind as you begin drafting your informative essay. As you draft, remember that effective informative writing depends on the clear presentation of information and ideas. Following the **Framework** at the right will help you achieve your purpose.

Framework for an Informative Essay

Introduction:
- Begin with an unusual fact or idea that will grab your reader's attention.
- Give any necessary background information.
- Include your thesis statement.

Body:
- Discuss the first idea that supports your thesis; discuss each other idea that supports your thesis, using the organizational structure you've chosen.
- Present the information you have learned, defining any terms your readers may not know.
- Keep your audience in mind, and adapt your word choice accordingly.

Conclusion:
- Remind your readers of your thesis.

Include Transitions

Good writers want to communicate information as clearly as possible. Writers leave signposts for their readers to follow so that they don't become confused. As you write, lead your readers through the essay with **transitional words and phrases**—specific words and phrases that will help readers follow your organizational strategy.

Chronological	Cause and Effect	Topical
first, later, then, eventually, before, after, finally, now	because, since, therefore, as a result, consequently, thus, for this reason	also, and, in addition, similarly, too, mainly, first, last, then

Transitional elements will help the reader follow the organizational plan you choose. Because they help you connect ideas from sentence to sentence, many transitional devices appear at the beginning of sentences.

Grammar Link **Punctuating Introductory Elements with Commas**

Punctuation can help your ideas and information flow clearly. Using commas to set off some introductory elements can make your writing smoother.

- You can use a comma after an introductory participial phrase.

  Returning to earlier practices, more and more theaters are building "thrust" stages, or arena stages.

- You can also use a comma after an introductory prepositional phrase.

  In this kind of theater, the audience once again sits on three or even four sides of the stage.

Learn more about using commas in the Language Handbook.

Writing Tip

Remember that in an informative essay you are not offering your opinion. Instead, you are conveying information. Avoid using sentences that begin with the words "In my opinion" or "I believe."

Your Turn

Draft Your Essay Follow your notes and organizational plan to create the first draft of your informative essay. As you draft, ask yourself:
- What does my audience need to know to understand this topic fully?
- How can I use transitional devices to help my reader follow the organizational structure of the essay? Which words are proper?

Peer Review

Review the chart at the right with a classmate. Then, read your draft aloud to him or her. Have your classmate take notes as you read. When you have finished reading aloud, allow your partner to offer suggestions about which sections work well and which could be improved. Repeat this process with your partner's essay.

Evaluating and Revising

Read and evaluate your informative essay at least twice to make sure you have covered the essentials of a good informative essay. Use the following chart as a guide to evaluating and revising your essay.

Informative Essay: Guidelines for Content and Organization

Evaluation Questions	Tips	Revision Techniques
1. Does the introduction catch the reader's attention?	**Underline** the attention-getting opening.	**Add** an appropriate anecdote, quotation, question, or fact.
2. Does the introduction include a clear statement of the main idea, or thesis, of the essay?	**Highlight** the thesis statement, or statement of the main idea.	**Add** a clear thesis statement that presents the main idea of the essay.
3. Do the paragraphs in the body support the thesis by providing facts, details, examples, and statistics?	**Put a star** by each idea that supports the thesis. **Put two stars** next to the information that supports each point.	**Add** supporting information, or **elaborate** on existing supporting information.
4. Is the essay well organized, using chronological order, cause and effect, or subtopics of the main topic?	**Label** the organizational technique. **Underline** the words that make the technique obvious. (For example, you might underline the word *because* if the strategy is cause and effect, or the word *first* if the strategy is chronological.)	**Rearrange** the information so that it follows a clear strategy. **Add** transitions that will help the reader follow ideas.
5. Are ideas connected by transitional words and phrases? Do they guide your readers through the information?	**Put parentheses** around transitional words and phrases.	**Add** transitional words and phrases to make clear the relationships between ideas.
6. Does the conclusion restate the thesis?	**Highlight** the sentence that restates the thesis.	**Add** a sentence restating the thesis.

Read this student draft, and notice the comments on its strengths as well as suggestions on how it could be improved.

Student Draft

Poverty in America

by Mary Keiser, Ashland Middle School

In 1964 President Lyndon Johnson declared war on poverty. In the more than forty years since then, the United States of America has spent seven trillion dollars to fight this war in our own land. Today there are still more than 37 million Americans who live in poverty. According to UNICEF, America has the second highest percentage of children in poverty in the developed world. Only Mexico rates higher than the United States in the number of citizens living below the poverty threshold. Three federal programs, Head Start, subsidized housing, and health care, have a positive influence on combating existing poverty and its long-lasting effects.

Mary uses surprising statistics to catch her readers' attention. Her introduction establishes the **topic** and **main idea** of her essay.

Created in 1965 to target children from birth to five years of age, the Head Start program strikes at a basic cause and result of poverty: the lack of prerequisite skills among preschool children. Poor children, who enter school without preschool educational programs, often have lower rates of high school completion and higher high school dropout rates than children from average or affluent homes.

In this paragraph, Mary provides background **details** about Head Start and gives information about how poverty affects education.

MINI-LESSON How to Add Specific Information

Mary's revision partner told her that she hadn't included enough information about the Head Start program. Mary had plenty of information she had not included in her draft. She consulted her notes and sources and decided to add more facts about the program. She also included the effect the program has on young children to enhance her cause-effect reasoning in the essay.

Mary's Revision

Created in 1965 to target children from birth to five years of age, the Head Start program strikes at a basic result of poverty: the lack of prerequisite skills among preschool children. ^*Head Start classes provide poor children with early instruction in the basic skills of reading and mathematics so that they can be ready to start school with their peers.* Poor children, who enter school without preschool educational programs like Head Start, have lower rates of high school completion and higher high school dropout rates than children from average or affluent homes.

Your Turn

Revise Your Draft Read your draft, and then ask yourself:

- Have I included enough specific information?
- What other notes and sources have information I could add to my draft?

Then, make revisions to your draft.

Informative Essay

In this paragraph, Mary gives **clear and accurate details and statistics,** and mentions the **source** of her information.

This paragraph introduces the connection between poverty and health, but the **evidence** is weak.

A striking quotation focuses Mary's **conclusion** on the importance of her issue and leaves readers with an emotional appeal.

Student Draft *continues*

Americans expect to have safe and affordable housing as a basic necessity of life. Without a decent place to live, people cannot be productive members of society. Children cannot learn and families cannot thrive. The U.S. Department of Housing and Urban Development website states that a worker earning a minimum wage salary cannot afford a two bedroom apartment at fair-market value in any city in the country. Out of 30 million households with housing problems, only 14.5 million qualify for government aid and only 4.1 million are receiving the aid that is available. The government currently has plans to expand community awareness of the availability of subsidized housing for America's poor.

Recent studies show that for every chronic health condition, for every disease, people who have lower incomes have a higher rate of illness and death. Those who have jobs are absent from work more frequently, losing income. Yet, it is also true that lots of Americans do not have health insurance and do not have access to preventative or routine care. Medicare and Medicaid are designed to meet the needs of America's poor.

"The moral test of society is how it ensures the needs of the most vulnerable, including those unable to provide for themselves and their families," said Reverend Larry Snyder, president of Catholic Charities USA. Without healthy and well-educated children, America will not have a bright future. We can meet the promise of the "war on poverty" declared so long ago. We have three successful federal programs that can help our nation's poor.

MINI-LESSON How to Make Information Credible

Mary used her facts, dates, and information well until her fourth paragraph. She failed to cite the source of her information and statistics that support her point about health care. She revised this paragraph to add specifics.

Mary's Revision of Paragraph Four

in The American Journal of Medicine

Recent studies ^ show that for every chronic health condition, for every disease, people who have lower incomes have a higher rate of illness and death. Those who have jobs are absent from work more frequently, losing income.

46 million

Yet, it is also true that ~~lots of~~ Americans do not have health insurance and do not have access to preventative or routine care. Medicare and Medicaid are designed to meet the needs of America's poor.

Your Turn

Revise Your Draft Review your draft and ask yourself:

- Are all of the details I include accurate?
- Do I provide enough support for each of the facts I present?
- Which parts of the essay could be stronger if I added one or two additional details?

Proofreading and Publishing

Proofreading

To prepare your essay for publishing, make sure to proofread and edit it carefully. Find and correct errors in grammar, usage, and mechanics, and correct spelling errors. Mistakes like these can keep readers from enjoying and learning from your informative essay.

Grammar Link Capitalizing Proper Nouns

Capital letters provide a kind of signpost: They tell readers when you are describing specific people, places, and things.

- Capitalize all proper nouns. Titles, such as Doctor and President, are capitalized when they precede someone's name.
  President Johnson   Doctor Benjamin Rush
- In proper nouns that have more than one word, do not capitalize articles, prepositions of fewer than five letters, or conjunctions unless they are the first word.
  U.S. Department of Housing and Urban Development
- Acronyms, formed from the first letters of a series of words, are in all capitals.
  UNICEF   FBI   CIA   AFL/CIO

Publishing

You have completed an informative essay on a topic that matters to you. To be informative, though, your essay has to be read by an audience. Here are some ways to share your informative essay with readers:

- Mail or e-mail your essay to others who share your interest.
- Send your essay to Web sites related to your topic.
- Compile a class book of essays. Use desktop publishing software to create a professional-looking final product.

Reflect on Your Informative Essay Thinking about how you wrote this essay can help you the next time you write. In your **RWN,** give short responses to these questions:

1. How did research and writing change your understanding of the topic?
2. Which stage was more satisfying—gathering information or writing the essay? Why?
3. What did you include to address what your audience wants or needs to know?

Proofreading Tip

Read your essay aloud slowly, focusing on each word to make sure every sentence is complete. Notice where you naturally pause—these pauses might indicate places where commas are missing.

Your Turn

Proofread and Publish As you are proofreading, make sure you have capitalized proper nouns and acronyms correctly. When you are satisfied that your work is error free, make a final copy of your informative essay, and publish it.

Scoring Rubric

Use one of the rubrics below to evaluate your informative essay or your response to the on-demand prompt on the next page. Your teacher will tell you which rubric to use.

6-Point Scale

Score 6 *Demonstrates advanced success*
- focuses consistently on a clear thesis
- shows effective organization throughout, with smooth transitions
- offers thoughtful, creative ideas
- develops ideas thoroughly, using examples, details, and fully elaborated explanation
- exhibits mature control of written language

Score 5 *Demonstrates proficient success*
- focuses on a clear thesis
- shows effective organization, with transitions
- offers thoughtful ideas
- develops ideas competently, using examples, details, and well-elaborated explanations
- exhibits sufficient control of written language

Score 4 *Demonstrates competent success*
- focuses on a clear thesis, with minor distractions
- shows effective organization, with minor lapses
- offers mostly thoughtful ideas
- develops ideas adequately, with a mixture of general and specific elaboration
- exhibits general control of written language

Score 3 *Demonstrates limited success*
- includes some loosely related ideas that distract from the writer's informative focus
- shows some organization, with noticeable gaps in the logical flow of ideas
- offers routine, predictable ideas
- develops ideas with uneven elaboration
- exhibits limited control of written language

Score 2 *Demonstrates basic success*
- includes loosely related ideas that seriously distract from the informative focus
- shows minimal organization, with major gaps in the logical flow of ideas
- offers ideas that merely skim the surface
- develops ideas with inadequate elaboration
- exhibits significant problems with control of written language

Score 1 *Demonstrates emerging effort*
- shows little awareness of the topic and purpose for writing
- lacks organization
- offers unclear and confusing ideas
- develops ideas in only a minimal way, if at all
- exhibits major problems with control of written language

4-Point Scale

Score 4 *Demonstrates advanced success*
- focuses consistently on a clear thesis
- shows effective organization throughout, with smooth transitions
- offers thoughtful, creative ideas
- develops ideas thoroughly, using examples, details, and fully elaborated explanation
- exhibits mature control of written language

Score 3 *Demonstrates competent success*
- focuses on a clear thesis, with minor distractions
- shows effective organization, with minor lapses
- offers mostly thoughtful ideas
- develops ideas adequately, with a mixture of general and specific elaboration
- exhibits general control of written language

Score 2 *Demonstrates limited success*
- includes some loosely related ideas that distract from the writer's informative focus
- shows some organization, with noticeable gaps in the logical flow of ideas
- offers routine, predictable ideas
- develops ideas with uneven elaboration
- exhibits limited control of written language

Score 1 *Demonstrates emerging effort*
- shows little awareness of the topic and purpose for writing
- lacks organization
- offers unclear and confusing ideas
- develops ideas in only a minimal way, if at all
- exhibits major problems with control of written language

Informative Essay

When you respond to a prompt asking you to write an informative essay—an essay that provides information—you can use what you have learned from this unit's selections, from writing your own informative essay, and from the rubric on page 1000. Use the steps below to guide your response to the following prompt.

Writing Prompt

Write an informative essay about the person you admire most. Inform your reader about the traits and accomplishments of this person. Be sure to include specific examples to support the information about this person in your informative essay.

Study the Prompt

Read the prompt carefully. Note that the key words are *informative essay, person you admire most,* and *traits and accomplishments*. The prompt requires that you include specific details and information. For this reason, you may be more successful writing about someone that you know personally rather than someone you know about through the media. Unless you have recently completed research on a person, choose someone you admire and know well. **Tip:** Spend about five minutes studying the prompt.

Plan Your Response

Writing an informative essay requires you to answer an implicit, or inherent, question: Why do I admire this person? Your answer will be in the form of the person's traits and accomplishments. A trait is a characteristic, such as *generosity* or *courage.* A web like the one pictured on the upper right can help you plan your informative essay.

First, write your subject's name in the center oval. Then, in each of the second-level ovals, write a trait or accomplishment you admire. Make sure you provide examples of these traits and achievements.

Tip: Spend about ten minutes planning your response.

Respond to the Prompt

Using your diagram, begin writing your essay. In the introduction, grab your reader's attention, and state the essay's thesis: whom you admire most, and why.

In the body of your essay, list and explain the traits and accomplishments of the person you admire. Provide examples and explanations to support your thesis. **Tip:** Spend about twenty minutes writing your draft.

Improve Your Response

Revising Go back to the key aspects of the prompt. Did you identify traits and accomplishments of the person you admire? If not, add those details.

Proofreading Take a few minutes to proofread your essay to correct errors in grammar, spelling, punctuation, and capitalization.

Checking Your Final Copy Before you turn your essay in, read it one more time to catch any errors you may have missed. **Tip:** Save ten minutes to improve your paper.

Listening & Speaking Workshop

Analyzing and Evaluating Speeches

Listen with a Purpose

Analyze and evaluate a historically significant speech to uncover its impact and effectiveness.

Think as a Reader/Writer As you know, listening is like reading: Both skills require that you absorb information. When you evaluate a speech that is being delivered, you're combining comprehension with sensory observation—of the voice and the actions of the speaker.

In this workshop, you'll have the opportunity to analyze a historically significant speech and determine what made it so effective.

Analyze the Content of a Speech

To find a historical speech, search your library, history textbook, or the Internet. Choose a speech on a topic that interests you, and try to find one that you can listen to and watch, instead of just read. Once you have selected a speech, analyze its content by listening for the elements listed below. As you do, think about their effectiveness.

- **Arguments** Begin your analysis by viewing a video of the speech. Identify key points and types of **arguments**, such as those featured in the chart below:

Types of Arguments	
causation	a cause-effect relationship supporting an opinion
analogy	a literal comparison between unlike things
appeal to authority	a reference to trustworthy experts
emotional appeal	language used to stir feelings in listeners
logical appeal	an idea aimed at listener's minds through the use of facts, statistics, anecdotes, and examples

- **Rhetorical Devices** To improve their arguments, speakers master rhetoric—ways of using language to make a message stand out and be persuasive. In the chart below, you'll find some **rhetorical devices** to look for as you analyze a speech.

Types of Rhetorical Devices	
allusion	an indirect reference to literature, history, or news
metaphor	an imaginative comparison between unlike things
repetition	repeating important words or phrases
diction	word choice creating specific audience reactions
parallelism	using the same phrase/sentence structure to highlight similar ideas and create a memorable rhythm

Reader/Writer Notebook

Use your **RWN** to complete the activities for this workshop.

Analyze Organization

Determine the organizational pattern of the speech by identifying which of two major approaches the speaker uses:

Deductive: In this pattern of organization, speakers present the thesis first, followed by reasons and support. Such speeches start with general ideas, then move to specific ones.

Inductive: In this pattern, speakers present reasons and support first, building to a thesis statement. Speakers using the inductive approach move from specific ideas to more general ones.

After determining the pattern of organization, evaluate how clearly and coherently the ideas are organized.

Speaker's Model

The following is an excerpt from a speech that President John F. Kennedy gave in 1962. Its message helped convince Americans to support the U.S. space program. The annotations in the model's margin identify arguments and rhetorical devices used in the speech.

If . . . history . . . teaches us anything, it is that man, in this quest for knowledge and progress, is determined and cannot be deterred. The exploration of space will go ahead whether we join it or not,[1] and it is one of the greatest adventures of all time. . . .[2]

Those who came before us made sure that this country rode the first waves of the industrial revolution,[3] the first waves of modern invention, and the first waves of nuclear power,[4] and this generation does not intend to founder in the backwash[5] of the coming age of space. We mean to be part of it—we mean to lead it. For the eyes of the world now look into space, to the moon and to the planets beyond, and we have vowed that we shall not see it governed by a hostile flag of conquest, but by a banner of freedom and peace.[6] We have vowed that we shall not see space filled with weapons of mass destruction, but with instruments of knowledge and understanding.[7]

1. causation
2. emotional appeal
3. metaphor
4. parallelism, repetition
5. diction, metaphor
6. emotional appeal
7. parallelism

A Good Analysis and Evaluation of a Speech

- notes the speaker's important points
- identifies and evaluates the speaker's arguments
- identifies and evaluates the rhetorical devices used by the speaker
- identifies the pattern of organization and assesses its clarity and effectiveness
- analyzes the speaker's delivery, including verbal and nonverbal techniques
- sums up with one paragraph of evaluation, incorporating the analysis and evaluation of the points above

Analyze the Delivery of a Speech

In addition to language, a speaker's **delivery,** or use of voice and body, helps set the tone and mood of the speech. **Tone** is the speaker's attitude toward the subject and audience. **Mood** is the impression the speech makes on the audience. Speakers use verbal and nonverbal techniques to convey tone and mood and to get their points across to an audience.

Listening Tips

As you listen to the speech, note any vocal emphases and pauses. Such highlighting can signal a rhetorical device or a key point of an argument. Note also the speaker's facial expressions and gestures to get a sense of his or her tone. If something is unclear, don't take long puzzling over it. Instead, listen to the next passage and come back to the difficult point later.

Listen for Verbal Techniques

The chart below lists and explains verbal techniques to note while listening to a speech.

Verbal Techniques	
Emphasis	The stress the speaker puts on certain words and phrases. Speakers emphasize key ideas in their speeches by saying those words with a little more volume or a different pitch.
Pauses	Small silences that a good speaker uses to let ideas soak in or to signal that what was just said or what is about to be said is important.
Enunciation	The clarity with which speakers pronounce their words. Good speakers always want their ideas to be clearly understood. Poor enunciation makes listeners strain.

Look for Nonverbal Techniques

In this chart, you'll find nonverbal techniques that you can observe while viewing a speech.

Nonverbal Techniques	
Posture	The way a speaker stands. A speaker standing straight and alert suggests confidence in his or her message; a slouching posture signals disinterest.
Facial Expressions	The look on a speaker's face clues listeners in to his or her feelings. For example, a smile can suggest warmth and sincerity, while a furrowed brow can show anger or impatience.
Gestures	Body movements that emphasize emotions or ideas. Good speakers use natural gestures, such as nodding their heads or pointing out at the audience.

Take Note

As you analyze each element of a speaker's delivery, take notes evaluating its effectiveness. You can quickly describe its impact and quality by jotting down a few words. The table on the next page will help you to better evaluate a speech.

MO **9.R.3.C.1.c** Use details from informational text: to analyze and evaluate the accuracy and adequacy of evidence **9.R.3.D.1** Read and apply multi-step directions to perform complex procedures and/or tasks **9.R.1.D.1.a** Read grade-level instructional text: with fluency, accuracy, comprehension and appropriate expression

Evaluate a Speech

The most important test of a successful persuasive speech is your own reaction. A speech should make you think more deeply about a subject and might even change your mind about an issue or prompt you to take action. Such successful speeches usually exhibit strong content and style and are delivered by seasoned speakers.

Question the Content and Delivery

Use the following questions to help you evaluate the effectiveness and quality of a persuasive speech, stating your own judgments about it.

Evaluating Persuasive Speeches

Content and Organization	Delivery
What **arguments** and **rhetorical devices** did the speaker use? Was there a variety of arguments and devices? Were the devices overused?	How did the speaker make good use of emphasis, enunciation, and pauses? Were his or her diction and syntax clear and effective?
What **evidence** (facts, statistics, or expert testimony) did the speaker provide to support his or her ideas?	Did the speaker use facial expressions, gestures, and posture to express tone and mood? If so, how would you describe the use of these nonverbal techniques?
Were the speaker's main points **clear** and **coherent**—connected to each other and to the main idea? What kind of organizational pattern was used?	Did the speaker's overall delivery capture your attention and help you understand the speech? What techniques contributed to the net effect?

Sum It Up

If you were telling a friend what you thought of a speech you saw on TV, you would briefly describe its content and explain why it worked or did not work. For the historical speech you chose, write a one paragraph evaluation of its effectiveness and quality. Incorporate your analysis of its content, style, and delivery.

Reflect

What listening skills did you find most useful when you analyzed a speech? Explain.

Writing Skills Review

Informative Essay **Directions:** Read this student's draft of an informative essay about building campfires. Note that the sentences are numbered. Then answer the questions.

My Father's Gift of Fire

(1) My interest in campfires all started because of a walk in a park in New York City. (2) When I was five, my family lived in New York City for one summer. (3) My father and I would go out early in the morning, when it was still cool, to walk the dog. (4) My dad would be dressed for work, his shoes walking along the asphalt path as I walked beside him to keep up.

(5) On one of these early-morning walks, my father was throwing sticks for the dog to fetch, and I started picking up sticks of my own. (6) Always ready to play and teach, my dad crouched down and said, "Here, let me show you how to build a campfire. (7) Once you learn how, you can build a fire in the middle of a tornado." (8) He looked over my sticks and helped me gather others, from twigs to heavy branches. (9) What he taught me continues to hold a fascination: the gift of fire.

(10) Starting a campfire, like most things, has a method, and that method works. (11) First, gather the smallest twigs available; often peeling dry bark may fleck small twigs, and this lights up just like paper. (12) Arrange these tiny twigs in a teepee shape atop dry ground or rock, adding paper or dry leaves to the "teepee floor." (13) The sticks tend to hold one another up, especially if they are no more than 10 inches in length. (14) After this kindling foundation is built, the next step is leaning larger sticks on the twigs. (15) A good campfire-builder knows that these sticks should not be tightly packed because that will prevent air from feeding the new-born fire. (16) Fires, like people, need plenty of oxygen. (17) After you have a good teepee built, strike a match and place its flaming head within the bottom of the cone. (18) It may take a few tries, but fire will come if the twigs are dry.

(19) If a camper's using the old noggin, he or she at this point will have two sizes of larger sticks, some heavy branches, and some logs or main branch parts waiting nearby. (20) All that remains is to carefully add another layer of wood, from smallest pieces to largest pieces. (21) Adding these pieces when the flames are strong will grow the campfire quickly and seamlessly.

(22) There are few things as quietly fascinating and comforting as staring into a roaring fire. (23) When I look at a fire I've help to build on a lonesome ocean shore or in the middle of a deep pine woods, I think of my father and his generous gift.

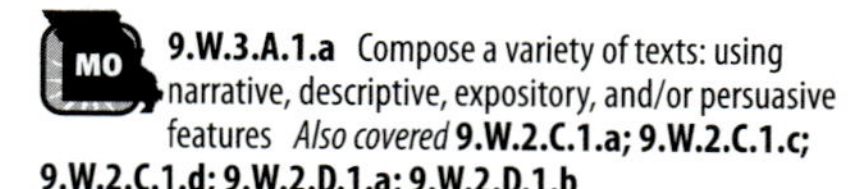

9.W.3.A.1.a Compose a variety of texts: using narrative, descriptive, expository, and/or persuasive features *Also covered* **9.W.2.C.1.a; 9.W.2.C.1.c; 9.W.2.C.1.d; 9.W.2.D.1.a; 9.W.2.D.1.b**

1. Which of the following sentences would *best* improve the introduction if used as a first sentence?

A Many people don't care about campfires, but I think they are missing out.

B While one could argue that campfires are not necessary, they are great fun.

C American essayist C.D. Warner said, "To poke a wood fire is more solid enjoyment than most anything else in the world."

D A fire can make camping tolerable.

9.W.2.C.1.a

2. Which of these words or phrases would *most* improve sentence 4 if they replaced both uses of the verb "to walk"?

A treading / quick-stepped

B stepping / moved

C moving / stepped faster

D grinding / skipped

9.W.2.D.1.a

3. Which of the following paragraph revisions would improve the organization of the essay?

A Start a new paragraph at sentence 3.

B Combine paragraphs 2 and 3.

C Combine paragraphs 4 and 5, deleting sentence 21.

D Start a new paragraph at sentence 14.

9.W.2.C.1.c

4. Which sentence pairs could be improved by adding a transitional phrase to the beginning of the second sentence?

A Sentences 8 and 9

B Sentences 12 and 13

C Sentences 19 and 20

D Sentences 22 and 23

9.W.2.C.1.d

5. Which sentence in the draft could be improved by revising the wording to maintain a consistent tone?

A Sentence 1: change "walk" to "leisurely stroll"

B Sentence 14: replace "After this kindling foundation is built," with "Once you got this part up and running,"

C Sentence 19: change "If a camper's using his or her noggin," to "If a camper is adequately prepared,"

D Sentence 23: replace "tastes better" to "has improved taste"

9.W.2.D.1.b

UNIT 5

Epic
Writers on Writing

Ian Johnston on the Epic

Ian Johnston was born in Chile and now lives in Canada, where he has worked as a writer, translator, and teacher. His compelling translations of the *Odyssey* and the *Iliad* make the passion and drive of ancient heroes accessible to modern readers.

"I first started reading epic poems because I loved the grand adventures of brave heroes in wild and often magical places. There is something immensely appealing about a world that is so large and so magically unpredictable. Gods and goddesses, monsters, and wild natural elements are always confronting and testing the hero in a setting quite different from the one in which I lived, where there was a rational explanation for everything.

At some point, I found that reading these poems made me ask myself some challenging questions: What would it be like to live in such a world, to accept a vision of reality so different from my own? What if there were gods and goddesses everywhere? How would that affect the way I acted in the world? What if the purpose of my life was to explore and challenge the world on the basis of such a changed understanding?

I remember that Homer's epics had a decisive effect on me, especially in giving me a new way of seeing myself. I loved the way his heroes faced the world with a strong sense of their own excellence and without any sense of guilt, deriving a purpose for their lives by testing their quality in confrontations with all aspects of experience. In a search for recognition and fame, Homeric heroes measured their value against the achievements of their comrades, past and present. And I loved the presence of a divine personality in every part of nature. Although this vision of life was quite different from what I had been taught to believe, I gradually realized, especially when I played team sports, that such a way of thinking was by no means foreign to me. All of a sudden, my understanding of the world and of myself was transformed.

So epic poems changed the way I viewed the past and present. I wasn't going to start roaming around the sea, acting like Odysseus, or start offering animal sacrifices to the gods. However, I could understand why Odysseus behaves the way he does, and I could sense the same imaginative possibilities in myself. So the past became intensely alive. It was not just a place full of old and irrelevant stories but brimming with fresh insights into what makes human beings what they are.

My translations of Homer are the product of this experience, a personal tribute to the transforming and enriching effects of ancient poetic visions, which can provide such stimulating nourishment for the modern imagination."

Think as a Writer

Ian Johnston says that reading about the lives of epic heroes helped him understand his own potential. Are there modern heroes, either real or fictional, with this type of power? If so, who? Explain.

Ulysses and the Sirens (detail) (3rd century A.D.). Roman Mosaic (130 cm x 344 cm).

COLLECTION 9

Epic and Myth

INFORMATIONAL TEXT FOCUS

Synthesizing Sources: Making Connections

"It is good to have an end to journey toward, but it is the journey that matters in the end."

—Ursula K. Le Guin

What Do You Think?

In what ways can life be thought of as a journey?

Learn It Online

Increase your knowledge of the vocabulary words in this collection with Word Watch, online at:

go.hrw.com L9-1011 

Literary Focus

by **Carol Jago**

What Elements Will You Find in Epics and Myths?

Are there long stories in your family or culture that go back several generations and are repeated over and over—perhaps stories about long journeys, fearsome obstacles, and extraordinary characters? Studying these stories can help us reflect upon our contemporary world. Since the earliest days, before writing was invented, human beings in nearly every culture have told stories, such as epics and myths, to explain the world.

Epic Literature

Elements of Epics Epics are long narrative poems that tell of the adventures of heroes who in some way embody the values of their civilizations. Epics are found in many cultures and share the following characteristics:

- a physically impressive hero of national or historical importance
- a vast setting
- a quest or journey undertaken in search of something of value
- the involvement of supernatural forces
- a basis in a specific culture or society
- characters struggling against fate

Oral Tradition Many ancient epics were sung or spoken by generations of anonymous storytellers and changed slightly with each retelling. Literary epics, on the other hand, were created by individuals. Most epics include poetic elements, such as figurative language and the repetition of certain images and phrases. Note the metaphor in this excerpt:

> When the young Dawn with fingertips of rose
> lit up the world . . .
> from the *Odyssey*, lines 297–298

Epic Characters The epic hero, who represents the values of the society, is at the center of every epic. **Epic heroes** are exceptional people who undertake difficult quests or journeys to achieve something of tremendous value to themselves or their people. They experience many obstacles, or **conflicts,** along the way. These conflicts are sometimes **external,** created by forces of nature or, as in many epics and myths, the gods. Epic heroes also experience **internal** conflict, in which they struggle to overcome their own feelings or fears.

> He saw the townlands
> and learned the minds of many distant men,
> and weathered many bitter nights and days
> in his deep heart at sea, while he fought only
> to save his life, to bring his shipmates home.
> from the *Odyssey*, lines 5–9

Character Foils Most epic heroes have a foil. A **foil** is a character that stands in stark contrast to another character. For example, Eurylochus's weakness of character contrasts with Odysseus's strength.

> Down to the ship Eurylochus came running
> to cry alarm, foul magic doomed his men!
> from the *Odyssey*, lines 577–578

MO 9.R.2.A.1 Analyze and evaluate the text features in grade-level text 9.R.2.A.1 Analyze and evaluate the text features in grade-level text 9.R.2.C.1.b Use details from text(s): to analyze character, plot, setting, point of view

Myths

Purposes of Myths **Myths** are stories that are nearly always religious. Most cultures have myths that explain natural phenomena such as seasonal changes, fire, lightning, drought, floods, and death. Myths also teach moral lessons, explain history, and express, as dreams do, the deepest fears and hopes of the human race. They describe rivalries among the gods and the consequences of disobedience to higher powers. In the following excerpt from "The Fenris Wolf," we learn how the deeds of Loki affected Norse society.

> Though Loki, the fire god, was handsome and ready-witted, his nature was really evil. He was, indeed, the cause of most of the misfortunes which befell the gods.
>
> from "The Fenris Wolf"

Mythic Characters In some myths, the characters have notable characteristics, or traits. For example, in Native American myths, Coyote is a trickster who is always causing trouble. Several myths also feature horrible animals and monsters with terrifying strength, which are difficult to escape from or subdue. One such creature is the Fenris Wolf of Norse mythology.

As in epics, many myths tell about gods and goddesses. These deities frequently interact with humans, sometimes testing or playing with humans as if they were chess pieces on a board.

> The goddesses arrived together, each in turn unveiling her beauty and each in turn offering a bribe.
>
> from "Paris and Queen Helen"

Your Turn Analyze Elements of Epics and Myths

Read the following excerpt from Virgil's *Aeneid,* a story of the founding of ancient Rome, and then answer the questions that follow.

Aeneas was a Trojan prince who escaped the destruction of Troy. He had a special destiny.

> Aeneas escaped from the flames of Troy, bearing his old father on his back . . . accompanied by a few friends and his little son Ascanius. He had been told in a dream that it was his destiny to found a nation in a country lying far to the west, Italy, to which divine guidance would eventually bring them. . . . Many years of wandering lay before them, at the end of which they would reach their new home.
>
> Passing Sicily, where lived the monster Polyphemus, who shouted terrible threats after them from the shore, they were met by a fearful storm sent by [the goddess] Hera, who hated all the Trojans but especially Aeneas, and had resolved that he should never reach Italy.
>
> from the *Aeneid* by Virgil

1. What qualities of the **epic hero** does Aeneas possess?
2. In this excerpt, which kind of **conflict—external** or **internal**—does Aeneas face?
3. What role do the gods play in this excerpt?

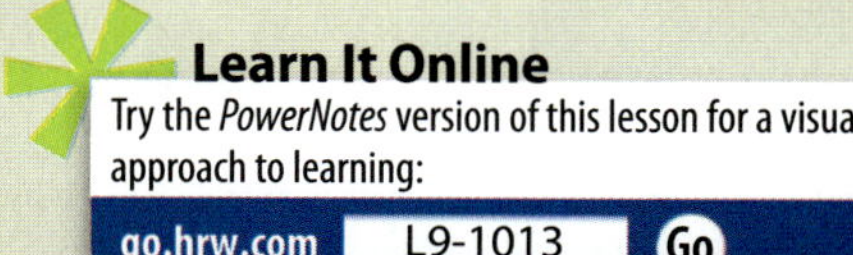

Learn It Online

Try the *PowerNotes* version of this lesson for a visual approach to learning:

go.hrw.com L9-1013 Go

Analyzing Visuals

What Elements of Epic and Myth Appear in Art?

Myths and epics are filled with heroes and villains whose grand adventures result in glory and violence. Artists' re-creations of moments from these tales are often larger than life. The works may include either noble characters or gods battling monsters twice their size or fanciful creatures in mystic settings. Epic scenes suggest matters of great importance or moments critical to the heroes' fate.

Analyzing Epic and Myth in Art

Use these guidelines to analyze art that has epic and mythic themes:

1. Identify the subject of the image. What makes this subject seem ordinary or extraordinary?
2. Look at the characters in the work. Which characters seem to embody virtuous or heroic qualities?
3. Consider the action taking place. Is there a conflict in progress? If so, does the struggle reflect a battle between good and evil?
4. Study the characters' clothing. What does their clothing tell you about their culture or time period?

Look at the details of the painting below to help you answer the questions on page 1015.

Details from *Andromeda Rescued from the Monster by Perseus Riding Pegasus.*

9.R.2.A.1 Analyze and evaluate the text features in grade-level text

Andromeda Rescued from the Monster by Perseus Riding Pegasus (c. 1410–1411).
French School (Fifteenth century), British Library, London, UK. Vellum.

1. In Greek mythology, Perseus rescues Princess Andromeda from a sea monster. How does the depiction of Perseus convey a sense of strength and bravery?

2. Myths sometimes combine natural and supernatural characters. How is this image an example of this kind of combination?

3. Epics and myths often feature the triumph of good over evil. How does the artist's use of color help emphasize those qualities?

4. What virtues does the figure of the woman seem to represent? How can you tell?

Your Turn Analyze Epic and Myth in Art

Myths often highlight the customs and beliefs of the culture or time period that created them. What does this image suggest about the role or status of women in ancient Greece?

Reading Focus

by **Kylene Beers**

What Skills Can Help You Understand Epics and Myths?

After you've read an epic or a myth, you want to be sure you understand the causes and effects—why certain events happened and how they affected the plot or the characters. Epics are long, and many epics and myths are complex. Keeping up with the characters and events as you read requires that you continually ask yourself if you understand what you are reading. It's a good idea to pause occasionally to write short statements that recap or summarize the events. Additionally, you can get more out of the story if you draw conclusions based on the details in the story and your own knowledge or experience.

Understanding Cause and Effect

Events in a narrative don't just happen by chance. Some events **cause** other things to happen. The result, or consequence, of a cause is called an **effect.** To understand an epic or a myth, it is important to pay attention to how the narrative is built on a series of causes and effects. For example, why do heroes fight monsters? What can happen as a result? Remember that not all effects have a single cause and that some causes have more than one effect.

Using a cause-and-effect chain like the one below will help you identify relationships between key events in epics and myths.

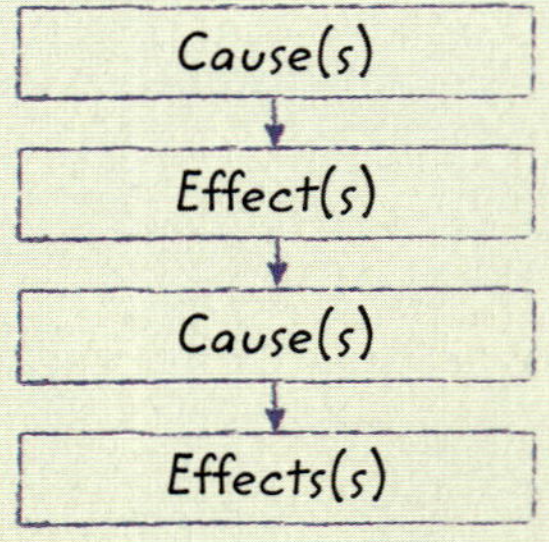

Summarizing

It can be challenging to keep track of the characters and events in a narrative, especially if it is a long narrative such as an epic. Summarizing after you read each section can help you see the big picture. As you read, you can **summarize** a plot by writing a statement about the narrative's most important events.

One very useful strategy for summarizing a story is called "Somebody Wanted But So." As you read, complete a chart like the following. Under "Somebody," write the character's name. Under "Wanted," describe the character's main goal. Under "But," describe what is preventing the character from achieving that goal. Write the outcome of the character's struggle under "So."

Somebody	Wanted	But	So
Odysseus	wanted to go home	Calypso wouldn't let him go.	Athena, a goddess, ordered her to do it.

9.R.3.C.1.a Use details from informational text: to identify and explain the organizational pattern **9.R.1.G.1.g** During reading, utilize strategies: to summarize **9.R.1.H.1.d** Apply post-reading skills to comprehend, interpret, analyze, and evaluate text: draw conclusions

Drawing Conclusions

Although it may be tempting to form an opinion about a work before examining all the evidence, try to wait until after you have finished reading to draw your final conclusions. When you **draw conclusions,** you sift through all the details in a narrative to make connections and form an opinion.

As you read, you will draw conclusions about the hero of an epic or a character in a myth. Follow these guidelines to help you formulate your conclusions:

Guidelines for Drawing Conclusions

Step One: Examine the characters' actions, and consider the effects of their actions.
Example: Odysseus sacrifices the lives of six men in order to save the rest of his crew.

Step Two: Make connections between what you've learned and what you know from life.
Example: Sometimes hard decisions have to be made for the greater good.

Step Three: Form a conclusion based on the clues in the epic or myth and your background knowledge.
Example: Odysseus is a good leader because he is trying to save the lives of as many crew members as he can.

Your Turn Apply Reading Skills

Read this selection from an American Indian myth. Then, complete the activities that follow.

Coyote and the Origin of Death

In the beginning of this world, there was no such thing as death. Everybody continued to live until there were so many people that the earth had no room for any more. The chiefs held a council to determine what to do. One man rose and said he thought it would be a good plan to have the people die and be gone for a little while, and then return.

As soon as he sat down, Coyote jumped up and said he thought people ought to die forever. He pointed out that this little world is not large enough to hold all of the people, and that if the people who died came back to life, there would not be food enough for all.

All the other men objected. They said that they did not want their friends and relatives to die and be gone forever, for then they would grieve and worry and there would be no happiness in the world. Everyone except Coyote decided to have people die and be gone for a little while, and then come back to life again.

1. **Summarize** each paragraph in a sentence.
2. What **caused** the chiefs to hold a council? What was the **effect** of the meeting?
3. In myths, the coyote is often a trickster. What **conclusions** can you **draw** about his character?

Now go to the Skills in Action: Reading Model

Learn It Online
Try the *PowerNotes* version of this lesson on:
go.hrw.com
L9-1017
Go

SKILLS IN ACTION

Reading Model

MYTH

Build Background

This retelling of a famous Greek myth explains the origin of the Trojan War, a devastating conflict between the people of Troy and an alliance of Greek kings. Priam (PRY uhm), the king of Troy, unsuccessfully demanded the release of his sister Hesione (heh SEE uh nee), who had been taken from Troy by Hercules. Paris, Priam's son, abducted Queen Helen of Sparta, thus starting the Trojan War. One of the Greek soldiers who fought in the Trojan War was Odysseus. The *Odyssey,* Homer's second epic, is the account of Odysseus's long journey home.

Read with a Purpose As you read this myth, pay attention to the consequences of the choices that the characters make.

Paris and Queen Helen

retold by **Robert Graves**

King Priam sulked on hearing the envoys' account of their visit to Salamis, and when his own son Paris ran away with Queen Helen of Sparta and brought her to Troy, the king refused to send her back. It was this decision that provoked the long, calamitous Trojan War, which benefited nobody, not even the conquerors.

Here is the story of Paris and Helen. Paris was Priam's son by Queen Hecuba who, just before his birth, dreamed that instead of a child she bore a blazing torch, from which wriggled countless fiery serpents. Priam asked Apollo's prophet Calchas what the dream meant. Calchas answered: "This child will be Troy's ruin. Cut his throat as soon as he is born!" Priam could not bring himself to kill any baby, especially his own son, but the warning frightened him; so he gave the child to his chief cattleman, saying: "Leave him behind a bush somewhere in the woods on Mount Ida, and don't go there again for nine days."

Literary Focus

Myth One frequent theme in myth, as in epic, is that of the lost son who is sent off at birth to be killed because of prophecies of doom. Inevitably, these children survive, with the help of foster parents, and grow up to fulfill the prophecy made at their birth.

The cattleman obeyed. But on the ninth day, passing through the busy valley in which Paris had been left, he found a she-bear suckling him. Amazed at this sight, the cattleman brought Paris up with his own children.

Paris grew to be tall, handsome, strong, and clever. He was always invited by the other cattlemen to judge bullfights. Almighty Zeus, watching from his palace on far-off Olympus, noticed how honestly he gave his verdict on such occasions and one day chose him to preside over a beauty contest at which he did not care to appear himself.

Reading Focus

Understanding Cause and Effect This part of the myth explains why Zeus chose Paris to judge the beauty contest.

The Abduction of Helen (1631) by Guido Reni (1575–1642). Oil on canvas (253 cm x 265 cm).

Analyzing Visuals

Viewing and Interpreting Which details in this painting suggest that Paris is a mythical character?

This is what happened. The goddess of quarrels, Eris by name, was not invited to a famous wedding (that of the sea-goddess Thetis and King Peleus of Phthia[1]), attended by all the other gods and goddesses. Eris spitefully threw a golden apple among the guests, after scratching on the peel: "For the Most Beautiful!" They would have handed the apple to Thetis, as the bride, but were afraid of offending the three far more important goddesses present: Hera, almighty Zeus's wife; Athene, his unmarried daughter, who was goddess not only of wisdom but of battle; and his daughter-in-law Aphrodite, goddess of love. Each of them thought herself the most beautiful, and they began quarreling about the apple, as Eris had intended. Zeus's one hope of domestic peace lay in ordering a beauty contest and choosing an honest judge.

So Hermes, herald of the gods, flew down with the golden apple

Reading Focus

Summarizing You can summarize this important story passage by saying "Eris deliberately caused a fight among the goddesses about who was the most beautiful."

1. **Phthia:** (THEE uh).

and a message for Paris from Zeus. "Three goddesses," he announced, "will visit you here on Mount Ida, and almighty Zeus's orders are that you shall award this apple to the most beautiful. They will all, of course, abide by your decision." Paris disliked the task but could not avoid it.

The goddesses arrived together, each in turn unveiling her beauty and each in turn offering a bribe. Hera undertook to make Paris Emperor of Asia. Athena undertook to make him the wisest man alive and victorious in all his battles. But Aphrodite sidled up, saying: "Darling Paris, I declare that you're the handsomest fellow I've seen for years! Why waste your time here among bulls and cows and stupid cattlemen? Why not move to some rich city and lead a more interesting life? You deserve to marry a woman almost as beautiful as myself—let me suggest Queen Helen of Sparta. One look at you, and I'll make her fall so deep in love that she won't mind leaving her husband, her palace, her family—everything, for your sake!" Excited by Aphrodite's account of Helen's beauty, Paris handed her the apple; whereupon Hera and Athena went off angrily, arm in arm, to plot the destruction of the whole Trojan race.

Literary Focus

Characters and Conflict Notice that in this passage the goddesses, who are jealous rivals, plot against their opponents in much the same way that humans do.

Next day, Paris paid his first visit to Troy, and found an athletic festival in progress. His foster-father, the cattleman, who had come too, advised him against entering the boxing contest which was staged in front of Priam's throne; but Paris stepped forward and won the crown of victory by sheer courage rather than skill. He put his name down for the foot race, too, and ran first. When Priam's sons challenged him to a longer race, he beat them again. They grew so annoyed, to think that a mere peasant had carried off three crowns of victory in a row, that they drew their swords. Paris ran for protection to the altar of Zeus, while his foster-father fell on his knees before Priam, crying: "Your Majesty, pardon me! This is your lost son."

Literary Focus

Hero Paris, like all heroes, is exceptionally courageous. He excels at sports and contests.

The king summoned Hecuba, and Paris's foster-father showed her a rattle left in his hands when he was a baby. She knew it at once; so they took Paris with them to the palace, and there celebrated a huge banquet in honor of his return. Nevertheless, Calchas and the other priests of Apollo warned Priam that unless Paris were immediately put to death, Troy would go up in smoke. He answered: "Better that Troy should burn, than that my wonderful son should die!"

Priam made ready a fleet to sail for Salamis and rescue Queen Hesione by force of arms. Paris offered to take command, adding:

"And if we can't bring my aunt home, perhaps I may capture some Greek princess whom we can hold as a hostage." He was of course already planning to carry off Helen, and had no intention of fetching his old aunt, in whom no Trojan but Priam took the least interest, and who felt perfectly happy at Salamis.

While Priam was deciding whether he should give Paris the command, Menelaus,[2] king of Sparta, happened to visit Troy on some business matter. He made friends with Paris and invited him to Sparta, which enabled Paris to carry out his plan easily, using no more than a single fast ship. He and Menelaus sailed as soon as the wind blew favorably and, on arrival at Sparta, feasted together nine days running. Under Aphrodite's spell, Helen loved Paris at first sight, but was greatly embarrassed by his bold behavior. He even dared to write "I love Helen!" in wine spilt on the top of the banqueting table. Yet Menelaus, grieved by news of his father's death in Crete, noticed nothing; and when the nine days ended, he set sail for the funeral, leaving Helen to rule in his absence. This was no more than Helen's due, since he had become king of Sparta by marrying her.

Literary Focus

Characters Aphrodite, the goddess of love, meddles in the affairs of humans and puts Helen under a spell.

That same night Helen and Paris eloped in his fast ship, putting aboard most of the palace treasures that she had inherited from her foster-father. And Paris stole a great mass of gold out of Apollo's temple, in revenge for the prophecy made by his priests that he should be killed at birth. Hera spitefully raised a heavy storm, which blew their ship to Cyprus; and Paris decided to stay there some months before he went home—Menelaus might be anchored off Troy, waiting to catch him. In Cyprus, where he had friends, he collected a fleet to raid Sidon, a rich city on the coast of Palestine. The raid was a great success: Paris killed the Sidonian king, and captured vast quantities of treasure.

Literary Focus

Hero Paris embarks on a perilous journey, in which he acquires both Helen and stolen treasure.

When at last he returned to Troy, his ship loaded with silver, gold, and precious stones, the Trojans welcomed him rapturously.[3] Everyone thought Helen so beautiful, beyond all comparison, that King Priam himself swore never to give her up, even in exchange for his sister Hesione. Paris quieted his enemies, the Trojan priests of Apollo, by handing them the gold robbed from the god's treasury at Sparta; and almost the only two people who took a gloomy view of what would now happen were Paris's sister Cassandra, and her twin brother Helenus, both of whom possessed the gift of prophecy. This

2. **Menelaus:** (mehn uh LAY uhs).

3. **rapturously:** joyfully.

they had won accidentally, while still children, by falling asleep in Apollo's temple. The sacred serpents had come up and licked their ears, which enabled them to hear the god's secret voice. Yet it did them no good, because Apollo arranged that no one would believe their prophecies. Time after time Cassandra and Helenus had warned Priam never to let Paris visit Greece. Now they warned him to send Helen and her treasure back at once if he wanted to avoid a long and terrible war. Priam paid not the least attention.

Reading Focus

Drawing Conclusions Based on the final sentence of the story, you can conclude that Priam is stubborn and that he has not taken the prophecy seriously.

Read with a Purpose Which character made the best choices? the worst choices? What were the consequences of each choice?

MEET THE WRITER

Robert Graves

(1895–1985)

Man of the World

Robert Graves was an English poet, novelist, critic, mythographer, translator, editor, and teacher. During his lifetime he wrote more than 120 books, including many volumes of poetry, several novels, and many nonfiction works. His novel *I, Claudius,* about the emperor of ancient Rome, became a famous television series. Perhaps one of his best-known books is *Goodbye to All That,* an autobiography filled with reminiscences of World War I. During that war, he fought alongside the poet Siegfried Sassoon and was wounded during the Battle of the Somme.

Poetry and the Gods

Graves considered himself a poet above all else, but he could not live on poetry. One of his most famous comments was the following: "There's no money in poetry, but then there's no poetry in money, either." During the 1940s, he became fascinated with mythology, history, and classical literature and went on to write several books about the ancient world. The most famous of these, *The White Goddess,* is still widely read today.

Think About the Writer Given what Graves says about poetry and money, why do you think he devoted so much of his time to writing?

SKILLS IN ACTION

Wrap Up

9.R.2.A.1 Analyze and evaluate the text features in grade-level text 9.R.2.C.1.b Use details from text(s): to analyze character, plot, setting, point of view 9.R.1.E.1.c Develop vocabulary through text: using glossary, dictionary and thesaurus

Into Action: Elements of Myth

Complete this chart to identify main elements of the myth you have just read. What elements does this myth share with epics?

Element of Myth	Example from "Paris and Queen Helen"
Purpose of the Myth	
Character Types	
Similarities to Epic	

Talk About . . .

Get together with a small group, and discuss "Paris and Queen Helen" by answering the following questions. Try to use each Academic Vocabulary word listed at the right at least once in your discussion.

1. How are the goddesses in this myth portrayed?
2. What destiny did the prophets predict for Paris when he was born?
3. Why do Hera and Athena have a mutual interest in getting back at Aphrodite?
4. How does Eris express her anger at not being invited to the party?

Write About . . .

Think about the impact of destiny in "Paris and Queen Helen." Could the Trojan War have been avoided if King Priam had killed his son Paris, or was there a greater destiny, where Paris was fated to survive and Troy to fall? Write a brief essay, and explain your answer.

Writing Focus

Think as a Reader/Writer

Find It In Your Reading In Collection 9, you will read a Norse myth and excerpts from a Greek epic. The Writing Focus activities throughout the collection will help you analyze elements of these genres and challenge you to use these elements in your own writing.

Academic Vocabulary for Collection 9

Talking and Writing About Epics and Myths

Academic Vocabulary is the language you use to write and talk about literature. Use these words to discuss the works you read in this collection. The words are underlined throughout the collection.

portrayed (pawr TRAYD) *v.:* showed. *The story portrayed Priam as stubborn.*

destiny (DEHS tih nee) *n.:* unavoidable future; fate. *Some myths describe how the destiny of its characters is fulfilled.*

mutual (MYOO choo uhl) *adj.:* done, said, or felt by each toward the other. *Helen and Paris had a mutual attraction.*

express (ehk SPREHS) *v.:* put into words; show feeling or emotion. *Priam chose to express his joy at Paris's return by hosting a feast.*

Your Turn

In your *Reader/Writer Notebook,* write a news report based on the myth you read. Use each Academic Vocabulary word above.

EPIC

Preparing to Read

from the ODYSSEY

by **Homer**

Ulysses Defying the Cyclos (1887) by T. Zeinberger.

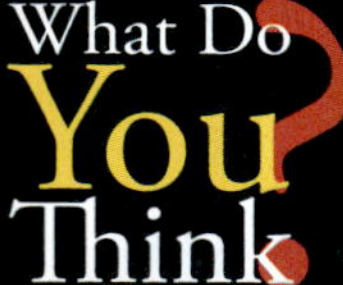

What difference can a journey make in a person's life?

QuickWrite

How could events in a journey reveal the heroic qualities in someone? Write down your opinions.

An **Introduction** to the Odyssey

by **David Adams Leeming**

Almost three thousand years ago, people who lived in the starkly beautiful part of the world we now call Greece were telling stories about a great war. The person credited with later gathering all these stories together and telling them as one unified epic is a man named Homer (*Homēros,* in Greek). Homer's great war stories are called, in English, the *Iliad* and the *Odyssey.* (In Greek, the *Iliad* is *Ilias* and the *Odyssey* is *Odysseia.*)

Homer's stories probably can be traced to historical struggles for control of the waterway leading from the Aegean Sea to the Sea of Marmara and the Black Sea. These battles might have taken place as early as 1200 B.C.—a time that was at least as long ago for Homer's audience as the Pilgrims' landing at Plymouth Rock is for us.

These battles might have taken place as early as 1200 B.C.—a time that was at least as long ago for Homer's audience as the Pilgrims' landing at Plymouth Rock is for us.

Homer's first epic was the *Iliad,* which tells of a ten-year war fought on the plains outside the walls of a great city called Troy (also known as Ilion). The ruins of Troy can still be seen in western Turkey. In Homer's story the Trojan War was fought between the people of Troy and an alliance of Greek kings (at that time each island and area of the Greek mainland had its own king). The *Iliad* tells us that the cause of the war was jealousy: The world's most beautiful woman, Helen, abandoned her husband, Menelaus, a Greek king, and ran off with Paris, a prince of Troy. (See "Paris and Queen Helen," page 1018.)

The *Odyssey,* Homer's second epic, is the story of the attempt of one Greek soldier, Odysseus, to get home after the Trojan War. All epic poems in the Western world owe something to the basic patterns established by these two stories.

Epics and Values

Epics are long narrative poems that tell of the adventures of heroes who in some way embody the values of their civilizations. For centuries the Greeks used the *Iliad* and the *Odyssey* in schools to teach Greek virtues. So it is not surprising that later cultures that admired the Homeric epics created their own epics, imitating Homer's style but conveying their own value systems.

Still, for all the epics written since Homer's time and for all the ones composed before it, when people in the Western world think of the word *epic*, they think primarily of the *Iliad* and the *Odyssey*. Rome's *Aeneid,* France's *Song of Roland,* Italy's *The Divine Comedy,* the ancient Mesopotamian tale of Gilgamesh, India's *Mahabharata* and *Ramayana,* Mali's *Sundiata*—all are great stories in the epic tradition. But Homer's epics are at the heart of the epic tradition.

The *Iliad* is the primary model for the epic of war. The *Odyssey* is the model for the epic of the long journey. The theme of the journey has been basic in Western literature—it is found in fairy tales, in such novels as *The Incredible Journey, Moby-Dick,* and *The Hobbit,* and in such movies as *The Wizard of Oz* and *Star Wars*. Thus, the *Odyssey* was probably Homer's most influential story.

The blind poet Homer. Detail from statue found near Naples (probably around 2nd century A.D.). British Museum, London.

The War-Story Background: Violence and Brutality

The background for Odysseus's story is found in the *Iliad,* which is set in the tenth and final year of the Trojan War. According to the *Iliad,* the Greeks attacked Troy to avenge the insult suffered by Menelaus, king of Sparta, when his wife, Helen, ran off with Paris, a young prince of Troy. The Greek kings banded together under the leadership of Agamemnon, the brother of Menelaus. In a thousand ships, they sailed across the Aegean Sea and laid siege to the walled city of Troy.

Analyzing Visuals

Viewing and Interpreting What does the image on the sail suggest about the Greeks, making their way to Troy?

The audience of the *Odyssey* would have known this war story. Listeners would have known that the Greeks were eventually victorious—that they gained entrance to Troy, reduced the city to smoldering ruins, and butchered all the inhabitants, except for those they took as slaves back to Greece. They would have known all about the greatest of the Greek warriors, Achilles, who died young in the final year of the war. The audience would probably have heard other epic poems (since lost) that told of the homecomings of the various Greek heroes who survived the war. They would especially have known about the homecoming of Agamemnon, the leader of the Greek forces, who was murdered by his unfaithful wife when he returned from Troy.

Finally, Homer's listeners might well have been particularly fascinated by another homecoming story—this one about a somewhat unusual hero, known as much for his brain as for his brawn. In fact, many legends had already grown up around this hero, whose name was Odysseus. He was the subject of Homer's epic, the *Odyssey.*

Odysseus: A Hero in Trouble

In Homer's day, heroes were thought of as a special class of aristocrats. They were placed somewhere between the gods and ordinary human beings. Heroes experienced pain and death, but they were always sure of themselves, always "on top of the world."

Odysseus is different. He is a hero in trouble. We can relate to Odysseus because like him we also face a world of difficult choices. Like Odysseus we have to cope with unfair authority figures. Like him we have to work very hard to get what we want.

The *Odyssey* is a story marked by melancholy and a feeling of postwar cynicism and doubt. Odysseus was a great soldier, but his war record is not of interest to the monsters that populate the world of his wanderings. Even the people of his home island, Ithaca, seem to lack respect for him. It is as if society were saying to the returning hero, "You were a great soldier once—or so they say—but times have changed. This is a difficult world, and we have more important things to think about than your record."

In the years before the great war, Odysseus had married the beautiful and ever-faithful Penelope, one of several very strong women in the masculine world of the Greek epic. (One writer and critic, Robert Graves, was so impressed by the unusual importance of women and home and hearth in the *Odyssey* that he believed Homer must have been a woman.)

One writer and critic, Robert Graves, was so impressed by the unusual importance of women and home and hearth in the *Odyssey* that he believed Homer must have been a woman.

Penelope and Odysseus had one son, Telemachus (tuh LEHM uh kuhs). He was still a baby when Odysseus was called by Agamemnon and Menelaus to join them in the war against Troy. But Odysseus was a homebody. He preferred not to go to war, especially a war fought for an unfaithful woman. Even though he was obligated under a treaty to go, Odysseus tried draft-dodging. It is said that when Agamemnon and Menelaus came to fetch him, he pretended to be insane and acted as if he did not recognize his visitors. Instead of entertaining them, he dressed as a peasant and began plowing a field and sowing it with salt. But the "draft board" was smarter than Odysseus. They threw his baby, Telemachus, in front of his oncoming plow. Odysseus revealed his sanity by quickly turning the plow aside to avoid running over his son.

Trojan Horse (16th century) by Niccolò dell' Abbate (c. 1512–1571). Tempera on wood panel.

The Wooden-Horse Trick

Once in Troy, Odysseus performed extremely well as a soldier and commander. It was he, for example, who thought of the famous wooden-horse trick that would lead to the downfall of Troy. For ten years the Greeks had been fighting the Trojans, but they were fighting outside Troy's massive walls. They had been unable to break through the walls and enter the city. Odysseus's plan was to build an enormous wooden horse and hide a few Greek soldiers inside its hollow belly. After the horse was built, the Greeks pushed it up to the gates of Troy and withdrew their armies, so that their camp appeared to be abandoned. Thinking that the Greeks had given up the fight and that the horse was a peace offering, the Trojans brought the horse into their city. That night the Greeks hidden inside the hollow belly came out, opened the gates of Troy to the whole Greek army, and began the battle that was to win the war.

> Odysseus and his family are people searching for the right relationships with one another and with the people around them.

The Ancient World and Ours

The world of Odysseus was harsh, a world familiar with violence. In a certain sense, Odysseus and his men act like pirates on their journey home. They think nothing of entering a town and carrying off all its worldly goods. The "worldly goods" in an ancient city might have been only pots and pans and cattle and sheep. The "palaces" the Greeks raided might have been little more than elaborate mud and stone farmhouses. Yet, in the struggles of Odysseus, Penelope, and Telemachus in their "primitive" society that had little in common with the high Athenian culture that would develop several centuries later, there is something that has a great deal to do with us.

A Search for Their Places in Life

Odysseus and his family are people searching for the right relationships with one another and with the people around them. They want to find their proper places in life. It is this **theme,** or central idea, that sets the tone for the *Odyssey* and determines the unusual way in which the poem is structured.

Instead of beginning at the beginning with Odysseus's departure from Troy, the story begins with his son, Telemachus. Telemachus is now twenty years old. He is threatened by rude, powerful men swarming about his own home, pressuring his mother to marry one of them. These men are bent on robbing Telemachus of his inheritance. Telemachus is a young man who needs his father, the one person who can put things right.

Meanwhile, we hear that his father is stranded on an island, longing to find a way to get back to his wife, child, and home. It is ten years since Odysseus sailed from Troy, twenty years since he left Ithaca to fight in Troy. While Telemachus is in search of his father, Odysseus is in search of a way out of what we might today call his midlife crisis. He is searching for inner peace, for a way to reestablish a natural balance in his life. The quests of father and son provide a framework for the poem and bring us into it as well—because we all are in search of our real identities, our true selves.

Myths are traditional stories, rooted in a particular culture, that usually explain a belief, a ritual, or a mysterious natural phenomenon.

Relationships with the Gods

This brings us to mythic and religious questions in the *Odyssey.* **Myths** are traditional stories, rooted in a particular culture, that usually explain a belief, a ritual, or a mysterious natural phenomenon. Myths are essentially religious because they are concerned with the relationship between human beings and the unknown or spiritual realm.

As you will see, Homer is always concerned with the relationship between humans and gods. Homer is religious: For him, the gods control all things. Athena, the goddess of wisdom, is always at the side of Odysseus. This is appropriate, because Odysseus is known for his mental abilities. Thus, in Homer's stories a god can reflect a hero's best or worst qualities. The god who works against Odysseus is Poseidon, the god of the sea, who is known for arrogance and a certain brutishness. Odysseus himself can be violent and cruel, just as Poseidon is.

Who was Homer?

No one knows for sure who Homer was. The later Greeks believed he was a blind minstrel, or singer, who came from the island of Chios. Some scholars feel there must have been two Homers; some think he was just a legend. But scholars have also argued about whether a man called Shakespeare ever existed. It is almost as if they were saying that Homer and Shakespeare are too good to be true. On the whole, it seems sensible to take the word of the Greeks themselves. We can at least accept the existence of Homer as a model for a class of wandering bards or minstrels later called rhapsodes (RAP sohdz).

These **rhapsodes,** or "singers of tales," were the historians and entertainers as well as the mythmakers of their time. There was probably no written history in Homer's day. There were certainly no movies and no television, and the Greeks had nothing like a Bible or a book of religious stories. So it was that the minstrels traveled about from community to community singing of recent events or of the doings of heroes, gods, and goddesses. The people in Homer's day saw no conflict among religion, history, and good fun.

Some scholars think Homer was just a legend. But scholars have also argued about whether a man called Shakespeare ever existed. It is almost as if they were saying that Homer and Shakespeare are too good to be true.

How Were the Epics Told?

Scholars have found that oral epic poets are still composing today in Eastern Europe and other parts of the world. These scholars suggest that stories like the *Iliad* and the *Odyssey* were originally told aloud by people who could not read and write. The stories followed a basic story line, but most of the actual words were improvised—made up on the spot—in a way that fit a particular rhythm or meter. The singers of these stories had to be talented, and they had to work very hard. They also needed an audience that could listen closely.

We can see from this why there is so much repetition in the Homeric epics. The oral storyteller, in fact, had a store of formulas ready in his memory. He knew formulas for describing the arrival and greeting of guests, the eating of meals, and the taking of baths. He knew formulas for describing the sea (it is "wine-dark") and for describing Athena (she is "gray-eyed Athena").

Formulas such as these had another advantage: they gave the singer and his audience some breathing time. The audience could relax for a moment and enjoy a familiar and memorable passage, while the singer could think ahead to the next part of his story.

When we think about the audience that listened to these stories, we can also understand the value of the extended comparisons that we today call **Homeric** or **epic similes.** These similes compare heroic or epic events to simple and easily understandable everyday events—events the audience would recognize instantly. For example, at one point in the *Iliad,* Athena prevents an arrow from striking Menelaus. The singer compares the goddess's actions to an action that would have been familiar to every listener:

> She brushed it away from his skin as lightly as when a mother
> Brushes a fly away from her child who is lying in sweet sleep.

Epic poets such as Homer would come to a city and would go through a part of their repertory while there. A story as long as the *Odyssey* (11,300 lines) could not be told at one sitting. We have to assume that if the singer had only a few days in a town, he would summarize some of his story and sing the rest in detail, in as many sittings as he had time for.

This is exactly what will happen in the selections from the *Odyssey* that are presented here. We'll assume that Homer wants to get his story told to us, but that his time is limited. We'll also assume that the audience, before retiring at the end of each performance, wants to talk about the stories they've just heard. You are now part of that audience.

Bard (singer) with lyre (10th–6th century B.C.). Geometric period. Minoan bronze figure. Location Archaeological Museum, Heraklion, Crete, Greece.

Homer is said to have accompanied his epic poems with a lyre, a type of stringed instrument.

A Live Performance

What was it like to hear a live performance of the *Odyssey?* We can guess what it was like because there are many instances in the epic itself in which traveling singers appear and sing their tales. In the court of the Phaeacian king, Alcinous (al SIHN oh uhs), in Book 8, for instance, there is a particularly wonderful singer who must make us wonder if the blind Homer is talking about himself. Let's picture the setting of a performance before we start the story.

Imagine a large hall full of people who are freshly bathed, rubbed with fine oils, and draped in clean tunics. Imagine the smell of meat being cooked over charcoal, the sound of voices. Imagine wine being freely poured, the flickering reflections of the great cooking fires, and the torches that light the room. A certain anticipation hangs in the air. People gossip that the blind minstrel Homer is in the city and that he has new stories about that long war in Troy. Will he appear and entertain tonight?

People and Places in the *Odyssey*

The following is a list of characters who take part in the sections of the *Odyssey* included in this book. Note that the Greeks in the *Odyssey* are often referred to as **Achaeans** (uh KEE uhnz) or **Argives** (AHR gyvz). *Achaeans,* the more general term, also includes the people of Ithaca, the island off the west coast of Greece where Odysseus ruled. The word *Achaeans* is taken from the name of an ancient part of northeastern Greece called Achaea. The name *Argives* usually refers to the Greeks who went to fight at Troy.

Penelope by John Roddam Spencer Stanhope (1829–1908). Oil on canvas. Private collection.

The Wanderings: Characters and Places

Aeaea (ee EE uh): home of Circe, the enchantress and goddess.

Alcinous (al SIHN oh uhs): king of Phaeacia. Odysseus tells the story of his adventures to Alcinous's court.

Calypso (ka LIHP soh): nymph goddess who keeps Odysseus on her island for seven years.

Charybdis (kuh RIHB dihs): female monster who sucks in water three times a day to form a deadly whirlpool. (Scholars believe the character is based on a real whirlpool in the Strait of Messina.)

Colossal head of Zeus (1st century B.C.) from Otricoli. Hellenistic. Location: Museo Pio Clementino, Vatican Museums, Vatican State.

Cicones (sih KOH neez): people living on the southwestern coast of Thrace who battle Odysseus and his men on their journey.

Circe (SUR see): enchantress and goddess who turns Odysseus's men into swine.

Cyclops: See **Polyphemus,** below.

Erebus (EHR uh buhs): dark area of the underworld where the dead reside.

Eurylochus (yuh RIHL uh kuhs): a member of Odysseus's loyal crew.

Lotus Eaters: people who feed Odysseus's men lotus plants to make them forget Ithaca.

Phaeacia (fee AY shuh): island kingdom ruled by King Alcinous. The Phaeacians are shipbuilders and traders.

Polyphemus (pahl uh FEE muhs): son of the sea god Poseidon and blinded by Odysseus. Polyphemus is a **Cyclops** (SY clops), one of a race of brutish one-eyed giants, the **Cyclopes** (sy CLOH peez), who live solitary lives as shepherds, supposedly on the island now known as Sicily.

Scylla (SIHL uh): female monster with six serpent heads, each head having a triple row of fangs.

Pensive Athena, a votive relief from the Acropolis (c. 470–450 B.C.). Acropolis Museum, Athens, Greece.

(Scholars believe this character is based on a dangerous rock in the Strait of Messina.)

Sirens: sea nymphs whose beautiful and mysterious music lures sailors to steer their ships toward dangerous rocks.

Teiresias (ty REE see uhs): famous blind prophet from the city of Thebes. Odysseus meets him in the Land of the Dead.

Thrinakia (thrih NAY kee uh): island where the sun god Helios keeps his cattle.

Ithaca: The People at Home

Antinous (an TIHN oh uhs): one of Penelope's main suitors; an arrogant and mean young noble from Ithaca.

Eumaeus (yoo MEE uhs): swineherd, one of Odysseus's loyal servants.

Eurycleia (yoo ruh KLEE uh): Odysseus's old nurse.

Eurymachus (yoo RIHM uh kuhs): suitor of Penelope.

Eurynome (yur IHN uh mee): Penelope's housekeeper.

Penelope (puh NEHL uh pee): Odysseus's faithful wife.

Philoeteus (fih LEE shee uhs): cowherd, one of Odysseus's loyal servants.

Telemachus (tuh LEHM uh kuhs): Odysseus's son.

The Gods

Apollo (uh PAHL oh): god of poetry, music, prophecy, medicine, and archery.

Athena (uh THEE nuh): favorite daughter of Zeus; the great goddess of wisdom as well as war and peace. She favored the Greeks during the Trojan War. She is often called Pallas Athena.

Cronus (KROH nuhs): **Titan** (giant god) who ruled the universe until his son Zeus overthrew him.

Helios (HEE lee ahs): sun god.

Hephaestus (hee FEHS tuhs): god of metalworking.

Hermes (HUR meez): messenger god.

Poseidon (poh SY duhn): god of the sea; brother of Zeus. Poseidon is called Earth Shaker because he is believed to cause earthquakes. He is an enemy of Odysseus.

Zeus (zoos): the most powerful god. His home is on Olympus.

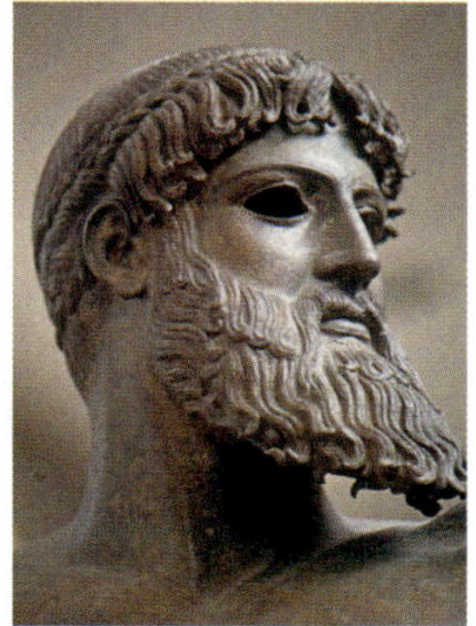

Poseidon. Detail from a bronze statue (5th century B.C.).

Mapping Odysseus's Journey

The map below illustrates Odysseus's travels. His journey begins in Troy, on the coast of Asia Minor (now Turkey). Much of Odysseus's journey takes place in and around the Aegean Sea, Sicily, Sardinia, and the Italian mainland, all of which made up the heart of Mediterranean Greco-Roman culture. Between 700 and 450 B.C., the ancient Greek city-states, such as Athens, Corinth, and Sparta, established many colonies in Sicily (called Magna Graecia, or Great Greece), as well as on the western coast of Asia Minor. Were Odysseus's journey to take place today, he would travel to parts of Italy, Greece, Turkey, and the continent of Africa.

1. Troy
2. Cicones
3. Lotus Eaters
4. Cyclops
5. Island of Aeolia
6. Laestrygonians
7. Circe
8. Sirens
9. Teiresias and the Land of the Dead
10. Circe
11. Charybdis
12. Scylla
13. Thrinakia
14. Calypso
15. Phaeacia
16. Ithaca

Preparing to Read

from the Odyssey, Part One

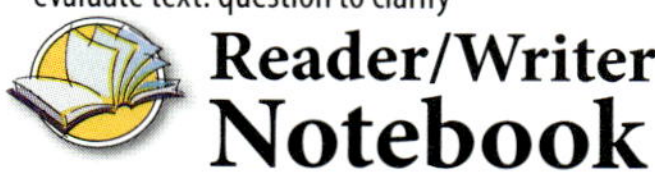

9.R.2.C.1.b Use details from text(s): to analyze character, plot, setting, point of view **9.R.1.G.1.f** During reading, utilize strategies: to paraphrase **9.R.1.G.1.g** During reading, utilize strategies: to summarize **9.R.1.H.1.b** Apply post-reading skills to comprehend, interpret, analyze, and evaluate text: question to clarify

Reader/Writer Notebook

Use your **RWN** to complete the activities for this selection.

Literary Focus

Epic Heroes and Conflict An "ordinary" hero saves children from a roaring river or rescues people from a burning building. An **epic hero** is larger than life and usually has the following character traits: uncommon strength and exceptional knowledge, cunning, courage, and daring. An epic hero often goes on a dangerous journey or quest of discovery. On his journey, the hero encounters **conflict** as he battles forces of nature, gods, and other beings who help or hinder his progress. As the hero faces conflict after conflict, he embodies or personifies the values of the society or civilization from which he sprang.

Literary Perspectives Apply the literary perspective described on page 1037 as you read this epic.

Reading Focus

Reading an Epic When you read a long work, it helps to use many strategies. If you are reading a complex passage, try **paraphrasing,** restating the content in your own words. To be sure you are following the sequence of events, **summarize** or briefly note each event in the order it occurred. **Ask questions** to monitor your comprehension.

Into Action As you read, use the *5W-How?* questions, like the ones below, to make sure you understand the epic.

- **Who** are the main characters?
- **What** has happened so far, and what might happen next?
- **Where** and **when** are the events taking place?
- **Why** are the events happening?
- **How** does the epic hero use his talents to resolve the conflict?

Writing Focus

Think as a Reader/Writer

Find It in Your Reading As you read, write in your *Reader/Writer Notebook* what you learn about Odysseus. Is he noble or selfish? wise or foolish? arrogant or humble?

Vocabulary

adversity (ad VUR suh tee) *n.:* hardship; great misfortune. *On his long journey Odysseus meets with adversity.*

formidable (FAWR muh duh buhl) *adj.:* awe-inspiring by reason of excellence; strikingly impressive. *The monster proved to be a formidable enemy.*

profusion (pruh FYOO zhuhn) *n.:* large supply; abundance. *Odysseus hid the weapon under a profusion of dung piles.*

adversary (AD vuhr sehr ee) *n.:* enemy; opponent. *The Cyclops was an adversary that was difficult to defeat.*

tumult (TOO muhlt) *n.:* commotion; uproar; confusion. *Looking out over the raging sea, the sailor saw waves in tumult.*

Language Coach

Related Words The adjective *adverse* means "harmful" or "unfavorable." Which two words on the list above are forms of the word *adverse?*

Learn It Online

Get a sneak peek of this selection by viewing the video introduction at:

go.hrw.com L9-1035 

MEET THE WRITER

Homer

(c. 8th century B.C.)

Who Was Homer?

No one knows for sure who Homer was. The later Greeks believed he was a blind minstrel, or singer, who came from the island of Chios. However, seven different cities claimed to be his birthplace, and if he was blind, then he must have been able to see at one time because his epics are so rich in visual imagery. Some scholars think there must have been two Homers; some think he was a legend; the English author Samuel Butler believed that Homer was a woman and wrote *The Authoress of the Odyssey* (1897) to prove his theory.

On the Road Again

If we accept the word of the Greeks themselves, then Homer was the model for a group of wandering bards or minstrels later called rhapsodes (RAP sohdz). He was a singer who traveled from community to community singing of the doings of heroes in battle, and the exploits of gods and goddesses. He was a historian, mythmaker, and entertainer. It is as if the author of the Book of Kings in the Bible, the writer of a history of World War II, and a famous pop singer were combined in one person.

Think About the Writer Do you think it matters that we don't know exactly who Homer was? Why or why not?

Marble bust portrait of Homer. Frontal view. 2nd century B.C. Hellenistic.

Preview the Selection

In the *Odyssey* you will meet **Odysseus,** an epic hero consumed with one goal: He wants to return home to his kingdom of Ithaca and his faithful wife **Penelope.**

Meet the Translator

Robert Fitzgerald (1910–1985)

After Robert Fitzgerald graduated from Harvard, he first worked as a reporter for a newspaper and then for *Time* magazine. He served in the Navy during World War II and then began teaching at a college. He published poetry and worked on his famous translation of the *Odyssey* while living in Italy for ten years. His translation has been called "the best and truest *Odyssey* in the English language."

Read with a Purpose Read to learn about the epic hero Odysseus and the journey that has inspired storytellers for centuries.

by **Homer**

translated by **Robert Fitzgerald**

Tell the Story

Homer opens with an invocation, or prayer, asking the Muse° to help him sing his tale. Notice how the singer gives his listeners hints about how his story is to end.

Sing in me, Muse, and through me tell the story
of that man skilled in all ways of contending,°
the wanderer, harried for years on end,
after he plundered the stronghold
on the proud height of Troy.
He saw the townlands
and learned the minds of many distant men,
and weathered many bitter nights and days
in his deep heart at sea, while he fought only
to save his life, to bring his shipmates home.
But not by will nor valor could he save them,
for their own recklessness destroyed them all—
children and fools, they killed and feasted on
the cattle of Lord Helios, the Sun,
and he who moves all day through heaven
took from their eyes the dawn of their return.

Of these adventures, Muse, daughter of Zeus,
tell us in our time, lift the great song again.
Begin when all the rest who left behind them
headlong death in battle or at sea
had long ago returned, while he alone still hungered
for home and wife. Her ladyship Calypso

° **Muse:** The Greeks believed that there were nine Muses, daughters of Zeus, the chief god. The Muses inspired people to produce music, poetry, dance, and all the other arts. Many epics begin with a poet requesting inspiration from a muse.

2. **contending** (kuhn TEHND ihng): fighting; dealing with difficulties.

Literary Perspectives

Analyzing Historical Context When applying this perspective, you will view a literary text within its historical context. Specific historical information—such as the time during which the author wrote, the time period in which the text is set, and the ways in which people of the period saw and thought about the world in which they lived—will be of key interest. As you read, be sure to notice the notes and questions at the bottom of the pages, which will guide you in using this perspective.

clung to him in her sea-hollowed caves—
a nymph, immortal and most beautiful,
who craved him for her own.
And when long years and seasons
wheeling brought around that point of time
ordained for him to make his passage homeward,
trials and dangers, even so, attended him
even in Ithaca, near those he loved.
Yet all the gods had pitied Lord Odysseus,
all but Poseidon, raging cold and rough
against the brave king till he came ashore
at last on his own land. . . . **A**

(*from* Book 1)

PART ONE:
The Wanderings

Calypso, the Sweet Nymph

Books 1–4 of the epic tell about Odysseus's son, Telemachus. Telemachus has been searching the Mediterranean world for his father, who has never returned from the ten-year Trojan War. (Today, Odysseus would be listed as missing in action.)

When we first meet Odysseus, in Book 5 of the epic, he is a prisoner of the beautiful goddess Calypso. The old soldier is in despair: He has spent ten years (seven of them as Calypso's not entirely unwilling captive) trying to get home.

The goddess Athena has supported and helped Odysseus on his long journey. Now she begs her father, Zeus, to help her favorite mortal, and Zeus agrees. He sends the messenger god Hermes to Calypso's island to order Odysseus released. Although Calypso is not described as evil, her seductive charms—even her promises of immortality for Odysseus—threaten to keep the hero away from his wife, Penelope.

No words were lost on Hermes the Wayfinder
who bent to tie his beautiful sandals on,

? **33–66.** *There is a great deal of nature* ***imagery*** *in this episode. Jot down some of the images that help you see Hermes' flight. What images describing Calypso's island appeal to your senses of sight, hearing, and smell?*

A **Reading Focus** **Summarizing** Read this invocation to the Muse aloud. What does Homer tell you about the hero and what is going to happen to him?

ambrosial,° golden, that carry him over water
or over endless land in a swish of the wind,
and took the wand with which he charms asleep—
or when he wills, awake—the eyes of men.
So wand in hand he paced into the air,
shot from Pieria° down, down to sea level,
and veered to skim the swell. A gull patrolling
between the wave crests of the desolate sea
will dip to catch a fish, and douse his wings;
no higher above the whitecaps Hermes flew
until the distant island lay ahead,
then rising shoreward from the violet ocean
he stepped up to the cave. Divine Calypso,
the mistress of the isle, was now at home.
Upon her hearthstone a great fire blazing
scented the farthest shores with cedar smoke
and smoke of thyme, and singing high and low
in her sweet voice, before her loom aweaving,
she passed her golden shuttle to and fro. **A**
A deep wood grew outside, with summer leaves
of alder and black poplar, pungent cypress.
Ornate birds here rested their stretched wings—
horned owls, falcons, cormorants—long-tongued
beachcombing birds, and followers of the sea.
Around the smooth-walled cave a crooking vine
held purple clusters under ply° of green;
and four springs, bubbling up near one another
shallow and clear, took channels here and there
through beds of violets and tender parsley.
Even a god who found this place
would gaze, and feel his heart beat with delight:
so Hermes did; but when he had gazed his fill
he entered the wide cave. Now face-to-face
the magical Calypso recognized him, **B**
as all immortal gods know one another
on sight—though seeming strangers, far from home.
But he saw nothing of the great Odysseus,

Analyzing Visuals

Viewing and Interpreting What does the portrayal of images from mythology on everyday objects, such as this vase, tell you about the values and beliefs of the ancient Greeks?

Ulysses and Calypso. Red-figured vase (5th century B.C.). Location: Museo Archeologico Nazionale, Naples, Italy.

35. ambrosial (am BROH zhuhl): fit for the gods; divine. Nectar and ambrosia are the drink and food that keep the gods immortal.

40. Pieria (py IHR ee uh): place in central Greece not far from Olympus; a favorite spot of Hermes'.

40–45. *To help his audience visualize Hermes dropping down and skimming the waves, Homer compares Hermes to a gull. This comparison between something the audience knows to something unknown is called an* ***epic simile****.*

60. ply: twisted strands.

A **Literary Perspectives** **Analyzing Historical Context** What do the characters of the gods reveal about the beliefs of the ancient Greeks?

B **Literary Focus** **Epic Heroes and Conflict** How does the natural beauty of Calypso's island contrast with the internal conflict that Odysseus is experiencing?

who sat apart, as a thousand times before,
and racked his own heart groaning, with eyes wet
scanning the bare horizon of the sea. . . .

Hermes tells Calypso that she must give up Odysseus forever. Now we are directly introduced to Odysseus. Notice what this great warrior is doing when we first meet him.

The strong god glittering left her as he spoke,
and now her ladyship, having given heed
to Zeus's mandate, went to find Odysseus
in his stone seat to seaward—tear on tear
brimming his eyes. The sweet days of his lifetime
were running out in anguish over his exile,
for long ago the nymph had ceased to please.
Though he fought shy of her and her desire,
he lay with her each night, for she compelled him.
But when day came he sat on the rocky shore
and broke his own heart groaning, with eyes wet
scanning the bare horizon of the sea.
Now she stood near him in her beauty, saying:

"O forlorn man, be still.
Here you need grieve no more; you need not feel
your life consumed here; I have pondered it,
and I shall help you go. . . ." **C**

Calypso promises Odysseus a raft and provisions to help him homeward without harm—provided the gods wish it. Now Odysseus and Calypso say goodbye.

Swiftly she turned and led him to her cave,
and they went in, the mortal and immortal.
He took the chair left empty now by Hermes,
where the divine Calypso placed before him
victuals° and drink of men; then she sat down
facing Odysseus, while her serving maids
brought nectar and ambrosia to her side.
Then each one's hands went out on each one's feast

96. victuals (VIHT uhlz): food.

C **Reading Focus** **Asking Questions** Calypso claims that it is her idea to release Odysseus. Why do you think she does this?

MUSIC LINK

Calypso, Then and Now

Modern songwriters have been inspired by the ancient tale of the *Odyssey*. Here are the lyrics to a song Suzanne Vega recorded and released in 2003.

My name is Calypso
And I have lived alone
I live on an island
And I waken to the dawn
A long time ago
I watched him struggle with the sea
I knew that he was drowning
And I brought him into me
Now today
Come morning light
He sails away
After one last night
I let him go.

My name is Calypso
My garden overflows
Thick and wild and hidden
Is the sweetness there that grows
My hair it blows long
As I sing into the wind
I tell of nights
Where I could taste the salt on his skin
Salt on the waves
And of tears
And though he pulled away
I kept him for years
I let him go.

My name is Calypso
I have let him go
In the dawn he sails away
To be gone forever more
And the waves will take him in again
But he'll know their ways now
I will stand upon the shore
With a clean heart
And my song in the wind
The sand will sting my feet
And the sky will burn
It's a lonely time ahead
I do not ask him to return
I let him go
I let him go.

Ask Yourself

From whose point of view is this song sung? What insights into Calypso does this song offer you?

The Departure of Ulysses from the Isle of Calypso (1848–1849) by Samuel Palmer (1805–1881). The Whitworth Art Gallery, the University of Manchester, U.K.

until they had had their pleasure; and she said:
"Son of Laertes,° versatile Odysseus,
after these years with me, you still desire
your old home? Even so, I wish you well.
If you could see it all, before you go—
all the adversity you face at sea—
you would stay here, and guard this house, and be
immortal—though you wanted her forever,
that bride for whom you pine each day.
Can I be less desirable than she is?
Less interesting? Less beautiful? Can mortals
compare with goddesses in grace and form?"

To this the strategist Odysseus answered:

"My lady goddess, there is no cause for anger.
My quiet Penelope—how well I know—
would seem a shade before your majesty,
death and old age being unknown to you,
while she must die. Yet, it is true, each day
I long for home, long for the sight of home. . . ." **D**

So Odysseus builds the raft and sets sail. But the sea god Poseidon is by no means ready to allow an easy passage over his watery domain. He raises a storm and destroys the raft. It is only with the help of Athena and a sea nymph that Odysseus arrives, broken and battered, on the island of Scheria (SKEE ree uh). *There he hides himself in a pile of leaves and falls into a deep sleep.*

A man in a distant field, no hearth fires near,
will hide a fresh brand° in his bed of embers
to keep a spark alive for the next day;
so in the leaves Odysseus hid himself,
while over him Athena showered sleep
that his distress should end, and soon, soon.
In quiet sleep she sealed his cherished eyes.

(*from* Book 5)

101. Laertes (lay UR teez).

120. brand: burning stick.

D **Reading Focus** **Summarizing** How does Odysseus say no to Calypso's offer of immortality and still not offend her?

Vocabulary **adversity** (ad VUR suh tee) *n.:* hardship; great misfortune.

"I am Laertes' son. . . ."

Odysseus is found by the daughter of Alcinous, king of the Phaeacians. That evening he is a guest at court (Books 6–8).

To the ancient people of Greece and Asia Minor, all guests were god-sent. They had to be treated with great courtesy before they could be asked to identify themselves and state their business. That night, at the banquet, the stranger who was washed up on the beach is seated in the guest's place of honor. A blind minstrel, or singer, is called, and the mystery guest gives him a gift of pork, crisp with fat, and requests a song about Troy. In effect, Odysseus is asking for a song about himself.

Odysseus weeps as the minstrel's song reminds him of all his companions, who will never see their homes again. Now Odysseus is asked by the king to identify himself. It is here that he begins the story of his journey.

Now this was the reply Odysseus made: . . .

"I am Laertes' son, Odysseus.
Men hold me
formidable for guile in peace and war:
this fame has gone abroad to the sky's rim. **A**
My home is on the peaked seamark of Ithaca
under Mount Neion's windblown robe of leaves,
in sight of other islands—Doulikhion,
Same, wooded Zakynthos—Ithaca
being most lofty in that coastal sea,
and northwest, while the rest lie east and south.
A rocky isle, but good for a boy's training;
I shall not see on earth a place more dear,
though I have been detained long by Calypso,
loveliest among goddesses, who held me
in her smooth caves, to be her heart's delight,
as Circe of Aeaea, the enchantress,
desired me, and detained me in her hall.
But in my heart I never gave consent.

A **Literary Focus** **Epic Heroes and Conflict** What does Odysseus's introduction of himself tell you about the traits that the Greeks admired in an epic hero?

Vocabulary **formidable** (FAWR muh duh buhl) *adj.:* awe-inspiring by reason of excellence; strikingly impressive.

HISTORY LINK

After the Trojan Horse by Henri Paul Motte. Engraving.

Unearthing Troy

The ancient Greeks and Romans had no doubt that the Trojan War really happened. They believed it took place around 1200 B.C. The Greek historian Thucydides (c. 460–c. 400 B.C.) believed the causes of the war were economic and political, not due to Helen of Troy's abduction by the Greeks. By the middle of the nineteenth century, however, most historians had dismissed the Trojan War as legend.

Enter Heinrich Schliemann (1822–1890). Schliemann was a wealthy German who developed an interest in archaeology. Armed with a copy of Homer's *Iliad,* he arrived in northwestern Turkey in 1871. A few miles from the Dardanelles, the sea lane that divides Europe from Asia, Schliemann began excavations at a small hill called Hissarlik, perched about a hundred feet above a wide plain.

After five long years, Schliemann made an electrifying discovery. He unearthed gold cups, bracelets, and a spectacular gold headdress. Homer had called Troy rich in gold, and Schliemann believed he had found the treasure of Priam, the last king of Troy. Despite his success, he was filled with doubt about whether or not he had really found Troy.

We now know that Schliemann's treasure came from a stratum, or layer of earth (called Troy II), that dated back to a thousand years before the Trojan War. Another level (Troy VIIA) showed violent destruction by fire around 1200 B.C. Could this have been Homer's Troy? During the 1930s, another team of archaeologists confirmed this theory. Despite the inconsistencies that remain, the hill of Hissarlik is widely accepted as the most likely location of the Trojan War.

Ask Yourself

Do you believe that the Trojan War actually occurred? How does your opinion influence your reading of Odysseus's adventures?

Where shall a man find sweetness to surpass
his own home and his parents? In far lands
he shall not, though he find a house of gold.

What of my sailing, then, from Troy?
What of those years
of rough adventure, weathered under Zeus?
The wind that carried west from Ilion°
brought me to Ismaros, on the far shore,
a strongpoint on the coast of the Cicones.
I stormed that place and killed the men who fought.
Plunder we took, and we enslaved the women,
to make division, equal shares to all—
but on the spot I told them: 'Back, and quickly!
Out to sea again!' My men were mutinous,
fools, on stores of wine. Sheep after sheep
they butchered by the surf, and shambling cattle,
feasting—while fugitives went inland, running
to call to arms the main force of Cicones. (B)
This was an army, trained to fight on horseback
or, where the ground required, on foot. They came
with dawn over that terrain like the leaves
and blades of spring. So doom appeared to us,
dark word of Zeus for us, our evil days.
My men stood up and made a fight of it—
backed on the ships, with lances kept in play,
from bright morning through the blaze of noon
holding our beach, although so far outnumbered;
but when the sun passed toward unyoking time,
then the Achaeans, one by one, gave way.
Six benches were left empty in every ship
that evening when we pulled away from death.
And this new grief we bore with us to sea:
our precious lives we had, but not our friends.
No ship made sail next day until some shipmate
had raised a cry, three times, for each poor ghost
unfleshed by the Cicones on that field.
Now Zeus the lord of cloud roused in the north
a storm against the ships, and driving veils

147. *The answer to this question becomes the epic tale.*

149. Ilion (IHL ee ahn): another name for Troy.

(B) Literary Focus **Epic Heroes and Conflict** In this conflict Odysseus loses control over his men. What does this tell you about his abilities as a leader?

of squall moved down like night on land and sea.
The bows went plunging at the gust; sails
cracked and lashed out strips in the big wind.
We saw death in that fury, dropped the yards,°
unshipped the oars, and pulled for the nearest lee:°
then two long days and nights we lay offshore
worn out and sick at heart, tasting our grief,
until a third Dawn came with ringlets shining.
Then we put up our masts, hauled sail, and rested,
letting the steersmen and the breeze take over.

184. yards: sails.

185. lee: place of shelter from the wind.

I might have made it safely home, that time,
but as I came round Malea the current
took me out to sea, and from the north
a fresh gale drove me on, past Cythera.°
Nine days I drifted on the teeming sea
before dangerous high winds." **C**

194. Cythera (sih THIHR uh).

(*from* Book 9)

The Lotus Eaters

"Upon the tenth
we came to the coastline of the Lotus Eaters,
who live upon that flower. We landed there
to take on water. All ships' companies
mustered° alongside for the midday meal.
Then I sent out two picked men and a runner
to learn what race of men that land sustained.
They fell in, soon enough, with Lotus Eaters,
who showed no will to do us harm, only
offering the sweet Lotus to our friends—
but those who ate this honeyed plant, the Lotus,
never cared to report, nor to return:
they longed to stay forever, browsing on
that native bloom, forgetful of their homeland.
I drove them, all three wailing, to the ships,
tied them down under their rowing benches,
and called the rest: 'All hands aboard;
come, clear the beach and no one taste

201. mustered: gathered; assembled.

C **Literary Perspectives** **Analyzing Historical Context** Much of this story involves sea travel. What concerns might a seagoing nation have?

the Lotus, or you lose your hope of home.'
Filing in to their places by the rowlocks
my oarsmen dipped their long oars in the surf,
and we moved out again on our seafaring. . . ." 

(*from* Book 9)

The Cyclops

In his next adventure, Odysseus describes his encounter with the Cyclops named Polyphemus, Poseidon's one-eyed monster son. Polyphemus may represent the brute forces that any hero must overcome before he can reach home. Now Odysseus must rely on his special intelligence. Odysseus is the cleverest of the Greek heroes because he is guided by the goddess of wisdom, Athena.

A Reading Focus **Asking Questions** Why does Odysseus tie down the three men? Based on Odysseus's actions, what can you infer about his attitude toward his crew?

The Cyclops (1914) by Odilon Redon (1840–1916). Oil on canvas (64 cm x 51 cm).

It is Odysseus's famed curiosity that leads him to the Cyclops's cave and that makes him insist on waiting for the barbaric giant.

Odysseus is still speaking to the court of King Alcinous.

"We lit a fire, burnt an offering,
and took some cheese to eat; then sat in silence
around the embers, waiting. When he came
he had a load of dry boughs on his shoulder
to stoke his fire at suppertime. He dumped it
with a great crash into that hollow cave,
and we all scattered fast to the far wall.
Then over the broad cavern floor he ushered
the ewes he meant to milk. He left his rams
and he-goats in the yard outside, and swung
high overhead a slab of solid rock
to close the cave. Two dozen four-wheeled wagons, **A**
with heaving wagon teams, could not have stirred
the tonnage of that rock from where he wedged it
over the doorsill. Next he took his seat
and milked his bleating ewes. A practiced job
he made of it, giving each ewe her suckling;
thickened his milk, then, into curds and whey,
sieved out the curds to drip in withy° baskets,
and poured the whey to stand in bowls
cooling until he drank it for his supper.
When all these chores were done, he poked the fire,
heaping on brushwood. In the glare he saw us.

'Strangers,' he said, 'who are you? And where from?
What brings you here by seaways—a fair traffic?
Or are you wandering rogues, who cast your lives
like dice, and ravage other folk by sea?'

We felt a pressure on our hearts, in dread
of that deep rumble and that mighty man.
But all the same I spoke up in reply:

237. withy: made from willow twigs.

A Literary Focus Epic Heroes and Conflict Epic heroes need a mighty opponent to show how resourceful they can be. How does Homer make it clear that Odysseus faces a formidable opponent in the Cyclops?

CULTURE LINK

Greek Hospitality

Today's visitors to Greece are often struck by the generous hospitality of its people. An ancient Greek tradition lies behind the traveler's welcome—and it is a tradition that was fundamentally religious before it became a part of social custom. Zeus, the king of the gods, demanded that strangers be treated graciously. Hosts had a religious duty to welcome strangers, and guests had a responsibility to respect them. This close interconnection and mutual respect between host and guest are reflected in the fact that the word *xenos* (ZEHN nohs) in ancient Greek can mean both "host" and "guest."

Ask Yourself

How has the tradition of hospitality been expressed in Homer's epic?

'We are from Troy, Achaeans, blown off course
by shifting gales on the Great South Sea;
homeward bound, but taking routes and ways
uncommon; so the will of Zeus would have it.
We served under Agamemnon,° son of Atreus°—
the whole world knows what city
he laid waste, what armies he destroyed.
It was our luck to come here; here we stand,
beholden for your help, or any gifts
you give—as custom is to honor strangers.
We would entreat you, great Sir, have a care
for the gods' courtesy; Zeus will avenge
the unoffending guest.' **B**

He answered this
from his brute chest, unmoved:
'You are a ninny,
or else you come from the other end of nowhere,

253. **Agamemnon** (ag uh MEHM nahn). **Atreus** (AY tree uhs).

B **Literary Perspectives** **Analyzing Historical Context** In this passage Odysseus informs the Cyclops that Zeus will punish the Cyclops if he injures or harms his guests. What can you infer about Greek society from this remark?

telling me, mind the gods! We Cyclopes
care not a whistle for your thundering Zeus
or all the gods in bliss; we have more force by far.
I would not let you go for fear of Zeus—
you or your friends—unless I had a whim to.
Tell me, where was it, now, you left your ship—
around the point, or down the shore, I wonder?'

He thought he'd find out, but I saw through this,
and answered with a ready lie:

'My ship?
Poseidon Lord, who sets the earth atremble,
broke it up on the rocks at your land's end.
A wind from seaward served him, drove us there.
We are survivors, these good men and I.'

Neither reply nor pity came from him,
but in one stride he clutched at my companions
and caught two in his hands like squirming puppies
to beat their brains out, spattering the floor.
Then he dismembered them and made his meal,
gaping and crunching like a mountain lion—
everything: innards, flesh, and marrow bones.
We cried aloud, lifting our hands to Zeus,
powerless, looking on at this, appalled;
but Cyclops went on filling up his belly
with manflesh and great gulps of whey,
then lay down like a mast among his sheep.
My heart beat high now at the chance of action, **C**
and drawing the sharp sword from my hip I went
along his flank to stab him where the midriff
holds the liver. I had touched the spot
when sudden fear stayed me: if I killed him
we perished there as well, for we could never
move his ponderous doorway slab aside.
So we were left to groan and wait for morning.

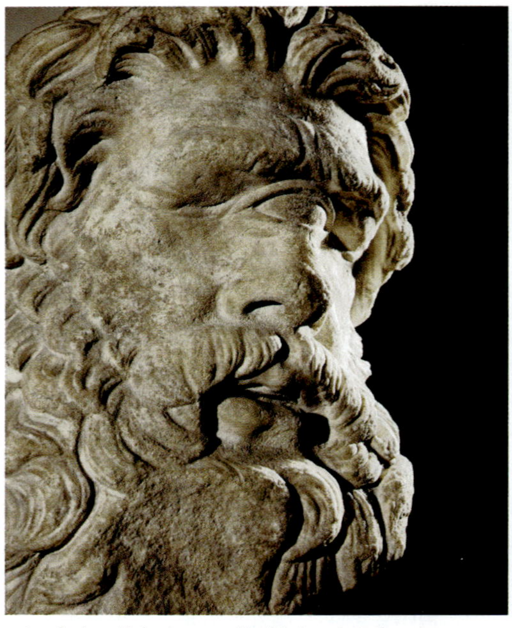

Cyclops Polyphemus. Marble head, 2nd century B.C. Location: Museum of Fine Arts, Boston, U.S.A.

C **Reading Focus** **Asking Questions** Why doesn't Odysseus kill the Cyclops at this moment? What must Odysseus consider in devising an escape plan?

When the young Dawn with fingertips of rose
lit up the world, the Cyclops built a fire
and milked his handsome ewes, all in due order,
putting the sucklings to the mothers. Then,
his chores being all dispatched, he caught
another brace° of men to make his breakfast,
and whisked away his great door slab
to let his sheep go through—but he, behind,
reset the stone as one would cap a quiver.°
There was a din of whistling as the Cyclops
rounded his flock to higher ground, then stillness.
And now I pondered how to hurt him worst,
if but Athena granted what I prayed for.
Here are the means I thought would serve my turn:

a club, or staff, lay there along the fold—
an olive tree, felled green and left to season
for Cyclops' hand. And it was like a mast
a lugger° of twenty oars, broad in the beam—
a deep-seagoing craft—might carry:
so long, so big around, it seemed. Now I
chopped out a six-foot section of this pole
and set it down before my men, who scraped it;
and when they had it smooth, I hewed again
to make a stake with pointed end. I held this
in the fire's heart and turned it, toughening it,
then hid it, well back in the cavern, under
one of the dung piles in profusion there. D
Now came the time to toss for it: who ventured
along with me? Whose hand could bear to thrust
and grind that spike in Cyclops' eye, when mild
sleep had mastered him? As luck would have it,
the men I would have chosen won the toss—
four strong men, and I made five as captain. E

302. brace: pair.

305. quiver: case for arrows.

314. lugger: type of sailboat.

D Reading Focus Paraphrasing What does Odysseus do with the stake? Explain in your own words.

E Literary Focus Epic Heroes and Conflict As the leader and hero, Odysseus could have simply chosen the men he wanted for the job. Why do you think he draws lots?

Vocabulary **profusion** (pruh FYOO zhuhn) *n.:* large supply; abundance.

At evening came the shepherd with his flock,
his woolly flock. The rams as well, this time,
entered the cave: by some sheepherding whim—
or a god's bidding—none were left outside.
He hefted his great boulder into place
and sat him down to milk the bleating ewes
in proper order, put the lambs to suck,
and swiftly ran through all his evening chores.
Then he caught two more men and feasted on them.
My moment was at hand, and I went forward
holding an ivy bowl of my dark drink,
looking up, saying:

'Cyclops, try some wine.
Here's liquor to wash down your scraps of men.
Taste it, and see the kind of drink we carried
under our planks. I meant it for an offering
if you would help us home. But you are mad,
unbearable, a bloody monster! After this,
will any other traveler come to see you?'

He seized and drained the bowl, and it went down
so fiery and smooth he called for more:

'Give me another, thank you kindly. Tell me,
how are you called? I'll make a gift will please you.
Even Cyclopes know the wine grapes grow
out of grassland and loam in heaven's rain,
but here's a bit of nectar and ambrosia!'

Three bowls I brought him, and he poured them down.
I saw the fuddle and flush come over him,
then I sang out in cordial tones:

'Cyclops,
you ask my honorable name? Remember
the gift you promised me, and I shall tell you.
My name is Nohbdy: mother, father, and friends,
everyone calls me Nohbdy.'

? **360.** *The Greek word for "nobody" is* outis, *which sounds somewhat like "Odysseus." Why do you think Odysseus says his name is Nohbdy?*

And he said:
'Nohbdy's my meat, then, after I eat his friends.
Others come first. There's a noble gift, now.'

Even as he spoke, he reeled and tumbled backward,
his great head lolling to one side; and sleep
took him like any creature. Drunk, hiccuping,
he dribbled streams of liquor and bits of men.

Now, by the gods, I drove my big hand spike
deep in the embers, charring it again,
and cheered my men along with battle talk
to keep their courage up: no quitting now.
The pike of olive, green though it had been,
reddened and glowed as if about to catch.
I drew it from the coals and my four fellows
gave me a hand, lugging it near the Cyclops
as more than natural force nerved them; straight
forward they sprinted, lifted it, and rammed it
deep in his crater eye, and I leaned on it
turning it as a shipwright turns a drill
in planking, having men below to swing
the two-handled strap that spins it in the groove.
So with our brand we bored that great eye socket
while blood ran out around the red-hot bar.
Eyelid and lash were seared; the pierced ball
hissed broiling, and the roots popped.

In a smithy°
one sees a white-hot axhead or an adze°
plunged and wrung in a cold tub, screeching steam—
the way they make soft iron hale and hard—
just so that eyeball hissed around the spike.
The Cyclops bellowed and the rock roared round him,
and we fell back in fear. Clawing his face
he tugged the bloody spike out of his eye,
threw it away, and his wild hands went groping;
then he set up a howl for Cyclopes
who lived in caves on windy peaks nearby.
Some heard him; and they came by divers° ways
to clump around outside and call:

The Blinding of Polyphemus. Greek black figure hydria (531-510 B.C.). Location: Museo Nazionale di Villa Guilia, Rome, Italy.

385. smithy: blacksmith's shop, where iron tools are made.

386. adze (adz): axlike tool with a long, curved blade.

396. divers (DY vuhrz): diverse; various.

'What ails you,
Polyphemus? Why do you cry so sore
in the starry night? You will not let us sleep.
Sure no man's driving off your flock? No man
has tricked you, ruined you?'

Out of the cave
the mammoth Polyphemus roared in answer:

'Nohbdy, Nohbdy's tricked me. Nohbdy's ruined me!'

To this rough shout they made a sage° reply:

'Ah well, if nobody has played you foul
there in your lonely bed, we are no use in pain
given by great Zeus. Let it be your father,
Poseidon Lord, to whom you pray.'

So saying
they trailed away. And I was filled with laughter
to see how like a charm the name deceived them.
Now Cyclops, wheezing as the pain came on him,

404. sage (sayj): wise.

Odysseus escaping from the cave of Polyphemus under the belly of the ram. Detail from a krater, a vessel for holding wine (c. 510 B.C.).

Analyzing Visuals

Viewing and Interpreting How well does this image express Homer's description of Odysseus's escape? Why do you think so?

fumbled to wrench away the great doorstone
and squatted in the breach with arms thrown wide
for any silly beast or man who bolted—
hoping somehow I might be such a fool.
But I kept thinking how to win the game: **F**
death sat there huge; how could we slip away?
I drew on all my wits, and ran through tactics,
reasoning as a man will for dear life,
until a trick came—and it pleased me well.
The Cyclops' rams were handsome, fat, with heavy
fleeces, a dark violet.

Three abreast

I tied them silently together, twining
cords of willow from the ogre's bed;
then slung a man under each middle one
to ride there safely, shielded left and right.
So three sheep could convey each man. I took
the woolliest ram, the choicest of the flock,
and hung myself under his kinky belly,
pulled up tight, with fingers twisted deep
in sheepskin ringlets for an iron grip.
So, breathing hard, we waited until morning.

When Dawn spread out her fingertips of rose
the rams began to stir, moving for pasture,
and peals of bleating echoed round the pens
where dams with udders full called for a milking.
Blinded, and sick with pain from his head wound,
the master stroked each ram, then let it pass,
but my men riding on the pectoral fleece°
the giant's blind hands blundering never found.
Last of them all my ram, the leader, came,
weighted by wool and me with my meditations.
The Cyclops patted him, and then he said:
'Sweet cousin ram, why lag behind the rest
in the night cave? You never linger so,
but graze before them all, and go afar
to crop sweet grass, and take your stately way

? **421–442.** *Explain Odysseus's trick. What do you* ***visualize*** *happening in this scene?*

439. pectoral fleece: wool on an animal's chest.

F **Literary Focus** **Epic Heroes and Conflict** What heroic character traits is Odysseus showing?

leading along the streams, until at evening
you run to be the first one in the fold.
Why, now, so far behind? Can you be grieving
over your Master's eye? That carrion rogue°
and his accurst companions burnt it out
when he had conquered all my wits with wine.
Nohbdy will not get out alive, I swear.
Oh, had you brain and voice to tell
where he may be now, dodging all my fury!
Bashed by this hand and bashed on this rock wall
his brains would strew the floor, and I should have
rest from the outrage Nohbdy worked upon me.'

He sent us into the open, then. Close by,
I dropped and rolled clear of the ram's belly,
going this way and that to untie the men.
With many glances back, we rounded up
his fat, stiff-legged sheep to take aboard,
and drove them down to where the good ship lay.
We saw, as we came near, our fellows' faces
shining; then we saw them turn to grief
tallying those who had not fled from death.
I hushed them, jerking head and eyebrows up,
and in a low voice told them: 'Load this herd;
move fast, and put the ship's head toward the breakers.'
They all pitched in at loading, then embarked
and struck their oars into the sea. Far out,
as far offshore as shouted words would carry,
I sent a few back to the adversary:

'O Cyclops! Would you feast on my companions?
Puny, am I, in a Caveman's hands?
How do you like the beating that we gave you,
you damned cannibal? Eater of guests
under your roof! Zeus and the gods have paid you!'

The blind thing in his doubled fury broke
a hilltop in his hands and heaved it after us.
Ahead of our black prow it struck and sank

451. carrion rogue: rotten scoundrel. Carrion is decaying flesh.

Vocabulary **adversary** (AD vuhr sehr ee) *n.:* enemy; opponent.

whelmed in a spuming geyser, a giant wave
that washed the ship stern foremost back to shore.
I got the longest boathook out and stood
fending us off, with furious nods to all
to put their backs into a racing stroke—
row, row or perish. So the long oars bent
kicking the foam sternward, making head
until we drew away, and twice as far.
Now when I cupped my hands I heard the crew
in low voices protesting:

'Godsake, Captain!
Why bait the beast again? Let him alone!'

'That tidal wave he made on the first throw
all but beached us.'

'All but stove us in!'
'Give him our bearing with your trumpeting,
he'll get the range and lob° a boulder.'

'Aye
He'll smash our timbers and our heads together!'

I would not heed them in my glorying spirit
but let my anger flare and yelled:

'Cyclops,
if ever mortal man inquire
how you were put to shame and blinded, tell him
Odysseus, raider of cities, took your eye:
Laertes' son, whose home's on Ithaca!' G

At this he gave a mighty sob and rumbled:

'Now comes the weird° upon me, spoken of old. H

498. lob: toss.

507. weird: fate.

G **Reading Focus** **Asking Questions** Odysseus's love of boasting is one of his traits. Is he wise in revealing his name to the Cyclops? Why or why not?

H **Literary Focus** **Epic Heroes and Conflict** Heroes and their opponents often have character flaws that can undo them. What character flaws have led to the Cyclops's downfall?

A wizard, grand and wondrous, lived here—Telemus,°
a son of Eurymus;° great length of days
he had in wizardry among the Cyclopes,
and these things he foretold for time to come:
my great eye lost, and at Odysseus' hands.
Always I had in mind some giant, armed
in giant force, would come against me here.
But this, but you—small, pitiful, and twiggy—
you put me down with wine, you blinded me.
Come back, Odysseus, and I'll treat you well,
praying the god of earthquake to befriend you—
his son I am, for he by his avowal
fathered me, and, if he will, he may
heal me of this black wound—he and no other
of all the happy gods or mortal men.'

Few words I shouted in reply to him:

'If I could take your life I would and take
your time away, and hurl you down to hell!
The god of earthquake could not heal you there!'

At this he stretched his hands out in his darkness
toward the sky of stars, and prayed Poseidon:

'O hear me, lord, blue girdler of the islands,
if I am thine indeed, and thou art father:
grant that Odysseus, raider of cities, never
see his home: Laertes' son, I mean,
who kept his hall on Ithaca. Should destiny
intend that he shall see his roof again
among his family in his fatherland,
far be that day, and dark the years between.
Let him lose all companions, and return
under strange sail to bitter days at home.' . . ." **I**

(*from* Book 9)

508. Telemus (TEHL uh muhs).
509. Eurymus (YOO ree muhs).

? **512.** *The Cyclops realizes that his fate, predicted by Telemus, has come true.*

Odysseus being given a drugged potion by Circe (late 5th century B.C.). Ceramic cup.

I **Reading Focus** **Summarizing** How has Odysseus handled himself in this dangerous situation?

Here we will imagine that Homer stops reciting for the night. The blind poet might take a glass of wine before turning in. The listeners would go off to various corners of the local nobleman's house. They might discuss highlights of the poet's tale among themselves and look forward to the next evening's installment.

The Enchantress Circe

After sailing from the Cyclops's island, Odysseus and his men land on the island of Aeolia. There the wind king, Aeolus (EE uh luhs), *does Odysseus a favor. He puts all the stormy winds in a bag so that they will not harm the Ithacans. The bull's-hide bag containing the winds is wedged under Odysseus's afterdeck. During the voyage, when the curious and suspicious sailors open the bag, thinking it contains treasure, the evil winds roar up into hurricanes that blow the ships back to Aeolia. Aeolus drives them away again.*

On the island of the Laestrygonians (lehs trihg OH nee uhnz), *gigantic cannibals, all the ships but Odysseus's are destroyed and their crews devoured. Odysseus's ship sails on, eventually arriving at Aeaea, the home of the enchantress and goddess Circe. Here a party of twenty-three men, led by Eurylochus, goes off to explore the island. Odysseus is still telling his story to Alcinous and his court.*

"In the wild wood they found an open glade,
around a smooth stone house—the hall of Circe—
and wolves and mountain lions lay there, mild
in her soft spell, fed on her drug of evil.
None would attack—oh, it was strange, I tell you—
but switching their long tails they faced our men
like hounds, who look up when their master comes
with tidbits for them—as he will—from table.
Humbly those wolves and lions with mighty paws
fawned on our men—who met their yellow eyes
and feared them.
In the entranceway they stayed
to listen there: inside her quiet house
they heard the goddess Circe. **A**

Odysseus pursuing Circe (5th century B.C.). Greek wine vase. Louvre, Paris, France.

A **Reading Focus** **Summarizing** What has happened so far in this episode?

Low she sang
in her beguiling voice, while on her loom
she wove ambrosial fabric sheer and bright,
by that craft known to the goddesses of heaven.
No one would speak, until Polites°—most
faithful and likable of my officers—said:

'Dear friends, no need for stealth:° here's a young weaver
singing a pretty song to set the air
atingle on these lawns and paven courts.
Goddess she is, or lady. Shall we greet her?'

So reassured, they all cried out together,
and she came swiftly to the shining doors
to call them in. All but Eurylochus—
who feared a snare—the innocents went after her.
On thrones she seated them, and lounging chairs,
while she prepared a meal of cheese and barley
and amber honey mixed with Pramnian wine,°
adding her own vile pinch, to make them lose
desire or thought of our dear fatherland.
Scarce had they drunk when she flew after them
with her long stick and shut them in a pigsty—
bodies, voices, heads, and bristles, all
swinish now, though minds were still unchanged.
So, squealing, in they went. And Circe tossed them
acorns, mast,° and cornel berries—fodder
for hogs who rut and slumber on the earth.

Down to the ship Eurylochus came running
to cry alarm, foul magic doomed his men!
But working with dry lips to speak a word
he could not, being so shaken; blinding tears
welled in his eyes; foreboding filled his heart.
When we were frantic questioning him, at last
we heard the tale: our friends were gone. . . ." **B**

(*from* Book 10)

Swineherd and Odysseus (470–460 B.C.) by the Pig Painter.

555. Polites (poh LY teez).

557. stealth: sneaky behavior.

567. Pramnian wine: strong wine from Mount Pramnos in ancient Greece.

575. mast: various kinds of nuts used as food for hogs.

B **Literary Focus** **Epic Heroes and Conflict** In what way does Eurylochus contrast with Odysseus? Does Eurylochus act as a hero would? Explain.

Odysseus leaves the ship and rushes to Circe's hall. The god Hermes stops him to give him a plant that will weaken Circe's power. (Homer calls it a moly; it might have been a kind of garlic.) Protected by the plant's magic, Odysseus resists Circe's sorcery. The goddess, realizing she has met her match, frees Odysseus's men. Now Circe, "loveliest of all immortals," persuades Odysseus to stay with her. Odysseus shares her meat and wine, and she restores his heart. After many seasons of feasting and other pleasures, Odysseus and his men beg Circe to help them return home.

She responds to their pleas with the command that Odysseus alone descend to the Land of the Dead, "the cold homes of Death and pale Persephone," queen of the underworld. There Odysseus must seek the wisdom of the blind prophet Teiresias.

The Land of the Dead

In the Land of the Dead, Odysseus seeks to learn his destiny. The source of his information is Teiresias, the famous blind prophet from the city of Thebes. The prophet's lack of external sight suggests the presence of true insight. Circe has told Odysseus exactly what rites he must perform to bring Teiresias up from the dead. Odysseus continues telling his story to Alcinous's court.

"Then I addressed the blurred and breathless dead,
vowing to slaughter my best heifer for them
before she calved, at home in Ithaca,
and burn the choice bits on the altar fire;
as for Teiresias, I swore to sacrifice
a black lamb, handsomest of all our flock. **A**
Thus to assuage the nations of the dead
I pledged these rites, then slashed the lamb and ewe,
letting their black blood stream into the well pit.
Now the souls gathered, stirring out of Erebus,
brides and young men, and men grown old in pain,
and tender girls whose hearts were new to grief;
many were there, too, torn by brazen lanceheads,
battle-slain, bearing still their bloody gear.

A Literary Perspectives **Analyzing Historical Context** Sacrificial offerings to the gods have been mentioned several times. Why might such a ritual have been important to the ancient Greeks?

From every side they came and sought the pit
with rustling cries; and I grew sick with fear.
But presently I gave command to my officers
to flay° those sheep the bronze cut down, and make
burnt offerings of flesh to the gods below—
to sovereign Death, to pale Persephone.°
Meanwhile I crouched with my drawn sword to keep
the surging phantoms from the bloody pit
till I should know the presence of Teiresias. . . . **B**

Soon from the dark that prince of Thebes came forward
bearing a golden staff; and he addressed me:

'Son of Laertes and the gods of old,
Odysseus, master of landways and seaways,
why leave the blazing sun, O man of woe,
to see the cold dead and the joyless region?
Stand clear, put up your sword;
let me but taste of blood, I shall speak true.'

At this I stepped aside, and in the scabbard
let my long sword ring home to the pommel silver,
as he bent down to the somber blood. Then spoke
the prince of those with gift of speech:

'Great captain,
a fair wind and the honey lights of home
are all you seek. But anguish lies ahead;
the god who thunders on the land prepares it,
not to be shaken from your track, implacable,°
in rancor for the son whose eye you blinded.
One narrow strait may take you through his blows:
denial of yourself, restraint of shipmates.
When you make landfall on Thrinakia first
and quit the violet sea, dark on the land
you'll find the grazing herds of Helios
by whom all things are seen, all speech is known.
Avoid those kine,° hold fast to your intent,
and hard seafaring brings you all to Ithaca.

601. flay: strip the skin from.

603. Persephone (puhr SEHF uh nee).

622. implacable (ihm PLAK uh buhl): unyielding; merciless.

? **623.** *To which god is Teiresias referring? How can you tell?*

630. kine: old term for cattle.

B **Reading Focus** **Asking Questions** What is happening here? Where is Odysseus?

Persephone, queen of the underworld, with her husband, Hades (4th century B.C.). Greek vase painting. British Museum, London.

Analyzing Visuals

Viewing and Interpreting Why do you think the gods were portrayed with human characteristics in Greek art?

But if you raid the beeves,° I see destruction
for ship and crew. Though you survive alone,
bereft of all companions, lost for years,
under strange sail shall you come home, to find
your own house filled with trouble: insolent men
eating your livestock as they court your lady.
Aye, you shall make those men atone in blood!
But after you have dealt out death—in open
combat or by stealth—to all the suitors,
go overland on foot, and take an oar,
until one day you come where men have lived
with meat unsalted, never known the sea,
nor seen seagoing ships, with crimson bows
and oars that fledge light hulls for dipping flight.
The spot will soon be plain to you, and I
can tell you how: some passerby will say,
"What winnowing fan° is that upon your shoulder?"
Halt, and implant your smooth oar in the turf
and make fair sacrifice to Lord Poseidon:
a ram, a bull, a great buck boar; turn back,
and carry out pure hecatombs° at home
to all wide heaven's lords, the undying gods,
to each in order. Then a seaborne death

632. beeves: another old term for cattle.

? **639–645.** ***Alliteration*** *is the repetition of consonant sounds in words close together. What instances of alliteration can you find in this passage? What effect does the use of this sound device create?*

648. winnowing fan: device used to remove the useless dry outer covering from grain. (These people would never have seen an oar.)

652. hecatombs (HEHK uh tohmz): sacrifices of groups of one hundred cattle to the gods. In Greek, *hekaton* means "one hundred."

Analyzing Visuals **Viewing and Interpreting** Are the Sirens in this portrayal what you imagined them to be? Explain.

Ulysses and the Sirens (1891) by John William Waterhouse (1849–1917). Oil on canvas (100 cm x 201.7 cm).

soft as this hand of mist will come upon you
when you are wearied out with rich old age,
your countryfolk in blessed peace around you.
And all this shall be just as I foretell.' . . ." **C**

(*from* Book 11)

The Sirens; Scylla and Charybdis

Odysseus and his men return to Circe's island, where Circe warns Odysseus of the perils that await him. In the following passage, Odysseus, quoting Circe, is still speaking at Alcinous's court.

"'Listen with care
to this, now, and a god will arm your mind.
Square in your ship's path are Sirens, crying
beauty to bewitch men coasting by;
woe to the innocent who hears that sound!
He will not see his lady nor his children

C **Reading Focus** **Summarizing** What does the prophecy reveal about Odysseus's destiny? How does the prophecy increase our suspense?

in joy, crowding about him, home from sea;
the Sirens will sing his mind away
on their sweet meadow lolling. There are bones
of dead men rotting in a pile beside them
and flayed skins shrivel around the spot.
Steer wide;
keep well to seaward; plug your oarsmen's ears
with beeswax kneaded soft; none of the rest
should hear that song.
But if you wish to listen,
let the men tie you in the lugger, hand
and foot, back to the mast, lashed to the mast,
so you may hear those Harpies'° thrilling voices;
shout as you will, begging to be untied,
your crew must only twist more line around you
and keep their stroke up, till the singers fade. . . .'" **A**

The next peril lies between two headlands. Circe continues delivering her warning.

"'. . . That is the den of Scylla, where she yaps
abominably, a newborn whelp's° cry,
though she is huge and monstrous. God or man,
no one could look on her in joy. Her legs—
and there are twelve—are like great tentacles,
unjointed, and upon her serpent necks
are borne six heads like nightmares of ferocity,
with triple serried° rows of fangs and deep
gullets of black death. Half her length, she sways
her heads in air, outside her horrid cleft,
hunting the sea around that promontory°
for dolphins, dogfish, or what bigger game
thundering Amphitrite° feeds in thousands.
And no ship's company can claim
to have passed her without loss and grief; she takes,
from every ship, one man for every gullet.

675. Harpies (HAHR peez): monsters, half bird and half woman, who are greedy for victims. Homer is referring to the Sirens as a type of Harpy.

? **679–694.** *Take a moment to **visualize** Scylla. Then, read on and locate the description of Charybdis (lines 695–703). Of the two, which seems more horrifying, or do you find them equally fearsome? Explain.*

680. whelp's: puppy's.

686. serried: crowded together; densely packed.

689. promontory (PRAHM uhn tawr ee): elevated area of land that juts out into a body of water.

691. Amphitrite (am fih TRYT ee): goddess of the sea and wife of Poseidon.

A **Literary Focus** **Epic Heroes and Conflict** From what you know about Odysseus, do you think he will try to avoid the conflict that lies ahead? Explain.

The opposite point seems more a tongue of land
you'd touch with a good bowshot, at the narrows.
A great wild fig, a shaggy mass of leaves,
grows on it, and Charybdis lurks below
to swallow down the dark sea tide. Three times
from dawn to dusk she spews it up
and sucks it down again three times, a whirling
maelstrom;° if you come upon her then
the god who makes earth tremble could not save you.
No, hug the cliff of Scylla, take your ship
through on a racing stroke. Better to mourn
six men than lose them all, and the ship, too. . . .
Then you will coast Thrinakia, the island
where Helios's cattle graze, fine herds, and flocks
of goodly sheep. The herds and flocks are seven,
with fifty beasts in each.
No lambs are dropped,
or calves, and these fat cattle never die. . . .

Now give those kine a wide berth, keep your thoughts
intent upon your course for home,
and hard seafaring brings you all to Ithaca.
But if you raid the beeves, I see destruction
for ship and crew. . . .'" **B**

The Ithacans set off. Odysseus does not tell his men of Circe's last prophecy—that he will be the only survivor of their long journey. Still speaking to Alcinous's court, Odysseus continues his tale.

"The crew being now silent before me, I
addressed them, sore at heart:

'Dear friends,
more than one man, or two, should know those things
Circe foresaw for us and shared with me,
so let me tell her forecast: then we die
with our eyes open, if we are going to die,
or know what death we baffle if we can. Sirens
weaving a haunting song over the sea
we are to shun, she said, and their green shore

702. maelstrom (MAYL struhm): large, violent whirlpool.

B Reading Focus Paraphrasing What dangers lie ahead? List them.

all sweet with clover; yet she urged that I
alone should listen to their song. Therefore
you are to tie me up, tight as a splint,
erect along the mast, lashed to the mast,
and if I shout and beg to be untied,
take more turns of the rope to muffle me.'

I rather dwelt on this part of the forecast,
while our good ship made time, bound outward down
the wind for the strange island of Sirens.
Then all at once the wind fell, and a calm
came over all the sea, as though some power
lulled the swell.
The crew were on their feet
briskly, to furl the sail, and stow it; then,
each in place, they poised the smooth oar blades

LITERATURE LINK

Odysseus and the Sirens (c. 5th century B.C.). Athenian earthenware red-figure stamnos vase by the Siren Painter. British Museum, London, U.K.

This poem, written in 1987, gives another perspective on the Sirens.

Siren Song

by Margaret Atwood

This is the one song everyone
would like to learn: the song
that is irresistible:

the song that forces men
to leap overboard in squadrons
even though they see the beached skulls

the song nobody knows
because anyone who has heard it
is dead, and the others can't remember.

Shall I tell you the secret
and if I do, will you get me
out of this bird suit?

I don't enjoy it here
squatting on this island
looking picturesque and mythical

with these two feathery maniacs,
I don't enjoy singing
this trio, fatal and valuable.

I will tell the secret to you,
to you, only to you.
Come closer. This song

is a cry for help: Help me!
Only you, only you can,
you are unique

at last. Alas
it is a boring song
but it works every time.

Now you know. Don't listen.

Ask Yourself

Who is the poem's speaker? What new idea about the Sirens does the poem express?

and sent the white foam scudding by. I carved
a massive cake of beeswax into bits
and rolled them in my hands until they softened—
no long task, for a burning heat came down
from Helios, lord of high noon. Going forward
I carried wax along the line, and laid it
thick on their ears. They tied me up, then, plumb° **C**
amidships, back to the mast, lashed to the mast,
and took themselves again to rowing. Soon,
as we came smartly within hailing distance,
the two Sirens, noting our fast ship
off their point, made ready, and they sang. . . .

The lovely voices in ardor appealing over the water
made me crave to listen, and I tried to say
'Untie me!' to the crew, jerking my brows;
but they bent steady to the oars. Then Perimedes°
got to his feet, he and Eurylochus,
and passed more line about, to hold me still.
So all rowed on, until the Sirens
dropped under the sea rim, and their singing
dwindled away.
My faithful company
rested on their oars now, peeling off
the wax that I had laid thick on their ears;
then set me free.
But scarcely had that island
faded in blue air when I saw smoke
and white water, with sound of waves in tumult—
a sound the men heard, and it terrified them.
Oars flew from their hands; the blades went knocking
wild alongside till the ship lost way,
with no oar blades to drive her through the water.

Well, I walked up and down from bow to stern,
trying to put heart into them, standing over
every oarsman, saying gently,

746. plumb: vertically.

755. Perimedes (pehr ih MEE deez).

C Reading Focus **Asking Questions** Why does Odysseus put wax in his men's ears?

Vocabulary **tumult** (TOO muhlt) *n.:* commotion; uproar; confusion.

'Friends,
have we never been in danger before this?
More fearsome, is it now, than when the Cyclops
penned us in his cave? What power he had!
Did I not keep my nerve, and use my wits
to find a way out for us?
Now I say
by hook or crook this peril too shall be
something that we remember.
Heads up, lads!
We must obey the orders as I give them.
Get the oar shafts in your hands, and lie back
hard on your benches; hit these breaking seas.
Zeus help us pull away before we founder.°

You at the tiller, listen, and take in
all that I say—the rudders are your duty;
keep her out of the combers° and the smoke;
steer for that headland; watch the drift, or we
fetch up in the smother,° and you drown us.'

That was all, and it brought them round to action.
But as I sent them on toward Scylla, I
told them nothing, as they could do nothing.
They would have dropped their oars again, in panic,
to roll for cover under the decking. Circe's **D**
bidding against arms had slipped my mind,
so I tied on my cuirass° and took up
two heavy spears, then made my way along
to the foredeck—thinking to see her first from there,
the monster of the gray rock, harboring
torment for my friends. I strained my eyes
upon that cliffside veiled in cloud, but nowhere
could I catch sight of her.
And all this time,
in travail,° sobbing, gaining on the current,
we rowed into the strait—Scylla to port

783. founder: sink.

786. combers (KOHM uhrz): large waves.

788. smother: commotion; violent action or disorder.

794. *Circe had warned Odysseus earlier that it was useless to bear arms against Scylla.*

795. cuirass (kwih RAS): armor for the breast and back.

802. travail (truh VAYL): hard, exhausting work or effort; tiring labor.

D Literary Focus Epic Heroes and Conflict Think about what kind of hero Odysseus is. What does he tell his men to reassure them? Why do you think he decides not to tell them everything he knows?

and on our starboard beam Charybdis, dire
gorge° of the salt sea tide. By heaven! when she
vomited, all the sea was like a caldron
seething over intense fire, when the mixture
suddenly heaves and rises.
The shot spume
soared to the landside heights, and fell like rain.

But when she swallowed the sea water down
we saw the funnel of the maelstrom, heard
the rock bellowing all around, and dark
sand raged on the bottom far below.
My men all blanched° against the gloom, our eyes
were fixed upon that yawning mouth in fear
of being devoured.
Then Scylla made her strike,
whisking six of my best men from the ship.
I happened to glance aft at ship and oarsmen
and caught sight of their arms and legs, dangling
high overhead. Voices came down to me
in anguish, calling my name for the last time.

A man surf-casting on a point of rock
for bass or mackerel, whipping his long rod

805. gorge: throat and jaws of a greedy, all-devouring creature.

814. blanched: grew pale.

Circe Pouring Poison into a Vase and Awaiting the Arrival of Ulysses (19th century) by Sir Edward Burne-Jones (1833–1898). Watercolor on paper.

Analyzing Visuals

Viewing and Interpreting How does the imagery in this painting of Circe contrast with the current action in the epic?

to drop the sinker and the bait far out,
will hook a fish and rip it from the surface
to dangle wriggling through the air;
so these
were borne aloft in spasms toward the cliff.

She ate them as they shrieked there, in her den,
in the dire grapple,° reaching still for me—
and deathly pity ran me through
at that sight—far the worst I ever suffered
questing the passes of the strange sea.
We rowed on.
The Rocks were now behind; Charybdis, too,
and Scylla dropped astern. **E**
Then we were coasting
the noble island of the god, where grazed
those cattle with wide brows, and bounteous flocks
of Helios, lord of noon, who rides high heaven.
From the black ship, far still at sea, I heard
the lowing of the cattle winding home
and sheep bleating; and heard, too, in my heart
the words of blind Teiresias of Thebes
and Circe of Aeaea: both forbade me
the island of the world's delight, the Sun. . . ."

(*from* Book 12)

829. dire grapple: terrible struggle.

The Cattle of the Sun God

Odysseus urges his exhausted crew to bypass Thrinakia, the island of the sun god, Helios. When the men insist on landing, Odysseus makes them swear not to touch the god's cattle. Odysseus is still speaking to Alcinous's court.

"In the small hours of the third watch, when stars
that shone out in the first dusk of evening
had gone down to their setting, a giant wind
blew from heaven, and clouds driven by Zeus
shrouded land and sea in a night of storm;
so, just as Dawn with fingertips of rose

? **844–852.** *Read through this passage, and find instances of* ***imagery****—language that appeals to our senses. Also, look for an example of* ***personification****, in which a nonhuman thing is described in human terms.*

E **Reading Focus** **Summarizing** What has happened? How have Odysseus and his crew managed to escape?

touched the windy world, we dragged our ship
to cover in a grotto, a sea cave
where nymphs had chairs of rock and sanded floors.
I mustered all the crew and said:

'Old shipmates,
our stores are in the ship's hold, food and drink;
the cattle here are not for our provision,
or we pay dearly for it.
Fierce the god is
who cherishes these heifers and these sheep:
Helios; and no man avoids his eye.' **A**

To this my fighters nodded. Yes. But now
we had a month of onshore gales, blowing
day in, day out—south winds, or south by east.
As long as bread and good red wine remained
to keep the men up, and appease their craving,
they would not touch the cattle. But in the end,
when all the barley in the ship was gone,
hunger drove them to scour the wild shore
with angling hooks, for fishes and sea fowl,
whatever fell into their hands; and lean days
wore their bellies thin.

The storms continued.
So one day I withdrew to the interior
to pray the gods in solitude, for hope
that one might show me some way of salvation.
Slipping away, I struck across the island
to a sheltered spot, out of the driving gale.
I washed my hands there, and made supplication°
to the gods who own Olympus, all the gods—
but they, for answer, only closed my eyes
under slow drops of sleep.
Now on the shore Eurylochus
made his insidious° plea:

875. supplication: humble requests; prayers.

879. insidious (ihn SIHD ee uhs): treacherous; more dangerous than is apparent.

A Reading Focus **Paraphrasing** What warning does Odysseus issue his men upon landing?

'Comrades,' he said,
'You've gone through everything; listen to what I say.
All deaths are hateful to us, mortal wretches,
but famine is the most pitiful, the worst
end that a man can come to.
Will you fight it?
Come, we'll cut out the noblest of these cattle
for sacrifice to the gods who own the sky;
and once at home, in the old country of Ithaca,
if ever that day comes—
we'll build a costly temple and adorn it
with every beauty for the Lord of Noon.
But if he flares up over his heifers lost,
wishing our ship destroyed, and if the gods
make cause with him, why, then I say: Better
open your lungs to a big sea once for all
than waste to skin and bones on a lonely island!' **B**

Thus Eurylochus; and they murmured 'Aye!'
trooping away at once to round up heifers.
Now, that day tranquil cattle with broad brows
were grazing near, and soon the men drew up
around their chosen beasts in ceremony.
They plucked the leaves that shone on a tall oak—
having no barley meal—to strew° the victims,
performed the prayers and ritual, knifed the kine
and flayed each carcass, cutting thighbones free
to wrap in double folds of fat. These offerings,
with strips of meat, were laid upon the fire.
Then, as they had no wine, they made libation°
with clear spring water, broiling the entrails° first;
and when the bones were burnt and tripes° shared,
they spitted the carved meat.
Just then my slumber
left me in a rush, my eyes opened,
and I went down the seaward path. No sooner
had I caught sight of our black hull, than savory
odors of burnt fat eddied around me;
grief took hold of me, and I cried aloud:

901. strew: scatter about.

906. libation (ly BAY shuhn): offering of wine or oil to the gods.

907. entrails: intestines; guts.

908. tripes: stomach parts.

B **Reading Focus** **Paraphrasing** What is Eurylochus's "insidious plea"?

'O Father Zeus and gods in bliss forever,
you made me sleep away this day of mischief!
O cruel drowsing, in the evil hour!
Here they sat, and a great work they contrived.' **C**

Lampetia° in her long gown meanwhile
had borne swift word to the Overlord of Noon:

'They have killed your kine.'

And the Lord Helios
burst into angry speech amid the immortals:

'O Father Zeus and gods in bliss forever,
punish Odysseus' men! So overweening,°
now they have killed my peaceful kine, my joy
at morning when I climbed the sky of stars,
and evening, when I bore westward from heaven.
Restitution or penalty they shall pay—
and pay in full—or I go down forever
to light the dead men in the underworld.' . . ." **D**

(*from* Book 12)

919. Lampetia (lam PEE shee uh): daughter of Helios. Lampetia guarded her father's herds of cattle.

924. overweening: excessively proud.

? **930.** *What happens here that increases our suspense?*

When Odysseus and his men set sail again, the crew are punished with death—a thunderbolt from Zeus destroys their ship, and all the men except Odysseus drown. Exhausted and nearly drowned, he makes his way to Calypso's island, where we met him originally, in Book 5.

Odysseus has brought us up to date. He can now rest and enjoy the comforts of Alcinous's court—but not for long. Ahead lies his most difficult task—reclaiming his own kingdom.

At this moment of suspense, Homer might have put aside his lyre until the next night.

C **Literary Focus** **Epic Heroes and Conflict** Odysseus takes the credit when things go well. Now, when a disaster occurs, he blames the gods. What does this reveal about his character?

D **Reading Focus** **Summarizing** What exactly happened to cause the gods' fury?

Applying Your Skills

MO 9.R.2.C.1.b Use details from text(s): to analyze character, plot, setting, point of view 9.R.1.H.1.b Apply post-reading skills to comprehend, interpret, analyze, and evaluate text: question to clarify 9.R.1.G.1.g During reading, utilize strategies: to summarize

from the Odyssey, Part One

Respond and Think Critically

Reading Focus

Quick Check

1. Whom does Homer ask to help him tell the epic?
2. From what war is Odysseus trying to return? What god causes Odysseus to lose course when he sets sail for home?
3. What does Odysseus learn about his destiny from blind Teiresias in the Land of the Dead?

Read with a Purpose

4. Based on what you have read so far, what makes Odysseus and his journey so memorable?

Reading Skills: Reading an Epic

5. Use your *5W-How?* answers to help you briefly summarize Odysseus's adventures in a chart.

Adventure	My Summary
Calypso	
Lotus Eaters	
Cyclops	
Sirens; Scylla and Charybdis	
Cattle of the Sun God	

Literary Focus

Literary Analysis

6. **Interpret** What do you think the land of the Lotus Eaters might symbolize? Cite lines from the episode to support your interpretation.
7. **Draw Conclusions** What conclusions about the deceptive nature of beauty can you draw from the Circe episode?
8. **Literary Perspectives** What have you learned about ancient Greek society from reading Part One of the *Odyssey*?

Literary Skills: Epic Heroes and Conflict

9. **Identify** What qualities does Odysseus embody? For example, is he generous, foolish, or quick-tempered? List three qualities, and give one example from the text that illustrates each.
10. **Analyze** Which characters are **foils,** contrasting with Odysseus? How does the use of foils heighten the heroic character of Odysseus?
11. **Evaluate** What sort of internal conflict does Odysseus undergo while he is with Calypso? Does this conflict make him seem less heroic? Explain.

Literary Skills Review: Foreshadowing

12. **Analyze** **Foreshadowing** is the use of clues to hint at events that will occur later. Re-read the Cyclops's prayer to Poseidon. What other troubles for Odysseus are hinted at by these lines? How does foreshadowing create suspense?

Writing Focus

Think as a Reader/Writer

Use It in Your Writing Use your notes on what Homer reveals about the character of Odysseus to write a brief character sketch of the hero. Keep in mind that Odysseus describes himself as "formidable for guile in peace and war."

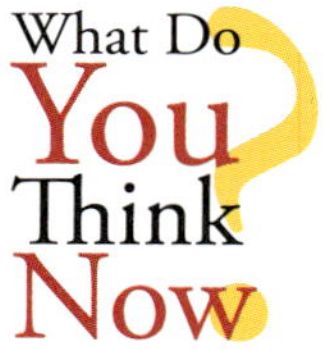

How do you think Odysseus's life will change as a result of his journey?

Applying Your Skills

MO 9.R.1.G.1.a During reading, utilize strategies: to determine meaning of unknown words 9.R.1.E.1.b Develop vocabulary through text: using context clues 9.R.1.E.1.c Develop vocabulary through text: using glossary, dictionary and thesaurus

from the Odyssey, Part One

Vocabulary Development

Vocabulary Check

Match each Vocabulary word with its definition.

1. **adversity** a. abundance
2. **adversary** b. enemy
3. **formidable** c. hardship
4. **profusion** d. confusion
5. **tumult** e. impressive

Vocabulary Skills: Epithets

An **epithet** (EP uh theht) is an adjective or phrase used to characterize someone. *Catherine the Great* and *baby boomers* are epithets used to characterize an empress and a generation. Homer uses epithets as formulas to characterize places, people, and gods. Zeus is called "father of gods and men" to remind us of how powerful he is. The epithet "faithful Penelope" instantly tells us her outstanding trait.

A Famous Epithet Mystery

One of Homer's famous epithets is "the wine-dark sea." Because wine is red or white or yellowish, and the sea is none of these hues, the description is puzzling. Some people say that the ancient Greeks diluted their wine with water and that the alkali in the water changed the color of the wine from red to blue. Others think the sea was covered with red algae. Robert Fitzgerald, the great translator of the *Odyssey*, was sailing on the Aegean Sea when he had this realization:

> The contrast of the bare arid baked land against the sea gave the sea such a richness of hue that I felt as though we were sailing through a bowl of dye. The depth of hue of the water was like the depth of hue of a good red wine.

Your Turn

Answer the following questions to test your knowledge of the italicized epithets.

1. Odysseus is called "*versatile* Odysseus," "*wily* Odysseus," "the *strategist*," and "the noble and *enduring* man." What does each italicized word mean?
2. Dawn is described as "*rosy-fingered*." What does this epithet help you see?
3. What epithets can you make up for these characters: Calypso, the Lotus Eaters, the Cyclops, Circe, and Scylla?

Language Coach

Related Words Earlier, you learned that *adverse, adversity,* and *adversary* are related words. Here are some more words from the epic. Copy these words down and list two related words for each.

- mortal (line 93)
- custom (line 258)
- magic (line 578)
- destruction (line 632)
- horrid (line 688)

Academic Vocabulary

Write About . . .

In a few paragraphs, outline the ways Homer portrays Odysseus as an epic hero. How does Homer express Odysseus's heroic qualities to his audience? Use the Academic Vocabulary in your response.

Preparing to Read

from the Odyssey, Part Two

9.R.2 Develop and apply skills and strategies to comprehend, analyze and evaluate fiction, poetry and drama from a variety of cultures and times
9.R.2.A.1 Analyze and evaluate the text features in grade-level text *Also covered* **9.R.2.B.2.d, 9.R.1.G.1.f, 9.R.1.G.1.g, 9.R.1.H.1.b**

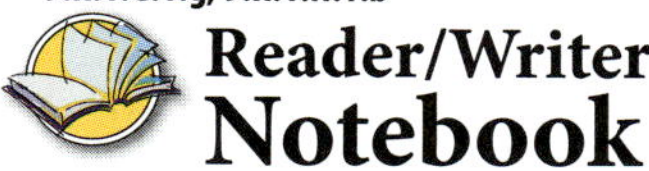

Use your **RWN** to complete the activities for this selection.

Literary Focus

Oral Tradition: Repetition and Similes Stories such as the *Odyssey* were retold over the centuries by traveling singers. Many epics follow a formula, which enabled the singers to describe everyday activities while they thought ahead to the next passage.

Another storytelling device from the oral tradition is the epic simile (also called Homeric simile). **Epic similes** extend comparisons between something that the audience cannot have seen—such as Scylla grabbing Odysseus's men and holding them high in the air—and something ordinary that they would know—such as a fisherman catching a fish and holding it in the air (lines 822–827).

Reading Focus

Reading an Epic Continue to read this epic, **paraphrasing, summarizing,** and **asking questions** as necessary.

Into Action Ask and answer questions such as these to check your understanding of the selections from Part Two of the *Odyssey*.

Questions to Ask	My Responses
Who are the main characters?	
What has happened so far?	
Where and when are the events taking place?	
Why did the events happen?	
How does the hero resolve the conflict?	

Writing Focus

Think as a Reader/Writer

Find It in Your Reading Write down in your *Reader/Writer Notebook* what you learn about Odysseus and other characters.

TechFocus As you read, consider how these adventures might form the basis for a computer game.

Vocabulary

candor (KAN duhr) *n.:* honesty; frankness. *Telemachus spoke with candor, unwilling to hide his true feelings.*

disdainful (dihs DAYN fuhl) *adj.:* scornful; regarding someone as beneath oneself. *The suitors were disdainful of one another, each thinking he would be the one to win Penelope's heart.*

glowered (GLOW urhd) *v.:* glared; stared angrily. *When he heard the bad news, Odysseus glowered at his men.*

lavished (LAV ihsht) *v.:* gave generously. *Athena, who loved Odysseus, lavished beauty upon him when he returned home.*

aloof (uh LOOF) *adj.:* unfriendly; at a distance. *Unsure of how to greet Odysseus on his return, Penelope appeared aloof at first.*

Language Coach

Word Origins The Latin verb *candere* means "to shine." *Candle* comes to us from that word. One of the words on the list above also is derived from *candere*. See if you can figure out which word it is.

Learn It Online
Use Word Watch to explore the meaning of vocabulary terms at:

go.hrw.com L9-1077 

Read with a Purpose Read the rest of the epic to discover how Odysseus uses both strength and cunning to reclaim his kingdom of Ithaca.

PART TWO:
Coming Home

In Book 13, Odysseus, laden with gifts, has returned in secret to Ithaca aboard a magically swift Phaeacian ship. In Ithaca, Athena appears to the hero. Because his home is full of enemies, she advises Odysseus to proceed disguised as a beggar. Now, Odysseus must succeed not only by physical power but also by intelligence.

In Book 14, Odysseus, in his beggar's disguise, finds his way to the hut of Eumaeus, his old and trusty swineherd. Eumaeus is the very image of faithfulness in a servant—a quality much valued in Homer's society. The introduction of members of the so-called servant class as important characters is unusual in epic poetry and reflects Homer's originality. Odysseus is politely entertained by Eumaeus, but the king remains disguised from his old servant.

In Book 15, Athena appears to Odysseus's son, Telemachus. The young man has gone to Pylos and Sparta to talk with old comrades of his father in hopes of finding out whether Odysseus is alive or dead. Athena advises him to return to Ithaca. His home—the palace of Odysseus—has been overrun by his mother's suitors. These arrogant men are spending money from Telemachus's inheritance on feasting and drinking, and they are demanding that his mother, Penelope, take one of them as a husband. Athena warns Telemachus that the suitors plan to ambush him. Telemachus boards a ship for home, lands secretly on Ithaca, and heads toward the hut of the swineherd.

The suspense increases as father and son move closer and closer together. Now Homer is ready to recount what could be the most dramatic moment in the epic. Remember that Odysseus has not seen his son for twenty years. Telemachus has been away from Ithaca for a year.

Analyzing Visuals

Viewing and Interpreting What clues in this tapestry let you know that the woman portrayed is Penelope, Odysseus's wife?

Penelope at Her Loom, a fragment from *The Story of Penelope and The Story of the Cimbri Women* (from the series, *The Stories of Virtuous Women*). French or Franco-Flemish, about 1480–83. Wool tapestry. 100 x 150 cm (39 3/8 x 59 1/16 in.).

Museum of Fine Arts, Boston. Maria Antoinette Evans Fund, 26.54.

The Meeting of Father and Son

But there were two men in the mountain hut—
Odysseus and the swineherd. At first light
blowing their fire up, they cooked their breakfast
and sent their lads out, driving herds to root
in the tall timber.
When Telemachus came,
the wolfish troop of watchdogs only fawned on him
as he advanced. Odysseus heard them go
and heard the light crunch of a man's footfall—
at which he turned quickly to say:
"Eumaeus,
here is one of your crew come back, or maybe
another friend: the dogs are out there snuffling
belly down; not one has even growled.
I can hear footsteps—"
But before he finished
his tall son stood at the door.
The swineherd
rose in surprise, letting a bowl and jug
tumble from his fingers. Going forward,
he kissed the young man's head, his shining eyes
and both hands, while his own tears brimmed and fell.
Think of a man whose dear and only son,
born to him in exile, reared with labor,
has lived ten years abroad and now returns:
how would that man embrace his son! Just so
the herdsman clapped his arms around Telemachus
and covered him with kisses—for he knew
the lad had got away from death. He said:

"Light of my days, Telemachus,
you made it back! When you took ship for Pylos°
I never thought to see you here again.
Come in, dear child, and let me feast my eyes;
here you are, home from the distant places!
How rarely, anyway, you visit us,
your own men, and your own woods and pastures!

957. Pylos (PY lohs): home of Nestor, one of Odysseus's fellow soldiers in the Trojan War. Telemachus had gone to see if Nestor knew anything about Odysseus's whereabouts.

Analyzing Visuals **Viewing and Interpreting** How can you tell which figure is Odysseus and which is Telemachus in this mosaic?

Odysseus and his son Telemachus (1st century A.D.). Mosaic (31.5 cm wide). Location: Kunsthistorisches Museum, Vienna, Austria.

Always in the town, a man would think
you loved the suitors' company, those dogs!" **A**

Telemachus with his clear candor said:

"I am with you, Uncle.° See now, I have come
because I wanted to see you first, to hear from you
if Mother stayed at home—or is she married
off to someone, and Odysseus' bed
left empty for some gloomy spider's weaving?"

966. Uncle: here, a term of affection.

A **Reading Focus** **Paraphrasing** What happens in this scene? Bring it to life in your own words.

Vocabulary **candor** (KAN duhr) *n.:* honesty; frankness.

Gently the forester replied to this:

"At home indeed your mother is, poor lady
still in the women's hall. Her nights and days
are wearied out with grieving."

Stepping back
he took the bronze-shod lance, and the young prince
entered the cabin over the worn door stone.
Odysseus moved aside, yielding his couch,
but from across the room Telemachus checked him:

"Friend, sit down; we'll find another chair
in our own hut. Here is the man to make one!"

The swineherd, when the quiet man sank down,
built a new pile of evergreens and fleeces—
a couch for the dear son of great Odysseus—
then gave them trenchers° of good meat, left over
from the roast pork of yesterday, and heaped up
willow baskets full of bread, and mixed
an ivy bowl of honey-hearted wine.
Then he in turn sat down, facing Odysseus,
their hands went out upon the meat and drink
as they fell to, ridding themselves of hunger. . . .° B

984. **trenchers** (TREHN chuhrz): wooden platters.

? **990.** *Hospitality—the welcoming of visitors—is a quality that Greeks held in high regard. Who is still in disguise in this scene? In what way do these characters display hospitality?*

Not realizing that the stranger is his father, Telemachus tries to protect him as best he can. He says that the beggar cannot stay in the palace hall because he will be abused by the drunken suitors.

The swineheard is sent to Penelope with news of her son's return. Now even Athena cannot stand the suspense any longer. She appears and turns to Odysseus, who is still in beggar's rags.

. . . She tipped her golden wand upon the man,
making his cloak pure white, and the knit tunic
fresh around him. Lithe° and young she made him,
ruddy with sun, his jawline clean, the beard

993. lithe (lyth): flexible; graceful.

B **Literary Perspectives** **Analyzing Historical Context** In Homer's time, slaves may very well have outnumbered the citizens. What do you think Homer is trying to say by having Odysseus make an alliance with a servant?

no longer gray upon his chin. And she
withdrew when she had done.
Then Lord Odysseus
reappeared—and his son was thunderstruck.
Fear in his eyes, he looked down and away
as though it were a god, and whispered:
"Stranger,
you are no longer what you were just now!
Your cloak is new; even your skin! You are
one of the gods who rule the sweep of heaven!
Be kind to us, we'll make you fair oblation°
and gifts of hammered gold. Have mercy on us!" C

The noble and enduring man replied:

"No god. Why take me for a god? No, no.
I am that father whom your boyhood lacked
and suffered pain for lack of. I am he."

Held back too long, the tears ran down his cheeks
as he embraced his son.
Only Telemachus,
uncomprehending, wild
with incredulity,° cried out:
"You cannot
be my father Odysseus! Meddling spirits
conceived this trick to twist the knife in me!
No man of woman born could work these wonders
by his own craft, unless a god came into it
with ease to turn him young or old at will.
I swear you were in rags and old,
and here you stand like one of the immortals!"

Odysseus brought his ranging mind to bear
and said:
"This is not princely, to be swept
away by wonder at your father's presence.
No other Odysseus will ever come,
for he and I are one, the same; his bitter

1003. oblation (ahb LAY shuhn): offering of a sacrifice. Telemachus thinks the stranger is a god.

1012. incredulity (ihn kruh DOO luh tee): disbelief.

C Reading Focus Asking Questions Why do you think Athena has suddenly changed Odysseus?

fortune and his wanderings are mine.
Twenty years gone, and I am back again
on my own island. . . ."

Then, throwing
his arms around this marvel of a father,
Telemachus began to weep. Salt tears
rose from the wells of longing in both men,
and cries burst from both as keen and fluttering
as those of the great taloned hawk,
whose nestlings° farmers take before they fly. D
So helplessly they cried, pouring out tears,
and might have gone on weeping so till sundown. . . .

(*from* Book 16)

1033. **nestlings:** young birds that are not ready to leave the nest.

The Beggar and the Faithful Dog

Telemachus returns to the family compound and is greeted tearfully by his mother, Penelope, and his old nurse, Eurycleia. A soothsayer has told his mother that Odysseus is alive and in Ithaca. However, Telemachus does not report that he has seen his father. The suspense builds as Odysseus, once again disguised as a beggar, returns to his home, accompanied only by the swineherd. He has been away for twenty years. Only one creature recognizes him.

While he spoke
an old hound, lying near, pricked up his ears
and lifted up his muzzle. This was Argos,
trained as a puppy by Odysseus,
but never taken on a hunt before
his master sailed for Troy. The young men, afterward,
hunted wild goats with him, and hare, and deer,
but he had grown old in his master's absence.
Treated as rubbish now, he lay at last
upon a mass of dung before the gates—
manure of mules and cows, piled there until
field hands could spread it on the king's estate.
Abandoned there, and half destroyed with flies,
old Argos lay.

Laconian hound scratching his head (c. 500 B.C.). Detail from an Attic red-figured ceramic scyphus, or drinking cup, by the Euergides Painter. Ashmolean Museum, Oxford, England.

Analyzing Visuals

Viewing and Interpreting Why do you think an artist would decorate a drinking cup with this design? Did the Greeks think of their dogs as we do ours today?

D Literary Focus Epic Similes What are Odysseus's and Telemachus's cries compared to during their tearful reunion? What aspect of their reunion does this simile emphasize?

But when he knew he heard
Odysseus' voice nearby, he did his best
to wag his tail, nose down, with flattened ears,
having no strength to move nearer his master.
And the man looked away,
wiping a salt tear from his cheek; but he
hid this from Eumaeus. Then he said: **A**

"I marvel that they leave this hound to lie
here on the dung pile;
he would have been a fine dog, from the look of him,
though I can't say as to his power and speed
when he was young. You find the same good build
in house dogs, table dogs landowners keep
all for style."

And you replied, Eumaeus:
"A hunter owned him—but the man is dead
in some far place. If this old hound could show
the form he had when Lord Odysseus left him,
going to Troy, you'd see him swift and strong.
He never shrank from any savage thing
he'd brought to bay in the deep woods; on the scent
no other dog kept up with him. Now misery
has him in leash. His owner died abroad,
and here the women slaves will take no care of him.
You know how servants are: without a master
they have no will to labor, or excel.
For Zeus who views the wide world takes away
half the manhood of a man, that day
he goes into captivity and slavery." **B**

Eumaeus crossed the court and went straight forward
into the megaron° among the suitors;
but death and darkness in that instant closed
the eyes of Argos, who had seen his master,
Odysseus, after twenty years. . . .

(*from* Book 17)

? **1049–1062.** *What* ***dramatic irony*** *is created in this passage? What do we know that the others don't know?*

? **1069–1076.** *In this passage, Argos, the faithful dog,* ***symbolizes*** *conditions in Ithaca. What can you infer about the state of Ithaca from the description of Argos?*

1078. megaron (MEHG uh rahn): great hall or central room.

A **Literary Focus** **Epic Heroes and Conflict** What do Odysseus's tears and comments about the dog reveal about Odysseus's character?

B **Reading Focus** **Paraphrasing** Restate this description of the dog's life. What point about life might Homer be making with this passage?

The Epic Continues

In the hall the "beggar" is taunted by the evil suitors, but Penelope supports him. She has learned that the ragged stranger claims to have news of her husband. Unaware of who the beggar is, she invites him to visit her later in the night to talk about Odysseus.

In Book 18, Penelope appears among the suitors and reproaches Telemachus for allowing the stranger to be abused. She certainly must have warmed her husband's heart by doing this and also by singing the praises of her lost Odysseus.

In Book 19, the suitors depart for the night, and Odysseus and Telemachus discuss their strategy. The clever hero goes as appointed to Penelope with the idea of testing her and her maids. (Some of the maids have not been loyal to the household and have been involved with the suitors.) The faithful wife receives her disguised husband. We can imagine the tension Homer's audience must have felt. Would Odysseus be recognized?

The "beggar" spins a yarn about his origins, pretending that he has met Odysseus on his travels. He cannot resist praising the lost hero, and he does so successfully enough to bring tears to Penelope's eyes. We can be sure that this does not displease her husband.

The storytelling beggar reveals that he has heard that Odysseus is alive and is even now sailing for home. Penelope calls for the old nurse and asks her to wash the guest's feet—a sign of respect and honor. As Eurycleia does so, she recognizes Odysseus from a scar on his leg.

Quickly Odysseus swears the old nurse to secrecy. Meanwhile, Athena has cast a spell on Penelope so that she has taken no notice of this recognition scene. Penelope adds to the suspense by deciding on a test for the suitors on the next day. Without realizing it, she has given Odysseus a way to defeat the men who threaten his wife and kingdom.

In Book 20, Odysseus, brooding over the shameless behavior of the maidservants and the suitors, longs to destroy his enemies but fears the revenge of their friends. Athena reassures him. Odysseus is told that the suitors will die.

Odysseus is recognized by Eurycleia. Detail from an Attic red-figured scyphus, or drinking cup. Museo Archeologico, Chiusi, Italy.

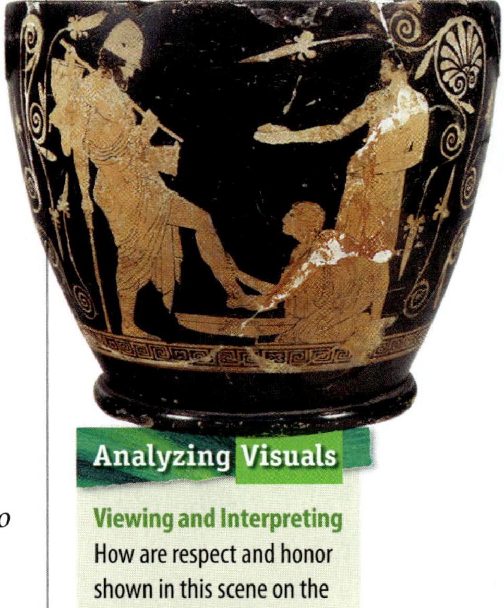

Analyzing Visuals

Viewing and Interpreting
How are respect and honor shown in this scene on the drinking cup? What does this tell you about the Greeks' sense of hospitality?

The Test of the Great Bow

In Book 21, Penelope, like many unwilling princesses of myth and fairy tale, proposes a seemingly impossible task for those who wish to marry her. By doing so, she causes the bloody events that lead to the restoration of her husband as Ithaca's leader. The test involves stringing Odysseus's huge bow, an impossible feat for anyone except Odysseus himself. Odysseus had left his bow home in Ithaca twenty years earlier.

Now the queen reached the storeroom door and halted.
Here was an oaken sill, cut long ago
and sanded clean and bedded true. Foursquare
the doorjambs and the shining doors were set
by the careful builder. Penelope untied the strap
around the curving handle, pushed her hook
into the slit, aimed at the bolts inside,
and shot them back. Then came a rasping sound
as those bright doors the key had sprung gave way—
a bellow like a bull's vaunt° in a meadow—
followed by her light footfall entering
over the plank floor. Herb-scented robes
lay there in chests, but the lady's milk-white arms
went up to lift the bow down from a peg
in its own polished bow case.

Now Penelope
sank down, holding the weapon on her knees,
and drew her husband's great bow out, and sobbed
and bit her lip and let the salt tears flow. **A**
Then back she went to face the crowded hall
tremendous bow in hand, and on her shoulder hung
the quiver spiked with coughing death. Behind, her
maids bore a basket full of ax heads, bronze
and iron implements for the master's game.
Thus in her beauty she approached the suitors,
and near a pillar of the solid roof
she paused, her shining veil across her cheeks,
her maids on either hand and still,
then spoke to the banqueters:

1091. vaunt (vawnt): boast.

A **Reading Focus** **Asking Questions** Why do you think Penelope is crying?

"My lords, hear me:
suitors indeed, you recommended this house
to feast and drink in, day and night, my husband
being long gone, long out of mind. You found
no justification for yourselves—none
except your lust to marry me. Stand up, then:
we now declare a contest for that prize.
Here is my lord Odysseus' hunting bow.
Bend and string it if you can. Who sends an arrow
through iron ax-helve sockets,° twelve in line?
I join my life with his, and leave this place, my home,
my rich and beautiful bridal house, forever
to be remembered, though I dream it only." . . .

Many of the suitors boldly try the bow, but not one man can even bend it enough to string it.

1118. ax-helve sockets: An ax helve is an ax handle; a socket is a hollow piece lined with iron at the end of the handle. Shooting an arrow through a line of ax-helve sockets would be a feat possible only for a superhero like Odysseus.

Analyzing Visuals

Viewing and Interpreting Penelope is known for her faithfulness and for being resourceful. How are those qualities conveyed in this painting?

Penelope with the Suitors (c. 1509) by Bernardino Pintoricchio.

Two men had meanwhile left the hall:
swineherd and cowherd, in companionship,
one downcast as the other. But Odysseus
followed them outdoors, outside the court,
and coming up said gently:

"You, herdsman,
and you, too, swineherd, I could say a thing to you,
or should I keep it dark? **B**

No, no; speak,
my heart tells me. Would you be men enough
to stand by Odysseus if he came back?
Suppose he dropped out of a clear sky, as I did?
Suppose some god should bring him?
Would you bear arms for him, or for the suitors?"

The cowherd said:

"Ah, let the master come!
Father Zeus, grant our old wish! Some courier°
guide him back! Then judge what stuff is in me
and how I manage arms!"

Likewise Eumaeus
fell to praying all heaven for his return,
so that Odysseus, sure at least of these,
told them:

"I am at home, for I am he. **C**
I bore adversities, but in the twentieth year
I am ashore in my own land. I find
the two of you, alone among my people,
longed for my coming. Prayers I never heard
except your own that I might come again.
So now what is in store for you I'll tell you:
If Zeus brings down the suitors by my hand
I promise marriages to both, and cattle,
and houses built near mine. And you shall be
brothers-in-arms of my Telemachus.
Here, let me show you something else, a sign

1135. courier (KUR ee uhr): guide or messenger.

B **Literary Focus** **Epic Heroes and Conflict** What internal conflict is Odysseus experiencing?

C **Reading Focus** **Summarizing** How do the swineherd and cowherd prove they can be trusted?

that I am he, that you can trust me, look:
this old scar from the tusk wound that I got
boar hunting on Parnassus°— . . ."
Shifting his rags
he bared the long gash. Both men looked, and knew
and threw their arms around the old soldier, weeping,
kissing his head and shoulders. He as well
took each man's head and hands to kiss, then said—
to cut it short, else they might weep till dark—

"Break off, no more of this.
Anyone at the door could see and tell them.
Drift back in, but separately at intervals
after me.
Now listen to your orders:
when the time comes, those gentlemen, to a man,
will be dead against giving me bow or quiver.
Defy them. Eumaeus, bring the bow
and put it in my hands there at the door.
Tell the women to lock their own door tight.
Tell them if someone hears the shock of arms
or groans of men, in hall or court, not one
must show her face, but keep still at her weaving.
Philoeteus, run to the outer gate and lock it.
Throw the crossbar and lash it." . . .

Now Odysseus, still in his beggar's clothes, asks to try the bow. The suitors refuse to allow a mere beggar to try where they have failed, but Penelope insists that the stranger be given his chance. The suspense is very great—by this act, Penelope has accepted her husband as a suitor.

Eumaeus, the swineherd, hands Odysseus the bow and tells the nurse to retire with Penelope and the maids to the family chambers and to bolt the doors. Odysseus had earlier told Telemachus to remove the suitors' weapons from the great hall. Now he takes the bow.

1154. Parnassus (pahr NAS uhs): As a young man, Odysseus had gone hunting on Parnassus, his mother's home, and was gored above the knee by a boar.

Analyzing Visuals

Viewing and Interpreting How does the artist let you know that shooting Odysseus's bow takes great physical effort?

Odysseus slaying the suitors. Detail from an Attic red-figured scyphus, or drinking cup, by the Penelope Painter, from Tarquinii, an ancient city in central Italy (c. 440 B.C.). Antikensammlung, Staatliche Museen zu Berlin, Berlin, Germany.

And Odysseus took his time,
turning the bow, tapping it, every inch,
for borings that termites might have made
while the master of the weapon was abroad.
The suitors were now watching him, and some
jested among themselves:
"A bow lover!"
"Dealer in old bows!"
"Maybe he has one like it
at home!"
"Or has an itch to make one for himself."

"See how he handles it, the sly old buzzard!"

And one disdainful suitor added this:

"May his fortune grow an inch for every inch he bends it!" **D**

But the man skilled in all ways of contending,
satisfied by the great bow's look and heft,
like a musician, like a harper, when
with quiet hand upon his instrument
he draws between his thumb and forefinger
a sweet new string upon a peg: so effortlessly
Odysseus in one motion strung the bow.
Then slid his right hand down the cord and plucked it,
so the taut gut vibrating hummed and sang
a swallow's note.
In the hushed hall it smote the suitors
and all their faces changed. Then Zeus thundered **E**
overhead, one loud crack for a sign.

? **1174–1220.** *As you read this scene, make notes about how you* ***visualize*** *it. Where are the various characters placed, and how are they reacting to Odysseus?*

D **Reading Focus** **Paraphrasing** What insults do the suitors throw Odysseus's way? Do you expect their inhospitality will go unpunished? Explain.

E **Literary Focus** **Epic Similes** Here, Odysseus's handling of the bow is described in terms of a master musician readying an instrument. What effect do Odysseus's effortless actions have on the suitors?

Vocabulary **disdainful** (dihs DAYN fuhl) *adj.:* scornful; regarding someone as beneath oneself.

And Odysseus laughed within him that the son
of crooked-minded Cronus° had flung that omen down.
He picked one ready arrow from his table
where it lay bare: the rest were waiting still
in the quiver for the young men's turn to come.
He nocked° it, let it rest across the handgrip,
and drew the string and grooved butt of the arrow,
aiming from where he sat upon the stool.
Now flashed
arrow from twanging bow clean as a whistle
through every socket ring, and grazed not one,
to thud with heavy brazen head beyond.
Then quietly
Odysseus said:
"Telemachus, the stranger
you welcomed in your hall has not disgraced you.
I did not miss, neither did I take all day
stringing the bow. My hand and eye are sound,
not so contemptible as the young men say.
The hour has come to cook their lordships' mutton—
supper by daylight. Other amusements later, F
with song and harping that adorn a feast."

He dropped his eyes and nodded, and the prince
Telemachus, true son of King Odysseus,
belted his sword on, clapped hand to his spear,
and with a clink and glitter of keen bronze
stood by his chair, in the forefront near his father.

(*from* Book 21)

1198. Cronus (KROH nuhs): father of Zeus. He is called crooked-minded because of his schemes to destroy his children.

1202. nocked (nahkt): fitted to the bowstring.

F **Reading Focus** **Asking Questions** What "amusements" do you think might be in store for the suitors?

LITERATURE LINK

An Ancient Gesture

by **Edna St. Vincent Millay**

I thought, as I wiped my eyes on the corner of my apron:
Penelope did this too.
And more than once: you can't keep weaving all day
And undoing it all through the night;
Your arms get tired, and the back of your neck gets tight;
And along towards morning, when you think it will never be light,
And your husband has been gone, and you don't know where,
for years,
Suddenly you burst into tears;
There is simply nothing else to do.

And I thought, as I wiped my eyes on the corner of my apron:
This is an ancient gesture, authentic, antique,
In the very best tradition, classic, Greek;
Ulysses° did this too.
But only as a gesture,—a gesture which implied
To the assembled throng that he was much too moved to speak.
He learned it from Penelope . . .
Penelope, who really cried.

13. Ulysses (yoo LIHS eez): Roman name for Odysseus.

Ask Yourself

Do you agree that only Penelope, not her husband, was emotionally overcome? Why or why not?

Penelope (detail) (1878) by Anthony Frederick Augustus Sandys (1829–1904). Colored chalk on paper.

Death at the Palace

The climax of the story is here, in Book 22. Although Odysseus is ready to reclaim his kingdom, he must first confront more than a hundred hostile suitors. The first one he turns to is Antinous. All through the story, Antinous has been the meanest of the suitors and their ringleader. He hit Odysseus with a stool when the hero appeared in the hall as a beggar, and he ridiculed the disguised king by calling him a bleary vagabond, a pest, and a tramp.

Now shrugging off his rags the wiliest fighter of the islands
leapt and stood on the broad doorsill, his own bow in his hand.
He poured out at his feet a rain of arrows from the quiver
and spoke to the crowd:

"So much for that. Your clean-cut game is over.
Now watch me hit a target that no man has hit before,
if I can make this shot. Help me, Apollo."°

He drew to his fist the cruel head of an arrow for Antinous
just as the young man leaned to lift his beautiful drinking cup,
embossed, two-handled, golden: the cup was in his fingers,
the wine was even at his lips, and did he dream of death?
How could he? In that revelry amid his throng of friends
who would imagine a single foe—though a strong foe indeed—
could dare to bring death's pain on him and darkness on his eyes?
Odysseus' arrow hit him under the chin
and punched up to the feathers through his throat.

Backward and down he went, letting the wine cup fall
from his shocked hand. Like pipes his nostrils jetted
crimson runnels,° a river of mortal red,
and one last kick upset his table
knocking the bread and meat to soak in dusty blood.
Now as they craned to see their champion where he lay
the suitors jostled in uproar down the hall,
everyone on his feet. Wildly they turned and scanned
the walls in the long room for arms; but not a shield,
not a good ashen spear was there for a man to take and throw. **A**
All they could do was yell in outrage at Odysseus:

"Foul! to shoot at a man! That was your last shot!"

"Your own throat will be slit for this!"

"Our finest lad is down!

? **1221–1303.** *As you read this action scene, imagine it as a film. What props might you need if you were filming the battle?*

? **1221–1303.** *How does this bloody episode relate to the epic's* ***theme*** *about the value of hospitality and about what happens to people who mock divine laws?*

? **1224–1263.** *Re-read this passage, and look for ways Homer assigns color to* ***symbolize*** *character qualities or emotions. What colors does Homer use to indicate rage and death? purity or nobility? jealousy? cowardice?*

1226. Help me, Apollo: Odysseus prays to Apollo because this particular day is one of the god's feast days. Apollo is also the god of archery.

1238. runnels (RUHN uhlz): streams.

A **Reading Focus** **Paraphrasing** Restate what happens in this passage.

You killed the best on Ithaca."

"Buzzards will tear your eyes out!"

For they imagined as they wished—that it was a wild shot,
an unintended killing—fools, not to comprehend
they were already in the grip of death.
But glaring under his brows Odysseus answered:

"You yellow dogs, you thought I'd never make it
home from the land of Troy. You took my house to plunder,
twisted my maids to serve your beds. You dared
bid for my wife while I was still alive.
Contempt was all you had for the gods who rule wide heaven,
contempt for what men say of you hereafter.
Your last hour has come. You die in blood."

As they all took this in, sickly green fear
pulled at their entrails, and their eyes flickered
looking for some hatch or hideaway from death.
Eurymachus alone could speak. He said:

"If you are Odysseus of Ithaca come back,
all that you say these men have done is true.
Rash actions, many here, more in the countryside.
But here he lies, the man who caused them all.
Antinous was the ringleader, he whipped us on
to do these things. He cared less for a marriage
than for the power Cronion° has denied him
as king of Ithaca. For that
he tried to trap your son and would have killed him.
He is dead now and has his portion. Spare
your own people. As for ourselves, we'll make
restitution of wine and meat consumed,
and add, each one, a tithe of twenty oxen
with gifts of bronze and gold to warm your heart.
Meanwhile we cannot blame you for your anger." **B**

1271. Cronion (KROH nee uhn): another name for Zeus, meaning "son of Cronus."

B **Literary Focus** **Epic Heroes and Conflict** In what way is Eurymachus a character foil to Odysseus? What does his speech reveal about his character?

Odysseus glowered under his black brows
and said:
"Not for the whole treasure of your fathers,
all you enjoy, lands, flocks, or any gold
put up by others, would I hold my hand.
There will be killing till the score is paid.
You forced yourselves upon this house. Fight your way out,
or run for it, if you think you'll escape death.
I doubt one man of you skins by." . . .

Telemachus joins his father in the fight. They are helped by the swineherd and cowherd. Now the suitors, trapped in the hall without weapons, are struck right and left by arrows, and many of them lie dying on the floor.

At this moment that unmanning thundercloud,
the aegis, Athena's shield,
took form aloft in the great hall.
And the suitors mad with fear
at her great sign stampeded like stung cattle by a river
when the dread shimmering gadfly strikes in summer,
in the flowering season, in the long-drawn days.
After them the attackers wheeled, as terrible as falcons
from eyries° in the mountains veering over and diving down
with talons wide unsheathed on flights of birds,
who cower down the sky in chutes and bursts along the
valley—
but the pouncing falcons grip their prey, no frantic wing
avails,
and farmers love to watch those beakèd hunters. **C**
So these now fell upon the suitors in that hall,
turning, turning to strike and strike again,
while torn men moaned at death, and blood ran smoking
over the whole floor. . . .

(*from* Book 22)

1295. eyries (AIR eez): nests built in high places.

C Literary Focus Epic Similes To what are the suitors compared? To what are the suitors' attackers compared?

Vocabulary glowered (GLOW urhd) *v.:* glared; stared angrily.

Odysseus and Penelope

Odysseus now calls forth the maids who have betrayed his household by associating with the suitors. He orders them to clean up the house and dispose of the dead. Telemachus then "pays" them by hanging them in the courtyard.

Eurycleia tells Penelope about the return of Odysseus and the defeat of the suitors. The faithful wife—the perfect mate for the wily Odysseus—suspects a trick from the gods. She decides to test the stranger who claims to be her husband.

Penelope by John Roddam Spencer Stanhope (1829–1908). Oil on canvas (168 cm x 81.3 cm). Private collection.

Analyzing Visuals

Viewing and Interpreting How would you describe the expression on Penelope's face? Based on what you know of Penelope, what do you imagine she is thinking about?

Crossing the doorsill she sat down at once
in firelight, against the nearest wall,
across the room from the lord Odysseus.

There

leaning against a pillar, sat the man
and never lifted up his eyes, but only waited
for what his wife would say when she had seen him.
And she, for a long time, sat deathly still
in wonderment—for sometimes as she gazed
she found him—yes, clearly—like her husband,
but sometimes blood and rags were all she saw. **A**
Telemachus's voice came to her ears:

"Mother,

cruel mother, do you feel nothing,
drawing yourself apart this way from Father?
Will you not sit with him and talk and question him?
What other woman could remain so cold?
Who shuns her lord, and he come back to her
from wars and wandering, after twenty years?
Your heart is hard as flint and never changes!"

Penelope answered:

"I am stunned, child.

I cannot speak to him. I cannot question him.
I cannot keep my eyes upon his face.
If really he is Odysseus, truly home,
beyond all doubt we two shall know each other
better than you or anyone. There are
secret signs we know, we two."

A smile

came now to the lips of the patient hero, Odysseus,
who turned to Telemachus and said:

"Peace: let your mother test me at her leisure.
Before long she will see and know me best.
These tatters, dirt—all that I'm caked with now—
make her look hard at me and doubt me still. . . ." **B**

? **1304–1321.** *Take notes as you read this episode. What might Penelope be thinking as she listens to Telemachus speak?*

A **Literary Focus** **Epic Heroes and Conflict** What internal conflicts do you imagine both Odysseus and Penelope are facing? Are these feelings mutual? Explain.

B **Literary Focus** **Epic Heroes and Conflict** What admirable qualities do both Odysseus and Penelope display here?

LITERATURE LINK

Constantine Cavafy, one of Greece's foremost poets, wrote this famous poem in 1911. Read it to learn his ideas about the importance of the journey.

Ithaka

by **C. P. Cavafy**
translated by **Edmund Keeley** *and* **Philip Sherrard**

When you set out for Ithaka,
pray that your road's a long one,
full of adventure, full of discovery.
Laistrygonians, Cyclops,
angry Poseidon—don't be scared of them:
you won't find things like that on your way
as long as your thoughts are exalted,
as long as a rare excitement
stirs your spirit and your body.
Laistrygonians, Cyclops,
wild Poseidon—you won't encounter them
unless you bring them along inside you,
unless your soul raises them up in front of you.

Pray that your road's a long one.
may there be many a summer morning when—
full of gratitude, full of joy—
you come into harbors seen for the first time;
may you stop at Phoenician trading centers
and buy fine things,
mother-of-pearl and coral, amber and ebony,
sensual perfumes of every kind,
as many sensual perfumes as you can;
may you visit numerous Egyptian cities
to fill yourself with learning from the wise.

Keep Ithaka always in mind.
Arriving there is what you're destined for.
But don't hurry the journey at all.
Better if it goes on for years
so you're old by the time you reach the island,
wealthy with all you've gained on the way,
not expecting Ithaka to make you rich.
Ithaka gave you the marvelous journey.
Without her you wouldn't have set out.
She hasn't anything else to give.

And if you find her poor, Ithaka won't have
fooled you.
Wise as you'll have become, and so experienced,
you'll have understood by then what an
Ithaka means.

Ask Yourself

What is Ithaka? Can Ithaka mean different things to different people? Explain.

Odysseus orders Telemachus, the swineherd, and the cowherd to bathe and put on fresh clothing.

Greathearted Odysseus, home at last,
was being bathed now by Eurynome
and rubbed with golden oil, and clothed again
in a fresh tunic and a cloak. Athena
lent him beauty, head to foot. She made him
taller, and massive, too, with crisping hair
in curls like petals of wild hyacinth
but all red-golden. Think of gold infused
on silver by a craftsman, whose fine art

Ulysses Deriding Polyphemus (detail) (1829) by J.M.W. Turner. Oil on canvas. Tate Gallery, London.

Hephaestus taught him, or Athena: one
whose work moves to delight: just so she lavished
beauty over Odysseus' head and shoulders.
He sat then in the same chair by the pillar,
facing his silent wife, and said:

"Strange woman,

the immortals of Olympus made you hard,
harder than any. Who else in the world
would keep aloof as you do from her husband
if he returned to her from years of trouble,
cast on his own land in the twentieth year?

Nurse, make up a bed for me to sleep on.
Her heart is iron in her breast."

Vocabulary **lavished** (LAV ihsht) *v.:* gave generously.
aloof (uh LOOF) *adj.:* unfriendly; at a distance.

Penelope
spoke to Odysseus now. She said:
"Strange man,
if man you are . . . This is no pride on my part
nor scorn for you—not even wonder, merely.
I know so well how you—how he—appeared
boarding the ship for Troy. But all the same . . .

Make up his bed for him, Eurycleia.
Place it outside the bedchamber my lord
built with his own hands. Pile the big bed
with fleeces, rugs, and sheets of purest linen."

With this she tried him to the breaking point,
and he turned on her in a flash, raging:

"Woman, by heaven you've stung me now!
Who dared to move my bed?
No builder had the skill for that—unless
a god came down to turn the trick. No mortal
in his best days could budge it with a crowbar.
There is our pact and pledge, our secret sign,
built into that bed—my handiwork
and no one else's!
An old trunk of olive
grew like a pillar on the building plot,
and I laid out our bedroom round that tree,
lined up the stone walls, built the walls and roof,
gave it a doorway and smooth-fitting doors.
Then I lopped off the silvery leaves and branches,
hewed and shaped the stump from the roots up
into a bedpost, drilled it, let it serve
as model for the rest, I planed them all,
inlaid them all with silver, gold, and ivory,
and stretched a bed between—a pliant° web
of oxhide thongs dyed crimson. **C**
There's our sign!
I know no more. Could someone else's hand

1384. pliant (PLY uhnt): flexible.

C **Reading Focus** **Paraphrasing** What trick does Penelope use to get Odysseus to prove who he is? How does Odysseus describe the bed?

have sawn that trunk and dragged the frame away?"

Their secret! as she heard it told, her knees
grew tremulous and weak, her heart failed her.
With eyes brimming tears she ran to him,
throwing her arms around his neck, and kissed him,
murmuring:
"Do not rage at me, Odysseus!
No one ever matched your caution! Think
what difficulty the gods gave: they denied us
life together in our prime and flowering years,
kept us from crossing into age together.
Forgive me, don't be angry. I could not
welcome you with love on sight! I armed myself
long ago against the frauds of men,
impostors who might come—and all those many
whose underhanded ways bring evil on! . . .
But here and now, what sign could be so clear
as this of our own bed?
No other man has ever laid eyes on it—
only my own slave, Actoris, that my father
sent with me as a gift—she kept our door.
You make my stiff heart know that I am yours." **D**

Now from his breast into his eyes the ache
of longing mounted, and he wept at last,
his dear wife, clear and faithful, in his arms,
longed for
as the sun-warmed earth is longed for by a swimmer
spent in rough water where his ship went down
under Poseidon's blows, gale winds and tons of sea.
Few men can keep alive through a big surf
to crawl, clotted with brine, on kindly beaches
in joy, in joy, knowing the abyss behind:
and so she too rejoiced, her gaze upon her husband,
her white arms round him pressed, as though forever. . . .
(*from* Book 23)

? **1408–1418.** *The journey ends with an embrace. What* ***simile*** *helps you understand the joy Odysseus feels in the arms of his wife?*

D **Reading Focus Summarizing** What key information are we given here?

Applying Your Skills

MO 9.R.2.A.1 Analyze and evaluate the text features in grade-level text 9.R.1.G.1.g During reading, utilize strategies: to summarize 9.R.1.H.1.b Apply post-reading skills to comprehend, interpret, analyze, and evaluate text: question to clarify *Also covered* 9.W.3.A.1.e

from the Odyssey, Part Two

Respond and Think Critically

Reading Focus

Quick Check

1. Why does Telemachus think Odysseus is a god?
2. How does Argos recognize Odysseus?
3. What is the contest of the bow, and how will Penelope reward the winner?
4. Before trying the bow, Odysseus reveals himself to two people. Why does he confide in them?
5. How does Penelope test Odysseus?

Read with a Purpose

6. How does Odysseus use his strength and cunning to overcome his enemies in Part Two?

Reading Skills: Reading an Epic

7. Use your *5W-How?* chart from page 1077 to help you summarize the various meetings, tests, and conflicts and resolutions in the chart below.

Episode	My Summary
The Meeting of Father and Son	
The Beggar and the Faithful Dog	
The Test of the Great Bow	
Death at the Palace	
Odysseus and Penelope	

Literary Focus

Literary Analysis

8. **Literary Perspectives** Epic heroes rarely deal with ordinary people, but Odysseus treats Eumaeus and the cowherd with respect. What idea about life does this episode convey?
9. **Analyze** What character traits does Penelope reveal in her interactions with Odysseus when he is disguised as a beggar?
10. **Infer** What does the interaction between Odysseus and Penelope in lines 1348–1418 tell you about their relationship?
11. **Evaluate** Do you think Odysseus's revenge on the suitors and maids is excessive? Explain.

Literary Skills: Epic Similes

12. **Analyze** What epic simile in lines 1031–1033 describes the feelings of father and son as they embrace after twenty years?
13. **Interpret** What is being compared in the epic simile in the final passage of Book 23? What effect does this simile create?

Literary Skills Review: Irony

14. **Analyze** **Situational irony** occurs when what happens is different from what we expect. Why is it ironic that Odysseus returns to Ithaca dressed as a beggar?

Writing Focus

Think as a Reader/Writer

Use It in Your Writing Now that you've read Part Two of the *Odyssey,* add another paragraph to your character sketch of Odysseus as an epic hero. Keep in mind his feelings toward Argos, the servants of his kingdom, his son, and Penelope.

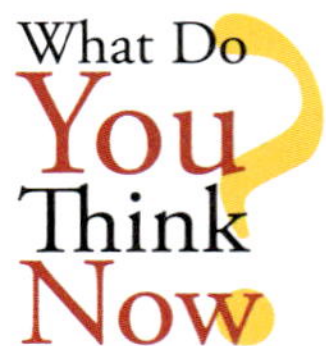

What do you think was the purpose of Odysseus's journey? What does his journey symbolize?

Applying Your Skills

from the Odyssey, Part Two

Vocabulary Development

Vocabulary Check

Answer true (T) or false (F) to the following items.

1. A secretive person usually displays **candor.**
2. You probably would not invite a person who was **disdainful** of you to your birthday party.
3. A person who **glowered** at me showed anger.
4. If someone were **lavished** with praise, he or she would feel ignored.
5. Someone who is **aloof** shows little interest in others.

Vocabulary Skills: Words from Myths

Myths are religious stories associated with a particular society. Myths often explain the mysteries of nature, the origins of rituals, and the relationships between gods and humans.

Many English words have their origins in Greek and Roman myths and epics. For example, a long, difficult journey in search of something of value is called an *odyssey,* like the epic you have just read.

Names from Greek and Roman Myths

Name	English Word	Name	English Word
aegis	aegis	Muses	museum; music
Ceres	cereal	Narcissus	narcissistic
Hector	hector	Olympia	Olympics
Jove	jovial	Siren	siren
Mentor	mentor	Tantalus	tantalize
Mercury	mercury	Titans	titanic
Helios	helium	Vulcan	volcano

Celestial Objects Named for Gods in Greek and Roman Myths			
Mercury	Mars	Saturn	Neptune
Venus	Jupiter	Uranus	Pluto

Your Turn

Words from Greek Myths Read the following information, and answer the questions about words derived from the Greek myths and epics. For help, look up the boldface words in a good dictionary.

1. Homer opens his epics with a prayer to the Muse. In mythology the nine Muses were goddesses who inspired people working in the arts and sciences.
   How is the meaning of **museum** *related to the Muses?*
2. The Sirens were island creatures with enchanting voices who lured sailors to steer their ships toward rocks.
   Why is the horn of an ambulance called a **siren?**
3. The aegis (EE jihs) was the great shield of Zeus, king of the gods. Anyone who acted "under the aegis" had Zeus's power and support.
   What do we mean when we say we live under the **aegis** *of the Constitution?*
4. Tantalus, a mortal son of Zeus, was sent to Hades for revealing his father's secrets. There he is forced to stand in water, with fruit hanging over his head. Whenever he tries to drink the water or eat the fruit, he cannot reach it.
   How is the word **tantalize** *related to Tantalus?*
5. Narcissus, son of a river god, was a handsome youth who was cold to all who loved him. To punish him, the gods doomed him to fall in love with his own reflection in the water. When Narcissus tried to embrace his beloved, the reflection in the water disappeared. After Narcissus died from grief, he was changed into a flower, which we call narcissus.
   What kind of person is **narcissistic?**

(*continued*)

MO **9.R.1.G.1.a** During reading, utilize strategies: to determine meaning of unknown words **9.R.1.E.1.a** Develop vocabulary through text: using roots and affixes **9.R.1.E.1.c** Develop vocabulary through text: using glossary, dictionary and thesaurus

Vocabulary Development

Words from Roman Myths The ancient Romans adopted many of the Greek myths but changed Greek names to Latin ones. Answer the following questions about words derived from Roman myths.

6. Mars was the Roman god of war (the Greek god Ares). The third month of the year is named in his honor, as is the planet Mars.
What happens when a peace-loving nation becomes **martial**?
7. Ceres was the Roman goddess of corn and grain, who also controlled fertility and the harvest. After Pluto (his Greek name was Hades) kidnapped her daughter, Proserpina (the Greek Persephone), Ceres stopped crops from growing. When Proserpina, goddess of spring, returns to Ceres for six months each year, crops grow again.
Why might people have given the name **cereal** *to a breakfast food?*
8. Vulcan was the Roman god of fire and metalworking. A blacksmith, he created beautiful things and instruments of war. He lived under various mountains. When he worked, smoke and fire spewed from the mountains.
How is the word **volcano** *related to the god Vulcan?*
9. Jove was another name for the Roman god Jupiter (the Greek god Zeus). According to those who believe the stars and planets influence our lives, people who are born under the sign of the planet Jupiter are jovial.
Why is it fun to have a **jovial** *guest at a party?*

Language Coach

Word Origins See if you can match these Latin words with the related words from the epic.

1. *brachium,* "arm" — **a.** pastures (line 962)
2. *pascere,* "to feed" — **b.** patient (line 1329)
3. *fors,* "chance" — **c.** trouble (line 1352)
4. *patiens,* "one who suffers" — **d.** fortune (line 1184)
5. *turba,* "crowd" — **e.** embrace (line 952)

Academic Vocabulary

Talk About . . .

Think about the final scene in Part Two of the *Odyssey*. Discuss the following questions with a partner, using the Academic Vocabulary words:

1. What do you think about the love between Odysseus and Penelope? Are their feelings mutual? Explain.
2. How is Odysseus's and Penelope's marriage bed portrayed? What do you think this description says about their marriage?

Applying Your Skills

from the **Odyssey, Part Two**

MO **9.W.3.A.1.e** Compose a variety of texts: including reflective writing **9.W.2.B.1.b** Compose text with: relevant specific details **9.W.3.A.1.a** Compose a variety of texts: using narrative, descriptive, expository, and/or persuasive features **9.W.2.E.1.c** In written text apply: standard usage *Also covered* **9.W.2.C.1.e; 9.W.1.A.1.d**

Grammar Link

Double Negatives

The *Odyssey* contains one of the most famous double negatives in all literature. When the blinded Cyclops is searching for Odysseus (who said his name is Nohbdy), he declares, "Nohbdy will not get out alive, I swear."

A double negative is a sentence construction in which two negative words are used where one is enough. In Shakespeare's time, double negatives were acceptable, but now they are considered nonstandard.

Nonstandard I had *not never* heard of a Cyclops.

Standard I had *never* heard of a Cyclops.

Nonstandard *Not nobody* can resist the Sirens' song.

Standard *Nobody* can resist the Sirens' song.

Here are common negative words: *neither, never, no, nobody, none, no one, not, nothing, nowhere,* and *hardly.* (As you can see, negative words in English often start with the letter *n.*)

Your Turn

In each sentence below, choose the correct word from the pair given in parentheses.

1. Penelope would not marry (*no, any*) suitor.
2. The men who ate the Lotus (*could, couldn't*) hardly remember their homeland.
3. Calypso wouldn't get (*anywhere, nowhere*) arguing with Hermes.
4. Odysseus doesn't say (*anything, nothing*) as he strings his bow.

Writing Applications Look through the writing you have done while answering questions about the *Odyssey*. Correct any faulty use of negatives you find in your work.

CHOICES

As you respond to the Choices, use these **Academic Vocabulary** words as appropriate: express, destiny, mutual, portrayed.

REVIEW

Describe Odysseus

Timed Writing In a brief essay, discuss at least four of Odysseus's character traits. Find examples in the epic that express each trait. In your final paragraph, sum up your opinion of Odysseus's character. Do you think he is admirable? To what extent would he be considered a hero today?

CONNECT

Create a Computer Game

TechFocus With several classmates, develop an outline for a computer game based on some of the episodes from the *Odyssey*. In your outline, indicate the characters who will appear in the game and their descriptions; the goal of the game; the sequence of events; and graphics that you will use. You might also include other Greek gods and goddesses who can influence the action in some way.

EXTEND

Write a Sequel

Suppose Odysseus soon gets bored with peace and inactivity in Ithaca and yearns to explore new regions. This time, however, Penelope demands to go with him. They leave Telemachus to govern Ithaca and set sail for unknown lands. Write a story describing where they go, who or what they meet, and how they use their skills to outwit deadly characters and escape dire situations.

MYTH

Preparing to Read

The Fenris Wolf

retold by **Olivia Coolidge**

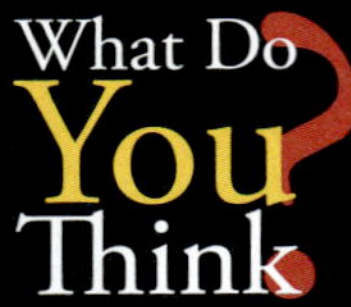

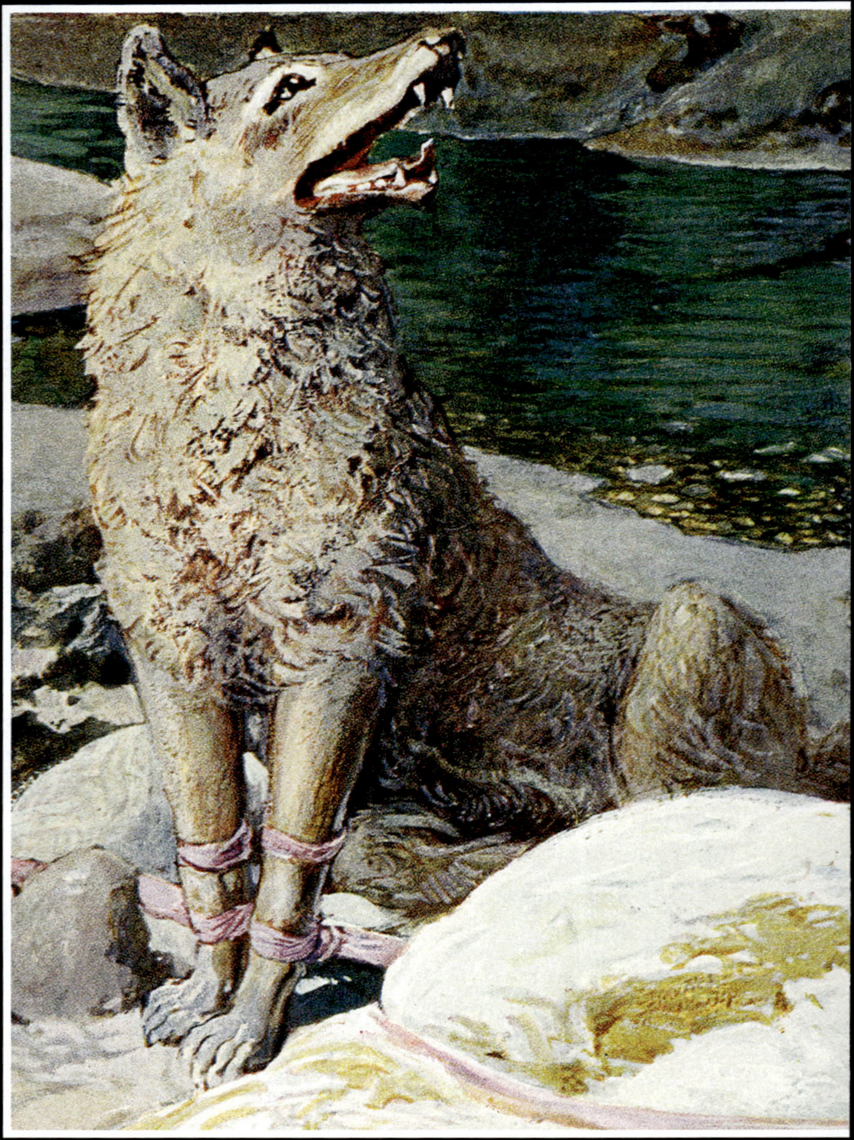

An illustration of the shackled Fenris Wolf.

What Do You Think? What kinds of journeys—either literal or figurative—are commonly the subject of myths?

QuickTalk

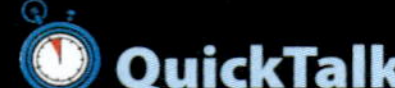

With a partner, brainstorm a list of myths you know. What kinds of journeys, such as a journey to the underworld or a quest to achieve a goal, do the characters in these myths undertake?

Use your **RWN** to complete the activities for this selection.

MO **9.R.2.A.1** Analyze and evaluate the text features in grade-level text **9.R.2.C.1.b** Use details from text(s): to analyze character, plot, setting, point of view **9.R.3.C.1.a** Use details from informational text: to identify and explain the organizational pattern

Literary Focus

Myths and Archetypes Every society has its **myths,** stories that are connected to the traditions and religion of the culture that created them. Myths tell people where they came from, where they are going, and how they should live. Many archetypes (AHR kuh typs) come from myths. **Archetypes** are patterns that recur in literature. They can be characters (the brave hero; the wise old man), plots or events (the heroic quest), settings (paradise; a dark forest), or images or things (a crystal ball; a trusty sword).

Reading Focus

Analyzing Causes and Effects Myths are narratives, which are built on a series of causes and effects. One event happens in a narrative, which causes another event to happen, which causes yet another event to happen. Identifying cause-and-effect relationships as you read will help you understand why actions were taken and the effects they trigger.

Into Action As you read this myth, record causes and their effects in a chart like the one below. Create as many boxes as you need.

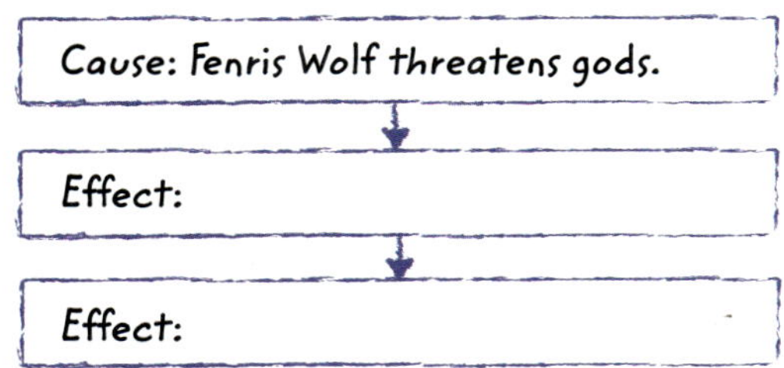

Writing Focus

Think as a Reader/Writer

Find It in Your Reading Traditional folk tales and myths often include events that happen in threes. As you read this myth, record in your *Reader/Writer Notebook* the things or events that come in threes.

Vocabulary

grisly (GRIHZ lee) *adj.:* horrible; terrifying; gruesome. *The Fenris Wolf is a grisly monster.*

reigned (raynd) *v.:* ruled. *Odin reigned over the other gods.*

sullenly (SUHL uhn lee) *adv.:* in a resentful, disagreeable, and unsociable manner. *The Fenris Wolf responds sullenly to the gods' request.*

writhing (RYTH ihng) *v.* used as *adj.:* twisting or turning, as in pain. *The writhing wolf struggles to break the chains.*

perish (PEHR ihsh) *v.:* be destroyed; die. *According to Norse mythology, the gods will ultimately perish.*

Language Coach

Word Derivations What do the words *solo* (meaning "performance by one person" as a noun and "alone" as an adverb), *solitude* ("state of being alone; seclusion"), and *desolate* ("lonely; uninhabited; deserted") all have in common? They are all derived from the same Latin word, *solus*, meaning "alone." Which word on the list above is also derived from *solus*?

Learn It Online
Find graphic organizers online to help you analyze cause and effect:

go.hrw.com  

MEET THE WRITER

Olivia Coolidge

(1908–2006)

An Uncommon Childhood

Although Olivia Coolidge's father, a newspaper columnist and a professor, worked in the cities of London and Oxford, England, he and Coolidge's mother chose to make their home in the country. Coolidge grew up in a house that lacked gas, electricity, central heating, and a hot-water system, and her family grew its own fruits and vegetables. Although Coolidge enjoyed the benefits of being allowed "to run wild," she once noted, "I used to wish hard when I was at school that my parents would act just a little bit more like ordinary people."

A Reteller of Tales

Coolidge is best known for her retellings of ancient Greek myths, specifically aimed at young adults. Her interest in ancient legends was evident at the start of her career. One of her earliest works, *Legends of the North*, is a collection of Norse myths that contains "The Fenris Wolf" and other tales of Northern gods. Coolidge also wrote highly praised biographies for young adults. These books describe people such as Abraham Lincoln, Tom Paine, and Gandhi. She once remarked, "I write about history, biography, and ancient legends for teens because I am more interested in values that always have been of concern to people than I am in the form we express them in at this moment."

Think About the Writer Explain why Coolidge focused on history, biography, and ancient legends during her career.

Build Background

"The Fenris Wolf" is a story from Norse mythology, the collection of myths that developed thousands of years ago among the peoples of Scandinavia and Germany. The oldest surviving written versions of these tales came from Iceland in the thirteenth century.

Preview the Selection

In a battle of strength and wit, the Norse gods, including **Odin, Tyr,** and **Thor,** confront the **Fenris Wolf,** the offspring of the god **Loki** and a giantess.

The Norse Gods from the Story:
Odin (OH dihn): also known as **Woden** (WOH dihn), god of wisdom and victory; leader of the family of gods.

Ve (vay) and **Vili** (VIHL ee): Odin's brothers.

Frigga (FRIHG uh) or **Frigg** (frihg): Odin's wife, goddess of marriage and motherhood.

Thor (thawr): Odin's oldest son, god of thunder and lightning.

Tyr (tihr) or **Tiu** (TEE oo): god of war; the bravest of the gods.

Loki (LOH kee): god of fire, mischief, and evil.

Read with a Purpose Read this myth to explore a conflict of dreadful proportions.

The Fenris Wolf
A NORSE MYTH

retold by **Olivia Coolidge**

The Norse god Tyr losing his hand to the Fenris Wolf (Eighteenth century) by Icelandic School. Pen and ink on paper.

Though Loki, the fire god, was handsome and ready-witted, his nature was really evil. He was, indeed, the cause of most of the misfortunes which befell the gods. He was constantly in trouble, yet often forgiven because the gods valued his cleverness. It was he who found ways out of difficulty for them, so that for a long time they felt that they could not do without him. **A**

In the early days Loki, though a god, had wedded a monstrous giantess, and the union of these two evil beings produced a fearful brood. The first was the great world serpent, whom Odin cast into the sea, and who became so large that he completely encircled the earth, his tail touching his mouth. The second was Hel, the grisly goddess of the underworld, who reigned in the horrible land of the dead. The third was the most dreadful of all, a huge monster called the Fenris Wolf.

When the gods first saw the Fenris Wolf, he was so young that they thought they could tame him. They took him to Asgard, therefore, and brave Tyr undertook to feed and train him. Presently, however, the black monster grew so enormous that his open jaws would stretch from heaven to earth, showing teeth as large as the trunks of oak trees and as sharply pointed as knives. The howls of the beast were so dreadful as he tore his vast meals of raw meat that the gods, save for Tyr, dared not go near him, lest he devour them.

At last all were agreed that the Fenris Wolf

A **Literary Focus** **Myths and Archetypes** A clever troublemaker, Loki is an archetypal trickster figure. What other tricksters in myths or folk tales can you name?

Vocabulary **grisly** (GRIHZ lee) *adj.:* horrible; terrifying; gruesome.
reigned (raynd) *v.:* ruled.

must be fettered[1] if they were to save their very lives, for the monster grew more ferocious towards them every day. They forged a huge chain, but since none was strong enough to bind him, they challenged him to a trial of strength. "Let us tie you with this to see if you can snap the links," said they. **B**

The Fenris Wolf took a look at the chain and showed all his huge white teeth in a dreadful grin. "Bind me if you wish," he growled, and he actually shut his eyes as he lay down at ease to let them put it on.

The gods stepped back, and the wolf gave a little shake. There was a loud cracking sound, and the heavy links lay scattered around him in pieces. The wolf howled in triumph until the sun and moon in heaven trembled at the noise.

Thor, the smith,[2] called other gods to his aid, and they labored day and night at the second chain. This was half as strong again as the first, and so heavy that no one of the gods could drag it across the ground. "This is by far the largest chain that was ever made," said they. "Even the Fenris Wolf will not be able to snap fetters such as these."

Once more they brought the chain to the wolf, and he let them put it on, though this time it was clear that he somewhat doubted his strength. When they had chained him, he shook himself violently, but the fetters held. His great, red eyes burned with fury, the black hair bristled on his back, and he gnashed his teeth until the foam flew. He strained heavily against the iron until the vast links flattened and lengthened, but did not break. Finally with a great bound and a howl he dashed himself against the ground, and suddenly the chain sprang apart so violently that broken pieces were hurled about the heads of the watching gods.

Now the gods realized in despair that all their strength and skill would not avail to bind the wolf. Therefore Odin sent a messenger to the dwarf people under the earth, bidding them forge him a chain. The messenger returned with a little rope, smooth and soft as a silken string, which was hammered on dwarfish anvils[3] out of strange materials which have never been seen or heard. The sound of a cat's footfall, the breath of a fish, the flowing beard of a woman, and the roots of a mountain made the metal from which it was forged. **C**

The gods took the tiny rope to the Fenris Wolf. "See what an easy task we have for you this time," they said.

"Why should I bother myself with a silken string?" asked the wolf sullenly. "I have broken your mightiest chain. What use is this foolish thing?"

"The rope is stronger than it looks," answered they. "We are not able to break it, but it will be a small matter to you."

"If this rope is strong by enchantment," said

1. **fettered:** (FEHT uhrd): chained.
2. **smith:** blacksmith, someone who works at a forge and makes and repairs metal objects, such as horseshoes.
3. **anvils** (AN vuhlz): iron or steel blocks on which hot metal objects are hammered into shape.

B Literary Focus **Myths and Archetypes** Think of other myths and folk tales you know. What archetypal plot element is described in this passage?

C Reading Focus **Analyzing Causes and Effects** What is the cause of the gods' despair? What action do they take as a result of their defeat?

Vocabulary **sullenly** (SUHL uhn lee) *adv.:* in a resentful, disagreeable, and unsociable manner.

CULTURE LINK

Hermod, son of the Norse god Odin (Eighteenth century), by Icelandic School. Pen and ink on paper. Manuscript. Royal Library, Copenhagen, Denmark.

Norse Mythology

Norse mythology presents a terribly gloomy worldview. According to one version of the Norse creation story, life began in the boundary between fire and ice. Eventually, the first gods were born from a family of giants. The gods Odin, Ve, and Vili created the earth and the first man and woman. They also created Asgard (AS gahrd), where the gods live, and Midgard (MIHD gahrd), where humans live. One of the most remarkable and tragic aspects of Norse mythology is its bleak prophecy about how the world will end. In this prophecy, giants and monsters led by the evil god Loki will do battle with the other gods and goddesses. All the gods and goddesses, giants, and monsters will slay each other, and the entire earth will be consumed by fire. This final struggle is called Ragnarok (RAG nuh rahk).

Ask Yourself

What details does "The Fenris Wolf" provide about Ragnarok?

the wolf in slow suspicion, "how can I tell that you will loosen me if I cannot snap it after all? On one condition you may bind me: You must give me a hostage from among yourselves."

"How can we do this?" they asked.

The Fenris Wolf stretched himself and yawned until the sun hid behind clouds at the sight of his great, red throat. "I will let you bind me with this rope," he said, "if one of you gods will hold his hand between my teeth while I do it."

The gods looked at one another in silence. The wolf grinned from ear to ear. Without a word Tyr walked forward and laid his bare hand inside the open mouth.

The gods bound the great wolf, and he stretched himself and heaved as before. This time, however, he did not break his bonds. He gnashed his jaws together, and Tyr cried out in pain as he lost his hand. Nevertheless, the great black wolf lay howling and writhing and helplessly biting the ground. There he lay in the bonds of the silken rope as long as the reign of Odin endured. The Fates declared, however, that in the last days, when the demons of ice and fire should come marching against the gods to the battlefield, the great sea would give up the serpent, and the Fenris Wolf would break his bonds. The wolf would swallow Odin, and the gods would go down in defeat: Sun and moon would be devoured, and the whole earth would perish utterly. **D**

D **Reading Focus** **Analyzing Causes and Effects** Why does Tyr place his hand in the wolf's mouth? What happens as a result? Do you believe this is the Fenris Wolf's destiny? Explain.

Vocabulary **writhing** (RYTH ihng) *v.* used as *adj.:* twisting or turning, as in pain.
perish (PEHR ihsh) *v.:* be destroyed; die.

Applying Your Skills

The Fenris Wolf

Respond and Think Critically

Reading Focus

Quick Check

1. Why are the gods afraid to go near the Fenris Wolf when it grows up?
2. What does Thor, with the help of other gods, create?
3. What does the Fenris Wolf demand in return for letting the gods bind him a third time?

Read with a Purpose

4. What does the conflict between the gods and the Fenris Wolf **symbolize,** or represent? Why might the myth emphasize the wolf's fierceness and strength as well as the difficulty the gods face in defeating him?

Reading Skills: Analyzing Causes and Effects

5. Review the cause-and-effect chart you filled in as you read. How do the gods' errors in judgment contribute to the conflict with the Fenris Wolf and to the series of causes and effects described in the myth?

Cause: Fenris Wolf threatens gods.
↓
Effect:
↓
Effect:

Literary Focus

Literary Analysis

6. **Connect** In what ways does Loki seem human? In what ways does he seem godlike?
7. **Compare and Contrast** What similarities and differences do you note between the Fenris Wolf and his father, Loki? Be sure to consider their relationship with the gods.

Literary Skills: Myths and Archetypes

8. **Analyze** In many Norse myths, heroes face terrible enemies with great courage, though they know they will be defeated in the end. How is such behavior displayed in "The Fenris Wolf"?
9. **Analyze** Which elements of "The Fenris Wolf" are archetypal? Consider the myth's plot and characters, and support your answer by drawing parallels to other stories you know.

Literary Skills Review: Imagery and Figures of Speech

10. **Analyze** The Fenris Wolf is presented as a larger-than-life figure. Explain how Olivia Coolidge uses **imagery** (language that appeals to our senses) and **similes** (comparisons between two unlike things, using words such as *like* or *as*) to convey the wolf's dreadfulness.

Writing Focus

Think as a Reader/Writer

Use It in Your Writing Review your notes on "The Fenris Wolf." Did you find the use of the pattern of threes effective? In what way does that pattern seem familiar? In what ways are the story's events unique? Write your thoughts in a brief essay.

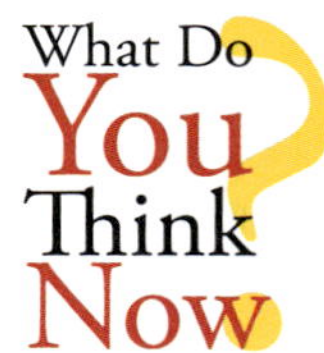

In what ways does the journey in this myth reflect the bleak outlook of Norse mythology?

9.R.2.A.1 Analyze and evaluate the text features in grade-level text **9.R.2.C.1.b** Use details from text(s): to analyze character, plot, setting, point of view *Also covered* **9.R.2.B.2.b; 9.R.2.B.2.d; 9.R.3.C.1.a; 9.W.3.A.1.d; 9.R.1.E.1.a; 9.R.1.E.1.c; 9.R.1.G.1.a**

Vocabulary Development

Vocabulary Check

grisly
reigned
sullenly
writhing
perish

Write the Vocabulary word that best completes the meaning of each sentence.

1. The queen __________ in England for many years.
2. I tried to hold the __________ dog still so that the veterinarian could examine her.
3. I had nightmares after seeing the __________ movie.
4. Many people will __________ if the ship sinks in the storm.
5. Because he did not get his way, the child behaved __________.

Vocabulary Skills: Words from Norse Myths

The English language that we speak today has been enriched over the centuries by contributions from many languages, among them German, Latin, Greek, French, and Spanish. Old English, the ancestor of our modern English, was the language spoken by Anglo-Saxon tribes who migrated to England from areas in what are now Germany, Denmark, and other northern European countries. Because they originated in northern Europe, the Anglo-Saxon people shared much of the culture from which Norse mythology sprang. In modern English we still use many terms that derive from that ancient culture.

Your Turn

1. Which days of the week are named for these gods: Odin, or Woden; Frigga, or Frigg; Tyr, or Tiu; and Thor? Use a dictionary to check your answers.
2. Refer to the story and to a dictionary for help answering the following questions:
   - **a.** To what Norse name is the word *hell* related?
   - **b.** What Norse god gave us our word *thunder*?

Language Coach

Word Derivations In a dictionary, information about the derivation of a word usually appears in brackets. The symbol < means "derived from," and the oldest form of the word appears last. *OE* stands for "Old English," *Gr* stands for "Greek," and *L* stands for "Latin." Always be sure, however, to check the meanings of the abbreviations used in a dictionary. Use a dictionary to determine the origin of these words: *grisly, reign, writhe,* and *perish.*

Academic Vocabulary

Write About . . .

1. Write a one-paragraph summary of what you believe will happen when the Fenris Wolf breaks free of his bonds. Will he fulfill his destiny? Explain.
2. Whom would you cast in a film of this myth? Why do you think those actors would portray these characters effectively?

Comparing Themes and Topics Across Genres

CONTENTS

This sign along the Rio Grande marks the boundary between Texas, in the United States, and Mexico.

How can your expectations affect what you find on a journey?

QuickWrite

Think about a journey you have taken, either long or short. What did you expect to find on your journey? Write down a few thoughts about how you felt before the journey began. Then, explain whether the journey lived up to your expectations.

Preparing to Read

9.R.2.C.1.c Use details from text(s): to analyze the development of a theme across genres
Also covered **9.R.1.H.1.a; 9.R.1.I.1.a**

Mexico Next Right / The Boy Left Behind

Reader/Writer Notebook

Use your **RWN** to complete the activities for these selections.

Literary Focus

Themes and Topics Across Genres Fiction writers use story elements to highlight important **themes,** or key insights about life. For example, a fictional story character may learn to embrace challenges rather than flee from them. Nonfiction writers, however, don't make up stories. Instead, they present information about a **topic,** or subject, and share insights about it.

Reading Focus

Comparing Details When comparing texts, begin by looking for obvious similarities and differences. For example, one of these selections is fiction, and the other is nonfiction; but they both tell about journeys. Don't stop there, however. Comparing details also helps you appreciate the subtle ways that two texts relate to each other. Key details you might consider are the main character(s) or person(s), setting, and **tone** (a writer's attitude toward his or her subject).

Into Action Use a chart like this one to collect notes about the selections.

	"Mexico Next Right"	"The Boy Left Behind"
Main Character	a young girl named Layla	
Setting	in a car driving to Mexico	
Tone		

Writing Focus

Think as a Reader/Writer

Find It in Your Reading Writers choose active, interesting verbs to create clear images of the actions that take place in the stories they write. Use your *Reader/Writer Notebook* to note specific verbs that Cisneros and Nazario have chosen.

Vocabulary

Mexico Next Right

vendors (VEHN duhrz) *n.:* sellers. *Vendors tempt customers with balloons, fresh fruit, and ice cream.*

The Boy Left Behind

idealize (y DEE uh lyz) *v.:* think of someone or something as perfect; ignore any flaws. *He tends to idealize mothers, imagining that they never make mistakes.*

incomprehensible (ihn kahm prih HEHN suh buhl) *adj.:* not able to be understood. *From the son's point of view, his mother's decision to leave was completely incomprehensible.*

scavenging (SKAV uhnj ihng) *v.:* searching through rubbish to find things that can be used or sold. *They were scavenging for scraps of food at the dump.*

salvation (sal VAY shuhn) *n.:* person or thing that protects others from harm. *Enrique believes that his mother will be his salvation.*

Language Coach

Suffixes The suffix *–ize* can turn a noun into a verb. What does *ideal* mean? How does the word's meaning change when you add *–ize*? Name three other verbs that have this ending.

Learn It Online

Elevate your vocabulary skills with Word Watch:

go.hrw.com L9-1115 

MEET THE WRITERS

Sandra Cisneros

(1954–)

Celebrating Cultural Differences

Sandra Cisneros writes stories, novels, and poems that often reflect her life as the daughter of a Mexican father and Chicana mother. Her family often made the trip between Chicago and Mexico City. In her writing, she explores how Latinos in the United States are similarly divided between strikingly different cultures. She frequently writes about the challenges facing young Latina women. "I am a woman and I am a Latina. Those are the things that make my writing distinctive. Those are the things that give my writing power. They are the things that give it *sabor* [flavor], the things that give it *picante* [spice]."

Sonia Nazario

(1960–)

The Real Story: Up Close and Personal

Sonia Nazario's journalism is personal; she looks for people whose lives reflect social trends. To investigate the experiences of Puerto Ricans in the United States, she wrote about one family. To learn about young children from Latin America who search for their parents in the United States, she focused on one boy named Enrique. She followed his dangerous, 12,000-mile path from Honduras to the United States and said of the journey: "Where he rode buses through Central America, I rode buses. And where he boarded the train in southern Mexico, I did, too." These firsthand experiences give her writing the sharp details that help readers feel that they, too, are following in Enrique's footsteps. Nazario won many awards, including the Pulitzer Prize, for her articles about Enrique, which she then expanded into the full-length book *Enrique's Journey.*

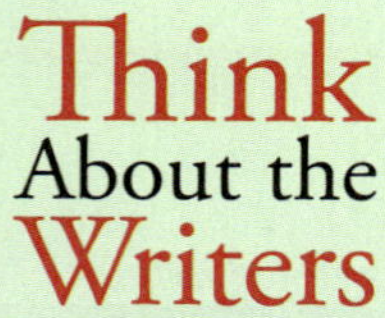

In what way do both Nazario and Cisneros draw on personal experience in their writing?

Preview the Selections

Sandra Cisneros describes the flood of feelings a young girl named **Layla** experiences when her family crosses the border from the United States to Mexico in "Mexico Next Right."

In "The Boy Left Behind," Sonia Nazario explains why **Enrique** decided to leave everything he knew to begin a frightening journey into the unknown.

SHORT STORY

MEXICO NEXT RIGHT

from *Caramelo* by **Sandra Cisneros**

Read with a Purpose

Read these works to find out how borders between countries can have very different effects on two young people's journeys.

Build Background

In the novel *Caramelo*, Sandra Cisneros tells the story of a teenager named Celaya Reyes, whose nickname is Layla. Like Cisneros, Layla is the only daughter of eight siblings. In this selection, the family travels from Chicago to Mexico City, and impressions of Mexico flood Layla's mind: She remembers bits and pieces of popular culture, from advertising jingles to uniquely Mexican foods. Cisneros uses many specific details—but you do not need to understand every reference to appreciate how Layla feels. Even if you've never seen a bottle of Lulú soda, Cisneros gives you enough details to help you understand how its bright colors affect Layla's emotions at the border crossing.

Not like on the Triple A atlas from orange to pink, but at a stoplight in a rippled heat and a dizzy gasoline stink, the United States ends all at once, a tangled shove of red lights from cars and trucks waiting their turn to get past the bridge. Miles and miles.

—Oh, my Got, Father says in his gothic English. —Holy cripes! says Mother, fanning herself with a Texaco road map.

I forgot the light, white and stinging like an onion. I remembered the bugs, a windshield spotted with yellow. I remembered the heat, a sun that melts into the bones like Bengay. I remembered how big Texas is. —Are we in Mexico yet? —No, not yet. [Sleep, wake up.] —Are we in Mexico yet? —Still Texas. [Sleep, wake up.] —Are we . . .

But the light. That I don't remember forgetting until I remember it. **A**

We've crossed Illinois, Missouri, Oklahoma, and Texas singing all the songs we know. "The Moon Men Mambo" from our favorite Rocky and Bullwinkle album. *Ah, ah, aaaah! Scrooch, doobie-doobie, doobie-do. Swing your partner from planet to planet when you dooooo the moon man mamboooo!* The *Yogi Bear* song. *He will sleep till noon, but before it's dark he'll have ev'ry picnic basket that's in Jellystone Park* . . . We sing TV commercials. *Get the blanket with the A, you can trust the big red A. Get the blanket made with ACRYLAN today . . . Knock on any Norge, knock on any Norge, hear the secret sound of quality, knock on any Norge! Years from now you'll be glad you chose Norge. CoCo Wheats, CoCo Wheats can't be beat. It's the creamy hot cereal with the cocoa treat* . . . Until Mother yells, —Will you shut your *hocicos* or do I have to shut them for you?!!!

But crossing the border, nobody feels like singing. Everyone hot and sticky and in a bad mood, hair stiff from riding with the windows open, the backs of the knees sweaty, a little circle

A **Reading Focus** **Comparing Details** What specific details does Cisneros use to describe the setting on the United States side of the border?

of spit next to where my head fell asleep; "good lucky" Father thought to sew beach towel slip-covers for our new car.

No more billboards announcing the next Stuckey's candy store, no more truck-stop donuts or roadside picnics with bologna-and-cheese sandwiches and cold bottles of 7-Up. Now we'll drink fruit-flavored sodas, tamarind, apple, pineapple; Pato Pascual with Donald Duck on the bottle, or Lulú, Betty Boop soda, or the one we hear on the radio, the happy song for Jarritos soda.

As soon as we cross the bridge everything switches to another language. *Toc,* says the light switch in this country, at home it says *click.*

Honk, say the cars at home, here they say *tán-tán-tán.* The *scrip-scrape-scrip* of high heels across *saltillo* floor tiles. The angry lion growl of the corrugated curtains when the shopkeepers roll them open each morning and the lazy lion roar at night when they pull them shut. The *pic, pic, pic* of somebody's faraway hammer. Church bells over and over, all day, even when it's not o'clock. Roosters. The hollow echo of a dog barking. Bells from skinny horses pulling tourists in a carriage, *clip-clop* on cobblestones and big chunks of horse *caquita* tumbling out of them like shredded wheat. **B**

Sweets sweeter, colors brighter, the bitter more bitter. A cage of parrots all the rainbow colors of Lulú sodas. Pushing a window out to open it instead of pulling it up. A cold slash of door latch in your hand instead of the dull round doorknob. Tin sugar spoon and how surprised the hand feels because it's so light. Children walking to school in the morning with their

B **Reading Focus** **Comparing Details** How does the speaker's tone change when she describes the Mexican side of the border?

Restaurant next to the fish market by the wharf in Ensenada, Mexico.

hair still wet from the morning bath.

Mopping with a stick and a purple rag called *la jerga* instead of a mop. The fat lip of a soda pop bottle when you tilt your head back and drink. Birthday cakes walking out of a bakery without a box, just like that, on a wooden plate. And the metal tongs and tray when you buy Mexican sweet bread, help yourself. Cornflakes served with *hot* milk! A balloon painted with wavy pink stripes wearing a paper hat. A milk gelatin with a fly like a little black raisin rubbing its hands. Light and heavy, loud and soft, *thud* and *ting* and *ping*. **C**

Churches the color of *flan*. Vendors selling slices of *jícama* with *chile*, lime juice, and salt. Balloon vendors. The vendor of flags. The corn-on-the-cob vendor. The pork rind vendor. The fried-banana vendor. The pancake vendor. The vendor of strawberries in cream. The vendor of rainbow *pirulís*, of apple bars, of *tejocotes* bathed in caramel. The meringue man. The ice cream vendor, —A very good ice cream at two *pesos*. The coffee man with the coffeemaker on his back and a paper cup dispenser, the cream-and-sugar boy scuttling alongside him.

Little girls in Sunday dresses like lace bells, like umbrellas, like parachutes, the more lace and froufrou the better. Houses painted purple, electric blue, tiger orange, aquamarine, a yellow like a taxicab, hibiscus red with a yellow-and-green fence. Above doorways, faded wreaths from an anniversary or a death till the wind and rain erase them. A woman in an apron scrubbing the sidewalk in front of her house with a pink plastic broom and a bright green bucket filled with suds. A workman carrying a long metal pipe on his shoulder, whistling *ffftttt-ffftttt* to warn people—Watch out!—the pipe longer than he is tall, almost putting out someone's eye, *ya mero*—but he doesn't, does he? *Ya mero, pero no.* Almost, but not quite. *Sí, pero no.* Yes, but no. **D**

Fireworks displays, *piñata* makers, palm weavers. Pens, —Five different styles, they cost us a lot! A restaurant called —His Majesty, the Taco. The napkins, little triangles of hard paper with the name printed on one side. Breakfast: a basket of *pan dulce*, Mexican sweet bread; hotcakes with honey; or steak; *frijoles* with fresh *cilantro; molletes;* or scrambled eggs with *chorizo;* eggs *a la mexicana* with tomato, onion, and *chile;* or *huevos rancheros.* Lunch: lentil soup; fresh-baked crusty *bolillos;* carrots with lime juice; *carne asada;* abalone; *tortillas.* Because we are sitting outdoors, Mexican dogs under the Mexican tables. —I can't stand dogs under the table when I'm eating, Mother complains, but as soon as we shoo two away, four others trot over.

The smell of diesel exhaust, the smell of somebody roasting coffee, the smell of hot corn *tortillas* along with the *pat-pat* of the women's hands making them, the sting of roasting *chiles* in your throat and in your eyes. Sometimes a smell in the morning, very cool and clean that makes you sad. And a night smell when the stars open white and soft like fresh *bolillo* bread.

Every year I cross the border, it's the same—my mind forgets. But my body always remembers. **E**

C **Literary Focus** **Themes and Topics Across Genres** What does the speaker's list of impressions suggest about her feelings for Mexico?

Vocabulary **vendors** (VEHN duhrz) *n.:* sellers.

D **Reading Focus** **Comparing Details** How would you describe the narrator's way of speaking? What does her word choice reveal about her?

E **Literary Focus** **Themes and Topics Across Genres** What idea is the narrator presenting in the final paragraph?

NONFICTION

The Boy Left Behind

from *Enrique's Journey* by **Sonia Nazario**

Preparing to Read for this selection is on page 1115.

Build Background

Honduras is the second-largest country in Central America. It shares borders with the countries of Guatemala, El Salvador, and Nicaragua and has coastlines on both the Caribbean Sea and the Pacific Ocean. Its capital is Tegucigalpa. Spanish is the dominant language, and about 90 percent of the population is *mestizo*, meaning they have both American Indian and European ancestry. Most of the population is Roman Catholic. The main exports from Honduras are bananas and coffee. Its economy, however, is weak and poverty is an enduring problem.

The boy does not understand.

His mother is not talking to him. She will not even look at him. Enrique has no hint of what she is going to do.

Lourdes knows. She understands, as only a mother can, the terror she is about to inflict, the ache Enrique will feel, and finally the emptiness.

What will become of him? Already he will not let anyone else feed or bathe him. He loves her deeply, as only a son can. With Lourdes, he is openly affectionate. "*Dame pico, mami.* Give me a kiss, Mom," he pleads, over and over, pursing his lips. With Lourdes, he is a chatterbox. "*Mira, mami.* Look, Mom," he says softly, asking her questions about everything he sees. Without her, he is so shy it is crushing. **A**

Slowly, she walks out onto the porch. Enrique clings to her pant leg. Beside her, he is tiny. Lourdes loves him so much she cannot bring herself to say a word. She cannot carry his picture. It would melt her resolve. She cannot hug him. He is five years old.

They live on the outskirts of Tegucigalpa, in Honduras. She can barely afford food for him and his sister, Belky, who is seven. She's never been able to buy them a toy or a birthday cake. Lourdes, twenty-four, scrubs other people's laundry in a muddy river. She goes door to door, selling tortillas, used clothes, and plantains.[1]

She fills a wooden box with gum and crackers and cigarettes, and she finds a spot where she can squat on a dusty sidewalk next to the downtown Pizza Hut and sell the items to passersby. The sidewalk is Enrique's playground.

They have a bleak future. He and Belky are not likely to finish grade school. Lourdes cannot afford uniforms or pencils. Her husband is gone. A good job is out of the question.

Lourdes knows of only one place that offers hope. As a seven-year-old child, delivering tortillas her mother made to wealthy homes, she glimpsed this place on other people's television screens. The flickering images were a far cry from Lourdes's childhood home: a two-room shack made of wooden slats, its flimsy tin roof weighted down with rocks, the only bathroom a

1. **plantains** (PLAN tuhnz): Green fruit that resembles bananas; plantains are a staple food in many tropical countries.

A **Reading Focus** **Comparing Details** What similarities in word choice are evident between the two selections?

To earn money, Enrique washes cars in Nuevo Laredo, Mexico.

Analyzing Visuals

Viewing and Interpreting Viewing this photograph of Enrique at age 16, what characteristics do you think he possesses?

clump of bushes outside. On television, she saw New York City's spectacular skyline, Las Vegas's shimmering lights, Disneyland's magic castle.

Lourdes has decided: She will leave. She will go to the United States and make money and send it home. She will be gone for one year—less, with luck—or she will bring her children to be with her. It is for them she is leaving, she tells herself, but still she feels guilty.

She kneels and kisses Belky and hugs her tightly. Then she turns to her own sister. If she watches over Belky, she will get a set of gold fingernails from *el Norte.*

But Lourdes cannot face Enrique. He will remember only one thing that she says to him: "Don't forget to go to church this afternoon."

It is January 29, 1989. His mother steps off the porch.

She walks away. **B**

"*¿Dónde está mi mami?*" Enrique cries, over

B **Literary Focus** **Themes and Topics Across Genres** Why has Enrique's mother decided that she has to leave her family?

and over. "Where is my mom?"

His mother never returns, and that decides Enrique's fate. As a teenager—indeed, still a child—he will set out for the United States on his own to search for her. Virtually unnoticed, he will become one of an estimated 48,000 children who enter the United States from Central America and Mexico each year, illegally and without either of their parents. Roughly two thirds of them will make it past the U.S. Immigration and Naturalization Service.

Many go north seeking work. Others flee abusive families. Most of the Central Americans go to reunite with a parent, say counselors at a detention center in Texas where the INS houses the largest number of the unaccompanied children it catches. Of those, the counselors say, 75 percent are looking for their mothers. Some children say they need to find out whether their mothers still love them. A priest at a Texas shelter says they often bring pictures of themselves in their mothers' arms. **C**

The journey is hard for the Mexicans but harder still for Enrique and the others from Central America. They must make an illegal and dangerous trek up the length of Mexico. Counselors and immigration lawyers say only half of them get help from smugglers. The rest travel alone. They are cold, hungry, and helpless. They are hunted like animals by corrupt police, bandits, and gang members deported from the United States. . . .

They set out with little or no money. Thousands, shelter workers say, make their way through Mexico clinging to the sides and tops of freight trains. Since the 1990s, Mexico and the United States have tried to thwart them. To evade Mexican police and immigration authorities, the children jump onto and off of the moving train cars. Sometimes they fall, and the wheels tear them apart.

They navigate by word of mouth or by the arc of the sun. Often, they don't know where or when they'll get their next meal. Some go days without eating. If a train stops even briefly, they crouch by the tracks, cup their hands, and steal sips of water from shiny puddles tainted with diesel fuel. At night, they huddle together on the train cars or next to the tracks. They sleep in trees, in tall grass, or in beds made of leaves.

Some are very young. Mexican rail workers have encountered seven-year-olds on their way to find their mothers. A policeman discovered a nine-year-old boy near the downtown Los Angeles tracks. "I'm looking for my mother," he said. The youngster had left Puerto Cortes in Honduras three months before. He had been guided only by his cunning and the single thing he knew about her: where she lived. He had asked everyone, "How do I get to San Francisco?"

Typically, the children are teenagers. Some were babies when their mothers left; they know them only by pictures sent home. Others, a bit older, struggle to hold on to memories: One has slept in her mother's bed; another has smelled her perfume, put on her deodorant, her clothes. One is old enough to remember his mother's face, another her laugh, her favorite shade of lipstick, how her dress felt as she stood at the stove patting tortillas.

Many, including Enrique, begin to idealize their mothers. They remember how their mothers fed and bathed them, how they walked them to kindergarten. In their absence, these mothers become larger than life. Although in the United

---

C **Reading Focus** **Comparing Details** For what purpose does Nazario cite statistics? How does the tone of this story differ from the tone of the fictional story?

Vocabulary **idealize** (y DEE uh lyz) *v.:* think of someone or something as perfect; ignore any flaws.

States the women struggle to pay rent and eat, in the imaginations of their children back home they become deliverance itself, the answer to every problem. Finding them becomes the quest for the Holy Grail.[2] **D**

CONFUSION

Enrique is bewildered. Who will take care of him now that his mother is gone? Lourdes, unable to burden her family with both of her children, has split them up. Belky stayed with Lourdes's mother and sisters. For two years, Enrique is entrusted to his father, Luis, from whom his mother has been separated for three years.

> They navigate by word of mouth or by the arc of the sun. Often, they don't know where or when they'll get their next meal.

Enrique clings to his daddy, who dotes on him. A bricklayer, his father takes Enrique to work and lets him help mix mortar. They live with Enrique's grandmother. His father shares a bed with him and brings him apples and clothes. Every month, Enrique misses his mother less, but he does not forget her. "When is she coming for me?" he asks.

Lourdes and her smuggler cross Mexico on buses. Each afternoon, she closes her eyes. She imagines herself home at dusk, playing with Enrique under a eucalyptus tree in her mother's front yard. Enrique straddles a broom, pretending it's a donkey, trotting around the muddy yard. Each afternoon, she presses her eyes shut and tears fall. Each afternoon, she reminds herself that if she is weak, if she does not keep moving forward, her children will pay.

Lourdes crosses into the United States in one of the largest immigrant waves in the country's history. She enters at night through a rat-infested Tijuana sewage tunnel and makes her way to Los Angeles. There, in the downtown Greyhound bus terminal, the smuggler tells Lourdes to wait while he runs a quick errand. He'll be right back. The smuggler has been paid to take her all the way to Miami.

Three days pass. Lourdes musses her filthy hair, trying to blend in with the homeless and not get singled out by police. She prays to God to put someone before her, to show her the way. Whom can she reach out to for help? Starved, she starts walking. East of downtown, Lourdes spots a small factory. On the loading dock, under a gray tin roof, women sort red and green tomatoes. She begs for work. As she puts tomatoes into boxes, she hallucinates that she is slicing open a juicy one and sprinkling it with salt. The boss pays her $14 for two hours' work. Lourdes's brother has a friend in Los Angeles who helps Lourdes get a fake Social Security card and a job.

She moves in with a Beverly Hills couple to take care of their three-year-old daughter. Their spacious home has carpet on the floors and mahogany panels on the walls. Her employers are kind. They pay her $125 a week. She gets

2. **the Holy Grail:** In medieval legends, knights searched for this cup from which Jesus drank at the Last Supper. The grail only appeared to a pure knight. Today, the "holy grail" is often used as a metaphor for the ultimate goal of a long, seemingly impossible search.

D Literary Focus **Themes and Topics Across Genres** How does the image of the Holy Grail help convey Nazario's attitude about children who immigrate to find their parents?

nights and weekends off. Maybe, Lourdes tells herself—if she stays long enough—they will help her become legal.

Every morning as the couple leave for work, the little girl cries for her mother. Lourdes feeds her breakfast and thinks of Enrique and Belky. She asks herself: "Do my children cry like this? I'm giving this girl food instead of feeding my own children." To get the girl to eat, Lourdes pretends the spoon is an airplane. But each time the spoon lands in the girl's mouth, Lourdes is filled with sadness.

In the afternoon, after the girl comes home from prekindergarten class, they thumb through picture books and play. The girl, so close to Enrique's age, is a constant reminder of her son. Many afternoons, Lourdes cannot contain her grief. She gives the girl a toy and dashes into the kitchen. There, out of sight, tears flow. After seven months, she cannot take it. She quits and moves to a friend's place in Long Beach. **E**

Boxes arrive in Tegucigalpa bearing clothes, shoes, toy cars, a Robocop doll, a television. Lourdes writes: Do they like the things she is sending? She tells Enrique to behave, to study hard. She has hopes for him: graduation from high school, a white-collar job, maybe as an engineer. She pictures her son working in a crisp shirt and shiny shoes. She says she loves him.

Enrique asks about his mother. "She'll be home soon," his grandmother assures him. "Don't worry. She'll be back."

But his mother does not come. Her disappearance is incomprehensible. Enrique's bewilderment turns to confusion and then to adolescent anger. . . .

Confused by his mother's absence, Enrique turns to his grandmother. Alone now, he and his father's elderly mother share a shack thirty feet square. María Marcos built it herself of wooden slats. Enrique can see daylight in the cracks. It has four rooms, three without electricity. There is no running water. Gutters carry rain off the patched tin roof into two barrels. A trickle of cloudy white sewage runs past the front gate. On a well-worn rock nearby, Enrique's grandmother washes musty used clothing she sells door to door. Next to the rock is the latrine—a concrete hole. Beside it are buckets for bathing.

The shack is in Carrizal, one of Tegucigalpa's poorest neighborhoods. Sometimes Enrique looks across the rolling hills to the neighborhood where he and his mother lived and where Belky still lives with their mother's family. They are six miles apart. They hardly ever visit.

Lourdes sends Enrique $50 a month, occasionally $100, sometimes nothing. It is enough for food but not for school clothes, fees, notebooks, or pencils, which are expensive in Honduras. There is never enough for a birthday present. But Grandmother María hugs him and wishes him a cheery *¡Feliz cumpleaños!* "Your mom can't send enough," she says, "so we both have to work."

Enrique loves to climb his grandmother's guayaba tree, but there is no more time for play now. After school, Enrique sells tamales and plastic bags of fruit juice from a bucket hung in the crook of his arm. "*¡Tamarindo! ¡Piña!*" he shouts.

Sometimes Enrique takes his wares to a service station where diesel-belching buses rumble into Carrizal. Jostling among mango and avocado vendors, he sells cups of diced fruit.

After he turns ten, he rides buses alone to

E **Literary Focus** **Themes and Topics Across Genres** What generalizations about living in the United States can you make based on Lourdes's experiences?

Vocabulary **incomprehensible** (ihn kahm prih HEHN suh buhl) *adj.:* not able to be understood.

David Velásquez, 13, (at left) and Roberto Gaytán, 17, are caught in Tapachula, Mexico, and wait to be jailed. The boys are from Guatemala and were headed for Los Angeles and North Carolina.

Analyzing Visuals **Viewing and Interpreting**
What emotions are captured in this photograph? Do you think the boys will try to cross the border again? Explain.

an outdoor food market. He stuffs tiny bags with nutmeg, curry powder, and paprika, then seals them with hot wax. He pauses at big black gates in front of the market and calls out, "*¿Va a querer especias?* Who wants spices?" He has no vendor's license, so he keeps moving, darting between wooden carts piled with papayas. Younger children, five and six years old, dot the curbs, thrusting fistfuls of tomatoes and chiles at shoppers. Others offer to carry purchases of fruits and vegetables from stall to stall in rustic wooden wheelbarrows in exchange for tips. "*Te ayudo?* May I help you?" they ask. Arms taut, backs stooped, the boys heave forward, their carts bulging. . . .

Grandmother María cooks plantains, spaghetti, and fresh eggs. Now and then, she kills a chicken and prepares it for him. In return, when she is sick, Enrique rubs medicine on her back. He brings water to her in bed. Two or three times a week, Enrique lugs buckets filled with drinking water, one on each shoulder, from the water truck at the bottom of the hill up to his grandmother's house.

Every year on Mother's Day, he makes a heart-shaped card at school and presses it into her hand. "I love you very much, Grandma," he writes.

But she is not his mother. Enrique longs to hear Lourdes's voice. Once he tries to call her collect from a public telephone in his neighborhood. He can't get the call to go through. His only way of talking to her is at the home of his mother's cousin María Edelmira Sánchez Mejía, one of the few family members who has a telephone. His mother seldom calls. One year she does not call at all. . . . **F**

For Enrique, each telephone call grows more strained. Because he lives across town, he is not often lucky enough to be at María Edelmira's house when his mother phones. When he is, their talk is clipped and anxious. Quietly, however, one of these conversations plants the seed of an idea. Unwittingly, Lourdes sows it herself.

> Lourdes does consider hiring a smuggler to bring the children but fears the danger.

"When are you coming home?" Enrique asks. She avoids an answer. Instead, she promises to send for him very soon.

It had never occurred to him: If she will not come home, then maybe he can go to her. Neither he nor his mother realizes it, but this kernel of an idea will take root. From now on, whenever Enrique speaks to her, he ends by saying, "I want to be with you."

"Come home," Lourdes's own mother begs her on the telephone. "It may only be beans, but you always have food here." Pride forbids it. How can she justify leaving her children if she returns empty-handed? Four blocks from her mother's place is a white house with purple trim. It takes up half a block behind black iron gates. The house belongs to a woman whose children went to Washington, D.C., and sent her the money to build it. Lourdes cannot afford such a house for her mother, much less herself.

But she develops a plan. She will become a resident and bring her children to the United States legally. Three times, she hires storefront immigration counselors who promise help. She pays them a total of $3,850. But the counselors never deliver. . . .

Lourdes wants to give her son and daughter some hope. "I'll be back next Christmas," she tells Enrique.

Enrique fantasizes about Lourdes's expected homecoming in December. In his mind, she arrives at the door with a box of Nike shoes for him. "Stay," he pleads. "Live with me. Work here. When I'm older, I can help you work and make money."

Christmas arrives, and he waits by the door. She does not come. Every year, she promises. Each year, he is disappointed. Confusion finally grows into anger. "I need her. I miss her," he tells his sister. "I want to be with my mother. I see so many children with mothers. I want that."

One day, he asks his grandmother, "How did my mom get to the United States?" Years later, Enrique will remember his grandmother's reply—and how another seed was planted: "Maybe," María says, "she went on the trains."

"What are the trains like?"

"They are very, very dangerous," his grandmother says. "Many people die on the trains."

When Enrique is twelve, Lourdes tells him yet again that she will come home.

"Sí," he replies. "*Va, pues.* Sure. Sure."

Enrique senses a truth: Very few mothers

F **Reading Focus** **Comparing Details** How do Enrique's relationships with his family members develop and change as he grows up?

ever return. He tells her that he doesn't think she is coming back. To himself, he says, "It's all one big lie."

The calls grow tense. "Come home," he demands. "Why do you want to be there?"

"It's all gone to help raise you." **G**

Lourdes has nightmares about going back, even to visit, without residency documents. In the dreams, she hugs her children, then realizes she has to return to the United States so they can eat well and study. The plates on the table are empty. But she has no money for a smuggler. She tries to go back on her own. The path becomes a labyrinth. She runs through zigzagging corridors. She always ends up back at the starting point. Each time, she awakens in a sweat. . . .

Lourdes does consider hiring a smuggler to bring the children but fears the danger. The coyotes, as they are called, are often alcoholics or drug addicts. Usually, a chain of smugglers is used to make the trip. Children are passed from one stranger to another. Sometimes the smugglers abandon their charges.[3]

Lourdes is continually reminded of the risks. One of her best friends in Long Beach pays for a smuggler to bring her sister from El Salvador. During her journey, the sister calls Long Beach to give regular updates on her progress through Mexico. The calls abruptly stop.

Two months later, the family hears from a man who was among the group headed north. The smugglers put twenty-four migrants into an overloaded boat in Mexico, he says. It tipped over. All but four drowned. Some bodies were swept out to sea. Others were buried along the beach, including the missing sister. He leads the family to a Mexican beach. There they unearth the sister's decomposed body. She is still wearing her high school graduation ring.

Another friend is panic-stricken when her three-year-old son is caught by Border Patrol agents as a smuggler tries to cross him into the United States. For a week, Lourdes's friend doesn't know what's become of her toddler.

Lourdes learns that many smugglers ditch children at the first sign of trouble. Government-run foster homes in Mexico get migrant children whom authorities find abandoned in airports and bus stations and on the streets. Children as young as three, bewildered, desperate, populate these foster homes. . . .

"Do I want to have them with me so badly," [Lourdes] asks herself of her children, "that I'm willing to risk their losing their lives?" Besides, she does not want Enrique to come to California. There are too many gangs, drugs, and crimes.

In any event, she has not saved enough. The cheapest coyote, immigrant advocates say, charges $3,000 per child. Female coyotes want up to $6,000. A top smuggler will bring a child by commercial flight for $10,000. She must save enough to bring both children at once. If not, the one left in Honduras will think she loves him or her less.

Enrique despairs. He will simply have to do it himself. He will go find her. He will ride the trains. "I want to come," he tells her.

Don't even joke about it, she says. It is too dangerous. Be patient. **H**

3. **charges:** people placed in the care of someone else.

G **Reading Focus** **Comparing Details** How does including dialogue affect the tone of Nazario's writing? How might the tone be different if all the events were reported without any dialogue?

H **Literary Focus** **Themes and Topics Across Genres** What idea about parent-child relationships does Nazario emphasize in this passage?

Buzzards and children compete for trash at the dump in Tegucigalpa.

REBELLION

. . . Her gifts arrive steadily. She sends Enrique an orange polo shirt, a pair of blue pants, a radio cassette player. She is proud that her money pays Belky's tuition at a private high school and eventually a college, to study accounting. In a country where nearly half live on $1 or less a day, kids from poor neighborhoods almost never go to college.

Money from Lourdes helps Enrique, too, and he realizes it. If she were here, he knows where he might well be: scavenging in the trash dump across town. Lourdes knows it, too; as a girl, she herself worked the dump. Enrique knows children as young as six or seven whose single mothers have stayed at home and who have had to root through the waste in order to eat. . . .

In one neighborhood near where Enrique's mother grew up, fifty-two children arrive at kindergarten each morning. Forty-four arrive barefoot. An aide reaches into a basket and

Vocabulary **scavenging** (SKAV uhnj ihng) *v.:* searching through rubbish to find things that can be used or sold.

places a pair of shoes into each one's hands. At 4 P.M., before they leave, the children must return the shoes to the basket. If they take the shoes home, their mothers will sell them for food.

Black rats and a pig root around in a ravine where the children play.

At dinnertime, the mothers count out three tortillas for each child. If there are no tortillas, they try to fill their children's bellies with a glass of water with a teaspoon of sugar mixed in. . . . I

AN EDUCATION

Enrique marks his sixteenth birthday. All he wants is his mother. One Sunday, he and his friend José put train riding to the test. They leave for *el Norte*.

At first, no one notices. They take buses across Guatemala to the Mexican border. "I have a mom in the United States," Enrique tells a guard.

"Go home," the man replies.

They slip past the guard and make their way twelve miles into Mexico to Tapachula. There they approach a freight train near the depot. But before they can reach the tracks, police stop them. The officers rob them, the boys say later, but then let them go—José first, Enrique afterward.

They find each other and another train. Now, for the first time, Enrique clambers aboard. The train crawls out of the Tapachula station. From here on, he thinks, nothing bad can happen.

They know nothing about riding the rails. José is terrified. Enrique, who is braver, jumps from car to car on the slow-moving train. He slips and falls—away from the tracks, luckily—and lands on a backpack padded with a shirt and an extra pair of pants.

He scrambles aboard again. But their odyssey comes to a humiliating halt. Near Tierra Blanca, a small town in Veracruz, authorities snatch them from the top of a freight car. The officers take them to a cell filled with MS gangsters, then deport them. Enrique is bruised and limping. . . . They find coconuts to sell for bus fare and go home.

GOOD-BYE

. . . Enrique fears he will end up on the streets or dead. Only his mother can help him. She is his salvation. "If you had known my mom, you would know she's a good person," he says to his friend José. "I love her."

Enrique has to find her.

Each Central American neighborhood has a smuggler. In Enrique's neighborhood, it's a man who lives at the top of a hill. For $5,000, he will take anyone to *los Estados*. But Enrique can't imagine that kind of money.

He sells the few things he owns: his bed, a gift from his mother; his leather jacket, a gift from his dead uncle; his rustic armoire,[4] where he hangs his clothes. He crosses town to say good-bye to Grandmother María. Trudging up the hill to her house, he encounters his father. "I'm leaving," he says. "I'm going to make it to the U.S." He asks him for money.

His father gives him enough for a soda and wishes him luck.

"Grandma, I'm leaving," Enrique says. "I'm going to find my mom."

4. **armoire** (ahr MWAHR): tall cupboard or wardrobe.

I **Reading Focus** **Comparing Details** What details does Nazario use to make the setting of the events powerfully clear?

Vocabulary **salvation** (sal VAY shuhn) *n.:* person or thing that protects others from harm.

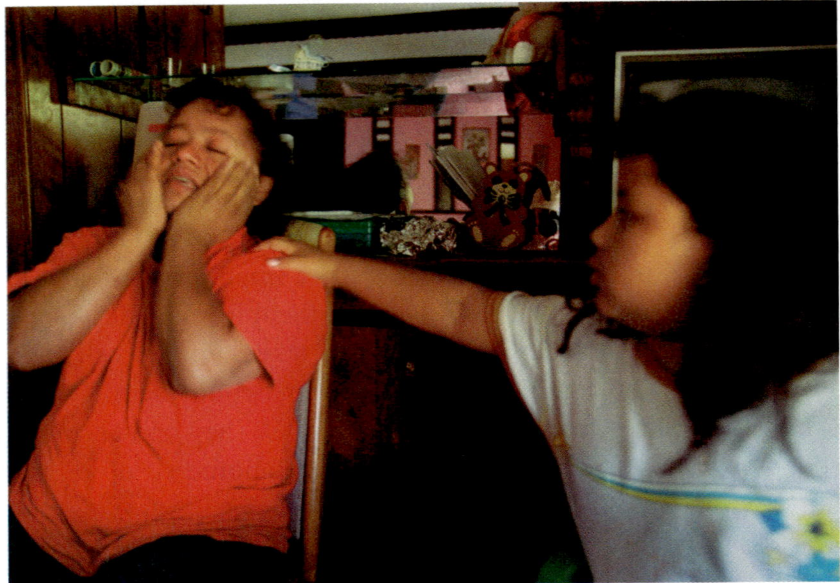

Enrique's mother Lourdes breaks down as she talks about her life and her separation from her son. Her daughter, Diana, 9, tries to comfort Lourdes.

Don't go, she pleads. She promises to build him a one-room house in the corner of her cramped lot. But he has made up his mind. **J**

She gives him 100 lempiras, about $7—all the money she has.

"I'm leaving already, sis," he tells Belky the next morning.

She feels her stomach tighten. They have lived apart most of their lives, but he is the only one who understands her loneliness. Quietly, she fixes a special meal: tortillas, a pork cutlet, rice, fried beans with a sprinkling of cheese. "Don't leave," she says, tears welling up in her eyes.

"I have to."

It is hard for him, too. Every time he has talked to his mother, she has warned him not to come—it's too dangerous. But if somehow he gets to the U.S. border, he will call her. Being so close, she'll have to welcome him. "If I call her from there," he says to José, "how can she not accept me?"

He makes himself one promise: "I'm going to reach the United States, even if it takes one year." Only after a year of trying would he give up and go back.

Quietly, Enrique, the slight kid with a boyish grin, fond of kites, spaghetti, soccer, and break dancing, who likes to play in the mud and watch Mickey Mouse cartoons with his four-year-old cousin, packs up his belongings: corduroy pants, a T-shirt, a cap, gloves, a toothbrush, and toothpaste.

For a long moment, he looks at a picture of his mother, but he does not take it. He might lose it. He writes her telephone number on a scrap of paper. Just in case, he also scrawls it in ink on the inside waistband of his pants. He has $57 in his pocket.

On March 2, 2000, he goes to his grandmother Águeda's house. He stands on the same porch that his mother disappeared from eleven years before. He hugs Maria Isabel and Aunt Rosa Amalia. Then he steps off.

J **Reading Focus** **Comparing Details** Why has Enrique decided to make his journey now? What does this decision tell you about him?

BOOK COVER

ENRIQUE'S JOURNEY

The STORY *of a* BOY'S DANGEROUS ODYSSEY *to* REUNITE *with his* MOTHER

Sonia Nazario

Winner of the Pulitzer Prize

Analyzing Visuals

Viewing and Interpreting What do you think the boy is doing in the photograph? How does the photo convey the idea of an *odyssey,* or epic journey? Based on the text excerpt you have just read and the book's cover, would you choose to read this book? Explain.

Build Background

Don't judge a book by its cover. Although this is good advice, many readers *do* consider a book's cover when deciding whether to read it. Publishers know this and use various techniques to entice readers, such as listing awards that the author or book has won and including endorsements (called blurbs) by writers who recommend the book.

Applying Your Skills

MO 9.R.2.C.1.c Use details from text(s): to analyze the development of a theme across genres 9.R.2.C.1.d Use details from text(s): to evaluate the effect of author's style 9.R.1.I.1.a Compare, contrast, analyze and evaluate connections: text to text 9.W.3.A.1.e Compose a variety of texts: including reflective writing *Also covered* 9.W.3.A.1.a; 9.R.1.G.1.a

Mexico Next Right / The Boy Left Behind

Respond and Think Critically

Reading Focus

Quick Check

1. What does Layla experience when she enters Mexico?
2. What events contribute to Enrique's decision to leave Honduras?

Read with a Purpose

3. How is the idea of a border different for Layla and Enrique?

Reading Skills: Comparing Details

4. You have explored specific details of character, setting, and tone as used by these authors. Now, add a row to your chart and describe the key similarities and differences between the two works.

	"Mexico Next Right"	"The Boy Left Behind"
Main Character	Layla experiences a different culture.	Enrique feels lonely without his mother.
Setting		
Tone		

Key similarities and differences:

Vocabulary Check

Match the Vocabulary words with their definitions.

5. **idealize**
6. **incomprehensible**
7. **salvation**
8. **scavenging**
9. **vendors**

a. sellers
b. sifting through rubbish
c. regard as perfect
d. not understandable
e. protector

Literary Focus

Literary Analysis

10. **Interpret** What does Layla mean when she crosses the border and says her "mind forgets" but her "body always remembers"?
11. **Infer** Enrique decides to leave behind a loving father and grandmother. Why might he have made this choice?
12. **Compare and Contrast** Both Enrique and his mother decide to leave Honduras. How are their decisions to journey to the United States similar and different?

Literary Skills: Themes and Topics Across Genres

13. **Interpret** What is the theme of "Mexico Next Right"?
14. **Analyze** What insights about immigration does Nazario share by focusing on the story of one boy from Honduras?

Literary Skills Review: Style

15. **Analyze** The unique way a writer uses language is called **style.** What are the most distinctive features of Nazario's writing style? What tools does she use to tell Enrique's story? How is Cisneros's style different from Nazario's?

Writing Focus

Think as a Reader/Writer

Use It in Your Writing Describe a journey—real or imaginary. Like Cisneros and Nazario, use active verbs to describe each stage of your journey.

COMPARING TEXTS

Wrap Up

Mexico Next Right / The Boy Left Behind

MO **9.W.3.A.1.a** Compose a variety of texts: using narrative, descriptive, expository, and/or persuasive features **9.W.3.A.1.d** Compose a variety of texts: including literary analysis **9.W.3.A.1.e** Compose a variety of texts: including reflective writing **9.R.1.D.1.a** Read grade-level instructional text: with fluency, accuracy, comprehension and appropriate expression *Also covered* **9.W.2.A.1.b; 9.R.1.E.1.c**

Writing Focus

Comparison-Contrast Essay

You have just read about two young people taking journeys. Now, write a comparison-contrast essay in which you focus on what these journeys have in common and what makes them different.

Prewriting Review the notes you took during and after reading. Look for details that highlight similarities and differences between the journeys. Choose one of these comparison structures for your essay.

Point-by-Point Organization	Block Organization
Point 1 Layla, Enrique	Layla's Journey Points 1, 2, and 3
Point 2 Layla, Enrique	Enrique's Journey Points 1, 2, and 3

Drafting Begin by drafting a thesis statement that makes the central point of your essay. Introduce your thesis in your opening paragraph. Then, develop your ideas in the body paragraphs.

Revising As you review your essay, look at the connections between ideas. Consider adding transitions to clarify your comparisons. Also, use quotations from the text to illustrate the points you made.

Proofread and Publish Read your essay carefully. Correct any errors you find in spelling, grammar, and punctuation.

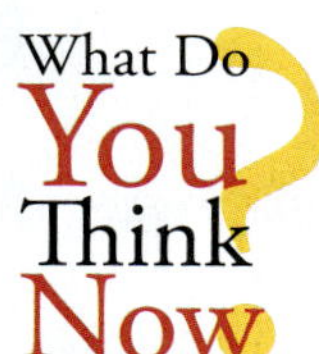

What do Layla and Enrique expect from the journeys? Of the two, who is more likely to be satisfied? Why?

CHOICES

As you respond to the Choices, use these **Academic Vocabulary** words as appropriate: portrayed, destiny, mutual, express.

REVIEW

Discuss Reading

Group Discussion With a group of classmates, discuss the two stories you have just read. Use the following to help guide your discussion:

- What is Enrique hoping to find at his journey's end? What is Layla hoping to find?
- What theme does Cisneros express in her story? What insights does Nazario express in hers?
- Which story did you find more moving? Which story did you find more entertaining?

CONNECT

Prepare an Interview

Listening and Speaking Imagine that you have the opportunity to interview Enrique and/or Sonia Nazario. Prepare a list of six questions you would like to ask, and try to create questions that will produce interesting and insightful answers. Ask a partner to play the role of Enrique and improvise his answers. Use your prepared questions, but look for opportunities to ask follow-up questions, too.

EXTEND

Write an Essay

Timed Writing Both "Mexico Next Right" and "The Boy Left Behind" focus on borders and journeys. Think about a time in your life when you journeyed across borders (it could be a trip to another state or even to another neighborhood). Write a personal essay describing this experience and how it affected you.

INFORMATIONAL TEXT FOCUS

Synthesizing Sources: Making Connections

CONTENTS

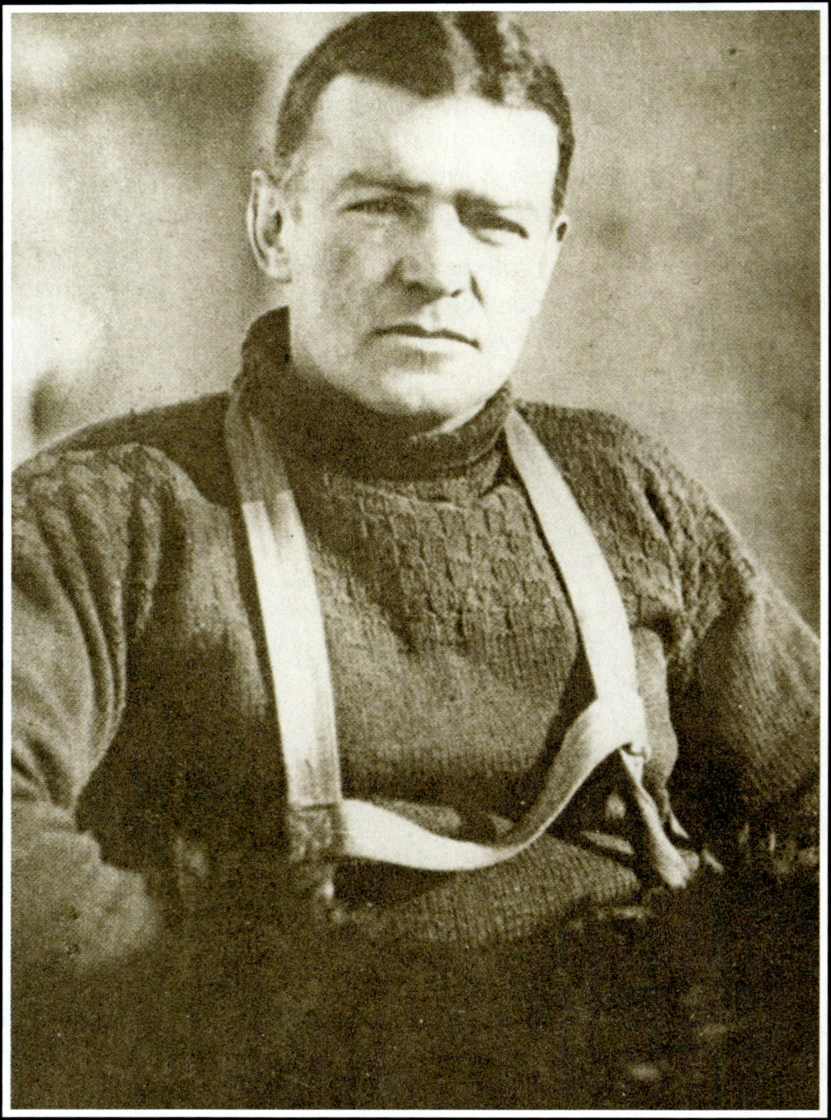

A photograph of Sir Ernest Shackleton.

What Do You Think?

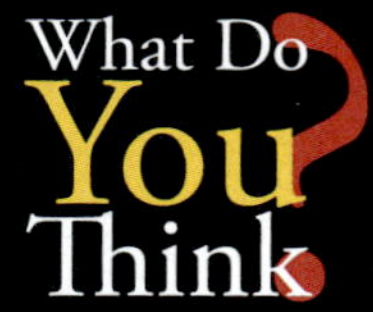

What does it take to be a successful leader of a dangerous expedition?

QuickTalk

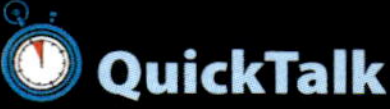

With a partner, discuss the heroic qualities that famous leaders exhibit in times of crisis. Write down your ideas.

BIOGRAPHY AND INTERVIEW

Preparing to Read

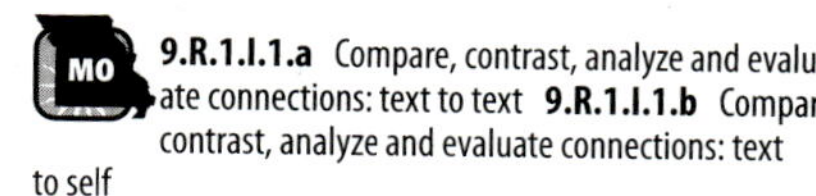

9.R.1.I.1.a Compare, contrast, analyze and evaluate connections: text to text 9.R.1.I.1.b Compare, contrast, analyze and evaluate connections: text to self

from Shipwreck at the Bottom of the World / Tending Sir Ernest's Legacy

Reader/Writer Notebook

Use your **RWN** to complete the activities for these selections.

Informational Text Focus

Synthesizing Sources: Making Connections When you **synthesize** information, you pull together what you have learned from various sources on one topic. You make connections between what you are reading and your own experiences.

Connecting and Comparing Whenever you read, you look for connections between what you are reading and the world you know. You think about how the subject **connects** with your own experience and ask yourself whether the work rings true.

You should also connect and compare your reading with other works you have read. For example, you might **compare** a courageous character in a novel with characters that perform heroically from other works. Each work you read on a subject will add to your overall understanding of the topic.

Into Action As you read the following biography and interview, ask yourself the following questions and respond to them:

Questions to Ask	My Responses
How are these sources similar? How are they different?	Both are about heroes; they are written by different authors.
What other works on this topic do these pieces remind me of?	
How have these sources added to my understanding of life?	

Writing Focus

Preparing for Constructed Response

Reading two sources about a related topic can challenge, support, or extend your own ideas about the topic. As you read the selections, write down in your *Reader/Writer Notebook* how the sources influence your own ideas.

Vocabulary

from Shipwreck at the Bottom of the World

provisions (pruh VIHZH uhnz) *n.:* supply or stock, especially of food. *The provisions from the* Endurance *were loaded onto the* James Caird.

plummeted (PLUHM ih tihd) *v.:* plunged or dropped. *When the storm came, the temperature plummeted.*

Tending Sir Ernest's Legacy

abandon (uh BAN duhn) *v.:* leave behind. *The crew had to abandon the ship once it became encased in ice.*

priority (pry AWR uh tee) *n.:* something deemed of utmost importance. *Shackleton's top priority was the rescue of his crew.*

Language Coach

Word Derivations The word *prior* means "coming first." In what way might a *priority* be something that has to come first? Check the definition above for help.

Learn It Online

To read more articles like this, go to the interactive Reading Workshops on:

go.hrw.com L9-1135 Go

BIOGRAPHY

from Shipwreck at the Bottom of the World

by **Jennifer Armstrong**

Sir Ernest Shackleton's ship *Endurance* is being crushed in the ice floes of Antarctica in 1916.

The Open Boat Journey: The First Ten Days

Read with a Purpose

Read this true account to see what odds one leader is willing to face in order to save the members of his crew.

Build Background

In 1915, Ernest Shackleton and his crew of 28 men were stranded in the Antarctic, the most treacherous environment on earth. Their ship, the *Endurance,* was caught in pack ice and frozen in place for the winter. When spring came, ice masses pushed the ship over and crushed it. The crew took to the sea in three lifeboats and made it to Elephant Island on April 16, 1916, after six days on the water. There was nothing on the island, and Shackleton knew that somebody had to get help from the whaling station on South Georgia Island or they would all perish. Shackleton picked five men besides himself to make up a relief party: Frank Worsley, captain of the *Endurance*; Tom Crean, second officer; Harry McNeish, the ship's carpenter; and seamen John Vincent and Timothy McCarthy. After McNeish refitted the lifeboat *James Caird* for the journey to South Georgia Island, the relief party set off.

On the morning of Monday, April 24, all hands were roused at six o' clock to help lash up and stow the *Caird*. As Wild[1] oversaw the preparation of the boat, Shackleton and Worsley climbed up a small hill they used as a lookout and surveyed the ocean. The ice was within five or six miles of the shore, drifting northeast. Large, grounded icebergs made wide gaps in the ice as they streamed past them. The rescue party would escape through one of those leads.

Below, the *Caird* was dragged down to the surf and loaded with the bags of ballast,[2] boxes of stores, a hand pump, a cook pot, six reindeer-skin sleeping bags, and the rest of the provisions. At noon the men heaved the laden boat out on the backwash of a breaking wave, and the remainder of the stores was ferried out on the *Stancomb Wills*. Shackleton and Worsley rejoined the group. There were handshakes all around. The six members of the relief party boarded the boat, and they shoved off. **A**

Behind on the beach, the remaining twenty-two men cheered and waved. "Good luck, Boss!" they shouted. Shackleton looked back once and raised his hand in farewell. Gentoo penguins porpoised along beside the boat as they raised the sail and plunged forward into the rolling waves. The Boss stood with one arm around the mast looking forward, directing Worsley at the helm around the ice.

They made good speed for two hours and then reached the loose belt of ice they had seen from the lookout. They turned east along it, searching for the leads that would let them through. Huge, lopsided remnant bergs bobbed and heaved in the waves, and small chunks of

1. **Wild:** Frank Wild, second-in-command of the *Endurance*.
2. **ballast** (BAL uhst): something heavy carried in a ship's hold to steady it.

A **Informational Focus** **Synthesizing Sources** Based on the supplies being loaded onto the *Caird,* what kind of trip do you expect the men to take?

Vocabulary **provisions** (pruh VIHZH uhnz) *n.:* supply or stock, especially of food.

broken floe[3] knocked and scraped along the sides of the *Caird*. The whole jumble of loose pack hissed and rustled as it rose to the swell. After an hour's run, they found an opening and turned north to sail through it. Just before dark they were on the other side, and when they looked over their shoulders they saw Elephant Island as a small shadow far astern.

Shackleton and Worsley had agreed that the safest plan was to get as far north as possible before heading east. For one thing, they would be glad to get away from the most frigid weather as soon as they could. Furthermore, they would be sailing day and night, and they needed to get beyond the limit of floating ice: if they rammed a chunk in the dark, their journey would be a short one. By 10:00 P.M. the water seemed relatively clear of ice, and their spirits rose: so far, so good. In the darkness, they steered by keeping an eye on the small blue pennant that streamed from the mast in the wind.

The living arrangements on board were uncomfortable and cramped. The men were divided into two watches: Shackleton, Crean, and McNeish steered, bailed, and pumped for four hours, while Worsley, Vincent, and McCarthy slept—or tried to. Then the watches traded places—watch and watch, every four hours. The sleeping bags were forward, under the improvised decking on the bow. To reach them, the men had to crawl on hands and knees over the stone ballast, then wriggle forward on their stomachs over the crates of stores. Then, with barely enough room to turn around, they wormed themselves into the sleeping bags and attempted to sleep as the boat bucked up and down through the heavy swell. At the end of each four-hour watch, the men would change places, wriggling past each other in the cramped space. **B**

It was a tossup which was worse—being pounded up and down in the bow of the boat in a sorry excuse for sleep, or huddling in the cockpit as icy seas swept across the thwarts[4] and gunwales.[5] There were no oilskins, and the men were dressed in wool, which got wet and stayed wet for the duration of the voyage. With temperatures below freezing, and no room to move around to get their blood stirred up, they were always cold. Miserably cold. Waves broke over the bows, where bucketfuls of water streamed through the flimsy decking. The bottom of the boat was constantly awash, and the two men on watch who weren't steering were always bailing or pumping. The reindeer-skin sleeping bags were soaking wet all the time, and beginning to rot. Loose reindeer hair found its way into the men's nostrils and mouths as they breathed, into their water and their food as they ate.

Crean had taken over as cook for the journey. In the pitching and rolling of the boat, preparing meals was a tricky business. Crean and Worsley would sit on opposite sides of the boat with their feet out, bracing the Primus camp stove. Crean would light the stove and begin

3. **floe** (floh): sheet of floating ice.

4. **thwarts:** rowers' seats extending across a boat.

5. **gunwales** (GUHN uhlz): upper edges of the sides of a boat.

B **Informational Focus** **Synthesizing Sources** What conditions do these explorers face? Why must they have four-hour watches for the boat?

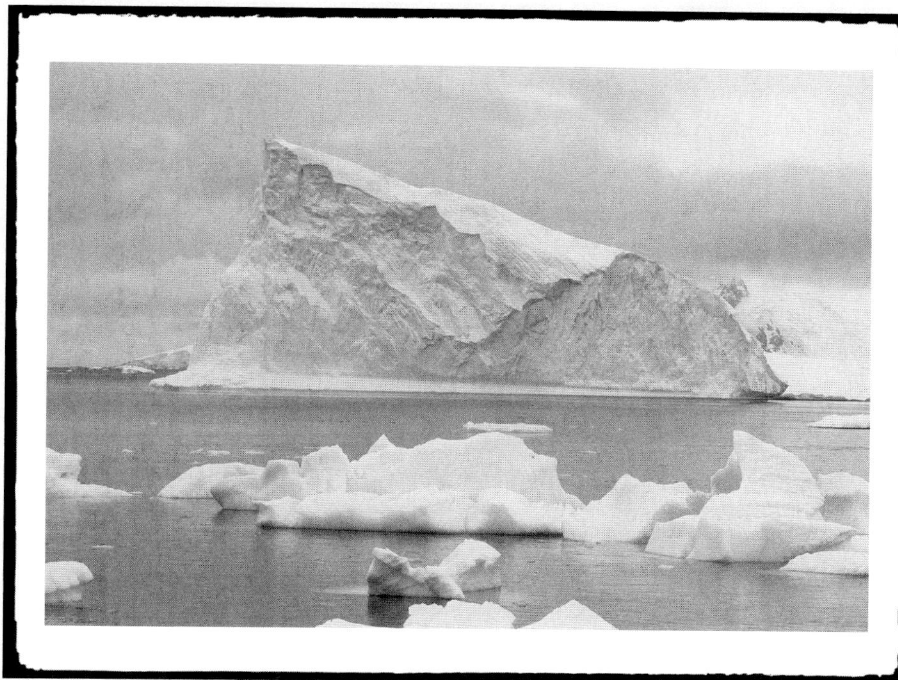

Icebergs in Paradise Bay, Antarctica.

stirring up chunks of sledging ration[6] in water as Worsley held the pot. With each dip and plunge of the boat, Worsley swooped the pot up in the air lest their precious hoosh[7] go slopping into the bilges.[8] When the hoosh was cooked, Crean doled it out into six bowls, and the men ate it scalding hot, hunched under the decking. Whoever finished first went out to relieve the man at the tiller[9] so that he could eat his hoosh before it cooled. In addition, Shackleton allowed hot milk and sugar at regular intervals: the only way to keep going was by fueling themselves constantly.

By the third day of sailing, the weather turned rotten. A gale blew up with snow squalls and heavy seas, and waves broke incessantly over the boat. The *James Caird* clawed its way up the face of one hissing wave and then plunged down the other side as spray lashed into the men's faces. The gale continued into the fourth day, finally blowing them north of the sixtieth parallel. Floating past them went two pieces of wreckage from a lost ship. The men watched it disappear, and hunched their shoulders and struggled to keep their little boat on course. As Shackleton put it, "So small was our boat and so great were the seas that often our sail flapped idly in the calm between the crests of two waves. Then we would climb the next slope, and catch the full fury of the gale where the wool-like whiteness of the breaking water surged around us."

For Worsley, navigating had ceased to be a

---

6. **sledging ration:** crew member's daily food allotment while on an Antarctic expedition.
7. **hoosh:** thick stew made from pemmican (mixture of dried meat, fat, and cereal), a thickener such as ground biscuits, and water.
8. **bilges** (BIHLJ ihz): bottom of a ship's hull.
9. **tiller:** bar or handle at the stern of a boat used for steering.

Shackleton and his men leaving Elephant Island.

science and had turned into a kind of sorcery. To get a sight of the sun meant Worsley had to kneel on the thwart, where Vincent and McCarthy would hug him around the waist to keep him from pitching out of the boat as it bucked and leaped over the waves. Then, while Shackleton stood by with the chronometer,[10] Worsley would wait until the boat reached the top of the wave and the horizon came into sight, then shout "Now!" as he shot the sun. His books were fast turning into useless pulp. His sun sights were the crudest of guesses, and to look up positions in the tables he had to peel apart the wet pages one by one. Making his calculations with a pencil became laughably impossible. The boat pitched and rolled so badly that he could barely read his own scribbles. The weather was so foul that in the whole journey he managed to take a sight of the sun only four times. **C**

Since leaving Elephant Island, the six men had been accompanied by an albatross, who soared and dipped through the air. The bird could have reached South Georgia in a matter of hours, if it chose, while the men in the *James Caird* were crawling like a beetle over the surface of the ocean. Each time Worsley calculated the number of miles they had put behind them, the bird seemed to mock their slow progress.

On their seventh day at sea, the wind again turned into a gale roaring up from the Pole; the

10. **chronometer** (kruh NAHM uh tuhr): clock or watch that keeps exact time and is used to determine longitude at sea.

C **Informational Focus** **Synthesizing Sources** Paraphrase this passage. What descriptive words and phrases help bring to life the crew's experiences?

temperature plummeted. The men began to fear that the sails would freeze up and cake with ice, becoming heavier and heavier until the boat toppled upside down. With the gale howling around their ears, they took down the sails and rolled them up, stuffing them into the cramped space below. Then they rigged a sea anchor, a canvas cone dragged through the water to keep the boat turned into the storm.

Throughout the night, waves crashed over the *James Caird* and quickly turned to ice. At first the crew was relieved, since it meant the flimsy decking was sealed against further leaks. But when they awoke on the eighth day, they felt the clumsy, heavy motion of the boat beneath them and knew they were in trouble: fifteen inches of ice encased the boat above the waterline, and she was rolling badly. "We saw and felt that the *James Caird* had lost her resiliency," Shackleton said later. "She was not rising to the oncoming seas. The weight of the ice was having its effect, and she was becoming more like a log than a boat."

The ice had to come off. Taking turns, the men crawled on hands and knees over the iced deck, hacking away with an ax. "First you chopped a handhold, then a kneehold, and then chopped off ice hastily but carefully, with an occasional sea washing over you," Worsley explained. Each man could stand only five minutes or so of this cold and perilous job at a time. Then it was the next man's turn. **D**

And the gale continued through the next day, too. As Shackleton crawled out to relieve Worsley at the tiller, a large wave slammed the skipper right in the face. Shackleton took the tiller ropes and commented, "Pretty juicy," and both men managed a weak laugh.

As the storm continued, a large buildup of ice on the sea anchor's rope had kept the line swinging and sawing against the stern. Before noon on the ninth day, the sea anchor broke away, and the boat lurched heavily as seas hit her broadside. Before the gale ended that afternoon, the men had had to crawl onto the deck three times to get rid of the boat's shell of ice. The men all agreed that it was the worst job any of them had ever been forced to do.

By the time the gale ended, everything below was thoroughly soaked. The sleeping bags were so slimy and revolting that Shackleton had the two worst of them thrown overboard. Even before the storm, however, the men had been suffering from the constant wet. "After the third day our feet and legs had swelled," Worsley wrote later, "and began to be superficially frostbitten from the constant soaking in seawater, with the temperature at times nearly down to zero; and the lack of exercise. During the last gale they assumed a dead-white color and lost surface feeling."

Exposure was beginning to wear the men down. In spite of two hot meals a day, they were hungry for fresh meat. Cape pigeons often darted and flitted around the boat, but the men couldn't bring themselves to kill the friendly birds, and ancient superstition forbade them from killing the albatross that still followed majestically above. But the men were in pain. They were cold, frostbitten, and covered with salt-water blisters. Their

---

D Informational Focus **Synthesizing Sources** The situation has taken a turn for the worse, according to these last two paragraphs. What similar situations have you read about or seen portrayed in film or on television?

Vocabulary **plummeted** (PLUHM ih tihd) *v.:* plunged or dropped.

legs were rubbed raw from the chafing of their wet pants. Conditions below were almost unbearable: the stinking, rotting sleeping bags made the air putrid, and the molting hairs choked the men as they tried to gasp for breath. Their bodies were bruised and aching from their pounding up and down in the bows, and they were exhausted from lack of sleep. McNeish, who was more than fifty, was beginning to break down. Vincent, who should have stood the conditions well, was also close to collapsing. Shackleton, Worsley, Crean, and McCarthy took up the slack. When someone looked particularly bad, the Boss ordered a round of hot milk for all hands. The one man he really wanted to get the hot drink into never realized that the break was for his benefit and so wasn't embarrassed, and all of the men were better off for having the warmth and nourishment. **E**

The night after the gale ended, Shackleton was at the tiller, crouched in a half-standing, half-sitting position against the thwart with his back hunched against the cold. He glanced back toward the south and saw a line of white along the horizon. "It's clearing, boys!" he shouted. But when he looked back again, he yelled, "For God's sake, hold on! It's got us!" Instead of a clearing sky, the white line to the south was the foaming crest of an enormous storm wave bearing down on them. Worsley was just crawling out of his sleeping bag when the wave struck, and for a few moments the entire boat seemed to be submerged.

Worsley, Crean, Vincent, McCarthy, and McNeish frantically pumped and bailed with anything they could find—the cook pot, dippers, their hands—anything that would get the water out of the boat. For an hour they labored to keep the water from capsizing the *Caird.* They could hardly believe they had not foundered,[11] and they prayed they would not see another wave like that one again.

On the tenth day, the sun showed its face long enough for Worsley to get a fix. He calculated that they had made 444 miles from Elephant Island, more than half the distance. The men rejoiced as the weather cleared and they had the first good weather of the passage. They brought wet sleeping bags and clothes up on deck and hung them from the masts, halyards, and rigging.[12] The sleeping bags and clothing didn't dry, but they were reduced from soaking wet to merely damp. All their spirits were lifted. They were more than halfway to South Georgia Island.

"We were a tiny speck in the vast vista of the sea," Shackleton wrote later. "For a moment the consciousness of the forces arrayed against us would be overwhelming. Then hope and confidence would rise again as our boat rose to a wave and tossed aside the crest in a sparkling shower like the play of prismatic colors at the foot of a waterfall." **F**

They had less than half the distance left to go.

Read with a Purpose What dangers did the rescue crew encounter?

---

11. **foundered:** sank.
12. **halyards** (HAL yuhrdz), **and rigging:** ropes used on a ship to raise or lower something, such as a flag or sail, or to support the masts, yards, and sails.

E **Informational Focus** **Synthesizing Sources** In what way do Shackleton's actions show his leadership abilities?

F **Informational Focus** **Synthesizing Sources** Judging by what Shackleton wrote, how would you describe his character?

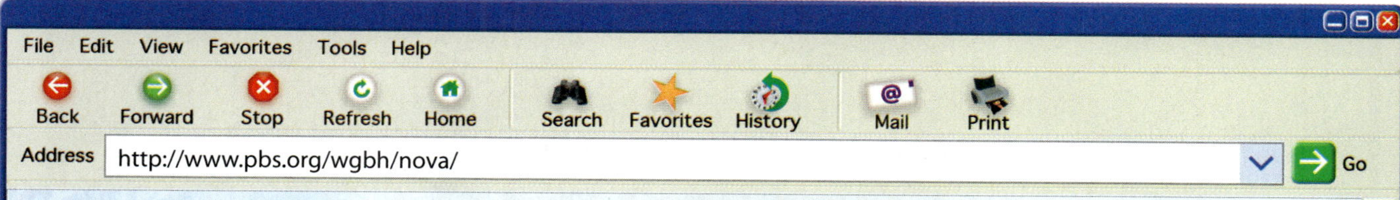

Read with a Purpose

Read this interview to get a family member's perspective on Sir Ernest Shackleton.

Tending Sir Ernest's Legacy:

An Interview with Alexandra Shackleton

from NOVA Online

Alexandra Shackleton, granddaughter of Antarctica explorer Sir Ernest Shackleton.

Sir Ernest could do far worse than have as his only granddaughter the Honorable Alexandra Shackleton. Life-president of the James Caird Society, which was founded to honor Shackleton and provide information about his expeditions, Ms. Shackleton looks after her grandfather's legacy about as well as the great man himself looked after his men.

Based in London, she has been instrumental in furthering Shackleton historical research, has contributed forewords to books on Antarctic exploration, and consulted for the Channel Four/First Sight Films television drama *Shackleton*, starring Kenneth Branagh. She has even had the honor to christen three ships: the Royal Navy's Ice Patrol ship, *HMS Endurance*; the trawler *Lord Shackleton*; and, most recently, the British Antarctic Survey ship, *RRS Ernest Shackleton*.

NOVA: What was really pushing your grandfather to do this expedition to cross Antarctica?

Shackleton: Well, the Pole had been attained, so he had to abandon that dream. I think he considered it the last great Antarctic adventure—to cross the Antarctic from the Weddell Sea to the Ross Sea, a distance of about 1,800 miles. Of course, in those days it was felt that it should be done by somebody British. All of the nationalities felt that. The Germans felt that. The Americans felt that. The French felt that. And he considered he was pretty well fitted to do it, having built up a reputation as a successful leader of the Nimrod Expedition

Vocabulary **abandon** (uh BAN duhn) *v.:* leave behind.

Analyzing Visuals

Viewing and Interpreting Do you think this photo was taken before the Antarctic expedition or after? What makes you think so?

The crew of the *Endurance* photographed on the bow of the ship.

[a 1907 attempt to reach the South Pole, to which he got within 100 miles before having to turn back]. **A**

NOVA: It was a pretty ambitious plan, given the stage of Antarctic exploration at that time. Was the monumental challenge part of the attraction?

Shackleton: It was ambitious, but I think he thought it was possible. He was a very practical person, and he would have never attempted anything that he thought could not be done. The main reason was that, above all, he had the lives of his men to consider.

NOVA: How do you think your grandfather felt at the moment when the *Endurance* was finally stuck in the ice, and he realized he would never attain his goal of crossing Antarctica?

“The realization gradually dawned on them that the ship was not going to get out.”

Shackleton: Well, when the ship got locked in the ice, it wasn't a sudden event, of course. The realization gradually dawned on them that the ship was not going to get out, that she was stuck—I think one of the crew members said "like an almond in toffee." Eventually, it became clear that she was being crushed by the ice and had no chance of rising above it. And my grandfather

A Informational Focus **Synthesizing Sources** What background information about Shackleton is provided in this passage?

said to the captain, Frank Worsley, "the ship can't live in this, skipper." Then he started making plans for what could be done when the ship finally had to be abandoned. He was a great planner who was always working out what to do in every conceivable eventuality.

For several weeks the ship had been letting out terrible creaking and groaning noises like a human in agony, and then eventually my grandfather called out, "she's going, boys," and they saw her disappear. He wrote in his diary, "I cannot write about it." He found it extremely distressing. Of course, it was the abandonment of his dream.

Yet he said to his men, quite calmly, "ship gone, stores gone, now we will go home." And he wrote in his diary, "a man must set himself to a new mark directly the old one goes." And what became his new mark was bringing every one of his 27 men home alive, from a part of the world where nobody knew they were. He knew there was no chance whatsoever of rescue. There were no communications. They might as well have been in space. **B**

NOVA: That was probably one of the toughest tests of his character, because he must have been bitterly disappointed.

Shackleton: Bitterly. Also, a ship is more to a sailor than just a floating home. It is a symbol. It's distressing for any captain, any leader of an expedition, to lose his ship.

NOVA: And yet he held himself together.

Shackleton: Indeed, and the men apparently felt reassured. After losing the ship, they felt rather adrift in every sense of the word, and yet he helped them to feel reassured. There was something to set themselves to do.

NOVA: How did you think he felt when he realized that his plan to travel over the ice was just not going to work?

Shackleton: When that method didn't work, I think he simply switched to the next method. He was extremely pragmatic,[1] and he always had many alternatives in his mind. Ernest Shackleton did not go in for soul-searching and self-recrimination.[2] He would have called it a complete waste of valuable time. **C**

NOVA: Now, on the journey to South Georgia aboard the *Caird*, how did your grandfather help the men cope with the horrendous conditions?

---

1. **pragmatic** (prag MAT ihk): practical.
2. **self-recrimination:** blaming oneself.

B **Informational Focus** **Synthesizing Sources** Paraphrase this passage. What new information does Shackleton's granddaughter reveal about Shackleton and his style of leadership?

C **Informational Focus** **Synthesizing Sources** Does Shackleton's attitude surprise you, or do you think that kind of thinking is to be expected in a leader? Explain.

Locked in an ice pack, the *Endurance* keels, or tips over.

Analyzing Visuals

Viewing and Interpreting
The *Endurance* was home to Shackleton's crew for more than a year. How do you think the men reacted when they had to leave their ship stranded in ice like this?

Shackleton: Well, he was well aware of the importance of a hot drink. Every man was fed every four hours, but if he noticed any member of the expedition failing slightly, he would order hot milk then and there, not just for him, but for everybody, so this man would not, as he put it, have doubts about himself. When he noticed one man suffering particularly from cold, he would rummage in the damp supplies and dig him out a pair of gloves. D

NOVA: How do you think your grandfather felt when South Georgia appeared on the horizon?

D **Informational Focus** **Synthesizing Sources** How does this passage support or expand on a similar passage from the biography?

> Because against almost impossible odds he brought his 27 men home safely.

Shackleton: When they saw South Georgia for the first time, and he realized that Worsley had accomplished his miracle of navigation, he felt huge relief, but sadly that was tempered[3] instantly by the fact they could not land. There was a lee shore,[4] and they were very nearly driven onto the reefs and sunk. It took two days of agonies of thirst before they could actually land.

While they were struggling to land, Worsley said he felt this almost detached resentment that no one would ever know what they had accomplished. They would just be sunk as if they had been sunk at the beginning of the journey.

NOVA: Even today that journey is seen as nothing short of miraculous.

Shackleton: Yes. They had accomplished what many regard as the greatest small boat journey in the world, 800 miles across the stormiest seas in the world in a little boat not even 23 feet long—all the while encountering extremely harsh weather and suffering gales, privations[5] of thirst, hunger, and everything. It was a colossal achievement, and when they saw the black peaks of South Georgia, they felt huge relief and happiness.

NOVA: Was the *Endurance* expedition the greatest achievement of his life?

Shackleton: I think so, because against almost impossible odds he brought his 27 men home safely. The boat journey to South Georgia was an epic in itself, and climbing across the uncharted, unmapped island of South Georgia with no equipment was remarkable. To this day, no one has ever beaten his record of 30 miles in 36 hours.

NOVA: What did your grandfather think were the most important qualities for a polar explorer to possess?

Shackleton: Well, he actually listed them. In order of priority, he said first optimism, second patience, third imagination (with which he coupled idealism), and fourth, courage. He thought every man had courage. E

Now, those are very practical qualities, and yet Ernest Shackleton was a very romantic man who wrote poetry. This was an era in which fine words abounded, and I might have thought he would have chosen qualities such as self-sacrifice or going for glory. After all, the search for the pole was likened to the search for the Holy Grail.[6] But his practical qualities did not war against his romantic

---

3. **tempered** (TEHM puhrd): counter-balanced; offset by.
4. **lee shore:** term used to describe a shoreline that is hard to reach by sea because of wind conditions.
5. **privations** (pry VAY shuhnz): lack of necessities.
6. **Holy Grail:** The Holy Grail was the cup or dish said to be used by Christ at the Last Supper. The quest for the Holy Grail formed the basis of many Arthurian legends.

E Informational Focus Synthesizing Sources In your opinion does Shackleton live up to his own expectations of the qualities an explorer should possess? Why or why not?

Analyzing Visuals

Viewing and Interpreting How does this photograph help you to see how dangerous the expedition was?

aspects. They made a harmonious whole, which I think was one of his strengths.

NOVA: What qualities do you think he possessed that made him such a compelling leader and instilled such loyalty in his crew?

Shackleton: I think that the fact that his men were so important. Leadership was a two-way thing for him. It wasn't a case of men following him just because he was the leader; he was devoted to them. It was a reciprocal, very close relationship. That's why any discord and disobedience he took personally. He was the ultimate leader because his men were his priority at all times. It took four attempts to rescue his men from Elephant Island and he visibly aged, particularly after the third one did not succeed. But when he got to Elephant Island, counted the heads frantically, and found all safe, all well, well, the years rolled away.

Frank Hurley, the expedition's photographer.

NOVA: Do you think he was happiest when he was in the Antarctic?

Shackleton: Grandfather was, I think, happiest in the Antarctic, yes. He wrote once to my grandmother, "I'm not much good at anything else but being an explorer." He loved her and he loved his home, but he chafed in the confines of this country. For a man who loved wide open spaces, Antarctica does get a grip of one. If one has never seen it, it's like nowhere else. He wrote once to a little sister, "you cannot imagine what it is like to tread where no man has trod before." F

—Interview conducted by Kelly Tyler, NOVA producer, "Shackleton's Voyage of Endurance"

Read with a Purpose How does this interview give you a more complete picture of Shackleton?

F **Informational Focus** **Synthesizing Sources** How well do these two accounts of Shackleton match up? Are they more similar or more different? Explain.

Vocabulary **priority** (pry AWR uh tee) *n.:* something deemed of utmost importance.

Internet

BIOGRAPHY AND INTERVIEW

Applying Your Skills

MO 9.R.1.I.1.a Compare, contrast, analyze and evaluate connections: text to text 9.R.1.I.1.b Compare, contrast, analyze and evaluate connections: text to self 9.R.1.G.1.a During reading, utilize strategies: to determine meaning of unknown words

from Shipwreck at the Bottom of the World / Tending Sir Ernest's Legacy

Practicing the Standards

Informational Text and Vocabulary

1. Which of the following points do *both* Jennifer Armstrong and Alexandra Shackleton make?
   - **A** Shackleton was angry because he failed to reach the Antarctic.
   - **B** Shackleton was mysterious and kept his ideas to himself.
   - **C** The entire crew survived the expedition because of Shackleton's leadership.
   - **D** Trying to reach Antarctica needlessly put people's lives at risk.

2. Which of the following statements highlights a key *difference* in the selections?
   - **A** The interview gives more details about the expedition.
   - **B** The interview contains more facts than the biography.
   - **C** Armstrong's biography lacks quotations.
   - **D** Armstrong's biography focuses more on the hardships of the journey to South Georgia Island.

3. Which statement **synthesizes** themes from the two selections?
   - **A** Good leaders put the well-being of their crew first.
   - **B** All people should strive to become leaders.
   - **C** All people can be leaders.
   - **D** Being a leader means being a hero.

4. The opposite of *plummeted* is —
   - **A** hiked
   - **B** rose
   - **C** stabilized
   - **D** inhaled

5. *Provisions* might include —
   - **A** a list of crew members
   - **B** steamboats
   - **C** a shoehorn
   - **D** cans of soup

6. A *priority* is something —
   - **A** that is difficult to do
   - **B** that needs to be done right away
   - **C** that tends to get ignored
   - **D** that provides a foundation

Writing Focus — Constructed Response

List the similarities and differences between the two works. Then, explain ways in which these texts enriched your ideas about leadership, bravery, and exploration.

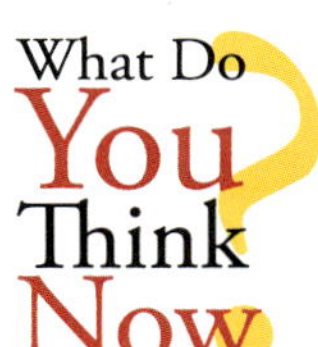

What heroic qualities did Shackleton display during the expedition to Antarctica?

FOCUS ON MISSOURI COURSE LEVEL EXPECTATIONS

Literary Skills Review

Myths **Directions:** Read the Cherokee myth below. Then, read and respond to the questions that follow.

Strawberries retold by **Gayle Ross**

Long ago, in the very first days of the world, there lived the first man and the first woman. They lived together as husband and wife, and they loved one another dearly.

But one day, they quarreled. Although neither later could remember what the quarrel was about, the pain grew stronger with every word that was spoken, until finally, in anger and in grief, the woman left their home and began walking away—to the east, toward the rising sun.

The man sat alone in his house. But as time went by, he grew lonelier and lonelier. The anger left him, and all that remained was a terrible grief and despair, and he began to cry.

A spirit heard the man crying and took pity on him. The spirit said, "Man, why do you cry?"

The man said, "My wife has left me."

The spirit said, "Why did your woman leave?"

The man just hung his head and said nothing.

The spirit asked, "You quarreled with her?" And the man nodded.

"Would you quarrel with her again?" asked the spirit.

The man said, "No." He wanted only to live with his wife as they had lived before—in peace, in happiness, and in love.

"I have seen your woman," the spirit said. "She is walking to the east toward the rising sun."

The man followed his wife, but he could not overtake her. Everyone knows an angry woman walks fast.

Finally, the spirit said, "I'll go ahead and see if I can make her slow her steps." So the spirit found the woman walking, her footsteps fast and angry and her gaze fixed straight ahead. There was pain in her heart.

The spirit saw some huckleberry bushes growing along the trail, so with a wave of his hand, he made the bushes burst into bloom and ripen into fruit. But the woman's gaze remained fixed. She looked neither to the right nor to the left, and she didn't see the berries. Her footsteps didn't slow.

And again, the spirit waved his hand, and one by one, all of the berries growing along the trail burst into bloom and ripened into fruit. But still, the woman's gaze remained fixed. She saw nothing but her anger and pain, and her footsteps didn't slow.

And again, the spirit waved his hand, and, one by one, the trees of the forest—the peach, the pear, the apple, the wild cherry—burst into bloom and ripened into fruit. But still, the woman's eyes remained fixed, and even still, she saw nothing but her anger and pain. And her footsteps didn't slow.

Then finally, the spirit thought, "I will create an entirely new fruit—one that grows very, very close to the ground so the woman must forget her anger and bend her head for a moment." So the spirit waved his hand, and a thick green carpet began to grow along the trail. Then the carpet became starred with tiny white flowers, and each flower gradually ripened into a berry that was the color and shape of the human heart.

As the woman walked, she crushed the tiny berries, and the delicious aroma came up through her nose. She stopped and looked down, and she saw the berries. She picked one and ate it, and she discovered its taste was as sweet as love itself. So she began walking slowly, picking berries as she went, and as she leaned down to pick a berry, she saw her husband coming behind her.

The anger had gone from her heart, and all that remained was the love she had always known. So she stopped for him, and together, they picked and ate the berries. Finally, they returned to their home, where they lived out their days in peace, happiness, and love.

And that's how the world's very first strawberries brought peace between men and women in the world, and why to this day they are called the berries of love.

---

1. What **conflict** is played out in the myth?

A An external conflict between nature and the wife

B An internal conflict between nature and the spirit

C An external conflict between husband and wife

D An internal conflict between the husband and the spirit

9.R.2.C.1.b

2. What types of **characters** appear in the myth?

A Gods and tricksters

B Humans and gods

C Spirits and humans

D Spirits and gods

9.R.2.C.1.b

3. What role does the mythical **character** of the spirit play in "Strawberries"?

A The healer

B The creator

C The trickster

D The peacemaker

9.R.2.C.1.b

Literary Skills Review CONTINUED

MO **9.R.2.A.1** Analyze and evaluate the text features in grade-level text *Also covered* **9.R.1.H.1.f; 9.R.2.B.1.d**

4. Myths often stem from **oral traditions** and sometimes contain **figurative language.** Which of the following quotations from "Strawberries" contains figurative language?

A "She discovered its taste was as sweet as love."

B "But one day, they quarreled."

C "Her footsteps didn't slow."

D "The anger had gone from her heart."

9.R.2.B.1.d

5. What natural origin does the myth explain?

A The creation of strawberries

B The beginning of marriage

C The presence of spirits

D The creation of man and woman

9.R.1.H.1.f

6. What **moral lesson** does "Strawberries" teach?

A Don't anger spirits.

B Husbands and wives should never fight.

C With love comes peace and forgiveness.

D Men and women cannot live together peacefully.

9.R.1.H.1.f

Constructed Response

7. Why do you think it was important for the spirit to intervene and reunite the husband and wife? What greater reason might the spirit have had for resolving their dispute?

9.R.1.H.1.f

FOCUS ON MISSOURI COURSE LEVEL EXPECTATIONS

Informational Skills Review

Synthesizing Sources: Making Connections

Directions: Read the following article and journal entry. Then, read and respond to the questions that follow.

The Appalachian Trail: A Hike Through History

from **World Almanac**

You hike a tree-lined pathway, along a trail thousands of miles long. As you progress across the mountain ridge, the sun rises and sets, its beams moving from one shoulder to the other. Let your imagination do the listening, and you can almost detect the whispers of early explorers.

The Appalachian Trail was built with imagination. Nearly 2,175 miles long, the Appalachian Trail was patched together from public and private land, a task that seemed nearly impossible at first. The trail now runs through 14 U.S. states, from Mount Katahdin in Maine to Springer Mountain in Georgia. It grew length by length, in a tremendous "citizen-led effort," says Caroline Dufour, lands resources coordinator for the Appalachian Trail Conservancy.

The Appalachian Trail follows the ridgeline of the Appalachian Mountains, from the White Mountains in the north to the Blue Ridge Mountains in the south. More than 9,000 hardy visitors claim to have hiked from end to end—5 million footsteps apiece.

The idea for the trail dates back to 1921—when a forester from Massachusetts outlined the concept in an architectural journal. Benton MacKaye envisioned thousands of miles of pathway connecting wilderness communities from New England to the South, providing an escape from modern living.

Though the wilderness communities never came to be, the first section of the trail was cleared in New York's Bear Mountain State Park in 1923. Two years later, the Appalachian Trail Conference, a collection of foresters, public officials, and outdoor enthusiasts, was formed. Workers scouted additional routes and marked new sections.

Activity slowed down, until Judge Arthur Perkins, of Connecticut, and Myron Avery, a Washington, D.C., lawyer, stepped in and established a network of new support. Volunteers worked with local, state, and federal government to get the job done, finishing in 1937.

The pathway fell apart during World War II, but reopened in 1951. In 1968, Congress declared the Appalachian a national scenic trail. In 2005, the conference was renamed the Appalachian Trail Conservancy, to highlight its changing mission.

The Appalachian Trail was conceived as a protected "trailway," with one-mile swaths on both sides. Conservators have also worked to protect the "viewshed," the land visible from the highest points. And now, the trail is being touted as a "megatransit," a means of monitoring[1] environmental health across the East.

"Basically, the concept is to use the Appalachian Trail as a way to not just measure but also frame the changes in the environment so that we can see what is happening and put it in context," says Dufour. Volunteers monitor air quality in a "citizen-led effort" that mirrors the trail's establishment.

"If you can say that half the year, the air quality is affected at the viewpoints, people will understand," says Dufour. And "if things improve along the Appalachian Trail, it means they are improving for a lot of people."

1. **monitoring:** watching, observing, or keeping a record for a set purpose.

Appalachian Trail Journal

by **Edward Burgess**

4/5 Neels Gap (Mile point 30.7)

Day 4—Today was very difficult but I did my first 10-mile day, not without a price. I have a blister on my right heel and a small one on the left foot as well. Despite the blisters, it was a great day. I left Big Cedar Mountain around 8:30 A.M., the sun was already heating up the day, and I took it pretty slow since it was so warm. It was a great morning with the bright sunshine and squirrels playing on the trail. They seemed so tame, like they expected me to pet them. Since I traveled so slow this morning, I arrived at the base of Blood Mountain about 2:00 this afternoon, which meant it was the hottest part of the day. However, I was determined to make it to Neels Gap this evening. It was a difficult climb, and the heat only made it worse. After signing the register at Blood Mountain Shelter, I decided to continue on down the trail.

A few yards beyond the shelter, I stepped out to view the beauty of the Georgia Mountains. It was awesome. After taking some photos, I continued down the mountain to Neels Gap. I think that two miles had to be the longest of the trail. It was as though it were never going to end—it just kept going. I finally arrived at the Walasi-Yi

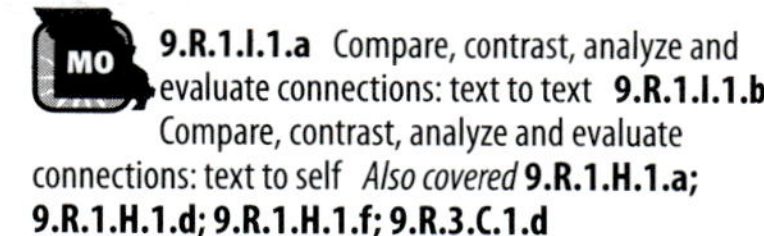
9.R.1.I.1.a Compare, contrast, analyze and evaluate connections: text to text 9.R.1.I.1.b Compare, contrast, analyze and evaluate connections: text to self *Also covered* 9.R.1.H.1.a; 9.R.1.H.1.d; 9.R.1.H.1.f; 9.R.3.C.1.d

Center.[1] Next on the agenda was to find a shower and a place to stay. Since the center was about to close for the night, I got a shuttle to Goose Creek Cabins with Jennifer, who was also waiting for a ride. When we arrived, we were informed they had no vacancies in any of the cabins. They had a mobile home they use as an overflow for hikers, and we could stay there for $25, so we agreed. We were driven to the mobile home, with all the comforts of home: complete kitchen, washer and dryer, satellite TV, microwave oven and even air conditioning. I watched the Weather Channel after taking a nice long shower, then did my laundry. As I lie here in my bed writing this, I am just overwhelmed with the entire trail experience. It is so much more than I ever imagined—the simple basic necessities of life and all the wonderful folks you meet. This is great, and I'm looking forward to tomorrow, even with the blisters. It is still my dream coming true.

1. **Walasi-Yi Center:** a rest stop and store for hikers in Georgia.

---

1. Which of the following sentences *best* expresses the **main idea** of "The Appalachian Trail: A Hike Through History"?

A Many people labored for many decades to create the Appalachian Trail.

B The Appalachian Trail is used for environmental research.

C The Appalachian Trail was formed from public and private lands.

D The trail spans the ridgeline of the Appalachian Mountains.

9.R.1.H.1.a

2. According to the article, what environmental purpose is served by the trail?

A It protects the nation's watershed.

B It provides means of monitoring air quality.

C It is a haven for endangered species.

D It helps preserve rolling farmland.

9.R.1.H.1.f

3. The *most likely* **purpose** for Burgess's journal entry is to —

A study the wildlife along the trail

B document his experience and feelings

C record changes in his health

D log how many miles he hikes each day

9.R.3.C.1.d

4. Based on Burgess's journal entry, what lesson is he taking away from his Appalachian Trail hike?

A Hiking alone can be lonely.

B Only trained athletes should climb the trail.

C Challenging yourself can change your outlook on life.

D Harsh weather can slow a hiker's pace.

9.R.1.H.1.d

Informational Skills Review CONTINUED

5. In *both* the article and the journal entry, we learn that —

A part of the trail runs through mountains in Georgia

B the trail offers hikers several thousand miles of wooded paths

C parts of the trail are difficult to climb

D shelter can be found at many points along the trail

9.R.1.I.1.a

6. Which statement *best* **synthesizes** the messages in the article and journal entry?

A Some challenges are better left alone.

B When people work together toward a common goal, anything is possible.

C It's possible to survive on only a few necessities.

D The Appalachian Trail is a national treasure that everyone should visit in his or her lifetime.

9.R.1.I.1.a

Constructed Response

7. Compare the article about the Appalachian Trail to the ideas Burgess presents in his trail journal. What do you learn from the article that you don't learn in the journal? What do you learn from the journal that you don't learn from the article? **Connect** the ideas from the article and journal with your real-life experiences. Finally, **synthesize** what you learned about life and nature from these two pieces.

9.R.1.I.1.a

FOCUS ON MISSOURI COURSE LEVEL EXPECTATIONS

Vocabulary Skills Review

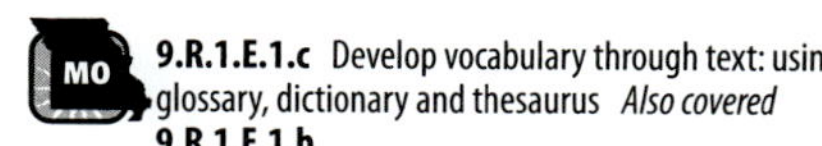

9.R.1.E.1.c Develop vocabulary through text: using glossary, dictionary and thesaurus *Also covered* **9.R.1.E.1.b**

Synonyms

Directions: Choose the word or phrase that is the *best* synonym of each italicized word taken from the selections in this collection.

1. In the Norse myth, Fenris the Wolf is described as a *grisly* monster.

A greasy
B horrible
C slimy
D smelly

9.R.1.E.1.b

2. The Trojans had a *profusion* of warriors to fight the battle.

A basket
B large amount
C bouquet
D scarcity

9.R.1.E.1.b

3. Sir Ernest Shackleton did not want his men to *abandon* hope.

A hang on to
B preserve
C give up
D store

9.R.1.E.1.b

4. Enrique tended to *idealize* his memories of times spent with his long-lost mother.

A analyze
B worship
C ogle
D criticize

9.R.1.E.1.b

5. Finding water was a *priority* for the survivors.

A main concern
B lark
C job
D affair

9.R.1.E.1.b

6. "Sorry, but all *vendors* require a permit at the craft fair."

A sellers
B waiters
C buyers
D manufacturers

9.R.1.E.1.b

7. The *hostile* weather conditions made it difficult for the explorers to reach safety.

A loving
B threatening
C ridiculous
D friendly

9.R.1.E.1.b

Academic Vocabulary

Directions: Choose the word that is the *best* synonym for each italicized Academic Vocabulary word.

8. The captain and his crew had a *mutual* love of adventure.

A fierce
B unnatural
C uncanny
D shared

9.R.1.E.1.b

9. In the biography of Shackleton, he is *portrayed* as a great leader.

A ridiculed
B depicted
C honored
D recommended

9.R.1.E.1.b

Read On

FICTION

The Pearl

In the tiny village of La Plata, a fisherman, Kino, is doing his best to support his wife, Juana, and their baby son, Coyotito. Times are tough, however, and money is scarce. Kino's discovery of a valuable pearl seems to be the answer to all his prayers. The only trouble is that everyone else in his village thinks so too, and Kino must make a perilous escape from would-be thieves in order to protect his family and his fortune. John Steinbeck's novella *The Pearl* is a heart-rending moral tale of greed and its consequences.

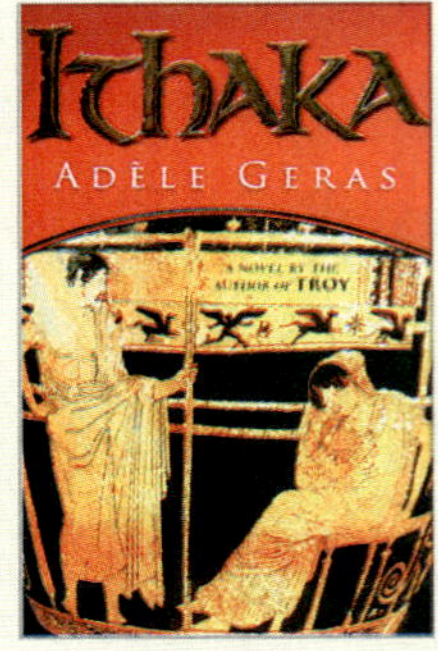

FICTION

Ithaka

The travels of Odysseus as he makes his way home after fighting in the Trojan War are well-known, but what was happening at home while Odysseus was away? Adèle Geras tells the other side of the story in *Ithaka* through the character of Klymene, a girl who pines for Telemachus and acts as a surrogate daughter for Penelope. Klymene witnesses Penelope's long wait for Odysseus and the raucous behavior of Penelope's suitors. The suitors have descended on Ithaka determined to win Penelope's hand in marriage, until the appearance of a mysterious stranger changes everything.

NONFICTION

Mythology

The author Edith Hamilton was one of our leading experts on classical myths, and her love of the subject can be found on every page of her reference collection *Mythology*. Most of the best-known Roman, Greek, and Norse myths are here—from the labors of Hercules to Jason's quest to the triumph of Perseus. Odysseus's long travels are also included, as are tales of Odin, Thor, and Loki. Hamilton's brisk retellings make each story an adventure with glorious heroes and monstrous villains.

NONFICTION

Kon-Tiki

Kon-Tiki is a real-life adventure story with a suspenseful plot that rivals anything in fiction or in film. Thor Heyerdahl journeyed 4,300 nautical miles across the Pacific Ocean—supported by nothing more than a handmade balsa-wood raft. Read this now-classic tale of Heyerdahl's voyage to experience the dangers that threatened the *Kon-Tiki* crew: encounters with strange "monsters," leaks in the raft, and life-or-death struggles with a treacherous sea.

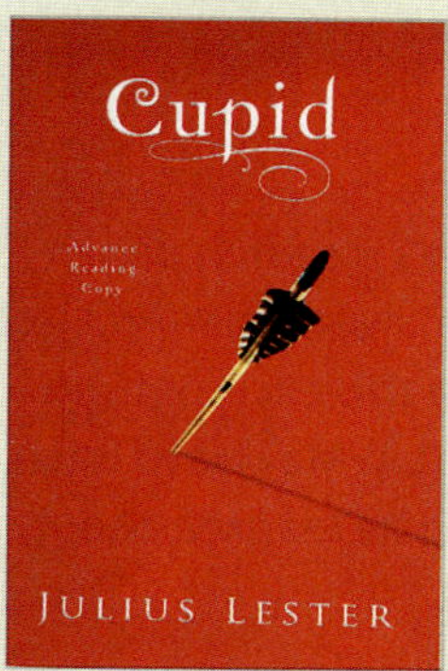

FICTION

Cupid

Cupid is the story of the god whose arrows make mortals fall in love. When Cupid falls in love himself, he discovers just how complicated love can be. He falls for Psyche, a woman so beautiful that Venus, Cupid's mother, is jealous of her. Venus gives Psyche four impossible tasks to perform. Psyche's jealous sisters get involved in the plot, and other gods also decide to meddle in the affair. Julius Lester tells the myth with humor that is cool and contemporary and with wisdom that is based on his own experiences with Cupid's arrows.

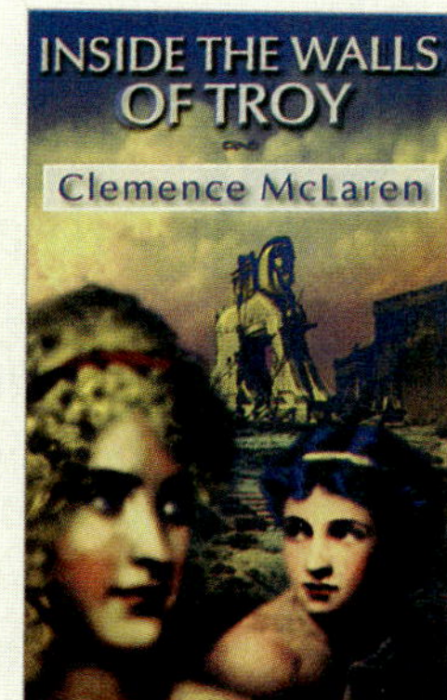

FICTION

Inside the Walls of Troy

What was it like to be the most beautiful woman in the world? Suppose you have visions of the future, but no one believes you? These questions are answered in Clemence McLaren's novel *Inside the Walls of Troy*. The story is told from the perspective of two women: Helen and Cassandra. Helen, who is married to the king of Sparta, abandons her husband and sails to Troy with Paris, a son of Priam, king of Troy. Cassandra is a daughter of Priam, and her visions foretell Troy's doom.

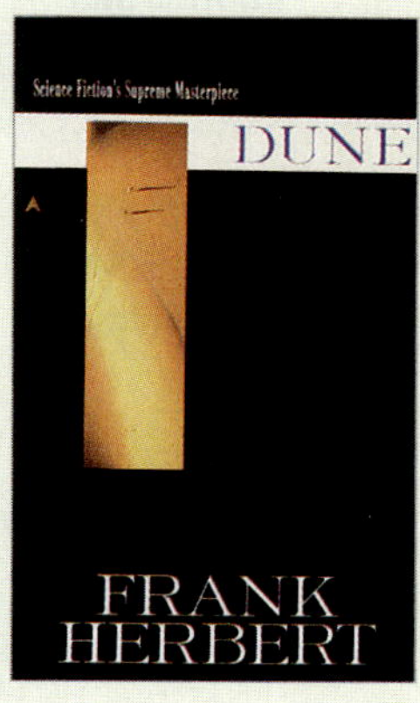

FICTION

Dune

Frank Herbert's classic science fiction novel *Dune* takes place on the strange desert planet Arrakis. There, under the shifting sands, live enormous worms that produce a precious life-sustaining spice valued throughout the universe. The young hero, Paul Atreides, must defend his noble family against rivals in a struggle for control of the spice.

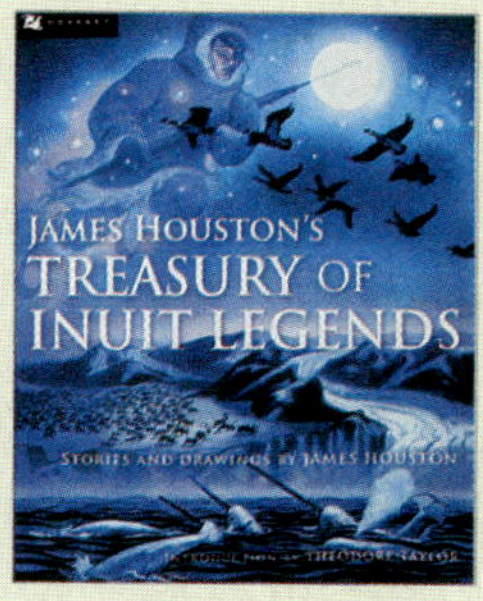

FICTION

Treasury of Inuit Legends

James Houston lived among the Inuit in the Canadian Arctic for fourteen years. He traveled the area by dogsled, camped with the Inuit, and learned their legends. In his collection, Houston tells four legends. In "Tiktaliktak," a young Inuit hunter is trapped on a drifting ice floe. In "The White Archer," Kanguq trains to become a great archer who can avenge his family. A boy and his grandfather make a dangerous journey in "Akavak." In "Wolf Run," a hunter competes with wolves to feed his family.

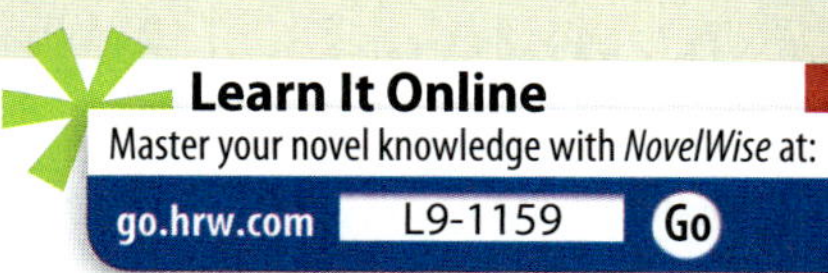

Writing Workshop

Research Paper

Write with a Purpose

Write a research paper in which you present documented evidence that supports a thesis. Your **purpose** is to research a topic thoroughly, draw conclusions, and then share your findings. Your **audience** is your classmates, teacher, and others interested in your topic.

A Good Research Paper

- has an introduction that includes a clear thesis statement
- supplies readers with background information on the topic
- has a body in which each main point is fully developed and supported with evidence
- presents main points and evidence in a logical order
- has a conclusion that restates the thesis and leaves readers with a closing thought
- identifies sources cited in the correct format

Use your **RWN** to complete the activities for this workshop.

Think as a Reader/Writer

When you write a research paper, you begin by asking questions and tracking down the answers; then, you tell others by writing a paper about your new knowledge. In this excerpt from an article in *National Geographic News,* "Delphic Oracle's Lip May Have Been Loosened by Gas Vapors," John Roach shares information he learned about the oracle of Delphi:

The oracle of Delphi in Greece was the telephone psychic of ancient times: People came from all over Europe to call on the Pythia at Mount Parnassus to have their questions about the future answered. Her answers could determine when farmers planted their fields or when an empire declared war.

← Roach introduces his **topic** with a surprising comparison.

The Pythia, a role filled by different women from about 1400 B.C. to A.D. 381, was the medium through which the god Apollo spoke. According to legend, Plutarch, a priest at the Temple of Apollo, attributed Pythia's prophetic powers to vapors. Other accounts suggested the vapors may have come from a chasm in the ground. . . .

← He provides **background information** about the oracle.

In 1927, French geologists surveyed the oracle's shrine and found no evidence of a chasm or rising gases. . . . Now, a four-year study of the area in the vicinity of the shrine is causing archaeologists . . . to revisit the notion that intoxicating fumes loosened the lips of the Pythia.

← Accurate **details** are presented in **chronological order.**

The study, reported in the August issue of *Geology,* reveals that two faults intersect directly below the Delphic temple. The study also found evidence of hallucinogenic gases rising from a nearby spring and preserved within the temple rock.

← The **source** of key information is identified.

Think About the Professional Model

With a partner, discuss the following questions about the model:

1. How does the opening capture readers' interest?
2. What is the effect of the specific dates, facts, and information the author cites?

MO **9.W.3.A.1.a** Compose a variety of texts: using narrative, descriptive, expository, and/or persuasive features

Prewriting

Select a Topic

With so many topics you can research, where should you start? First, consider the task you will be undertaking—thoroughly researching a topic and writing a detailed report on your findings. Because you'll spend considerable time and energy on this task, the topic of your research paper should be something that interests you and will also interest others. Here are ways to generate ideas for a topic:

- **Follow current events.** Consider any topic that catches your attention, such as legislation affecting teenagers or a new scientific breakthrough.
- **Dream up a vacation.** Look over maps or visit Web sites for a location you'd like to visit. Learn all you can about the people, geography, and attractions in the area.
- **Make a list of your personal interests.** Consider hobbies, sports, music, or other interests you already have. Make your research paper assignment a way to learn more about one of your pastimes or to get involved in a new area of interest.
- **Think about historical or literary figures.** You've learned about many interesting people in this class and in others. Which historical or literary figure interests you?

Form a Research Question What do you want and need to know about your topic? Develop a question that will focus your project and help keep you on track as you gather information. This **research question** should pinpoint what you want to find out from your research. To get started, ask yourself the questions shown in the left-hand column of the chart below. One writer's responses to those questions are shown in the right-hand column. Notice that the writer's research questions cannot be answered with a single word—they require investigation.

Questions	My Answers
What is my topic?	*the Cuban Missile Crisis*
What do I hope to learn from my research?	*I want to know how President Kennedy avoided nuclear war.*
What is my research question?	*What did President Kennedy do to avoid nuclear war during the Cuban Missile Crisis?*

Idea Starters

- Jamaica: past and present
- soccer in the United States
- the life of Albert Einstein
- effects of pollution on rivers
- history and workings of satellite radio

Writer's Tip

Look for a topic that is broad enough to support a full-length research paper, but not too broad to cover well. Narrow broad topics by focusing on one part. Instead of writing about mammals, for example, you might research group behavior in lions. Expand narrow ideas by looking for larger connections. For example, instead of limiting yourself to how a printing press works, you might write about how the printing press changed the world immediately after its invention.

Your Turn

Choose a Topic and Research Question List three or four **topic** ideas in your **RWN,** and evaluate which one would be best for your essay. Then, develop a **research question** that focuses your search for information.

Learn It Online
For an interactive example of a research paper, go to the writer's model online:

go.hrw.com L9-1161 Go

Write Related Questions Next, let your research question lead you to form other, more detailed questions. These detailed questions, in turn, will help you find the specific evidence you need for your paper. The student writer created these detailed questions:

- *Why did the former Soviet Union have missiles in Cuba?*
- *How did the United States respond to this situation?*
- *Why did Khrushchev agree to remove the missiles?*

Think About Your Audience and Purpose

Why Are You Writing? Before you head to the library or search on the Internet, think about why you are researching this topic and who will be reading your findings. The **purpose** of your research paper is to discover information from various sources. You'll **synthesize,** or combine, the information you gather from multiple sources, draw conclusions based on your research, and then inform others about your findings.

Who Is Your Audience? The others that you'll inform are your **audience,** such as your classmates, your teacher, and anyone else with whom you wish to share your research. For your audience to understand you, you must first understand them. Ask yourself these questions about your audience so you can tailor your research to anticipate and address their wants and needs:

- What information will my readers already have about my topic?
- What questions will they expect me to answer about it?
- How can I clear up any misunderstandings or biases they might have?
- What unfamiliar terms or technical notations will I need to define for my readers?

Find Sources

Types of Information To find answers to your research questions, you'll need to gather information from both primary and secondary sources. **Primary sources** contain original firsthand information that is usually unfiltered and unedited, such as legal documents, letters, diaries, and eyewitness accounts. **Secondary sources** provide other people's interpretations of primary material, in the form of encyclopedia entries, newspaper articles, documentaries, and biographies.

Starting Your Search Begin your search for sources at the school library, but plan on also visiting your community library and any nearby college or university library. At the left is a list of resources that might be available in your area libraries or through other community resources.

Library Resources

1. **Card or Online Catalog** These list library holdings by title, author, and subject.
2. ***Readers' Guide to Periodical Literature*** Use this to find articles in magazines and journals.
3. **Online Databases** These include encyclopedias, biographical references, atlases, and almanacs.
4. **Reference Books** Look at these to find indexes and back issues of major newspapers, such as *The New York Times*.
5. **Online Services** Search to find articles, interviews, pictures, videos, and sound recordings as well as to access to the Library of Congress and other libraries.

Community Resources

1. **Local, State, and National Government Agencies** At these offices you can request the voting records of government officials and find out about recent or pending legislation.
2. **Local Newspaper Office** Visit to find accounts of local events and historical information.
3. **Museums, Historical Societies, Service Groups** Go to these to find records of historical events, scientific achievements, art and artists, and experts on your topic.

Your Turn

Get Ready to Research In your **RWN,** write at least three detailed questions about your topic. Then, complete these sentences:

- My purpose for writing is to explain ______.
- The audience for my research paper is ______.

Evaluate Sources

As you begin to find sources of information, you have to determine the extent to which you can trust each one. Ask these questions of your sources:

1. **Is the source up-to-date?** Information is generated so quickly now that it is easy to find current material. If information on your topic is constantly changing, you must be sure that your sources are up-to-date.
2. **Does the source seem factual?** Check against your own knowledge of the topic and against other sources. If you find a **discrepancy,** or difference, between sources, check additional sources to determine which information is the most accurate or most useful.
3. **Does the source provide explanations?** Look for explanations that help you and your readers understand the **complexities** of the topic.
4. **Do the sources cover different perspectives?** Some sources may be biased, or slanted, toward one point of view. You want to find balanced sources that present varying **perspectives** on the same subject.

Prepare Source Cards

Since your paper will include a *Works Cited* list, which is a list of all the sources you use in your paper, you need to keep track of all your information. One way is to write down information about each source on a 3- x 5-inch index card and number each card. If you keep track of your sources on a computer, create a separate file, or record, for each source. Keeping your source cards or files separate will ensure that you don't get confused about where a piece of information came from. By compiling this information, you'll also begin building your *Works Cited* list. The guidelines below follow the recommendations of the Modern Language Association (MLA); your teacher may require a different format. As you fill out your source cards, refer to these guidelines, and note the special uses of punctuation.

Guidelines for Recording Source Information
Books. Write the author's name, last name first; book title; place of publication; name of publishing company; and year of publication. George, Alice L. *Awaiting Armageddon: How Americans Faced the Cuban Missile Crisis.* Chapel Hill: U of North Carolina P, 2006.
Magazine or Newspaper Articles. Write author's name, last name first; article title; magazine or newspaper name; day, month, and year of publication; edition; and beginning page number. Frankel, Max. "Learning from the Missile Crisis." *Smithsonian*. 1 Oct. 2002: 53.
Online sources. Write author's name, last name first (if listed); title of document; title of site or database; date of electronic publication (if available); name of sponsoring institution or organization; date information was accessed; <URL> or name of online service. "The Cuban Missile Crisis, 1962: The 40th Anniversary." *National Security Archive*. George Washington U. 9 Sept. 2009 <http://www.gwu.edu/~nsarchiv/nsa/cuba_mis_cri/>.

Writing Tip

Closely evaluate your Internet sources. Oftentimes you may not know who created a site and where the person or institution found its information. Your teacher may have strict rules about the kinds of online sources you can use. For example, many teachers do not accept wikis as sources for research papers.

Preparing a *Works Cited* List

1. Put your *Works Cited* list on a separate page at the end of your draft. Center the words *Works Cited* at the top of the page.
2. Follow the correct format for each source. See the guidelines to the left, the most recent edition of the *MLA Handbook,* or other style guides suggested by your teacher.
3. List your sources in alphabetical order by the authors' last names (or by the title for a work with no author listed). Ignore *A, An,* and *The.*
4. Begin each entry on a separate line, aligned with the left margin; additional lines have a hanging indent of one-half inch. Double-space all entries.

Your Turn

Carry Out a Research Plan To begin your research, list at least four **resources** you will use. As you read, **evaluate** each source you locate. Prepare a **source card** for each source you decide to use.

Research Paper

Writer's Tip

To add variety and interest to your paper, consider using these types of evidence:

- **scenarios:** descriptions of potential events or common situations
- **commonly held beliefs:** broad ideas that most people accept
- **hypotheses:** educated guesses about causes or outcomes
- **definitions:** objective explanations of unfamiliar terms

Writing Tip

Expert interviews can be valuable primary sources and often can direct you to other useful sources. Be sure to prepare questions in advance and to arrive on time. Conduct yourself in a mature and respectful way. Remember, this person is providing you with priceless help. Finally, compile the most useful responses while they are still fresh in your mind.

Your Turn

Take Notes Complete **note cards** to help you recall the most interesting and important information you find in the sources you have decided to use. If you choose to make notes on a computer, record the information from each source in a separate file.

Encyclopedia Article. Write author's name, last name first (if provided); article title; encyclopedia name; edition number, followed by the abbreviation *ed.*; and year of publication.

"Cuban Missile Crisis." *Encyclopædia Britannica*. *ed.* 2007.

Radio or Television Program. Write episode or segment title; program name; series title (if any); network name; local station call letters and city (if any); and date of broadcast.

"10 Presidents, One Dictator: U.S.-Cuba Policy." *Morning Edition*. National Public Radio. 4 Aug. 2006.

Film, Audio, or Video. Write title; director or artist, first name first; distributor; and year of release. When citing an audio or video recording, include the original release date (if relevant) and the medium, if other than CD (for example, audiocassette, DVD).

13 Days. Dir. Roger Donaldson. 2000. DVD. New Line, 2001.

Interviews. Write interviewee's name, last name first; interview type (personal, telephone, e-mail); and the date.

Deal, R. B. E-mail interview. 21 June 2009.

Take Notes

Take **accurate and coherent notes** of information and ideas you find in your sources. You'll use these facts and details as evidence to support your thesis. Note specific data, facts, and ideas that seem significant and will provide valuable support to answer your questions. Take notes on each piece of information by using one of the following methods:

- **Quote** the information directly, writing down the author's exact words.
- **Paraphrase** the information by restating all the author's ideas in your own words.
- **Summarize** the information by briefly restating only the author's main idea and most important details.

Keep Separate Cards for Notes Write direct quotations, paraphrases, and summaries on **note cards** or in a computer file. In the upper left-hand corner of each card or file, write a keyword or phrase as the **card heading** so that you can tell at a glance what the note is about. In the upper right-hand corner, write the **source number** (from your source cards) to show where you found the information. Then, write the **text** of the note. Finally, in the bottom right-hand corner, record the **page number** (when appropriate).

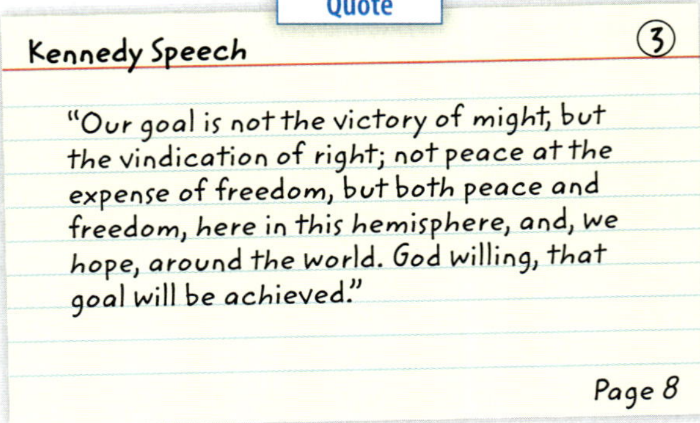

Quote
Kennedy Speech
3
"Our goal is not the victory of might, but the vindication of right; not peace at the expense of freedom, but both peace and freedom, here in this hemisphere, and, we hope, around the world. God willing, that goal will be achieved."
Page 8

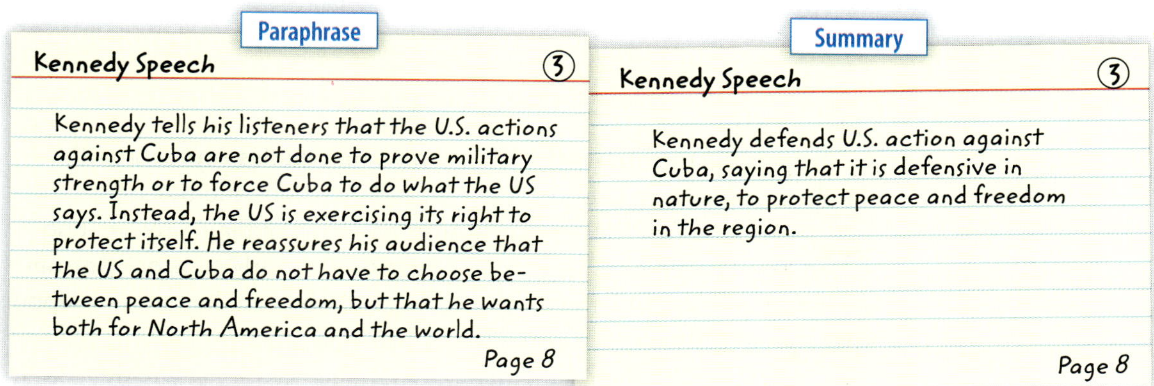

Paraphrase
Kennedy Speech
3
Kennedy tells his listeners that the U.S. actions against Cuba are not done to prove military strength or to force Cuba to do what the US says. Instead, the US is exercising its right to protect itself. He reassures his audience that the US and Cuba do not have to choose be-tween peace and freedom, but that he wants both for North America and the world.
Page 8
Summary
Kennedy Speech
3
Kennedy defends U.S. action against Cuba, saying that it is defensive in nature, to protect peace and freedom in the region.
Page 8

Write a Thesis Statement

Your **thesis** is the main idea of your report and the answer to your original research question. Try to turn your original research question into a statement, adding the information that answers the question. Here's an example of a **preliminary thesis statement.** Refer to the student model (page 1169) to see how the writer fine-tuned this statement into her final thesis.

Original Question: How was the Cuban Missile Crisis averted?
Preliminary Thesis: President John F. Kennedy was the main force in averting catastrophe during the Cuban Missile Crisis.

Since you want your readers to take your ideas seriously, be sure that your thesis statement has a formal tone that reflects confidence in what you say. You will use this **formal tone** throughout your paper. That means you should avoid slang words, contractions, and first-person pronouns, such as *I* or *we*. You should also use correct grammar. Use technical terms where appropriate, defining or thoroughly explaining them for readers.

Organize Information

Next, you'll have to organize all the information you have gathered. Begin by reviewing your note cards (or files) and then sorting them into groups with similar headings. If one group doesn't have enough note cards to provide adequate support for its heading, you may decide to omit that group or do additional research for more support.

Organize the groups of cards into the order in which you will present the information in your paper. Choose the method that best fits your topic:

- **Chronological order** presents events in the order that they happened.
- **Logical order** groups related ideas together—explaining the parts of a whole or comparing two subjects, for example.
- **Order of importance** places the most important ideas first and moves to the least important (or vice versa).

You can combine orders in your report if doing so will make your information clearer. For example, you could arrange your main points in logical order but organize the support for those points chronologically.

Peer Review

Your entire research paper will connect to your thesis statement, so you want to craft a statement that is effective, interesting, and appropriate. Read your thesis statement aloud to a classmate, and ask for comments about its clarity. Does your classmate know what your paper will discuss?

Your Turn

Create a Thesis Statement and Organization Transform your research question into a **thesis statement,** following the suggestions on this page. Be sure that your tone is appropriate. Then, choose an **organization** that makes sense for your paper. Arrange your note cards to consider at least two different organization strategies, and choose the one that will be most effective.

Create an Outline

An outline for a research paper is like a map that guides you. Your outline should include the answers to your detailed questions and the important facts and details that support those answers. Begin outlining by creating an early plan based on your sorted note cards. This early plan, or **informal outline,** should include the major headings and broad categories of support from your notes.

You will use this informal outline as a guide to create a more detailed **formal outline.** In a formal outline, you plan the arrangement of more specific information from your notes and show the hierarchy of ideas using a formal structure. As you create your formal outline, use letters and roman and arabic numbers to identify main points (headings), supporting ideas (subheadings), and details (facts and examples).

This format is shown in the following student outline:

I. Introduction
  A. Thesis statement: Kennedy's wise response to the Soviet Union helped avoid nuclear devastation during the Cuban Missile Crisis.
  B. Background information—explanation of situation
II. Body
  A. United States first responds to threat.
    1. Kennedy alerts the public after one week.
    2. America prepares for the worst.
      a. Officials try to improve civil defense.
      b. Troops prepare for battle.
  B. Cuba and the Soviet Union respond.
    1. Cubans are scared, knowing bombs are real.
    2. The Soviet Union denies that bombs are real.
  C. The United States and the Soviet Union make their moves.
    1. Kennedy states his plan to blockade area around Cuba.
      a. Kennedy makes a national speech.
      b. Kennedy orders navy vessels and aircraft carriers to the Caribbean.
    2. Khrushchev responds, weakening over time.
III. Conclusion
  A. Restatement of thesis

Writer's Tip

Watch for opportunities to include graphs, charts, maps, and time lines in your paper, and note on your outline where to place them. Visuals such as these can help your readers understand important ideas. Word-processing programs often include features that make it simple for you to include visuals in your paper.

Your Turn

Create an Outline First, jot down an informal outline in your **RWN**. This outline will present the main headings. Then, use this structure to help you create a **formal outline** that presents your information in a logical organization. To prepare for drafting, arrange your note cards in the order in which you will present facts in your paper.

Drafting

Use your outline to guide your draft. Review the **Writer's Framework** at the right to be sure you include the key elements of a research paper.

Document Sources

In a research paper, you will use information from outside sources. Give credit by citing sources in the body of your paper and supplying them at the end in a *Works Cited* list. By doing so you will avoid the serious academic offense of **plagiarism,** or claiming someone's else's ideas as your own. If the same information can be found in several easy-to-find sources, it is considered common knowledge. You do not have to document such information.

How to Credit One of the most widely used methods to credit a source within your paper is called **parenthetical citation.**

Guidelines for Giving Credit Within a Paper	
Source with one author	Last name of the author, followed by the page number (if any) of the work cited: (George 158)
Source with no author	Title, or shortened form of it, followed by the page number (if any): ("10 Presidents")
Source with two or more authors	Last names of all authors, followed by the page number (if any): (Allison and Zelikow 14)
An indirect source	Abbreviation *qtd in* [quoted in] before the source, followed by the page number (if any): (qtd in George 73)
Author's name given in sentence	Page number only: (14)

Use correct punctuation when including titles in your text, in parenthetical citations, or in a *Works Cited* list.

Grammar Link Punctuating Titles

Use the following guidelines to punctuate any titles you include in your research paper:

Underline (or **italicize**) titles of books, encyclopedias, plays, films, magazines, newspapers, journals, CDs and albums, works of art, TV and radio programs, and Web sites.

Use quotation marks for newspaper, encyclopedia, and magazine articles, short poems; short stories; essays and chapters in books; songs; TV episodes; radio segments; and Web pages.

Notice the magazine title from the professional model on page 1160 and the magazine article and magazine used in the *Works Cited* list in the student model on page 1169-1170.

The study, reported in the August issue of *Geology*, reveals that two faults . . .

Frankel, Max. "Learning from the Missile Crisis." Smithsonian. 1 Oct. 2002: 53.

Framework for a Research Paper

Introduction

- Grab the reader's attention.
- Supply background information on the topic.
- Include a clear thesis statement.

Body

- Develop each point from your outline in a separate paragraph.
- Support each main point with evidence—facts and details.
- Arrange main points and evidence in a logical order.

Conclusion

- Restate your thesis.
- Leave readers with a closing thought.

Your Turn

Draft Your Paper Follow your outline and note cards to create the first draft of your research paper. Also think about these questions:

- What background does my audience need?
- How does each of my main ideas connect to my thesis statement? How can I make these connections clear?

Peer Review

Working with a partner, review the chart to the right. Then, ask your partner to read your paper before you begin revising. He or she may be able to point out places where you need more evidence to support a main point.

Writer's Tip

You can create and hold reader interest by using a variety of sentences. Include a mixture of simple, compound, and complex sentences.

Simple: Both countries stood on the brink of nuclear war.

Compound: The crisis was averted, but tensions remained.

Complex: Although the Soviets denied that they were hiding missiles, the Cubans knew the bombs were authentic.

Evaluating and Revising

The following chart will help you evaluate and revise the content and organization of your draft. Ask yourself the questions in the left-hand column. If you need help answering them, use the tips in the middle column. Then, make the changes suggested in the right-hand column.

Research Paper: Content and Organization Guidelines

Evaluation Questions	Tips	Revision Techniques
1. Is the thesis clearly stated? Does it answer a specific research question?	**Underline** the thesis statement. **Draw a box** around the part that answers a specific research question.	**Add** a thesis statement or **replace** an existing statement with one that clearly answers the research question.
2. Is each main point supported with evidence—facts and details in the form of direct quotations, summaries, and paraphrases?	**Highlight** each main point with a different colored marker. Then, **highlight** evidence with the color of its corresponding main point.	**Add** additional evidence for any main points that have too little support.
3. Are direct quotations smoothly integrated into the paper?	**Draw an arrow** from each direct quotation to the words that introduce the quotation.	**Reword** the text around quotations so that the flow of ideas is not disrupted.
4. Are all sources given proper credit within the paper?	**Review** all highlighted direct quotations, paraphrases, and summaries. **Place check marks** by their parenthetical citations.	**Add** parenthetical citations for direct quotations, paraphrases, or summaries from sources.
5. Does the conclusion restate the thesis and give the readers a closing thought?	**Underline** the restatement of the thesis. **Put a wavy line** under the closing thought.	**Add** a restatement of the thesis. **Leave** readers with an idea or point to ponder.
6. Does a *Works Cited* list correctly indicate sources used to document information in the paper?	Put a **check mark** next to each source used in your paper and in your *Works Cited* list.	**Add** an entry to the *Works Cited* list for each source mentioned in your paper. **Delete** any entries that are not mentioned in your paper.

Read the following portions of a student draft; note the comments on its strengths and suggestions on how it could be improved.

Student Draft

The Cuban Missile Crisis

by Nicole Dagata, Don Estridge High Tech Middle School

"Our goal is not the victory of might, but the vindication of right; not peace at the expense of freedom, but both peace and freedom, here in this hemisphere, and, we hope, around the world. God willing, that goal will be achieved" (Kennedy 8). This famous quote, taken from John F. Kennedy's address to the nation on October 22, 1962, inspired millions to stand strong and remain calm as Americans and Cubans alike were catapulted into the terrifying event known as the Cuban Missile Crisis. For thirteen days, Cubans and Americans gazed into the eyes of nuclear missiles. Both countries stood on the brink of nuclear war. President Kennedy's wise actions prevented this nuclear devastation.

The episode, for the United States, began with a meeting between Kennedy and EXCOMM. They gathered to discuss recent reconnaissance photographs they had taken a mere twenty-four hours before. Kennedy explained in his address that the photographs showed "medium range ballistic missiles capable of carrying a nuclear warhead a distance more than 1,000 nautical miles . . . capable of striking Washington, D.C." The photos also showed construction of sites for intermediate range missiles, with twice the range, and of jet bombers capable of carrying nuclear weapons. (Kennedy 3).

← Nicole's **introduction** uses a quotation to set the historical period and introduce the **topic** of her paper.

← The final sentence presents her **thesis statement.**

← She presents information in the **body** in **chronological order,** beginning with the first event.

MINI-LESSON How to Revise for Accuracy

Your descriptions and explanations must provide enough detail to give readers a clear and accurate understanding of your topic. When she reviewed her draft, Nicole realized that her readers needed more information about EXCOMM. Her draft did not clearly explain who the EXCOMM was. Readers might also get the impression that the EXCOMM took the surveillance photos. She added information, shown in blue type, to correct that impression.

Nicole's Revision of Paragraph 2:

The episode, for the United States, began with a meeting between Kennedy and ~~EXCOMM. They~~ *a small group of advisors. The group, known as the EXCOMM (Executive Committee of the National Security Council),* gathered to discuss recent reconnaissance photographs ~~they had taken,~~ *acquired by U.S. spy planes* a mere twenty-four hours before.

Your Turn

Edit for Thoroughness and Accuracy Read your draft and then ask yourself:

- What information and support have I provided about each idea?
- Are all of my statements accurate? How can I prevent any misinterpretations?

Make any revisions to ensure the accuracy of information in your paper.

Student Draft *continues*

Nicole provides background information about the event.

In 1961, the Bay of Pigs invasion—a plan to overthrow Cuban president Fidel Castro—had failed miserably for the United States and Cuban exiles. A year later, the Soviet Union began to secretly smuggle missiles in cargo ships to Cuba, a newly communist country. Immediately and hastily, the ballistic missiles launch sites were constructed and aimed toward America. Soviet soldiers and technicians were convinced that the missiles wouldn't be detected under the thick palm trees of Cuba (Frankel 14). They were wrong.

Nicole uses parenthetical citations to identify sources.

Eight days after the discovery of the missile sites, Kennedy relayed the horrifying news to the public. Americans began to prepare for the worst.

Under the potential threat of nuclear missiles, American officials began to question the civil defense policy and worked long hours to improve their system (George 1). I know that U.S. troops were really psyched for battle and were required to learn new war tactics and review strategic plans. Families were totally scared and knew they'd have to come up with their own solutions, things like drills for rushing to fallout shelters during an emergency.

This partial *Works Cited* list gives full credit for each source listed in the portions of Nicole's draft shown here.

Works Cited

Frankel, Max. "Learning from the Missile Crisis." Smithsonian. 1 Oct. 2002: 53.

George, Alice L. Awaiting Armageddon: How Americans Faced the Cuban Missile Crisis. Chapel Hill: U of North Carolina P, 2006.

Kennedy, John F. "Cuban Missile Crisis Address to the Nation." 22 Oct. 1962. American Rhetoric. 2006. Transcript. 10 Sept. 2009 <http://www.americanrhetoric.com/speeches/jfkcubanmissilecrisis.html>.

MINI-LESSON How to Revise for a Formal Tone

Because a research paper reaches a wide audience and provides documentation, you should maintain a formal tone throughout the essay. Avoid first-person pronouns (*I, me, my, we, us, ours*), contractions, and slang. Nicole made adjustments to her fifth paragraph to maintain a formal tone.

Nicole's Revision

~~I know that~~ U.S. troops *prepared themselves mentally* ~~really psyched up~~ for battle and were required to learn new war tactics and review strategic plans. *Frightened* Families *also developed* ~~were totally scared and knew they'd have to come up with~~ their own *tactics and* solutions, *such as* ~~things like~~ drills for rushing to fallout shelters during an emergency.

Your Turn

Review Your Tone Read your draft and ask yourself these questions:

- Have I avoided first-person pronouns, contractions, and slang?
- Is my language formal enough to earn my reader's confidence?
- Are any of my sentences so formal that they sound stiff and awkward?

Proofreading and Publishing

Proofreading

Before you prepare the final copy of your research paper, **edit** it to make sure it's free of grammar, spelling, and punctuation errors. In particular, watch out for errors in integrating quotations from your sources.

Grammar Link Integrating Quotations

Use these guidelines to ensure that you have punctuated quotations correctly in your paper:

Type of Quotation	Example
Place **quotations shorter than four lines** within your own sentences, and enclose in quotation marks	Kennedy explained that "the greatest danger of all would be to do nothing."
For **quotations longer than four lines,** introduce the quotation in your own words, followed by a colon. Indent the entire quotation, and do not use quote marks.	Kennedy told the nation: It shall be the policy of this Nation to regard any nuclear missile launched from Cuba against any nation in the Western Hemisphere as an attack by the Soviet Union on the United States, requiring a full retaliatory response upon the Soviet Union.

Publishing

Now that you have completed a research paper, consider some ways to share your information with readers. Here are some suggestions:

- Locate a group or organization that would have an interest in your research. See if the group would like to publish your paper in a newsletter or on its Web site, or give an oral presentation at one of its meetings.
- Collect your classmates' papers for a special display in your school library, in your classroom, or on a shared Web site. Use publishing and graphics software to heighten your display's appeal.
- Send your paper to any professional you may have interviewed.

Reflect on Your Research Paper

In your **RWN,** give short responses to these questions:

1. What difficulties did you encounter while writing this paper?
2. How might you use the research skills you've acquired in this workshop in your other classes?

Proofreading Tip

Scan your paper for quotation marks and parentheses—if you are working on a computer, use the Find function. Each time you find these, check to make sure you've correctly punctuated and integrated quotations and parenthetical citations.

Your Turn

Proofread and Publish

Proofread your paper to make sure it is free of errors. Be sure to correctly integrate quotations. When your review is complete, make a final copy of your research paper and publish it.

Scoring Rubric

Use one of the rubrics below to evaluate your research paper or your response to the on-demand prompt on the next page. Your teacher will tell you to use either the six- or the four-point rubric.

6-Point Scale

Score 6 *Demonstrates advanced success*

- focuses consistently on a clear definition
- shows effective organization throughout, with smooth transitions
- offers a thoughtful, creative, and insightful approach to the definition
- develops the definition throughly, using specific, fully developed details
- exhibits mature control of written language

Score 5 *Demonstrates proficient success*

- focuses on a clear definition
- shows effective organization, with transitions
- offers a thoughtful approach to the definition
- develops the definition competently, using specific details and explanation
- exhibits sufficient control of written language

Score 4 *Demonstrates competent success*

- focuses on a clear definition, with minor distractions
- shows effective organization, with minor lapses
- offers a mostly thoughtful approach to the definition
- develops the definition adequately, using some details and explanation
- exhibits general control of written language

Score 3 *Demonstrates limited success*

- includes some loosely related ideas that distract from the definition
- shows some organization, with noticeable gaps in the logical flow of ideas
- offers a routine, predictable approach to the definition
- develops the definition with uneven use of details and explanation
- exhibits limited control of written language

Score 2 *Demonstrates basic success*

- includes loosely related ideas that seriously distract from the definition
- shows minimal organization, with major gaps in the logical flow of ideas
- offers a definition that merely skims the surface
- develops the definition with inadequate use of details and explanation
- exhibits significant problems with control of written language

Score 1 *Demonstrates emerging effort*

- shows little awareness of the topic and purpose for writing
- lacks organization
- offers an unclear and confusing definition
- develops the definition in only a minimal way, if at all
- exhibits major problems with control of written language

4-Point Scale

Score 4 *Demonstrates advanced success*

- focuses consistently on a clear definition
- shows effective organization throughout, with smooth transitions
- offers a thoughtful, creative, and insightful approach to the definition
- develops the definition throughly, using specific, fully developed details
- exhibits mature control of written language

Score 3 *Demonstrates competent success*

- focuses on a clear definition, with minor distractions
- shows effective organization, with minor lapses
- offers a mostly thoughtful approach to the definition
- develops the definition adequately, using some details and explanation
- exhibits general control of written language

Score 2 *Demonstrates limited success*

- includes some loosely related ideas that distract from the definition
- shows some organization, with noticeable gaps in the logical flow of ideas
- offers a routine, predictable approach to the definition
- develops the definition with uneven use of details and explanation
- exhibits limited control of written language

Score 1 *Demonstrates emerging effort*

- shows little awareness of the topic and purpose for writing
- lacks organization
- offers an unclear and confusing definition
- develops the definition in only a minimal way, if at all
- exhibits major problems with control of written language

Extended Definition Essay

When responding to a prompt asking you to write an extended definition essay, use what you have learned from this unit's selections, your own experiences, and the rubric on page 1172. Use the steps below to guide your response to the following prompt.

Writing Prompt

A good businessperson is usually a good leader. Strong leadership, however, is a rare quality that combines many individual characteristics.

Write an essay in which you write an extended definition of the word *leadership.* Also describe the qualities that leaders should exhibit.

Study the Prompt

Read carefully through the prompt again. Circle or underline key terms that you need to address in your essay, such as *extended definition, characteristics,* and *qualities.*

First, think of words and phrases that describe the idea of leadership. Also think of words and phrases that describe things a leader should *not* be. Then, identify a person who displays good leadership. What qualities make this person so effective? **Tip:** Spend about five minutes studying the prompt.

Plan Your Response

Referring to a person you know will help you elaborate on your definition of *leadership.* Make a list of all the qualities that you think make that person a good leader. For each quality you list, write down a specific event or detail from the person's life that illustrates this quality. For example, when describing your subject's bold thinking, you might describe a time he or she decided to enter your sports team in a state competition. Use a chart like the one at the top right as you gather details.

Definition of *Leadership*

Quality	Example from Real Life
Boldness	Made a decision to enter our team in the state championships

Tip: Spend about fifteen minutes planning your response.

Respond to the Prompt

Using your list, start writing your extended definition essay. Keep the following guidelines in mind:

- In your introduction, introduce your topic: exploring the definition of *leadership.*
- The body of your essay will expand on this statement, thoroughly defining the qualities of a good leader. Each time you describe a specific quality of leadership, give at least one example that demonstrates it.

Tip: Spend about twenty minutes writing your draft.

Improve Your Response

Revising Revisit the key aspects of the writing prompt. Have you clearly explained what qualities you think make a good leader? Did you provide specific examples of these qualities? If not, take time to do so now.

Proofreading Be sure you proofread your essay to correct errors in grammar, spelling, punctuation, and capitalization. Check your edits to ensure they are neat, and erase any stray marks.

Checking Your Final Copy Before you turn your essay in, read it one more time to catch any errors you may have missed. **Tip:** Save ten minutes to improve your paper.

Presenting Research

Speak with a Purpose

Adapt the information from a written research paper to effectively deliver it in an oral presentation.

Use your **RWN** to complete the activities for this workshop.

Think as a Reader/Writer Just as writing involves making choices about how to convey information, speaking requires that you make communication choices, too. When presenting research orally, you should ask yourself, "What is the best way to state this idea for listeners who cannot re-read my sentence?" and "How can I make this interesting to an audience of my classmates?"

Adapt Your Research Paper

The main information in your oral presentation will most likely be the same as that in your paper. However, you will need to adapt your written ideas so you can deliver them effectively as a speaker. To get started, consider the following suggestions:

- **Shorten and Simplify** Make your points directly, keeping your words and ideas simple so that listeners don't get lost. Use standard English and avoid slang. If you must use unfamiliar words, technical terms, or notations, define them carefully and clearly.
- **Preview and Repeat** Break the information in your presentation into small units; then, prepare a one- or two-sentence preview of each section so listeners know what to expect. At the end of each section, sum up the ideas you have given. Previews and repetition help listeners absorb and remember information.
- **Drop Clues** Listeners need to know where you are leading them. Help them by presenting your ideas in a logical, easy-to-follow order. Do not stray too far from the simplest, most straightforward uses of chronological order and order of importance. Insert transitional words and phrases, such as *first, second, next, most important,* and *finally,* to help make the organization of your ideas crystal clear.
- **Anticipate Your Listeners' Reactions** Be prepared to deal with listeners who may misunderstand you or have a bias against your subject. You should be able to restate or paraphrase information if your listeners look confused. Refer to your facts when handling doubters. Remember to respect their ideas, but also express confidence in your research.

MO **9.R.1.D.1.a** Read grade-level instructional text: with fluency, accuracy, comprehension and appropriate expression **9.W.1.A.1.c** Follow a writing process to: revise in response to feedback **9.W.2.C.1.a** Compose text with: effective beginning, middle, and end **9.W.1.A.1.e** Follow a writing process to: share writing **9.R.1.D.1.a** Read grade-level instructional text: with fluency, accuracy, comprehension and appropriate expression

Show and Tell

As you review your material, check to be sure that it has a clear introduction, body, and conclusion. Use the chart below to review each section.

ORGANIZING SPEECH CONTENT	
Introduction	• Plan to grab listeners' attention with a "hook," or startling statement; an interesting and relevant anecdote; or a connection that interests your listeners. • Consider incorporating your original research question into your introduction.
Body	• Support your thesis with only the most relevant and significant evidence from your paper. • Use ideas from both primary and secondary sources to show breadth of perspective. • Keep your ideas logically organized in either chronological order or order of importance. • State your sources. Introduce information by saying something like "Chemist Philippe Petit says . . ."
Conclusion	• Summarize your main points. • Pose a relevant and interesting thought or question to keep listeners thinking after the presentation.

A Good Oral Research Presentation

- engages attention from the start with a good "hook"
- supports the thesis with only the most relevant evidence
- uses primary and secondary sources
- uses a clear pattern of organization, with helpful transitional words and phrases
- delivers a conclusion that summarizes key points and offers a thought-provoking close

Deliver Your Research Presentation

Use Verbal Techniques

Remember to speak in a sufficiently loud voice. Try to vary your tone of voice to stress key ideas. Before stating a key point, give a brief pause to set off that idea. Above all, don't rush; maintain a steady pace.

Use Nonverbal Techniques

You can make your presentation clearer and more interesting by using gestures and facial expressions. You might also consider using technology available at your school to include **visuals**—such as charts, maps, graphs, or short video clips. Also think about using props. For example, you could display various balls to indicate the different sizes of planets.

Take Note

As you give your presentation, use brief notes to help you stay on track and to ensure that your presentation is clear. Make notecards with short reminder phrases, and arrange the cards in their correct order.

Speaking Tips

Rehearse the presentation to become familiar with its structure and information. Memorizing key passages will enable you to make eye contact with your audience more frequently.

Learn It Online

Learn how to make your presentation more compelling by visiting MediaScope at:

Writing Skills Review

Research Paper

Directions: Read the following excerpt from a student's research paper. Then, answer the questions about it.

(1) Invented around 1900, the first commercially produced radios, introduced in 1920, altered the way people learned about world events. (2) For the first time in history, everyone could receive the same information simultaneously. (3) In the 1920s, sociologists Robert and Helen Lynd said, "With but little equipment one can call the life of the rest of the world from the air. . . ." (4) My great-grandfather told me that each night his family listened to radio news programs. (5) In fact, according to the researcher Phyllis Stark, most people at the time learned of historic events from radio broadcasts.

(6) In 1888, a German physicist named Heinrich Rudolf Hertz was the first scientist to create radio waves in a controlled way. (7) Hertz confirmed earlier theories that radio radiation exhibited the properties of waves. (8) Using these electromagnetic signals, which are still called Hertz waves, the physicist transmitted basic radio waves. (9) A few years later Nikola Tesla, who was born in the Austrian Empire but who later became an American citizen, patented a means to reliably produce radio frequency currents. (10) In 1900, from his New York City lab, Tesla submitted a U.S. patent for a System of Transmission of Electrical Energy. (11) In it, Tesla declared that "the apparatus which I have shown will have many other valuable uses—as for instance, when it is desired to transmit intelligible messages to great distances. . . ."

(12) In radio's history, the name Guglielmo Marconi stands alongside that of Tesla. (13) As of 1894, the Italian engineer was working on the transmission of radio waves for the purpose of communication. (14) In 1895, Marconi transmitted radio signals for a mile in Bologna, Italy. (15) After moving to the United States, he filed a patent two years later on a two-circuit system for the "transmission and reception of Hertzian waves." (16) While credited for wireless communication on ships and for the first British short-wave service, Marconi may be best known for receiving the first transatlantic radio signal.

(17) In 1906, Reginald Fessenden transmitted the first audio radio broadcast on AM from Brant Rock, Massachusetts. (18) Ships at sea heard him playing "Silent Night" on his violin. (19) Widespread radio was on its way.

MO **9.W.3.A.1.a** Compose a variety of texts: using narrative, descriptive, expository, and/or persuasive features **9.W.2.B.1.b** Compose text with: relevant specific details *Also covered* **9.W.2.B.1.a; 9.W.2.C.1.b; 9.IL.1.A.1; 9.IL.1.D.1**

1. Which sentence in this excerpt presents the controlling idea, or thesis statement?

A Sentence 1

B Sentence 2

C Sentence 3

D Sentence 4

9.W.2.B.1.a

2. To improve the coherence of the first paragraph, which sentence could be deleted?

A Sentence 2

B Sentence 3

C Sentence 4

D Sentence 5

9.W.2.C.1.b

3. If the student wanted to add a quotation from another primary source, which of these sources would be appropriate?

A The autobiography of a radio pioneer

B An analysis of statistics on early radio audiences

C A Web site dedicated to a famous radio star

D A documentary on popular music in the 1920s

9.IL.1.B.1.a

4. What information would be the *best* addition to sentence 16?

A An explanation of the term "wireless"

B The date on which Marconi received the radio signal

C Marconi's date of birth

D A map showing the radio signal's path

9.W.2.B.1.b

5. Which of the following research questions is *best* answered by the excerpt?

A What events led to the invention of the radio?

B What advances brought about mass communication in the twentieth century?

C How did Nobel laureate Guglielmo Marconi invent the radio?

D How did radio lead to TV?

9.IL.1.A.1

6. To credit the source materials for the information on Fessenden, you could —

A insert the title of the source name in the margin

B include a parenthetical citation at the end of sentence 17

C put an asterisk next to Fessenden's name

D include a parenthetical citation at the end of the report

9.IL.1.D.1

Consumer and Workplace Documents

Writers on Writing

Carol Jago

Carol Jago wrote an education column for the *Los Angeles Times* and is the author of nine books for teachers.

Carol Jago on Consumer and Workplace Documents

"A few months ago my best friend and I were out on our usual jog through the neighborhood. It was a beautiful summer day. As we crossed the street in front of a large yellow truck, cheerfully chatting about this and that, a sanitation worker accidentally dropped the high-pressure hose he was holding in his hands. Before the man could bring what seemed like a massive live snake back under control, the two of us were sprayed from head to toe in raw sewage. Twice.

Needless to say it was a nasty business. We ran back to my friend's house, showered under the hottest water we could stand, and dumped the clothes we were wearing into the trash. As soon as we were dry and wrapped in bathrobes, we sat down to write.

Together we composed a complaint to the Los Angeles Sanitation Department. We didn't threaten to sue the city or in any way suggest that the man with the hose was at fault. It was an accident. We explained that though the incident was truly unpleasant, it had not resulted in any lasting physical harm or injury. What we did claim was that the city owed us for our discarded clothes.

Now the cost of two tee shirts and two pairs of shorts is a small thing, but writing that letter helped us feel a lot better. Setting out our complaint on paper got the bad taste out of our mouths—yes, the water from the hose got into our mouths along with in our eyes and ears—and allowed us to begin to laugh about it all.

When our $30 checks from the Sanitation Department arrived in the mail, we cheered. This time around, the pen was mightier than the hose."

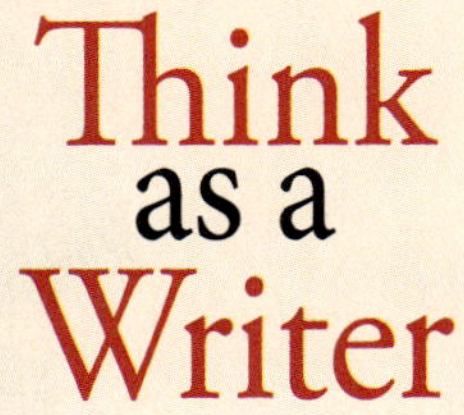

Think of a situation where you might want to write a letter of complaint. What would you say?

COLLECTION 10

Reading for Life

INFORMATIONAL TEXT FOCUS

Consumer, Workplace, and Public Documents

"Ninety percent of leadership is the ability to communicate something people want."

—Dianne Feinstein

What Do You Think? What does it take to succeed in the world?

Learn It Online

Let *PowerNotes* introduce you to reading for life the interactive way online:

go.hrw.com  L9-1181  Go

Informational Text Focus

by **Carol Jago**

Documents for Life

Have you ever tried to read an instruction manual and found yourself utterly confused? Sometimes texts that are meant to provide us with important information can be difficult to understand. Good readers know not to panic. They slow down the pace of their reading, identify and look up critical vocabulary, and prepare to re-read passages several times. Here are some of the functional documents you may encounter in your everyday life.

Consumer Documents

A **consumer** is someone who buys or uses something. You, your parents, and your classmates are all consumers. Most of the things you buy—even a backpack—come with **consumer documents.** An advertisement, for example, may have convinced you to try a particular backpack, or you may have read the features on a tag attached to it and have now decided to purchase the item. The more complicated the product is, the more complex the documents that come with it. Here are some consumer documents you may find with a video computer game.

- **Product information** is often found on the box or label. It tells you if the product has the features you are looking for.
- **Instruction manuals** usually include more detailed product information. They also tell you how to set up and use the product.
- **Warranties** explain what happens if the product does not work as guaranteed and what you have to do to get it repaired or replaced.
- **Contracts** give information on the legal use of the product.

Public Documents

Simply stated, a **public document** is any document that is made public—for all to read. For example, when a government agency develops new regulations that affect consumers or citizens, the agency announces the information to the public. Other public documents inform citizens of decisions, responsibilities, and schedules of events or services. Government agencies, schools, libraries, fire and police departments, transit departments, even movie theaters all produce public documents. Public documents come in many forms. Here are some that may be familiar to you:

- Newspaper items
- Fliers or posters
- Legal records
- Product recalls
- Emergency evacuation guidelines
- Travel advisories
- Congressional proceedings

MO **9.R.3.A.1** Explain, analyze and evaluate the author's use of text features to clarify meaning **9.R.3.D.1** Read and apply multi-step directions to perform complex procedures and/or tasks

Workplace Documents

Documents that are created for and by employees are called **workplace documents.** When you look for a job, for example, you may write a **business letter** in which you state your qualifications and ask for an interview. You might include a **résumé,** a formal list of your educational and work experience, or fill in an **application** supplied by the employer. The graphic organizer below shows the documents you may encounter when you apply for a job.

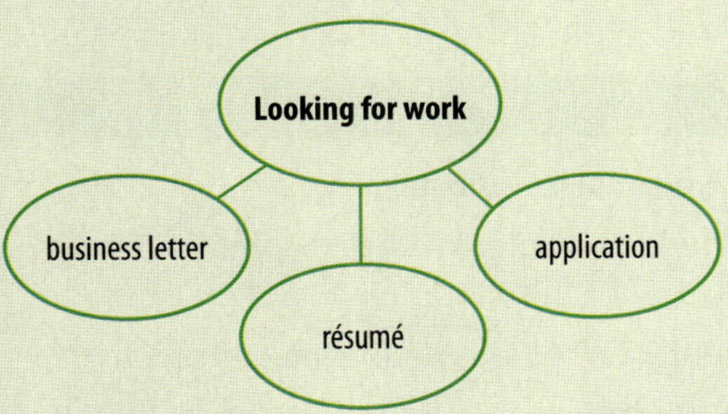

When you are hired, you might be asked to sign an employment **contract.** Your employer may give you an **employee manual,** which spells out rules and instructions related to your job. **User guides** will show you how to use the office equipment. On the job, you will communicate with others using **e-mail, memorandums,** often called memos, and **reports.**

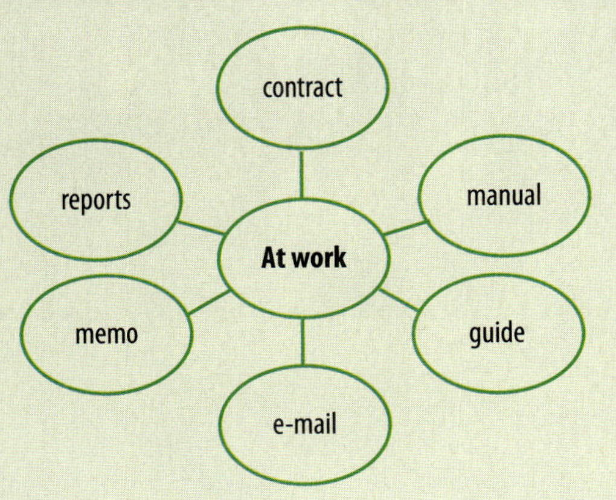

Technical Directions

You often follow directions when you cook, play music or sports, exercise, or dance. When the instructions are for assembling or using a mechanical or electronic device or for performing a scientific activity, they are called **technical directions.** You want to follow all directions carefully, especially technical directions. If you make a mistake and skip a step or perform one out of order, the device or experiment may not work.

Well-written directions often have **numbered steps** and clear **diagrams** that make them easy to follow. These tips can help you follow technical directions:

1. Read through *all* the directions.
2. Follow each step in order.
3. Compare what you are doing with the drawings and illustrations.

Your Turn Analyze Documents

Create a chart like this one in your *Reader/Writer Notebook*. Then, fill in at least two examples for each category. Try to use examples from real life.

	Examples
Consumer documents	
Public documents	
Workplace documents	
Technical directions	

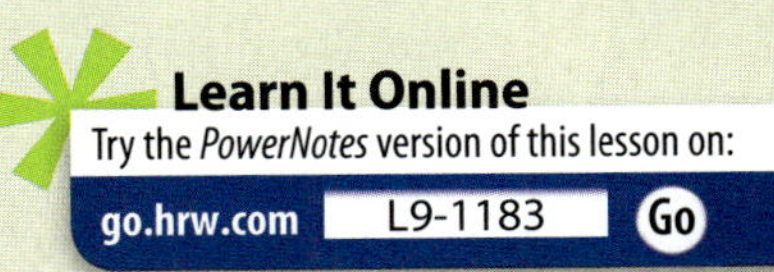

Learn It Online
Try the PowerNotes version of this lesson on:
go.hrw.com
L9-1183
Go

Analyzing Visuals

How Is Information for the Public Communicated in Art?

A well-crafted poster for an art exhibit is a thing of beauty. It gives you information on who, what, when, and where, but it is also designed to lure you to the exhibit to see the art firsthand. Museum staff, graphic artists, and sponsors—the organizations that fund the exhibit—all have a say in what is included on the poster. A graphic artist will then weave text and images together to create an appealing poster.

Analyzing a Poster

Use these guidelines to help you analyze a poster:

1. Study the text—its size, style, and color. What text commands your attention?
2. Look at the images presented. What idea do the images convey?
3. Analyze the use of color. What impact does the color create?
4. Think about the relationship between the text and images. What is the focus of the poster?

Study the detail of the poster below. Use it to help you answer the questions on the next page.

MUSEUM OF MODERN ART
11 WEST 53 STREET N. Y. C.
AN EXHIBITION PREPARED BY THE INDIAN ARTS AND CRAFTS BOARD U.S. DEPT OF THE INTERIOR
MADE BY NEW YORK CITY W.P.A. ART PROJECT

9.R.3.A.1 Explain, analyze and evaluate the author's use of text features to clarify meaning

Indian Art of the United States (c. 1941) by Pistchal. Exhibition poster. WPA artwork.

1. Which element of the poster catches your eye the most? Why?

2. Why do you think the poster designer chose to use the two different sizes of type in the title of the exhibition?

3. What effect does the use of color, both in the image and in the type, create?

4. Why do you think the poster designer chose to use a smaller type size to convey information about the museum's location?

Your Turn Write About the Poster

If you saw this poster on the street, would it catch your eye? Why or why not? What changes would you make if you were in charge of designing this poster?

Reading Focus

by **Kylene Beers**

What Skills Help You Read Functional Documents?

Since so many of the things you will want to do in life—such as make purchases, find a job, or create and market a new product—require functional documents, you need to know how to read them. Some you will want to read quickly to find the information you are seeking. Others you will want to read slowly and carefully. Below are some skills that will help.

Skimming and Scanning

These two skills with similar-sounding names can help you preview a document to find the information you need without wasting time.

Skimming helps you get an overview of the document. You look through it quickly by reading the title, heads, and subheads. You also read the first line or two of each paragraph to decide if it is a document you want to read more carefully.

Scanning helps you find particular information in a document. You look for boldface or italic terms, key words or phrases, or any other important details that relate to your topic. When you find them, you read those sections more carefully to learn what they say about your topic.

Skimming gives you a broad view.

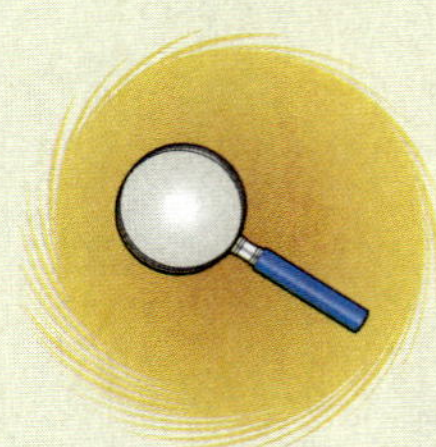

Scanning gives you a focused view.

Taking Notes

Functional documents often contain important information that you want to remember, so it is a good idea to make note of it. There are many different ways of **taking notes.** You might keep notes

- in a **notebook,** like your *Reader/Writer Notebook*
- on **notecards,** such as index cards
- on **self-adhesive notes** that you attach to the document
- in the **margins**—if you own the book or document
- as **highlighted** important phrases, sentences, or paragraphs—again, if you own the book or document
- on a **computer**

When taking notes, be sure to write down *all* the important information you will need. If you are recording facts and statistics, make certain they are accurate. If you are quoting an author, note the quotation exactly as written. Also, include any information necessary to help you find the material again. Include the source title, author, publisher, and page number or URL, as appropriate.

MO **9.R.1.F.1.b** Apply pre-reading strategies to aid comprehension: preview **9.R.1.G.1.b** During reading, utilize strategies: to self-monitor comprehension **9.R.1.H.1.b** Apply post-reading skills to comprehend, interpret, analyze, and evaluate text: question to clarify **9.R.1.D.1.b** Read grade-level instructional text: adjusting reading rate to difficulty and type of text

Adjusting Reading Rate

When reading functional documents, you must learn how to **adjust your reading rate.** When you skim and scan, for example, you read quickly. Then, when you find the information you are looking for, you slow down and read more carefully. While taking notes, you have to read slowly and thoroughly to be sure the information in your notes is correct.

You might read quickly through a newspaper article or an advertisement, but you need to slow down when reading product information or an employee manual. You will first want to read technical directions quickly to get a general idea about what is included. Then, read them carefully a second time as you follow the steps. Legal documents such as contracts and warranties require a slow, precise reading so you will know exactly what you can expect—and what is expected of you.

Reading Rate	Documents
quick	newspaper articles; advertisements
slower	product information; employee manual; business letters; schedules
slowest	technical directions; contracts; warranties

Asking Questions

Good learners **ask questions** to grasp new information, to get answers, and to critique a text. Here are some of the many questions you might ask when reading functional documents:

- Does this product have the features I want?
- Is this advertisement telling the truth?
- What are the hidden costs of this service?
- What is this document *not* telling me?
- What exactly is covered in this warranty?
- What am I responsible for in this contract?
- Are these directions presented logically?

Your Turn Read Functional Documents

Read this train timetable, and answer the questions that follow.

Depart	*Arrive*	*Notes*
Georgeville	**Allendale**	
8:00 A.M.	9:15 A.M.	Track 1: Express
9:00 A.M.	9:35 A.M.	Track 5: Local
9:30 A.M.	10:45 A.M.	Track 5: Sunday only
10:00 A.M.	11:15 A.M.	Track 1: Express

Fares:	**Adults:**	$12.00 one way	$20.00 round trip
	Children:	$4.00 one way	$6.00 round trip
	Seniors:	$8.00 one way	$12.00 round trip

1. Would you skim or scan to find the train that departs at 10:00? Explain.
2. Which information on the timetable would you read slowly and carefully?
3. What questions might you have that are *not* answered here?

Now go to the Skills in Action: Reading Model

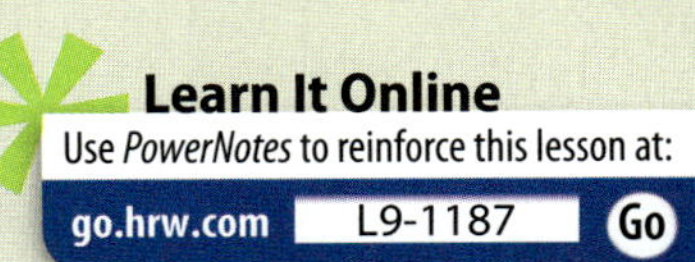

Learn It Online
Use *PowerNotes* to reinforce this lesson at:
go.hrw.com
L9-1187
Go

SKILLS IN ACTION

Reading Model

DOCUMENTS

Read with a Purpose Read to learn what consumer documents are all about.

Consumer Documents

From the Manufacturer to You

Picture before you an unopened box. In it is the latest and greatest computer game console. In your hurry to get it out of the box, you let a sheaf of papers slide to the floor. There they lie in danger of being thrown out with all the packing materials. Be sure you retrieve and read them carefully. These **consumer documents** can make a big difference in how much you enjoy your new game.

Reading Focus

Skimming Skimming through the information on this page informs you that the text is about the types, elements, and features of consumer documents.

Elements and Features of Consumer Documents

Here are some types of consumer documents and the **elements,** or types of information, that each document provides:

- **product information**—descriptions of what the product will do
- **instruction manual**—information on how to use the product
- **warranty**—details of company and owner responsibilities if the product does not work

Consumer documents itemize, or detail, the unique **features** of each product. Here are some samples.

Product Information

WYSIWYGAME ARTS

CPU	800MHz
Video card	250 MHz GPU
Resolution	1920 × 1080 maximum
Memory	128 MB
Storage	Memory Card—Hard Drive
Sound card	64 Channels
DVD	Yes
Media	12 × DVD-ROM 6.2 GB Capacity
Hard drive	8 GB
Modem	Yes
Ethernet port	Yes
Controllers	4

Safety Information

Please follow these safeguards regarding the installation and use of your game console:

1. When installing your game console, be certain that the unit receives proper ventilation. Vents in the console covering are provided for this purpose. Never block or cover these vents with any objects, such as fabric, books, or magazines.
2. Do not install your game console in a bookcase or entertainment rack where it cannot receive proper ventilation.
3. Do not place the game console in direct sunlight or near a heat source, such as a radiator or hot-air duct.
4. Do not set the game console on a soft surface, such as a bed, sofa, or rug, since doing so may result in damage to the appliance.
5. Unplug this appliance from the wall outlet, and contact a qualified service person under the following conditions:
   a. The power-supply cord or plug is damaged.
   b. Liquid has been spilled on, or objects have fallen into, the game console.
   c. The game console has been exposed to rain or water.
   d. The game console does not operate normally after you follow the operating instructions.
   e. The game console has been dropped, or the cabinet has been damaged.
   f. The game console exhibits a distinct change in performance.

Do not attempt to service this product yourself. Opening or removing the outside covers may expose you to dangerous voltage or other hazards. All service must be done by qualified service personnel.

Reading Focus

Adjusting Reading Rate You probably read through the product information rather quickly. If you are seriously considering buying a video computer game, you should slow down and pay careful attention to the features listed in the product information. This way you will be sure to buy a product that has what you need.

Taking Notes You might want to take note of features you care most about and compare them with the product information on other game packages.

Informational Text Focus

Consumer Documents This page from an instruction manual lists safety information. Specific instructions include the need to ventilate the console and to keep it stable and dry.

Informational Text Focus

Consumer Documents Instruction manuals often include important warnings. Be sure to read—and heed—them carefully.

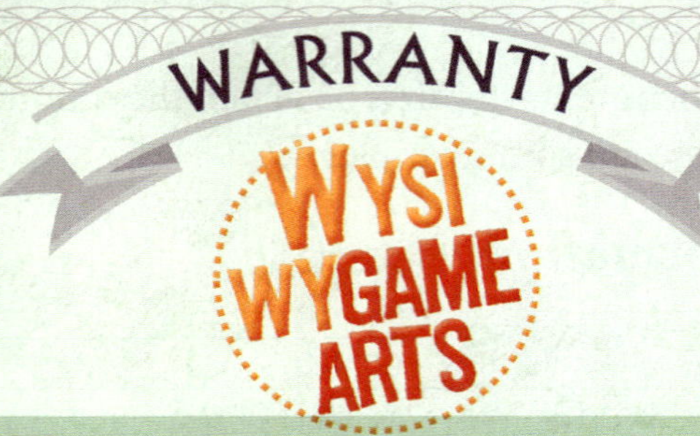

Limited Warranty

WYSIWYGame Arts makes the following limited warranties. These limited warranties extend to the original consumer purchaser or any person receiving this product as a gift from the original consumer purchaser and to no other purchaser or transferee.

Limited Ninety [90] Day Warranty

WYSIWYGame Arts warrants this product and its parts against defect in materials and workmanship for a period of ninety [90] days after the dated or original retail purchase. During this period, WYSIWYGame Arts will replace any defective product or part without charge to you. For replacement you must deliver the entire product to the place of purchase.

Limited One [1] Year Warranty of Parts

WYSIWYGame Arts further warrants the parts of this product against defects in materials or workmanship for a period of one [1] year after the date of original retail purchase. During this period, WYSIWYGame Arts will replace a defective part without charge to you, except that if a defective part is replaced after ninety [90] days from the date of original purchase, you pay labor charges involved in the replacement. You must also deliver the entire product to an authorized WYSIWYGame Arts service station. You pay all transportation and insurance charges for the product to and from the service station.

Owner's Manual and Warranty Registration

Read the owner's manual thoroughly before operating this product. WYSIWYGame Arts does not warrant any defect caused by improper installation or operation. Complete and mail the attached registration card within fourteen [14] days; the warranty is effective only if your name, address, and date of purchase are on file as the new owner of a WYSIWYGame Arts product.

Informational Text Focus

Consumer Documents Warranties all share certain elements, such as eligibility, time limits, parts warranties, and disclaimers. Two specific features of this warranty are that only the original purchaser or gift recipient is eligible for the warranty and that the company will replace defective parts without charge for a period of ninety days after purchase.

Reading Focus

Asking Questions One question you may ask here is, "How do I make sure that this company receives the registration card?"

SKILLS IN ACTION

Wrap Up

9.R.3.A.1 Explain, analyze and evaluate the author's use of text features to clarify meaning 9.R.1.H.1.b Apply post-reading skills to comprehend, interpret, analyze, and evaluate text: question to clarify *Also covered* 9.R.3.D.1; 9.R.1.F.1.b; 9.R.1.G.1.b; 9.R.1.D.1.b

Into Action: Features of Consumer Documents

In a chart like the one below, describe the types of information presented in the three consumer documents you have just read.

Document	Type of Information Presented
Product information	
Safety information	
Warranty	

Talk About . . .

1. With a partner, talk about the ease or difficulty of understanding these consumer documents. How well was the information presented? Was it easy to find? Try to use each Academic Vocabulary word listed at the right at least once in your discussion.

Write About . . .

Use the underlined Academic Vocabulary words in your answers to the following questions. Definitions appear at the right.

2. What is the function of workplace documents?
3. Why is it important that technical directions be coherent?
4. What might be the consequences of poorly written directions?
5. What type of information might be specified in a warranty.

Writing Focus

Think as a Reader/Writer

In Collection 10, you will read functional documents like those you will encounter in life. The Writing Focus activities on the Preparing to Read pages help you recognize how each document presents information. On the Practicing the Standards pages, you will check your understanding of these documents.

Academic Vocabulary for Collection 10

Talking and Writing About Functional Documents Academic Vocabulary is the language you use to write and talk about functional documents. Use these words to discuss the documents you read in this collection. The words are underlined throughout the collection.

consequences (KAHN suh kwehns ehz) *n. pl.:* results; outcomes. *The consequences of poorly written directions could be confusion and despair!*

function (FUHNGK shuhn) *n.:* typical action of something. *The function of consumer documents is to inform consumers about products or services.*

coherent (koh HIHR uhnt) *adj.:* clear; connected logically; understandable. *It is usually easy to understand a coherent document.*

specify (SPEHS uh fy) *v.:* state in detail. *Product information on clothing labels may specify the size, material, and laundry instructions.*

Your Turn

Copy the Academic Vocabulary words into your *Reader/Writer Notebook.* Write sentences in which you use each of the four words correctly.

INFORMATIONAL TEXT FOCUS

Following Technical Directions

Why is it so important to understand the way things work?

QuickWrite

If you were building a home on a desert island, what directions or instruction manuals would you find useful? Write down your ideas.

USER'S MANUAL

Preparing to Read

Following Technical Directions

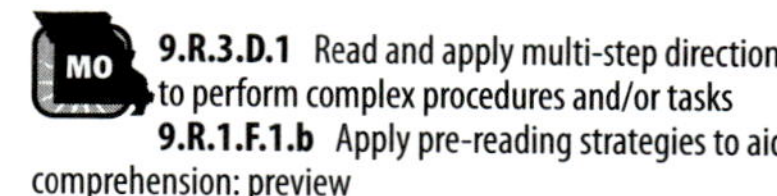

9.R.3.D.1 Read and apply multi-step directions to perform complex procedures and/or tasks **9.R.1.F.1.b** Apply pre-reading strategies to aid comprehension: preview

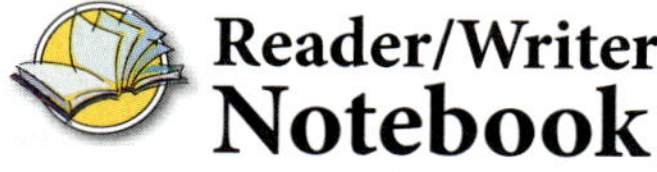

Reader/Writer Notebook

Use your **RWN** to complete the activities for this selection.

Informational Text Focus

Following Technical Directions Instructions for using computers as well as other scientific, mechanical, and electronic products and activities are called **technical directions.** You follow technical directions when you read instructions on how to do an experiment in a chemistry lab, fix a flat tire on your bicycle, program the remote control for your television, operate your new microwave oven, or install software on your computer. Technical directions may seem complicated at first, but if you pay attention and follow each step carefully, you can accomplish the task.

Reading Focus

Skimming and Scanning These skills can help you when you first encounter an informational document.

- **Skimming** helps you get an overview of the document. You glance at titles, heads, and subheads and read the first line or two of each paragraph to get a general idea of what information is provided.
- **Scanning** helps you locate information in the document. You search for boldface or italic terms, graphics, and other important details for specific pieces of information.

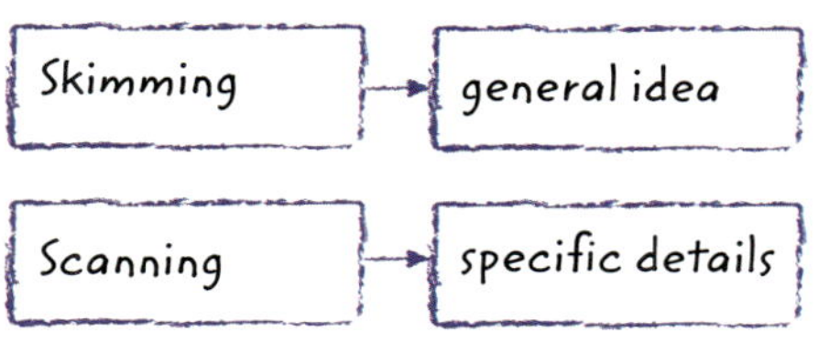

Into Action As you read the directions that follow, skim to get the general idea and scan to find specific information.

Writing Focus

Preparing for **Constructed Response**

When you read the following technical directions, jot down any steps that confuse you in your *Reader/Writer Notebook*.

Vocabulary

scan (skan) *v.:* copy text or graphics from paper into a computer file. *You can scan any picture on paper into your computer to use in your documents or multimedia presentations.*

image (IHM ihj) *n.:* visual illustration; graphic. *Most presentations are improved by the addition of an interesting image.*

options (AHP shuhnz) *n.:* choices. *Computer menus offer you many options for creating documents.*

Language Coach

Multiple-Meaning Words The Vocabulary words above are defined in ways that relate to computers, but they all have other meanings as well. Challenge yourself to find at least one more meaning for each Vocabulary word. Use a dictionary if you need help.

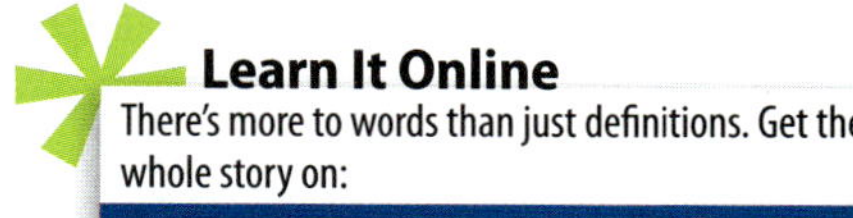

Learn It Online

There's more to words than just definitions. Get the whole story on:

go.hrw.com L9-1193

Read with a Purpose

Read the following technical directions from a user's manual to become familiar with the format of instructions.

Adding Graphics to Your Web Site

The following technical directions show how to *scan*, edit, and save an *image* for your Web site using a made-up photo-editing program called PhotoEdit. The directions assume you have a scanner and it is set up properly to work with your computer. Reading through these instructions will make you familiar with the process of following **technical directions** so that when you choose your own picture-editing program, you'll have no trouble getting the results you want. Ⓐ

Setting Up

1. Make sure the scanner is turned on.
2. Place your image in the scanner. The image should lie face down on the glass, aligned according to the page-size indicators on the scanner.
3. Open up the PhotoEdit program.

Ⓐ Reading Focus Skimming What does a quick read of the title and first paragraph tell you about the topic of this document?

Vocabulary **scan** (skan) *v.:* copy text or graphics from paper into a computer file.
image (IHM ihj) *n.:* visual illustration; graphic.

Scanning

4. In PhotoEdit, under the File menu, choose Import; then select your scanner's name under the list of options. This will open up a scanning dialogue box within PhotoEdit. A preview of your picture will also appear. **Do not remove original image from the scanner.** B

5. With the cursor, select the area of the image you want scanned.

6. Set the size and resolution of the image. In general, scan your image at a larger size than the original (such as 200%) to provide more options for editing later on. For Web use, it is best to set the resolution to 72 dpi (dots per inch).

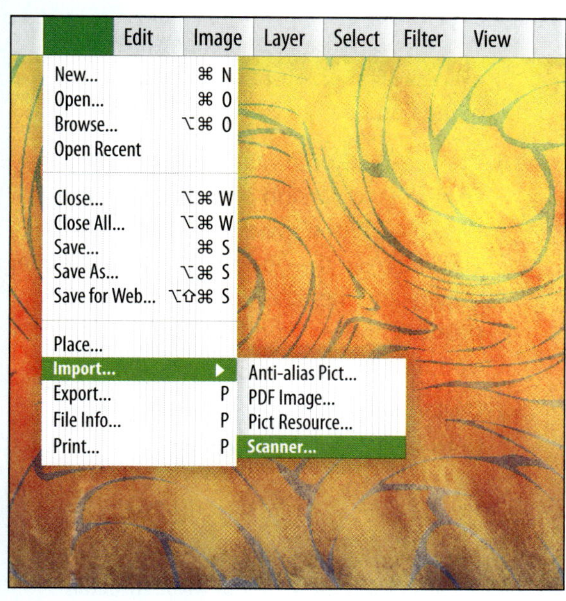

7. Click on SCAN. Your image will now open as an untitled document in PhotoEdit, ready to be edited.

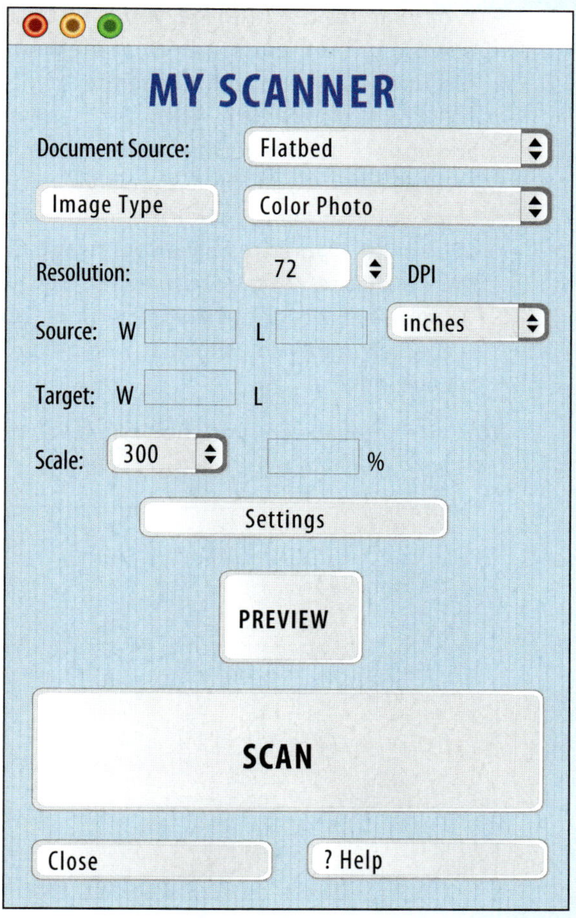

B Informational Focus Technical Directions
Why is this statement boldface?

Vocabulary **options** (AHP shuhnz) *n.:* choices.

Editing

8. You may now perform any number of edits to ready your image for Web use. You can crop, adjust the color, retouch, and sharpen the image in PhotoEdit.

9. In order to resize the image, you must decide how big you want it to appear on the Web page. First, make sure you are viewing the image at 100% (actual size). Next, go to the Image menu and choose the Image Size option. A dialogue box will open. If you want your image to be large, you may set the pixel size to 800 width x 600 height. If you would like your image to be a thumbnail size, set the width to a size of around 180 pixels. If the "Constrain proportions" option is enabled in this box, the image height will be set automatically.

10. Once you have entered the desired values, hit OK. You will now see the resized image. **C**

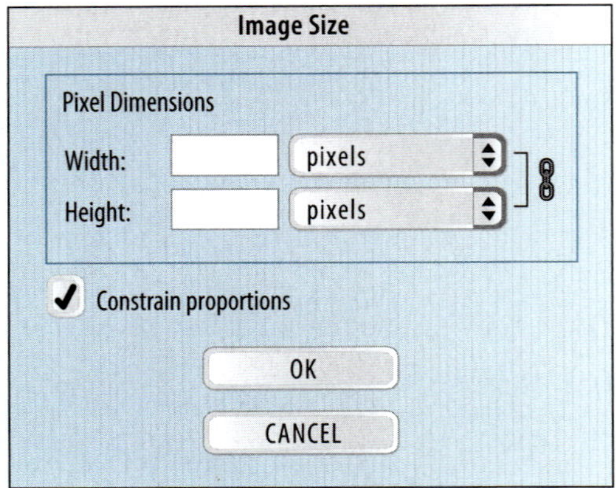

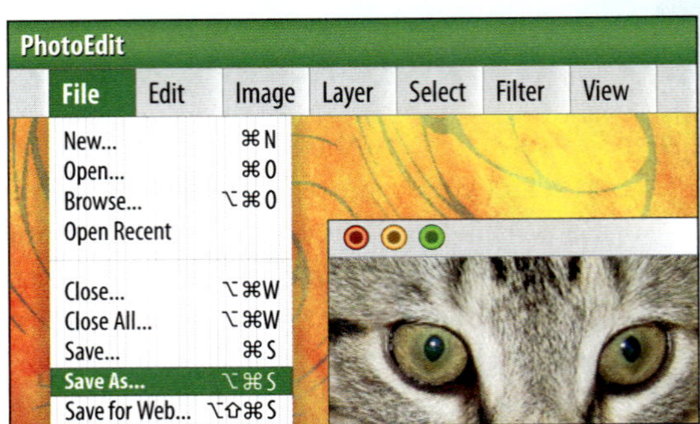

Saving

11. When you are satisfied with the way your image looks, go to the File menu and select Save As.

12. When you name your file, be sure not to exceed 31 characters, including the file extension.

13. Choose JPEG under file format (a JPEG is a compressed version of the file, suitable for Web use). When saving an image as a JPEG, you will have the option of setting the image quality and file size. For the Internet, it is best to choose a "medium" setting for these options.

14. Click OK. Your image is now ready to be uploaded onto your Web site.

Read with a Purpose What organizational pattern did the writer of these directions follow?

C **Reading Focus** **Scanning** If you were scanning through the headers to find out how to edit your image, what steps would you read carefully?

Applying Your Skills

MO 9.R.3.D.1 Read and apply multi-step directions to perform complex procedures and/or tasks 9.R.1.G.1.a During reading, utilize strategies: to determine meaning of unknown words

Following Technical Directions

Practicing the Standards

Informational Text and Vocabulary

1. After you have placed your image in the scanner and opened up PhotoEdit, what is the first thing you need to do in order to scan the image?
   A Input a resolution of 72 dpi.
   B Change the image's size.
   C Choose Save As from the File menu.
   D Choose Import from the File menu.

2. It is wise to scan your image at a larger size than the original because —
   A it is easier to see the image
   B it allows for more editing options
   C it will appear smaller on the Internet
   D you can't save the image if it's too small

3. For Web use, you should set the resolution to —
   A 200 dpi
   B 800 dpi
   C 7.2 dpi
   D 72 dpi

4. When you *scan* a document into a computer, you —
   A copy it
   B read it
   C skim it
   D delete it

5. Another word for *options* is —
   A opportunities
   B advantages
   C orders
   D choices

6. When you talk about computers or publications, *images* can also be called —
   A ideas
   B articles
   C graphics
   D headers

Writing Focus Constructed Response

Write instructions explaining how to perform a task that involves a machine or tool. You may, for example, choose to write directions for retrieving phone messages, sending an instant message on a cell phone, or using a compass. Make sure that your steps are clear and easy to follow.

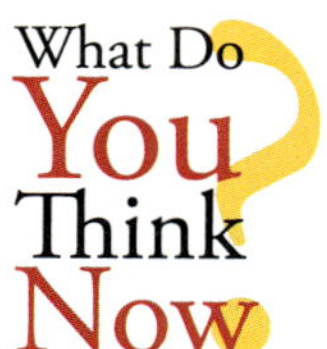

How can understanding technical directions help you communicate with others?

INFORMATIONAL TEXT FOCUS

Citing Internet Sources

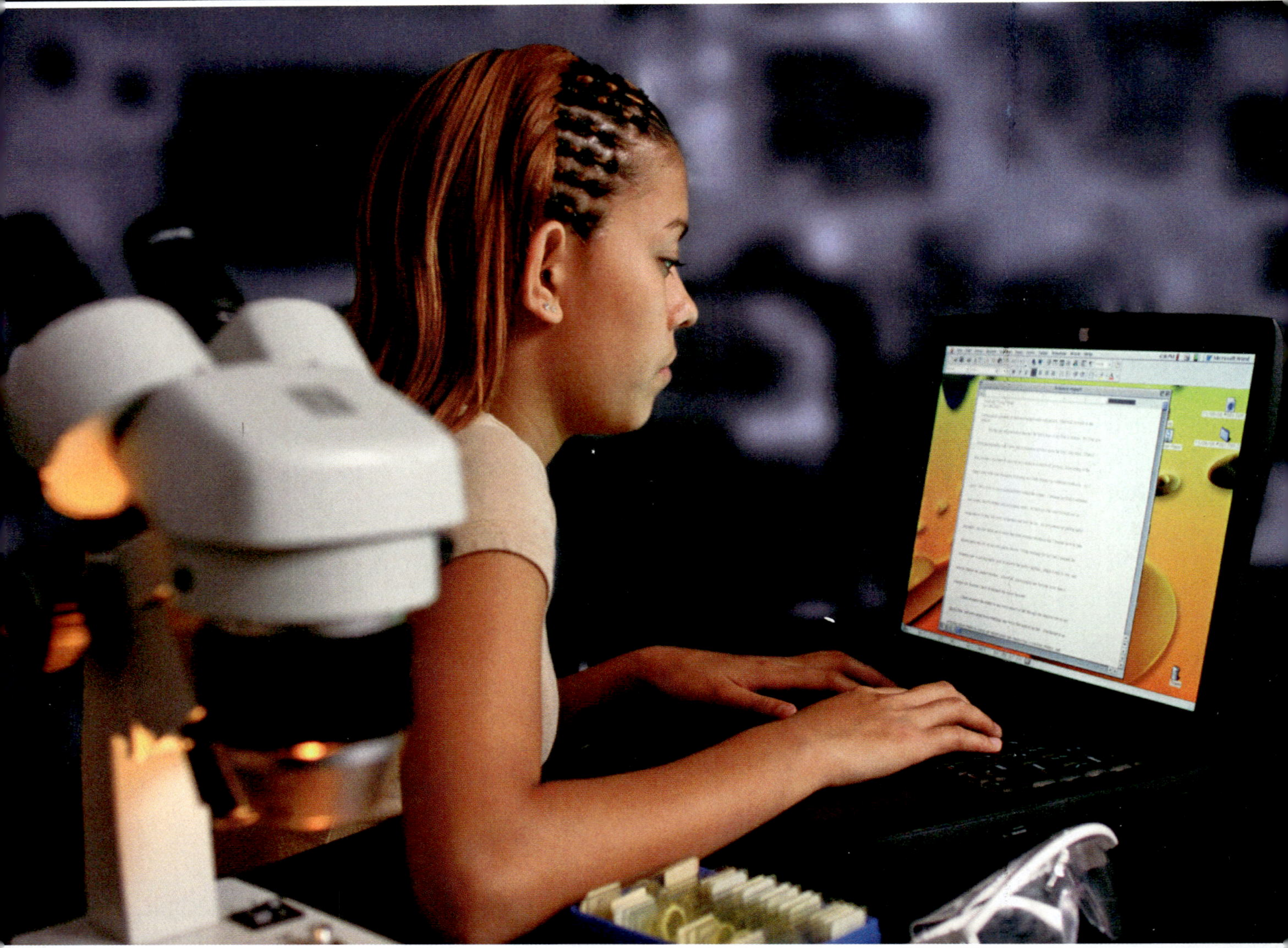

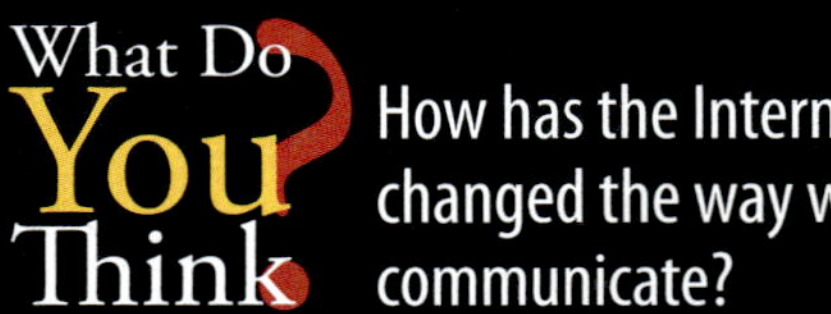

What Do You Think? How has the Internet changed the way we communicate?

QuickTalk

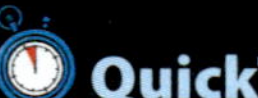

Think of past essays, reports, and biographies that you've written. Were any of your sources from the Internet? When you searched for information on the Internet, where did you go to find it? Share your sources with the class.

STYLE MANUAL

Preparing to Read

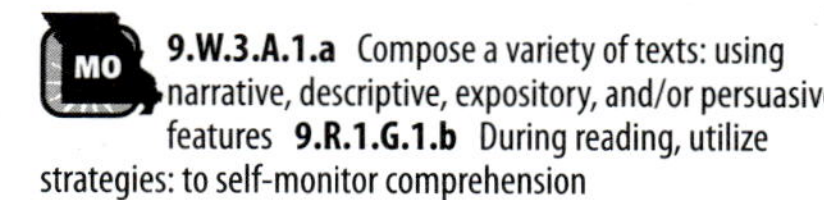

9.W.3.A.1.a Compose a variety of texts: using narrative, descriptive, expository, and/or persuasive features **9.R.1.G.1.b** During reading, utilize strategies: to self-monitor comprehension

Citing Internet Sources

Reader/Writer Notebook

Use your **RWN** to complete the activities for this selection.

Informational Text Focus

Citing Internet Sources You've probably been asked at some point to write a report or essay for which you've had to research a subject. Before you hand in your report, you must include a ***Works Cited*** list. This list of the sources you've used enables others to find and read them. Because online information is updated often (in some cases, daily), citing **Internet sources** requires more information than citations of print materials.

Reading Focus

Taking Notes A good way to keep track of the sources you've used in your research is to use **notecards.** Your notecards can contain as much detailed information as you wish, but they must contain certain basic information.

Into Action Record information about Internet sources on notecards like the one below.

Description of Source	Essay
Author(s)	Dr. Luther Agons
Title	"Greek Military Tactics"
URL:	http://www.ancientworlds.com/articles/Agons1

Writing Focus

Preparing for **Constructed Response**

As you look at example citations, pay attention to the formatting, especially the order in which the information appears.

Vocabulary

expansive (ehk SPAN sihv) *adj.:* covering many things; spread out; broad. *The World Wide Web is so large that it has become an expansive source of knowledge.*

expedient (ehk SPEE dee uhnt) *adj.:* very helpful in the pursuit of a goal or desire; advantageous. *Because the Internet is so easy to access, going online to find information is expedient.*

Language Coach

Related Words Once you know one form of a word, you can more easily understand related words. For example, if you know the meaning of the verb *generate,* you can guess at the meaning of related words, such as *generation, regenerate,* and *generator*.

See if you can sort these words into the appropriate columns of the chart below: *expand, expanse, expeditious, expandable, expedite, expansively, expediential*.

Words Related to *Expansive*	Words Related to *Expedient*

Learn It Online
Master these words. Visit Word Watch at:
go.hrw.com
L9-1199
Go

Read with a Purpose Read this style manual to find out how we use and refer to information found on the Internet.

Chapter 11

Guide to Citing Internet Sources

Recently, with the explosion of the World Wide Web, the Internet has become an expansive source of information. You may even find yourself doing most of your research online rather than using print media. In fact, in researching cutting-edge technologies, such as the video game industry, it may be more expedient to look for your information online. For example, if you want to find the latest news on graphics technology, or advances in hardware and software components, the frequently updated Internet would be your best bet.

After you have found your online sources, you need to cite them in any report you write, just as you would offline sources (books, magazines, newspapers). Since online information is easily updated, citing Internet sources requires more information than you may be used to providing in citation of print materials. You are *not,* of course, responsible for changes made in a site between the time you make your notation and the time your reader goes there to find the work. You *are* responsible for giving your reader as much information as you have. In particular, it is crucial that you reproduce the URL (uniform resource locator)—the site's Internet address—exactly, so that a reader may access the site.

General Format for an Online Source

Author's Last Name, Author's First Name (if known). "Title of Work." Title of Web Site or Database. Date of electronic publication. Name of Sponsoring Institution. Date information was accessed <URL>. **A**

Note: If an electronic address, or URL, must be broken at the end of a line, break the address immediately after one of the slash marks. Do not add a hyphen or any other mark of punctuation to indicate a division of an address.

A Reading Focus Taking Notes Why would you want to copy this general format onto a notecard?

Vocabulary **expansive** (ehk SPAN sihv) *adj.:* covering many things; spread out; broad.
expedient (ehk SPEE dee uhnt) *adj.:* very helpful in the pursuit of a goal or desire; advantageous.

The box below shows the types of information you will need to include in an online citation. It includes examples of citations for **consumer, public,** and **workplace documents** you might find on the Internet. (Some of the sites are made up; some are real.) The examples follow the Modern Language Association (MLA) style. When you prepare a list of sources, which style you follow is less important than choosing one style and sticking to it. Ask your teacher which style you should follow.

You may confuse online citations with parenthetical citations. A parenthetical citation briefly cites the source of specific information at the point where it is cited. The Works Cited list includes all the sources cited in the full text of the research paper. It is placed at the end of the research paper.

Sample Citations for Consumer, Public, and Workplace Documents

Product Information from a Commercial Site

"About the New WYSIWYGame Arts Console." WYSIWYGame Arts Console Page. 7 June 2001. WYSIWYGame Arts. 27 July 2001 <http://wysiwgame.com/console/index/asp>.

Article from an Online Nonprofit Magazine Dedicated to Protecting Consumers

Sleuthing, I. B. "And the Winner Is—Testing Today's Game Consoles." Digital. 25 June 2001. 7 Aug. 2001 <http://www.digital.org/main/article/gamcon/1.html>.

Article from a Reference Database (Encyclopedia)

"Programming Language." Electronic Library Presents: Encyclopedia.com. The Columbia Electronic Encyclopedia, Sixth Ed. 2000. Columbia UP. 15 July 2001 <http://encyclopedia.com/articlesnew/10538biblio.html>. **B**

Part of an Online Book Found on a Public-Library Site (Also Available in Print)

Case, Loyd. "Chapter 4—Graphics." Building the Ultimate Game PC. Indianapolis: Macmillan, 2000. netLibrary. 3 Aug. 2001 <http://emedia.netlibrary.com/nlreader/dll?bookid=38549&filename=Page_v.html>.

Copyright Forms from the Library of Congress (Government Office)

United States. Library of Congress. US Copyright Office. Form VA—For a Work of the Visual Arts. Washington: GPO, 1999. 2 Aug. 2001 <www.loc.gov/copyright/forms/formva.pdf>.

Information from a Company's FAQ Page

"Resource Code Game Software Developers May Use When Programming for Our Products." ShellGame, Inc. 7 June 2001 <http://www.shellgame.com/corp/faqs/faqslist.html>.

Posting to a Discussion List (Message Board)

Game Dawg. "Why More Polygons Mean Awesome Graphics." Online postage. 23 June 2001. Way Kool Net. 16 Aug. 2001 <http://www.waykoolnet.com/mboards/boards.cgi?board=prgm&read=9218>.

Quotation from an E-mail Communication

Nguyen, W. "Re: WYSIWYGame Arts Graphics." E-mail to the author. 21 Aug. 2001.

B Informational Focus Internet Sources What differences do you find in the first three examples of Internet citations?

Using Notecards

Ready to try a few Internet citations on your own? When you are researching on the Internet, it is a good idea to record your sources on three-by-five-inch cards like the ones at the right. (Most of these are made-up sources.)

Source Type: Consumer information
What it is: Online magazine article
Author(s): Art C. Graphic
Title: "Writing Game Software Without Writing Code"
Other Information: from Click magazine, printed 1/17/07. I found it on 8/5/07.
URL: http://www.clickmag.com/main/articles/artg/1.html

Source Type: Workplace document
What it is: Company software instruction manual
Author(s): V. Phat
Title: "User's Manual for Compiler Version 2.2"
Other Information: There is no print version (they change it too often). You have to print from the WYSIWYGame Arts company intranet. It had last been updated 6/27/07 when I accessed the info on 7/3/07.
URL: http://www.wysiwygame.com/manuals.compiler2.2.html

Source Type: Public document
What it is: Government information service
Author(s): Federal Consumer Information Service, a division of the U.S. General Services Administration
Title: "Recalls"
Other Information: Note to myself: This is where I found out about the computer-chip recall from the company that WYSIWYGame Arts was considering switching to for its chips. I found the recall on 8/3/07 using my usual search engine. There was no notation of when the site had last been updated.
URL: http://www.pueblo.gsa.gov/recallsdesc.html

Formatting Your *Works Cited* List

The last step in writing a report is to compile all the sources you have cited in a *Works Cited* list (see page 1170). Follow these formatting steps:

- At the top of the page, center the title "Works Cited."
- Alphabetize your sources by the author's last name. If no author is listed, alphabetize a source by the first two words in the title, ignoring *A*, *An*, and *The*.
- If two or more sources are by the same author, use the author's full name in the first entry only. For the other entries, type three dashes in place of the name, followed by a period and the rest of the citation.
- Double-space the list, and begin each entry at the left margin. If an entry runs longer than one line, indent the following lines five spaces. C

Read with a Purpose What new information did you learn by reading this style manual?

C **Informational Focus** **Internet Sources** What differences do you find in the first three examples of Internet citations? What function does each type of source serve?

STYLE MANUAL

Applying Your Skills

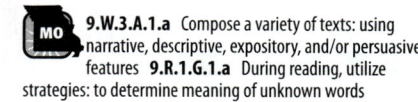

9.W.3.A.1.a Compose a variety of texts: using narrative, descriptive, expository, and/or persuasive features 9.R.1.G.1.a During reading, utilize strategies: to determine meaning of unknown words

Citing Internet Sources

Practicing the Standards

Informational Text and Vocabulary

1. The purpose of a ***Works Cited*** list is to —

A document the sources used in your research
B enable your readers to access your sources
C neither of the above
D both of the above

2. On a ***Works Cited*** list an author's name appears —

A after the title of the work cited
B last, at the end of the citation
C first, with the first name first
D first, with the last name first

3. The most crucial information to reproduce accurately in an Internet citation is the —

A URL
B date you accessed the site
C title of the site
D author of the site

4. According to the MLA style, what is the correct way to cite a URL in a ***Works Cited*** list?

A hrw.com
B www.hrw.com
C http://www.hrw.com
D <http://www.hrw.com>

5. In your ***Works Cited*** list, how would you alphabetize an entry that does not have an author?

A Use *Anonymous* as the author's name.
B Alphabetize by the first two words in the title, ignoring *A, An,* or *The.*
C Type two dashes and a period, and then alphabetize by the title.
D Alphabetize by the month you accessed the Web site.

6. Something that is *expansive* —

A covers many things
B is very flexible
C costs a lot of money
D is in another country

7. Something that is *expedient* is —

A expansive
B useful
C ancient
D faraway

Writing Focus Constructed Response

Why do you think formatting guidelines for Internet sources have been developed? What purpose do they serve?

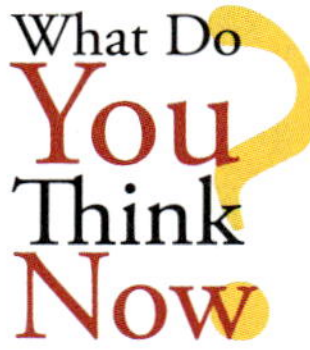

What information is required when citing Internet sources?

INFORMATIONAL TEXT FOCUS

Analyzing Functional Workplace Documents

CONTENTS

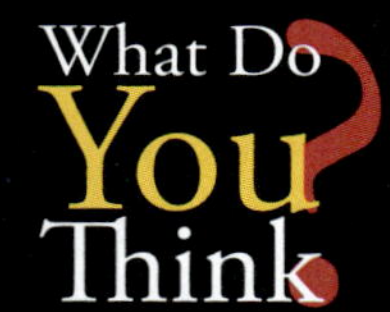

What Do You Think? How does the look of a document affect your ability to use it?

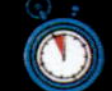

QuickTalk
With a partner, discuss informational material whose appearance made you want to read it. Discuss instances when the appearance of a document distracted or confused you.

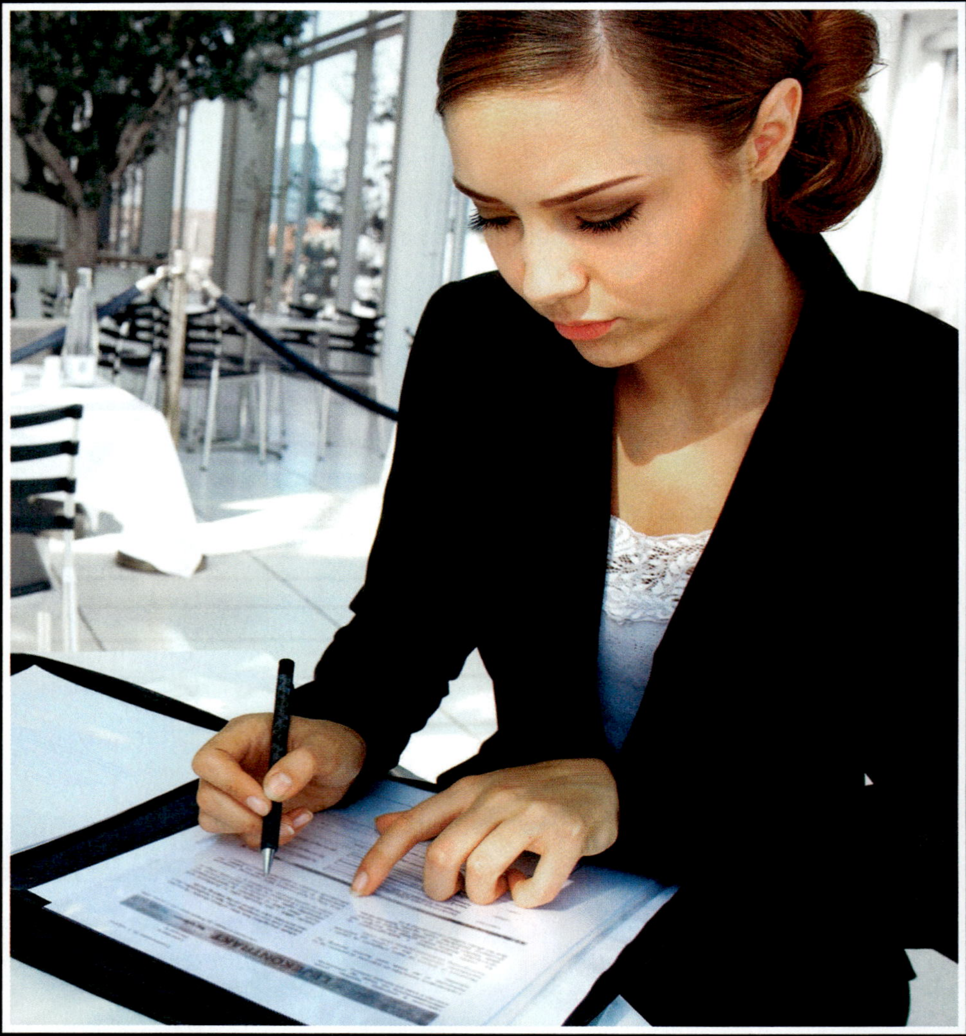

FUNCTIONAL WORKPLACE DOCUMENTS

Preparing to Read

9.R.3.A.1 Explain, analyze and evaluate the author's use of text features to clarify meaning
9.R.1.D.1.b Read grade-level instructional text: adjusting reading rate to difficulty and type of text

Business Letter / E-mail Message / Web Site / Contract

Reader/Writer Notebook

Use your **RWN** to complete the activities for these selections.

Informational Text Focus

Analyzing Functional Workplace Documents Some workplace documents follow a specific **structure** and **format.** For instance, in writing a business letter or memorandum, you should use a specific style for the heading. Contracts usually have short, numbered sections with boldface headers. User guides and technical directions often include **graphics** such as **charts, diagrams,** and **illustrations.** Web sites have many different structures and formats and often include attention-grabbing graphics features such as icons and colorful type.

Reading Focus

Adjusting Reading Rate When you read workplace documents, you will probably find yourself **adjusting your reading rate.** You may quickly skim the address on a business letter and slow down to pay attention to its content. You will glance quickly through a user guide until you find the information you want. When you find it, you will slow down to learn what you need to know. You should always read contracts and other legal documents very slowly and carefully.

Into Action As you read the documents in this section, jot down notes about your reading rate. Here is an example.

Business letter—read heading and closing quickly; slowed down to pay attention to body of letter

Shareware agreement—

Game description—

Writing Focus

Preparing for **Constructed Response**

When you view the page from the WYSIWYGame Arts Web site, write in your *Reader/Writer Notebook* whether you find the structure and format of the site effective.

Vocabulary

diligent (DIHL uh juhnt) *adj.:* hard-working. *A diligent student puts in a lot of time studying.*

differentiate (dihf uh REHN shee ayt) *v.:* distinguish by creating a difference between. *An interesting cast of characters will differentiate your game from all others.*

en route (ahn ROOT) *adv.:* along the way. *You may discover many adventures en route to your destination.*

Language Coach

Oral Fluency Sometimes, the letter combination *di–* has a long *i* sound, such as in *diary* and *diet*. In two words in the Vocabulary list, however, that letter combination has a short *i* sound.

Sort these words that begin with *di–* into their proper categories in the chart below.

digress	digest	distinct
dissent	dissect	diction
dimension	disperse	dispose

Long i Sound	Short i Sound

Learn It Online

Learn more about e-mail and Web sites at MediaScope online:

go.hrw.com L9-1205 

Read with a Purpose
Read the following documents to help you better understand their different uses.

March 10, 2009

Ms. Donna Pulsipher
Senior Editor
GearTroll Magazine
5100 South Nixom Lane
Grand Rapids, MI 49503

Dear Ms. Pulsipher:

For the past several months, I have been designing a computer game, and I have recently created a new Web site to promote it. Because you know so much about this industry, I wonder if you would be willing to offer your opinion. I want the site to be clear, interesting, and easy to use, and I would love to hear your ideas and suggestions.

I am a diligent student, and I like to spend my spare time developing my design and programming skills. I want to create new video games that will appeal to young adults like me. Now I have developed a game that I think can be very successful, and I want to make it available to users all over the world.

If you have any time available, I would also enjoy the opportunity to meet with you in person to discuss the Web site and my project. Please feel free to contact me at any time. You can reach me at the above address or at gdesigner@wysiwygames.com.

Again, thank you so much for your help. I am very much looking forward to your insight. **A**

Sincerely,

G. Designer

G. Designer

A **Reading Focus** **Adjusting Reading Rate** What is the main idea of this letter? Did you need to adjust your reading rate to find the main idea? Explain.

Vocabulary **diligent** (DIHL uh juhnt) *adj.:* hardworking.

E-MAIL

From: Donna Pulsipher
To: G. Designer
Cc: Aaron Kravitz
Subject: Web site review (B)

Hello G. Designer,

It was my pleasure to look at your Web site. I think that overall, it is easy to use and will be appealing to your users.

Here are a few suggestions:

- I would try to improve your graphics. You want graphics that will grab gamers and players and get them interested in your game and that will also differentiate your game from all others.
- Think about adding a page where users can make suggestions or comments.
- Finally, I would add a legal document called a Shareware Agreement. This is an agreement between you and the user that protects your software. I have attached an example.

I would be happy to meet with you to discuss your projects further. I have copied my assistant on this e-mail. If you call the office, he will be happy to arrange an appointment.

Best of luck!

Donna Pulsipher
555-555-0177

(B) **Informational Focus** **Workplace Documents** How does this heading structure add clarity to an e-mail message?

Vocabulary **differentiate** (dihf uh REHN shee ayt) *v.:* distinguish by creating a difference between.

WEB SITE

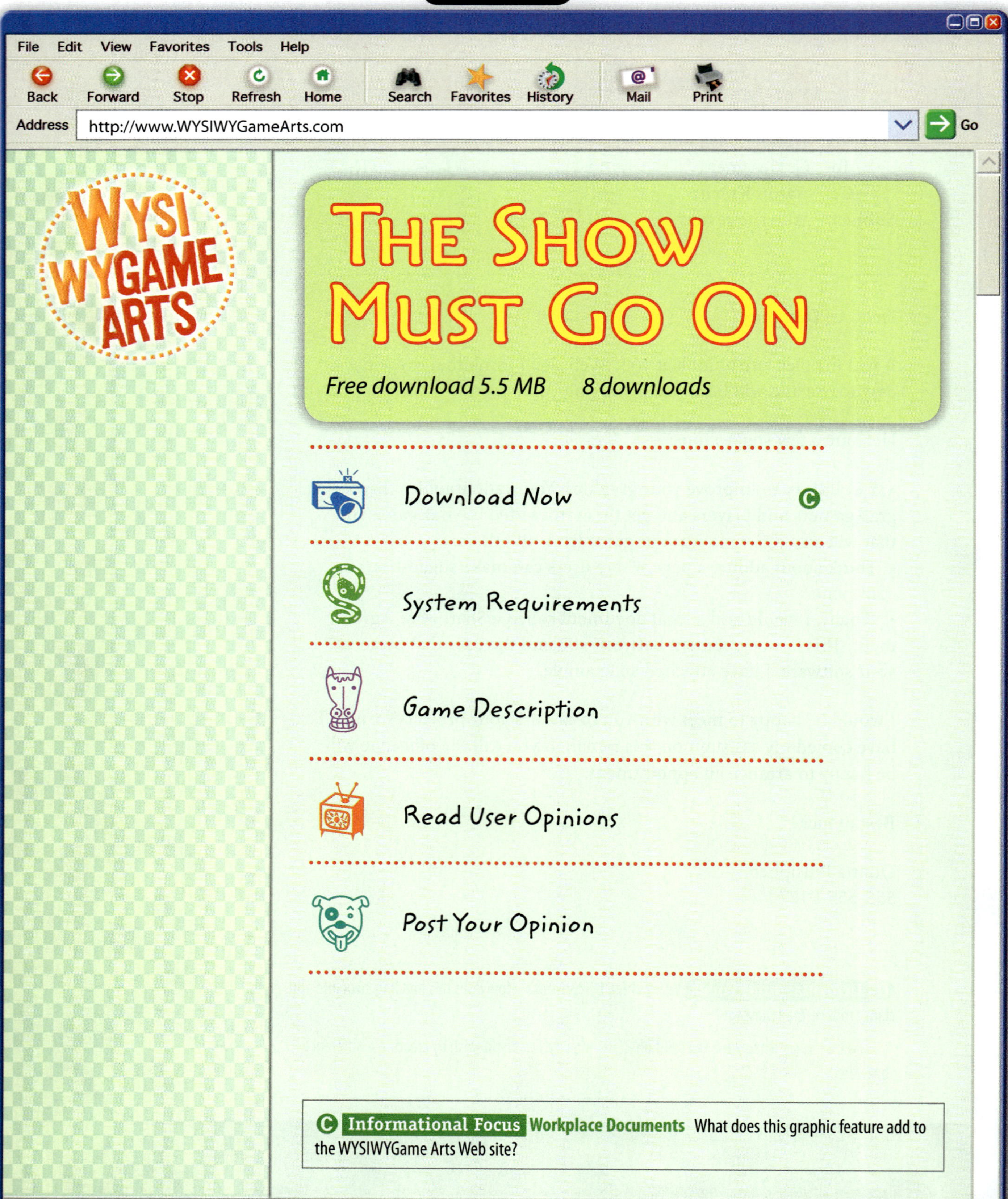

C **Informational Focus** **Workplace Documents** What does this graphic feature add to the WYSIWYGame Arts Web site?

Game Description

You, Candy Rapper, are trying to get to the stadium to sing at the big benefit concert to aid the farmworkers. En route, though, you are stopped by different characters—Terry Techno and Coyote Cowboy, for example—who demand that you play them *their* songs before they let you pass. With a quick check of the playlist, you dial up a song on your boombox. If you play the right song, you gain points and move on toward the stadium. If not, you lose points and have to stay until you find the right song. Can you make it to the stadium in time? If you do, you perform to a standing ovation accompanied by a fireworks display. D

Would you recommend this game?

 YES  NO  Post My Opinion

Game Facts

Version 1.0

Ages: 10–16

Date added: April 6, 2009

File size: 5.5 MB

Approximate download time: 13 min. at 56 kbps

Downloads: 8

Opinions (5): 80% YES; 20% NO

Licensee: Shareware

 Download Now

Read with a Purpose What did you learn about posting a game to a Web site?

D **Reading Focus** **Adjusting Reading Rate** The game description will help you decide if you want to play this game. What reading rate would you use to read the description?

Vocabulary **en route** (ahn ROOT) *adv.:* along the way.

Internet

File Edit View Favorites Tools Help

Back Forward Stop Refresh Home Search Favorites History Mail Print

Address http://www.WYSIWYGameArts.com Go

Shareware Agreement

This is a legal agreement between you, the end user, and WYSIWYGame Arts, the proprietor. By using the WYSIWYGame Arts software [hereafter called the SOFTWARE], you indicate your acceptance of these terms.

1. **GRANT OF LICENSE** WYSIWYGame Arts grants you the right to use the SOFTWARE on a single computer. The SOFTWARE is considered in use on a computer when it is loaded into RAM or installed in permanent memory.

2. **PROPRIETARY RIGHTS** The SOFTWARE is owned exclusively by WYSIWYGame Arts. This license does not transfer any ownership rights of the SOFTWARE to you.

3. **RESTRICTIONS** You may not translate, reverse program, decompile, disassemble, or otherwise reverse engineer the SOFTWARE.

4. **NO WARRANTY** This SOFTWARE is licensed to you "as is" and without any warranty of any kind, expressed or implied, including but not limited to warranties of merchantability and fitness for a particular purpose.

5. **LIMITATIONS OF LIABILITY** In no event shall WYSIWYGame Arts' liability related to any of the SOFTWARE exceed the license fees, if any, actually paid by you for the SOFTWARE. WYSIWYGame Arts shall not be liable for any damage whatsoever arising out of, or related to, the use or inability to use the SOFTWARE, including but not limited to direct, indirect, special, incidental, or consequential damages. E

E **Informational Focus** **Workplace Documents** In a step-by-step sequence, the steps have to be followed in order. In a point-by-point sequence, the points can be taken in any order. Which sequence is followed in this contract?

Internet

Applying Your Skills

9.R.3.A.1 Explain, analyze and evaluate the author's use of text features to clarify meaning **9.R.1.G.1.a** During reading, utilize strategies: to determine meaning of unknown words

Business Letter / E-mail Message / Web Site / Contract

Practicing the Standards

Informational Text and Vocabulary

1. On the WYSIWYGame Arts Web site, the name of the computer game is displayed —

A in a long paragraph
B next to the company logo
C under the "Download Now" icon
D next to the "Read User Opinions" icon

2. A repeated **graphic** icon on the Web site draws the reader's attention to —

A the download icon
B the search icon
C the company logo
D the game's name

3. The Web site uses the structural element of a list to —

A describe the game
B repeat the company name
C provide game facts
D identify internal links

4. The Web site uses all of the following elements of **structure** and **format** *except* —

A bold and colored print
B graphics and bullets
C step-by-step sequence
D text placed in sections

5. When you *differentiate* ideas, you —

A show how they are the same
B point out their differences
C disagree with their theses
D come up with additional ones

6. A *diligent* student is —

A hardworking
B duty bound
C direct
D respectful

7. Something discovered *en route* is found —

A under a tree
B on a highway
C faraway
D along the way

Writing Focus — Constructed Response

Choose three structural, formatting, or graphic features of the WYSIWYGame Arts Web site, and describe how each contributes to the designer's purpose in creating the site.

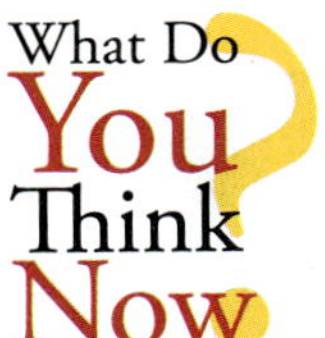

How did the appearance—the structure and format—of these documents affect your ability to use or understand them?

INFORMATIONAL TEXT FOCUS

Evaluating the Logic of Functional Documents

CONTENTS

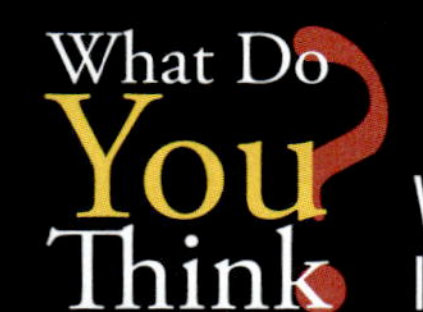

Why is it important to be logical in your writing?

QuickTalk

With a group of classmates, brainstorm examples of rules or situations that made no sense or were confusing or even contradictory. Compare your reactions to those situations.

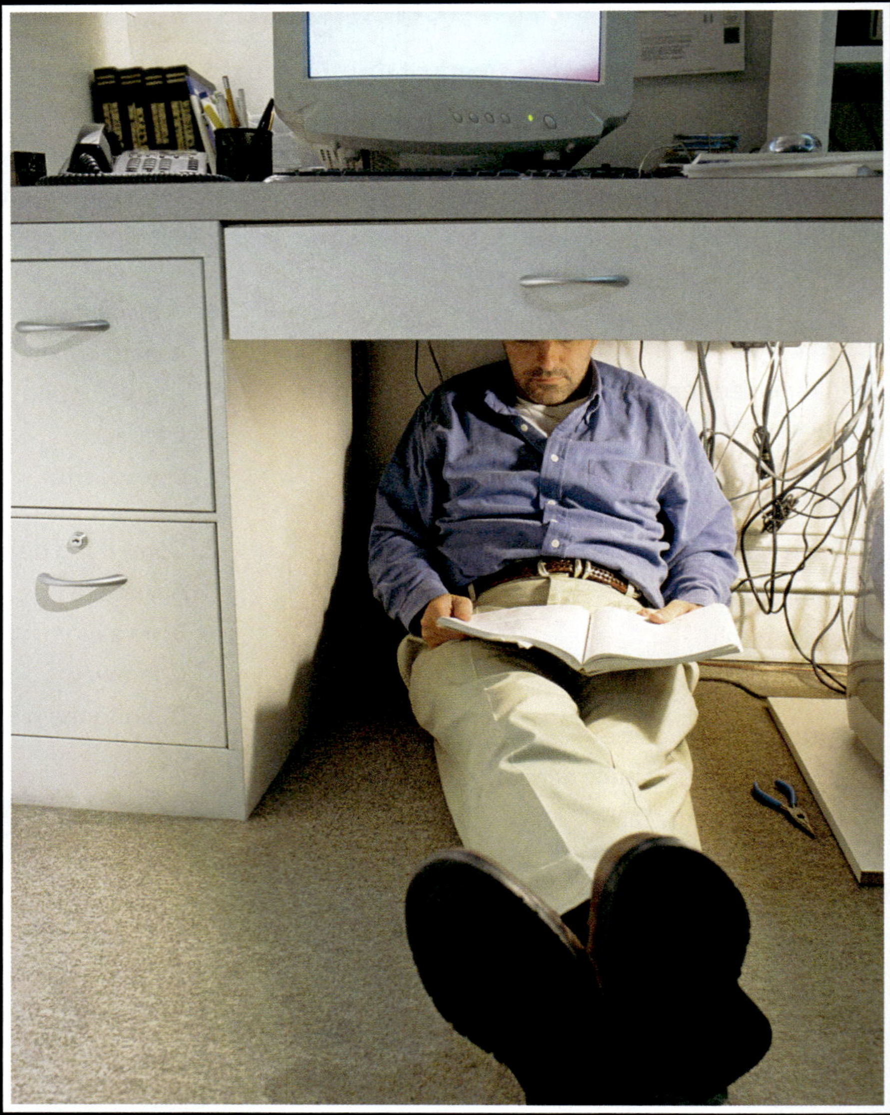

FUNCTIONAL DOCUMENTS

Preparing to Read

MO **9.R.3.A.1** Explain, analyze and evaluate the author's use of text features to clarify meaning **9.R.1.G.1.c** During reading, utilize strategies: to question the text

What Is Wrong with This Document? / WYSIWYGame Arts: The Show Must Go On

Informational Text Focus

Evaluating the Logic of Functional Documents Functional documents have to make sense. When they are clear and logical, they help people get things done. By contrast, documents that are illogically sequenced or are missing steps are useless. In writing or evaluating functional documents, remember that **logical sequencing** requires that

- all the steps be there
- the steps appear in the correct order

Reading Focus

Asking Questions It is a good idea to **ask questions** of any text you are reading, but especially when evaluating the logic of informational text. Here are some of the types of questions you might ask:

- Does this information agree with what I already know about the topic?
- What seems to be missing in this text?
- Is all the information in the correct sequence?

Into Action Use a chart like the one below to keep track of your questions and their answers.

Document	My Questions	My Answers
Instruction manual	Are these steps in the right order?	
Technical directions		

Writing Focus

Preparing for **Constructed Response**

You will soon be reading some technical directions. In your *Reader/Writer Notebook,* note what is logical or illogical about the document.

Reader/Writer **Notebook**

Use your **RWN** to complete the activities for these selections.

Vocabulary

"What Is Wrong with This Document?"

critical (KRIHT uh kuhl) *adj.:* essential; important. *Directions are hard to follow if a critical piece of information is left out.*

flawlessly (FLAW lihs lee) *adv.:* without error; perfectly. *She flawlessly followed the directions for installing the software.*

WYSIWYGame Arts

decompression (dee kuhm PREHSH uhn) *n.* used as *adj.:* here, having the ability to expand a compressed file. *You can use decompression software to restore your compressed files and play your game.*

Language Coach

Affixes Do you recognize a familiar word in the middle of *decompression?* The word *press* is surrounded by **affixes**—two prefixes and a suffix. Adding *com–* changes the word's meaning to "press together." Adding *–sion* changes the meaning to "act of pressing together." And adding *de–* changes the meaning to "undo the act of pressing together."

What other word in the Vocabulary list has a familiar word inside it? How do the affixes change the meaning of that familiar word?

Learn It Online

There's more to words than just definitions. Get the whole story on:

go.hrw.com L9-1213 

MAGAZINE ARTICLE

What Is Wrong with This Document?

by Juan T. Presso

Read with a Purpose Read these selections to evaluate the logic of informational documents.

When you are downloading a software game, putting together your young cousin's new swing set, or following the prompts on the ATM or voice-mail system, you are using functional documents. "Wait a minute!" you are probably saying. "Aren't documents pieces of paper? Can on-screen or voice prompts be considered documents?" Yes, they can, if you remember this: Someone wrote the words and decided on the sequence of the procedure that you see on the ATM screen or hear when you reach a voice-mail system.

When functional documents are well written, they are easy to follow. When they are not well written, they can cause serious misunderstanding. When a functional document is poorly written, chances are that either a critical piece of the information you need has been left out or the information is not presented in a logical, step-by-step sequence. Either way, you end up scratching your head and thinking, "Huh?" A

Missing a Step

Let's say, for example, that you are installing memory chips in a laptop computer that has been

A **Informational Focus** **Evaluating Logic** What happens when documents are poorly written?

Vocabulary **critical** (KRIHT uh kuhl) *adj.:* essential; important.

designed to let you do this. The first step tells you, in big block letters, to unplug the computer and remove the battery. You follow each of the next twenty steps flawlessly. The illustrations actually match what you see, and you are confident that you have done everything correctly. The last step tells you to turn the computer on. You take a deep breath, press the On switch, and . . . nothing. No lights, no whirring, no little *chucka-chucka-chucka* sounds. Finally, you think, "Duh. Plug it in."

We've all been there. The instructions omitted that vital step. As obvious as the step may have seemed to the person who wrote the document, it is still necessary to tell you when it's safe to plug the computer back in, especially after you've been instructed to unplug it. Such a failure in logic creates confusion, and creating confusion is not what a functional document should do.

A Step Out of Order

Let's take a look at a page from an instruction manual to see what happens when a step is not in the correct sequence.

Did you notice that step 7 is clearly out of order? If you were trying to follow these directions, you'd have to decide whether it should go after step 3, 4, or 5. Logic will tell you that it should go after step 3, since you will need a connection to the wireless system in order to turn it on. But wouldn't it have been nice if the instructions had told you that?

Installing Your Wireless Access

1. Your new wireless system will use your existing cable-modem service to access the Internet. Test to see whether the cable connection is working by going to your home page in the usual way. If the connection is working, go on to steps 2–7.
2. Shut down your computer.
3. Unplug the cable modem from your computer.
4. Turn the wireless system on. **B**
5. Restart your computer.
6. Check to see that the wireless system has taken you back to your home page.
7. Plug the cable modem you unplugged from your computer into the wireless system.

B **Reading Focus** **Asking Questions** What question might you ask here?

Vocabulary **flawlessly** (FLAW lihs lee) *adv.:* without error; perfectly.

Build Background

G. Designer wants the instructions on how to download software from the WYSIWYGame Arts Web site to be easy and clear for readers to follow. Below are the instructions provided by the technical support crew at WYSIWYGame Arts. Critique the logic and clarity of their instructions.

The Show Must Go On

FIVE EASY STEPS TO DOWNLOADING SOFTWARE

1. Click on Download Now.
2. Decompress your download on a PC.
3. Install the game software on the hard drive of your PC.
4. Clean up your desktop directory.
5. Download decompression software.

STEP 1 . . .
Click on Download Now 

a. The download window will appear.
b. Click on OK for the download to begin.
c. Your browser will automatically download the file to the folder you have specified.

STEP 2 . . .
Decompress Your Download on a PC

NOTE: This game has been compressed for faster file downloading. PC files will download in .zip format.

a. Double-click on the game icon with the .zip extension. Your decompression software will automatically load.
b. Click on Extract.
c. Select the destination folder, and click on Extract again. The file will appear in that folder.

STEP 3 . . .
Install the Game Software on the Hard Drive of Your PC

a. Click on Install on the button bar, or click on Next as prompted.
b. Follow the prompts.

STEP 4 . . .
Clean up Your Desktop Directory

Delete the compressed file ending in .zip, and empty the trash or recycle bin. Once the game software has been installed, you will no longer need this file.

STEP 5 . . .
Download Decompression Software

Click here for .zip, .arc, .arj, .gz, and .z files.

Files that end in .exe or .sea do not need compression software. 

Read with a Purpose Which set of directions, the instruction-manual page within the magazine article or the technical directions, was clearer? Was either set of directions error-free? Explain.

Ⓐ **Reading Focus** **Asking Questions** What questions might you ask here?

Ⓑ **Informational Focus** **Evaluating Logic** Are steps 4 and 5 logical? Why or why not?

Vocabulary **decompression** (dee kuhm PREHSH uhn) *n.* used as *adj.:* here, having the ability to expand a compressed file.

FUNCTIONAL DOCUMENTS

Applying Your Skills

MO **9.R.3.A.1** Explain, analyze and evaluate the author's use of text features to clarify meaning **9.R.1.G.1.a** During reading, utilize strategies: to determine meaning of unknown words

What Is Wrong with This Document? / WYSIWYGame Arts

Practicing the Standards

Informational Text and Vocabulary

1. In the WYSIWYGame Arts technical directions, which step is out of sequence?

A Step 1
B Step 2
C Step 3
D Step 5

2. Where *should* the step that is out of sequence be placed?

A After step 1
B After step 2
C After step 3
D After step 4

3. The *most* logical order for giving instructions in any functional document is —

A alphabetical order
B order of importance
C step-by-step order
D spatial order

4. Step 2 will probably leave an inexperienced computer user *most* uncertain about which question?

A I'm supposed to double-click on *what*?
B *What* do I have to do to make the decompression software load?
C *How* do I select a destination folder (and what is it)?
D *Why* exactly did I think I wanted this computer game anyway?

5. A dance move performed *flawlessly* is done —

A awkwardly
B gracefully
C perfectly
D pointlessly

6. When software undergoes *decompression*, it —

A expands to normal size
B is compressed inward
C changes its shape
D becomes much smaller

7. A *critical* piece of information is —

A judgmental
B mean
C useless
D essential

Writing Focus Constructed Response

Write a brief evaluation of the WYSIWYGame Arts technical directions. Are the steps in a logical order? Is the information clear and easily understood? What possible misunderstandings could occur? How could misunderstandings be prevented? Write your suggestions for changes.

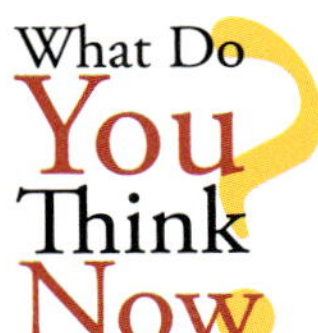

What have these documents shown you about the importance of logic in our everyday lives?

Informational Skills Review

Documents for Life **Directions:** Read the following selection. Then, read and respond to the questions that follow. Questions 6–18 are general questions about functional documents.

Employee Manual
Using the Office Defibrillator

Basic Information

Defibrillators are devices that treat irregular heart rhythms with electrical shock. The first successful use of a modern defibrillator was in 1947, when Dr. Claude Beck used an electrical shock device he designed to revive a dying heart patient in an operating room. Since then, defibrillators have been improved on and produce everyday miracles.

A defibrillator consists of a generator, leads, and electrodes. The generator provides power and houses the controls. It is a small computer that runs on a battery and generates a pulse. The electrodes are used to deliver a correcting electrical shock through the skin to the patient's heart. The device can assess a patient's needs and respond in kind. When the electrodes are placed on the patient, the computer that controls the device reads the heart rhythm and determines its type. The device then provides a personalized level of power and shock. If no need is detected, the device will not allow shock to be administered.

Emergency Model

Emergency defibrillators, such as the one in our office, are portable and can often be found hanging on the walls of public places. Ours hangs to the right of the door inside our cafeteria.

Some devices have metal paddles with insulated handles. Ours has adhesive electrodes. They are a bit slower to use but minimize steps and reduce the risk of shock to the operator, because the operator can stand several feet away. To make certain that no one else receives a shock, operators must make certain that no one is touching the patient when the shock is delivered.

Placing the Electrodes

The proper placement of the electrodes is important. This is the one element the device cannot control itself, and it is critical to an effective rescue.

For long-term assessment and treatment:

1. One electrode is placed over the lower part of the chest, in front of the heart, at the patient's left side.
2. The second electrode is placed on the patient's back, behind the heart and between the scapula (the two flat, triangular bones in the back of the shoulders).

When the first method is inconvenient:

1. One electrode is placed at the patient's right, below the clavicle (collarbone).
2. The second electrode is placed at the patient's left, below and left of the pectoral muscle (large chest muscle).

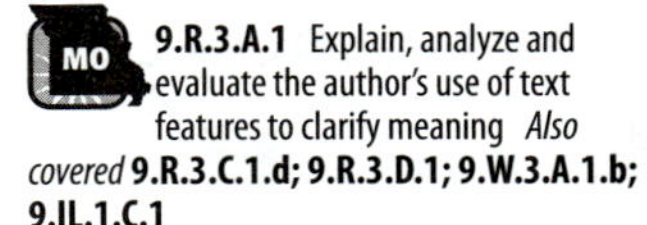

9.R.3.A.1 Explain, analyze and evaluate the author's use of text features to clarify meaning *Also covered* **9.R.3.C.1.d; 9.R.3.D.1; 9.W.3.A.1.b; 9.IL.1.C.1**

1. The **purpose** of this document is to —

A explain business practices
B provide technical directions
C describe office equipment
D detail a public policy issue

9.R.3.C.1.d

2. The **text features** in the document include —

A key words in boldface
B boldface headers
C graphic illustrations
D bulleted lists

9.R.3.A.1

3. The directions for placing the electrodes are —

A given at the beginning of the document
B shown in numbered lists
C called out with boldface type
D shown in reverse order

9.R.3.A.1

4. The directions for placing the electrodes could be made clearer by —

A numbering the steps
B reordering the steps
C adding extra steps
D including illustrations

9.R.3.A.1

5. If you needed to use the defibrillator right away, which of the following would you do?

A Take notes in the margins
B Scan the document for directions
C Ask question to critique the text
D Slowly read the defibrillator's history

9.R.3.D.1

6. Which **consumer document** is *most* likely to help you if you have trouble figuring out how to operate a device?

A A contract
B An instruction manual
C A warranty
D Product information

9.R.3

7. The purpose of a **limited warranty** is to provide —

A some protection if a product is defective
B a lifetime provision for repair of a product
C directions for operating a product
D a lifetime guarantee of a product

9.R.3

8. For most product **warranties** to be effective, the manufacturer usually requires that the purchaser —

A mail a registration card to the manufacturer
B pay full price, not a reduced price, for the product
C wait at least thirty days before requesting repairs
D sign a legal contract with the manufacturer

9.R.3

9. Which of these **consumer documents** would *most* likely tell you how many phone numbers you can store in a cell phone's memory?

A A warranty
B Product information
C Safety information
D A contract

9.R.3

Informational Skills Review CONTINUED

10. A **shareware agreement** is a type of —

A software program
B contract
C warranty
D Web browser

9.R.3

11. A ***Works Cited*** list is different from a **parenthetical citation** because it lists —

A the Internet sources consulted
B all the sources cited in the paper
C the most important sources consulted
D sources in logical order

9.IL.1.C.1

12. In preparing a ***Works Cited*** list, you should —

A divide a URL only after a period
B divide a URL only after a slash
C divide a URL anywhere in the address as long as you use a hyphen
D not divide a URL at all

9.IL.1.C.1

13. According to MLA style, what is the correct way to cite a URL?

A Within parentheses
B Within slash marks
C Within angled brackets
D Within dashes

9.IL.1.C.1

14. Which of the following is *not* an example of a **public document**?

A A coupon for a haircut
B A police brochure about avoiding theft
C A government memo about flu shots
D A train schedule for the summer

9.R.3

15. A set of **technical directions** is badly flawed if it —

A omits a step
B puts a step in the wrong order
C does either of the above
D does none of the above

9.R.3.D.1

16. The **purpose** of a workplace document is to —

A eliminate some jobs
B increase paperwork
C make a task easier
D decrease unemployment

9.R.3

17. An **employee manual** will tell you —

A how to find a new job
B how to get along with others
C about federal employment policies
D about workplace rules and policies

9.R.3

Constructed Response

18. Think about a product you've used recently, and write a **business letter** to the manufacturer that states and explains your praises or complaints. Be sure to include all six parts of the business-letter format.

9.W.3.A.1.b

FOCUS ON MISSOURI COURSE LEVEL EXPECTATIONS

Vocabulary Skills Review

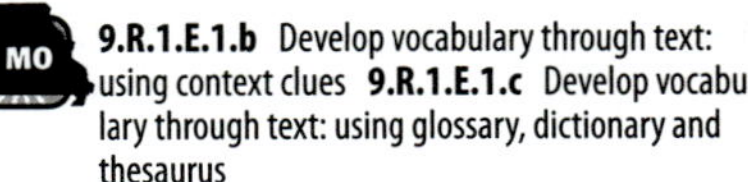

9.R.1.E.1.b Develop vocabulary through text: using context clues **9.R.1.E.1.c** Develop vocabulary through text: using glossary, dictionary and thesaurus

Context Clues

Directions: For questions 1–6, use the context clues in the sentences to help you identify the meaning of the italicized Vocabulary words. For questions 7–8, choose the correct definition for each italicized Academic Vocabulary word.

1. It is easier to *scan* color photos with this new hardware. In this sentence, to *scan* is to —

A copy into a computer file
B edit in a computer program
C paste into a different file
D delete from a computer

9.R.1.E.1.b

2. When you choose your character in the game, you have several *options*. In this sentence, *options* are —

A games
B places
C choices
D openings

9.R.1.E.1.b

3. The Internet is an *expansive* source of good information. In this sentence, *expansive* means —

A unreliable
B complicated
C broad
D reluctant

9.R.1.E.1.b

4. To find the latest information, it is more *expedient* to look online. In this sentence, *expedient* means —

A useful
B extreme
C up-to-date
D reliable

9.R.1.E.1.b

5. I am a *diligent* student, and I plan to go to college. In this sentence, *diligent* means —

A graduating
B straight-A
C hardworking
D intelligent

9.R.1.E.1.b

6. Using attractive graphics will *differentiate* your computer game from all the others. In this sentence, *differentiate* means —

A distinguish
B discover
C display
D designate

9.R.1.E.1.b

Academic Vocabulary

7. What are the *consequences* of arriving late to school?

A Merits or benefits
B Punishments
C Effects; results
D Aspects

9.R.1.E.1.b

8. The advertisement does not *specify* the product's ingredients.

A Clearly state
B List
C Emphasize
D Criticize

9.R.1.E.1.b

Read On

WEB SITE

National Safety Council

To "educate and influence people to prevent accidental injury and death," is the goal of the National Safety Council. Its Web site contains hundreds of tips on how to make home, driving, and work safer. From "22 Safety Items No Home Should Be Without" to defensive driving for teens to the unsafe decibel level of pig squeals (85–115), it's hard to find a safety category not covered. Because more than 100,000 deaths occur from accidents each year in the United States, www.nsc.org is a Web site that everyone should visit.

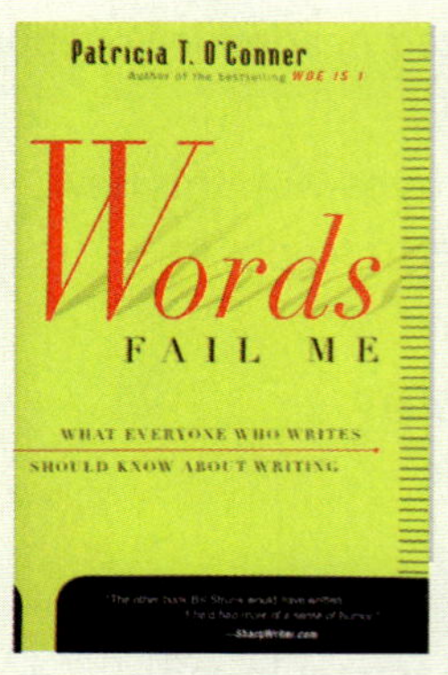

NONFICTION

Words Fail Me

If you think books on writing and grammar are boring, think again. In *Words Fail Me*, Patricia T. O'Conner takes a comedic approach to writing. O'Conner covers all the basic rules of writing while still managing to make her reader laugh. In short, snappy chapters, she covers topics such as "Pronoun Pileups," "Verbs That Zing," and "What to Do When You're Stuck." Next time you're having trouble with a report or a letter, page through this book and you'll find that it isn't your average writing book.

WEB SITE

Ben's Guide

This is Ben, as in Benjamin Franklin: Founder, inventor, and kite flyer. His Web site is devoted to giving you numerous facts and figures about state and federal government. Here you can learn how to write members of Congress from your state and discover state mottoes, songs, birds, and flowers. You can investigate important historical documents such as the Federalist Papers and the U.S. Constitution. Learn how laws are made and what career opportunities there are in the government. The site even includes games and activities. For all this and more, go to http://bensguide.gpo.gov.

WEB SITE

Youth@Work

Suppose you've gotten a summer job, but now you think you are a victim of discrimination by your boss or a co-worker. Go to Youth@Work, a Web site run by the Equal Employment Opportunity Commission, a federal agency whose goal is to eliminate discrimination from the workplace. This Web site explains that, as an employee, you have the right to work free of discrimination and harassment. It tells you how to file a complaint without fear of punishment. It includes real cases, such as one about a store that refused to hire two young men because they were hearing impaired. For more, visit http://youth.eeoc.gov.

WEB SITE

Consumer Action

This very useful government Web site contains information on such topics as locating your local Better Business Bureau, buying a home, understanding credit, getting a mortgage, and protecting your identity from theft. It has brief articles on consumer news from the Federal Drug Administration and on the Internal Revenue Service. It tells you how to stop junk mail and how to write a complaint letter (complete with sample). You can even order a free copy of the *Consumer Action Handbook* to have this information available for easy reference. Visit http://www.consumeraction.gov.

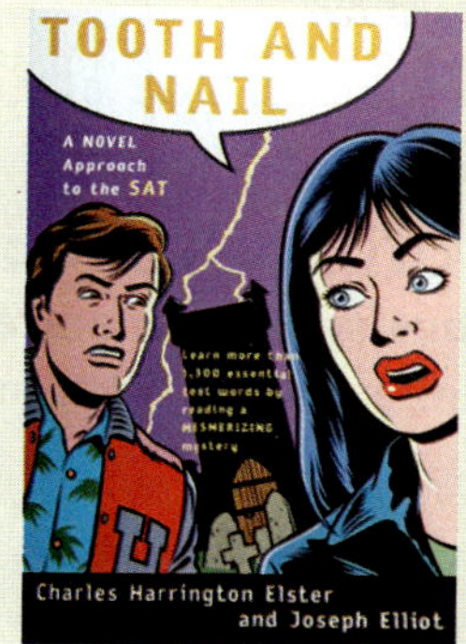

FICTION

Tooth and Nail

Like mystery novels? Need to begin studying for the Student Aptitude Test (SAT)? You can do both at the same time by reading *Tooth and Nail* by Charles Harrington Elster and Joseph Elliot. This book is a lively mystery novel that contains more than 1,200 highlighted SAT vocabulary words. Not only will you enjoy a great story, but you'll also prepare yourself for college.

WEB SITE

United States Government Web Portal

At http://www.usa.gov, you'll find links to Web sites under such headings as "Science and Technology" or "Travel and Recreation." For example, under the heading "Reference and General Government," you can access sites dealing with libraries (including lists of all of the books in the Library of Congress), data and statistics (download the federal budget, and see where our tax dollars go), and government news (such as where to find the cheapest gasoline).

WEB SITE

Consumer Reports

Consumer Reports is a monthly magazine that reviews thousands of products and rates them from "excellent" to "poor." The annual issue that rates cars from best to worst is a major event. The magazine will even give you advice on how to negotiate for the best deal when buying a new or used car. The magazine and Web site (http://www.consumerreports.org) also review appliances such as refrigerators and vacuum cleaners, computers, and electronics such as cell phones and TVs.

Writing Workshop

Business Communications

Write with a Purpose

Write a variety of business communications to an **audience** that is comprised of a company, individual, group, or organization with whom you have a specific reason for communicating. Your **purpose** is to provide accurate information necessary for accomplishing your goals.

Think as a Reader/Writer

Knowing how to write a variety of **business communications** is an important skill. Here are a sample business letter using block format and minutes for a related meeting:

5271 Lodgepole Drive
Alpine, AL 35014
March 18, 2009

← Sender's address
← Date

Rosa Gonzales, Town Council Member
3434 Tenth Street
Alpine, AL 35014

← Recipient's address

Dear Ms. Gonzales:

← Salutation

I am writing to you to ask the city to keep the high school's field open after school hours. There are few places to play sports in town. Teenagers like me need a place to exercise. Please consider my request at the next City Council meeting.

← Body includes purpose and supporting details

Sincerely,
Jeffrey Peyton
Jeffrey Peyton

← Closing signature

Alpine Town Council Meeting, May 5, 2009

← Heading

Present: Tim Jones, Marisol Ortega, Phoebe White, Anton Moore, Rosa Gonzales

← List of Attendees

Call to order: Tim Jones, President of the Town Council, called the meeting to order at 7:00 P.M.

← Starting time of meeting

Business conducted: Rosa Gonzales made a motion to keep the high school field open after school hours. The motion passed unanimously. Anton Moore suggested placing new traffic lights at major intersections on Main Street. Council agreed to study matter further.

← Report of business conducted

A Good Business Communication

- follows the specified format
- is purposeful, clear, and brief
- uses a respectful and formal tone
- provides all necessary information
- is grammatically correct and free of errors

Reader/Writer Notebook

Use your **RWN** to complete the activities for this workshop.

Think About the Models

What is the goal of each communication? How does each achieve its goal?

MO 9.W.2.E.1.c In written text apply: standard usage 9.W.2.D.1.a Compose text using: precise and vivid language 9.W.1.A.1.c Follow a writing process to: revise in response to feedback 9.W.3.A.1.b Compose a variety of texts: in various formats, including workplace communication

Prewriting

Gather Ideas for a Business Communication

Business Letter There are many reasons to write a business letter—even if you are not in business. The Idea Starters show some reasons. Once you have decided to whom you are writing, do your research. You might need to find out how a company handles complaints or get some facts about the person to whom you are writing. Make a chart like the one below, and answer these questions:

Knowledge What do I need to know about the person or company to which I am writing?	I know that . . .
Purpose What is my purpose for writing the letter? What do I hope to achieve?	I am writing this letter because . . .
Details What information should I include to help me achieve my purpose?	I will include . . .

Meeting Notes Find a meeting you can attend. Consider groups in your community, as well as local councils and school boards. Contact organizers to find out where and when the meeting will happen. Prepare a chart to help you to be ready to take notes, also known as meeting minutes. Adapt the basic model below as needed.

Name of Organization	
Date of Meeting	
People Attending	
Call to Order	
Business Conducted	

Think About Purpose and Audience

Before you draft any kind of business communication, think about your purpose and audience. You should know as much information as you can about your **audience,** including facts about a business or group so that you can focus your communication. Your **purpose** is to convey or solicit information that you need to fulfill your goals.

Idea Starters

Here are some situations that might prompt a business communication:

- Write a business to praise or complain about a service or product.
- Write a company to inquire about a job or internship.
- Write a school about a scholarship or loan.
- Write an organization about becoming a member.
- Write an author, business leader, or government official requesting an interview.
- Take minutes at a meeting of your club, school organization, or another group to which you belong.

Your Turn

Create Planning Charts Choose a topic for your business letter, and **gather ideas** in a chart like the one on this page. Then, find a meeting to attend and **prepare a note-taking chart** so you will be ready during the meeting.

Learn It Online
Use the interactive graphic organizer to help gather and formulate your ideas:

go.hrw.com L9-1225 

Business Communications

Writer's Tips

Here are a few things to keep in mind when you are writing a business letter:

- Use a formal form of address.
- Follow the salutation with a colon (:).
- If you do not know the name of the person to whom you are writing, use "To Whom It May Concern" followed by a colon.
- Use a standard closing, such as "Sincerely," followed by a comma.
- Leave spaces so that there is room to sign your name.
- Underneath, type your full name.

Your Turn

Organize and Format Business Communications Each type of business communication has a purpose and a format. Gather information for a business letter. Also gather information for meeting notes.

Planning a Business Letter Use the following format to help you decide how to organize the information in your business letter.

Introduction: State your purpose (why you are writing the letter).

Body: Give information relevant to your goal, including questions and information about your background.

Conclusion: Express appreciation to the recipient in advance for taking the time to deal with your request.

Follow the Proper Format

Remember that the body is just one part of a business letter. To make a good impression, you will need to use the **proper format** and conventional **style** for a business letter. A business letter has six parts:

1. **heading,** or sender's address, and the **date,** with month spelled out
2. **inside address,** or recipient's address
3. **salutation,** followed by a colon. Be sure to use a formal form of address, such as "Dear Sir" or "Dear Ms. Gonzales." If you do not know the name of the person to whom you are writing, use "To Whom It May Concern."
4. **body** of the letter
5. **closing,** such as "Sincerely," followed by comma
6. **signature,** hand written: Leave spaces so there is room to sign your name and also to type your name out.

If you use **block-style format,** have all six parts of the letter align at the left margin. See the model on page 1224 for an example of the block-style format. If you use a **modified-block-style format,** indent the heading, closing, and signature. The letter on page 1229 uses the modified-block style.

Taking Meeting Notes

Be prepared to listen well when you attend a meeting for the purpose of taking notes. You may even ask if you may use a recording device during the meeting so you can listen to the meeting discussion again. As you take notes about the business conducted, pay attention to the following points:

- What is the focus of the discussion? What issues or points do the meeting participants discuss at length? These are probably the most important points to include in your notes.
- What is the final decision or outcome concerning the issues discussed during the meeting?
- What are the next steps agreed upon by the meeting participants?

Drafting

Draft Your Business Letter

As you write, keep in mind the essentials of a good business communication (page 1224), and follow your outline for the body of the letter. Make sure to include all six parts of a business letter, as shown on pages 1224 and 1226.

Draft Minutes of a Meeting

Taking notes of what is said at a meeting may not seem to be a problem because you take notes in classes every day. But minutes, or meeting notes, are different from classroom notes, even though both involve listening carefully and noting important information.

When you are writing the minutes, however, you'll be writing a **formal report** (no slang or informal language) in complete sentences. In your minutes you'll **summarize** in a sentence or two each speaker's main ideas. Also include the outcome of any votes. You'll report information **clearly, briefly,** and **accurately,** covering the complete meetings in **chronological order.** You'll also include certain **formal conventions,** such as the names of those who attended and those who were unable to attend, the person who chaired (ran) the meeting, and the time that the meeting began and ended.

Make sure to include all the elements of good minutes for a meeting, listed in item 2 at right. Then, look at the professional model on page 1224 and the student model on page 1230 to see examples of the correct **format** for presenting the minutes of a meeting.

Maintain Accuracy

When writing any type of business communication, be sure to use abbreviations and acronyms correctly. Maintaining accuracy will make your business letter or meeting notes more credible, or believable.

Grammar Link **Abbreviations and Acronyms**

Use abbreviations and acronyms accurately in formal writing.

- Abbreviations are shortened forms of words. They usually end in a period.
  Mister —> Mr. Avenue —> Ave. Corporation —> Corp.
- Acronyms are words from the initial letters of several words in a name. They are written in capital letters without periods.
  National Aeronautics and Space Administration NASA
- When writing long proper nouns, you may wish to spell out the noun when it first appears and then use its acronym later in the letter or notes.
  Young Writer's Workshop (*first appearance*)
  YWW (later appearances)

Your Turn

Draft Your Business Communication

1. Follow your notes and organization plan to create the draft of your business letter. Keep these questions in mind:

- How can I make my writing appropriate for the person to whom I am writing?
- How can I state my purpose clearly and directly?

2. Take notes at a meeting. Then, draft your minutes. Your meeting notes should follow the order in which things happened at the meeting. Consider these questions:

- What happened first?
- What topics were discussed?
- What was the outcome of the discussion?
- How can I describe what happened for someone who wasn't there?

Peer Review

Working with a partner, review the chart at the right. Ask your classmate to read your letter as if it were addressed to him or her. Discuss whether or not your purpose is clear and if the letter is persuasive.

Then, ask your partner to read your meeting notes and discuss whether or not they are clear and written in an appropriately formal style. Finally, change papers with your partner and repeat the process with his or her business communications.

Evaluating and Revising

Read and evaluate your business letter and minutes at least twice. First, make sure you have covered the essentials of a good business letter and minutes. Then, on your second reading, focus on your **style**—the way you express yourself.

Business Communications: Guidelines for Content and Organization

Evaluation Questions	Tips	Revision Techniques
1. In the letter, is the purpose clearly stated in the introduction?	**Underline** the statement that indicates why you are writing the letter.	**Add** a purpose statement, or **replace** an existing statement with more precise wording.
2. Does the body provide appropriate and relevant information about you and your goals for writing?	**Put brackets** around the body sentences that state information about you and your goals in writing.	**Add** or **replace** information about your background and your goals.
3. Have you written using the appropriate, formal tone? Is the writing courteous, even if you are expressing complaints or reporting conflicts?	**Put a star** next to casual phrasing or slang. **Underline** phrases that sound rude.	**Reword** any informal or rude phrases. **Add** thanks to the recipient for taking time with your written request. (Remember that you are writing in a business environment.)
4. Does your business letter follow proper formatting style?	In the letter, **put a check mark** near your address, the date, the inside address, the salutation, the body of the letter, the closing and your signature.	**Add** any of the parts that are missing.
5. Do your meeting notes accurately convey the content of the meeting?	**Put a check mark** next to the topics discussed, decisions made, and plans for further action. **Put a star** near the meeting name, list of attendees, time the meeting started and ended, and the name of the person taking the minutes.	**Add** information that summarizes topics discussed, decisions made, and plans for next steps.

Read this student draft of a business letter; note the comments on its strengths and suggestions on how it could be improved.

Student Draft

35 Oakdale Rd.
Parma, OH 44131
May 5, 2009

Evan Thomas
Young Writers' Workshop
10902 Payne Avenue
Cleveland, OH 45101

Dear Mr. Thomas:

I love reading and writing poetry. I enjoy writing collaborative poetry with my stepmother, Tamesa Williams. She went to the Young Writers' Workshop when she was younger and told me about it. I would very much like to take part in your poetry workshop.

At school, the best part of the year is when we finally get around to the poetry unit. I would like to get lots better at poetry. The Young Writers' Workshop could be my way to go. At YWW, I could get other students' opinions of all sorts of things. I cannot get that anywhere else.

Thank you for considering me for the poetry workshop. I am looking forward to the chance to join the group at YWW.

Yours truly,

James Kolditz

James Kolditz

← James includes the proper information in the header of his letter, using the **modified-block-style format.**

← In the introduction, he describes his **purpose**—to take part in the Young Writers' Workshop.

← In the body, James explains why he is a good candidate for the workshop.

← Throughout, the letter conveys a respectful **tone** and ends on a cordial note.

MINI-LESSON How to Use Precise Language

When James reviewed his draft, he noticed that some of his language was vague and informal. He took care to revise his words so that they say exactly what he meant to say. He knew that his letter would be much more effective if his language was direct and precise.

James' Revision of Paragraph Two

At school, ~~the best~~ *my favorite* part of the year is ~~when we finally get around to~~ the poetry unit. I would like to ~~get lots better at poetry~~ *improve my poetry skills*. The Young Writers' Workshop could ~~be the way to go~~ *start me down that path*. At YWW, I could get other students' opinions of ~~all sorts of things~~ *my work*. I cannot get that anywhere else.

Your Turn

Review Your Business Letter Read the draft of your business letter, and then ask yourself:

- Have I used precise language to describe what happened?
- Are there vague or unclear sections I can improve?

Business Communications

Now read James's draft of a meeting's minutes, along with comments and suggestions for improvement.

The meeting notes, or minutes, include the correct information about the **date, time,** and **attendees.**

Discussions are described, including the votes taken and their outcome.

The **time** the meeting ended is noted as well as the name of the person writing the minutes.

Student Draft

YWW Planning Committee

Attendees: Evan Thomas, Rachel Ortiz, Ben Lovitz, Aliki Kheelan, James Kolditz

Meeting Date: June 15, 2009

Meeting Called to Order 6:30 P.M. by Aliki Kheelan

Business Conducted:

1. Aliki Kheelan suggested that participants hold a Poetry Reading on Friday, July 11. Ben Lovitz seconded motion. Motion passed.
2. Rachel Ortiz discussed the possibility of theme dinners to inspire writers. Others argued they would be a distraction. No vote was taken.
3. Evan Thomas made a motion that participants be required to keep a journal to be read by staff throughout their stay. Motion did not pass.

Adjournment: Meeting was adjourned at 7:20 P.M. Minutes prepared by James Kolditz.

MINI-LESSON How to Check Formatting of Meeting Minutes

When James reviewed his minutes, he noticed he did not always follow a standard format. He also noticed that he had used boldface type inconsistently. He then made these changes:

- He spelled out the name of the organization in the heading and added the word "Minutes."
- He moved the meeting date to just below the main heading.
- He set the subhead "Attendees" in boldface.
- He put the names of attendees in alphabetical order (except his own, which, as notetaker, should appear last).
- He placed a colon after the subhead "Meeting Called to Order."

Here is James's final version of the heading. Notice how his changes make the information easier to read.

James's Revision

Young Writers' Workshop Planning Committee Minutes

Meeting Date: June 15, 2009

Attendees: Aliki Kheelan, Ben Lovitz, Rachel Ortiz, Evan Thomas, James Kolditz

Meeting Called to Order: 6:30 P.M. by Aliki Kheelan

Your Turn

Check Your Formatting and Organization Review the draft of your minutes and ask yourself:

- Have I followed the standard format correctly?
- Did I follow the chronological order of the discussion without leaving out anything?
- Can I make any formatting choices, such as boldfacing headings, to make the minutes easier to read?

Proofreading and Publishing

Proofreading

Before you mail your business letter or submit your meeting notes, read aloud slowly to locate any errors in grammar, usage, and mechanics. Mistakes like these can keep readers from taking your writing seriously. In business communications it's especially important to use correct grammar.

Grammar Link **Correcting Sentence Fragments**

A **sentence fragment** is a word group that is missing a subject or a verb or that does not express a complete thought. Here are two ways to correct a sentence fragment:

- Add words that will make the thought complete.

  Fragment: Suggested that I join the YWW.
  Sentence: My stepmother suggested that I join the YWW.

- Attach the fragment to a sentence that comes before or after it.

  Fragment: Joining the YWW would improve my poetry. Develop my communication skills, too.
  Sentence: Joining the YWW would improve my poetry and develop my communication skills, too.

Publishing

Consider these strategies to share your completed writing:

- Send your letter to the addressee. Note the response you receive. Did you achieve your purpose?
- Compile a book of your letters with your classmates.
- Copy your minutes, and distribute them to everyone who was at the meeting. Also make copies available to people who are interested in joining the group. Ask for feedback on the accuracy and thoroughness of your notes.

Reflect on Your Business Communications

Think about the processes you used to write the business communications in this Writing Workshop. In your **RWN,** answer the following questions:

1. What strategies helped you find the correct tone for your business letter?
2. How did writing the meeting minutes affect the way you paid attention during a meeting?
3. What did you learn from doing business communications that also applies to other types of writing?

Proofreading Tip

Try this double proofreading strategy: Review your letter and minutes twice.

- First, focus on the sentences. Make sure each one is complete and punctuated correctly.
- Then, focus on the words. Check your spelling and use of abbreviations and acronyms.

Your Turn

Proofread and Publish Proofread your business communications carefully for any errors in grammar, mechanics, and usage. Look carefully for errors in sentence fragments. Errors in business communications can keep you from achieving the purpose of your communication. When you are satisfied that your work is error free, make a final copy of your business communication, and send or give it to the recipient.

Scoring Rubric

Use one of the rubrics below to evaluate your response to the on-demand prompt on the next page. Your teacher will tell you to use either the four- or the six-point rubric.

6-Point Scale

Score 6 *Demonstrates advanced success*
- focuses consistently on a process appropriate to the prompt
- shows effective, step-by-step organization throughout, with smooth transitions
- offers a thoughtful, creative explanation of the process
- explains each step of the assigned process thoroughly, using examples and specific, detailed instructions
- exhibits mature control of written language

Score 5 *Demonstrates proficient success*
- focuses on a process appropriate to the prompt
- shows effective, step-by-step organization, with transitions
- offers a thoughtful explanation of the process
- explains the steps of the process competently, using examples and specific instructions
- exhibits sufficient control of written language

Score 4 *Demonstrates competent success*
- focuses on an appropriate process, with minor distractions
- shows effective, step-by-step organization, with minor lapses
- offers a mostly thoughtful explanation of the process
- explains the process adequately, with a mixture of general and specific instructions
- exhibits general control of written language

Score 3 *Demonstrates limited success*
- includes some loosely related material that distracts from the writer's how-to focus
- shows noticeable gaps in the step-by-step presentation of the process
- offers a routine, predictable explanation of the process
- explains the process with uneven elaboration
- exhibits limited control of written language

Score 2 *Demonstrates basic success*
- includes loosely related material that seriously distracts from the writer's how-to focus
- shows major gaps in the step-by-step presentation of the process
- offers explanation that merely skims the surface
- explains the process with inadequate elaboration
- exhibits significant problems with control of written language

Score 1 *Demonstrates emerging effort*
- shows little awareness of the topic and purpose for writing
- lacks organization
- offers unclear and confusing explanation
- develops the explanation in only a minimal way, if at all
- exhibits major problems with control of written language

4-Point Scale

Score 4 *Demonstrates advanced success*
- focuses consistently on a process appropriate to the prompt
- shows effective, step-by-step organization throughout, with smooth transitions
- offers a thoughtful, creative explanation of the process
- explains each step of the assigned process thoroughly, using examples and specific, detailed instructions
- exhibits mature control of written language

Score 3 *Demonstrates competent success*
- focuses on an appropriate process, with minor distractions
- shows effective, step-by-step organization, with minor lapses
- offers a mostly thoughtful explanation of the process
- explains the process adequately, with a mixture of general and specific instructions
- exhibits general control of written language

Score 2 *Demonstrates limited success*
- includes some loosely related material that distracts from the writer's how-to focus
- shows some organization, with noticeable gaps in the step-by-step presentation of the process
- offers a routine, predictable explanation of the process
- explains the process with uneven elaboration
- exhibits limited control of written language

Score 1 *Demonstrates emerging effort*
- shows little awareness of the topic and purpose for writing
- lacks organization
- offers unclear and confusing explanation
- develops the explanation in only a minimal way, if at all
- exhibits major problems with control of written language

How-to Essay

When responding to a prompt asking you to write a how-to essay, use what you have learned from your own writings and the rubric on page 1232. Use the steps below to guide your response to the following prompt.

Writing Prompt

Documents explaining how to complete a task are useful to a wide audience. In an essay, explain how to conduct research for a research paper or an informative essay.

Study the Prompt

Be sure to read the prompt and identify all parts of the task. Your essay should clearly explain the process of conducting research in a way that any reader can understand. Think about the way you researched your topic in your own research paper or informative essay. Recall the steps you went through during your research. Note that this prompt does not ask you to explain how to write the paper but how to conduct the research. **Tip:** Spend about five minutes studying the prompt.

Plan Your Response

The most important aspect of a how-to essay is its organization. Your instructions should be written in the order that they will be performed. Make sure your instructions are clear and specific by using the following strategies:

- Make a brief outline breaking the process down into individual steps.
- Come up with examples and specific, detailed instructions for each step. Consider creating visuals to illustration steps or key points.

Tip: Spend about ten minutes planning your response.

Respond to the Prompt

Using your outline, draft your how-to essay. Follow these guidelines:

- In the introduction, explain what it is you want your audience to accomplish by reading and following your how-to essay.
- In the body of your essay, organize your information in chronological order. Be sure that each step of your process is clearly explained, using examples and detailed instructions. Use transitions to take the reader smoothly from point to point. Consider using bulleted lists and numbered lists to highlight important steps and ideas.
- Include illustrations or sketches if they help to clarify the process you are explaining.
- Close with a short paragraph that points out the usefulness of your process.

Tip: Spend about twenty minutes writing your draft.

Improve Your Response

Revising Go back to the key aspects of the prompt. Is your essay organized clearly? Have you provided enough specific examples to illustrate your steps? If not, add more details.

Proofreading Take a few minutes to proofread your essay to correct errors in grammar, spelling, punctuation, and capitalization. Make sure all your edits are neat, and erase any stray marks.

Checking Your Final Copy Before you turn your essay in, read it again carefully to catch any errors you may have missed. **Tip:** Save ten minutes to improve your paper.

Listening & Speaking Workshop

Debating an Issue

Speak with a Purpose

With other students, conduct a debate in which two teams present opposite sides of an issue.

Think as a Reader/Writer Debating an issue is part discussion, part persuasive essay. To write a good persuasive essay, you must support your thesis with convincing evidence put forth in a logical argument. Debating an issue draws on similar skills. Instead of supporting a thesis, a debate focuses on a narrow issue, the **proposition.** The proposition is worded as a **resolution,** a positive statement calling for a change.

Even though a **debate** is a balanced argument covering opposing sides of an issue, discussions about controversial topics may break down for several reasons. Perhaps one person is long-winded. Perhaps another gets angry. A debate, however, has rules that keep the discussion from breaking down.

Prepare to Debate: Define the Proposition

Usually a debate's proposition will be chosen for you and will involve a topic with strong arguments on both sides. Here's a sample resolution:

> Resolved: That Johnston High School should turn an existing classroom into a computer lab.

Take Sides

A traditional debate requires a chairperson and two teams of two people each. Debate participants work within the following roles and conditions:

- **Affirmative Team** This side, which speaks first, argues *for* the proposition. Because this team is arguing for a change in the current state of things, it has the **burden of proof.** The team's task is to prove why the change must be made.
- **Negative Team** This side argues that the proposal of the affirmative side should be rejected—that things are fine the way they are.
- **Chairperson** The chairperson directs the debate and ensures that rules and time limits are followed. If a debater thinks an opponent has broken a rule, he or she may appeal to the chairperson.
- **Team Assignments** Participants in a debate are generally assigned to a team, regardless of how each member personally feels about an issue. You might think it's better to argue for the position you support, but sometimes it's easier to argue for the other side because you know the weaknesses in the case. Whichever side of the resolution you are on, you should present arguments that are easy to follow and understand.

Use your **RWN** to complete the activities for this workshop.

9.W.1.A.1.e Follow a writing process to: share writing 9.R.3.C.1.c Use details from informational text: to analyze and evaluate the accuracy and adequacy of evidence 9.W.2.A.1.b Compose text: choosing a form and point of view appropriate to purpose and audience 9.R.1.D.1.a Read grade-level instructional text: with fluency, accuracy, comprehension and appropriate expression

Research the Proposition

To prepare for a debate, you must research the proposition fully. Identify the **key issues**—the main differences between your position and that of the opposing side. Key issues often involve the following questions:

- Does a problem exist? If so, what is causing the problem?
- Will this proposition resolve the problem?

Your research should answer these questions. Use the answers to develop reasons that support your side of the proposition. Reasons, even those that include rhetorical devices, must be supported by evidence, or **proof.**

A Good Debate Team

- analyzes the problem at hand
- researches the proposition thoroughly
- develops sound reasons to back its position
- gathers solid proof, based on specific instances, testimony, facts, and statistics
- tests the evidence to ensure that it is valid, credible, and relevant

Gather Proof

Proof can make or break an argument in a debate. If you have relevant and credible proof, you can make a convincing argument. Here are four of the most common types of proof:

PROOF USED IN DEBATES

Type of Proof	Example
Specific Instances: examples that illustrate a point	Many Johnston High students have so little computer experience that they can't even do basic research tasks using the Internet.
Testimony: comments from someone who has already studied or experienced the problem	According to Philip Martin, a former Johnston student, "I felt ill-prepared when I entered college because my computer skills were so far behind those of my classmates."
Facts: statements that can be proved true	The school board voted not to buy computers for classrooms.
Statistics: facts presented as numerical information	While 976 students are enrolled at Johnston, the current computer lab has space for only 30 students per class period.

Test the Proof

To meet the standard tests for evidence, your proof must be

- **credible,** that is, from a recognized and nonbiased authority on the subject.
- **valid** so that it clearly supports the position it claims to support.
- **relevant,** with a close, logical relationship to the reason it supports.

Tip

As you gather proof, record it on index cards. Then, when you test for evidence you can discard any cards containing invalid information.

Tip

As you find information that could be used against your position, note it on index cards. Then, on those cards, jot down how you might counter such evidence. You can refer to those cards in your debate.

Planning Tips

Plan your rebuttal speeches in advance, before you hear what the other side says about your argument. The time allowed for rebuttal speeches is short, so you must focus only on the opposing team's most important points. Don't try to address every point they have made.

Be sure to take notes on the evidence that might be used against your position as well as evidence that supports your position. If you know what proof the other team might present, you'll be better prepared to respond to their arguments. Once you've researched your topic, organize your evidence into three categories:

- **Constructive arguments,** which support your side
- **Refutations,** which attack the other side
- **Rebuttals,** which reply to challenges to your side

Prepare Debate Speeches

An effective structure for persuasive speeches is the **classical speech** form—a brief and engaging introduction, smooth transitions, a concise body, and a strong conclusion. In a debate, there are two types of speeches you'll need to organize in this manner. The first, **constructive speeches,** are delivered in the first part of a debate. The second, **rebuttal speeches,** are delivered in response to constructive speeches.

- **Affirmative constructive speeches** build the argument in favor of the proposition. A constructive speech for the affirmative side should present two to four reasons in support of the position. Each reason should be supported by strong evidence.
- **Negative constructive speeches** build the argument against the proposition. They should also present two to four reasons, each supported by strong evidence.
- **Rebuttal speeches** respond to the constructive speeches. They have two objectives: refutation and rebuttal. During a **refutation** you attack the other side's argument by questioning the quantity and quality of their evidence and the logic of their reasoning. During a **rebuttal** you rebuild your argument after the other team has attacked it.

Conduct the Debate

Present Yourself

When it's time for you to present your constructive and rebuttal speeches, speak clearly and naturally. Use your **voice, facial expressions,** and **gestures** to make your message expressive. For example, speak at a volume loud enough to be heard and at a rate that is not too fast or too slow. Make eye contact with your audience and with members of the other team, and use hand gestures in a natural way.

Follow Debate Rules

The chairperson conducts the debate. He or she should state the proposition, enforce time limits for speakers, and oversee the rules of **etiquette** (agreed-upon manners).

In traditional debates, each team member gives one constructive and one rebuttal speech. The following table shows a debate structure. Intermission is held between the first and second parts.

TRADITIONAL DEBATE SCHEDULE	
Part I: Constructive Speeches (10 minutes each)	**Part II: Rebuttal Speeches** (5 minutes each)
1st Affirmative Team Speaker	1st Negative Team Speaker
1st Negative Team Speaker	1st Affirmative Team Speaker
2nd Affirmative Team Speaker	2nd Negative Team Speaker
2nd Negative Team Speaker	2nd Affirmative Team Speaker

Judge a Debate

Win or Lose

Unlike a baseball game, debates do not always have clear winners. Normally, to determine a winner, three appointed judges listen to the debate and evaluate how well each speaker met certain standards. If you are judging a debate, it may help to keep in mind the following questions:

Content

- Did the team prove that a significant problem does/does not exist? How thorough was the team's analysis of the problem?
- How did the team convince you that the proposition is/is not the best solution to solving the problem?
- How effectively did the team present reasons and evidence supporting the case? Was the evidence credible, valid, and relevant?
- How well did the team refute and rebut arguments made by the opposing team?

Delivery

- Did the speakers seem confident and well prepared? Explain.
- Did the speakers make eye contact and speak at a good volume and pace? Explain.
- Did the speakers observe proper debate etiquette? Explain.

As you listen to the debaters, try to assess the logic and evidence cited in each argument. Note any vocal emphases and pauses. Such highlighting can signal a rhetorical device or a key point of an argument. Note also the speaker's facial expressions and gestures to get a sense of his or her tone.

Writing Skills Review

Business Letter **Directions:** Read the following business letter. Then, answer the questions on the next page.

Renata Martínez
1612 Finklore Avenue
Los Angeles, CA 98990

September 22, 2009

Sam Miyamoto
Temple Drake Media
Paramount Drive
N. Hollywood, CA 99988

Dear Mr. Miyamoto:

(1) Thank you in advance for your time and attention. (2) I am one of nine students in the Marshall High Audiovisual Lab, an ongoing elective project on video production and editing at our school. (3) We all share an interest in CGI effects and computer graphics.

(4) I am writing in hopes that you would grant us a formal tour of Temple Drake's computer-graphic imagery studio. (5)The opportunity to see your facility and team at work would be awesome.

Sincerely,

Renata Martinez

Renata Martínez

9.W.3.A.1.b Compose a variety of texts: in various formats, including workplace communication *Also covered* 9.W.2.C.1.f; 9.W.2.E.1.c

1. Which of the following is an error that should be corrected in the inside address?

A The name of the company should appear before the addressee's name.

B The street address should be completed to include the numbers for the address.

C The abbreviation CA should be spelled out as *California*.

D The zip code should be deleted since it's only necessary on the envelope.

9.W.3.A.1.b

2. Which of the following revisions would improve the presentation of information in the body of the business letter?

A Switch the order of sentences 1 and 2.

B Move sentence 1 to the end of the first paragraph.

C Revise the salutation to *Dear Sam*.

D Move sentence 1 to the end of the second paragraph.

9.W.3.A.1.b

3. Which of the following edits would improve the **tone** of the letter?

A Replace the words *I am* with the contraction *I'm* in sentences 2 and 4.

B Add the words *some of whom are my friends* after the word *students* in sentence 2.

C Replace the word *awesome* in the sentence 5 with the phrase *very enlightening*.

D Change the closing from *sincerely* to *Talk to you soon*.

9.W.2.C.1.f

4. Which of the following changes should be made to the letter's format?

A Add space between the addressee's name and his business address.

B Delete the sender's name from the sender's address and move up the date to join this address.

C Move the closing signature to the far right of the page.

D Indent the salutation line.

9.W.3.A.1.b

5. Which of the following changes should be made to the letter's format?

A Move the recipient's address, or heading, to the far right of the page.

B Delete the sender's address.

C Delete the two paragraph indents so the letter is in block format.

D Delete the date.

9.W.2.E.1.c

Resource Center

Handbook of Literary Terms

For more information about a topic or to see related entries, turn to the page(s) indicated with each entry. On another line are cross-references to entries in this handbook that provide closely related information. For instance, at the end of *Alliteration* is a cross-reference to *Assonance*.

ALLEGORY **A narrative in which characters and settings stand for abstract ideas or moral qualities.** In addition to the literal meaning of the story, an allegory contains a symbolic, or **allegorical,** meaning. Characters and places in allegories often have names that indicate the abstract ideas they stand for: Justice, Deceit, Vanity. George Orwell's novel *Animal Farm* is a well-known modern allegory.

See pages 320, 373.

ALLITERATION **Repetition of the same or very similar consonant sounds, usually at the beginnings of words that are close together in a poem.** In this example the sound "fl" is repeated in line 1, and the "s" sound is repeated in line 2:

> Open here I flung the shutter, when with many
> a flirt and flutter,
> In there stepped a stately Raven of the
> saintly days of yore.
>
> *from* "The Raven" by
> Edgar Allan Poe

See pages 619, 694.
See also *Assonance*, *Onomatopoeia*, *Rhyme*.

ALLUSION **Reference to a statement, a person, a place, or an event from literature, history, religion, mythology, politics, sports, science, or pop culture.** In calling one of his stories "The Gift of the Magi" (page 363), O. Henry uses an allusion to the wise men from the East called the Magi, who presented the infant Jesus with the first Christmas gifts.

AMBIGUITY **An element of uncertainty in a text, in which something can be interpreted in a number of different ways.** Ambiguity adds a layer of complexity to a story, for it presents us with a variety of possible interpretations, all of which are valid. Edgar Allan Poe's "The Cask of Amontillado" (page 286) is ambiguous because we don't know if we should trust the narrator's claims. **Subtleties,** or fine distinctions in meaning, in a text help create ambiguity. The significance of these subtleties is open to question.

See page 321.

"I think I'll wait for the next elevator."

Drawing by Chas. Addams. ©1988 The New Yorker Magazine, Inc.

ANALOGY **Comparison made between two things to show how they are alike in some respects.** During the Revolutionary War the writer Thomas Paine drew an analogy between a thief breaking into a house and the king of England interfering in the affairs of the American Colonies (*The Crisis*, No. 1). **Similes** are a kind of analogy. However, an analogy usually clarifies something, while a simile shows imaginatively how two different things are alike in some unusual way.

See page 541.

ANECDOTE **Very, very brief story, usually told to make a point.** Historians and other writers of nonfiction often use anecdotes to clarify their texts or to provide human interest.

ASIDE **Words that are spoken by a character in a play to the audience or to another character but that are not supposed to be overheard by the others onstage.** Stage directions usually tell when a speech is an aside. For example, in Shakespeare's *Romeo and Juliet* (page 807), there are two asides in the opening scene. Sampson speaks to Gregory in an aside, and Gregory responds to him in another aside as they pick a fight with the servants of the house of Montague. Sampson and Gregory hear each other's asides, and so do we in the audience, but Montague's servants do not.

See page 752.

ASSONANCE **Repetition of similar vowel sounds that are followed by different consonant sounds, especially in words that are close together in a poem.** The words *base* and *fade* and the words *young* and *love* contain examples of assonance. The lines that follow are especially musical because of assonance:

> Seeing the snowman standing all alone
> In dusk and cold is more than he can bear.
> The small boy weeps to hear the wind prepare
> A night of gnashings and enormous moan.
>
> *from* "Boy at the Window"
> by Richard Wilbur

See pages 619, 694.
See also *Alliteration, Onomatopoeia, Rhyme.*

AUTHOR **The writer of a literary work.**

AUTOBIOGRAPHY **An account of the writer's own life.** An example of a book-length autobiography is *Life on the Mississippi* by Mark Twain (see page 447).

See also *Biography.*

BALLAD Song that tells a story. Folk ballads are composed by unknown singers and are passed on for generations before they are written down. **Literary ballads,** on the other hand, are poems composed by known individuals and are written in imitation of the old folk ballads. "Ballad of Birmingham" by Dudley Randall (page 714) is a modern literary ballad. Ballads usually tell sensational stories of tragedy or adventure. They use simple language and a great deal of repetition and usually have regular rhythm and rhyme schemes, which make them easy to memorize.

See pages 616, 711.

BIOGRAPHY **An account of a person's life, written or told by another person.** A classic American biography is Carl Sandburg's multivolume life of Abraham Lincoln. Today biographies are written about movie stars, TV personalities, politicians, sports figures, self-made millionaires, even underworld figures. Biographies are among the most popular forms of contemporary literature. On page 298 is an excerpt from Kenneth Silverman's biography of Edgar Allan Poe.

See pages 434–435.
See also *Autobiography.*

BLANK VERSE **Poetry written in unrhymed iambic pentameter.** *Blank* means the poetry is not rhymed. *Iambic pentameter* means that each line contains five iambs, or metrical feet that consist of an unstressed syllable followed by a stressed syllable (˘ ʹ). Blank verse is the most important poetic form in English epic and dramatic poetry. It is the major verse form used in Shakespeare's plays.

See pages 802, 855.
See also *Iambic Pentameter, Meter.*

CHARACTER **Person in a story, poem, or play.** Sometimes, as in George Orwell's novel *Animal Farm,* the characters are animals. In myths the characters are divinities or heroes who have superhuman powers, such as Poseidon and Athena and Odysseus in the *Odyssey* (page 1037). Most often a character is an ordinary human being, like Mme. Loisel in Guy de Maupassant's "The Necklace" (page 351).

The process of revealing the personality of a character in a story is called **characterization.** A writer can reveal a character by

1. letting us hear the character speak
2. describing how the character looks and dresses
3. letting us listen to the character's inner thoughts and feelings
4. revealing what other characters in the story think or say about the character
5. showing us what the character does—how he or she acts
6. telling us directly what the character's personality is like: cruel, kind, sneaky, brave, and so on

The first five ways of revealing a character are known as **indirect characterization.** When a writer uses indirect characterization, we have to use our own judgment to decide what a character is like, based on the evidence the writer gives us. But when a writer uses the sixth method, known as **direct characterization,** we don't have to decide for ourselves; we are told directly what the character is like.

Characters can be classified as static or dynamic. A **static character** is one who does not change much in the course of a story. By contrast, a **dynamic character** changes as a result of the story's events.

Characters can also be classified as flat or round. A **flat character** has only one or two traits, and these can be described in a few words. Such a character has no depth, like a piece of cardboard. A **round character,** like a real person, has many different character traits, which sometimes contradict one another.

Static and flat characters often function as **subordinate characters** in a story. This means that they may play important roles in a story, but they are not the main actors in the plot.

The fears or conflicts or needs that drive a character are called **motivation.** A character can be motivated by many factors, such as vengeance, fear, greed, love, even boredom.

See pages 124, 145.

CLIMAX **Moment of great emotional intensity or suspense in a plot.** The major climax in a story or play usually marks the moment when the conflict is decided one way or another.

See pages 4, 804.

COMEDY **In general, a story that ends happily.** The hero or heroine of a comedy is usually an ordinary character who overcomes a series of obstacles that block what he or she wants. Many comedies have a boy-meets-girl plot, in which young lovers must face obstacles to their marrying. At the end of such comedies, the lovers marry, and everyone celebrates, as in Shakespeare's play *A Midsummer Night's Dream*. In structure and characterization, a comedy is the opposite of a **tragedy.**

See pages 755, 774
See also *Comic Relief*, *Drama*, *Tragedy*.

COMIC RELIEF **Comic scene or event that breaks up a serious play or narrative.** Comic relief allows writers to lighten the tone of a work and show the humorous side of a dramatic theme. In Shakespeare's tragedy *Romeo and Juliet* (page 807), the nurse and Mercutio provide comic relief.

CONFLICT **Struggle or clash between opposing characters or opposing forces.** In an **external conflict,** a character struggles against an outside force. This outside force might be another character, or society as a whole, or something in nature. "The Most Dangerous Game" by Richard Connell (page 19) is about the external conflict between the evil General Zaroff and the hunter Rainsford. By contrast, an **internal conflict** takes place entirely within a character's own mind. An internal conflict is a struggle between opposing needs or desires or emotions within a single person. In James Hurst's "The Scarlet Ibis" (page 333), the young narrator struggles with an internal conflict—between love for his brother and hatred of his brother's disabilities. Many works, especially longer ones, contain both internal and external conflicts, and an external conflict often leads to internal problems.

See pages 4–5, 55, 774, 1012, 1035.

CONNOTATION **All the meanings, associations, or emotions that have come to be attached to some words, in addition to their literal dictionary definitions, or denotations.** For example, *skinny* and *slender* have the same literal definition, or **denotation**—"thin." But their connotations are completely different. If you call someone skinny, you are saying something unflattering. If you call someone slender, you are paying him or her a compliment. The British philosopher Bertrand Russell once gave a classic example of the different connotations of words: "I am firm. You are obstinate. He is a pigheaded fool." Connotations, or the suggestive power of certain words, play an important role in creating **mood** or **tone.**

See pages 285, 373, 669, 685.
See also *Diction*, *Mood*, *Tone*.

COUPLET **Two consecutive lines of poetry that rhyme.** Alexander Pope wrote this sarcastic couplet for a dog's collar (Kew is a place in England):

> I am his Highness' dog at Kew;
> Pray tell me, Sir, whose dog are you?
>
> by Alexander Pope

Couplets work nicely for humor and satire because the punch line comes so quickly. However, they are most often used to express a completed thought. In Shakespeare's plays an important speech or scene often ends with a couplet.

See pages 638, 802.

DESCRIPTION **Type of writing intended to create a mood or emotion or to re-create a person, a place, a thing, an event, or an experience.** Description is one of the four major techniques used in writing. (The others are **narration, exposition,** and **persuasion.**) Description works by creating images that appeal to the senses of sight, smell, taste, hearing, or touch. Writers use description in all forms of fiction, nonfiction, and poetry.

See also *Imagery*.

DIALECT **Way of speaking that is characteristic of a particular region or a particular group of people.** Dialects may have a distinct vocabulary, pronunciation system, and grammar. In a sense, we all speak dialects; but one dialect usually becomes dominant in a country or culture and becomes accepted as the standard way of speaking. In the United States, for example, the formal language is known as standard English. (This is what you usually hear spoken by TV newscasters on the national channels.)

See page 535.

DIALOGUE **The conversation between characters in a story or play.** Dialogue is an important factor in characterization and in moving the plot forward. Dialogue forms the structure of most plays. The following dialogue is taken from Edgar Allan Poe's "The Cask of Amontillado" (page 286):

> "You do not comprehend?" he said.
> "Not I," I replied.
> "Then you are not of the brotherhood."
> "How?"
> "You are not of the Masons."
> "Yes, yes," I said, "yes, yes."
> "You? Impossible! A Mason?"
> "A Mason," I replied.
> "A sign," he said.
> "It is this," I answered, producing a trowel from beneath the folds of my roquelaure.
> "You jest," he exclaimed, recoiling a few paces. "But let us proceed to the amontillado."

DICTION **A writer's or speaker's choice of words.** Diction is an essential element of a writer's style. Some writers use simple, down-to-earth, or even slang words (*house*, *home*, *digs*); others use ornate, official-sounding, or even flowery language (*domicile*, *residence*, *abode*). The **connotations** of words are an important aspect of diction.

See page 435.
See also *Connotation*, *Tone*.

DRAMA **Story that is written to be acted for an audience.** The action of a drama is usually driven by a character who wants something and takes steps to get it. The elements of a dramatic plot are **exposition, complications, climax,** and **resolution.** The term *drama* is also used to describe a serious play that is neither a **comedy** nor a **tragedy.**

See pages 752–759.
See also *Comedy*, *Tragedy*.

DRAMATIC MONOLOGUE **A poem in which a speaker addresses one or more silent listeners, often reflecting on a specific problem or situation.** Though the person addressed in a dramatic monologue does not speak, we often can discover something about the listener or listeners—as well as the speaker—by paying close attention to the speaker's words. The speaker in Edgar Lee Masters's dramatic monologue "Lucinda Matlock" is an outspoken old woman who addresses the younger generation from the graveyard in Spoon River:

> What is this I hear of sorrow and weariness,
> Anger, discontent, and drooping hopes?
> Degenerate sons and daughters,
> Life is too strong for you—
> It takes life to love Life.

See pages 752–759.

EPIC **Long story told in elevated language (usually poetry), which relates the great deeds of a larger-than-life hero who embodies the values of a particular society.** Most epics include elements of myth, legend, folk tale, and history. Their tone is serious and their language is grand. Most epic heroes undertake quests to achieve something of tremendous value to themselves or their people. Often parts of the hero's quest are set in both heaven and hell. Homer's *Iliad* and *Odyssey* (page 1037) are the best-known epics in Western civilization. The great epic of ancient Rome is Virgil's *Aeneid*, which, like the *Iliad* and *Odyssey*, is based on events that happened during and immediately after the Trojan War. The great epic of India is the *Mahabharata*. The great epic of Mali in Africa is *Sundiata*. Spain's epic is *El Cid*.

See Pages 1012–1017.

EPITHET **Adjective or descriptive phrase that is regularly used to characterize a person, place, or thing.** We speak of "Honest Abe," for example, and "America the Beautiful." Homer created so many epithets in his *Iliad* and *Odyssey* that his name is permanently associated with a type of epithet. The **Homeric epithet** in most English translations consists of a compound adjective that is regularly used to modify a particular noun. Three famous examples from the *Odyssey* are "*wine-dark* sea," "*rosy-fingered* dawn," and "the *gray-eyed* goddess Athena."

See page 1076.

ESSAY **Short piece of nonfiction that examines a single subject from a limited point of view.** Most essays can be categorized as either **personal** or **formal.**

A **personal essay** (sometimes called an **informal essay**) generally reveals a great deal about the writer's personality and tastes. Its tone is often conversational, sometimes even humorous.

A **formal essay** is usually serious, objective, and impersonal in tone. Its purpose is to inform its readers about some topic of interest or to persuade them to accept the writer's views. The statements in a formal essay are supported by facts and logic.

EXPOSITION **Type of writing that explains, gives information, defines, or clarifies an idea.** Exposition is one of the four major techniques used in writing. (The others are **narration, description,** and **persuasion.**) We find exposition in news articles, in histories, in biographies (and even in cookbook recipes). In fact, each entry in this Handbook of Literary Terms is an example of exposition.

Exposition is also the term for that beginning part of a plot that gives information about the characters and their problems or conflicts.

See pages 4, 804.
See also *Plot.*

FABLE **Very brief story in prose or verse that teaches a moral, or a practical lesson about how to get along in life.** The characters in most fables are animals that behave and speak like human beings. Some of the most popular fables are those attributed to Aesop, who scholars believe was a slave in ancient Greece.

See also *Folk Tale, Tall Tale.*

FIGURE OF SPEECH **Word or phrase that describes one thing in terms of another and is not meant to be understood on a literal level.** Most figures of speech, or **figurative language,** involve some sort of imaginative comparison between seemingly unlike things.

Some 250 different types of figures of speech have been identified. The most common are the **simile** ("I wandered lonely as a cloud"), the **metaphor** ("Fame is a bee"), and **personification** ("The wind stood up and gave a shout").

See also pages 617, 674.
See also *Metaphor, Personification, Simile.*

FLASHBACK **Scene in a movie, play, short story, novel, or narrative poem that interrupts the present action of the plot to flash backward and tell what happened at an earlier time.** That is, a flashback breaks the normal time sequence of events in a narrative, usually to give the readers or viewers some background information that helps them make sense of a story. Much of the *Odyssey* (page 1037) is told in the form of a flashback, as Odysseus describes his previous adventures to the Phaeacian court of King Alcinous.

Flashbacks are extremely common storytelling devices in movies. In fact, the word *flashback* comes from film criticism, and it has spread to the rest of literature.

See pages 4, 41.

FLASH-FORWARD **A scene in a movie, play, short story, novel, or narrative poem that interrupts the present action of the plot to shift into the future.** Writers may use a flash-forward to create **dramatic irony.** By means of the flash-forward, we know the future, but the story characters do not.

FOIL **Character who is used as a contrast to another character.** A writer uses a foil to accentuate and clarify the distinct qualities of two characters. The word *foil* is also used for a thin sheet of shiny metal that is placed beneath a gem to intensify its brilliance. A character who is a foil, like the metal behind the gem, sets off or intensifies the qualities of another character. In Shakespeare's *Romeo and Juliet* (page 807), the cynical, sophisticated Mercutio is a foil to the romantic, naive Romeo.

See pages 754, 1012.

FOLK TALE **Story that has no known author and was originally passed on from one generation to another by word of mouth.** Unlike myths, which are about gods and heroes, folk tales are usually about ordinary people. Folk tales tend to travel, and you'll often find the same motifs—elements such as characters, images, and story lines—in the tales of different cultures. For example, there are said to be nine hundred versions of the folk tale about Cinderella.

See also *Fable, Tall Tale.*

FORESHADOWING **The use of clues to hint at events that will occur later in a plot.** Foreshadowing is used to build suspense and, sometimes, anxiety in the reader or viewer. In a drama the gun found in a bureau drawer in Act I is likely to foreshadow violence later in the play. In "The Cask of Amontillado" (page 286), Poe uses foreshadowing skillfully. For example, when Montresor produces a trowel from beneath his cloak, Poe is foreshadowing the means Montresor will use to murder his enemy. When later he begins to build a wall around Fortunato, we remember that trowel.

See pages 5, 17.

FREE VERSE **Poetry that does not have a regular meter or rhyme scheme.** Poets writing in free verse try to capture the natural rhythms of ordinary speech. To create its music, free verse may use **internal rhyme,**

alliteration, onomatopoeia, refrain, and **parallel structure.** For an example of a poem written in free verse, read "Daily" (page 650).

See pages 616, 694.
See also *Meter, Rhythm.*

GENRE (ZHAHN ruh) **The category in which a work of literature is classified.** Five major genres in literature are nonfiction, fiction, poetry, drama, and myth. Collections 7, 8, and 9 of this book are organized by genre: by poetry, by drama, and by epic and myth.

See page 1115.

HAIKU **Japanese verse form consisting of three lines and, usually, seventeen syllables (five in the first line, seven in the second, and five in the third).** The writer of a haiku uses association and suggestion to describe a particular moment of discovery or enlightenment. A haiku often presents an image of daily life that relates to a particular season.

See pages 616, 634.

HYPERBOLE (hy PUR buh lee) **Figure of speech that uses exaggeration to express strong emotion or to create a comic effect.** Writers often use hyperbole, also called **overstatement,** to intensify a description or to emphasize the essential nature of something. If you say that a limousine is as long as an ocean liner, you are using hyperbole.

IAMBIC PENTAMETER **Line of poetry that contains five iambs.** An **iamb** is a metrical foot, or unit of measure, consisting of an unstressed syllable followed by a stressed syllable (˘ ′). *Pentameter* comes from the Greek *penta* (five) and *meter* (measure). Here is one iamb: *ărı́se*. Here is a line measuring five iambs:

> Bŭt sóft! Whăt lı́ght thrŏugh yóndĕr wı́ndŏw
> bréaks?
>
> from *Romeo and Juliet*
> by William Shakespeare

Iambic pentameter is by far the most common verse line in English poetry.

See pages 638, 802.
See also *Blank Verse, Meter.*

IDIOM **Expression peculiar to a particular language that means something different from the literal meaning of each word.** "It's raining cats and dogs" and "We heard it through the grapevine" are idioms of American English. One of the difficulties of translating a work from another language is translating the idioms.

See pages 456, 683.

IMAGERY **Language that appeals to the senses.** Most images are visual—that is, they create pictures in the reader's mind by appealing to the sense of sight. Images can also appeal to the senses of hearing, touch, taste, or smell or even to several senses at once. Imagery is an element in all types of writing, but it is especially important in poetry. The following lines contain images that make us see, hear, and even smell what the speaker experiences as he travels to meet someone he loves.

> Then a mile of warm sea-scented beach;
> Three fields to cross till a farm appears;
> A tap at the pane, the quick sharp scratch
> And blue spurt of a lighted match . . .
>
> *from* "Meeting at Night"
> by Robert Browning

See pages 616, 629.
See also *Description.*

INVERSION **Reversal of the normal word order of a sentence.** The elements of a standard English sentence are subject, verb, and complement, and in most sentences that is the order in which they appear. (*Ray rowed the boat.*) Writers use inversion for emphasis and variety. They may also use it for more technical reasons—to create end rhymes or to accommodate a given meter. In a statement about Ulysses S. Grant and Robert E. Lee, the historian Bruce Catton wrote, "Daring and resourcefulness they had too. . . ." Catton inverts the order of the parts of the sentence so that the important words (*daring* and *resourcefulness*) come first.

IRONY **Contrast between expectation and reality—between what is said and what is really meant, between what is expected to happen and what really does happen, or between what appears to be true and what is really true.**

In **verbal irony**, a writer or speaker says one thing but really means something completely different. If you call a clumsy basketball player the new Michael Jordan, you are using verbal irony. The murderer in Edgar Allan Poe's "The Cask of Amontillado" (page 286) is using verbal irony when he says to his unsuspecting victim, "Your health is precious."

Situational irony occurs when there is a contrast between what would seem appropriate and what really happens or when there is a contradiction between what we expect to happen and what really does take place.

Dramatic irony occurs when the audience or the reader knows something important that a character in a play or story does not know. In Shakespeare's *Romeo and Juliet* (page 807), we know, but Romeo does not, that when he finds Juliet in the tomb, she is drugged, not dead. Thus we feel a terrible sense of dramatic irony as we watch Romeo kill himself upon discovering her body.

See pages 321, 349, 361.
See also *Satire*, *Tone*.

LYRIC POETRY **Poetry that does not tell a story but is aimed only at expressing a speaker's emotions or thoughts.** Most lyrics are short, and they usually imply, rather than directly state, a single strong emotion. The term *lyric* comes from Greek. In ancient Greece, lyric poems were recited to the accompaniment of a stringed instrument called a lyre. Today poets still try to make their lyrics "sing," but they rely only on the musical effects they create with words (such as **rhyme, rhythm,** and **onomatopoeia**).

See pages 616, 642.
See also *Sonnet*.

METAPHOR **Figure of speech that makes a comparison between two unlike things, in which one thing becomes another thing without the use of the word *like, as, than,* or *resembles.*** The poet Robert Burns's famous comparison "O my love is like a red, red rose" is a simile. If he had written, "O my love is a red, red rose" or "O my love bursts into bloom," he would have been using a metaphor.

Notice that the comparison in the second metaphor above is implied, or suggested, rather than directly stated, as it is in the first metaphor. An **implied metaphor** does not tell us directly that one thing is something else. Instead, it uses words that suggest the nature of the comparison. The phrase "bursts into bloom" implies that the feeling of love is like a budding flower.

An **extended metaphor** is a metaphor that is extended, or developed, over several lines of writing or even throughout an entire poem.

A **dead metaphor** is a metaphor that has been used so often that we no longer realize it is a figure of speech—we simply skip over the metaphorical connection it makes. Examples of dead metaphors are *the roof of the mouth*, *the eye of the storm*, *the heart of the matter*, and *the arm of the chair*.

A **mixed metaphor** is the inconsistent mixture of two or more metaphors. Mixed metaphors are a common problem in bad writing, and they are often unintentionally funny. You are using a mixed metaphor if you say, "Put it on the back burner and let it germinate" or "Let's set sail and get this show on the road."

See pages 617, 679, 950.
See also *Figure of Speech*, *Personification*, *Simile*.

METER **Generally regular pattern of stressed and unstressed syllables in poetry.** When we want to indicate the metrical pattern of a poem, we mark the stressed syllables with the symbol (′) and the unstressed syllables with the symbol (˘). Indicating the metrical pattern of a poem in this way is called **scanning** the poem, or **scansion** (SKAN shuhn). Notice the pattern of stressed and unstressed syllables in the first four lines of this poem:

> Slówly̆, sílĕntly̆, nów thĕ móon
> Wálks thĕ níght ĭn hĕr sílvĕr shóon;
> Thís wăy, ănd thát, shé peérs, ănd seés
> Sílvĕr frúit ŭpŏn sílvĕr trées. . . .
>
> "Silver" by Walter de la Mare

See pages 618, 685.
See also *Blank Verse*, *Iambic Pentameter*, *Rhythm*.

MOOD **A story's atmosphere or the feeling it evokes.** Mood is often created by a story's setting. A story set in a wild forest at night, with wolves howling in the distance, will probably convey a mood of terror, tension, or uneasiness. A story set in a cozy cottage or garden full of sunlight and the chirps of birds will probably create a mood of peace.

See pages, 5, 435, 674.
See also *Setting*.

MYTH **Traditional story that is rooted in a particular culture, is basically religious, and usually serves to explain a belief, a ritual, or a mysterious natural phenomenon.** Most myths grew out of religious rituals, and almost all of them involve the influence of gods on human affairs. Every culture has its own mythology. For many centuries the myths of ancient Greece and Rome were very influential in the Western world.

"The Fenris Wolf" (page 1109) is a story from Norse mythology, the system of myths developed thousands of years ago by the people of Scandinavia. The myths were part of an oral tradition; the oldest surviving written versions of these ancient tales came from Iceland in the thirteenth century. There are variations in the Norse myths, as there are in the myths of most cultures.

See pages 953, 1012–1013.

NARRATION **Type of writing or speaking that tells about a series of related events.** Narration is one of the four major techniques used in writing. (The others are **description, exposition,** and **persuasion.**) Narration can be any length, from a brief paragraph to an entire book. It is most often found in short stories, novels, epics, and ballads. But narration is also used in any piece of nonfiction that relates a series of events that tell what happened—such as a biography, an essay, or a news story—and even in a scientific analysis or a report of a business meeting.

See also *Point of View.*

NARRATOR **The voice telling a story.** The choice of a narrator is very important in storytelling. For example, Edgar Allan Poe chose the murderer himself to tell the story "The Cask of Amontillado" (page 286). This choice of a narrator not only increases our sense of horror but also raises many questions, which make us uneasy. For one thing we wonder whether this narrator is telling the truth. We also wonder whom the narrator is talking to as he relates the details of his crime.

See also *Point of View*.

NONFICTION **Prose writing that deals with real people, things, events, and places.** The most popular forms of nonfiction are **biography** and **autobiography**. Other examples include essays, newspaper stories, magazine articles, historical writing, scientific reports, and even personal diaries and letters.

NOVEL **Fictional prose narrative usually consisting of more than fifty thousand words.** In general, the novel uses the same basic literary elements as the short story (**plot, character, setting, theme,** and **point of view**) but develops them more fully. Many novels have several subplots, for instance. Modern writers often do away with one or more of the novel's traditional elements. Some novels today are basically character studies, with only the barest, stripped-down story lines.

ONOMATOPOEIA (ahn uh maht uh PEE uh) **Use of a word whose sound imitates or suggests its meaning.** Onomatopoeia is so natural to us that we begin using it instinctively as children. *Crackle, pop, fizz, click,* and *zoom* are examples of onomatopoeia. Onomatopoeia is an important element in the music of poetry.

> And in the hush of waters was the sound
> Of pebbles, rolling round;
> Forever rolling, with a hollow sound:
> And bubbling seaweeds, as the waters go,
> Swish to and fro
> Their long cold tentacles of slimy gray. . . .
>
> *from* "The Shell"
> by James Stephens

See pages 472, 619.
See also *Alliteration*, *Assonance*, *Rhyme*.

PARADOX **Statement or situation that seems to be a contradiction but reveals a truth.** Paradoxes in literature are designed to make readers stop and think. They often express aspects of life that are mysterious, surprising, or difficult to describe. When O. Henry, in "The Gift of the Magi" (page 363), refers to the impoverished Della and Jim as "one of the richest couples on earth," he is stating a paradox.

PARALLELISM **Repetition of words, phrases, or sentences that have the same grammatical structure or that state a similar idea.** Parallelism, or parallel structure, helps make lines rhythmic and memorable and heightens their emotional effect.

> It was the best of times, it was the worst of times, it was the age of wisdom, it was the age of foolishness, it was the epoch of belief, it was the epoch of incredulity, it was the season of Light, it was the season of Darkness, it was the spring of hope, it was the winter of despair, we had everything before us, we had nothing before us, we were all going direct to Heaven, we were all going direct the other way. . . .
>
> from *A Tale of Two Cities*
> by Charles Dickens

See pages 699, 705.

PERSONA **Mask or voice assumed by a writer.** Authors often take on other identities in their works. In a short story a writer may assume a persona by using a first-person narrator. When a poet is not the speaker of a poem, the poet is creating a persona.

See page 705.
See also *Point of View*, *Speaker.*

PERSONIFICATION **Kind of metaphor in which a nonhuman thing or quality is talked about as if it**

were human. Here are a few lines in which poetry itself is personified—that is, it is described as behaving and feeling the way people do:

> This poetry gets bored of being alone,
> it wants to go outdoors to chew on the winds,
> to fill its commas with the keels of rowboats. . . .
>
> *from* "Living Poetry"
> by Hugo Margenat

See pages 617, 669.
See also *Figure of Speech, Metaphor.*

PLOT **Series of related events that make up a story or drama.** Plot is what happens in a story, novel, or play. An outline showing the "bare bones" of a plot would include the story's **basic situation,** or **exposition;** the **conflict,** or problem; the **main events** (including **complications**); the final **climax,** or moment of great emotional intensity or suspense, when we learn what the outcome of the conflict is going to be; and the **resolution,** or **denouement.**

See pages 4–5, 77.

POETRY **Type of rhythmic, compressed language that uses figures of speech and imagery to appeal to the reader's emotions and imagination.** The major forms of poetry are the **lyric poem** and the **narrative poem.** Two types of narrative poetry are the **epic** and the **ballad.** One popular type of lyric poetry is the **sonnet.** Beyond this, poetry is difficult to define, though many readers feel it is easy to recognize. The poet Wallace Stevens, for example, once described poetry as "a search for the inexplicable."

See also *Ballad, Epic, Lyric Poetry, Sonnet.*

POINT OF VIEW **Vantage point from which a writer tells a story.** In broad terms there are three possible points of view: omniscient, first person, and third-person limited.

In the **omniscient** (or "all-knowing") **point of view,** the person telling the story knows everything there is to know about the characters and their problems. This all-knowing narrator can tell us about the past, the present, and the future of all the characters. He or she can even tell us what the characters are thinking. The narrator can also tell us what is happening in other places. In the omniscient point of view, the narrator is not in the story at all. In fact, the omniscient narrator is like a god telling the story.

In the **first-person point of view,** one of the characters is telling the story, using the pronoun *I*. We get to know this narrator very well, but we can know only what this character knows, and we can observe only what this character observes. All of our information about the events in the story must come from this one character. When a story is told from the first-person point of view, readers often must ask if the narrator is unreliable. An **unreliable narrator** does not always know what is happening in the story, or he or she might be lying or telling us only part of the story.

In the **third-person-limited point of view,** the narrator, who plays no part in the story, zooms in on the thoughts and feelings of just one character. With this point of view, we observe the action through the eyes and with the feelings of this one character.

See pages 220–221, 245.
See also *Narrator, Persona.*

PROTAGONIST **Main character in fiction or drama.** The protagonist is the character we focus our attention on, the person who sets the plot in motion. The character or force that blocks the protagonist is the **antagonist.** Most protagonists are rounded, dynamic characters who change in some important way by the end of the story, novel, or play. The antagonist is often but not always the villain in the story. Similarly, the protagonist is often but not always the hero.

See page 124.

PUN **Play on the multiple meanings of a word or on two words that sound alike but have different meanings.** Most often puns are used for their humorous effects; they are used in jokes all the time. ("What has four wheels and flies?" Answer: "A garbage truck.") Shakespeare was one of the great punsters of all time. The servants in *Romeo and Juliet* (page 807) make crude puns as they clown around at the start of the play. Later, Romeo and his friend Mercutio trade wits in

"Does the doctor make mouse calls?"

Drawing by Bernard Schoenbaum, ©1991 The New Yorker Magazine, Inc.

a series of more sophisticated puns. Since word meanings change so quickly, some of Shakespeare's puns are barely understandable to us today, just as puns popular today may be puzzling to people a hundred years from now.

See page 950.

REFRAIN **Repeated word, phrase, line, or group of lines.** Though refrains are usually associated with songs and poems, they are also used in speeches and other forms of literature. Refrains are most often used to build rhythm, but they may also provide commentary or build suspense.

See page 711.

RHYME **Repetition of accented vowel sounds, and all sounds following them, in words that are close together in a poem.** *Choice* and *voice* are rhymes, as are *tingle* and *jingle*.

End rhymes occur at the ends of lines. In this poem the words *defense/tense, know/go,* and *Spain/Maine* are end rhymes:

Old Mary
My last defense
Is the present tense.
It little hurts me now to know
I shall not go
Cathedral-hunting in Spain
Nor cherrying in Michigan or Maine.

by Gwendolyn Brooks

Internal rhymes occur in the middle of a line. This line has an internal rhyme (*dreary* rhymes with *weary*):

Once upon a midnight dreary, while I
pondered, weak and weary

from "The Raven"
by Edgar Allan Poe

When two words have some sound in common but do not rhyme exactly, they are called **approximate rhymes** (or **half rhymes, off rhymes,** or **slant rhymes**). In Brooks's poem on this page, the words *now* and *know* are approximate rhymes.

The pattern of end rhymes in a poem is called a **rhyme scheme.** The rhyme scheme of a stanza or a poem is indicated by the use of a different letter of the alphabet for each new rhyme. For example, the rhyme scheme of Brooks's poem is *aabbcc*.

See pages 618–619, 689.

RHYTHM **Musical quality in language produced by repetition.** Rhythm occurs naturally in all forms of spoken and written language. The most obvious kind of rhythm is produced by **meter,** the regular repetition of stressed and unstressed syllables found in some poetry. But writers can also create rhythm by using rhymes, by repeating words and phrases, and even by repeating whole lines or sentences. This stanza by Walt Whitman is written in free verse and so does not follow a metrical pattern. Yet the lines are rhythmical because of Whitman's repeated use of certain sentence structures, words, and sounds.

Give me the splendid silent sun with all his
beams full-dazzling,
Give me juicy autumnal fruit ripe and red
from the orchard,
Give me a field where the unmowed grass
grows,
Give me an arbor, give me the trellised grape,
Give me fresh corn and wheat, give me
serene-moving animals teaching content,
Give me nights perfectly quiet as on high
plateaus west of the Mississippi, and I
looking up at the stars. . . .

from "Give Me the Splendid
Silent Sun"
by Walt Whitman

See pages 618–619.
See also *Free Verse, Meter*.

SATIRE **Type of writing that ridicules something—a person, a group of people, humanity at large, an attitude or failing, a social institution—in order to reveal a weakness.** Most satires are an attempt to convince us of a point of view or to persuade us to follow a course of action. They do this by pointing out how the opposite point of view or action is ridiculous or laughable. Satire often involves **exaggeration**—the act of overstating something to make it look worse than it is.

See also *Irony, Tone*.

SCENE DESIGN **Sets, lights, costumes, and props, which bring a play to life onstage.** Sets are the furnishings and scenery that suggest the time and place of the action. **Props** (short for *properties*) are all the objects that the actors use onstage, such as books, telephones, and suitcases.

See page 753.

SETTING **The time and place of a story or play.** Most often the setting of a narrative is established early in the story. For example, in the fourth paragraph of "The Cask of Amontillado" (page 286), Edgar Allan Poe tells his readers, "It was about dusk, one evening during the supreme madness of the carnival season. . . ." Setting often contributes to a story's emotional effect. In "The Cask of Amontillado" the descriptions of the gloomy Montresor palace, with its damp catacombs full of bones, help create the story's mood of horror. Setting can also contribute to the conflict in a story, as the harsh environment does in Eugenia W. Collier's "Marigolds" (page 259). Setting can also be used to reveal character, as it does in Truman Capote's "A Christmas Memory" (page 177).

See pages 5, 77.
See also *Mood*.

SHORT STORY **Short, concentrated, fictional prose narrative.** Some say Edgar Allan Poe was the first short-story writer. He was also one of the first to attempt to define the short story. He said "unity of effect" is crucial, meaning that a short story ought to concentrate on a single purpose. Short stories are usually built on a plot that consists of these "bare bones": the **basic situation,** or **exposition; complications; climax;** and **resolution.** Years ago, most short stories were notable for their strong plots. Today's short-story writers tend to be more interested in character.

SIMILE **Figure of speech that makes a comparison between two unlike things, using a word such as *like, as, resembles*, or *than*.** Shakespeare, in one of his famous sonnets, uses a simile with an ironic twist, comparing two things that are *not* alike:

> My mistress' eyes are nothing like the sun

We would expect a love poem to compare the light in a lover's eyes to the bright sun. But instead, Shakespeare puts a twist into a common comparison—in order to make a point about the extravagant similes found in most love poems of his day.

See pages 459, 669.
See also *Figure of Speech*, *Metaphor*.

SOLILOQUY **Long speech in which a character who is onstage alone expresses his or her thoughts aloud.** The soliloquy is a very old dramatic convention, in which the audience is supposedly overhearing the private thoughts of a character. Perhaps the most famous soliloquy is the "To be or not to be" speech in Shakespeare's play *Hamlet*. There are also several soliloquies in *Romeo and Juliet*, including Friar Laurence's soliloquy at the opening of Act II, Scene 3; Juliet's at the end of Act IV, Scene 3; and Romeo's in Act V, Scene 3.

SONNET **Fourteen-line lyric poem that is usually written in iambic pentameter and that has one of several rhyme schemes.** The oldest kind of sonnet is called the **Italian sonnet,** or **Petrarchan sonnet,** after the fourteenth-century Italian poet Petrarch. The first eight lines, or **octet** or **octave,** of the Italian sonnet pose a question or problem about love or some other subject. The concluding six lines, or the **sestet,** are a response to the octet. The octet has the rhyme scheme *abba abba*; the sestet has the rhyme scheme *cde cde*.

Another important sonnet form, widely used by Shakespeare, is called the **Shakespearean sonnet.** It has three four-line units, or **quatrains,** followed by a concluding two-line unit, or **couplet**. The most common rhyme scheme for the Shakespearean sonnet is *abab cdcd efef gg*.

See page 638.
See also *Lyric Poetry*.

SPEAKER **Voice that is talking to us in a poem.** Sometimes the speaker is identical with the poet, but often the speaker and the poet are not the same. The poet may be speaking as a child, a woman, a man, a whole people, an animal, or even an object. For example, the speaker of Maya Angelou's poem "Woman Work" (page 499) is a hardworking woman with several children, who cuts cane and cotton and lives in a hut—not Maya Angelou at all.

See pages 616, 679, 705.
See also *Persona*.

STANZA **Group of consecutive lines in a poem that form a single unit.** A stanza in a poem is something like a paragraph in prose: It often expresses a unit of thought. A stanza may consist of any number of lines. The word *stanza* is Italian for "stopping place" or "place to rest." Emily Dickinson's poem "'Hope' is the thing with feathers" (page 666) consists of three four-line stanzas, or **quatrains,** each one expressing a unit of thought.

STYLE **The particular way in which a writer uses language.** Style is created mainly through diction (word choice), use of **figurative language,** and sentence patterns. Style can be described as plain, ornate, formal, ironic, conversational, and so on.

See pages 434–435.

SUSPENSE **Uncertainty or anxiety the reader feels about what is going to happen next in a story.** In "The Most Dangerous Game" (page 19), our curiosity is aroused at once when we hear about Ship-Trap Island and sailors' fear of it. When Rainsford lands on that very island and is hunted by the sinister General Zaroff, suspense keeps us on the edge of our seats. We wonder: Will Rainsford be another victim who is hunted down and killed by the evil and weird Zaroff?

See also *Foreshadowing*, *Plot*.

SYMBOL **Person, place, thing, or event that stands for itself and for something beyond itself as well.** For example, a scale has a real existence as an instrument for measuring weights, but it also is used as a public symbol of justice. Other familiar public symbols are the cross that symbolizes Christianity, the six-pointed star that symbolizes Judaism, the star and crescent that symbolizes Islam, and the bald eagle that symbolizes the United States. These are public symbols that most people know, but in literature, writers sometimes create new, private symbols that can be understood only from their context. One of the great symbols in literature is Herman Melville's great white whale, used as a symbol of the mystery of evil in the novel *Moby-Dick*.

See pages 320–321, 331, 349.

TALL TALE **Exaggerated, far-fetched story that is obviously untrue but is told as though it should be believed.** Most tall tales are humorous. Tall tales are especially popular in the United States. As tall tales are passed on, they often get taller and taller—more and more exaggerated. The tales told about Paul Bunyan, the superheroic logger of the Northern forests, are tall tales.

See also *Fable*, *Folk Tale*.

THEME **Central idea of a work of literature.** A theme is not the same as a subject. The subject of a work can usually be expressed in a word or two: love, childhood, death. The theme is the idea the writer wishes to reveal *about* that subject. The theme is something that can be expressed in at least one complete sentence. For example, one theme of Shakespeare's *Romeo and Juliet* (page 807) might be stated in this way: "Love is more powerful than hatred." Theme is not usually stated directly in a work of literature. Most often, the reader has to think about all the elements of the work and use them to make an inference, or educated guess, about what its theme is. Some themes are so commonly found in the literature of all cultures and all ages that they are called **universal themes.** Here are some universal themes found in stories throughout the ages and expressed in the *Odyssey* (page 1037): "Heroes must undergo trials and endure losses before they can claim their rightful kingdom." "Arrogance and pride can bring destruction." "Love will endure and triumph over evil."

See pages 331, 383, 1115

TONE **Attitude a writer takes toward a subject, a character, or the audience.** Tone is conveyed through the writer's choice of words and details. For example, Gary Soto's "The Grandfather" (page 469) is affectionate and nostalgic in tone.

See pages 221, 524, 679.
See also *Connotation*, *Diction*, *Irony*, *Satire*.

TRAGEDY **Play that depicts serious and important events in which the main character comes to an unhappy end.** In a tragedy the main character is usually dignified and courageous. His or her downfall may be caused by a character flaw, or it may result from forces beyond human control. The tragic hero usually wins some self-knowledge and wisdom, even though he or she suffers defeat, perhaps even death.

See pages 754, 804.
See also *Comedy*, *Drama*.

VOICE **The writer's or speaker's distinctive use of language in a text.** Voice is created by a writer's tone and choice of words. Some writers have such a distinctive voice that you can identify their works on the basis of voice alone. The detached, objective tone and simple language in "Old Man at the Bridge" (page 130), for example, make it instantly recognizable as one of Ernest Hemingway's short stories.

See pages 221, 269.

Handbook of Reading and Informational Terms

For more information about a topic, turn to the page(s) indicated with most entries. The words in **boldface** are other key terms, with definitions provided in context. On another line there are cross-references to entries in this handbook that provide closely related information. For instance, *Logic* contains a cross-reference to *Logical Order*.

ARGUMENT **A series of statements in a text designed to convince us of something.** What the writer or speaker wants to prove is called the **claim** (or the **opinion**). An argument might appeal to both our reason and our emotions. An argument in a scientific or historical journal, for instance, would probably present only **logical appeals,** which include sound reasons and factual evidence. An argument in a political text would probably also include **emotional appeals,** which are directed more to our "hearts" than to our minds. Some arguments use **loaded words** (words loaded with emotional connotations) and **anecdotes** (brief, personal stories) that also appeal to our feelings. It is important to be able to recognize emotional appeals used in arguments—and to be aware of how they can trick an audience.

Arguments can be found in editorials, magazine articles, political speeches, professional journals, and primary source material.

See pages 524, 535, 541, 549.

CAUSE AND EFFECT **A text structure that shows how or why one thing leads to another.** The **cause** is the reason that an action takes place. The **effect** is the result or consequence of the cause. A cause can have more than one effect, and an effect may have several causes. Writers may explain causes only or effects only.

A text may be organized in a cause-effect chain. One cause leads to an effect, which causes another effect, and so on. Notice the cause-effect chain in the following paragraph from "An Arctic Floe of Climate Questions":

> But some alarm bells did ring, because there is growing concern that we humans are fouling things up through our burning of gas, oil, and coal, which releases so-called greenhouse gases such as carbon dioxide into the air. These gases, which trap heat, may be causing the world's temperature to steadily creep higher and higher. And an absence of ice at the North Pole seemed like one more ominous sign of impending trouble.

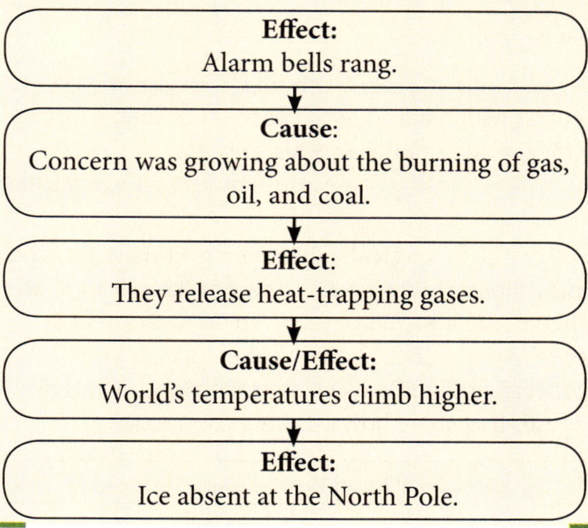

Effect:
Alarm bells rang.
Cause:
Concern was growing about the burning of gas, oil, and coal.
Effect:
They release heat-trapping gases.
Cause/Effect:
World's temperatures climb higher.
Effect:
Ice absent at the North Pole.

Writers use the cause-effect pattern in both narrative and informational texts. In most short stories, events in the plot are connected in a cause-effect chain. Some words and phrases that signal the cause-effect pattern are *because*, *depended on*, *inspired*, *produced*, *resulting in*, *led to*, and *outcome*. Never assume, either in your reading or in real life, that one event causes another just because that event happened before the other.

See pages 324, 373.
See also *Text Structures*.

CHRONOLOGICAL ORDER **The arrangement of details in time order, that is, in the order in which they occurred.** Chronological order is used in a narrative, which describes a series of events, and in texts that explain the steps in a process.

See also *Text Structures*.

CLAIM **The idea or opinion that a writer tries to prove or defend in an argument.** The claim is stated as a **generalization,** a broad statement or conclusion that covers many situations (or follows from the evidence). The following statements are examples of claims stated as generalizations:

> Edgar Allan Poe died as a result of rabies poisoning. ("Poe's Death is Rewritten as Case of Rabies, Not Telltale Alcohol," page 302)
>
> War and and its consequences continue because humans have an ingrained mistrust and fear of one another. ("The Arms Race" from *Einstein on Peace,* page 403)

The author of the argument then supports the claim with either logical appeals (reasons backed by factual evidence), emotional appeals, or both.

See also *Argument*, *Generalization*.

COHERENT **Logically integrated, consistent, and understandable.** A text is **coherent** (koh HIHR uhnt) when its ideas are arranged in an order that makes sense to the reader. To aid in coherence, writers help readers follow a text by using **transitions,** words and phrases that show how ideas are connected.

Common Transitional Words and Phrases	
Comparing Ideas also, and, too, moreover, similarly, another	**Contrasting Ideas** although, still, yet, but, on the other hand, instead
Showing Effect for, since, as a result, therefore, so that, because	**Showing Importance** first, last, to begin with, mainly, more important
Showing Location above, across, over, there, inside, behind, next to, through, near	**Showing Time** before, at last, now, when, eventually, at once, finally

COMPARISON/CONTRAST **A method of organizing information by showing similarities and differences among various groups of details.**

See pages 397, 1135.
See also *Text Structures*.

CONSUMER DOCUMENTS **Informative texts, such as a warranties, contracts, instruction manuals.** Here are some points to keep in mind when you read consumer documents:

1. Try to read the consumer document before you buy the product. Then, you can ask the clerk to explain anything you don't understand.
2. Read all of the pages in whatever language comes most easily to you. (Many documents are printed in two or three languages.) You will often find important information where you least expect it, such as at the end of the document.
3. Read the fine print. Fine, here, means "tiny and barely readable." Some fine-print statements in documents are required by law. They are designed to protect you, the consumer, so the company may not be interested in emphasizing these points.
4. Don't expect the document to be interesting or easy to read. If you don't understand a statement and you can't ask someone at the store that sold you the product, call or write to the company that made it. You should complain to the company if you find its consumer document confusing.
5. Before you sign anything, read everything on the page, and be sure you understand what you're agreeing to. Ask to take the document home, and have your parent or guardian read it. If you are not of legal age, an adult may be responsible for whatever you've signed. Make a copy of any document that you've signed—and keep the copy in a place where you can find it.

See pages 1182–1183.

CONTEXT CLUES **The words and sentences surrounding a word.** Context clues can sometimes help you guess at the meaning of an unfamiliar word. You will find examples that follow of three types of context clues. In the examples, the unfamiliar word appears in boldface. The context clue is underlined.

Definition Look for words that define the unfamiliar word, often by giving a synonym or a definition for it.

Mathilde brought no **dowry** to her marriage—no property or money to give her marriage a good start.

Example Look for examples that reveal the meaning of the unfamiliar word.

She wanted **tapestries** on her walls, like those beautiful embroidered hangings that decorated her friend's home.

Contrast Find words that contrast the unfamiliar word with a word or phrase you already know.

M. Loisel was **distracted**, but Mathilde was fully involved in the party.

See page 841.

CREDIBILITY **The believability of a writer's argument.** To evaluate credibility, you first need to determine the author's claim, or opinion. Then you need to look at the **reasons** (statements that explain *why* the author holds the opinion) and the **evidence** (information that supports each reason). To be credible, evidence must be **relevant,** that is, directly related to the argument; **comprehensive,** that is, sufficient to be convincing; and **accurate,** that is, from a source that can be trusted as factually correct or otherwise reliable. The writer's **intent** should also be considered. If you're reading an opinion essay, for instance, be sure to note any credentials or background information about the writer. Does the writer work for an institution that represents a particular point of view? Has the writer published a book on the same topic? Do emotional appeals and fallacious reasoning reveal a bias even though the writer pretends to be fair to both sides of the argument?

Notice the **tone** of the text. An argument that is based on logical appeals will usually have a serious, sincere tone. An angry or self-righteous tone might make you question the credibility of the argument.

See pages 351, 525.
See also *Argument*.

DICTIONARY You use a dictionary to find the precise meaning and usage of words. The elements of a typical entry are explained below.

1. **Entry word.** The entry word shows how the word is spelled and divided into syllables. It may also show capitalization and other spellings.
2. **Pronunciation. Phonetic symbols** (such as the *schwa*, ə) and **diacritical marks** (such as the *dieresis*, ä) show how to pronounce the entry word. A key to these symbols and marks usually appears at the bottom of every other page of a dictionary.
3. **Part-of-speech label.** This label tells how the entry word is used. When a word can be used as more than one part of speech, definitions are grouped by part of speech. The sample entry shows three definitions of *indulge* as a transitive verb (*vt.*) and one as an intransitive verb (*vi.*).
4. **Other forms.** Sometimes the spellings of plural forms of nouns, principal parts of verbs, and comparative and superlative forms of adjectives and adverbs are shown.
5. **Word origin.** A word's origin, or **etymology** (eht uh MAHL uh jee), shows where the word comes from. *Indulge* comes from the Latin *indulgere*, which probably comes from the prefix *in–*, meaning "not," added to the Greek *dolichos*, "long," and the Gothic *tulgus*, "firm."
6. **Examples.** Phrases or sentences show how the entry word is used.
7. **Definitions.** If a word has more than one meaning, the meanings are numbered or lettered.
8. **Special-usage labels.** These labels identify special meanings or special uses of the word. Here, *Archaic* indicates an outdated meaning.
9. **Related word forms.** Other forms of the entry word are listed. Usually these are created by the addition of suffixes.
10. **Synonyms and antonyms. Synonyms** (words similar in meaning) and **antonyms** (words opposite in meaning) may appear at the end of the entry.

A dictionary is available as a book, a CD-ROM, or part of a word-processing program or Web site.

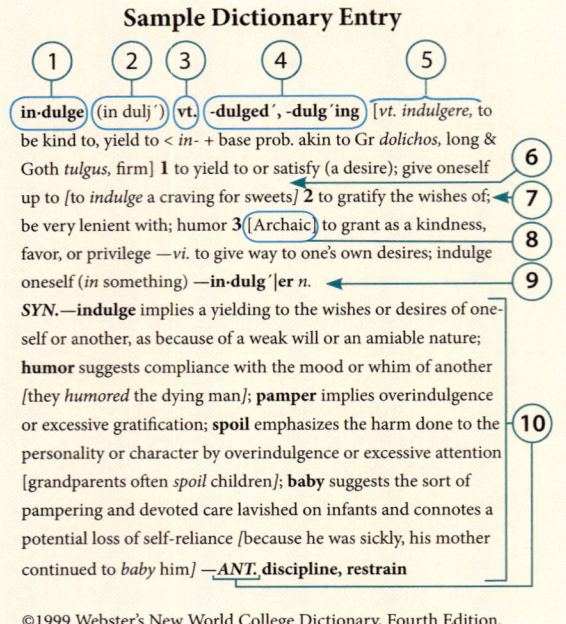

Sample Dictionary Entry

(1) **in·dulge** (2) (in dulj′) (3) **vt.** (4) **-dulged′, -dulg′ing** (5) [*vt. indulgere,* to be kind to, yield to < *in-* + base prob. akin to Gr *dolichos,* long & Goth *tulgus,* firm] **1** to yield to or satisfy (a desire); give oneself up to [to *indulge* a craving for sweets] (6) **2** to gratify the wishes of; be very lenient with; humor (7) **3** [Archaic] (8) to grant as a kindness, favor, or privilege —*vi.* to give way to one's own desires; indulge oneself (*in* something) —**in·dulg′er** *n.* (9)

SYN.—**indulge** implies a yielding to the wishes or desires of oneself or another, as because of a weak will or an amiable nature; **humor** suggests compliance with the mood or whim of another [they *humored* the dying man]; **pamper** implies overindulgence or excessive gratification; **spoil** emphasizes the harm done to the personality or character by overindulgence or excessive attention [grandparents often *spoil* children]; **baby** suggests the sort of pampering and devoted care lavished on infants and connotes a potential loss of self-reliance [because he was sickly, his mother continued to *baby* him] —*ANT.* **discipline, restrain** (10)

See also *Text Structures*.

EVIDENCE **Specific information or proof that backs up the reasons in an argument. Factual evidence** includes statements that can be proved by direct observation or by checking reliable reference sources. **Statistics** (facts in the form of numbers) and **expert testimony,** statements from people who are recognized as experts or authorities on an issue, may all be considered factual evidence.

In fields where discoveries are constantly being made, such as in astronomy and genetics, facts need to be checked in a recently published source. Remember that a Web site on the Internet may be current, but it may not be reliable. Anybody can post a statement on the Internet. If you suspect that a statement presented as a fact is not true, try to find the same fact in another source.

See pages 106, 297, 524–525.

FALLACIOUS REASONING **Faulty reasoning, or mistakes in logical thinking.** (The word *fallacious* comes from a Latin word meaning "deceptive" or "tricky." The word *false* comes from the same root word, as does the word *fallacy*.) Fallacious reasoning leads to false or incorrect conclusions. Here are some types of fallacious reasoning:

1. **Begging the question,** also called **circular reasoning,** assumes the truth of a statement before it has been proved. You appear to be giving a reason to support your opinion, but all you're doing is restating your opinion in different words.

   All students in the ninth grade need to get a laptop computer because it's essential for every ninth-grader to have one.

2. **Name-calling** uses labels to attack a person who holds an opposing view instead of giving reasons or evidence to attack the opposing view itself. This fallacy includes criticizing the person's character, situation, or background.

   Why should I listen to someone who doesn't even know who won the World Series?

3. **Stereotyping** gives all members of a group the same (usually undesirable) characteristics. It assumes that everyone (or everything) in that group is alike. (The word *stereotype* comes from the word for a metal plate that was used to print the same image over and over.) Stereotypes are often based on misconceptions about racial, social, religious, gender, or ethnic groups.

   Small towns are boring.
   Cats are self-centered.

4. **Hasty generalization** is a broad, general statement or conclusion that is made without sufficient evidence to back it up. A hasty generalization is often made on the basis of one or two experiences or observations.

   Insufficient evidence: I read about a healthy eighty-eight-year-old woman who smokes a pack of cigarettes every day. My grandfather smokes, too, and he's in great shape physically.

   Hasty generalization: Smoking does not affect your health.

If any exceptions to the conclusion can be found, the generalization is not true.

5. **Either/or fallacy** assumes that there are only two possible choices or solutions (usually extremes), even though there may be many.

   Either I get a cell phone, or you're never going to know where I am after school.

6. **False cause and effect** occurs when one event is said to be the cause of another event just because the two events happened in sequence. You cannot assume that an event caused whatever happened afterward.

> Her grades improved when she got a job after school.

See page 579.

GENERALIZATION **A broad statement that applies to or covers many individuals, experiences, situations, observations, or texts.** A **valid generalization** is a type of conclusion that is drawn after considering as many of the facts as possible. Here are some specific facts from "The Next Green Revolution" (page 551) and a generalization based on them. Notice that each fact is one piece of evidence. The generalization then states what the evidence adds up to, drawing a conclusion that applies to all members of the group.

> **Specific facts:** One alternative to the traditional automobile is the hybrid car, which burns far less gasoline. There is plenty of renewable energy, which can be tapped from many sources, including wind and water.

> **Generalization:** Many alternative energy sources are available today.

A generalization jumps from your own specific experiences and observations to a larger, general understanding.

GRAPHS **Graphic depiction of information. Line graphs** generally show changes in quantity over time. **Bar graphs** usually compare quantities within categories. **Pie graphs,** or **circle graphs,** show proportions by dividing a circle into different-sized sections, like slices of a pie.

How to Read a Graph

1. **Read the title.** The title will tell you the subject and purpose of the graph.
2. **Read the headings and labels.** These will help you determine the type of information presented.
3. **Analyze the details.** Read numbers carefully. Note increases or decreases. Look for the direction or order of events and trends and for relationships.

See pages 1205, 1271.

INFERENCE **A guess based on observation and prior experience.** When you make inferences about a literary work, you use evidence from the text as well as from other texts you have read and from your own prior experience. One way to analyze a character, for instance, is to consider what the person says and how he or she interacts with other characters. In the story "Thank You, M'am" (page 137), after the woman is almost mugged, she says to the boy who tried to steal her pocketbook:

> "You ought to be my son. I would teach you right from wrong. Least I can do right now is to wash your face. Are you hungry?"

From these statements, you can infer that the woman is strong and not easily intimidated. You can infer that she is also kind, that she understands why the boy tried to steal from her. Values are important to her, and she is determined to do what she can to help him.

When you're writing about a story or an informational text, you must be sure your inferences are supported by details in the text. **Supported inferences** are based directly on evidence in a text that you can point to and on reasonable prior knowledge. Some interpretation of the evidence is possible, but you cannot ignore or contradict facts that a writer gives you.

See pages 128, 145, 758.

INFORMATIVE TEXTS **Texts that communicate information and data.** When you're reading informative texts, you need to read slowly, looking for main ideas and important details. Slow and careful reading is especially important when you're trying to get meaning from consumer, workplace, and public documents. These documents are often not written by professional writers, so they may be difficult to read.

See also *Consumer Documents*, *Public Documents*, *Workplace Documents*.

LOGIC **Correct reasoning.** A logical text presents reasons supported by evidence (facts and examples). A text is illogical when it does not provide reasons backed by evidence. Notice how each sentence in this text, from "A Country Divided," gives evidence that supports the sentence that precedes it.

> Through the long years of British rule, the Irish fought for their freedom. They fought with what weapons they had, in rebellions great and small—rebellions that the vast British army always put down. The Irish fought with words as well as weapons. They organized and signed petitions, held massive nonviolent protests, and after Catholics regained the vote in 1829, they lobbied in the English Parliament for their freedom.

See pages 535, 579, 1213.
See also *Logical Order*.

LOGICAL ORDER **A method of organizing information by putting details into related groupings.** Writers use logical order most often when they want to classify information, that is, to examine a subject and its relationship to other subjects. When you classify, you can divide a subject into its parts (for example, presenting research from various sources about plagiarism and memory in "Kaavya Syndrome" (page 583).

See page 1213.
See also *Text Structures*.

MAIN IDEA **The writer's most important point, opinion, or message.** The main idea may be stated directly, or it may be only suggested or implied. If the idea is not stated directly, it's up to you to look at the details and decide on the idea that they all seem to support. Try to restate the writer's main idea in your own words.

In an argument, the main idea (the generalization that the writer is trying to prove) is called the **claim,** or **opinion.**

> **Main idea of essay:** Animals have a sixth sense about approaching natural disasters (for "Did Animals Sense Tsunami Was Coming?" page 107).
>
> **Claim of argument:** Power can be nurturing—it does not have to come at the price of another's well-being (for "Cinderella's Stepsisters," page 543).

See pages 99, 297.

MAPS **A drawing showing all or part of the earth's surface or of bodies in the sky. Physical maps** illustrate the natural landscape of an area, using shading, lines, and color to show landforms and elevation. **Political maps** show political units, such as states and nations. They usually also show borders and capitals and other major cities. **Special-purpose maps** present specific information, such as the routes of the explorers. The special-purpose map on page 1034 shows the route of Odysseus's journey. Use these guidelines to help you read the map on the right.

How to Read a Map

1. **Determine the focus of the map.** The map's title and labels tell you its focus—its subject and the geographical area it covers.
2. **Study the legend.** The **legend,** or **key,** explains the symbols, lines, colors, and shadings used in the map.
3. **Check directions and distances.** Maps often include a **compass rose,** a diagram that shows north, south, east, and west. If there isn't one, assume that north is at the top, west to the left, and so on. Many maps also include a scale that relates distances on the map to actual distances.
4. **Look at the larger context.** The **absolute location** of any place on earth is given by its **latitude** (the number of degrees north or south of the equator) and its **longitude** (the number of degrees east or west of the **prime meridian,** or 0 degrees longitude). Some maps also include **locator maps,** which show the area depicted in relation to a larger area.

OPINION **A statement of a person's belief, idea, or attitude.** A **fact** is something that can be verified or proved by direct observation or by checking a reliable reference source. An **opinion** cannot be proved to be either true or false—even when it is supported by facts. The following statement is an unsupported opinion:

> William Shakespeare is the greatest writer that the world has ever known.

A **valid opinion** is an opinion that is supported by verifiable facts. In the following example, the verifiable facts are underlined:

> I think that William Shakespeare was a great writer because most of his plays and poems are still read and enjoyed today, four hundred years after they were written.

When you read a persuasive text, remember that statements of opinion can't be proved, but they can and should be supported by facts and logical reasoning.

See pages 557, 579.

ORDER OF IMPORTANCE **A means of organizing information by ranking details in the order of their importance.** Writers of persuasive texts have to decide whether to give the strongest reason first or to present the weakest reason first and end with the strongest point. Informational texts such as news articles always begin with the most important details because they want to grab the readers' attention immediately. The structure of a news article looks like an upside-down triangle, with the least important details at the bottom.

See pages 524, 601.
See also *Text Structures*.

OUTLINING **A way of organizing information to show relationships among key details in a text.** You can use outlining as a writer and as a reader. Outlining puts main ideas and details in a form that you can review quickly. An **informal outline,** sometimes called a working outline, should have at least three main ideas. You put supporting details under each main idea, like this:

Informal Outline
- I. First main idea
  - A. First detail supporting first main idea
  - B. Second detail supporting first main idea
  - C. Third detail supporting first main idea
- II. Second main idea
  - [etc.]

A **formal outline** is especially useful if you're writing a research paper. You might start with a working outline and then revise it into a formal one. Your teacher may ask you to submit a formal outline with your completed research paper.

Formal outlines use Roman numerals (I, II, III), capital letters (A, B, C) and Arabic numerals (1, 2, 3) to show order, relationship, and relative importance of ideas. The headings in a formal outline should have the same grammatical structure, and you must be consistent in your use of either phrases or sentences. (You can't move back and forth between them.) There should always be at least two divisions under each heading or none at all.

PARAPHRASING **Restating each sentence of a text in your own words.** Paraphrasing is usually done only for difficult texts. Paraphrasing a text helps you to be certain you understand it. When you paraphrase, you follow the author's sequence of ideas. You carefully reword each line (if it's a poem) or sentence (if it's prose) without changing the author's ideas or leaving anything out. You restate each figure of speech to be sure you understand the basis of the comparison. If sentences are missing words or if the words are wrenched out of the usual order, you rephrase the sentence.

See pages 297, 397.

PRIMARY SOURCE **An original, firsthand account.** Primary sources may include an autobiography; an eyewitness testimony; a letter, speech, or literary work; a historical document; or information gathered from firsthand surveys or interviews. For example, Albert Einstein's "Letter to President Roosevelt" (page 399) is a primary source. It's important to use primary sources wherever they are available on a topic, but you need to research widely to make sure that a primary source is not biased.

Be sure to keep track of your primary sources by numbering each source and recording the necessary publishing information. If you quote directly from the primary source, be sure to use quotation marks and to give credit to your source.

See pages 199, 973.
See also *Secondary Source.*

PUBLIC DOCUMENTS **Informative texts put out by the government or public agencies. Public documents include political platforms, public policy statements, speeches, and debates.** These documents inform the public about government policy, laws, municipal codes, records, schedules, and the like.

See page 1182.

RESEARCH QUESTIONS **Questions that are focused on a specific subject, which the researcher searches to answer.** Such questions are essential tools for focusing your research.

One way to generate research questions is to use the *5W-How?* questions: *Who? What? When? Where? Why?* and *How?* As you seek primary and secondary source information at libraries and museums, in various electronic media (Internet, films, tapes), and from personal interviews, you will come up with more research questions. Always remember to keep your questions focused on the specific subject you have chosen.

See pages 721, 1161.

ROOTS, PREFIXES, SUFFIXES
English words are often made up of two or more word parts. These words parts include—

- **roots,** which carry a word's core meaning
- **prefixes,** added onto the beginning of a word or in front of a word root to form a new word
- **suffixes,** added onto the end of a word or after a word root to form a new word

Most word roots come from Greek and Latin. Prefixes and suffixes come from Greek, Latin, and Anglo-Saxon.

Greek Roots	Meaning	Examples
–dem–	people	**dem**ocracy, epi**dem**ic
–hydr–	water	de**hydr**ate, **hydr**ogen
–psyche-	mind, soul	**psych**ic, **psych**ology
–syn–, –sym–	together	**syn**thesize, **sym**phony

Latin Roots	Meaning	Examples
–cog–	think, know	in**cog**nito, re**cog**nize
–dic–, –dict–	say, speak	**dict**ion, inter**dict**
–juven–	young	**juven**ile, re**juven**ate
–mar–	war	**mar**tial, **mar**tinet
–somn–	sleep	**somn**olent, **som-n**ambulate

Greek Prefixes	Meaning	Examples
a–	lacking, without	**a**moral, **a**typical
neo–	new	**neo**classic, **neo**natal

Latin Prefixes	Meaning	Examples
e–, ef–, ex–	away, from, out	**ef**face, **ex**punge
retro–	back	**retro**active, **retro**spective

Anglo-Saxon/ Old English Prefixes	Meaning	Examples
be–	around	**be**friend, **be**grime
over–	above	**over**bite, **over**see
mis–	badly, not	**mis**hap, **mis**copy

Greek Suffixes	Meaning	Examples
–logue	speech	dia**logue,** epi**logue**
–ism	act, manner	critic**ism**, ostrac**ism**

Latin Suffixes	Meaning	Examples
–esce	become, grow	coal**esce**, efferv**esce**
–tude	quality of being	apti**tude,** multi**tude**

Anglo-Saxon/ Old English Suffixes	Meaning	Examples
–less *–ful* *–en*	lacking full of, marked by become	aim**less**, rest**less** rest**ful**, wonder**ful** strength**en**, light**en**

SECONDARY SOURCE **A secondhand account written by a writer who did not participate directly in the events he or she interprets, relates, or analyzes.** Secondary sources may include encyclopedias, magazine articles, textbooks, biographies, and technical journals. The news feature "Dear Juliet" (page 974) is an example of a secondary source. A research paper may include both primary and secondary sources.

See page 973.

SPATIAL ORDER **A means of organizing information by showing where things are located.** (The word *spatial* is related to the word *space*. Spatial order shows where things are located in space.) Spatial order is often used in descriptive writing. Here is an example from "The Most Dangerous Game" (page 19). Phrases showing spatial order are underlined.

> The baying of the hounds drew nearer, then still nearer, nearer, ever nearer. On a ridge Rainsford climbed a tree. Down a water course, not a quarter of a mile away, he could see the bush moving.

See also *Text Structures*.

SYNTHESIZING **Putting all the different sources of information together in a process that gives you a better understanding of the whole subject.** In order to synthesize information, you first gather information about a topic from several sources. Then you find each writer's main ideas. Paraphrasing ideas, restating them in your own words, can help you understand difficult texts. Next you examine the ideas in each source, and you compare and contrast the ideas you've found. To synthesize what you have learned, you draw conclusions about the information you have gathered .

See pages 199, 397.
See also *Generalization*.

TEXT STRUCTURES **Any organizational patterns that writers use to make their meaning clear.** In imaginative literature, text structures range from the plot structures in stories and dramas to the sonnet structure in poetry.

In nonfiction and informational texts, the writer's intent or purpose in creating the text determines how the text will be organized. Don't expect writers of informational texts and nonfiction to use the same structure throughout an entire text. Most writers switch from one type of structure to another and may even combine structures. Ideas or details in nonfiction and informational texts are arranged in four basic ways:

1. **Chronological order, time order, or sequence**—putting events or steps in the order in which they occur. Most narrative and historical texts are written in chronological order. Chronological order is also found in writing that explains a process such as technical directions and recipes. This type of chronological order is called **step-by-step order.**
2. **Spatial order**—the order that shows where things are located. This pattern is used in descriptive writing. It is especially useful in helping readers visualize setting. See the first paragraph of "Teaching Chess, and Life" (page 205).
3. **Order of importance**—ranking details from most important to least important or from least important to most important. Writers of persuasive texts in particular have to decide which order makes the strongest impact: putting the strongest reason first and the weaker ones later or saving the strongest reason for last. News articles always begin with the most important details because they want to grab the readers' attention immediately.
4. **Logical order**—classifying details into related groups. One type of logical order is the **comparison-and-contrast** text structure, which shows similarities and differences among various groups.

Other methods used to organize texts include:

- **cause and effect**—showing how events happen as a result of other events.
- **problem-solution**—explaining how a problem may be solved.
- **question-answer**—asking questions, then giving the answers. See "Did Animals Sense Tsunami Was Coming?" (page 107).

Recognizing these structures will help you understand the ideas in a text. The following guidelines can help you recognize text structures:

1. Search the text for the main idea. Look for clue words **(transitions)** that signal a specific pattern of organization. Also note colors, special type, headers, numbered lists, and icons that may be used to highlight terms or indicate text structure.
2. Analyze the text for other important ideas. Think about how the ideas connect, and look for an obvious pattern.
3. Remember that a writer might use one organizational pattern throughout a text or combine two or more patterns.
4. Draw a graphic organizer that maps how the text is structured. Some common graphic organizers are a **causal chain** (for the cause-effect text structure), a **flowchart** (showing chronological sequence), and a **Venn diagram** (showing similarities and differences).

See pages 524–525, 1182–1183.
See also *Chronological Order, Logical Order, Order of Importance, Spatial Order*.

WORKPLACE DOCUMENTS **Job-related texts, such as job applications, memos, instructional manuals, and employee handbooks.** When you read workplace documents, keep these points in mind (in addition to the points about reading consumer documents cited on page 1188):

1. Take all the time you need to read and understand the document. Don't be rushed or think that a document is unimportant or just a formality.
2. Read technical directions carefully before you start. Ask questions if you're not sure how to proceed. Don't try anything out before you know what will happen next.
3. The employee handbook contains the "rules of the game" at that particular business. It tells you about holidays, work hours, break times, and vacations as well as other important company policies. Read the employee handbook from cover to cover.

See page 1183.
See also *Consumer Documents*.

Writer's Handbook

The Writing Process

Good writing doesn't just appear, ready-made, out of nowhere. The writer of an enjoyable piece uses a process to create it. The writing process has four stages, each with several steps. The chart below lists what happens during each stage.

Stages of the Writing Process	
Prewriting	• Choose your topic. • Identify your purpose and audience. • Generate ideas, and gather information about the topic. • Begin to organize the information. • Draft a sentence that expresses your main point and your perspective on the topic.
Drafting	• Grab your readers' attention in the introduction. • Provide background information. • State and support your main points, and elaborate on them. • Follow a plan of organization. • Wrap up with a conclusion.
Evaluating and Revising	• Evaluate your draft. • Revise the draft's content, organization, and style.
Proofreading and Publishing	• Proofread, or edit, your final draft. • Publish, or share your finished writing with readers. • Reflect on your writing experience.

You can always return to an earlier stage in the process to improve your writing. For example, if in revising you find that you need more information, you can return to prewriting to gather ideas and then draft a new paragraph.

As you progress through the stages of the writing process, make sure you do the following:

- **Keep your ideas focused.** Your writing should be **coherent,** with ideas clearly connected to one another. To keep your writing on track, pin down the specific purpose you want the piece to achieve and establish a coherent thesis. Every idea in a piece must support your thesis or the controlling impression you want to create. Eliminate anything that doesn't fit your distinct perspective or that might detract from a tightly reasoned argument. Your focus should be clear and consistent throughout a piece of writing.
- **Use a consistent tone.** To unify the ideas in a piece of writing, keep your tone consistent. Avoid jumping from a serious, formal tone to a casual

or sarcastic tone midway through a piece. Choose your tone by thinking about your specific audience. What tone would they appreciate? Does that tone fit your topic?

- **Plan to publish.** Develop each piece as though it might be published, or shared with an audience. When you proofread, use the following questions to guide you. The numbers in parentheses indicate the sections in the Language Handbook that contain instruction on these topics.

Guidelines for Proofreading
1. Is every sentence complete, not a fragment or run-on? (9a, b)
2. Are punctuation marks used correctly? (12a–r, 13a–j, 14a–o)
3. Are the first letters of sentences and proper nouns and adjectives capitalized? (11a, d)
4. Does each verb agree in number with its subject? (2a) Are verb forms and tenses used correctly? (3a–e)
5. Are subject and object forms of personal pronouns used correctly? (4a–e) Does every pronoun agree with a clear antecedent in number and gender? (4i)

To mark proofreading corrections, use the symbols below.

Proofreading Symbols

Symbol	Example	Meaning of Symbol
≡	Fifty-first street	Capitalize a lowercase letter.
/	Jerry's Aunt	Lowercase a capital letter.
^	the capital ^of Ohio	Insert a missing word, letter, or punctuation mark.
^—	beside the ~~river~~ lake	Replace a word.
ℓ	Where's the ~~the~~ key?	Delete a word, letter, or punctuation mark.
∽	thier	Change the order of letters.
¶	¶ "Hi," he smiled.	Begin a new paragraph.

Paragraphs

A **paragraph** is made up of sentences grouped together for a reason—usually to present and support a single idea. Each paragraph in a composition is like a member of a team, working with other paragraphs to develop ideas. Think of a paragraph as a link in a chain connecting ideas.

Paragraphs are used to divide an essay into blocks of separate thoughts or to divide a story into a series of events. Paragraphs signal readers that a new thought or a new speaker is coming. They also allow readers to pause to digest what they've read so far.

Parts of a Body Paragraph

Although some paragraphs—especially in narrative writing—do not have a central focus, most paragraphs do emphasize one **main idea.** Paragraphs like this, often called **body paragraphs,** usually have three major parts: a **topic sentence,** which states the paragraph's main idea; additional **supporting sentences** that elaborate on and support the topic sentence; and (often, but not always) a concluding **clincher sentence.**

THE MAIN IDEA AND TOPIC SENTENCE Together, the sentences in a paragraph make its main idea clear. Many paragraphs express the main idea in a single sentence, called a **topic sentence.**

Although a topic sentence can be placed at any point in the paragraph, it often appears as the first or second sentence. A topic sentence at the beginning of a paragraph helps a reader know what to expect in the rest of the paragraph. The diagram below shows the typical three-part structure of a body paragraph that begins with a topic sentence.

Tip Although many paragraphs you read will not have topic sentences, it's a good idea to use them in your own writing to keep you focused on your main idea and to organize your support.

Typical Body Paragraph Structure

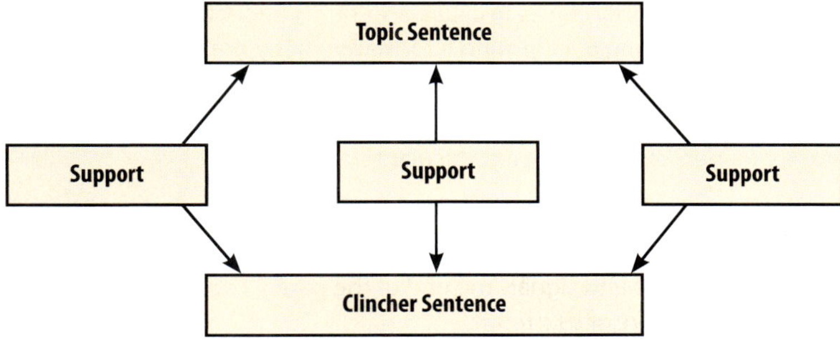

A topic sentence placed at the end of a paragraph can be an effective way to create surprise or summarize ideas. As you read the following paragraph, notice how the writer sews all the details together with a topic sentence at the very end.

> In the summer, hosts of big red-and-yellow grasshoppers, with heads shaped like horses, will descend and eat holes in all the softer leaves. Walking sticks fly like boomerangs. Shining brown leaf-shaped palmetto bugs scurry like cockroaches. Spiders like tiny crabs hang in stout webs. The birds snap at small moths and butterflies of every kind. A blue racer, the snake that moves across the cleared land like whiplash, will with one flick destroy the smooth, careful cup of the ant lion in the hot sand. The whole world of the pines and of the rocks hums and glistens and stings with life.
>
> from *The Everglades: River of Grass* by Marjory Stoneman Douglas

Tip Supporting sentences don't just provide evidence, but also elaborate on it. Every piece of support must clearly relate to the main idea; you may need to use supporting sentences to explain this connection or simply to explain a piece of evidence to make it more clear.

SUPPORTING SENTENCES To make your main idea clear and interesting, **elaborate** on it, or develop it in detail. Use supporting sentences to give the types of specific evidence below for the main idea.

Sensory Details Details collected through the senses of sight, hearing, smell, touch, or taste are called **sensory details.**

Facts and Statistics A **fact** is a statement that can be proved true. A **statistic** is a fact based on numbers, such as "During the Civil War, the South lost about 260,000 soldiers, and the North lost about 360,000." Choose facts and statistics from reliable, unbiased sources.

Examples An **example** is a specific instance or illustration of a general idea. A cow is an example of an animal.

Other Types of Supporting Evidence Some types of supporting evidence are useful only in certain kinds of writing.

- **Scenarios** are general descriptions of potential events or common situations. They can support ideas in persuasive writing and in cause-and-effect or problem-solution essays.
- **Commonly held beliefs** help support appeals in persuasive pieces. For example, to encourage voter registration, you could note the commonly held belief that everyone's vote should count. You could also grab attention at the beginning of a research report by stating a commonly held belief that your research disproves.
- **Hypotheses** are unproven theories that serve as the basis for investigation. They can support ideas in cause-and-effect papers or in research reports by providing background information or by presenting possible results of events or situations.
- **Definitions** provide support in expository and persuasive pieces by clarifying for readers exactly what a particular term means.

THE CLINCHER SENTENCE Some paragraphs, especially long ones, end with a **clincher**—a sentence that emphasizes the paragraph's main idea. A clincher pulls together details and signals the end of the paragraph, often using a transition such as *therefore* or *as a result.*

The Makings of a Good Paragraph

A good paragraph has **unity** and **coherence.** Use the following guidelines to give your own writing these two important qualities.

UNITY When a paragraph has **unity,** all its sentences work together as a unit to express or support one main idea. Sentences can work as a unit by supporting a main idea that is either stated or implied, or by expressing a related series of actions. Sentences that interrupt the consistent focus of a paragraph destroy its unity.

COHERENCE A paragraph lacking **coherence** fails to make clear how the ideas it presents fit together. Create coherence by using a clear **order,** or structure, of ideas and by making strong **connections** between ideas.

Order of Ideas How you structure ideas in a paragraph can help your readers follow those ideas. Here are four ways to organize a paragraph:

- Use **chronological order,** relating events in the order they happened, to explain a process, tell a story, or explain a cause-and-effect sequence.

- Use **spatial order,** describing things according to where they are located in relation to one another or to a viewer (for example, moving from nearest to farthest or from left to right) for descriptive writing.
- Use **order of importance,** showing the importance of details in relation to one another, to build up to or down from your most important point. Place that point prominently—first or last.
- Use **logical order,** grouping related ideas together, to **compare and contrast subjects** (explaining how they are alike and different) or to **define a subject.** The paragraph below defines *mummies.*

> A mummy is the preserved body of a human being or an animal, by any means, either deliberate or accidental. Mummies survive from many ancient cultures, some preserved in a wet state, others dry. The bog bodies of northern Europe, such as the 2,000-year-old Lindow Man, found in Cheshire, England, in 1984, belonged to people who had either fallen, or been thrown, into wet, marshy places. The exclusion of oxygen and acidity in the peat of the bog effectively preserved their bodies. Most mummies, though, were preserved by being dried, or desiccated. Many civilizations, including the Egyptian, Chinese, and some South American cultures, tried to achieve this artificially.
>
> *Mummies, Myth and Magic in Ancient Egypt* by Christine El Mahdy

Definition

Specific example

Details

Details

Details

Connections Between Ideas Along with putting ideas in an order that makes sense, you create coherence in a paragraph by showing how ideas are connected. You can show connections by using **direct references** and by using **transitional words and phrases.**

- **Direct References** Use **direct references** to link ideas by referring to a noun or pronoun used earlier in a paragraph. You can make direct references by using a noun or pronoun that refers to a noun used earlier, by repeating a word used earlier, or by using a word or phrase with the same meaning as one used earlier.
- **Transitional Words and Phrases** A **transitional expression**—whether a word, a phrase, or a sentence—shows *how* ideas are connected, often by using a conjunction or preposition. The chart below shows transitions that fit certain types of writing.

Tip Direct references and transitional words and phrases can make connections *between* paragraphs as well as *within* paragraphs.

Transitional Words and Phrases

Comparing Ideas	also and	another moreover	similarly too
Contrasting Ideas	although however	in spite of instead	on the other hand, yet
Showing Cause and Effect	as a result because consequently	for since so	so that thus therefore

Showing Chronological Order	after at last before	eventually finally first	meanwhile next then
Showing Spatial Order	above across around behind	beyond down here inside	into next to over under
Showing Importance	first last	mainly more important	then to begin with

YOUR TURN Draft a paragraph on a topic of your choice. First, identify your main idea. As you write, give your paragraph a clear topic sentence, several types of support for your main idea, and a clincher sentence; unity and coherence, with all ideas creating a controlling impression; and an easy-to-follow structure with clear connections between ideas.

The Writer's Language

Revising to Improve Style

When you revise a draft, be sure to look at your **style**—the way you express your ideas. Consider your **audience** and **purpose,** and examine your draft for **precise language, action verbs, sensory details, appropriate modifiers,** and the **active voice.**

WHO AND WHY As you re-read your draft, answer these questions:

- **What is my purpose?** Ask yourself *why* you are writing this piece and what you hope it will achieve. Make sure your **tone**—your attitude toward your topic—fits this purpose.
- **Who is my audience? Does my essay speak directly to them?** Consider whether your **level of formality** is appropriate. Avoid making your writing too formal or too informal for your audience.

THE FINER POINTS When revising, consider your **word choice**—particularly precise language, action verbs, sensory details, and appropriate modifiers. Also, use the **active voice** as much as possible. Read this example:

> I was hungry. I went home after school. Thoughts of eating were starting to come into my mind. I opened the refrigerator door and looked inside. There was nothing good to eat. The loud refrigerator door closed. Then I saw exactly what I wanted to eat—food that had been made for my mother for her birthday. I ate it all and then had to replace it.

Because it lacks stylistic elements such as precise language and sensory detail, this paragraph fails to create a complete picture.

Precise Language To paint a clear picture of a subject, use **precise verbs, nouns,** and **adjectives.** For example, the phrase "nothing good to eat" doesn't show what is in the refrigerator. Are there moldy green leftovers? a wilted head of lettuce? Create a vivid picture for readers.

Action Verbs Avoid overusing dull verbs, such as *be, go, have,* and *do.* To improve the dull sentence "I went home after school," try substituting the more vivid *ran, galloped, dragged,* or *hurried* for the verb *went.* **Action verbs** such as these *show* what happened. When revising, replace dull verbs, especially *be* verbs, with more vivid action verbs.

Sensory Details Words and phrases that appeal to the senses— sight, hearing, taste, touch, and smell—are called **sensory details.** For example, noting the sound of the narrator's growling stomach would help readers experience his or her hunger.

Appropriate Modifiers Use **appropriate modifiers** to clearly relate to the correct word. For example, in the paragraph on page 1268, the use of "loud" as an adjective implies that the refrigerator door is loud all by itself. Instead, the adverb *loudly* should modify the verb *closed.* Also, consider whether you really *need* a modifier; a more precise noun or verb is often a better solution, as in the revised sentence, "I slammed the refrigerator door."

Active Voice Use the **active** rather than the **passive voice** whenever possible in your writing. The phrase "food that had been made for my mother" is in the passive voice. The action just "happens" to the subject. To show *who* performed the action, the phrase should be turned around: "food I had made for my mother." To find passive constructions in your writing, first look for *be*-verbs. Then, decide whether the action of the sentence is being done *by* the subject or to the subject. If the subject is receiving the action, revise.

Read the following revision of the passage from page 1268. Notice how precise language, action verbs, sensory details, appropriate modifiers, and the active voice make the writing more vivid and entertaining.

A Writer's Model

My stomach growled, and I galloped home from school—all I could think about was food. I opened the refrigerator door and peeked inside. A wilted head of lettuce stared back at me, along with a mysterious something, squishy and greenish brown in a plastic bag. "Yuck," I thought, hungrier than ever. I slammed the refrigerator door. Suddenly, my mouth watered as I saw just what I wanted to eat on the kitchen counter. The muffins I had made for my mother for a birthday breakfast were irresistible. By the time I thought about what I was doing, I had wolfed down all of them. Now I had to figure out how to replace the birthday treat before my mother got home!

Action verbs

Precise language and sensory detail

Action verb

Precise language and active voice

YOUR TURN **Revise the following paragraph to improve its style. Make up details as needed.**

A collection of American Indian items is on display at a museum in town. They have arrowheads, blankets, and cooking pots. Some of the arrowheads are small, and some are larger. The blankets are colorful, and the cooking pots are interesting. One of the pots can be touched. A lecture is given. The exhibit is unique.

Designing Your Writing

No matter how well-written a document's content might be, if it looks confusing or hard to read, it won't make a strong impact on the audience. Some readers may give up trying to read a badly designed document. Others may assume that a writer who is careless about design is also careless about facts. Use the suggestions in this section to get your ideas across clearly.

Page Design

EASY ON THE EYES If you want your documents to make a good impression, make sure they are visually appealing and easy to read. You can improve the readability and impact of your papers by using some of the design elements below, whether you create those documents by hand or by using a word-processing program.

Design Elements

Element	Definition	Purpose
Bullets	A *bullet* (•) is an icon used to make information stand out.	Bullets are most often used for lists.
Captions	A *caption* is text printed beneath an illustration.	Captions explain photos, maps, and graphs.
Columns and blocks of text	*Columns* arrange text in two or more separate sections printed side by side. A *block* is a section of text shorter than a page—for example, one story would fill a rectangular block on the front page of the newspaper. Columns and blocks of text are separated from each other by white space.	Columns and blocks make text easier to read.
Headings and subheadings	A *heading* gives readers a general idea of what a section of text, such as a chapter, will be about. A *subheading* is used to indicate subsections of the text.	Headings and subheadings give readers clues about the content and organization of the document.
Leading	*Leading* (rhymes with *heading*) is the amount of white space *between* lines of text. This text is single-spaced.	For school papers, use double-spaced text, which gives your teacher space to comment on your ideas.
Margins	*Margins* are the white space at the top, bottom, and both sides of a page.	Page margins of about one inch create a visual break for readers and make text easier to read.

A CAPITAL IDEA Your choice of type can affect a document's readability and attractiveness. You can vary the **case** of type (from the usual **lowercase,** or small type) to add interest to a document and make it easier to navigate.

- **Uppercase,** or all capital, letters attract readers' attention and may be used in headings or titles. Words in uppercase letters can be difficult to read. Use uppercase letters for emphasis, not for large bodies of text.
- **Small caps** are uppercase letters that are reduced in size. Usually they appear in abbreviations of time, such as 9:00 A.M. and A.D. 1500.

FONT-ASTIC! A **font** is one complete set of characters (such as letters, numbers, and punctuation marks) of a given size and design. Here are the types of fonts. (The chart below uses a sans serif font.)

Types of Fonts

Category	Explanation	How They Are Used
decorative, or **script**, fonts	elaborately designed characters that convey a distinct mood or feeling	Decorative fonts are difficult to read and should be used sparingly for an artistic effect.
serif fonts	characters with small strokes (serifs) attached at each end	Because the strokes on serif characters guide the reader's eyes from letter to letter, serif type is often used for large bodies of text.
sans serif fonts	characters formed of neat straight lines, with no serifs at the ends of letters	Sans serif fonts are easy to read and are used for headings, subheadings, callouts, and captions.

Graphics and Visuals

THE BIG PICTURE Some information is difficult to communicate in words but easy to communicate visually. Fortunately, advanced publishing software has made creating many kinds of visuals easy. A graphic program may allow you to enter your information and choose the most appropriate type of visual. You can also create nearly any type of graphic by hand.

Choosing the right visual to show a piece of information will help you avoid confusing your readers. Include a **caption** or **title** that explicitly tells readers what they are to see in the visual and why it is there. Use **color** sparingly to emphasize ideas, not as decoration. The following pages explain some useful types of visuals.

Charts show relationships among ideas or data. Two types of charts you are likely to use are flowcharts and pie charts. A **flowchart** uses geometric shapes linked by arrows to show the sequence of events in a process.

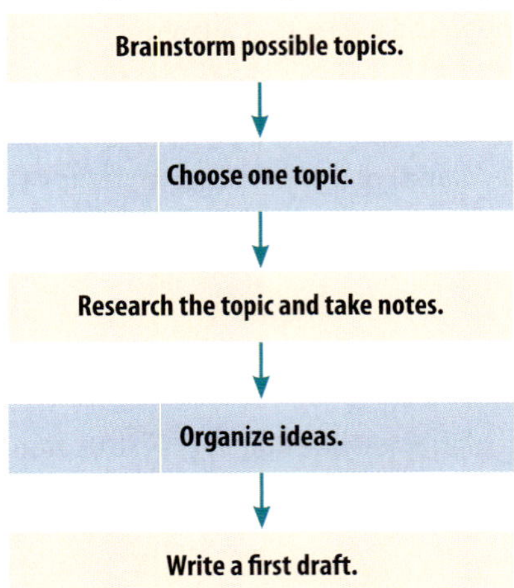

A **pie chart** shows the parts of a whole. This type of chart is a circle that is divided into wedges. Each wedge represents a certain percentage of the total. A legend tells what idea or characteristic of the whole is represented by each wedge color.

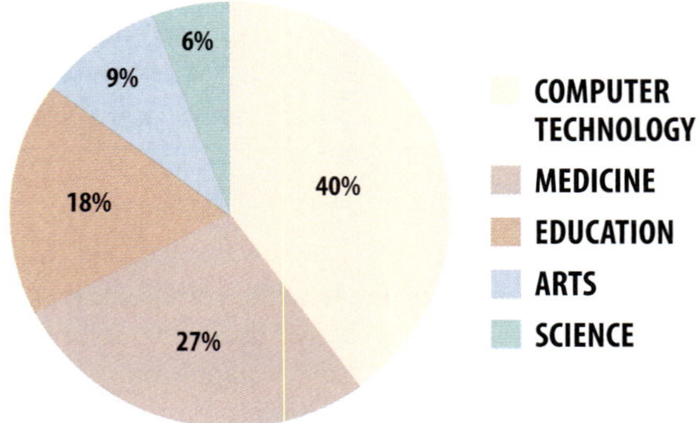

Graphs use numbers to present facts and figures. There are two types of graphs, both used to show how one thing changes in relation to another. A **bar graph** can be used to compare quantities at a glance, to show trends or changes over time, or to indicate the parts of a whole. Bar graphs, such as the example at the top of the next page, are formed along a vertical and horizontal axis.

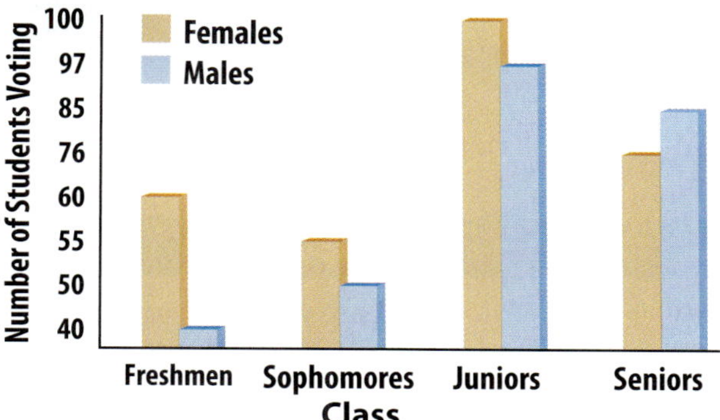

A **line graph** can be used to show changes or trends over time, to compare trends, or to show how two or more variables interact.

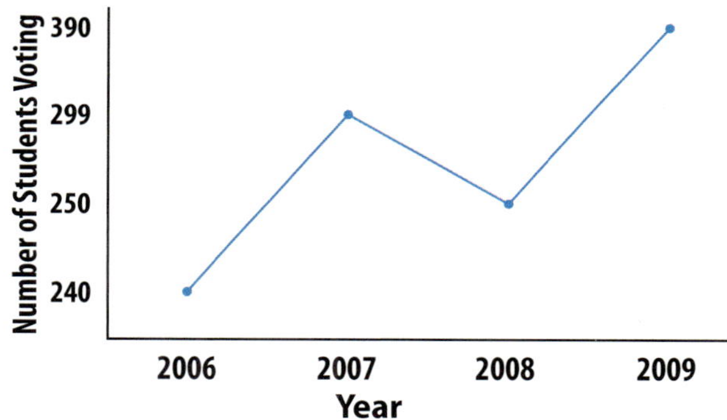

- **Maps** represent part of the earth or space. Maps of the earth may show geographical features, roads, cities, and other important locations.

Other types of visuals you might use to present information include **illustrations** showing your subject, **diagrams** clarifying a process you explain, and **time lines** pinpointing historical events you discuss.

YOUR TURN Choose the visual you think would most effectively communicate the information below. Then, use the guidelines in this section to create the visual.

Diameters of selected solar system planets in kilometers:

Mercury 4,878
Earth 12,756
Jupiter 142,800
Neptune 49,528

Language Handbook

1. The Parts of Speech

Part of Speech	Definition	Examples
NOUN	Names a person, place, thing, or idea	captain, swimmers, Maria Tallchief, team, London, "The Scarlet Ibis," justice
PRONOUN	Takes the place of a noun or pronoun	
personal	Refers to the one(s) speaking (first person), spoken to (second person), or spoken about (third person)	I, me, my, mine, we, us, our, ours you, your, yours he, him, his, she, her, hers, it, its they, them, their, theirs
reflexive	Refers to and directs the action of the verb back to the subject	myself, ourselves, yourself, yourselves, himself, herself, itself, themselves
intensive	Refers to and emphasizes a noun or pronoun	(Same as reflexive.)
demonstrative	Refers to specific one(s) of a group	this, that, these, those
interrogative	Introduces a question	what, which, who, whom, whose
relative	Introduces subordinate clause and refers to noun or pronoun outside the clause	that, which, who, whom, whose
indefinite	Refers to one(s) not specifically named	all, any, anyone, both, each, either, everybody, many, none, nothing
ADJECTIVE	Modifies a noun or pronoun by telling *what kind, which one, how many,* or *how much*	**an old, flea-bitten** dog, **that** one, **the twelve red** roses, **more** water
VERB	Shows action or state of being	
action	Expresses physical or mental activity	paint, jump, write, know, imagine
linking	Connects subject with word identifying or describing it	appear, be, seem, become, feel, look, smell, sound, taste
helping (auxiliary)	Combines with another verb to form a verb phrase	be, do, have, may, can shall, will, would
ADVERB	Modifies a verb, adjective, or adverb by telling *how, when, where,* or *to what extent*	drives **carefully,** arrived **there late, shortly afterward, quite** dangerous
PREPOSITION	Relates a noun or pronoun to another word	across, between, into, near, of, on, with, aside from, instead of, next to

Part of Speech	Definition	Examples
CONJUNCTION	Joins words or word groups	
coordinating	Joins words or word groups used similarly	and, but, for, nor, or, so yet
correlative	A pair of conjunctions that join parallel words or word groups	both . . . and, either . . . or, neither . . . nor, not only . . . but (also)
subordinating	Begins a subordinate clause and connects it to an independent clause	as though, because, if, since, so that, than, when, where, while
INTERJECTION	Expresses emotion	hey, oops, ouch, wow

Your Turn Determining Parts of Speech

The way a word is used in a sentence determines the word's part of speech:

The fine feathers of birds are called **down.** [noun]
She wore a **down** vest. [adjective]
We watched him **down** the milk in gulps. [verb]
Her poster fell **down.** [adverb]
We coasted **down** the hill. [preposition]

Write three sentences using the word *water* as a noun, as a verb, and as an adjective.

2. Agreement

Agreement of Subject and Verb

2a. A verb should always agree with its subject in number. Singular subjects take singular verbs. Plural subjects take plural verbs.

SINGULAR **She searches** for the necklace.
PLURAL **They search** for the necklace.

SINGULAR The flower **garden was destroyed.**
PLURAL The **marigolds were destroyed.**

COMPUTER NOTE Some word-processing programs can identify problems in subject-verb agreement. You can use such a program to help you search for errors when you are proofreading your writing. If you are not sure if a problem identified by the program is actually an error, check it in this section of the Language Handbook.

2b. The number of the subject is not changed by a phrase following the subject.

SINGULAR The **sign** near the glass doors **explains** the theme of the exhibit.
PLURAL Several **paintings** by Emilio Sánchez **were hanging** in the gallery.

SINGULAR **Romeo,** together with Benvolio and Mercutio, **goes** to Lord Capulet's party.
PLURAL The **combs** made of pure tortoise shell **were** expensive.

The number of the subject is not changed by a negative construction following the subject.

A **human being**, not a tiger nor any other animal, **is** the prey hunted by General Zaroff.

2c. The following indefinite pronouns are singular: *anybody, anyone, anything, each, either, everybody, everyone, everything, neither, nobody, no one, nothing, one, somebody, someone, something.*

Each of the poems **was written** by Gary Soto.
Has anyone in your study group **read** *The Skirt*?

2d. The following indefinite pronouns are plural: *both, few, many, several.*

Both of the poems **were written** by Gary Soto.
How many in your study group **have read** *The Skirt*?

2e. The indefinite pronouns *all, any, most, none,* and *some* are singular when they refer to singular words and are plural when they refer to plural words.

SINGULAR **Some** of the show **was** funny.
PLURAL **Some** of the skits **were** funny.

SINGULAR **All** of the house **looks** clean.
PLURAL **All** of the houses **look** clean.

2f. A *compound subject,* which is two or more subjects that have the same verb, may be singular, plural, or either.

(1) Subjects joined by *and* usually take a plural verb.
Leslie Marmon Silko and **Mari Evans are** poets.

A compound subject that names only one person or thing takes a singular verb.

My **pen pal and best friend is** my cousin.
Macaroni and cheese makes a good side dish.

(2) Singular subjects joined by *or* or *nor* take a singular verb.

Either the **principal** or the **coach has** to approve it.
Neither **Della** nor **Jim was** disappointed.

(3) When a singular subject and a plural subject are joined by *or* or *nor*, the verb agrees with the subject nearer the verb.

Neither the losers nor the **winner was** happy with the outcome of the match.
Neither the winner nor the **losers were** happy with the outcome of the match.

NOTE If such a construction sounds awkward, revise the sentence to give each subject its own verb.

The **losers were** not happy with the outcome of the match, and neither **was** the **winner.**

2g. *Don't* and *doesn't* must agree with their subjects.

With the subjects *I* and *you* and with plural subjects, use *don't (do not)*.

I **don't** know.
You **don't** seem happy.
Some people **don't** care.

With other subjects, use *doesn't* (*does not*).

He **doesn't** drive.
Donna **doesn't** work.
It **doesn't** have one.

2h. **A collective noun takes a singular verb when the noun refers to the group as a unit and takes a plural verb when the noun refers to the individual parts or members of the group.**

A ***collective noun*** is singular in form but names a group of persons or things.

SINGULAR The class **has** elected its officers. [class = a unit]
PLURAL The class **have** completed their reports. [class = individual students]

Common Collective Nouns			
army	club	group	public
assembly	committee	squad	majority
audience	couple	jury	staff
crew	class	flock	pair
cast	crowd	number	team
chorus	family	pack	troop

2i. **A verb agrees with its subject, not with its predicate nominative.**

SINGULAR The main **attraction is** the marching bands.
PLURAL The marching **bands are** the main attraction.

2j. **A verb agrees with its subject even when the verb precedes the subject, as in sentences beginning with *here* or *there* and in questions.**

SINGULAR Here **is** my **drawing** of the Cyclops.
PLURAL Here **are** my **drawings** of the Cyclops.

NOTE Contractions such as *here's, there's,* and *where's* should be used only with singular subjects.

2k. **An expression of an amount (a length of time, a statistic, or a fraction, for example) is singular when the amount is thought of as a unit or when it refers to a singular word and is plural when the amount is thought of as many parts or when it refers to a plural word.**

SINGULAR **Twenty dollars was** the amount Della received for her hair. [Twenty dollars is the single amount Della receives.]
PLURAL **Twenty dollars were** hidden in the book. [Twenty dollar bills were hidden.]

SINGULAR **Half** of the barrel **is** full. [*Half* refers to *barrel.*]
PLURAL **Half** of the barrels **are** full. [*Half* refers to *barrels.*]

2l. **The title of a creative work (such as a book, song, film, or painting) or the name of an organization, a country, or a city (even if it is plural in form) takes a singular verb.**

"Marigolds" is a story by Eugenia W. Collier.
Friends of the Earth was founded in 1969.
The Netherlands has thousands of canals.

2m. **A few nouns, although plural in form, take singular verbs.**

The **news was** reported in all the media.

Some nouns that end in *–s* take a plural verb even though they refer to a single item.

The **scissors need** to be sharpened.
Were these **pants** on sale?

AGREEMENT OF PRONOUN AND ANTECEDENT

A pronoun usually refers to a noun or another pronoun. The word that a pronoun refers to is called its ***antecedent.***

2n. **A pronoun agrees with its antecedent in number and gender. A few singular personal pronouns indicate gender: feminine, masculine, or neuter. No plural pronouns indicate gender.**

masculine	he	him	his	himself
feminine	she	her	hers	herself
neuter	it	it	its	itself

Juliet stabs **herself.** [singular, feminine]
General Zaroff thinks that Rainsford has escaped **him.** [singular, masculine]
After eating the Lotus plant, the **men** did not want to return to **their** homeland. [plural]

2o. **A singular pronoun is used to refer to *anybody, anyone, anything, each, either, everybody, no one, nothing, one, somebody, someone,* or *something.* The gender of any of these pronouns can sometimes be determined by a word in a phrase following the pronoun.**

Each of the **boys** held some pebbles in **his** hand.
Everyone on the **girls'** tennis team won **her** match.

When the antecedent is unclear, use both a masculine and feminine pronoun connected by *or.*

Everybody shared **his** or **her** opinion.

2p. **A singular pronoun is used to refer to two or more singular antecedents joined by *or* or *nor.***

Paula or **Janet** will present **her** report next.
Neither **Richard** nor **Bob** has finished **his** report.

If a sentence sounds awkward when the antecedents are of different genders, revise it.

AWKWARD Either **Ben** or **Maya** will read **his** or **her** report on O. Henry.

REVISED Either **Ben** will read **his** report on O. Henry, or **Maya** will read **hers.**

2q. **A plural pronoun is used to refer to two or more antecedents joined by *and.***

Romeo and Juliet marry despite the feud between **their** families.
Because **Doodle and his brother** spent much time together, **they** became very close.

2r. **The number of a relative pronoun (such as *who, whom, whose, which,* or *that*) depends on the number of its antecedent.**

Aretha is a **friend who** always keeps her word.
Many who volunteer **find their** experiences rewarding.

Your Turn Eliminating *His* or *Her* Construction

When an antecedent can be either masculine or feminine, you can avoid the *his or her* construction by using plural nouns and pronouns. Revise each of the following sentences to eliminate the *his or her* construction.

1. Each person had to hide his or her talents.
2. Could anyone take off his or her handicap bag?
3. Everybody had to be equal to his or her neighbor.
4. Did Harrison or the dancer realize his or her fate?
5. Neither he nor she wore his or her handicaps.

3. Using Verbs

The Principal Parts of Verbs

3a. The four principal parts of a verb are the *base form,* the *present participle,* the *past,* and the *past participle.* These principal parts are used to form all the different verb tenses. The present and past participles are always used with helping verbs—forms of *be* or *have.* If you are unsure about the principal parts of a verb, you can find them in a dictionary.

Common Regular Verbs

BASE FORM	PRESENT PARTICIPLE	PAST	PAST PARTICIPLE
ask	(is) asking	asked	(have) asked
raise	(is) raising	raised	(have) raised
plan	(is) planning	planned	(have) planned
try	(is) trying	tried	(have) tried

Common Irregular Verbs

BASE FORM	PRESENT PARTICIPLE	PAST	PAST PARTICIPLE
be	(is) being	was, were	(have) been
begin	(is) beginning	began	(have) begun
bring	(is) bringing	brought	(have) brought
drink	(is) drinking	drank	(have) drunk
eat	(is) eating	ate	(have) eaten
fall	(is) falling	fell	(have) fallen
find	(is) finding	found	(have) found
go	(is) going	went	(have) gone
keep	(is) keeping	kept	(have) kept
lay	(is) laying	laid	(have) laid
lead	(is) leading	led	(have) led
lie	(is) lying	lay	(have) lain
ride	(is) riding	rode	(have) ridden
set	(is) setting	set	(have) set
shake	(is) shaking	shook	(have) shaken
sing	(is) singing	sang	(have) sung
sit	(is) sitting	sat	(have) sat
steal	(is) stealing	stole	(have) stolen
swim	(is) swimming	swam	(have) swum
tear	(is) tearing	tore	(have) torn

3b. A *regular verb* forms its past and past participle by adding *–ed* to the base form.

3c. An *irregular verb* forms its past and past participle in a way other than adding *–ed* to the base form.

TENSE

3d. The *tense* of a verb indicates the time of the action or the state of being expressed by the verb. Verbs in English have six tenses: *present, past, future, present perfect, past perfect,* and *future perfect.* The tenses are formed from the verb's principal parts.

(1) The ***present tense*** is used mainly to express an action or a state of being that is occurring now.

The car **turns** into the driveway.
They **like** my idea for a science project.

The present tense is also used—

- to show a customary action or state of being
  Every November she **bakes** fruitcakes for her friends.
- to express a general truth—something that is always true
  The sun **sets** in the west.
- to make historical events seem current (such use is called the ***historical present***)
  In 1905, Albert Einstein **proposes** his theory of relativity.
- to discuss a literary work (such use is called the ***literary present***)
  Maya Angelou's *I Know Why the Caged Bird Sings* **tells** the story of her childhood.
- to express future time
  Finals **begin** next week.

(2) The ***past tense*** is used to express an action or a state of being that occurred in the past but that is not occurring now.

Jim **gave** Della a set of combs.
The children **annoyed** Miss Lottie.

A past action or state of being can also be shown with the verb *used* followed by an infinitive.

We **used to live** in Chicago.

(3) The ***future tense*** (formed with *will* or *shall* and the verb's base form) is used to express an action or a state of being that will occur.

I **shall play** the part of Romeo.
They **will arrive** soon.

A future action or state of being can also be shown in other ways.

They **are going to win.**
We **leave** for the theater **in an hour.**

(4) The ***present perfect tense*** (formed with *have* or *has* and the verb's past participle) is used to express an action or a state of being that occurred at some indefinite time in the past.

Doodle **has learned** how to walk.
We **have read** the *Odyssey*.

The present perfect tense is also used to express an action or a state of being that began with the past and continues into the present.

We **have lived** in the same house for nine years.

(5) The ***past perfect tense*** (formed with *had* and the verb's past participle) is used to express an action or a state of being that was completed in the past before some other past action or event.

Lizabeth regretted what she **had done.** [The doing occurred before the regretting.]
When you called, I **had** already **eaten** supper. [The eating occurred before the calling.]

(6) The ***future perfect tense*** (formed with *will have* or *shall have* and the verb's past participle) is used to express an action or a state of being that will be completed in the future before some other future occurrence.

When Mom returns, I **will have done** my chores. [The doing will be completed before the returning.]
He **will have finished** his Hebrew lessons before his bar mitzvah. [The finishing will be completed before the bar mitzvah.]

Each of the six verb tenses has an additional form called the ***progressive form.*** The progressive form expresses a continuing action or state of being. It consists of the appropriate tense of *be* plus the verb's present participle. For the perfect tenses, the progressive form includes one or more helping verbs.

Progressive Form of *Give*	
Present	am, are, is giving
Past	was, were giving
Future	will be giving
Present Perfect	has, have been giving
Past Perfect	had been giving
Future Perfect	will have been giving

3e. Do not change needlessly from one tense to another.

INCONSISTENT Jim **sold** his watch and **buys** Della a set of combs.

CONSISTENT Jim **sold** his watch and **bought** Della a set of combs.

ACTIVE AND PASSIVE VOICE

3f. A verb in the *active voice* expresses an action done by its subject. A verb in the *passive voice* expresses an action received by its subject.

A verb in the passive voice is always a verb phrase that includes a form of *be* and the main verb's past participle.

ACTIVE VOICE Rainford **surprised** General Zaroff. [The subject, *Rainsford*, performs the action.]

PASSIVE VOICE General Zaroff **was surprised** by Rainsford. [The subject, *General Zaroff*, receives the action.]

3g. Use the passive voice sparingly.

The passive voice is not any less correct than the active voice, but it is less direct, less forceful, and less concise. As a result, a sentence written in the passive voice can often sound awkward or weak.

AWKWARD PASSIVE Mme. Forestier's necklace **was borrowed** by Mme. Loisel.

ACTIVE Mme. Loisel **borrowed** Mme. Forestier's necklace.

The passive voice is useful, however, in certain situations:

(1) when you do not know the performer of the action

The Globe Theatre **was built** in 1599.

(2) when you do not want to reveal the performer of the action

Mistakes **were made**.

(3) when you want to emphasize the receiver of the action

Abraham Lincoln **was elected** president in 1860.

COMPUTER NOTE Some software programs can identify and highlight passive-voice verbs. If you use such a program, keep in mind that it can't tell why you used the passive voice. If you did so for one of the reasons listed in 3g, you may want to leave it.

Your Turn Changing Verb Tense

Change the verb tenses in each sentence to make them consistent.

1. Before he went away, they are going to the ocean.
2. I am eating dinner, and I will have taken a nap.
3. What he drank is a glass of milk.
4. She writes ghost stories and was superstitious.
5. He was grateful for the help she will offer.

4. Using Pronouns

Case

Case is the form that a pronoun takes to indicate its use in a sentence. In English, there are three cases: *nominative, objective,* and *possessive.* Most personal pronouns have a different form for each case.

PERSONAL PRONOUNS			
Singular			
	NOMINATIVE	OBJECTIVE	POSSESSIVE
FIRST PERSON	I	me	my, mine
SECOND PERSON	you	you	your, yours
THIRD PERSON	he, she, it	him, her, it	his, her, hers, its
Plural			
	NOMINATIVE	OBJECTIVE	POSSESSIVE
FIRST PERSON	we	us	our, ours
SECOND PERSON	you	you	your, yours
THIRD PERSON	they	them	their, theirs

The Nominative Case

4a. A subject of a verb is in the nominative case.

She was glad that **they** were elected. [*She* is the subject of *was; they* is the subject of *were elected.*]

Are **Della** and **he** disappointed? [*Della* and *he* are the compound subject of *are.*]

4b. A predicate nominative is in the nominative case.

A ***predicate nominative*** follows a linking verb and explains or identifies the subject of the verb.

The woman who borrows the necklace is **she.** [*She* identifies the subject *woman.*]

The main characters are **he** and his **brother** Doodle. [*He* and *brother* identify the subject *characters.*]

The Objective Case

4c. *A direct object* of a verb is in the objective case.

A ***direct object*** follows an action verb and tells *whom* or *what.*

Lizabeth destroyed **them.** [*Them* tells *what* Lizabeth destroyed.]

Friar Laurence helps **him.** [*Him* tells *whom* Friar Laurence helps.]

4d. An indirect object of a verb is in the objective case.

An **indirect object** comes before a direct object and tells *to whom* or *to what* or *for whom* or *for what.*

Buddy gave **her** a kite. [*Her* tells *to whom* Buddy gave a kite.]

Molly made **him** and **me** a CD. [*Him* and *me* tell *for whom* Molly made a CD.]

4e. An object of a preposition is in the objective case.

An ***object of a preposition*** comes at the end of a phrase that begins with a preposition.

Mme. Loisel borrows a necklace from **her.**

This gift is for **them.**

SPECIAL PRONOUN PROBLEMS

4f. The pronoun *who (whoever)* is in the nominative case. The pronoun *whom (whomever)* is in the objective case.

NOMINATIVE **Who** wrote *Black Boy*? [*Who* is the subject of *wrote.*]

OBJECTIVE From **whom** did Mme. Loisel borrow the necklace? [*Whom* is the object of the preposition *from.*]

When choosing between *who* and *whom* in a subordinate clause, be sure to base your choice on how the pronoun functions in the subordinate clause.

The sniper learned **who** his enemy had been. [*Who* is the predicate nominative identifying the subject *enemy.*]

The sniper learned the identity of the man **whom** he had shot. [*Whom* is the direct object of *had shot.*]

4g. **An appositive is in the same case as the noun or pronoun to which it refers.**

An ***appositive*** is a noun or pronoun placed next to another noun or pronoun to identify or explain it.

The main characters, **Romeo and Juliet,** are lovers. [The appositive, *Romeo and Juliet,* identifies the subject, *characters.*]

The teacher did not say a word to either of the boys, **Ned or Sam.** [The appositive, *Ned or Sam,* identifies an object of a preposition, *boys.*]

Sometimes the pronouns *we* and *us* are used with noun appositives.

We cast members have a dress rehearsal tonight. [The pronoun *we* is the subject of *have.*]

The principal praised **us** members of the Ecology Club. [The pronoun *us* is in the direct object of *praised.*]

4h. **A pronoun following *than* or *as* in an incomplete construction is in the same case as it would be if the construction were completed.**

I wrote you more often than **he** [wrote you].
I wrote you more often than [I wrote] **him.**

Did you help Ada as much as **I** [helped Ada]?
Did you help Ada as much as [you helped] **me**?

Clear Pronoun Reference

4i. **A pronoun should refer clearly to its antecedent.**

An ***antecedent*** is the word a pronoun stands for.

(1) Avoid an ***ambiguous reference,*** which occurs when a pronoun can refer to any one of two or more antecedents.

AMBIGUOUS Miss Lottie saw Lizabeth when she was in the garden. [*She* can refer to either Miss Lottie or Lizabeth.]

CLEAR When **Miss Lottie** was in the garden, **she** saw Lizabeth.

CLEAR When **Lizabeth** was in the garden, Miss Lottie saw **her.**

(2) Avoid a ***general reference,*** which occurs when a pronoun refers to a general idea rather than to a specific antecedent.

GENERAL Rainsford had escaped. This annoyed General Zaroff. [*This* has no specific antecedent.]

CLEAR That Rainsford had escaped annoyed General Zaroff.

(3) Avoid a ***weak reference,*** which occurs when a pronoun refers to an implied antecedent.

WEAK Ralph enjoys writing poetry, but he never shows **them** to anyone else. [*Them* most likely refers to the unstated plural *poems,* but the writer has used the singular word *poetry.*]

CLEAR Ralph enjoys writing poetry, but he never shows his poems to anyone else.

(4) Avoid using an ***indefinite reference,*** which occurs when a pronoun (such as *you, it,* or *they*) refers to no particular person or thing.

INDEFINITE In the owner's manual, they explain how to program the DVD player.

CLEAR The owner's manual explains how to program the DVD player.

NOTE The indefinite use of *it* is acceptable in familiar expressions such as *It is snowing.*

Your Turn Using *Whom* in a Sentence

Insert *whom* where it is appropriate in each of these sentences. Make other changes as needed for the sentence to sound correct.

1. The girl they admired was reading.
2. Do you know boys like the ones he speaks of?
3. They talked about the woman each of them would marry.
4. The other boy Gary Soto wrote of said that he would go to school.
5. The field of carpentry appealed to the boy that kind of work was easy for.

5. Using Modifiers

What Is a Modifier?

A ***modifier*** is a word or group of words that limits the meaning of another word or group of words. The two kinds of modifiers are *adjectives* and *adverbs.* An ***adjective*** limits the meaning of a noun or a pronoun. An ***adverb*** limits the meaning of a verb, an adjective, or another adverb.

Adjective or Adverb?

Not all adverbs end in *–ly,* and not all words that end with *–ly* are adverbs. Some adjectives also end in *–ly.* You can't tell whether a word is an adjective or adverb simply by looking for the *–ly* ending.

Adverbs not Ending in *–LY*

arrive **soon** sit **here** run **loose**

Adjectives Ending in *–LY*

daily diet **holy** place **silly** joke

Some words can be used as adjectives or adverbs.

Adjectives	Adverbs
He is an **only** child.	She has **only** one sister.
I have an **early** class.	I get up **early.**
We caught the **last** bus.	We left **last.**

COMPARISON OF MODIFIERS

5a. **The forms of modifiers change to show comparison.**

The three degrees of comparison are *positive, comparative,* and *superlative.*

Regular Comparison

(1) Most one-syllable modifiers form the comparative and superlative by adding *–er* and *–est.*

(2) Some two-syllable modifiers form the comparative and superlative by adding *–er* or *–est*. Some form the comparative and superlative with *more* and *most.*

(3) Modifiers of more than two syllables form the comparative and superlative by using *more* and *most.*

(4) All modifiers show decreasing degrees of comparison by using *less* and *least.*

Positive	Comparative	Superlative
deep	deeper	deepest
gentle	gentle	gentlest
careful	more careful	most careful
important	more important	most important
common	less common	least common

Irregular Comparison

(5) Some modifiers form the comparative and superlative in other ways.

Positive	Comparative	Superlative
bad	worse	worst
good/well	better	best
little	less	least
many/much	more	most

Use of Comparative and Superlative Forms

5b. **Use the comparative degree when comparing two things. Use the superlative degree when comparing more than two.**

COMPARATIVE Rainsford was **more resourceful** than Zaroff thought he would be.

SUPERLATIVE This was the **most suspenseful** story I have ever read.

5c. **Include *other* or *else* when comparing one thing with others in the same group.**

ILLOGICAL Ruth is more agile than any member of her gymnastics team. [Ruth is a member of her team; she cannot be more agile than herself.]

LOGICAL Ruth is more agile than any **other** member of her gymnastics team.

ILLOGICAL Carlos ran faster than everyone. [*Everyone* includes Carlos; he cannot run faster than himself.]

LOGICAL Carlos ran faster than everyone **else.**

Gerunds and Gerund Phrases

6d. **A *gerund* is a verb form ending in *–ing* that is used as a noun. A *gerund phrase* consists of a gerund and all the words related to the gerund.**

Violently destroying the marigolds was Lizabeth's last act of childhood. [The gerund phrase is the subject of *was.*]
They enjoy **making fruitcakes together.** [The gerund phrase is the direct object of *enjoy.*]
Rainsford escaped from Zaroff by **leaping into the sea.** [The gerund phrase is the object of the preposition *by.*]

Do not confuse a gerund with a present participle used as an adjective or as part of a verb phrase.
Following her coach's advice, she was **planning** to go on with her **training.**[*Following* is a present participle modifying *she*. *Planning* is part of the verb phrase *was planning. Training* is a gerund used as the object of the preposition *with.*]

NOTE When preceding a gerund, a noun or pronoun should be in the possessive form.
Pedro's constant practicing improved **his** playing.

Infinitives and Infinitive Phrases

6e. **An *infinitive* is a verb form, usually preceded by *to,* that can be used as a noun, an adjective, or an adverb. An *infinitive phrase* consists of an infinitive and all the words related it.**

NOUN **To proofread your writing carefully** is important. [The infinitive phrase is the subject of *is.*]
Why did she finally decide **to buy that video?** [The infinitive phrase is the direct object of *decide.*]
Zaroff's plan was **to hunt Rainsford.** [The infinitive phrase is the predicate nominative identifying the subject *plan.*]

ADJECTIVE Friar Laurence's plan **to help Romeo and Juliet** failed. [The infinitive phrase modifies the noun *plan.*]

ADVERB Fortunato was eager **to taste the amontillado.** [The infinitive phrase modifies the adjective *eager.*]

Sometimes the *to* of the infinitive is omitted.
You should go [to] get a warmer jacket.

NOTE Do not confuse an infinitive with a prepositional phrase that begins with *to.*
Doodle and he went **to the creek** [prepositional phrase] **to swim** [infinitive].

6f. **An infinitive may have a subject, in which case it forms an *infinitive clause.***

Juliet trusted Friar Laurence and asked **him to help her.** [The infinitive clause is the direct object of *asked. Him* is the subject of the infinitive to *help; her* is its direct object.]

Note that a pronoun functioning as the subject of an infinitive clause takes the objective form.

APPOSITIVES AND APPOSITIVE PHRASES

6g. **An *appositive* is a noun or a pronoun placed beside another noun or pronoun to identify it or explain it. An *appositive phrase* consists of an appositive and its modifiers.**

Kurt Vonnegut wrote the story **"Harrison Bergeron."** [The appositive identifies the noun *story.*]
Odysseus blinded Cyclops, **the one-eyed giant.** [The appositive phrase explains the noun *Cyclops.*]

An appositive phrase usually follows the noun or pronoun it refers to. For emphasis, however, it may come at the beginning of a sentence.
A noble leader of his people, Chief Joseph spoke with quiet dignity.

Appositives and appositive phrases are usually set off by commas. However, if the appositive is necessary for identifying the preceding noun or pronoun, it should not be set off by commas.
My brother **Richard** goes to college. [The writer has more than one brother, and the appositive identifies which brother goes to college.]
My brother, **Richard,** goes to college. [The writer has only one brother; therefore, the appositive is not necessary to identify him.]

Your Turn Forming Verbal Phrases

Combine each of the following pairs of sentences by using the predicate of one sentence to form a verbal or verbal phrase that can be added to the other sentence. Revise your sentence as needed to make it clear and concise.

1. N. Scott Momaday often rode his horse. For him, this activity was "an exercise of the mind."
2. He rode his horse, Pecos, over the hills of New Mexico. Along the way, he liked to imagine that he was traveling with Billy the Kid.
3. Sometimes he and Billy saved a wagon train in trouble. Such a rescue was one of Momaday's favorite adventures.
4. Pecos could outrun the other horses in Jemez. Momaday was proud of his horse's ability.
5. Scents of pine and cedar smoke filled the air. A fresh, cold wind carried them from the canyon.

7. Clauses

7a. **A *clause* is a group of words that contains a verb and its subject and is used as part of a sentence.**

KINDS OF CLAUSES

7b. **An *independent* (or *main*) *clause* expresses a complete thought and can stand by itself as a sentence.**

Della gives Jim a watch chain, and **Jim gives Della a set of combs.**

When I wrote my report on William Shakespeare, **I quoted from *Hamlet* and *Macbeth*.**

7c. **A *subordinate* (or *dependent*) *clause* does not express a complete thought and cannot stand alone.**

Because I told him the truth, Dad wasn't too angry about the broken window.

Stephanie wants to know **what the show is about.**

7d. **An *adjective clause* is a subordinate clause that modifies a noun or pronoun.**

An adjective clause always follows the word it modifies and usually begins with a ***relative pronoun,*** such as *who, whom, whose, which,* or *that.*

Della and Jim, **who are deeply in love,** make sacrifices to buy gifts for each other. [The adjective clause modifies *Della* and *Jim.*]

Not all the stories **that Edgar Allan Poe wrote** deal with horror or terror. [The adjective clause modifies *stories.*]

I read about Sequoyah, **whose invention of a written language aided other Cherokees.** [The adjective clause modifies *Sequoyah.*]

A relative pronoun is sometimes left out of an adjective clause.

Was *The Miracle Worker* the first play [**that**] **William Gibson wrote?**

The mechanic [**whom**] **you recommended** fixed my stepfather's motorcycle.

Occasionally, an adjective clause begins with the ***relative adverb*** *where* or *when.*

We visited the town **where Shakespeare was born.**

Summer is the season **when I feel happiest.**

7e. **An *adverb clause* is a subordinate clause that modifies a verb, an adjective, or an adverb.**

An adverb clause, which may come before or after the word it modifies, tells *how, when, where, why, to what extent (how much),* or *under what condition.* An adverb clause begins with a **subordinating conjunction,** such as *although, because, if,* or *so that.*

Because we did so well in the discussion, our teacher did not assign any homework. [The adverb clause modifies the verb and tells *why.*]

I wrote a poem about war **after I read "The Sniper."** [The adverb clause modifies the verb and tells *when.*]

If Harry moves, he may disturb the sleeping snake. [The adverb clause modifies the verb and tells *under what condition.*]

His pitching arm is stronger today **than it ever was.** [The adverb clause modifies an adjective and tells *to what extent.*]

7f. **A *noun clause* is a subordinate clause used as a subject, a predicate nominative, a direct object, an indirect object, or an object of a preposition.**

The words commonly used to begin noun clauses include *that, what, whether, who,* and *why.*

SUBJECT	**What Odysseus did** was clever.
PREDICATE NOMINATIVE	The captains are **who pick the players for their teams.**
DIRECT OBJECT	The sniper discovered **that his brother was the enemy.**
INDIRECT OBJECT	The clerk should tell **whoever asks** the sale prices.
OBJECT OF PREPOSITION	He knew the price of **whatever they requested.**

The word that introduces a noun clause may or may not have a function within the noun clause.

Lizabeth regretted **what she had done.** [*What* is the direct object of *had done.*]

Mme. Loisel learned **that the necklace was fake.** [*That* has no function in the clause.]

Sometimes the word that introduces a noun clause is not stated, but its meaning is understood.

His mother said [**that**] **he could go to the concert.**

Your Turn Using Adjective and Adverb Clauses

Using adjective and adverb clauses can help make your writing smoother. Use these clauses to combine each of the following pairs of short, choppy sentences.

1. Many people do not have homes. They wander the cities.
2. Ann appears in this article. She is one of these homeless people.
3. Ann lost her job. She lost her house, too.
4. Now she has only a coat. The coat is dirty and creased.
5. People like Ann need help, not labels. Their lives are hard.

8. Sentence Structure

Sentence or Sentence Fragment?

8a. **A *sentence* is a group of words that contains a subject and a verb and expresses a complete thought.**

A sentence should begin with a capital letter and end with a period, a question mark, or an exclamation point. A group of words that does not contain a subject and verb or does not express a complete thought is called a ***sentence fragment.***

FRAGMENT Romeo banished from Verona?
SENTENCE Was Romeo banished from Verona?

FRAGMENT What a clever plan!
SENTENCE What a clever plan it was!

FRAGMENT When the families learned of the deaths of Romeo and Juliet.
SENTENCE When the families learned of the deaths of Romeo and Juliet, they ended their feud.

COMPUTER NOTE Many word-processing programs can identify sentence fragments. If you have access to such a program, use it to help you evaluate your writing. Revise each fragment to make sure that all your sentences are complete.

SUBJECT AND PREDICATE

8b. **A sentence consists of two parts: the *subject* and the *predicate*. The subject tells *whom* or *what* the sentence is about. The predicate tells something *about* the subject.**

In the following examples, all the words labeled *subject* make up the ***complete subject,*** and all the words labeled *predicate* make up the ***complete predicate.***

SUBJECT | PREDICATE
Tybalt | was Juliet's cousin.

SUBJECT | PREDICATE
Two of Prince Escalus's kinsmen | died.

PREDICATE | SUBJECT | PREDICATE
Why did | Juliet | take the sleeping potion?

The Simple Subject

8c. **The *simple subject* is the main word or words that tell *whom* or *what* the sentence is about.**

An **excerpt** from Maya Angelou's *I Know Why the Caged Bird Sings* appears in this book. [The complete subject is *An excerpt from Maya Angelou's* I Know Why the Caged Bird Sings.]

The talented **Georgia O'Keeffe** is known for her paintings of huge flowers. [The complete subject is *The talented Georgia O'Keeffe.*]

The Simple Predicate

8d. **The *simple predicate* is the main word or words that tell something about the subject.**

A simple predicate may be a single word or a ***verb phrase*** (a verb with one or more helping verbs).

Montresor **led** Fortunato to the catacombs. [The complete predicate is *led Fortunato to the catacombs.*]

Did Mme. Loisel **find** the necklace? [The complete predicate is *did find the necklace.*]

NOTE In this book, the term *subject* refers to the simple subject and the term *verb* refers to the simple predicate unless otherwise indicated.

The Compound Subject and the Compound Verb

8e. **A *compound subject* consists of two or more subjects that are joined by a conjunction—usually *and* or *or*—and have the same verb.**

Does **Rainsford** or **Zaroff** win the game?

Romeo, Benvolio, and **Mercutio** attend the Capulets' party.

8f. **A *compound verb* consists of two or more verbs that are joined by a conjunction—usually *and, but,* or *or*—and that have the same subject.**

Della **sold** her hair and **bought** Jim a watch chain.

Timber **looked** for the snake but **did** not **find** it.

Finding the Subject of a Sentence

8g. To find the subject of a sentence, ask "Who?" or "What?" before the verb.

The price of those videos seems high. [What seems high? The price seems high. *Price* is the subject.]

(1) The subject of a sentence is never in a prepositional phrase.

Her **garden** of marigolds was ruined. [What was ruined? *Garden* was ruined. *Marigolds* is the object of the preposition *of.*]

On the rooftop crouched the **sniper.** [Who crouched? The *sniper* crouched. *Rooftop* is the object of the preposition *on.*]

(2) The subject of a sentence expressing a question usually follows the verb or a part of the verb phrase. Turning the question into a statement may help you find the subject.

QUESTION Did **she** give Buddy a kite?
STATEMENT **She** did give Buddy a kite.

QUESTION Is the ***Odyssey*** an epic?
STATEMENT The ***Odyssey*** is an epic.

(3) The word *there* or *here* is never the subject of a sentence.

There are your **keys.** [What are there? *Keys* are.]
Here is your **pencil.** [What is here? *Pencil* is.]

(4) The subject of a sentence expressing a command or request is always understood to be *you.*

[**You**] Listen carefully to this question.

The subject of a command or request is *you* even when the sentence contains a ***noun of direct address,*** a word naming the one or ones spoken to.

Ellen, [**you**] please read the part of Juliet.

COMPLEMENTS

8h. A *complement* is a word or group of words that completes the meaning of a verb.

Three kinds of complements are the *subject complement,* the *direct object,* and the *indirect object.*

The Subject Complement

8i. A *subject complement* is a word or word group that completes the meaning of a linking verb and identifies or modifies the subject.

The two types of subject complements are the *predicate nominative* and the *predicate adjective.*

(1) A ***predicate nominative*** is a noun or pronoun that follows a linking verb and renames or identifies the subject of the verb.

"The Necklace" is a classic **story.** [The noun *story* identifies the subject "*The Necklace.*"]

The only people in line were **they.** [The pronoun *they* renames the subject *people.*]

(2) A ***predicate adjective*** is an adjective that follows a linking verb and that modifies the subject.

The necklace was **inexpensive**. [The adjective *inexpensive* modifies the subject *necklace.*]

The corn tasted **sweet** and **buttery.** [The adjectives *sweet* and *buttery* modify the subject *corn.*]

The Direct Object and Indirect Object

8j. A *direct object* is a noun or pronoun that receives the action of a verb or that shows the result of the action. It tells *whom* or *what* after a transitive verb.

The sniper killed his own **brother.** [*killed* whom? *brother*]

Shakespeare wrote not only **plays** but also beautiful **sonnets.** [*wrote* what? *plays* and *sonnets*]

8k. An *indirect object* is a noun or pronoun that precedes the direct object and that usually tells *to whom* or *for whom* (or *to what* or *for what*) the action of the verb is done.

Sheila read the **children** a story by Truman Capote. [*read* to whom? *children*]

Frank gave the **Red Cross** a donation. [*gave* to what? *Red Cross*]

NOTE A complement may precede the subject and the verb.

DIRECT OBJECT What a good **friend** Buddy has!
PREDICATE ADJECTIVE How **happy** Della is!

CLASSIFYING SENTENCES ACCORDING TO PURPOSE

8l. Sentences may be classified as *declarative, imperative, interrogative,* or *exclamatory.*

Classification	Purpose	Punctuation	Example
Declarative	Makes a statement	Period	My favorite story is "Thank You, M'am."
Imperative	Makes a request or gives a command	Period or exclamation point	Please open your books. Stop that right now!
Interrogative	Asks a question	Question mark	What did Romeo do when he saw Juliet?
Exclamatory	Expresses strong feeling	Exclamation point	What a mess we're in now!

CLASSIFYING SENTENCES ACCORDING TO STRUCTURE

8m. Sentences may be classified as *simple, compound, complex,* or *compound-complex.*

Classification	Structure	Example
Simple sentence	One independent clause and no subordinate clauses	*Frankenstein* was written in the nineteenth century.
Compound sentence	Two or more independent clauses but no subordinate clause	Rita wanted to see a serious film, but Carlos preferred a comedy. Harriet Tubman led people to freedom; she was a leader of the Underground Railroad.
Complex sentence	One independent clause and at least one subordinate clause	On Shakespeare's gravestone is an inscription that places a curse on anyone who moves his bones.
Compound-complex sentence	Two or more independent clauses and at least one subordinate clause	William Golding published *Lord of the Flies*, which is his best-known novel, in 1954, and he received the Nobel Prize in 1983.

Your Turn Using a Variety of Sentence Structures

The following paragraph is composed of simple sentences. Revise the paragraph, using a variety of sentence structures.

[1] "The Most Dangerous Game" begins with a conversation about hunting. [2] Rainsford is the protagonist. [3] He and Whitney are on a yacht in the Caribbean. [4] They're near the eerie Ship-Trap Island. [5] Rainsford loves hunting. [6] He thinks that sympathy for the hunted animal is foolish. [7] Later Rainsford falls overboard. [8] He swims to the island. [9] He meets General Zaroff at the general's chateau. [10] Zaroff hunts human beings for sport. [11] Soon Rainsford the hunter becomes the hunted.

9. Writing Complete Sentences

Sentence Fragments

9a. **Avoid using a *sentence fragment*—a part of a sentence that has been punctuated as if it were a complete sentence.**

Here are two ways to correct a sentence fragment.

(1) Add words that will make the thought complete.

FRAGMENT Shortly after his birth, was baptized in a small church in Stratford. [The subject is missing.]

SENTENCE Shortly after his birth, **Shakespeare** was baptized in a small church in Stratford.

FRAGMENT Odysseus a great hero of the Greeks. [The verb is missing.]

SENTENCE Odysseus **became** a great hero of the Greeks.

(2) Attach the fragment to a sentence that comes before or after it.

FRAGMENT When she takes off her coat. [fragment] Mme. Loisel discovers that she is no longer wearing the necklace. [sentence]

REVISED **When she takes off her coat,** Mme. Loisel discovers that she is no longer wearing the necklace.

FRAGMENT Odysseus figured out a way for his men and him. [sentence] To escape from the Cyclops. [fragment]

REVISED Odysseus figured out a way for his men and him **to escape from the Cyclops.**

RUN-ON SENTENCES

9b. **Avoid using a *run-on sentence*—two or more complete sentences that run together as if they were one complete sentence.**

There are two kinds of run-on sentences.

- A ***fused sentence*** has no punctuation between the complete sentences.

  Della sold her hair to buy Jim a watch chain Jim sold his watch to buy Della combs for her hair.

- A ***comma splice*** has only a comma between the complete sentences.

  Della sold her hair to buy Jim a watch chain, Jim sold his watch to buy Della combs for her hair.

COMPUTER NOTE The style-checking feature in a word processing program can help you evaluate your writing for the use of clear, complete sentences. Many programs can identify and highlight sentence fragments. Additionally, you can use the "Find" or "Search" command to identify comma splices. Search for commas, and make sure that they do not separate complete sentences. This command can also be used to identify sentences in which you've used a comma and a coordinating conjunction—one search for each different conjunction. These searches can help you make sure that the ideas you've combined in a compound sentence are complete, closely related, and equally important.

FIVE WAYS TO FIX A RUN-ON SENTENCE		
1.	Make two sentences.	Della sold her hair to buy Jim a watch chain**.** Jim sold his watch to buy Della combs for her hair.
2.	Use a comma and a ***coordinating conjunction***—*and, but, or, yet, for, so,* or *nor.*	Della sold her hair to buy Jim a watch chain**, and** Jim sold his watch to buy Della combs for her hair.
3.	Use a semicolon.	Della sold her hair to buy Jim a watch chain**;** Jim sold his watch to buy Della combs for her hair.
4.	Use a semicolon and a ***conjunctive adverb,*** such as *therefore, instead, meanwhile, also,* or *however.*	Della sold her hair to buy Jim a watch chain**; however,** Jim sold his watch to buy Della combs for her hair.
5.	Change one of the complete thoughts into a subordinate clause.	Della sold her hair to buy Jim a watch chain, **while Jim sold his watch to buy Della combs for her hair**.

Your Turn Revising Run-on Sentences and Sentence Fragments

Revise each of the following run-on sentences and sentence fragments.

1. Doodle and his brother had an active fantasy world, they created stories and imaginary plans.
2. Doodle was afraid of being left behind, he cried when his brother started to leave.
3. Brother taught Doodle to walk. Was ashamed of Doodle.
4. Doodle didn't think that he could walk after much help and practice, he did.
5. He could walk. Even run.

10. Writing Effective Sentences

Sentence Combining

10a. Combine related sentences by taking a key word (or by using another form of the word) from one sentence and inserting it into another.

ORIGINAL Edgar Allan Poe led a short life. His life was tragic.

COMBINED Edgar Allan Poe led a short, **tragic** life.

ORIGINAL Edgar Allan Poe wrote strange stories. He wrote stories of suspense.

COMBINED Edgar Allan Poe wrote strange, **suspenseful** stories.

10b. Combine related sentences by taking (or creating) a phrase from one sentence and inserting it into another.

ORIGINAL *A Fire in My Hands* is a collection of poems. The poems were written by Gary Soto.

COMBINED *A Fire in My Hands* is a collection of poems **by Gary Soto**. [prepositional phrase]

ORIGINAL Romeo kills Tybalt. Tybalt is Juliet's cousin.

COMBINED Romeo kills Tybalt, **Juliet's cousin.** [appositive phrase]

10c. Combine related sentences by using a coordinating conjunction (*and, but, or,* or *nor*) to make a compound subject, a compound verb, or both.

ORIGINAL After lunch Doodle went to Horsehead Landing. His brother went, too.

COMBINED After lunch **Doodle and** his **brother** went to Horsehead Landing. [compound subject]

ORIGINAL Ernesto Galarza's family immigrated to the United States. They eventually settled in Sacramento, California.

COMBINED Ernesto Galarza's family **immigrated** to the United States **and** eventually **settled** in Sacramento, California. [compound verb]

10d. Combine related sentences by creating a compound sentence.

You can form a compound sentence by linking two or more independent clauses with a comma and a coordinating conjunction, a semicolon, or a semicolon and a conjunctive adverb.

ORIGINAL Buddy makes his friend a kite. She makes him one, too.

COMBINED Buddy makes his friend a kite, **and** she makes him one, too. [comma and coordinating conjunction]

COMBINED Buddy makes his friend a kite**;** she makes him one, too. [semicolon]

COMBINED Buddy makes his friend a kite**; meanwhile,** she makes him one, too. [semicolon and conjunctive adverb]

10e. Combine related sentences by creating a complex sentence.

You can form a complex sentence by joining one independent clause with one or more subordinate clauses.

ORIGINAL Gwendolyn Brooks often wrote about Chicago. She won a Pulitzer Prize for her poetry.

COMBINED Gwendolyn Brooks, **who won a Pulitzer Prize for her poetry,** often wrote about Chicago. [adjective clause]

ORIGINAL Zaroff turned on the light. He saw Rainsford.

COMBINED	**When Zaroff turned on the light,** he saw Rainsford. [adverb clause]
ORIGINAL	The snake in "Poison" is just an illusion on Harry's part. Many readers think this.
COMBINED	Many readers think **that the snake in "Poison" is just an illusion on Harry's part.** [noun clause]

IMPROVING SENTENCE STYLE

10f. Use the same grammatical form (*parallel structure*) to express equal ideas.

NOT PARALLEL	Buddy and she liked baking fruitcakes and to fly kites. [gerund phrase paired with infinitive phrase]
PARALLEL	Buddy and she liked **baking fruitcakes** and **flying kites.** [two gerund phrases]
NOT PARALLEL	Harry received help from not only Timber but also from Ganderbai. [noun paired with prepositional phrase]
PARALLEL	Harry received help not only **from Timber** but also **from Ganderbai.** [two prepositional phrases]

10g. Avoid using stringy sentences—sentences that have too many independent clauses strung together with coordinating conjunctions like *and* or *but.*

The fire alarm rang, and everyone started to file out of school, but then our principal came down the hall, and he said that the bell was a mistake, and we went back to our classes.

There are two ways to revise a stringy sentence.

(1) Break the sentence into two or more sentences.

The fire alarm rang, and everyone started to file out of school. Then our principal came down the hall to say that the bell was a mistake. We went back to our classes.

(2) Turn some of the independent clauses into subordinate clauses or into phrases.

When the fire alarm rang, everyone started to file out of school. Then our principal came down the hall. He said that the bell was a mistake, and we went back to our classes.

COMPUTER NOTE Whenever you revise your writing on a computer, you can use functions such as "Copy," "Paste," "Cut," and "Move" to experiment with your sentences. Try a variety of sentence beginnings and structures. Then, decide which ones work best with the other sentences in a particular paragraph.

10h. Avoid using unnecessary words.

Here are three tips for avoiding wordiness.

(1) Don't use more words than you need to use.
(2) Don't use difficult words where simple ones will do.
(3) Don't repeat yourself unless it's absolutely necessary.

WORDY	Fortunato is a wine connoisseur who has much knowledge of and great appreciation for fine wines.
REVISED	Fortunato is a connoisseur of fine wines.

10i. Use a variety of sentence beginnings.

The basic structure of an English sentence is a subject followed by a verb. The following examples show how you can revise sentences to avoid beginning with the subject every time. Notice that a comma follows the introductory word, phrase, or clause in each revision.

BASIC	Della excitedly opened her present.
REVISED	**Excitedly,** Della opened her present. [adverb first]
BASIC	You must study to make good grades.
REVISED	**To make good grades,** you must study. [infinitive phrase first]
BASIC	Romeo fell in love with Juliet as soon as he saw her.
REVISED	**As soon as he saw her,** Romeo fell in love with Juliet. [adverb clause first]

Your Turn Combining Sentences

Combine each of these pairs of related sentences into one sentence.

1. Mrs. Johnson's husband moved to Oklahoma. He studied religion.
2. The cotton gin would not hire her. Neither would the lumber mill.
3. She didn't want to become a servant. She saw another possibility.
4. The cotton gin and lumber workers walked to her stand. They bought lunch.
5. In time, syrup and canned goods were sold at the store. Mrs. Johnson had a good business.

11. CAPITALIZATION

11a. Capitalize the first word in every sentence.

The two boys discussed their plans.
Look at this!

(1) Capitalize the first word of a direct quotation.
Maria asked, "**H**ave you written your report yet?"

(2) Traditionally, the first word of a line of poetry is capitalized.

Two roads diverged in a wood, and I—
I took the one less traveled by,
And that has made all the difference.
—Robert Frost, "The Road Not Taken"

NOTE Some writers do not follow these practices. When you are quoting, use capital letters exactly as they are used in the source for the quotation.

11b. Capitalize the first word both in the salutation and in the closing of a letter.

To Whom It May Concern:
Dear Ann, **D**ear Sir:
Sincerely, **Y**ours truly,

11c. Capitalize the pronoun *I* and the interjection *O*.

EXAMPLES
Mom says that **I** can go this weekend.
"**O** Romeo, Romeo! Wherefore art thou Romeo?"

11d. Capitalize proper nouns and proper adjectives.

A ***common noun*** is a general name for a person, a place, a thing, or an idea. A ***proper noun*** names a particular person, place, thing, or idea. A ***proper adjective*** is formed from a proper noun.

Common Nouns	Proper Nouns	Proper Adjectives
poet	**H**omer	**H**omeric simile
planet	**M**ars	**M**artian landscape

In proper nouns that are more than one word, do *not* capitalize articles (*a, an, the*), prepositions of fewer than five letters, coordinating conjunctions, or *to* in an infinitive unless they are the first word.

Society **f**or **t**he Prevention **o**f Cruelty **t**o Animals
National Campers **a**nd Hikers Association
"Writing **a** Paragraph **t**o Inform"

(1) Capitalize the names of persons and animals.

PERSONS	**S**andra **C**isneros	**L**angston **H**ughes
ANIMALS	**O**ld **Y**eller	**B**rer **R**abbit

Abbreviations such as *Ms., Mr., Dr.,* and *Gen.* should always be capitalized.

Mr. James Thurber **Dr.** Mary McLeod Bethune

Capitalize the abbreviations *Jr.* and *Sr.* after a name, and set them off with commas.

Gen. Daniel James**, Jr.,** was the first African American four-star general in the U.S. Air Force.

(2) Capitalize geographical names.

Type of Name	Examples	
Towns and Cities	**S**an **F**rancisco	**S**t. **C**harles
Counties, Townships, and Parishes	**H**ayes **T**ownship **U**nion **P**arish	**K**ane **C**ounty **M**anhattan
States and Territories	**F**lorida **G**uam	**N**orth **C**arolina **N**orthwest **T**erritory
Countries	**C**anada	**U**nited **S**tates of **A**merica
Continents	**A**frica	**N**orth **A**merica
Islands	**L**ong **I**sland	**I**sle of **P**alms
Mountains	**R**ocky **M**ountains **M**ount **M**cKinley	
Other Landforms and Features	**C**ape **H**atteras **K**alahari **D**esert	**N**iagara **F**alls **M**ammoth **C**ave
Bodies of Water	**P**acific **O**cean **C**ross **C**reek	**G**ulf of **M**exico **B**lue **S**prings
Parks	**Y**ellowstone **N**ational **P**ark **C**leburne **S**tate **R**ecreation **A**rea	
Regions	the **N**orth **N**ew **E**ngland	the **M**idwest the **G**reat **P**lains
Roads, Streets, and Highways	**R**oute 66 **G**ibbs **D**rive	**P**ennsylvania **T**urnpike **T**hirty-fourth **S**treet

NOTE Words such as *north, west,* and *southeast* are not capitalized when they indicate direction.

north of town traveling **s**outheast

NOTE In a hyphenated number, the second word is not capitalized.

Twenty-**o**ne people came to dinner.

NOTE Words like *city, river, street,* and *park* are capitalized only when they are part of a name.

across the **r**iver across the Pecos **R**iver

(3) Capitalize the names of organizations, teams, business firms, institutions, buildings and other structures, and government bodies.

Type of Name	Examples
Organizations	**U**nited **N**ations **N**ational **B**asketball **A**ssociation
Teams	**T**ampa **B**ay **B**uccaneers **M**innesota **T**wins
Business Firms	**Q**uaker **O**ats **C**ompany **A**luminum **C**ompany of **A**merica
Institutions	**U**nited **S**tates **N**aval **A**cademy **B**ethune-**C**ookman **C**ollege
Buildings and Other Structures	**A**pollo **T**heater **T**aj **M**ahal **G**olden **G**ate **B**ridge
Government Bodies	**F**ederal **B**ureau of **I**nvestigation **H**ouse of **R**epresentatives

NOTE Capitalize words such as *democratic* or *republican* only when they refer to a specific political party.

The new leaders promised **d**emocratic reforms.

The **D**emocratic candidate for mayor held a rally.

(4) Capitalize the names of historical events and periods, special events, holidays, and calendar items.

Type of Name	Examples	
Historical Events and Periods	**F**rench **R**evolution **B**oston **T**ea **P**arty	**M**iddle **A**ges **M**esozoic **E**ra
Special Events	**I**nterscholastic **D**ebate **T**ournament **K**ansas **S**tate **F**air	
Holidays and Calendar Items	**S**aturday **F**ourth of **J**uly	**D**ecember **N**ational **B**ook **W**eek

NOTE Do not capitalize the name of a season unless it is being personified or used in the name of a special event.

I'm on the committee for the **W**inter Carnival.

Soon **A**utumn will paint the leaves in bright colors.

(5) Capitalize the names of ships, trains, aircraft, spacecraft, monuments, awards, planets, and other particular places, things, or events.

Type of Name	Examples
Ships and Trains	***M**ayflower* ***S**ilver **M**eteor*
Aircraft and Spacecraft	***S**pirit of **S**t. **L**ouis* **L**ockheed ***P**ioneer 10* **C**-5A **G**alaxy **H**ubble **S**pace **T**elescope
Monuments and Memorials	**W**ashington **M**onument **S**tatue of **L**iberty **V**ietnam **V**eterans **M**emorial
Awards	**P**ulitzer **P**rize **C**ongressional **M**edal of **H**onor **S**tanley **C**up **K**ey **C**lub **A**chievement **A**ward
Planets, Stars, and Constellations	**M**ercury **D**og **S**tar **L**ibra **V**enus **B**ig **D**ipper **R**igel

NOTE The word *earth* is not capitalized unless it is used along with the names of other heavenly bodies that are capitalized. The words *sun* and *moon* are not capitalized.

The **m**oon is a satellite of the **e**arth.

Venus is closer to **E**arth than **M**ars is.

(6) Capitalize the names of nationalities, races, and peoples.

Greek **H**ispanic **C**herokee

(7) Capitalize the brand names of products but not the common nouns that follow the name.

Ford **t**ruck Teflon **p**an

11e. **Do *not* capitalize the names of school subjects, except for languages or course names followed by a number.**

algebra **E**nglish **B**iology I

11f. **Capitalize titles.**

(1) Capitalize the title of a person when it comes before the person's name.

President Bush **S**enator Kennedy

Usually, do not capitalize a title that is used alone or following a person's name, especially if the title is preceded by *a* or *the.*

Cleopatra became the **q**ueen of Egypt in 51 B.C.

When a title is used alone in direct address, it is usually capitalized.

I think, **S**enator, that the issue is critical.

(2) Capitalize words showing family relationship when used alone or with a person's name but *not* when preceded by a possessive.

Aunt **C**lara my **m**other Harold's **g**randmother

(3) Capitalize the first and last words and all important words in titles.

Type of Title	Examples
Books	_**T**he **P**earl_ _**I K**now **W**hy the **C**aged **B**ird **S**ings_
Periodicals	_**T**he **A**tlantic **M**onthly_ _**F**ield and **S**tream_
Poems	"**T**he **R**oad **N**ot **T**aken" "**T**he **G**irl **W**ho **L**oved the **S**ky"
Stories	"**T**he **C**ask of **A**montillado" "**T**he **M**ost **D**angerous **G**ame"
Essays and Speeches	"**T**he **D**eath of a **T**ree" "**W**ork and **W**hat **I**t's **W**orth"
Plays	_**T**he **M**iracle **W**orker_ _**T**he **P**hantom of the **O**pera_
Historical Documents	**D**eclaration of **I**ndependence **E**mancipation **P**roclamation
Movies	_**D**ances with **W**olves_ _**S**tand and **D**eliver_
Radio and Television Programs	_**A**ll **T**hings **C**onsidered_ _**S**tar **T**rek: **T**he **N**ext **G**eneration_ _**N**ova_
Works of Art	_**A**merican **G**othic_ _**T**he **T**hinker_
Musical Compositions	"**T**he **T**ennessee **W**altz" "**T**he **F**light of the **B**umblebee"
Cartoons	_**C**alvin and **H**obbes_ _**T**he **N**eighborhood_

NOTE Unimportant words in a title are articles (*a, an, the*), prepositions of fewer than five letters (such as *for* and *from*), and coordinating conjunctions (*and, but, so, nor, or, yet, for*). **NOTE** When *a, an,* or *the* are written before a title, they are capitalized only if they are part of the official title. The official title of a book is found on the title page. The official title of a newspaper or periodical is found on the masthead, which is usually on the editorial page.

The Autobiography of Malcolm X

the Austin American-Statesman

***A** Tale of Two Cities*

(4) Capitalize the names related to religions.

Type of Name	Examples	
Religions and Followers	**J**udaism **T**aoism	**Q**uaker **M**uslim
Holy Days and Celebrations	**P**assover **R**amadan	**G**ood **F**riday **L**ent
Holy Writings	**B**ible **K**oran	**U**panishads **T**orah
Specific Deities	**A**llah **B**rahma **Z**eus	

Your Turn Correcting Errors in Capitalization

Rewrite this letter to correct the errors in capitalization.

dear mr. Hargrove,

Thank you for sending me a copy of moby-dick. i have always enjoyed books about the sea. Last week i read a novel about captain horatio hornblower. As you know, I live in the midwest and have never seen an ocean. I think that it must be exciting to sail on the atlantic ocean, which is known for its violent storms. I am looking forward to reading about the adventures of new england sailors on a great whaling ship.

sincerely,
Tom Wayne

12. Punctuation

END MARKS

Sentences

End marks—*periods, question marks,* and *exclamation points*—are used to indicate the purpose of a sentence.

12a. A statement (or declarative sentence) is followed by a period.

Dorothy M. Johnson wrote "A Man Called Horse**.**"

12b. A question (or interrogative sentence) is followed by a question mark.

Did Penelope recognize Odysseus**?**

NOTE Be sure to distinguish between a declarative sentence that contains an indirect question and an interrogative sentence, which asks a direct question.

INDIRECT QUESTION He asked **what was worrying her.**

DIRECT QUESTION What is worrying her**?**

A direct question may have the same word order as a declarative sentence. Since it *is* a question, however, it is followed by a question mark.

A cat can see color**?** The plane was late**?**

12c. An exclamation is followed by an exclamation point.

Wow**!** What a great play *The Miracle Worker* is**!**

12d. A command or request (or imperative sentence) is followed by either a period or an exclamation point.

A request or a mild command is followed by a period. A strong command is followed by an exclamation point.

Please be quiet**.** [request]
Turn off your radio**.** [mild command]
Be quiet**!** [strong command]

Sometimes a command or request is stated in the form of a question. Because of its purpose, however, the sentence is really an imperative sentence and should end with a period or an exclamation point.

Could you please send me twenty-five copies**.**
Will you stop that**!**

Abbreviations

12e. An abbreviation is usually followed by a period.

Types of Abbreviations	Examples
Personal Names	A. E. Housman Eugenia W. Collier
Organizations and Companies	Assn. Co. Inc. Ltd. Corp.
Titles Used with Names	Mr. Mrs. Jr. Dr.
Times of Day	A.M. P.M.
Years	B.C. (written after the date) A.D. (written before the date)
Addresses	Ave. St. Blvd. Pkwy.
States	Calif. Mass. Tex. N. Dak.

NOTE Two-letter state abbreviations without periods are used only when the ZIP Code is included.

Cincinnati, OH 45233

NOTE In most cases, an abbreviation is capitalized only if the words it stands for are capitalized. If you are unsure whether to capitalize an abbreviation or to use periods with it, check a recent dictionary.

If a statement ends with an abbreviation, do not use an additional period as an end mark. However, do add a question mark or an exclamation point if the sentence should have one.

Mrs. Tavares will be arriving at 3 P.M**.**
Can you go to meet her at 3 P.M.**?**

Abbreviations for government agencies and international organizations and some other frequently used abbreviations are written without periods. Abbreviations for most units of measurement are commonly written without periods, especially in science books.

CD, DVD, FM, IRS, TV, UFO
cm, kg, lb, ml

NOTE Use a period with the abbreviation for *inch* (*in.*) so that it will not be confused with the word *in.*

COMMAS

12f. **Use commas to separate items in a series.**

Homer wrote about Troy, Achilles, and Odysseus.
We can meet before school, at lunch, or after school.

(1) Some words—such as *bread and butter, rod and reel,* and *law and order*—are used in pairs and may be considered one item in a series.

My favorite breakfast is milk, **biscuits and gravy,** and fruit.

(2) Independent clauses in a series are generally separated by semicolons. Short independent clauses, however, may be separated by commas.

The sky darkened, branches swayed, the cold deepened, and snow fell.

12g. **Use commas to separate two or more adjectives preceding a noun.**

Montresor leads Fortunato to the dark, cold vault below the palazzo.

When the last adjective in a series is thought of as part of the noun, the comma before the adjective is omitted.

The Loisels bought an expensive **diamond necklace.**

12h. **Use commas before *and, but, or, nor, for, so,* and *yet* when they join independent clauses.**

General Zaroff was confident he would kill Rainsford, but the hunt did not go as he had planned.

You may omit the comma before *and, but, or,* or *nor* if the clauses are very short and there is no chance of misunderstanding.

12i. **Use commas to set off nonessential clauses and nonessential participial phrases.**

A **nonessential** (or **nonrestrictive**) clause or participial phrase adds information that is not needed to understand the main idea in the sentence.

NONESSENTIAL CLAUSE Langston Hughes, **who was a key figure in the Harlem Renaissance,** often used jazz rhythms in his poetry.

Omitting the adjective clause in this example would not change the main idea of the sentence.

An ***essential*** (or ***restrictive***) clause or phrase provides information that is needed to understand the sentence, and commas are *not* used.

ESSENTIAL PHRASE Actors **missing more than two rehearsals** will be replaced.

The participial phrase tells *which* actors. Omitting it would affect the meaning of the sentence.

12j. **Use commas after certain introductory elements.**

Introductory Element	Example
A word such as *next, yes,* or *no*	**Yes,** I've read "Salvador Late or Early."
An interjection, such as *ah, well, oops, why*	**Ah,** there's nothing like lemonade on a hot day!
A participial phrase	**Having passed Penelope's last test,** Odysseus reclaims his home and his kingdom.
The last of two or more prepositional phrases	**Of all of his novels,** Charles Dickens liked *David Copperfield* best.
An adverb clause	**Until he meets Juliet,** Romeo is madly in love with Rosaline.

12k. **Use commas to set off elements that interrupt a sentence.**

Element That Interrupts	Example
Appositive or appositive phrase	The storm**, the worst this winter,** raged for days.
Words used in direct address	**Linda,** please read the part of Juliet.
Parenthetical expressions (side remarks)	He was not angry and**, on the contrary,** was actually glad that you pointed out the error.
A contrasting expression introduced by *not* or *yet*	It is the spirit of the giver**, not the cost of the gift.**

NOTE An appositive that tells which one(s) of two or more is a ***restrictive appositive*** and should not be set off by commas.

The TV special is about Graham Greene the British writer, not Graham Greene the Canadian actor.

12l. Use commas in certain conventional situations.

NOTE Do not use a comma to separate a two-letter state abbreviation and a ZIP Code.

EXAMPLE

Our new address is 25 Peralta Road**,** Oakland**,** CA 94611.

Conventional Situation	Example
To separate items in dates and address	My family moved to Oakland**,** California**,** on Wednesday**,** December 5**,** 1993.
After the salutation of a friendly letter and the closing of any letter	Dear Ms. Chen**,** Dear Amy**,** Yours truly**,** Sincerely yours**,**
To set off such abbreviations as *Jr., Sr.,* or *M.D.*	Dr. Martin Luther King**,** Jr.**,** made that speech.

SEMICOLONS

12m. Use a semicolon between independent clauses if they are not joined by *and, but, or, nor, for, so,* or *yet.*

I enjoyed reading *The Miracle Worker***;** it tells what Helen Keller's youth was like.

12n. Use a semicolon between independent clauses joined by a conjunctive adverb—such as *however, therefore,* and *furthermore*—or a transitional expression, such as *for instance, in fact,* and *that is.*

Sherlock Holmes is a fictional character**; however,** it's easy to think that he actually did exist.

My parents are strict**; for example,** I can watch TV only on weekends.

Notice in the two examples above that a comma always follows a conjunctive adverb or a transitional expression that joins independent clauses.

12o. Use a semicolon (rather than a comma) before a coordinating conjunction to join independent clauses that contain commas.

Doodle's mother, father, and brother went back inside the house**; but** Doodle remained outside to bury the scarlet ibis.

12p. Use a semicolon between items in a series if the items contain commas.

I have postcards from Paris, France**;** Rome, Italy**;** Lisbon, Portugal**;** and London, England.

COLONS

12q. Use a colon to mean "note what follows."

(1) In some cases a colon is used before a list of items, especially after the expressions *the following* and *as follows.*

The reading list includes the following titles**:** "The Gift," "The Sniper," and "The Necklace."

Do not use a colon before a list that follows a verb or a preposition

INCORRECT The list of literary terms includes: *conflict, climax,* and *resolution.*

CORRECT The list of literary terms includes *conflict, climax,* and *resolution.*

INCORRECT In the past five years, my family has lived in: Texas, Oregon, and Ohio.

CORRECT In the past five years, my family has lived in Texas, Oregon, and Ohio.

(2) Use a colon before a long, formal statement or a long quotation.

O. Henry had this to say about Della and Jim**:** "But in a last word to the wise of these days, let it be said that of all who give gifts, these two were the wisest."

12r. Use a colon in certain conventional situations.

Conventional Situation	Example
Between the hour and the minute	9:30 A.M. 8:00 P.M.
After the salutation of a business letter	Dear Ms. Gomez: Dear Sir or Madam: To Whom It May Concern:
Between chapter and verse in referring to passages from the Bible	Esther 3:5 Exodus 1:6–14 Colossians 3:18–23
Between a title and a subtitle	"Shakespeare and His Theater: A Perfect Match"

Your Turn Correcting Punctuation Errors

Correct the punctuation errors in these sentences.

1. Langston Hughes's "Luck" my favorite poem is brief but powerful.
2. My sister an avid reader is partial to the poems of Emily Dickinson.
3. Mary please give me that copy of the book.
4. Dickinson a complex person wrote poems that can be hard to understand
5. Her poems are complex and layered with meanings not simple and straightforward

13. Punctuation

ITALICS

When writing or typing, indicate italics by underlining. If your composition were to be printed, the typesetter would set the underlined words in italics. The Color Purple would be set as *The Color Purple.*

COMPUTER NOTE If you use a computer, you can set words in italics yourself. Most word-processing software and printers can produce italic type.

13a. Use underlining (italics) for titles of major works and objects.

Type of Title	Examples
Books	*Black Boy* *Odyssey*
Plays	*The Miracle Worker*
Films	*Jurassic Park*
Periodicals	*National Geographic*
Works of Art	*Mona Lisa*
Recordings	*Two Worlds, One Heart*
Long Musical Works	*The Magic Flute* *Rhapsody in Blue*
Television Series	*The Simpsons*
Trains and Ships	*Orient Express* U.S.S. *Nimitz*
Aircraft and Spacecraft	*Spirit of St. Louis* *Apollo 13*

NOTE The articles *a, an,* and *the* before a title are italicized only when they are part of the official title. The official title of a book appears on the title page. The official title of a newspaper or periodical appears on the masthead, usually found on the editorial page.

We subscribe to ***The** Wall Street Journal* and **the** *Austin American-Statesman.*

13b. Use underlining (italics) for numbers, letters, and words referred to as such and for foreign words not yet a part of English vocabulary.

The word *excellent* has two *l*'s.
The *3* on that license plate looks like an *8*.
The *corrido* is a fast-paced ballad.

QUOTATION MARKS

13c. Use quotation marks to enclose a *direct quotation*—a person's exact words.

She asked, **"**How much does the necklace cost?**"**

Do not use quotation marks for indirect quotations.

DIRECT QUOTATION	She asked, **"**How much does the necklace cost?**"**
INDIRECT QUOTATION	She asked how much the necklace cost.

An interrupting expression is not a part of a quotation and should not be inside quotation marks.

"Let's go,**"** **Ellen urged,** **"**it's starting to rain."

Use one set of quotation marks for two or more sentences by the same speaker quoted together.

Brennan said, **"**I'm making a fruitcake. Do you like fruitcake?**"**

13d. **A direct quotation begins with a capital letter.**

Mrs. Perez asked, "**W**ho is Mercutio?

NOTE If a quotation is a fragment of the original quotation, it should begin with a lowercase letter.

To Romeo, Juliet is "**a** winged messenger of heaven."

13e. **When a quoted sentence is divided into two parts by an interrupting expression, the second part begins with a lowercase letter.**

"I wish," she said, "**t**hat we went to the same school."

If the second part of a quotation is a new sentence, a period follows the interrupting expression, and the second part begins with a capital letter.

"I requested an interview," the reporter said. "She told me she was too busy."

13f. **When used with quotation marks, other marks of punctuation are placed according to the following rules.**

Rule	Example
Commas and periods go inside closing quotation marks.	"I haven't seen the film**,**" said Jane, "but people say it's excellent**.**"
Semicolons and colons go outside closing quotation marks.	Find examples of the following figures of speech in "I Wandered Lonely as a Cloud"**:** simile, personification, and alliteration.
A question mark or exclamation point goes inside closing quotation marks if the quotation is a question or exclamation; otherwise, it goes outside.	"Did you read this book?" he asked**.** "I love it!" she exclaimed. Who said "parting is such sweet sorrow"? It's *not* an insult to be called a "bookworm"!

13g. **When you write dialogue (a conversation), begin a new paragraph every time the speaker changes.**

"Come quickly**!**" Ann shouted, breathlessly.

"What's happened**?** What's wrong?" Colby asked, ready to give whatever help was needed.

13h. **When a quoted passage consists of more than one paragraph, put quotation marks at the beginning of each paragraph and at the end of only the last paragraph.**

"At nine o'clock this morning," read the news story, "someone entered the Millford Bank by the back door, broke into the vault, and escaped with sixteen bars of gold.

"No arrests have yet been made, but state and local police are confident the case will be solved within a few days.

"FBI agents are expected later today."

13i. **Use single quotation marks to enclose a quotation within a quotation.**

"Do you agree with O. Henry that Della and Jim 'were the wisest'?" asked Greg.

13j. **Use quotation marks to enclose titles of smaller works and parts of works.**

Type of Title	Examples
Articles	"Computers in the Classroom"
Short Stories	"Thank You, M'am"
Essays	"How to Name a Dog"
Poems	"The Raven"
Songs	"Lean on Me"
TV Episodes	"Farewell, Friends"
Chapters and Other Parts of Books and Periodicals	"Life in the First Settlements" "The Talk of the Town" "Laughter, the Best Medicine"

NOTE Neither italics nor quotation marks are used for the titles of major religious texts or for the titles of legal or historical documents.

RELIGIOUS TEXTS

New Testament Koran Rig-Veda

LEGAL AND HISTORICAL DOCUMENTS

Declaration of Independence

EXCEPTION

Names of court cases are usually italicized.

Brown v. Board of Education of Topeka

Your Turn Revising Dialogue

Revise the following dialogue by adding quotation marks and paragraph breaks, where necessary. In addition, underline words to indicate any necessary italics.

[1] You know what really bothers me about a lot of stories? said Kyle. [2] What? inquired Erin. [3] I can never figure out if a story is fiction or if it really happened, he said. [4] Yeah, she nodded, I know what you mean. That reminds me of the story A Man Called Horse. Did it really happen or not? [5] I don't know, he answered When I saw the movie, I thought it did, but now I'm not so sure. And what about that book Twenty Days to Sunrise, Erin asked. Do you think it is based on a true story?

14. PUNCTUATION

APOSTROPHES

Possessive Case

The ***possessive case*** of a noun or pronoun shows ownership or relationship

OWNERSHIP **Mme. Forestier's** necklace
RELATIONSHIP **Buddy's** friend

14a. **To form the possessive case of a singular noun, add an apostrophe and an *s*.**

Miss Lottie**'s** marigolds a bus**'s** wheel

NOTE For a proper name ending in *s*, add only an apostrophe if adding *'s* would make the name awkward to pronounce.

West Indies' climate Mrs. Saunders' class

14b. **To form the possessive case of a plural noun ending in *s*, add only the apostrophe. For a plural noun that does not end in *s*, add an apostrophe and an *s*.**

birds' feathers Capulets' party children**'s** shoes

14c. **Possessive personal pronouns—*my, mine, your, yours, his, her, hers, its, our, ours, their,* and *theirs*—do not require an apostrophe.**

This is **our** plant. This plant is **ours.**

14d. **Indefinite pronouns, such as *everybody* and *neither*, in the possessive case require an apostrophe and an *s*.**

nobody**'s** wish another**'s** viewpoint

14e. **In compound words, names of groups or businesses, and word groups that show joint possession, only the last word is possessive.**

brother-in-**law's** gift City **Garage's** tow trucks
United **Fund's** drive Della and **Jim's** home

14f. **When two or more persons possess something individually, each of their names is possessive in form.**

Poe's and **Dahl's** stories

Contractions

14g. **Use an apostrophe to show where letters, words, or numerals have been omitted in a contraction.**

let's [let us] **you're** [you are] **'02** [2002]

Ordinarily, the word *not* is shortened to *-n't* and added to a verb with no change in the verb's spelling.

are not | are**n't** has not | has**n't**

EXCEPTIONS will not | wo**n't** cannot | ca**n't**

Do not confuse contractions with possessive pronouns.

Contractions	Pronouns
Who's [Who is] at bat?	**Whose** bat is that?
It's [It is] roaring.	Listen to **its** roar.
You're [You are] late.	**Your** friend is late.
There's [There is] a kite.	That kite is **theirs.**
They're [They are] here.	**Their** bus is here.

PLURALS

14h. **Use an apostrophe and an *s* to form the plurals of all lowercase letters, some capital letters, numerals, and some words used as words.**

Grandma always tells me to mind my *p*'**s** and *q*'**s**.
Those *U*'**s** look like *V*'**s**.
His *hi*'**s** are always cheerful.

HYPHENS

14i. **Use a hyphen to divide a word at the end of a line.**

"The Most Dangerous Game" is suspenseful.

When you divide a word at the end of a line, keep in mind the following rules.

(1) Do not divide one-syllable words.

(2) Divide a word only between syllables.
fi-an-cé   wor-thy

(3) Words with double consonants may usually be divided between those two consonants.
rib-bon   man-ners

EXCEPTION Words that end in double consonants followed by a suffix are divided before the suffix.
fall-ing   sniff-ing

(4) Usually a word with a prefix or a suffix may be divided between the prefix or suffix and the base word (or root).

pro-gressive   govern-ment

(5) Divide a hyphenated word only at a hyphen.
man-of-war   daughter-in-law

(6) Do not divide a word so that one letter stands alone.

NOTE If you need to divide a word and are not sure about its syllables, look it up in a recent dictionary.

14j. **Use a hyphen with compound numbers from *twenty-one* to *ninety-nine* and with fractions used as adjectives.**

twenty-four chairs   one-half cup

14k. **Use a hyphen with the suffix *-elect* and with any prefix before a proper noun or proper adjective.**

president-elect   pre-Revolutionary

14l. **Hyphenate a compound adjective that precedes the noun it modifies.**

a well-written book   a world-famous skier

Do not use a hyphen if one of the modifiers is an adverb that ends in *-ly*.
a **bitterly cold** day

NOTE Some compound adjectives are always hyphenated, whether they precede or follow the nouns they modify.
an up-to-date dictionary
a style that is up-to-date

If you're not sure if a compound adjective should be hyphenated, check a recent dictionary.

DASHES

14m. **Use a dash to indicate an abrupt break in thought or speech or an unfinished statement or question.**

Judy—Ms. Lane, I mean—will be your new coach.

14n. **Use a dash to mean *namely, that is, in other words,* and similar expressions.**

Dr. Ganderbai considered using an anesthetic—ether or chloroform. [namely]
William Sydney Porter—O. Henry—is my favorite writer. [that is]

NOTE When you use a typewriter or computer, you can indicate a dash by using two hyphens. Leave no space before, between, or after the hyphens. Most software programs will automatically convert two hyphens into a dash. When you write by hand, use an unbroken line about as long as two hyphens.

PARENTHESES

14o. **Use parentheses to enclose material that is not of major importance in a sentence.**

Richard Wright (1908–1960) wrote *Black Boy.*

Capitalize and use end punctuation for parenthetical matter that stands alone as a sentence. Do not capitalize and use end punctuation for parenthetical matter contained within a sentence.
Complete the form. (Please print or type.)
The protagonist (not named by the author) is a sniper.

Your Turn Adding Apostrophes

Add apostrophes wherever they are needed in these sentences.

1. As on your report card are great, but Bs are good, too.
2. Helens computer was on the fritz.
3. Business letters formats are usually easy to follow.
4. The *10s* in this chart indicate the highest scores.
5. Dont you think the instructions are clear?

15. Spelling

Spelling

Many English words are made up of roots and affixes (prefixes and suffixes). The ***root*** of a word is the part that carries the word's core meaning. A ***prefix*** is a word part added to the beginning of a word or root to create a new word. A ***suffix*** is a word part added to the end of a word or root to create a new word. Learning how to spell and combine commonly used word parts can help you spell thousands of words.

Commonly Used Roots

ROOTS	MEANINGS	EXAMPLES
–aud–, –audit–	hear	audible, auditorium
–chron–	time	chronological, synchronize
–cycl–	circle, wheel	cyclone, bicycle
–dem–	people	democracy, epidemic
–gen–	birth, kind, origin	generate, generic, generous
–graph–	write, writing	autograph, geography
–log–, –logue–	study, word	logic, mythology, dialogue
–phil–	like, love	philanthropic, philosophy
–phon–	sound	phonograph, euphony
–port–	carry, bear	export, important
–psych–	mind	psychology, psychosomatic
–verse–, –vert–	turn	reverse, convert
–vid–, –vis–	see	television, evident

Commonly Used Prefixes

PREFIXES	MEANINGS	EXAMPLES
anti–	against, opposing	antipathy, antithesis
bi–	two	bimonthly, bisect
de–	away, off, down	defect, desert, decline
dis–	away, off, opposing	dismount, dissent
hyper–	excessive, over	hyperactive, hypertension
inter–	between, among	intercede, international
mis–	badly, not, wrongly	misfire, misspell
over–	above, excessive	oversee, overdo
post–	after, following	postpone, postscript
re–	back, backward, again	revoke, reflect, reforest
tra–, trans–	across, beyond	traffic, transport
un–	not, reverse of	untrue, unfold

Commonly Used Suffixes		
–able	able, likely	capable, changeable
–cy	state, condition	accuracy, normalcy
–er, –or	doer	baker, director
–ful	full of, marked by	thankful, masterful
–ion	action, result, state	union, fusion, dominion
–ish	suggesting, like	smallish, childish
–ist	doer, believer	artist, capitalist
–ly	like, characteristic of	friendly, cowardly
–ness	quality, state	softness, shortness
–ous	marked by, given to	religious, furious
–tion	action, condition	selection, relation
–tude	quality, state	fortitude, multitude

SPELLING RULES

ie and *ei*

15a. **Write *ie* when the sound is long e, except after *c*.**

achi**e**ve chi**e**f c**e**iling rec**e**ive

EXCEPTIONS **ei**ther, l**ei**sure, n**ei**ther, s**ei**ze, prot**ei**n

15b. **Write *ei* when the sound is not long e.**

for**ei**gn forf**ei**t h**ei**ght h**ei**r r**ei**gn

EXCEPTIONS anc**ie**nt, consc**ie**nce, fr**ie**nd, misch**ie**f, v**ie**w

–cede, *–ceed*, and *–sede*

15c. **The only English word ending in *–sede* is *supersede.* The only words ending in *–ceed* are *exceed, proceed,* and *succeed.* Most other words with this sound end in *–cede.***

inter**cede** re**cede** pre**cede** se**cede**

Adding Prefixes

15d. **When adding a prefix, do not change the spelling of the original word.**

im + mortal = **im**mortal mis + step = **mis**step
re + elect = **re**elect over + run = **over**run

Adding Suffixes

15e. **When adding the suffix *–ness* or *–ly,* do not change the spelling of the original word.**

fair + ness = fair**ness** sure + ly = sure**ly**

EXCEPTIONS

For many words ending in *y,* change the *y* to *i* before adding *–ness* or *–ly:*

empty—empti**ness** easy—easi**ly**

However, most one-syllable words ending in *y* follow rule 15e.

dry + ness = dry**ness** sly + ly = sly**ly**

15f. **Drop the final silent e before a suffix beginning with a vowel.**

hope + ing = hop**ing** strange + est = strang**est**

EXCEPTIONS Keep the final silent **e**

- in words ending in *ce* or *ge* before a suffix that begins with *a* or *o:* knowledg**eable,** outrag**eous**
- in *dye* and in *singe*, before *–ing;* dy**eing,** sing**eing**
- in *mile* before *–age:* mil**eage**

15g. **Keep the final silent *e* before a suffix beginning with a consonant.**

nine + ty = nine**ty** entire + ly = entire**ly**

EXCEPTIONS

nine + th = nin**th** judge + ment = judg**ment**
awe + ful = aw**ful** argue + ment = argu**ment**

15h. **For words ending in *y* preceded by a consonant, change the *y* to *i* before any suffix that does not begin with *i.***

fifty + eth = fift**ieth**
mystery + ous = myster**ious**

15i. **For words ending in *y* preceded by a vowel, simply add the suffix.**

joy + ful = joy**ful**
boy + hood = boy**hood**

EXCEPTIONS

day + ly = da**ily** pay + ed = pa**id**
say + ed = sa**id** lay + ed = la**id**

15j. **Double the final consonant before a suffix that begins with a vowel if the word *both* (1) has only one syllable or has the accent on the last syllable *and* (2) ends in a single consonant preceded by a single vowel.**

drop + ing = dro**pping** occur + ence =occu**rrence**
strum + ed = stru**mmed** thin + er = thi**nner**

Forming Plurals of Nouns

15k. To form the plurals of most nouns, add *-s*.

boats houses nickels Lincolns

15l. To form the plurals of other nouns, follow these rules.

(1) For nouns ending in *s, x, z, ch,* or *sh,* add *-es.*
glasses boxes waltzes beaches Bushes

(2) For nouns ending in *y* after a consonant, change the *y* to *i* and add *-es.*
armies babies skies mysteries
EXCEPTION For proper nouns, add *-s:* Hardys

(3) For nouns ending in *y* after a vowel, add *-s.*
joys keys Momadays

(4) For some nouns ending in *f* or *fe,* add *-s.* For others, change the *f* or *fe* to *v* and add *-es.*
beliefs roofs safes giraffes
calves wives leaves shelves
EXCEPTION For proper nouns, add *-s*: Radcliffs, Rolfes

(5) For nouns ending in *o* after a vowel, add *-s.*
radios patios stereos Marios

(6) For nouns ending in *o* after a consonant, add *-es.*
echoes heroes vetoes tomatoes
EXCEPTIONS tacos pianos cellos Sotos

(7) The plurals of a few nouns are formed irregularly.
children feet men teeth mice

(8) For a few nouns, the singular and the plural forms are the same.
deer Japanese Navajo sheep trout series

(9) For a compound noun written as one word, form the plural of only the last word of the compound.
Iceboxes blackberries businesspeople

(10) For a compound noun that is hyphenated or written as separate words, form the plural of the noun that is modified.
sisters-in-law runners-up music boxes

(11) For some nouns borrowed from other languages, the plurals are formed as in the original languages.
crisis—crises phenomenon—phenomena

A few nouns borrowed from other languages have two plural forms.
appendix—appendices *or* appendixes
formula—formulas *or* formulae

COMPUTER NOTE The spell-checking software on many computers can help you proofread your writing. However, even the best spell-checking program is not foolproof. Most do not identify words that are spelled correctly but are used incorrectly, such as *affect* for *effect*. Always make sure your spelling is error-free.

Your Turn Using Prefixes and Suffixes

Create new words by adding prefixes and suffixes to the following words. You may have to add extra letters for some words.

pull, amuse, respect, use, sincere, rude, sudden, teach, nerve

Prefixes	*Suffixes*
un–	–ing
dis–	–ful
re–	–er
mis–	–ous
	–ly
	–ness

16. Glossary of Usage

The Glossary of Usage is an alphabetical list of words, expressions, and special terms with definitions, explanations, and examples. Some examples have usage labels. *Standard* or *formal* usages are appropriate in serious writing and speaking, such as compositions and speeches. *Informal* words and expressions are standard English usages appropriate in conversation and in informal writing. *Nonstandard* usages do not follow the conventions of standard English.

accept, except *Accept* is a verb that means "receive." *Except* may be a verb or a preposition. As a verb, *except* means "leave out." As a preposition, *except* means "excluding."

We **accept** your apology.
Present company **excepted.** [verb]
Everyone **except** me has read the book. [preposition]

advice, advise *Advice* is a noun meaning "suggestion about what to do." *Advise* is a verb meaning "offer a suggestion; recommend."

He gave me some excellent **advice.**
She **advised** me to finish high school.

affect, effect *Affect* is a verb meaning "influence." As a verb, *effect* means "accomplish." As a noun, *effect* means "result (of an action)."

What he said did not **affect** my decision.
The new mayor has **effected** many changes. [verb]
What **effect** will it have on the environment? [noun]

ain't Avoid using this word in speaking and in all writing other than dialogue; it is nonstandard English.

all together, altogether *All together* means "everyone or everything in the same place." *Altogether* is an adverb meaning "entirely."

When we were **all together,** we voted.
He was **altogether** wrong.

a lot Do not write the expression *a lot* as one word.

Edgar Allan Poe also wrote **a lot** [*not* alot] of poetry.

anyways, anywheres Use these words (and others like them, such as *everywheres, somewheres,* and *nowheres*) without the final *s*.

I have to babysit tonight **anyway.**
The Loisels could not find the necklace **anywhere.**

at Do not use *at* after *where.*

NONSTANDARD Where was Romeo at?
STANDARD **Where** was Romeo?

bad, badly *Bad* is an adjective. *Badly* is an adverb. Only *bad* should follow a linking verb, such as *feel, look, sound, taste, or smell,* or forms of *be.*

The band played **badly.**
She felt **bad** about leaving.

being as, being that Use *since* or *because* instead of these expressions.

Because [*not* Being as] President Clinton admired Maya Angelou's writing, he invited her to write a poem for his inauguration.

beside, besides *Beside* is a preposition that means "by the side of" or "next to." As a preposition, *besides* means "in addition to" or "other than." As an adverb, *besides* means "moreover."

His rifle lay **beside** him. [preposition]
I don't want to go; **besides,** it's snowing. [adverb]

between, among Use *between* when you are referring to two things at a time, even though they may be part of a group consisting of more than two.

The feud was **between** the two families.
The woman couldn't decide which of the three cars to buy, because there wasn't much difference **between** them. [Although there are three cars, each is being compared to the others separately.]

Use *among* when referring to a group rather than to separate individuals.

We had only ten dollars **among** the four of us.

bust, busted Avoid using these words as verbs. Instead, use a form of *burst* or *break.*

The balloon **burst** [*not* busted] loudly.
The firefighters **broke** [*not* busted] a window.

consul, council, counsel *Consul* is a noun meaning "representative of a foreign country." *Council* is a noun meaning "group called together to accomplish a job." As a noun, *counsel* means "advice." As a verb, it means "give advice."

The French **consul** outlined his government's plan.
The city **council** will debate the issue.
I'm grateful for your **counsel.** [noun]
Did the doctor **counsel** her to get more rest? [verb]

discover, invent *Discover* means "be the first to find or learn about something that already exists." *Invent* means "be the first to do or make something."

Marguerite Perey **discovered** the element francium.
The zipper was **invented** in 1893.

double negative A double negative is two negative words when one is enough. Avoid double negatives.

Common Negative Words

barely	never	no one	not (–n't)
hardly	no	nowhere	nothing
neither	nobody	none	scarcely

double subject Do not use an unnecessary pronoun—*he, she, it, they*—after the subject.

NONSTANDARD Miss Lottie she likes her garden.
STANDARD Miss Lottie likes her garden.

etc. *Etc.* is the abbreviation of *et cetera,* meaning "and other things." Do not use *and* with *etc.*

My sister collects stickers, bottle caps, string, **etc.** [*not* and etc.]

fewer, less *Fewer* tells "how many"; it is used with plural nouns. *Less* tells "how much"; it is used with singular nouns.

There were **fewer** mosquitoes this summer.
Reading the *Odyssey* took **less** time I thought.

good, well *Good* is an adjective. *Well* may be used as an adjective or an adverb. Never use *good* to modify a verb; instead, use *well* as an adverb meaning "capably" or "satisfactorily."

Sandra Cisneros writes **well** [not good].

As an adjective, *well* means "healthy" or "satisfactory" in appearance or condition.

Lying in his bed, Harry did not look **well.**
He assured me that all was **well.**

NOTE *Feel good* and *feel well* mean different things. *Feel good* means "feel happy or pleased." *Feel well* means "feel healthy."

The news made her feel **good.**
I didn't feel **well,** so I went home.

hisself, theirselves Do not use these words for *himself* and *themselves.*

imply, infer *Imply* means "suggest indirectly." *Infer* means "interpret" or "draw a conclusion."

Doug **implied** that he will vote for me.
From Doug's remark, I **inferred** that I had his vote.

its, it's *Its* is the possessive form of *it. It's* is the contraction of *it is* or *it has.*

The bird stopped **its** singing.
It's [it is] an easy problem.
It's [it has] been raining since noon.

kind of, sort of In formal situations, avoid using these terms to mean *somewhat* or *rather.*

INFORMAL Zaroff was kind of surprised to see that Rainsford was still alive.
FORMAL Zaroff was **rather** surprised to see that Rainsford was still alive.

kind of a, sort of a Avoid using *a* after *kind of* and *sort of* in formal situations.

INFORMAL What kind of a snake was it?
FORMAL What **kind of** snake was it?

kind(s), sort(s), type(s) Use *this* or *that* with the singular form of each of these nouns. Use *these* or *those* with the plural form.

I like **this kind** of tea better than **those** other **kinds.**

learn, teach *Learn* means "acquire knowledge." *Teach* means "instruct" or "show how."

Doodle **learns** to walk.
His brother **teaches** him to walk.

leave, let *Leave* means "go away" or "depart from." *Let* means "allow." Avoid using *leave* for *let.*

Let [not *Leave*] her speak if she wants.

lie, lay The verb *lie* means "rest" or "stay, recline, or remain in a certain position." *Lie* never takes an object. Its principal parts are *lie, lying, lay, lain.* The verb *lay* means "put in a place." Its principal parts are *lay, laying, laid, laid. Lay* usually takes an object.

Is there really a snake **lying** on Harry's stomach?
He **laid** his books on the table.

like, as In formal English, use *like* to introduce a prepositional phrase, and use *as* to introduce a subordinate clause.

Does Juliet look **like** Rosaline? [*Like* introduces the phrase *like Rosaline.*]
Juliet does **as** Friar Laurence suggests. [*As* introduces the clause *as Friar Laurence suggests.*]

like, as if In formal situations, use the compound conjunction *as if* or *as though* instead of *like.*

Juliet looks **as though** [*not* like] she is alive.

moral, morale As an adjective, *moral* means "good; virtuous." As a noun, it means "lesson." *Morale* is a noun meaning "spirit; mental condition."

People are governed by **moral** standards. [adjective]
The **moral** of the story is: "Don't give up." [noun]
The employees' **morale** is high.

of *Of* is a preposition. Do not use *of* in place of *have* after verbs such as *could, should, would, ought (to), might,* and *must.* Also, do not use *had of* for *had.*

NONSTANDARD If I had of known it was your birthday, I would of sent you a card.
STANDARD If I **had** known it was your birthday, I **would have** sent you a card.

Also, do not use *of* after other prepositions such as *inside, off,* or *outside.*

The sniper's enemy fell **off** [*not* off of] the roof.
He hid **inside** [*not* inside of] the shack.

ought Unlike other verbs, *ought* is not used with *had.*

Doodle's brother **ought** [*not* had ought] to be more patient; he **ought not** [*not* hadn't ought] to push Doodle so hard.

peace, piece *Peace* means "calmness; absence of war or strife." *Piece* means "part of something."

After the long war, **peace** was welcome.
May I borrow a **piece** of paper?

principal, principle As a noun, *principal* means "the head of a school." As an adjective, it means "main or most important." *Principle* is a noun meaning "a rule of conduct" or "a general truth."

Ted had a long talk with the **principal.** [noun]
Winning is not our **principal** goal. [adjective]
My friends have high **principles.**
I don't know the **principles** of physics.

rise, raise The verb *rise* means "go up" or "get up." *Rise* almost never takes an object. Its principal parts are *rise, rising, rose, risen.* The verb *raise* means "cause to rise" or "lift up." *Raise* usually takes an object. Its principal parts are *raise, raising, raised, raised.*

Everyone **rose** when the judge entered the courtroom. [no object]
The witness **raised** her right hand. [object]

sit, set The verb *sit* means "rest in a seated position." *Sit* almost never takes an object. Its principal parts are *sit, sitting, sat, sat.* The verb *set* means "put in a place." *Set* usually takes an object. Its principal parts are *set, setting, set, set.*

The campers were **sitting** around the fire. [no object]
Ganderbai **set** the bag on a chair. [object]

some, somewhat In formal situations, do not use *some* to mean "to some extent" or "slightly." Instead, use *somewhat.*

INFORMAL My spelling has improved some.
FORMAL My spelling has improved **somewhat.**

than, then *Than* is a conjunction used in comparisons. *Then* is an adverb meaning "at that time" or "next."

This box is heavier **than** that one.
The sniper knew **then** who his enemy was.
First, I read *Romeo and Juliet;* **then**, I saw the film.

their, there, they're *Their* is a possessive form of *they.* As an adverb, *there* means "at that place." *There* is also used to begin a sentence. *They're* is the contraction of *they are.*

Their daughter, Juliet, was in love with a Montague.
Harry Pope lay **there** quietly.
There is a conflict in the *Odyssey.*
They're throwing pebbles at Miss Lottie's flowers.

Your Turn Correcting Usage

Revise the incorrect or nonstandard usage in the paragraph below.

Dog owners should train there pets to behave proper in public. Dogs that steal food or dig up gardens are kind of annoying. People should learn there pets to come when called. They should be sure that they're animals do not jump on people. Like I have said, people had ought to train their dogs to act good.

Glossary

The glossary that follows is an alphabetical list of words found in the selections in this book. Use this glossary just as you would use a dictionary—to find out the meaning of unfamiliar words. (Some technical, foreign, and more obscure words in this book are not listed here but instead are defined for you in the footnotes that accompany many of the selections.)

Many words in the English language have more than one meaning. This glossary gives the meanings that apply to the words as they are used in the selections in this book. Words closely related in form and meaning are usually listed together in one entry (for instance, *cower* and *cowered*), and the definition is given for the first form.

The following abbreviations are used:

adj.	adjective
adv.	adverb
n.	noun
v.	verb

Each word's pronunciation is given in parentheses. For more information about the words in this glossary or for information about words not listed here, consult a dictionary.

A

abandon (uh BAN duhn) *v.:* leave behind.
abundance (uh BUHN duhns) *n.:* full supply; plenty.
acclaimed (uh KLAYMD) *v.:* greeted with strong approval; applauded.
admonitions (ad muh NIHSH uhnz) *n.:* scoldings; warnings.
adulation (aj uh LAY shuhn) *n.:* intense or excessive admiration and praise.
adversary (AD vuhr sehr ee) *n.:* enemy; opponent.
adversity (ad VUR suh tee) *n.:* hardship; great misfortune.
affluent (AF loo ehnt) *adj.:* wealthy.
aghast (uh GAST) *adj.:* horrified; greatly dismayed.
agile (AJ uhl) *adj.:* moving with ease.
agitation (aj uh TAY shuhn) *n.:* state of being troubled or worried; excitement.
alignment (uh LYN muhnt) *n.:* arranged in a straight line; condition of having the parts of something coordinated or in the proper relationship.
aloof (uh LOOF) *adj.:* unfriendly; at a distance.
annihilate (uh NY uh layt) *v.:* destroy; wipe out.
anonymity (an uh NIHM uh tee) *n.:* namelessness; lack of individuality.
anticipate (an TIHS uh payt) *v.:* expect; to look forward to.
appease (uh PEEZ) *v.:* make calm or quiet; satisfy.
apprehensive (ap rih HEHN sihv) *adj.:* feeling alarm; afraid, anxious, or worried.
arbitrary (AHR buh trehr ee) *adj.:* based on one's preferences; capricious.
ardent (AHR duhnt) *adj.:* passionate; extremely enthusiastic.
armored (AHR muhrd) *adj.:* covered with defensive or protective covering, as on animals or plants.
articulate (ahr TIHK yuh layt) *v.:* clearly express.
artless (AHRT lihs) *adj.:* simple; innocent.
aspired (uh SPYRD) *v.:* wanted to achieve something; sought.
austere (aw STIHR) *adj.:* sober; solemn.

B

barren (BAR uhn) *adj.:* empty; deserted.
blithe (blyth) *adj.:* cheerful; happy.
bounds (bowndz) *v.:* leaps or springs forward.
brandished (BRAN dihsht) *v.:* waved in a threatening manner.

C

candor (KAN duhr) *n.:* honesty; frankness.
canopy (KAN uh pee) *n.:* in a forest, the leafy layer formed by the tops of trees.
caprice (kuh PREES) *n.:* sudden idea or change of mind, often made with little reason.
caress (kuh REHS) *v.:* touch gently in an affectionate manner.
ceremonial (sehr uh MOH nee uhl) *adj.:* having to do with a rite or ceremony.
charisma (kuh RIHZ muh) *n.:* personal charm.
chronic (KRAHN ihk) *adj.:* constant; frequently occurring.
client (KLY uhnt) *n.:* person or group for which a professional person or service works.
collaborate (kuh LAB uh rayt) *v.:* work together.
collective (kuh LEHK tihv) *adj.:* of or as a group.
compassion (kuhm PASH uhn) *n.:* sympathy; pity.
compelling (kuhm PEHL ihng) *adj.:* interesting; engaging.
comply (kuhm PLY) *v.:* act in agreement with

something; obey.
conceivable (kuhn SEE vuh buhl) *adj.:* capable of being imagined or understood.
condolences (kuhn DOH luhns ihz) *n.:* expressions of sympathy.
confronted (kuhn FRUHNT ihd) *v.:* came face to face with someone.
consoled (kuhn SOHLD) *v.:* comforted; calmed; cheered up.
conspicuous (kuhn SPIHK yoo uhs) *adj.:* remarkable; notable.
constrain (kuhn STRAYN) *v.:* confine; restrict.
contrition (kuhn TRIHSH uhn) *n.:* deep feelings of regret and repentance.
corroded (kuh ROH dihd) *v.* used as *adj.:* slowly worn away or decayed, especially by rust or chemicals.
coveted (KUHV iht ihd) *v.* used as *adj.:* longed-for.
cowered (KOW uhrd) *v.:* drew back in fear; cringed.
cowering (KOW uhr ihng) *v.:* drawing back, crouching, or trembling in fear.
critical (KRIHT ih kuhl) *adj.:* essential; important.
cross (kraws) *adj.:* angry.

D

decompression (dee kuhm PRESH uhn) *adj.:* here, something that expands a compressed file.
deflect (dih FLEHKT) *v.:* turn aside.
deliberate (dih LIHB uhr iht) *adj.:* done with careful thought or method in mind.
delirium (dih LIHR ee uhm) *n.:* extreme mental disturbance, often accompanied by hallucinations (seeing things that are not there).
demure (dih MYUR) *adj.:* seeming more modest and proper than one really is.
desolate (DEHS uh liht) *adj.:* deserted; lonely; not lived in; gloomy; producing a feeling of loneliness and sadness.
desperados (dehs puh RAH dohz) *n.:* reckless criminals.
differentiate (dih fuhr EHN shee ayt) *v.:* create a difference between; distinguish.
dilapidated (duh LAP uh day tihd) *adj.:* shabby; falling apart.
diligent (DIHL uh gehnt) *adj.:* hardworking.
diminish (duh MIHN ihsh) *v.:* lessen; reduce.
din (dihn) *n.:* loud, continuous noise.
disarming (dihs AHR mihng) *adj.:* removing suspicion or fear; charming.
disconsolate (dihs KAHN suh liht) *adj.:* causing sadness or depression; very unhappy.
discreet (dihs KREET) *adj.:* careful; showing good judgment.
disdainful (dihs DAYN fuhl) *adj.:* scornful; regarding someone as beneath oneself.
disposition (dihs puh ZIHSH uhn) *n.:* usual frame of mind; temperament.
disputed (dihs PYOOT ihd) *v.* used as *adj.:* subject of an argument.
distracted (dih STRAKT ihd) *adj.:* not able to concentrate; unfocused.
domestic (duh MEHS tihk) *adj.:* not wild; tame.

E

eerie (IHR ee) *adj.:* causing fear; strange.
elation (ih LAY shuhn) *n.:* great joy.
elect (ih LEHKT) *v.:* choose as a course of action.
emigrated (EHM uh gray tihd) *v.:* moved to another country.
eminence (EHM uh nuhns) *n.:* rank of distinction; fame.
en route (ahn ROOT) *adv.:* along the way.
enabled (ehn AY buhld) *v.:* make able; provide with means, opportunity, power, or authority.
encompass (ehn KUHM puhs) *v.:* include; contain.
endure (ehn DUR) *v.:* put up with something difficult; suffer.
enduring (ehn DUR ihng) *adj.:* strong and lasting.
enlisted (ehn LIHS tihd) *v.:* secured the services of.
enveloped (ehn VEHL uhpt) *v.:* wrapped around; surrounded.
eradicate (ih RAD uh kayt) *v.:* eliminate completely; get rid of.
evolved (ee VAHLVD) *v.:* developed or changed gradually.
exasperated (ehg ZAS puh ray tuhd) *adj.:* irritated and angry.
exasperation (ehg zas puh RAY shuhn) *n.:* state of great annoyance.
exorbitant (ehg ZAWR buh tuhnt) *adj.:* much greater than is reasonable.
expansive (ehk SPAN sihv) *adj.:* covering many things; spreading out; broad.
expedient (ehk SPEE dee uhnt) *adj.:* very helpful in the pursuit of a goal or desire; advantageous.
expendable (ehk SPEHN duh buhl) *adj.:* not worth saving; unnecessary.
exuberance (ehg ZOO buhr uhns) *n.:* overflowing joy or enthusiasm.
exuberant (ehg ZOO buhr uhnt) *adj.:* joyful; high-spirited.

F

facilitator (fuh SIHL uh tay tuhr) *n.:* person who assists.
flawlessly (FLAW lehs lee) *adv.:* without error; perfectly.
forging (FAWRJ ihng) *v.:* making; forming.
formidable (FAWR muh duh buhl) *adj.:* awe-inspiring by reason of excellence; strikingly impressive.
forward (FAWR wuhrd) *v.:* send on to a new destination or address.
frail (frayl) *adj.:* thin and weak; delicate.
futile (FYOO tuhl) *adj.:* useless; hopeless; in vain.

G

gleam (gleem) *n.:* shining; glow; flash of light.
glee (glee) *n.:* great delight; merriment.
glowered (GLOW urhd) *v.:* glared; stared angrily.
grisly (GRIHZ lee) *adj.:* horrible; terrifying; gruesome.
gurgle (GUR guhl) *v.:* to flow or run with a bubbling sound.

H

haunches (HAWN chuhz) *n.:* the hindquarters of an animal; the part of the body around the hips.
hindrances (HIHN druhns ihzs) *n.:* obstacles; things that restrain or prevent an activity.
hovered (HUHV uhrd) *v.:* stayed suspended over something.

I

idealize (y DEE uh lyz) *v.:* think of someone or something as perfect; ignore any flaws.
image (IHM ihj) *n.:* visual illustration; graphic.
imminent (IHM uh nuhnt) *adj.:* near; about to happen.
impaled (ihm PAYLD) *v.* used as *adj.:* pierced with something pointed.
impending (ihm PEHN dihng) *adj.:* about to happen; looming.
implore (ihm PLAWR) *v.:* beg.
impose (ihm POHZ) *v.:* (used with *upon*) take advantage of.
imposing (ihm POH zihng) *adj.:* large and impressive looking.
impoverished (ihm PAHV uhr ihsht) *v.* used as *adj.:* poor; poverty-stricken.
impression (ihm PREHSH uhn) *n.:* idea; notion.
imprudent (ihm PROO duhnt) *adj.:* unwise; foolish.
impunity (ihm PYOO nuh tee) *n.:* freedom from punishment or harm.
inadvertent (ihn ad VUR tuhnt) *adj.:* unintentional, accidental; not done on purpose.
inaugurating (ihn AW gyuh ray tihng) *v.:* formally beginning.
inception (ihn SEHP shuhn) *n.:* start of something; beginning.
inciting (ihn SY tihng) *v.* used as *n.:* provoking; stirring up.
incomprehensible (ihn kahm prih HEHN suh buhl) *adj.:* not able to be understood.
inconsolable (ihn kuhn SOHL uh buhl) *adj.:* unable to be comforted; brokenhearted.
incredulous (ihn KREHJ uh luhs) *adj.:* doubting; here, prompting disbelief.
indifferently (ihn DIHF uhr uhnt lee) *adv.:* in an uncaring way.
indignation (ihn dihg NAY shuhn) *n.:* anger at something unworthy, unjust, unfair, or mean.
indispensable (ihn dih SPEHN suh buhl) *adj.:* absolutely necessary; essential.
indulged (ihn DUHLJD) *v.:* gave way to one's desires.
indulgent (ihn DUHL juhnt) *adj.:* giving in to someone else's wishes.
infallibility (ihn fal uh BIHL uh tee) *n.:* inability to make a mistake.
infamous (IHN fuh muhs) *adj.:* having a bad reputation; notorious.
infatuated (ihn FACH oo ay tihd) *adj.:* carried away by shallow or foolish love.
ingeniously (ihn JEE nyuhs lee) *adv.:* in a clever way; brilliantly.
inhabit (ihn HAB iht) *v.:* live in.
innovative (IHN uh vay tihv) *adj.:* new and original; groundbreaking.
inoffensive (ihn uh FEHN sihv) *adj.:* harmless; not objectionable in any way.
insensible (ihn SEHN suh buhl) *adj.:* not fully conscious or aware.
insistently (ihn SIHST uhnt lee) *adv.:* in a demanding manner; persistently.
intact (ihn TAKT) *adj.:* with no missing parts; whole.
intent (ihn TEHNT) *n.:* purpose; goal.
intermission (ihn tuhr MIHSH uhn) *n.:* a pause between periods of activity.
internalized (ihn TUR nuh lyzd) *v.:* adopted as one's own.
invariably (ihn VAIR ee uh blee) *adv.:* without exception.
iridescent (ihr uh DEHS uhnt) *adj.:* rainbowlike; displaying a shifting range of colors.
isolated (Y suh layt ihd) *v.* used as *adj.:* alone; separated.

J

judicious (joo DIHSH uhs) *adj.:* showing good judgment; wise.
justifying (JUHS tuh fy ihng) *v.:* proving that something is correct or valid.

K

kin (kihn) *n.:* family members; relatives.

L

lavished (LAV ihsht) *v.:* gave generously.
legitimate (luh JIHT uh miht) *adj.:* complying with the law.
literally (LIHT uhr uh lee) *adv.:* taking words at their exact meaning.
loathsome (LOHTH suhm) *adj.:* hateful; disgusting.
lurched (lurcht) *v.:* swayed suddenly.
lurked (lurkt) *v.:* lay in wait, ready to attack.

M

malevolent (muh LEHV uh luhnt) *adj.:* evil; harmful.
malicious (muh LIHSH uhs) *adj.:* showing a desire to harm another; spiteful.
malignant (muh LIHG nuhnt) *adj.:* evil; cruel.
mar (mahr) *v.:* damage; spoil.
marauders (muh RAW duhrz) *n.:* people who roam in search of loot, or goods to steal; raiders.
martyrs (MAHR tuhrz) *n.:* people who choose to die rather than give up their beliefs.
matured (muh CHURD) *v.:* learned more about life; developed more fully.
meager (MEE guhr) *adj.:* thin; small; inadequate.
menacing (MEHN ihs ihng) *v.* used as *adj.:* threatening.
mentorship (MEHN tuhr shihp) *n.:* advice or lessons from a mentor, or wise teacher.
meticulously (meh TIHK yuh luhs lee) *adv.:* carefully; with great attention to detail.
missives (MIHS ihvz) *n.:* written messages, such as letters.
monotony (muh NAHT uh nee) *n.:* lack of variety.
mortal (MAWR tuhl) *adj.:* here, very intense; severe.
mourning (MAWR nihng) *adj.:* indicating sorrow.

N

noncommittal (nahn kuh MIHT uhl) *adj.:* not agreeing or disagreeing.
nuzzled (NUHZ uhld) *v.:* rubbed gently with the nose.

O

obstinate (AHB stuh nuht) *adj.:* stubborn.
ominous (AHM ih nuhs) *adj.:* unfavorable.
options (AHP shuhnz) *n.:* choices.

P

pacifist (PAS uh fihst) *n.:* person who believes that conflicts should be resolved by peaceful means and not by war or violence.
pauper (PAW puhr) *n.:* very poor person.
pensive (PEHN sihv) *adj.:* thoughtful in a serious manner; reflective.
perennial (puh REHN ee uhl) *adj.:* year-round; continual.
perish (PEHR ihsh) *v.:* be destroyed; die.
permit (puhr MIHT) *v.:* allow.
perseverance (pur suh VIHR uhns) *n.:* sticking to a purpose, never giving up.
placid (PLAS ihd) *adj.:* quiet; still and peaceful.
pliant (PLY uhnt) *adj.:* easily bendable.
plummeted (PLUHM ih tihd) *v.:* plunged or dropped.
precipice (PREHS uh pihs) *n.:* rock face that projects out, such as a cliff; the brink of a dangerous or disastrous situation.
priority (pry AWR uh tee) *n.:* something deemed of utmost importance.
profusion (pruh FYOO zhuhn) *n.:* large supply; abundance.
provisions (pruh VIHZH uhnz) *n.:* supply or stock, especially of food.
prowled (prowld) *v.:* hunted; stalked.
prudence (PROO duhns) *n.:* caution; good judgment.
pursued (puhr SOOD) *v.:* followed or chased.

R

radical (RAD uh kuhl) *adj.:* extreme; thorough.
rampaging (RAM pay jihng) *v.* used as *adj.:* rushing widely about.
rancid (RAN sihd) *adj.:* having a disgusting smell or taste.
rationalizations (rash uh nuh luh ZAY shuhnz) *n.:* excuses made for behavior.
receding (rih SEED ihng) *v.* used as *adj.:* moving into the distance.
reconciliation (rehk uhn sihl ee AY shuhn) *n.:* friendly end to a quarrel.
reigned (raynd) *v.:* ruled.
reiterated (ree IHT uh rayt uhd) *v.:* repeated.
resiliency (rih ZIHL ee uhn see) *n.:* ability to spring back.
resolve (rih ZAHLV) *n.:* determination; fixed purpose.

resort (rih ZAWRT) *v.:* turn to something when in need.
retribution (reh truh BYOO shuhn) *n.:* punishment for a wrong; justice; revenge.
revoke (rih VOHK) *v.:* cancel; withdraw.
robust (roh BUHST) *adj.:* sturdy; healthy and strong.
rouse (rowz) *v.:* wake up.

S

sacred (SAY krihd) *adj.:* here, set aside for or dedicated to one person or use.
salvation (sal VAY shuhn) *n.:* person or thing that protects others from harm.
scan (skan) *v.:* copy text or graphics from paper into a computer file.
scavenging (SKAV uhnj ihng) *v.:* searching through rubbish to find things that can be used or sold.
scrutiny (SKROO tuh nee) *n.:* close inspection.
sensibilities (sehn suh BIHL uh teez) *n.:* ability to respond emotionally.
shard (shahrd) *n.:* a small bit or broken piece of something.
shriveled (SHRIHV uhld) *v.* used as *adj.:* shrunken and wrinkled, often as a result of being dried out.
solace (SAHL ihs) *n.:* comfort; easing of grief.
solitude (SAHL uh tood) *n.:* being alone; isolation.
spare (spair) *v.:* give up the use or possession of; part with.
sparse (spahrs) *adj.:* growing or spaced wide apart; small in quantity and thinly spread.
splayed (splayd) *v.* used as *adj.:* spread out.
spontaneous (spahn TAY nee uhs) *adj.:* arising naturally; unplanned.
sprawled (sprawld) *v.:* lying down with limbs spread out awkwardly.
sprightly (SPRYT lee) *adj.:* lively; full of spirit.
stark (stahrk) *adj.:* complete; absolute.
suffice (suh FYS) *v.:* to be enough; be adequate.
sulked (suhlkt) *v.:* showed resentment and ill-humor.
sullenly (SUHL uhn lee) *adv.:* in a resentful, disagreeable, and unsociable manner.
surmounted (suhr MOWN tihd) *v.:* overcame.
susceptible (suh SEHP tuh buhl) *adj.:* easily affected or influenced.
sustain (suh STAYN) *v.:* support; nourish.
sustainable (suh STAY nuh buhl) *adj.:* able to be maintained.
synchronizing (SIHNG kruh ny zihng) *v.:* causing to occur at the same time or rate; coordinating.

T

tenuous (TEHN yoo uhs) *adj.:* slight; flimsy.
tolling (TOHL ihng) *v.:* ringing slowly at regular intervals.
tramp (tramp) *n.:* person who goes about on foot, sometimes doing odd jobs or begging for a living.
transforming (trans FAWRM ihng) *v.:* changing from one thing into another.
transient (TRAN shuhnt) *adj.:* quickly passing; fleeting.
transmitted (trans MIHT ihd) *v.:* passed on.
trepidation (trehp uh DAY shuhn) *n.:* fear; nervous dread.
tumult (TOO muhlt) *n.:* commotion; uproar; confusion.
turmoil (TUR moyl) *n.:* confusion; disturbance.
twilight (TWY lyt) *n.:* soft light just after sunset; period between sunset and night.

U

unalterable (uhn AWL tuhr uh buhl) *adj.:* not able to be changed.
unconventional (uhn kuhn VEHN shun nuhl) *adj.:* not conforming to customary, formal, or accepted practices.
unmitigated (uhn MIHT uh gay tihd) *adj.:* absolute; not lessened in any way.
unrelenting (uhn rih LEHN tihng) *adj.:* not letting up or weakening.

V

vendors (VEHN duhrz) *n.:* sellers.
vigilance (VIHJ uh luhns) *n.:* state of being alert; watchfulness.
vigilant (VIHJ uh luhnt) *adj.:* watchful.
vile (vyl) *adj.:* disgusting; offensive.
vital (VY tuhl) *adj.:* very important.
vivacious (vy VAY shuhs) *adj.:* spirited; full of life.
vulnerable (VUHL nuhr uh buhl) *adj.:* defenseless; likely to give in to a force or desire.

W

writhing (RYTH ihng) *v.* used as *adj.:* twisting or turning, as in pain.

Z

zeal (zeel) *n.:* great enthusiasm or devotion to an ideal or goal.

Spanish Glossary

A

abandonar *v.* dejar atrás.
absoluto *adj.* total.
abundancia *sust.* gran cantidad.
acariciar *v.* tocar suavemente en demostración de afecto.
acatar *v.* actuar de acuerdo con algo; obedecer.
acechar *v.* esperar, preparado para atacar.
aclamar *v.* recibir con gran aprobación; aplaudir.
adinerado *adj.* rico.
adulación *sust.* admiración y alabanzas excesivas o intensas.
adversario *sust.* enemigo; oponente.
adversidad *sust.* dificultad; desgracia grande.
agazaparse *v.* agacharse para ocultarse o protegerse de algo.
ágil *adj.* que se mueve con facilidad.
aislado *adj.* solo; separado.
alineación *sust.* disposición en línea recta; estado de coordinación o relación apropiada entre las partes de algo.
amenazante *adj.* que indica que algo malo o desagradable va a suceder.
amenazante *adj.* que indica que algo malo o desagradable va a suceder.
amonestación *sust.* reprimenda; advertencia.
anca *sust.* cada una de las partes traseras de un animal.
aniquilar *v.* destruir; eliminar por completo.
anonimato *sust.* condición de no tener nombre; falta de individualidad.
anticipar *v.* esperar, ansiar.
apaciguar *v.* calmar o tranquilizar.
aprensivo *adj.* que se siente en peligro; temeroso, ansioso o preocupado.
aprovecharse *v.* sacar beneficio de algo o algui*en.*
arbitrario *adj.* basado en las propias preferencias; caprichoso.
ardiente *adj.* apasionado.
arrasar *v.* avanzar destrozando lo que se encuentra al paso.
articular *v.* expresar claramente.
asistente *sust.* persona que ayuda.
aspirar *v.* querer lograr algo.
austero *adj.* sobrio; sencillo.
autorizar *v.* permitir.

B

barullo *sust.* ruido fuerte, continuo y confuso.
bastar *v.* ser suficiente; ser adecuado.
blandir *v.* agitar de manera amenazante.
blindado *adj.* cubierto con un material protector.
brincar *v.* dar saltos hacia adelante.

C

camino a *loc. adv.* en el trayecto a un lugar.
candor *sust.* honestidad, franqueza.
capricho *sust.* idea o apetencia repentina, en general sin pensar demasiado en ella.
carácter *sust.* estado de ánimo habitual de una persona; temperamento.
carisma *sust.* encanto personal.
cautivador *adj.* que elimina la sospecha o el miedo; encantador.
ceremonial *adj.* relativo a un rito o una ceremonia.
cliente *sust.* persona que usa los servicios de un profesional o una empresa.
codiciar *adj.* desear.
colaborar *v.* trabajar juntos.
colectivo *adj.* relativo a un grupo.
comerciante *sust.* vendedor.
compasión *sust.* lástima; piedad.
completo *adj.* absoluto; total.
concebible *adj.* capaz de ser imaginado o entendido.
confrontar *v.* hacer frente a algui*en.*
consentir *v.* permitir los gustos y deseos.
consolar *v.* tranquilizar, aliviar.
contorsionarse *v.* retorcerse, por ejemplo de dolor.
contrición *sust.* sentimiento profundo de culpa y arrepentimiento.
conveniente *adj.* que sirve de ayuda para alcanzar un objetivo o un deseo; ventajoso.
convincente *adj.* interesante; que atrae.
corroerse *v.* desgastarse o degradarse, especialmente a causa del óxido o de productos químicos.
crepúsculo *sust.* luz débil que permanece después de la puesta del Sol.
crítico *adj.* esencial; de gran importancia.
crónico *adj.* constante; que ocurre con frecuencia.
cúpula *sust.* en un bosque, la capa de hojas que forman las copas de los árboles.

D

delirio *sust.* alteración mental extrema, a menudo acompañada de alucinaciones (ver cosas que no son reales).
descompresión *sust.* aquí, proceso de expandir un archivo comprimido.
desconsolado *adj.* triste y deprimido; muy infeliz.
desdeñoso *adj.* despectivo; que menosprecia o considera inferiores a los demás.
desolado *adj.* desierto; solitario; que no está habitado; que provoca un sentimiento de soledad y tristeza.
desorden *sust.* confusión; agitación.
despatarrarse *v.* acostarse o sentarse con las piernas extendidas de manera poco elegante.
despertar *v.* interrumpir a alguien el sueño.
desplomarse *v.* caer en picado.
despreocupadamente *adv.* sin interés, de manera indiferente.
desviar *v.* apartar, alejar.
detestable *adj.* odioso; desagradable.
diferenciar *v.* establecer una diferencia entre dos o más cosas para distinguirlas.
diligente *adj.* trabajador.
discreto *adj.* cuidadoso; que tiene buen criterio.
disminuir *v.* reducir; hacer más pequeño.
distante *adj.* poco amigable; alejado.
distraído *adj.* incapaz de concentrarse; descentrado.
doméstico *adj.* que no es salvaje; domesticado.

E

efímero *adj.* que pasa rápidamente; fugaz.
emigrar *v.* mudarse a otro país.
eminencia *sust.* rango de distinción; fama.
empobrecer *v.* llegar a un estado de pobreza.
encapricharse *v.* dejarse llevar por un amor superficial o poco sensato.
enfadado *adj.* enojado.
enfurruñarse *v.* mostrar resentimiento y mal humor.
englobar *v.* abarcar; contener.
enlutado *adj.* con signos exteriores de pena y duelo por la muerte de una persona.
envolver *v.* cubrir totalmente un objeto.
erradicar *v.* eliminar completamente; deshacerse de algo.
escanear *v.* hacer que un texto o un gráfico pase del papel a un archivo en la computadora.
escaso *adj.* disperso, diseminado; en poca cantidad.
escrutinio *sust.* examen riguroso y minucioso.
espeluznante *adj.* horrible; aterrador.
espontáneo *adj.* que surge naturalmente; que no está planeado.
estorbo *sust.* obtáculo; cosas que frenan o impiden una actividad.
estremecedor *adj.* que causa miedo; inquietante.
estropear *v.* dañar; arruinar.
euforia *sust.* estado de gran alegría.
euforia *sust.* alegría o entusiasmo desbordante.
evasivo *adj.* que no da su opinión, que no se compromete.
evolucionar *v.* desarrollarse o cambiar gradualmente.
exasperación *sust.* gran irritación.
exasperante *adj.* que causa irritación y enojo.
exiguo *adj.* insuficiente; escaso.
exorbitante *adj.* mucho más de lo que es razonable.
expansivo *adj.* que abarca muchas cosas; que se esparce o propaga; amplio.
exultante *adj.* lleno de alegría; entusiasmado.

F

fervor *sust.* entusiasmo o devoción hacia un ideal o un objetivo.
forajido *sust.* delincuente que huye de la justicia.
forjar *v.* fabricar; formar.
formidable *adj.* que inspira respeto y temor por su excelencia; impresionante.
frágil *adj.* débil; delicado.
fragmento *sust.* un trozo de algo roto, en especial de cerámica o vidrio.
fulgor *sust.* luz brillante y resplandeciente.
fulminar *v.* mirar intensamente con enojo.
fútil *adj.* inútil; sin importancia.

G

gorgotear *v.* fluir un líquido haciendo ruido.

H

habitar *v.* vivir en un lugar.
hocicar *v.* frotar suavemente con la nariz.
horrorizado *adj.* aterrorizado; muy consternado.
hoscamente *adv.* con resentimiento, de una manera desagradable e insociable.
hurgar *v.* revolver entre cosas para buscar algo, por ejemplo, entre la basura para encontrar cosas que se pueden usar o vender.

I

idealizar *v.* pensar que alguien o algo es perfecto; ignorar los defectos.
imagen *sust.* ilustración; gráfico.
impecablemente *adv.* sin errores; perfectamente.

implacable *adj.* que no disminuye ni se debilita.
implorar *v.* rogar.
imponente *adj.* grande y de aspecto impresionante.
impresión *sust.* idea; noción.
imprudente *adj.* insensato; alocado.
impunidad *sust.* falta de castigo.
inalterable *adj.* que no se puede cambiar.
inaugurar *v.* comenzar formalmente.
incitar *v.* promover, estimular a hacer algo.
incomprensible *adj.* que no se puede entender.
inconsciente *adj.* que no se da cuenta de algo.
inconsolable *adj.* que no se puede tranquilizar; destrozado.
incrédulo *adj.* que duda; que no cree con facilidad.
indigente *sust.* persona muy pobre.
indignación *sust.* enojo ante una injusticia, una maldad o algo impropio.
indispensable *adj.* absolutamente necesario; esencial.
indulgente *adj.* que cede a los deseos de los demás.
infalibilidad *sust.* sin posibilidad de cometer un error.
infame *adj.* que tiene mala reputación.
ingenio *sust.* inteligencia.
ingenuo *adj.* simple; inocente.
inicio *sust.* comienzo de algo.
inminente *adj.* que está a punto de suceder.
inminente *adj.* cercano; que está a punto de ocurrir.
innovador *adj.* nuevo y original; novedoso.
inofensivo *adj.* que no puede hacer daño.
inquietud *sust.* estado de agitación o preocupación.
insistentemente *adv.* de manera exigente; persistentemente.
intacto *adj.* que no le faltan partes; entero.
intención *sust.* propósito; objetivo.
interiorizar *adj.* adoptar como propio.
intervalo *sust.* una pausa entre períodos de actividad.
invariablemente *adv.* sin cambios.
involuntario *adj.* sin intención, accidental; que no se hace a propósito.
iridiscente *adj.* que muestra o refleja los colores del arco iris; que brilla o produce destellos.

J

júbilo *sust.* gran alegría; regocijo.
justificación *sust.* excusa para un comportamiento.
justificar *v.* demostrar que algo es correcto o válido.

L

legítimo *adj.* conforme a la ley.
literalmente *adv.* según el significado exacto de las palabras.

M

madurar *v.* aprender más sobre la vida; desarrollarse por completo.
maleable *adj.* que se dobla fácilmente.
maleantes *sust.* personas que merodean en busca de un botín o bienes para robar.
malicioso *adj.* que muestra deseos de hacer daño a otros; ruin.
maligno *adj.* malo; cruel; malvado; dañino.
marchitarse *v.* encogerse y arrugarse, a menudo como resultado del resecamiento.
mártir *sust.* persona que prefiere morir antes que renunciar a sus creencias.
meditabundo *adj.* que está pensando seriamente; reflexivo.
merodear *v.* ir por un sitio para espiar, observar o buscar algo.
meticulosamente *adv.* cuidadosamente; prestando mucha atención a los detalles.
misivas *sust.* mensajes escritos.
monotonía *sust.* falta de variedad.
mortal *adj.* aquí, muy intenso; grave.

N

notorio *adj.* llamativo; evidente.

O

obstinado *adj.* testarudo.
opción *sust.* posibilidad de elección.
optar *v.* elegir una forma de actuar.

P

pacifista *sust.* persona que cree que los conflictos deben resolverse mediante soluciones pacíficas y no con guerras y violencia.
parientes *sust.* miembros de la familia; familiares.
pausado *adj.* lento; metódico.
pena *sust.* castigo por un delito cometido.
perdurable *adj.* fuerte y duradero.
perecer *v.* ser destruido; morir.
perenne *adj.* que dura todo el año; continuo.
perforar *v.* agujerear con un objeto punzante.
perseguir *v.* seguir a alguien para cogerle o hacer por conseguir una cosa.
perseverancia *sust.* constancia en mantener un objetivo y no rendirse.

pésame *sust.* expresión de compasión.
plácido *adj.* calmado y tranquilo.
polémico *adj.* que es objeto de discusión.
posibilitar *v.* hacer que algo pueda suceder; proporcionar los medios, la oportunidad, el poder o la autoridad.
precipicio *sust.* parte vertical o que cuelga de un grupo de rocas, como un acantilado; situación peligrosa cercana.
prescindible *adj.* que no vale la pena guardar; innecesario.
prescindir *v.* abstenerse de usar o poseer algo; privarse de algo.
prioridad *sust.* algo que se considera de suma importancia.
prodigar *v.* dar generosamente.
profusión *sust.* abundancia; gran cantidad.
provisiones *sust. pl.* suministros o reservas, especialmente de comida.
prudencia *sust.* precaución; buen criterio.

R

radical *adj.* extremo.
rancio *adj.* que tiene olor o gusto desagradable.
recatado *adj.* que parece más modesto y más correcto de lo que es en realidad.
reclutar *v.* conseguir los servicios de alguien.
reconciliación *sust.* fin amistoso de una pelea.
recular *v.* echarse atrás, especialmente por miedo.
recurrir *v.* acudir o apelar a algo en caso de necesidad.
reinar *v.* gobernar.
reiterar *v.* repetir.
remitir *v.* enviar a un destino nuevo o a otra dirección.
resolución *sust.* determinación; decisión.
restringir *v.* limitar.
retirarse *v.* alejarse.
revocar *v.* cancelar; retirar.
risueño *adj.* alegre; feliz.
robusto *adj.* macizo y sólido; saludable y fuerte.
rompedor *adj.* que no sigue las costumbres aceptadas, formales o tradicionales.
ruinoso *adj.* en mal estado; destrozado.

S

sagrado *adj.* aquí, dedicado a una persona o separado para un uso especial.
salvación *sust.* persona o cosa que protege a otros del daño y el sufrimiento.
sensato *adj.* que tiene buen criterio; prudente.
sensibilidad *sust.* capacidad para responder emocionalmente.
sincronizar *v.* hacer que dos o más cosas ocurran al mismo tiempo o al mismo ritmo; coordinar.
siniestro *adj.* desfavorable.
solaz *sust.* consuelo; alivio de la pena.
soledad *sust.* falta de compañía; aislamiento.
soportar *v.* tolerar algo difícil; padecer.
sostenible *adj.* que se puede mantener.
superar *v.* vencer.
susceptible *adj.* vulnerable; que las cosas le afectan con facilidad.
suspender *v.* colgar por encima de algo.
sustentar *v.* mantener, alimentar.

T

tambalearse *v.* moverse a un lado y al otro, como a punto de caerse.
tañer *v.* tocar un instrumento despacio a intervalos regulares.
temor *sust.* miedo.
tenderse *adj.* estirarse.
tenue *adj.* ligero; de poca intensidad.
transformar *v.* cambiar una cosa o estado a otro.
transmitir *v.* pasar.
tumulto *sust.* confusión; alboroto; agitación.
tutoría *sust.* conjunto de lecciones o consejos de un mentor o un maestro sabio.

V

vagabundo *sust.* persona que va a pie y a veces hace trabajos pequeños o mendiga para vivir.
vigilancia *sust.* estado de alerta; estado de atención.
vigilante *adj.* alerta.
vil *adj.* desagradable; ofensivo.
vital *adj.* muy importante.
vivaz *adj.* con energía; lleno de vida; alegre.
vulnerable *adj.* que no se puede defender; que tiende a ceder ante una fuerza o un deseo.

Y

yermo *adj.* vacío; desierto.

Academic Vocabulary Glossary

English/Spanish

The Academic Vocabulary Glossary in this section is an alphabetical list of the Academic Vocabulary words found in this textbook. Use this glossary just as you would use a dictionary—to find out the meanings of words used in your literature class to talk about and write about literary and informational texts and to talk about and write about concepts and topics in your other academic classes.

For each word, the glossary includes the pronunciation, part of speech, and meaning. A Spanish version of the glossary immediately follows the English version. For more information about the words in the Academic Vocabulary Glossary, please consult a dictionary.

English

A

appeal (uh PEEL) *v.* attract; interest.
associate (uh SOH shee ayt) *v.* mentally make a link; connect in thought.
attitude (AT uh tood) *n.* way of thinking, acting, or feeling; outlook.

C

coherent (KOH hehr ehnt) *adj.* clear, logical, connected, understandable.
complex (KAHM plehks) *adj.* having more than one part or aspect; complicated.
consequences (KAHN she kwehn sehz) *n.* results, outcomes.
convention (kuhn VEHN shuhn) *n.* standard technique.
convey (kuhn VAY) *v.* suggest; communicate.
counter (KOWN tuhr) *v.* oppose or take issue with.

D

destiny (DEHS tuh nee) *n.* unavoidable future; fate.
distinct (dihs TIHNGKT) *adj.* obviously different; unique.

E

effect (uh FEHKT) *n.* result.
elaborate (ih LAB uh rayt) *v.* go into greater detail about something.
embody (ehm BAHD ee) *v.* give form to something abstract.
enhance (ehn HANS) *v.* make greater; improve.
establish (ehs TAB lihsh) *v.* set up; create.
evoke (ih VOHK) *v.* bring a memory or feeling to mind.
excerpt (EHK surpt) *n.* passage; part of a longer work.
express (ehk SPREHS) *v.* put into words; show feeling or emotion.

F

function (FUHNGK shuhn) *n.* typical action of something.

I

imply (ihm PLY) *v.* suggest; hint at.
impression (ihm PREHSH uhn) *n.* overall effect.
incident (IHN suh duhnt) *n.* something that took place; event.
influence (IHN floo uhns) *v.* persuade or affect someone.
insight (IHN syt) *n.* clear understanding.
interpretation (ihn tur pruh TAY shuhn) *n.* portrayal that conveys a particular understanding of a work.

L

literal (LIHT uhr uhl) *adj.* based on the ordinary meaning of the actual words.

M

mutual (MYOO choo uhl) *adj.* done, said, or felt by each toward the other.

N

nuances (NOO ahns ihz) *n.* shades of difference in meaning or feeling.

O

observation (ahb zuhr VAY shuhn) *n.* statement based on what one sees.
outcome (OWT kuhm) *n.* result; ending.

P

portray (pawr TRAY) *v.* describe with words or other means; show.
production (pruh DUHK shuhn) *n.* presentation of a play; performance.

S

significant (sihg NIHF uh kuhnt) *adj.* important.
specify (spehs ih FY) *n.* state in detail.
support (suh PAWRT) *v.* back up; strengthen by giving evidence.

V

valid (VAL ihd) *adj.* supported by facts; true.
verify (VEHR uh fy) *v.* prove something to be true.

Spanish

A

actitud *sust.* modo de pensar, actuar o sentir; perspectiva.
ambiguo *adj.* que no está definido de manera clara; que puede tener dos resultados distintos.
asociar *v.* establecer mentalmente una relación.

C

cautivar *v.* atraer; interesar.
coherente *adj.* claro; comprensible.
complejo *adj.* que se compone de varios elementos; complicado.
consecuencias *sust.* resultados, efectos.
convención *sust.* técnica estándar.

D

desarrollar *v.* explicar algo en detalle.
destino *sust.* futuro inevitable.
distinto *adj.* diferente; único.

E

efecto *sust.* resultado.
especificar *v.* exponer en detalle.
establecer *v.* crear.
evocar *v.* traer a la memoria un recuerdo o un sentimiento.
expresar *v.* poner en palabras; demostrar un sentimiento o una emoción.

F

función *sust.* acción que realiza algo o alguien normalmente.

I

impresión *sust.* efecto o sensación general que causa algo o alguien.
incidente *sust.* algo que ocurre; suceso.
influir *v.* producir un efecto sobre alguien.
inminente *adj.* cercano; que está a punto de ocurrir.
insinuar *v.* sugerir; dar a entender.
interpretación *sust.* forma de expresar algo para que se entienda un siginificado específico de una palabra.

L

literal *adj.* según el significado habitual de las palabras.

M

matices *sust.* gradaciones en los significados o sentimientos.

O

observación *sust.* afirmación basada en lo que uno ve.

P

pasaje *sust.* fragmento; parte de un texto más largo.
perspicacia *sust.* entendimiento claro.
plasmar *v.* dar forma a algo abstracto.
producción *sust.* presentación de una obra; desempeño.

R

realzar *v.* mejorar.
rebatir *v.* oponerse con argumentos a algo.
recíproco *adj.* que se hace, dice o siente de manera mutua entre dos o más personas.
representar *v.* describir; mostrar.
respaldar *v.* apoyar con pruebas.
resultado *sust.* efecto; desenlace.

S

significativo *adj.* importante.

T

transmitir *v.* sugerir; comunicar.

V

válido *adj.* respaldado por hechos; verdadero.
verificar *v.* demostrar que algo es verdadero.

ACKNOWLEDGMENTS

For permission to reprint copyrighted material, grateful acknowledgment is made to the following sources:

Roger Ebert's review of *4 Little Girls* by Spike Lee, from *Chicago Sun Times*, October 24, 1997. Copyright © 1997 by Roger Ebert. Reproduced by permission of **Andrews McMeel Publishing.**

"Advice for a Stegosaurus" by Jessica Goodheart from *The Best American Poetry* (originally appeared in *The Antioch Review*, vol. 63, no. 4). Copyright © 2005 by **The Antioch Review, Inc.** Reproduced by permission of the publisher's editors.

"Legal Alien" and "Extranjera legal" from *Chants* by Pat Mora. Copyright © 1984 by Pat Mora. Published by **Arte Público Press–University of Houston, Houston, TX, 1985, 2000.** Reproduced by permission of the publisher.

"In the Family" by María Elena Llano, translated by Beatriz Teleki from *Short Stories by Latin American Women: The Magic and the Real*, edited by Celia Correas de Zapata. Copyright © 1990 by **Arte Público Press, University of Houston, Houston, TX.** Reproduced by permission of the publisher.

"Poe's Death Is Rewritten as Case of Rabies, Not Telltale Alcohol" from *The New York Times*, September 15, 1996. Copyright © 1996 by **The Associated Press.** All rights reserved. Reproduced by permission of the copyright holder.

Slightly adapted from "Spielberg Collection Is Found to Contain Stolen Rockwell Art" as it appears in *The New York Times*, March 4, 2007. Copyright © 2007 by **The Associated Press.** Reproduced by permission of the publisher.

"The Courage That My Mother Had" from *Collected Poems* by Edna St. Vincent Millay. Copyright © 1954, 1982 by Norma Millay Ellis. All rights reserved. Reproduced by permission of **Elizabeth Barnett, Literary Executor.**

"Rabies Death Theory" by R. Michael Benitez from *The New York Times*, Editorial Desk, September 30, 1996. Copyright © 1996 by **R. Michael Benitez.** Reproduced by permission of the author.

"Liberty" by Julia Alvarez. Copyright © 1996 by Julia Alvarez. First published in *Writer's Harvest 2*, edited by Ethan Canin, published by Harcourt Brace and Company, 1996. All rights reserved. Reproduced by permission of **Susan Bergholz Literary Services, New York, NY and Lamy, NM.**

"Papa Who Wakes Up Tired in the Dark" from *The House on Mango Street* by Sandra Cisneros. Copyright © 1984 by Sandra Cisneros. Published by Vintage Books, a division of Random House, Inc., and in hardcover by Alfred A. Knopf in 1994. All rights reserved. Reproduced by permission of **Susan Bergholz Literary Services, New York, NY and Lamy, NM.**

"Geraldo No Last Name" from *The House on Mango Street* by Sandra Cisneros. Copyright © 1984 by Sandra Cisneros. Published by Vintage Books, a division of Random House, Inc., and in hardcover by Alfred A. Knopf in 1994. All rights reserved. Reproduced by permission of **Susan Bergholz Literary Services, New York, NY and Lamy, NM.**

"Mexico Next Right" from *Caramelo* by Sandra Cisneros. Copyright © 2002 by Sandra Cisneros. Published by Alfred A. Knopf, a division of Random House, Inc., 2002. Reproduced by permission of **Susan Bergholz Literary Services, New York, NY and Lamy, NM.**

"Tiburón" from *Trumpets from the Islands of Their Evictions* by Martín Espada. Copyright © 1987 by Bilingual Review Press. Reproduced by permission of **Bilingual Press/Editorial Bilingüe, Hispanic Research Center, Arizona State University, Tempe, AZ.**

"The Gift" from *Rose: Poems* by Li-Young Lee. Copyright © 1986 by Li-Young Lee. Reproduced by permission of **BOA Editions, Ltd.**

"The Most Dangerous Game" by Richard Connell. Copyright © 1924 by Richard Connell; copyright renewed © 1952 by Louise Fox Connell. Reproduced by permission of **Brandt & Hochman Literary Agents, Inc.** Any electronic copying or distribution of this text is expressly forbidden.

Adapted from "Day 4" from *Appalachian Trail Journal* by Edward Burgess. Copyright © 1999 by **Edward Burgess.** Reproduced by permission of the author.

From "Teaching Chess, and Life" by Carlos Capellan from *The New York Times*, September 3, 2000. Copyright © 2000 by **Carlos Capellan.** Reproduced by permission of the author.

"Paris and Queen Helen" from *The Siege and Fall of Troy* by Robert Graves. Text copyright © 1962 by International Authors N.V. Reproduced by permission of **Carcanet Press Limited** and electronic format by permission of **A. P. Watt, Ltd.**

Slightly adapted from "The Secret Latina" by Veronica Chambers from *Becoming American: Personal/Essays by First Generation Immigrant Women*. Copyright ©2000 By **Veronica Chambers.** Reproduced by permission of the author.

"Letter to Juliet" by Charlotte Schein from *The Juliet Club*. Copyright © 1994 by **Club de Giulietta.** Reproduced by permission of the publisher.

"Essay" by **Judith Ortiz Cofer.** Copyright © 2007 by Judith Ortiz Cofer. Reproduced by permission of the author.

Slightly adapted from "Marigolds" by Eugenia W. Collier from *Negro Digest*, November 1969. Copyright © 1969 by **Eugenia W. Collier.** Reproduced by permission of the author.

"The Golden Kite, the Silver Wind" by Ray Bradbury from *Epoch*, Winter 1953. Copyright © 1953 by Epoch Associates; copyright renewed © 1981 by Ray Bradbury. Reproduced by permission of **Don Congdon Associates, Inc.**
no web allowed

"A Sound of Thunder" by Ray Bradbury from *Collier's*, June 28, 1952. Copyright © 1952 by the Crowell-Collier Publishing Co.; copyright renewed © 1980 by Ray Bradbury. Reproduced by permission of **Don Congdon Associates, Inc.**
no web allowed

"Country Scene" from *Spring Essence, The Poetry of Hô Xuân Hu'o'ng*, edited and translated by John Balaban. Copyright © 2000 by John Balaban. Reproduced by permission of **Copper Canyon Press.**

"On the Abolition of the Threat of War" from *Ideas and Opinions* by Albert Einstein. Copyright © 1954 and renewed © 1982 by **Crown Publishers, Inc., a division of Random House, Inc., www.randomhouse.com.** Reproduced by permission of the publisher.

"The Open Boat Journey: The First Ten Days" from *Shipwreck at the Bottom of the World: The Extraordinary True Story of Shackleton and the Endurance* by Jennifer Armstrong. Copyright © 1998 by Jennifer M. Armstrong. Reproduced by permission of **Crown Publishers, a division of Random House, Inc., www.randomhouse.com.**

"Prologue: How to Eat a Guava" from *When I Was Puerto Rican* by Esmeralda Santiago. Copyright © 1993 by Esmeralda Santiago. Reproduced by permission of **Da Capo Press, a member of Perseus Books, L.L.C.**

"Harrison Bergeron" from *Welcome to the Monkey House* by Kurt Vonnegut, Jr. Copyright © 1961 by Kurt Vonnegut, Jr. Reproduced by permission of **Dell Publishing, a division of Random House, Inc., www.randomhouse.com** and CD-ROM format by permission of **Donald C. Farber, Attorney for Kurt Vonnegut, Jr.**

"The Road Block" ("Get out of my road") by Miura Chora from *An Introduction to Haiku* by Harold G. Henderson. Copyright © 1958 by Harold G. Henderson. Reproduced by permission of **Doubleday, a division of Random House, Inc., www.randomhouse.com.**

"The Girl Who Loved the Sky" from *At the Helm of Twilight* by **Anita Endrezze.** Copyright © 1988 by Anita Endrezze. Published by Broken Moon Press, 1992. Reproduced by permission of the author.

From the lyrics to "Moon Men Mambo," words and music by Paul Parnes. Copyright © by Fairyland Music (ASCAP). All rights reserved. Reproduced by permission of **Fairyland Music.**

Slightly adapted from pp 33–45 (from "The Bicycle and the Sweet Shop," "The Great Mouse Plot," and "Mr. Coombes") from *Boy: Tales of Childhood* by Roald Dahl. Copyright © 1984 by Roald Dahl. Reproduced by permission of **Farrar, Straus and Giroux, LLC.**

"To Da-Duh, In Memoriam" from *Reena and Other Stories* by Paule Marshall. Copyright © 1983 by Paule Marshall. Reproduced by permission of **The Feminist Press at The City University of New York, www.feministpress.org.**

From "Book 1: A Goddess Intervenes" (retitled "Tell the Story") from *The Odyssey* by Homer, translated by Robert Fitzgerald. Copyright © 1961, 1963 by Robert Fitzgerald; copyright renewed © 1989 by Benedict R. C. Fitzgerald, on behalf of the Fitzgerald Children. Reproduced by permission of **Benedict R. C. Fitzgerald.**

From "Book 5: Sweet Nymph and Open Sea" from *The Odyssey* by Homer, translated by Robert Fitzgerald. Copyright © 1961, 1963 by Robert Fitzgerald; copyright renewed © 1989 by Benedict R. C. Fitzgerald, on behalf of the Fitzgerald children. Reproduced by permission of **Benedict R. C. Fitzgerald.**

From "Book 9: New Coasts and Poseidon's Son" from *The Odyssey* by Homer, translated by Robert Fitzgerald. Copyright © 1961, 1963 by Robert Fitzgerald; copyright renewed © 1989 by Benedict R. C. Fitzgerald, on behalf of the Fitzgerald children. Reproduced by permission of **Benedict R. C. Fitzgerald.**

From "Book 10: The Grace of the Witch" from *The Odyssey* by Homer, translated by Robert Fitzgerald. Copyright © 1961, 1963 by Robert Fitzgerald; copyright renewed © 1989 by Benedict R. C. Fitzgerald, on behalf of the Fitzgerald children. Reproduced by permission of **Benedict R. C. Fitzgerald.**

From "Book 11: A Gathering of Shades" from *The Odyssey* by Homer, translated by Robert Fitzgerald. Copyright © 1961, 1963 by Robert Fitzgerald; copyright renewed © 1989 by Benedict R. C. Fitzgerald, on behalf of the Fitzgerald Children. Reproduced by permission of **Benedict R. C. Fitzgerald.**

From "Book 12: Sea Perils and Defeat" from *The Odyssey* by Homer, translated by Robert Fitzgerald. Copyright © 1961, 1963 by Robert Fitzgerald; copyright renewed © 1989 by Benedict R. C. Fitzgerald, on behalf of the Fitzgerald children. Reproduced by permission of **Benedict R. C. Fitzgerald.**

From "Book 16: Father and Son" from *The Odyssey* by Homer, translated by Robert Fitzgerald. Copyright © 1961, 1963 by Robert Fitzgerald; copyright renewed © 1989 by Benedict R. C. Fitzgerald on behalf of the Fitzgerald children. Reproduced by permission of **Benedict R. C. Fitzgerald.**

From "Book 17: The Beggar at the Manor" from *The Odyssey* by Homer, translated by Robert Fitzgerald. Copyright © 1961, 1963 by Robert Fitzgerald; copyright renewed © 1989 by Benedict R. C. Fitzgerald, on behalf of the Fitzgerald Children. Reproduced by permission of **Benedict R. C. Fitzgerald.**

From "Book 21: The Test of the Bow" from *The Odyssey* by Homer, translated by Robert Fitzgerald. Copyright © 1961, 1963 by Robert Fitzgerald; copyright renewed © 1989 by Benedict R. C. Fitzgerald, on behalf of the Fitzgerald Children. Reproduced by permission of **Benedict R. C. Fitzgerald.**

From "Book 22: Death in the Great Hall" from *The Odyssey* by Homer, translated by Robert Fitzgerald. Copyright © 1961, 1963 by Robert Fitzgerald; copyright renewed © 1989 by Benedict R. C. Fitzgerald, on behalf of the Fitzgerald Children. Reproduced by permission of **Benedict R. C. Fitzgerald.**

From "Book 23: The Trunk of the Olive Tree" from *The Odyssey* by Homer, translated by Robert Fitzgerald. Copyright © 1961, 1963 by Robert Fitzgerald; copyright renewed © 1989 by Benedict R. C. Fitzgerald, on behalf of the Fitzgerald Children. Reproduced by permission of **Benedict R. C. Fitzgerald.**

"The Great Escape" by **Thomas Fleming** from *Boys' Life*, March 1997. Copyright © 1997 by **Thomas Fleming.** Reproduced by permission of the author.

Slightly adapted from "Kaavya Syndrome" by Joshua Foer from *Slate.com*, accessed on May 22, 2006 at http://www.slate.com/toolbar.aspx?action=print&id=2140685. Copyright © 2006 by **Joshua Foer.** Reproduced by permission of the author.

From Chapter 1 from *And Words Can Hurt Forever: How to Protect Adolescents from Bullying, Harassment, and Emotional Violence* by James Garbarino, Ph.D. and Ellen deLara, Ph.D. Copyright © 2002 by Dr. James Garbarino and Dr. Ellen deLara. Reproduced by permission of **The Free Press, a division of Simon & Schuster, Inc.**

"Fifteen" from *The Way It Is: New & Selected Poems* by William Stafford. Copyright © 1966, 1998 by the Estate of William Stafford. Reproduced by permission of **Graywolf Press.**

"The Frog Prince" from *Three Children's Tales* by David Mamet. Copyright © 1982 by David Mamet. Reproduced by permission of **Grove/Atlantic, Inc.** and audio format by permission of **Abrams Artists Agency.**

"Women" from *Revolutionary Petunias & Other Poems* by Alice Walker. Copyright © 1970 and renewed © 1998 by Alice Walker. Reproduced by permission of **Harcourt, Inc.** and electronic format by permission of **The Wendy Weil Agency, Inc.** This material may not be reproduced in any form or by any means without the prior written permission of the publisher.

"The Happy Man's Shirt" from *Italian Folktales, Selected and Retold by Italo Calvino*, translated by George Martin. Copyright © 1956 by Giulio Einaudi editore, s.p.a.; translation copyright © 1980 by Harcourt, Inc. Reproduced by permission of **Harcourt, Inc.** and electronic format by **The Wylie Agency, Inc.**

Excerpt (retitled "Poe's Final Days") from *Edgar A. Poe: Mournful and Never-Ending Remembrance* by Kenneth Silverman. Copyright © 1991 by Kenneth Silverman. Reproduced by permission of **HarperCollins Publishers. Inc.**

"Initiation" from *Johnny Panic and the Bible of Dreams* by Sylvia Plath. Copyright © 1952, 1953, 1954, 1955, 1956, 1957, 1960, 1961, 1962, 1963 by Sylvia Plath. Copyright © 1977, 1979 by Ted Hughes. Reproduced by permission of **HarperCollins Publishers, Inc.** and electronic format by **The Wylie Agency, Inc.**

"Possum Crossing" from *Quilting the Black-Eyed Pea* by Nikki Giovanni. Copyright © 2002 by Nikki Giovanni. All rights reserved. Reproduced by permission of **HarperCollins Publishers, Inc.**

Chapter 1 from *Understanding Comics: The Invisible Art* by Scott McCloud. Copyright © 1993 by Scott McCloud. Reproduced by permission of **HarperCollins Publishers, Inc.**

"Fame is a fickle food" from *The Poems of Emily Dickinson*, edited by Thomas H. Johnson, J1659. Copyright © 1951, 1955, 1979, 1983 by the President and Fellows of Harvard College. Published by The Belknap Press of Harvard University Press, Cambridge, MA. Reproduced by permission of **Harvard University Press and the Trustees of Amherst College.**

Essay by Joyce Carol Oates. Copyright © 2007 by Joyce Carol Oates. Reproduced by permission of **John Hawkins & Associates, Inc.**

From "Einstein's interview with George Sylvester Viereck" from *Einstein on Peace*, edited by Otto Nathan and Heinz Norden. Copyright © 1960 by Otto Nathan. Reproduced by permission of **The Albert Einstein Archives, The Hebrew University of Jerusalem, Israel.**

"Letter to President Roosevelt" from *Dr. Einstein's Warning to President Roosevelt* by Albert Einstein. Copyright © 1939 by Albert Einstein. Reproduced by permission of **The Albert Einstein Archives, The Hebrew University of Jerusalem, Israel.**

"Einstein's remarks to Eleanor Roosevelt, February 13, 1950" (retitled "The Arms Race") from *Einstein on Peace*, edited by Otto Nathan and Heinz Norden. Copyright © 1960 by Otto Nathan. Reproduced by permission of **The Albert Einstein Archives, The Hebrew University of Jerusalem, Israel.**

"Thank You, M'am" from *Short Stories* by Langston Hughes. Copyright © 1996 by Ramona Bass and Arnold Rampersad. All rights reserved. Reproduced by permission of **Hill and Wang, a division of Farrar, Straus and Giroux, LLC.**

From pages 158–165 from *Cyrano de Bergerac* by Edmond Rostand, translated by Brian Hooker. Copyright 1951 by Doris Hooker. Reproduced by permission of **Henry Holt and Company, LLC.**

"Once by the Pacific" from *The Poetry of Robert Frost*, edited by Edward Connery Lathem. Copyright 1936, 1951, © 1956 by Robert Frost; copyright © 1964 by Lesley Frost Ballantine; copyright 1923, 1928, © 1969 by **Henry Holt and Company, LLC.** Reproduced by permission of the publisher.

From "Graphic Novels 101: FAQ" by Robin Brenner from *The Horn Book Magazine*, March/April 2006. Copyright © 2006 by **The Horn Book, Inc.** Reproduced by permission of the publisher.

"The Fenris Wolf" from *Legends of the North* by Olivia E. Coolidge. Copyright © 1951 and renewed © 1979 by Olivia E. Coolidge. All rights reserved. Reproduced by permission of **Houghton Mifflin Company.**

"The Scarlet Ibis" by James R. Hurst from *The Atlantic Monthly*, July 1960. Copyright © 1960 by **James R. Hurst.** Reproduced by permission of the author.

From "Internment History" by Satsuki Ina from *Children of the Camps: Internment History*. Copyright © 1999 by **Satsuki Ina, Ph.D.** All rights reserved. Reproduced by permission of the author.

"Cinderella's Stepsisters" by Toni Morrison from *Ms. Magazine*, September, 1979. Copyright © 1979 by Toni Morrison. Reproduced by permission of the **International Creative Management, Inc.**
print only—NO audio, no web, no CDs, no CD-ROMS; no alterations.

Essay by Ian Johnston. Copyright © 2007 by **Ian Johnston.** Reproduced by permission of the author.

"The Wife's Story" from *The Compass Rose: Short Stories* by Ursula K. Le Guin. Copyright © 1982 by Ursula K. Le Guin. Reproduced by permission of **Virginia Kidd Literary Agency.**

"Mother to Son" from *The Collected Poems of Langston Hughes*. Copyright © 1994 by The Estate of Langston Hughes. Reproduced by permisison of **Alfred A. Knopf, a division of Random House, Inc.** and electronic format by permission of **Harold Ober Associates Incorporated.**

"Internment" from *Hilo Rains* by Juliet S. Kono. Copyright © 1988 by **Juliet S. Kono.** Reproduced by permission of the author.

"Disguises" by Jean Fong Kwok from *Story*, 1997. Copyright © 1997 by **Jean Fong Kwok.** Reproduced by permission of the author.

Slightly adapted from "On Writing *Persepolis*" (from "Why I Wrote *Persepolis*," "Writing a Graphic Novel is Like Making a Movie," and "What I Wanted to Say") by Marjane Satrapi from *Pantheon Graphic Novels*. Reproduced by permission of **L'Association, Paris, France.**

Graphic panel from *Persepolis* by Marjane Satrapi. Copyright © 2003 by **L'Association, Paris, France.** Reproduced by permission of the publisher.

Essay by Andrew Lam. Copyright © 2007 by **Andrew Lam.** Reproduced by permission of the author.

"In the Current" from *The Boys of My Youth* by Jo Ann Beard. Copyright © 1997 by Jo Ann Beard. Reproduced by permission of **Little, Brown and Company, Inc.**

From the lyrics to "Coco Wheats Jingle." Coco Wheats is a registered trademark of Little Crow Milling Co., Inc., Warsaw, Indiana. "Coco Wheats Jingle" copyrighted to Little Crow Foods. Reproduced by permission of **Little Crow Foods.**

in Just-" from *Complete Poems: 1904–1962* by E. E. Cummings, edited by George J. Firmage. Copyright 1923, 1951, © 1991 by the Trustees for the E. E. Cummings Trust; copyright © 1976 by George James Firmage. Reproduced by permission of **Liveright Publishing Corporation.**

"Those Winter Sundays" from *Collected Poems of Robert Hayden*, edited by Frederick Glaysher. Copyright © 1966 by Robert Hayden. Reproduced by permission of **Liveright Publishing Corporation.**

From the lyrics to "Norge" appliances jingle. Reproduced by permission of **Maytag Corporation.**

"Sanctuary" from *Museum of Absences* by Luis H. Francia. Copyright © 2004 by Luis H. Francia. Reproduced by permission of **Meritage Press, San Francisco, CA.**

"Did Animals Sense Tsunami Was Coming?" by Maryann Mott from *National Geographic News*. Copyright © 2005 by **National Geographic Society.** Reproduced by permission of the publisher.

"Delphic Oracle's Lips May Have Been Loosened by Gas Vapors" by John Roach from *National Geographic News*. Copyright © 2001 by **National Geographic Society.** Reproduced by permission of the publisher.

Slightly adapted from "Coping With Cliques" (reviewed by D'Arcy Lyness, August, 2005) from *KidsHealth*. Copyright © 1995–2007 by The Nemours Foundation. Reproduced by permission of **KidsHealth and The Nemours Foundation,** one of the largest resources online for medically reviewed health information written for parents, kids, and teens, www.KidsHealth.org or www.TeensHealth.org.

From "Look Who's in the Kitchen Dishing Out Advice" by Sarah Lyall from *The New York Times*, April 23, 2005. Copyright © 2005 by **The New York Times Company.** Reproduced by permission of the publisher.

"Glorious Food? English Schoolchildren Think Not" by Sarah Lyall from *The New York Times*, October 18, 2006. Copyright © 2006 by **The New York Times Company.** Reproduced by permission of the publisher.

From "'Dear Juliet': Seeking Succor From a Veteran of Love" by Dinitia Smith from *The New York Times*, March 27, 2006. Copyright © 2006 by **The New York Times Company.** Reproduced by permission of the publisher.

"I Got It: Mentoring Isn't For the Mentor" by Jane Armstrong from *Newsweek Magazine*, June 5, 2000. Copyright © 2005 by **Newsweek, Inc.** Reproduced by permission of the publisher.

"Alcyone and Ceyx" from *Metamorphoses: A Play* by Mary Zimmerman. Copyright © 2002 by Mary Zimmerman. Reproduced by permission of **Northwestern University Press.**

"Daily" from *Hugging the Jukebox* by Naomi Shihab Nye. Copyright © 1982 by **Naomi Shihab Nye.** Reproduced by permission of the author.

"Ambush" from *The Things They Carried* by Tim O'Brien. Copyright © 1990 by **Tim O'Brien.** Reproduced by permission of the author.

"My Father's Song" by Simon J. Ortiz. Originally published in *Woven Stone*, 1992, University of Arizona Press, Tuscon. Copyright © 1992 by **Simon J. Ortiz.** Reproduced by permission of the author.

From *Barefoot in the Park* by Neil Simon. Copyright © 1964, 2002 by Paramount Pictures. All rights reserved. Reproduced by permission of **Paramount Pictures.**

"The Sniper" from *Spring Sowing* by Liam O'Flaherty. Copyright © 1924 by The Estate of Liam O'Flaherty. Reproduced by permission of **The Peters Fraser & Dunlop Group Limited (www.pfd.co.uk) on behalf of The Estate of Liam O'Flaherty.**

From "Being Prey" by Val Plumwood from *UTNE Reader*, July/August 2000. Copyright © 2000 by **Val Plumwood.** Reproduced by permission of the author.

"If Only Poe Had Succeeded When He Said Nevermore to Drink" by Burton R. Pollin from *The New York Times*, Editorial Desk, September 23, 1996. Copyright © 1996 by **Burton R. Pollin.** Reproduced by permission of the author.

"Ballad of Birmingham" from *Cities Burning* by Dudley Randall. Copyright © 1968 by **Broadside Press.** Reproduced by permission of the publisher.

"Woman Work" from *And Still I Rise* by Maya Angelou. Copyright © 1978 by Maya Angelou. Reproduced by permission of **Random House, Inc., www.randomhouse.com.**

"New Directions" from *Wouldn't Take Nothing For My Journey Now* by Maya Angelou. Copyright © 1993 by Maya Angelou. Reproduced by permission of **Random House, Inc., www.randomhouse.com.**

From *I Know Why the Caged Bird Sings* by Maya Angelou. Copyright © 1969 and renewed 1997 by Maya Angelou. Reproduced by permission of **Random House, Inc., www.randomhouse.com.**

"Caged Bird" from *Shaker, Why Don't You Sing?* by Maya Angelou. Copyright © 1983 by Maya Angelou. Reproduced by permission of **Random House, Inc., www.randomhouse.com.**

A Christmas Memory by Truman Capote. Copyright © 1956 by Truman Capote. Reproduced by permission of **Random House, Inc.** and electronic format by permission of **The Truman Capote Literary Trust, Alan U. Schwartz, Trustee.**

"The Car" from *Ultra-Marine* by Raymond Carver. Copyright © 1986 by Raymond Carver. Reproduced by permission of **Random House, Inc., www.randomhouse.com.**

From "Peter and Rosa" from *Winter's Tales* by Isak Dinesen. Copyright 1942 by Random House, Inc.; copyright renewed © 1970 by Johan Philip Thomas Ingerslev, c/o The Rungstedlund Foundation. Reproduced by permission of **Random House, Inc.** and electronic by permission of **Judith Buckner, Literary Agent for the Rungstedlund Foundation.**

From "The Boy Left Behind" from *Enrique's Journey* by Sonia Nazario. Copyright © 2006 by Sonia Nazario. Reproduced by permission of **Random House, Inc., www.randomhouse.com.**

"Homeless" from *Living Out Loud* by Anna Quindlen. Copyright © 1988 by Anna Quindlen. Reproduced by permission of **Random House, Inc.** and electronic format by permission of **International Creative Management.**

"Strawberries" retold by Gayle Ross from *Homespun: Tales from America's Favorite Storytellers*, edited by Jimmy Neil Smith. Copyright © 1988 by **Gayle Ross.** Published by Crown Publishers, 1988. Reproduced by permission of the author.

From Foreword by Pierre Salinger from *Where Were You When President Kennedy Was Shot? Memories and Tributes to a Slain President as Told to Dear Abby*. Foreword copyright © 1993 by **Pierre Salinger.** Reproduced by permission of the author.

From "Travis's Dilemma" by Charlie LeDuff, Patricia Smith, and David Leonhardt from *The New York Times Upfront*, vol. 139, no. 6, November 27, 2006. Copyright © 2006 by **Scholastic, Inc.** Reproduced by permission of the publisher.

"Lost at Sea: The Story of Ceyx and Alcyone" from *Favorite Greek Myths* by Mary Pope Osborne. Copyright © 1989 by Mary Pope Osborne. Reproduced by permission of **Scholastic Inc.**

"Old Man at the Bridge" from *The Short Stories of Ernest Hemingway*. Copyright 1938 by Ernest Hemingway; copyright renewed © 1966 by Mary Hemingway. Reproduced by permission of **Scribner, an imprint of Simon & Schuster Adult Publishing Group.**

Excerpt (retitled "The History Behind the Ballad") from *Parting the Waters: America in the King Years, 1956–63* by Taylor Branch. Copyright © 1988 by Taylor Branch. Reproduced by permission of **Simon & Schuster Adult Publishing Group.**

From the lyrics to "ACRYLAN Jingle." ACRYLAN is a registered trademark of Solutia, Inc. for acrylic fibers and textiles. Reproduced by permission of **Solutia, Inc.**

Slightly adapted from "StoryCorps Do It Yourself Interview" from *StoryCorps*. Reproduced by permission of **Sound Portraits Productions, Inc.**

Slightly adapted from "About StoryCorps" from *StoryCorps*. Reproduced by permission of **Sound Portraits Productions, Inc.**

"The Next Green Revolution" by Alex Nikolai Steffen from *Wired Magazine*, May 2006. Copyright © 2006 by **Alex Nikolai Steffen.** Reproduced by permission of the author.

"The Trailblazer" (retitled "Jackie Robinson") by Henry Aaron from *American Legends: From the Time 100*. Copyright © 2001 by **Time Inc.** Reproduced by permission of the publisher.

"A morning glory" by Chiyo from *Zen Art for Meditation* by Stewart W. Holmes and Chimoyo Horioka. Copyright © 1973 by **Tuttle Publishing, a member of the Periplus Publishing Group.** All rights reserved. Reproduced by permission of the publisher.

"The old pond" by Matsuo Bashō from *Zen Art for Meditation* by Stewart W. Holmes and Chimoyo Horioka. Copyright © 1973 by **Tuttle Publishing, a member of the Periplus Publishing Group.** All rights reserved. Reproduced by permission of the publisher.

"A dragonfly!" by Kobayashi Issa from *Zen Art for Meditation* by Stewart W. Holmes and Chimoyo Horioka. Copyright © 1973 by **Tuttle Publishing, a member of the Periplus Publishing Group.** All rights reserved. Reproduced by permission of the publisher.

"Airport" by Pauline Kaldas from *Dinarzad's Children*, edited by Pauline Kaldas and Khaled Mattawa. Copyright © 2004 by **University of Arkansas Press, c/o The Permissions Company.** Reproduced by permission of the publisher.

Slight adaptation of "American History" from *The Latin Deli: Prose and Poetry* by Judith Ortiz Cofer. Copyright © 1993 by Judith Ortiz Cofer. Reproduced by permission of **The University of Georgia Press.**

"Starfish" from *Emplumada* by Lorna Dee Cervantes. Copyright © 1981 by Lorna Dee Cervantes. Reproduced by permission of **University of Pittsburgh Press.**

"The Grandfather" from *A Summer Life* by Gary Soto (Dell 1991). Copyright © 1990 by University Press of New England. Reproduced by permission of **University Press of New England** and electronic format by permission of **Gary Soto.**

"First Lesson" from *Relations: New and Selected Poems* by Philip Booth. Copyright © 1957 by Philip Booth. Reproduced by permission of **Viking Penguin, a division of Penguin Group (USA) Inc.**

From the lyrics to "Yogi Bear Song" by Joseph Barbera, William Hanna, and Hoyt Curtin. Copyright © 1960, 1967 by Barbera-Hanna Music. Copyright renewed. Yogi Bear is a trademark of and copyrighted by Hanna-Barbera Productions, Inc. Reproduced by permission of **Warner Bros. Publications.**

"Essay" by Anna Deavere Smith. Copyright © 2007 by Anna Deavere Smith. Reproduced by permission of **Anna Deavere Smith and the Watkins/Loomis Agency.**

From "A 'Staggering Genius' Talks About Writing, Fame, and ...Trout. An Interview With Dave Eggers" from *Writing Magazine*, vol. 27, no. 4, January 2005. Copyright © 2005 by Weekly Reader Corporation. All rights reserved. Reproduced by permission of **Weekly Reader Corpration.**

Slightly adapted from "Kaavya Viswanathan: Unconscious Copycat or Plagiarist?" by Sandhya Nankani from *WORD: Official Blog of Read and Writing* magazines, Friday, April 28, 2006. Reproduced by permission of **Weekly Reader Corporation.**

"A Blessing" from *Collected Poems* by James Wright. Copyright © 1963, 1971 by James Wright. Reproduced by permission of **Wesleyan University Press, www.wesleyan.edu/wespress.**

From "Tending Sir Ernest's Legacy: An Interview with Alexandra Shackleton" by Kelly Tyler from *NOVA Online* Web site, 2002, accessed May 17, 2007 at http://www.pbs.org/wgbh/nova/shackleton/1914/alexandra.html. Copyright © 2002 by **WGBH Educational Foundation.** Reproduced by permission of the publisher.

From "John Fitzgerald Kennedy" by Eric Sevareid from *The World Book Encyclopedia*, vol. 11, pp. 266-268. Copyright © 2001 by **World Book, Inc., www.worldbook.com.** Reproduced by permission of the publisher.

"Pronunciation Key" from *World Book Online Reference Center* at www.worldbook.com. Reproduced by permission of **World Book, Inc.**

PICTURE CREDITS

The illustrations and photographs on the Contents pages are picked up from pages in the textbook. Credits for those can be found either on the textbook page on which they appear or in the listing below.

Cover (c), ©Macduff Everton/The Image Bank/Getty Images; (bkgd), ©Bill Stevenson/Aurora/Getty Images; (b), ©Sot/Photodisc/Getty Images; (inset), ©Jason Horowitz/zefa/CORBIS; (bc), ©Siede Preis/Photodisc/Getty Images; **iii** (bl), Sam Dudgeon/HRW Photo; (tl), Sam Dudgeon/HRW Photo; (bc), Sam Dudgeon/HRW Photo; (tr), Sam Dudgeon/HRW Photo; (br), Sam Dudgeon/HRW Photo; **iv** (bl), Sam Dudgeon/HRW Photo; (tl), Courtesy of Hector Rivera; (bc), Sam Dudgeon/HRW Photo; (tr), Courtesy of Eric Cooper; (br), Sam Dudgeon/HRW Photo ; **v** (l), Sam Dudgeon/HRW Photo; (cl), Sam Dudgeon/HRW Photo; (cr), Courtesy of Margaret McKeown; (r), Courtesy of Mabel Rivera; **vi** (l), Sam Dudgeon/HRW Photo ; (cl), Sam Dudgeon/HRW Photo; (cr), Sam Dudgeon/HRW Photo; (r),Sam Dudgeon/HRW Photo; **vii** (tm), ©Andrew Lam; (tr), ©University of Georgia/Peter Frey; (bl), ©Peter Kramer/Getty Images; (bm), Courtesy of Ian Johnston; (br),HRW Photo; **A4,** ©Paul Sierra; **A5** (inset), ©Brooke/Stringer/Getty Images; (b),©Demetrio Carrasco/Getty Images; **A6–A7** (b), Ras Ishi Butcher; **A7** (l), ©Deborah Davis/Alamy; **A8,** *Rampaging Wolves Attacking*, illustration from *The Hobbit*, by J.R.R Tolkien (1892–1973), edition published 1976 (engraving), Belomlinsky, Mikhail (Contemporary Artist)/Private Collection/Bridgeman Art Library; **A9** (l), *Girl in Red*, 1992 (oil on canvas) Willis, Tilly (Contemporary Artist)/Private Collection/The Bridgeman Art Library International; (r), ©Crawford Municipal Art Gallery, Cork, Ireland,/The Bridgeman Art Library International; **A10,** ©SuperStock; **A11** (t), Réunion des Musées Nationaux/Art Resource, NY. *A Soiree*. 1878. Oil on canvas. Photo: H. Lewandowski. ©2007 Artists Rights Society (ARS), New York/ ADAGP, Paris; (b), ©age fotostock/SuperStock; **A12,** ©age fotostock/SuperStock; **A13,** ©AP IMAGES/TITO HERRERA; **A14,** first tier (left to right): "Kelly" 2006 by Dan Goldman, "Glam" 2007 by Pedro Camargo, "Sack of Puppies" 2007 by Nikki Cook, second tier (left to right): "Hutch Owen" 2007 by Tom Hart, Sir Ernest Shackleton in "The Voyage of the *James Caird*," 2006 by Nick Bertozzi, "Hebi No Hada" 2006 by Rami Efal, third tier (left to right): "Panorama" 2002 by Michel Fiffe, "On the Beautiful Blue Danube" 2002 by Megan Kelso [top], "Billy Dogma in Fear, My Dear," 2007 by Dean Haspiel [bottom]; "What's the Difference?" 2005 by Josh Neufeld; **A15** (t), ©Marcell/CORBIS; (b), ©Stephanie Dalton/Art Image LA; **A16** (t), ©Kunin/Woman on the Stair/Art Image LA; (b), ©CORBIS; **A16–17** (bkgd), ©YVA MOMATIUK/JOHN EASTCOTT/Minden Pictures; **A18** (l), ©J Silver/SuperStock; **A18–19** (r), Smithsonian American Art Museum, Washington, DC/Art Resource, NY; **A20,** ©Content Mine International/Alamy; **A21** (inset), ©blickwinkel/Alamy; (b), 2002 Production of *Romeo and Juliet*/Foreground: Claire Jullien as Juliet and Graham Abbey as Romeo. Background: Patrick Galligan as Paris and Julia Donovan as Lady Capulet. Photo by Terry Manzo/Courtesy of the Stratford Shakespeare Festival Archives; **A22,** ©British Library Board. All Rights Reserved/The Bridgeman Art Library Nationality/Copyright status: French/out of Copyright; **A23,** Scala/Art Resource, NY; **A24,** ©Roger Ressmeyer/CORBIS; **A25,** Masterfile Royalty Free (RF); **A36** (bl), ©Jeff Greenberg/PhotoEdit; (tr), ©Radius Images/Alamy; (cr), ©StockConnection Distribution/Alamy; (tl), ©John Powell Photographer/Alamy; **A37** (tr), ©Dinodia Images/Alamy; (l), ©M Stock/Alamy; **A36–A37** (bkgd), Peter Dazeley/Photodisc/Getty Images; ©Steven Raniszewski/Design Pics/CORBIS; **1,** (bkgd), ©Radius Images/Alamy; (bl), Cover image from *Big Mouth & Ugly Girl* by Joyce Carol Oates. Copyright ©2002 by The Ontario Review, Inc. Reproduced by permission of **HarperCollins Publishers, Inc.;** (br), Cover image from *The Faith of a Writer* by Joyce Carol Oates. Copyright ©2003 by The Ontario Review, Inc. Reproduced by permission of **HarperCollins Publishers; 2–3,** ©Tom Collicott/Masterfile; **3,** ©PhotoDisc; **11,** ©Brooke/Stringer/Getty Images; **14** (inset), ©Bettmann/CORBIS; (bkgd), ©MedioImages; **18** (l), Brandt & Hochman Literary Agents, Inc.; (r), Masterfile Royalty Free; **22,** ©VStock/Alamy; **27,** ©VStock/Alamy; **29,** ©Winfried Wisniewski/zefa/CORBIS; **33,** ©VStock/Alamy; **42** (l), Photo by Shauna Angel Blue; **42** (bkgd), ©Royalty Free; **43,** ©ArkReligion.com/Alamy; **44,** ©Demetrio Carrasco/Getty Images; **47,** ©Patrik Giardino/CORBIS; **49,** ©Kurt Scholz/SuperStock; **50–51,** ©Lucidio Studio Inc./CORBIS; **52,** ©Corey Wise/Alamy; **54,** ©Bo Zaunders/CORBIS; **56** (l), ©Theo Westenberger (1995); **56** (bkgd), Harcourt HRW owned; **59,** ©Raul Touzon/National Geographic/Getty Images; **61,** ©Jerry Shulman/SuperStock; **62,** ©Geri Lavrov/SuperStock; **68** (bl), ©Getty Images; **68** (br), ©CORBIS; **73** ©Darren Winter/CORBIS; **78** (t), ©Steven Georges/Press-Telegram/CORBIS; **78** (b), Courtesy of Val Plumwood; **91,** ©Genevieve Vallee/Alamy; **93,** ©Arco Images/Alamy; **94,** ©Randy Olson/National Geographic Image Collection; **98,** ©Eric Nguyen/CORBIS; **103** (b), Ian Le Sueur Collection; (t), Jonathan F. Vance, Canada Research Chair, The University of Western Ontario; (c), Jonathan F. Vance, Canada Research Chair, The University of Western Ontario; **108,** ©M.A. Pushpa Kumara/epa/CORBIS; **109** (l), ©AP IMAGES/GEMUNU AMARASINGHE; (r), ©KAMAL KISHORE/Reuters/CORBIS; **110,** ©AP IMAGES/DITA ALANGKARA; **120** (bl), Cover image from *Gifts* by Ursula K. Le Guin. Copyright ©2004 by Ursula K. Le Guin. Reproduced by permission of **Harcourt Inc.;** (tl), Cover image from *The Hobbit* by J. R.R. Tolkien, Cover art by Peter Sís. Copyright renewed ©1994 by Christopher R. Tolkien, John F.R. Tolkien and Priscilla M.A.R. Tolkien; Copyright restored ©1996 by the Estate of J.R.R. Tolkien. Reproduced by permission of **Houghton Mifflin Company;** (tr), Cover image from *Apollo 13* by Jim Lovell and Jeffrey Kluger; Copyright ©1994 by Jim Lovell and Jeffrey Kluger. Reproduced by permission of **Houghton Mifflin Company;** (br), Cover image from *Woodsong* by Gary Paulsen. Copyright ©1990 by Gary Paulsen. Reproduced by permission of **Simon & Schuster Books for Young Readers, an imprint of Simon & Schuster Children's Publishing Company; 121** (tl), Cover image from Kindred (25th Anniversary Edition) by Octavia E. Butler Copyright © 1979 by Octavia E. Butler. Reproduced by permission of **Beacon Press;** (br), Cover image from *Gorillas in the Mist* by Dian Fossey. Copyright ©1983 by Dian Fossey. Reproduced by permission of **Houghton Mifflin Company;** (tr), Cover image from *Before We Were Free* by Julia Alvarez. Copyright © 2005 by Julia Alvarez. Reproduced by permission of **Random House Children's Books;** (bl), Cover image from *Help Wanted* by Gary Soto. Copyright © 2005 by Gary Soto. Reproduced by permission of **Harcourt, Inc.; 130,** ©Hulton-Deutsch Collection/CORBIS; **132,** ©POPPERFOTO/Alamy; **136** (l), Henri Cartier-Bresson/Magnum Photos; **136** (r), ©Bernd Obermann/CORBIS; **139,** ©Underwood & Underwood/CORBIS; **146** (bl), ©Daniela Zedda; (br), ©Steve Skjold/Alamy; **148,** ©Dennis Cooper/zefa/CORBIS; **154–155,** ©Atlantide Phototravel/CORBIS; **158,** ©Deborah Davis/Alamy; **160,** ©Elmtree Images/Alamy; **162** (bl), Photo by Sortino; (cr), ©Bettmann/CORBIS; (br), ©age fotostock/SuperStock; **164** (inset), Bruce Davidson/Magnum Photos; (bkgd), ©2007 Corbis/Jupiterimages Corporation; **167,** ©Blend Images/Alamy; (bkgd) ©2007 Corbis/Jupiterimages Corporation; **169** (inset) ©Time Life Pictures; **169** (bkgd) ©2007 Corbis/Jupiterimages Corporation; **174,** ©Stock Connection Distribution/Alamy; **176** (br), Debra P. Hershkowitz; **179,** ©Grace/zefa/CORBIS; **182,** Sam Ang/FoodPix/Jupiterimages; **186–187,** ©Tiit Veermae/Alamy; **188,** ©Nordic Photos/Nils-Johan Norenlind/Getty Images; **192** (cl), ©Prints & Photographs Division, Library of Congress, LC-USZ62-43606; (tl), ©Ulf Andersen/Getty Images; (bl), SCHOMBURG CENTER/The New York Public Library/Art Resource, NY; **198,** Debra P. Hershkowitz; **200,** ©AP IMAGES/SUSAN RAGAN; **201,** ©Urbano Delvalle/Time Life Pictures/Getty Images; **203,** ©Meiko Arquillos; **204** (r), ©steve bly/Alamy; (tl), ©AP IMAGES/SUSAN RAGAN; **205,** ©PhotoDisc; **206** (bl), Daily News L.P.; (tr), ©Getty Images; **216** (tr), Cover image from *Hitch* by Jeanette Ingold. Copyright © 2005 by Jeanette Ingold. Reproduced by permission of **Harcourt, Inc.;** (tl), Cover image from *A Tree Grows in Brooklyn* by Betty Smith. Copyright ©1943, 1947 by Betty Smith; Copyright renewed ©1971 by Betty Smith (Finch). Reproduced by permission of **HarperCollins Publishers, Inc.;** (bl), Cover image from *Black Boy*, 60th Anniversary Edition, by Richard Wright. Copyright © 1937, 1942, 1944, 1945 by Richard Wright; Copyright renewed ©1973 by Ellen Wright. Reproduced by permission of **HarperCollins Publishers;** (br), Cover image from *Life of Pi* by Yann Martel, Cover illustration by Andy Bridge. Copyright © 2001 by Yann Martel. Reproduced by permission of **Harcourt, Inc.; 217** (tl), Cover image from *I, Robot* by Isaac Asimov. Copyright © 1950, 1977 by the Estate of

Isaac Asimov. Cover Copyright © 2004 by Twentieth Century Fox Film Corporation. All rights reserved. Reproduced by permission of **Bantam Dell, a division of Random House, Inc., www.randomhouse.com;** (tr), Cover image from *The Young Landlords* by Walter Dean Myers. Copyright © 1989 by Walter Dean Myers. Reproduced by permission of **Viking Penguin, a division of Penguin Group (USA), Inc.;** (bl), Cover image from *America Street: A Multicultural Anthology of Stories*, edited by Anne Mazer. Copyright © 1993 by Anne Mazer. Reproduced by permission of **Persea Books, Inc.;** (br), Cover image from *April and the Dragon Lady* by Lensey Namioka. Copyright © 1994 by Lensey Namioka. Reproduced by permission of **Harcourt, Inc.; 234** (bl), ©Time Life Pictures/Getty Images; **234** (br), ©Trevor Smithers ARPS/ Alamy; **246** (bl), ©Bettmann/CORBIS; (br), Courtesy of Peter K. Steinberg; **248–249,** ©Stephen Oliver/Alamy; **253,** ©Angelo Hornak/ CORBIS; **254,** ©Spencer Grant/PhotoEdit; **258** (r), ©Mark Gibson/Index Stock Imagery, Inc.; (l), Courtesy of Eugenia W. Collier; **263,** ©Photodisc/Fotosearch; **268,** ©John Warden/SuperStock; **270** (bl), ©Dan Tuffs/Getty Images; (br), ©FogStock/Alamy; **271,** ©SuperStock; **273,** Miguel Angel Muñoz/AGE fotostock; **274,** ©Tim Davis/CORBIS; **276,** ©Prints & Photographic Division, Library of Congress, LC-USZ62-10610; **278** (l), ©Bettmann/CORBIS; (tr), ©Prints & Photographs Division, Library of Congress, LC-USZ62-62322; **279** (tr), Debra P. Hershkowitz; **281** (l), Debra P. Hershkowitz; (r), Courtesy of the Edgar Allan Poe Museum, Richmond, Virginia; **282** (bkgd), Rebecca Floyd/ Images.com; **287,** ©Jim Zuckerman/Alamy; **288,** ©Steve Allen/Alamy; **291,** Copyright Scala/Art Resource, NY; **298,** Photography by Chris Semtner, Courtesy of Edgar Allan Poe Museum, Richmond, Virginia; **300,** Rebekah F. Owens, Westminister Preservation Trust, Inc.; **303,** R. Kubner/RobertStock.com; **316** (tl), Cover image from *To Kill A Mockingbird* by Harper Lee. Copyright ©1960 by Harper Lee. Reproduced by permission of **Warner Books, Inc., a subsidiary of Hachette Books, Inc.;** (bl), Cover image from *The Circuit* by Francisco Jimenez. Copyright ©1997 by Francisco Jimenez. Reproduced by permission of **University of New Mexico Press;** (br), Cover image from *Graphic Classics: Edgar Allan Poe* (Volume One, Third Edition, 2006). Copyright ©2006 by **Eureka Productions.** Reproduced by permission of the publisher; (tr), Cover image from *A Separate Peace* by John Knowles. Copyright ©1959 and renewed ©1987 by John Knowles, Inc. Reproduced by permission of **Scribner, a division of Simon & Schuster; 317** (bl), Cover image from *Girl Sleuth: Nancy Drew and the Women Who created Her* by Melanie Rehak. Copyright ©2005 by Melanie Rehak. Reproduced by permission of **Harcourt, Inc.;** (tl), Cover image from *Odd Girl Out* by Rachel Simmons. Copyright ©2002 by Rachel Simmons. Reproduced by permission of **Harcourt, Inc.;** (tr), Cover image from *Seabiscuit: An American Legend* by Laura Hillenbrand. Copyright ©2001 by Laura Hillenbrand. Reproduced by permission of **Random House, Inc., www.randomhouse.com;** (br), Cover image from *Where the Broken Heart Still Beats* by Carolyn Meyer. Copyright ©1992 by Carolyn Meyer. Reproduced by permission of **Harcourt, Inc.; 326–327,** ©Nik Wheeler/CORBIS; **328** (bkgd), Artville; **330,** ©age fotostock/SuperStock; **333,** ©age fotostock/SuperStock; **334,** ©James Randklev/Photographer's Choice/Getty Images; **336,** ©age fotostock/ SuperStock; **341,** ©age fotostock/SuperStock; **344,** ©Image Source/ PunchStock; **348** (inset), ©Bonhams, London, UK, Private Collection/ Bridgeman Art Library; **350** (br), ©Iconotec/Alamy; **356,** ©Bonhams, London, UK, Private Collection/Bridgeman Art Library; **362** (bl), ©Bettmann/CORBIS; **362** (br), ©Alinari Archives/The Image Works; **363,** ©Brand X Pictures/PunchStock; **367,** ©Andrew Sadler/Alamy; **374** (bl), ©Douglas Kirkland/CORBIS; **374** (br), Harcourt Owned; **379,** ©PhotoDisc; **384** (t), ©Lorraine Chittock/*Saudi Aramco World*/padia; **384** (b), ©Time & Life Pictures/Getty Images; **387,** ©ColorBlind Images/ Getty Images; **388,** ©Dave Bartruff/CORBIS; **390,** ©age fotostock/J.D. Dallet; **392** (bkgd), ©Photodisc Green/Getty Images; **396,** ©POPPERFOTO/Alamy; **399,** ©Farm Security Administration and Office of War Information Collection, Prints & Photographs Division, Library of Congress, LC-USZ62-15185; **400,** ©CORBIS; **401** (r), Philippe Halsman/ Magnum Photos; (l), ©CORBIS; (b), ©Bettmann/CORBIS; **402,** Courtesy of Tokue Kasaoka/Hiroshima Peace Memorial Museum; **403,** ©CORBIS; **404,** ©CORBIS; **414** (tl), Cover image from *The Little Prince* by Antoine de Saint-Exupéry. Copyright ©1943 by **Harcourt Inc.;** Copyright renewed ©1971 by Consuelo de Saint-Exupéry. Reproduced by permission of Harcourt Inc.; (bl), Cover image from *A Northern Light* by Jennifer Donnelly. Copyright ©2003 by Jennifer Donnelly. Reproduced by permission of **Harcourt, Inc.;** (tr), Cover image from *My World and Welcome To It* by James Thurber. Copyright ©1942 by James Thurber; Copyright renewed ©1970 by Helen W. Thurber and Rosemary Thurber Sauers. Reproduced by permission of **Harcourt Inc.;** (br), Cover image from *East* by Edith Pattou. Copyright ©2003, 2005 by Edith Pattou. Reproduced by permission of **Harcourt Inc.; 415** (tl), Cover image from *Peak: A Novel* by Roland Smith. Copyright ©2007 by Roland Smith. Reproduced by permission of **Harcourt, Inc.;** (bl), Cover image from *Come Juneteenth* by Ann Rinaldi. Copyright ©2007 by Ann Rinaldi. Reproduced by permission of **Harcourt Inc.;** (tr), Cover image from *The Giver* by Lois Lowry. Copyright ©1993 by Lois Lowry. Reproduced by permission of **Random House Children's Books;** (br), Cover image from *True Grit* by Charles Portis. Copyright ©1968 by; Charles Portis. Reproduced by permission of **The Overlook Press; 430** (inset), ©Andrew Lam; (bkgd), ©imagebroker/Alamy; **430** (bl), Cover image from *Perfume Dreams* by Andrew Lam. Copyright ©2005 by Andrew Lam. Reproduced by permission of **Heyday Books; 432–33,** ©Mark Wilson/Getty Images; **433,** ©Dennis MacDonald/Alamy; **440–41** (inset), ©Jon Arnold Images/Alamy; ©Jon Arnold Images/Alamy; **442** (bl), ©Frank Cantor; (cl), Front jacket Cover from *When I Was Puerto Rican* by Esmeralda Santiago. Used by permission of **Vintage Books, a division of Random House, Inc.; 446** (l), ©North Wind Picture Archives/Alamy; (r), ©Lee Snider/Photo Images/CORBIS; **447,** ©Index Stock/Alamy; **451,** ©Gary Braasch/CORBIS; **453,** ©Owen Franken/ CORBIS; **458,** ©AP IMAGES/TITO HERRERA; **460** (r), ©Alan Schein/ Alamy; (l), Anna Williams/Fresh Stock USA; **461,** ©Danny Lehman/ CORBIS; **462–63,** ©AP IMAGES/TITO HERRERA; **464,** ©AP IMAGES; **468** (l), Courtesy of Gary Soto; (r), ©Lake County Museum/CORBIS; **469,** Ron Giling/Peter Arnold, Inc.; **474,** ©age fotostock/SuperStock; **476** (l), ©Topham/The Image Works; **477,** ©age fotostock/SuperStock; **478,** ©Stockbyte/Getty Images; **479,** ©James Cotier/Getty Images; **480,** ©age fotostock/SuperStock; **482–83,** ©Hulton Archive/Getty Images; **486,** ©AP IMAGES/WF; **488** (l), ©Syracuse Newspapers/Frank Ordonez/ The Image Works; (r), ©Michael Ochs Archives/CORBIS; **489,** ©GARY HERSHORN/Reuters/CORBIS; **490–91,** ©Brand X Pictures/Jupiterimages Corporation; **493,** ©Library of Congress, Prints & Photographs Division, FSA/OWI Collection, LC-USF33-006029-M[P&P]; **496,** ©Eudora Welty/ CORBIS; **498–99,** ©MARC ROMANELLI/Alamy; **502,** ©AP IMAGES/ MANUEL BALCE CENETA; **504–05,** ©Andrew Holbrooke/CORBIS; **504 & 507,** StoryCorps; **506,** ©AP IMAGES/JAMES A. FINLEY; **508** (l), ©TRBfoto/Photodisc; **508** (c), ©PhotoDisc; (r), ©PhotoDisc; **520** (tl), Cover image from *In Search of Our Mothers' Gardens: Womanist Prose* by Alice Walker. Copyright ©1974 by Alice Walker. Reproduced by permission of **Harcourt Inc.;** (bl), Cover image from *The Chosen* by Chaim Potok. Copyright © by **Holt, Rinehart and Winston.** Reproduced by permission of the publisher; (tr), Cover image from *The Member of the Wedding* by Carson McCullers. Copyright ©1946 and renewed ©1973 by Carson McCullers. Reproduced by permission of **Bantam Books, a Division of Random House, Inc.;** (br), Cover image from *Down the Rabbit Hole* by Pas de Deux. Copyright ©2005 by Pas de Deux. Reproduced by permission of **HarperCollins Publishers. Inc.; 521** (tl), Cover image from *Grayson* by Lynne Cox. Copyright ©2007 by Lynne Cox. Reproduced by permission of **Harcourt Inc.;** (tr), Cover image from *Let It Shine: Stories of Black Women Freedom Fighters*, illustrations by Stephen Alcorn. Text Copyright ©2000 by Andrea Davis Pinkney. Reproduced by permission of **Harcourt, Inc.;** (br), Cover image from *Pilgrim at Tinker Creek* by Annie Dillard. Copyright ©1974 by Annie Dillard. Reproduced by permission of **HarperCollins Publishers, Inc.;** (bl), Cover image from *The Endurance* by Caroline Alexander. Copyright ©1998 by Caroline Alexander. Reproduced by permission of **Alfred A. Knopf, a division of Random House, Inc., www.randomhouse.com; 522–23,** ©AP IMAGES/PETROS KARADJIAS; **523,** ©AP IMAGES/PETROS KARADJIAS; **530–31,** ©Marcell/CORBIS; **532** (inset), ©Frank and Frances Carpenter Collection, Prints & Photographs Division, Library of Congress, LC-USZ62-132047; (bkgd), ©Heeb/age fotostock/SuperStock; **536** (r), Courtesy Willard Library; (l), Prints & Photographs Division, Library of Congress, LC-USZ62-119343; **540,** ©AP IMAGES/DAVID UMBERGER; **542** (l), ©Deborah Feingold/CORBIS; (r), ©Adam Jones/Getty Images; **548,** ©Reuters/CORBIS; **550** (l), ©Doug DuBois; (r), ©PhotoDisc; **551,** ©Mark Boulton/Alamy; **553,** Thomas Nilsen/Photo Researchers,Inc.; **554,** ©PhotoDisc/Getty Images; **556,** first tier (left to right): "Kelly" 2006 by Dan Goldman, "Glam" 2007 by Pedro Camargo, "Sack of Puppies" 2007 by Nikki Cook, second tier (left to right): "Hutch Owen" 2007 by Tom Hart, Sir Ernest Shackleton in "The Voyage of the *James Caird*," 2006 by Nick Bertozzi, "Hebi No Hada" 2006 by Rami Efal, third tier (left to right): "Panorama" 2002 by Michel Fiffe, "On the Beautiful Blue Danube" 2002 by Megan Kelso [top], "Billy Dogma in Fear, My Dear," 2007 by Dean Haspiel [bottom]; "What's the Difference?" 2005 by Josh Neufeld; **558** (l), ©AP IMAGES/GINO DOMENICO; (r), ©Iconotec/Alamy; **561,** ©Ray Manley/SuperStock; **564** (t), Courtesy of Scott McCloud; (b), Courtesy of Robin Brenner; **565,** Scott McCloud; (bkgd), Scott McCloud; **566–67** (bkgd), Scott McCloud; **566,** Scott McCloud; **567,** Scott McCloud; **568–69** (bkgd), Scott McCloud; **568,** Scott McCloud; **569,** Scott McCloud; **570–71** (bkgd), Scott McCloud; **570,** Scott McCloud; **571,** Scott McCloud; **572,** Scott McCloud; (bkgd), Scott McCloud; **574–75,** ©AP IMAGES/MIKE YODER; **578,** ©Bob Daemmrich/The Image Works; **580,** ©Weekly Reader Corporation; **583,** ©Jodi Hilton/The New York Times/Redux; **585,** ©age fotostock/SuperStock; **586** (bkgd), ©age fotostock/SuperStock; **596** (bl), Cover image from *An Inconvenient Truth* by Al Gore. Copyright © 2006 by Al Gore. Reproduced by permission of **Rodale, Inc.;** (br), Cover image from *Sweet Summer: Growing Up With and Without My Dad* by Bebe Moore Campbell. Copyright ©1989 by Bebe Moore Campbell. Reproduced by permission of **Penguin Group (USA),Inc.;** (tr), Cover image from *Merlin's Tour of the Universe* by Neil de Grasse Tyson. Copyright ©1989, 1997 by Neil de Grasse Tyson. Reproduced by permission of **Doubleday, a division of Random House, Inc.; 597** (tl), Cover image from *Animal Farm* by George Orwell. Copyright ©by **Holt, Rinehart and Winston.** Reproduced by permission of the publisher.; (bl), Cover image from *Persepolis: The Story of a Childhood* by Marjane Satrapi. Translation Copyright ©2003 by **L'Association Paris, France.** Reproduced by permission of the publisher.; (tr), Cover image from *Invisible Cities* by Italo Calvino. Translation Copyright ©1974 by **Harcourt, Inc.** Reproduced by permission of the publisher.; (br), Cover image from *Long Walk to Freedom* by Nelson Mandela. Copyright © by **Holt, Rinehart and Winston.** Reproduced by permission of the publisher.; **602,** Sam Dudgeon/HRW; **612** (inset), ©University of Georgia/Peter Frey; (bkgd), ©AP IMAGES/ROSARIO ESPOSITO; **615,** ©James Urbach/SuperStock; **624,** ©W. Perry Conway/CORBIS; **625,** ©Angelo Cavalli/zefa/CORBIS; **626** (b), ©Tom Stewart; **630** (t), Photo by Bryce Milligan ©2005; **630** (b), ©AP IMAGES; **631,** ©Stockbyte; (inset), ©Stockbyte; **632,** ©Paul A. Souders/CORBIS; **635,** ©Tibor Bognar/CORBIS; **639** (l), ©CORBIS; (r), ©JUPITERIMAGES/Creatas/Alamy; **640,** ©age fotostock/SuperStock; **644,** ©Tim Page/CORBIS; **647** (b), Nancy Kaszerman/zuma/Newscom; (t), ©Sophie Bassouls/CORBIS SYGMA; **648,** ©age fotostock/SuperStock; **649,** ©age fotostock/SuperStock; **650,** ©Paul Barton/CORBIS; **653** (l), ©Photo by Carol Bly; (r), ©Danita Delimont/Alamy; **654–55,** ©YVA MOMATIUK/JOHN EASTCOTT/Minden Pictures; **660** (t), ©Bettmann/CORBIS; (b), ©Time & Life Pictures/Getty Images; **661,** ©Morton Beebe/CORBIS; **662,** ©Robert Postma/Getty Images; **665** (tr), ©AP IMAGES/DENNIS VANDAL; **666,** ©J Silver/SuperStock; **667,** ©Brand X Pictures/Alamy; **670,** (t), ©AP IMAGES/KEVIN GUTTING; (b), ©AP IMAGES; **671,** ©Richard Cummins/SuperStock; **672,** ©age fotostock/SuperStock; **675,** (t), ©Photo by David B. Lee; **676,** ©Seattle Post-Intelligencer Collection; Museum of History and Industry/CORBIS; **677,** ©David Turnley/CORBIS; **680** (l), Justin Sullivan/Getty Images; (r), Masterfile Royalty Free (RF); **681,** ©Artistic photographs Collected by Frances Benjamin Johnston in the Frances Benjamin Johnston Collection, Prints & Photographs Division, Library of Congress, LC-USZC2-6125; **686** (r), E A Bowness/AA World Travel/Topfoto/The Image Works; **687,** ©A Curtis/Alamy; **690** (b), ©Roxane Auer; **691** (b), ©Kunin/*Woman on the Stair* /Art Image LA; (t), ©Richarda Hellner; **692,** ©blickwinkel/Alamy; **695** (t), photograph by Donna Lee; (b), ©E.A. Kennedy III/The Image Works ; **696** (bkgd), ©RubberBall/Alamy; **697,** ©Robert Harding Picture Library Ltd/Alamy; **700** (l), ©CORBIS; (c), Feinberg-Whitman Collection, Prints & Photographs Division, Library of Congress, LC-DIG-ppmsca-07531; (r), Feinberg-Whitman Collection, Prints & Photographs Division, Library of Congress, LC-DIG-ppmsca-07541; **701** (inset), ©Atlantide Phototravel/CORBIS; (bkgd), Digital Vision/Getty Images; **706** (l), ©Cheron Bayna; (r), ©Jan Butchofsky-Houser/CORBIS; **707,** ©Jason Horowitz/zefa/CORBIS; **710,** ©AP IMAGES/BILL HUDSON; **712** (c), Courtesy of the Dudley Randall Literary Estate; (t), Getty Images for *Meet the Press*; (b), Frank Capri/Hulton Archive/Getty Images; **714–15,** Courtesy of The Birmingham Public Library Archives, Neg. [85.1.20]; **716,** ©AVolker Steger/Peter Arnold, Inc.; **722,** Courtesy of the Federal Bureau of Investigation (FBI); ©Social Studies Technology Group/Royalty Free/CORBIS; **723,** ©AP IMAGES/TOM GANNAM; **732** (tl), Cover image by Claudine Guerguerian from *The Discovery of Poetry* by Frances Mayes. Copyright ©2001 by Frances Mayes. Reproduced by permission of **Harcourt, Inc.;** (bl), Cover image from *Talking to the Sun*, selected and introduced by Kenneth Koch and Kate Farrell. Copyright ©1985 by **Henry Holt and Company, LLC.** Reproduced by permission of the publisher; (tr), Cover image from *Native Guard* by Natasha Trethewey. Copyright ©2006 by Natasha Trethewey. Reproduced by permission of **Houghton Mifflin Company; 733** (tr), Cover image from *I Am the Darker Brother*, edited by Arnold Adoff. Copyright ©1997 by Aladdin Paperbacks, an imprint of Simon & Schuster Children's Publishing Division. Reproduced by permission of **Simon & Schuster;** (bl), Cover image from *Boris* by Cynthia Rylant. Copyright ©2005 by Cynthia Rylant. Reproduced by permission of **Harcourt, Inc.;** (br), Cover image from *Extra Innings: Baseball Poems*, compiled by Lee Bennett Hopkins. Compilation Copyright ©1993 by Lee Bennett Hopkins. Reproduced by permission of **Harcourt, Inc.;** (tl), Cover image from *A Fire in My Hands* by Gary Soto. Copyright ©1999, 2006 by Gary Soto. Reproduced by permission of **Harcourt, Inc.; 738,** Sam Dudgeon/HRW; **738,** Sam Dudgeon/HRW; **748** (inset), ©Peter Kramer/Getty Images; (bkgd), ©Michael Prince/CORBIS; (bl), PLAYBILL ® All rights reserved. Used by permission; (bc), Cover image from *Letters to a Young Artist* by Anna Deavere Smith. Copyright ©2006 by Anna Deavere Smith. Reproduced by permission of **Anchor Books, a division of Random House, Inc., www.randomhouse.com;** (br), PLAYBILL ® All rights reserved. Used by permission; **750–751,** Sheila Burnett/ArenaPAL© ArenaPal/Topfoto/The Image Works; **751,** J. A. Kraulis/Masterfile; **756** (l), ©Sara Krulwich/*The New York Times*/Redux; (c), ©Sara Krulwich/*The New York Times*/Redux; (r), ©Sara Krulwich/*The New York Times*/Redux; **757,** ©Sara Krulwich/*The New York Times*/Redux; **760,** HACHETTE/CAMERA 1/FILMS A2/DD PROD/UGC/THE KOBAL COLLECTION; **762,** ©Orion Classics/courtesy Everett Collection; **765,** ©Orion Classics/courtesy Everett Collection; **766,** ©Orion Classics/courtesy Everett Collection; **771,** ©Content Mine International/Alamy; **772** (inset), ©Mary Evans Picture Library/The Image Works; (bkgd), ©Hemis/Alamy; **774** (b), ©blickwinkel/Alamy; (t), ©Alleycat Productions/Brand X/CORBIS; **776** (l), ©AP IMAGES/FRANCESCO PROIETTI; (r), ©Stock Montage/Index Stock; **777,** ©Alleycat Productions/Brand X/CORBIS; **778,** Theater in the Open, Newburyport, Massachusetts; **780,** Theater in the Open, Newburyport, Massachusetts; **786–87,** Theater in the Open, Newburyport, Massachusetts; **790,** Theater in the Open, Newburyport, Massachusetts; **793,** ©Alleycat Productions/Brand X/CORBIS; **796,** 2002 Production of *Romeo and Juliet*/ Foreground: Claire Jullien as Juliet and Graham Abbey as Romeo. Background: Patrick Galligan as Paris and Julia Donovan as Lady Capulet. Photo by Terry Manzo/Courtesy of the Stratford Shakespeare Festival Archives; **797,** ©Time Life Pictures/Getty Images; **798,** ©National Portrait Gallery/SuperStock; **799,** ©Roger de la Harpe/CORBIS; **800,** ©Adam Woolfitt/CORBIS; **802,** ©Dana White/PhotoEdit; **806,** TM & Copyright © 20th Century Fox FilmCorp. All rights reserved./Everett Collection; (border), ©1999 Image Farm Inc.; **810,** 2002 Production of *Romeo and Juliet*/Tim Campbell as Abram and Aaron Franks as Gregory with members of the Festival Company. Photo by Terry Manzo/Courtesy of the Stratford Shakespeare Festival Archives; **820,** 2002 Production of *Romeo and Juliet*/Caleb Marshall as Benvolio and Graham Abbey as Romeo. Photo by Terry Manzo/Courtesy of the Stratford Shakespeare Festival Archives; **832,** 2002 Production of *Romeo and Juliet*/Claire Jullien as Juliet. Photo by Michael Cooper/Courtesy of the Stratford Shakespeare Festival Archives; **835,** 2002 Production of *Romeo and Juliet*/Graham Abbey as Romeo. Photo by Michael Cooper/Courtesy of the Stratford Shakespeare Festival Archives; **838,** 2002 Production of *Romeo and Juliet*/Foreground: Claire Jullien as Juliet and Graham Abbey as Romeo. Background: Scott Wentworth as Capulet, Patrick Galligan as Paris, Julia Donovan as Lady Capulet, Courtenay J. Stevens as Peter, and Nicolas Van Burek as Tybalt. Photo by Michael Cooper/Courtesy of the Stratford Shakespeare Festival Archives; **842,** ©ArenaPal/Topham/The Image Works; (border), ©1999 Image Farm Inc.; **847,** 2002 Production of *Romeo and Juliet*/Graham Abbey as Romeo and Claire Jullien as Juliet. Photo by Terry Manz/Courtesy of the Stratford Shakespeare Festival Archives; **854,** 2002 Production of *Romeo and Juliet*/Graham Abbey as Romeo and Keith Dinicol as Friar Laurence. Photo by Terry /Courtesy of the Stratford Shakespeare Festival Archives; **865,** 2002 Production of

Romeo and Juliet/Claire Jullien as Juliet and Lally Cadeau as Juliet's Nurse. Photo by Michael Cooper/Courtesy of the Stratford Shakespeare Festival Archives; **868,** 2002 Production of *Romeo and Juliet*/Graham Abbey as Romeo, Keith Dinicol as Friar Laurence and Claire Jullien as Juliet. Photo by Michael Cooper/Courtesy of the Stratford Shakespeare Festival Archives; **872,** ©Tristram Kenton/Lebrecht Music; (border), ©1999 Image Farm Inc.; **876,** 2002 Production of *Romeo and Juliet*/ Foreground: Wayne Best as Mercutio and Nicolas Van Burek as Tybalt. Background: Caleb Marshall as Benvolio and Graham Abbey as Romeo. Photo by Michael Cooper/Courtesy of the Stratford Shakespeare Festival Archives; **887,** 2002 Production of *Romeo and Juliet*/Claire Jullien as Juliet. Photo by Terry Manzo/Courtesy of the Stratford Shakespeare Festival Archives; **897,** 2002 Production of *Romeo and Juliet*/Graham Abbey as Romeo and Claire Jullien as Juliet. Photo by Terry Manzo/Courtesy of the Stratford Shakespeare Festival Archives; **903,** 2002 Production of *Romeo and Juliet*/Julia Donovan as Lady Capulet. Photo by Michael Cooper/Courtesy of the Stratford Shakespeare Festival Archives; **908,** ©Michal Daniel, 2004; (border), ©1999 Image Farm Inc.; **912,** 2002 Production of *Romeo and Juliet*/ Claire Jullien as Juliet and Keith Dinicol as Friar Laurence. Photo by Terry Manzo/Courtesy of the Stratford Shakespeare Festival Archives; **917,** 2002 Production of *Romeo and Juliet*/Claire Jullien as Juliet, Julia Donovan as Lady Capulet, and Lally Cadeau as Juliet's Nurse. Photo by Terry Manzo/Courtesy of the Stratford Shakespeare Festival Archives; **921,** ©20th Century Fox/courtesy Everett Collection; **930,** Everett Collection; **944,** 2002 Production of *Romeo and Juliet*/Centre Stage: Graham Abbey as Romeo and Claire Jullien as Juliet. From left to right: Keith Dinicol as Friar Laurence, Patrick Galligan as Paris, David Kirby as Friar John, Caleb Marshall as Benvolio with members of the Company. Photo by Terry Manzo/Courtesy of the Stratford Shakespeare Festival Archives; **954** (t), ©AP IMAGES/JESSICA HILL; (b), ©Scott Gries/ ImageDirect/Getty Images; **955,** Usher, D./Peter Arnold, Inc.; **956,** ©National Museum and Gallery of Wales,Cardiff/The Bridgeman Art Library International; **958,** ©Mary Evans Picture Library/The Image Works; **972,** ©Rupert Sagar-Musgrave/Alamy; **975,** Courtesy of Club di Giulietta; **977** (t), Courtesy of Club di Giulietta; (b), ©Hemis/Alamy; (inset), ©Hemis/Alamy; (t), (border) ©1999 Image Farm Inc.; **978** (t), "1973 Love Stamp" image reprinted with permission of the United States Postal Service. All Rights Reserved.; **990** (tl), Cover image from *Romeo and Juliet/West Side Story*. Copyright ©1965 by Dell Publishing Co. Inc. Reproduced by permission of **Bantam Books, a Division of Random House, Inc.;** (tr), Cover image from *The Miracle Worker* by William Gibson. Copyright ©1956, 1957 by William Gibson. Reproduced by permission of **Bantam Books, a Division of Random House, Inc.;** (bl), Cover image from *A Midsummer Night's Dream* by William Shakespeare. Copyright ©by **Holt, Rinehart and Winston.** Reproduced by permission of the publisher; (br), Cover image from *Favorite Stories for Performance*. Copyright © by **Holt, Rinehart and Winston.** Reproduced by permission of the publisher; **991** (tl), Cover image from *The Time Machine and The War of the Worlds* by H. G. Wells. Copyright © by **Holt, Rinehart and Winston.** Reproduced by permission of the publisher; (br), Cover image from *Letters to a Young Artist* by Anna Deavere Smith. Copyright ©2006 by Anna Deavere Smith. Reproduced by permission of **Anchor Books, a division of Random House, Inc., www.randomhouse.com;** (bl), Cover image from *Letters to Juliet* by Lise Friedman and Ceil Friedman. Copyright ©2006 by Lise Friedman and Ceil Friedman. Reproduced by permission of **Stewart, Tabori & Chang, an imprint of Harry N. Abrams, Inc.;** (tr), Cover image from Wanda Hickey's *Night of Golden Memories and Other Disasters* by Jean Shepherd. Copyright ©1971 by Jean Shepherd. Reproduced by permission of **Random House, Inc., www. randomhouse.com; 826–27,** 2002 Production of *Romeo and Juliet*/ Members of the Festival Company as Masquers. Photo by Michael Cooper/Courtesy of the Stratford Shakespeare Festival Archives; **880–81,** 2002 Production of *Romeo and Juliet*/Foreground: Julia Donovan as Lady Capulet, Nicolas Van Burek as Tybalt, Wayne Best as Mercutio, and Wyatt Best as Mercutio's Page. Background left to right: Adrienne Gould as Citizen, Martha Farrell as Citizen, Patrick Galligan as Paris, Sarah Dodd as Lady Montague, John Dolan as Montague, Philip Griffith Pace as Citizen, Raymond O'Neill as Escalus, the Prince of Verona, Phillip Hughes as Balthasar, and Courtenay J. Stevens as Peter. Photo by Terry Manzo/Courtesy of the Stratford Shakespeare Festival Archives; **926–27,** 2002 Production of *Romeo and Juliet*/Julia Donovan as Lady Capulet, Claire Jullien as Juliet, and Scott Wentworth as Capulet. Photo by Terry Manzo/Courtesy of the Stratford Shakespeare Festival Archives; **930** (border), ©1999 Image Farm Inc.; **938–39,** 2002 Production of *Romeo and Juliet*/Graham Abbey as Romeo and Claire Jullien as Juliet. Photo by Terry Manzo/Courtesy of the Stratford Shakespeare Festival Archives; **961, 964, 969,** ©Mary Evans Picture Library/The Image Works; **996,** Sam Dudgeon/HRW; **1008** (inset), Courtesy of Ian Johnston; (bkgd), ©Perry Mastrovito/CORBIS; (bl), Cover image from *The Iliad* by Homer, translated by Ian Johnston. Copyright ©2006 by **Richer Resources Publications.** Reproduced by permission of the publisher; (tr), Cover image from *The Odyssey* by Homer, translated by Ian Johnston. Copyright ©2006 by **Richer Resources Publications.** Reproduced by permission of the publisher; **1010–11,** Musee du Bardo, Tunis, Tunisia, Giraudon/The Bridgeman Art Library International; **1022** (inset), ©Time & Life Pictures/Getty Images; (bkgd), ©JUPITERIMAGES/Brand X/Alamy; **1036** (r), ©Yiorgos Depollas/ SuperStock; **1049,** ©AP IMAGES/PETROS KARADJIAS; **1108** (l), Courtesy of Houghton Mifflin Company; (r), Digital Stock ; **1114,** ©Arcaid/Alamy; **1116** (t), ©Ulf Andersen/Getty Images; (b), ©William Regensburger; **1118,** ©Thomas Shjarback/Alamy; **1121,** *Los Angeles Times* Photo by Don Bartletti; **1125,** *Los Angeles Times* Photo by Don Bartletti; **1128,** *Los Angeles Times* Photo by Don Bartletti; **1130,** *Los Angeles Times* Photo by Don Bartletti; **1131,** *Los Angeles Times* Photo by Don Bartletti; **1134,** Royal Geographical Society; **1136,** ©Bettmann/ CORBIS; **1139,** ©Joseph Sohm; Visions of America/CORBIS; **1140,** ©Underwood & Underwood/CORBIS; **1143,** Helen Atkinson; (bkgd), ©PhotoLink; **1144,** Frank Hurley/Royal Geographical Society; **1146,** Frank Hurley/Royal Geographical Society; **1148,** Frank Hurley/Royal Geographical Society; **1158** (bl), Cover image from *Mythology* by Edith Hamilton. Copyright 1942 by Edith Hamilton; Copyright renewed ©1969 by Dorian Fielding Reid and Doris Fielding Reid. Reproduced by permission of **Little, Brown and Company, Inc.; 1158** (tl), Cover image from *The Pearl* by John Steinbeck. Copyright 1945 by John Steinbeck; Copyright renewed ©1973 by Elaine Steinbeck, John Steinbeck IV, and Thom Steinbeck. Reproduced by permission of **Penguin Group (USA), Inc.;** (bl), Cover image from *Mythology* by Edith Hamilton. Copyright 1942 by Edith Hamilton; copyright renewed ©1969 by Dorian Fielding Reid and Doris Fielding Reid. Reproduced by permission of **Little, Brown and Company, Inc.;** (br), Cover image from *Kon-Tiki* by Thor Heyerdahl.; (tr), Cover image from *Ithaka* by Adäle Geras. Copyright ©2005 by Adäle Geras. Reproduced by permission of **Harcourt, Inc.;** 1159 (tl), Cover image from *Cupid* by Julius Lester. Copyright ©2006 by Julius Lester. Reproduced by permission of Harcourt, Inc.; (tr), Cover image from *Inside the Walls of Troy* by Clemence McLaren. Copyright ©1996 by Clemence McLaren. Reproduced by permission of **Simon & Schuster Adult Publishing Group;** (bl), Cover image from *Dune* by Frank Herbert. Copyright ©1965 by Frank Herbert. Reproduced by permission of **G. P. Putnam's Sons, a division of Penguin Group (USA), Inc.;** (br), Cover image from James Houston's *Treasury of Inuit Legends* by James Houston. Copyright ©2006 by Saumik LLC. Reproduced by permission of **Harcourt Inc.; 1168,** Sam Dudgeon/HRW; **1178** (inset), HRW Photo; (bkgd), ©Supapixx/Alamy; **1180–1181,** Masterfile Royalty Free (RF); **1181,** Masterfile Royalty Free (RF); **1185,** ©CORBIS; **1192,** ©Roger Ressmeyer/CORBIS; **1198,** ©David Young-Wolff/Alamy; **1204,** ©Formcourt (Form Advertising)/Alamy; **1212,** Photographer's Choice/ Getty Images; **1214,** ©Digital Vision/Alamy; **1215,** ©Myrleen Ferguson Cate/PhotoEdit; **1222** (bl), ©Bloomimage/CORBIS; (br), ©Photodisc/ Getty Images; (tl), ©Image Source/CORBIS; **1223** (bl), ©Lawrence Manning/CORBIS; (tr), Cover image from *Tooth and Nail: A Novel Approach to the SAT* by Charles Harrington Elster and Joseph Elliot. Copyright ©2004 by Charles Harrington Elster and Joseph Elliot. Reproduced by permission of **Harcourt, Inc.;** (tl), ©Photodisc/Getty Images; (br), ©Image Source/CORBIS; **1228,** Sam Dudgeon/HRW; **1240,** ColorBlind Images/Getty Images; **1241,** Courtesy of Tee and Charles Addams Foundation;

INDEX OF SKILLS

The boldface numbers indicate an extensive treatment of the topic.

The Index of Skills is divided into the following categories:

LITERARY SKILLS

INFORMATIONAL TEXT SKILLS

READING SKILLS

VOCABULARY SKILLS

WRITING SKILLS

STANDARDIZED TEST PRACTICE

LANGUAGE (GRAMMAR, USAGE, AND MECHANICS) SKILLS

LISTENING AND SPEAKING SKILLS

READ ON

INDEX OF AUTHORS AD TITLES

The italicized page numbers indicate thges on which author biographies appear.